# Assessing Trauma in Forensic Contexts

Rafael Art. Javier • Elizabeth A. Owen
Jemour A. Maddux
Editors

# Assessing Trauma
# in Forensic Contexts

 Springer

*Editors*
Rafael Art. Javier
Psychology
St. John's University
Queens, NY, USA

Elizabeth A. Owen
Columbia University/Teachers College
New York, NY, USA

Jemour A. Maddux
Lamb & Maddux, LLC
Hackensack, NJ, USA

ISBN 978-3-030-33105-4      ISBN 978-3-030-33106-1   (eBook)
https://doi.org/10.1007/978-3-030-33106-1

This Springer imprint is published by the registered company Springer Nature Switzerland AG
The registered company address is: Gewerbestrasse 11, 6330 Cham, Switzerland

**Rafael Art. Javier**
*I dedicate this book to the NYSPA Forensic Division for providing me the opportunity to engage in this important topic and, also, to all those suffering the consequences of traumas in all its permutations*

**Jemour A. Maddux**
*For my wife, Ponnie, and children, Daniel, Isabel, and Ryan*

**Elizabeth A. Owen**
*To HP for always supporting me, even when I pushed you away*

# Foreword

## Why Lawyers and Forensic Mental Health Professionals Must be Trauma-Informed

Thirty years ago, there was nothing (that is not hyperbole) in the legal literature that discussed trauma in the context of forensic psychology or psychiatry. Before 1991, there were but two cases that even mentioned both trauma and any aspect of forensic mental health.[1] When I offered a course at New York Law School in the late 2000s on "Trauma and Mental Disability Law," it was—to the best of my knowledge—the first such course ever offered at any US law school.

Times have changed. A simple WESTLAW search for 2019 alone[2] reveals over 80 secondary sources (law review articles and learned treatise chapters) and over 20 cases that mention (in some cases multiple times) this relationship. An article in an American Bar Association journal is clear: "The need for forensic experts and mental health professionals in trauma cases ... is acute" (Gwyn & Strack, 2019, p. 3). Within the last year, expert witnesses have regularly testified about this relationship in the context of cases arising in criminal law (e.g., *State v. Beck, 2019)*, parental rights (e.g., *Interest of N.S.,* 2019), custody (e.g., *Hamtyon v. Williams*, 2019) and juvenile dependency (e.g., *In re A.C.)*, false arrest and false imprisonment (e.g., *Gonzales v. First Food HFDC, Inc, 2019)*, and civil tort actions for interfamilial sexual abuse (e.g., *Iino v. Spalter, 2019)*. In short, times have changed, and it has become essential that lawyers, forensic witnesses, and clinicians begin to take seriously these connections.[3]

In an insightful article, Professors Sarah Katz and Deeya Haldar suggest that lawyers incorporate trauma-informed practice in their skill set. Trauma-informed

---

[1] WESTLAW search <trauma /s forensic /p psychiat! Psychol! "mental health> conducted Sept. 21, 2013.

[2] Search conducted Sept. 23, 2019.

[3] This is not solely a domestic issue, but an international one as well. See, e.g., Gallagher &. Perlin, 2018; Perlin, 2018).

practice recognizes the impact of trauma on systems and individuals. Trauma-informed practice ensures that clients have access to trauma-focused interventions during all routine practice. These interventions incorporate an assessment of trauma and trauma symptoms and endeavor to treat the consequences of traumatic stress. Instead of asking, "What is wrong with you?" a trauma-informed practitioner asks, "What happened to you?" (see Cucolo & Perlin, 2017, p. 324, discussing Katz & Halder, 2016). In this context, Professors Sarah Katz and Deeya Haldar have underscored, "The trauma experiences of clients have a direct relationship to how they relate to their attorneys and the courts, because trauma has a distinct physiological effect on the brain, which in turn affects behavior in the short-term and long-term" (Katz & Halder, 2016, p. 366).

Tardily, we have begun to realize, variously, the impact of posttraumatic stress disorder on persons who have been the victims of domestic violence and trafficking, and of veterans who have served in the recent wars in the Middle East (Perlin, 2015), on the traumatic outcomes of shaming processes in juvenile court matters (Perlin & Lynch, 2018),[4] on how factors such as trauma may lead to behavior that results in a death sentence (Perlin, 2016), on how trauma from sexual violence may lead to psychiatric disability requiring long-term institutionalization (Perlin & Cucolo, 2017), and the need for trauma-informed care in mental health courts (Weinstein & Perlin, 2018). And all of these realizations call out—better, *scream* out—for greater awareness of these phenomena on the part of forensic witnesses.

This masterful book, edited by Rafael Art. Javier, Elizabeth Owen, and Jemour A. Maddux, is a refreshing, original, and thoughtful response to these needs, demonstrating—beyond any doubt—why lawyers and forensic mental health professionals must be trauma-informed in all of their relevant work. This book does not simply fill a gap; it creates a high bar for any other authors who seek to enter this complex territory that spans the intersection of law and psychology. We are fortunate that they have chosen this path.

The book is extensive, and it is comprehensive. After an initial part, setting out a conceptual framework (one that focuses both on issues of law such as competency to stand trial and sentencing mitigation, and on issues of psychology (focusing on how trauma issues are at the heart of forensic developmental psychology, and on the critically *under*considered issues that involve culture and linguistic differences in assessing trauma), it moves on to a host of *civil* forensic matters (many of which deal with issues that focus on children and juveniles, but also matters involving employment and injuries), and then on to a similar range of *criminal* matters (in addition to the ones in the opening part noted above, including sexual offenses, juvenile delinquency, intimate partner violence, and, so especially important, the role of problem-solving (diversion) courts). Finally, in the concluding part, the

---

[4] See *id.,* p. 80 at 80, quoting, Coyne, 2012, p. 557, quoting Read, 2012:

The director of a mental health program for juveniles has directly criticized the shaming approach, stating that "[a]ll of our mental health programs end up having more and more people come in with trauma at the hands of humiliation ... the behavior [will] show up in different ways ... [and] unfortunately, the morgue may see that person."

chapter authors consider best practice models, case studies of criminal cases "ripped from the headlines," and a return to a special kind of diversion court, a veterans' court, in a chapter written by a NY state judge who presides over problem-solving courts.

Each section of the book—each chapter—is replete with challenges to the forensic mental health professional.[5] In their introductory chapter, two of the editors—Javier and Owen—highlight one of these challenges: "to be able to determine the extent to which an individual's earlier attachment experience is implicated in future responses to difficult conditions that become the subject of the assessment" (p. xx). They note, accurately, that "not everyone who experienced early trauma ends up involved in the justice system as defendants or victims" (*id.*). But the statistics they share with us are unnerving: a child exposed to five or more "significant adverse experiences" before age 4 is **15 times more likely than others to attempt suicide, and 3–4 times more likely to become an alcoholic"** (p. xy; emphasis added). All witnesses in cases involving trauma—and all lawyers involved in trauma-focused litigation—need to familiarize themselves with such frightening information.

Consider also the chapter by Daneille Neal, James Garabino, and Caitlin Prater on how trauma is at the "heart" of forensic developmental psychology. The data that they present—on the "strong associations between traumatic experiences and criminal behavior" (p. zz)—is essential for anyone trying to understand why some offenders do what they do, especially when adverse childhood experiences (ACE) are examined (p. zzz). Lawyers and forensic mental health professionals must all understand the significance of this data in their representation and evaluations of this population. Given the recent focus by the US Supreme Court on juvenile sentencing issues (especially in the context of brain development), see, for example, *Miller v. Alabama,* 2012; for a consideration of all relevant issues, see Steinberg, 2017), their finding that young offenders are *thirteen* times less likely to have reported no early traumatic experiences, and four times more likely than the general population to have experienced four or more such experiences (p. zzzz) is of profound significance to all who work in this aspect of the forensic justice system.

It will be no surprise to most readers that, per the chapter by Corey Leidenfrost and Daniel Antonius, those who are incarcerated—be they men, women, young or old—have had "alarming rates of trauma experience" (p. qqq). This trauma, which generally began pre-incarceration, continues during the period of incarceration and after release, when it may have a pointedly negative impact on any post-incarceration treatment (p. qqq). The authors stress that identification of past trauma must start with initial admission and screening procedures, something that is not done at all in many correctional facilities. (*id.*) Again, for those working with this population—as lawyers, as clinicians, or as expert witnesses—this information is mandatory.

In his chapter on sentence mitigation, Thomas Caffrey offers a blueprint for the defense lawyer and the expert witness in death penalty cases (on the need for a

---

[5] In this foreword, I focus solely on a few chapters. The reader should not take this to mean that these are the only ones I found to be of value. I found them *all* of value, but am simply offering these as examples of their values to different cohorts of potential readers.

mitigation specialist in such cases, see American Bar Association, 2003).[6] Here, he focuses on how forensic experts must be able to explain to fact-finders how an external event "traumatically affected the subject, and how that effect—psychological and, or with probability, physiological—within the subject, affected the subject's behavior at the time he or she committed the crime" (p. aaa). This may seem intuitive to many reading this, but it is not done in many, many cases,[7] as often, counsel is not even aware that this is worth exploring (see generally, on the abysmal work done by lawyers in so many death penalty cases, Perlin, Harmon & Chatt, 2019).

I need to emphasize that there is much here for the lawyer and the witness who is never involved in criminal work, but who stays solely in the civil court systems. Think, for example, about the law as it relates to child protection matters. In their chapter on this topic, Susan Cohen Esquilin and Denise M. Williams Johnson focus both on personal and *racial* trauma as those phenomena relate to all the loss of a child to foster care via the child protection system. They note that the significance of race-based trauma is often misunderstood by system decision-makers, a misunderstanding that often results in "seriously negative consequences for both parents and children" (p. bbb). Trauma, they note accurately, is "central to the lives of many parents involved in the child welfare system" (p. bbbbb); without a full understanding of this trauma—and its roots—evaluations of parental fitness are "potentially harmful to the parent and the child" (*id.*). The authors suggest a series of helpful steps to make it more likely that the evaluator, in taking a thorough history, will be able to identify past traumatic experiences, to "assess whether trauma sequelae are present in the current symptom picture, and to offer treatment suggestions" (*id.*).

The relationship between parental rights, child custody, and trauma history also matters in such areas as juvenile delinquency prevention (Amanda Zelechoski, Rachel Lindsay, and Lori Heusel, concluding that any forensic psychological evaluation must be performed through a trauma-informed lens as the best possible strategy for preventing negative long-term outcomes) and immigration status (Yosef Amrami and Javier, seeking to focus our attention on the trauma of family separation in the migration and deportation processes). Both chapters need to be read

---

[6]On the need for a mitigation specialist in such cases, see, e.g., American Bar Association, Guidelines *for the Appointment and Performance of Defense Counsel in Death Penalty Cases*, 31 HOFSTRA L. REV. 913, 1007-08 (2003)

[7]For an almost grotesque example in which counsel did not explore mitigation avenues at trial, see *Hammond v. Scott*, 1994, p. *4 n. 12):

According to Hammond's brief, this information included evidence that his father constantly beat his mother, abused his brothers, and raped and sexually abused his sisters (at least one time in front of Hammond) and that he was also beaten by his father and mother, many times in front of other people, causing his psychological trauma. When Hammond was nine, the father was beating the mother and an older brother shot and killed the father in the presence of Hammond and other family members. The brother then used a razor to mutilate the father's body. After this, Hammond began to have nightmares, hallucinations (primarily about "Ozzie" who directs Hammond to harm others) and to abuse drugs. There was also some proof that Hammond is borderline mentally retarded (IQ 77) and suffers from severe psychopathology as well as paranoia and post-traumatic stress disorder. Anti-psychotic drugs have reduced the delusions, but Hammond was unable to obtain those drugs at the time of the crime.

hand-in-glove with that of Mary Kelly Persyn and Owen on the "toxic stress" of the asylum process on refugee children, noting that lawyers are often not provided for children in cases that arise out of these processes, creating even more need for forensic mental health professionals to be involved in such cases.

In their chapter, Zelechoski and her colleagues also point out the potential cost-savings of addressing areas of risk and need before delinquent behavior is manifested (p. ggg), an often-hidden value in identifying, assessing, and combatting trauma. In theirs, Amrami and Javier tackle one of the major political issues of the day, stressing the "significant psychological, social and economic hardships the children face upon separation" (p. mmm). And in their chapter, Persyn and Owen make clear how the shortcomings of the legal system—in not mandating counsel and expert assistance—fail the children at risk and exacerbate their traumas. In all of these examples, the authors teach us that traumatic experiences have lifelong outcomes and that they cannot be isolated from the political system in which we live.

Again, these are just a sample of chapters in this magnificent work. In each of these—and the others—the authors demonstrate how the poison of trauma has permeated all of society, and how necessary it is for those who involve themselves in the legal/forensic system to grasp this, and to begin to figure out how these experiences can be responded to and ameliorated to the greatest extent possible. The editors have done a brilliant job in putting this together. We all owe them a great debt.

New York, NY, USA                                                                              Michael L. Perlin

# References

American Bar Association (2003). Guidelines for the appointment and performance of defense counsel in death penalty cases. *Hofstra Law Review, 31,* 913-1090.

Coyne, L. (2012). Can shame be therapeutic? *Arizona Summit Law Review, 7,* 539–561.

Cucolo, H.E. & Perlin, M.L. (2017). Promoting dignity and preventing shame and humiliation by improving the quality and education of attorneys in Sexually Violent Predator (SVP) civil commitment cases. *Florida Journal of Law and Public Policy, 28.* 291–328.

Gallagher. M. & Perlin, M.L. (2018). "The pain I rise above": How international human rights can best realize the needs of persons with trauma-related mental disabilities. *Florida Journal of International Law, 29,* 271–301.

Gonzales v. First Food HFDC, Inc., 64 Misc.3d 1206(A),2019 WL 260868 (Civil Ct. 2019).

Gwinn C. & Strack, G., (Jan.-Feb.2019). Legal incubators: Pathways to justice and hope for survivors of violence and abuse. *GPSolo, 36.* 30–33.

Hammond v. Scott, 35 F. 3d 559, 1994 WL 499681 (5th Cir. 1994).

Hampton v. Williams, 2019 WL 4410320 (Ill. App. Ct. 2019).

Iino v. Spalter, — A. 3d —, 2019 WL 4251293 (Conn. App. Ct. 2019).

*In re* A.C., 2019 WL 3408698 (Cal. Ct. App. 2019).

Interest of N.S., 2019 WL 1872346 (Pa. Super. Ct. 2019).

Katz, S. & Haldar, D. (2016). *The pedagogy of* trauma *informed lawyering. Clinical Law Review, 22,* 359–393.

Miller v. Alabama, 567 U.S. 460 (2012).

Perlin, M.L. (2018). "Your old road is/Rapidly agin": International human rights standards and
their impact on forensic psychologists, the practice of forensic psychology, and the conditions of institutionalization of persons with mental disabilities. *Washington University Global
Studies Law Review, 17,* 79–111.

Perlin, M.L. (2016). "Your corrupt ways had finally made you blind": Prosecutorial misconduct
and the use of "ethnic adjustments" in death penalty cases of defendants with intellectual disabilities. *American University Law Review, 65,* 1437–1459.

Perlin, M.L. (2015). "*I expected it to happen/I knew he'd lost control": The impact of PTSD on
criminal sentencing after the promulgation of DSM-5. Utah Law Review, 2015, 881–927.*

Perlin, M.L. & Cucolo, H.E. (2017). "Tolling for the aching ones whose wounds cannot be nursed":
The marginalization of racial minorities and women in institutional mental disability law.
*Journal of Gender, Race and Justice, 20,* 431–457.

Perlin, M.L. & Lynch, A.J. (2018). "She's nobody's child/the law can't touch her at all": Seeking
to bring dignity to legal proceedings involving juveniles. *Family Court Review, 56,* 79–90.

Perlin, M.L., Harmon, T.R. & Chatt, S. (2019; forthcoming). "A world of steel-eyed death":
An empirical evaluation of the failure of the *Strickland* standard to ensure adequate counsel to defendants with mental disabilities facing the death penalty. *University of Michigan
Journal of Law Reform* (draft copy accessible at https://papers.ssrn.com/sol3/papers.
cfm?abstract_id=3332730).

Read, T. (Dec. 31, 2012, 12:00 AM). Most influential: Judge Cicconetti's alternative sentences
leave impression (with video). *News-Herald* (accessible at https://www.news-herald.com/
news/most-influential-judge-michael-cicconetti-s-alternative-sentences-leave-impression/
article_3afd711b-7755-5492-bb41-1ac0c7f2ac3a.html).

State v. Beck, — S.W. 3d —, 2019 WL 1904931 (Mo. Ct. App. 2019).

Steinberg, L. (2017). Adolescent brain science and juvenile justice policymaking. *Psychology,
Public Policy and Law, 23,* 410–420.

Weinstein, N.M. & Perlin, M.L. (2018). "Who's pretending to care for him?" How the endless jail-
to-hospital-to-street-repeat cycle deprives persons with mental disabilities the right to continuity of care. *Wake Forest Journal of Law and Policy, 8,* 455–502.

# Editors' Acknowledgments

**Rafael Art. Javier**

This book is the result of a long journey whose seed was planted at the NYSPA Forensic Division Annual Conference several years ago where the issue of trauma in forensic contexts was the organizing theme. But if it had not been for the active involvement of my coeditors, Elizabeth Owen and Jemour Maddux, this book would have been relegated to "it could have been" and the victim of yet one more good idea never realized. The active collaborations among the coeditors provided a wonderful opportunity to identify relevant topics to include that could be of benefit to our forensic community. In our capacity as president and past presidents of the NYSPA Forensic Division, we saw as our responsibility to contribute to the forensic profession by addressing core issues in forensic psychology and by providing training opportunities that can serve as guide to the discipline. Writing this book is meant to serve that very purpose. The decision to focus the book on trauma was guided by our recognition that trauma is ubiquitous to all human experiences and likely to be front and center in many forensic situations. I want to thank my coeditors for their determination to prepare a book that included contributions from well-established scholars and forensic professionals with many years of experience. Although we were unable to cover all possible ways trauma may be present in a forensic issue under consideration, our readers can rest assured that the material included are likely to show in forensic practices in some shape or form.

I want to thank my students whose assistance in the various stages of the book preparation became so critical. I am referring to Yosef Amrami, Marko Lamela, Alexis Kachersky, Devesh Permanan, and Shaianne Innocent. Two of these students ended up coauthoring some of the chapters (Yosef and Marko), while Alexis Kachersky deserves special mention for her excellent and professional manner with which she was able to help prepare the tables of different crimes that are listed at the end of the book as part of the "Case Study" section (Chap. 21). A heartfelt thank should also go to Evelyn Falcone, Lauren Euell, and Diane Spitz for providing the necessary secretarial structure throughout the process. Ms. Falcone should be particularly recognized for always looking after my office to ensure that we have the appropriate group of students assigned to assist us in our work. But none of that could have been possible without the active support of Dr. William Chaplin, our chair, whose different decisions have benefitted our office and have helped provide crucial assistance in the preparation of this book and beyond .

Finally, I would like to thank all my forensic clients for providing me with many opportunities to assess more intimately the extent to which trauma and its consequences may have been involved in the forensic issues under assessment.

**Jemour A. Maddux**

Most importantly, I would like to acknowledge my coeditors, particularly Rafael Art. Javier for his commitment to his colleagues and the specialty of forensic psychology. I would also like to acknowledge my research assistant on this project, Grishma Ghelani; my coauthors, Amy Jane Agnew and I. Bruce Frumkin; and my colleagues from the American Academy of Forensic Psychology, the New York State Psychological Association, and the American Professional Society on the Abuse of Children for their willingness to assist with this project and many others. Lastly, I must acknowledge Michelle Maddux and Joe Yazdian for calling my attention to the importance of this publication.

**Elizabeth A. Owen**

I would like to thank Timothy Strode, Michael Ledereich, and Edmund Dalton for taking the time to read, and sometimes reread, to provide much appreciated suggestions. Co-writing a chapter can be complex and stressful work, but not with the likes of Alan Perry, Devora Scher, and Mary Kelly Persyn not to mention Rafael Javier and Jemour Maddux who helped to make this a wonderful learning experience. Thanks also to the Forensic Division of the New York Psychological Association, whose conference on trauma in forensic settings was the inspiration for this book, and, lastly, and in many ways most importantly, to Susan Owen, who kept me sane these past few months.

# Contents

# About the Editors

**Rafael Art. Javier, Ph.D., ABPP** is a professor of psychology and the director of Inter-agencies Training and Research Initiatives, director of the Post-Graduate Professional Development Programs, and the director of the Postdoctoral Certificate Programs in Forensic Psychology at St. John's University. He also functioned as the first director of the Center for Psychological Services and Clinical Studies at St. John's University for almost 20 years. He was on the faculty and a supervisor at New York University Medical Center, Department of Psychiatry. He is currently a faculty and supervisor at the Object Relations Institute. Prior to joining St. John's University, he was the head of psychology at Kingsboro Psychiatric Center and on the faculty at Downstate Medical Center.

Dr. Javier has presented at national and international conferences including Spain, Italy, Germany, England, Greece, Vienna, Brussels, Argentina, Venezuela, Mexico, Costa Rica, Cuba, Chile, Ecuador, etc., on psycholinguistic and psychoanalytic issues in research and treatment and on ethnic and cultural issues in psychoanalytic theories and practice, including on issues of violence and the impact on general cognitive and emotional functioning. He has published extensively on the subject including several co-edited books: *Reaching Across Boundaries of Culture and Class*, *Domestic Violence*, and *Personality Development and Psychotherapy in Our Diverse Society: A Source Book* all published by Jason Aronson. The *Patterns of Desire: Sexual Diversity in Psychoanalysis*, coauthored with Dr. William Herron, was published by Nova Science Publishers, Inc. in the spring 2006. Early in 2007, he was the senior editor for the *Handbook of Adoption: Implication for Researchers, Practitioners and Families* co-edited with Amanda Baden, Frank Biafora, and Alina Camacho-Gingerich, published by Sage Publications. His book *The Bilingual Mind: Thinking, Feeling and Speaking in Two Languages* was published in 2007 by Springer Publications. In 2015, he published with Oxford University Press *The Specialty Competencies in Psychoanalysis in Psychology* written with Dolores Morris and William Herron. His most recent book *Understanding Domestic Violence: Theories, Challenges, Remedies*, co-edited and authored with William Herron was published in 2018 by Rowman and Littlefield. He has been in forensic practice for more than twenty five years and testified in multiple courts.

He is on the editorial board of the *Journal of Psycholinguistic Research*, the *Journal of Social Distress and the Homeless*, and the *Journal of Infant, Child and Adolescent Psychotherapy*. He is the editor-in-chief for the *Journal of Psycholinguistic Research* and the past co-editor of the *Journal of Social Distress and the Homeless*. His current research activities include issues of violence and moral development, suicide in adolescents and young adults, and bilingualism. He is in private practice. He holds a diplomate in clinical psychology by the American Board of Professional Psychology and another diplomate in psychoanalysis by the same board. He is a visiting professor at the Universidad de la Cuenca del Plata, in Corrientes, Argentina, and appointed "Profesor Honorario" by that university in 2016. He was the president of the Forensic Division of the New York State Psychological Association 2017–2018 and the past vice-president of the Association of Hispanic Mental Health Professionals. He was appointed as Special Advisor to the Executive Board of the New York State Psychological Association.

**Elizabeth A. Owen** is a graduate of Columbia University with a Ph.D. in clinical psychology. She is a past president of the Forensic Division of the New York State Psychological Association. Dr. Owen has worked in the area of mental illness in the criminal justice system since 1997 and has published articles in the *Journal of the American Academy of Psychiatry and the Law*, the *International Journal of Law and Psychiatry*, and the *Journal of Forensic Psychology Practice*. She is a sought-after speaker and has presented at international conferences, national and local conferences, legal and medical schools and institutions, and is currently or has held academic positions at Columbia University's Teachers College, SUNY Downstate Medical School, Adelphi University, Brookdale Medical School, and St. John's University. Dr. Owen has a private forensic psychology practice including performing evaluations for competency not responsible due to mental disease or defect (insanity), and disputed confessions and has been deemed an expert in multiple criminal, supreme, federal, and immigration courts in New York.

**Jemour A. Maddux, Psy.D., ABPP** is the managing director of Lamb and Maddux, LLC. He is board certified in forensic psychology by the American Board of Professional Psychology. He is a fellow of the American Academy of Forensic Psychology. His areas of interest include the assessment of harm, risk and various abilities in family, civil, and police and public safety contexts. Primarily focused upon forensic practice, Dr. Maddux is an experienced evaluator having completed over 3,000 evaluations and affidavits in federal and state cases. He has served on multiple national committees charged with developing various policy statements, amicus briefs, and practice guidelines used by legal professionals and forensic practitioners throughout the United States. Dr. Maddux is a board member of the American Professional Society on the Abuse of Children (APSAC), which is the nation's leading professional organization for child-maltreatment professionals. He is also a past President of the Forensic Division of the New York State Psychological Association.

# Contributors

**Amy Jane Agnew** devotes her law practice to representing victims of constitutional and civil rights violations in federal courts. For five years, Ms. Agnew served as the Graduate Fellow in Constitutional Law and Legal History at Rutgers School of Law – Newark.

**Yosef Amrami** is a doctoral student in clinical psychology at St. John's University in Queens, NY. Yosef has researched the psycholinguistic underpinnings of how people convey stress and depression while speaking. In addition, he has been trained as a psychotherapist in hospital centers and foster care agencies across New York City. Within these roles, Yosef has treated and assessed children and families from diverse linguistic and cultural backgrounds.

**Daniel Antonius** is an associate professor and the director of the Division of Forensic Psychiatry and the Division of Psychology in the Department of Psychiatry at University at Buffalo. Additionally, he is the chief psychologist at the Erie County Forensic Mental Health Services. Dr. Antonius oversees the University at Buffalo's Psychiatry Department's forensic faculty and staff, the forensic programs, and the forensic psychology training program. He also conducts psychological and forensic evaluations that address psychological and legal questions in local, state, and federal courts. His research program focuses on (1) enhancing mental health-care delivery services in adult correctional and forensic settings, with emphasis on assessment and treatment of psychopathology and substance use, and reduction of recidivism; (2) developing and implementing diversion models for mentally ill individuals/offenders in crisis; and (3) expanding effective mental health-care models into the juvenile justice system. Dr. Antonius has published numerous journal articles, book chapters, and books on aggression, violence, emotions, mental illness, psychological assessment, forensic issues, psychometrics, and terrorism. Dr. Antonius is the recipient of several awards and grants, including from the Erie County Department of Mental Health, New York State Office of Mental Health, New York State's Sheriff's Association, Association for Threat Assessment

Professionals, International Society for Research on Aggression, and the American Psychological Foundation.

**Amy Beebe, Psy.D.** is a licensed psychologist in the state of New York. She received a doctorate in clinical psychology from the Chicago School of Professional Psychology in Chicago, IL. She has been conducting pre-employment evaluations and providing crisis intervention and trauma debriefing services for the New York City Police Department (NYPD) for three-and-a-half years. Her areas of interest include trauma, systems theory, and psychological assessment.

**Monique Bowen** received a Ph.D. in clinical psychology from The Graduate Center, CUNY. She is Associate Department Chair and core faculty at Antioch University New England. She has nearly a decade of experience in forensic psychology beginning with predoctoral training at Kings County Hospital, and later in her postdoctoral training and professional work with the forensic psychiatric evaluation court clinics serving Kings, Queens, and Richmond counties of New York. Her forensic evaluation and assessment experience spans competency to stand trial to sentencing competency, as well as expertise with specialized populations through dedicated treatment courts, including Drug and Veterans Courts, and a mental health court – precursor to an *Enhanced Treatment Track* for co-occurring psychiatric disorders. Dr. Bowen is also clinical instructor at SUNY Downstate Medical Center and co-principal investigator of a chart review study of court-involved cases of family violence in NYC. She has published on clinical issues with diverse populations and psychodynamic psychotherapy with children and families, including in the *Journal of Child and Adolescent Psychotherapy* and in *Psychoanalytic Psychology*. Her scholarly interests include family and interpersonal violence, coping and resilience in childhood and adolescence, and the application of psychoanalytic ideas to social problems.

**Thomas A. Caffrey, Ph.D.** grew up, began his education, and taught high school for 3 years in the Midwest. He moved to New York City and received his Ph.D. in clinical psychology at the psychoanalytically inclined program at City College of The City University of New York. In spite of the excellent mentoring provided by such professors as Irving Paul, Max Hertzman, Jerome Singer, and Paul Wachtel, Tom gravitated toward the Tavistock group consulting work of Larry Gould and program intervention and development work of David Twain. He wrote his dissertation on determinants of assaultive behavior among prisoners. Of the predictors he tested, maternal rejection stood out as most predictive of assault.

When he graduated, in 1974, a prison psychiatrist wedged Tom into the federal prison where she worked, as its first psychologist. Soon he was the Chief, Psychology Services, at New York City's federal Metropolitan Correctional Center. His group and systems work with Gould and Twain served to help him develop the psychology department as an integral part of the institution. In addition to establishing an institution-wide suicide prevention program that in its first year halved the number of suicidal and assaultive incidents, he consulted to the food services department, trained correctional counselors to meet with inmates' families, increased mental health staff in the department, and conducted crisis intervention with prisoners. In 1980, Tom began a private practice that specialized in helping the staff of the Southern District of New York Court to evaluate and provide mental health and substance abuse treatment to defendants facing adjudication, recently convicted, or being released from prison. For the next 35 years, he consistently received "Excellent" ratings for the consultations he provided to the court's staff and the evaluations and psychotherapy he provided to the patients.

Overlapping his years working for the Southern District were 20 years conducting custody and visitation evaluations for the family courts of New York City. These evaluations were long, thorough, and investigative. Tom was an early, active member of the New York State Psychological Association's Forensic Division, and served as its president in 2010. He followed this by helping Dr. Rafael Javier launch the postgraduate program in Basic and Advanced Postdoctoral Forensic Expertise at St. John's University. He then joined the program and graduated in its first class.

**Michelle Casarella, Psy.D.** is a New York State–licensed psychologist who practices in Westchester County. She received a doctorate in clinical psychology from the California School of Professional Psychology at Alliant International University in Sacramento, CA. Dr. Casarella has been conducting pre-employment evaluations for the New York City Police Department for over 3 years. She began a forensic private practice in August 2018 with a focus on immigration evaluations. Her areas of interest include trauma, cultural and immigration issues, women's issues, and human trafficking.

**Sarah DeMarco, Psy.D.** received her Psy.D. in clinical psychology from the Philadelphia College of Osteopathic Medicine. She previously received an M.A. in forensic psychology from John Jay College of Criminal Justice, where she later became an adjunct professor. Dr. DeMarco is a licensed psychologist in New York and New Jersey, where she currently works in private practice. Dr. DeMarco conducts a wide range of clinical and clinical-forensic mental health assessments in criminal, civil, and administrative matters. Of particular note, Dr. DeMarco has extensive experience conducting violence and sexual violence risk assessments with both adult and adolescents. Dr. DeMarco has worked in a variety of clinical-forensic and correctional settings, such as a forensic psychiatric hospital, state prisons, inpatient and outpatient substance abuse treatment centers, and a juvenile detention center.

**Susan Cohen Esquilin** is a licensed psychologist, trained in developmental and clinical psychology at the University of Chicago, with a diplomate in clinical psychology from the American Board of Professional Psychology. She has served on the faculties of Montclair State, Rutgers, and University of Medicine and Dentistry of NJ. Dr. Esquilin has testified as an expert in criminal, family court, and civil matters. She was part of a faculty that developed and taught a decade-long course sponsored by Rutgers School of Social Work and the NJ Department of Children and

Families that trained psychologists and psychiatrists to function as expert evaluators in child protection matters. She is the author of curricula developed for staff of the state child protective agency on cultural competency, on child traumatic stress, and on facilitating relationships between birth and resource parents. Dr. Esquilin has presented at both state and national conferences, and regularly teaches continuing education programs at Rutgers School of Social Work for the NJ Children's System of Care through University Behavioral HealthCare in NJ and for Court Appointed Special Advocates in Essex County. She serves on the Model Court Committee in Essex County and is a member of its Equity and Fairness as well as Child Well-Being Subcommittees. Dr. Esquilin is a past president of the New Jersey Chapter of the American Professional Society on the Abuse of Children. She was named Psychologist of the Year for 2017 by the New Jersey Psychological Association, serves on its Committee on Diversity and Inclusion, is the co-chair of the Immigration Emergency Action Group, and is currently president of the Essex-Union County Association of Psychologists.

**William E. Foote** has been a forensic psychologist in private practice in Albuquerque, New Mexico, since 1979. He is an affiliate faculty member of the University of New Mexico Department of Psychology and has taught in the UNM School of Law. He has held a number of professional offices including the president of the New Mexico Psychological Association, representative on APA Council, member and chair of the APA Committee on Legal Issues, member and chair of the APA Committee on Professional Practice and Standards, president of Division 31, president of Division 41, and president of the American Board of Forensic Psychology. He is the author of many peer-reviewed professional articles and book chapters, and is the co-author, with Jane Goodman-Delahunty of two books on psychological evaluation in sexual harassment and employment discrimination cases. Dr. Foote enjoys singing first tenor in the acapella men's group DeProfundis, playing guitar and mandolin, traveling, hiking, and fly fishing.

**I. Bruce Frumkin** is board-certified in clinical and forensic psychology from the American Board of Professional Psychology. He is a nationally recognized expert in the areas of capacity to waive Miranda rights and false/coerced confessions. Dr. Frumkin is director of Forensic and Clinical Psychology Associates with offices in New York, Miami, Philadelphia, and Chicago.

**James Garbarino, Ph.D.** holds the Maude C. Clarke Chair in Humanistic Psychology and was founding director of the Center for the Human Rights of Children at Loyola University Chicago. Among the books he has authored are *Listening to Killers: Lessons Learned from My 20 Years as a Psychological Expert Witness in Murder Cases (2015), Miller's Children: Why Giving Teenage Killers a Second Chance Matters for All of Us (2018), and Lost Boys: Why Our Sons Turn Violent and How We Can Save Them (1999)*. In 1989, he received the American Psychological Association's Award for Distinguished Professional Contributions to Public Service.

**Robert Geffner, PhD, ABPP** is President and Founder of IVAT, a nonprofit international resource, training, and direct service center, formerly known as the Family Violence & Sexual Assault Institute (FVSAI). He was a Professor of Psychology at the University of Texas at Tyler and is now a Distinguished Research Professor of Psychology at Alliant International University in San Diego and Editor of four professional peer-reviewed journals (including the *Journal of Child Sexual Abuse, Journal of Child & Adolescent Trauma, Journal of Child Custody,* and *Journal of Aggression, Maltreatment & Trauma*).

He has a Diplomate in Clinical Neuropsychology from the American Board of Professional Neuropsychology and is Board Certified in Couple and Family Psychology from the American Board of Professional Psychology. He is a Licensed Clinician (Psychologist in CA and in TX and Marriage and Family Therapist in CA) and directed a full-service private practice mental health clinic in East Texas for over 15 years prior to relocating to California 20 years ago. He has written, edited, coauthored, or coedited over 100 published professional books, chapters, journal articles, and technical reports on a variety of topic areas related to violence, child abuse, sexual assaults, victimization, and trauma.

He is a Founding Member and Past President of the American Psychological Association Division of Trauma Psychology, Founding Co-chair and Immediate Past President of the National Partnership to End Interpersonal Violence Across the Lifespan (NPEIV), and Past President of the American Academy of Couple and Family Psychology. He has been a Researcher, Trainer, Practitioner, and Consultant for about 40 years.

**Hannah L. Geller, Ph.D.** received her M.S. in psychology from the Moscow State University in Russian Federation. She immigrated to the USA and continued her education, earning an M.A. and a Ph.D. in clinical psychology from the Long Island University in Brooklyn, N.Y. Dr. Geller completed predoctoral and postdoctoral training in neuropsychology and is interested in the intersection of neurological and psychological conditions, especially in the forensic context. Dr. Geller is an adjunct professor at the John Jay University of Criminal Justice, where she teaches neuropsychology, psychopathology, and clinical interviewing. Dr. Geller evaluates sex offenders for civil management for the New York State Office of Mental Health. An additional special interest of Dr. Geller is transgender health. She has a private practice in New York City, where she offers psychological and neuropsychological assessments, as well as psychotherapy. Dr. Geller volunteers some of her time to provide free evaluations for asylum seekers in the USA. In her free time, she enjoys museums, horses, and travel.

**Lori Heusel, B.A.** received a Bachelor of Arts degree in Psychology, with a minor in Criminal Justice, from Indiana University-Purdue University Indianapolis (IUPUI) in 2017. She is nearing completion of a Master of Arts degree in Clinical Mental Health Counseling at Valparaiso University and will soon begin her counseling career in both school and correctional settings. As a member of the Psychology, Law, and Trauma Lab at Valparaiso University, Ms. Heusel's research interests include trauma-based therapy, specifically related to working with adolescents in the juvenile justice system. Her clinical interests include working with incarcerated juveniles and adults, youth in school settings, and addictions.

**Marcia P. Hirsch** is an Acting Justice of the Queens County Supreme Court, Criminal Term, in the 11th Judicial District of New York. She was appointed to this position in 2005. She received her undergraduate degree from Union College and her JD degree from Syracuse Law School in 1978. In the same year, she became Assistant Counsel to the New York State Higher Education Services Corp. The following year, she worked as an Administrative Law Judge for the NYS Department of Social Services. In 1980, she became an Associate of the law firm of *Mandell & Mandell* and then worked as Counsel to RKM Enterprise in 1983 and 1984. She was in private practice from 1984 to 1990 and was a partner of the firm *Horing Welikson & Rosen, P.C.* from 1990 to 1995. In 1995, she became Acting General Counsel to the NYS Division of Housing and Community Renewal and General Counsel to this division from 1997 until her judicial appointment in 2005.

**Raina V. Lamade** received her Ph.D. in clinical psychology with a concentration in forensic psychology from Fairleigh Dickinson University and completed her internship at the Northport Veterans Affairs Medical Center. She was trained at forensic, inpatient, and outpatient settings in the New York Metropolitan area and completed postdoctoral training programs in forensic psychology at St. John's University. Dr. Lamade completed a four-year research postdoctoral fellowship where she managed a national study funded by the Department of Justice SMART Office grant that developed and pilot tested an intervention to treat college students found responsible of sexual misconduct. Dr. Lamade has conducted psychological evaluations for various Problem-Solving Courts in New York City, and competency to stand trial evaluations in criminal court for New York City Health and Hospitals Corporation. Dr. Lamade is an assistant professor of psychology at the University of Massachusetts Dartmouth and maintains a private forensic assessment practice. She serves as an ad hoc reviewer for two professional journals, has published in professional journals, and has presented at various conferences.

**Marko Lamela** is a third-year doctoral candidate at St. John's University under the supervisions of Dr. Rafael A. Javier and Dr. Robin Wellington. His research interests include social justice in relation to psychological treatment, psychological treatment in minority groups, and the possible moderating factors of dementia. He can be contacted at marko.lamela17@stjohns.edu.

**Rachel M. Lee** is a licensed mental health counselor with a master's degree from Hunter College. Rachel is an adjunct lecturer at Hunter College, as well as a psychotherapist with background specializations in criminal justice, substance abuse, career counseling, and trauma. Rachel has coordinated several SAMHSA grants and participated in problem-solving courts, as well as outpatient substance abuse settings, community mental health clinics, and private practice.

**Melissa C. Leeolou** graduated from Fordham University in 2016 with a BS in Psychology and a BA in Theology.

**Corey M. Leidenfrost** is a research assistant professor and the associate training director of the Psychology Doctoral Internship Program in the Department of Psychiatry at University at Buffalo. He is a psychologist with Erie County Forensic Mental Health Services where he conducts forensic evaluations and works with individuals with serious mental illness and suicidality in a large county jail system. Dr. Leidenfrost also serves as the unit chief for a psychiatric intensive care unit, working with individuals who are high risk for violence due to acute symptoms of serious mental illness. His research interests include the efficacy of mental health services, along with reducing recidivism for individuals with serious mental illness in a correctional setting and violence among individuals with serious mental illness. Dr. Leidenfrost has published several journal articles and a book chapter on psychological well-being among an incarcerated seriously mentally ill population, the efficacy of treatment in jail, and the associations between substance use and crime. He has presented at several local-, state-, and national-level professional conferences.

**Rachel Lindsay, B.A.** received a Bachelor of Arts degree in Psychology from Northern Illinois University in 2017. As an undergraduate student, Ms. Lindsay was a member of several research teams and primarily studied emotional regulation in children and various trauma-exposed populations. She is nearing completion of a Master of Arts degree in Clinical Mental Health Counseling at Valparaiso University and will soon begin a position as a staff counselor at Behavior Specialists of Indiana in Valparaiso, IN. During her time at Valparaiso University, Ms. Lindsay was a member of the Psychology, Law, and Trauma lab, served as the Psychology Department graduate student research assistant, and co-founded Valparaiso University's first Counselors for Social Justice chapter. Ms. Lindsay's clinical interests include working with individuals with intellectual and developmental disabilities, children, and adolescents.

**Gene McCullough** is a psychiatric nurse practitioner in the Department of Psychiatry at Mount Sinai West Hospital, New York. He has over 30 years experience evaluating and treating patients in psychiatric and substance abuse settings. He has conducted research in the areas of psychiatry and forensics and has published in the *Journal of the American Academy of Psychiatry and the Law, Psychiatric Annals,* and the *International Journal of Law and Psychiatry*

**Danielle Nesi, M.A.** is a doctoral student in the Developmental Psychology program at Loyola University Chicago. Her general research interests include forensic developmental psychology and issues related to juvenile justice. Danielle's most current work investigates risk and resiliency in adolescents and emerging adults and interventions to promote positive outcomes for justice-involved individuals.

**Cheryl Paradis** received her Psy.D. in clinical psychology from Yeshiva University. She is a professor at Marymount Manhattan College and a psychologist with the Manhattan Forensic Psychiatric Evaluation Court Clinic. She has approximately 30 years experience evaluating defendants in several areas including competency to stand trial, competency to waive Miranda rights, and mental state at the time of the offense. She is also trained in psychodiagnostic and neuropsychological testing. Dr. Paradis has conducted research in the areas of forensic psychology, neuropsychology, and cross-cultural issues. She has published in journals including *The Journal of the American Academy of Psychiatry and the Law, Psychiatric Annals*, and the *International Journal of Law and Psychiatry*. In 2010, she published a forensic casebook entitled *The Measure of Madness: Inside the Disturbed and Disturbing Criminal Mind*.

**Alan Perry** is an Associate Professor of Psychology and the Deputy Chair of the Department of Psychology at the Lander College for Men and has a private forensic psychology consulting practice. He earned his PhD from Fordham University. Over the years, he has been the Director of Psychological Services at Kings County Hospital and Clinical Assistant Professor of Psychiatry at Downstate Medical Center as well as Deputy Director of Mental Health Services at Rikers Island.

**Mary Kelly Persyn** is an attorney, author, and children's advocate in San Francisco, California. She is the owner of Persyn Law & Policy and serves as senior director, Legal & Strategy at New Teacher Center; chair of the Board of Directors of the Center for Youth Wellness; member of the Amicus and Policy Committee of the American Professional Society on the Abuse of Children (2018 Special Recognition Award); member of the California Campaign to Counter Childhood Adversity; and member of the Leadership Council of Children Now. She has published articles on childhood adversity in *Poverty & Race*, the journal of the Poverty & Race Research Action Council (PRRAC), and has represented the American Professional Society on the Abuse of Children as *amicus curiae* in cases involving childhood adversity and maltreatment in the Second, Fourth, and Ninth Circuit Courts of Appeal and the United States Supreme Court. Prior to her current roles, Persyn was a government enforcement and appellate associate at law firms in Boston and San Francisco and served as a judicial law clerk in the US Court of Appeals for the Ninth Circuit. Driven by compassion, integrity, justice, and a fierce love of children, Persyn's work raises public awareness of childhood adversity and advocates for the interventions that strengthen resilience and improve lifetime outcomes for children who have experienced trauma. Persyn received a Ph.D. in English Literature from the University of Washington and a J.D. from Columbia Law School.

**Caitlin Prater, B.A.** is a graduate from Loyola University Chicago with a Psychology Major and a Philosophy Minor. She worked on the psychology poster CaLM: Children Learning Mindfulness Strategies for Self-regulation in Head Start Classrooms based on Lab Research. She was a Medical and Legal Advocate for Resilience (or also known as Rape Victim Advocates (RVA)), and now, she is a police officer for the city of Alpharetta in Georgia. Her dream is to work with the Federal Bureau of Investigations to stop child molesters and focus on finding missing children. She continues to expand her education in order to help children who have experienced traumatic situations.

**Gimel Rogers, PsyD** is a Licensed Psychologist and the Training Director of the Professional Clinical and Forensic Services Department at the Institute on Violence, Abuse, and Trauma (IVAT). She earned her doctorate from Pepperdine University and has provided trauma-focused care with clients from the Children of the Night Program, the Ventura Youth Correctional Facility, the FCI Terminal Island, and community programs serving survivors of intimate partner violence.

She presently works with survivors who are recovering from emotional, physical, and sexual abuse. Additionally, she assists clients who are involved in criminal, family, and civil cases involving a broad range of forensic issues. Having published in the areas of culture, coping, spirituality, and trauma, she is an Adjunct Professor at Pepperdine University and Point Loma Nazarene University.

**Devora Panish Scher** is a doctoral student in school psychology at the Graduate School of Applied and Professional Psychology at Rutgers University. As a forensic extern at the Kings County Hospital Center, Devora received training in evaluating defendants' competencies to stand trial, spotlighting for her the crucial need for early and effective clinical treatment. Formerly a middle school teacher, Devora has more recently pursued clinical and school externships at the Queens Hospital Center, New York Presbyterian, and Cresskill Public Schools (New Jersey). She is interested in dialectical behavior therapy, working with youth experiencing emotional dysregulation and those impacted by trauma. Her doctoral research focuses on self-regulated learning and examines the effects of DBT STEPS-A on urban, low-income school populations.

**Morgan Shaw, PsyD** is a Licensed Clinical and Forensic Psychologist. She currently serves as the Director of Professional Services at the Institute on Violence, Abuse, and Trauma. She provides trauma-informed therapeutic services to a variety of adolescent and adult clients and specializes in working with individuals who have a history of child abuse. She also conducts comprehensive forensic evaluations and provides expert witness testimony in criminal, family, and civil cases involving a broad range of forensic issues.

She also serves as the Coeditor in Chief for the *Journal of Aggression, Maltreatment & Trauma, Journal of Child Sexual Abuse,* and *Journal of Child Custody*, as well as the Publications Coordinator for the *Journal of Child and Adolescent Trauma.*

**Harold Takooshian, PhD** has been on the faculty of Fordham University since 1975, where he is Professor of Psychology, Urban Studies, and Organizational Leadership. He completed his Ph.D. in Psychology in 1979 at the City University of New York with Stanley Milgram and Florence L. Denmark. He is a researcher, teacher, consultant, and U.S. Fulbright Scholar, whose work is described in Marquis' *Who's Who in the World*. He has taught at 12 institutions in 6 nations. At Fordham, he has co-taught Law and Psychology annually since 1979, with attorneys Robert Emmons and Jon David Sherry. The URL of his website is https://takooshian.social-psychology.org/

**Denise M. Williams Johnson, Ph.D.INC.** received her Ph.D. in clinical psychology from Emory University in Atlanta Georgia. She is a New Jersey–licensed psychologist who has been in private practice for over 25 years. Her office is currently located in West Orange, NJ.

Dr. Johnson has had a contract to provide psychological services to the New Jersey Division of Child Protection and Permanency (DCP&P) for the past 25 years. Those services have included psychotherapy, consultation, psychological evaluations for case planning, and psychological and bonding evaluations for Termination of Parental Rights litigation. Dr. Johnson has provided psychological and bonding evaluations for about 15 years to the New Jersey Law Guardian's Office, and to the New Jersey Office of Adult Representation. She has also served as an expert witness in child protective service cases and in other forensic cases.

Some of Dr. Johnson's other professional experiences include psychological services to a primarily inner-city, African descent population; supervision, consultation, and presentations about cultural and spiritual issues in evaluations and treatment; and performance consultation to professional sports organizations, high school/college athletes, and business executives.

For the past 5 years, Dr. Johnson has also had her own radio show, aired in the Atlanta GA and Washington DC areas, that integrates spirituality, cultural issues, and emotional wellness.

**Amanda D. Zelechoski, J.D., Ph.D., ABPP** is a licensed clinical and forensic psychologist and attorney. Dr. Zelechoski received her B.A. from the University of Notre Dame, her M.S. and Ph.D. from Drexel University, and her J.D. from Villanova University School of Law. She completed a postdoctoral fellowship at The Trauma Center at Justice Resource Institute (Brookline, MA) and is board certified in Clinical Child and Adolescent Psychology. She has worked clinically with adults, children, and families in inpatient, outpatient, and forensic settings. Currently, Dr. Zelechoski is an associate professor of psychology at Valparaiso University. She teaches a wide variety of psychology and counseling courses and provides clinical supervision to graduate students. As the director of the Psychology, Law, and Trauma Lab, her primary research interests include trauma in at-risk and delinquent youth and forensic mental health assessment. In addition, Dr. Zelechoski is an associate editor for *Law and Human Behavior*, a risk management consultant for The Trust, and provides training and consultation to numerous mental health, law enforcement, and correctional agencies.

# Chapter 1
# Trauma and its Vicissitudes in Forensic Contexts: An Introduction

Rafael Art. Javier and Elizabeth A. Owen

## On the Pervasiveness of Trauma: Its Normal and Pathologial Trajectory

Trauma is an experience that, depending on how it is defined, can be considered pervasive and ubiquitous to all human experiences, although it is not unique to human beings. In its simplest form, it is a reaction of the organism/individual to unexpected changes in its otherwise reasonably predictable environment (Hartmann, 1958; Russell, 1998) that causes a temporary or permanent disruption of functions in those affected and forces some kind of action. An example from the botanical world is of a plant whose growth may become compromised if the soil composition is changed due to lack of water or the presence of serious contaminants in the environment that challenge the plant's ability to thrive/survive. We can also find a number of examples in pet animals (like dogs) whose response to inhospitable environment that is characterized by serious and prolonged mistreatment and abuse could be one of fear of human interactions; once in that state, these animals may show antagonistic reactions to any human approaching/invading their space, which could include growling or outright vicious attack (attempts at biting to repel the object of the threat); such a maneuver can be considered more defensive than offensive in nature. It could also include a partial or total surrender out of exhaustion as if in the midst of an anaclitic depression.

In the case of humans, there are various reactions to real or perceived conditions that we may experience as threatening and unsafe. These could include physiological and psychological reactions, such as heart palpitation, sweating, tightening of

R. A. Javier (✉)
Psychology, St. John's University, Queens, NY, USA
e-mail: javierr@stjohns.edu

E. A. Owen
Columbia University/Teachers College, New York, NY, USA

© Springer Nature Switzerland AG 2020
R. A. Javier et al. (eds.), *Assessing Trauma in Forensic Contexts*,
https://doi.org/10.1007/978-3-030-33106-1_1

1

muscles, loss of appetite, anxiety, fear, dread, panic, and all the typical range of emotions associated with PTSD. The ultimate goal of these reactions is to force us to act and to find a more secure and predictable situation; in the process, we end up developing strategies (coping schemes) that are meant to ensure that the conditions which created the threat are kept under control at whatever cost; that may also include avoiding and developing phobic reactions to any situation where the possibility of being hurt is even remotely possible. We can observe these types of reactions in a case of a child who gets badly hurt while playing with his friends, resulting in serious bruises and a broken arm; as a result, he is now forced to wear a brace that renders him unable to play for a while and thus disrupting (hopefully, only temporarily) future enjoyable outings with his friends; lingering fear may include the possibility of reinjuring the same arm or breaking the other if he is not careful enough, thus forcing the child to change the ways of interacting with the environment and friends out of the need to protect him/herself from future harms. That could mean no bicycle, no sports, no taking airplanes, or traveling in general, etc. The fear then sometimes develops into a psychological scar, representing the physical wound that, in the child's mind, could become reopened if faced with similar or remotely similar situations.

This concept of a 'psychological scar' likely to be left by the 'wounds' resulting from traumatic experiences can be more clearly seen in another example of a young man who is assaulted by three masked young men with knives in the front foyer of his building (considered a safe haven), and who threatened to do great harm to him if he did not cooperate and comply. He felt the sharp edge of these knives by his neck and thigh, while hearing/feeling the heavy breathing of these men on him, who have managed to put him in a lock hold from behind, making him unable to move freely. It was clear that they meant business. They stripped him of all his belonging (e.g., watch, cash, etc.) and then threatened to take him to a more isolated place (his own apartment) to complete their deeds. Feeling quite alone and abandoned to his own destiny, somehow he was able to escape physically unharmed, but became overwhelmed with recurrent and lingering fear that it could happen again. Most immediately, he became suspicious (hyper vigilant) about everyone he did not recognize for fear that these men, whose faces he could not see because of the masks, were still watching him to complete the job they started. His suspiciousness went as far as wondering whether someone who knew him was also involved in the assault. Even years later, he would still become overtaken by tremendous tension and trepidation whenever approaching the front of his building where it all happened. The whole experience was now engrained in his body-memory (sensory organization), which would become activated even when inside his apartment, thinking of what could have happened if they had succeeded in their goal. He was now saddled with a recurrent fear of pending danger and hyper vigilance that were generalized to other similar conditions/situations.

These last two examples represent the kind of physical and psychological impact on functioning which may result when something unexpected and dangerous happens in an individual's life that forces a reconsideration of previously safe way of dealing with the world. These types of experiences are likely to prompt necessary changes in one's previous behavioral repertoire. We are aware that, although our reactions to disruptions and traumatic and threatening events are normally guided by the same evolutionary and biologically influenced need for self-preservation, there are specific personal qualities that determine the ultimate resolution of traumatic events. We are referring to those personal qualities that are developed in the course of our early developmental trajectory and that have been found to determine the different ways we are likely to react to stressful/threatening conditions in general (Allen & Fonagy, 2017). According to some authors, these personal qualities are developed in the context of our early attachment reactions in relationship with our caretakers (Mikulincer & Shaver, 2017).

Several scholars have taken great pains to describe the processes involved in our becoming a fully developed and capable organism able to organize, categorize, and remember experiences of things/situations that occur; this ability is expected to ensure our psychological and physical survival. There are optimal conditions for the development of these important developmental milestones. Under these conditions, the individual can typically develop a strong and solid sense of self as a secure, loved, relevant, capable, and efficacious individual; able to modulate/regulate and use emotions that are appropriate to the circumstances; able to adapt to different situations; and whose ability to think remains flexible and goal directed. That is, a well-integrated individual is expected to emerge out of an interpersonal environment where he/she is guided to venture and engage with that environment and feels protected (Ainsworth & Bell, 1970; Ainsworth, Blehar, Waters, & Wall, 1978; Mahler, Pine, & Bergman, 1975; Sullivan, 1955). However, when the interpersonal environment is not optimal, when that environment is fraught with disruptions, something else happens that has been found to disrupt development and complicate the individual's quality of life and his/her ability to develop healthy relationships.

Several studies have highlighted how different types of complicated attachments are developed as a consequence of types of environments that cause severe disruptions in interpersonal relationships with others during the early developmental process and subsequently. According to these authors, a disruption can occur at various times during the individual's developmental trajectory with different degrees of implications. The earlier and more severe the disruption, the more likely to detour and/or seriously compromise any possibility for a viable sustainability in the future for some individuals (Ainsworth & Bell, 1970; Bowlby, 1988), while for others with well-developed resilience, this effect is less disruptive and debilitating, if present at all. The development of personality characteristics and behavioral disorders (e.g., borderline personality disorders, psychopathic tendencies, etc.) have been found to be influenced by the quality of these earlier experiences (Allen & Fonagy, 2017; Garbarino, 2015), and associated with the development of different attachment constellations in these individuals (e.g., secure, avoidant, resistant, disorganized, and disordered attachments) (Ainsworth et al., 1978; Bowlby, 1988; Mikulincer & Shaver, 2017). These constellations can be described as different cognitive and affective organizations profoundly ingrained in the person's psychic structure that later guide his/her general relationship with the world (e.g., whom to trust and to fear, what situation to avoid, how to select friends and romantic partners, etc.). A *secure attachment* is found in individuals who develop in the context of an environment sensitive and responsive to their needs. Someone with a secure attachment is more likely to be able to face different challenges and stresses from the environment with equanimity and a general sense that things will ultimately be okay. That is, that they do not become emotionally and cognitively disorganized, and if they do, it is only briefly. This is someone who is able to develop confidence and trust in others, and able to tolerate and engage intimacy. Several authors have elucidated the conditions (e.g., the nature/quality of the response/intervention by the caretaker during critical developmental moments) that have been found to moderate the effect of psychological injuries (or traumatic conditions) on the individual that result in the development of healthy attachment reaction (Ainsworth & Bell, 1970; Ainsworth et al., 1978; Mahler et al., 1975; Sullivan, 1955).

Someone with an *insecure attachment*, on the other hand, tends to develop a relationship style where the bond with others can become easily contaminated by fear; this is normally expressed in difficulties dealing with mixed emotions and these individuals become particularly sensitive to any real or perceived rejections. Individuals with an insecure attachment have been found to be at risk for intimate partner violence and other interpersonal difficulties (Allen & Fonagy, 2017; Almeida, Ramalho, Fernandez, & Guarda, 2019). An *avoidant attachment* is found to develop in the context of an insensitive or overly neglectful environment; those with this type of attachment are prone to denial and isolation of affect under stress. These are individuals who tend not to feel comfortable with emotions and consequently they are apt to deny their feelings, particularly in cases of negative and disruptive emotions (such as anger, fear, etc.). They are liable to have trouble with intimacy and trust, and great difficulty tolerating intense emotions; the tendency is to break away and demand distance from their partners, blaming them for becoming too clinging and demanding. They do better in situations that allow for contained, predictable, shallower, and not too intimate or intense romantic connections.

A *resistant attachment* tends to develop in the context of an insensitive or overly intrusive environment (characterized by expressed anger or passivity or passive-aggression mode). These are individuals who are very sensitive to separation, normally experienced as profound personal rejection. The tendency is then to remain emotionally removed from others based on their experience of a caretaker who was unable to be available to meet basic needs whether physical or emotional. Individuals with borderline personality organizations have been described as showing these qualities of relating (Kernberg, 1975). A *disorganized attachment* tends to develop in the context of a fearful or frightening-abusive and unpredictable and fragmented environment. These individuals tend to understand others' intentions as purposely and intentionally attempting to do them harm and hence their need to remain ready to defend themselves. There is a tendency toward dissociation. Individuals with a paranoid organization have been described as showing these qualities of relating (Kernberg, 1975). Finally, a *disordered attachment* tends to develop in the context of an absent or profoundly neglectful environment where the individual is left alone to make sense out of the world around and unable to negotiate because they have been deprived of the role model normally played by the caregiver and are left without a point of reference.

## Trauma and Its Pervasive Presence in Forensic Issues

Trauma has been found to permeate the lives of many notorious criminals in our society. In Table 1.1, we can see early histories of abuse and neglect, abandonment, history of substance abuse and criminality even in parents or caretakers (an early trauma history), all suggesting the necessary conditions for the development of some types of attachment disorders preceding their history of criminality (Garbarino, 2015). To that point, we have put together a list of case studies (Chap. 21 – Trauma and Its Criminal Trajectory) of individuals who have engaged in different types of criminal acts over the years (from fraud, to serial killings, to school shootings, sexual predators, etc.), where the reader is able to look at the personal trauma histories, the types of attachments likely to have developed in these individuals, and the crimes they committed. It is clear that the different attachment styles, once developed, have been found to affect the individuals' response to future traumatic experiences; these attachment styles have been found to be intimately implicated in the development of personality disorders and many criminal behaviors (Allen & Fonagy, 2017; Garbarino, 2015; Mikulincer & Shaver, 2017).

The challenge to the forensic professional is to be able to determine the extent to which an individual's earlier attachment experience is implicated in future responses to difficult conditions (Smith & Stover, 2016) that become the subject of the assessment. This is particularly the case in view of the fact that, although traumatic conditions permeate the lives of many in our society and are inescapable components of the lives of many individuals (Richardson, Freeh, & Acierno, 2010; Rojas-Flores, Clements, Koo, & London, 2017), not everyone who has experienced early trauma ends up involved in the justice system as defendants or victims. When we consider the number of victims of assaults and random shootings in subways, movie theaters, malls, entertainment centers, school grounds, places of worship, one's communities, at a restaurant, and even at one's own living quarters (https://www.ncjrs.gov/pdffiles1/bjs/104274.pdf), it is not unusual to hear that most of us have been affected. To that, we can add anti-immigrant sentiments, racism, and discrimination that many in our society are forced to endure and the frequent acts of terrorism within the country and many parts of the world. When we consider all these threats, it may feel to many that we are not safe and should remain vigilant at all times. However, the reactions to these situations are likely to be influenced by the quality of early and subsequent personal experiences.

Statistics supporting the general sense of unsafety are found in a recent report by the Bureau of Justice Statistics (2019) that focuses on school settings. In this report, we find that there were 827,000 of total victimizations (e.g., theft and nonfatal violent victimization) at school and 503,800 total victimizations away from school among students aged 12–18; there were 153 killed or wounded in active shooting incidents at elementary and secondary schools, and 143 casualties in active school shooting incidents in postsecondary institutions. Also reported is the concern of gang activities in school, with 20% of students between the ages 12–18 reporting that they were bullied at school during the school year, and with 16% of students in grades 9–12 deciding to carry a weapon to defend themselves (e.g., a gun, knife, or

**Table 1.1** Life trajectory of some of notorious/convicted criminals (created by the authors)

| Name | Early history | Crime committed |
|------|---------------|-----------------|
| Aileen Wuornos: The Florida Highway Killer | Abandoned by her mother as babies, Aileen and her brother, Keith, grew up with their grandparents Lauri and Britta Wuornos who adopted them. | Wuornos' crimes spanned from 1989 to 1990. |
| | She believed they were her parents until the age of 11. Her biological father was Leo Pittman. He was a child molester who killed himself in prison. | She continued her work as a prostitute on the highways of Florida, killing seven men between ages 41–65. |
| | As a child, she claimed to have been beaten and whipped often by her grandfather. Reportedly, she was forced to lay face down and naked, telling her she was "evil," "wicked," "worthless," and that she should have never been born; that she wasn't worthy of the air she breathed. | Aileen procured victims by hitchhiking and all were victims of opportunity. |
| | As a teenager, Aileen was known for her temper characterized by unpredictable anger outbursts and usually unprovoked. | She killed her victims with multiple 0.22 caliber rounds. There were 2–9 gunshots per victim and at least three were left nude. |
| | She was thrown out of parties for being vulgar, drunk, and starting fights. | She would leave the bodies in wooded areas near state or interstate highways. |
| | She performed sexual acts with boys for cigarettes and money. | The victims' cars were left miles away from their bodies, sometimes in different counties. Money or personal belongings were stolen from almost her victims. |
| | At age 14, she had a baby and gave him up for adoption. It was unclear who the father was. | She pleaded no contest to the murders of Dick Humphreys, Troy Burress, and David Spears and maintained that Richard Mallory had violently raped her as the reason for killing him and claimed that the others only tried to rape her. Wuornos was given three death sentences. |
| | Once her grandmother died she was displaced from her grandparents' home, ending up in Florida at 16 where she began working as a prostitute. | Wuornos also pleaded guilty to the killing of Charles Carskaddon for which she received another death sentence. |
| | At 20, she married a 70-year-old man. The marriage lasted a month, as Aileen's husband filed for a divorce and a restraining order against her for beating him with his own cane. | In 1993, she pleaded guilty to the death of Walter Jeno Antonio, and received yet another death sentence. |
| | | In the case of Peter Siems, the body was never found, and she could not be tried for his murder. |
| | | She was killed by lethal injection on October 9, 2002, in Florida State Prison. |
| | | Arrigo and Griffin (2004), Broomfield (2014), Myers, Gooch, and Meloy (2005). |

| Name | Early history | Crime committed |
|---|---|---|
| Albert Fish | Born on May 19, 1870, in Washington, D.C., and abandoned by his parents (father ages 75 years old, and mother 32) lived in an orphanage until the age of 9 years old.<br><br>Fish lived a brutal life in the orphanage. Reportedly, he was beaten regularly and exposed to sadistic acts of brutality; reportedly he was unmercifully whipped and observed other boys engaged in wrong activities.<br><br>When he was only 12, he was introduced to urolagnia (drinking urine) and coprophagy (eating feces). These acts uncovered Fish's paraphilic tendencies through the humiliation of himself or his partner, and the intense sexual urges associated with the thought of urine.<br><br>He later spent a great amount of his weekends lurking public baths, where he would watch other boys undressed. This uncovered his voyeuristic affinities (also known as peeping or onlooking).<br><br>Fish's paraphilic impulses eventually led him to an obsession with mutilation of self and other. | Most serious criminal history started in 1919 when Fish's obsession with torture and cannibalism – eating raw meat for dinner, and occasionally feeding his children the raw meat as well – that led him to plan an actual murder.<br><br>Fish molested mostly boys under the age of six. He would also expose himself to his victims. Fish often targeted vulnerable children, and paid boys to obtain other children for him. He eventually tortured, molested, mutilated, and murdered several young children.<br><br>In looking for boys to torture, Albert Fish found 10-year-old Grace Budd after putting up an ad in the news in May of 1928 in the hopes of "hiring" a boy for his farm. Upon visiting the Budd family to interview their son, daughter Grace Budd fell victim to Fish at first sight. Fish seemed like the typical "loving grandfather" whom occasionally bore gifts. Grace was invited by Fish to a children's party, along with brother Edward, and the unsuspecting parents accepted.<br><br>It wasn't until 6 years later that a grotesque letter sent by Fish to the Budd house described the rape, mutilation, and consumption of grace Budd, after drinking her blood. Fish was caught, arrested, and immediately began confessing to the killing, mutilation, and molestation of Grace and hundreds of other children.<br><br>The jury found him sane, and guilty, and was executed by the electric chair on January 16, 1936 at Sing Prison in New York.<br><br>Blanco (2017), Fink (2015), Montaldo (2018), Peters (2017), Serena (2018). |

(continued)

**Table 1.1** (continued)

| Name | Early history | Crime committed |
|---|---|---|
| Charles Manson | Charles Manson was born November 12, 1934, in Cincinnati Ohio.<br><br>Mother was 16 at the age of his birth and he never knew his father.<br><br>His mother was described as an alcoholic and a criminal. She was arrested for armed robbery when he 9 years old forcing him to move in with his Aunt and Uncle in West Virginia.<br><br>He was sold as a child by his mother for a pitch of beer, and was under the care of multiple people who all were bad experiences.<br><br>He would often get into trouble at school.<br><br>He engaged in petty crimes when he was younger.<br><br>1947 –at 12 years old, Manson is sent to Gibault School for stealing. Over the next 20 years he was in and out of reform schools & prison. | Manson exited his first juvenile facility at the age of 10 and attempted to live with his mother again; this was unsuccessful.<br><br>His crime picked up after this event, and he was eventually sent to Indiana's' Boys School, a reformatory school where he escaped 3 days later.<br><br>Manson was paroled at age 19 in 1954 but by 1961 he was serving a 10-year sentence for check forgery.<br><br>1956–1966 he was in and out of prison:<br>  Stole cars, probation revoked, pimping, stealing checks, committing crimes cross state lines.<br><br>During this prison stay, he began to study various religious teachings including Scientology, as well as continue to study music.<br><br>In this period, he began to desire to become a superstar and was heavily influenced by the Beatles and the effects they had on the world.<br><br>Manson was released after 7 years on Parole and made his way to San Francisco.<br><br>He became heavily involved in psychedelic drugs and the Counter Culture (Hippie) movement, which provided him with a platform to attract his followers.<br><br>Carried out more than 30 killings with his followers<br><br>First known murder: Gary Hinman on July 25, 1969.<br><br>August 9, 1969, Manson told followers to kill actress Sharon Tate (who was pregnant at the time) & her husband director Roman Polanski, along friend visitors who were at the house. Sentenced to death. When the death penalty was ruled unconstitutional in 1972, he was resentenced to life.<br><br>Died in prison on November 19, 2017<br><br>A&E (2018), Altman (2015), Bullis (1985), Charles Manson: Helter skelter and beyond (n.d.), Charles Manson (1995), Guinn (2014), Linder (2007). |

| | | |
|---|---|---|
| Colin Ferguson | Born on January 14th, 1958 in Kingston, Jamaica | In 1992, his ex-wife filed a complaint stating Ferguson pried open the trunk of her car. |
| | His father, Von Herman Ferguson, was a wealthy and influential pharmacist who was described by Time magazine as "one of the most prominent businessman in Jamaica." | In February of 1992, Ferguson was arrested and charged for harassing a woman on the subway. |
| | Lived luxuriously in a large home with nannies and housekeepers. | The woman, who was white, tried to sit next to Ferguson when he started to scream at her and press his elbow and leg against her. |
| | Described as a well-rounded student that played sports such as cricket and soccer while also performing at the top of his class consistently. | Police came to the scene and pinned him down; he attempted to escape the police while shouting for help. |
| | In 1978, Ferguson's father died in a car crash and his mother died of cancer a few years later. | Claimed police brutality which was investigated and then dismissed. |
| | This destroyed his family's fortune and also deeply disturbed Ferguson | Moved to California in April 1993 for a new career, but was unsuccessful after applying for several jobs. However, he purchased a pistol there which would become the crime weapon. |
| | Ferguson left for America in 1982 with a Visitor's Visa. | Moved back to New York City a month later. |
| | According to family and friends, he had a hard time dealing with racism as well as not getting any meaningful jobs. | According to his landlord and neighbors, he was becoming increasingly mentally unstable. |
| | Married Audrey Warren in May 13, 1986; that marriage was soon in trouble as they fought a lot and sometimes police were involved | He began talking about a revolution in the future where black people would rise up and strike their oppressors. |
| | Got divorced 2 years later, Colin stating they had "different social views," while Audrey stating that he was "too aggressive and antagonistic." | On December 7, 1993, Ferguson purchased a ticket at Penn Station and boarded the third car of an eastbound LIRR 5:33 train. |
| | He attended Nassau Community College where he was disciplined for being over aggressive towards a teacher. | He sat at the back of the train car with his handgun and a bag filled with about 160 rounds of ammunition. |
| | He then transferred to Adelphi University where he regularly spoke out against coexistence of blacks and whites and called for a revolution. He also accused those around him of being racist. | As the trains was approaching the Merillon Avenue Station, Ferguson got up, drew his gun, and started to open fire at random. |
| | He was suspended in June 1991 for yelling, "Kill everybody white!" and threatening violence against those that spoke against him. | It was said that he would approach each person for a brief second before firing and moving forward. |
| | | He was quoted as saying, "I'm going to get you" over and over again while walking down the aisle. |
| | | He told the judge and the media that he wanted to call a number of witnesses including a handwriting expert and President Clinton. |
| | | Had several bizarre defenses such as a computer chip was implanted in his brain by the government, a white man stole his gun while on the train, etc. |
| | | Was convicted on February 17, 1995. He received a sentence of 315 years and 8 months to life. |
| | | Blanco (n.d.). |
| | | Eugene, Or.: Wipf and Stock. |
| | | Ewing and McCann (2006), Grier and Cobbs (2000), Ramsland (2005) |

a club). Additionally, 6% of 12–18-year-old students reported being called hate-related words. There was also evidence of a high percentage of teachers in elementary and secondary public school who reported being threatened with injury or being physically attacked, with 6% having been physically attacked by students from their school in 2015–16, an increase from previous years.

These findings reflect similar trends reported in such sources as National Center for Mental Health and Youth Violence Prevention (2012), JAMA Pediatrics (2013), and U.S. Department of Health and Human Services (2012). According to these sources, 60% of adults reported experiencing abuse and other difficult family circumstances during childhood; 26% of children in the U.S. witnessed or experienced a traumatic event before age four; nearly 14% of children repeatedly experienced maltreatment by a caregiver; 13% reported being physically bullied, 1 in 3 reporting that they have been emotionally bullied; 39% of children aged 12–17 reported witnessing violence; 17% reported being victims of physical assault; and 8% reported being the victim of sexual assault. It was also highlighted that 60% of 17-year-old youth or younger reported having been exposed to crime, violence, and abuse, either directly or indirectly; and that 30% of elementary and middle school children in inner city communities have witnessed stabbing, with 26% having witnessed a shooting. An important finding in these statistics is that of those young children exposed to five or more significant adverse experience in the first 3 years of childhood were estimated to face the following challenges:

- A 76% likelihood of having one or more delays in their language and emotional or brain development
- Fifteen times more likely to attempt suicide
- Three–four times more likely to become alcoholic
- More likely to:
  - Develop a sexually trasmitted disease
  - Inject drugs
  - Be absent from work
  - Experience depression
  - Have serious job problems (recognizetrauma.org, 2019).

Regarding possible trauma experience in terms of domestic and relational violence, there was a serious concern of victimizations reported by the National Coalition Against Domestic Violence (2017), which also summarized findings from several sources, discussed by Javier and Herron (2018). We find in these reports that 1 in 3 women and 1 in 4 men experience intimate partner physical violence, intimate partner sexual violence, and/or intimate partner stalking in their lifetime; that 1 in 4 women and 1 in 7 men experience severe physical intimate partner violence in their lifetime; and that 1 in 7 women and 1 in 18 men have been stalked by an intimate partner during their lifetime to the point which they felt very fearful or believed that they or someone close to them would likely be harmed or killed. The report also highlights that, on average, nearly 20 people per minute are being physically abused by an intimate partner in the United States; and that for a single year, this equates to more than ten million women and men. In the end, the core finding in this report is that across all types of violence examined, lifetime estimates for women ranged from 11.4–29.2% for rape; 28.9–58% for sexual violence other than rape; and 25.3–49.1% for combined rape, physical violence, and/or stalking by an intimate partner. For men, lifetime estimates ranged from 10.8–33.7% for sexual violence other than rape; and 17.4–41.2% for combined rape, physical violence, and/or stalking by an intimate partner (Black et al., 2011; Walters, Chen, & Breiding, 2013).

The scientific community has been hard at work attempting to identify the various responses likely to emerge as a consequence of these and similar traumatic events. They found that these types of events result in changes in our internal and external environments at the cellular, physiological, and neurological levels (Fan et al., 2009; Kemeny, 2003; Solms & Turnbull, 2002); and that they also result in changes in behavioral and psychological patterns (Allen & Fonagy, 2017) that emerge as a function of temporary or prolonged traumatic conditions. Considering the range of responses discussed by these scholars, the greatest and most difficult challenges for the forensic professional who is asked to provide an assessment of psychological damage in relationship to conditions that become the subject of a legal action are: (a) How to identify the specific causal link(s) in relationship to a specific event or a series of events/incidents that are found to cause physical and/or psychological damage to an individual; (b) to be able to tease out from previous traumatic reactions the individuals may have experienced in reference to different sets of circumstances, only those that apply to the situation that is the object of the assessment; and (c) to be able to do so sufficiently clear to be of help to the court, that is ultimately responsible to make a reasonably accurate adjudication of damage or culpability.

## Trauma and Its Trajectory

One of the most important considerations to understanding trauma and its consequences is that once it occurs, it leaves an indelible mark in those affected, physically and psychologically (Russell, 1998). Something fundamentally happens to the individual cognitively and affectively as a result of exposure to a severe traumatic experience. That includes a fundamental shift in perceptions where the world is not experienced the same as before the trauma. This realization is reflected in the diagnostic descriptions included in the DSM nomenclature of trauma-related disorders, particularly regarding PTSD (APA, 2013). Evolutionary scholars have contributed a great deal to our understanding of that process and the mechanism solidly engrained in the human organism to ensure its physical and psychological survival (Belsky, 2019). Some of the components of this mechanism have been described in reference to domestic violence (Javier & Herron, 2018) and, in that context, the work of Tomkins (1962, 1978) and Solms and Turnbull (2002) provide an important and relevant framework. We will now expand a bit more on that subject, particularly on the link to the physiological and psychological changes that are normally part of the reaction to trauma.

Our point of departure is the fact that we are biologically equipped, and guided by an evolutionary necessity, to organize our experiences with and reactions to the world around us and retain them in memory to be able to compare among future experiences with similar valence. This organization takes place initially *sensorially* and then more *cognitively* when our neurological development becomes more sophisticated (i.e., when the myelination of neurons is complete, which makes them more efficient in retaining information and data from the environment). The extent to which we can pay attention to, and keep in mind, what is happening in our surroundings will ensure our ability to survive and thrive in that environment. This is particularly important in the context of environments that are inhospitable and threatening to the organism.

Our purpose in including this information in the introductory chapter is (1) to highlight both the normal, abnormal, and complex nature of the way we automatically react when confronted with situations in our environment that are experienced/perceived as threatening physically and/or psychologically; (2) to highlight that these reactions are initially adaptive for the most part but that they can become counterproductive or maladaptive when deployed inappropriately to situations/individuals not justified by the condition 'on the ground'; and (3) to help the forensic professional recognize that once developed, these reactions are organized into shortcuts or personal scripts that become difficult to tease out when attempting to assess a traumatic reaction (PTSD) to specific situations assumed to have caused harm to the individual that we are asked to assess. The chapters included in this volume are meant to provide the readers with an examination of some of the typical conditions that require the involvement of a forensic professional and where variations in trauma manifestations and their consequences may need to be considered and factored in the forensic assessment.

We start our discussion by looking at the series of physiological mechanisms that are normally (automatically) activated when we are faced with dangerous and threatening situations, specifically designed for the protection and preservation of the organism. This follows a discussion of the more psychological and, at times, less obvious reactions to stressful conditions that have been associated with traumatic situations (e.g., guilt, disgust, shame, anger, etc.) (Allen & Fonagy, 2017; Friedman, Resick, & Keane, 2007). The consideration of more psychological and internally based reactions is not clearly listed under PTSD in the DSM-5, although they were in previous editions of the DSM. Nevertheless, we find it critical to understand the more complex trauma reactions we observe in some of the forensic clients for whom a forensic assessment is requested.

## The Physiological Face of Trauma

An environment found to be implicated in traumatic condition is experienced as stressful and out of the ordinary because it triggers the kind of physiological and evolutionarily based response associated with danger to the organism. We have a sophisticated and complex nervous system that allows us not only to organize but also to categorize the various information we derive from our environment (and registered in and by our senses) and that we need to survive. When dealing with a threatening situation, we have a mechanism (the *autonomic nervous system-* or ANS) that alerts us to be prepared for action (Nevid, Rathus, & Greene, 2018). That is done through increased physiological activity, which involves two interrelated systems: The sympathetic (SNS) and the parasympathetic nervous systems (PNS). The operation of the first system (SNS) allows us to be prepared to deal with any threat/danger we may experience in our internal or external environment. In that context, there is gland activation (responsible for hormonal secretions) and a series of increased involuntary physiological activities (such as heart rate, breathing, salivation, digestion, muscle tone, dilation of pupils, etc.). These reactions have been found to be implicated in the development of indigestion in some situations and/or emotional responses, such as fear and anxiety (Nevid et al., 2018); in fact, there is evidence that the organism will shut down any function that will divert energy to the threat at hand, and activates only those operations that are necessary for preparing a response. Fear and anxiety serve as *amplifiers* to communicate the seriousness of the situation at hand and thus function as an important signal for the individual to draft a response that also alleviates those affects.

Under normal conditions, our body is expected to return to its pre-traumatic condition through the operation of our *parasympathetic nervous system*, whose function is to normalize physiological operations. As a result, the heart rate, breathing, muscle tone, salivation, digestion, etc., are returned to their normal levels, thus allowing the whole system to relax; it allows the body then to engage in replenishing its energy reserves (Nevid et al., 2018).

This whole process is efficiently synchronized by The *General Adaptation Syndrome (GAS)*, which is responsible for organizing all these functions so that the SNS and PNS are adapting at the level required by the level and nature of the threats to the organism. This is accomplished through the operation of three basic and interrelated stages (alarm reaction, resistance, and exhaustion) which function in concert to ensure its ultimate goal, the preservation and protection of the organism. The *alarm reaction stage* is characterized by heightened sympathetic activity, during which our body is mobilized to prepare for the challenge triggered by the threat experience. This is followed by the *resistance stage*, or an adaptation stage, where the organism remains alert but not as high as when in the alarm stage; this stage allows the organism to renew spent energy and repair whatever damage may have occurred in the previous stage. Finally, in the *exhaustion stage* our whole system is then managed and maneuvered by the parasympathetic system, whose basic function is to bring down (a deceleration of) heart rate, respiration, etc., and eventually, an opportunity to return to homeostasis (Nevid et al., 2018).

When the individual is forced to live in situations that requires the organism to remain at a constant alert (highly tense and life threatening, like when living in a war zone, domestic violence, repressive governments, etc.), it can result in damage to those parts of the body which are now forced to operate without the necessary resources normally distributed through the blood supply which has been interrupted by the emergency decree operating in the whole system. This condition has been referred to a *Disease of Adaption* that comes about when the source of stress persists, resulting from mild (allergic reaction) to more serious conditions (such as heart disease and even death, compromised perceptions about others' motivations, and other serious psychological conditions, etc.) (Nevid et al., 2018).

In a recent paper, Belsky (2019) reaffirmed this very view, already amply discussed in her earlier publications (Belsky, Steinberg, & Draper, 1991) of how the organism develops adaptation strategies to even most difficult early-life adversities, guided by evolutionary-based goals. That the individual will do whatever it takes to survive, even developing strategies that, in the mind of others not living in the midst of these individuals' situations, may seem counterproductive. In the end, the author suggests that although, an adaptation strategy is developed because of its "beneficial effect on the dispersion of genes in future generation…" and may have an evolutionary adaptation benefit, "… [it] may or may not be considered psychologically or culturally beneficial" (p. 241). One of the consequences of the evolutionary adaptation is that it may or may not accelerate child and adolescent development and promote reproductive fitness, depending upon how extreme the developmental conditions are. If the environmental conditions are so extreme to the point of threatening survival itself, the energy and resources of the organism are then used primarily for maintenance purposes, rather than growth and reproduction. Under adverse/high-risk conditions (e.g., growing up in a high-risk environment, financially unstable household, absent parents due to death, abandonment or imprisonment; a family environment characterized by sexual, physical, and or verbal abuse, etc.), development can become accelerated because "this should increase the chance of reproduction, the ultimate goal of all living things, before dying or having one's mate quality seriously compromised" (Belsky, 2019, p. 242); this is done in an effort to ensure a future for that person's gene pool, only when it is not too extreme. Such a tendency may explain the various behaviors we find in individuals living in high-risk environments, including children and adolescents engaging in "adult-like behaviors earlier…. (e.g., drinking, smoking, sex)" (p.241) than compared with others of similar age range not living in the same threatening conditions. An example of developments not being accelerated because the conditions are too extreme are findings of delayed puberty development in cases of "early-life deprivation (e.g., physical and emotional neglect, food insecurity), but not in threat exposure (e.g., child abuse, domestic violence)" (Sumner, Colich, Uddin, Armstrong, & McLaughlin, 2019, as cited by Belsky, 2019, p. 242). Young children suffering from severe deprivation (a form of intense trauma) were found to become totally withdrawn and apathetic to their environments when left unattended without or very limited and/or unpredictable human contacts (Spitz, 1946); again, this suggests that an internal biological mechanism is at play from the very beginning, where withdrawal of function is used as an attempt to preserve the limited available personal resources.

Findings from several studies looking at the effect of stress on the body have provided us with sufficient data to keep us vigilant about the effects of stressful conditions. For instance, prolonged stress has been found to weaken the body's immune system (Fan et al., 2009; Kemeny, 2003) and be implicated in the development of cancer of various organs, heart conditions, digestive difficulties, hypertension, diabetes, sleep disorders, memory difficulties, anxiety and depression, Alzheimer's Disorder, and in some, neurocognitive disorders, etc. (Alzheimer's Risk Gene, 2011; Nevid et al., 2018). (We say 'implicated' because there are likely other genetic and physical factors involved in some of these conditions). It has been implicated indirectly in the development of Wernicke's Disease (and Korsacoff syndrome) normally triggered as a consequence of alcoholism and the resulting depletion of vitamin B1 from the brain (Charness, 2009; Nevid et al. 2018). That is the case when the alcoholism is initially triggered in an attempt to respond to a traumatic condition. Most recently, for instance, posttraumatic symptoms were found to contribute to alcohol misuse and hazardous drinking in a group of trauma-exposed Latinx, a behavior related to maladaptive emotion dysregulation (Paulus et al., 2019).

Similarly, there are other conditions when stressful and inhospitable conditions that have introduced anxiety and depression in the developing child/adolescent (e.g., mother's infection, substance abuse, and family conflicts during pregnancy and subsequently, etc.) have been found to be implicated in the development and/or maintenance of mental disorders (e.g., particularly anxiety and depression), learning disabilities, attention-deficit disorders, and even suicide (APA, 2000, 2013; Blanchard, Gurka, & Blackman, 2006; Dervic, Brent, & Oquendo, 2008; Einfeld et al., 2006; Essex et al., 2006; Fergusson & Woodward, 2002; Kilpatrick et al., 2003; McGillivray & McCabe, 2006; Nevid et al., 2018; NIMH, 2003; Pelkonen & Marttunen, 2003; Weissman et al., 2006).

Finally, trauma reactions have also been found to occur from TBI or assault (Teasdale & Engberg, 2003) from sport (football, soccer, hockey, baseball, etc.) (Schwarz, Penna, & Novack, 2009; Small et al., 2013), or because of domestic violence (Banks, 2018). There is some evidence that progressive dementia due to traumatic brain injury is more likely to result from multiple head traumas than from a single blow or head trauma (McCrea et al., 2003). Yet, several scholars have emphasized that even a single head trauma can have psychological effects, and if severe enough, can lead to physical disability or death. It was also found that the specific changes in personality vary with the site and extent of the injury following traumatic injury to the brain (Nevid et al., 2018).

## *A Cognitive/Affective Face of Trauma*

Several scholars coming from different theoretical persuasions have provided explanations of the cognitive and affective mechanisms normally implicated in our responses to traumatic and inhospitable conditions (Allen & Fonagy, 2017; Beck, 2009, 2019; Bowlby, 1973, 1980, 1982; Ellis, Abrams, & Abrams, 2009: Freud, 1894, 1896; Kernberg, 1975; Luyten, Mayes, Fonagy, Target, & Blatt, 2017; Mahler et al., 1975; Morris, Javier, & Herron, 2015; Solms & Turnbull, 2002; Sullivan, 1955; etc.). These inhospitable conditions have been found to be implicated in the development of psychopathology in general, including personality and character disorders. As indicated earlier, these conditions (e.g., trauma-related disorders, substance use disorders, personality disorders, etc.) are found in the DSM nomenclature and in clients involved in the justice system (APA, 2013; Garbarino, 2015). Since the common denominator of these different views is the involvement of strong emotions and the individual's difficulty to negotiate these emotions, we will use the work of Solms and Turnbull (2002), Tomkins (1962, 1978), Demos (1998) and Allen and Fonagy (2017) to guide our analysis. We find that their views tend to incorporate not only a close evolutionary-based connection between emotions and neuroanatomy in processing and responding to unusual/traumatic latent conditions in the individual's internal and external environment, but also offer other explanatory models that provide additional enrichment to our understanding of the phenomenon.

According to these authors, the processes described earlier guided by the operation of the central nervous system that makes possible for us to receive/organize information about our environment through our senses (Luria, 1973; Solms & Turnbull, 2002), also prepares us for much more sophisticated development. That is, the ability to organize information into good, bad, or neutral, based on our physiological reactions that are strongly linked to our basic affective physiological reactions to this information. Tomkins (1962, 1978) has identified eight physiological-based rudimentary affective reactions (affects) involved in that organization (e.g., enjoyment, interest, distress, anger, fear, startle, disgust, and shame); Solms and Turnbull (2002), on the other hand, were only able to identify (based on their neuropsychological studies) four basic affects that are implicated in the organization of our reactions to the world around (e.g., seeking, rage, fear, and panic). According to these authors, these basic emotions are organized as part of what they called *basic-emotion command systems*, which is normally deployed to respond to different internal and/or external demands (threats). Most importantly, these authors were able to identify specific neurologically based functions implicated in the operation of these different affective responses to environmental demands, particularly in cases of high importance for the individual's physical and emotional survival.

It is presumed that these neurological functions become particularly operational in traumatic conditions and are involved in the development of specific organized structures that encapsulate the organization of different experiences into specific categories or personal scripts, as a function of the emotions they elicit in us. These are experiences that elicit and are then organized around personal scripts characterized by fear, joy, shame, bewilderment, disgust, anger, or panic, etc. Demos (1998) defines scripts as "sets of ordering rules for the interpretation, evaluation, prediction, production, or control of scenes," or experiences in the world (p. 82). By that she meant that,

> Inherent in the script is the specific way of responding to the demands of the scene (e.g., run away, get ready to fight back, or to remain quiet) that the individual has already incorporated into [his] her repertoire and that tends to guide that individual's behavior when relating in [his]her surroundings…once traumatized by abuse, the individual may not only feel threatened by the components of the event related to the abuse…by remembering the content of the communication surrounding the event and/or other components of the abusive

experience… the time of the event…the quality of the perpetrator's voice preceding the abuse…The victim may remember the items of clothing as well…the time and place of the occurrence…In a final analysis, the purpose of these scripts (or schemas) is to allow and guide the organism to respond to the environmental demands in a parsimonious, efficient, and historically contextual manner, the ways that are consistent with one's… history. (Javier & Herron, 2018, p. 14)

In other words, these personal scripts function as shortcuts that are deployed automatically as part of the *sympathetic nervous system* mechanism for the protection of the individual when an experience triggers feelings and emotions initially and historically associated with development of specific scripts. Warburton and Anderson (2018) provide an excellent description of the development and automatic deployment of these personal scripts, and which they suggest are normally operationalized through associative conditioning, instrumental conditioning, and social learning. An important point made by these authors is that the associative activation depends also upon unique personality characteristics (e.g., highly anxious, fearful prone, with borderline characteristics, etc.), as well as mental resources of the victim (e.g., whether the person feels he/she has what it takes to address the threat). These personal resources are what are referred to as 'self-efficacy,' 'ego strength,' or 'resilience' in various literature (Bellak & Goldsmith, 1984; Blanck & Blanck, 1974). According to Warburton and Anderson (2018), although strongly anchored in the individual's personal behavioral repertoire, these scripts can be altered through systematic and sustained intervention, so their deployment becomes more appropriate to the situation at hand and more a function of conscious and volitional decision on part of the individual than mere reflexive reaction.

The fact that personal scripts, once developed, are so endemically present in all human behaviors creates a challenge to the forensic professional who is asked to assess a specific consequence of an event presumed to have caused damage to an individual. It requires an examination of personal information related to a developmental period that precedes the forensic issue under consideration and that may be directly or indirectly implicated in the forensic issue. As we stated earlier, several scholars have looked at specific and critical conditions that have been found to be implicated in the development of one's personal scripts and emphasize the period of early development of attachment as being most critical. The works of Bowlby (1973, 1982) and Ainsworth et al. (1978), and later further expanded by Allen and Fonagy (2017), provide us with a wealth of empirical findings on the role earlier attachments could play in and impact on further functioning; included in that impact is the development of particular psychopathologies found to be present in individuals involved in the justice system (Garbarino, 2015).

An extreme disruption of a healthy attachment development is captured in the concept of *Attachment Disorder* or *Reactive Attachment Disorder* (Steele & Steele, 2017) described in the DSM. It refers to a constellation of disturbed behavior developed as a response to an extreme variation from the average expectable environment. It applies to individuals (normally children) whose behavior is characterized by extreme withdrawal from social interaction or where, if there is an interaction, it is characterized by a shallow and superficial investment in relations with multiple others (Luyten et al., 2017). The development of this type of reactive attachment condition is considered a sign of core deficits in self and social development that tend to occur in children and other individuals who have suffered extreme neglect and maltreatment over a sustained period.

Bowlby (1944) was able to identify problems with attachment in criminal behavior in his study of 44 juvenile thieves at the London Child Guidance Clinic during 1936–1939. This is something that he considered a reenactment later in life of early patterns of attachment disruptions. He found that these youths' quality of their early attachment histories was consistently unstable and problematic. During that same period, Spitz (1946) observed the development of what he called *anaclitic depression* in orphaned children deprived of human interactions. This was followed by the seminar work of Mahler and her associates who delineated, through careful observational studies, the early contexts of the development of these scripts as a function of the quality of the early environment (Mahler et al., 1975). These seminal works provide us with empirical contexts to understand how the transformative effect of earlier relationships (good or bad) with one's human environment reverberates throughout the person's overall relationship/interaction with their surroundings. When the nature and quality of those early relationships were found to be positive, it led to a good outcome of a healthy, stable, and socially well-integrated and productive citizen. When the early environment was less than ideal, it was found to lead to behavioral difficulties and even criminal behaviors (Garbarino, 2015).

Blatt was able to identify anaclitic (or dependent) depression in adult clients as well (Blatt, 2004), a condition normally associated with inhospitable/neglectful family environment during early developmental history. Anaclitic depression is characterized by feelings of loneliness, helplessness, weakness, intense and chronic fears of being abandoned and left unprotected and uncared for. There are deep, unfulfilled longings to be loved, nurtured, and protected. Those with this condition are unable to internalize the experience of satisfaction (indicating a problem with mentalizing). The relationship with others is found to be valued based on what they can derive from these individuals in terms of immediate care and comfort provided (Blatt, 2017). Unlike the typical experience of depression, anaclitic depression is more profound in nature and quality and reflects a serious problem with self-concept and self-efficacy.

In explaining past trauma (particularly related to early experience of bullying and cyberbullying), several scholars have also suggested a 'Developmental Cascades Model' to explain its effect; such a model is very much in keeping with findings already discussed earlier in this chapter. This model posits that there are cumulative consequences of past problems and past traumatic events that reverberate throughout the individual's developmental trajectory and predict difficulties in adulthood and across systems and generations (Lereya, Copeland, Costello, & Wolke, 2015; Masten & Cicchetti, 2010). This model was used by Indellicati (2019) to look at the effect of childhood and adolescent peer victimization on academic, social, and emotional adjustment in college students as part of her doctoral dissertation.

## Sources of Trauma in Forensic Contexts and Its Diagnostic Challenges

From a forensic perspective, any condition which impacts the normal developmental trajectory and/or functioning of the individual and whose impact is sufficiently serious as to cause a traumatic condition that derails temporarily/permanently the individual's future, can be of interest to the forensic professional. Again, the challenge here is how to determine and distinguish the immediate causal link to the damage being examined, as well as being able to identify those responsible (Koch, Douglas, Nicholls, & O'Neill, 2006); most importantly, to determine whether the principle of *mens rea* applies. For that to be the case, the person/entity identified as responsible (e.g., the landlord in case of lead poisoning of children inhabitants of that landlord's property; a driver in case of car accident; a mechanic/dealer in case of a malfunctioned vehicle involved in a deadly accident; a tobacco industry in case of lung cancer caused by first or second-hand smokers; a police officer/prison personnel in a case of death while apprehending or while in custody, etc.) has to be found to have "intentionally committed an act, violent or otherwise, with a guilty or wrongful purpose" (Huss, 2014, p. 98), and thus violated established norms. Although simply defined, it is a lot more complicated to prove intentionality. A case in point may be when legal responsibility for an act may become unenforceable if the one responsible is found to be mentally incapable or insane at the time of the identified incident.

### *The First Complication Is One of Definition*

Koch et al. (2006) make the point that it is not enough to define a situation as 'stressful-related emotional condition' (resulting from real or imagine threats or injuries); they argue that to be legally bound when it becomes the subject of personal injury compensation claim or criminal injury compensation, it should include causation by a third party, substantial economic costs, lack of productivity, mental illness, increase in substance abuse, depression, etc. (Koch et al., 2006). According to these authors, we should add the issue of how to determine degree of compensation and level of culpability/causation in the context of other possible factors which may be involved, such as psychological vulnerability factors (or preexistence conditions).

### *Issue of Accuracy of Diagnosis*

We also run into the problem of being able to accurately diagnose whether PTSD, as defined in DSM-5, can apply. This very issue was seriously challenged by Allen and Fonagy (2017) in their recent publication on trauma and also discussed in this book by Caffrey (Chap. 5). They make the point that unlike the DSM-IV, the new diagnostic category for PTSD does not consider subjective experience of what could be considered extreme distress at the time of a traumatic event. According to these authors, by only focusing on an objective delineation of observable physical injury and behaviors, the DSM-5 is missing from serious considerations a whole range of psychological or emotionally laden situations that have been found to be profoundly damaging to many (e.g., such as situations that are humiliating and sadistic or when the individual is submitted to psychological neglect or act of terrorism and mental torture) (Bifulco, Moran, Baines, Bunn, & Stanford, 2002; Erickson & Egeland, 1996 as cited by Allen & Fonagy, 2017).

This is further complicated by the findings that exposure to objectively defined trauma events has (at times) not been found to be sufficient to produce PTSD (Rasmussen, Verkuilen, Jayawickreme, Wu, & McCluskey, 2019; Rosen & Lilienfeld, 2008); meaning that just because one is exposed to a trauma event, they will not necessarily develop a diagnosable PTSD. The fact that the symptom clusters of PTSD are sometimes evident even in the absence of objectively defined traumatic event (like in Criteria A) makes the diagnosis of PTSD in the context of DSM-5 more problematic. For instance, PTSD syndrome has been found in relationship to seemingly ordinary stressors, such as family problems, parental divorce, occupational difficulties, deaths of loved-ones, or serious loses, etc., where it was reported that the more severe the stressor, the more the likelihood of developing PTSD (Friedman et al., 2007; Gold, Marx, Soler-Baillo, & Sloan, 2005 as cited by Allen & Fonagy, 2017). In the end, these authors conclude that there is enough evidence to raise "appropriate questions about the precise etiological role of traumatic event…in PTSD" (p. 167). This means that a traumatic reaction may still be present in an individual even when a PTSD diagnosis, as defined by the DSM current nomenclature, may not totally apply. Rasmussen, Verkuilen, Jayawickreme, Wu, and McCluskey's recent article (2019) confirm this argument and concluded that it is clear from the literature that it is difficult to identify clear diagnostic items that are unique to posttraumatic stress disorder because many of the items utilized to assess PTSD also overlap with requirements for other diagnostic categories, such as anxiety and depression. They conclude that it is important to keep in mind that PTSD is not one thing, and that re-experience and avoidance are the only two factors that meet standards for construct validity. They even suggest a radical solution to the problem with DSM diagnosing of PTSD, which is to address the conceptual flaw by focusing on measuring what is uniquely PTSD separate and apart from any overlap with other diagnoses related to negative emotions. To that point, Malaktaris and Lynn (2019) recently looked at the relevance of flashbacks to the PTSD diagnosis by comparing three groups of individuals with PTSD or subthreshold PTSD symptoms (or PTSS) with or without flashbacks to a trauma-exposed control and control participants without trauma exposure. They found that individuals with PTSD reported "significantly greater sleep disturbances, experiential avoidance, and lower mindfulness than those without PTSS…"; also, that "individuals without PTSD underestimated the vividness, emotional intensity, distress, and functional impact associated with flashbacks…" (p. 249); no fragmentation of flashbacks was found in individuals with PTSS. That is, individual with PTSS, with or without flashbacks, reported significantly more psychological symptoms compared to individuals without PTSS; there was an increase in sleep disturbances in individuals with PTSS.

A similar example is provided by Koch and associates (2006) who examined the role of dissociation found to be involved in the diagnosis of two interrelated diagnostic conditions since the DSM-IV, namely PTSD and Acute Stress Disorder (ASD). According to these authors, this condition may require two diagnoses (PTSD and ASD) to capture the reality of some individuals who are found to have suffered trauma and who may meet criteria for PTSD one-month post-trauma but not ASD. They concluded that such a decision de facto "arbitrarily dichotomizes a naturally occurring continuum" (p. 13). They also suggested, in this regard, that considering the often-strong comorbidity of PTSD with diagnoses of anxiety and mood disorders, personality disorders, substance abuse, etc., and the fact that our understanding of our beliefs about emotionality may lead to vastly different responses across cultures, to consider placing PTSD as part of a larger construct such as a "negative affectivity" construct (p. 10). In the end, however, it leaves us with a lingering question regarding the determination and adjudication of responsibility when "the relationship between traumatic event and PTSD is mediated by attributional style, cognitive processing, and emotionality, which differs across developmental stages…[and where] the prevalence, course, and expression might differ as well" (Koch et al., 2006, p. 12).

Allen and Fonagy (2017) suggest with regard to the DSM-5 that it would be more appropriate, and more in keeping with the data on the ground, to consider a broader diagnostic category to include a "multitude of symptoms, relationship and identity disturbance, as well as patterns of self-harming behavior than can stem from repeated and severe trauma, including childhood abuse and neglect" (p. 167). According to these authors, this was initially suggested by Herman in 1992 and 1993 under the concept *Complex PTSD* to be diagnosed as "disorders of extreme distress not otherwise specified" (p. 167), and further developed by Courtois and Ford (2009), Ford and Courtois (2009), and Courtois (2016) with the concept of *Complex Psychological Trauma* and *Complex Traumatic Stress Disorders.* Allen and Fonagy (2017) conclude that we are in a better, and more accurately and empirically based position, when defining and/or assessing the impact of trauma on an individual's function by considering that "…traumatic stress makes some substantial-albeit individually variable-contribution, in conjunction with a host of other etiological factors" (p.168). They further suggest that we should consider that to be the case for 'simple' and for 'complex' PTSD. Koch and associates (2006) also suggest that the event itself is not the most important predictor of PTSD but that individual characteristics and perception of the event are the most relevant factors in this regard. This is not to say that the nature, quality, and intensity of the trauma event should not be carefully examined, because they should.

The description of complex trauma and its effect that emerged from the work by Courtois and Ford (2009) and Ford and Courtois (2009) has three basic requirements: The first one (1), that it has to be related to an early experience of abandonment and or harm at a time the individual was most vulnerable (e.g., childhood or adolescence); (2) that the condition was repetitive or prolonged; and finally (3), that it was caused by an individual considered important and crucial for the physical and/or psychological survival/wellbeing of the victim (e.g., primary caregivers or other responsible adults). Also important is the multifaceted impact that it causes in the individual's overall functioning. That is, "the changes in mind, emotions, body, and relationships" (p. 13) that are experienced in connection with complex psychological trauma, and that it results in "severe problems with dissociation, emotional dysregulation, somatic distress, or relational or spiritual alienation" (p. 13). Such a description eloquently highlights the complex nature of the phenomenon while at the same time provides a framework for the development of an intervention that is in keeping with that complexity.

## *Trauma in Its Multiple Contexts*

Following Courtois and Ford's conceptualization and the seminal work by Bowlby, Ainsworth, Mahler and her associates, as well as more recent contributions by Koch and associates, Allen and Fonagy, and others, we can now appreciate and recognize the multiple contexts where trauma may be present and where there may be a request for an assessment of its effect for general psychological, educational, or forensic purposes. For the latter, we have included several chapters in this book (see section below on 'faces of trauma in this book') specifically dedicated to the exploration of some forensic areas that forensic psychologists are more likely to encounter. The areas covered are by no means exhaustive of situations in which forensic psychologists may be asked for their professional opinion. The central point that we are emphasizing, regardless of the area of forensic practice one is engaged in, is the importance to carefully consider the possible role a traumatic experience may play in the condition under assessment.

Also, recognizing that forensic involvement is made possible by what is required by case laws and statues, it is possible that areas not initially considered within the purview of forensic psychology at a point in time may become so in the future. An example of that is the one discussed by Suk (2010) regarding the legal and still controversial standing of 'abortion trauma' where a woman who decides on an abortion and later feels 'regret', resulting in "severe depression and loss of esteem" (p. 1200), could be admissible in court. Although extremely controversial because of its implications for both sides of the abortion discourse, nevertheless, a forensic psychologist may become involved in such cases. Forensic psychology played a part in the defense of Lorena Bobbitt's successful acquittal in 1994 (for cutting off her abusive husband's penis) where she was presented as someone suffering from a battered woman syndrome "…whose act was attributable to psychological trauma from an unwanted abortion" and being a victim of sustained domestic violence (Suk, 2010, p. 1200).

With those caveats in mind, we can now explore several areas that could be of forensic interest, some of which to be more fully covered in the various chapters listed in this book. This list may include such areas as to what happens when a developing fetus and/or child is negatively impacted as a function of inhospitable prenatal environment. Such an eventuality has been found when a mother's pregnancy is characterized by alcohol and drug abuse and the child comes into this world suffering from fetal alcoholism (Burns, Breen, & Dunlop, 2014; Waterman, Pruett, & Caughey, 2013), resulting in compromised development. Another example is when the home environment exposes a child to lead poisoning (plumbism) resulting in neurodevelopmental difficulties and seriously complicating the early developmental trajectory of the child (Bellinger & Needleman, 2003; Canfield et al., 2003; Needleman, McFarland, Ness, Fienberg, & Tobin, 2002). That condition has been found to cause neurodevelopment and executive function difficulties even in children with a lead concentration level below 10 µg/dL *and as low as* 5 µg/dL *(the level suggested in 2012)* (https://www.cdc.gov/nceh/lead/data/definitions.htm). Some of the effects include disruption in normal language development, behavioral, and affect dysregulation, "deficits in attention and concentration, visual-special skills, fine-motor coordination, balance, and social-emotional modulations" (American Academy of Pediatrics, 2005, p. 15; Pocock, Smith & Baghurst, 1994; Sciarillo, Alexander, & Farrell, 1992); it was also found to contribute to a propensity to antisocial behavior and juvenile delinquency (Bellinger & Needleman, 2003; Dietrich et al., 2000; Dietrich, Ris, Succop, Berger, & Bornschein, 2001; Needleman et al., 2002). At the physiological level, it has been found to cause recurrent headaches, abdominal pain, loss of appetite, and constipation, as well as clumsiness, and agitation; it may even proceed to vomiting, stupor, and convulsion (American Academy of Pediatrics, 1998; 2005; CDC, 2002). Although we have noticed improvement in this area, the issue of plumbism and mercury exposure continues to be a factor in the lives of many children still living in old dwellings (Blackman, 2006; Patel et al., 2019). In some of the cases evaluated by one of the authors of this chapter over the last 20 or so years, the lead intoxication was found to be as high as 70 µg/dL in some children suffering from severe learning disability and behavioral disorders, particularly attention-deficit hyperactivity and conduct disorders.

Although chelation therapy with *ethylenediaminetetraacetic acid* (EDTA) has been found to be effective in reducing the lead level in blood (CDC, 2002), with some positive reversal at least physically, the damage to a child who has lived with the condition for many years to the point of infiltration (bone calcification) tends to be more lasting once the earlier developmental educational/social/emotional trajectory has been seriously derailed for a prolonged period. This situation is further compounded by the challenges the parents and the rest of the family face when having to negotiate a not always adequate school environment to secure special educational intervention for the resulting developmental and learning disabilities, and behavioral disorders in affected children (Hou et al., 2013; Landrigan, Schecter, Lipton, Fahs, & Schwartz, 2002).

Another example of inhospitable environment is a family environment characterized by domestic violence (Javier & Herron, 2018) and child abuse and neglect (Centers for Disease Control and Prevention, 2014; Moylan et al., 2010) as discussed earlier. And as if these conditions are not challenging enough, financial and political instabilities can also contribute to creating an environment of disruptions, characterized by a sense of unpredictability and fear. This is particularly the case when these conditions contribute to making more likely the individual will hear, witness, or be the victim of assault (by gun/knife/etc.) or sexual acts, act of community terrorism, identity thefts, cases of domestic violence, school shootings, and acts of blatant and subtle discrimination (macro and micro aggression) on the basis of race or religion, gender, cultural backgrounds, etc. (Bureau of Justice Statistics, 2017; Daniels, Bradley, & Hays, 2007; Harrell, 2019; Morgan & Truman, 2018; Oudekerk, Musu, Zhang, Wang, & Zhang, 2019; Sue et al., 2007).

Again, these disruptions can be temporary or more permanent, causing tremendous psychological impact in the individual's overall functioning, depending on where he/she is in the developmental trajectory. That fact brings us to another source of trauma that we can categorize under 'bullying' and 'cyberbullying,' a phenomenon whose devastating effects have created havoc in the educational, social, and emotional lives of those affected (Javier, Dillon, DaBreo, & Mucci, 2013). Several prominent scholars have concentrated their research effort to tease out the major consequences experienced by those who are victims and/or are forced to witness (bystanders) bullying behavior in school or outside school (Espelage & Swearer, 2008; Hinduja & Patchin, 2012). There are legal cases emerging against school personnel, perpetrators, and parents/family of perpetrators that include assessment of culpability and of damage for failing to create a secure learning school environment.

Bullying has been found to also be experienced by the elder population. This is the case when the elder may experience violence/neglect at the hands of family members or by employees of nursing homes, and thus reducing them to a life of fear and submission after an active and full life of financial and physical independence (Dahlkemper, 2016). We can get a sense of the pervasiveness of traumatic conditions in the elder population from findings discussed in Dong's report (2017).

Similarly, there are more and more reports emerging from many sources, and now part of the public discourse, related to sexual and physical abuse at the hands of members of religious institutions, medical professions, teachers, etc. The 2015 film "Spotlight", about child abuse cases by priests in the Boston Dioceses, contributed to the public display of consternation and outcry that now permeate many sectors of our society and that propelled justice systems in many countries throughout the world to bring indictments against priests, bishops, religious and church personnel, sport coaches and administrators, etc., many resulting in jail terms (Death, 2013, 2018; McCluskey, 2000; O'Reilly & Chalmers, 2014; Trothen, 2012). Findings from different sources  profound traumas have been hidden, have resulted in eroding/destroying those victims from within even decades after the abuse occurred. It is the protracted and stubborn denials of the abuse, the sense of profound betrayal, and the sense of shame and confusion that have resulted from the ways members of those institutions responsible for the protection, religious, and moral teaching of what it is meant to be a member, have historically responded to the allegations. The victims of the Olympic gymnastics sexual predator, doctor Larry Nassar, considered one of "the most prolific known sex criminal in American sport history" (Pesta, 2019, p. 48), relate similar pain of abuse, denigration, and betrayal by their coach John Geddert and others in the institution who were supposed to look after their well-being and safety. For some of these victims, the diagnosis of 'complex trauma' may apply, considering how their lives devolved, including the excessive use of drug and alcohol, sexual promiscuity and sexual confusion, the development of psychiatric disorders, and even suicide.

And the list goes on and on. We find traumatic situations in wide variety of systems: the workplace, in the military, law enforcement, justice, medical and health delivery, transportation, border patrols, etc. In all these situations, the question for the forensic professional is whether *mens rea* can be applied and whether the discipline can provide the necessary tool of assessment for these conditions to fulfill the various standards of evidence operating in different jurisdictions. We are referring to the *Frye Standard* (that refers to the importance for the professional to rely on tools generally accepted by the discipline...that is, it must be sufficiently established and have gained general acceptance in the particular field it belongs), or the *Daubert Standard* (that refers to the importance to rely on scientific evidence on which the forensic professional opinion should be based. It should be scientifically reliable, relevant, and valid; also, that the application of such standards requires from the professional specialized knowledge) (Huss, 2014).

## Faces of Trauma in This Book

Recognizing the central role that trauma and its consequences have played in history of psychology (Beck, 2009, 2019; Ellis et al., 2009; Freud, 1894, 1896; Greenberg & Mitchell, 1983; Sullivan, 1955), and being cognizant of the growing role of psychology as a discipline and scientific enterprise in the forensic arena, it has become abundantly clear that it was now time to organize a forensic book where trauma was centrally addressed. Our goal is to include thoughtful and informative discussions on the various ways trauma is implicated in many areas of forensic practice; also to prepare a volume that can be used as part of a forensic course at upper undergraduate or graduate levels; and finally, as a resource for forensic professionals and those in the legal systems interested in getting a better understanding of the role of trauma in criminal behavior, in sentencing adjudication, risk assessment and management, and in the nature of treatment in forensic contexts. This book requires at least a basic exposure to forensic psychology, and it is not meant as a textbook for a basic forensic course.

With that in mind, we divide the book into four sections with the first section (Part I: Six chapters) dedicated to addressing Conceptual Framework, covering examination of trauma from a forensic developmental lens (Chap. 2 by Nesi, Garbarino, & Praeter); the role of trauma in the evaluation of various competencies (Chap. 3 by Owen, Perry, & Scher); the challenges addressing issues related to individuals who are mentally ill, with a serious history of multiple traumas, and incarcerated (Chap. 4 by Leindenfrost & Antonius); issues related to the complexity of what is involved in considering trauma as an important factor in sentencing mitigation (Chap. 5 by Caffrey); the role of trauma in propelling individuals to become activists and thus turning a bad experience into a force for positive changes on what they refer to as 'homicide activism' (Chap. 6 by Tookoshian & Leeolou); and finally, challenges related to issues of individuals who are unable to communicate due to limited, if any, knowledge of English; individuals with low educational background and who are cognitively compromised; and individuals who are coming from different cultural contexts, and whose understanding of the work and special terms used by the court is limited at best (Chap. 7 by Javier & Lamela).

The second section (Part II: Seven chapters) is dedicated to the exploration of a number of core, relevant, and current topics likely to emerge in forensic practice related to civil matters (issues related to children/adolescents where the forensic question involves protective custody issues, child custody) (Chaps. 8 by Esquilin & Johnson, and 9 by Zelechoski, Rachel, & Heusel); immigration and termination of parental rights (Chaps. 10 by Persyn & Owen, and 11 by Amrami & Javier, respectively); issues of pre-employment and fitness for duty, personal injury and employment discrimination, including law enforcer personnel (Chaps. 12 Casarella & Beebe, 13 by Foote and Chap. 14 by Maddux, Agnew, & Frumkin). The section to follow (Part III: Six chapters) is dedicated to the exploration of trauma in cases of criminal matters. In this context, the reader finds the examination of trauma in the context of intimate partner violence (Chap. 15 by Paradis, Bowen, & McCullough), among the Veterans who find themselves involved in the justice system (Chap. 19 by Lamade & Lee), and in sex offenders (Chaps. 16 by Lamade, and 17 by DeMarco & Geller). Also included in this section is a chapter by Shaw, Rogers, and Gefner (Chap. 18) who seeks to address an issue that is in the mind of many when dealing with criminal or unlawful behaviors. We are referring to the fact that not everyone whose life experience is characterized by an unfortunate course of events and trauma ends up involved with the legal system or engaged in criminal behavior and legal situations. The factors normally associated with that eventuality are what are referred to as resilience factors that serve as buffer against the likely effect of noxious and traumatic events (Ungar, 2013). It is an important chapter that is meant to tease out those components of the personal life that can be helpful in keeping the person away from having to engage with the legal system as defendant or become paralized by the negative effect of personally experienced traumatic events. The book concludes with another section (Part IV: three chapters) dedicated to a general discussion of the emerging issues raised throughout the book and a discussion of specific prescriptions for the forensic professionals (Chap. 20 by Javier, Owen, & Maddux). In that context, it also includes a chapter on 'Trauma and its Trajectory in Criminal Behaviors' (Chap. 21 by Javier, Owen, & Jemour); and another and final chapter by Hon. Hirsch (Chap. 22) that provides a case study of how a justice system that considers the multiplicity of factors (including traumatic experiences) that are normally involved in the commission of a crime, can be meaningfully considered in the deliberation and adjudication of the crime by the court while still affirming the defendants' personal accountability.

Each chapter in the book has been structured to encourage ongoing active participation from those interested in further and careful exploration of trauma issues addressed in the book. In this context, the readers will find that each chapter in the book poses a series of questions/and activities that they can use to further their understanding and making them more personally relevant. Additionally, we also dedicate a chapter (Chap. 21) to listing a series of different types of crimes in a form of 'Case Studies' which features not only the specific (notorious) crimes committed over the course of history but also some personal history (biographies) of those involved in these crimes. It is set up as a separate chapter to facilitate the use of that section as a teaching tool for class assignments. Finally, on the back section of the book (Appendices), the readers will find a series of resources about each topic covered in the book, all in the spirit of encouraging them to further explore the issues addressed in the different chapters.

In the end, the readers will find that the material presented is written by individuals not only knowledgeable of various aspects of forensic practice but who also show a clear determination and passion to make sure that trauma information is given its important and rightful place in all aspects of the forensic endeavor. This is evident throughout the book.

## Concluding Thoughts

In this book, we discuss the complex nature of trauma and its consequences in the general context, while also including more specific forensic foci. Ultimately, while widening the scope of inquiry regarding the nature of trauma in general, our goal is to provide the forensic professional with the necessary tools to examine and make a reasonable determination of what aspects of the traumatic condition presented by their clients can be directly linked to the specific event that is the subject of the forensic assessment; and to be able to do so, while following the standards of practice guiding the profession. The ultimate goal is to provide as clear and concise assessment of trauma in relationship to the forensic issues at hand so that adjudication of accountability can be clearly established, if present. The emphasis is on providing specific recommendations for the professional when addressing the challenges in considering the role of trauma in forensic contexts. There is a recurrent theme throughout the book, an invitation to those interested in trauma to recognize its pervasive and damaging nature, as well as to recognize the difficulty in assessing its true nature and impact on individuals, and what it would take to develop intervention approaches that are more likely to succeed. There are no easy answers, but there are directions provided by empirically derived information that we can now follow in our attempt to address the complexity of considering trauma in forensic contexts.

In preparing this volume, it became patently clear that there are more forensic contexts where trauma is implicated that we are covering or could possibly cover in a single volume. Our hope is that, perhaps, some of our readers may be inclined and encouraged to continue the exploration of trauma in other forensic contexts, with a focus on providing specific trauma-sensitive assessment/intervention recommendations. This is our hope and our invitation.

## Questions/Activities for Further Exploration

1. Identify one difficult/stressful situation in your life where you felt particularly affected for a long time and another less stressful situation that affected you only for a brief period.
2. Identify in both conditions what was it that made it particularly stressful or not, how did you know, what you felt physically and emotionally, what part of your life was affected, in what way, and for how long.
3. Identify what helped, if anything, to make you feel better.
4. Discuss the personal history of trauma in someone involved in criminal behavior, whether already known to the justice system or not, and what pushed that person into a criminal act while others with similar experience did not engage in criminal behavior.
5. What do you consider criminal behavior and why?
6. What role should trauma experience play, if any, in determining culpability for a crime, in sentencing, etc., and your view of how intervention could be helpful and when it may be counterproductive?
7. Select a convicted inmate to get to know more about his/her life trajectory, the context of the crimes, role of trauma, if any, etc.

## References

A&E. (2018, May 14). Charles Manson. Retrieved November 13, 2018, from https://www.biography.com/people/charles-manson-9397912
Ainsworth, M. D., & Bell, S. (1970). Attachment, exploration, and separation: Illustrated by the behavior of one-year-olds in a strange situation. *Child Development, 41*, 49–67.
Ainsworth, M. D., Blehar, M. C., Waters, E., & Wall, S. (1978). *Patterns of attachment: A psychological study of strange situation*. Hillsdale, NJ: Erlbaum.
Allen, J. G., & Fonagy, P. (2017). Trauma. In P. Luyten, L. C. Mayes, P. Fonagy, M. Target, & S. Blatt (Eds.), *Handbook of psychodynamic approaches to psychopathology* (pp. 165–198). New York, NY/London: The Guilford Press.
Almeida, I., Ramalho, A., Fernandez, M. B., & Guarda, R. (2019). Adult attachment as a risk factor for intimate partner violence. *Annals of Medicine, 51*(1), 1–5.
Altman, R. (2015). Sympathy for the devil: Charles Manson's exploitation of California's 1960s counter-culture. Undergraduate honors theses. 907. https://scholar.colorado.edu/honr_theses/90
Alzheimer's Risk Gene disrupts brain's wiring 50 years before the disease hits (2011, May 16). Science Daily. Retrieved from http://www.sciencedaily.com;
American Academy of Pediatrics. (1998). Committee on Environmental Health. Screening for elevated blood lead levels. *Pediatrics, 101*, 1072–1078.
American Academy of Pediatrics. (2005). Lead exposure in children: Prevention, detection, and management-Committee on Environment Health. *Pediatrics, 116*(4), 1036–1046; http://doi.org/10.1542/peds.2005-1947.
American Psychiatric Association (2000). Diagnostic and Statistical Manual of Mental Disorders (4th edition), Washington DC: APA.
American Psychiatric Association. (2013). *Diagnostic and statistical manual of mental disorders* (5th ed.). Washington, D.C.: Author.

Arrigo, B. A., & Griffin, A. (2004). Serial murder and the case of Aileen Wuornos: Attachment theory, psychopathy, and predatory aggression. *Behavioral Sciences & the Law, 22*(3), 375–393. https://doi.org/10.1002/bsl.583

Banks, M. E. (2018). Victimized and disabled: Neuropsychological issues at the intersection of gender and ethnicity. In R.A. Javier & W.G.Herron (Eds.), Understanding domestic violence: Theories, challenges, and remedies (Pp.265–285). New York/London: Rowman & Litttlefield;

Beck, A. T. (2009). Cognitive aspects of personality disorders and their relation to syndromal disorders. A psychoevolutionary approach. In C. R. Cloninger (Ed.), *Personality and psychopathology* (pp. 411–429). Washington, D.C.: American Psychological Association.

Beck, A. T. (2019). A 60-year evolution of cognitive theory and therapy. *Perspective on Psychological Science, 14*(1), 16–20.

Bellak, L., & Goldsmith, L. (1984). *The broad scope of ego function assessment.* New York, NY: Wiley.

Bellinger, D. C., & Needleman, H. L. (2003). Intellectual impairment and blood levels [letter]. *New England Journal of Medicine, 349,* 500–502.

Belsky, J., Steinberg, L., & Draper, P. (1991). Childhood experience, interpersonal development,and reproductive strategy: an evolutionary theory of socialization. Child Dev, 62(4), 647–70.

Belsky, J. (2019). Early-life adversity accelerates child and adolescent development. *Current Directions in Psychological Science, 28*(3), 241–243.

Bifulco, A., Moran, P. M., Baines, R., Bunn, A., & Stanford, K. (2002). Exploring psychological abuse in childhood: II. Association with other abuse and adult clinical depression. *Bulletin of the Menninger Clinic, 66*(3), 241–258. https://doi.org/10.1521/bumc.66.3.241.23366

Black, M. C., Basile, K. C., Breiding, M. J., Smith, S. G., Walters, M. L., Merrick, M. T., … Spivak, H. R. (2011). *The National Intimate Partner and Sexual Violence Survey (NISVS): 2010 summary report.* Atlanta, GA: National Center for Injury Prevention and Control, Centers for Disease Control and Prevention. Retrieved from http://cdc.gov/violenceprevention/pdf/nisvs_report2010-a.pdf.

Blackman, T. (2006). *Placing health: Neighbourhood renewal, health improvement and complexity.* Bristol, UK: Policy Press.

Blanchard, L., Gurka, M., & Blackman, J. (2006). Emotional, developmental, and behavioral health of American children and their families: A report from the 2003 National Survey of Children's Health. *Pediatrics, 11*(7), e1202–e1212.

Blanco, J. I. (2017, June 4). Albert Hamilton fish. Retrieved from http://murderpedia.org/male.F/f/fish-albert.htm.

Blanco, J. I. (n.d.). Retrieved from http://murderpedia.org/male.F/f/ferguson-colin.htm

Blanck, G., & Blanck, R. (1974). *Ego psychology: Theory and practice.* New York, NY: Columbia University Press.

Blatt, S. J. (2004). *Experiences of depression: Theoretical, clinical, and research perspectives.* Washington, D. C.: American Psychological Association.

Blatt, S. J. (2017). Depression. In P. Luyten, L. C. Mayes, P. Fonagy, M. Target, & S. Blatt (Eds.), *Handbook of psychodynamic approaches to psychopathology* (pp. 131–151). New York, NY/London: The Guilford Press.

Bowlby, J. (1944). Forty-four juvenile thieves: Their characters and home life. *International Journal of Psychoanalysis, 25*(19–52), 107–127.

Bowlby, J. (1973). *Attachment and loss: Vol. 2. Separation: Anxiety and anger.* New York, NY: Basic Books.

Bowlby, J. (1980). *Attachment and loss: Vol. 3. Loss: Sadness and depression.* New York, NY: Basic Books.

Bowlby, J. (1982). *Attachment and loss: Vol. 1. Attachment* (2nd ed.). New York, NY: Basic Books.

Bowlby, J. (1988). *A secure base: Clinical applications of attachment theory.* London, UK: Routledge.

Broomfield, N. (Director). (2014, September 18). *Aileen Wuornos: The selling of a serial killer* [Video file]. Retrieved from https://www.youtube.com/watch?v=oPD2hd6y_C8

Bullis, J. E. (1985). A social-psychological case history: The Manson incident. Dissertations and Theses. Paper 3564.

Bureau of Justice Statistics (2017). www.bing.com/search?q=2017+crime+rate+united+states&F
 ORM=RSFD3.

Bureau of Justic Statistics (2019). http://bjs.gov/index.cfm?=pbdetail&iid=6646.

Burns, L., Breen, C., & Dunlop, A. J. (2014). Prevention of fetal alcohol spectrum disorders must
 include maternal treatment. *Medical Journal of Australia, 200*(7), 392.

Canfield, R. L., Henderson, C. R., Jr., Cory-Slechta, D. A., Cox, C., Jusko, T. A., & Lanphear,
 B. (2003). Intellectual impairment in children with blood lead concentrations below 10μg per
 deciliter. *New England Journal of Medicine, 348*, 1517–1526.

Centers for Disease Control and Prevention. (2002). *Managing elevated blood levels among
 young children: Recommendations from Advisory Committee on Childhood Lead Poisoning
 Prevention.* Atlanta, GA: Center for Disease Control and Prevention. www.cdc.gov/nceh/lead/
 CaseManagement/CaseManage_main.htm. Retrieved June 12, 2019.

Centers for Disease Control and Prevention. (2014). *Intimate partner violence: Consequences.*
 Retrieved from http://www.cdc.gov/violenceprevention/intimatepartnerviolence/conse-
 quences.html

Charles Manson: Helter skelter and beyond. (n.d.). Place of publication not identified: Filiquarian
 Pub. LLC.

Charness, M. E. (2009). Functional connectivity in Wernike Encephalopathy. Journal
 Watch Neurology. Retrieved from http://neurology.watch.jwatch.org/cgi/content/
 full/2009/623/4?q=etoc_jwneuro;

Courtois, C. A. (2016). Complex development trauma in adults: Innovation in integrated treatment.
 Paper presented at the 2016 ABPP Annual Convocation-APA Annual Convention, Denver, CO,
 4–7 Aug 2016.

Courtois, C. A., & Ford, J. (Eds.). (2009). *Treating complex traumatic stress disorders: An evidence-based guide.* New York, NY: The Guildford Press.

Dahlkemper, T. R. (2016). *Caring for older adults holistically* (6th ed.). Philadelphia, PA: Terri
 Wood Allen.

Daniels, J. A., Bradley, M. C., & Hays, M. (2007). The impact of school violence on school
 personnel: Implications for psychologists. *Professional Psychology: Research and Practice,
 38*(6), 652–659. https://doi.org/10.1037/0735-7028.38.6.652

Death, J. (2013). Identity, forgiveness, and power in the management of child abuse by personnel
 in Christian institutions. *International Journal of Crime and Justice, 2*(1), 82–97.

Death, J. (2018). *Governing child abuse, voices, and victimization. The use of public inquiry into
 child abuse in Christian institutions.* New York, NY: Routledge.

Demos, E. V. (1998). Differentiating the repetition compulsion from trauma through the lens
 of Tomkins's script theory: A response to Russell. In J. G. Teicholz & D. Kriegman (Eds.),
 *Trauma, repetition & affect regulation: The work of Paul Russell* (pp. 67–104). New York, NY:
 The Other Press.

Dervic, K., Brent, D., & Oquendo, M. (2008). Completed suicide in childhood. *The Psychiatric
 Clinics of North America, 31*(2), 271–291.

Dietrich, K. N., Berger, O., & Bhattacharya, A. (2000). Symptomatic lead poisoning in infancy: A
 prospective case analysis. *The Journal of Pediatrics, 137*, 668–571.

Dietrich, K. N., Ris, M. D., Succop, P. A., Berger, O. G., & Bornschein, R. L. (2001). Early exposure to lead and juvenile delinquency. *Neurotoxical Teratol, 23*, 511–518.

Dong, X. (2017). *Elder abuse: Research, practice, and policy.* London/New York, NY: Springer.

Einfeld, S. L., Piccinin, A. M., Mackinnon, A., Hofer, S. M., Taffe, J., Gray, K. M., … Tonge,
 B. J. (2006). Psychopathology in young people with intellectual disability. *JAMA, 296*(16),
 1981–1989.

Ellis, A., Abrams, M., & Abrams, L. (2009). *Personality theories: Critical perspectives.* Los
 Angeles, CA/London: Sage.

Erickson, M. F., & Egeland, B. (1996). Child neglect. In J. Briere, L. Berliner, J. A. Bulkley,
 C. Jenny, & T. Reid (Eds.), *The APSAC handbook on child maltreatment* (pp. 4–20). Thousand
 Oaks, CA: Sage Publications.

Espelage, D., & Swearer, S. (Eds.). (2008). *Bullying in American schools: Social-ecological perspectives on prevention and intervention.* London/Mahwah, NJ: Lawrence Erlbaum Associates.

Essex, M. J., Kraemer, H. C., Armstrong, J. M., Boyce, W. T., Goldsmith, H. H., Klein, M. H., … Kupfer, D. J. (2006). Exploring risk factors for the emergence of children's mental health problems. *JAMA Psychiatry, 63*(11), 1246–1256.

Ewing, C. P., & McCann, J. T. (2006). *Minds on trial: Great cases in law and psychology*. Oxford, UK: Oxford University Press.

Fan, J., Gu, X., Guise, K. G., Liu, X., Fossella, J., Wang, H., & Posner, M. I. (2009). Testing the behavioral interaction and integration of attentional networks. *Brain and Cognition, 70*(2), 209–220. https://doi.org/10.1016/j.bandc.2009.02.002

Fergusson, D., & Woodward, L. (2002). Mental health, educational and social role outcomes of adolescents with depression. *Archives of General Psychiatry, 59*(3), 225–231.

Fink, K. (2015, Jan 21). The 8 scariest psychopaths in history. Retrieved from https://medium.com/@JeriFink/the-8-scariest-psychopaths-in-history-b5f13b9d9aa2.

Finkelhor, D., Turner, H. A., Shattuck, A., & Hamby, S. L. (2013). Violence, crime, and abuse exposure in a national sample of children and youth: An update. *JAMA Pediatrics, 167*(3), 614–621.

Ford, J. D., & Courtois, C. A. (2009). Defining and understanding complex trauma and complex traumatic stress disorders. In C. A. Courtois & J. D. Ford (Eds.), *Treating complex traumatic stress disorders: An evidence-based guide* (pp. 13–30). New York, NY: Guilford Press.

Freud, S. (1894). Neuropsychosis of defense. Standard Edition. London: Hogarth Press.

Freud, S. (1896). Further remarks on the neuropsychosis of defense. Standard edition. London: Hogarth Press.

Friedman, M. J., Resick, P. A., & Keane, T. M. (Eds.). (2007). *Handbook of PTSD: Science and practice*. New York, NY: Guilford Press.

Garbarino, J. (2015). *Listening to killers: Lessons learned from my twenty years as a psychological expert in murder cases*. Los Angeles, CA: University California Press.

Gold, S. D., Marx, B. P., Soler-Baillo, J. M., & Sloan, D. M. (2005). Is life stress more traumatic than traumatic stress? *Journal of Anxiety Disorders, 19*, 687–698.

Greenberg, J. R., & Mitchell, S. A. (1983). *Object relations in psychoanalytic theory*. Cambridge, MA: Harvard University Press.

Grier, W. H., & Cobbs, P. M. (2000). Black rage.

Guinn, J. (2014). *Manson the life and times of Charles Manson*. New York, NY: Simon & Schuster.

Harrell, E. (2019, January 8). Victims of identity theft, 2016. *Bureau of Justice Statistics*. http://www.bjs.gov/index.cfm?ty=pbdetail&iid=6467. Retrieved 12 June 2019.

Hartmann, H. (1939/1958). *Ego psychology and the problem of adaptation*. New York, NY: International University Press.

Herman, J. L. (1992). Complex PTSD: A syndrome in survivors of prolonged and repeated trauma. *Journal of Traumatic Stress, 5*, 377–391.

Herman, J. L. (1993). Sequalae of prolonged and repeated trauma: Evidence for a complex post-traumatic syndrome (DESNOS). In J. R. T. Davidson & E. B. Foa (Eds.), *Posttraumatic stress disorder: DSM IV and beyond* (pp. 213–228). Washington, D.C.: American Psychological Association.

Hinduja, S., & Patchin, J. W. (2012). *School climate 2.0. Preventing cyberbullying and sexting one classroom at a time*. London, UK: Sage Publications.

Hou, S., Yuan, L., Jin, P., Ding, B., Qin, N., Li, L., … Deng, Y. (2013). A clinical study of the effects of lead poisoning on the intelligence and neurobehavioral abilities of children. *Theoretical Biology & Medical Modelling, 10*, 13. https://doi.org/10.1186/1742-4682-10-13

Huss, M. T. (2014). *Forensic psychology. Research, clinical practice, and applications* (2nd ed.). Hoboken, NJ: Wiley.

Indellicati, A. (2019). Effects of childhood and adolescent peer victimization on academic, social, and emotional adjustment in college students. Doctoral dissertation, St. John's University.

Javier, R. A., Dillon, J., DaBreo, C., & Mucci, D. (2013). Bullying and its consequences: In search of solutions – Part II. *Journal of Social Distress and Homeless, 22*(2), 59–72. https://doi.org/10.1179/1053078913Z.0000000008

Javier, R. A. & Herron, W.G. (2018). Understanding Domestic Violence: Theories, challenges, and remedies. New York/London: Rowman & Littlefield.

Kemeny, M. E. (2003). The psychobiology of stress. *Current Directions in Psychological Science, 12*(4), 124–129. https://doi.org/10.1111/1467-8721.01246

Kernberg, O. (1975). *Borderline conditions and pathological narcissism.* New York, NY: Jason Aronson.

Kilpatrick, D. G., Ruggiero, K. J., Acierno, R., Saunders, B. E., Resnick, H. S., & Best, C. L. (2003). Violence and risk of PTSD, major depression, substance abuse/dependence, and comorbidity: Results from the national survey of adolescents. *Journal of Consulting and Clinical Psychology, 71*(4), 692–700.

Koch, W. J., Douglas, K. S., Nicholls, T. L., & O'Neill, M. L. (2006). *Psychological injuries: Forensic assessment, treatment, and law.* New York, NY/London: Oxford University Press.

Landrigan, P. J., Schecter, C. B., Lipton, J. M., Fahs, M. C., & Schwartz, J. (2002). Environmental pollutants and disease in American children: Estimates of morbidity, mortality, and costs for lead poisoning, asthma, cancer, and developmental disabilities. *Environ Health Perspective, 110,* 721–728.

Lereya, S. T., Copeland, W. E., Costello, E. J., & Wolke, D. (2015). Adult mental health consequences of peer bullying and maltreatment in childhood: Two cohorts in two countries. *Lancet Psychiatry, 2,* 524–531. https://doi.org/10.1016/S2215-0366(15)00165-0

Linder, D. (2007). The Charles Manson (Tate-Labianca Murder) trial. Available at SSRN: https://ssrn.com/abstract=1029399 or https://doi.org/10.2139/ssrn.1029399

Luria, A. (1973). *The working brain: An introduction.* New York, NY: Basic Books.

Luyten, P., Mayes, L. C., Fonagy, P., Target, M., & Blatt, S. (Eds.). (2017). *Handbook of psychodynamic approaches to psychopathology.* New York, NY/London: The Guilford Press.

Mahler, M., Pine, F., & Bergman, A. (1975). *The psychological birth of the human infant: Symbiosis and individuation.* New York, NY: Basic Books.

Malaktaris, A. L., & Lynn, S. J. (2019). The phenomenology and correlates of flashbacks in individuals with posttraumatic stress symptoms. *Clinical Psychological Science, 7*(2), 249–264. https://doi.org/10.1177/2167702618805081

Manson, C. [Interview by D. Sawyer]. (1995). *ABC News.*

Masten, A. S., & Cicchetti, D. (2010). Developmental cascades. *Development and Psychopathology, 22,* 491–495. https://doi.org/10.1017/S0954579410000222

McCluskey, U. (2000). Abuse in religious institutions: An exploration of the psychosocial dynamics in the Irish context. In U. McCluskey & C. A. Hooper (Eds.), *Psychodynamic perspectives on abuse: The cost of fear.* London/Philadelphia, PA: Jessica Kingsley Publishers.

McCrea, M., Guskiewicz, K. M., Marshall, S. W., Barr, W., Randolph, C., Cantu, R. C., … Kelly, J. P. (2003). Acute effects and recovery time following concussion in collegiate football players: The NCAA concussion study. *JAMA, 290*(19), 2556–2563.

McGillivray, J. A., & McCabe, M. P. (2006). Early detection of depression and associated risk factors in adults with mild/moderate intellectual disability. *Research in Developmental Disabilities, 28*(1), 59–70.

Mikulincer, M., & Shaver, P. R. (2017). Attachment-related contributions to the study of psychopathology. In P. Luyten, L. C. Mayes, P. Fonagy, M. Target, & S. Blatt (Eds.), *Handbook of psychodynamic approaches to psychopathology* (pp. 27–46). New York, NY/London: The Guilford Press.

Montaldo, C. (2018, August 23). Biography of serial killer Albert Fish. Retrieved from https://www.thoughtco.com/serial-killer-albert-fish-973157.

Morgan, R. E., & Truman, J. (2018, December 21). Criminal victimization, 2017. *Bureau of Justice Statistics.* http://www.bjs.gov/index.cfm?ty=pbdetail&iid=6466. Retrieved 12 June 2019.

Morris, D. O., Javier, R. A., & Herron, W. G. (2015). *Specialty competencies in professional psychology. Specialty competencies in psychoanalysis in psychology.* New York, NY: Oxford University Press.

Moylan, C., Herrenkohl, T., Sousa, C., Tajima, E., Herrenkohl, R., & Russo, M. (2010). The effects of child abuse and exposure to domestic violence on adolescent internalizing and externalizing behavior problems. *Journal of Family Violence, 25*(1), 53–63. https://doi.org/10.1007/s10896-009-9269-9

Myers, W. C., Gooch, E., & Meloy, J. R. (2005). The role of psychopathy and sexuality in a female serial killer. *Journal of Forensic Sciences, 50*(3), 1–6. https://doi.org/10.1520/jfs2004324

National Center for Mental Health Promotion and Youth Violence Prevention. (2012). http://www.promoteprevent.org/sites/www.promoteprevent.org/files/resources/childhood%20trauma_brief_in_final.pdf. Retrieved 8/12/19

National Coalition Against Domestic Violence. (2017). http://ncadv.org/learn-more/statistics. Retrieved 8/9/2017

National Institute of Mental Health (NIMH) (2003). Suicide facts. Retrieved from http://www.nimh.nih.gov/research/suifact.cfm;

Needleman, H. L., McFarland, C., Ness, R. B., Fienberg, S. E., & Tobin, M. J. (2002). Bone lead levels in adjudicated delinquents: A case control study. *Neurotoxicology and Teratology, 24*, 711–717.

Nevid, J. S., Rathus, S.A., & Greene, B. (2018). *Abnormal Psychology in a Changing World*. N.Y.: Pearson.

O'Reilly, J., & Chalmers, M. P. (2014). *The clergy sex abuse crisis and the legal responses*. New York, NY: Oxford University Press.

Oudekerk, B.A., Musu, L., Zhang, A., Wang, K., & Zhang, J. (2019). *Bureau of Justice Statistics*. http://www.bjs.gov/index.cfm?ty=pbdetail&iid=6526. Retrieved 12 June 2019.

Patel, N. B., Xu, Y., McCandless, L. C., Chen, A., Yolton, K., Braun, J., … Lanphear, B. P. (2019). Very low-level prenatal mercury exposure and behaviors in children: The Home Study. *Environmental Health, 18*(4). https://ehjournal.biomedcentral.com/articles/10.1186/s12940-018-0443-5. Retrieved August 20, 2019.

Paulus, D. J., Tran, N., Gallagher, M. W., Viana, A. G., Bakhshaie, J., Garza, M., … Zvolensky, M. J. (2019). Examining the indirect effect of posttraumatic stress symptoms via emotion dysregulation on alcohol misuse among trauma-exposed Latinx in primary care. *Cultural Diversity and Ethnic Minority Psychology, 25*, 55–64. https://doi.org/10.1037/cdp0000226

Pelkonen, M., & Marttunen, M. (2003). Child and adolescent suicide epidemiology, risk factors, and approaches to prevention. *Pediatric Drugs, 5*(4), 243–265.

Pesta, A. (2019, July 29). Time, *194*(4), 48–52. www.time.com

Peters, L. (2017, July 13). Eight suspected psychopaths from history whose stories are still chilling in 2017. Retrieved from https://www.bustle.com/p/8-suspected-psychopaths-from-history-whose-stories-are-still-chilling-in-2017-70014.

Pocock, S. J., Smith, M., & Baghurst, P. (1994). Environmental lead and children's intelligence: A systematic review of the epidemiological evidence. *BMJ, 309*, 1189–1197.

Ramsland, K. M. (2005). *Inside the minds of mass murderers: Why they kill*. Westport (Conn.): Praeger.

Rasmussen, A., Verkuilen, J., Jayawickreme, N., Wu, Z., & McCluskey, S. T. (2019). When did posttraumatic stress disorder get so many factors? Confirmatory factor models since DSM-5. *Clinical Psychological Science, 7*(2), 234–248.

Recognizetrauma. (2019). http://recognizetrauma.org/index.php. Retrieved 1/26/2019.

Richardson, L., Freeh, B. C., & Acierno. (2010). Prevalence estimates of combat-related PTSD: A critical review. *Australian and New Zealand Journal of Psychiatry, 44*(1), 4–19.

Rojas-Flores, L., Clements, M. L., Hwang Koo, J., & London, J. (2017). Trauma and psychological distress in Latino citizen children following parental detention and deportation. *Psychological Trauma: Theory, Research, Practice, and Policy, 9*(3), 352–361. https://doi.org/10.1037/tra0000177

Rosen, G. M., & Lilienfeld, S. O. (2008). Posttraumatic stress disorder: An empirical evaluation of core assumptions. *Clinical Psychology Review, 28*, 837–868.

Russell, P. L. (1998). The role of paradox in repetition compulsion. In J. G. Teicholz & D. Kriegman (Eds.), *Trauma, repetition compulsion, and affect regulation: The work of Paul Russell* (pp. 1–22). New York, NY: The Other Press.

Schwarz, L., Penna, S., & Novack, T. (2009). Factors contributing to performance on the Rey Complex Figure Test in individuals with traumatic brain injury. *The Clinical Neuropsychologist, 23*(2), 255–267. https://doi.org/10.1080/13854040802220034

Sciarillo, W. G., Alexander, G., & Farrell, K. P. (1992). Lead exposure and child behavior. *American Journal of Public Health, 82*, 1356–1360.

Serena, K. (2018, Jan 30). The gruesome crimes of Albert Fish, the Brooklyn Vampire. Retrieved from https://allthatsinteresting.com/albert-fish.

Small, G. W., Kepe, V., Siddarth, P., Ercoli, L. M., Merrill, D. A., Donoghue, N., ... Barrio, J. R. (2013). PET scanning of brain tau in retired National Football League players: Preliminary findings. *American Journal of Geriatric Psychiatry, 21*(2), 138–144.

Smith, L. S., & Stover, C. S. (2016). The moderating role of attachment on the relationship between history of trauma and intimate violence victimization. *Violence Against Women, 22*(6), 745–764.

Solms, M., & Turnbull, O. (2002). *The brain and the inner world: An introduction to the neuroscience of subjective experience*. New York, NY: Karnac Books.

Spitz, R. A. (1946). Anaclitic depression: An inquiry into the genesis of psychiatric conditions in early childhood. *Psychoanalytic Study of the Child, 2*, 313–342.

Steele, M., & Steele, H. (2017). Attachment disorders. In P. Luyten, L. C. Mayes, P. Fonagy, M. Target, & S. Blatt (Eds.), *Handbook of psychodynamic approaches to psychopathology* (pp. 426–444). New York, NY/London: The Guilford Press.

Sue, D. W., Capodilupo, C. M., Torino, G. C., Bucceri, J. M., Holder, A. M. B., Nadal, K. L., & Esquilin, M. (2007). Racial microaggression in everyday life: Implications for clinical practice. *American Psychologist, 62*(4), 271–286.

Suk, J. (2010). The trajectory of trauma: Bodies and minds of abortion discourse. *Columbia Law Review, 110*(5), 1193–1252. Downloaded from 149.68.240.133 on Fri, 23, March 2018 16:57:57 UTC http://about.jstor.org/terms.

Sullivan, H. S. (1955). *Interpersonal theories of psychiatry*. New York, NY: Tavistock Publications.

Sumner, J. A., Colich, N. L., Uddin, M., Armstrong, D., & McLaughlin, K. A. (2019). Early experiences, of threat, but not deprivation, are associated with accelerated biological aging in children and adolescents. *Biological Psychiatry, 85*, 268–278. https://doi.org/10.1016/j.biopsych.2018.09.008

Teasdale, T. W., & Engberg, A. W. (2003). Cognitive dysfunction in young men following head injury in childhood and adolescence: A population study. *Journal of Neurological and Neurosurgical Psychiatry, 4*(7), 933–936.

Tomkins, S. (1962). *Affect, imagery, consciousness (vol. 1): The positive affects*. New York, NY: Springer.

Tomkins, S. (1978). Script theory: Differential magnification of affects. In H. E. Howe Jr. & R. A. Dunstbier (Eds.), *Nebraska symposium on motivation* (pp. 201–236). Lincoln, NB: University of Nebraska Press.

Trothen, T. J. (2012). Shattering the illusion. In *Child sexual abuse in Canadian religious institutions*. Waterloo, ON: Wilfrid Laurier University Press.

U.S. Department of Health & Human Services. (2012). Child maltreatment, 2011. https://www.acf.hhs.gov/sites/default/files/cb/cm11.pdf. Retrieved 8/12/19

Ungar, M. (2013). Resilience, trauma, context, and culture. *Trauma, Violence, & Abuse, 14*(3), 255–266.

Walters, M., L. Chen, & Breiding, M. J. (2013). *The National Intimate Partner and Sexual Violence Survey*. Retrieved from http://www.cdc.gov/violenceprevention/pdf/nisvs_sofings.pdf

Warburton, W. & Anderson, C. A. (2018). On the clinical applications of the General Aggression Model to understanding domestic violence. In R. A. Javier & W.G. Herron (Eds.). Understanding domestic violence: Thories, challlenges, and remedics. (Pp. 71–106). New York/London:Rowman & Littlefield.

Waterman, E. H., Pruett, D., & Caughey, A. B. (2013). Reducing fetal alcohol exposure in the United States. *Obstet Gynecol Survey, 68*(5), 367–378. https://doi.org/10.1097/OGX.0b013e31828736d5

Weissman, M. M., Wickramarante, P., Nomura, Y., Warner, V., Pilowsky, D., & Verdeli, H. (2006). Offspring of depressed parents: 20 years later. *American Journal of Psychiatry, 163*(6), 1001–1008.

# Part I
# Conceptual Framework

**Rafael Art. Javier, Elizabeth A. Owen, and Jemour A. Maddux**

## Introduction

We begin with a series of chapters as part of the "Conceptual Framework" section (Part I) meant to set the stage for the kinds of examinations we intend to engage in the other more specific forensic issues we explore in chapters included in Parts II, III, and IV. For instance, the chapter by Nesi and Garbarino (Chap. 2) looks at trauma from a forensic developmental psychology lens and provides a framework to understand that even in most vicious criminals, there may be a traumatic condition and personal vulnerability that can come across in transformed (criminal) behavior, but that whose debilitating and disorganizing effects continue to haunt them while in prison, and to the end of their natural life. The following chapter by Owen and Perry (Chap. 3) then examines the role of trauma in the evaluation of competency to stand trial where they make the point that properly assessing competency in individual accused of a crime is at the bedrock of the commitment to a fair trial. That goal is quite challenging as there are so many factors and obstacles that can derail the adequate competency evaluation. These obstacles and challenges are a function of the population for which competency evaluation is normally requested: from individuals who are mentally ill, with a serious history of multiple traumas and incarcerated; to individuals who are cognitively compromised and who are unable to communicate due to limited, if any, knowledge of English; to individuals who are coming from different cultural contexts and whose understanding of the work and

R. A. Javier
Psychology, St. John's University, Queens, NY, USA

E. A. Owen
Columbia University/Teachers College, New York, NY, USA

J. A. Maddux
Lamb and Maddux, LLC, Hackensack, NJ, USA

special terms used by the court is limited at best. In the end, it challenges the forensic professional to be thorough and steadfast in their determination to ensure competency evaluation for those individuals whose trauma experience may also be affecting their attention, concentration, and reality testing.

The chapter by Leidenfrost and Antonious (Chap. 4) offers another insightful and important examination of trauma, but more specifically in the context of the incarceration experience. This chapter provides a comprehensive review of the literature on trauma and incarceration, with focus on trauma experienced both before and during incarceration, and its impact on post-release. Part of the authors' concerns is the understanding that exposure to trauma increases the risk for the development of a multitude of problems for incarcerated individuals, including violence and other disciplinary issues; development or worsening of mental illness; death through suicide; and criminal recidivism post-release. In this chapter, they examine the various ways a system that is supposed to encourage positive changes in inmates, paradoxically becomes a catalyst for additional trauma experience in these individuals and, in the end, making things worse both for the individual and for the society that it is expected to protect. The chapter by Caffrey (Chap. 5) challenges the reader by providing another look at the complexity of what is involved in considering trauma as an important factor in sentencing mitigation. It includes an examination of the history of how the presence of trauma was eventually allowed in court proceedings with the acceptance of the PTSD diagnosis, and the current challenge in determining what conditions are now allowable components of a PTSD-DSM- 5 diagnosis. This chapter then offers an empirically supported exploration of the different physiological and psychological manifestations of trauma and their possible role in sentence mitigation. Finally, guided by the principle of best practice, this chapter provides a meticulous step-by-step method to assess trauma in this context and the specific laws that guide that process.

This section concludes with two other important chapters: Chap. 6 by Takooshian and Leeolou that addresses an area not often considered in a discussion of trauma ("homicide activism") and Chap. 7 by Javier and Lamela that focuses on the serious challenges faced by even the most experienced and knowledgeable forensic professional related to the reliability and validity of psychological instruments when applied to a forensic population whose composition and diversity continue to change. More specifically, the chapter by Takooshian and Leeolou (Chap. 6) highlights the role of trauma on what they refer to as "homicide activism" which has had a tremendous impact on a few changes in laws. In this context, they describe instances in which an experience of trauma related to the loss of loved ones due to negligence has propelled some individuals to become activists and thus turning a bad experience into a force for positive changes; examples of these changes are the introduction of the Amber Alerts, Megan's Law, and the formation of Mothers Against Drunk Driving. Again, raising the issue of the different ways the effect of trauma can be experienced and that not everyone whose life is affected by a traumatic experience ends up engaged in the justice system as a defendant. How and what personal and environmental conditions are involved in making that possible is a question whose answer we attempt to address in the various chapters of this book.

Finally, the chapter by Javier and Lamela (Chap. 7) focuses on the importance of considering culturally and linguistically specific issues in trauma evaluation of individuals from diverse populations who are involved in the justice system. This chapter examines specific ways language deficiencies in English, low educational background, the specific ways emotions are expressed, and how the development of one's personality are culturally influenced. Also explored in this chapter is the issue of competency raised in Chap. 3, raising the issue that it is not enough to use translation or interpreters when examining these types of individuals. The recommendation is that specific strategies and considerations should be followed to ensure that the forensic assessment does not become seriously compromised for its lack of reliability and validity when assessing individuals from different cultural and linguistic communities. This does not only refer to individuals whose primary language is not the one used for the assessment, like the case for immigrants, but also members of the deaf and mute community who do not know American Sign Language. Part of the complication in these situations is the unique language of the court which may not be easily understood and translatable to another language (e.g., the Miranda Rights, plead, plea bargain, etc.) and thus possibly compromising the defendants' ability to understand the charges against them and their consequences, and let alone being able to assist in their own defense (Vernon, Steinberg, & Montoya, 1999).

The reader is then invited to engage in an exploration on specific ways trauma permeates individuals across the developmental spectrum and life experiences and within various involvements with our legal system. In that context, the reader has a unique opportunity to explore specific trauma likely to emerge in civil and criminal contexts.

# Reference

Vernon, M., Steinberg, A. G., & Montoya, L. A. (1999). Deaf murderers: Clinical and forensic issues. *Behavioral Sciences and the Law, 17*, 495–516.

# Chapter 2
# Trauma at the Heart of Forensic Developmental Psychology

**Danielle Nesi, James Garbarino, and Caitlin Prater**

## Introduction

Trauma is the result of encountering experiences that are characterized by "overwhelming negative cognitions" (i.e., where the idea of what is happening violates normal standards of reality, such as when you witness people being killed or you are physically attacked with potentially lethal violence) and "overwhelming negative arousal" (i.e., when you are so terrified that normal emotional coping is disrupted, when "your emotional circuits are blown").

Effects of trauma in the short run include disrupted sleep and normal activities of life, emotional deadening and disconnection ("dissociation"), hypersensitivity to events and stimuli that are associated with the traumatic event(s), and other psychological symptoms of what has come to be known as post-traumatic stress disorder (PTSD). In the long run, effects can include problems with prosocial behavior and moral development. These problems should be addressed therapeutically because they are generally remediable.

While all human beings are vulnerable to being traumatized, children are particularly vulnerable (especially elementary school-aged children who are old enough to realize what is happening around them and yet who are not mature enough to process overwhelming arousal effectively) (Carpenter & Stacks, 2009; Cohen, Mannarino, & Deblinger, 2006; Lieberman & Knorr, 2007). One of the most important variables in understanding trauma is whether it is a single incident ("acute" trauma) or it is an ongoing pattern of experience ("chronic" trauma). Acute trauma

D. Nesi · J. Garbarino (✉)
Loyola University Chicago, Department of Psychology, Chicago, IL, USA
e-mail: dnesi@luc.edu; jgarbar@luc.edu

C. Prater
Loyola University Chicago, Chicago, IL, USA
e-mail: cprater@luc.edu

© Springer Nature Switzerland AG 2020
R. A. Javier et al. (eds.), *Assessing Trauma in Forensic Contexts*,
https://doi.org/10.1007/978-3-030-33106-1_2

is amenable to resolution through some combination of "psychological first aid" in the form of reassurance and the passage of time as things return to normal. Chronic trauma (like war zones trauma) is not so amenable to resolution because there is no possibility of a simple therapy of reassurance, as a "return to normal" is not a solution because the problem is the normal. "War zones" exist as neighborhoods with high levels of community violence that afflict children and youth with such chronic trauma. Of special concern is chronic trauma that is severe and occurs during the first few years of life when the basic building blocks of human development are being assembled in a child's brain.

Beyond the chronic adversity individuals experienced as a child (e.g., lack of food and consistent care giving), many traumatized children and adolescents are plagued by intrusive traumatic images in the community (e.g., witnessing a shooting, being shot at, and being beaten up) and in the family (e.g., seeing a mother repeatedly beaten and witnessing relatives assault each other). Each of these experiences is the kind of "classic" traumatic experience that would elicit "psychological first aid" – psychotherapeutic intervention (counseling and therapy) – were it to occur to a "mainstream" child living in a high-resource family and community. But given the realities of American life, namely, that trauma is particularly prevalent among low-income and minority populations, such trauma often is not dealt with therapeutically, as these groups experience greater barriers to accessing mental health care evidenced by lower rates of mental health service use (Marrast, Himmelstein, & Woolhandler, 2016).

What is more, it would appear that such families often do not provide the kind of informal processing of experiences (i.e., open and nurturing opportunities to report his or her experiences, empathic listening, and "clarifying" adult responses) that has been found to reduce the traumatic effect of such experiences. For example, in research on Palestinian children dealing with the trauma associated with war zone living, we found that mothers who were open and available to discuss frightening experiences helped children cope with political violence in the community (Garbarino & Kostelny, 1996).

Research has demonstrated that frequent exposure to trauma in childhood can have effects on the development of the brain, affecting two crucial elements in effective, prosocial decision-making, namely, "executive function" (see Aas et al., 2012; Beers & De Bellis, 2002; El-Hage, Gaillard, Isingrini, & Belzung, 2006; Majer, Nater, Lin, Capuron, & Reeves, 2010; Navalta, Polcari, Webster, Boghossian, & Teicher, 2006; Nolin & Ethier, 2007; Zou et al., 2013) and "emotional regulation" (Erickson, Egeland, & Pianta, 1989; Pollak, 2008; Shields, Cicchetti, & Ryan, 1994). Chronic trauma tends to lead to the overdevelopment of the more primitive parts of the brain (e.g., amygdala) that processes emotions (particularly anger and fear) to the detriment of the more sophisticated parts of the brain (e.g., the cortex) that are involved in reasoning. This negative effect is most clear when chronic trauma is experienced in early childhood, but given the malleability of the brain (even in adulthood), adolescents who experience chronic trauma can also be affected, as is evident in the lives of violent youth (Garbarino, 1999; Garbarino, 2015; Garbarino, 2018). This chapter explores these issues of experiencing trauma and developing in its wake, as they are relevant to issues on forensic psychology.

## *A Case Study of Aileen Wuornos*

Trauma not only causes destruction in the current state of a child's mind, but it can cause long-term effects such as violent acts and aggressive behavior for the remainder of the child's life. For example, at one point in time, the names of Lyle and Erik Menendez, Jeffrey Dahmer, Ted Bundy, Aaron Thomas, Mary Bell, Aileen Wuornos, and many others were written into history for mass murder, rape, and sexual assault against a child. They became famous based on the horrific crimes that they committed. However, these convicted criminals were once victims themselves of chronic and/or catastrophic trauma.

Let us look at one example: Aileen Wuornos, convicted for the murders of seven men between 1989 and 1990 (Myers, Gooch, & Meloy, 2005). Her biological father abused alcohol and committed suicide while serving a life sentence in a Kansas prison for raping a 7-year-old girl (Wuornos vs. Florida, 1994). Wuornos' mother was physically abused during her pregnancy with Aileen, and following Aileen's birth, she soon abandoned her children (Wuornos vs. Florida, 1994). When Wuornos and her brother Keith were discovered, they were found alone in an attic covered with feces and flies (Wuornos vs. Florida, 1994). Wuornos and her brother eventually came to live with their grandparents (Wuornos vs. Florida, 1994; Wuornos vs. Florida, 1996). There, conditions remained dire. Like her father, her grandparents also abused alcohol (Wuornos vs. Florida, 1994) and Wuornos sustained emotional, physical, and sexual abuse from her grandfather, including physical beatings without intervention from her passive grandmother who was also emotionally abusive (Myers et al., 2005).

Wuornos' early life was plagued with behavioral problems (Myers et al., 2005). During the early years of her childhood, Wuornos had an "explosive temper," making it harder to create friendships, and by age 9 Wuornos began stealing from family and friends (Myers et al., 2005, p. 2). By age 9, she became infatuated with fire, set fire to her home at age 9, the school bathroom at age 13, and a field at age 14 (Myers et al., 2005). When she was 13 years old, Wuornos was raped and became pregnant (Smith, 2005). She tried to hide her pregnancy, but once her grandfather became aware, she was forced to complete her pregnancy in a home for unwed mothers and give her child up for adoption (Smith, 2005). After returning to her grandparents, Wuornos could no longer stand the abuse and ran away. At the age of 14, she was living on the streets and exploiting drugs and alcohol leading into prostitution (Smith, 2005).

Around the age of 20, Aileen married a man of 69 years which ended due to physical abuse (Myers et al., 2005). During the same time frame, her brother Keith passed away from cancer and her abusive grandfather committed suicide (Myers et al., 2005). Wuornos attempted suicide twice: once by a gunshot in the stomach and later by an overdose of tranquilizers (Myers et al., 2005).

Given this detailed past of abuse and neglect, when and how did Aileen Wuornos transition from victim to perpetrator? It appeared to start with wanting a gun for self-protection. She described to police that, "I've been beat up so bad you couldn't describe me" throughout her prostitution career (Brief Challenging Death Sentences in Three Murder Cases, supra note 32, at 61 (quoting from appellate record, at 593)). Shortly after buying a firearm, she killed her first victim (Wuornos vs. Florida, 1994). Initially, Wuornos was reportedly more interested in the thrill of robbing these men than she was in killing them. It escalated, however, to the point where she did not want witnesses to her crime, and shot the men to prevent them from reporting her actions. In her words:

> "I had no intentions of killing anybody . . . it wasn't intentional killing. It wasn't just kill somebody. It was because they physically attacked me . . . I was afraid that if I shot 'em one time and they survived, my face and all that, description of me. Would be all over the place and the only way I could make money was to hustle. And I knew these guys would probably . . . rat on me if they survived . . . I was hoping . . . that I wouldn't of had gotten caught for it because I figured that these guys deserved it. Because these guys were gonna either rape, kill-I don't know what they were gonna do to me . . ." (Brief Challenging Death Sentences in Three Murder Cases, supra note 32, at 61 (quoting from appellate record, at 593)).

Female serial killers (FSKs) "[kill] for money, power, revenge, and even notoriety and excitement" (Harrison, Murphy, Ho, Bowers, & Flaherty, 2015, p. 397). These women often suffer from mental illness or abuse drugs and/or alcohol (Harrison et al., 2015) and many experienced early trauma. It has been reported that one in ten FSKs experienced severe childhood illness or trauma and these women demonstrate considerably higher rates of childhood physical and/or sexual abuse than other children (Harrison et al., 2015). In addition to her extensive history of emotional, physical, and sexual abuse, Wuornos had issues with drugs and alcohol abuse since age 14. In 1970, her school made efforts to warn her grandparents and make them aware that Aileen needed psychological counseling as soon as possible. The need for psychological counseling is not atypical for FSKs; it has been reported that 40% of FSKs experience mental illness (Harrison et al., 2015), suggesting that mental illness contributes to later violence perpetration. In the case of Aileen Wuornos, we can see evidence of the shift from victim to perpetrator, which was heavily influenced by early trauma and resulting psychological damage.

## Prevalence of Trauma Among Offenders

Research has demonstrated that there are strong associations between traumatic experiences and criminal behavior (Ardino, 2011; Foy, Furrow, & McManus, 2011; Weeks & Widom, 1989, 1998) such that offenders have higher prevalence of post-traumatic stress disorder and PTSD symptoms as compared to non-offenders (Wright, Borrill, Teers, & Cassidy, 2006). A review by Vermeiren (2003) found that the prevalence of PTSD among sentenced prisoners ranged from 4% (Brink, Doherty, & Boer, 2001) to 21.4% (Butler, Levy, Dolan, & Kaldor, 2003). The rate of PTSD may be even higher when considering lifetime PTSD criteria. For example, work by Powell, Holt, and Fondacaro (1997) found that 21% of their sample met 6-month criteria for PTSD and 33% met lifetime PTSD criteria. These rates are far higher than those observed among the general population. In the United States, research by the National Comorbidity Survey Replication (NCS-R) estimated the lifetime prevalence of PTSD among adult Americans to be 6.8% (Kessler et al., 2005), (3.6% for men and 9.7% for women) and the 12-month prevalence was esti-mated to be 3.5% (Kessler, Chiu, Demler, Merikangas, & Walters, 2005), 1.8% among men and 5.2% among women (National Comorbidity Survey, 2005). However, other estimates suggest even lower rates of PTSD among the general pop-ulation in the United States. For example, work by Helzer, Robins, and McEvoy (1987) and Davidson, Hughes, Blazer, and George (1991), both using the DSM-III criteria and the Diagnostic Interview Schedule (DIS) (Robins, Helzer, Croughan, Williams, & Spitzer, 1981) to assess PTSD, reported lifetime rates of 1.0 and 1.3%, respectively.

It is possible that the lower rates found by Helzer et al. (1987) and Davidson et al. (1991) may be attributed to their use of the DIS, which has faced criticism because the traumatic event and PTSD are not independently assessed. Rather, the events that induct PTSD symptomology are required to be subjectively perceived as being related to the traumatic event that predated the symptoms. This could explain why, when omitting that requirement and estimating signs and symptoms of PTSD irrespective of traumatic events, Resnick, Kilpatrick, Dansky, Saunders, and Best (1993) reported a lifetime DSM III-R (American Psychiatric Association [APA], 1987) defined prevalence of 12.3% in women and Kessler, Sonnega, Bromet, Hughes, and Nelson (1995) found an overall prevalence rate of 7.8% (10.4% in women and 5.0% in men), which is similar to that observed by Breslau et al. (1998) who observed an average lifetime prevalence of 8.3%. It is also important to note that changing diagnostic criteria may also account for differences in PTSD rates over time. The lifetime prevalence rate of 6.8% (e.g., Kessler, Berglund, et al., 2005), 7.8% (Kessler et al., 1995), and 8.3% (Breslau et al., 1998) were found using DSM IV (1994). However, when we consider the lifetime prevalence rates of PTSD among women, it seems they may vary depending on diagnostic criteria of different versions of PTSD. Specifically, using the DSM III-R, Resnick et al. (1993) reported a lifetime prevalence of PTSD among women of 12.3%, whereas Kessler et al. (1995) found a lifetime prevalence among females to be 10.4% when using the DSM IV. Thus, it is possible that changes in diagnostic criteria may influence the observed rates of PTSD (e.g., changes from DSM IV and DSM III-R PTSD criteria).

The high rates of PTSD among offenders are not surprising when considering the high rates of trauma and adversity faced by offenders. One way of conceptualizing the level of trauma and/or adversity a person has experienced is through the use of the Adverse Childhood Experiences scale (ACE). Originally developed by the Kaiser Permanent Medical Care Program in San Diego, CA through a longitudinal study involving over 17,000 patients, the ACE incorporated preexisting research on traumatic events leading to adverse future adjustment as adults into a single assess-ment (Anda et al., 1999). The ACE questionnaire includes items that inquire about prior experiences of abuse (physical, sexual, and emotional), neglect (physical and emotional), and household dysfunction (the experience of having a battered mother, parental abandonment, or having had a substance abusing, mentally ill, or incarcerated household member) in childhood, defined as the first 18 years of life

(Anda et al., 1999). Using the ACE is useful, as it can provide a way to understand the severity of trauma an individual has experienced.

One research exploring the prevalence of ACEs among offenders was done by Reavis, Looman, Franco, and Rojas (2013), who explored the prevalence of ACEs among groups of offenders (nonsexual child abusers, domestic violence offenders, sexual offenders, and stalkers). Overall, offenders had 3.73 (*SD* = 2.69) ACEs, which is consistent with other work including that by Moore and Tatman (2016) who found an average ACE score of 4.03 (*SD* = 2.61) among a sample of offenders (male and female) on probation and parole from a Midwestern community-based corrections agency. In this study, only 9.3% reported no ACEs, while nearly half reported experiencing four or more ACE factors. In contrast, 38% of the normative sample had experienced no ACEs and only 12.5% reported having four or more ACEs. Overall, it was found that when compared with a normative group of adult males, the offenders in this study had much higher rates of traumatic events or experiences. Four times as many subjects endorsed four or more adverse experiences in their early lives as compared to the normative sample. In fact, every ACE Questionnaire item, apart from a history of neglect, was found at significantly higher rates among the sample of offenders. Although nearly all ACE factors were more prevalent among offenders, certain ACE factors were especially pervasive among this population, including physical abuse (52.3% vs. 7.6% in normative sample), parental criminality (20.5% vs. 4.1% in normative sample), and household substance abuse (47.7% vs. 23.8% in normative sample).

Another interesting finding of Reavis et al. (2013)'s study was the information regarding ACE prevalence among antisocial individuals engaged in different offending behaviors. Specifically, it was reported that there was a difference in the number of ACEs reported by the groups: more sexual offenders reported having four or more ACEs (68.9%) than did child abusers (22.9%) and perpetrators of domestic violence were more likely to report no ACEs (17.8%) than sexual offenders (3.3%). When comparing rates of individual ACE items across offender types, significant differences were observed in the prevalence of sexual abuse. Sexual offenders and child abusers demonstrated higher than expected rates of sexual abuse, whereas stalkers were found to have lower than expected rates.

Additional studies using the ACE have found that childhood adversity is also common among other antisocial populations, including female offenders and juvenile offenders of both sexes. Previous studies have found that incarcerated women are more likely to report extensive histories of trauma, including emotional, physical, and sexual abuse, with estimates ranging from 77% to 90% (Jordan et al., 2002; Jordan, Schlenger, Fairbank, & Caddell, 1996; Langan & Pelissier, 2001; Messina, Burdon, Hagopian, & Prendergast, 2006; Messina, Burdon, & Prendergast, 2003; Peters, Strozier, Murrin, & Kearns, 1997; Pollock, 2002). Again, as with work done on male offenders, the Adverse Childhood Experiences questionnaire has been used as a means to quantify the amount of childhood trauma experienced by female offenders.

Previous work using the ACE with female offenders includes work by Messina and Grella (2006), who interviewed approximately 500 incarcerated women in

California using an ACE framework and asked female offenders about their experiences of eight types of childhood trauma, including prior experiences involving abuse and neglect (emotional abuse and neglect, physical neglect, physical abuse, and sexual abuse) and experiences involving household dysfunction (e.g., family violence, parental separation/divorce, incarcerated family member, and out-of-home placement) as compared to a comparison population of females (sample derived from a health maintenance organization). As expected, incarcerated women had far higher levels of adversity as compared to women in the comparison group. For example, only 15.7% of incarcerated females reported having no traumatic experiences in childhood as compared to 31.3% of women in the comparison group and a majority of women in the comparison group (55%) reported having zero or one traumatic experience, as compared to less than a third of incarcerated women (32.4%). Overall, incarcerated women were much more likely to report high levels of adversity; more than one-fifth (21.2%) of women reported five or more traumatic experiences, as compared to only 12.5% among the comparison group. Among adjudicated murderers, one study found that the average ACE score was seven (Garbarino, 2018).

Other work exploring the prevalence of ACEs among incarcerated females includes work by De Ravello, Abeita, and Brown (2008), who administered the ACE questionnaire to a sample of incarcerated Native American women in New Mexico and found that all but one individual reported having at least one ACE and the majority (81%) were found to have an ACE score of two or more. Among this sample, the most frequently endorsed traumas were having a household family member have an alcohol or drug problem (75.0%), witnessing violence in the home (72.2%), having an immediate family member be incarcerated (69.4%), and a history of sexual abuse (52.8%). In the study by Moore and Tatman (2016), no significant differences were found in ACE scores among females ($M = 4.04$, $SE = 3.11$) and males ($M = 4.02$, $SE = 2.93$). Thus, it seems that childhood trauma is pervasive among both male and female adult offenders.

Unsurprisingly, high rates of trauma and adversity are also found among juvenile offenders. Work by Baglivio et al. (2014) extrapolated ACE scores from the standardized assessment tool used within the Florida Department of Juvenile Justice (FDJJ) and found an average composite ACE score of 4.29 for females and 3.48 for male offenders (difference was statistically significant at $p < 0.001$) and nearly all juvenile offenders surveyed had experienced at least on traumatic event (96–97%), indicating that both male and female juvenile offenders have high rates of childhood trauma. To put these numbers in context, Baglivio et al. (2014) compared their results to those observed in the original ACE study conducted by Felitti and colleagues (Felitti et al., 1998). Their results indicate that young offenders are 13 times less likely to report having no early traumatic experiences (i.e., an ACE score of 0) (2.8% compared to 36%) and they are four times more likely to report having experienced four our more ACEs (50% compared to 13%) (Baglivio et al., 2014).

In regard to gender differences among adversity and trauma experiences by young offenders, the findings of Baglivio et al. (2014) do appear to indicate that female juvenile offenders are especially likely to have experienced high rates of trauma. Although the most commonly endorsed items were the same for both male and female juvenile offenders (family violence, parental separation or divorce, incarceration of a household member) and the rank order of individual ACE item prevalence was the same across genders, with the exception of sexual abuse (which was reported 4.4 times more frequently by females than by males (31% in females, 7% in males), females had a higher prevalence than males on every ACE questionnaire item. The findings of Baglivio and colleagues are consistent with previous studies which have found high rates of early trauma among young offenders, such as that by Grevstad (2010) who found that juvenile offenders had approximately three times more ACEs than the population reported by Felitti et al. (1998). Again, though early trauma is common among both male and female young offenders and both genders share some similarities in traumatic histories, particularly in the number of traumatic experiences they have encountered and in the types of trauma to which they have been exposed, it seems clear that the major distinction between the traumatic histories of young male and female offenders lies in prior experience of sexual abuse, as studies consistently report far higher rates of sexual abuse among young female offenders (e.g., Baglivio et al., 2014; Cauffman, Feldman, Waterman, & Steiner, 1998; Dierkhising et al., 2013; Ford, Chapman, Hawker, & Albert, 2007; Wood, Foy, Layne, Pynoos, & James, 2002).

Beyond identifying the prevalence and type of trauma offenders are exposed to, other research has explored *when*, or at what developmental stage, offenders experience trauma. Research indicates that trauma is ongoing for these individuals, oftentimes beginning in early life or childhood and continuing through adulthood. Previously, we have discussed findings that demonstrate that adverse childhood experiences (ACEs) are consistently found to occur at high rates among offenders, indicating that many have experienced trauma during the first 18 years of their life (unfortunately, less is known about the time frame of traumatic experiences over the course of childhood and adolescence, as measures such as the ACE questionnaire ask respondents to indicate whether a certain traumatic event occurred during the first 18 years of life, but does not ask respondents to indicate at what specific age those events took place). Trauma is not confined to childhood for offenders, however, as research has found that both experienced (direct) and witnessed (indirect) trauma often continues into adulthood (Wolff & Shi, 2012). Prior work by Widom, Czaja, and Dutton (2008) found all types of childhood trauma (physical, sexual, and neglect) elevated one's risk of lifetime re-victimization and this pattern is also observed among offenders. It has been reported that a significant minority of trauma experiences continue into adulthood, but such events are lower than found in childhood apart from being threatened or harmed by a gun or knife, which occurs at roughly the same rate during childhood and adulthood (Wolff & Shi, 2010). Perhaps unsurprisingly, for some incarcerated males, traumatic experiences persist during confinement; among male inmates, six-month prevalence rates of inmate- and staff-on-inmate physical victimization have been estimated at 21% and 25%, respectively (Wolff, Shi, & Siegel, 2009).

Finally, it is also important to note that the high rate of early trauma among offenders is not unique to the United States. Rather, numerous international studies have demonstrated that high rates of trauma are common among antisocial youths and adults globally. Work by Matsuura, Hashimoto, and Toichi (2009) in Japan found high rates of trauma among a sample of juvenile females in a correctional facility in Japan (Mean ACE score 1.914, $SD = 1.96$, range 0–9). Similarly, European prevalence studies demonstrate higher rates of PTSD symptoms among prison populations than in clinical or community samples (Ardino, 2012). A German study evaluating PTSD among delinquents detained in forensic psychiatric institutions found a lifetime prevalence of 36% and a point prevalence of 17% (Spitzer et al., 2001) and research on offenders in Switzerland found a point prevalence of PTSD that was conservatively estimated at 27% (Urbaniok, Endrass, Noll, Vetter, & Rossegger, 2007).

## How Do Traumatic Experiences Affect Individual Development?

In considering how people develop in the face of adversity, a common theme for work done in the field of trauma has been to distinguish different types of trauma. Specifically, acknowledging the variations in outcomes among people who have had trauma, researchers have increasingly realized that not all traumatic experiences are equal, that some types of traumatic events are comparatively more traumatic, leading to worse outcomes among those who have had such experiences. Part of this discussion has been to categorize and label various trauma experiences in order to better understand how people may respond to various types of traumas.

In their analysis of trauma, Ford and Courtois (2009) provide a definition of complex trauma and complex traumatic stress disorders. In this chapter, they provide background, including a discussion on the history of trauma and its conceptualization. They note that originally, psychological trauma was considered to be an abnormal experience (i.e., "outside the range of normal human experience" in DSM-III (APA, 1980)), but following an accumulation of epidemiological evidence demonstrating that a majority of adults (e.g., Kessler et al., 1995) and a substantial minority of children (Costello, Erklani, Fairbank, & Angold, 2002) are exposed to traumatic events, a shift has taken place toward defining psychological trauma without any qualifications about its normality or abnormality (Ford & Courtois, 2009).

They note that people who have never encountered trauma do not expect trauma to occur in their (or their families' or communities') lives, an idea reminiscent of the optimism bias "it won't happen to me," wherein people believe that they are less likely to experience negative events in comparison to others. However, after psychological trauma has occurred, a person is both "more likely objectively to experience subsequent traumatic events and more prone subjectively to expect trauma to be a possibility" (Ford & Courtois, 2009, p. 15). Thus, the experience of trauma fundamentally changes a person as they are more likely to experience a subsequent traumatic episode, and they experience changes in their cognition, such that they are more likely to expect trauma. In a sense, the experience of trauma primes a person for future trauma, both emotionally and cognitively.

Ford and Courtois make an additional point that the very nature of trauma itself has changed over time. Thus, it is not just that the conceptualization and appraisal of trauma have changed overtime, but the very nature of trauma has changed. Specifically, they write that with the increasing diffusion of virtually instantaneous information through the many forms of electronic and other media, people's awareness of traumatic events has been greatly heightened, even if these events never happen to them or to anyone they know personally (e.g., Silver, Holman, McIntosh, Poulin, & Gil-Rivas, 2002).

Early research distinguished between two different types of trauma: Type I and Type II trauma (Terr, 1991). According to Terr, Type I trauma is defined as a single-incident trauma (e.g., an event that is "out of the blue" and therefore, is unexpected, such as a traumatic accident, natural disasters, terrorist attack, or a single episode of abuse or assault, or witnessing violence. Type II trauma (also referred to as complex trauma) involves chronic, repeated, and ongoing exposure to traumatic events (e.g., ongoing abuse, domestic violence, war, genocide, community violence, etc.). Generally, Type II trauma is more prevalent than perhaps typically recognized and more often occurs in combination or cumulatively (i.e., "poly-victimization" Finkelhor, Ormrod, & Turner, 2007). For example, the National Survey of Adolescents found that 20% of all youth had experienced more than one type of victimization (Saunders, 2003) and the National Survey of Children's Exposure to Violence II found that 48% of youth had experienced two or more of 50 types of victimization surveyed (Finkelhor, Turner, Shattuck, & Hamby, 2013). Moreover, another unique feature of Type II trauma is that because it is often perpetrated by someone known by, or related to the victim, it often involves a fundamental betrayal of trust within primary relationships (Ford & Courtois, 2009).

Overall, evidence suggests that the effects of Type II trauma are far more severe, as it is associated with a much higher risk for development of PTSD (e.g., 33–75+% risk vs. 10–20% for individuals who have experienced Type I trauma; Copeland, Keeler, Angold, & Costello, 2007; Kessler et al., 1995). Moreover, it seems that Type II trauma may compromise, or alter, a person's psychobiological and socio-emotional development when such trauma occurs at critical developmental stages (Ford & Courtois, 2009). It has been suggested that such "developmentally adverse interpersonal traumas" (Ford, 2005) are "complex" because they leave a person at risk for recurrent anxiety (e.g., PTSD, other anxiety disorders) as well as interruptions and breakdown in "the most fundamental outcomes of healthy psychobiological development: the integrity of the body, the development of a healthy identity and coherent personality, and secure attachment, leading to the ability to have healthy and reciprocal relationships (Cook et al., 2005; van der Kolk, 2005)" (Ford, 2009, p. 18–19).

In addition to "Type II" trauma, other terms have been used to describe pervasive psychological trauma. Herman (1992) proposed the term "complex trauma" as a means to distinguish a "complex form of post-traumatic disorder in survivors of prolonged, repeated trauma" (p. 378) from traditional forms of PTSD, of which previous diagnostic formulation was largely derived from "observations of survivors of relatively circumscribed traumatic events: combat, disaster, and rape" (p.3 377). Moreover, similar to Type II trauma, others have used the term "developmental trauma" to refer to a type of stressful event that occurs repeatedly and cumulatively, usually over a period of time, and within specific relationships and contexts (Courtois, 2004). This nomenclature reinforces the theme that traumatic experiences can fundamentally alter a person's development in profound ways.

## *Severe Chronic Trauma in the First 1000 Days of Life*

Extending the work of Terr (1991), Solomon and Heide (1999) sought to extend the previously identified typology of trauma survivors in a way that addressed the finding that chronic, repeated exposure to traumatic events may be especially damaging when such traumas occur during particular developmental ranges. This led to Solomon and Heide (1999) to propose subdividing Terr's (1991) Type II trauma into two categories: Type II and Type III. In this model, Type III trauma is defined as the result of "multiple and pervasive violent events beginning at an early age and continuing for years" (p. 204). According to Solomon and Heide, Type III trauma is more extreme than other types of trauma. Individuals who experience Type III trauma are typically child victims of multiple perpetrators, one or more of whom are close relatives (p. 204). Moreover, the abusive events experienced by individuals with Type III trauma are "likely frequent, yet unpredictable" with force being a frequent component (Solomon & Heide, 1999, p. 204). The abuse experienced by these individuals has a "sadistic quality" and may have included threats of "torture or death, or death of a loved one" (Solomon & Heide, 1999, p. 204).

The basis for Solomon and Heide's (1999) three-tier conceptualization of psychological trauma was due to the fact that individuals who experienced these types of trauma had markedly different outcomes. This difference can be observed in the reactions and presentations of individuals who have experienced these different types of trauma which are vastly different. For example, they write that when clients who have experienced Type I trauma come into contact with mental health professions, these individuals typically report experiences and describe them in some detail. Frequently, brief therapy techniques, such as behavioral strategies, Neurolinguistic Programming (NLP), or Eye Movement Desensitization and Reprocessing (EMDR), can be used to quickly and effectively resolve trauma for these individuals (O'Hanlon & Weiner-Davis, 1989; Shapiro, 1995). In contrast, they explain, individuals who have experienced Type II trauma generally come to treatment with histories of "moderate depression, dependency and trust issues, and relationship problems" (p. 204). Diagnostic characteristics frequently observed among Type II trauma victims include "poor self-esteem, feeling of shame, and difficulties trusting others" (p. 204) and these individuals oftentimes repress or interject feelings of anger, which may be experienced "only as depression" (Solomon & Heide, 1999, p. 204). Moreover, these individuals develop maladaptive defense strategies, such as denial, repression, and dissociation (Solomon & Heide, 1999).

Though the outcomes and developmental trajectories observed among individuals who have experienced Type II trauma are far worse than those observed among Type I trauma survivors, Solomon and Heide (1999) explain "skilled, well-trained therapist[s] can effectively treat these individuals" (p. 204). Thus, individuals with either Type I or Type II trauma can be rehabilitated.

## But Type III?

Distinguishing Type III trauma survivors from their counterparts is that their outcomes appear far worse than those observed among other trauma survivors. Solomon and Heide (1999) explain that when these individuals present for treatment, they typically feel suicidal and hopeless and do not know why they have these feelings. Interestingly, these individuals may initially describe their childhoods and parents very positively (Solomon & Heide, 1999). These characterizations indicate a deep fracture between the traumatic histories these individuals have faced and their cognitions regarding such events and suggest that these individuals may have been unable to process earlier traumas. Beyond feelings of suicidality or depression, these individuals have numerous widespread negative effects. In total, these individuals typically experience 20 adverse effects including chronic depression, self-injury, eating disturbances, high anxiety, narcissism, impulsivity, identity confusion, dissociative symptoms, affective dysregulation, and a foreshortened sense of future (Solomon & Heide, 1999). To put this into context, you can compare these outcomes to those observed for individuals who have experienced less extreme trauma. For example, of the 20 maladaptive effects observed among Type III trauma survivors, individuals who have experienced Type I typically demonstrate one effect (e.g., PTSD symptoms) and individuals who have experienced Type II trauma typically demonstrate five effects (e.g., PTSD symptoms, poor self-esteem/self-concept, interpersonal distrust, feelings of shame, and dependency).

## Abuse Versus Neglect

In addition to the severity and age at which a youth experiences trauma, there is also research that demonstrates that certain types of trauma may differentially impact a youth's likelihood of engaging in antisocial behavior. In other words, not all types of trauma have the same impact on youth's development of antisocial behavior. A large body of research has demonstrated that childhood abuse and neglect is a predictor of adult criminal behavior (Kingree, Phan, & Thompson, 2003; Maxfield & Widom, 1996; Smith & Thornberry, 1995; Widom & Ames, 1994; Widom & Maxfield, 2001) and that childhood maltreatment and neglect is a predictor of future recidivism (Cottle, Lee, & Heilbrun, 2001). Interestingly, however, work by Dembo et al. (1998) found that childhood neglect was a stronger predictor of future recidivism as compared to childhood abuse. Overall, these findings demonstrate that early adverse childhood experiences have a large impact on future life outcomes (Moore & Tatman, 2016), but also imply that certain adverse experiences may be especially damaging for youth.

Dembo et al.'s (1998) finding that childhood neglect more strongly predicted future recidivism than childhood abuse is unsurprising in regard to developmental theories of attachment and prior work demonstrating the importance of parental acceptance for positive youth development (see meta-analysis by Khaleque & Rohner, 2002). Attachment theorists, such as Bowlby (1973), emphasized that parents' sensitivity and responsiveness causes children to form mental representations, or internal working models, of the parent as reliable and trustworthy, which allows the youth to view themselves as worthy of love. When parents are inconsistent and a secure attachment between the child and parent is not formed, the parental rejection makes a child hesitant, aggressive, and hostile toward others because of fear of rejection. Moreover, the rejection makes a child feel unworthy of love, which results in impaired self-esteem, depressive feelings, a negative worldview, and other maladaptive orientations (Rohner, 2004). Thus, it may be that parental neglect operates similarly to parental rejection and poor parental attachment, which may account for why parental neglect appears to be more damaging to children than child abuse.

## Response to Trauma Among the General Public and Among Offenders

It is important to note, however, that trauma is not an experience unique to antisocial populations. Though universal rates of PTSD may be generally low, as previously discussed, trauma and adversity are common features of the human experience. In the National Comorbidity Survey, more than 60% of American adults reported experiencing at least one traumatic event over the courses of their lives (Kessler et al., 1995) and more recent work by Kilpatrick et al. (2013) indicates that rates of trauma may be far higher, as they found that nearly 90% of individuals had experienced traumatic event exposure using DSM-5 criteria. Moreover, the study by Kilpatrick et al. (2013) found that exposure to multiple traumatic event types is normative, confirming previous findings (e.g., Breslau, Davis, Peterson, & Schultz, 2000; Copeland et al., 2007; Kessler et al., 1995; Norris, 1992).

Although initially striking, it is not altogether surprising that so many individuals experience at least some form of trauma over the course of their lifetimes. As noted by Bonanno (2004), as people progress through the life cycle, "they are also increasingly confronted with the deaths of close friends and relatives" (p. 20). Thus, over the course of a lifetime and with increasing age, it is almost inevitable that people will undergo trauma or other profound loss. Though trauma and loss are normative, common to nearly all people, the way people respond to trauma is more variable. As Bonanno (2004) explains, not everyone copes with potentially disturbing events the same way. For example, some individuals experience acute distress from which they are never able to recover, while others suffer less intensely and for a much shorter periods of time. Still, others recover quickly, Bonanno (2004) writes, but later begin to experience unexpected health problems or difficulties concentrating or enjoying life the way they had previously.

Generally, research has focused on the relationship between trauma and antisocial behavior and less research has focused on the developmental trajectories that connect trauma and PTSD to criminal behavior (Ardino, 2012). However, in recent years, several possible explanations have emerged to explain the mechanisms through which repeated trauma early in life can lead to antisocial behaviors.

## *Impact on Executive Functioning and Affective Regulation*

One such explanation focuses the effect trauma has on fundamentally altering brain structure and functioning. Through advances in neuroscience, researchers have been able to explore how the experience of trauma affects neuropsychological functioning (De Bellis & Putnam, 1994; van der Kolk, 1996). Among adults, PTSD has been found to be associated with deficits across many mental processes, including impaired working memory and ability to sustain attention, as well as impairment in the right brain and frontal lobe (Newport & Nemeroff, 2000). It is believed that the impact of traumatic experiences may be particularly detrimental for children and adolescents, whose brains and neural networks are still developing (De Bellis, 2001; Ford, 2005). Indeed, a large body of research has demonstrated structural and functional brain abnormalities among individuals who have experienced early trauma. Youth who meet the criteria for PTSD have been found to have smaller intracranial and cerebral volumes as compared to non-maltreated youths, and it was found that intracranial volume is positively correlated with the age of onset of maltreatment and negatively correlated with the duration of abuse (De Bellis et al., 1999).

Moreover, structural changes related to trauma include differences in the left and total lateral volumes, which were found to be positively associated with maltreatment duration, while the duration of abuse was found to be negatively associated with the total corpus collosum and its middle and posterior region volumes. Due to these changes, it is thought that the impact of trauma on the developing brain may alter the exchange of information between brain hemispheres and the capacity of sensory information to be integrated (Teicher et al., 2003).

In addition, other brain regions that appear especially impacted by trauma include the hippocampus, which is involved in memory and the regulation of emotions, including fear and aggression (Cellini, 2004; Gould & Tanapat, 1999; Kim, Song, & Kosten, 2006), and the regions of the prefrontal lobe (Ishikawa & Raine, 2003). The relation of trauma to prefrontal deficits is important when considering the role of the orbitofrontal cortex, part of the prefrontal cortex, in mental processes related to emotion processing, emotion regulation, interpersonal communication, and moral reasoning (Schore, 2003). Thus, orbitofrontal deficits may impact an individuals' propensity to engage in socially appropriate responses when faced with stressful situations, or in situations where one's behavioral inhibition is reduced (Giancola, 1995; Schore, 2003).

Beyond affecting structure and functioning of the brain and its regions, there is also evidence that trauma can affect the body's biological stress systems in ways that influence antisocial behavior. Evidence has found that youth with PTSD exhibit elevated levels of norepinephrine and dopamine and excrete greater concentrations of cortisol, and the levels of these neurochemicals have been found to correlate with the duration of trauma and with PTSD symptoms, including intrusive thoughts, avoidance, and hyperarousal (De Bellis et al., 1999). Consequently, youth with PTSD symptoms may have dysregulated biological stress systems and may demonstrate hyperarousal and overactive responses when faced with stressors (De Bellis, 2001; Heim, Meinlschmidt, & Nemeroff, 2003) as well as emotional dysregulation and problems with impulse control (Gollan, Lee, & Coccano, 2005). As noted by Kerig and Becker (2010), these factors may contribute to a propensity to easy provocation, misappraisal of situations as more threatening than they are, and to act impulsively, all responses which increase the risk of antisocial behavior.

As discussed previously, trauma can impact affective regulation through physiological mechanisms whereby long-standing trauma may serve to alter the brain's physical structural as well as the body's biological stress symptoms which can negatively impact emotion regulation. There are other ways, however, in which repeated trauma can hinder affect regulation. As discussed by Kerig and Becker (2010), parents play an important role in the development of emotion regulation strategies as well as in their children's recovery following traumatic experiences, as parents lend "auxiliary emotional regulation mechanism[s]" for their children to borrow (p. 9). However, they explain, when parents are unavailable, whether due to their own trauma, or when a child experiences chronic and/or pervasive trauma, the development of emotional regulation capacities may be impaired in the long term. Parents who reject, ignore, or punish a child's distress signals leave him or her in a prolonged and intolerable emotional state and fail to assist a child in developing internal strategies with which to regulate distress (Izard & Kobak, 1991). Thus, the child fails to develop strategies for modulating emotions in response to challenging stimuli, and this poor modulation may be expressed in the form of internalizing and/or externalizing behaviors (Cole & Zahn-Waxler, 1992). Consequently, trauma can impair emotional regulation by preventing children from acquiring successful coping strategies for managing emotions, either directly or indirectly, by preventing parents from transmitting these skills to their children.

In addition to impacting an individual's capacity, or ability, to regulate and manage emotions, trauma has also been likened to deficits in executive functioning (see meta-analyses by Morgan & Lilienfeld, 2000, Ogilvie, Stewart, Chan, & Shum, 2011). Previous work has demonstrated that EF deficits are pervasive among antisocial populations (Morgan & Lilienfeld, 2000), leading many researchers to conclude that such deficits are important risk factors for, or correlates of, antisocial behavior (Elliott, 1978; Gorenstein, 1982; Raine, 1997). Executive functioning can be understood as "an umbrella term that refers to the cognitive processes that allow for future, goal-oriented behavior" (Morgan & Lilienfeld, 2000, p. 114). Broadly, executive functions refer to the management of cognitive processes that guide complex behavior (Banich, 2009; Miller & Cohen, 2001) and EF is critical for activating, maintaining, and selecting different courses of action necessary to carry out complex behaviors required to achieve various goals (Miyake & Friedman, 2012). It has been suggested that, compared to the general population, individuals with EF deficits are less able to override inclinations toward maladaptive responses required to maintain more appropriate and personally beneficial behavior (Zeier, Baskin-Sommers, Hiatt Racer, & Newman, 2011). Moreover, it is believed that EF deficits may contribute to deviant behavior by decreasing impulse inhibition, sensitivity to reward and punishment, and the ability to plan and formulate behaviors that correspond with social demands (Ishikawa & Raine, 2003; Raine, 2002; Séguin, 2004). Models explaining the relationship between EF deficits and antisocial behavior suggest that compared to the general population, these individuals are less able to override inclinations toward maladaptive responses required to maintain more appropriate and personally beneficial behavior (Zeier et al., 2011), and consequently, individuals with EF deficits are at a high risk for persistent rule breaking and violent behavior (Zeier et al., 2011).

## War Zone Mentality

One way to summarize the overall development that occurs among youth who are repeatedly exposed to trauma and violence in early life is what has been called a "war zone mentality" (Garbarino, 2015). This term explains how individuals engage in violent and antisocial behavior that seems unfathomable to others, but these behaviors make sense in the mind of perpetrators. In essence, a childhood full of trauma and violence leads to a "damaged sense of reality," (Garbarino, 2012) wherein their behaviors make sense and are justified, even logical. In very much the same way as soldiers operate in battle, youth exposed to high levels of trauma and adversity, where violence and antisocial behavior is normative, come to believe that such behaviors are adaptive or necessary. These individuals "view the world as if they [were] soldiers confronting a hostile environment that they perceive to be full of enemies" (Garbarino, 2012, para. 7).

The idea that traumatized individuals develop a "war zone mentality" in response to an accumulation of traumatic experiences mirrors others who have proposed that delinquency, or antisocial behavior, is in a sense an adaptation developed in the face of adversity, that such behavior is actually a form of coping for some individuals, as it has an "adaptive intent" (Kerig & Becker, 2010, p. 18). Latzman and Swisher (2005) proposed that youth violence may comprise a functional as well as intentional, or active, response to a violent environment, for example, by generating a fear-provoking reputation that may deter future victimization.

In regard to the cognitions that accompany a war zone mentality, many individuals appear to develop a sense of futurelessness, wherein a person begins to believe that there is no point in considering the consequences of actions because there is no future in which those consequences might transpire. In experiences as a forensic expert witness by one of the co-authors, it is not uncommon for individuals to say that they did not think they would make it to 21, 25, or 30 years old. This sense of futurelessness is common among individuals who have high levels of trauma. For example, work with children with PTSD found that many did not believe they would marry, have children of their own, or live a normal life span (Saigh, 1992).

The consequence of this lack of belief in a future and a focus on only the present moment leads youth to engage in higher risk-taking, reckless behavior, and a disregard of consequences that can push youth to engage in delinquency; after all, there is little reason for being law abiding or planning and working toward a future if one does not believe in the existence of such future. Indeed, work done by Borowsky, Ireland, and Resnick (2009) found that among a nationally representative sample of adolescents, the nearly 15% of youth who believed that they would not live past the age of 35 were at the highest risk for engaging in risky behaviors, including arrest, substance abuse, unsafe sexual activity, suicide attempts, and fight-related injuries.

In addition to a foreshortened sense of the future, another cognitive adaptation that may be related to the development of a war zone mentality is Bandura'a concept of moral disengagement, which has also been posited as a mechanism by which children who have been traumatized develop a worldview that justifies and legitimizes perpetration of violence (Kerig & Becker, 2010). According to Bandura, Barbaranelli, Caprara, and Pastorelli (1996), there are eight mechanisms of moral disengagement through which an immoral act can be made more acceptable, including attributing it to a higher purpose (i.e., moral justification), blaming others (i.e., displacement of responsibility), and belittling the victim (i.e., dehumanizing). Bandura (1997) proposes various mechanisms through which moral disengagement can occur; however, a common theme in these processes is that they are not instantaneous; rather, the change is usually achieved through the gradual weakening of self-sanctions, during which people may not be cognizant of changes in their morality. Generally, however, moral disengagement occurs as individuals engage in delinquent acts that disregard the rights of others and then desensitize themselves to such behavior and develop self-justifications, which foster the perpetration of more offensive behaviors (Wilkinson & Carr, 2008). In regard to the link between trauma and moral disengagement, it seems that trauma may interrupt moral development, or lead to an altered morality that justifies the victimization of others (Garbarino, 1999) and may account for the perpetration of violence and other forms of antisocial behavior observed among individuals with histories of trauma.

## Conclusion

The finding that many individuals either do not develop PTSD following exposure to trauma or recover expeditiously is important for two reasons. For one, it indicates that negative responses are not inevitable, as many individuals who experience traumatic events are resilient. Secondly, it is important to distinguish what factors may cause some individuals to have more negative reactions to trauma, while others are able to respond more favorably. This is why we believe that a complete understanding of trauma will move beyond the narrow conception of post-traumatic stress disorder to embrace the concept of post-traumatic stress development. Therein lies the future for a complete understanding of the complex role of trauma in forensic psychology.

## Questions/Activities for Further Exploration

1. In what ways can experiencing trauma make someone more likely to engage in aggressive or antisocial behavior?
2. What factors make a traumatic experience(s) more damaging in regard to individuals' development? In other words, why is it that some individuals may experience trauma and have no adverse implications, whereas others who experience trauma demonstrate maladjustment, including aggression and violence.
3. Compare Type I, Type II, and Type III traumas. What outcomes are experienced by individuals who have experienced each type of trauma?
4. In light of evidence suggesting that early trauma may be particularly damaging for individuals, including in facilitating the development of antisocial behavior, what are ways we can address the prevalence of traumatic exposure among children in society? What types of interventions could be useful for children exposed to higher levels of trauma in their communities and/or in their home.

## References

Aas, M., Steen, N. E., Agartz, I., Aminoff, S. R., Lorentzen, S., Sundet, K., … Melle, I. (2012). Is cognitive impairment following early life stress in severe mental disorders based on specific or general cognitive functioning? *Psychiatry Research, 4*, 2–6.
American Psychiatric Association [APA]. (1980). *Diagnostic and statistical manual of mental disorders* (3rd ed.). Arlington, VA: Author.
American Psychiatric Association [APA]. (1987). *Diagnostic and statistical manual of mental disorders* (3rd ed., revised). Washington, D.C.: Author.
American Psychiatric Association [APA]. (1994). *Diagnostic and statistical manual of mental disorders* (4th ed.). Washington, D.C.: Author.
Anda, R. F., Croft, J. B., Felitti, V. J., Nordenberg, D., Giles, W. H., Williamson, D. F., & Giovino, G. A. (1999). Adverse childhood experiences and smoking during adolescence and adulthood. *JAMA, 282*(17), 1652–1658.
Ardino, V. (2011). Post-traumatic stress in antisocial youth: A multifaceted reality. In V. Ardino (Ed.), *Post-traumatic syndromes in children and adolescents* (pp. 211–229). Chichester, UK: Wiley/Blackwell Publishers.
Ardino, V. (2012). Offending behaviour: The role of trauma and PTSD. *European Journal of Psychotraumatology, 3*, 1–4.
Baglivio, M., Epps, N., Swartz, K., Huq, M. S., Sheer, A., & Hardt, N. S. (2014). The prevalence of Adverse Childhood Experiences (ACE) in the lives of juvenile offenders. *Journal of Juvenile Justice, 3*(2), 1–23.

Bandura, A. (1997). *Self-efficacy: The exercise of control*. New York, NY: Freeman.

Bandura, A., Barbaranelli, C., Caprara, G. V., & Pastorelli, C. (1996). Mechanisms of moral disengagement in the exercise of moral agency. *Journal of Personality and Social Psychology, 71*, 364–374.

Banich, M. T. (2009). Executive function: The search for an integrated account. *Current Directions in Psychological Science, 18*, 89–94.

Beers, S. R., & De Bellis, M. D. (2002). Neuropsychological function in children with maltreatment- related posttraumatic stress disorder. *American Journal of Psychiatry, 159*, 483–486.

Bonanno, G. A. (2004). Loss, trauma, and human resilience: Have we underestimated the human capacity to thrive after extremely aversive events? *American Psychologist, 59*(1), 20–28.

Borowsky, I. W., Ireland, M., & Resnick, M. D. (2009). Health status and behavioral outcomes for youth who anticipate a high likelihood of early death. *Pediatrics, 124*(1), e81–e88.

Bowlby, J. (1973). *Attachment and loss, vol. 2. Separation: Anxiety and anger*. New York, NY: Basic.

Breslau, N., Davis, G. C., Peterson, E. L., & Schultz, L. (2000). A second look at comorbidity in victims of trauma: The posttraumatic stress disorder–major depression connection. *Biological Psychiatry, 48*, 902–909.

Breslau, N., Kessler, R. C., Chilcoat, H. D., Schultz, L. R., Davis, G. C., & Andreski, P. (1998). Trauma and posttraumatic stress disorder in the community: The 1996 Detroit Area Survey of Trauma. *Archives of General Psychiatry, 55*(7), 626–632.

Brief. Challenging Conviction and Sentence in Richard Mallory Case, supra note 32, at 16.

Brief. Challenging Death Sentences in Three Murder Cases, supra note 32, at 11–12.

Brink, J. H., Doherty, D., & Boer, A. (2001). Mental disorder in federal offenders: A Canadian prevalence study. *International Journal of Law and Psychiatry, 24*(4–5), 339–356.

Butler, T., Levy, M., Dolan, K., & Kaldor, J. (2003). Drug use and its correlates in an Australian prisoner population. *Addiction Research & Theory, 11*(2), 89–101.

Carpenter, G. L., & Stacks, A. M. (2009). Developmental effects of exposure to intimate partner violence in early childhood: A review of the literature. *Children and Youth Services Review, 31*(8), 831–839.

Cauffman, E., Feldman, S., Waterman, J., & Steiner, H. (1998). Posttraumatic stress disorder among female juvenile offenders. *Journal of the American Academy of Child and Adolescent Psychiatry, 37*(11), 1209–1216.

Cellini, H. R. (2004). Child abuse, neglect, and delinquency: The neurobiological link. *Juvenile and Family Court Journal, 55*(4), 1–14.

Cohen, J. A., Mannarino, A. P., & Deblinger, E. (2006). *Treating trauma and traumatic grief in children and adolescents*. New York, NY: Guilford Press.

Cole, P. M., & Zahn-Waxler, C. (1992). Emotional dysregulation in disruptive behavior disorders. In D. Cicchetti & S. L. Toth (Eds.), *Rochester symposium on developmental psychopathology: Vol. 4. Developmental perspectives on depression* (pp. 173–210). Rochester, NY: University of Rochester Press.

Cook, A., Spinazzola, J., Ford, J., Lanktree, C., Blaustein, M., Cloitre, M., … Van der Kolk, B. (2005). Complex trauma in children and adolescents. *Psychiatric Annals, 35*(5), 390–398.

Copeland, W. E., Keeler, G., Angold, A., & Costello, E. J. (2007). Traumatic events and posttraumatic stress in childhood. *Archives of General Psychiatry, 64*(5), 577–584.

Costello, E. J., Erklani, A., Fairbank, J., & Angold, A. (2002). The prevalence of potentially traumatic events in childhood and adolescence. *Journal of Traumatic Stress, 15*(2), 99–112.

Cottle, C., Lee, R., & Heilbrun, K. (2001). The prediction of criminal recidivism in juveniles: A meta- analysis. *Criminal Justice and Behavior, 28*(3), 367–394.

Courtois, C. A. (2004). Complex trauma, complex reactions: Assessment and treatment. *Psychotherapy: Theory, Research, Practice, Training, 41*(4), 412–425.

Davidson, J. R., Hughes, D., Blazer, D. G., & George, L. K. (1991). Posttraumatic stress disorder in the community: An epidemiological study. *Psychological Medicine, 21*(3), 713–721.

De Bellis, M. D. (2001). Developmental traumatology: The psychobiological development of maltreated children and its implications for research, treatment, and policy. *Development and Psychopathology, 13*(3), 539–564.

De Bellis, M. D., Baum, A. S., Birmaher, B., Keshavan, M. S., Eccard, C. H., Boring, A. M., … Ryan, N. D. (1999). Developmental traumatology part I. Biological stress systems. *Biological Psychiatry, 45*(10), 1259–1270.

De Bellis, M. D., Keshavan, M. S., Clark, D. B., Casey, B. J., Giedd, J. N., Boring, A. M., … Ryan, N. D. (1999). Developmental traumatology part II: Brain development. *Biological Psychiatry, 45*, 1271–1284.

De Bellis, M. D., & Putnam, F. W. (1994). The psychobiology of childhood maltreatment. *Child and Adolescent Psychiatric Clinics of North America, 3*(4), 663–677.

De Ravello, L., Abeita, J., & Brown, P. (2008). Breaking the cycle/mending the hoop: Childhood experiences among incarcerated American Indian/Alaska Native women in New Mexico. *Health Care for Women International, 29*(3), 300–315.

Dembo, R., Schmeidler, J., Nini-Gough, B., Sue, C. C., Borden, P., & Manning, D. (1998). Predictors of recidivism to a juvenile assessment center: A three year study. *Journal of Child and Adolescent Substance Abuse, 7*(3), 57–77.

Dierkhising, C. B., Ko, S. J., Woods-Jaeger, B., Briggs, E. C., Lee, R., & Pynoos, R. S. (2013). Trauma histories among justice-involved youth: Findings from the National Child Traumatic Stress Network. *European Journal of Psychotraumatology, 4.* https://doi.org/10.3402/ejpt.v4i0.20274

El-Hage, W., Gaillard, P., Isingrini, M., & Belzung, C. (2006). Trauma-related deficits in working memory. *Cognitive Neuropsychiatry, 11*(1), 33–46.

Elliott, F. (1978). Neurological aspects of antisocial behavior. In W. H. Reid (Ed.), *The psychopath: Comprehensive study of antisocial disorders and behaviors* (pp. 146–189). New York, NY: Bruner/Mazel.

Erickson, M., Egeland, B., & Pianta, R. (1989). The effects of maltreatment on the development of young children. In D. Cicchetti & V. Carlson (Eds.), *Child maltreatment: Theory and research on the causes and consequences of child abuse and neglect* (pp. 647–684). New York, NY: Cambridge University Press.

Felitti, V. J., Anda, R. F., Nordenberg, D., Williamson, D. F., Spitz, A. M., Edwards, V., … Marks, J. S. (1998). Relationship of childhood abuse and household dysfunction to many of the leading causes of death in adults: The Adverse Childhood Experiences (ACE) Study. *American Journal of Preventive Medicine, 14*(4), 245–258.

Finkelhor, D., Ormrod, R., & Turner, H. (2007). Poly-victimization: A neglected component in child victimization. *Child Abuse and Neglect, 31*(1), 7–26.

Finkelhor, D., Turner, H. A., Shattuck, A., & Hamby, S. L. (2013). Violence, crime, and abuse exposure, in a national sample of children and youth: An update. *JAMA Pediatrics, 167*(7), 614–621.

Ford, J. D. (2005). Treatment implications of altered neurobiology, affect regulation and information processing following child maltreatment. *Psychiatric Annals, 35*(5), 410–419.

Ford, J. D. (2009). *Posttraumatic stress disorder: Scientific and professional dimensions* (1st ed.). San Diego, CA: Elsevier Academic Press.

Ford, J. D., Chapman, J. F., Hawker, J., & Albert, D. (2007). Trauma among youth in the juvenile justice system: Critical issues and new directions. National Center for Mental Health and Juvenile Justice. Retrieved September 9, 2013, from http://www.ncmhjj.com/pdfs/publications/trauma_and_youth.pdf.

Ford, J. D., & Courtois, C. A. (2009). Defining and understanding complex trauma and complex stress disorders. In C. A. Courtois & J. D. Ford (Eds.), *Treating complex traumatic stress disorders: Scientific foundations and therapeutic models* (pp. 13–30). New York, NY: The Guilford Press.

Foy, D. W., Furrow, J., & McManus, S. (2011). Exposure to violence, post-traumatic symptomatology, and criminal behaviors. In V. Ardino (Ed.), *Post-traumatic syndromes in children and adolescents* (pp. 199–210). Chichester, UK: Wiley/Blackwell Publishers.

Garbarino, J. (1999). *Lost boys: Why our sons turn violent and how we can save them.* New York, NY: Free Press.

Garbarino, J. (2012, December 19). How a boy becomes a killer. *CNN*. Retrieved from https://www.cnn.com/2012/12/19/opinion/garbarino-violence-boys/index.html

Garbarino, J. (2015). *Listening to killers: Lessons learned from my twenty years as a psychological expert witness in murder cases*. Oakland, CA: University of California Press.

Garbarino, J. (2018). *Miller's children: Why giving teenage killers a second chance matters for all of us*. Oakland, CA: University of California Press.

Garbarino, J., & Kostelny, K. (1996). The effects of political violence on Palestinian children's behavior problems: A risk accumulation model. *Child Development, 67*(1), 33–45

Giancola, P. R. (1995). Evidence for dorsolateral and orbital prefrontal cortical involvement in the expression of aggressive behavior. *Aggressive Behavior, 21*(6), 431–450.

Gollan, J. K., Lee, R., & Coccano, E. F. (2005). Developmental psychopathology and neurobiology of aggression. *Development and Psychopathology, 17*(4), 1151–1171.

Gorenstein, E. E. (1982). Frontal lobe functions in psychopaths. *Journal of Abnormal Psychology, 91*(5), 368–379.

Gould, E., & Tanapat, P. (1999). Stress and hippocampal neurogenesis. *Biological Psychiatry, 46*(11), 1472–1479.

Grevstad, J. A. (2010). Adverse childhood experiences and juvenile justice. PowerPoint delivered to Washington State Family Policy Council June 8, 2010.

Harrison, M. A., Murphy, E. A., Ho, L. Y., Bowers, T. G., & Flaherty, C. V. (2015). Female serial killers in the United States: Means, motives, and makings. *The Journal of Forensic Psychiatry & Psychology, 26*(3), 383–406.

Heim, C., Meinlschmidt, G., & Nemeroff, C. B. (2003). Neurobiology of early-life stress. *Psychiatric Annals, 33*(1), 18–26.

Helzer, J. E., Robins, L. N., & McEvoy, L. (1987). Post-traumatic stress disorder in the general population. Findings of the epidemiologic catchment area survey. *New England Journal of Medicine, 317*(26), 1630–1634.

Herman, J. L. (1992). Complex PTSD: A syndrome in survivors of prolonged and repeated trauma. *Journal of Traumatic Stress, 5*(3), 377–391.

Initial Brief of Appellant at 12, Wuornos v. Florida, 644 So. 2d 1012 (Fla. 1994).

Initial Brief of Appellant at 16, Wuornos v. Florida, 644 So. 2d 1000 (Fla. 1994) (No. 79,484).

Initial Brief of Appellant at 6, Wuornos v. Florida, 676 So. 2d 972 (Fla. 1996) (No. 81,498).

Ishikawa, S., & Raine, A. (2003). Prefrontal deficits and antisocial behavior: A causal model. In B. Lahey, T. Moffitt, & A. Caspi (Eds.), *Causes of conduct disorder and juvenile delinquency* (pp. 277–304). New York, NY: Guilford Press.

Izard, C. E., & Kobak, R. R. (1991). Emotions systems functioning and emotional regulation. In J. Garber & K. A. Dodge (Eds.), *The development of emotion regulation and dysregulation* (pp. 303–321). Cambridge, UK: Cambridge University Press.

Jordan, B. K., Federman, E. B., Burns, B. J., Schlenger, W. E., Fairbank, J. A., & Caddell, J. M. (2002). Lifetime use of mental health and substance abuse treatment services by incarcerated women felons. *Psychiatric Services, 53*(3), 317–325.

Jordan, B. K., Schlenger, W. E., Fairbank, J. A., & Caddell, J. M. (1996). Prevalence of psychiatric disorders among incarcerated women: Convicted felons entering prison. *Archives of General Psychiatry, 53*(6), 513–519.

Kerig, P. K., & Becker, S. P. (2010). From internalizing to externalizing: Theoretical models of the processes linking PTSD to juvenile delinquency. In S. J. Egan (Ed.), *Posttraumatic stress disorder (PTSD): Causes, symptoms and treatment* (pp. 33–78). Hauppauge, NY: Nova Science Publishers.

Kessler, R. C., Berglund, P., Delmer, O., Jin, R., Merikangas, K. R., & Walters, E. E. (2005). Lifetime prevalence and age-of-onset distributions of DSM-IV disorders in the National Comorbidity Survey Replication. *Archives of General Psychiatry, 62*(6), 593–602.

Kessler, R. C., Chiu, W. T., Demler, O., Merikangas, K. R., & Walters, E. E. (2005). Prevalence, severity, and comorbidity of 12-month DSM-IV disorders in the National Comorbidity Survey Replication. *Archives of General Psychiatry, 62*(6), 617–627.

Kessler, R. C., Sonnega, A., Bromet, E., Hughes, M., & Nelson, C. B. (1995). Posttraumatic stress disorder in the National Comorbidity Survey. *Archives of General Psychiatry, 52*(12), 1048–1060.

Khaleque, A., & Rohner, R. P. (2002). Perceived parental acceptance-rejection and psychological adjustment: A meta-analysis of cross-cultural and intracultural studies. *Journal of Marriage and Family, 64*(1), 54–64.

Kilpatrick, D., Resnick, H., Milanak, M., Miller, M., Keyes, K., & Friedman, M. (2013). National estimates of exposure to traumatic events and PTSD prevalence using DSM-IV and DSM-5 criteria. *Journal of Traumatic Stress, 26*(5), 537–547.

Kim, J. J., Song, E. Y., & Kosten, T. A. (2006). Stress effects in the hippocampus: Synaptic plasticity and memory. *Stress, 9*(1), 1–11.

Kingree, J. B., Phan, D., & Thompson, M. (2003). Child maltreatment and recidivism among adolescent detainees. *Criminal Justice and Behavior, 30*(6), 623–643.

Langan, N. P., & Pelissier, B. M. (2001). Gender differences among prisoners in drug treatment. *Journal of Substance Abuse, 13*(3), 291–301.

Latzman, R., & Swisher, R. (2005). The interactive relationship among adolescent violence, street violence, and depression. *Journal of Community Psychology, 33*(3), 355–371.

Lieberman, A. F., & Knorr, K. (2007). The impact of trauma: A development framework for infancy and early childhood. *Psychiatric Annals, 37*(6), 416–422.

Majer, M., Nater, U. M., Lin, J. M., Capuron, L., & Reeves, W. C. (2010). Association of childhood trauma with cognitive function in healthy adults: A pilot study. *BMC Neurology, 10*, 61–71.

Marrast, L., Himmelstein, D. U., & Woolhandler, S. (2016). Racial and ethnic disparities in mental health care for children and young adults: A national study. *International Journal of Health Services, 46*(4), 810–824.

Matsuura, N., Hashimoto, T., & Toichi, M. (2009). Correlations among self-esteem, aggression, adverse childhood experiences and depression in inmates of a female correctional facility in Japan. *Psychiatry and Clinical Neurosciences, 63*(4), 478–485.

Maxfield, M. G., & Widom, C. S. (1996). The cycle of violence: Revisited 6 years later. *Archives of Pediatrics & Adolescent Medicine, 150*(4), 390–395.

Messina, N. P., Burdon, W., Hagopian, G., & Prendergast, M. (2006). Predictors of prison TC treatment outcomes: A comparison of men and women participants. *American Journal of Drug Alcohol Abuse, 32*(1), 7–28.

Messina, N. P., Burdon, W. M., & Prendergast, M. L. (2003). Assessing the needs of women in institutional therapeutic communities. *Journal of Offender Rehabilitation, 37*(2), 89–106.

Messina, N. P., & Grella, C. (2006). Childhood trauma and women's health outcomes in a California prison population. *American Journal of Public Health, 96*(10), 1842–1848.

Miller, E. K., & Cohen, J. D. (2001). An integrative theory of prefrontal cortex function. *Annual Review of Neuroscience, 24*, 167–202.

Miyake, A., & Friedman, N. P. (2012). The nature and organization of individual differences in executive functions: Four general conclusions. *Current Directions in Psychological Science, 21*(1), 8–14.

Moore, M. D., & Tatman, A. W. (2016). Adverse Childhood Experiences and offender risk to re-offend in the United States: A quantitative examination. *International Journal of Criminal Justice Sciences, 11*(2), 148–158.

Morgan, A. B., & Lilienfeld, S. O. (2000). A meta-analytic review of the relation between antisocial behavior and neuropsychological measures of executive function. *Clinical Psychology Review, 20*(1), 113–136.

Myers, W. C., Gooch, E., & Meloy, J. R. (2005). The role of psychopathy and sexuality in a female serial killer. *Journal of Forensic Sciences, 50*(3), 1–6.

National Comorbidity Survey. (2005). NCS-R appendix tables: Table 1. Lifetime prevalence of DSM- IV/WMH-CIDI disorders by sex and cohort. Table 2. Twelve-month prevalence of DSM- IV/WMH-CIDI disorders by sex and cohort. Accessed at: http://www.hcp.med.harvard.edu/ncs/publications.php

Navalta, C. P., Polcari, A., Webster, D. M., Boghossian, A., & Teicher, M. H. (2006). Effects of childhood sexual abuse on neuropsychological and cognitive function in college women. *Journal of Neuropsychiatry and Clinical Neuroscience, 18*(1), 45–53.

Newport, D. J., & Nemeroff, C. B. (2000). Neurobiology of posttraumatic stress disorder. *Current Opinion in Neurobiology, 10*(2), 211–218.

Nolin, P., & Ethier, L. (2007). Using neuropsychological profiles to classify neglected children with or without physical abuse. *Child Abuse and Neglect, 31*(6), 631–643.

Norris, F. H. (1992). Epidemiology of trauma: Frequency and impact of different potentially traumatic events on different demographic groups. *Journal of Consulting and Clinical Psychology, 60*(3), 409–418.

O'Hanlon, W., & Weiner-Davis, M. (1989). *In search of solutions: A new direction in psychotherapy*. New York, NY: W.W. Norton.

Ogilvie, J. M., Stewart, A. L., Chan, R. C. K., & Shum, D. H. K. (2011). Neuropsychological measures of executive function and antisocial behavior: A meta-analysis. *Criminology, 49*(4), 1063–1107.

Peters, R. H., Strozier, A. L., Murrin, M. R., & Kearns, W. D. (1997). Treatment of substance-abusing jail inmates. Examination of gender differences. *Journal of Substance Abuse Treatment, 14*(4), 339–349.

Pollak, S. D. (2008). Mechanisms linking early experience and the emergence of emotions: Illustrations from the study of maltreated children. *Current Directions in Psychological Science, 17*(6), 370–375.

Pollock, J. (2002). *Women, prison, and crime* (2nd ed.). Belmont, CA: Wadsworth Thomson Learning.

Powell, T. A., Holt, J. C., & Fondacaro, K. M. (1997). The prevalence of mental illness among inmates in a rural state. *Law and Human Behavior, 21*(4), 427–438.

Raine, A. (1997). Antisocial behavior and psychophysiology: A biosocial perspective and a prefrontal dysfunction hypothesis. In D. M. Stoff, J. Breiling, & J. D. Maser (Eds.), *Handbook of antisocial behavior* (pp. 289–304). New York, NY: Wiley.

Raine, A. (2002). Annotation: The role of prefrontal deficits, low autonomic arousal, and early health factors in the development of antisocial and aggressive behavior in children. *Journal of Child Psychology and Psychiatry, 43*(4), 417–434.

Reavis, J. A., Looman, J., Franco, K. A., & Rojas, B. (2013). Adverse childhood experiences and adult criminality: How long must we live before we possess our own lives. *The Permanente Journal, 17*(2), 44–48.

Resnick, H. S., Kilpatrick, D. G., Dansky, B. S., Saunders, B. E., & Best, C. L. (1993). Prevalence of civilian trauma and posttraumatic stress disorder in a representative national sample of women. *Journal of Consulting and Clinical Psychology, 61*(6), 984–991.

Robins, L. N., Helzer, J. E., Croughan, J. L., Williams, J. B. W., & Spitzer, R. L. (1981). *NIMH diagnostic interview schedule, version III*. Rockville, MD: NIMH, Public Health Service.

Rohner, R. P. (2004). The parental "acceptance-rejection syndrome": Universal correlates of perceived rejection. *American Psychologist, 59*(8), 827–840.

Saigh, P. (1992). *Posttraumatic stress disorder: A behavioral approach to diagnosis and treatment*. Needham Heights, MA: Allyn and Bacon.

Saunders, B. E. (2003). Understanding children exposed to violence: Toward an integration of overlapping fields. *Journal of Interpersonal Violence, 18*(4), 356–376.

Schore, A. N. (2003). Early relational trauma, disorganized attachment, and the development of a predisposition to violence. In M. F. Solomon & D. J. Siegel (Eds.), *Healing trauma: Attachment, mind, body, and brain* (pp. 107–167). New York, NY: W. W. Norton.

Séguin, J. R. (2004). Neurocognitive elements of antisocial behavior: Relevance of an orbitofrontal cortex account. *Brain and Cognition, 55*(1), 185–197.

Shapiro, F. (1995). *Eye movement desensitization and reprocessing: Basic EMDR principles, protocols, and procedures*. New York, NY: Guilford Press.

Shields, A., Cicchetti, D., & Ryan, R. (1994). The development of emotional and behavioral self-regulation and social competence among maltreated school-age children. *Development and Psychopathology, 6*(1), 57–75.

Silver, R. C., Holman, E. A., McIntosh, D. N., Poulin, M., & Gil-Rivas, V. (2002). Nationwide longitudinal study of psychological responses to September 11. *Journal of the American Medical Association, 288*(10), 1235–1244.

Smith, A. (2005). The "Monster" in all of us: When victims become perpetrators. *Suffolk University Law Review, 39*, 367–394. Retrieved May 30, 2018, from http://suffolklawreview.org/wp-content/uploads/2005/03/SmithFinal.pdf

Smith, C., & Thornberry, T. (1995). The relationship between childhood maltreatment and adolescent involvement in delinquency. *Criminology, 33*(4), 451–477.

Solomon, E. P., & Heide, K. M. (1999). Type III trauma: Toward a more effective conceptualization of psychological trauma. *International Journal of Offender Therapy and Comparative Criminology, 43*(2), 202–210.

Spitzer, C., Dudeck, M., Liss, H., Orlob, S., Gillner, M., & Freyberger, H. J. (2001). Post-traumatic stress disorder in forensic inpatients. *Journal of Forensic Psychiatry, 12*(1), 63–77.

Teicher, M. H., Andersen, S. L., Polcari, A., Anderson, C. M., Navalta, C. P., & Kim, D. M. (2003). The neurobiological consequences of early stress and childhood maltreatment. *Neuroscience & Biobehavioral Reviews, 27*(1–2), 33–44.

Terr, L. C. (1991). Childhood traumas: An outline and overview. *The American Journal of Psychiatry, 148*(1), 10–20.

Urbaniok, F., Endrass, J., Noll, T., Vetter, S., & Rossegger, A. (2007). Posttraumatic stress disorder in a Swiss offender population. *Swiss Medical Weekly, 137*(910), 151–156.

van der Kolk, B. A. (1996). The body keeps the score: Approaches to the psychobiology of post-traumatic stress disorder. In B. A. van der Kolk, A. C. McFarlane, & L. Weisaeth (Eds.), *Traumatic stress: The effects of overwhelming experience on mind, body, and society* (pp. 214–241). New York, NY: Guilford.

van der Kolk, B. A. (2005). Developmental trauma disorder: Toward a rational diagnosis for children with complex trauma histories. *Psychiatric Annals, 35*(5), 401–408.

Vermeiren, R. (2003). Psychopathology and delinquency in adolescents: A descriptive and developmental perspective. *Clinical Psychology Review, 23*(2), 277–318.

Weeks, R., & Widom, C. S. (1989). Child abuse, neglect, and adult behavior: Research design and findings on criminality, violence, and child abuse. *American Journal of Orthopsychiatry, 59*(3), 355–367.

Weeks, R., & Widom, C. S. (1998). Self-reports of early childhood victimization among incarcerated adult male felons. *Journal of Interpersonal Violence, 13*(3), 346–361.

Widom, C. S., & Ames, M. A. (1994). Criminal consequences of childhood sexual victimization. *Child Abuse & Neglect, 18*(4), 303–318.

Widom, C. S., Czaja, S. J., & Dutton, M. A. (2008). Childhood victimization and lifetime revictimization. *Child Abuse & Neglect, 32*(8), 785–796. https://doi.org/10.1016/j.chiabu.2007.12.006

Widom, C. S., & Maxfield, M. G. (2001). *An update on the "cycle of Violence"* (p. 184894). Washington, D.C.: US Department of Justice, Office of Justice Programs, National Institute of Justice.

Wilkinson, D. L., & Carr, P. J. (2008). Violent youths' responses to high levels of exposure to community violence: What violent events reveal about youth violence. *Journal of Community Psychology, 36*(8), 1026–1051.

Wolff, N., & Shi, J. (2010). Trauma and incarcerated persons. In C. L. Scott (Ed.), *The handbook of correctional mental health* (2nd ed., pp. 277–320). Arlington, VA: American Psychiatric Publishing.

Wolff, N., & Shi, J. (2012). Childhood and adult trauma experiences of incarcerated persons and their relationship to adult behavioral health problems and treatment. *International Journal of Environmental Research and Public Health, 9*(5), 1908–1926.

Wolff, N., Shi, J., & Siegel, J. (2009). Patterns of victimization among male and female inmates: Evidence of an enduring legacy. *Violence & Victims, 24*(4), 469–484. https://doi.org/10.1891/0886-6708.24.4.469

Wood, J., Foy, D. W., Layne, C., Pynoos, R., & James, C. B. (2002). An examination of the relationships between violence exposure, posttraumatic stress symptomatology, and delinquent activity: An "ecopathological" model of delinquent behavior among incarcerated adolescents. *Journal of Aggression, Maltreatment, Trauma, 6*(1), 127–147.

Wright, L., Borrill, R., Teers, R., & Cassidy, T. (2006). The mental health consequences of dealing with self-inflicted death in custody. *Counselling Psychology Quarterly, 19*(2), 165–180.

Wuornos v. Florida, 644 So. 2d 1000, 1003–04 (Fla. 1994)

Wuornos v. Florida, 676 So. 2d 972 (Fla. 1996).

Zeier, J. D., Baskin-Sommers, A. R., Hiatt Racer, K. D., & Newman, J. P. (2011). Cognitive control deficits associated with antisocial personality disorder and psychopathy. *Personality Disorders: Theory, Research, and Treatment, 3*(3), 283–293.

Zou, Z., Meng, H., Ma, Z., Deng, W., Du, L., Wang, H., … Hu, H. (2013). Executive functioning deficits and childhood trauma in juvenile violent offenders in China. *Psychiatry Research, 207*(3), 218–224.

# Chapter 3
# Trauma in Competency to Stand Trial Evaluations

**Elizabeth A. Owen, Alan Perry, and Devora Panish Scher**

## Introduction

The competency to stand trial evaluation (CST) has long been identified as the most important inquiry in the area of criminal mental health (Grisso, 1986; Melton et al., 2018; Perlin, 2003, 2008; Perlin, Champine, Dlugacz, & Connell, 2008; Stone, 1975), as it is part of the bedrock of commitment to the right to a fair trial. Certainly, it is the most frequently ordered and performed criminal evaluation with the often-cited number of 60,000 evaluations performed a year (Bonnie & Grisso, 2000). This number was based on data published in the early to mid-1990s (Hoge, Bonnie, Poythress, & Monahan, 1992; Poythress, Bonnie, Hoge, Monahan, & Oberlander, 1994) and did not include misdemeanor or federal cases. In the last two decades, the rate of incarceration in general and of those with mental illness has grown substantially such that the estimate of CST evaluations in the United States is now 90,000 (Fuller, et al., 2017). Our own calculations, based partially on national rates of incarceration at the pre-conviction level (Sawyer & Wagner, 2019) and rate of severe mental illness in that population, place the number at a conservative 94,000.

The concept of competency to proceed to trial has its roots in English law, dating back to the seventeenth century. Justice Blackstone (in Prest, 2008) notes that the "mad" defendant cannot "make his defense." This idea carried over to the American courts as well. In 1835, the individual who made an attempt on President Andrew

E. A. Owen (✉)
Teachers College/Columbia University, New York, NY, USA
e-mail: eao8@tc.columbia.edu

A. Perry
Lander College for Men/Touro University System, New York, NY, USA

D. P. Scher
Doctoral Candidate School Psychology, Rutgers University,
New Brunswick, Newark and Camden, NJ, USA

© Springer Nature Switzerland AG 2020
R. A. Javier et al. (eds.), *Assessing Trauma in Forensic Contexts*,
https://doi.org/10.1007/978-3-030-33106-1_3

Jackson's life was thought unfit to proceed and in Drope vs Missouri [420 US, 162, 172 (1975), Dusky vs US 362 US, 462 (1960)], it was thought to move a person deemed 'insane' to trial was a violation of due process. Further, to quote Pate v. Robinson, "The conviction of a defendant while mentally incompetent violates due process" (383 U.S 375, 378; 1966).

The 6th and 14th amendments in the Bill of Rights are the legal basis for CST. The 6th amendment guarantees the accused effective counsel and the ability to confront their accusers, as well as present evidence in their defense, while the 14th amendment addresses the right to due process. An incompetent person is thought to be unable to assist her/his attorney and participate effectively in a trial. Those defendants deemed by the court unfit to proceed and unable to participate in their defense are permitted a delay of trial to restore competency via psychiatric treatment and psycho-legal education, or movement to adjudication of charges lodged against them. Competency, therefore, like insanity, is a legal construct, albeit one with strong psychological underpinnings.

## *Definition of Competency to Stand Trial*

On the federal level, and in most states, the legal standard, or definition of competency, follows that laid out in Dusky v. U.S. (1960) "that it is not enough for the district judge to find that 'the defendant [is] oriented to time and place and [has] some recollection of events,' but that the test must be whether he has sufficient present ability to consult with his lawyer with a reasonable degree of rational understanding and whether he has a rational as well as factual understanding of the proceedings against him" [p. 362 U.S. 402]. In practice, this is often reduced to whether the defendant knows the charges, roles of key court personnel (defense attorney, district attorney, and judge), and the process of trial (role of a jury, possible outcomes).

It is vital that "(t)he accused must be able to perform the functions which 'are essential to the fairness and accuracy of a criminal proceeding'" (Wilson v U.S. 391 F.2d 460, 1968, at 463). While the CST criteria in Dusky are viewed as a notoriously low bar ("Somebody described 'competent' once as knowing the difference between a judge and a grapefruit," ADA Cheryl Coleman, People v Tortoricci), other, state-defined criteria, suggest a more contextual approach to competency. "The central issue remains whether on *all the facts and circumstances of a particular case* (emphasis added) the determination as to 'capacity' is compatible with fundamental fairness" (People v Valentino, 1974). (Capacity, or the ability to be competent, is differentiated from the willingness to do so.)

This complexity is often overlooked in competency evaluations, but in addition to being part of the Dusky opinion, it is also promoted by theorists and researchers in forensic psychology (Roesch, Zapf, Golding, & Skeem, 1999). "Mere presence of severe disturbance (a psychopathological criterion) is only a threshold issue--it must be further demonstrated that such severe disturbance in this defendant, facing these charges, in light of existing evidence, anticipating the substantial effort of a particular attorney with a relationship of known characteristics, results in the defendant being unable to rationally assist the attorney or to comprehend the nature of the proceedings and their likely outcome" (Golding & Roesch, 1988, p. 79). These different approaches to competency evaluations (criteria-based verses contextual) is likely one of the factors behind the vast difference in range of findings of incompetence – 1–99% (Cochrane, Grisso, & Frederick, 2001; Cooper & Zapf, 2003; Grisso, 1986; Mossman et al., 2007; Nicholson & Kugler, 1991; Paradis et al., 2016; Roesch & Golding, 1980; Skeem, Golding, Cohn, & Berge, 1998; Warren et al., 2006; Zapf & Roesch, 2006; personal communication, 2019) found in defendants being found not fit to proceed.

Individual states (via common law found in decisions on the local or state level) may proffer their own more specific guideline criteria for competency to proceed. One such example is People v Valentino, (78 Misc. 2d 678. N.Y. Misc. 1974) that delineated six areas of concern:

> (1) Is the defendant oriented as to time and place? ("[T]he defendant must have a minimal contact with reality. This encompasses the basic human functions that are automatic to all but the seriously mentally ill. An accused must appreciate his presence in relation to time, place and things." Bennett, Competency to Stand Trial: A Call for Reform, 59 J. Crim. L. C. & P. S. 569, 574–575)

> (2) Can the defendant perceive, recall, and relate? These abilities should be familiar as three of the four necessary qualifications of witnesses. (Bacon, Incompetency to Stand Trial: Commitment to an Inclusive Test, 42 So. Cal. L. Rev. 444, 450, *supra*.) Recollection is used not as pertaining to the events underlying the charge, a question covered in *People v. Francabandera*, but in the more basic sense of the ability to recall sensory perceptions from one moment to the next.

> (3) Does the defendant have at least a rudimentary understanding of the process of trial and the roles of the Judge, jury, prosecutor, and defense attorney? (See *People v. Posey*, 74 Misc.2d 149)

> (4) Can the defendant, if he wishes, establish a working relationship with his attorney? ("If the accused is so delusional or paranoid that he will not trust the counsel or tell him the true facts, then he would be incompetent." Bennett, *supra*, p. 574, and see *People v. Francabandera*, 33 N.Y.2d 429, 435–436)

> (5) Does the defendant possess sufficient intelligence and judgment to listen to the advice of counsel and, based on that advice, appreciate (without necessarily choosing to adopt it) that one course of conduct may be more beneficial to him than another? (Bacon, *supra*, p. 446; Bennett, p. 575.)

> (6) Is the defendant's mental state sufficiently stable to enable him to withstand the stresses of the trial without suffering a serious, prolonged, or permanent breakdown? Will the trial be long, complex, short, or simple? (See *People v. Swallow*, 60 Misc.2d 171, 175–177) Are adjustments required in the manner of trial rather than a finding of incapacity? (See *Matter of Russell*, 126 Vt. 240.)

These address more explicitly the psychological underpinnings of the legal definition of competency to stand trial, giving evaluators specifics to address in their evaluations and reports.

## Racial Disparities

Considering that jails and prisons are the "de facto" largest providers of mental health services in the United States (Kinsler & Saxman, 2007) and that our jails and prisons are disproportionately filled with the poor, often marginalized segments of our population (Rabuy & Kopf, 2015), it is intuitive that there is an increased likelihood of encountering someone in a CST evaluation who is expressing symptoms of mental illness (James & Glaze, 2006), is acutely mentally ill (Fuller et al., 2017), and who has experienced a traumatic experience if not multiple traumas (Byrne, 2000; Kinsler & Saxman, 2007). Indeed, simply being arrested, being incarcerated, or experiencing the conditions of being mentally ill while incarcerated can induce trauma symptoms. With mentally ill inmates sometimes "locked away in fetid cells" for "therapeutic seclusion" (Biesecker, 2011), trauma may become evident only after incarceration. Data on inmates were obtained from the Bureau of Justice Statistics' "Indicators of Mental Health Problems Reported by Prisoners and Jail Inmates, 2011–12," the National Inmate Survey conducted in 233 states and federal prisons, 358 jails, and 15 special facilities between February 2011 and May 2012. Inmates were assessed for serious psychological distress using the Kessler 6 (K6) nonspecific psychological distress scale and self-report data were obtained regarding mental health history. The percentages of prison and jail inmates assumed to meet the threshold for serious psychological distress were 14 and 26, respectively. When compared to the general population, based on the National Survey on Drug Use and Health data, prison and jail inmates were three to five times as likely to have met the threshold for serious psychological distress as adults in the general United States population in the past 30 days. Furthermore, based on the Bureau of Justice Statistics' data, only half of prisoners (50%) and a third of jail inmates (36%) either did not meet threshold for serious psychological distress or had not been told in the past that they had a mental health disorder (Bronson & Berzofsky, 2017). The disproportionate number of individuals in the forensic system who are mentally ill can partly be attributed to the criminalization hypothesis. This theory posits that as a result of the release of patients from mental institutions and stricter commitment laws, large numbers of mentally ill people, particularly in urban centers, remain in the community. The lack of treatment and supervision at times results in erratic behavior by these individuals, which may lead to an increase in their criminal arrests (Gibbs, 1987).

Torrey, Kennard, Eslinger, Lamb, and Pavle (2010) determined that in the year 2004–2005 the odds of a seriously mentally ill individual being in jail or prison compared to a hospital was 3.2–1. This also means that throughout the United States that year, there were three times more people with serious mental illnesses in jails and prisons than in hospitals (Torrey et al., 2010). Furthermore, an overwhelming amount of research demonstrates that the criminal justice forensic system exacerbates mental health symptomatology and that jail inmates experience substantially more deleterious consequences than prison inmates do. Several factors reflecting the role of local jails may explain these higher rates. The psychological toll of incarceration includes both high levels of uncertainty regarding their own incarceration and the conditions of the respective facilities (Yi, Turney, & Wildeman, 2017). Even without having a history of mental health problems, a high proportion of inmates are found to experience mental health disorders upon incarceration. In fact, of the mentally ill inmates whom James and Glaze (2006) studied, a higher proportion of them did not have a mental health *history*. However, among jail inmates with mental health problems, James and Glaze found that a significant percentage had experienced trauma, including living in a foster home and past physical or sexual abuse. (By definition, jails have a higher turnover rate than prisons, which also contributes to inmates' lack of stability and poorer mental health.) Another explanation for the greater percentage of psychopathology in jail inmates is possible behaviors prior to incarceration including drug use and the relatively recent interruption in those behaviors on the part of jail inmates. The differences in inmate numbers, budget, and turnover rate also determine the availability and quality of on-site physical and mental health services, resulting in limited and inferior facilities servicing jail inmates (Yi et al., 2017).

While the impact of trauma in general on CST is now only coming to the fore, it is remiss not to consider the broader sociocultural influences impacting the processing and disclosing of trauma, which are often minimized and/or neglected. In many contexts, perspectives of individuals of authority (e.g., evaluators) or those from privileged backgrounds (e.g., those from majority culture) are amplified while those perspectives of less powerful (e.g., defendants) or less privileged (e.g., those from more marginalized groups) are weighted less and considered differently. At times, voices from underprivileged individuals can be stifled or ignored, sometimes based on biases. Both evaluators and defendants are subject to biases, as are all individuals. Evaluators' assumptions and beliefs about an individual's cultural background are important to keep in mind. A specific important sociocultural component to consider is that of stigma or even an awareness that symptoms may be mental (and not physical or spiritual) in nature. Some groups are more ashamed of mental illness than others are and perceive it as a shortcoming. Individuals from these groups may be more reluctant or unable to share information. A heightened awareness of different groups' feelings toward mental illness and differential access to mental health services is helpful and perhaps necessary to consider in the CST process.

Regardless of race, the prevalence of trauma and PTSD are particularly elevated in urban, low-income communities, with nearly one in four adults in these types of neighborhoods experiencing PTSD (Breslau, Davis, Andreski & Peterson, 1991; Goldmann et al., 2011). It is individuals from these same socially disadvantaged communities who have a disproportionately increased likelihood of both experiencing trauma and involvement with the criminal justice system (Golembeski & Fullilove, 2008; Hartney & Vuong, 2009; Nicosia, MacDonald, & Arkes, 2013).

In a segment of the PBS News Hour aired on May 15, 2014, Sarah Varney reported the following:

> For many of those inmates (those with mental illness), their path to incarceration started in childhoods marked by trauma and poverty.

Inmates with mental health problems are much more likely to have experienced or witnessed traumatic events during adolescence: "They grow up in homes witnessing violence and sexual abuse, and caregivers going in and out of jail," said Dana DeHart, an assistant dean for research support at the College of Social Work at DeSaussure College in Columbia, South Carolina. "Victimization leads to or exacerbates mental health problems like depression, anxiety and PTSD."

As they grow up, their conditions worsen, DeHart explained, and these fragile men and women turn to drugs or alcohol to soothe their anxiety or numb their pain. To pay for their addictions, they often get involved in property crimes and prostitution, and then escalate to violent offenses.

But jail and prison are particularly bad places to be mentally ill. Men and women with behavioral disorders and mental illness end up in stressful prison environments – many are put in seclusion for long stretches of time – that further exacerbate their conditions, researchers say. Inmates with mental illness are much more likely to be injured in prison fights. The Department of Justice reported that 20 percent of inmates with mental illness were injured in jailhouse fights compared to 10 percent of inmate without mental illness. In local jails, inmates with mental illness are three times as likely to be injured.

Research generally indicates that race is not a significant factor in defendants being referred for CTS evaluations (Harris & Weiss, 2018), or in the results of these evaluations (Cooper & Zapf, 2003; Hart & Hare, 1992; Kois, Pearson, Chauhan, Goni, & Saraydarian, 2013; Melton et al., 2018; Paradis et al., 2016). However, the percentage of non-Whites incarcerated in the United States is much higher than the percentage of non-Whites in the general population (65.8% versus 28.9%, respectively) (Humes, Jones, & Ramirez, 2011; West, 2010), and in plea offers, there has been shown to be a racial/ethnic difference in who is offered lower pleas and whose charges are dismissed outright (Berdejó, 2018). Therefore, while there does not seem to be a bias in either people being referred for a CST evaluation, or in the outcome of the evaluation when looking at CST evaluations, there is clearly a social/institutional bias in who is arrested, charged, and incarcerated (Schwartz & Feisthamel, 2009).

There is also, a racial disparity when it comes to diagnosing. Schwartz and Blankenship (2014) found a "clear and pervasive pattern" (p. 133) of minorities being diagnosed with psychotic disorders at a higher rate than their Caucasian counterparts (3–4 times higher for African Americans and 3 times higher for Latinx/Hispanics). (For an overview, see Moreno-Kustner, Martin, & Pastor, April 12, 2018. Prevalence of psychotic disorders and its association with methodological issues. A systematic review and meta-analyses, PLOS, https://doi.org/10.1371/journal.pone.0195687).

## Competency and Mental Illness

While mental disease or defect (hereafter referred to as a mental health disorder) is not explicitly mentioned in Dusky, most courts, and professional standards, indicate that a mental health disorder should be directly tied to the reasons the defendant is unfit (Mossman et al., 2007; Zapf & Roesch, 2009). The cleanest way to achieve this for the examiner (as the evaluation is not a diagnostic one) is to link specific symptoms the defendant is displaying to specific competency criteria. For example, it may not be possible to discriminate schizophrenia from schizoaffective disorder in one interview, but we certainly can state that psychotic symptoms (e.g., paranoia, hallucinations) are interfering with the defendant's ability to work with an attorney and assist in a defense. In conveying this to the court, the more specific the description of the defendant, the better. For example, stating that the defendant's psychotic paranoia prevents him from being able to work with his attorney is not as effective as stating that the defendant believes he is royalty and warring factions, including his attorney, want to dethrone him. In this example, there well may also be symptoms of mania and the examiner must use critical thinking and sound judgment to determine which symptoms are primary (paranoia, delusion, or mania) in incapacitating the defendant. As a result, unless records are available positively confirming a more specific diagnosis, most reports will conclude that a defendant is suffering from an "unspecified" form of a disorder.

A psychotic break from reality both intuitively and factually is linked to being unfit to stand trial. This is not to suggest that psychosis indicates incompetence (one can be fit and still experience psychotic symptoms), rather that incompetence is most often attributed to psychotic symptoms. Psychotic symptomatology may very well render an individual unfit (Colwell & Gianesini, 2011; Cooper & Zapf, 2003; Hart & Hare, 1992; Kois et al., 2013; Nicholson & Kugler, 1991; Paradis et al., 2016; Pirelli et al., 2011; Warren et al., 2006), because the psychotic process can prevent a defendant from examining his legal case in a rational fashion. In addition, the presence of a psychotic process may render the defendant inaccessible to counsel, perhaps making it difficult for him or her to develop and maintain a working relationship or examine their legal options and the ramification thereof with their attorney in a reasonable fashion. Prelli, Gottdiener, and Zapf (2011) found "those diagnosed with a psychotic disorder were nearly eight times more likely to be found incompetent than those without the diagnosis" (p. 29).

Regardless of psychosis, trauma plays a large part in the psychological experience of jail inmates. The route to incarceration, for many inmates, "started in childhoods marked by trauma and poverty" (Varney, May 15, 2014). Having a history of trauma results in an increased likelihood of being involved with the criminal justice system for both majority and minority populations (Baglivio et al., 2014; English, Widon, & Brandford, 2002; Gabarino, 2015; Gabarino, 2017; Howell, Cater, Miller-Graff, Schwartz, & Graham-Bermann, 2017; Roos et al., 2016; Wolff & Shi, 2012).

## General Procedures in Competency to Stand Trial

The competence to stand trial evaluation is performed by one or two neutral professionals (psychologist, psychiatrist, social worker, or experienced nurse), or by committee (Mossman et al., 2007). Reports based on the examination indicating the examiner's opinions are sent to the Court and the Court makes the final determination.

While the Court agrees with the opinions of the examiners over 90 percent of the time (Acklin & Gowensmith, 2015; Cox & Zapf, 2004; Cruise & Rogers, 1998; Freckleton, 1996; Goldstein & Stone, 1977; Hart & Hare, 1992; Paradis et al., 2016; Poythress & Stock, 1980; Reich & Tookey, 1986; Rosenfeld & Ritchie, 1998; Zapf, Hubbard, Cooper, Wheeles, & Ronan, 2004) either party (defense or prosecution), prior to the final determination, can contest the opinions in the reports. (Often, the contesting party will hire a private evaluator.) In states where there are two evaluators, when they do not agree in their opinion if the defendant is competent or not, typically a third neutral evaluator is assigned, and a hearing is held to put the specific issues of the competency, or lack thereof, on the record and to aid the Court in making the final determination.

A competency to stand trial evaluation of a criminal defendant is ordered by the Court, usually based on a request from the defense attorney (although any interested party can request one). According to People v. Burson, it must be based on a "bona fide doubt" of the defendant's competency. However, there are instances where attorneys will request an evaluation as a 'fishing expedition' to see if any possible mental health issues exist, or as a way of avoiding the cost of hiring an expert to reveal to the court possible mitigating factors (however, this goes against the spirit of CST evaluations as neutral and nonadversarial). Some prosecutors view competency examiners, and evaluations, as inherently biased in favor of the defendant and view them as a way of delaying trial, obtaining information favorable to the defendant, and generally obstructing prosecution. Therefore, with many possible deviations on both sides from the spirit of CST, much depends on the relationships among the attorney, the prosecutor, the court, and the examiners as to the adversarial level of the process. If all parties are invested in a just outcome and not just a 'leg up' for one side or the other, the process is one similar to being a "master teacher," educating the court about possible mental health issues related to competency in the particular defendant (Brodsky, 1999, p. 52). Even during competency hearings, where each side will want to 'score points' during questioning, the role of the expert should be only to describe the defendant to the Court utilizing their expertise. Keeping this in mind will help protect the expert from becoming defensive on the stand.

The evaluation can be ordered any time during the process, from arraignment up to the sentencing phase, at the judge's discretion. Unlike insanity, which is based on the accused individual's state of mind in the past (at the time of the incident), competency is based on a defendant's current state of mind, which can change as medications are taken or refused, as symptoms wax and wane or are exacerbated by confinement, as the reality of the situation starts to set in, or any number of reasons humans' presentation change from day to day, week to week, or month to month. External events can also disrupt a defendant's competency to stand trial such as the death of a loved one, a divorce, a new medical diagnosis, or even incidents unrelated to the defendant or the case such as tragedies which impact the entire community (e.g., the attack on the World Trade Center of 9/11, hurricanes Katrina and Sandy, political disruption). Needless to say, there are times when a judge is loath to delay (prior to the start of a trial) or interrupt a trial for a variety of case-relevant (or sometimes not case-relevant) issues.

If the defendant is deemed fit to proceed, the case continues. If the defendant is deemed not fit to proceed, one of two outcomes are possible. The defendant may be sent to a psychiatric or other appropriate facility for restoration of competence or, in some cases, the defendant is civilly committed, and the charges are dismissed (in misdemeanor cases, in some states). In the first instance, while hospitalized, the treatment team may petition the Court for treatment over objection if the defendant is refusing medication. However, usually, treatment over objection is not allowed when the defendant is held in a jail. Medication over objection is controversial, as the defendant may not meet civil commitment criteria, usually immediate harm to self or others, thereby not meeting civil criteria for medication over objection. The legal justification then, to violate a defendant's right to refuse treatment, is decided on a case-by-case basis using specific criteria set forth in *Sell v. United States*, 539 U.S. 166 (2003). As a result, some defendants are forced into treatment during restoration hospitalization but then refuse treatment after being returned to the holding facility. Also relevant to consider in findings of incompetence is the possibility a defendant may, in fact, be innocent. "The gravest injustice is inflicted upon a person by criminal law commitment upon a finding of unfitness to proceed when it later turns out that he had not committed any criminal act" (Silving, 1967, p. 168).

## The Evaluation

Who performs CST evaluations? Typically, states require a psychiatrist or psychologist to perform the evaluations. Some states will allow a physician, nurse, or social worker, and a few states have a team, examination board, or facility complete the evaluation. Most states and the Federal Courts (34) require one examiner; eight states require two examiners; four states and the military require a team, board, or facility to perform the examinations; two states designate one, two, or three depending on whether the case is a misdemeanor or felony; and three states have no specifications as to the number of examiners (Mossman et al., 2007). In all states, Federal and military courts, it is the judge (or sometimes a special jury) who decides the issue of competency, as it is a legal and not a mental health construct. All states have provisions for hearings, although in most cases it is left to the judge's discretion (except in cases where the two or more examiners disagree, or a private examiner comes to a different conclusion).

A combination of examination procedures is used to arrive at an opinion on an individual's competency to proceed. The cornerstone of the evaluation is an interview of the defendant including current mental status, bio-psycho-social-legal history, as well as a discussion of the charges, court processes, and legal options available for resolution of the charges. Defense attorneys may be present (which gives the examiner an opportunity to observe how the attorney and client communicate and work together), as well as an interpreter, if needed. Additional sources of information may be required if the examiners are unable to arrive at an opinion or if their state/district or other policy requires it. These include, but are not limited to, rap sheets, treatment records, collateral contacts, and audio and/or video recordings of the defendant which exist prior to the evaluation. Also, psychological or psycho-legal testing may be needed as part of the evaluation. The former can include tests for cognitive functioning (IQ and/or neuro-psychological), personality, effort (feigning), and tests specifically created to address the issue of competency. The latter include the Fitness Interview Test – Revised (FIT-R; Roesch, Webster, & Eaves, 1984), *The MacArthur Competence Assessment Tool - Criminal Adjudication (MacCAT-CA;* Poythress et al., 1999), and the Competence Assessment for Standing Trial for Defendants with Mental Retardation (CAST-MR; Everington, 1990), to name a few. One caution: No single test or measure is adequate for forming an opin-ion on competency and any results should be taken in consideration with other sources of information (Mossman et al., 2007; Zapf & Roesch, 2009).

Clinically, many competency to proceed to trial exams focus on the presence or absence of psychotic symptoms (in addition to a general mental status). However, just as we are encouraged not to rely on one test or measure, we should also not rely on one diagnostic category or one source of information. The cases below demon-strate how obtaining more contextual information can significantly alter the evalua-tor's conclusions. For example, acting out or otherwise unreasonable behavior on the part of the defendant, if not attributed to psychosis, may be thought to be directly referable to a personality disorder (Case #1), the fabrication or exaggeration of psy-chotic symptoms (Case #2), cultural issues (Case #3), or even the defendant having been traumatized by the very event which led to his/her incarceration (Case #4) when in fact, they may be attributable to the experience of trauma. We have pro-vided these deidentified four cases in which trauma ultimately were grounds for findings of unfitness.

## Case Examples

### *Case #1: The Bad Boy?*

A good example of a case in which trauma directly impacts on the issue of compe-tency involved a 24-year-old African-American male who was charged with a fel-ony assault, in that it was alleged that he punched a nurse in the face while being treated as an inpatient on a psychiatric unit of municipal hospital, causing her to sustain serious facial injuries. In addition, he was facing serious violent felony charges in another county. Although staff in the court clinic assigned to assess com-petency attempted to see the defendant several times, he refused.

During one attempt to see the defendant, staff went to the holding cells in the back of the courtroom, where the defendant was observed banging on the door with his fists. His attorney attempted to calm him down but was unable to do so. He reported his client told him "all I want to do is die." Correction Department person-nel informed that the defendant was a known slasher, having cut at least 12 inmates and was recorded on jail phone conversations asking friends and family to bring him contraband. In another attempt to see the defendant, he refused to leave the holding area, despite his attorney and the forensic examiners, as well as the judge himself, imploring the defendant to come into the courtroom. He was again observed banging on the door and chanting. He later was reported to have destroyed a light fixture in the room.

Records from the municipal hospital, where the defendant had been an inpatient several months before, revealed that the defendant had not been cooperative with psychological testing. He was referred from jail after making a maneuver at self-harm by ingesting large amounts of hoarded anti-depressants. He was discharged after 2 weeks with a diagnosis of adjustment disorder with a disturbance of emotions and conduct as a result of "suicide attempts and averse legal situations." Soon after discharge, he was returned to the hospital from jail twice, after again making maneuvers at self-harm, and each time was returned to jail after a few hours with a diagnosis of adjustment disorder and antisocial personality disorder.

A conversation with the defendant's mother revealed that the defendant had been diagnosed with bipolar disorder and treated as an inpatient on a psychiatric ward of a local private hospital between the ages of 11 and 13. She was charged with neglect of her son in Family Court because she did not want him medicated. He had been prescribed Seroquel and Ritalin, but she would not let him take these medications on an outpatient basis. When the defendant was 15 years old, he spent 2 months in a state psychiatric facility after attacking his mother's abusive boyfriend. His mother confirmed that she was in an abusive relationship for 16 years and the defendant would repeatedly witness this man beating and verbally abusing her. He was also in a juvenile detention facility during these years and repeatedly refused psychotropic medications.

It was the opinion of the forensic examiners that as opposed to struggling with an adjustment disorder or having an antisocial personality disorder, the defendant was beset by a long-standing posttraumatic stress disorder (chronic) which caused him to act out violently. This extreme acting out violent behavior was seen by examiners to be directly referable to PTSD which did not permit him, in their opinion, to consider his legal options reasonably or able to establish a working relationship with counsel. It was thought that a period of hospitalization with a provision of counseling and psychotropic medication would render the defendant more accessible to counsel.

Here is a case of an individual who on the surface appeared to be merely "a bad actor" and just "carrying on." His history of witnessing abuse of his mother at an early age, however, was thought to account for his legal incapacitation. He was ultimately adjudicated unfit to proceed, received a regimen of psychotropic medication, and individual and group therapy in a secure state psychiatric facility. These treatment modalities addressed his anger issues surrounding trauma. He was found fit to proceed within 3 months of admission to the hospital and discharged back to court where he went on to successfully deal with his charges in an appropriate and effective manner.

## Case #2: Feigning and Incompetent

Fabrication or exaggeration of symptoms in criminal cases, while substantially less than in civil cases (Mittenberg, Patton, Canyock, & Condit, 2002 indicate 19% in criminal cases compared to over 30% in civil cases), is still an issue which can impact competency to stand trial evaluations – but not always in the way we expect. For example, in a case that spanned many months, a young man initially presented with intellectual deficits, unusual hallucinations, and symptoms of panic attacks. During the initial competency evaluation where he had been brought to (but not admitted to) an inpatient forensic psychiatric unit, his petite stature was accessorized with heavy black framed glasses with extremely thick lenses held together with duct tape, reinforcing the image of vulnerability. He walked in a halting manner and generally seemed confused about where he was and why. Responding better to simple language, the evaluation took significantly longer than usual and was still inconclusive. Eventually, it was decided to have him admitted for observation and treatment (if needed). When informed, his speech became wonderfully fluid with good vocabulary and it was clear that he had a good understanding of what was happening. He "confessed" he was just "playing at" being intellectually limited and in no circumstances wanted to be admitted. Even with that explanation, some things just did not seem to add up and he was admitted for observation, assessment, and possibly treatment.

During the course of his first admission in an acute-care forensic hospital, he exhibited signs of dramatic emotionality, possible psychotic confusion, manipulation, and anxiety. He was medicated and engaged – sometimes – in psychotherapy, primarily discussing his murder charge. After several gestures at suicide, he was placed in a cell by himself directly across from the nurses' station where he loudly began to insist he be sent back to the main jail. Eventually, the treatment team yielded and returned him. Within 2 months, he was sent back to the hospital after increasing the seriousness of his self-harm. Medications and therapy resumed with some good effect but no real improvement in insight. He would become bored, said he was no longer interested in harming himself, and ask to be sent back. This back and forth happened several times. During one therapy session, in an attempt to break through his resistance, the statement and question were posed to him: "Something is going on – something I believe you want help with but can't ask for. What can we do for you?" His response (with a twinkle in his eye): "Send flowers to my grave." On another occasion when he was hospitalized, he was discovered with feces smeared on his body and cell walls. This was a new and disturbing behavior. However, upon close examination, the feces were in two delineated stripes on his face, four on his chest and several on his lower legs. His white underwear was pristine and when his glasses started to slip down his nose, he very carefully used the (clean) back of his hands to push them up. Clearly, the feces smearing behavior was a new manipulation, frustrating the treatment team, competency evaluation team, and Department of Corrections team alike. However, this also seemed to mark a shift in the defendant's behavior. Once allowed to shower, in the subsequent individual therapy session, he revealed that he had been sexually abused repeatedly as a child, including being drugged to make him more compliant. The murder victim in the instant offence was one of the men who had abused the defendant and who was now targeting the defendant's younger brother.

In this case, the manipulative behaviors and instances of clear feigning were the means by which he protected himself from very raw and painful traumatic symptoms. A diagnosis of PTSD was finally made – along with Personality Disorder with Borderline features – and he was determined to be Not Competent to Proceed due to an inability to trust his attorney (or anyone in authority) and not being stable enough to withstand the stresses of what promised to be a long and complicated trial. A period of long-term hospitalization with an adjustment in medication and treatment was successful in helping him cope with the reality of his past and (likely) future. He was eventually returned to jail where he was able to manage his symptoms, develop and maintain a working relationship with his attorney, consider his legal options in a clear and reasonable manner, and resolve his case. (This is an example of Roger's, 1990 Pathogenic model of malingering.)

## Case #3: You Wouldn't Understand

In another very interesting case, the trauma was of a much different nature and related to cultural issues rather than direct symptoms of a trauma-related disorder. As this individual did not complain of and did not present with mental health symptoms, his apparent inability to consider rationally his legal options was perplexing. He was a middle-aged, intelligent, proud (some would even say narcissistic) married man with three children who had allegedly been swindling people for years via property fraud with losses in the hundreds of thousands of dollars. He had been under investigation for many years. As a result, by the time he was arrested, there was a wealth of evidence against him. For several years, he was held in jail while cases were solidified, motions made, trial preparation conducted, and plea offers made and rejected. These pre-trial measures lasted so long that eventually an offer was made of time served. Of course, he would have had to acknowledge guilt in a public forum and lose his right to appeal, which he seemed to understand. When he consistently refused this offer, a competency evaluation was ordered.

During the evaluation (over the course of 4 sessions), the defendant claimed that he was a devoted family man and was in considerable distress at having not been with his wife and not having seen his children for several years. With an offer which would mean he could immediately return to his family, albeit with supervised release, his refusal to even consider this course of action was incomprehensible and hinted at possible underlying serious mental health issues despite no obvious signs or symptoms. He refused to even explain his thought and decision-making processes. That is, until the last session. Then, through a steady stream of stoic tears, he indicated his family, who lived in another country, were of high social standing, and well respected (and successful) in business. Even with this knowledge, his logic for declining the offer of time served was lost on the evaluators. Eventually, he spelled it out for us. He was not worried about his own future and diminished opportunities to support his family in the United States; his concern was for his family of origin and extended family, most of whom had not immigrated to America. The shame he would have brought on his family still in their home country would ruin their social standing, respectability, and ability to continue in their business ventures because they would be viewed as pariahs. His only options for saving face, and thereby his family's economic and social health, would be to never admit wrongdoing. This would allow his family to assert that he was innocent all along and had been caught in a corrupt injustice. This avoidance of culturally bound trauma, potentially having intergenerational consequences, was now understood as a rational thought process behind his legal decision. He was found fit and remained incarcerated for several more years, having been denied parole, as he continued to refuse to acknowledge his guilt. In cases of seemingly extreme beliefs, it is important to differentiate them from psychosis in part by asking questions and keeping an open mind (Owen & Weissman, 2018).

## Case #4: Who Are You?

In our last example involving the issue of trauma and competency, a 50-year-old South American male was charged with murdering his wife and son by stabbing them to death and slitting their throats. The defendant claimed that he did not slaughter his family but rather his alter ego, Diego, did it. He reported no history of prior psychiatric hospitalization because "Diego would not allow" him to be hospitalized. He was enrolled in the past in an anger management course at the behest of his employer because "Diego was threatening people." The defendant reported Diego often "taking over and talking," but he felt powerless to intervene and take control of the situation. Of particular note is the fact the first time the defendant remembered experiencing Diego's presence was when as a child he saw his godfather beating his godmother savagely with a belt while she was naked. The defendant remembers witnessing these beatings on an ongoing basis. He reported when these incidents occurred he would hear Diego tell him, "See what he is doing. You can't allow that." He added that this same godmother who was beaten so brutally would discipline him in turn by beating him with a belt to such an extent that she would leave welts on his body.

Regarding the issue of competency, the diagnosis of dissociative identity disorder was considered. The defendant might have been considered fit to proceed, save for suicidal feelings he was experiencing, stemming from the awareness of the horrendous nature of the charges against him and the torment he expressed because of the sudden and uncontrolled emergence of his alter ego. He was ultimately adjudicated unfit to proceed because of the risk to suicide he posed. At the heart of the psychogenesis of the suspected dissociative identity disorder was his history of witnessing as a youngster the beatings of his godmother and his failure to protect her and her subsequent beatings of him. His competency was eventually restored and his charges resovled.

## Additional Considerations

Specific issues involving trauma that are timely and consequential must also inform forensic examiners when making decisions related to CST. One example is asylum seekers who are leaving countries of origin where they are often subjected to or witness extreme violence. These individuals are also being placed in detention and separated from families, exacerbating trauma. They are then expected to participate in legal proceedings that will determine whether or not they can stay in the country. If the issue of CST is considered by an immigration judge, when the undocumented individual is set to move forward on asylum issues, should not the effects of the immigrant's history of trauma be seriously considered? How, for example, might the trauma of witnessing family or friends being killed or raped, or the individual him or herself subjected to rape, torture, or separation from children or parents impact the ability to assist counsel during legal proceedings? The perilous sojourns of immigrants in an attempt to seek asylum must be taken into consideration when an examiner is asked to do a CST evaluation. Similar issues may be raised when performing a criminal CST evaluation for a defendant who may be deported after the conclusion of their case.

Furthermore, we are all painfully aware of current concerns with mass shootings. We awake many mornings to the headlines of newspapers questioning the motives of mass shooters. All too often, the issue of trauma falls by the wayside when an individual charged with a heinous crime is often prejudged in a harsh light by the media. The history of such an individual ordered to undergo a CST evaluation is often overlooked. Despite the media circus that all too often accompanies these cases and the social pressure to hold the defendant responsible for the alleged crimes, the forensic evaluator tasked with doing a comprehensive and fair CST must consider the trauma background of the defendant in rendering a legal opinion. It is the individual defendant, not the crime itself, which must be evaluated.

This issue is also relevant when working with a sex offender. At times, the accused sex offender is a victim of abuse (physical, sexual, emotional, neglect, etc.). It is the job of the forensic examiner to consider a history of abuse and how it presently impacts on the individual's ability to work with an attorney. Sometimes, anger and acting out behavior that is mistaken for character pathology may be directly referable to a history of abuse, physical or sexual.

Finally, the plight of battered women (or any gender) raises a particularly thorny question when examining the issue of CST. Specifically, while from a common-sense perspective the actions of the accused woman with a history of abuse who is charged with retaliating against her partner may be offered as defense, often the abuse she has suffered at the hands of her partner may prevent her from fully assessing her legal options in a rational manner due to trauma symptoms. The motives of her retaliation and thought processes may be more complex and thus should be considered before opining such a woman fit to proceed.

In sum, trauma may pervade many cases which we, as forensic evaluators, conduct and as such should not be overlooked when we are called upon to opine on fitness.

# Conclusion

While it is well established that those with mental illness and those arrested have a significantly higher rate of trauma history, and the mere fact of incarceration, especially at the local jail level, can in itself be traumatizing, trauma is frequently overlooked in competency to stand trial (CST) evaluations. As CST evaluation are by far the most frequent mental health evaluations ordered for those facing criminal charges, and the fact psychosis is the primary reason defendants are deemed unfit to stand trial, there is a dearth of assessment of trauma in these evaluations as well as in the literature. A search of the terms "trauma" and "competence to stand trial" reveals a number of articles discussing traumatic brain injury and amnesia, but precious few related to psychological trauma and related symptoms as important factors in CTS. Trauma symptoms can, and do, vary significantly, and are not always identified as reactions to trauma by the defendant. Evaluators are encouraged to presume a history of trauma and make due diligence in assessment to ensure that trauma symptoms are not interfering with their constitutional rights to a fair trial.

# Questions/Activities for Further Exploration

1. What is the difference between a criterion-based and a contextual CTS evaluation? What are the pros and cons of each? How could a trauma history impact each?
2. What impact could the trauma of arrest and incarceration have on the outcome of a CTS evaluation?
3. How could cultural issues impact the expression of trauma in a CTS evaluation?
4. How does the evaluator manage his or her feelings toward the sex abuser in considering a history of trauma and its effect on competency?
5. The issue of memory often plays a part in competency. How might trauma affect memory or other cognitive issues?

# References

Acklin, M., & Gowensmith, K. (2015). Examiner agreement and judicial consensus in forensic mental health evaluations. *Journal of Forensic Psychology Practice, 15*(4), 318–343.

American Bar Association, (1994). Judicial Administration Division, in Standards Relating to Appellate Courts (Vol. 3).

Baglivio, M., Epps, N., Swartz, K., Huq, M., Sheer, A., & Hardt, N. (2014). The prevalence of adverse childhood experiences (ACE) in the lives of juvenile offenders. *Journal of Juvenile Justice, 3*(2), 1–17. https://www.prisonpolicy.org/scans/Prevalence_of_ACE.pdf

Berdejó, C. (2018). Criminalizing race: Racial disparities in plea bargaining. *Boston College Law Review, 59*(4), 1187–1249.

Biesecker, M. (2011, November 19). Central prison's warden steps down after scathing report. Ashville Citizen (B3).

Bonnie, R., & Grisso, T. (2000). Adjudicative competence and youthful offenders. In T. Grisso & R. Schwartz (Eds.), *Youth on trial: A developmental perspective on juvenile justice* (pp. 73–103). Chicago, IL: University of Chicago Press.

Brodsky, S. (1999). *The expert expert witness.* Washington, D.C.: The American Psychological Association.

Breslau, N., Davis, G. C., Andreski, P., & Peterson, E. (1991). Traumatic events and posttraumatic stress disorder in an urban population of young adults. *Archives of General Psychiatry, 48*(3), 216–222.

Bronson, J., & Berzofsky, M. (2017, June). Indicators of mental health problems reported by prisoners and jail inmates, 2011–12. *Bureau of Justice Statistics.*

Byrne, M. K. (2000). Trauma reactions in the offender. Understanding Post-Traumatic Conditions: Medico-legal seminar papers (pp. 1-32). Bondi Junction, Australia: LAAMS Publications.

Cochrane, R. E., Grisso, T., & Frederick, R. I. (2001). The relationship between criminal charges, diagnoses, and psycholegal opinions among federal pretrial defendants. *Behavioral Sciences & The Law, 19*(4), 565–582.

Colwell, L. H., & Gianesini, J. (2011). Demographic, criminogenic, and psychiatric factors that predict competency restoration. *Journal of the American Academy of Psychiatry and the Law Online, 39*(3), 297–306.

Cooper, V. G., & Zapf, P. A. (2003). Predictor variables in competency to stand trial decisions. *Law and Human Behavior, 27*(4), 423–436.

Cox, M. L., & Zapf, P. A. (2004). An investigation of discrepancies between mental health professionals and the courts in decisions about competency. *Law & Psychology Review, 28*, 109.

Cruise, K. R., & Rogers, R. (1998). An analysis of competency to stand trial: An integration of case law and clinical knowledge. *Behavioral Sciences & the Law, 16*(1), 35–50.

Dusky V. United States, 362 U.S. 402 (1960).

English, D., Widon, C., & Brandford, C. (2002). Childhood victimization and delinquency, adult Criminality, and violent criminal behavior: A replication and extension, final report. US Department of Justice unpublished document No.: 192291. https://www.ncjrs.gov/App/Publications/abstract.aspx?ID=192291

Everington, C. T. (1990). The competence assessment for standing trial for defendants with mental retardation (CAST-MR): A validation study. *Criminal Justice and Behavior, 17*(2), 147–168.

Freckleton, I. (1996). Rationality and flexibility in assessment of fitness to stand trial. *International Journal of Law and Psychiatry, 19*, 39–59.

Fuller, D., Sinclair, E., Lamb, H., Cayce, J., & Snook, J. (2017). *Emptying the 'new asylums': A beds capacity model to reduce mental illness behind bars.* Arlington, VA: Treatment Advocacy Center. http://www.treatmentadvocacycenter.org/storage/documents/emptying-new-asylums.pdf

Gabarino, J. (2015). *Listening to killers.* Berkley, CA: University of California Press.

Gabarino, J. (2017). ACEs in the criminal justice system. *Academic Pediatrics, 17*(7), S32–S33. https://www.academicpedsjnl.net/article/S1876-2859(16)30419-3/fulltext

Gibbs, J. (1987). Symptoms of psychopathology among jail prisoners: The effects of exposure to the jail environment. *Criminal Justice and Behavior, 14*(3), 288–310. https://doi.org/10.1177/0093854887014003003

Golding, S. L., & Roesch, R. (1988). Competency for adjudication: An international analysis. In D. N. Weisstub (Ed.), Law and mental health: International perspectives, Vol. 4, pp. 73–109). Elmsford, NY, US: Pergamon Press.

Goldmann, E., Aiello, A., Uddin, M., Delva, J., Koenen, K., Gant, L. M., & Galea, S. (2011). Pervasive exposure to violence and posttraumatic stress disorder in a predominantly African American urban community: The Detroit Neighborhood health study. *Journal of Traumatic Stress, 24*(6), 747–751.

Goldstein, R. L., & Stone, M. (1977). When doctors disagree: differing views on competency. *The Bulletin of the American Academy of Psychiatry and the Law, 5*(1), 90–97.

Golembeski, C., & Fullilove, R. (2008). Criminal (in)justice in the city and its associated health consequences. American Journal of Public Health, 98 (Supplement_1), S185-S190.

Grisso, T. (1986). *Evaluating competencies: Forensic assessments and instruments.* New York, NY: Plenum.

Harris, S., & Weiss, R. (2018). The impact of defendants' race in competency to stand trial referrals. *International Journal of Law and Psychiatry, 57*, 85–90.

Hart, S., & Hare, R. (1992). Predicting fitness to stand trial: The relative power of demographic, criminal, and clinical variables. *Forensic Reports, 5*(1), 53–65.

Hartney, C., & Vuong, L. (2009). Created equal: Racial and ethnic disparities in the US criminal justice system. National Council on Crime and Delinquency.

Hoge, S., Bonnie, R., Poythress, N., & Monahan, J. (1992). Attorney-client decision making in criminal cases: Client competence and participation as perceived by their attorneys. *Behavioral Sciences & the Law, 10*, 385–394.

Howell, K., Cater, A., Miller-Graff, L., Schwartz, L., & Graham-Bermann, S. (2017). The relationship between types of childhood victimization and young adulthood criminality. *Criminal Behaviour and Mental Health, 27*(4), 341–353.

Humes, K., Jones, N., & Ramirez, R. (2011, March). Overview of race and hispanic origin: 2010. *United States Census Bureau.* https://www.census.gov/prod/cen2010/briefs/c2010br-02.pdf

James, D., & Glaze, L. (2006). *Mental health problems of prison and jail inmates (Rev. 12/14/06.).* Washington, D.C.: U.S. Dept. of Justice, Office of Justice Programs, Bureau of Justice Statistics. https://www.bjs.gov/content/pub/pdf/mhppji.pdf

Kinsler, P. J., & Saxman, A. (2007). Traumatized offenders: Don't look now, but your jail's also your mental health center. *Journal of Trauma & Dissociation, 8*(2), 81–95.

Kois, L., Pearson, J., Chauhan, P., Goni, M., & Saraydarian, L. (2013). Competency to stand trial among female inpatients. *Law and Human Behavior, 37*(4), 231–240.

Melton, G., Petrila, J., Poythress, N., Slobogin, C., Otto, R., Mossman, D., & Condie, L. (2018). *Psychological evaluations for the courts: A handbook for mental health professionals and lawyers* (4th ed.). New York, NY: Guilford Press.

Mittenberg, W., Patton, C., Canyock, E. M., & Condit, D. C. (2002). Base rates of malingering and symptom exaggeration. *Journal of Clinical and Experimental Neuropsychology, 24*(8), 1094–1102.

Mossman, D., Noffsinger, S., Ash, P., Frierson, R., Gerbasi, J., Hackett, M., ... Zonana, H. (2007). AAPL practice guideline for the forensic psychiatric evaluation of competence to stand trial. *Journal of the American Academy of Psychiatry and the Law, 35*(4), S3–S72.

Nicosia, N., MacDonald, J. M., & Arkes, J. (2013). Disparities in criminal court referrals to drug treatment and prison for minority men. *American Journal of Public Health, 103*(6), e77-e84.

Nicholson, R. A., & Kugler, K. E. (1991). Competent and incompetent criminal defendants: A quantitative review of comparative research. *Psychological Bulletin, 109*(3), 355–370.

Owen, E., & Weissman, E. (2018). Standby or advisory counsel. In E. Kelly (Ed.), *Representing people with mental disabilities: A practical guide for criminal defense lawyers.* Chicago, IL: American Bar Association.

Paradis, C., Owen, E., Solomon, L., McCullough, G., Lane, B., Gulrajani, C., … McCullough, G. (2016). Competency to stand trial evaluations in a multicultural population: Associations among psychiatric, demographic, and legal factors. *International Journal of Law and Psychiatry, 47,* 79–85.

Pate v. Robinson, 383 U.S. 375 (1966).

People v. Valentino, 78 Misc.2d 678 (1974).

Perlin, M. (2003). Beyond Dusky and Godinez: Competency before and after trial. *Behavioral Sciences & the Law, 21,* 297–310.

Perlin, M. L. (2008). Representing Criminal Defendants in Incompetency and Insanity Cases: Some Therapeutic Jurisprudence Dilemmas. SSRN Electronic Journal

Perlin, M., Champine, P., Dlugacz, H., & Connell, M. (2008). *Competence in the law: From legal theory to clinical application.* Hoboken, NJ: Wiley.

Pirelli, G., Gottdiener, W., & Zapf, P. (2011). A meta-analytic review of competency to stand trial research. *Psychology, Public Policy, and Law, 17,* 1–53.

Poythress, N. G., & Stock, H. V. (1980). Competency to stand trial: A historical review and some new data. *The Journal of Psychiatry & Law, 8*(2), 131–146.

Poythress, N., Bonnie, R., Hoge, S., Monahan, J., & Oberlander, L. (1994). Client abilities to assist counsel and make decisions in criminal cases: Findings from three studies. *Law and Human Behavior, 18,* 437–452.

Poythress, N., Nicholson, R., Otto, R. K., Edens, J. F., Bonnie, R. J., Monahan, J., & Hoge, S. K. (1999). *The MacArthur competence assessment tool—Criminal adjudication: Professional manual.* Odessa, FL: Psychological Assessment Resources.

Prelli, G., Gottdiener, W., & Zapf, P. (2011). A meta-analytic review of competency to stand trial research. *Psychology, Public Policy, and Law, 17,* 1–53.

Prest, W. (2008). *William Blackstone: Law and letters in the eighteenth century.* Oxford, UK: Oxford University Press. ISBN 978-0-19-955029-6.

Rabuy, B., & Kopf, D. (2015). Prisons of poverty: Uncovering the pre-incarceration incomes of the imprisoned. Prison Policy Initiative, 9.

Reich, J. H., & Tookey, L. (1986). Disagreements between court and psychiatrist on competency to stand trial. *The Journal of Clinical Psychiatry, 47*(1), 29–30.

Roesch, R., & Golding, S. L. (1980). *Competency to stand trial.* Urbana, IL: University of Illinois Press.

Roesch, R., Webster, C. D., & Eaves, D. (1984). *The fitness interview test: A method for assessing fitness to stand trial.* Toronto, Canada: University of Toronto Centre of Criminology.

Roesch, R., Zapf, P., Golding, S., & Skeem, J. (1999). Defining and assessing competency to stand trial. In I. B. Weiner & A. K. Hess (Eds.), *Handbook of forensic psychology* (2nd ed., pp. 327–349). New York, NY: Wiley.

Rogers, R. (1990). Development of a new classificatory model of malingering. *The Bulletin of the American Academy of Psychiatry and the Law, 18*(3), 323–333.

Roos, L. E., Afifi, T. O., Martin, C. G., Pietrzak, R. H., Tsai, J., & Sareen, J. (2016). Linking typologies of childhood adversity to adult incarceration: Findings from a nationally representative sample. *American Journal of Orthopsychiatry, 86*(5), 584–593. https://doi.org/10.1037/ort0000144

Rosenfeld, B., & Ritchie, K. (1998). Competence to stand trial: Clinician reliability and the role of offense severity. *Journal of Forensic Science, 43*(1), 151–157.

Sawyer, W., & Wagner, P. (2019). Mass incarceration: The whole pie 2019. *Prison Policy Initiative.* https://www.prisonpolicy.org/reports/pie2019.html

Schwartz, R., & Blankenship, D. (2014, December 22). Racial disparities in psychiatric disorder diagnosis: A review of empirical literature. *World Journal of Psychiatry, 4*(4), 133–140. https://doi.org/10.5498/wjp.v4.i4.133

Schwartz, R., & Feisthamel, K. (2009). Disproportionate diagnosis of mental disorders among African American versus European American clients: Implications for counseling theory, research, and practice. *Journal of Counseling and Development, 87*(3), 295–301. https://doi.org/10.1002/j.1556-6678.2009.tb00110.x

Silving, H. (1967). *Essays on mental incapacity and criminal conduct*. Florida, IL: Charles C Thomas.

Skeem, J. L., Golding, S. L., Cohn, N. B., & Berge, G. (1998). Logic and reliability of evaluations of competence to stand trial. *Law and Human Behavior, 22*(5), 519–547.

Stone, A. (1975). *Mental health and the law: A system in transition*. Rockville, MD: National Institute of Mental Health.

Torrey, E. F., Kennard, A. D., Eslinger, D., Lamb, R., & Pavle, J. (2010). *More mentally ill persons are in jails and prisons than hospitals: A survey of the states*. Arlington, VA: Treatment Advocacy Center.

Varney, S. (2014, May 15). By the numbers: Mental illness behind bars. *PBS News Hour*. https://www.pbs.org/newshour/health/numbers-mental-illness-behind-bars

Warren, J. I., Murrie, D. C., Stejskal, W., Colwell, L. H., Morris, J., Chauhan, P., & Dietz, P. (2006). Opinion formation in evaluating the adjudicative competence and restorability of criminal defendants: A review of 8,000 evaluations. *Behavioral Sciences & the Law, 24*(2), 113–132.

West, H. (2010). Prison inmates at midyear 2009– statistical tables. U.S. Department of Justice Office of Justice Programs Bureau of Justice Statistics. https://www.bjs.gov/content/pub/pdf/pim09st.pdf

Wolff, N., & Shi, J. (2012). Childhood and adult trauma experiences of incarcerated persons and their relationship to adult behavioral health problems and treatment. *International Journal of Environmental Research and Public Health, 9*(5), 1908–1926.

Yi, Y., Turney, K., & Wildeman, C. (2017). Mental health among jail and prison inmates. *American Journal of Men's Health, 11*(4), 900–909. https://doi.org/10.1177/1557988316681339

Zapf, P., & Roesch, R. (2009). *Evaluation of competence to stand trial*. New York, NY: Oxford University Press.

Zapf, P. A., & Roesch, R. (2006). Competency to stand trial: A guide for evaluators. *The handbook of forensic psychology*, 305–331.

Zapf, P. A., Hubbard, K. L., Cooper, V. G., Wheeles, M. C., & Ronan, K. A. (2004). Have the courts abdicated their responsibility for determination of competency to stand trial to clinicians?. *Journal of Forensic Psychology Practice, 4*(1), 27–44.

# Chapter 4
# Incarceration and Trauma: A Challenge for the Mental Health Care Delivery System

Corey M. Leidenfrost and Daniel Antonius

## Introduction

More than 11 million people are incarcerated worldwide (Walmsley, 2018). The rates of the incarcerated population vary widely by country with 53% of countries reporting incarceration rates below 150 per 100,000 people and 15 countries reporting rates exceeding 400 per 100,000 people (Walmsley, 2018). The United States has the highest incarceration rate exceeding 650 per 100,000 residents (Bureau of Justice Statistics, 2018; Sawyer & Wagner, 2019; Walmsley, 2018). Since year 2000, the global incarceration rate has increased on pace with the 24% global population increase, with some geographical differences: Europe has decreased their incarcerated population by 22%, while the Oceania region has increased their incarcerated population by 86% (Walmsley, 2018). Although the correctional population in the United States has seen some decline over the past decade (Bureau of Justice Statistics, 2018), the same population has quadrupled since the 1970s and it continues to account for about one quarter of the world's total incarcerated population (National Research Council, 2014).

Racial disparity is apparent in incarceration rates in the United States (National Research Council, 2014; Sawyer & Wagner, 2019). Although incarceration rates for minorities have always been disproportionate to White offenders (National Research Council, 2014), the difference has increased over time. In 2010, African Americans and Hispanics were incarcerated at six to seven times the rates of White offenders (National Research Council, 2014), with African Americans making up approximately 40% of the total incarcerated population (Sawyer & Wagner, 2019).

C. M. Leidenfrost (✉) · D. Antonius
Department of Psychiatry, University at Buffalo, State University of New York, Buffalo, NY, USA

Erie County Forensic Mental Health Services, Buffalo, NY, USA
e-mail: coreylei@buffalo.edu

© Springer Nature Switzerland AG 2020
R. A. Javier et al. (eds.), *Assessing Trauma in Forensic Contexts*,
https://doi.org/10.1007/978-3-030-33106-1_4

Trauma histories are widespread amongst incarcerated individuals. Studies consistently find alarming rates of trauma symptoms and posttraumatic stress disorder (PTSD) in incarcerated individuals (DeHart, Lynch, Belknap, Dass-Brailsford, & Green, 2014; Goff, Rose, Rose, & Purves, 2007; Green, Miranda, Daroowalla, & Siddique, 2005; Greenberg & Rosenheck, 2009; Lynch, DeHart, Belknap, & Green, 2013; Prins, 2014; Wolff, Huening, Shi, & Frueh, 2014), with the trauma event occurring prior to incarceration (Blaauw, Arensman, Kraaij, Winkel, & Bout, 2002; Clements-Nolle, Wolden, & Bargmann-Losche, 2009; Gunter, Chibnall, Antoniak, Philibert, & Black, 2013; Komarovskaya, Booker Loper, Warren, & Jackson, 2011; Maschi, Gibson, Zgoba, & Morgen, 2011; Morrissey, Courtney, & Maschi, 2012; Zgoba, Jennings, Maschi, & Reingle, 2012), though individuals may become further traumatized, or traumatized for the first time, through the conditions in prisons and jails (Beck & Harrison, 2008; Crisanti & Frueh, 2011; National Research Council, 2014; Struckman-Johnson, Struckman-Johnson, Rucker, Bumby, & Donaldson, 1996; Wolff, Blitz, & Shi, 2007). The experience of trauma either prior to or during incarceration is associated with post-release outcomes, including increased recidivism rates (Brennen, 2007; Kubiak, 2004; Morrissey et al., 2012; Zgoba et al., 2012). The consequences of not treating trauma are significant (Clements-Nolle et al., 2009; Kubiak, 2004; Maschi, Viola, & Morgen, 2013; Salina, Lesondak, Razzano, & Weilbaecher, 2007).

The rate of PTSD among incarcerated individuals is significantly higher than in the general population, with research reporting PTSD rates up to 55% (Kubiak, 2004), compared to 3.5% in the general population (APA, 2013). Also, many offenders experience trauma (Komarovskaya et al., 2011) and develop PTSD (Goff et al., 2007) while incarcerated.

The presence of trauma and PTSD has been widely linked to increased risk for mental health problems, including among incarcerated populations. For example, the destabilizing impact of early childhood trauma can make individuals less psychologically equipped to remain resilient when coping with stressors associated with incarceration (e.g., National Research Council, 2014). Inmates with trauma histories are at increased risk for suicide attempts (Blaauw et al., 2002; Clements-Nolle et al., 2009; Gunter et al., 2013; Mandelli, Carli, Roy, Serretti, & Sarchiapone, 2011; Moloney, van den Bergh, & Moller, 2009; National Research Council, 2014), further victimization (Bradley & Davino, 2002; Crisanti & Frueh, 2011), violence (Green et al., 2005; Neller, Denney, Pietz, & Thomlinson, 2006), and other general disciplinary problems while incarcerated (Komarovskaya et al., 2011). Trauma histories may serve as a predictor of incidence and severity of violence in jails and prisons, reflecting a continuation of similar behavior in the community (Neller et al., 2006).

The purpose of this chapter is to provide a comprehensive review of the empirical and theoretical literature that examines the problem of trauma in incarcerated individuals. The focus is on trauma experienced both before and during incarceration, and its impact on post-incarceration. The various types of trauma experience, including sexual, physical, and emotional trauma, as well as the multitude of demographic factors, such as age, ethnicity, gender, and sexual identity, and its impact on the diverging rates of incarcerations will be critically reviewed. Additionally, the importance of treatment of trauma among incarcerated individuals is examined in the context of different types of interventions, as well as building resilience and psychological well-being. Lastly, the chapter will, in the context of trauma treatment, discuss the challenges the mental health care delivery system faces in adapting and creating new approaches to work within a correctional health care system often fraught with obstacles, while also adapting these new approaches to the larger integrated, continuity-of-care-focused model.

## Trauma and Gender Differences

### Trauma and Men

There is a disparate gender focus in trauma research among inmates. Anecdotally, trauma and PTSD have been considered more prevalent and problematic in women. However, literature suggests similarly high rates of PTSD for each gender, with male prisoners being exposed to similar degrees of trauma as female prisoners (Prins, 2014). Identifying the ubiquitous magnitude of the problem, Wolff et al. (2014) concluded that "trauma was a universal experience" for incarcerated men (p. 715).

Studies (Table 4.1) examining the incidence of trauma and PTSD among incarcerated men consistently find rates much higher than among the general population where 1.8% of men meet criteria for current PTSD (symptoms within the past 12 months; Harvard Medical School, 2007a) and 3.6% meet criteria for lifetime PTSD (symptoms at any time during a lifetime; Harvard Medical School, 2007b). Beyond the high rates of diagnosable PTSD, the rates of any trauma exposure are often much higher (Table 4.2), though not always. Disparity of reported trauma rates exist in the literature, with a relative low rate of 35% for at least one lifetime traumatic event in a sample of incarcerated men (Gibson et al., 1999), to rates as high as 96% of surveyed incarcerated men experiencing or witnessing trauma (Neller et al., 2006). Research suggests that many incarcerated men experience their first traumatic event as a teenager, with trauma-related symptoms lasting over a decade following the event (Gibson et al., 1999). One study described incarcerated men's history of traumatic events as "violent, interpersonal, sudden and life threatening" (Wolff et al., 2014, p. 716). Compared to some community samples, incarcerated men tend to have higher rates of assault victimization (96% in one study) and rape histories (Gibson et al., 1999; Wolff et al., 2014) (Tables 4.1 and 4.2).

Incarcerated men exposed to trauma or diagnosed with PTSD are likely to experience comorbid mental health problems, including major depressive disorder, obsessive compulsive disorder, and generalized anxiety disorder (Gibson et al., 1999; Wolff et al., 2014). Trauma and incarceration are also associated with higher incidence of aggression in men. Sarchiapone, Carli, Cuomo, Marchetti, and Roy (2009)

**Table 4.1** Studies reporting on current and lifetime posttraumatic stress disorder (PTSD)[a] rates among incarcerated men and women

| Study | N | Gender | Sample description | Current PTSD[b] | Lifetime PTSD[c] |
|---|---|---|---|---|---|
| Gibson et al. (1999) | 213 | Men | Randomly selected men in jails (n = 95) and prison (n = 118) in rural New England | 21% | 33% |
| Lynch et al. (2013) | 491 | Women | Randomly selected women in rural and urban jails from four geographic regions in the U.S. | 28% | 53% |
| Hutton et al. (2001) | 177 | Women | Volunteer sample of women in a minimum- to maximum-security prison in Maryland | 15% | 33% |
| DeHart et al. (2014) | 115 | Women | Randomly selected women in jail from four geographic regions in the U.S. | ** | 51% |
| Green et al. (2005) | 100 | Women | Convenience sample of female inmates in jail in Maryland | 22% | ** |
| Salina et al. (2007) | 283 | Women | Women with co-occurring disorders on a specialized treatment program in prison in Washington state | ** | 75% |
| Komarovskaya et al. (2011) | 239 | Men (125) and Women (114) | Randomly selected men and women in prisons in a Midwestern state | ** | 12.5% (men) 40.2% (women) |
| Kubiak (2004) | 199 | Men (139) and Women (60) | Volunteer sample of men and women in prison in a residential substance abuse treatment program | ** | 53% (men) 60% (women) |

*Notes.* ** Rate not examined in study
[a]Studies were using DSM-III (Gibson et al., 1999), DSM-IV (DeHart et al., 2014; Green et al., 2005; Hutton et al., 2001; Lynch et al., 2013; Salina et al., 2007), or DSM-IV-TR (Komarovskaya et al., 2011; Kubiak, 2004) criteria
[b]Current PTSD refers to individuals who have experienced symptoms within the past 6 or 12 months. Not all studies specify what timeframe "current" refers to
[c]Lifetime PTSD refers to individuals who have experienced symptoms at any point during their life

found that high levels of lifetime aggression among male prisoners were linked to higher trauma scores. This, in turn, is concerning, as increased risk for violence perpetration impacts behaviors associated with criminal conduct. Also, individuals who are exhibiting trauma-associated aggression are likely to have difficulty adjusting to the correctional environment and trauma can serve as a predictor of who tends to exhibit violence while incarcerated, though having a diagnosis of PTSD may mediate this relationship (Sarchiapone, Carli, Cuomo, et al., 2009).

Not all studies have found a clear association between trauma, aggression, and other behavioral problems. Cuomo, Sarchiapone, Di Giannantonio, Mancini, and Roy (2008) examined the relationship between trauma, aggression, personality traits,

**Table 4.2** Studies reporting on any history of trauma exposure[a] among incarcerated men and women

| Study | N | Gender | Sample description | Any trauma history |
|---|---|---|---|---|
| Gibson et al. (1999) | 213 | Men | Randomly selected men in jails ($n = 95$) and prison ($n = 118$) in rural New England | 35% |
| Neller et al. (2006) | 93 | Men | Convenience sample of men from a maximum-security detention center in the Midwest | 96% |
| Wolff et al. (2014) | 269 | Men | Randomly selected men in a high-security prison in Pennsylvania | 96% |
| Green et al. (2005) | 100 | Women | Convenience sample of women in jail in Maryland | 98% |
| Bradley and Davino (2002) | 65 | Women | Randomly selected and volunteer sample of women in a medium-security prison in a southeastern state | 95% |
| DeHart et al. (2014) | 115 | Women | Randomly selected women in jail from four geographic regions in the U.S. | 86% |

[a]Any trauma history includes the nine trauma events from the Diagnostic Interview Schedule for the DSM-III-R (Gibson et al., 1999), experiencing or witnessing 11 types of trauma from the Trauma Events Questionnaire (Neller et al., 2006), 24 life-threatening or traumatizing experiences from the Trauma History Questionnaire (Wolff et al., 2014), 12 categories of trauma from the trauma screening measure from the National Comorbidity Survey (Green et al., 2005), sexual violence or physical abuse as measured by the Conflict Tactics Scale (Bradley & Davino, 2002), and any sexual violence history (DeHart et al., 2014)

and substance abuse in male prisoners. Interestingly, they found no overall trauma difference between the total sample and a subsample of male prisoners abusing substances. However, those with substance abuse problems were more likely to report experiences of emotional abuse and physical neglect as children.

## Trauma and Women

An abundance of research has examined trauma and PTSD in incarcerated women. Studies find high rates of female inmates meeting current criteria for PTSD and/or lifetime criteria for PTSD (see Table 4.1), and rates are significantly higher than reported rates among the general population where 5.2% meet current criteria for PTSD (Harvard Medical School, 2007a) and 9.7% meet lifetime criteria (Harvard Medical School, 2007b).

Additionally, and similarly to findings in male inmates, the prevalence of any trauma exposure among incarcerated women is high (Table 4.2). Research shows that the majority of incarcerated women experience trauma as both a child and an adult, with the most common types being intimate partner violence (Green et al., 2005) and sexual and physical abuse (Bradley & Davino, 2002; DeHart et al., 2014). When considering histories of sexual abuse in female prisoners, prevalence rates are proportionally significantly higher compared to community samples of women (Bradley & Davino, 2002; DeHart et al., 2014). The presence of trauma in incarcerated women is also associated with a multitude of other problems (Hutton et al., 2001; Lynch et al., 2013), and the psychological and behavioral impact only increases with cumulative trauma (Messina & Grella, 2006). Messina and Grella (2006) found that the presence of five or more childhood adverse experiences was associated with a myriad of medical, substance use, and behavioral issues in a convenience sample of 500 incarcerated women involved in a prison-based substance abuse program. A higher number of childhood adverse experiences were associated with earlier involvement in drug use, criminal behavior, and more arrests. Furthermore, higher numbers of childhood adverse experiences were associated with adolescent conduct problems, homelessness, drug and alcohol problems, and higher likelihood of involvement in prostitution, having eating disorders, increased rates of sexually transmitted diseases, and overall gynecological problems. Additionally, Messina and Grella (2006) reported that these women were more likely to have previous mental health and substance abuse treatment.

A high rate of problematic substance abuse among female inmates with trauma histories is a common finding in the literature (Driessen, Schroeder, Widman, Schonfeld, & Schneider, 2006). For these women, the abuse of substances may serve several purposes, including a means to self-medicate and numb the emotional distress related to past trauma experiences (Brady, 2001; Khantzian, 1985; Quina & Brown, 2007). Similar to male inmates, substance abuse among female inmates may, in itself, increase the risk of incarceration for drug-related offenses and behavior associated with unlawfully obtaining illicit or prescription drugs.

Risky sexual behaviors among incarcerated women, and subsequent health concerns, have been linked to trauma and a diagnosis of PTSD. Studies show that women with PTSD or trauma histories are more likely to engage in risky sexual practices, such as prostitution or being less likely to practice safe sex and use a condom, which increase their risk for exposure to sexually transmitted infections and diseases, along with higher risk for experiencing further trauma (Green et al., 2005; Hutton et al., 2001; Messina & Grella, 2006; Salina et al., 2007).

A less researched area is the effects of trauma experiences on parenting skills. Women with trauma histories tend to have poor parenting skills (Green et al., 2005). Poor parenting may increase the risk of further violence exposure on children, resulting in higher likelihood of trauma, and perpetuating a cycle of incarceration. There is also evidence of an intergenerational transference of trauma (Lev-Wiesel, 2007; Schwerdtfeger & Goff, 2007). The negative influence of trauma on parenting skills and parent–child attachment in mothers can result in the children not only inheriting trauma-altered genes, but the children also experience their own trauma through maltreatment, neglect, and other forms of abuse. Thereby, the cycle of criminal behavior and incarceration is ongoing. Evidence suggests a similar route of transmission for fathers (Dekel & Goldblatt, 2008).

## Gender Differences

In the general population, women experience PTSD at twice the rate of men (APA, 2013). This difference is smaller and more complicated for incarcerated men and women where gender differences exist in the experience of and coping with trauma, as well as the development of PTSD (Miller & Najavits, 2012). Men tend to exhibit externalizing behaviors as a reaction to trauma through substance use, violence, and crime, while women tend to exhibit internalizing behaviors to trauma through self-injurious behaviors, eating disorders, and avoidance. Additionally, incarcerated men are more likely to experience interpersonal nonsexual trauma and witnessing harm, while women tend to experience interpersonal sexual trauma (Komarovskaya et al., 2011). For other forms of trauma, such as physical neglect, witnessing family violence, and separation from caregivers, there are limited gender differences (Messina, Grella, Burdon, & Prendergast, 2007).

Some studies show that men are exposed to more traumatic events as a child or adolescent than women (Komarovskaya et al., 2011), while other studies find that men experience more traumatic events in the 12 months preceding study participation (Kubiak, 2004). Conversely, research indicates greater repeated episodes of trauma and more trauma-related symptoms in women compared to men (Komarovskaya et al., 2011; Kubiak, 2004). These gender differences may result in disparate negative developmental trajectories that contribute to a myriad of mental health, substance use, and conduct problems. In fact, research suggests that predictors of symptom severity vary based on gender, with nonsexual trauma for men and sexual trauma for women predicting higher levels of symptom severity (Komarovskaya et al., 2011). In men, the early nonsexual trauma influences the development of conduct problems, along with exposure to further violence as an adolescent (Komarovskaya et al., 2011). In women, who experience more sexual trauma at all stages of life (Komarovskaya et al., 2011; Messina et al., 2007), repeated exposure to sexually traumatizing events, along with other forms of trauma, has a negative effect, with more childhood adverse experiences being associated with early onset of and more extensive mental health history, as well as more serious problems with drugs and crime (Messina et al., 2007).

Concerns have been raised about the accuracy of gender differences in trauma experiences among incarcerated individuals. Many studies rely on self-reported trauma history and symptoms, which may be biased based on how questions are worded (Crisanti & Frueh, 2011), failure to remember incidents of trauma (Gibson et al., 1999), unwillingness to disclose trauma to correctional staff (Grella & Greenwell, 2007), or not considering the experience as out of the ordinary (Moses, Reed, Mazelis, & D'Ambrosio, 2003). Moreover, findings of higher incidents of trauma among women may be biased by extensively more research on trauma among incarcerated women compared to men (Komarovskaya et al., 2011), misleadingly suggesting that trauma is more prevalent in that population.

# Trauma and Unique Populations

## *Trauma and Incarcerated Older Adults*

From 1980 to 2010, the United States experienced an increase of 222% in incarceration rates, much of which has been linked to lengthier prison sentences (National Research Council, 2014). As of 2010, one in nine prisoners faced life sentences and a third of those had no chance of parole. Subsequently, rates of incarcerated older adults—usually defined as individuals 55 years and older—have increased fivefold since 1990 (Aday, 2003). More recently, Carson and Sabol (2016) found that rates of incarcerated older adults increased by 400% from 1993 to 2013. This population now represents the largest-growing segment of prisoners in not only the United States, but in many other countries (Psick, Ahalt, Brown, & Simon, 2017).

As with studies examining younger people, incarcerated older adults appear to experience trauma at greater rates than the general population (Maschi, Morgen, Zgoba, Courtney, & Ristow, 2011). Given the higher probability of longer incarcerations and repeated prison sentences, risk for in-facility trauma is greater. Prior victimization also predicts increased risk for victimization while incarcerated (Morrissey et al., 2012), while trauma experienced while incarcerated may exacerbate old traumas. Incarcerated older adults have been found to have a greater risk for reemergence of trauma-related symptoms compared to younger prisoners (Maschi, Morgen et al., 2011).

Many older adult inmates have experienced at least one type of trauma in their lifetime, often occurring before 16 years of age and commonly a physical or sexual assault (Maschi et al., 2013; Morrissey et al., 2012; Zgoba et al., 2012). There may be less of a cumulative effect for trauma experiences among older inmates, compared to younger inmates, as recent subjective distress appears to have a greater impact on trauma symptoms compared to the number of traumas experienced. Resilience factors and the impact of positive coping may help to stave off negative effects of trauma among older inmates who have been found to report higher rates of well-being (Maschi et al., 2013).

Research contrasting younger and older prisoners shows similarities between the two groups on the experience of physical assault occurring during any stage of life, with older adults having experienced slightly more physical assaults during adolescence (Maschi, Gibson et al., 2011). Also, older adult inmates are more likely to have witnessed a sexual assault and to have lived in a violent neighborhood, while younger inmates are more likely to have witnessed someone physically assaulted and experienced a human-made disaster such as a plane crash (Maschi, Gibson et al., 2011).

Some racial differences among incarcerated older individuals have been found. Older African-American and Hispanics prisoners report significantly lower trauma symptoms, compared to older Caucasian prisoners (Zgoba et al., 2012).

## *Trauma and Incarcerated Youthful Offenders*

Determining accurate and reliable rates of PTSD among incarcerated youth is difficult as many studies have small samples (Abram et al., 2004) or have samples that include *all* justice involved youth (e.g., both incarcerated youth and non-incarcerated criminal justice involved youth), resulting in disparate estimates of PTSD (see Table 4.3). Regardless of these differences, the rates of PTSD, as well as any type of trauma among criminal justice involved youth, are alarming. As noted in Table 4.3, research has found PTSD rates as high as 45.7% among criminal justice involved youth. However, rates of any type of trauma experience are even higher. In a youth detention sample, 92.5% had experienced at least one trauma event, 84% had experienced more than one event, and 56.8% had experienced six or more events (Abram et al., 2004). In a nationally representative sample of criminal justice-involved youth, 90% had experienced multiple forms of trauma events, with

**Table 4.3** Studies reporting on current posttraumatic stress disorder (PTSD)[a] rates among justice-involved youth

| Study | N | Gender | Sample description | Current PTSD[b] |
|---|---|---|---|---|
| Dierkhising et al. (2013) | 658 | Boys (355) and Girls (303) | A national sample of adolescents, 13–18 years, referred for trauma-focused treatment and who had criminal justice system contact within the last 30 days | 23.6% |
| Abram et al. (2004) | 898 | Boys (532) and Girls (366) | Randomly selected youth, aged 10–18 years, incarcerated in a youth detention center in Cook County, Illinois | 11.2% |
| Ford, Hartman, Hawke, and Chapman (2008) | 264 | Boys (193) and Girls (71) | Youths aged 10–17 years admitted to a pretrial juvenile detention center in the State of Connecticut. | 5% |
| Wasserman and McReynolds (2011) | 9819 | Boys (5201) and Girls (4618) | Youth (average age 16 years) entering a juvenile justice agency (e.g., probation or family court intake, detention centers or correctional facility) from 57 sites in 19 states | 3.7% |
| Rosenberg et al. (2014) | 350 | Boys (262) and Girls (83) | Youth aged 11–17 years who were incarcerated, in a residential treatment facility or involved in family court in New Hampshire ($n = 269$) and Stark County, Ohio ($n = 81$) | 45.7% |

[a]Studies were using DSM-IV (Abram et al., 2004; Rosenberg et al., 2014; Wasserman & McReynolds, 2011), DSM-IV-R (Ford et al., 2008), or DSM-IV-TR (Dierkhising et al., 2013) criteria
[b]Current PTSD refers to individuals who have experienced symptoms within the past month (Ford et al., 2008; Dierkhising et al., 2013; Rosenberg et al., 2014; Wasserman & McReynolds, 2011) or 12 months (Abram et al., 2004)

an average of almost five different events of trauma, including a significant loss or separation from a caregiver (61.2%), domestic violence (51.6%), and physical abuse (38.6%; Dierkhising et al., 2013) (Table 4.3).

Few studies on incarcerated youth have focused on the age of trauma exposure. Dierkhising et al. (2013) reported that a third of their national sample of criminal justice involved youth had been exposed to a traumatic event within the first year of their life as reported by a caregiver. By 5 years of age, 62.14% of the sample had been exposed to at least one trauma event, while a third had experienced multiple trauma events. In another sample of incarcerated youth, most participants had experienced their worst traumatic event in the past 2 years prior to the study and age of trauma onset was associated with more severe traumatic events among incarcerated girls, while it was associated with higher numbers of traumatic events and more externalizing and internalizing problems in both girls and boys (Abram et al., 2004).

## Trauma and Veterans

A 2012 report from the U.S. Department of Justice found that veterans accounted for about 8% of the total prison population in the United States (Bronson, Carson, Noonan, & Berzofskym, 2015). This is a substantial decrease from 24% in 1978, corresponding with less military veterans in the general population. Only a minority of the incarcerated veterans has seen combat (25% in prison and 31% in jail; Bronson et al., 2015).

The rate of PTSD among incarcerated veterans is much higher than in the general population (Greenberg & Rosenheck, 2009; Saxon et al., 2001). Saxon et al. (2001) found that 39% of incarcerated veterans met criteria for PTSD and most of the sample had experienced at least one traumatic event (87%). The most common precipitating event to developing PTSD was seeing someone badly injured or killed, and those with PTSD tended to have a myriad of other problems as well, including a wider variety of traumas, more substance use problems, more psychiatric problems, worse health, and a more severe legal history (Saxon et al., 2001). While Saxon et al. (2001) noted that these veterans had PTSD rates similar to other incarcerated individuals, Bronson et al. (2015) found in a separate national sample of veterans twice the rate of PTSD among incarcerated veterans (23%), compared to incarcerated non-veterans (11%).

While the rate of PTSD is high among incarcerated veterans, trauma may not necessarily be the causative factor in arrest and incarceration. In a sample of non-incarcerated veterans, those who met criteria for PTSD and reported problems with anger and irritability were more likely to have more criminal arrests than those with only PTSD, while combat exposure was not found to be a significant predictor of criminal arrest (Elbogen et al., 2012). Military experience and related trauma may play less of a role in criminal behavior as compared to other common risk factors, such as drug abuse, exposure to domestic violence, and younger age.

## *Trauma and Sex Offenders*

Individuals who commit sexual offenses tend to have been exposed to multiple childhood adverse experiences, including victimization, at rates much higher than the general population and even other offenders (Levenson & Socia, 2016; Levenson, Willis, & Prescott, 2014). In one study, 45% of sex offenders reported four or more childhood adverse experiences, compared to only 12.5% in the general population (Levenson & Socia, 2016). Also, sex offenders often have high rates of physical and sexual abuse as children (Morrissey et al., 2012; Weeks & Widom, 1998), with one study revealing three times the rate of sexual abuse and two times the rate of physical abuse among sex offenders compared to other offenders (Levenson et al., 2014). Another study of only incarcerated female sexual offenders reported that 69% of the participants had been sexually abused and 57% had been physically abused as a child (Turner, Miller, & Henderson, 2008).

Consistent with findings among other populations, childhood traumas in sex offenders, combined with the negative cumulative effects of other risk factors, are associated with broad criminal behaviors, not only sexual offending, as well as subsequent incarceration (Levenson & Socia, 2016). Among incarcerated sex offenders, emotional neglect from mothers has been associated with intrafamilial child molesters, while unsympathetic and abusive fathers have been linked to stranger rapists (Smallbone & Dadds, 1998). Research suggests that various risk factors, such as insecure childhood attachments, interpersonal deficits, and emotional dysregulation, are related to deviant sexual behavior, in which certain combinations of traumatic childhood experiences may relate more specifically to different kinds of sexual offending (Levenson & Socia, 2016; Smallbone & Dadds, 1998).

## Trauma During Incarceration

Much has been written about whether the experience of incarceration is inherently traumatic (National Research Council, 2014). Bonta and Gendreau (1990) concluded that the experience of incarceration is not in itself necessarily traumatic. However, there are certain risk factors that may place some individuals at higher risk for victimization and traumatization. Further, harsher prison environments may increase risk for negative outcomes. For example, policy changes through the 1980s and beyond led to the creation of more maximum-security conditions and the advent of "supermax" facilities (National Research Council, 2014). These settings established a more punitive approach to incarceration that emphasized dehumanization and isolation. Some states, like Arizona, have passed specific legislation that arguably increases the harshness of the prison environment by reducing programming and using attack dogs to extract prisoners (Lynch, 2010).

Research has reported that the experience of incarceration may exacerbate existing trauma or cause trauma for prisoners (Miller & Najavits, 2012; Moloney et al., 2009 ; National Research Council, 2014). A literature review found rates ranging from 4% to 21.4% for PTSD developed during incarceration among prisoners across the world (Goff et al., 2007), while other research emphasizes higher rates of incarceration-related PTSD in the United States compared to the rest of the world (National Research Council, 2014).

Studying the exposure of trauma that develops over the course of incarceration is rife with challenges. Often, there is a wide disparity between official reports of abuse versus inmate self-report, which creates challenges for accuracy and reliability (Byrne, 2011). Inmates may be reluctant to reveal incidents of trauma for multiple reasons, including a lack of trust in clinical staff (Grella & Greenwell, 2007; Struckman-Johnson et al., 1996), they may consider their experiences as normal (Moses et al., 2003), reluctance to "snitch" on staff or other inmates, and concerns about negative stereotypes or judgment (e.g., it is unmanly to reveal vulnerability; Goff et al., 2007). Some inmates may fail or be reluctant to disclose trauma in order to hide their sexual identity or hide psychiatric symptoms to avoid unwanted attention (Miller & Najavits, 2012).

Gibson et al. (1999) raised the possibility of underreporting of sexual assaults during incarceration. In their prison sample, 50% of the respondents indicated that the first time they reported sexual victimization was at the time of the study survey. Only 29% of the sample reported a sexual assault to the prison administration. Also, the accuracy of sexual victimization rates may differ based on instruments used to measure trauma-related symptoms, as well as the skill level of the assessors (Goff et al., 2007).

Gender differences is a major concern, especially since the United States correctional system is designed on a male model, and incarcerated women may be particularly vulnerable to trauma in these settings (Moloney et al., 2009). By design, the system may recreate aspects of past abuse, including elements of power and control, humiliation, and lack of privacy (Moloney et al., 2009; National Research Council, 2014). Women (and men) with trauma histories are more vulnerable to re-experience trauma in a correctional system (Miller & Najavits, 2012) and research suggests that past trauma experiences can weaken a woman's resilience and ability to cope with the stressors associated with incarceration, including interacting with male staff (Gilfus, 2002; Moloney et al., 2009; Van Voorhis, Salisbury, Wright, & Bauman, 2008).

Research on incarcerated women in female correctional settings has shown that there are fewer services available compared to male correctional settings, including services that specifically address the unique medical needs of women (Moloney et al., 2009). Further, preexisting trauma histories may interfere with women's ability to benefit from these programs, when offered (Miller & Najavits, 2012).

Despite the increased risk for victimization within a correctional facility, some research has pointed out that women are actually less likely to be victimized in prison compared to the community (Loper, 2002; Miller & Najavits, 2012). In fact, some studies show that women feel subjectively *safer* in the prison environment than in the community (Bradley & Davino, 2002;Loper, 2002 ; Miller & Najavits, 2012). Bradley and Davino (2002) described that while a portion of their sample of incarcerated women believed that prison was safer, they did not prefer incarceration over freedom. Further, it is important to note that the perception of *safer* is not equal to *safe*. Many incarcerated women have a global perspective that the world is unsafe, including prison. However, women with histories of sexual and physical abuse as a child or adult perceive no environment as safer, including prison (Bradley & Davino, 2002).

In contrast, men encounter higher risk of victimization while incarcerated than in the community (Miller & Najavits, 2012). In a self-report study, men were more likely to have been exposed to trauma during incarceration than women who were more likely to be exposed prior to incarceration (Kubiak, 2004).

One may question whether general exposure to a correctional environment can cause trauma symptoms, or whether one has to experience an actual traumatic event in prison before symptoms of PTSD are evident. Results of one study suggest that development of trauma-related symptoms is more likely to be associated with actual trauma exposure during incarceration than simply being in a general prison environment (Kubiak, 2004). Also, other factors associated with an oppressive and punitive prison environment may serve as triggers to already vulnerable individuals, who will repeat dysfunctional patterns already long present in their life (Miller & Najavits, 2012). Studies appear to confirm that punitive measures to address behavioral concerns are largely ineffective (Andrews, Bonta, & Hoge, 1990; Landenberger & Lipsey, 2005). Experts argue that the punitive approach in the criminal justice system has led to "a wide range of social costs" and has had a "highly uncertain" effect on reducing crime while doing little to act as a deterrent (National Research Council, 2014, p. 339).

## Sexual Victimization During Incarceration

Data from the U.S. Bureau for Justice Statistics on 80,600 incarcerated people indicate that 4% of prison inmates and 3.2% of jail inmates have experienced in-facility sexual victimization (Beck, Berzofsky, Caspar, & Krebs, 2014). Further, 2% of inmates and 2.4% of staff were reported to be perpetrators. A small number of victims (0.4%) were perpetrated by both inmates and staff. In a gender comparison study, rates for inmate-to-inmate sexual victimization were higher for women than men (Beck et al., 2014). This study also found that the rate of sexual victimization in prisons has decreased from 2007 (4.5%) to 2012 (4%), while rates remained steady for jails (Beck et al., 2014).

Rates of sexual victimization vary based on demographic variables and instrumentation differences (e.g., wording of questions; Wolff, Blitz, Shi, Bachman, & Siegel, 2006). For example, studies that average rates of sexual victimization and limit analysis to particular types of sexual victimization may leave out important and crucial data (Beck et al., 2014; Wolff et al., 2006). Moreover, inadequate designs of surveys or other instrumentation limitations may set limits on perceptions of victimization severity and associated problems. One study noted that some respondents actually added higher rating items to their Likert scales (Struckman-Johnson et al., 1996).

Sexual victimization in female correctional facilities is greater than in most male facilities (Beck et al., 2014; Wolff et al., 2006), though there are conflicting reports

(Struckman-Johnson et al., 1996). Struckman-Johnson et al.'s (1996) sample of incarcerated men and women reported sexual victimization rates of 22% and 7%, respectively.

Research has speculated that male correctional officers may use their position of authority or otherwise use frisk requirements or room searches as opportunities to sexually assault women. While some sources suggest that women's greatest risk comes from male correctional officers (Human Rights Watch, 1996), other data suggest that there may be an even greater risk from other inmates (Beck et al., 2014; Wolff et al., 2006). Wolff et al. (2006) found that the rate of inmate-to-inmate sexual victimization was two times higher in female correctional facilities than in male facilities. Women with histories of being the victim of domestic violence or sexual assault are at increased risk for sexual violence while incarcerated (Beck et al., 2014; Human Rights Watch, 1996). Other vulnerable individuals include lesbian and transgendered prisoners, along with women who have attempted to shed light on the abuses that are occurring (Human Rights Watch, 1996). A U.S. Bureau of Justice Statistics report (Beck et al., 2014) found much higher rates of sexual victimization between non-heterosexual inmates, with rates of 12.2% for prison inmates and 5.4% for jail inmates.

Surveys of inmates and staff within correctional facilities find similar reported rates of pressured and forced sexual contact compared to officially reported incidents (approximately 20%; Struckman-Johnson et al., 1996). These findings illustrate that both inmates and staff are aware of sexual victimization occurring in correctional settings. Individuals who are sexually assaulted in a correctional facility are prone to becoming victimized multiple times and research has found that some victims are victimized by up to four different perpetrators (Struckman-Johnson et al., 1996). Men may be at higher risk of "gang rape" compared to women, with most offenders being male and the most severe incidents (e.g., forced rape) being perpetrated by another inmate about half the time and prison staff about 20% of the time (Struckman-Johnson et al., 1996). Vulnerability factors for sexual victimization include being older, white, bisexual, a sex offender, and an inmate with a longer prison sentence (Beck et al., 2014; National Institute of Corrections, 2007; Struckman-Johnson et al., 1996).

The magnitude and consequence of sexual victimization in correctional settings are a major concern that results in increased risk for a variety of medical and mental health problems (Wolff et al., 2006), including depression and suicidal ideation (Struckman-Johnson et al., 1996). Moreover, considering research findings on long-term effects, the trauma related to sexual victimization is likely to increase the risk for criminal recidivism.

## *Serious Mental Illness and Trauma During Incarceration*

Serious mental illness is more prevalent in jails and prisons than in the general population, with some reports indicating that the rate of seriously mentally ill inmates is somewhere between 15% and 20%, if not higher (Treatment Advocacy

Center, 2016). Moreover, adding to the complexity, the proportion of seriously mentally ill inmates to other inmates has grown at a troublesome rate over the past couple of decades, bringing with it challenges to both administrators and treatment providers who work in a system not built to house and treat large populations of seriously mentally ill individuals.

There is a dearth of research on the victimization of seriously mentally ill inmates and exact rates of victimization are difficult to determine (Crisanti & Frueh, 2011). Extant research reports that incarcerated individuals with serious mental illness experience higher rates of sexual violence (Wolff et al., 2007) and physical assaults than other inmates (Blitz, Wolff, & Shi, 2008). Understanding the extent of psychological and other problems among the incarcerated mentally ill is complicated by factors unique to these individuals. For example, compared to non-mentally ill inmates, individuals with serious mental illness may be more distrustful of staff, not know how to report problems, or may experience acute psychiatric symptoms that interfere with their ability to report problems, all contributing to underreporting of trauma (Crisanti & Frueh, 2011). One study speculated that among inmates who refused to participate in a survey was a subset of individuals with paranoid schizophrenia (Treatment Advocacy Center, 2016). Crisanti and Frueh (2011) concluded that while actual rates remain unclear, people diagnosed with serious mental illness are at an increased risk for any type of victimization in jails and prisons, compared to other non-mentally ill incarcerated individuals.

## Trauma and Suicide During Incarceration

A number of studies have highlighted the association between trauma and increased risk of suicide attempts among people who are incarcerated (Blaauw et al., 2002; Mandelli et al., 2011; Sarchiapone, Carli, Di Giannantonio, & Roy, 2009; Sarchiapone, Jovanović, Roy, et al., 2009). Suicidal behavior is often a result of a multitude of problems that can develop as a direct consequence of not being able to cope with a traumatic experience or as a means to escape ongoing trauma occurring in a correctional facility (National Research Council, 2014).

Inmates who exhibit suicidal behaviors typically have more traumatic life events, such as sexual abuse, physical and emotional maltreatment, abandonment and suicide attempts of significant others, than those without suicide histories (Blaauw et al., 2002; Clements-Nolle et al., 2009). Additionally, disruption of interpersonal social networks early in life (Blaauw et al., 2002) and cumulative effects of negative life events occurring in all phases of life (Clements-Nolle et al., 2009) have been associated with higher levels of suicide risk. A link between childhood trauma and suicidal behavior has also been established in Italian prisoners (Mandelli et al., 2011; Sarchiapone, Jovanović, Roy, et al., 2009) and findings indicate that, with the exception of sexual abuse, all forms of trauma are associated with younger age of first suicide attempt (Mandelli et al., 2011). Sexual abuse is associated with an increased risk for repeated suicide attempts (Mandelli et al., 2011), which is consistent with other research showing that about a third of victims of sexual assault in prison experience suicidal ideation (Struckman-Johnson et al., 1996).

There is limited research on trauma and personality risk factors among inmates presenting with suicidal behavior. However, consistent with other literature on personality traits (Brezo, Paris, & Turecki, 2006), personality features such as trait-level impulsive aggression, overall aggression, and neuroticism have been linked to suicidal behavior among inmates (Sarchiapone, Carli, Di Giannantonio, & Roy, 2009). Though traumatic experiences are likely to exacerbate problematic personality features, more research is warranted to determine the specific link between trauma, personality traits, and suicidal behavior in inmates.

## Impact of Trauma

### *Trauma and Increased Incarceration Risk*

Exposure to trauma, particularly repeated exposure, starting at an early age has clear implications on the development of emotional regulation systems in the brain and increased risks for impulsivity and aggression (e.g., Braquehais, Oquendo, Baca-Garcia, & Sher, 2010; Mandelli et al., 2011; Morrissey et al., 2012; Sergentanis et al., 2014). Problems regulating emotions and disruptions in the behavioral disinhibition system increase risk for impulsive behaviors, which in turn may contribute to engaging in risky behavior and novelty seeking, thus resulting in drug use (Sergentanis et al., 2014) and other conduct problems. Long-term, these individuals are more likely to engage in criminal behaviors that result in incarceration. Underlying neurobiological alterations caused by early trauma also increase the risk for developing psychopathology (Teicher, Andersen, Polcari, Anderson, & Navalta, 2002).

While incarcerated women have high rates of trauma, determination of a causal relationship is difficult. Does trauma increase risk of incarceration or are other mediating variables responsible? Widom (2000) found that women who were abused as children were twice as likely to be arrested. However, DeHart et al. (2014) did not find that a PTSD diagnosis was predictive of any type of offending. Instead, DeHart et al. (2014) described that some forms of abuse were more frequently associated with certain types of offending. For example, the experience of intimate partner violence was associated with property crime, drug offending, and prostitution, whereas witnessing violence was associated with property crime, violence, and use of weapons (DeHart et al., 2014). In examining the trajectory of trauma to incarceration, Lynch et al. (2013) speculated that child and adult trauma histories result in an exacerbation of mental health problems, which subsequently, but not necessarily directly, elevates the risk for increased legal involvement. In other words, trauma in itself may not have a causative effect on the commission of crime leading to incarceration; however, it may lead to development of other associated psychological, personality and social problems that can have an impact on criminal behavior. For example, a woman may flee abuse as a teenager, putting her at risk for homelessness and stress, which increases substance abuse risk (Covington & Bloom, 2007; Tompsett, Domoff, & Toro, 2013). In turn, they may engage in risky behaviors that lead to criminal offending (Harris & Fallot, 2001). Some research indicates an intricate link between women with sexual abuse histories and criminal behaviors (Brennen, 2007) and arrests (Hubbard, 2002).

## *Trauma and Recidivism*

The exact relationship between recidivism and trauma is complex, especially considering that trauma may have occurred before, during, and after an incarceration. Also, as explored above, traumatic events that occur while incarcerated may exacerbate existing trauma problems. Since women tend to experience more trauma in the community, re-entering the community may mean continued risk of exposure to further trauma or reminders of past trauma, which may increase their risk for returning to behaviors that resulted in incarceration previously (Kubiak, 2004).

Whether a diagnosis of PTSD in itself accounts for a higher risk for recidivism is unclear. One study found that a greater portion of men with PTSD recidivated (17%) compared to men without such a diagnosis (6%); however, the difference was not statistically significant (Kubiak, 2004). Conversely, findings from the same study showed that women without a PTSD diagnosis were more likely to recidivate than those with a PTSD diagnosis (Kubiak, 2004). Those with a PTSD diagnosis, however, had a higher likelihood of a drug relapse after incarceration. Kubiak (2004) surmised that the trauma symptoms act as a destabilizing factor, thus increasing the risk for future drug use. This hypothesis is consistent with reports from other literature (e.g., Najavits, Gastfriend, & Barber, 1998; Najavits, Weiss, & Shaw, 1997; Ouimette, Brown, & Najavits, 1998) suggesting that the use of drugs serves a self-medicating role for trauma symptoms, while also resulting in behaviors that increase the risk for re-incarceration.

## Treatment and Management of Trauma in Incarcerated Populations

Addressing preexisting trauma, along with traumatic experiences during incarceration, presents significant challenges for mental health professionals in correctional settings. As reviewed above, it is essential to consider a host of complex factors in implementing any form of treatment to incarcerated individuals with trauma-related symptoms. For example, mental health professionals must consider issues related to gender, race, age, veteran status, presence of serious mental illness, and substance abuse, among other factors. A one-size-fits-all approach to treating trauma is likely to be inadequate. Furthermore, failing to address and treat trauma can result in higher lethality risk, disciplinary problems, vulnerability to further victimization, worsening of clinical symptoms, and increased risk for recidivism. Appropriate treatment of trauma-related symptoms, including targeting factors associated with increased suicide risk while incarcerated and after, through skill and resilience-building, has been linked to a reduction in recidivism and suicide risk (Blaauw et al., 2002; Clements-Nolle et al., 2009; Zgoba et al., 2012). Thus, substantial resource allocation toward the treatment and prevention of trauma may have significant benefits, especially long term. However, obtaining valuable resources needed to offer additional programming that targets trauma-related issues is a challenge, given the current sparse resources available for mental health care in the correctional system.

An important aspect of treatment to consider is the negative impact trauma may have on the treatment of other problems (Salina et al., 2007). For example, the success of substance abuse treatment may be negatively impacted by a history of trauma. Similarly, Miller and Najavits (2012) noted that the efficacy of cognitive behavioral treatment may be affected by active trauma symptoms. Trauma-informed care has been highlighted as essential in any programming offered to inmates; however, it is particularly difficult to attain in a correctional setting (Miller & Najavits, 2012).

Inmates with serious mental illness pose multiple additional issues for treatment. For example, it is well known that many of these individuals have histories of trauma that need treatment attention; however, they are also susceptible to victimization which should be another goal of treatment and programming to reduce or minimize this risk (Crisanti & Frueh, 2011), along with strengthening psychological health and well-being (Leidenfrost et al., 2016).

Not surprisingly, it is crucial to identify trauma experiences and symptoms of PTSD early in incarcerated youth. In fact, incarceration may serve as an opportunity for early intervention and treatment, which should occur with proper assessment and development of appropriate treatment planning. It is important that detention facilities work to avoid further traumatizing these youth. Thus, placing youth in facilities designed and modeled after adult correctional environment, or with adult male inmates, may have detrimental effects.

Identification of trauma starts with initial admission and screening procedures. A high number of prisons and jails inadequately screen for trauma histories or are not asking about it at all (Maschi, Morgen et al., 2011), let alone taking a gender-sensitive approach. Staff who are conducting mental health and trauma screens should have education about how to assess for trauma, including being able to consider individual differences in presentation, and they should be trauma-informed trained, which includes a comprehensive understanding of how trauma may impact an inmate's presentation in the correctional facility.

Mental health professionals involved in admission and screening assessment may also need to confront personal attitudes about the danger of addressing trauma in correctional setting and beliefs that it is unsafe, since it has been shown that the cost of not addressing trauma-related problems is too great (Miller & Najavits, 2012). At the same time, "delivering these services in an environment that is known for being predatory, harsh, and violent will require sensitivity to privacy, confidentiality, and safety" (Wolff et al., 2014, p. 718).

Mental health professionals have steep obstacles to overcome in order to be able to effectively treat trauma in incarcerated men and women. Treatment of trauma should focus on both short- and-long term aspects of trauma (Maschi et al., 2013). Trauma treatment that focuses more on present aspects of treatment (e.g., active coping, addressing current emotions), versus the past, may offer the best way to provide treatment in a "safe" manner (Miller & Najavits, 2012). Although exposure techniques have been found to be effective in certain populations, it is likely better to avoid exposure interventions in a correctional setting to avoid re-traumatizing and destabilizing people, and instead there should be a focus on improving coping skills (Maschi et al., 2013).

Unfortunately, staff, including mental health staff, may be woefully unprepared to address trauma among incarcerated offenders. As has been discussed throughout this chapter, it is abundantly clear that an overwhelming number of inmates have experienced various degrees of trauma. Without proper training and supervision, working with populations with such overwhelming trauma histories may leave staff susceptible to developing vicarious trauma (Miller & Najavits, 2012). Staff may require diverse and extensive training to become equipped to address trauma. Any efforts to affect institutional change, such as implementing trauma-informed approaches and programming, require substantial buy-in from correctional administration and staff (Miller & Najavits, 2012).

Extant literature acknowledges that treating trauma in incarcerated populations is crucial. Most of the literature on treatment, however, focuses on women, while there is a dearth of studies on treatment programming in incarcerated men. There is also a paucity of studies on treatment modalities available for older adults and ethnically diverse populations (Maschi et al., 2013). While various treatment modalities exist that are designed for delivering treatment for trauma in the community (e.g., eye movement desensitization and reprocessing, and the Sanctuary Model), caution should be made in assuming that these interventions will translate to the unique needs of a correctional environment. Also, limited assumptions can be made that treatments developed for younger people will translate to the needs of older adults. Developing reliable and efficacious treatment programs that target the needs of men, older adults, and other diverse populations is paramount. These treatment programs need to be gender-sensitive and consider the unique aspects of getting men to report and discuss trauma in a correctional setting (Wolff et al., 2014). Treatment programs that focus on women with trauma have been more widely studied and one such program found to be efficacious in correctional settings is *Seeking Safety*.

## *Seeking Safety*

Seeking Safety is one of the few evidenced-based treatment modalities for incarcerated women that address trauma history in a correctional environment. Specifically, Seeking Safety is a manual-based treatment that uses a cognitive behavioral treatment strategy to address PTSD and substance abuse issues (Najavits, 2002). The program is described as follows:

The treatment consists of 25 topics (e.g., asking for help, coping with triggers) that addresses the cognitive, behavioral, interpersonal, and case management needs of persons with SUD [substance use disorder] and PTSD. *Seeking Safety* is a first-stage therapy, emphasizing stabilization, coping skills, and the reduction of self-destructive behavior. Therefore, the primary goals of treatment are abstinence from substances and personal safety (p. 100; Zlotnick, Najavits, Rohsenow, & Johnson, 2003).

The efficacy of Seeking Safety has been examined in specialized treatment units and in the general prison population within correctional settings, finding mostly positive results; however, not all studies had a control group (e.g., Zlotnick et al., 2003) or showed improvements in both the experimental and wait-list control group (Lynch, Heath, Mathews, & Cepeda, 2012). Women who participate in the Seeking Safety program appear to experience a decrease in PTSD-related symptoms, with a significant portion (about 50% in some studies) no longer meeting criteria for PTSD after completion of the program (Gatz et al., 2007; Lynch et al., 2012; Wolff, Frueh, Shi, & Schumann, 2012; Zlotnick et al., 2003), along with decreases in depressive symptoms, improvement in interpersonal functioning, coping skills (Gatz et al., 2007; Lynch et al., 2012), and marked decreases in substance use 6 weeks post-release (Zlotnick et al., 2003). Examination of the reception of the treatment by participants generally appears positive and shows superior retention rates compared to other forms of treatment (Gatz et al., 2007; Wolff et al., 2012). Follow-up examinations of the positive effects of Seeking Safety indicate that the remission of trauma symptoms remains longer term, though there is limited evidence of any impact on recidivism (Zlotnick et al., 2003). Overall, Seeking Safety appears to be a promising treatment model for incarcerated individuals, though it is in need of further research.

# Conclusion

High rates of trauma histories appear ubiquitous in incarcerated populations. Many of these individuals have been diagnosed with PTSD prior to incarceration and many others go on to develop it during the course of incarceration. Unfortunately, most current treatment models for incarcerated populations are not designed to specifically address trauma, and some models may even exacerbate associated problems.

Failing to address trauma among incarcerated populations may lead to significant consequences, including worsening mental health, problems adapting to the correctional environment, recidivism, and increased risk of death through suicide. Correctional administration and mental health professionals are charged with delivering appropriate care to imprisoned individuals. Efforts must start with screening for trauma, taking a gender-sensitive approach that considers a myriad of factors, including age-related concerns, gender identity, sexual orientation, and the presence of serious mental illness.

While addressing and treating trauma symptoms in incarcerated individuals may be resource-intensive, the risk of not doing so may result in greater resource utilization later. Also, focusing on individuals at high risk for multiple problems fits the risk-need-responsivity model. That is, resources should primarily be devoted to those individuals with the highest degree of need. Screening may help identify the at-risk individuals.

Few specific evidence-based treatment approaches exist for addressing trauma in a correctional environment. Those that do – such as *Seeking Safety* – have been developed for women. While adapting existing trauma treatments may be a good place to start, caution should be made in assuming that they will apply to a correctional environment without modification. For women, *Seeking Safety* has been found to be efficacious.

A large portion of the incarcerated population presents with a complex set of issues, including mental health and substance use issues that may be associated with a history of trauma exposure. These factors contribute to criminal offending behavior and repeated incarceration. While many of these individuals may best be treated in the community, incarceration offers an opportunity to implement appropriate treatment interventions. Failing to do so may lead to long-term consequences, including repeated incarcerations. Mental health professionals have an obligation to treat inmates while incarcerated, though clearly face substantial obstacles from a lack of resources to administrative buy-in. Until the trend of mass incarceration changes, the mental health delivery system must find ways to identify and treat trauma among incarcerated individuals in jails and prisons.

## Questions/Activities for Further Exploration

1. A history of exposure to trauma is associated with increased risk of violence in male inmates. Consider and discuss how trauma may impact violence risk for some inmates in a correctional setting.
2. Research suggests that women have a lower risk of victimization in correctional settings compared to the community. Men appear to have an increased risk for victimization during incarceration. What are the implications of these findings?
3. Individuals with serious mental illness are at a higher risk for victimization within correctional settings compared to other inmates. Consider and discuss factors that may contribute to this problem.
4. Various treatment modalities exist for treating trauma-related symptoms in the community, but there are few developed specifically for correctional settings. Discuss the potential pitfalls and challenges in adapting these interventions for a correctional environment.

## References

Abram, K. M., Teplin, L. A., Charles, D. R., Longworth, S. L., McClelland, G. M., & Dulcan, M. K. (2004). Posttraumatic stress disorder and trauma in youth in juvenile detention. *Archives of General Psychiatry, 61*, 403–410.

Aday, R. H. (2003). *Aging prisoners: Crisis in American corrections.* Westport, CT: Praeger.

American Psychiatric Association. (2013). *Diagnostic and statistical manual of mental disorders* (5th ed.). Arlington, VA: American Psychiatric Publishing.

Andrews, D. A., Bonta, J., & Hoge, R. D. (1990). Classification for effective rehabilitation: Rediscovering psychology. *Criminal Justice and Behavior, 17*, 19–52.

Beck, A. J., Berzofsky, M., Caspar, R., & Krebs, C. (2014). *Sexual victimization in prisons and jails reported by inmates, 2011–12*. (Reported No. NCJ 241399). Retrieved from Bureau of Justice Statistics https://www.bjs.gov/content/pub/pdf/svpjri1112.pdf

Beck, A. J., & Harrison, P. M. (2008). *Sexual victimization in state and federal prisons reported by inmates, 2007*. (Report No. NCJ 219414). Retrieved from Bureau of Justice Statistics https://www.bjs.gov/content/pub/pdf/svsfpri07.pdf

Blaauw, E., Arensman, E., Kraaij, V., Winkel, F. W., & Bout, R. (2002). Traumatic life events and suicide risk among jail inmates: The influence of types of events, time period and significant others. *Journal of Traumatic Stress, 15*, 9–16.

Blitz, C. L., Wolff, N., & Shi, J. (2008). Physical victimization in prison: The role of mental illness. *International Journal of Law and Psychiatry, 31*, 85–393.

Bonta, J., & Gendreau, P. (1990). Reexamining the cruel and unusual punishment of prison life. *Law and Human Behavior, 14*, 347–372.

Bradley, R. G., & Davino, K. M. (2002). Women's perceptions of the prison environment: When prison is "the safest place I've ever been". *Psychology of Women Quarterly, 26*, 351–359.

Brady, K. T. (2001). Comorbid posttraumatic stress disorder and substance use disorders. *Psychiatric Annals, 31*, 313–319.

Braquehais, M. D., Oquendo, M. A., Baca-Garcia, E., & Sher, L. (2010). Is impulsivity a link between childhood abuse and suicide? *Comprehensive Psychiatry, 51*, 121–129.

Brennen, T. (2007). *Institutional assessment and classification of women offenders: From robust beauty to person-centered assessment*. Boulder, CO: Northpointe Institute.

Brezo, J., Paris, J., & Turecki, G. (2006). Personality traits as correlates of suicidal ideation, suicide attempts, and suicide completions: A systematic review. *Acta Psychiatrica Scandinavica, 113*(3), 180–206.

Bronson, J., Carson, E. A., Noonan, M., & Berzofskym, M. (2015). *Veterans in prison and jail, 2011–12*. (Report No. NCJ 249144). Retrieved from Bureau of Justice Statistics http://www.bjs.gov/content/pub/pdf/vpj1112. pdf

Bureau of Justice Statistics. (2018). *U.S. correctional population declined for the ninth consecutive year*. Retrieved from Bureau of Justice Statistics https://www.bjs.gov/content/pub/press/cpus16pr.cfm

Byrne J. (2011). *Commission on safety and abuse in America's prisons: Summary of testimony*. Retrieved from Vera Institute of Justice http://www.prisoncommission.org/statements/byrne_james_m.pdf.

Carson, E. A., & Sabol, W. J. (2016). *Aging of the state prison population, 1993–2013*. (Report No. NCJ 248766). Retrieved from National Criminal Justice Reference Services https://www.ncjrs.gov/App/Publications/abstract.aspx?ID=270871

Clements-Nolle, K., Wolden, M., & Bargmann-Losche, J. (2009). Childhood trauma and risk for past and future suicide attempts among women in prison. *Women's Health Issues, 19*, 185–192.

Covington, S. S., & Bloom, B. E. (2007). Gender responsive treatment and services in correctional settings. *Women & Therapy, 29*, 9–33.

Crisanti, A. S., & Frueh, B. C. (2011). Risk of trauma exposure among persons with mental illness in jails and prisons: What do we really know? *Current Opinion in Psychiatry, 24*, 431–435.

Cuomo, C., Sarchiapone, M., Di Giannantonio, M., Mancini, M., & Roy, A. (2008). Aggression, impulsivity, personality traits, and childhood trauma of prisoners with substance abuse and addiction. *The American Journal of Drug and Alcohol Abuse, 34*, 339–345.

DeHart, D., Lynch, S., Belknap, J., Dass-Brailsford, P., & Green, B. (2014). Life history models of female offending: The roles of serious mental illness and trauma in women's pathways to jail. *Psychology of Women Quarterly, 38*, 138–151.

Dekel, R., & Goldblatt, H. (2008). Is there intergenerational transmission of trauma? The case of combat veterans' children. *American Journal of Orthopsychiatry, 78*, 281–289.

Dierkhising, C. B., Ko, S. J., Woods-Jaeger, B., Briggs, E. C., Lee, R., & Pynoos, R. S. (2013). Trauma histories among justice-involved youth: Findings from the National Child Traumatic Stress Network. *European Journal of Psychotraumatology, 4*, 1–12.

Driessen, M., Schroeder, T., Widman, B., Schonfeld, C., & Schneider, F. (2006). Childhood trauma, psychiatric disorders, and criminal behavior in prisoners in Germany: A comparative study in incarcerated women and men. *Journal of Clinical Psychiatry, 67*, 1486–1492.

Elbogen, E. B., Johnson, S. C., Newton, V. M., Straits-Troster, K., Vasterling, J. J., Wagner, H. R., & Beckham, J. C. (2012). Criminal justice involvement, trauma, and negative affect in Iraq and Afghanistan war era veterans. *Journal of Consulting and Clinical Psychology, 80*, 1097.

Ford, J. D., Hartman, J. K., Hawke, J., & Chapman, J. F. (2008). Traumatic victimization, post-traumatic stress disorder, suicidal ideation, and substance abuse risk among juvenile justice-involved youth. *Journal of Child & Adolescent Trauma, 1*, 75–92.

Gatz, M., Brown, V., Hennigan, K., Rechberger, E., O'Keefe, M., Rose, T., & Bjelajac, P. (2007). Effectiveness of an integrated, trauma-informed approach to treating women with co-occurring disorders and histories of trauma: The Los Angeles site experience. *Journal of Community Psychology, 35*, 863–878.

Gibson, L. E., Holt, J. C., Fondacaro, K. M., Tang, T. S., Powell, T. A., & Turbitt, E. L. (1999). An examination of antecedent traumas and psychiatric comorbidity among male inmates with PTSD. *Journal of Traumatic Stress, 12*, 473–484.

Gilfus, M. E. (2002). *Women's experiences of abuse as a risk factor for incarceration.* Retrieved from Penn State University http://citeseerx.ist.psu.edu/viewdoc/download?doi=10.1.1.208.744 3&rep=rep1&type=pdf

Goff, A., Rose, E., Rose, S., & Purves, D. (2007). Does PTSD occur in sentenced prison populations? A systematic literature review. *Criminal Behaviour and Mental Health, 17*, 152–162.

Green, B. L., Miranda, J., Daroowalla, A., & Siddique, J. (2005). Trauma exposure, mental health functioning, and program needs of women in jail. *Crime & Delinquency, 51*, 133–151.

Greenberg, G. A., & Rosenheck, R. A. (2009). Mental health and other risk factors for jail incarceration among male veterans. *Psychiatric Quarterly, 80*, 41–53.

Grella, C. E., & Greenwell, L. (2007). Treatment needs and completion of community-based aftercare among substance-abusing women offenders. *Women's Health Issues, 17*, 244–255.

Gunter, T. D., Chibnall, J. T., Antoniak, S. K., Philibert, R. A., & Black, D. W. (2013). Childhood trauma, traumatic brain injury, and mental health disorders associated with suicidal ideation and suicide-related behavior in a community corrections sample. *Journal of the American Academy of Psychiatry and the Law Online, 41*, 245–255. Retrieved from https://pdfs.semanticscholar.org/1491/88fe023ec1b29cc918cd72cc570cbbb7452f.pdf

Harris, M., & Fallot, R. (2001). *Using trauma theory to design service systems.* San Francisco, CA: Jossey-Bass.

Harvard Medical School. (2007a). *National Comorbidity Survey twelve-month prevalence estimates.* Retrieved from https://www.hcp.med.harvard.edu/ncs/index.php.

Harvard Medical School. (2007b). *National Comorbidity Survey lifetime prevalence estimates.* Retrieved from https://www.hcp.med.harvard.edu/ncs/index.php

Hubbard, D. J. (2002). *Cognitive-behavioral treatment: An analysis of gender and other responsivity characteristics and their effects on success in offender rehabilitation.* (Doctoral dissertation). Retrieved from https://etd.ohiolink.edu/

Human Rights Watch. (1996). *All too familiar: Sexual abuse of women in U.S. state prisons.* New York, NY: Human Rights Watch.

Hutton, H. E., Treisman, G. J., Hunt, W. R., Fishman, M., Kendig, N., Swetz, A., & Lyketsos, C. G. (2001). HIV risk behaviors and their relationship to posttraumatic stress disorder among women prisoners. *Psychiatric Services, 52*, 508–513.

Khantzian, E. J. (1985). The self-medication hypothesis of addictive disorders: Focus on heroin and cocaine dependence. *American Journal Psychiatry, 142*, 1259–1264. Retrieved from https://www.researchgate.net/profile/Edward_Khantzian/publication/19256427_The_self_medication_hypothesis_of_addictive_disorders_Focus_on_heroin_and_cocaine_dependence/

links/54ad98fb0cf24aca1c6f6792/The-self-medication-hypothesis-of-addictive-disorders-Focus-on-heroin-and-cocaine-dependence.pdf

Komarovskaya, I. A., Booker Loper, A., Warren, J., & Jackson, S. (2011). Exploring gender differences in trauma exposure and the emergence of symptoms of PTSD among incarcerated men and women. *Journal of Forensic Psychiatry & Psychology, 22*, 395–410.

Kubiak, S. P. (2004). The effects of PTSD on treatment adherence, drug relapse, and criminal recidivism in a sample of incarcerated men and women. *Research on Social Work Practice, 14*, 424–433.

Landenberger, N. A., & Lipsey, M. W. (2005). The positive effects of cognitive-behavioral programs for offenders: A meta-analysis of factors associated with effective treatment. *Journal of Experimental Criminology, 1*, 451–476.

Leidenfrost, C. M., Calabrese, W., Schoelerman, R. M., Coggins, E., Ranney, M., Sinclair, S. J., & Antonius, D. (2016). Changes in psychological health and subjective well-being among incarcerated individuals with serious mental illness. *Journal of Correctional Health Care, 22*, 12–20.

Levenson, J. S., & Socia, K. M. (2016). Adverse childhood experiences and arrest patterns in a sample of sexual offenders. *Journal of Interpersonal Violence, 31*, 1883–1911.

Levenson, J. S., Willis, G., & Prescott, D. (2014). Adverse childhood experiences in the lives of male sex offenders and implications for trauma-informed care. *Sexual Abuse: A Journal of Research and Treatment, 28*, 340–359.

Lev-Wiesel, R. (2007). Intergenerational transmission of trauma across three generations: A preliminary study. *Qualitative Social Work, 6*, 75–94.

Loper, A. B. (2002). Adjustment to prison of women convicted of possession, trafficking, and non-drug offenses. *Journal of Drug Issues, 32*, 1033–1050.

Lynch, M. (2010). *Sunbelt justice: Arizona and the transformation of American punishment.* Stanford, CA: Stanford University Press.

Lynch, S. M., DeHart, D. D., Belknap, J., & Green, B. (2013). *Women's pathways to jail: Examining mental health, trauma, and substance use.* (Report No. NCJ 241045). Retrieved from Bureau of Justice Statistics https://www.bja.gov/Publications/WomensPathwaysToJail.pdf

Lynch, S. M., Heath, N. M., Mathews, K. C., & Cepeda, G. J. (2012). Seeking safety: An intervention for trauma-exposed incarcerated women? *Journal of Trauma & Dissociation, 13*, 88–101.

Mandelli, L., Carli, V., Roy, A., Serretti, A., & Sarchiapone, M. (2011). The influence of childhood trauma on the onset and repetition of suicidal behavior: An investigation in a high risk sample of male prisoners. *Journal of Psychiatric Research, 45*, 742–747.

Maschi, T., Gibson, S., Zgoba, K. M., & Morgen, K. (2011). Trauma and life event stressors among young and older adult prisoners. *Journal of Correctional Health Care, 17*, 160–172.

Maschi, T., Morgen, K., Zgoba, K., Courtney, D., & Ristow, J. (2011). Age, cumulative trauma and stressful life events, and post-traumatic stress symptoms among older adults in prison: Do subjective impressions matter? *The Gerontologist, 51*, 675–686.

Maschi, T., Viola, D., & Morgen, K. (2013). Unraveling trauma and stress, coping resources, and mental Well-being among older adults in prison: Empirical evidence linking theory and practice. *The Gerontologist, 54*, 857–867.

Messina, N., & Grella, C. (2006). Childhood trauma and women's health outcomes in a California prison population. *American Journal of Public Health, 96*, 1842–1848.

Messina, N., Grella, C., Burdon, W., & Prendergast, M. (2007). Childhood adverse events and current traumatic distress: A comparison of men and women drug-dependent prisoners. *Criminal Justice and Behavior, 34*, 1385–1401.

Miller, N. A., & Najavits, L. M. (2012). Creating trauma-informed correctional care: A balance of goals and environment. *European Journal of Psychotraumatology, 3*, 17246. https://doi.org/10.3402/ejpt.v3i0.17246

Moloney, K. P., van den Bergh, B. J., & Moller, L. F. (2009). Women in prison: The central issues of gender characteristics and trauma history. *Public Health, 123*, 426–430.

Morrissey, M. B., Courtney, D., & Maschi, T. (2012). Sexual abuse histories among incarcerated older adult offenders: A descriptive study. In E. A. Kalfoglu & R. Faikoglu (Eds.), *Sexual abuse: Breaking the silence* (pp. 21–32). Rijeka, Croatia: InTech.

Moses, D. J., Reed, B. G., Mazelis, R., & D'Ambrosio, B. (2003). Creating trauma services for women with co-occurring disorders . Retrieved from Substance Abuse and Mental Health Services Administration https://www.samhsa.gov/sites/default/files/wcdvs-lessons.pdf

Najavits, L. M. (2002). *Seeking safety: A treatment manual for PTSD and substance abuse.* New York, NY: Guilford Press.

Najavits, L. M., Gastfriend, D., & Barber, J. (1998). Cocaine dependence with and without PTSD among subjects in the National Institute on Drug Abuse Collaborative Cocaine Treatment Study. *American Journal of Psychiatry, 155,* 214–219. Retrieved from https://ajp.psychiatry-online.org/doi/full/10.1176/ajp.155.2.214

Najavits, L. M., Weiss, R., & Shaw, S. (1997). The link between substance abuse and posttraumatic stress disorder in women. *American Journal on Addictions, 6,* 273–283.

National Institute of Corrections. (2007). *Report to the congress of the United States on activities of the Department of Justice in relation to the Prison Rape Elimination Act (Public Law 108–79).* Washington, D.C.: US Department of Justice.

National Research Council. (2014). *The growth of incarceration in the United States: Exploring causes and consequences.* Washington, D.C.: The National Academies Press.

Neller, D. J., Denney, R. L., Pietz, C. A., & Thomlinson, R. P. (2006). The relationship between trauma and violence in a jail inmate sample. *Journal of Interpersonal Violence, 21,* 1234–1241.

Ouimette, P. C., Brown, P. J., & Najavits, L. M. (1998). Course and treatment of patients with both substance use and posttraumatic stress disorders. *Addictive Behaviors, 23,* 785–796.

Prins, S. J. (2014). Prevalence of mental illnesses in US state prisons: A systematic review. *Psychiatric Services, 65,* 862–872.

Psick, Z., Ahalt, C., Brown, R. T., & Simon, J. (2017). Prison boomers: Policy implications of aging prison populations. *International Journal of Prisoner Health, 13,* 57.

Quina, K., & Brown, L. S. (2007). Introduction. *Journal of Trauma Dissociation, 8,* 1–7.

Rosenberg, H. J., Vance, J. E., Rosenberg, S. D., Wolford, G. L., Ashley, S. W., & Howard, M. L. (2014). Trauma exposure, psychiatric disorders, and resiliency in juvenile-justice-involved youth. *Psychological Trauma: Theory, Research, Practice, and Policy, 6,* 430.

Salina, D. D., Lesondak, L. M., Razzano, L. A., & Weilbaecher, A. (2007). Co-occurring mental disorders among incarcerated women: Preliminary findings from an integrated health treatment study. *Journal of Offender Rehabilitation, 45,* 207–225.

Sarchiapone, M., Carli, V., Cuomo, C., Marchetti, M., & Roy, A. (2009). Association between childhood trauma and aggression in male prisoners. *Psychiatry Research, 165,* 187–192.

Sarchiapone, M., Carli, V., Di Giannantonio, M., & Roy, A. (2009). Risk factors for attempting suicide in prisoners. *Suicide and Life-threatening Behavior, 39,* 343–350.

Sarchiapone, M., Jovanović, N., Roy, A., Podlesek, A., Carli, V., Amore, M., … Marušič, A. (2009). Relations of psychological characteristics to suicide behaviour: Results from a large sample of male prisoners. *Personality and Individual Differences, 47,* 250–255.

Sawyer, W., & Wagner, W. (2019). *Mass incarceration: The whole pie 2019.* Retrieved from Prison Policy Initiative https://www.prisonpolicy.org/reports/pie2019.html

Saxon, A. J., Davis, T. M., Sloan, K. L., McKnight, K. M., McFall, M. E., & Kivlahan, D. R. (2001). Trauma, symptoms of posttraumatic stress disorder, and associated problems among incarcerated veterans. *Psychiatric Services, 52,* 959–964.

Schwerdtfeger, K. L., & Goff, B. S. N. (2007). Intergenerational transmission of trauma: Exploring mother–infant prenatal attachment. *Journal of Traumatic Stress, 20,* 39–51.

Sergentanis, T. N., Sakelliadis, E. I., Vlachodimitropoulos, D., Goutas, N., Sergentanis, I. N., Spiliopoulou, C. A., & Papadodima, S. A. (2014). Does history of childhood maltreatment make a difference in prison? A hierarchical approach on early family events and personality traits. *Psychiatry Research, 220,* 1064–1070.

Smallbone, S. W., & Dadds, M. R. (1998). Childhood attachment and adult attachment in incarcerated adult male sex offenders. *Journal of Interpersonal Violence, 13*(5), 555–573.

Struckman-Johnson, C., Struckman-Johnson, D., Rucker, L., Bumby, K., & Donaldson, S. (1996). Sexual coercion reported by men and women in prison. *Journal of Sex Research, 33,* 67–76.

Teicher, M. H., Andersen, S. L., Polcari, A., Anderson, C. M., & Navalta, C. P. (2002). Developmental neurobiology of childhood stress and trauma. *Psychiatric Clinics of North America, 25*, 397–426.

Tompsett, C., Domoff, S., & Toro, P. (2013). Peer substance use and homelessness predicting substance abuse from adolescence through early adulthood. *American Journal of Community Psychology, 51*, 520–529.

Treatment Advocacy Center. (2016). *Serious mental illness (SMI) prevalence in jails and prisons.* Retrieved from https://www.treatmentadvocacycenter.org/storage/documents/backgrounders/smi-in-jails-and-prisons.pdf

Turner, K., Miller, H. A., & Henderson, C. E. (2008). Latent profile analyses of offense and personality characteristics in a sample of incarcerated female sexual offenders. *Criminal Justice and Behavior, 35*(7), 879–894.

Van Voorhis, P., Salisbury, E., Wright, E., & Bauman, A. (2008). *Achieving accurate pictures of risk and identifying gender responsive needs: Two new assessments for women offenders.* (Report No. 022844). Retrieved from National Institute of Corrections https://nicic.gov/achieving-accurate-pictures-risk-and-identifying-gender-responsive-needs-two-new-assessments-women

Walmsley, R. (2018). *World prison population list.* (12th ed.). Retrieved from Institute for Criminal Policy Research http://www.prisonstudies.org/sites/default/files/resources/downloads/wppl_12.pdf

Wasserman, G. A., & McReynolds, L. S. (2011). Contributors to traumatic exposure and posttraumatic stress disorder in juvenile justice youths. *Journal of Traumatic Stress, 24*, 422–429.

Weeks, R., & Widom, C. S. (1998). Self-reports of early childhood victimization among incarcerated adult male felons. *Journal of Interpersonal Violence, 13*, 346–361.

Widom, C. S. (2000). Childhood victimization and the derailment of girls and women to the criminal justice system. In B. E. Richie, K. Tsenin, & C. S. Widom (Eds.), *Research on women and girls: Plenary papers of the 1999 conference on criminal justice research and evaluation—Enhancing policy and practice through research* (pp. 27–36). Retrieved from https://www.ncjrs.gov/pdffiles1/nij/180973.pdf

Wolff, N., Blitz, C. L., & Shi, J. (2007). Rates of sexual victimization in prison for inmates with and without mental disorders. *Psychiatric Services, 58*, 1087–1094. Retrieved from https://ps-psychiatryonline-org.gate.lib.buffalo.edu/doi/full/10.1176/ps.2007.58.8.1087#

Wolff, N., Blitz, C. L., Shi, J., Bachman, R., & Siegel, J. A. (2006). Sexual violence inside prisons: Rates of victimization. *Journal of Urban Health, 83*, 835–848.

Wolff, N., Frueh, B. C., Shi, J., & Schumann, B. E. (2012). Effectiveness of cognitive–behavioral trauma treatment for incarcerated women with mental illnesses and substance abuse disorders. *Journal of Anxiety Disorders, 26*, 703–710.

Wolff, N., Huening, J., Shi, J., & Frueh, B. C. (2014). Trauma exposure and posttraumatic stress disorder among incarcerated men. *Journal of Urban Health, 91*, 707–719.

Zgoba, K., Jennings, W. G., Maschi, T., & Reingle, J. M. (2012). An exploration into the intersections of early and late sexual victimization and mental and physical health among an incarcerated sample of older male offenders. *Best Practices in Mental Health, 8*, 82–98. Retrieved from https://www.researchgate.net/profile/Tina_Maschi/publication/249997835_An_Empirical_Assessment_of_the_Overlap_Between_Sexual_Victimization_and_Sex_Offending/links/546e01f10cf29806ec2e695e/An-Empirical-Assessment-of-the-Overlap-Between-Sexual-Victimization-and-Sex-Offending.pdf

Zlotnick, C., Najavits, L. M., Rohsenow, D. J., & Johnson, D. M. (2003). A cognitive-behavioral treatment for incarcerated women with substance abuse disorder and posttraumatic stress disorder: Findings from a pilot study. *Journal of Substance Abuse Treatment, 25*, 99–105.

# Chapter 5
# PTSD in Sentence Mitigation

Thomas A. Caffrey

## Mental Health as Mitigating: a Neglected Reality

As this chapter was going to press, federal District Judge T. S. Ellis III sentenced the highest-ranking convicted appointee of President Donald Trump, Paul Manafort, to less than 4 years in prison – even though the Federal Guidelines recommended 19–24 years for his crimes. Pundits and scholars have been abuzz about the politics, racial bias, and judicial unpredictability that led to this sentence. The event reflects both the leeway judges now have when sentencing, following the *Booker* decision of 2005, and the importance of the sentencing phase of the criminal judicial process. Like politics and racial bias, forensic mental health findings can play a decisive part in sentencing decisions.

According to Law Professor (Emeritus) Michael Perlin, an advocate for recognizing defendants' mental disabilities in court decisions, "Remarkably little has been written about the impact of mental disability on the sentencing process" (Perlin, 2015). For example, a thorough, 32-chapter review of specific legal cases relevant to mental health law contains no chapter or subheading on sentence mitigation and no mention of "mitigation" or "sentence mitigation" in its glossary (Thenor, 2004). On the ground, practicing attorneys and mental health practitioners too often fail to demonstrate to courts that convicted individuals' mental and emotional difficulties should play a role in sentencing decisions.

T. A. Caffrey (✉)
Private Practice of Psychology, New York, NY, USA

© Springer Nature Switzerland AG 2020
R. A. Javier et al. (eds.), *Assessing Trauma in Forensic Contexts*,
https://doi.org/10.1007/978-3-030-33106-1_5

## Historical Context

A practicing defense attorney recently posted the following on his website:

> Years ago, judges were legally required to sentence criminal defendants to a sentence
> within the guideline range of imprisonment. Cases such as *Booker*, *Apprendi*, *Hughes* and
> others changed that. Now a [federal] sentencing judge can consider information outside of
> the United States Sentencing Guidelines in determining an appropriate sentence. The judge
> can consider the nature and circumstances of the offense, your personal history, the need to
> protect the public from you, the need to provide you with vocational or rehabilitative
> services and other factors. This change in the law provides your lawyer with a great
> opportunity to show the sentencing judge positive information about you that is not included
> in the Pre-Sentence Report. Your lawyer can include this information in a Sentencing
> Memorandum that he or she can prepare and present to the judge in advance of the
> sentencing hearing (Speaks, 2018).

"Years ago" refers to the years before the 2005 *Booker* case, during which the US
Sentencing Commission's strict Guidelines largely determined how federal judges
calculated the sentences of convicted defendants. In its *Booker* decision, the
Supreme Court ruled that judges were no longer required to follow the Guidelines
(United States v. Booker, 2005). 18 U.S.C. § 3553 (a), the federal code that emerged
from the *Booker* and other cases, became the ruling source of guidance. After 2005,
as Speaks advertises, the defendant's attorney may submit a sentencing memorandum
that cites aspects of the defendant's life, or life circumstances, that may have been
overlooked, or underemphasized, in the federal probation officer's presentence report.

The 2005 change was far from new in federal judicial practice. It constituted a
restoration of the practices that preceded the establishment of the US Sentencing
Commission. Prior to the Commission's founding, judges entertained all information
about offenders and their offenses, mitigating circumstances as well as aggravating.
Moreover, when Congress founded the Commission, the wording of its founding
Sentencing Reform Act [SRA] (US House of Representatives, 1984), within the
overall Crime Control Act signed into law by President Reagan in 1984, included
the following directive: "No limitation shall be placed on the information concerning
the background, character, and conduct of a person convicted of an offense which a
court of the United States may receive and consider for the purpose of imposing an
appropriate sentence" (18 U.S.C. § 3661).

However, in its own *Federal Sentencing: The Basics*, the US Sentencing
Commission, typically defined as "an independent agency in the judicial branch of
government" (United States Sentencing Commission, 2018), sounds a more
constraining note:

> Before the SRA [Sentencing Reform Act] went into effect on November 1, 1987, federal
> judges imposed "indeterminate" sentences with virtually unlimited discretion within broad
> statutory ranges of punishment, and the United States Parole Commission would thereafter
> decide when offenders were actually released from prison on parole. The Supreme Court
> has recognized that "the broad discretion of sentencing courts and parole [officials] had led
> to significant sentencing disparities among similarly situated offenders." As found by
> members of Congress who enacted the SRA: "[E]ach judge [was] left to apply his own
> notions of the purposes of sentencing. . . . As a result, every day federal judges mete[d] out

an unjustifiably wide range of sentences to offenders with similar histories, convicted of similar crimes, committed under similar circumstances." (United States Sentencing Commission, 2015, p. 1)

Thus, seeds of conflict have been evident from the start. Congress, and judicial practice before them, stood for openness to information about mitigating as well as aggravating conditions and circumstances. The Commission itself, however, viewed its role as reining in "virtually unlimited discretion" by judges, reducing "significant sentencing disparities," and narrowing "an unjustifiably wide range of sentences" "meted out" by judges. From their implementation in 1987 till the 2005 undoing of their mandatory force, the Sentencing Guidelines served as a rigid formula of weighted values of offender and offense characteristics – mostly aggravating – and the corresponding prescribed months (e.g., "96 months," rather than 8 years) of prison time that constrained judges' discretionary authority.

It was the Sixth Amendment to the Constitution, a defendant's right to trial by jury, that led to the 2005 change. In two preceding cases, *Apprendi v New Jersey* (2000) and *Blakeley v Washington* (2004), the Supreme Court, in upholding defendants' jury rights, ruled against using postconviction information that had not been established, jury-like, "beyond reasonable doubt," to enhance a defendant's sentence. With these precedents having established and clarified what kind of information could *not* be included (without the stamp of "beyond reasonable doubt") in a sentencing determination, when *Booker* came along, the Supreme Court simply severed the mandatory characteristic of the Guidelines from the Guidelines' founding Federal Sentencing Act, leaving the Guidelines as something sentencing judges must *consider*, but locating the ultimate decision as to whether or not to *follow* a given guideline with the sentencing judge.

Following the Supreme Court's removal of the Guidelines' mandatory authority, many judges, after years of following them, continued to follow the Guidelines as if still mandatory. In some instances, there were appeals. Several appeals made it back to the Supreme Court. In one instance, *Nelson v United States* (2009), the sentencing judge had explained, during sentencing, that under a Fourth Circuit precedent, "the Guidelines are considered presumptively reasonable." When the defendant appealed, on the grounds that the judge had given too much weight to the Guidelines, the appellate court, also citing the Fourth Circuit precedent, sided with the sentencing judge. However, the Supreme Court corrected the lower courts, admonishing them for allowing that the sentencing judge "presume" that Guidelines are "reasonable." The Supreme Court asserted, "The Guidelines are not only *not mandatory* on sentencing courts; they are also not to be *presumed* reasonable." (In the case cited by the sentencing judge and the Fourth Circuit [Rita v U.S.], the same Fourth Court of *Appeals* had been allowed to make that presumption about a lower court's deliberation; but the Supreme Court's resolution of *Booker* precluded frontline (*trial*) court judges from thinking or speaking that way.) After *Booker*, it was the wording of § 3553 (a), the bulk of which is cited in Appendix A, that ruled; the Guidelines were no longer determinative, or, as *Nelson v United States* indicates, even allowed at the trial court level to be *presumed* to be *reasonable*.

Among the four "considerations" required of sentencing judges, it is notable that the first listed includes the words, "history and characteristics of the defendant." Since *Booker*, judges are required to "consider" the "history and characteristics of the defendant," a phase that clearly includes a defendant's possible PTSD. It is also noteworthy that the requirement that the Guidelines be considered is listed fourth among the four considerations, a place in line that at least suggests that the history and characteristics of the defendant are to be treated in judicial deliberations as at least as significant as are the formerly mandatory Guidelines. (The exact wording of the post-2005 law, *Title 18, § 3553 (a)*, can be found in Appendix A.) To sum up, *Booker* was revolutionary. It raised the stuff of mitigation ("… circumstances of the offense and the history and characteristics of the defendant") to the level of the formerly mandatory Guidelines. From 2005 on, *both* "shall" be "considered" by the sentencing judge.

## Thwarting Efforts

In years to follow, there was a concerted effort by the Sentencing Commission to thwart Congressional intent and judicial discretion *during* the mandatory period of its rules and policy statements and the Supreme Court's intent *since* 2005 (when those rules and policy statements had been ruled only advisory). A 200-page 2011 study is instructive: *No More Math Without Subtraction: Deconstructing the Guidelines' Prohibitions and Restrictions on Mitigating Factors* (Baron-Evans & Coffin, 2011). With exacting detail, the authors show how from the beginning of the Commission's formation, and down into the twenty-first century, the Commission has persisted, through political and public relations channels, and by means of its training across the country of judges and probation staff, to buttress its own authoritative role over against judges' deliberations, and while doing so, curtailing the place of mitigating factors, and fortifying that of aggravating factors within the deliberations. For instance, the Commission secured a kind of statutory authority for the policy statements that it generated and then, through many of the policy statements (23 of which the authors "deconstruct"), imposed limits on what, prior to 1984, had been viewed as factors for possible sentence mitigation. Two sections of this study are especially pertinent to mitigation-related evaluations: Mental and Emotional Conditions (pp. 74–87; and Diminished Capacity, pp. 169–178).

Given the Commission's tenacious grip on its recently softened prerogatives, a tenacity often joined by Justice Department advocates, today's defense attorneys are counseled to prepare for Commission-grounded objections when submitting the kind of sentencing memoranda cited by Clarke, above. This is especially true recently, following the appointment of an attorney general (removed in November of 2018) who "ordered all federal prosecutors across the nation to seek the most extreme charges possible against criminal defendants, regardless of extenuating circumstances, and without any consideration of whether the specific case justifies the penalty sought" (Cole, 2018, p. 16).

## *State Guidelines*

Many states have formulated their own guidelines, with Minnesota leading the way in 1978. In 2008, the National Center for State Courts reviewed 21 states' sentencing guideline practices (Kauder & Ostrom 2008). Some proved more mandatory than others. Other states launched guidelines more recently, including New York whose guidelines are explicitly advisory. Some states modeled their guidelines after the federal 1984 guidelines. More importantly, the federal Supreme Court upholds and overturns state court decisions and rules on the constitutionality of state guideline policies and practices.

In an early account of lessons learned by state guideline commissions, Frase (1995) listed 5 good characteristics that the first 17 commissions shared with one another, and that tended to contrast with the then increasingly unpopular federal guidelines:

> Some of the most important features of state systems also serve to distinguish them from the federal guidelines. First, state guidelines tend to permit more judicial discretion (especially in the assessment of offender characteristics) and are less constrained by mandatory minimum sentencing statutes. Second, all state guideline systems (as well as the recently revised ABA Sentencing Standards [ABA, 1994]) reject routine sentence enhancements based on unconvicted, "real offense" factors [the factors lacking "beyond reasonable doubt" credibility that led eventually to Booker]. Third, state guideline reforms are increasingly motivated by a desire to gain better control over escalating prison populations; several states (and the ABA Standards) directly link guideline sentences to available correctional resources. Fourth, the focus on prison capacity limits has encouraged state reformers to give increasing emphasis to the development and structuring of non-prison sanctions, especially for non-violent or first offenders. Fifth, as a result of the above features and other policy decisions, state guideline systems have generally achieved broad acceptance by judges and attorneys. (Frase, 1995, p. 39)

Knapp and Hauptly (1991–1992) show how the then state guidelines' use of the "typical case" differed from, and was superior to, what they described as the federal guidelines' "mechanistic, elemental" approach. My own metaphor for that difference is a sphere representing a state's typical case of a crime; and, for the federal guidelines, a stack of coins. The bottom coin represents the points assigned when, as Knapp and Hauptly put it, "the barest elements [are present] of the offense that must be shown for a conviction" (685). The upper coins represent point-values added because of aggravating conditions. The sphere, by contrast, already represents the *typical* instance of a crime and, as spherical, lends itself equally to aggravating conditions above, mitigating conditions below, and more neutral conditions at the sides.

Finally, in my own work with persons convicted of federal crimes (1974–2016), I was repeatedly told of the impregnability of the federal prosecutorial system. I rarely spoke with convicted persons who had "gone to trial" with his or her offense; instead, I regularly heard a judgment of "insane" leveled against those who tried. The Guidelines' grid of months to be served in prison for given offenses included the "upper coins" described above. These could be added or overlooked by a prosecutor, depending on the probability of a conviction at trial. This month-dealing was regularly used by prosecutors as a threat, and thus as means of securing a guilty plea from a defendant. One statistic showed that in 1983 (prior to the Guidelines' launch), federal defendants pleaded guilty 83% of the time; by 2003, that rate had jumped to 95% (Devers, 2011). A perusal of the US Justice Department's 666-page Sourcebook of Criminal Justice Statistics reveals that, in 2001, of the 66,112 defendants charged with felonies, 60,467 (or 91.5%) were convicted; of those 60,467 convicted defendants, 58,039 (or 96%) were convicted by means of a "guilty plea" (Pastore & Maguire, 2003, p. 418). In 2018, a Chief Clerk of a mid-western federal court region estimated that the rate had climbed to 97% (Dries, 2018). It appears that, in spite of *Booker*, prosecutors have successfully carried forward the Guidelines' bias toward aggravating circumstances. Pfaff (2017) argues that it has been primarily prosecutorial charging decisions that have driven the rise in the nation's prison population in the final decades of the twentieth century, and not longer sentences or more frequent arrests. Hence the relevance of, and need for, an increased focus on sentencing deliberations and decisions.

## Posttraumatic Stress Disorder (PTSD)

With the relatively recent medical acknowledgment of PTSD as a diagnosis – in DSM-III (1980) – courts may view the condition as something recent, lacking in seasoned science, and therefore as of questionable weight in judicial decision-making. Forensic examiners should therefore be able to speak of the length and breadth of the condition's history, as well as, more specifically, of its germinal presence in the pages of the earliest of the American psychiatric diagnostic manuals.

## *The Evolution of the PTSD Diagnosis*

### Fright, Shock, and Abuse

Young (2016) cites Birmes and Bui (2016) and Ford, Grasso, Elhai, and Courtois (2015) as having documented trauma and reactions to it that go back 5000 years. In the English-speaking world, well before the seventeenth century, Bethlem Hospital in London, known by then as "Bedlam," came to house severely mentally ill persons; in 1630, for instance, "cryings, screechings, roarings, brawlings, shaking of chains, swearings, frettings, [and] chaffings" were heard at the institution (Andrews et al., 1997). In 1766, John Munro, who headed Bedlam till 1791, kept a casebook about his private mental patients. As causes of their illnesses, he listed "impoverishment, upset, bereavement, love, fright, shock, rejection and physical and verbal abuse … [and the] lunar cycle" (Stewart, 2003). The eighteenth-century fright, shock, and abuse predate today's Criterion A sources of PTSD by 250 years.

## Railway Spine and Shell Shock

Exactly one hundred years after Munro's report, physician John Erichsen wrote *On Railway and Other Injuries of the Nervous System* (1866), in which he coined the term, "railway spine." Originating in the "jars, shakes, shocks, or concussions" sustained in accidents in railway construction, or in passengers' mishaps, the railway spine would manifest itself in damaged memories, thoughts, temper, or sleep (Smith, 2011). Erichsen's tort victories for these damages triggered opposing arguments. Herbert Page argued that the claimed railway spine was little more than a "nervous spine," and one arising from a fearful, "nervous temperament" (muting thereby the external source's liability) (ibid, 6). German neurologist Hermann Oppenheim coined "traumatic neurosis" for the illness and looked to mental or emotional sources for it, namely, "terror" or "emotional shock" (Lerner, 2001). His claim was met by Charcot in France, who asserted that "traumatic neurosis" was nothing other than hysteria. Other terms followed, including "traumatic neurasthenia" (American, George Beard), "traumatic memory," and, finally, early during WWI, "shell shock," a term probably coined by British psychologist C. S. Myers in 1915 (Shephard, 2000). Like Erichsen's railway spine, shell shock introduced an external event as causing a mental illness.

## DSM and Posttraumatic Stress Disorder Diagnosis

George Raines was the Chair of the American Psychiatric Association's Mental Hospital Service's Committee on Nomenclature and Statistics, the organization that published the 1952 work, *Diagnostic and Statistical Manual [of] Mental Disorders* (DSM-I) (American Psychiatric Association, 1952). In his forward to the manual, Raines explains how WWII motivated the text's development. Army and VA psychiatrists had been forced to apply to 90% of the military patients they saw diagnoses framed for patients in public mental hospitals. For example, "The 'psychoneurotic label' had to be applied to men reacting briefly with neurotic symptoms to considerable stress"; they also used "psychopathic personality" to categorize minor personality disorders (vii). But more to our purposes, Raines stated, "No provision existed for diagnosing psychological reactions to the stress of combat, and terms had to be invented to meet this need" (*id.*). Hence, the need arose at the time for the *diagnostic manual itself*, DSM-I. As with DSM-II (American Psychiatric Association, 1968) after it, DSM-I satisfied the need to categorize combat stress. It accomplished this within its general category of "Transient situational personality disturbance" (p. 7). The personality disturbance stemming from combat stress was listed as "Gross stress reaction."

   Though its publication in 1968 followed two World Wars and occurred in the midst of the US's involvement in the Vietnam War, DSM-II's 119 pages of psychiatric "nomenclature" included no explicit reference to "Post-Traumatic Stress Disorder (PTSD)," to "Shell Shock," or to other pre-PTSD terminology.

Nonetheless, as in DSM-I, in DSM-II *seeds* of PTSD can be detected. They are found in one of the three examples provided therein, of "Adjustment reaction of adult life" (1968, p. 48). The example is worded as, "Fear associated with military combat and manifested by trembling, running and hiding" (p. 49). This and the other adjustment reactions are listed under "Transient Situational Disturbances" and are all explained as representing "an acute reaction to overwhelming environmental stress" (p. 48).

The expectation then was that "with good adaptive capacity," the patient's "symptoms usually recede as the stress diminishes" (DSM-II, p. 48). However, if "symptoms persist after the stress is removed, the diagnosis of another mental disorder is indicated" (*id.*). In today's world, that other mental disorder would likely be PTSD. Strikingly, the DSM-II of 1968 predicted more recent research. For instance, Piechowski (2015) asserts that PTSD is a "pathological response" and "is not the expected response." She cites Brunello's research as indicating that of those exposed to trauma as defined in DSM-5, 10%–20% develop PTSD (Brunello et al., 2001). Young (2016, p. 247), after reviewing multiple studies, concludes to a general estimate at the low end of Brunello's range, or 10%. (Conditions, such as predisposing factors and severity of the *experience* of trauma, can increase the 10% figure; but overall, 10% of those exposed to true trauma come to sustain chronic PTSD.). Hence, there was prognostic consistency from DSM-II through DSM-5. Fact-finders (judges or juries) can rest with the knowledge that professional American psychiatric conclusions about PTSD and PTSD-like conditions reach back to 1952 ("Gross stress reaction") and 1968 ("acute reaction to overwhelming environmental stress"); that is, diagnostic conclusions of more than 65 years, and prognostic of more than 50.

What is newer is the mental health community's explicit focus on PTSD. Beginning with DSM-III (American Psychiatric Association, 1980), the term, posttraumatic stress disorder (PTSD), came into official use. It emerged as one of the anxiety disorders. With DSM-III's introduction of the multiaxial classification system, the clinician was advised to identify the external stressor, and its intensity, on Axis IV, while using Axis I for the diagnosis itself. The Axis IV focus *outside* the individual patient echoed DSM-I's "situational … disturbance" and DSM-II's "… environmental stress." In DSM-III, the "external" marker, Category A, was described broadly: Existence of a recognizable stressor that would evoke significant symptoms of distress in almost everyone (DSM-III, p. 238).

As noted, DSM-III brought the diagnosis PTSD into the world of mental health. Seven years later, the DSM-III-R (American Psychiatric Association, 1987) framed Category A much more specifically, with a specificity that continued, with changes, through DSM-IV (American Psychiatric Association, 1994) and DSM-5 (American Psychiatric Association, 2013):

> A. The person has experienced an event that is outside the range of usual human experience and that would be markedly distressing to almost anyone, e.g., serious threat to one's life or physical integrity; serious threat or harm to one's children, spouse, or other close relatives and friends; sudden destruction of one's home or community; or seeing another person who has been or is being, seriously injured or killed as the result of an accident or physical violence (DSM-III-R, p. 250).

*DSM-III-R* performed a further service. It clarified PTSD's symptom categories (B, C, and D). It did so by sorting the 4, 7, and 6 subcategories, respectively, into 3 rationally distinct categories. The categories came to reflect the three general ways in which the affected person responds to current stressors: (1) by re-experiencing the original traumatic event in some way; (2) by avoiding (current) reminders of the event, including by numbing himself/herself; and (3) by experiencing physiological arousal of some kind in the face of a current stressor (p. 250–251). Again, whether in memory of the original stressor, or in actual perception of a reminder of the original stressor, there is an *external* element (the original stressor) that is intrinsic to the PTSD experience and diagnosis.

Reflecting their layout in the DSM-III-R edition, the symptom categories of re-experiencing, avoidance, and arousal reappear in DSM-IV, again as parts B, C, and D of PTSD's now 6-part (A–F) criteria. Criterion F, added in DSM-IV, requires that significant emotional distress or functional impairment be present, in addition to the A–E criteria of DSM-III-R.

The first two of the manuals that identified PTSD as a separate disorder – DSM-III and DSM-III-R – dedicated just 3 pages to the condition. DSM-IV dedicated 9 pages. In all three of these editions, PTSD is listed among the given manual's "Anxiety Disorders," as one diagnosis listed among the chapter's 11 anxiety disorders. By contrast, *DSM-5* (2013) dedicated a 26-page chapter to a whole new category: Trauma and Stressor-Related Disorders. It was as if the diagnosis PTSD had sprouted relatives that emerged to populate the chapter. Like PTSD itself, each of the relatives requires, as a criterion of itself, "Exposure to a traumatic or stressful event" (p. 265). The new diagnoses include reactive attachment disorder, disinhibited social engagement disorder, and adjustment disorders. This newly promulgated multiplicity of trauma-based diagnoses stems, the authors explain, from the "variable expressions" (*id.*) of distress exhibited by persons who have been exposed to trauma or stress.

## *Trauma's Causal Importance in DSM-5*

The DSM-5 authors are less explicit about what appears to be a second motive for the new multiplicity of diagnoses. That motive appears to be the authors' growing awareness of, and sensitivity to, the pivotal, causal role that trauma plays in a widening circle of diagnosed conditions. For instance, DSM-5's placing of two diagnosed results of social neglect (reactive attachment disorder and disinhibited social engagement disorder) among PTSD's "relatives" *removes* them from their previous, less causally defined, place among childhood disorders. This move, under the umbrella of social neglect, changes the disorders from conditions that are floating freely among childhood disorders to disorders now anchored in, and flowing from, trauma-inducing parental, or other guardian, behavior. The authors cite social neglect as an example of a stressor with diverse clinical outcomes, and as exemplifying their stated reason for the new multiplicity of stressor-based diagnoses. They convincingly explain that the neglect can result variously in a child with internalizing, dysphoric (depressive) mood and self-presentation, to be diagnosed with reactive attachment disorder, or in a child with externalizing, impulsive, uninhibited behavior, to be diagnosed with disinhibited social engagement disorder. Moreover, as noted, the conditions are no longer "floating" on their own, as they had been in DSM-IV's section of childhood disorders.

The authors' rooting the two childhood disorders in an external trauma (neglect), along with their refraining from drawing causal lines from one kind of neglect to one of the disorders, and another to the other, is all supported by research. For example, Croft et al. (2018) longitudinally studied the trauma of a sample of 4433 children, from birth through 17 years of age, and found that all kinds of trauma appear to result, at age 18, in increases in psychotic experiences. Increases in the psychotic experiences occurred when the trauma was repeated, when there were many kinds of trauma, and when subjects' exposure to trauma was short-range. But these were quantitative effects, not effects stemming from specific *kinds* of trauma. The longitudinal study of Copeland et al. (2007) had had similar findings: one childhood trauma almost never resulted in childhood or adolescent PTSD symptoms, whereas many, especially if violent and/or sexual in nature, resulted in increased PTSD symptomatology. Among the study's conclusions is that "the effects of trauma are not symptom specific" (p. 583). That is, childhood trauma could result in anxiety, increased trauma experiences, break-downs in living, *or* diverse PTSD symptoms. Ninety-four percent of the Copeland sample's 1420 children were interviewed up to 4 more times, until they were 30 years old, for a second study (Copeland et al., 2018). In this study, also prospective, the earlier-recorded childhood trauma was found to cast a "long and wide-ranging shadow" (p. 7) over adulthood, a shadow that adversely affects adult health, criminality, finances, and social life. Again, it is not one kind of trauma yielding a specific kind of outcome; rather, a greater amount and intensity of childhood trauma yields more severely compromised adult outcomes. "There may indeed be some outcome specificity to the effects of individual events, but the strongest and most pervasive patterns of associations are established when considering children's total trauma history" (id., p. 8).

In DSM-5, PTSD and its relatives, in their multiplicity, reflect a "horizontally" expanded influence of trauma. The expansion has also been "vertical": trauma or stress has come to be seen as a defining, causal factor in conditions previously categorized under banners other than "Trauma and Stressor-Related Disorders." By bringing "outside" diagnoses (like reactive attachment disorder) into the Trauma and Stressor-Related Disorders chapter, the authors identify a causal link between trauma and the previously less anchored conditions, and highlight the importance of the causal link.

As noted earlier within the legal context of a mitigation inquiry, the causal link should not be assumed. On the one hand, DSM-5's explication of diverse kinds of

PTSD, among adults *and* children, along with its identification of diverse Criteria A as sources of the condition (including the guardian neglect and/or abuse implied in the two varieties of childhood stress disorders), provides the evaluator with an authoritative, articulated diagnostic framework within which to locate a given subject's condition. On the other, as cautioned by Smith (2011), the causal link between the identified source and the subject's condition needs to be buttressed, when possible, with credible confirmatory findings.

There is a further development that DSM-5 brings to trauma-related disorders. The authors of DSM-5 note that the new Trauma and Stressor-Related chapter is related to and therefore located among "surrounding chapters on [other] anxiety disorders, obsessive-compulsive and related disorders, and dissociative disorders" (p. 265). Given the buttressing the Trauma and Stressor-Related chapter has given to the place of trauma in the overall world of mental health, this comment about the related chapters suggests that when DSM-6 is formulated, PTSD's relatives could come to include a yet larger group of diagnosed conditions. Mental disorders may become separated into "trauma-based" and "nontrauma-based." Given their growth in importance from DSM-I through DSM-5, it is clear that trauma-based conditions will be serving increasingly as the stuff of forensic deliberations, including those about sentence-mitigation.

## Clinical Benefits and Legal Caution

Clinical, or medical, benefits follow from this inclusion of the external element as an essential part of the PTSD diagnosis. It serves to identify the condition's originating event(s). This identification is useful in justifying the diagnosis and in framing eventual exposure therapy. Moreover, a focus on the external element serves to ease a subject's sensitivity to being viewed as defective, abnormal, or crazy. The external, Axis IV focus can allow the evaluee to look outward and thereby view himself or herself as an ordinary recipient of the stressor(s) focused upon. This also allows the evaluee to more readily provide specific information about the origins – internal as well as external – of his or her possible PTSD condition.

But legally, as Smith (2011) argues, the inclusion of the external event as causal within an authoritative AMA-sanctioned diagnosis lends pseudo-credence to the actuality both of the event itself and of its causal link to the mental illness. Smith's caution pertains to deliberations about criminal responsibility and mitigation, as well as about personal injury. The caution would be that Erichsen's, Oppenheim's, or Myers' condition, however labeled (railway spine, traumatic neurosis, or shell shock), remain disjoined from its claimed "cause" until the trier of fact establishes the external event and its causal role. Her concern is that courts too often allow undue influence to the medical authority carried by a diagnosis (PTSD) that *assumes* the link.

# Physiological Effects of Trauma

## *Physiological "History and Characteristics"*

The "history and characteristics of the defendant" (§3553 [A][1]) include the physiological as well as the psychological. Chronic, excessive firing of hormonal responses, as a result of prolonged stress or trauma, can cause toxic central nervous system (CNS) effects. These effects, in addition to psychological effects, and how they affect a subject's criminal or other behavior, can play a critical role in the discussion and conclusions sections of a forensic report, and during testimony. "Your Honor, not only has the defendant learned, in the usual sense of learning – as a result of years-long abusive treatment as a child – to react, as demonstrated, too immediately to perceived threats. It is likely that in addition to that usual, associative learning, the defendant's years of being subjected to the described abuse also brought about changes to the section of his brain known as the amygdala, thereby *physiologically* locking in his 'too immediate' negative reactions." Such physiological causes of PTSD-based behavior are given central stage in Young's comprehensive, 3-part treatment of PTSD in court (2016, 2017a, 2017b). PTSD's grounding in biological causes has so withstood experimental replication, Young asserts (2016), that (citing five studies from 2014 alone [2017a, 4]) it could be called a "neurobiological disorder." Adding social risk and other social factors, he later (2017b) casts PTSD as a "biopsychosocial" disorder – rather than as a purely mental one. In a summary introductory statement to his 3-part study, Young states that a "biopsychosocial, multicausal model best encompasses the multifactorial causality of PTSD" (2016, p. 238).

## *Normal and Destructive Trauma*

On its Psychology Help Center web page, The American Psychological Association (2018) lays out how a trauma elicits a cognitive experience that, through the CNS, triggers the HPA axis (hypothalamic-pituitary-adrenal axis) to release its respective hormones (from the hypothalamic gland to the pituitary, and thence to the adrenal gland). These releases, occurring closely on the heels of the cognitive experience, come to constitute the biological and emotional fabric of the individual's experience. The hormonal emissions signal other metabolic processes, such as the closing down of the autoimmune and inflammatory responses. They also mobilize the individual (especially as a result of the adrenal's release of ACTH) for physical action (such as a child running from a dog; a police officer chasing down a dangerous suspect). In their detailed review of the above "neurobiological" processes, Gunnar and Quevedo (2007) repeatedly note that the hormonal and other physiological changes that take place under normal circumstances are natural, and at times necessary for survival (pp. 146, 152, 162, & 164).

For *destructive trauma,* Danese and Baldwin (2017) explain "childhood maltreatment" as including "sexual, physical, and emotional abuse as well as physical and emotional neglect" (p. 519). They base their summary of the destructive neurological effects of childhood maltreatment, or of trauma, on the "comprehensive reviews" of Danese and McEwen (2012), Lim et al. (2014), Lupien et al. (2009), McCrory et al. (2010), Nusslock and Miller (2016), Teicher and Samson (2016), and Tottenham and Sheridan (2009). For their summary of the neurological effects of childhood maltreatment, Danese and Balwin use the framework of the Research Domain Criteria (RDoC) of Insel (2014) and Kaufman et al. (2015). In doing so, they focus on three of the changes that take place in brain function: changes in cognition, in positive valence, and in negative valence.

## Cognition-in-Life: Prefrontal Lobe Effects

When the trauma is major, or remains emotionally unresolved, or continues over a significant period of time (as in chronic child maltreatment) – the repeated trauma referred to earlier – the activation of the HPA axis can also become chronic, rather than normal or ad hoc, with toxic effects on the brain and brain function. These lasting toxic effects carry more than strictly cognitive consequences. That is, the effects have been found to detract from one's IQ (Pechtel & Pizzagalli, 2011) and from what is known as one's declarative memory (Danese & McEwen 2012) – both cognitive human functions. But they also detract, by their effects on the prefrontal lobe of the brain, from executive function (Danese & McEwen 2012) – that is, from one's ability to choose between acting and refraining from acting; from one's ability to plan, to follow through with plans, to keep the separate parts of a plan in order, to prioritize, in importance as well as chronologically, which plan, or part of a plan, to follow, and when. These functions go beyond the exclusively cognitive. This is cognition-in-life, the stuff of sound practical judgment. It entails common sense, prudence (wisdom in the moment), and appropriate human action that flows from common sense and prudence. That is, it is the kind of functioning often deficient in persons brought before criminal justice authorities.

## Positive and Negative Valence: The Amygdala Effects

For those familiar with the literature on emotional intelligence (EI), the amygdala serves as EI's neurological heart. The amygdala, like the prefrontal lobe, gets harmed by overactivation of the HPA axis. One result is a person's lesser sensitivity to rewards, or lesser responsiveness to what are called reward-predicting cues (Dillon et al., 2009, Guyer et al. 2006, Mehta et al. 2010). This reduced sensitivity would understandably reduce one's motivation to make positive choices and to initiate the kind of constructive planning and prudent action cited above.

On the negative side, the overactivation of the HPA axis results in a hypersensitivity to threat. Maltreated children were found to be biased in how they perceived others' emotions. They tend to see angry faces where there are none, a reflection of negative bias (Leppanen & Nelson, 2009; Pollak & Kistler, 2002). Thus, the overactivation of the HPA axis can negatively affect one's view of the outside world by falsely heightening an expectation of being punished. Again, the individual's practical judgment and executive function are compromised. As with the compromised prefrontal lobe, so with the harmed amygdala: compromised positive and negative feelings and expectations (valence) result in deficiencies in sound judgment – and crimes get committed. Young (2016) cautions that the research on these physiological effects is so far limited to *group* research and should therefore not be used, as yet, to make judgments about individual defendants.

## Assessing the Subject

### *The Court's Rheostat*

When addressing a competency, or sanity at the time of the crime, question, the evaluator usually concludes with the equivalent of a yes or no opinion. When addressing a sentence mitigation question, the evaluator faces something more fluid. In effect, the evaluator is being invited to join the court in its deliberations about possibly adjusting its sentencing "rheostat." The evaluator therefore focuses on the *extent* and *quality* of the subject's assumed sanity or, more generally, the subject's human capacity: *how* "sane" was he or she when she or he acted? *How* "equipped," or "capable" – cognitively, emotionally, practical judgmentally, interpersonally – was he or she? "How much" or "how seriously" were a subject's capabilities compromised, if at all? And, by implication, how serious an adjustment, if any, to an expected sentence might be in order?

Further, *what* precisely *motivated* the subject to commit the crime? What were the motivating factors, *before*, and *when*, the crime was committed? *To what extent* was the defendant acting from within his or her own planning and motivation, and to what extent did the action stem from past or current pressures, from inside or outside the defendant? What earlier-life factors may have affected the defendant's capacity for self-directed, as opposed to other-directed or compliant, action, or action driven by defective thinking, or thinking clouded by excessive emotion? What other actions or events in the defendant's life might shed light on these questions, such as instances of focused self-direction or instances of fragmented, broken-down, aborted plans? What *kind* of practical judgment did the subject have at the time of the crime? What was its *quality* or *capacity*? Thus, without offering specific sentencing recommendations – unless asked to do so – by framing the evaluative mitigation report against the backdrop of a rheostat (how much, or how serious, if at all, were the defendant's capabilities compromised?), and by adhering to the conclusion of Berger et al., that "in most jurisdictions, a showing of a direct connection between PTSD and the offense is required" (Berger et al., 2012, p. 519), the evaluator should be able to help the fact-finder coordinate a multiplicity of events, circumstances, and conditions (including the defendant's diversely neurologically affected condition) to arrive at an appropriate sentence for the subject.

## *Clear Thinking about Trauma*

In order to develop a viable trauma-based mitigation report, the evaluator needs to think and communicate clearly about trauma. Four (4) separate steps are suggested:

1. Mere words on a checklist of possible Criterion A events: for example, "Life-threatening illness or injury" (#12 on LEC-5 or Life Event Checklist); such words are referred to by Gray et al. (2004) as PTEs, or potentially traumatic events; at this point, neither real events nor real evaluees are at issue; it is no more than words, ideas, and generalities.
2. An actual traumatic event: this would be a *conclusion* made by an evaluator after assessing a subject's past *experience of* one or more of the PTEs on a page; in terms of DSM-5, this conclusion would establish Criterion A as applying to the subject; given that, as noted, roughly 70% of adults have been found to have had this kind of actual traumatic experience, qualifying for Criterion A is common.
3. PTSD (posttraumatic stress disorder): this diagnostic conclusion narrows the 70% Criterion A qualifiers down, roughly, to 50%, 3 months after the event; 15%, 18 months post-event; and 10% thereafter; this last is the "disorder," and not the relatively brief "trauma" that 70% of adults experience.
4. When possible, the evaluator establishes that the subject's PTSD *resulted from* the Criterion A event established in #2 above. Identifying this link is complex: it needs to be differentiated from both predisposing risk factors and post-trauma events; and, given that just one Criterion A event seldom results in PTSD, that circumstance should increase an evaluator's caution. In either event, if the evaluator can be clear about #s1–3 above – perhaps by labeling them, respectively, as *ideas* of trauma, *actual* trauma, and PTS *disorder* – she or he should be better focused in evaluating a subject, and clearer in communicating findings to a court.

When summarizing their findings about courts' responses to evidence of mitigating circumstances, Berger et al. stated:

> . . .in cases in which PTSD played a role in an offense but did not meet the standard for an exculpating defense [i.e., NGRI], courts have found it [PTSD] to be a mitigating circumstance that permits a reduction in sentencing [mitigation]. In such cases, a wide range of PTSD phenomena have been found to be applicable, including hyperarousal symptoms, impaired impulse control, overestimation of danger, and dissociative phenomena. (2012, p. 519)

## Empathic History-Taking

To provide a useful mitigation report, the evaluator needs a thorough knowledge and understanding of the subject, and – if that knowledge includes a diagnosis of PTSD – a grasp of the condition's relationship to the crime at issue. Thorough, empathic history-taking, as noted, is one avenue to the requisite knowledge. Empathy is needed during this phase because the evaluator seeks personal information that illuminates the subject's decisions and actions, such as the subject's habitual view of and expectations for him/herself, critical others' understood expectations for the subject, and objectives, expectations, fears, and other motive-relevant factors that immediately preceded the crime. To fully assess grounds for mitigation, it is essential to grasp these in-subject mental and emotional factors and, when found to be remarkable, to show how the subject's traumatized condition played a part in bringing the mental and emotional factors about. The empathic eliciting of these factors can be complemented by the structural inclusion of possibly overlooked factors. Screening and interviewing instruments provide this complement.

## Screening for Criterion A

The heart of *DSM-5*'s definition of PTSD's Criterion A is the following *precis*: "Exposure to actual or threatened death, serious injury, or sexual violence" (p. 271). This summary of Criterion A traumas is supported by research beyond the formulation of DSM-5 (Goldstein et al., 2016; Benjet et al., 2016, both cited in Young, 2016, p. 245). These authors have found that the most frequently identified trauma categories include childhood sexual assault, intimate partner violence and revictimization, and threatened or actual severe personal injury, especially injury in motor vehicle accidents (MVAs) – all of which are summarized in the DSM-5 Criterion A *precis*.

The Life Event Check List for DSM-5 (LEC-5), in its Extended Version or Interview Version (Weathers et al., 2013b; rev ed 2018), is one of a few tools available that can help assess the extent to which a traumatic experience meets the requirements of Criterion A. The instrument, readily available online, is designed to focus on a subject's identified "worst-event." It has served since 1995 to assess subjects' experiences. It routinely accompanies the CAPS-5 (the "gold standard in [overall] PTSD assessment"). And it has "adequate temporal stability, and good convergence with an established measure of trauma history – the Traumatic Life Events Questionnaire (TLEQ; Kubany et al., 2000)" (Gray et al., 2004). Gray (p. 337) adds that the LEC tends to emphasize military traumatic events, lacks inquiry into intimate partner abuse and childhood physical abuse, and provides less inquiry into sexual assault than does the TLEQ; subjects with one of these areas of potential traumatic events, he suggests, might better be screened with the TLEQ.

For a more accurate outcome, it is suggested that the second worst case be considered in addition to the first. A recent study (Bardeen & Benfer, 2018) showed that using only a subject's worst case, as does the LEC, results in finding adequate Criterion A severity only about 56% of the time. However, close inquiry by the evaluator into the second worst event of subjects whose worst events did not meet Criterion A requisites led, in the study, to a 24% increase of the 56% identification rate, for a total rate of 80%. Thus, when an initially identified worst event fails to meet Criterion A requirements, the evaluator is advised to inquire into the possible severity of that subject's second worst event. This should not be difficult, given that the LEC-5's recent Extended Version includes close questioning on any of the 17 checklist items receiving a positive response. Bardeen et al. found that the identified secondary events had a severity that was equivalent to that of initially identified worst events. The total rate of 80% should not be considered high: the population evaluated is already suspected of having had a Criterion A experience; and, as noted, there is already a 70% lifetime exposure prevalence among adults (Young, 2016, p. 245, citing Goldstein, and Benjet).

In addition to determining that a subject's reported traumatic experience has been found to meet Criterion A requirements, the evaluator needs to determine whether or not the subject's current condition 1) in fact *constitutes* a condition of PTSD (#3, above, "Clear thinking"); and, if so, 2) results *from* the Criterion A experience (#4, above). At this point, as noted, the prevalence drops precipitously, from a 70% expectation of trauma *exposure* to a 10% expectation of a chronic *condition* of PTSD. After reviewing a myriad of studies on PTSD prevalence, with rates found below and above the 10% level, Young (2016, p. 247) concluded, as noted earlier, that the 10% lifetime estimate is reasonable. Studies found higher rates shortly after exposure (35% after 3 months; Miller, 2015), with the rates dropping (15% after 18 months; Dyeregrov & Regel, 2012) – until the 10% rate for chronic PTSD is reached.

The *PCL-5*, the PTSD Check List, can serve as a first step, or screening instrument, in the task of determining whether a subject suffers from PTSD (Weathers, Litz, et al., 2013). It is a 10–15-minute self-report measure, based on the 20 symptoms of PTSD listed in DSM-5. A cut-off score of 33 (of possible 80) or above suggests the administration of a more thorough instrument, like the CAPS-5. Both the LEC-5 and PCL-5 are readily available online at the Veterans Administration's National Center for PTSD.

The *CAPS-5* (Weathers et al., 2013a) is a 30-item structured interview that takes 45 minutes to an hour to administer. A structured instrument like the CAPS-5 can help prevent the evaluator from overlooking potentially critical information relevant to a PTSD inquiry. The National Center for PTSD characterizes the CAPS-5 as "the gold standard in PTSD assessment" (National Center for PTSD, citing Gray, p. 335, "The CAPS is widely considered the gold standard in PTSD assessment [e.g., Zayfert, Becker, Unger, & Shearer, 2002]"). Its 30 items include the 20 symptoms screened in PCL-5, but with inquiries, along with further Criterion A inquiries and questions aimed at "overall response validity, overall PTSD severity, and specifications for the dissociative subtype (depersonalization and derealization)" (ibid.). Severity ratings (from 0 = absent to 4 = extreme/incapacitating) are made for each of the items after inquiry. A score of at least 2 ("moderate/threshold") on at least one symptom in each of DSM-5's Criteria B and C and on at least two symptoms in each of Criteria D and E, along with Criteria F and G being met, supports a PTSD diagnosis. A 4-hour, free, online training course in administering the CAPS-5 is available to mental health clinicians with at least a master's degree.

## Other Instruments

Other widely accepted PTSD screening and assessing instruments, in addition to the LTEQ, include the following: the Posttraumatic Cognitions Inventory (PTCI) (Foa et al., 1993) [Young, 2016, p. 248]; the Detailed Assessment of Posttraumatic Stress (DAPS) (Briere, 2001) [Young, 2016, p. 249]; and, for a "nonstigmatizing," indirect, self-report measure, the Pittsburgh Sleep Quality Index Addendum for PTSD (PSQI-A) (Buysse et al., 1989), an index whose "disruptive nocturnal behaviors" scores correlate well with measures of PTSD in male military veterans (Insana et al., 2013). Young (2017b, pp. 88–89) provides a review of the instruments described above, and others. For a list and brief description of each of 12 interview and self-report instruments for assessing PTSD, including several of those described above, see the American Psychological Association Practice Directorate's "Clinical Practice Guideline for the Treatment of Posttraumatic Stress Disorder (PTSD)" (American Psychological Association, 2017). DeAngelis (2017) points out that input for the Guideline stemmed from a "multidisciplinary panel of experts" that included primary care, psychiatry, and social work, in addition to psychology. This suggests an applicability of the guidelines beyond psychology.

## The Forensic Element

The terms effort, response style, feigning, and malingering, all refer, in increasingly censuring ways, to a subject's way of responding, to an interviewer or to an assessment instrument. Within a forensic context, a subject's way of responding is critical. Young (2017b, pp. 89–90) provides a list of reviews and findings about tests one can use to evaluate feigned or malingered PTSD. He reports, too, that in his own earlier overview of surveys of the instruments (2014a), he concluded, first, "Not one instrument was recommended across the board" (2017b, p. 91) and, second, the MMPI-2-RF was "a most useful tool in evaluating malingered PTSD" (id.; 2014a). Suhr (2015) concurred, adding the PAI to the MMPI-2-RF, with a specific focus on PTSD credibility. It should be noted that it was the most recent, or "RF," version of the MMPI (*not* its predecessor, the MMPI-2) whose validity scales Young found "promising," and that Suhr supported. Young based his judgment on the findings of ten studies conducted between 2005 and 2015 (2017b, p. 91).

## Negative Response Style

Young has listed nine (9) assessment instruments aimed to test a subject's "negative response bias" with respect to PTSD, or tendency to claim more PTSD symptomatology than is credible (Young, 2014). These include some already discussed here (the CAPS and the DAPS). Other well-known instruments (e.g., the SIRS, SIRS-2, and M-FAST) also probe for feigned psychopathology, but not specifically for feigned PTSD.

## The Full Picture

Forensic psychological experts concur that a professionally scientific and ethical approach to assessing a subject includes a variety of kinds of sources of information (e.g., interview, structured instrument, and collateral reports); a variety of sources within the different kinds (e.g., more than one interview; two or more structured instruments; medical and school records, as well as family and work associates' reports); and a bias toward hypotheses *contrary to* those emerging from the data. The American Psychological Association Practice Directorate's "Specialty Guidelines for Forensic Psychology" (American Psychological Association, 2012) puts it this way:

> 1.02 Impartiality and Fairness:
>
> . . . .Forensic practitioners recognize the adversarial nature of the legal system and strive to treat all participants and weigh all data, opinions, and rival hypotheses impartially.
>
> 9.01 Use of Appropriate Methods:
>
> . . . .When performing examinations, treatment, consultation, educational activities or scholarly investigations, forensic practitioners seek to maintain integrity by examining the issue or problem at hand from all reasonable perspectives and seek information that will differentially test plausible rival hypotheses (American Psychological Association, 2012).

Within this outlook, data that support a "feigning" conclusion, for instance, need to be counterbalanced by possible explanations to the contrary. Conversely, from the standpoint of an examiner preparing a mitigation report sought by a defense attorney, data supporting a "credible" conclusion need too to be counterbalanced. The virtual absence of feigning data does not establish with certainty, for instance, that the subject has been speaking "nothing but the truth" throughout the evaluation.

## Specific Case Law

In a thorough review of specific judicial decisions both before and after *Booker*'s return of judicial discretion to federal judges, Perlin (2015) cited NGRI and competency decisions, as well as sentence mitigation decisions. He found that judges sometimes (because of "sanist" or "ordinary common sense" thinking) decided that defendants' compromised emotional conditions were reason for *upward* departures from the Guidelines (more severe sentences). He also found specific instances of judges not merely "considering" the Guidelines, as directed to do by *Booker*, but rather ruling as if the Guidelines were still mandatory. Finally, he found that in spite of persuasive evidence of PTSD as a relevant causal factor to a crime, a defendant's level of violent propensity (understandably, for the protection of the public) can outbalance PTSD-based sentence mitigation (2015). Four years before Judge Ellis sentenced Paul Manafort to much less prison time than the Guidelines recommended, Perlin worried that judges were too reluctant to "embrace the right to be discretionary":

> What is not clear is the extent to which judges will consider the DSM-5's expanded definition of PTSD in subsequent litigation in light of their demonstrated reluctance to embrace the right to be discretionary (2015, p. 904).

On the more promising side, there is a post-*Booker*, 2009, Supreme Court decision (*Porter v. McCollum*). Porter had been convicted of murder and sentenced to death. The federal Supreme Court criticized a Florida state sentencing court, Florida's Supreme Court, and the Eleventh (federal) Judicial Circuit Court for having allowed for Porter's defense attorney's failure to include Porter's Korean War service as mitigation in his presentence argument. The Supreme Court noted that the lower courts' deliberations overlooked "the intense stress and mental and emotional toll that combat took on Porter." The Supreme Court's decision included the following explanation of how a proper consideration of Porter's battlefield trauma could well have elicited from the jury something less than a sentence of death:

> This is not a case in which the new evidence "would barely have altered the sentencing profile presented to the sentencing judge" Strickland (*Strickland v Washington*, 1984), supra, at 700. The judge and jury at Porter's original sentencing heard almost nothing that would humanize Porter or allow them to accurately gauge his moral culpability. They learned about Porter's turbulent relationship with Williams, his crimes, and almost nothing else. Had Porter's counsel been effective, the judge and jury would have learned of the "kind of troubled history we have declared relevant to assessing a defendant's moral culpability" Wiggins, supra, at 535. They would have heard about (1) Porter's heroic military service in two of the most critical—and horrific—battles of the Korean War, (2) his struggles to regain normality upon his return from war, (3) his childhood history of physical abuse, and (4) his brain abnormality, difficulty reading and writing, and limited schooling. (See *Penry v. Lynaugh* 1989: "[E]vidence about the defendant's background and character is relevant because of the belief, long held by this society, that defendants who commit criminal acts that are attributable to a disadvantaged background ... may be less culpable"). Instead, they heard absolutely none of that evidence, evidence which "might well have influenced the jury's appraisal of [Porter's] moral culpability" Williams (*Williams v Taylor*, 2000), 529 U. S., at 398. (Porter v. McCollum, 2009)

The Supreme Court reversed the federal Court of Appeals' (Circuit Court's) decision, and sent the case back to be re-heard "consistent with this opinion" – that is, re-heard taking into account the above Supreme Court explanation of its ruling.

## Conclusion

PTSD's official roots reach back to the start of official diagnostic classification in this country. Trauma's place in diagnostic classification has been growing. Since PTSD's war-related roots in DSM-I and DSM-II, diagnoses rooted in traumatic events have multiplied. DSM-IV and DSM-5 have come to include events such as "threat to the physical integrity of others," a Category A criterion that would include a child's witnessing, over a period of years, a father's rage expressed so intensely toward his mother that each time it erupts the child is certain that if his father *acts* on the rage he will kill his mother. In addition to their quantitative growth, traumatic events have grown in their importance as the causal, or explanatory, base of diverse psychiatric conditions. Previously isolated childhood conditions, for instance, have now found roots in traumatic, often abusive, experiences.

The PTSD diagnosis includes, as an element *essential* to itself, an *outside* causal reference – an element usually *independent* of the agency of the subject being evaluated. This external factor can soften deliberations about individual responsibility. Case law teaches, nevertheless, that the forensic examiner must demonstrate both how the external event traumatically affected the subject and how that effect – psychological and, or with probability, physiological – within the subject affected the subject's behavior at the time he or she committed the crime. Though it is too soon to predict trends in judges' responses to mitigation arguments, *Porter* has shown that when information relevant to mitigating a sentence finds its way to the attention of a court, the court can respond with pointed understanding.

## Questions/Activities for Further Exploration

1. Devers lists "involving both judges and defense attorneys in the charge bargaining process" (2011, p. 4) as one way to counterbalance prosecutorial influence in the early phase of a defendant's path through the criminal justice system. Suggest another remedy to excessive prosecutorial influence.
2. In light of the notoriously brief sentence recently given to Paul Manafort – convicted of millions of dollars fraudulently obtained and of lying to Congress regarding his close relationships with countries in conflict with the United States – should the Sentencing Guidelines be reinstated as mandatory?
3. Because of your widely known forensic competence, and especially because of the transparent impartiality and objectivity you show in your forensic evaluations, a defense attorney selects you to evaluate her client, telling you that a

traumatic experience her client underwent could, with your help, improve her client's chances of winning a downward departure (mitigation) from his probation officer's sentence recommendation. How would you respond to the attorney? Then, if you go forward with the evaluation, what would you especially watch for?

4. Role play. Based on a fictional instance of armed robbery on US Government property by a recently traumatized assailant, (a) choose a classmate to serve first as defendant, with you as prosecutor, then you as defendant, and she/he as prosecutor and then (b) join a second pair of students, with one of them serving as defense attorney reading her/his psychologist's brief mitigation report about the defendant, and the other serving as the ruling District Judge in the case; c) hold a mock presentence hearing about the report; d) then reverse the pairs' roles, with the other pair serving as prosecutor/defendant, your pair as defense attorney/judge, and hold another mock hearing. Adjust crime, roles, and pairings to taste.

5. Interview a defense attorney – private or employed by Legal Aid Society. Learn (a) the decision process that leads to her/his inclusion, or noninclusion, of sentence mitigation possibilities that are related to defendants' mental and emotional condition; (b) the steps she/he takes when she/he decides *to* include possible mitigation in her/his defense strategy; and (c) how she/he explores with a defendant her/his possibly traumatic background and its possible relevance to the crime at issue.

## Appendix A. Title 18: Crimes and Criminal Procedure

## § 3553. Imposition of a Sentence

(a) *FACTORS TO BE CONSIDERED IN IMPOSING A SENTENCE. The court shall impose a sentence sufficient, but not greater than necessary, to comply with the purposes set forth in paragraph (2) of this subsection. The court, in determining the particular sentence to be imposed, shall consider—*

    (1) *the nature and circumstances of the offense and the history and characteristics of the defendant;*
    (2) *the need for the sentence imposed –*

        (A) *to reflect the seriousness of the offense, to promote respect for the law, and to provide just punishment for the offense;*
        (B) *to afford adequate deterrence to criminal conduct;*
        (C) *to protect the public from further crimes of the defendant; and*

(D) *to provide the defendant with needed educational or vocational training, medical care, or other correctional treatment in the most effective
manner;*

(3) *the kinds of sentences available;*

(4) *the kinds of sentence and the sentencing range established for – (A) the
applicable category of offense committed by the applicable category of
defendant as set forth in the guidelines – (i) issued by the Sentencing
Commission pursuant to sect. 994(a)(1) of title 28, United States Code,
subject to any amendments made to such guidelines by act of Congress
(regardless of whether such amendments have yet to be incorporated by the
Sentencing Commission into amendments issued under sect. 994(p) of title
28); and (ii) that, except as provided in sect. 3742(g), are in effect on the
date the defendant is sentenced (U.S. House of Representatives, 2005).*

# References

ABA House of Delegates. (1994). *ABA standards for criminal justice: sentencing* (3rd ed.). Chicago: American Bar Association. *"Sentencing"* is a chapter, revised in 1993 and published in 1994, in ABA Criminal Justice Section. (1993). *ABA standards for criminal justice: Prosecution function and defense function; 3rd Edition.* Chicago: American Bar Association.

American Psychiatric Association. (1952). *Diagnostic and statistical manual. Mental disorders.* (DSM). American Psychiatric Association. Mental Hospital Service. Washington, 6, D.C.

American Psychiatric Association. (1968). *Diagnostic and statistical manual of mental disorders* (2nd ed.). (DSM-II). American Psychiatric Association. Washington, D.C. 2009.

American Psychiatric Association. (1980). *Diagnostic and statistical manual of mental disorders* (3rd ed.). (DSM-III). American Psychiatric Association. Washington, DC

American Psychiatric Association. (1987). *Diagnostic and statistical manual of mental disorders* (3rd ed. – revised). (DSM-III-R). American Psychiatric Association. Washington, DC

American Psychiatric Association. (1994). *Diagnostic and statistical manual of mental disorders* (4th ed.). (DSM-IV). American Psychiatric Association. Washington, DC

American Psychiatric Association. (2013). *Diagnostic and statistical manual of mental disorders* (5th ed.). (DSM-5). American Psychiatric Publishing. A Division of American Psychiatric Association. Washington, DC. London, England.

American Psychological Association (2012). Specialty guidelines for forensic psychology. Retrieved, 3/14/2019, from https://www.apa.org/practice/guidelines/forensic-psychology. Also, (2013). *American Psychologist, 68*(1), 7–19. https://doi.org/10.1037/a0029889.

American Psychological Association. (2017). *Clinical practice guideline for the treatment of posttraumatic stress disorder (PTSD).* Retrieved, Nov 2018, from https://www.apa.org/ptsd-guideline

American Psychological Association. (2018). Stress effects on the body. Psychology Help Center web page. Retrieved, 7/21/2019, from https://www.apa.org/helpcenter/stress/index

Andrews, J., Briggs, A., Porter, R., Tucker, P., & Waddington, K. (1997). *The history of Bethlem.* London/New York: Routledge. ISBN 0415017734.

Apprendi v. New Jersey. 530 U.S. 466 (2000).

Bardeen, J. R., & Benfer, N. (2018). Methodological considerations for assessing trauma history via self-report. *Psychological Trauma: Theory, Research, Practice, and Policy.* http://psycnet.apa.org/doiLanding?doi=10.1037%2Ftra0000398

Baron-Evans, A., & Coffin, J. N. (2011). *No More Math Without Subtraction: Deconstructing the Guidelines' Prohibitions and Restrictions on Mitigating Factors.* Retrieved in October 2018, from https://fln.fd.org/files/training/no-more-math-without-subtraction.pdf

Benjet, C., Bromet, E., Karam, E. G., Kessler, R. C., McLaughlin, K. A., Ruscio, A. M., … Koenen, K. C. (2016). The epidemiology of traumatic event exposure worldwide: Results from the world mental health survey consortium. *Psychological Medicine, 46*, 327–343.

Berger, O., McNiel, D. E., & Binder, R. L. (2012). PTSD as a criminal defense: a review of case law. *Journal of the American Academy of Psychiatry and Law, 40*, 509–521.

Birmes, P. J., & Bui, E. (2016). PTSD in history: From Uruk to Bagdad. In C. R. Martin, V. R. Preedy & V. B. Patel (Eds.), *Comprehensive guide to post-traumatic stress disorders* (pp. 3–19). Springer International Publishing. Cham, Switzerland.

Briere, J. (2001). Detailed Assessment of Posttraumatic Stress. Professional manual. *Psychological Assessment Resources.* Lutz, FL.

Blakeley v. Washington. 542 U.S. 296 (2004).

Brunello, N., Davidson, J. R., Deahl, M., Kessler, R. C., Mendlewicz, J., Racagni, G., … Zohar, J. (2001). Posttraumatic stress disorder: Diagnosis and epidemiology, comorbidity and social consequences, biology and treatment. *Neuropsychobiology, 43*, 150–162.

Buysse, D. J., Reynolds, C. F., Monk, T. H., Berman, S. R., & Kupfer, D. J. (1989). The Pittsburgh Sleep Quality Index (PSQI): A new instrument for psychiatric research and practice. *Psychiatry Research, 28*, 193–213.

Cole, D. (2018). Trump's inquisitor. *The New York Review of Books, 65*(7), 16–18. 4/19/2018.

Copeland, W., Keeler, G., Angold, A., & Costello, E. J. (2007). Traumatic events and posttraumatic stress in children. *Archives of General Psychiatry, 64*, 577–584.

Copeland, W. E., Shanahan, L., Hinesley, J., Chan, R. F., Aberg, K. A., Fairbank, J. A., … Costello, E. J. (2018). Association of childhood trauma exposure with adult psychiatric disorders and functional outcomes. *JAMA Network Open, 1*(7), e184493. https://doi.org/10.1001/jamanetworkopen.2018.4493

Croft, J, Heron, J, Teufel, C., et al. (2018). Association of trauma type, age of exposure, and frequency in childhood and adolescence with psychotic experiences in early adulthood. *JAMA Psychiatry* (3155), published online November 21, 2018.

Danese, A., & Baldwin, J. R. (2017). Hidden wounds? Inflammatory links between childhood trauma and psychopathology. *Annual Review of Psychology, 68*, 517–544.

Danese, A., & McEwen, B. S. (2012). Adverse childhood experiences, allostasis, allostatic load, and age-related disease. *Physiology & Behavior, 106*(1), 29–39.

DeAngelis, T. (2017). PTSD guideline ready for use. In *Monitor on Psychology.* Washington, D.C.: American Psychological Association.

Devers, L. (2011). *Plea and Charge Bargaining: Research Summary.* Washington, D.C.: Bureau of Justice Assistance, U. S. Department of Justice.

Dillon, D. G., Holmes, A. J., Birk, J. L., Brooks, N., Lyons-Ruth, K., & Pizzagalli, D. A. (2009). Childhood adversity is associated with left basal ganglia dysfunction during reward anticipation in adulthood. *Biological Psychiatry, 66*(3), 206–213.

Dries, S. (2018). Personal communication, June 17, 2018.

Dyregrov, A., & Regel, S. (2012). Early interventions following exposure to traumatic events: Implications for practice from recent research. *Journal of Loss and Trauma, 17*, 271–291.

Foa, E. B., Ehlers, A., Clark, D. M., Tolin, D. F., & Orsillo, S. M. (1993). The posttraumatic cognitions inventory (PTCI): Development and validation. *Psychological Assessment, 11*, 303–314.

Ford, J. D., Grasso, D. A., Elhai, J. D., & Courtois, C. A. (2015). *Posttraumatic stress disorder: scientific and professional dimensions* (2nd ed.). Academic Press. San Diego, CA.

Frase, R. (1995). Lessons of State Guideline Reforms. *Federal Sentencing Reporter, 8*(1), 39–41. Retrieved July, 2018, from: http://scholarship.law.umn.edu/faculty_articles

Goldstein, R. B., Smith, S. M., Chou, S. P., Saha, T. D., Jung, J., Zhang, H., … Grant, B. F. (2016). The epidemiology of DSM-5 posttraumatic stress disorder in the United States: Results from the National Epidemiological Survey on Alcohol and Related Conditions-III. *Social Psychiatry and Psychiatric Epidemiology, 51*, 1137–1148.

Gray, M., Litz, B., Hsu, J., & Lombardo, T. (2004). Psychometric properties of the Life Events Checklist. (PDF). *Assessment, 11*, 330–341. https://doi.org/10.1177/1073191104269954. PILOTS ID: 26825.

Gunnar, M., & Quevedo, K. (2007). The neurobiology of stress and development. *Annual Review of Psychology, 58*, 145–173.

Guyer, A. E., Kaufman, J., Hodgdon, H. B., Masten, C. L., Jazbec, S., et al. (2006). Behavioral alterations in reward system function: The role of childhood maltreatment and psychopathology. *Journal of the American Academy of Child and Adolescent Psychiatry, 45*(9), 1059–1067.

Insana, S. P., Hall, M., Buysse, D. J., & Germain, A. (2013). Validation of the Pittsburgh Sleep Quality Index Addendum for posttraumatic stress disorder (PSQI-A) in U.S. male military veterans. *Journal of Trauma Stress., 26*(2), 192–200. https://doi.org/10.1002/jts.21793. Epub 2013 Mar 19.

Insel, T. R. (2014). The NIMH Research Domain Criteria (RDoC) project: Precision medicine for psychiatry. *American Journal of Psychiatry, 171*(4), 395–397.

Kauder, N. B., & Ostrom, B. J. (2008). *State sentencing guidelines: Profiles and continuum.* National Center for State Courts. Public Safety Performance Project of the Pew Charitable Trust's Center on the States. Retrieved, Nov 2018, from https://www.pewtrusts.org/-/media/legacy/uploadedfiles/wwwpewtrustsorg/reports/sentencing_and_corrections/ncsc20sentencing20guidelines20profiles20july202008pdf.pdf

Kaufman, J., Gelernter, J., Hudziak, J. J., Tyrka, A. R., & Coplan, J. D. (2015). The Research Domain Criteria (RDoC) project and studies of risk and resilience in maltreated children. *Journal of the American Academy of Child and Adolescent Psychiatry, 54*(8), 617–625.

Knapp, K. A., & Hauptly, D. J. (1992). State and Federal Sentencing Guidelines: Apples and Oranges. *University of California Davis Law Review, 25*, 679–694. Retrieved, 18 Nov 2018, from HeinOnline.

Kubany, E. S., Leisen, M. B., Kaplan, A. S., Watson, S. B., Haynes, S. N., Owens, J. A., & Burns, K. (2000). Development and preliminary validation of a brief broad-spectrum measure of trauma exposure: The traumatic life events questionnaire. *Psychological Assessment, 12*, 210–224.

Lerner, P. (2001). From traumatic neurosis to male hysteria: The decline and fall of Hermann Oppenheim. In M. S. Micale & P. Lerner [Eds.], *Traumatic Pasts: History, Psychiatry, and Trauma in the Modern Age* (pp. 1870–1930). Cambridge University Press: Cambridge, United Kingdom.

Leppanen, J. M., & Nelson, C. A. (2009). Tuning the developing brain to social signals of emotions. *Nature Reviews Neuroscience, 10*(1), 37–47.

Lim, L., Radua, J., & Rubia, K. (2014). Gray matter abnormalities in childhood maltreatment: A voxel-wise meta-analysis. *American Journal of Psychiatry, 171*(8), 854–863.

Lupien, S. J., McEwen, B. S., Gunnar, M. R., & Heim, C. (2009). Effects of stress throughout the lifespan on the brain, behaviour and cognition. *Nature Reviews Neuroscience, 10*(6), 434–445.

McCrory, E. J., DeBrito, S. A., & Viding, E. (2010). Research review: The neurobiology and genetics of maltreatment and adversity. *Journal of Child Psychology and Psychiatry, 51*(10), 1079–1095.

Mehta, M. A., Gore-Langton, E., Golembo, N., Colvert, E., Williams, S. C. R., & Sonuga-Burke, E. (2010). Hyporesponsive reward anticipation in basal ganglia following severe institutional deprivation early in life. *Journal of Cognitive Neuroscience, 22*(10), 2316–2325.

Miller, L. (2015). *PTSD and forensic psychology: Applications to civil and criminal law.* Cham, Switzerland: Springer International Publishing.

Nelson v. United States. 555 U. S. (2009).

Nusslock, R., & Miller, G. E. (2016). Early-life adversity and physical and emotional health across the lifespan: Neuroimmune network hypothesis. *Biological Psychiatry, 80*, 23–32.

Pastore, A. & Maguire, K. (Eds.). (2003). *Sourcebook of Criminal Justice Statistics: 2002.* Washington, D.C.: U. S. Government Printing Office. Retrieved, on 3/12/2019, from https://www.ncjrs.gov/pdffiles1/Digitization/208756NCJRS.pdf

Pechtel, P., & Pizzagalli, D. A. (2011). Effects of early life stress on cognitive and affective function: An integrated review of human literature. *Psychopharmacology, 214*(1), 55–70.

Penry v. Lynaugh. 492 U. S. 302, 219 (1989).

Perlin, M. (2015). "I expected it to happen/I knew he'd lost control": The impact of PTSD on criminal sentencing after the promulgation of DSM-5. *Utah Law Review,* 4, Symposium legal borders and mental disorders: The challenge of defining mental illness, Article 14, 889.

Pfaff, J. (2017). *Locked in: The true causes of mass incarceration – And how to achieve real reform.* New York, NY: Basic Books.

Piechowski, L. D. (2015). *Disability and workers' compensation.* Course presented as segment of postdoctorate certificate program in forensic psychology, St. John's University, New York, NY

Pollak, S. D., & Kistler, D. J. (2002). Early experience is associated with the development of categorical representations for facial expressions of emotions. *PNAS, 99*(13), 9072–9076.

Porter v. McCullum. 558 U. S. 30, 42-44. (2009).

Shephard, B. (2000; rev ed 2003). *A war of nerves: Soldiers and psychiatrists in the twentieth century.* Cambridge: Harvard University Press.

Smith, D. M. (2011). Diagnosing liability: the legal history of posttraumatic stress disorder. *Temple Law Review, 84*(1), 4–5. Retrieved Oct 2018, from https://papers.ssrn.com/sol3/papers.cfm?abstract_id=1794180

Speaks, R. C. (2018) *R. Clarke Speaks Website.* http://www.speakslaw.com/faqs/what-is-involved-in-a-sentencing-in-a-federal-criminal-case-.cfm. Retrieved 18 Nov 2018.

Stewart, H. (2003). Sheer Bedlam. *The Guardian.* May 3, 2003. Review of Andrews, J, & Scull, A. *Customers and patrons of the mad-trade: The management of lunacy in eighteenth-century London.* Country: U Cal Press. https://www.theguardian.com/books/2003/may/03/featuresreviews.guardianreview18 Retrieved 24 Nov 2018.

Strickland v. Washington. 466 U. S. 668 (1984).

Suhr, J. A. (2015). *Psychological assessment: A problem-solving approach.* New York, NY: Guilford Press.

Teicher, M. H., & Samson, J. A. (2016). Annual research review: Enduring neurobiological effects of childhood abuse and neglect. *Journal of Child Psychology and Psychiatry, 57,* 241–266.

Thenor, F. (2004). *Civil and criminal mental health law. A companion reference for forensic experts and attorneys. The essential cases.* Balboa Island, CA: ACFP Press.

Tottenham, N., & Sheridan, M. S. (2009). A review of adversity, the amygdala and the hippocampus: A consideration of developmental timing. *Frontiers in Human Neuroscience, 3,* 68.

United States House of Representatives. Office of the Law Revision Counsel. (1984). *Sentencing Reform Act of 1984 (H.R.5773). 98th congress of the United States (1983–1984).* Washington, D.C.: Government Publishing Office.

United States House of Representatives. Office of the Law Revision Counsel. (2005). *United States code. Title 18. Crimes and criminal procedure. #3553 imposition of a sentence.* Washington, D.C.: Government Publishing Office.

United States Sentencing Commission. (2018). See "About," on the Commission's 2018 website.

United States Sentencing Commission. Office of General Counsel and the Office of Education and Sentencing Practice. (2015). *Federal sentencing: The basics* (49 pp). Washington, D.C.: United States Sentencing Commission. Retrieved, Oct 2018, from https://www.ussc.gov/guidelines/primers/federal-sentencing-basics

United States v. Booker, 543 U. S. 220 (2005).

Weathers, F.W., Blake, D.D., Schnurr, P.P., Kaloupek, D.G., Marx, B.P., & Keane, T.M. (2013a). *The clinician-administered PTSD scale for DSM-5 (CAPS-5).* Interview available from the National Center for PTSD at www.ptsd.va.gov

Weathers, F.W., Blake, D.D., Schnurr, P.P., Kaloupek, D.G., Marx, B.P., & Keane, T.M. (2013b; rev ed 2018). *The life events checklist for DSM-5 (LEC-5).* Instrument available from the National Center for PTSD at www.ptsd.va.gov

Weathers, F.W., Litz, B.T., Keane, T.M., Palmieri, P.A., Marx, B.P., & Schnurr, P.P. (2013). *The PTSD checklist for DSM-5 (PCL-5).* Scale available from the National Center for PTSD at www.ptsd.va.gov.

Williams v. Taylor. 529 U. S. 362, 396 (2000).

Young, G. (2014). *Malingering, feigning, and response bias in psychiatric/psychological injury: Implications for practice and court.* Dordrecht, Netherlands: Springer Science + Business Media.

Young, G. (2016). PTSD in court I: Introducing PTSD for court. *International Journal of Law and Psychiatry, 49*, 238–259.

Young, G. (2017a). PTSD in court. Part II. Risk factors, endophenotypes, and biological underpinnings. *International Journal of Law and Psychiatry, 51*, 1–21.

Young, G. (2017b). PTSD in court. Part III. Malingering, assessment/testing, and the law. *International Journal of Law and Psychiatry, 52*, 81–102.

# Chapter 6
# Homicide Activism: A Call for Research on a Neglected Phenomenon

**Melissa C. Leeolou and Harold Takooshian**

To live in hearts we leave behind is not to die – Thomas Campbell

Over 17,000 men, women, and children are victims of homicide in the United States each year ("Uniform Crime Reporting Program," 2018). Yet "as staggering as that figure is, it does not begin to indicate the toll of suffering that homicide extracts. If one estimates that each of its victims is survived by a minimum of five loved ones for whom the violent death will produce deep and bitter grief, the annual casualty rate escalates to nearly 85,000 individuals. And if one appreciates the intensity and duration of the trauma suffered by these survivors, we can conservatively estimate that we have three quarters of a million people in our midst who are wounded and scarred Americans, all victims of the murders of just the past decade" (Violent Crime Victim Services [VCVS], 2000).

In this review, we are careful to probe not one but two aspects of this trauma: (1) not just the intense anguish and anger following homicide but, equally important, (2) the heroic activism that often results from this trauma. This review pulls together many timely exemplars of a new concept of "homicide activism" (in Table 6.1), then discusses this concept, and calls for future research to more squarely examine this often overlooked phenomenon.

M. C. Leeolou (✉)
Fordham University, New York, NY, USA

H. Takooshian
Department of Psychology, Fordham University, New York, NY, USA

© Springer Nature Switzerland AG 2020
R. A. Javier et al. (eds.), *Assessing Trauma in Forensic Contexts*,
https://doi.org/10.1007/978-3-030-33106-1_6

**Table 6.1** Created by the authors. A compendium of 40 examples of US homicide activism

| Year | Homicide victim | Homicide survivor | Action |
|---|---|---|---|
| 1932 | Charles Lindbergh Jr. | Charles Lindbergh | Lindbergh Law, Federal Kidnapping Act |
| 1973 | Joan D'Alessandro | Rosemarie D'Alessandro | Joan's Law (1997), Justice for Victims (2000) |
| 1974 | Mike Mayborne | Terry Mayborne | Support for Homicide Survivors (SHS) |
| 1977 | Stacy Moskowitz | Jerry, Neysa Moskowitz | Son of Sam Law |
| 1978 | Lisa Hullinger | Robert, Charlotte Hullinger | Parents Of Murdered Children (POMC) |
| 1979 | Etan Patz | Stanley, Julie Patz | National Missing Children's Day; milk carton campaigns |
| 1980 | Cari Lightner | Candy Lightner | Mothers Against Drunk Driving (MADD) |
| 1980 | Sunny von Bulow | Ala Isham, Alexander Auersberg | National Center for Victims of Crime |
| 1981 | Adam Walsh | John Walsh | National Center for Missing and Exploited Children (MCMEC); America's Most Wanted; National Toll Free Hotline; Missing Children's Assistance Act; Adam Walsh Child Protection and Safety Act |
| 1982 | Dominique Dunne | Ellen Griffin Dunne | Justice for Victims of Homicide |
| 1983 | Gertrude McCabe | Jane Alexander | Citizens Against Homicide; victim rights |
| 1983 | Marsy Nicholas | Henry Nicholas | Marsy's Law, to notify homicide survivor families |
| 1986 | Jennifer Levin | Ellen Levin | Jennifer Dawn Levin Victim Memorial Fund |
| 1986 | Jeanne Clery | Connie, Howard Clery | Clery's Law, campus reporting of crimes |
| 1988 | Robert Cushing | Renny Cushing | MVFHR, Murder Victims' Families for Human Rights |
| 1988 | Pan Am Flight 103 | Families of 269 dead | Witness to Justice Act; Victim Rights Clarification Act |
| 1988 | Mickey Thompson; Trudy Thompson; Scott Campbell | Colleen Campbell | MOVE, Memory of Victims Everywhere; Victims' Rights Advocate |
| 1989 | Jacob Wetterling | Jerry & Patty Wetterling | Jacob Wetterling Foundation; Jacob Wetterling Crimes Against Children and Sexually Violent Offender Registration Act |
| 1991 | Michael Dunahee | Bruce, Crystal Dunahee | Child Find |
| 1993 | Polly Klaas | Marc Klaas | Polly Klaas Foundation, murdered children |
| 1994 | Megan Kanka | Richard, Maureen Kanka | Megan's Law (Amendment to the Sexual Offender Act); Megan Nicole Kanka Foundation |
| 1994 | Renee Rondeau | Elaine, Gordon Rondeau | Renee Olubunmi Rondeau Peace Foundation |

(continued)

**Table 6.1** (continued)

| Year | Homicide victim | Homicide survivor | Action |
|------|-----------------|-------------------|--------|
| 1995 | Tariq Khamisa | Azim Khamisa | Tariq Khamisa Foundation; four published books |
| 1996 | Amber Hagerman | Donna Norris | PROTECT Act; Amber Alert |
| 1997 | Levi Frady | Justin Frady | Levi's Call, Georgia child alert system |
| 1998 | Matthew Shepard | Dennis, Judy Shepard | Matthew Shepard Foundation; Angel Action |
| 1998 | Suzanne Lyall | Mary, Doug Lyall | Suzanne's Act (Amendment to the Child Search Assistance Act) |
| 2001 | Stephen Siller | Siller family | Tunnel to Towers Foundation |
| 2002 | Daniel Pearl | Judea, Ruth Pearl | Daniel Pearl Foundation |
| 2005 | Natalee Holloway | Beth Holloway | International Safe Travels Foundation; Natalee Holloway Resource Center |
| 2008 | Darnell Donerson; Jason Hudson; Julian King | Jennifer Hudson | Hudson-King Foundation for Families of Slain Victims |
| 2008 | Leandra Rosado | Rosado family | Leandra's Law, drunk driving with child passengers |
| 2010 | Ally Zimmerman | Zimmerman family | Ally's Law (2010) against distracted driving |
| 2010 | Josh Wilkerson | Laura Wilkerson | Enforce The Law, Angel Moms |
| 2010 | Tyler Clementi | Jane and Joseph Clementi | Tyler Clementi Foundation, against bullying |
| 2014 | James W. Foley | Diane Foley | James Foley Foundation, hostages advocacy |
| 2014 | Peter Kassig | Edward, Paula Kassig | Peter Kassig Foundation |
| 2015 | Kayla Mueller | Carl and Marsha Mueller | Kayla's Hands, global humanitarian work |
| 2015 | Kate Steinle | Jim Steinle | Kate's Law, illegal alien killers |
| 2016 | Taylor Force | Force family | Taylor Force Act, stops US aid to overseas terrorists |

## Homicide Anguish

What can be more traumatic than suddenly losing a loved one to homicide? "It is an event for which no one can adequately prepare, but which leaves in its wake tremendous emotional pain and upheaval" (Tischendorf, 2015, p. 167). As one survivor said, "I didn't want it to take over my life but it has. When they murder your loved one, they murder you" (Collins, 2008). The term "homicide survivors" may seem contradictory but accurately refers to those left behind to mourn the devastating loss of their loved one (Torch, 2006).

To clarify, the victim of a homicide is first and foremost the deceased, yet as Hertz, Prothrow-Smith, and Chery (2005) write, "there are two categories of victims in every homicide, however: the direct victims who are murdered and the associated victims who are the surviving family, friends, and loved ones, the survivors." These associated victims, or homicide survivors, are often overlooked, yet homicide survivorship is qualitatively different from survivorship of other violent crimes (Hertz et al., 2005). Although homicide grief responses have similarities to victims of other crimes, the deliberate and malicious death at the hands of a perpetrator is a circumstance unique to homicide survivors. After a homicide, survivors typically find themselves "entangled in a complex web of emotions and reactions" ("Grief: Coping with the Death of a Loved One," 1999). The death of a loved one is "sudden, violent, incomprehensible," and the effects of loss are "articulated through the practice of grief" (Network of Victim Assistance [NOVA], 2016). The founders of Parents Of Murdered Children explain that the "grief caused by murder does not follow a predictable course. It does not neatly unfold in stages" (Canadian Resource Centre for Victims of Crime [CRCVC], 2005, p. 1). "When a loved one's life is deliberately and maliciously taken, survivors have had no time to prepare emotionally for the loss or feel anticipatory grief" (CRCVC, 2005, p. 1). Their mourning does not follow the well-known five stages of grief outlined by Dr. Elisabeth Kübler-Ross in her 1969 book, *On Death and Dying*.

Hertz et al. (2005) proposed five central reasons why homicide survivors have a unique grief experience: first, homicides are often highly publicized and expose survivors to intrusive media coverage; second, the perpetrator may be a friend or family member, which strains social support; third, survivors may have increased fear of retaliation or further violent crimes toward their loved ones; fourth, the anger following a homicide might include overwhelming revenge fantasies; and fifth, that grief is complicated by involvement with the criminal justice system. As one survivor recalls, "the wounds keep being reopened. There is no chance to heal or move on. A state of limbo exists. Lawyers, courts, judges, and a live criminal blessed with civil rights control your life" (CRCVC, 2005, p. 12). Notably, in some cases, a perpetrator is not found, further compounding a lack of justice and deepening a survivor's anguish (King, 2004).

According to the Network of Victim Assistance, "factors which may complicate the grieving process for homicide survivors have to do with the ongoing exposure they have to homicide-related material – such as autopsy reports, crime scene photos, repairing or cleaning up the crime scene, trying to obtain the victim's personal effects (which may have been held as evidence), and other potentially trauma-inducing events" (2016). Redmond (1989) also noted other factors that contribute to homicide survivors' grief, including "the ages of the survivor and the victim at the time of the homicide; the survivors' physical and/or emotional state before the murder; their prior history of trauma; the way in which their loved one died; and whether or not the survivor has, and can make use of, social support systems" (p. 45). Therefore, dealing with the aftermath of a homicide is a process unique to each survivor; grief is a lasting consequence of traumatic ordeals that provokes reactions such as anger, guilt, isolation, and powerlessness (Zinzow, Rheingold, Hawkins, Saunders, & Kilpatrick, 2009; Justice for Homicide Victims, 2014).

## Homicide Activism

Back in the 1980s, when lecturing about his pioneering classic, *Victims of Crime* (Bard & Sangrey, 1979), forensic psychologist Morton Bard often noted that all crime victims are faced with a choice – to remain victimized or to somehow transform their tragedy into a growth experience. (Psychoanalysts like Bard saw this as an example "sublimation" – the ego's transformation of negative into positive energy.) Bard found this was especially true of homicide survivors that he interviewed. It is natural for homicide survivors to feel so much anguish and rage – at society, the criminal justice system, religious figures, and the offender – that emotions can be frightening. Yet Bard found surprisingly many survivors somehow found relief from their intense anguish and rage by transforming this into intense activism. Bard noted how it is too easy for us to see the anguish and overlook the activism. In fact, one is hard-put to find any published research on posthomicide activism (Graham, 2008). But in the 35 years since Bard and Sangrey's book appeared in 1979, we can now see a clear and ample evidence, in a series of powerful examples of "homicide activists" who transformed society, as noted in Table 6.1.

Homicide activism can be defined here as a redirection of a survivor's anguish and rage into a positive energy intended to create beneficial social change and give some meaning to their loved one's meaningless death. In proportion to their affection for their lost loved ones, the survivors somehow draw on the energy of their lost loved one, to create changes they feel would have benefitted that person and can now benefit others like him/her. These survivors draw strength from the loved one they lost and feel righteous as they refuse to take "no" for an answer in their determination to transform society to reduce future victimizations.

Tom McDermott found this by speaking at schools, conferences, and public hearings where he "transferred his hatred, bitterness and white hot anger into something positive" (Reno, Fisher, Robinson, Brennan, & Turman, 1998, p. 14). Survivors often "transcend [their] personal grievance against the perpetrator [and]... connect the fate of others to their own. Thus, in addition to wanting the individual offender brought to justice, they might work to ensure that victims are given the support they need or to fight the social conditions that may have contributed to the crime" (Reno et al., 1998, p. 14). The pursuit of justice serves a dual purpose, both to alleviate individual suffering and to address the broader impact of the crime (Reno et al., 1998). For example, Candy Lightner started Mothers Against Drunk Driving (MADD) 4 days after the tragedy that ended her daughter Cari's life on May 3, 1980. She was told that this repeat offender, although he had been caught, would likely receive no time in jail for the crime. Enraged at this injustice, Candy recalls, "I promised myself on the day of Cari's death that I would fight to make this needless homicide count for something positive in the years ahead" (Martin, 1994, p. 75). Now, four decades later, her efforts have forced society in general and courts in particular to recognize impaired driving as a serious felony – as this homicide activist powerfully transformed her anger into constructive social action.

One parent says he learned to release his rage because he did not want the memory of his beloved son to be marred by anger. His love for his son was what he wanted to hold onto more than anything else. He shares that his outlook on life has also changed: "I don't dislike people anymore. I don't have the energy for it. Losing my son helped me see the beauty in life" (Collins, 2008).

"Some homicide survivors experience intense guilt, as if they somehow could have stopped the tragedy, or they may have unresolved conflict with the deceased" (CRCVC, 2005, p. 4). Guilt additionally sets in when, at some point, survivors begin to make new decisions and lifestyle changes that are different than when their loved one was still alive. Family members may wonder if they are being "disloyal to their relationship with the deceased" (NOVA, 2016). Activism as related to the homicide victim suppresses these feelings of guilt; the survivors feel that even though they are moving on with their lives, their loved one is still immensely valued and has not been forgotten (Reno et al., 1998). In this way, survivors build a new life dedicated to the memory of their loved one. They continue living because they can, and even more so, because their loved one cannot.

It is common for homicide survivors to feel like outcasts from society ("Grief: Coping with the Death of a Loved One," 1999). It is difficult, if not impossible, for others to fathom what they are going through, and social relationships are further strained if the perpetrator was a friend or family member. People often distance themselves from tragedy, leaving the survivors feeling alienated and without vital social support (Bostrom, 1998). One way to regain social connection is through activism and advocating a particular cause. Dennis and Judy Shepard, for example, found support from their community when they started the Matthew Shepard Foundation for their son after he was brutally murdered in October of 1998 (Matthew Shepard Foundation, 2014). Maureen Kanka, a mother who fought for new legislation, says that her deceased daughter Megan became "everybody's child, a poignant symbol of the obligation that each of us has to make sure that children are safe in their own community" (Megan Nicole Kanka Foundation, 2014). Community involvement can help overcome feelings of isolation and loneliness. The process of reestablishing ties with others, confronting and overcoming challenges, striving for justice, and giving back to the community provides immense benefits (Reno et al., 1998).

## *Reconnecting Is a Balm for Trauma Recovery*

Homicide survivors cannot easily relate to those who have not faced a similar tragedy, so support groups specific to homicide survivors are an effective means of gradually achieving social involvement (CRCVC, 2005, p.17). Participation in a group enables survivors to validate their grieving processes and minimize feelings of isolation. The members of homicide survivor groups are highly diverse ages and backgrounds, but they all share a commonality: they are loved ones left behind from a murder, not by any fault of their own, but by a tragic circumstance (NOVA, 2016). There is a unique understanding that facilitates sharing and allows them to appreciate that others are experiencing and coping with the same complexity and depth of emotions (NOVA, 2016). Through providing and receiving support, survivors begin to heal and are motivated to continue and expand upon helping others. Such was the case for Robert and Charlotte Hullinger. After their daughter Lisa was murdered in 1978, they held the first meeting of Parents Of Murdered Children right at their home. With a "humble beginning of five parents, including themselves, the Hullingers' determination to survive and to help others survive soon grew into a national organization" and today, Parents Of Murdered Children has over 100,000 members (Parents of Murdered Children, n.d.). See also MADD, Mothers Against Drunk Driving (2014).

Individuals may find ways to reconnect with others while regaining their internal sense of power. Davidson and Doka (1998) explain, "murder is a violation of everything we have been taught to be right, honest, fair, or expected in life" (p. 59). The New Mexico Survivors of Homicide (2014) asserts, "the murderer violates the fundamental right to life; the criminal justice system violates the survivors' right to information about the crime; and the media violate the survivors' right to privacy. Homicide survivors report more feelings of abandonment, loss of control, and powerlessness in greater frequency, intensity, and duration than any other bereaved group. This is even more exaggerated when the murderer is not identified and there is no sense of closure to the death." To regain a sense of power, homicide survivors often become more active and productive members of society. They may work to assist other survivors, become more active participants in the criminal justice system, lobby for victims' rights, advocate for tougher laws, or write letters to the parole board so that the offender is not released (Reno et al., 1998). Brian Giesing, whose son and stepson were murdered in May 2006, actively advocates for tougher gun laws. "If I could save one person from having to sit in this [court] room," he says, "it would all have been worthwhile" (Collins, 2008). Homicide survivors regain a sense of control when they find that they are capable of affecting social or legislative change.

Similarly, homicide survivors search for some sense of validation; they need to know that their loved one's life had meaning and purpose. This pursuit is further compounded when the addition of cruelty to a loved one's death escalates the loss and sorrow with feelings of injustice, as well as if the victim is survived by parents or grandparents, and the expected sequence of life is destroyed. Donna Norris calls the Amber Alert system "the right legacy" for her daughter, Amber Hagerman. "It feels good when some child is brought home and our baby helped. You just look up to heaven and say, 'You did it again, baby.'" Donna also says she can "take solace in her legacy" (Krajicek, 2010). Likewise, John and Reve Walsh were devastated when their beloved 6-year-old son Adam disappeared on July 27, 1981, and was soon found murdered and decapitated. But the Walsh's rose up to pursue legislative change after their son Adam was kidnapped and murdered. The Adam Walsh Protection and Safety Act, signed on July 27, 2006, commemorates the worst day of their lives but also brings hope to families seeking justice (America's Most Wanted, n.d.). As of August 2014, John Walsh's activism through his TV programs, including America's Most Wanted, has resulted in the capture of over 1200 fugitives (America's Most Wanted, n.d.).

Another powerful example of this phenomenon of homicide activism is the tragic terrorist crash of Pan Am Flight 103 over Lockerbie Scotland on December 21, 1998. Many of these 259 victims of terrorism were Syracuse University students returning from Europe to their families for Christmas holidays. These families quickly and powerfully organized a corporation to take diplomatic as well as legal action. By their count, "400 parents lost a son or a daughter, 46 parents lost their only child, 65 women were widowed, 11 men lost their wives, 140 children lost a parent, and 7 children lost both parents" (Victims of Pan Am Flight 103, Inc., 2014). These outraged parents and families became a righteous force that literally forced scores of reluctant officials in several governments to identify and apprehend Libyan terrorist Abdel Basset Ali al-Megrahi, who was successfully extradited, convicted, and imprisoned for his crime.

Following the 9–11 terrorist attack on New York City on September 11, 2001, no fewer than 20 self-help or activist groups formed to change society for the better. One of these is the annual Tunnel to Towers Foundation (T2T) organized by the family of intrepid firefighter Stephen Siller, who perished after selflessly running alone from Brooklyn to Manhattan, to help his colleagues cope with the massive tragedy they faced that Tuesday morning (Tunnel to Towers Foundation, 2014).

As with any tragedy, an individual's faith is tried. Some turn to God or a Higher Power for comfort and inspiration. One example of this is Azim Khamisa, who "carries his inspirational message of forgiveness, peace and hope into a world in desperate need of each" (Khamisa, 2014). After his son Tariq was murdered in 1995, Azim established the Tariq Khamisa Foundation (www.TKF.org) in order to spread a message of love and forgiveness. This "forgiveness movement" has reached millions of people through Azim's advocacy. Azim engages through public speaking, workshops, and video and audio recordings and has four published books, including the award-winning *From Murder to Forgiveness: A Father's Journey* (2012).

The same faith affirmation is clear with UCLA Professor Judea Pearl, the father of beheaded *Wall Street Journal* reporter Daniel Pearl. Judea's family co-founded the Daniel Pearl Foundation in February 2002, "to continue Daniel's life-work of dialogue and understanding, and to address the root causes of his tragedy" (Daniel Pearl Foundation, 2014). Pearl's family heeded the Biblical injunction, "Do not be overcome by evil, but overcome evil with good" (Romans 12:21). The Foundation now provides scholarships to Moslem and other journalists. Judea and Ruth Pearl co-edited the inspiring, award-winning volume based on their beloved son's final three words before his beheading, *I am Jewish: Personal reflections inspired by the last words of Daniel Pearl* (Pearl & Pearl, 2004). In August 2014, when US journalist Jim Foley was beheaded by Islamic State in Iraq/Syria (ISIS) fanatics in Iraq,

Jim's father John Foley immediately joined US President Barrack Obama, to pledge whatever he could do to further his son's passion "to promote peace in that troubled region" (Landay, 2014).

## Other Perspectives on Homicide Activism

Many homicide survivors experience symptoms of posttraumatic stress disorder. In fact, 29% reported behavioral changes such as insomnia, hyperarousal, reoccurring dreams, and emotional numbness, all consistent with standard PTSD characteristics (Davidson & Foa, 1993, p. 27). Although therapy may be the most effective and beneficial means to dealing with PTSD, activism may also provide relief. Hypervigilance, for example, might contribute to a homicide survivor's zeal and emphatic pursuit of justice.

On the other hand, "some victims of crime, though able to lead normal lives, may never feel prepared to deal with the pain of others or the frustrations of advocacy efforts" and moreover, "advocating for legislative reform or helping others before coming to terms with their own trauma may impede some victims' recovery" (Reno et al., 1998, p. 19). Advocacy is not a necessary part of the trauma recovery process, and therefore could be provided as an option for those who chose to get involved (Reno et al., 1998, p. 19).

In addition to the frustrations of advocacy, Reno et al. (1998) recognize how "certain types of activism may cause victims to feel exploited, potentially re-victimizing them and setting back their recovery. For example, some victims who have spoken out through television and other news media feel that they have been taken advantage of—that their messages were misrepresented or their words cut or edited to alter their meaning. In an attempt to make a story more compelling, some journalists recast victim activists' identities, portraying them as powerless and piti-able rather than empowered and brave" (p. 20). Media interactions should be care-fully considered by survivors who tell their story.

## Conclusion

Homicides are as life-altering for survivors as they are life-ending for victims (Collins, 2008). Survivors must, in their own time, come to accept that life can and does go on. "Survivors face a long period of emotional struggle to reconstruct a devastated life. Most survivors feel that they never recover from the impact of the murder, but many still report reconstructing their lives to create some positive mean-ing out of their tragedy" (VCVS, 2000). As survivor David Sunshine said, "you try to rebuild your life on a scorched landscape. You can feel so completely alone. There's no more life the way it was. You just do the best you can with what's left"

(Collins, 2008). Survivors must redefine who they are as their whole lives change, and activism helps homicide survivors build a new future while still maintaining concentration on the memory of their loved one. In this way, homicide survivors reconstruct a new life without their loved one, but only in a way where they feel the loved one is still with them. "The mourner must somehow find a place for their loved one within their emotional life which can, at the same time, permit them to go on in the world" (NOVA, 2016). This is likely the final stage of healing for homicide survivors, yet even if accomplished, the scars of trauma never fade.

While homicide survivors often consume themselves in activities in memory of their loved one to help cope with and overcome their tremendous emotional pain, the toll that homicide extracts is vast and profound. Outstanding survivors have gone on from their overwhelming sorrow to regain a sense of power through advocating victims' rights issues, sentencing laws, and supporting new legislation. Although positive social reforms have been achieved by intractable homicide survivors, the losses are nonetheless devastating. No amount of justice, compassion, restitution, or prayer will ever bring a loved one back. Although "the law seeks to give opportunity to close this chapter of their lives, the pain of their loss lives on, and always will" (America's Most Wanted, n.d.). At the same time, society is no longer the same because of the heroic energies of homicide activists who have rechanneled their anguish and rage into positive changes that will lessen the number of future victims of crime and homicide.

Since 1979, much evidence has now emerged to support Morton Bard's early observations about crime victims and what we can now recognize as homicide activism. This includes the many social changes that would never have occurred, if not for dynamic homicide survivors bent on inserting some "meaning" into the meaningless death of their loved one. For victimologists, therapists, and behavioral scientists among us, more qualitative and quantitative research is useful, on two levels: (1) To better understand the complex psychic dynamics of this phenomenon of homicide activism, and (2) to learn what clinical applications this might offer in the healthy readjustment of crime victims in general.

## Questions/Activities for Further Exploration

1. How common is homicide activism among thousands of families that lost a loved one to criminal violence?
2. Why do some survivors become activists, while most do not?
3. Is activism therapeutic? How often does it become dysfunctional?
4. When people suffer a loss, can a self-help group or course on homicide activism be helpful?
5. How do traditional theorists explain homicide activism – Freud (sublimation) and Jung and Adler (will to perfection) – behaviorism, and self-psychology?
6. Is homicide activism a global phenomenon?
7. How would U.S. society be different if it were not for these 40+ homicide activists?

# References

America's Most Wanted. (n.d.). *About John Walsh*. Retrieved from http://www.amw.com/?home=1

Bard, M., & Sangrey, D. (1979). *The crime victim's book*. New York, NY: Basic Books.

Bostrom, S. (1998). Dealing with insensitivity. *Survivors of Homicide Newsletter*. Retrieved from www.azhomicidesurvivors.org

Canadian Resource Centre for Victims of Crime. (2005). *Homicide survivors – dealing with grief*. Retrieved from http://crcvc.ca/en

Collins, D. (2008, November 2). Ground zero for grief and healing. *The Day*. Retrieved from http://www.theday.com/article/20081102/DAYARC/311029879

Daniel Pearl Foundation (2014). *Our mission*. Retrieved from http://www.danielpearl.org/

Davidson, J., & Doka, K. J. (1998). *Living with grief: Who we are, how we grieve*. Abingdon, UK: Routledge.

Davidson, J. R., & Foa, E. B. (1993). *Posttraumatic stress disorder: DSM-IV and beyond*. Washington, D.C.: American Psychiatric Press.

Graham, C. (2008). A call to action: Families of victims of homicide and their response to murder. Unpublished manuscript, Fordham University, New York, NY.

Grief: Coping with the Death of a Loved One. (1999). Retrieved from http://victimsofcrime.org/help-for-crime-victims/get-help-bulletins-for-crime-victims/grief-coping-with-the-death-of-a-loved-one

Hertz, M. F., Prothrow-Stith, D., & Chery, C. (2005). Homicide survivors: Research and practice implications. *American Journal of Preventive Medicine, 29*(5), 288. https://doi.org/10.1016/j.amepre.2005.08.027. Retrieved from http://www.sciencedirect.com

Justice for Homicide Victims. (2014). *Discover jhv*. Retrieved from http://www.justiceforhomicidevictims.net/index.html

Khamisa, A.N. (2014). *Man of forgiveness*. Retrieved from http://www.azimkhamisa.com/

King, K. (2004). It hurts so bad: Comparing grieving patterns of the families of murder victims with those of families of death row inmates. *Criminal Justice Policy Review, 15*(2), 193–211. https://doi.org/10.1177/0887403404263625

Krajicek, D. (2010, January 17). *The story behind the 'amber alert.'* Retrieved from http://www.annoyatorium.com/tm.aspx?m=351740

Kubler-Ross, E. (1969). *On death and dying*. London: Routledge.

Landay, J. S. (2014, August 19). *Journalist James Foley beheaded by Islamic State*. Retrieved from http://www.stripes.com/news/middle-east/journalist-james-foley-abducted-in-syria-beheaded-by-islamic-state-1.299050

Martin, M. W. (1994). *Virtuous giving: Philanthropy, voluntary service, and caring*. Bloomington, IN: Indiana University Press.

Matthew Shepard Foundation. (2014). *Embracing diversity*. Retrieved from http://www.matthewshepard.org/

Megan Nicole Kanka Foundation. (2014). *Our mission*. Retrieved from http://www.megannicolekankafoundation.org/mission.htm

Mothers Against Drunk Driving. (2014). *Cari Lightner's story* Retrieved from http://www.madd.org/

Network of Victim Assistance (2016). *Homicide*. Retrieved from http://www.novabucks.org/otherinformation/homicide/

New Mexico Survivors of Homicide, Inc. (2014). *Survivors of Homicide: Complications of bereavement*. Retrieved from http://www.nmsoh.org/complications_of_breavement.htm

Pearl, J., & Pearl, R. (2004). (Eds.). *I am Jewish: Personal reflections inspired by the last words of Daniel Pearl*. Woodstock, VT: Jewish Lights. Retrieved http://www.jewishlights.com/page/product/978-1-58023-259-3

Redmond, L. M. (1989). *Surviving: When someone you love was murdered: A professionals guide to group grief therapy for families & friends of murder victims*. Clearwater, FL: Psychological Consultation and Education Services.

Reno, J., Fisher, R. C., Robinson, L., Brennan, N., & Turman, K. M. (1998). *From pain to power: Crime victims take action.* Washington, D.C.: Office for Victims of Crime, U.S. Department of Justice. Retrieved from http://www.ncjrs.gov/ovc_archives/reports/fptp/fptp.pdf

Parents Of Murdered Children Inc. (n.d.). *History of POMC.* Cincinnati, OH. Retrieved from http://www.pomc.com

Tischendorf, J. (2015). *Unfair advantage (a murder in Oklahoma).* Place of publication not identified: J Tischendorf Services.

Torch, P. (2006, March 6). *Loss of a loved one.* Retrieved from http://www.murdersurvivors.com/index.html

Tunnel to Towers Foundation. (2014). *Our mission.* Retrieved from http://tunnel2towers.org/

"Uniform Crime Reporting (UCR) Program." Criminal Justice Information Services, Federal Bureau of Investigation, 10 Sept 2018. www.fbi.gov/services/cjis/ucr

Victims of Pan Am Flight 103, Inc. (2014). *Call for action.* Retrieved from https://www.victimsofpanamflight103.org/node/86

Violent Crime Victim Services. (2000). *Homicide facts.* Tacoma, WA. Retrieved from http://vcvs.org/index.php?nid=168122&s=hm

Zinzow, H., Rheingold, A. A., Hawkins, A., Saunders, B. E., & Kilpatrick, D. G. (2009). Losing a loved one to homicide: Prevalence and mental health correlates in a national sample of young adults. *Journal of Traumatic Stress, 22*(1), 20. https://doi.org/10.1002/jts.20377. Retrieved from http://www.ncbi.nlm.nih.gov/pmc/articles/PMC2829865/

# Chapter 7
# Cultural and Linguistic Issues in Assessing Trauma in a Forensic Context

**Rafael Art. Javier and Marko Lamela**

## Immigration and Its Trauma Contexts

Sociopolitical and socioeconomic instabilities in many countries of the world have created a tremendous influx of immigrants who are forced to flee their countries of origin in search of safer and more economically and politically predictable conditions (United Nations, 2017). We have evidence of this influx of immigrants engaged in desperate and dangerous journeys to seek asylum from many countries of Europe (from Italy, Spain, France, Germany, England, Greece, Turkey, Demark, Rumania, Hungry, Austria, Australia, etc.), the United States, and Latin and South America (like Columbia, Mexico, Brazil, Chile, and Argentina) (United Nations, 2017). In Europe, the influx of immigrants has been fueled by sectarian wars in countries like Afghanistan, Iraq, Libya, Lebanon, Yemen, Nigeria, etc. (Hammer, 2015; O'Malley, 2018), including the emergence of ISIL and Boko Haram in some of these countries. In Latin American, this influx is fueled by political and economic instabilities in Venezuela, Cuba, Haiti, Honduras, Nicaragua, Guatemala, El Salvador, and Mexico (Edwards et al., 2019; Rojas-Flores, Hwang Koo, & Vaughn, 2019). Another additional contributing factor for these latter countries is the threats coming from the proliferation of vicious gang activities which seems to operate with impunity, partly due to the high level of corruptions in the very institutions responsible for securing the safety of their citizens (Guillermoprieto, 2010; Rojas-Flores et al., 2019).

In the end, these individuals have decided that it was better to gamble into conditions with no guarantee of a successful outcome than to remain in places where they and/or their families were not safe and in constant threat of physical and/or psychological harm and even death. There are horrific stories reported by those individuals

R. A. Javier (✉) · M. Lamela
St. John's University, Office of Postgraduate Professional Development Programs,
Queens, NY, USA
e-mail: javierr@stjohns.edu; marko.lamela17@stjohns.edu

© Springer Nature Switzerland AG 2020
R. A. Javier et al. (eds.), *Assessing Trauma in Forensic Contexts*,
https://doi.org/10.1007/978-3-030-33106-1_7

lucky enough to have had a receptive country that have provided at least a temporary refuge (Edwards et al., 2019; Rojas-Flores et al., 2019). Stories of many who have lost their lives in the process have witnessed others who have lost their lives or, at the very least, have been victims of physical and sexual assaults, and psychological manipulation, after leaving everything known to them for a chance to have a better life, a paradoxical and ironic outcome to a reasonable dream (Keygnaert, Vettenburg, & Temmerman, 2012; Haskins, 2017; Pineteh & Muly, 2016).

These are the conditions that have been associated with the development of trauma with the resulting cognitive and emotional sequelae in those affected (American Psychiatric Association, 2013). These are the types of conditions affecting many of the immigrants also coming into the United States and Europe (United Nations, 2017; Zayas, 2015). To add complication to an already traumatic condition for these immigrants, the influx of immigrants has had a variety of responses in the host countries, from a welcoming and humanitarian approach (e.g., securing lodging and safe haven) to an increase of nationalistic and anti-immigrant responses (Scherer, Altman, & Miller, 2017; Walt, 2019), which have resulted in adding additional upheaval and uncertainty in the lives of these immigrants and their families (Buchanan, Abu-Rayya, Kashima, Paxton, & Sam, 2018; Halpern & McKibben, 2014; Sadeghi, 2019).

The success of anti-immigrant political platforms has led to a rise in right-wing nationalist parties in the European Union, countries such as the Philippines, Russia, Italy, Turkey, Hungary, France, and here in the United States, and the success of nationalist initiatives such as Brexit in the United Kingdom (Walt, 2019; Edwards et al., 2019; Scherer, Altman, & Miller, 2017).

There are many challenges created by the immigrant influx, from challenges to housing, education, health and mental health systems, to challenges to the court and justice systems, etc. It requires the host countries to prepare their citizens to absorb and incorporate these individuals by addressing their various needs. The negative anti-immigrant rhetoric currently influencing these services has managed to create a toxic environment for these individuals, many of whom find themselves detained and in deportation centers (Vick, 2018). The fear is that the immigrant influx is threatening the very heart and soul of these countries and how they have defined themselves. To assuage the tremendous anxiety verbalized by the most vocal critics in these countries, many have resorted to demonizing the immigrants as rapists, thieves, terrorists, drug addicts, child predators, and hardened criminals sent to destroy our families and countries. In the process, it has managed to trigger from those willing and ready to entertain such a view, the most primitive fears. Once these fears are unleashed, it makes possible the evolutionarily based responses guided by the need for self-preservation (well described by Solms & Trumbull, 2002) and provides the justification for the inhumane treatments received by the immigrants, including the separation of children from their parents (American Psychological Association [APA], 2018; Ayon, 2018; Ball, 2018; Gibbs, 2018). For many, such decisions have resulted in further compounding the trauma already experienced in the countries of origin. This condition is what has been referred to as "complicated trauma" (Ford & Courtois, 2009) which has been found to result in devastating cognitive and emotional consequences for the individuals affected

(Allen & Fonagy, 2017). These are the complications likely to be encountered by the forensic professional who is now asked to engage in assessing and/or providing services to this population. The fact that these individuals come from different cultural, linguistic, socioeconomic, and sociopolitical conditions presents a particular challenge to mental health and forensic professionals who are called to provide these services. The purpose of this chapter is to highlight and examine some of these challenges and offer some remedies/recommendations to ensure objective and as accurate as possible assessment outcomes. We examine the situation in the United States as an example of the issues to consider when providing services to immigrant population with a trauma history, which may also apply to situations in Europe and other parts of the world (Wells, Wells, & Lawsin, 2015).

## *Defining the Terms*

Before proceeding with our discussion, it is vital to define a few key terms most often used when referring to individuals with different cultural background (e.g., race, ethnicity, and culture). The importance of defining these terms stems from our concern to ensure an agreed-upon reference point regarding terminology in order to avoid confusion. For instance, race has several different definitions, ranging from physical, biologically based appearance (Rowe, 2002), to a social construct used to maintain established sociopolitical hierarchy (Clauss-Ehlers, Chiriboga, Hunter, Roysircar, & Tummala-Narra, 2019). Racial categories are often used to refer to the physical characteristics of an individual, but doing so, often fails to account for the considerable variation these labels encompass (Weiss & Rosenfeld, 2012).

   Some scholars suggest focusing instead on the term ethnicity because it emphasizes critical components or commonalities (such as values, customs, and traditions) that allow an individual to experience and organize a sense of identification, meaning, and belonging (Helms, Jerrigan, & Mascher, 2005; Markus, 2008). A number of these commonalities are developed in the context of one's culture, a term that refers to the behavioral and ideological norms that define a group's identity (Alarcon, 2009). Culture includes variables such as language, traditions, values, religious beliefs, moral thoughts and practices, gender and sexual orientation, socioeconomic status, economic philosophies, and realities imposed by technological advances (Alarcon, 2009). These different components have been referred to as the intersectionality of multiple identities (Greene, 2006) that influence the individual's overall psychological makeup and which create a tremendous challenge to the forensic professional when in the process of addressing a forensic question. Part of the challenge is created by the unconscious way the forensic professional negotiates his/her personal feelings or bias (unconsciously derived reaction toward the client) about their clients' multiple cultural and linguistic identities (Morris, Javier, & Herron, 2015). Sue and associates (2007) provide us with ample examples of ways our personal reactions may come into play when face-to-face with individuals whose multiple identities are different from ours (see Table 7.1). In this context, they identified several types of microaggressions (e.g., microassault, microinsult,

**Table 7.1** Instances of microaggressions

| Extension of the nine categories of microaggression themes Initially identified by Sue and associates (2007) |
| --- |
| • *Alien in one's own land*: Relate to culturally/linguistic different clients emphasizing that "you speak with an accent" or being asked "where are you from?" |
| • *Ascription of intelligence*: Thinking/making statements suggesting that the client's cultural group is intellectually inferior: "You are a credit to your group or race," or "I am impressed, I did not expect that you will know that, considering where you come from." "How is that you have not learned English?" |
| • *Color blindness*: In an attempt to appear fair, the examiner may think/communicate to the client that "I don't see color/race when I see you." |
| • *Criminality/assumption of criminal status*: Not recognizing the traumatic effect of being made to feel like a criminal when the client relates stories of going to stores or walking in the street and being followed or stopped by the police as part of the "Stop-and-frisk." "You are too sensitive," "You look different…it is reasonable/not surprising for someone to be suspicious." |
| • *Denial of individual racism/classism*: Making comments to communicate open-mindedness… "We are all the same in the eyes of God"; "I am not a racist or a bigot, I have good friends who look like you." |
| • *Myth of meritocracy*: Telling the client that "In the end, anyone who works hard can succeed in this society." |
| • *Pathologizing cultural values/communication styles*: Saying to the client that what they describe sounds "weird" or "Do all your people tend to be so loud when having a normal conversation?" |
| • *Second-class status*: A person of color being mistaken for a service worker. |
| • *Environmental invalidation*: Overabundance of liquor stores/overcrowded schools in community of colors. |

and microinvalidation) that can seriously derail the objectivity of the evaluation and reflect negative bias toward the client.

Another critical term to consider is "acculturation," which reflects the extent to which the client is assimilated into a new cultural and linguistic context. It refers to the degree to which the individual adopts the customs and linguistic characteristics of the host society (Dana, 1996). From our perspective, we will use acculturation to include assimilation to the host society, familiarity with cultural norms of the host country, length of time spent in the new culture, and the fluency with the host culture and language (Weiss & Rosenfeld, 2012).

One final interrelated term to consider is the concept of bilingualism. An individual is defined as bilingual when he/she knows and uses more than one language to communicate (Bialystok, Craik, & Luk, 2008; 2012; Grosjean, 2010; Javier, 2007), the nature and quality of which requires different levels of cultural and linguistic proficiencies. This is an important consideration, in view of what forensic psychologists are likely to encounter when examining individuals who are coming from different cultural and linguistic contexts with various degrees of linguistic proficiency in the language of the host country. In many of these situations, the concept of bilingualism may not apply because the client may have little, if any, knowledge of the language of the host country. We will resume this discussion later in the chapter under the section on the "Role of Culture and Language in the Development and Presentation of Emotions."

## Challenges in the Assessment of Culturally and Linguistically Diverse Individuals

The ubiquitousness of cultural and linguistic factors in a person's overall functioning has been found to impact on every aspect of the assessment process, beginning during the initial contact with the client (Javier & Herron, 1998; Malgady & Costantino, 1998; Weiss & Rosenfeld, 2012). Concerned with this impact, Richard Dana (1993) put together an important volume dedicated specifically to delineating and identifying those very factors in psychological services that are still relevant today. He explored a series of unique aspects to consider when treating and evaluating clients coming from African-American, Asian, Hispanic, and Native Americans cultures, particularly the different components of worldviews that guide the behavior of individuals from these different cultural and linguistic backgrounds. The 2013 second edition compendium edited by Paniagua and Yamada should also be considered for its comprehensiveness of cultural influences in the development of multisectionality of identities in various cultural groups. West (2018), El-Jamil and Abi-Hashem (2018), and Clauss-Ehlers, Millan, and Zhao (2018) most recently also explored and expanded further many of the general themes identified by Dana and by Paniagua and Yamada, particularly with Arab-Middle Easterners (El-Jamil & Abi-Hashem, 2018). An important consideration to keep in mind that emerges from these explorations is moderator variables in the different cultural and linguistic groups related to "Emic" (culturally indigenous and idiographic) and "Etic" (universal, nomothetic, and cross-culturally comparable) perspectives that are likely to be operating during the assessment (Draguns, 1998, 1999). For example, while in some cultures a handshake may be appropriate for a first greeting, in others it may not. Eye contact may be seen as a typical way to communicate attention to and by a client in some cultures; in others, it may be seen as a threat, sign of untrustworthiness, or lack of respect. This was the case of a client hospitalized in an inpatient unit who in the midst of a psychotic decompensation decided to divest herself of all her clothing and now was standing star naked in the middle of the community room with the rest of the other psychiatric patients. When approached by the unit supervisor, she remained where she was standing but now with her eyes downcast as if embarrassed for being approached by someone in authority. The supervisor attempted to make eye contact with the patient and even asked her to look at him, only to be responded to with further evasive moves to avoid connecting with the eyes of the supervisor while saying "I am not supposed to look you in your eyes… it would be disrespectful." She was referring to her culturally ingrained behavioral expectation of how to deal with a person in authority that was part of her self-definition and was guiding her behavior even in the midst of a psychotic break.

It is clear from this example the importance of considering the pervasiveness of culture throughout the assessment process but particularly to be explored during the initial encounter/interview with the client. We need to consider, in this context, the specific ways the client's cultural identity is interwoven in his/her developmental history (Lu, Lim, & Mezzich, 1995); that includes consideration of the client's country of origin, family structure, customs, values, beliefs, and attitudes toward medicine and psychology. It also includes consideration of the linguistic and cultural contexts, as well as educational and social developments during the client's crucial developmental history (see Table 7.2). In the end, the forensic evaluation should consider the client's level of acculturation at the time of the examination because it will determine the extent to which the tools (tests) selected for the evaluation are linguistically and culturally appropriate. In the case of a recent immigrant client, there is an additional consideration of how to best assess the possible trauma history related to separation, losses, alienation, displacements, or disappoints, domestic and gang violence exposure, etc. (Lu et al., 1995; Weiss & Rosenfeld, 2012), which may be implicated in the decision to immigrate.

There are specific cultural factors that may make it difficult for the professional to elicit symptoms or understand their cultural significance (Lu et al., 1995). Both culture and society are involved in shaping the meanings and expressions people give to their various emotions and can determine which symptoms or signs are normal or abnormal, help define what comprises illness, and shape the illness behavior and help-seeking behavior (Kirmayer & Ryder, 2016; Lu et al., 1995; Wells et al., 2015). Culture can play a significant role as a trigger of psychopathology (pathogenic role) and/or as a buffer (resilience) against challenging conditions and thus can contribute to higher or lower levels of severity of psychiatric symptoms (Alarcon, 2009). It can represent a unique expression of clinical symptoms,

**Table 7.2** Brief assessment guide questions

**List of possible areas to inquiry during assessment**
*Questions regarding basic medical/developmental history*:
  *When did the assessee reach the basic developmental milestones (i.e., walking, language, toilet training, etc.)? This is particularly important in children.*
  *Was there any history of trauma, illnesses, etc. that could have affected the subject's cognitive and linguistic development? Is there a history of lead intoxication and other contaminants, prenatal substance abuse, exposure to domestic violence and child abuse, terrorism, bullying, etc.? Again, this is particularly important in children.*
*General questions:*
  *What level of education, level of cognitive/scholastic achievement proficiency did the subject reach in the native language?*
  *In what language and cultural context did the subject have the early schooling?*
  *What level of professional accomplishment did the subject reach in the country of origin?*
  *At what age did the subject learn the second language?*
  *How long has the subject been in the linguistic/cultural context of the language of the evaluation?*
  *What level of proficiency has the subject reached in the second language in*
    *speaking?*
    *reading?*
    *writing?*
    *thinking?*
  *What language does the subject use now for intellectual/school-related material?*
  *In what language does the subject dream?*
  *What language does the subject prefer when upset or dealing with emotions?*

reflecting the general themes of the period in which the illness occurs, as well as culturally idiosyncratic manifestations in these individuals' behavioral repertoire.

Cultural factors may also affect how the client relates to the professional. There is evidence that some cultures may be more open to relying on the professional for help and thus be more forthcoming due to their higher cultural value bestowed in that community to communicating one's psychological anguish and questions to professionals (Langman, 1997; Mojaverian, Hasimoto, & Kim, 2013). This is in contrast to other cultures, such as some western cultures, where independence is valued and reliance on others may be construed as a weakness (Langman, 1997). This sort of contrast is likely to affect and determine the strategies that a professional would need to use in order to complete the assessment successfully.

A culturally competent (or intelligent) forensic professional should be cognizant of how various cultural factors may influence the assessment and describes not just that the identified disorder goes against cultural norms but explains how it does (Lu et al., 1995) and what harm, if any, can be adjudicated in relationship to the specific events (e.g., a physical assault, sexual harassment, employment discrimination, etc.) being examined. The challenge in forensic cases is how best to assess the extent of a psychological harm (e.g., trauma) following these events when there are so many factors to consider (including cultural and linguistic factors, as well as those related to intersectionality, etc.) that can shape the way those being evaluated process and communicate their personal response to these events. Wells et al. (2015) suggested, in this regard, that we should be careful in how we go about gathering our evidence of the presence or absence of psychological disorders from someone coming from a diverse cultural and linguistic context. According to these authors, these individuals may or may not endorse the relevant items of the PTSD scales or the Beck Depression Inventory (BDI) but may still be suffering from a trauma or depression. Another possibility is that individuals may be diagnosed with PTSD and/or depressive disorder based on the endorsement of these items, whose meanings and relevance have been taken out of their cultural/linguistic contexts. They reported evidence, in this regard, from a study by Nicolas and Whitt (2012) of Haitian women not identifying items in the BDI as expressions of distress, something that can be avoided by contextualizing the items (criterion validity), and taking into consideration the specific ways the impact of distress becomes evident in these individuals' cultural contexts (e.g., by emphasizing somatic symptoms).

## *Role of Culture and Language in the Development and Presentation of Emotions*

It is, therefore, vital for the professional to recognize common cultural-specific ways that individuals may experience, express, and cope with their feelings of distress (Desai & Chaturvedi, 2017; Durà-Vilà & Hodes, 2012; Kleinman, 1987, 1988; Nichter, 1981). To that point, it is important to identify the primary idioms of distress that the symptoms reflect, as well as the meaning and perceived severity of these symptoms in relation to the norms of the original culture of the client being assessed. In this context, it is also important to obtain information about the different local illness categories used by the individual's community to identify illness and distress, the perceived causes or explanatory models that the individual and members of the original culture use to explain illnesses in general, and their view and nature of past experiences with mental health professionals (Kleinman, 1987/1988; Maeda & Nathan, 1999; Rogler & Cortes, 1993; Schwartz, 2002; Singh, et al. 2016).

When trying to conceptualize culture-bound assessment, Lu and associates (1995) proposed two methods: The first is through the use of an "interpersonal grid," which assesses the client's worldview through a system variable. According to these authors, this can only be accomplished by including in the assessment information about demographics, status, affiliations, and the behaviors, expectations, and values associated with these factors. Such a consideration allows the professional to understand, contextualize, and interpret specific behavior within the individual's cultural meaning.

The second method is through the use of what they referred to as "a multicultural cube." The multicultural cube allows for the addition of multiple dimensions of "cultural identity development" process and how the culturally diverse individual sees himself/herself in respect to the host culture. According to Lu and associates, the least advanced level of cultural identity development is found in individuals engaged in blind acceptance or conformity or what they describe as a "compliant position." A more developed "dissonance position" is found in individuals who are in conflict with their cultural identity and that of society as a whole. When the individual is engaged in rejecting all of the new culture, a "resistance position" is thought to be at play. An individual can also progress into a "introspection position," where he/she comes to accept that both cultures, the original and new, can coexist but that the new culture is irrelevant. The final level is "integrative awareness," which finds the individual accepting both the best and worst parts of both cultures. Other scholars have described similar processes in reference to an individual's identity development when multidimensional aspects of one's experiences (multiple and overlapping components of identities) are involved and required to negotiate the resulting multisectionality of their identities (Baden & Steward, 2007; Greene, 2006; Grotevant, Dunbar, Kohler, & Esau, 2007).

Hinton and Kleinman (1990) offer a practical method with three basic rules that they found useful (and still relevant today) to develop a culturally appropriate approach in assessment of individuals from diverse populations. The first rule is to show empathy throughout the interview and then elicit the client's perspective on the illness. The second rule is to assess the client's experience in the context of the client's family, workplace, health-care systems, and community. The final rule is to diagnose the illness through both DSM categories and the client's cultural idioms of distress, such as *susto* or *ataque de nervios*. These authors seem to be following and emphasizing the gold standards for the most effective ways to conduct a clinical interview amply discussed by McWilliams (2004), Safran (2012), and Weiner and Bornstein (2009).

Alarcon (2009) makes similar recommendations to ensure adequate assessment of clients from culturally and linguistically diverse communities: The first is to make sure to include cultural variables, which contain specific information about language, religion and spirituality, migration history, level of acculturation, and other family dynamics, child-rearing practices, rituals, etc. The gathering of all these data is meant to provide information about modalities used in child-rearing practices, familial roles or hierarchies, the types of activities that instilled their values, eating habits, social interactions, and help-seeking behaviors. Professionals are then encouraged to direct their focus onto what Alarcon refers to as "pathoplastic factors" or the uniqueness of the symptom's expression. This is accomplished by comparing the different descriptions of symptoms provided by clients and relatives, the words and terms used, and the context in which these symptoms tend to emerge. Of particular importance to consider is how the environment affects the form of the symptoms. In the end, the cultural identity of the person, their ethnic and cultural reference groups, should take front and center in these assessments (Center for Substance Abuse Treatment, 2014). These elements should also include the differences in culture and social status between client and professional, as well as how these differences may affect the diagnosis and treatment process.

This information becomes particularly important when deciding the appropriateness of testing norms in the host country to be applied to clients from diverse communities. It requires determining the level of competency in the host language and in how they navigate the tasks of learning to live in the culture of the host country. According to Lu and associates (1995), this can be assessed by examining not only how many years the client has spent in the host culture, the age at immigration, and exposure to the host culture in their original culture but also how successful the client is in securing housing, employment, childcare, and mastery of the public transportation system, etc.

Another way to measure level of acculturation is to examine how the family relates in the new culture. Lee (1990) suggests several family patterns whose specific family dynamics tend to complicate the interaction among their members once immigrated to a different cultural and linguistic context. Lee suggests, in this context, that "traditional families" that were born and raised in their country of origin and only speak their native language at home, live in ethnic enclaves, or have a rural background may tend to approach their problems in a concrete and functional fashion. In the case of traditional families in which the children are better acculturated than their parents (Lee, 1990), an interesting phenomenon tends to develop; the parents are forced to remain dependent on their children to navigate the linguistic and cultural demands of the new environment. According to some findings, these sorts of families tend to present more parent-child conflicts, role confusion, and marital difficulties (Lee, 1990) as compared to more integrated families. Some findings have also highlighted that these types of families tend to suffer from conflict resulting from the dislodging of the parents' position of authority by their dependency on their children for linguistic and cultural translation (Lee, 1990). In the case of a "bicultural family" where parents are professionals or business owners and speak primarily English (Lee, 1990), parental authority tends to be more egalitarian as opposed to patriarchal; these families tend to live in suburban areas and are more stable than the previous family types.

## Issues in the Assessment of Trauma in Cultural Contexts

We will now discuss some of the culturally specific organizations to express distress that have been identified in various publications, with the understanding that our presentation is only meant to highlight this important phenomenon and not intended to compile and offer an extensive and complete list. We want to encourage those engaged in assessing the impact of traumatic experience in culturally and linguistically diverse populations to explore with their clients the specific and unique ways that are relevant to the client being assessed. This is guided by the fact that cultural factors are shown to influence the presentation of psychiatric disorders (Balhara, 2011; Fabrega, 1987), which then may complicate the forensic picture to be examined. These culture-specific conditions are better known as a "culture-bound syndrome" (CBS) and are a broad range of behavioral, affective, and cognitive manifestations that are seen in specific cultures (Balhara, 2011; Mehta, De, & Balachandran, 2009) (see Paniagua & Yamada, 2013 for other examples). They are recurrent and specific patterns of aberrant behavior and troubling experiences that may not be linked to any specific disorder. These sorts of behavior manifestations are atypical of others in their original culture and are seen both as a reflection and as a source of distress (Balhara, 2011).

Paniagua and Yamada (2013)'s recent book provides an extensive and thoughtful analysis of the multiple challenges likely to face the professional when assessing the linguistically and culturally diverse populations. These authors make particular reference to cultural-bound syndromes used to communicate personal reactions to difficult events in their environments. These are unique syndromes whose descriptions suggest strong reactions and discomfort that the individuals had difficulty handling and that these scripts or schemas provide a way to organize that reaction. Let's take a look at some of the most relevant syndromes related to trauma expression: "*Amok*" is a violent and aggressive outburst normally directed at people and/or object. It is found to be associated with syndromes such as amnesia, exhaustion, and persecutory ideas. It is normally found in Malaysians, Laotians, Filipinos, Polynesians, Padua, New Guineans, and Puerto Ricans. "*Boufée Délirante*," usually found in Haitians and people from West Africa, is described as "sudden outburst of aggression, or agitation associated with cognitive confusion, psychomotor excitement, and symptoms resembling a Brief Psychotic Disorder" (also including visual and auditory hallucinations and paranoid ideations) (p. 26). "*Pibloktoq*," normally found among Arctic and Subarctic Eskimos, is described as an emotional reaction characterized by excitement, coma, and convulsive seizures resembling a dissociative episode. While in the midst of that reaction, the individual may show the presence of "withdrawal, amnesia, irritability, irrational behaviors" (e.g., breaking furniture, eating feces, obscenities, etc.) (p. 27). "*Susto*" (also referred to as Pasmo, Espanto, and Miedo) is found among the Hispanic populations and is described as "general weaknesses resulting from frightening and startling experiences" (p. 28). A related reaction also found among the Hispanic populations is "*Ataque de Nervios*," also referred to as the "*Puerto Rican Syndrome*" (Ghali, 1982; Godoy, 1995; Moitra, Duarte-Velez, Lewis-Fernandez, Weisber & Keller, 2018). This condition is characterized by epileptic-like reactions, including attacks of crying, trembling, uncontrollable shouting, physical and verbal agitation, normally followed by a temporary loss of consciousness, particularly in situations of high emotional intensity. Two conditions found among African Americans are "*Falling-out*" and "*Brain Fag*." The first one is characterized by "seizure-like symptoms resulting from traumatic events" (p. 26) and hence bearing some resembling to the "*Ataque de Nervio*." The latter one is normally found among high school and university students struggling with school demands. It is characterized by concentration and thinking problems, head and neck pain, blurred vision, burning, and general somatic, somatoform, depressive, and anxiety disorders.

## *Language*

Language identifies and codifies an individual's experience, which cannot be translated from one language to another without some distortion (Lu et al., 1995). Due to the nature of culturally diverse patients sometimes speaking more than one language, it is important to determine the individual's primary language prior to the evaluation. That is because a bilingual individual may vary on aspects of second language (L2) proficiency, age of L2 acquisition and processing emotional words (Baum & Titone, 2014; Bialystok, Craik, & Luk, 2008; Chen, Lin, Chen, Lu, & Guo, 2015), degree of L2 proficiency and fluency (Francis, Tokowicz, & Kroll, 2014; Gollan, Starr, & Ferreira, 2015), and the context of L2 learning (de Bruin, Bak, & Della Sala, 2015; Green, 2011). In that context, the forensic professional is likely to encounter clients who are considered beginners of the language or what we refer to as "subordinate bilingual" (Diller, 1974). These types of clients are quite deficient in the second language and tend to process whatever is going on with them through the lens of their first language, although they may be using words and phrases in the second language in ways that appear that they understand more than it is actually the case. There is enough evidence of the possibility for serious inaccuracies in the assessment of these individuals, giving rise to different conclusions of the nature of the psychological difficulties, depending on the language of the assessment. For instance, psychiatric assessments in the second language resulted in much more severe diagnosis of psychopathology, as compared with the assessment in the first/native language, in a sample of subordinate bilinguals (Javier, 2007; Marcos, Urcuyo, Kesselman, & Alpert, 1973).

We may also encounter another type of client that seems to have more knowledge and proficiency in the second language, having learned the second language either while in their country of origin or during their years in the host country, but in a different context from the first language. These individuals may have developed a coordinate linguistic organization and, as such, could be considered "coordinate bilinguals" (Lambert, 1972; Javier, 2007). Depending on the level of proficiency, there are challenges likely to emerge in the assessment of these individuals as well. Some of these challenges have been amply discussed by Javier, Barroso, and Munoz

(1993); Javier (2007); and most recently by Itzhak, Vingron, Baum, and Titone (2017). It has also been highlighted in a series of research findings in our lab (Acevedo et al., 2017; Amrami, Lamela, Maskit, Bucci, & Javier, 2019) that assessed qualitative and quantitative differences in the communication of events, memory of events, emotional reactions, etc. in a sample of coordinate bilinguals. Our concern for this group is the assumption of accuracy in communication, particularly with regard to communicating emotionally laden material. There is some evidence that with material related to too strong emotions (likely to be the case with individuals with a history of early trauma related to experience prior to immigration), important details of the event may not be that clearly available in the language of the assessment (Javier, 1996/2007).

More concretely, if a client uses the more limited secondary language, he/she may not be able to present their history accurately. The client may lose the more vibrant aspects of communication such as humor, assertiveness, expressions of displeasure, frustration, love, and trauma. Lacking this richness may lead to misdiagnosis or misconceptualization of the case (Lu et al., 1995). This issue was eloquently examined most recently by Itzhak et al. (2017) in their examination of how proficiency, emotion, and personality in L2 can impact communication. According to these authors, the higher a bilingual individual's L2 proficiency, the more likely that he/she is able to get by on L2 (Itzhak et al., 2017), because higher L2 proficiency may mean that the individual may have a greater L2 vocabulary (Hellman, 2011) when compared with L1 (the person's first language). However, this bilingual may still lack the specific vocabulary needed to fully express himself/herself in different contexts. This may result in the individual attempting to communicate his/her message via gestures or through the swapping of words (Itzhak et al., 2017). High L2 can also mislead an assessor into thinking the individual has a greater understanding of what is being communicated to him/her than is actually the case. In this context, the authors reported the difficulty of Low L2 proficiency (subordinate) bilinguals to convey important details of their personal history or presenting problem; their overall demeanor was found to be guarded and deferent with the evaluator that added to the perception or misperception of these individuals' level of difficulties (Itzhak et al., 2017).

These authors also provided confirmation that processing and communication of emotional content are dependent on language as emotion is not always processed the same way across all languages (Itzhak et al., 2017). This is particularly the case with emotionally laden communication. For example, some studies have found that phrases such as "I love you," "shame on you," or swear words have a greater emotional response based on their L1 as compared to their L2 (Dewaele, 2004, 2008), a finding supported by a study using an objective measure (e.g., skin conductance) (Harris, Aycicegi, & Gleason, 2003). These findings suggest that L2 has a weaker link to basic emotions than does L1. However, these findings become complicated when the factors of L2 proficiency and age of L2 acquisition are considered. Some studies have found that weaker emotionality is related to L2 proficiency factors and showed a weaker effect of emotion in L2 compared to L1 (Harris et al., 2003; Segalowitz, Trofimovich, Gatbonton, & Sokolovskaya, 2008) when subjects showed less proficiency in L2. However, there are some studies that found similar levels of emotion processing in L1 and L2 when there is a higher L2 proficiency or earlier acquisition (Conrad, Reccio, & Jacobs, 2011; Eilola, Havelka, & Sharma, 2007; Ferre, Garcia, Fraga, Sanchez-Casas, & Molero, 2010; Sutton, Altarriba, Gianico, & Basnight-Brown, 2007). One explanation for these findings may stem from how different language patterns are used across emotionally charged social contexts (Altarriba, 2003, 2008; Caldwell-Harris, 2015; Harris, Gleasson, & Aycicegi, 2006). That means that a word needs to be experienced during a real-life emotionally charged situation (Segalowitz et al., 2008) to be bound to the language used in the experience; this finding was supported by an emotional processing advantage with positive words in L2 but not negative ones (Sheikh & Titone, 2016). Based on these findings, it is possible for two equally proficient L2 speakers to express and understand emotion in L2 differently based on the experiences they have had (Caldwell-Harris, 2015).

Presentation of personality may also be affected by the language that is used, with bilinguals appearing to switch personalities based on the language they use (Itzhak et al., 2017). In a 2006 study of this phenomenon, Pavlenko found that two main themes arose when bilinguals were asked open-ended questions about how they felt like when speaking different languages. The first theme that emerged in almost two thirds of bilinguals was a feeling of change in self-image. The second theme was of a feeling that the L1 reflected their true and natural personality, whereas L2 reflected an "artificial self." These findings were supported by a second study that found a consistent shift in the way bilinguals perceived aspects of their own personality across their languages (Dewaele & Nakano, 2013). Dewaele and Nakano (2013) found that bilinguals expressed being less logical, serious, and emotional while being more unauthentic when not using their L1. This finding can only be understood if we also consider the close interconnection of language and culture. Some studies have found that psychological personality tests have had different results based on modifications to test administration that reflected the assessee's respective culture and language (Chen & Bond, 2010; Ramirez-Esparza, Gosling, Benet-Martinez, Potter, & Pennebaker, 2006; Veltkamp, Recio, Jacobs, & Conrad, 2013).

A related issue is that bilinguals may alternate between both known languages throughout the day in different aspects of their lives depending on context (Itzhak et al., 2017), a phenomenon we refer to as "code switching" (Javier & Marcos, 1989). One example may be when the bilinguals use their learned language at work while using their native language (L1) at home. There are many factors involved in language switching that could be at play in a forensic evaluation, and hence, the reader is encouraged to keep in mind and explore the possible factors that may be involved when present in the assessment process. Code switching has been found to be triggered by uncomfortable and trauma-related emotions (Javier, 1996, 2007; Perez-Foster, 1996) and as expression of social status (Itzhak et al., 2017). Ultimately, our concern is the implications for the forensic practice.

These findings highlight the difficult challenge a forensic psychologist may face when evaluating these types of individuals using psychological tests considered the gold standards of the discipline. This is true even if the test is in the language of the person being evaluated and with test tools that have been supposedly normed with a culturally relevant sample. According to these findings, we are left with what we actually get in terms of assessing the nature and extent of trauma that may have been processed in one or both languages. The fact that there are different contents of experience between which code-switching operates reflects not only that these individuals have developed different context-specific registers that are now encapsulated in their languages but that relevant information needed for the full forensic assessment of the condition under consideration may not be easily accessible in the language of the assessment.

### Nonverbal

Another complication is related to the issue that communication is not just limited to verbal methods of communication, as it also includes nonverbal communication (Lu et al., 1995). Culturally influenced eye contact, touch, and forms of gesticulation as well as body language, facial expressivity, and grooming are all aspects that may provide important information to be considered in the forensic evaluation.

## Some Remarks on the Use of Tests/Questionnaires in Forensic Contexts

The nature of linguistic and cultural issues delineated earlier make clear the serious challenge faced by the forensic psychologists in using standardized test material. Even translating a construct, however faithfully, may interfere with its reliability or validity (Camino & Bravo, 1994; Javier, 2007; Javier, Vasquez, & Marcos, 1998). For an assessment to follow proper standards, all measures must be reliable and valid, and the interpretation should consider the individual and group differences (Haas, Boyes, Cheng, MacNeil, & Wirove, 2016). While APA standards for forensic assessment (January 2013) make it clear that we have an ethical responsibility to ensure that measures are used relatively unbiasedly and in a culturally sensitive manner (Haas et al., 2016), this continues to be a difficult challenge for the discipline when dealing with culturally and linguistically diverse populations and where there are no sufficient and adequately standardized measures available.

A significant concern in these types of assessments is that of test equivalence, as tests may vary between cultural groups, particularly the case with migrant and refugee populations (Davidson, Murray, & Schweitzer, 2010). Equivalence (or degree of comparability between measurement outcomes) is a function of test validity across different cultural groups. The validity of a test refers to the soundness and defensibility of the interpretation, projections, and application of test results and that the extent to which the same construct is being assessed (Haas et al., 2016). It requires a structural equivalence, the similarity of meaning, and dimensional organization of the psychological construct across different cultural groups. It is a measurement of equivalence or the similarity of both the item content and formal psychometric properties across cultural groups.

Test bias is another concern because it involves the existence of external sources of variance unrelated to the valid variance held by the construct of interest (Byrne et al., 2009). Test bias can exist in two forms, namely construct bias and item bias. Construct bias occurs when a test does not accurately measure an identical construct among different groups; when an issue with item content or formatting influences the individual's responses in unexpected or unintended ways, item bias is suspected to be at play (Geisinger, 2003; Matsumoto & van de Vijver, 2011).

Finally, Byrne et al. (2009) raised a serious concern with the issue of data interpretation, particularly when the individual findings are found to be nested within a culture. According to these authors, by ignoring the nested structure of cross-cultural data, a single-level focus occurs that creates interpretive errors at both the individual and group levels. This can create an unfortunate condition resulting in a failure to detect the cross-cultural validity of the data. Different constructs may be required to test individual- and group-level differences because there are not many constructs that are statistically level-invariant. Van de Vijver and Poortinga described this in their 2002 paper which found that the multitude of outcomes can be reduced into three possibilities in terms of suitability and unsuitability of individual- and country-level differences. The first occurs when items show a different, but meaningful clustering on the individual and country levels (van de Vijver & Poortinga, 2002). Some tests may find correlated factors within country but may show differences between countries. In these cases, different constructs would be needed to describe these sort of differences. The second possibility occurs when a meaningful structure only occurs on one level (van de Vijver & Poortinga, 2002). This can occur when either within-country or between-country data yield a theoretically expected structure, but the converse within-country or between-country data structure cannot be interpreted. This shows the unsuitability of such an instrument for cross-cultural comparison. The third is a full agreement of individual- and country-level solutions, which may occur after a few items have been omitted from the comparison (van de Vijver & Poortinga, 2002).

Several scholars have attempted to provide recommendations for the selection of test material that consider the client's level of acculturation and linguistic proficiency in the context of the specific cultural and linguistic demands of these tests. The "Bio-Ecological Assessment System or Bio-Cultural Model of Cognitive Functioning" suggested by Armour-Thomas and Gopaul-McNicol (1997) attempts to address that issue head on with the recommendation that all relevant information emerging from all sources about the individual's cognitive and emotional ability be meaningfully included in the assessment. Richard Dana's work (1993) on "Multicultural Assessment Perspectives for Professional Psychology" is worth mentioning in this regard as his work represents one of the earliest and most serious attempts to include concerns of the role of culture and language in psychological assessments. The work of Giuseppe Costantino and his colleagues (Costantino, Dana, & Malgady, 2007; Costantino, Malgady, & Rogler, 1985) is also worth mentioning because of the unique culturally specific approach to capture and assess emotional difficulties in culturally diverse populations. These authors contributed to the creation of Tell-Me-A-Story (TEMAS) test and CUENTO (Story Telling) therapy that allow the evaluator to examine the nature and quality of the psychological problems presented by individuals from culturally, ethnic, and racially diverse communities. In the case of TEMAS, they developed a series of cultural/ethnically and racially sensitive scenarios guided by the Murray's Thematic Apperception Test (1938) but now populated by cultural-racial-ethnic characters and the scenarios reflecting relevant real-life situations for these individuals. It has a more carefully designed scoring system that has been adopted with several cultural, ethnic, and linguistic groups in various parts of the world (Costantino et al., 2007). CUENTO therapy is a method of using culturally relevant material and heroes and/or important characters in the folklore of the target group to address different psychological difficulties the person may be suffering from. It allows the person to anchor his/her personal processing of the nature of the psychological problems within his/her culturally relevant contexts. It has been found to be effective in working with juvenile delinquent populations and trauma victims (Costantino et al., 1985).

The contribution by Flannigan, McGrew, and Ortiz (2000) is also worth consideration. Their extensive work offers very specific analysis/recommendations of the cultural and linguistic loadings in these tests. We have discussed this issue more fully in an earlier publication (Javier, 2007) and hence will only summarize it here. The most important point for our purpose is the need to consider a cross-battery approach to assessment where specific tests are selected based on the client's expected linguistic and cultural demands and ability to respond to them. They predict that clients who are deficient in the second language and are very low in acculturation are likely to do poorly in tests assessing verbal knowledge. Thus, they are likely to fail any test that requires the subject to have a high-to-moderate linguistic and cultural knowledge to do relatively well. From that perspective, they suggest that the following subtests should be selected based on these demands and the best conditions likely to offer the most accurate information about the individual's true cognitive ability:

- *High in linguistic and cultural demands*

  - Similarities
  - Vocabulary
  - Information
  - Comprehension (Listening/Oral/Verbal comprehension)

- *High in linguistic and moderate in cultural demands*

  - Incomplete words
  - Sound blending
  - Memory for words
  - Auditory attention
  - Decision speed

- *High in linguistic and low in cultural demands*

  - Concept formation
  - Analysis synthesis
  - Auditory working memory
  - Pair cancellation

- *Moderate in linguistic and high in cultural demands*

  - Oral vocabulary
  - Picture vocabulary

- *Moderate in linguistic and cultural demands*

  - Visual auditory learning
  - Delayed recall-visual auditory learning
  - Retrieval fluency
  - Rapid picture naming
  - Arithmetic

- *Moderate in linguistic and low in cultural demands*

  - Digit span

- *Low linguistic and moderate cultural demands*

  - Object assembly
  - Picture recognition
  - Visual closure

- *Low linguistic and cultural demands*

  - Geometric design

In the case of a recently emigrated individual or someone who has limited knowledge of the language/culture of the assessment tool used (e.g., subordinate bilingual), subtests that have low linguistic and cultural loadings will likely offer the best condition for the purpose of the evaluation.

The Bender Gestalt has also been suggested as a nonverbal cognitive functioning screener to assess visual maturity, visual motor and spatial-motor integration skills, visual memory, response style and reaction to frustration, ability to correct mistakes, planning and organizational skills, and motivation (Kaufman & Lichtenberger, 2001; Koppitz, 1975). The newly re-normed Bender Gestalt II has been found to have good psychometric properties (e.g., reliability, concurrent validity, criterion-group validity, and construct validity) (Campbell, Brown, Cavanagh, Vess, & Segall, 2008).

There are specific tests that have been suggested for the assessment of trauma in diverse populations. Although these tests have not necessarily being validated in forensic samples, most have been found to retain good statistical properties when translated and used in languages other than English with other linguistically and culturally different populations. Listed under this category are the Clinically Administered PTSD Scale for DSM-5 (CAPS-5), the PTSD Checklist for DSM-5

(PCL-5), the Life Event Check List, 5th edition (LEC-5), and Minnesota Multiphasic Personality Inventory-2 (MMPI-2).

Typically considered the gold standard of PTSD interviews, the CAPS-5 is a 30-item structured interview that can be used to make a current and lifetime diagnosis of PTSD and assess PTSD symptoms over the past week (Weathers et al., 2013a). The CAPS-5 examines the onset and duration of symptoms, subjective distress, impact of symptoms on social and occupational functioning, improvement in symptoms since past CAPS assessment, PTSD severity, and PTSD subtype along with the 20 DSM-5 PTSD symptoms. Previous versions of the CAPS had been translated into other languages such as Chinese, German, Swedish, and Bosnian with high levels of validity, reliability, and correlation to the original English version (Charney & Keane, 2007; Chu, 2004; Paunovic & Ost, 2005; Schnyder & Moergeli, 2002; Wu & Chan, 2004; Wu, Chan, & Yiu, 2008). Research is ongoing on the validity of the translated versions of the CAPS-5 with versions translated into Turkish and German showing high levels of validity (Boysan et al., 2017; Müller-Engelmann et al., 2018).

The PCL-5 is a 20-item self-report measure that assesses the 20 DSM-5 symptoms of PTSD (Weathers et al., 2013). The PCL-5 can be used as a way to monitor symptoms change during and after treatment, screening for PTSD, and making a tentative PTSD diagnosis. Previous versions of the PCL have been translated into other languages such as Chinese and Spanish and with high levels of validity, reliability, and correlation to the original English version (Marshall, 2004; Miles, Marshall, & Schell, 2008; Orlando & Marshall; Wu et al., 2008). Since the development of the latest version, research into the validity of translated versions are ongoing. Currently, studies show high levels of validity for versions in Arabic, certain Kurdish dialects, Brazilian Portuguese, and French (Ashbaugh, Houle-Johnson, Herbert, El-Hage, & Brunet, 2016; de Paulo Lima et al., 2016; Ibrahim, Ertl, Catani, Ismail, & Neuner, 2018).

The LEC-5 is a self-report measure designed to screen for potentially traumatic events in the assessee's lifetime (Weathers et al., 2013b). The LEC-5 accomplishes this by assessing exposure to 16 known life events that potentially result in PTSD or distress. Current studies have found that other languages, such as Korean or Brazilian Portuguese, have found high levels of reliability and validity of the LEC when translated (Bae, Kim, Koh, Kim, & Park, 2008; de Paulo Lima et al., 2016).

Finally, the MMPI-2 is a personality and psychopathology measure that consists of 567 self-report items that reflect 8 Validity Scales, 10 Clinical Scales, and 15 Content Scales (Butcher, Dahlstrom, Graham, Tellegen, & Kaemmer, 1989). These scales include measures that may relate to aspects of trauma such as depression, paranoia, anxiety, fears, obsessions, depression, demoralization, low positive, emotions, and more.

An issue to keep in mind with regard to framing the diagnosis of PTSD following a DSM-5 is that serious questions have been raised with regard to the possible accuracy of the diagnosis using the criteria delineated in the DSM-5 nomenclature. According to Allen and Fonagy (2017), a traumatic reaction may still be present in an individual even when PTSD, as defined by the DSM-5, may not totally apply.

We also should keep in mind that although several of these scales showed good validity and reliability properties with their English version, it is not clear if construct validity was also assessed. In order to assess for construct validity, an assessment of the structural equivalence across different cultural groups is required.

## Conclusion

The primary goal of this chapter was to provide the reader with the necessary context to determine the extent to which assessment and intervention for individuals coming from diverse cultural and linguistic communities have followed the standard of practice of the profession. By that we mean that all efforts are made to ensure accuracy of information within that context when deciding on the presence of trauma in these individuals and the extent to which their overall functions are compromised. Although we discussed areas to keep in mind and types of test material to consider for this group based on the linguistic ability of these individuals and their understanding of cultural expectations (acculturation), this has to be preceded by a careful history taking of the individual history from the country of origin to the present. This is particularly important in assessing the presence of early trauma and the implication for the developmental trajectory with regard to the cognitive and emotional functioning that is the subject of the evaluation. In that context, gathering careful and relevant information about developmental history and kinds of early attachment, medical complications, school functioning, work history, family history, legal history, trauma exposure, etc., both in the country of origin and currently, are important; they provide the necessary context to understand the nature of the condition under assessment. The reader is encouraged to develop this mental set and approach to ensure the most ethical approach to the forensic assessment of this population.

## Questions/Activities for Further Exploration

1. Select an individual from a diverse cultural group and identify as many different ways stress is experienced and strategies utilized to address it.
2. Discuss how standard assessment tools can provide inaccurate information about the person being assessed in terms of cognitive abilities and emotional difficulties when cultural and linguistic factors are not considered.
3. List five important components to include in an assessment of culturally and linguistically diverse clients to ensure the most appropriate and ethical practice.
4. Identify the most important components to include in best practice curriculum to train future forensic professionals to address culturally and linguistically relevant issues in their clients.

# References

Acevedo, A., Buitrago Cohen, M. H., Amrami, Y., Lamela, M., Maskit, B., Bucci, W., & Javier, R. A. (Spring 2017). Language of the experience's influence on narrative specificity and emotion in Spanish-English Bilinguals. Presented at St. John's University Research Date.

Alarcon, R. D. (2009). Culture, cultural factors, and psychiatric diagnosis: Review and projections. *World Psychiatry, 8*, 131–139.

Allen, J. G., & Fonagy, P. (2017). Trauma. In P. Luyten, L. C. Mayes, P. Fonagy, M. Target, & S. Blatt (Eds.), *Handbook of psychodynamic approaches to psychopathology* (pp. 165–198). New York/London: The Guilford Press.

Altarriba, J. (2003). Does cariño equal "liking"? A theoretical approach to conceptual nonequivalence between languages. *The International Journal of Bilingualism, 7*, 305–322.

Altarriba, J. (2008). Expressions of emotion as mediated by context. *Bilingualism: Language and Cognition, 11*, 165–167.

American Psychiatric Association. (2013). *Diagnostic and statistical manual of mental disorders* (5th ed.). Arlington, VA: Author.

American Psychological Association. (January 2013). Specialty guidelines for forensic psychology. *American Psychologist, 68*(1), 7–19. https://doi.org/10.1037/a002988

American Psychological Association. (2018). Statement on the effects of deportation and forced separation on immigrants, their families, and communities. *The American Journal of Community Psychology, 62*, 3–12. https://doi.org/10.1002/ajcp.12256

Amrami, Y., Lamala, M., Makit, B., Bucci, W., & Javier, R. (2019). Language of the experience on emotional content and specificity in bilingal autobiographical narratives. Presented at the Eastern Psychological Association Annual Meeting in New York, March 2019.

Armour-Thomas, E., & Gopaul-McNicol, S. (1997). In search of correlates of learning underlying "learning disability" using a bio-ecological assessment system. *Journal of Social Distress and Homeless, 6*(1), 143–159.

Ashbaugh, A. R., Houle-Johnson, S., Herbert, C., El-Hage, W., & Brunet, A. (2016). Psychometric validation of the English and French versions of the posttraumatic stress disorder checklist for DSM-5 (PCL-5). *PLoS One, 11*(10), e0161645. https://doi.org/10.1371/journal.pone.0161645

Ayon, C. (2018). Immigrants in the U.S.: Detention, discrimination, and intervention. *Race and Social Problems, 10*(4), 273–274.

Baden, A. L., & Steward, R. J. (2007). The cultural-racial identity model: A theoretical framework for studying transracial adoptees. In R. A. Javier, A. L. Baden, F. A. Biafora, & A. Camacho-Gingerich (Eds.), *Handbook of adoption: Implications for researchers, practitioners, and families* (pp. 90–112). Thousand Oaks, CA: Sage Publications.

Bae, H., Kim, D., Koh, H., Kim, Y., & Park, J. S. (2008). Psychometric properties of the life events checklist-Korean version. *Psychiatry Investigation, 5*, 163–167. https://doi.org/10.4306/pi.2008.5.3.163

Balhara, Y. P. S. (2011). Culture-bound syndrome: Has it found its right niche. *Indian Journal of Psychological Medicine, 33*(2), 210–215.

Ball, M. (July 2, 2018). Trump's inhumane border policy tests America. *TIME Magazine, 192*(1), 32–33.

Baum, S., & Titone, D. (2014). Moving toward a neuroplasticity view of bilingualism, executive control, and aging. *Applied PsychoLinguistics, 35*, 857–894.

Bialystok, E., Craik, F., & Luk, G. (2008). Cognitive control and lexical access in younger and older bilinguals. Journal of Experimental Psychology: *Learning, Memory, and Cognition, 34*, 859–873.

Bialystok, E. Craik, F, & Luk, G, (2012). Bilingualism: Consequences for mind and brain. *Trends Cognitive Science, 16*(4), 240–250. https://doi.org/10.1016/j.tics.2012.03.001

Boysan, M., Ozhemir, P., Yilmaz, E., Selvi, Y., Özdemir, O., & Kefeli, M. (2017). Psychometric properties of the Turkish version of the clinician-administered PTSD scale for diagnostic and statistical manual of mental disorders, fifth edition. *Psychiatry and Clinical Psychopharmacology., 27*(2), 173–184.

Buchanan, Z. E., Abu-Rayya, H. M., Kashima, E., Paxton, S. J., & Sam, D. L. (2018). Perceived discrimination, language proficiencies, and adaptation: Comparisons between refugee and non-refugee immigrant youth in Australia. *International Journal of Intercultural Relations, 63*, 105–112. https://doi.org/10.1016/j.ijintrel.2017.10.006

Butcher, J. N., Dahlstrom, W. G., Graham, J. R., Tellegen, A., & Kaemmer, B. (1989). *Minnesota Multiphasic Personality Inventory–2 (MMPI-2): Manual for administration and scoring.* Minneapolis, MN: University of Minnesota Press.

Byrne, B. M., Oakland, T., Leong, F. T. L., van de Vijver, F. J. R., Hambleton, R. K., Cheung, F. M., & Bartram, D. (2009). A critical analysis of cross-cultural research and testing practices: Implications for improved education and training in psychology. *Training and Education in Professional Psychology, 3*(2), 94–105.

Caldwell-Harris, C. L. (2015). Emotionality differences between a native and foreign language: Implications for everyday life. *Current Directions in Psychological Science, 24*, 214–219.

Camino, G., & Bravo, M. (1994). The adaptation and testing of diagnostic and outcome measure for cross-cultural research. *International Review of Psychiatry, 6*, 281–286.

Campbell, J. M., Brown, R. T., Cavanagh, S. E., Vess, S. F., & Segall, M. J. (2008). Evidence-based assessment of cognitive functioning in pediatric psychology. *J Pediatr Psychol, 33*(9), 999–1014. Published online 2008 Jan 13. https://doi.org/10.1093/jpepsy/jsm138

Center for Substance Abuse Treatment (US). (2014). *Appendix E, cultural formulation in diagnosis and cultural concepts of distress. Improving cultural competence (Treatment Improvement Protocol [TIP] Series, No. 59.).* Rockville, MD: Substance Abuse and Mental Health Services Administration (US). Available from: https://www.ncbi.nlm.nih.gov/books/NBK248426/

Charney, M. E., & Keane, T. M. (2007). Psychometric analyses of the clinician-administered PTSD scale (CAPS)--Bosnian Translation. *Cultural Diversity and Ethnic Minority Psychology, 13*(2), 161–168.

Chen, P., Lin, J., Chen, B., Lu, C., & Guo, T. (2015). Processing emotional words in two languages with one brain: ERP and fMRI evidence from Chinese-English bilinguals. *Cortex, 71*, 34–48.

Chen, S. X., & Bond, M. H. (2010). Two languages, two personalities? Examining language effects on the expression of personality in a bilingual context. *Personality and Social Psychology Bulleting, 36*, 1514–1528.

Chu, L. Y. (2004). *Coping, appraisal and post-traumatic stress disorder in motor vehicle accident.* Unpublished master's thesis. Hong Kong, China: University of Hong Kong.

Clauss-Ehlers, C. S., Chiriboga, D. A., Hunter, S. J., Roysircar, G., & Tummala-Narra, P. (2019). APA multicultural guidelines executive summary: Ecological approach to context, identity, and intersectionality. *American Psychologist, 74*(2), 232–244.

Clauss-Ehlers, C. S., Millan, F., & Zhao, C. J. (2018). Understanding domestic violence within the Latino/Hispanic/Latinx context: Environmental, culturally relevant assessment tool. In R. A. Javier & W. G. Herron (Eds.), *Understanding domestic violence- theories, challenges, and remedies* (pp. 237–262). New York/London: Rowman & Littlefield.

Conrad, M., Reccio, G., & Jacobs, A. M. (2011). The time course of emotion effects in first and second language processing: A cross cultural ERP study with German-Spanish bilinguals. *Frontiers in Psychology, 2*, 351.

Costantino, G., Dana, R. H., & Malgady, R. G. (2007). *TEMAS (Tell-Me-A-Story). Assessment in multicultural societies.* Mahwah, N.J: Lawrence Erlbaum.

Costantino, G., Malgady, R. G., & Rogler, L. H. (1985). *Cuento therapy – Folktales as culturally sensitive psychotherapy for Puerto Rican children. HRC Monograph No 2.* Maplewood, N.J: Waterfront Press.

Dana, R. (1993). *Multicultural assessment perspectives for professional psychology.* Boston/London: Allyn and Bacon.

Dana, R. (1996). Assessment of acculturation in Hispanic populations. *Hispanic Journal of Behavioral Sciences, 18*, 317–328.

Davidson, G., Murray, K., & Schweitzer, R. (2010). Review of refugee mental health assessment: Best practices and recommendations. *Journal of Pacific Rim Psychology, 4*(1), 72–85. https://doi.org/10.1375/prp.4.1.72

de Bruin, A., Bak, T. H., & Della Sala, S. (2015). Examining the effects of active versus inactive bilingualism on executive control in a carefully matched non-immigrant sample. *Journal of Memory and Language, 85*, 15–26.

Desai, G., & Chaturvedi, S. (2017). Idioms of distress. *Journal of Neurosciences in Rural Practice, 8*(5), S094. https://doi.org/10.4103/jnrp.jnrp_235_17

Dewaele, J. M. (2004). The emotional force of swear words and taboo words in the speech of multilinguals. *Journal of Multilingual and Multicultural Development, 25*, 204–222.

Dewaele, J. M. (2008). The emotional weight of I love you in multilinguals' languages. *Journal of Pragmatics, 40*, 1753–1780.

Dewaele, J. M., & Nakano, S. (2013). Multilinguals' perceptions of feeling different when switching languages. *Journal of Multilingual and Multicultural Development, 34*, 107–120.

Diller, K. C. (1974). "Compound" and "coordinate" bilingualism: A conceptual artifact. *Word, 26*, 254–261.

Draguns, J. G. (1998). Cultural influences on psychopathology. In R. A. Javier & W. G. Herron (Eds.), *Personality development and psychotherapy in our diverse society* (pp 13–43). North\vale, N.J/London: Jason Aronson, Inc.

Draguns, J. G. (1999). Clinical psychology is cultural: Its present state and future prospects. *Contemporary Psychology, 44*(3), 242–244.

Durà-Vilà, G., & Hodes, M. (2012). Cross-cultural study of idioms of distress among Spanish nationals and Hispanic American migrants: Susto, nervios and ataque de nervios. *Social Psychiatry & Psychiatric Epidemiology, 47*(10), 1627–1637. https://doi.org/10.1007/s00127-011-0468-3

Edwards, H. S., Baker, A., Chan, M., Lull, J., Martinez, G., Traff, T., ... Walt, V. (2019). Dividing lines. (Cover story). *Time Magazine, 193*(4/5), 22–47.

Eilola, T. M., Havelka, J., & Sharma, D. (2007). Emotional activation in the first and second language. *Cognition and Emotion, 21*(5), 1064–1076. https://doi.org/10.1080/02699930601054109

El-Jamil, F., & Abi-Hashem, N. (2018). Family maltreatment and domestic violence among Arab Middle Easterners: A psychological, cultural, religious, and legal examination. In R. A. Javier & W. G. Herron (Eds.), *Understanding domestic violence: Theories, challenges, and remedies* (pp. 179–212). Lanham, MD: Rowman & Littlefield.

Fabrega, H. (1987). Psychiatric diagnosis: A cultural perspective. *Journal of Nervous and Mental Disease, 175*(7), 383–394.

Ferre, P., Garcia, T., Fraga, I., Sanchez-Casas, R., & Molero, M. (2010). Memory for emotional words in bilinguals: Do words have the same emotional intensity in the first and in the second language? *Cognition and Emotion, 24*, 760–785.

Flannigan, D. P., McGrew, K. S., & Ortiz, S. O. (2000). *The Wechsler intelligence scales and Gf-Gc theory: A contemporary approach to interpretation.* Boston: Allyn & Bacon.

Ford, J. D., & Courtois, C. A. (2009). Defining and understanding complex trauma and complex traumatic stress disorders. In C. A. Courtois & J. D. Ford (Eds.), *Treating complex traumatic stress disorders: An evidence-based guide* (pp. 13–30). New York, NY: Guilford Press.

Foster, R. (1996). Assessing the psychodynamic function of language in the bilingual patient. In R. Foster, M. Moskowitz, & R. Javier (Eds.), *Reaching across boundaries of culture and class: Widening the scope of psychotherapy* (pp. 243–263). Northvale, NJ: Jason Aronson.

Francis, W. S., Tokowicz, N. M., & Kroll, J. F. (2014). The consequences of language proficiency and difficulty of lexical access for translation performance and priming. *Memory & Cognition, 42*, 27–40.

Ghali, S. B. (1982). Understanding Puerto Rican traditions. *Social Work (January), 27*, 98–102.

Gibbs, N. (Nov 12, 2018). The only way forward. *TIME Magazine, 192*(20), 24–25. https://howlingpixel.com/i-en/Time_(magazine)

Geisinger, K. F. (2003). Testing and assessment in cross-cultural psychology. In R. J. Graham & A. J. Naglieri (Eds.), *Assessment psychology: Handbook of psychology* (pp. 99–117). Hoboken, NY: Wiley.

Godoy, I. (1995). El rol de los objetos transicionales en el proceso de separación de la tierra madre: Un estudio realizado con mujeres Latinas imigrantes. Tesis doctoral, Pontificia Universidad Catolica del Ecuador, Quito, Ecuador.

Gollan, T. H., Starr, J., & Ferreira, V. S. (2015). More than use it or lose it: The number-of-speakers effect on heritage language proficiency. *Psychonomic Bulletin & Review, 22*, 147–155.

Greene, B. (2006). How difference makes a difference: Social privilage, disadvantage, and multiple identities. In J. C. Muran (Ed.), *Dialogues on difference: Studies in diversity in therapeutic relationships* (pp. 47–63). Washington, D.C.: American Psychological Association Press.

Green, D. W. (2011). Language control in different contexts: The behavioral ecology of bilingual speakers. *Frontiers in Psychology, 2*, 103.

Grosjean, F. (2010). *Bilingual life and reality*. Boston, MA: Harvard University Press.

Grotevant, H. D., Dunbar, N., Kohler, J. K., & Esau, A. M. L. (2007). Adoptive identity: How contexts within and beyond the family shape developmental pathways. In R. A. Javier, A. L. Baden, F. A. Biafora, & A. Camacho-Gingerich (Eds.), *Handbook of adoption: Implications for researchers, practitioners, and families* (pp. 77–89). Thousand Oaks, CA: Sage Publications.

Guillermoprieto, A. (2010). The murderers of Mexico. *New York Review of Books, 57*(16), 46–48.

Haas, A. M., Boyes, A., Cheng, J., MacNeil, A., & Wirove, R. (2016). An introduction to the issues of cross-cultural assessment inspired by Ewert v. Canada. *Journal of Threat Assessment and Management, 3*(2), 65–75.

Halpern, S., & McKibben, B. (2014). Amid the heated debates, Iraqi immigrants struggle to make a living in Arizona. *Smithsonian, 45*(5), 1.

Hammer, J. (2015). S.O.S. *Outside, 40*(10), 62–104.

Harris, C. L., Aycicegi, A., & Gleason, J. B. (2003). Taboo words and reprimands elicit greater autonomic reactivity in a first language than in a second language. *Applied PsychoLinguistics, 24*, 561–579.

Harris, C. L., Gleasson, J. B., & Aycicegi, A. (2006). When is a first language more emotional? Psycho-physiological evidence from bilingual speakers. In A. Pavlenko (Ed.), *Bilingual minds: Emotional experience, expression, and representation* (pp. 257–283). New York: Multilingual Matters.

Haskins, J. (2017). Migrant, refugee youth face dangers on Mediterranean migration routes. *Nation's Health, 47*(9), 15.

Hellman, A. D. (2011). Vocabulary size and depth of word knowledge in adult-onset second language acquisition. *International Journal of Applied Linguistics, 21*, 162–182.

Helms, J. E., Jerrigan, M., & Mascher, J. (2005). The meaning of race in psychology and how to change it: A methodological perspective. *American Psychologist, 60*, 27–36.

Hinton, L., & Kleinman, A. (1990). Cultural issues and international psychiatric diagnosis. In I. C. De Silva & C. Nadenson (Eds.), *International Review of Psychiatry* (pp. 111–129). Washington, DC: American Psychiatric Press.

Ibrahim, H., Ertl, V., Catani, C., Ismail, A. A., & Neuner, F. (2018). The validity of posttraumatic stress disorder checklist for DSM-5 (PCL-5) as screening instrument with Kurdish and Arab displaced populations living in the Kurdistan region of Iraq. *BMC Psychiatry, 18*(1), 259. https://doi.org/10.1186/s12888-018-1839-z

Itzhak, I., Vingron, N., Baum, S. R., & Titone, D. (2017). Bilingualism in the real world: How proficiency, emotion, and personality in a second language impact communication in clinical and legal settings. *Translational Issues in Psychological Science, 3*(1), 48–65.

Javier, R. A. (1996). In search of repressed memories in bilingual individuals. In R. Pérez Foster, M. Moskowitz, & R. A. Javier (Eds.), *Reaching across boundaries of culture and class: Widening the scope of psychotherapy* (pp. 225–241). Lanham, MD: Jason Aronson.

Javier, R. A. (2007). *The bilingual mind: Thinking, feeling and speaking in two languages*. New York: Springer Science + Business Media.

Javier, R. A., & Herron, W. H. (1998). *Personality development and psychotherapy in our diverse society: A sourcebook*. Northdale, NJ: Jason Aronson.

Javier, R. A., & Marcos, L. R. (1989). The role of stress on the language-independence and code-switching phenomena. *Journal of Psycholinguistic Research, 18*, 449–472.

Javier, R.A., Barroso, F. & Munoz, M. (1993). Autobiographical memories in bilinguals. *Journal of Psycholinguistic Research, 2*, 319–338.

Javier, R. A., Vasquez, C. I., & Marcos, L. R. (1998). Common errors by interpreters in communicating with linguistically diverse patients. In R. A. Javier & W. H. Herron (Eds.), *Personality development and psychotherapy in our diverse society: A sourcebook* (pp. 521–534). Northdale, NJ: Jason Aronson.

Kaufman, A. S., & Lichtenberger, E. O. (2001). *Assessing adolescent and adult intelligence.* Boston: Allyn and Bacon.

Keygnaert, I., Vettenburg, N., & Temmerman, M. (2012). Hidden violence is silent rape: Sexual and gender-based violence in refugees, asylum seekers and undocumented migrants in Belgium and the Netherlands. *Culture, Health & Sexuality, 14*(5), 505–520.

Kirmayer, L. J., & Ryder, A. G. (2016). Culture and psychopathology. *Current Opinion in Psychology, 8*, 143–148. https://doi.org/10.1016/j.copsyc.2015.10.020

Kleinman, A. (1987). Anthropology and psychiatry. The role of culture in cross-cultural research on illness. *British Journal of Psychiatry, 179*, 1–3.

Kleinman, A. (1988). *The illness narratives: Suffering, healing, and the human condition.* New York, NY: Basic Books.

Koppitz, E. M. (1975). *The bender gestalt test for young children* (Vol. 2). New York: Grune and Stratton.

Lambert, W. (1972). Language, psychology, and culture (pp. 330–331). Stanford, CA: Stanford University Press.

Langman, P. F. (1997). White culture, Jewish culture and the origins of psychotherapy. *Psychotherapy, 34*(2), 207–218.

Lee, E. (1990). Assessment and treatment of Chinese-American immigrant families. In G. W. Saba, B. M. Karrer, & K. Hardy (Eds.), *Minorities and family therapy* (pp. 99–122). New York, NY: Hawthorth.

de Paulo Lima, E., Vasconcelos, A., Berger, W., Kristensen, C., Nascimento, E., Figueira, I., & Mendlowicz, M. (2016). Cross-cultural adaptation of the posttraumatic stress disorder checklist 5 (PCL-5) and life events checklist 5 (LEC-5) for the Brazilian context. *Trends in Psychiatry and Psychotherapy, 38*, 207–215. https://doi.org/10.1590/2237-6089-2015-0074

Lu, F. G., Lim, R. F., & Mezzich, J. E. (1995). Issues in the assessment and diagnosis of culturally diverse individuals. *American Psychiatric Press Review of Psychiatry, 14*, 477–510.

Maeda, F., & Nathan, J. H. (1999). Understanding taijin kyofusho through its treatment, morita therapy. *Journal of Psychosomatic Research, 46*(6), 525–530.

Malgady, R. G., & Costantino, G. (1998). Symptom severity in bilingual Hispanics as a function of clinician ethnicity and language of interview. *Psychological Assessment, 10*(2), 120–127. https://doi.org/10.1037/1040-3590.10.2.120

Marcos, L. R., Urcuyo, L., Kesselman, M., & Alpert, M. (1973). The language barrier in evaluating Spanish-American patients. *Archives of General Psychiatry, 29*(5), 655–659.

Markus, H. (2008). Pride, prejudice, and ambivalence: Toward a unified theory of rce and ethnicity. *American Psychologist, 63*(8), 651–670.

Marshall, G. N. (2004). Post-traumatic stress disorder symptom checklist: Factor structure and English-Spanish measurement invarience. *Journal of Traumatic Stress, 17*(3), 223–230.

Matsumoto, D. R., & van de Vijver, F. J. R. (2011). *Cross-cultural research methods in psychology.* New York: Cambridge University Press.

McWilliams, N. (2004). *Psychoanalytic psychotherapy: A practitioner's guide.* New York: Guilford Press.

Mehta, V., De, A., & Balachandran, C. (2009). Dhat syndrome: A reappraisal. *Indian Journal of Dermatology, 54*(1), 89–90. https://doi.org/10.4103/0019-5154.49002

Miles, J. N., Marshall, G. N., & Schell, T. L. (2008). Spanish and English versions of PTSD checklist-Civilian version (PCL-C): Testing for differential item functioning. *Journal of Traumatic Stress, 21*, 369–376.

Moitra, E., Duarte-Velez, Y., Lewis-Fernández, R., Weisber, R. B., & Keller, M. B. (2018). Examination of ataque de nervios and ataque de nervios like events in a diverse simple of adults with anxiety disorders. *Depression and Anxiety, 35*(12), 1190–1197. https://doi.org/10.1002/da.22853

Mojaverian, T., Hashimoto, T., & Kim, H. S. (2013). Cultural differences in professional help seeking: A comparison of Japan and U.S. Front Psychol. 2013 Jan 11;3:615. https://doi.org/10.3389/fpsyg.2012.00615.ecollection2012.

Morris, D. O., Javier, R. A., & Herron, W. G. (2015). *Specialty competencies in professional psychology. Specialty competencies in psychoanalysis in psychology.* New York: Oxford University Press.

Müller-Engelmann, M., Schnyder, U., Dittmann, C., Priebe, K., Bohus, M., Thome, J., … Steil, R. (2018). Psychometric properties and factor structure of the German version of the clinician-administered PTSD scale for DSM-5. *Assessment*, 1073191118774840. https://doi.org/10.1177/10731911187774840

Murray, H. A. (1938). *Explorations in personality.* Oxford, England: Oxford University Press.

Nichter, M. (1981). Idioms of distress: Alternatives in the expression of psychosocial distress: A case study from South India. *Culture, Medicine and Psychiatry, 5*(4), 379–408.

Nicolas, G. & Whitt, C. (2012). Conducting qualitative research with Black immigrant sample. Understanding depression among Haitian immigrant women. In D. K. Nagata, L. Kohn-Wood, & L. Suzuki (Eds.), Qualitative strategies for ethnocultural research (pp 199–217). Washington, D.C.: American Psychological Association Press. https://doi.org/10.10:3037/13742-011

O'Malley, P. (2018). Migration and conflict. *New England Journal of Public Policy, 30*(2). Retrieved from https://scholarworks.umb.edu/nejpp/vol30/iss2/14

Paniagua, F. A., & Yamada, A. M. (2013). *Handbook of multicultural mental health: Assessment and treatment of diverse populations* (2nd ed.). Amsterdam, Boston, London, San Francisco, New York: Elsevier.

Pavlenko, A. (2006). Bilingual selves. In A. Pavlenko (Ed.), *Bilingual minds: Emotional experience, expression, and representation* (Vol. 56, pp. 1–33). Clevedon: Multilingual Matters.

Paunovic, N., & Ost, L. (2005). Psychometric properties of a Swedish translation of the clinician-administered PTSD scale-diagnostic version. *Journal of Traumatic Stress, 18*(2), 161–164.

Pineteh, E. A., & Muly, T. N. (2016). Tragic and heroic moments in the lives of forced migrants. Memories of polical asylum-seekers in post-apartheid South Africa. *Refuge: Canada's Journal of Refugees, 32*(3), 63–72. Retrieved from https://refugejournals.yorku.ca/index.php/refuge/article/view/40285

Ramirez-Esparza, N., Gosling, S. D., Benet-Martinez, V., Potter, J. P., & Pennebaker, J. W. (2006). Do bilinguals have two personalities? A special case of cultural frame switching. *Journal of Research in Personality, 40*, 99–120.

Rogler, L. H., & Cortes, D. E. (1993). Help-seeking pathways: A unifying concept in mental health care. *The American Journal of Psychiatry, 150*(4), 554–561.

Rojas-Flores, L., Hwang Koo, J., & Vaughn, J. M. (2019). Protecting US-citizen children whose central American parents have temporary protected status. *International Perspectives in Psychology: Research, Practice, Consultation, 8*(1), 14–19.

Rowe, D. C. (2002). IQ, birth weight, and number of sexual partners in White, African American, and mixed-race adolescents. *Population, 23*, 513–524.

Sadeghi, S. (2019). Racial boundaries, stigma, and the re-emergence of "always being foreigners": Iranians and the refugee crisis in Germany. *Ethnic & Racial Studies, 42*(10), 1613–1631. https://doi.org/10.1080/01419870.2018.1506145

Safran, J. (2012). *Psychoanalysis and the psychoanalytic therapies.* Washington, DC: American Psychological Association.

Scherer, M., Altman, A., & Miller, Z. J. (2017). Bigots, boosted by the bully pulpit. *Time Magazine, 190*(8), 30–35.

Schnyder, U., & Moergeli, H. (2002). German version of clinician-administered PTSD scale. *Journal of Traumatic Stress, 15*(6), 487–492.

Schwartz, P. Y. (2002). Why is neurasthenia important in Asian cultures? *The Western Journal of Medicine, 176*(4), 257–258.

Segalowitz, N., Trofimovich, P., Gatbonton, E., & Sokolovskaya, A. (2008). Feeling affect in a second language: The role of word recognition automaticity. *The Mental Lexicon, 3*, 47–71.

Sheikh, N. A., & Titone, D. (2016). The embodiment of emotional words in a second language: An eye-movement study. *Cognition and Emotions, 30*, 488–500.

Singh, A., Tripathi, A., Gupta, B., & Agarwal, V. (2016). Pathways to care for Dhat (semen loss anxiety) syndrome: A study from North India. *International Journal of Mental Health, 45*(4), 253–261. https://doi.org/10.1080/00207411.2016.1238741

Solms, M., & Trumbull, O. (2002). *The brain and the inner world: An introduction to the neuroscience of subjective experience*. New York: Karnac Books.

Sue, D. W., Capodilupo, C. M., Torino, G. C., Bucceri, J. M., Holder, A. M. B., Nadal, K. L., & Esquilin, M. (2007). Racial microaggressions in everyday life: Implications for clinical practice. *American Psychologist, 62*(4), 271–286.

Sutton, T. M., Altarriba, J., Gianico, J. L., & Basnight-Brown, D. M. (2007). The automatic access of emotion: Emotional Stroop effects in Spanish-English bilingual speakers. *Cognition and Emotions, 21*, 1077–1090.

United Nations, Department of Economic and Social Affairs, Population Division. (2017). International Migration Report 2017 (ST/ESA/SER.A/403).

van de Vijver, F. J. R., & Poortinga, Y. H. (2002). Structural equivalence in multilevel research. *Journal of Cross-Cultural Research, 33*, 141–156.

Veltkamp, G. M., Recio, G., Jacobs, A. M., & Conrad, M. (2013). Is personality modulated by language? *The International Journal of Bilingualism, 17*, 496–504.

Vick, K. (2018, July 2). A reckoning after Trump's border separation policy: What kind of country are we? Times Magazine retrieved from https://abc13.com>timemagazine-cover-features-trump-imigration-girl

Walt, V. (2019). The plot against Europe. (Cover story). *Time Magazine, 193*(15), 26–33.

Weathers, F.W., Blake, D.D., Schnurr, P.P., Kaloupek, D.G., Marx, B.P., & Keane, T.M. (2013a). The clinician-administered PTSD scale for DSM-5 (CAPS-5).

Weathers, F.W., Blake, D.D., Schnurr, P.P., Kaloupek, D.G., Marx, B.P., & Keane, T.M. (2013b). The life events checklist for DSM-5 (LEC-5).

Weathers, F.W., Litz, B.T., Keane, T.M., Palmieri, P.A., Marx, B.P., & Schnurr, P.P. (2013). The PTSD checklist for *DSM-5* (PCL-5).

Weiner, I. B., & Bornstein, R. F. (2009). *Principles of psychotherapy: Promoting evidence-based psychodynamic practice*. Hoboken, NJ: Wiley.

Weiss, R. A., & Rosenfeld, B. (2012). Navigating cross-cultural issues in forensic assessment: Recommendations for practice. *Professional Psychology: Research and Practice, 43*(3), 234–240.

Wells, R., Wells, D., & Lawsin, C. (2015). Understanding psychological responses to trauma among refugees: The importance of measuring validity in cross-cultural settings. *Journal and Proceedings of the Royal Society of New South Wales, 148*(455–456), 60–69.

West, C. M. (2018). Crucial considerations in the understanding and treatment of intimate partner violence in African American couples. In R. A. Javier & W. G. Herron (Eds.), *Understanding domestic violence- theories, challenges, and remedies* (pp. 213–235). New York/London: Rowman & Littlefield.

Wu, K. K., & Chan, K. S. (2004). Psychometric properties of the Chinese version of impact of event scale - revised (IES-R). *Hong Kong Journal of Psychitry, 14*, 2–8.

Wu, K. K., Chan, S. K., & Yiu, V. F. (2008). Psychometric properties and confirmatory factor analysis of the posttraumatic stress disorder checklist (PCL) for Chinese survivors of motor vehicle accidents. *Hong Kong Journal of Psychiatry, 18*, 144–151.

Zayas, L. (2015). *Forgotten citizens: Deportation, children, and the making of American exiles and orphans*. New York/London: Oxford University Press.

# Part II
# Presence of Trauma in Civil Matters

**Rafael Art. Javier, Elizabeth A. Owen, and Jemour A. Maddux**

## 1.1   Introduction

Within the realm of civil proceedings (Part II), the reader finds a number of contributions focusing primarily on the world of children and adolescents, some of the most vulnerable members of our society and for whom the nature and quality of their developmental trajectories will have serious consequences for their future functioning. To that end, we include a chapter by Esquilin and Johnson (Chap. 8) that takes a closer look at the significance of contextual, personal, and racial trauma on forensic evaluations of parents in child protection matters; while the contribution by Zelechoski, Lindsay, and Heusel (Chap. 9) examines issues of prevention of delinquency by exploring the role of trauma-informed evaluation in child custody. By exploring the connection between exposure to family conflict and engaging in delinquent behavior, these authors provide a convincing empirically based argument of the extent to which a thorough family assessment can serve as a form of triage and, ultimately, prevention for negative long-term outcomes and re-traumatization of all involved parties.

The purpose of the next two chapters by Persyn and Owen (Chap. 10) and Amrami and Javier (Chap. 11) is to highlight further complications likely to emerge when assessing trauma in children/adolescent cases but now specifically related to the immigrant experience. This is a growing concern in forensic practice as there are increased demands for forensic psychologists to provide appropriate assessment related to refugee requests, deportation proceedings, termination of parental rights,

R. A. Javier
Psychology, St. John's University, Queens, NY, USA

E. A. Owen
Columbia University/Teachers College, New York, NY, USA

J. A. Maddux
Lamb & Maddux, LLC, Hackensack, NJ, USA

etc., following the standards of the discipline. These are thorny issues with major implications for those involved and for which there is a call for more involvement from the scientific/forensic professional community to provide clearer guidelines for assessment and intervention in the context of the immigration experience. There are too many issues to consider, not only about the specific assessment tools to assess requests for asylum seekers and in cases of deportation procedures but also the assessment of the consequences for the detainees, of the family left behind (e.g., young children, elderly parents, etc.), as well as the assessment of trauma and personal safety in the country to where the immigrants are being deported.

These chapters provide a good example of the kind of challenges that anyone is likely to face when taking the steps to immigrate to another country; thus, the issues raised in these chapters do not only apply to a particular group of immigrants. We are aware that those crossing the border through Mexico are not the only individuals coming from Central and Latin America (Rojas-Flores, Clements, Hwang Koo, & London, 2017), but also people coming from Africa, the Middle East, and other parts of Europe (UNHCR, 2018, 2019), in much the same way that those crossing different European borders also come from many different countries of the Middle East and Africa. Part of the complication has to do with having to assess a trauma history which may have occurred before the immigration, during the immigration, and following the immigration experience where sufficient documentation may not be available. The chapter by Persyn and Owen (Chap. 10) provides an examination of the various ways the immigration experience functions as a toxic environment, producing intense stress in the lives of migrant children seeking refuge from an environment where their safety and lives are constantly threatened because of political and socioeconomic conditions in their countries of origin. According to these authors, although their journey is fraught with much danger every step of the way, for these children/youth seeking asylum in other countries is the only viable solution for their safety. For some, that trauma history could include having to endure termination or even the threat of termination of parental rights, an issue addressed by Amrami and Javier in Chap. 11. The serious implications of being physically disconnected from direct parental connections already highlighted in the attachment literature are further addressed in this chapter, including the potential for the development of psychopathology and criminality. This chapter also provides specific recommendations for a forensically sound assessment where the possibility for termination of parental rights is involved.

Included in this section are also two chapters dedicated to examining the intersection of trauma and police work (Chaps. 12 by Casarella and Beebe and 14 by Maddux). The fact of the matter is everybody who comes in contact with the judicial system as defendants or law enforcement officers brings their personal history that guides their behavior and the decisions they make. For some, that history may include severe traumatic experiences. With that in mind, we thought it is necessary and relevant to include an exploration of trauma in relation to fitness for duty and pre-employment evaluations of law enforcement personnel (Chap. 12), a discussion of the litigation challenges faced by victims of police misconduct, and our evaluation procedures for assessing their trauma and other psychological injuries in civil rights and personal injury litigation (Chap. 14).

Considering the pernicious and insidious ways trauma can complicate one's functioning, individuals coming into law enforcement careers are likely to find themselves face-to-face with the traumatic conditions in those seeking/needing their interventions. The officer's personal familiarity with these intense and violent situations from their own histories may trigger in these officers a traumatic reaction and a job performance issue that could be harmful to the officer and/or a member of the community. The potential for inappropriate responses to these situations by police officers (e.g., excessive use of force) becomes more likely when these officers are not given the opportunity to explore and manage their own personal trauma histories and the conditions that may have triggered a reactivation of old traumas. Complicating things even more, excessive use of force problems disproportionately befall communities that have experienced historical, race-based, and other forms of trauma; these conditions have produced a distrust and poor relations with police, thereby, creating a volatile situation when being policed by officers with unaddressed trauma. In other words, there could be an intersection of traumatic stress between officers and civilians (adults and juveniles), particularly, within minority communities in disadvantaged neighborhoods.

The chapter by Foote (Chap. 13) in this section is meant to bring to the attention of the reader that even in cases of employment, we find trauma raising its ugly head, related to personal injury and discrimination. For this purpose, the reader finds the contribution by Foote who uses his extensive experience on personal injury and employment discrimination to provide the reader with comprehensive and clear guidelines to follow when involved in forensic assessments of these types of cases. This chapter is very specific about the steps to follow and issues to consider in order to provide an appropriate forensic assessment. It includes a discussion of specific tests that are considered the gold standards of forensic practice for those situations. This issue is also explored in the contribution by Maddux (Chap. 14) who looks at an application of this work in the police misconduct civil rights litigation context.

# References

Rojas-Flores, L., Clements, M. L., Hwang Koo, J., & London, J. (2017). Trauma and psychological distress in Latino citizen children following parental detention and deportation. *Psychological Trauma: Theory, Research, Practice, and Policy*, *9*(3), 352–361. https://doi.org/10.1037/tra0000177

UNICEF. (2018). *Child displacement*. Retrieved from https://data.unicef.org/topic/child-migration-and-displacement/displacement/

UNICEF. (2019). *Child refugees and migrants*. Retrieved from https://www.unicefusa.org/mission/emergencies/child-refugees

# Chapter 8
# Forensic Evaluations of Parents in Child Protection Matters: The Significance of Contextual, Personal, and Racial Trauma

**Susan Cohen Esquilin and Denise M. Williams Johnson**

## Introduction

Forensic evaluations of parents in child protection matters are typically conducted at two points. Early in the life of the case, the focus is on risk and protective factors to recommend services to achieve parent–child reunification. At the permanency stage, the question is whether the parents have been sufficiently rehabilitated for their children to be safely returned. The impact of trauma is frequently underestimated at both stages. Multiple sources of trauma can be in operation, particularly for African–American parents: interaction with the child protective service agency; the psychological evaluation process; the parent's personal trauma history; and the family's multigenerational experience of racial trauma. Unless psychologists identify and understand these contextual, personal, and racial sources of trauma, the parent's symptoms and self-protective behaviors may be unwittingly escalated. The result is misdiagnosis, inadequate or inappropriate therapeutic interventions, and the ultimate loss of children permanently.

## Contextual Trauma

### Parental Reactions to Child Welfare System Involvement

For parents, involvement with the child welfare system is highly stressful, if not traumatic (Dumbrill, 2006; Morrison, 1996; Tuttle, Knudson-Martin, Levin, Taylor, & Andrews, 2007). Parents describe fear of the caseworker's power, and feelings of

S. C. Esquilin (✉)
ABPP-Clinical, Independent Practice, Verona, NJ, USA

D. M. Williams Johnson
Independent Practice, West Orange, NJ, USA

© Springer Nature Switzerland AG 2020
R. A. Javier et al. (eds.), *Assessing Trauma in Forensic Contexts*,
https://doi.org/10.1007/978-3-030-33106-1_8

being out of control, and victimized. Many removals are made on an emergency basis. The process of the removal itself may be frightening to both parents and children, particularly if there has been no preparation. Some removals involve physical altercations and the presence of police officers. If the child is placed in a setting unknown to the birth parent, anxiety is generated about the welfare of the child in this anonymous home.

Parents are typically angry at the child protective agency but are simultaneously asked to cooperate with the agency. While the removal of a child can trigger motivation in parents to do everything possible to regain custody, many parents become immobilized and overwhelmed with the multiple demands that are made in the wake of their abject emotional pain. The absence of the child is likely to trigger intense sadness, while being viewed as an "unfit" parent is experienced as shameful. The presence of fear, anxiety, anger, sadness, shame, and being overwhelmed can easily interfere with the parent's ability to comply with expectations in an optimal manner. Rather than blaming parents for their predicament, acute distress, or difficult presentation, affording them the same sensitivity that is offered to other traumatized populations may de-escalate their situational, normal response to separation from their children.

## *The Psychological Evaluation Process*

Parents are often required to undergo psychological evaluations involving interviews and testing. For the parent, the psychologist and the evaluation will be perceived as extensions of the child protective agency. As such, the response of the traumatized and overwhelmed parent will be one of self-protection, and/or an exacerbation of their trauma symptoms. Psychologists must consider the real possibility that the parent's behavior during an evaluation reflects a reaction to the trauma of the child's removal and not the parent's typical functioning. For example, a parent who reacts to an interview with minimal responses for fear of saying the wrong thing can be seen as not introspective and not likely to benefit from treatment. A parent who seems angry toward the psychologist or the evaluation process may be considered to have an impulse-control or mood problem, and, by extension, pose a potential danger to her children.

## Impact of Personal Trauma

Maternal mental illness is present in a significant percentage of cases open for investigation of child maltreatment (Westad & McConnell, 2012). Research suggests a range of mental health problems (Gonzalez, 2014). Substance abuse is typically recognized, but many of these parents have co-occurring mental health conditions (Stromwall et al., 2008). Histories of trauma often play a significant but unrecognized role in these conditions. Even in the absence of diagnosable mental health conditions, a history of personal trauma can play a major role in parenting and child maltreatment.

## *Trauma Sequelae and Serious Mental Illness*

Child protective workers typically refer parents for evaluations if they have psychotic symptoms or serious problems with affect regulation. However, the role of trauma histories in these clients is often overlooked, and comorbid Posttraumatic Stress Disorder (PTSD) is often not diagnosed. Studies repeatedly indicate that the rates of both trauma exposure and PTSD in clients with severe mental illness are significantly higher than such rates in the general population (Alsawy, Wood, Taylor, & Morrison, 2015; Neria et al., 2008; O'Hare, Shen, & Sherrer, 2013). The trauma exposure in these studies does not seem to be the result of the psychotic symptoms but appears to predate psychotic symptoms. A history of interpersonal violence specifically was very common (Neria et al., 2008). These findings have been supported in multiple countries (Álvarez et al., 2012; Quarantini et al., 2010). When parents are diagnosed with severe mental illness, recommendations typically focus on ensuring compliance with medication and the trauma history is not addressed. This is an inadequate level of treatment.

As is generally true for clients with psychosis, individuals with Bipolar Disorder also have higher rates of diagnosable PTSD than the general population (Assion et al., 2009; Hernandez et al., 2013). A review of several studies (Otto et al., 2004) found that the rate of PTSD among Bipolar patients is roughly double the rate in the general population. Goldberg and Garno (2005) found diagnosable PTSD in about one-quarter of the patients with Bipolar Disorder they studied. Again, within child protective service evaluations, a diagnosis of Bipolar Disorder often results in a focus on medication compliance and an absence of treatment for trauma.

Patients with Bipolar Disorder *and* PTSD have significantly worse social functioning (Neria et al., 2002) than those with Bipolar Disorder only. This comorbidity is associated with greater likelihood of the presence of a substance use disorder, lower likelihood of being in recovery, elevated rates of suicide attempts, lower role attainment, and more problematic quality of life (Otto et al., 2004). Certain problems associated with PTSD may be particularly responsible for these negative life outcomes. For example, triggers associated with traumatic histories can lead to distress and panic, making the patient generally more emotionally labile. In addition, the chronic overarousal and difficulty sleeping associated with PTSD can put patients with Bipolar Disorder at risk for new episodes. Avoidance of stimuli that elicit trauma reactions can also result in the avoidance of activities and situations that could result in an improved quality of life. While many individuals with Bipolar Disorder alone can be managed quite well with medication and can appropriately parent children, the additional presence of PTSD makes the parent more unstable and more likely to engage in behavior that could put a child at risk of harm.

Childhood trauma appears to be a significant factor for clients with Bipolar Disorder, as it is for clients with psychosis generally. Clients with Bipolar Disorder are particularly likely to have PTSD when there was a history of severe childhood abuse, especially sexual abuse (Goldberg & Garno, 2005). Maniglio (2013) studied the specific presence of a history of child sexual abuse among patients with Bipolar Disorder in a review of studies. The conclusion was that the trauma of child sexual abuse was associated with a more severe form of Bipolar Disorder that was strongly related to PTSD. In addition, the presence of a history of child sexual abuse was associated with more suicide attempts, substance use, and psychotic level symptoms. The presence of these additional difficulties puts the parent at greater risk of child protective service involvement and the permanent loss of children.

When only Bipolar Disorder or psychosis is identified in the psychological evaluation without recognition of a trauma history, the ensuing treatment will typically not address those aspects of the history that may trigger episodic dyscontrol or acute trauma sequelae. Thus, even if the parent is compliant with medication, the continued episodic dyscontrol is viewed as only the result of the psychosis or mood disorder and is not understood as connected to trauma. Without a focus on treating trauma as well as the comorbid condition, the likely outcome is an assessment that this parent will never be able to care for the child safely due to the comorbid condition, when the real issue is often an untreated trauma history.

## *Complex Trauma and Borderline Personality Disorder*

Many parents in child protection cases have histories of chronic abuse and neglect as children. Complex Trauma is identified as "the experience of multiple, chronic and prolonged, developmentally adverse traumatic events, most often of an interpersonal nature and early-life onset" (van der Kolk, 2005, p. 401). The developing brain of the young child is impacted by these experiences in ways that scholars are now describing as "Developmental Trauma Disorder" (van der Kolk, 2005). These early experiences can have a lifelong impact in the areas of attachment, affect regulation, behavior control, biology, cognition, dissociation, and self-concept (Cook, Blaustein, Spinazzola, & van der Kolk, 2003). A child who is not treated for these difficulties becomes an adult with impaired ways of coping that can negatively impact parenting. It is therefore important that a psychological assessment of a parent include an assessment of the parent's own early childhood history as a potential source of the parenting difficulty that has emerged.

"Betrayal trauma" refers to the experience of trauma caused by someone very close to a victim. In the case of children, it typically refers to abuse by parents and is thus related to the concept of Complex Trauma or Developmental Trauma Disorder. High levels of dissociation are associated with betrayal trauma as well as Complex Trauma and are further heightened in mothers who are then revictimized in adulthood (Hulette et al., 2011). Dissociation makes these women less aware of interpersonal threats to themselves and their children, and thus, they are more likely to be revictimized. The children of those women who were revictimized in adulthood were more likely to experience interpersonal victimization themselves as compared with the children of women who had not been revictimized as adults. In addition, betrayal trauma also appears to be related to the development of Borderline Personality Disorder. DeGregorio (2013) argues that the neuropsychological mechanisms impacted by serious and chronic childhood abuse create deficits in social, cognitive, emotional, and behavioral domains that are linked not only to the development of Borderline Personality Disorder but are also linked to problems in parenting. Parents with Borderline Personality Disorder experience problems with stress and reactivity, the ability to regulate affect, and effective attunement to their child's emotional states.

A recent review raises the question of whether Borderline Personality Disorder is really a disorder of Complex Trauma (MacIntosh, Godbout, & Dubash, 2015), as the core components of Borderline Personality Disorder contain features that have been described as consequences of chronic childhood trauma: affect dysregulation, problems with relational adjustment, and problems with identity integration (including dissociation). It is these features that may be core to an understanding of the psychological difficulties that can result in child maltreatment.

Studies that specifically examine a child protective service population appear to provide further support for the relationship between Complex Trauma and Borderline Personality Disorder. A comparison of birth mothers involved with child protective services with a community control group found that mothers involved with child protective services had a higher rate of reported maltreatment in their own childhoods, as well as more features of Borderline Personality Disorder (Perepletchikova, Ansell, & Axelrod, 2012). Those with the most Borderline Personality features also had the most severe histories of maltreatment. However, it was the presence of Borderline Personality features, rather than the maltreatment history or even the presence of substance abuse, which predicted involvement with child protective services. These parents appear to have more difficulty maintaining a risk-free environment for children, even if they do not abuse or neglect their children.

## Trauma and Substance Use

Many people with traumatic histories, both children and adults, never receive the treatment they need in the aftermath of those experiences. Without adequate treatment and support, trauma often results in long-term subjective suffering from which people frequently seek to escape. A large and growing literature has found a positive relationship between histories of trauma and substance use problems (Keyser-Marcus et al., 2015). The presence of emotional dysregulation following child abuse seems to play a major role in the development of adult substance abuse (Mandavia, Robinson, Bradley, Ressler, & Powers, 2016). Parents who have used substances to self-medicate subjective distress produced by trauma often find themselves in further difficulty economically, socially, and legally, as well as in their capacity to parent in a reliable and consistent manner. As is true for serious mental illness, there is a tendency in child protective service evaluations to focus on compliance with drug treatment and with a cessation of drug use, without identifying and addressing the underlying trauma that stimulated the substance abuse. Thus, when parents continue to relapse, they are blamed for not being ready to live in recovery, not having sufficient self-control, or not loving their children enough, when the real problem is often going back into a trauma-filled environment or not sufficiently quelling the symptoms associated with the original trauma.

## Trauma and Parenting

Trauma from any source and its psychological consequences can impact parenting. Discussions of transgenerational trauma, intergenerational transmission of trauma, and historical trauma began in earnest in psychology with the examination of the impact of the European Holocaust on children of survivors. The idea that traumatic experiences of parents individually or communities of people collectively can impact subsequent generations continues to be the subject of considerable interest from psychological, historical, and biological perspectives.

Studies on the impact of parental PTSD specifically suggest an impairment in the parent–child relationship (van Ee, Kleber, & Jongmans, 2016). Several relational patterns are found in traumatized parents: less emotional availability; a more negative perception of their children; more easily dysregulated/distressed children. These relational patterns are like those of depressed and anxious parents. Caregivers substantiated for child abuse or neglect with a trauma history were found to have higher scores on the Child Abuse Potential Inventory than those without such a reported history (Craig & Sprang, 2007).

Trauma also appears to have an indirect effect upon parenting, in that there are elevated rates of postpartum depression in woman with a history of childhood trauma. Postpartum depression can affect the interaction and attachment between the child and mother and is associated with subsequent problems in the child (Choi et al., 2017). If a parent–child dyad with problematic interactions and attachment is the subject of a forensic evaluation, it is important to assess for both a history of parental trauma and of postpartum depression. This will provide the opportunity for an appropriate level of treatment that will assist each member of the dyad in the present and also serve a preventative function should the parent become pregnant again.

## Intergenerational Transmission of Child Abuse

The literature is generally supportive of the concept of an "intergenerational transmission of abuse" (Bartlett, Kotake, Fauth, & Easterbrooks, 2017). However, the degree of this transmission and the factors that provide protection are subject to continuing research.

There have been findings that suggest "type-to-type" correspondence in transmission, that is, parents who were neglected tend to be neglectful and parents who were physically abused tend to become physically abusive (Kim, 2009). A recent study (Bartlett et al., 2017) found that mothers who had experienced some type of maltreatment as children were much more likely to have maltreated their children in some manner, as compared with mothers who had not had this experience. They concluded, "As expected, although type-to-type (homotypic) transmission of neglect was strongly predicted across generations, when mothers had childhood histories of abuse *and* neglect, the likelihood of their own children experiencing multiple types of maltreatment, even by preschool age, increased sharply" (Bartlett et al., 2017, p. 92).

The presence of multiple types of maltreatment seems critical in the production of mental health problems that could lead to transmission of child abuse. Edwards, Holden, Felitti, and Anda (2003) studied a large sample of adults in a health maintenance organization and found that the number of types of abusive experiences (physical, sexual, witnessing maternal battering) was associated with poorer mental health. Furthermore, emotional abuse (e.g., being called names by a parent, feeling hated by a parent) had a significant main effect on mental health as an adult, and its presence heightened the impact of other types of abuse.

The presence of trauma symptoms in parents plays a mediational role in the intergenerational transmission of risk for physical abuse. Milner (2010) found that individuals with problems with self-reference (identity confusion) and with tension reduction behavior demonstrated heightened risk. Both problems are particularly associated with histories of Complex Trauma. High levels of defensive avoidance, a symptom typically associated with PTSD, was also predictive of heightened risk of intergenerational transmission of physical abuse.

Similarly, dissociation, a common consequence of repeated trauma, has also been implicated in the intergenerational transmission of child abuse. Focusing again on physical abuse, Narang and Contreras (2005) found that elevated dissociation was associated with higher physical abuse potential. Furthermore, parents who were physically abused and were also raised in a family environment characterized as uncohesive, unexpressive, and conflictual had higher levels of dissociation. Dissociation is often not identified during forensic evaluations unless the examiner inquires about it directly or it is manifested during the interview. When manifested, it can easily be misunderstood as a lack of interest in the content of the discussion, resulting in a parent being seen as uninvested in the process. Neglecting to identify dissociation can easily result in a client's lack of improvement when services are offered.

Another study confirmed emotional dysregulation and negative affect in mothers who experienced physical abuse as children to be mediators of the intergenerational transmission of child physical abuse (Smith, Cross, Winkler, Jovanovic, & Bradley, 2014). Emotional dysregulation and negative affect are likely to be identified in a forensic evaluation. However, if they are not understood as related to trauma, they can be easily misunderstood as general hostility and resistance.

## Racial Trauma

Although multiple authors cite the importance of identifying trauma, few recognize the existence and importance of racial trauma, especially for African–American parents within the context of child protective services and related forensic psychological evaluations.

A disproportionate number of African–American children across the country are placed in foster care and eventually freed for adoption through child protective service involvement (Dettlaff & Rycraft, 2010; Miller & Ward, 2008; Roberts, 2002). Factors that contribute to the disproportionality are: poverty; living in an urban poor neighborhood; institutional racism in the form of policy and procedures; a lack of staff cultural awareness and competence; staff fear of liability; high caseloads; and ineffective service delivery.

Bias in legal and mental health services was also reported to contribute to the disproportionality for African–Americans in the child welfare system. Several sources (Dettlaff & Rycraft, 2010; Miller & Ward, 2008) report disproportionality stemming from legal services to include the following issues: the quality of legal representation; inequity in child protective agency and court decisions; and the tendency to use middle-class standards for family reunification. Roberts (2002) reported that court decisions where parenting capacity is considered irrelevant to the issue of the child's "best interests" and the court's tendency to rely on forensic evaluations produced by the child welfare agency rather than attorneys for parents and children contribute to disproportionality. Dettlaff & Rycraft (2010) reported mental health services to be insensitive to the needs and worldview of African–American parents. In addition, Roberts (2002) reported mental health services contribute to disproportionality for African–Americans by: legitimizing the ongoing separation of parents and children; interpreting parental poverty and cultural issues as indicative of psychological deficiency; giving mental health providers monetary incentives to render opinions that side with the child welfare agency; giving the child welfare agency incentives to choose mental health providers that agree with them; and penalizing parents when they disagree with or question child protective service actions or child removal. Thus, for African–American parents, involvement with child protective services mirrors the race-based discrimination and oppression they experience in the larger society. This increases the likelihood that they will have a negative response to the child protective service system. This negative response reflects their lived experience of racism.

"Racial trauma," the repeated exposure to the chronic stressor of racism, has a cumulative effect on the individual and across multiple generations in a manner that is similar to the symptoms and sequelae noted in PTSD and Complex Trauma (Carlson, 1997; Carter, 2007; Comas-Diaz, Hall, & Neville, 2019; DeGruy, 2017; Ford, 2008; Franklin, Boyd-Franklin, & Kelly, 2006; Helms, Nicolas, & Green, 2012; Holmes, Facemire, & DaFonseca, 2016; Watson, Deblaere, Langrehr, Zelaya,

& Flores, 2016). Symptoms resulting from racial trauma include: reexperiencing; hyperarousal; hypervigilance; avoidance; dissociation; memory impairment; denial; limited emotional range; emotional reactivity; helplessness; anxiety; depression; anger/rage; self-blame; shame/guilt; poor self-concept; identity confusion; adoption of the belief system of the oppressor; self-defeating or overcompensating behaviors; poor/unstable relationships; inability to protect the self and others from situations that signal racism; exhaustion; and a high incidence of immune system and other medical problems (Carlson, 1997; Carter, 2007; DeGruy, 2017). As is true for more traditional forms of trauma, when racial trauma is also not identified and treated, parents will be at a higher risk for continuing to experience symptoms that will negatively impact their treatment success, functioning, and child protective service case.

Several studies have found a relationship between race-based stressors, trauma symptoms, mental health, and well-being. A direct relationship has been found between the level of racial discrimination and the level of dissociation (Polanco-Roman, Danies, & Anglin, 2016). Experiencing microaggressions has been found to be associated with depression and somatic symptoms (Holmes et al., 2016). Lastly, experiences with racial discrimination, and/or the frequency of racial discrimination, was found to predict PTSD diagnostic status, and was also found to be related to poorer general functioning in African–Americans (Sibrava et al., 2019). These studies demonstrate that, in order to be "culturally competent," attempts to address mental health and well-being among African–Americans must include a component that identifies and addresses racial trauma.

Racial trauma also impacts patterns of parent–child interaction and discipline. In comparison to white middle-class populations, African–American parenting styles often appear harsh and are more likely to include physical discipline (Dodge, McLoyd, & Lansford, 2005). African–American parents are often judged negatively during observations with their children and are frequently referred to parenting classes and family therapy. These negative characterizations often reflect a lack of recognition that the parenting styles, attitudes, and discipline patterns of African–American parents are adaptive and serve as a protective factor for many African–American children. Dodge et al. (2005) reported the parenting styles of African–Americans demonstrate the following strengths: these styles protect children from encounters with racism and from the dangers of the street; African–American children typically view strict discipline as a sign of family love and caring; greater African–American parental control and supervision were related to increased child well-being and higher grades in low-income neighborhoods. Within the African–American community, physical discipline is not necessarily seen as a sign of aggression. When African–American parents use culturally appropriate levels of physical discipline, it is done within the context of unqualified love and acceptance for the child, at levels that are far below the threshold for physical abuse (Dodge et al., 2005).

# Assessment Process

## *Parent Interview*

The goal of the parent interview is more than just collecting data. It is the psychologist's opportunity to demonstrate sensitivity toward the traumatized, anxious, upset parent, and demonstrate sensitivity to the power inequity and sociopolitical context of the evaluation. Psychologists can start the clinical evaluation by asking the parent several questions:

- How the parent feels about the interview
- Whether the parent has concerns about the evaluation
- What the parent's perceptions are regarding experiences with child protective services and the court

In addition to the above questions, the psychologist should also:

- Communicate awareness of the possibility of cultural, racial, and disproportionality issues in the evaluation and child protective service process;
- Establish the parent as the expert regarding these issues;
- Verbalize an openness to learn about and discuss these issues with the parent.

This approach provides the opportunity for the parent to feel empowered, decrease some of their self-protective behaviors, and to be more open and cooperative during the interview. It also allows the psychologist to demonstrate empathy, join with the client, and potentially be viewed as an ally.

During the evaluation, many parents will not identify their experiences as "traumas" or "maltreatment." Therefore, traumatic experiences can be elicited through questions that would produce a more general narrative about the parent's history. Parental narratives are likely to clarify themes of significance to the parent. It is important for the psychologist to be alert to the kinds of persistent interactions and misuse of power that characterize homes with chronic emotional abuse and domestic violence. Trauma narratives should include information about:

- Recollections of losses and separations
- Reasons for changes of residence
- Parenting practices in the parents' childhoods and with their own children
- Histories of conflicts in the home and in the community
- Sexual activity
- Experiences of coercion in adolescence and adulthood

The literature indicates that it is imperative to ask African–American parents specifically about their racial trauma histories. As recommended above for general traumas, the psychologist should also elicit narratives from the parent about their lifespan experiences with racism and discrimination. Examples of areas of inquiry include:

- The parents' experiences with racism and discrimination over their lifetime
- Specific instances of racism and discrimination that have had the most impact on them
- How these experiences shape who they are today
- What these experiences taught them
- What strategies they use to combat or counter their experience of racism and discrimination
- Whether these discrimination experiences and coping strategies manifested themselves during the current child protective service case

The nuance and richness of the parent narratives during the clinical interview far surpasses the type of information gleaned from merely having parents fill out impersonal personality and parenting inventories. This approach is especially critical for African–American parents, as it will produce a more accurate assessment and better prepare parents to engage in treatment.

## *Formal Testing*

For the child protection agency and the court, psychological testing is viewed as a benign and objective way to determine the presence of problems. Unfortunately, the history of testing shows it to be far from impartial. Rather, psychological tests, psychological theories, and the use of standardized norms have a history of being employed to legitimize bias and the social control of oppressed groups (Franklin, 1991; Kamin, 1974; Sue & Sue, 2016). The standards of functioning are based upon the attitudes, behavior, and performance of a white middle-class population. This does not recognize that the culture of oppressed parents imbues them with a different set of attitudes, behaviors, strengths, and worldviews that are adaptive for them (Boyd-Franklin, 2003; Kamin, 1974; McLoyd et al., 2005; Ramseur, 1991; Sue & Sue, 2016).

In addition to standard techniques, psychologists should consider using tests designed specifically to assess traumatic experiences and sequelae. Some of these tests include the Trauma Symptom Inventory -2 (Briere, 2011) and the Inventory of Altered Self-Capacities (Briere, 1998). Atkins (2014) provides a critique of 16 instruments used to measure perceived racial discrimination. Of the 16 instruments that were studied, only the adult Index of Race-Related Stress (IRRS) (Utsey & Ponterotto, 1996) was found to have all its racism subscales confirmed via factor analysis (Cultural, Institutional, Individual, and Collective Racism). The IRRS is a 46-item test that measures the frequency with which African–Americans encounter discrimination on a 5-point Likert scale. The IRRS also comes in a brief 22-item version (Utsey, 1999). In addition, a study by Sibrava et al. (2019) utilized the Everyday Discrimination Scale (Williams & Mohammed, 2009; Williams, Yu, Jackson, & Anderson, 1997), which was reported to be a 9-item scale with good psychometric properties that has been used in the United States and internationally.

## *Written Report*

Being treated with dignity and respect is very important for all parents, particularly for those of African descent (Boyd-Franklin, 2003; DeGruy, 2017; Sue & Sue, 2016). However, a lack of respect is often evident in the written psychological report. Parents may see the document and feel misunderstood, demeaned, over-pathologized, or even re-traumatized. This emotional harm contributes to difficulties completing services, including cooperation with future evaluations. The written report should offer a balanced view of the parent, where strengths, survival skills, and cultural issues, as well as problem areas are noted. Parents' statements should not be transcribed in broken English, which contributes to the parent appearing intellectually limited and incompetent. Surnames and not first names should be used to refer to adult clients.

### Testing Section

The testing section of the written report should discuss the ways in which the parent differs, if at all, from the predominant normative group of any psychological tests administered, including cognitive, personality, or parenting instruments. This section should outline what the literature says about performance differences between respective groups, and the cautions indicated by these differences. Any suggestion that IQ or other test scores are absolute or immutable or are more than a sample of behavior, with a related margin of error, should be avoided. If an adaptive behavior measure was not given, a diagnosis of Intellectual Disability cannot be used (American Psychiatric Association, 2013).

### Diagnostic Issues

The presence of diagnoses in a forensic psychological report often suggests to child protective services staff and the court that the client cannot parent. These professionals typically do not understand that having a mental health diagnosis does not necessarily indicate that parents are low functioning in comparison to the general population. The inappropriate portrayal of parents as pathological increases the likelihood that their children will not be returned to their care. When using diagnoses in child welfare cases, it is particularly important that the evaluator identify not only whether treatment is indicated, but also what the specific child safety risks are, if any, from such a diagnosis.

There are symptoms associated with trauma, particularly flashbacks, that may be misunderstood as symptoms of psychotic-level conditions. This kind of misdiagnosis has disastrous consequences for providing appropriate treatment as well as for child welfare outcomes. In addition, if there are comorbid diagnoses like Posttraumatic Stress Disorder, Complex Trauma, or other trauma sequelae, these are associated with a more complicated clinical picture. As stated earlier, without the recognition of trauma in the diagnostic assessment, progress in treatment of comorbid conditions may be significantly impaired. It is critical that trauma symptoms and issues be identified.

Despite the similarities between the symptoms of racial trauma and PTSD, the *Diagnostic and Statistical Manual of Mental Disorders - Fifth Edition (DSM-5)* (American Psychiatric Association, 2013) does not specifically recognize race-based trauma in its diagnostic nomenclature (Carter, 2007; DeGruy, 2017; Ford, 2008; Franklin et al., 2006; Helms et al., 2012; Holmes et al., 2016; Watson et al., 2016). A PTSD diagnosis requires an index event described as "actual or threatened death, serious injury or sexual violence" (American Psychiatric Association, 2013, p. 271). Most race-based events will not meet this criterion, despite the high level of victim suffering (Carter, 2007; Helms et al., 2012; Franklin et al., 2006; Watson et al., 2016), unless there is the threat of serious physical injury.

In cases where a race-based traumatic event does reach the threshold for a diagnosis of PTSD, there is a question as to whether giving a diagnosis is appropriate. Diagnoses presuppose pathology in the individual, rather than recognizing racial trauma symptoms to be a normal response to a malevolent environment (Carter, 2007; Franklin et al., 2006; Holmes et al., 2016). This becomes important in child welfare cases because a treatment plan for an individual with PTSD would be one of the trauma-informed therapies, whereas a treatment plan for racial trauma could simply involve some type of system intervention or client education. Within this context, a PTSD diagnosis may serve to further stigmatize the parent and cause child protective services to view the parent as more impaired than warranted. This could result in a longer mandate for services than is warranted, and result in a delay in family reunification.

African–Americans are typically inappropriately overdiagnosed, overmedicated, and undertreated in comparison to white middle-class populations (US Public Health Service, Office of the Surgeon General, Center for Mental Health, National Institute of Mental Health, 1999). This finding supports the authors' observation for African–American parents in child welfare cases to be more likely to be erroneously diagnosed with psychosis, Bipolar Disorder, or a Personality Disorder. Diagnostic differences may be due in part to the cultural insensitivity inherent in psychological tests and among many evaluators. However, it may also be due to the misinterpretation of sequelae of racial trauma as symptoms of clinical pathology rather than normal cultural variants. For example, African–American parents may be diagnosed as "paranoid" when they verbalize that "the system is against" them or be considered "religiously preoccupied" or "psychotic" because they admit "God frequently talks" to them. They may also be diagnosed with Bipolar Disorder because they present as "angry" during the interview. After being inappropriately diagnosed, it is not unusual for African–American parents to refuse to participate in the prescribed treatment. This refusal is typically labeled as "noncompliance" by the child protective service agency and the subsequent forensic psychologist, which in turn limits the likelihood that the child will be returned to the parent's care.

## Service Recommendations

There is a timetable within which parents must successfully complete services before their children can be returned to their care. There are often problems with the timeliness, the availability, the quality, the cultural appropriateness, and the breadth of services available through child protection agencies, particularly those provided to African–American parents (Dettlaff & Rycraft, 2010; Miller & Ward, 2008; Roberts, 2002). If parents do not complete services and improve, they may be deemed either unwilling or unable to correct the factors that are thought to be responsible for harm to their children.

When parents are not considered sufficiently rehabilitated, they are typically blamed for their lack of progress when many other factors may have played a role. The multiple external variables that pose problems are rarely recognized. For example, if a serious mental illness is diagnosed, the primary recommendation is typically medication. However, if Posttraumatic Stress Disorder and other trauma sequelae are present and not diagnosed, psychopharmacology may be inappropriate or insufficient. Other barriers to treatment include: no money for transportation to services; services that are far away from the parent's community; no childcare; scheduling services during the parent's work hours; not sufficiently explaining the rationale for services; poor communications with parents about appointment dates, times, and addresses; frequent turnover in service staff; the excessive use of group rather than individually oriented services; generic services that do not address the specific facts of the parent's child protective case; overscheduling parents with an excessive amount of services at one time; a lack of specialized mental health services; and not adequately addressing rapport, client resistance, and cultural preferences. Under these circumstances, parents are not likely to demonstrate significant improvements even when they attempt compliance with the recommended interventions. In contrast, clients who receive effective psychosocial interventions that target their trauma sequelae are much more likely to be able to manage their affective reactivity, create stability for their children, and achieve a positive child protective service outcome. Finally, it is important for psychologists to differentiate between suggestions for continued services that might be generally helpful and those that are required for a child to be safe, because suggestions for further treatment are often interpreted as necessary for reunification.

The literature suggests treating Posttraumatic Stress Disorder directly, once it is diagnosed, even when clients have comorbid diagnoses (Grubaugh et al., 2016). Similarly, it is recommended that those with histories of both psychological trauma and substance abuse problems be treated in an integrated manner (Dass-Brailsford & Myrick, 2010), as these clients tend to relapse quickly when treatment for either trauma or substance abuse is delayed.

When the symptom picture suggests borderline pathology or Complex Trauma, typically associated with histories of chronic trauma dating to childhood, Dialectical Behavior Therapy (DBT) should be considered. It should be noted, however, that evidence-based treatments are likely to require modification or time extensions, due to the number of multiple current stressors impacting these parents. Many parents involved in the child welfare system are also struggling with the chronic difficulties associated with concentrated poverty, like adequate housing, income, problematic schools, safety, and health issues. In addition, current approaches to the treatment of Complex Trauma suggest a three-stage model (safety, stabilization, and engagement; trauma memory and emotion processing; application to present and future), particularly for those with impaired relationships. This model involves considerably more time than treatments designated for simple trauma and classic PTSD (Courtois & Ford, 2013). Therefore, psychological evaluations should also include clear recommendations about what will be required to offer reasonable, adequate, and appropriate interventions. Furthermore, the psychologist should describe the kinds of positive changes that are likely to result from appropriate treatment.

Special consideration regarding interventions is also necessary as it pertains to domestic violence. A parent living in a situation characterized by intimate partner violence may well be traumatized by those experiences. The general tendency in child protection cases is to focus on eliminating the violence from the child's life. It is important to remember, however, that even when the violence stops, a parent who has been traumatized by these and other experiences may be struggling with trauma sequelae that can negatively affect parenting. Such parents may remain highly anxious, depressed, dissociative, and/or affectively labile. They can misperceive benign situations with children as very threatening or, conversely, be nonresponsive. Often, the perpetrator is underserved once removed from the home, and there are minimal services geared toward clinically appropriate and safe family reunification. Generic parenting or anger-control classes that do not address the trauma triggers inherent in the parent's interactions with the child or partner, or that do not address the specific characteristics of the parent's interactions with the specific child or partner, will be minimally effective.

As is true for personal trauma, African–American parents will only make partial improvements if racial trauma is not identified and incorporated into treatment. African–American parents need providers who possess an understanding of cultural issues and who will help them respond to racism in a manner that will facilitate rather than sabotage the return of their children. Trauma treatments like Eye Movement Desensitization and Reprocessing (EMDR), focused directly on memories of racial events and symptoms, have been useful in processing trauma across a variety of cultural issues (Nickerson, 2017). Numerous authors (Anderson & Stevenson, 2019; Coard & Sellers, 2005; DeGruy, 2017; Helms et al., 2012; Polanco-Roman et al., 2016; Sue & Sue, 2016; Sue et al., 2019) offer other techniques that forensic psychologists can also recommend for therapists to use to help African–American parents decrease racial trauma:

- Preemptive and anticipatory conversations with clients about race and racism
- Helping the client develop the ability to accurately read racist encounters
- Helping the client develop a repertoire of active strategies to implement during racist encounters
- Helping the client develop the ability to process or rewrite racist encounters in a positive manner

- Helping the client develop cultural pride and a positive racial identity
- Moving beyond client survival and coping toward concrete strategies that clients, bystanders, and allies can perform in response to perpetrators

The literature reports the above strategies have the potential to decrease dissociation and mitigate the effects of racial distress in African–American populations (Anderson & Stevenson, 2019; Coard & Sellers, 2005; DeGruy, 2005; Helms et al., 2012; Polanco-Roman et al., 2016; Sue & Sue, 2016; Sue et al., 2019). Therefore, it is incumbent upon mental health professionals to incorporate issues regarding positive racial coping, racial identity, and racial socialization into their work with African–Americans, as well as refer clients to African-centered community-based organizations.

Finally, given the socioeconomic conditions of many of these parents, it is sometimes necessary for child protective services to help with housing, vocational development, and employment opportunities. However, poverty is not a legitimate reason for removing children or terminating parental rights, and problems in economic and housing stability, endemic in poor communities, should not be the reason a psychologist finds a parent unfit for reunification.

## Conclusion

Trauma is central to the lives of many parents involved in the child welfare system. This chapter has reviewed ways in which trauma can affect a parent's psychological status, although its significance and impact are often under-recognized and misconstrued. Inquiries into the client's current perspective about the child welfare system and the psychological evaluation process, the client's personal trauma exposure, and the client's experiences of racial trauma are all necessary. Without a full understanding of the existence of trauma and its impact, it is likely that the findings of the evaluation will be limited at best and potentially harmful to the parent and child. Therefore, it is incumbent upon the evaluator to take steps to develop rapport with the parent, to take a thorough history with particular attention to traumatic experiences (including racially traumatic experiences), to assess whether trauma sequelae are present in the current symptom picture, and to offer treatment suggestions and plans that take traumatic histories, culture, and the context into account.

## Questions/Activities for Further Exploration

1. Why is it important to understand the context in which a forensic evaluation occurs? What is the impact on parents of being evaluated in the context of a child protection case?
2. What measures can psychologists take to minimize the impact of contextual trauma?

3. What is the role of trauma in the intergenerational transmission of child abuse?
4. What is meant by "racial trauma"? How does racial trauma affect African–American parents and child welfare forensic psychological evaluations?
5. Consider the relationship between the experience of separation from children for African–American parents today with the legacy of forced removal of children from enslaved Africans historically. How might that legacy impact parents involved in the child welfare system? Are there other groups who have experienced or are experiencing similar family disruptions by governmental agencies?
6. What are some techniques psychologists can employ to assess histories of trauma in parents?
7. How is the accurate identification of trauma and its sequelae important in recommending services for parents involved in child protection cases? What are the likely outcomes when trauma is not identified?
8. What are some specific strategies that psychological evaluations can recommend to help African–American parents decrease racial trauma?

# References

Alsawy, S., Wood, L., Taylor, P. J., & Morrison, A. P. (2015). Psychotic experiences and PTSD: Exploring associations in a population survey. *Psychological Medicine, 45*(13), 2849–2859.

Álvarez, M., Roura, P., Foguet, Q., Osés, A., Solà, J., & Arrufat, F. (2012). Posttraumatic stress disorder comorbidity and clinical implications in patients with severe mental illness. *Journal of Nervous and Mental Disease, 200*(6), 549–552.

American Psychiatric Association. (2013). *Diagnostic and statistical manual for mental disorders* (5th ed.). Washington, D.C.: American Psychiatric Publishing.

Anderson, R. E., & Stevenson, H. C. (2019). RECASTing racial stress and trauma: Theorizing the healing potential of racial socialization in families. *American Psychologist, 74*(1), 63–75.

Assion, H., Brune, N., Schmidt, N., Aubel, T., Edel, M., Basilowski, M., ... Frommberger, U. (2009). Trauma exposure and post-traumatic stress disorder in bipolar disorder. *Social Psychiatry and Psychiatric Epidemiology, 44*(12), 1041–1049.

Atkins, R. (2014). Instruments measuring perceived racism/racial discrimination: Review and critique of factor analytic techniques. *International Journal of Health Services, 44*(4), 711–734.

Bartlett, J. D., Kotake, C., Fauth, R., & Easterbrooks, M. A. (2017). Intergenerational transmission of child abuse and neglect: Do maltreatment type, perpetrator, and substantiation status matter? *Child Abuse and Neglect, 63*, 84–94.

Briere, J. (1998). Inventory of Altered Self-Capacities. Lutz, FL: Psychological Assessment Resources, Inc.

Briere, J. (2011). Trauma Symptom Inventory-2. Lutz, Fl: Psychological Assessment Resources, Inc.

Boyd-Franklin, N. (2003). *Black families in therapy* (2nd ed.). New York: Guilford Press.

Carlson, E. B. (1997). *Trauma assessments: Clinician's guide*. New York, NY: Guilford Press.

Carter, R. T. (2007). Racism and psychological and emotional injury: Recognizing and assessing race-based traumatic stress. *The Counseling Psychologist, 35*(1), 13–105.

Choi, K. W., Sikkema, K. J., Vythilingum, B., Geerts, L., Faure, S. C., Watt, M. H., ... Stein, D. J. (2017). Maternal childhood trauma, postpartum depression, and infant outcomes: Avoidant affective processing as a potential mechanism. *Journal of Affective Disorders, 211*, 107–115.

Coard, S., & Sellers, R. (2005). African American families as a context for racial socialization. In V. C. McLoyd, N. E. Hill, & K. A. Dodge (Eds.), *African American family life: Ecological and cultural diversity*. New York, NY: Guilford Press.

Comas-Díaz, L., Hall, G. N., & Neville, H. A. (2019). Racial trauma: Theory, research, and healing: Introduction to the special issue. *American Psychologist, 74*(1), 1–5.

Cook, A. Blaustein, M., Spinazzola, J., & van der Kolk, B. (Eds.) (2003). Complex trauma in children and adolescents. National Child Traumatic Stress Network. https://www.nctsn.org/resources/complex-trauma-children-and-adolescents. Accessed 31 May 2018.

Courtois, C. A., & Ford, J. D. (2013). *Treatment of complex trauma: A sequenced, relationship-based approach*. New York, NY: Guilford Press.

Craig, C. D., & Sprang, G. (2007). Trauma exposure and child abuse potential: Investigating the cycle of violence. *American Journal of Orthopsychiatry, 77*(2), 296–305.

Dass-Brailsford, P., & Myrick, A. C. (2010). Psychological trauma and substance abuse: The need for an integrated approach. *Trauma, Violence, and Abuse, 11*(4), 202–213.

DeGregorio, L. J. (2013). Intergenerational transmission of abuse: Implications for parenting interventions from a neuropsychological perspective. *Traumatology, 19*(2), 158–166.

DeGruy, J. (2005). Post Traumatic Slave Syndrome. Milwaukie, Oregon: Uptone Press.

DeGruy, J. (2017). *Post traumatic slave syndrome: America's legacy of enduring injury and healing*. Portland, OR: Joy DeGruy Publications Inc.

Dettlaff, A. J., & Rycraft, J. R. (2010). Factors contributing to disproportionality in the child welfare system: Views from the legal community. *Social Work, 55*(3), 213–224.

Dodge, K. A., McLoyd, V. C., & Lansford, J. E. (2005). The cultural context of physically disciplining children. In V. C. McLoyd, N. E. Hill, & K. A. Dodge (Eds.), *African American family life: Ecological and cultural diversity* (pp. 245–263). New York, NY: Guilford Press.

Dumbrill, G. C. (2006). Parental experience of child protection intervention: A qualitative study. *Child Abuse and Neglect, 30*(1), 27–37.

Edwards, V. J., Holden, G. W., Felitti, V. J., & Anda, R. F. (2003). Relationship between multiple forms of childhood maltreatment and adult mental health in community respondents: Results from the adverse childhood experiences study. *American Journal of Psychiatry, 160*(8), 1453–1460.

Ford, J. (2008). Trauma, posttraumatic stress disorder, and ethnoracial minorities: Towards diversity and cultural competence in principles and practice. *Clinical Psychology: Science and Practice, 15*(1), 62–67.

Franklin, V. P. (1991). Black social scientists and the mental testing movement. In R. Jones (Ed.), *Black psychology* (pp. 207–224). Berkeley, CA: Cobb and Henry Publishers.

Franklin, A. J., Boyd-Franklin, N., & Kelly, S. (2006). Racism and invisibility: Race-based stress, emotional abuse, and psychological trauma for people of color. *Journal of Emotional Abuse, 6*(2–3), 9–30.

Goldberg, J. F., & Garno, J. L. (2005). Development of posttraumatic stress disorder in adult bipolar patients with histories of severe childhood abuse. *Journal of Psychiatric Research, 39*(6), 595–601.

Gonzalez, M. J. (2014). Mental health care of families affected by the child welfare system. *Child Welfare, 93*(1), 7–57.

Grubaugh, A. L., Clapp, J. D., Frueh, B. C., Tuerk, P. W., Knapp, R. G., & Egede, L. E. (2016). Open trial of exposure therapy for PTSD among patients with severe and persistent mental illness. *Behaviour Research and Therapy, 78*, 1–12.

Helms, J., Nicolas, G., & Green, C. (2012). Racism and ethnoviolence as trauma: Enhancing professional and research training. *Traumatology, 18*(1), 65–74.

Hernandez, J. M., Cordova, M. J., Ruzek, J., Reiser, R., Gwizdowski, I. S., Suppes, T., & Ostacher, M. J. (2013). Presentation and prevalence of PTSD in a bipolar disorder population: A STEP-BD examination. *Journal of Affective Disorders, 150*(2), 450–455.

Holmes, S. C., Facemire, V. C., & DaFonseca, A. M. (2016). Expanding criterion A for posttraumatic stress disorder: Considering the deleterious impact of oppression. *Traumatology, 22*(4), 314–321.

Hulette, A., Kaehler, L., & Freyd, J. (2011). Intergenerational associations between trauma and dissociation. *Journal of Family Violence, 26*(3), 217–225.

Kamin, L. J. (1974). *The science and politics of IQ*. New York, NY: Routledge, Taylor and Francis Group.

Keyser-Marcus, L., Alvanzo, A., Rieckmann, T., Thacker, L., Sepulveda, A., Forcehimes, A., … Svikis, D. S. (2015). Trauma, gender, and mental health symptoms in individuals with substance use disorders. *Journal of Interpersonal Violence, 30*(1), 3–24.

Kim, J. (2009). Type-specific intergenerational transmission of neglectful and physically abusive parenting behaviors among young parents. *Children and Youth Services Review, 31*(7), 761–767.

MacIntosh, H. B., Godbout, N., & Dubash, N. (2015). Borderline personality disorder: Disorder of trauma or personality, a review of the empirical literature. *Canadian Psychology/Psychologie Canadienne, 56*(2), 227–241.

Mandavia, A., Robinson, G. N., Bradley, B., Ressler, K. J., & Powers, A. (2016). Exposure to childhood abuse and later substance use: Indirect effects of emotion dysregulation and exposure to trauma. *Journal of Traumatic Stress, 29*(5), 422–429.

Maniglio, R. (2013). The impact of child sexual abuse on the course of bipolar disorder: A systematic review. *Bipolar Disorders, 15*(4), 341–358.

McLoyd, V. C., Hill, N. E., & Dodge, K. A. (Eds.). (2005). *African American family life: Ecological and cultural diversity*. New York, NY: Guilford Press.

Miller, O. A., & Ward, K. J. (2008). Emerging strategies for reducing racial disproportionality and disparate outcomes in child welfare: The results of a national breakthrough series collaborative. *Child Welfare, 87*(2), 211–240.

Milner, J. S., Thomsen, C. J., Crouch, J. L., Rabenhorst, M. M., Martens, P. M., Dyslin, C. W., … Merrill, L. L. (2010). Do trauma symptoms mediate the relationship between childhood physical abuse and adult child abuse risk? *Child Abuse and Neglect, 34*(5), 332–344.

Morrison, T. (1996). Partnership and collaboration: Rhetoric and reality. *Child Abuse and Neglect, 20*(2), 127–140.

Narang, D. S., & Contreras, J. M. (2005). The relationships of dissociation and affective family environment with the intergenerational cycle of child abuse. *Child Abuse & Neglect, 29*(6), 683–699.

Neria, Y., Bromet, E. J., Sievers, S., Lavelle, J., & Fochtmann, L. J. (2002). Trauma exposure and posttraumatic stress disorder in psychosis: Findings from a first-admission cohort. *Journal of Consulting and Clinical Psychology, 70*(1), 246–251.

Neria, Y., Olfson, M., Gameroff, M. J., Wickramaratne, P., Pilowsky, D., Verdeli, H., & Weissman, M. M. (2008). Trauma exposure and posttraumatic stress disorder among primary care patients with bipolar spectrum disorder. *Bipolar Disorders, 10*(4), 503–510.

Nickerson, M. (Ed.). (2017). *Cultural competence and healing culturally based trauma with EMDR therapy: Innovative strategies and protocols*. New York: Springer Publishing Company.

O'Hare, T., Shen, C., & Sherrer, M. (2013). Differences in trauma and posttraumatic stress symptoms in clients with schizophrenia spectrum and major mood disorders. *Psychiatry Research, 205*(1–2), 85–89.

Otto, M. W., Perlman, C. A., Wernicke, R., Reese, H. E., Bauer, M. S., & Pollack, M. H. (2004). Posttraumatic stress disorder in patients with bipolar disorder: A review of prevalence, correlates, and treatment strategies. *Bipolar Disorders, 6*(6), 470–479.

Perepletchikova, F., Ansell, E., & Axelrod, S. (2012). Borderline personality disorder features and history of childhood maltreatment in mothers involved with child protective services. *Child Maltreatment, 17*(2), 182–190.

Polanco-Roman, L., Danies, A., & Anglin, D. M. (2016). Racial discrimination as race-based trauma, coping strategies, and dissociative symptoms among emerging adults. *Psychological Trauma: Theory, Research, Practice, and Policy, 8*(5), 609–617.

Quarantini, L. C., Miranda-Scippa, Â., Nery-Fernandes, F., Andrade-Nascimento, M., Galvão-de-Almeida, A., Guimarães, J. L., … Koenen, K. C. (2010). The impact of comorbid posttraumatic stress disorder on bipolar disorder patients. *Journal of Affective Disorders, 123*(1–3), 71–76.

Ramseur, H. (1991). Psychologically healthy Black Americans. In R. Jones (Ed.), *Black psychology*. Berkeley, CA: Cobb and Henry Publishers.

Roberts, D. (2002). *Shattered bonds: The color of child welfare*. New York: Basic Civitas Books.

Sibrava, N. J., Bjornsson, A. S., Pérez Benítez, A. C. I., Moitra, E., Weisberg, R. B., & Keller, M. B. (2019). Posttraumatic stress disorder in African American and Latinx adults: Clinical course and the role of racial and ethnic discrimination. *American Psychologist, 74*(1), 101–116.

Smith, A. L., Cross, D., Winkler, J., Jovanovic, T., & Bradley, B. (2014). Emotional dysregulation and negative affect mediate the relationship between maternal history of child maltreatment and maternal child abuse potential. *Journal of Family Violence, 29*(5), 483–494.

Stromwall, L. K., Larson, N. C., Nieri, T., Holley, L. C., Topping, D., Castillo, J., & Ashford, J. (2008). Parents with co-occurring mental health and substance abuse conditions involved in child protection services: Clinical profile and treatment needs. *Child Welfare, 87*(3), 95–113.

Sue, D. W., Alsaidi, S., Awad, M. N., Glaeser, E., Calle, C. Z., & Mendez, N. (2019). Disarming racial microaggressions: Microintervention strategies for targets, white allies, and bystanders. *American Psychologist, 74*(1), 128–142.

Sue, D. W., & Sue, D. (2016). *Counseling the culturally diverse: Theory and practice* (7th ed.). New York, NY: Wiley.

Tuttle, A. R., Knudson-Martin, C., Levin, S., Taylor, B., & Andrews, J. (2007). Parents' experiences in child protective services: Analysis of a dialogical group process. *Family Process, 46*(3), 367–380.

Utsey, S. O. (1999). Development and validation of a short form of the Index of Race-Related Stress (IRRS)–Brief Version. *Measurement and Evaluation in Counseling and Development, 32*(3), 149–167.

Utsey, S. O., & Ponterotto, J. G. (1996). Development and validation of the Index of Race-Related Stress (IRRS). *Journal of Counseling Psychology, 43*(4), 490–501.

U.S. Public Health Service, Office of the Surgeon General, Center for Mental Health, National Institute of Mental Health. (1999). *Mental health: A report of the surgeon general*. Rockville, MD: U.S. National Institute of Mental Health.

van der Kolk, B. A. (2005). Developmental trauma disorder: Toward a rational diagnosis for children with complex trauma histories. *Psychiatric Annals, 35*(5), 401–408.

van Ee, E., Kleber, R. J., & Jongmans, M. J. (2016). Relational patterns between caregivers with PTSD and their nonexposed children: A review. *Trauma, Violence, and Abuse, 17*(2), 186–203.

Watson, L. B., Deblaere, C., Langrehr, K., Zelaya, D. G., & Flores, M. J. (2016). The influence of multiple oppressions on women of color's experiences with insidious trauma. *Journal of Counseling Psychology, 63*(6), 656–667.

Westad, C., & McConnell, D. (2012). Child welfare involvement of mothers with mental health issues. *Community Mental Health Journal, 48*(1), 29–37.

Williams, D. R., & Mohammed, S. A. (2009). Discrimination and racial disparities in health: Evidence and needed research. *Journal of Behavioral Medicine, 32*(1), 20–47.

Williams, D.R., Yu, Y., Jackson, J.S., & Anderson, N.B. (1997). Racial differences in physical and mental health: Socioeconomic status, stress, and discrimination. *Journal of Health Psychology, 2*, 335–351.

# Chapter 9
# Trauma-Informed Child Custody Evaluation as Delinquency Prevention

**Amanda D. Zelechoski, Rachel Lindsay, and Lori Heusel**

## Introduction

It is well established that child custody evaluations are among the most complex and high-risk types of forensic mental health assessments to conduct (Melton et al., 2018). There are typically many individuals involved in the evaluation process (including parties and third-party collaterals) and the evaluator's findings and recommendations are often weighted heavily by the legal decision-maker. When a child custody evaluator becomes involved, it is usually after a period of intense family conflict, which can have long-standing adverse impacts on children's well-being and put them at risk for future problem behavior. The focus of this chapter is how such family conflict can be a risk factor for later delinquent behavior, and how custody evaluations can potentially serve as a protective factor. After discussing the empirical relationship between family conflict and delinquency, we provide a brief overview of the typical child custody evaluation process and offer ideas about how to incorporate more of a delinquency prevention framework into child custody evaluations. Given the robust efficacy of trauma-informed approaches, particularly in the area of juvenile delinquency prevention, we then highlight specific ways child custody evaluators can be trauma-informed and more prevention-oriented throughout the evaluation process. We follow this with a brief case example that demonstrates some of the concepts included in this chapter and conclude with a discussion of additional policy and implementation considerations.

A. D. Zelechoski (✉) · R. Lindsay · L. Heusel
Valparaiso University, Valparaiso, IN, USA
e-mail: amanda.zelechoski@valpo.edu; rachel.lindsay@valpo.edu; lori.heusel@valpo.edu

© Springer Nature Switzerland AG 2020
R. A. Javier et al. (eds.), *Assessing Trauma in Forensic Contexts*,
https://doi.org/10.1007/978-3-030-33106-1_9

## Overview of the Relationship Between Family Conflict and Juvenile Delinquency

As far back as documentation exists, scholars have been fascinated with and concerned about the relationship between family structure and long-term societal and individual outcomes. The constellation of the "typical" American family has seen dramatic fluctuation over the last several centuries related to what or who comprises a nuclear family, whether either or both parents work outside the home, and how child-rearing responsibilities are allocated (Sanburn, 2010). Part of this evolution is attributable to broader societal trends, such as lower marriage rates, higher cohabitation and remarriage/blended family rates, and increased racial, ethnic, and sexual orientation diversity within families (Melton et al., 2018). As the family structure landscape has changed over time, so has our understanding about the impact of parental conflict and separation on children.

Over the last century, a robust body of research has accumulated regarding the relationship between parental separation or divorce and negative outcomes for children, the most extreme of which may be juvenile delinquency. Though parental conflict and separation is, undoubtedly, a time of adjustment and disruption, many children demonstrate resilience, proving that long-term negative consequences are not necessarily inevitable (Kelly & Emery, 2003). However, there have also been numerous studies that found children from divorced families have a greater likelihood of engaging in delinquent behavior (e.g., Burt, Barnes, McGue, & Iacono, 2008; Demuth & Brown, 2004; Price & Kunz, 2003). As Price and Kunz (2003) noted in their comprehensive meta-analysis, this could be due to a myriad of factors that include differential processing by the juvenile justice system for children from "broken" versus "intact" homes, and not just due to the circumstances surrounding parental conflict and separation. Their results generally supported the abundance of research that establishes a link between parental separation and delinquency, but also cautions that divorce may not be the primary or the only factor in this relationship.

It is complex and, to some extent, impossible to establish a direct causal relationship between family conflict and delinquency, given the numerous moderating, mediating, and confounding factors that play a role, as well as the inability to carry out various types of controlled and randomized experiments in this domain due to ethical issues. Additional variables that could simultaneously be serving as risk factors for delinquency include increased financial pressure as a result of the parental separation; frequency and intensity of pre-separation conflict; presence of domestic violence, abuse, or neglect; instability or displacement due to the separation, nature, and quality of each parent's relationship with the child; each parent's ability to monitor, manage, nurture, and appropriately discipline the child; poor academic achievement or motivation; and other preexisting or exacerbated mental health issues of the parents and/or child (Melton et al., 2018; Price & Kunz, 2003). However, what seems clear is that there is, indeed, a relationship between parental conflict and adverse outcomes for children, even if the nature of that relationship is not quite understood (Zelechoski, 2015).

It is also unclear whether parental separation itself serves as a risk or protective factor and under what circumstances. For many children, the parental separation or divorce is the culmination of a long period of exposure to other risk factors, such as ongoing parental conflict, domestic violence, and instability in the home. Following the parental separation, additional risks may emerge, such as reduced or lost connections to important relationships, relocation and displacement, and increased economic pressures. Numerous studies confirm that divorce increases the risk for adjustment problems and Kelly and Emery (2003) noted that "the largest effects are seen in externalizing symptoms, including conduct disorders, antisocial behaviors, and problems with authority figures and parents" (p. 355). These types of post-divorce or separation outcomes are consistent with common emotional and behavioral precursors to juvenile justice involvement (Li & Lerner, 2011).

However, for some children, the parental separation can serve as a protective factor in mitigating risk for long-term adverse outcomes. This may be due to increased environmental stability, such as a reduction in exposure to daily conflict and establishment of a consistent custodial arrangement and schedule. It may also be due to improved relationships and support, including increased quality (as opposed to frequency) of time spent with each parent and increased parenting competence following separation (Kelly & Emery, 2003). These are just some examples that highlight the importance of remaining cognizant of the ways in which the process of parental separation can both increase and decrease risk for future negative outcomes, including delinquency.

## Systemic Involvement and Overlap

There are three systems that frequently overlap or interact when substantial family conflict is present: the family court system, the child welfare system, and the juvenile justice system. The family court system handles cases involving family matters such as custody, paternity, support, visitation, adoption, and divorce cases (Schepard & Bozzomo, 2003). The child welfare system is charged with ensuring children's safety and healthy development and handles reports of abuse and neglect (Child Welfare Information Gateway, 2013). The juvenile justice system is responsible for the processing and (depending on the jurisdiction's guiding philosophy) rehabilitation or punishment of youth charged with delinquent offenses (Snyder & Sickmund, 1999). Thus, another layer to consider is the complex role played by systemic involvement and how it factors into children's adjustment following parental separation.

The original inspiration for the underlying premise of this chapter was a conversation between the first author and a local judge in which the judge noted that, for many of the adults who come before her on serious criminal charges, she is acutely aware that she could walk down the hall to family court and likely find past case records related to that individual and his/her family. We wondered together why, then, do we fail to consider early family court involvement as potentially predictive of later juvenile justice system involvement in the same way that we devote much scholarship and policy-related resources to understanding and serving "crossover youth" (i.e., youth with concurrent involvement in the child welfare and juvenile justice systems)?

An example of one approach to address this overlapping system involvement for high-conflict families is "unified family courts," in which all cases involving the same family remain with the same judge (Belgrad, 2003). Often referred to as a "one judge-one family" model, this includes potentially handling any child custody, child support, abuse or neglect allegations, domestic violence allegations, and juvenile delinquency charges (Geraghty & Mlyniec, 2002). There have been many benefits cited by jurisdictions utilizing this approach, including service and intervention coordination, more effective and efficient case processing, and cost savings (Danziger, 2003). However, there have also been criticisms and concerns expressed about confidentiality, due process, and potential judicial conflicts of interest in unified family courts (Greacen, 2008). Notwithstanding these critiques, finding ways to coordinate multiple system involvement remains an important step toward prevention of long-term risk for juvenile delinquency and other adverse outcomes.

## Child Custody Evaluation as Prevention

Though laws related to parental rights and the legal status of children have evolved substantially over several centuries, it has only been in the last 50 or so years that mental health professionals have become directly involved in the family court decision-making process (Guy & Zelechoski, 2017). This is primarily due to the predominant shift toward a "best interests of the child" standard and the court's need to obtain information related to the child's relationship with each parent in order to make a best interests determination (Kelly, 1994). The specific role played by mental health professionals in these child custody matters has varied over time, but tends to primarily fall in the realm of psychological evaluation of the family, addressing domains such as parent–child attachment, the mental and physical health of some or all of the parties, co-parenting and communication dynamics between the parents, and specific needs of the child(ren). Though there is ongoing debate in the field regarding whether and to what extent child custody evaluations are valid, empirically supported, or even useful to the trier of fact, they continue to be requested by family law courts, particularly for the highest-conflict families (Lund, 2015; Melton et al., 2018).

Much has been written about procedures, methods, and best practices in forensic mental health assessment, of which child custody evaluation is one type (e.g., American Psychological Association [APA], 2010; Association of Family and Conciliation Courts [AFCC], 2006; Grisso, 2003; Heilbrun, 2001). Forensic mental health assessments are typically conducted at the request of an attorney or a court to provide information related to the facts at issue in a legal matter. This is distinguished from psychological assessment in therapeutic contexts, in which the mental health professional's role is to assess a client's current symptoms and functioning in order to determine the appropriate course of treatment (Greenberg & Shuman, 2007). In the family law context, child custody evaluations are used to assist judges, lawyers, and families in decision-making about the legal and physical custody arrangements for the child (Saini, 2008). Though child custody evaluation is perhaps the most underdeveloped and least empirically-grounded type of forensic mental health assessment (Emery, Otto, & O'Donohue, 2005), there are numerous guiding principles (e.g., AFCC, 2006; APA, 2010; Luftman, Veltkamp, Clark, Lannacone, & Snooks, 2005) and professional resources (e.g., Ackerman, 2006; Fuhrmann & Zibbell, 2012; Gould & Martindale, 2007; Zelechoski, Fuhrmann, Zibbell, & Cavallero, 2012) available to guide evaluators.

The standard child custody evaluation process is as follows. When the level of conflict between parents is high and alternative dispute resolution methods (e.g., mediation) have failed, one or both of the parents' attorneys may request or the judge may order that the family participates in an evaluation. Historically, each party would retain his/her own evaluator and a "battle of the experts" would ensue (Emery et al., 2005). Now, it is much more common and preferred for the court to order a single mental health professional to conduct the evaluation as a neutral, objective expert (Melton et al., 2018). The scope of the evaluation can vary widely and might include a request for information about the developmental needs of the child, psychological functioning of the parents, presence of child maltreatment or inappropriate disciplinary practices, or the potential impact of various custodial or visitation arrangements (Melton et al., 2018).

Depending on the specific referral question(s), the evaluator would then use multiple methods to gather data that forms the basis of recommendations provided in a final report to the court and/or the parties. The evaluator typically uses direct methods of data collection, such as psychological testing, clinical interview, parent-child observation, and collateral interviews, as well as indirect methods, such as reviewing school, medical, childcare, police, and legal records (APA, 2010). There is widespread disagreement in the field about whether and to what extent psychological testing should be utilized in this type of forensic mental health assessment and, if so, which tests are appropriate and provide valid, relevant information (Emery et al., 2005). Despite this debate, the use of both traditional psychological assessments and specialized parenting assessment measures occurs often in practice (Ackerman & Pritzl, 2011; Quinnell & Bow, 2001).

The child custody evaluation process then typically concludes with the preparation and submission of a final report to the court and/or the parties, which includes specific recommendations. Another common area of dispute within the field is related to the types of recommendations and opinions included in this final report. There is some disagreement in the forensic mental health assessment field generally about whether forensic evaluators should provide opinions about the "ultimate issue" or the specific legal issue to be decided by the trier of fact (Melton et al., 2018).

Research suggests that the vast majority of forensic experts believe it is not appropriate to opine about the ultimate issue, even if requested to do so by the court, though perspectives vary depending on the type of referral question and basis for rendering such an opinion (Buchanan, 2006).

Similarly, in the child custody realm, evaluators are cautioned against providing specific conclusions about how the judge should decide the custody matter. Rather, evaluators are encouraged to distinguish between descriptive information, interpretations, and recommendations, to tailor recommendations to the referral question(s), and to ensure that any conclusions drawn are closely and explicitly tied to the data on which they were based (Melton et al., 2018). Melton et al. (2018) provide the following examples of potential recommendations child custody evaluators might provide:

> Examples of recommendations include coparenting coordination and other conflict management services, emotional support services, community supports, respite options for mentally ill or overwhelmed parents, self-help services, anger management referrals, trauma therapy, substance abuse rehabilitation services, domestic violence safety resources, risk management, after-school resources, parent mentoring and support services for parents with cognitive limitations, and identification of visitation supervisory resources or supervision centers. Recommendations are most helpful when they include examples of existing services in the community. (p. 553).

However, child custody evaluation reports often stop short of this degree of breadth and only provide recommendations presumed to be relevant to the overall custodial determination or visitation schedule (Fuhrmann & Zibbell, 2012). For example, Bow and Quinnell (2001) found that there tend be minimal or no recommendations in child custody evaluation reports for supplemental intervention for any of the parties, such as individual therapy for one or both of the parents, individual therapy for the child, or parenting classes. They noted that, even when evaluators rated domestic violence as one of the most important criteria on which to base custody decisions, they rarely included recommendations for domestic violence programs in their evaluation reports.

As noted, child custody evaluations tend to be ordered by the court when there is extremely high parental conflict or when the parties have reached an impasse in mediation or settlement negotiations (Saini, 2008). The final child custody evaluation report is typically submitted directly to the court and/or to the parties' respective attorneys and the evaluator does not have further contact with the family unless or until he/she is called to testify about the evaluation in a subsequent court proceeding.

With this overview in mind, we now discuss why these two procedural elements, namely, ordering an evaluation as a last resort and not allowing post-evaluation feedback or clarification, miss important opportunities for prevention. We argue, among other things, that child custody evaluations should be utilized much earlier in the process as a form of triage, and that evaluators can play a more substantial role in future delinquency prevention by providing more comprehensive recommendations and feedback to families throughout the evaluation process.

## *Triage*

For many families, meeting with a child custody evaluator may be their first encounter with a mental health professional, particularly if there has never been prior child welfare involvement. Depending on the nature and specificity of the court's referral question(s), the child custody evaluator is presented with a unique opportunity to identify and triage the individual needs of each child, as well as to assess each parent's ability to meet those needs and make recommendations about what additional services or interventions might be necessary. The term "triage" is more often used in medical contexts and refers to the process of determining how to sort and allocate treatment to patients based on the severity of their conditions. In this context, conceptualizing a child custody evaluation as an indirect way to detect and prioritize the family's areas of risk and vulnerability can help the court and the parties with decision-making related to the child(ren)'s best interests.

In some cases, issues such as a child's learning difficulties or medical vulnerabilities may have already been identified by school personnel or a pediatrician and play a central role in the custody evaluation and decision-making process. However, depending on the child's age, the child custody evaluator might be the first to detect initial warning signs or symptoms of emotional or behavioral issues for a child, given the comprehensive nature of these types of family evaluations and the evaluator's access to and synthesis of multiple sources of data. Accordingly, the child custody evaluator is in the unique position of not only being able to identify and contextualize any special concerns or needs of the child, but also to prioritize the issues and make specific recommendations for intervention, when necessary and appropriate to do so (or to refer the family for further evaluation).

Another way that child custody evaluators can serve a triage role is to consider each child independently when conducting a child custody evaluation for families with multiple children about which custodial decisions are being made. Often, courts are tasked with having to make decisions that are in the best interests of the "children," and, thus, consider multiple children in a family as a collective entity for which a single custodial plan is created. For most referral questions, child custody evaluators should be evaluating each child's needs independently and providing analysis, triage, and recommendations specific to each child, and relative to each parent's ability to meet those needs.

A final way that child custody evaluators can serve a triage function is related to their ability to identify existing or emerging patterns that are indicative of risk for future problems. In most cases, the extensive training and experience of mental health professionals positions them to identify warning signs and indicators of potential domestic violence, abuse, neglect, traumatic stress responses, developmental delay, mental health symptoms, and alcohol or substance abuse patterns. Accordingly, the thorough data gathered by the child custody evaluator can reveal areas of concern, which might be the first recognition of potential harm or risk by anyone outside the family unit (Jaffe, Johnston, Crooks, & Bala, 2008). For example, the child custody evaluator might be the first to recognize signs of increasing anxiety in the child, which could be exacerbated by an unpredictable or inconsistent parenting time schedule. In that case, the evaluator could note this area of emerging risk and make recommendations to the court that increase stability in the parenting time schedule in order to reduce the child's anxiety.

## *Prevention*

Estimates vary across studies, but one study found that over 75% of family law cases that had custody evaluations settled before trial (Maccoby & Mnookin, 1992). In her seminal article (2015), Lund argued that custody evaluations should be a catalyst for peacemaking, rather than ongoing litigation and stated, "All family law professionals should be challenged to develop the knowledge and skills for using custody evaluations in the parallel tracks toward probable settlement by parents themselves and possible decision by a judge" (p. 407). She presented a number of justifications for this position, including the fact that the custody evaluation process presents a unique opportunity to provide parents with helpful information about their children's needs and how best to meet those needs, which can empower and motivate them to work toward mutually agreeable parenting plans and settlement, rather than incurring further expenses and leaving the decisions up to a third party. According to Lund, the very process of child custody evaluation, if done through a peacemaking framework, can be a form of prevention by reducing further parental conflict and expediting resolution of the custody matter in a way that parents are more likely to follow.

Accordingly, if evaluators enter the process from a potentially peacemaking framework, they are likely to approach and conduct the evaluation differently, using more of a prevention approach. Using a prevention lens means that evaluators consider and articulate ways that the child can develop in positive, prosocial, healthy, and developmentally appropriate manner, as well as ways that the parents and other caregivers can create environments that support healthy development (Substance Abuse and Mental Health Services Administration [SAMHSA], 2016). So, instead of just identifying for the court the current "fires" that need to be extinguished, the evaluator also considers how he/she can aid the decision-maker in reducing risk and preventing additional crises in the future.

One of the seemingly most obvious ways to do this is to conduct the evaluation in a manner that yields concrete and specific recommendations to address current and future issues that are likely to arise for the child(ren), as well as the collective family unit. For example, in the course of conducting a standard custody evaluation to determine parental visitation, the evaluator learns from the childcare provider that a young child is demonstrating problem behaviors in daycare that might be indicative of future emotion regulation or attention and concentration issues in school. In addition to addressing the identified referral question regarding visitation, the evaluator can provide some specific recommendations for further psychological evaluation of these emerging concerns, potential intervention strategies or resources for parents and teachers to collaboratively manage the child's behavior, and identification of transitions or challenges that might exacerbate the behaviors (e.g., moving to a new school, frequent disruption in the child's routine). In providing these types of recommendations, it is critically important for evaluators to be informed about the nature and availability of such resources in the family's community and to make recommendations that are both concrete and scalable. It is not helpful to families, attorneys, or judicial officers to make a long, comprehensive list of recommendations for services that are neither feasible nor available for a family to pursue. Thus, evaluators should consider how to offer recommendations in ways that can be prioritized, adopted gradually or in varying doses, and not always contingent on significant financial resources.

Another way that evaluators can use a prevention approach in conducting a child custody evaluation is to focus as much on identifying strengths and protective factors as they do on identifying risk factors and areas of concern. Writing for the Strengthening Families Approach, Harper Browne (2014) quoted Judy Langford (2011) addressing this paradigm shift:

> If we could mobilize [child welfare systems] to be prevention agents and early warning responders, we could impact millions of children. And by focusing on positive outcomes and healthy development, we could engage more families much more easily than prevention programs based on identifying "at risk" families. (p. 7)

Both Harper Browne and Langford were focused primarily on child welfare and maltreatment contexts, but their call to mental health professionals, childcare providers, and educators to consider and emphasize areas of strength for children and families is equally important in the family court decision-making situation. Whereas a risk factor is something that increases the likelihood of a problematic outcome, a protective factor is something that supports positive developmental outcomes or an ability to overcome adversity (Fraser, 2004). Though there are varying models and theoretical explanations regarding the ways that risk and protective factors interact and influence each other, there is strong empirical support for the importance of identifying protective factors toward prevention and intervention (Mallett & Stoddard Dare, 2009). This shift toward evaluating both risk and protective factors in the family law context is consistent with similar calls for a movement toward "preventive justice" or risk management as the goal in juvenile justice (Slobogin, 2016).

A final way that child custody evaluations can serve a prevention function is by educating the parties about the moderating and mediating roles played by numerous other factors in the relationship between parental conflict and long-term negative outcomes. Though it is well established that parental divorce is a consistent predictor of delinquent behavior (Amato, 2001; Amato & Keith, 1991), there is a robust body of research that unpacks this association with more nuance and depth, minimizing the notion that future delinquency is a clear or inevitable outcome of parental separation or divorce (e.g., Burt et al., 2008; van de Weijer, Thornberry, Bijleveld, & Blokland, 2015; Warmuth, Cummings, & Davies, 2018). For example, there are a number of studies that have found that family conflict impacts school readiness and adjustment (e.g., Harland, Reijneveld, Brugman, Verloove-Vanhorick, & Verhulst, 2002), which, in turn, impacts delinquency (e.g., Li & Lerner, 2011). Conversely, there is research that suggests that parental divorce can serve as a protective factor when maltreatment has occurred (e.g., Mallett & Stoddard Dare, 2009). Helping all parties (including parents, attorneys, and judges) understand the importance of targeting some of these other factors, in addition to minimizing the child's exposure to further family conflict, can serve to prevent or reduce future risk of delinquent behavior.

## *Procedural Justice*

In addition to using specific triage and prevention strategies, the child custody evaluation process has the potential to increase procedural justice for all involved parties. Procedural justice is the notion of fairness in dispute resolution and legal decision-making (Thibaut & Walker, 1975). Specifically, the degree to which parties report satisfaction with the legal outcome depends on their perception of whether the process was fair, even if the outcome is not necessarily in their favor (Lind & Tyler, 1988). In one of the only studies specifically examining procedural justice in child custody disputes, Kitzmann and Emery (1993) emphasized the importance of parties feeling a sense of control over the process and the ultimate decision, as well as feeling respected and acknowledged.

For many children (as well as parents), the child custody dispute is their first interaction with the legal system, which can significantly shape their attitudes and beliefs about authority and law. This process of "legal socialization"(Tyler & Trinker, 2017) is heavily influenced by parents' experiences and attitudes toward legal processes and personnel, which can have long-term implications for children's future interactions with the law (see, e.g., Cavanagh & Cauffman, 2015; Piquero, Fagan, Mulvey, Steinberg, & Odgers, 2005; Wolfe, McLean, & Pratt, 2017). Accordingly, if all parties feel that they were heard, respected, and treated fairly throughout the process (regardless of outcome), children's likelihood of future interaction with the juvenile and criminal justice systems is reduced (Bryan, 2006).

Beyond ensuring that parents and children feel acknowledged throughout the child custody evaluation process (specific strategies are discussed in the subsequent section), another way to increase procedural justice is to increase parents' perceptions of the evaluator's legitimacy. Lund (2015) stated, "It is vitally important that parents in conflict view the evaluator as neutral and unbiased, as well as expert, if the parents are to accept the evaluator's opinion about the needs of their children" (p. 411). Given the adversarial nature of the process, family law attorneys use a myriad of strategies to prepare their clients for participation in a child custody evaluation, which may include efforts to undermine or discredit the evaluator's credentials or experience and coaching a parent on how to minimize his/her areas of risk or deficit. Lund went on to emphasize that "The way clients are prepared for a custody evaluation, the way a custody evaluator is portrayed to them, and the way an evaluation report is discussed will have an influence on parenting and co-parenting and shortening the time of conflict" (p. 411). Accordingly, if a child custody evaluation can be a means to improve parent behavior and communication, which then improves children's outcomes, the parents must accept the evaluator as a legitimate expert and authentically commit to and participate in the process. In order to do so, they need to feel that the evaluator actually got to know the strengths and risks of each member of the family and obtained an accurate depiction of how the family functions.

## *Therapeutic Jurisprudence*

The final link to delinquency prevention is the notion of child custody evaluation as a form of therapeutic jurisprudence, which is a focus on "the law as therapeutic agent" and the legal system's ability to impact participants' emotional and psychological well-being (Wexler, 2000). Sometimes referred to as therapeutic justice, the emphasis is on applying the law in ways that are humanizing and produce positive change, while also examining negative unintended consequences. Weinsten (1997) was one of the first to consider how adopting a therapeutic jurisprudence approach in family law would go much further to advance the best interests of the children than the ways in which the current adversarial structure tends to exacerbate family conflict and traumatic stress for children and parents.

Rather than depict the child custody evaluation to parents as a ploy to expose and exploit any sign of purported weakness, perhaps the process could be reframed as an important opportunity to assess the child's needs and how each parent can best meet those needs. One way to do this would be for the evaluator to prepare the report with the goals of prevention, psychoeducation, and alternative dispute resolution in mind. Citing Pickar and Kaufman (2013), Lund (2015) argues that "[t] here need not be a contradiction between the kind of evaluation report that satisfies forensic guidelines, with the court as primary client, and for clients themselves because careful presentation of information based on sound procedures and research-based analysis are important for both" (p. 413) and that "information from evaluations is likely to be a key component of an evaluation's impact on positive parenting and co-parenting, and the possibility of settlement increases if information is presented in a way that the parent can understand and in a context that may counteract the predisposition to disregard information not consistent with self-protective attitudes" (p. 412, citing Taylor, Peplau, & Sears, 2006).

Accordingly, the more evaluators and family law attorneys can shift the paradigm to assist parents with understanding the purpose, process, reasoning, and recommendations of the child custody evaluation, the more parents are going to be able to use that information to develop a mutually agreeable parenting plan and move forward amicably (Babb, 1997). When parents and children feel heard and when evaluation reports are written clearly and thoughtfully, without clinical jargon and with parents in mind as the primary audience, the recommendations are much more likely to be implemented. This can include information and resources related to parenting strategies, child behavior management, appropriate developmental expectations, mental health treatment recommendations, common responses to domestic violence, child maltreatment, or other traumatic exposure, and ways to increase safety, predictability, and structure for the child. Ideally and when appropriate, a post-evaluation feedback or debriefing session could be an opportunity for the evaluator to provide additional information and context for the recommendations and would provide parents and attorneys with an chance to ask questions or seek clarification about the findings (Lund, 2015).

An additional method of increasing therapeutic jurisprudence in family court is the intentional incorporation of trauma-informed decision-making. Knowlton (2014) implored family court judges to remember that:

> Divorce can be a traumatic experience for adults, and research shows a connection between parental conflict and increased risk of emotional, behavioral, and psychological problems in children. New evidence-based practices emerging from the juvenile justice system suggest that courts and judges must understand the role of traumatic exposure, in order to better interact with victims of trauma and to determine appropriate processes and intervention strategies. [Family courts] that do not practice trauma-informed decision making may inadvertently increase the level of trauma that families experience. (p. 10)

As child custody evaluations are intended to aid the court, the more trauma-informed the evaluation process and final report, the more trauma-informed the ultimate legal decision-making is likely to be. To this end, we now offer specific considerations and suggestions for conducting trauma-informed child custody evaluations.

# Trauma-Informed Child Custody Evaluation

In order to utilize a trauma-informed (and, by extension, preventive) approach to child custody evaluation, the evaluator has to have adequate training and experience in understanding the impact and common manifestations of trauma, as well as how to conduct evaluations in a trauma-responsive manner. Kerig (2013) noted that, despite the robust research on the association between trauma and delinquency, many clinicians who conduct psychological evaluations for courts have not had training on how to be trauma-informed and do not typically incorporate trauma assessment into their forensic evaluation process. Accordingly, she argued that a critical first step toward being a trauma-informed evaluator is to "ensure that all mental health professionals who perform court-ordered evaluations are knowledgeable, skilled, and specifically trained in the assessment of trauma..." (p. 2). Given that exposure to extreme parental conflict is, by its very nature, typically considered traumatic for children, it seems critically necessary for forensic mental health professionals conducting child custody evaluations to have such training and experience.

But, what would that training and experience look like? What sort of background might be necessary in order to consider one's forensic mental health assessment process "trauma-informed?" At the most basic level, trauma-informed assessment involves conducting an evaluation in a manner that considers how one's functioning might be impacted by his/her traumatic experiences (Kerig, 2013). Delving deeper, one needs to have an understanding of each family members' individual traumatic experiences and how these experiences have impacted them, both individually and collectively. This involves assessing not only history of traumatic exposure, but also posttraumatic stress and related symptoms. Trauma-informed assessment, particularly when the focus is children or families, requires an understanding of trauma symptom manifestations beyond the standard posttraumatic stress disorder (PTSD) diagnostic criteria, including complex trauma (Cook et al., 2005) and developmental trauma disorder (van der Kolk, 2005) frameworks. It also requires familiarity with the literature on the intergenerational transmission of trauma (Spatz Widom, Czaja, & DuMont, 2015), the impact of historical trauma (Kirmayer, Gone, & Moses, 2014), and the influence of culture-specific trauma experiences and responses (Substance Abuse and Mental Health Services Administration [SAMHSA], 2014). Finally, all of this information is gathered, understood, and interpreted through the lens of the evaluator's own potentially traumatic or complex familial experiences; thus, the evaluator must remain cognizant of how that perspective might bias his/her opinions, conclusions, and recommendations (APA, 2013).

## *Informed Consent*

In addition to being trauma-informed, there are a number of specific ways that child custody evaluators can conduct the evaluation using trauma-responsive strategies. The first consideration is the manner in which the informed consent process is conducted. As noted previously, for many families, meeting with a child custody evaluator may be their first encounter with a mental health professional. Depending on a parent or child's individual or cultural beliefs about mental health providers, or even medical providers in general, they may be coming in with a formidable set of assumptions, fears, or reservations about divulging personal information to a stranger. In addition, attorneys representing the parents may have prepared them for the evaluation in a myriad of ways and parents themselves may have discovered the wide range of information available online about the child custody evaluation process. For example, a quick Internet search yielded the following information about meeting with a child custody evaluator: "Reasonable people should be nervous and fearful that some allegedly unbiased and professional individual has the power to make a life-altering recommendation and assess your ability to be a parent – after what usually amounts to less than 10 total hours of time spent with you, you're [*sic*] ex-spouse (or soon-to-be ex-spouse), and your children" ("Understanding What to Expect: Custody Evaluation Introduction," n.d.).

Given the high-stakes nature of the evaluation outcome, and the likelihood of a significant degree of conflict present to warrant such an evaluation, parties are not likely to be overly cooperative or enthusiastic about participating in the evaluation process. Parents and children may initially present to the evaluator as hesitant, skeptical, fearful, and even hostile. Accordingly, the child custody evaluator must recognize this context and be prepared to explain his/her role in and purpose of the child custody process and address any questions or concerns that parties may have during the informed consent stage. This would include clearly describing to each party one's role as being neutral, objective, and distinct from a therapeutic role, identifying the types of situations that would warrant an immediate, mandated report to authorities, and explaining the general lack of confidentiality, given that all information will ultimately be compiled and reported to the court. It is also necessary to provide the same type of explanation to the child(ren) in developmentally-appropriate language.

An additional aspect of the informed consent process that can be particularly critical for individuals who have experienced trauma is to provide as much information as possible about the steps in the evaluation process and what to expect at each stage. For example, the evaluator can describe the general timeline and process of a child custody evaluation, including whom the evaluator plans to interview and why, when, and for how long, what additional information will be gathered (e.g., psychological testing, record review) and for what purposes, and what will be done with all of the information (e.g., a report written and provided to the judge). The more predictable and transparent the evaluator can be throughout the process, the smoother and less traumatizing the evaluation will be for all of the involved parties, including the children. In approaching informed consent in this manner, the evaluator incorporates a fundamental tenet of trauma-informed assessment, which is to acknowledge that you are asking people to provide very sensitive information outside of an established trusting relationship, but that you will do your best to help them feel comfortable and safe in order to avoid re-traumatization.

## Clarity and Communication

Beyond the initial informed consent process, the evaluator should maintain consistency and predictability by striving for equitable and transparent communication with all parties throughout the entirety of the evaluation process. One way to do this is to ensure that parents and children understand what is meant by various terms or clinical jargon, including what the evaluator meanswhen asking about things like "trauma," "abuse," "inappropriate touching," or "harsh discipline," for example. In addition to using developmentally-appropriate explanations for children, it is important to recognize that parents, too, may have limited or inaccurate conceptions of what is meant by such terms, which can be subjective or culture-bound. Ensuring that the individual being evaluated understands exactly what is being asked increases the likelihood of obtaining more accurate and useful information and decreases the likelihood of accusations of factual inaccuracies in the evaluation report. It also serves a related goal of trauma-informed assessment, which is to ensure that all parties feel heard throughout the evaluation process and that they had an adequate opportunity to provide the evaluator with their perspectives.

Consistent with this goal of transparent communication is the notion that the evaluator should carry that goal through to the end of the evaluation process, which includes having a feedback or debriefing session with the parties after the evaluation report is completed. Though there are certainly some risks and role boundaries to consider in structuring such a final meeting, giving parents and their attorneys an opportunity to seek clarification, ask questions, and express concerns could empower them to more effectively work toward settlement and increase their ability to actually implement the evaluator's recommendations, rather than seeking to simply discredit an unfavorable report (Lund, 2015).

## *Contextualization and Psychoeducation*

As noted several times throughout this chapter, there is a substantial emphasis in forensic mental health assessment on distinguishing one's role from that of a therapeutic interaction with the person being evaluated (Greenberg & Shuman, 2007). This objective, neutral, and detached stance, though critical, can be difficult to reconcile with many of the trauma-informed assessment elements we have discussed thus far. However, one way to strike somewhat of a balance is to use a trauma lens to place the behavior and response styles of individuals being evaluated in appropriate context. There are obvious reasons that parents or children may not be forthcoming or truthful with various types of information in a child custody evaluation, not the least of which is the desire to put one's best foot forward in order to not be perceived as impaired or deficient in ways that could negatively impact the custodial decision-making. Parents may have been coached by their attorneys and children may have been coached by parents to provide or withhold specific information.

However, there are a host of other trauma-related reasons that individuals might be hesitant to engage with the evaluator or disclose aspects of their current or past experiences. For example, if domestic violence has occurred, the victimized parent might be too afraid to report the abuse to the evaluator out of fear of retaliation by a partner who has a history of coercive-control behavior patterns (Saunders, 2015). A parent might have had an early childhood experience of not being believed when disclosing abuse and, thus, is reluctant to discuss these experiences now out of fear or shame. A parent or child may not recall aspects of past trauma because of repression or dissociative experiences. For the child, after he is informed about the purpose of the evaluation and how the information will be reported, he may be unwilling to discuss his parents' shortcomings or his custodial preferences out of fear of serious repercussions. Yet another example might be a parent's fears that she will be judged or presumed to be a bad parent because of her history of traumatic experiences or posttraumatic stress symptoms. Accordingly, seeking to understand how and why individuals present the way they do from a trauma-informed perspective can provide critical context for the evaluator's overall case conceptualization and formulation of recommendations.

Likewise, evaluators can play an important role in both short- and long-term prevention by providing varying degrees of psychoeducation to parents and children throughout the child custody evaluation process. For example, when asking parents about their potentially traumatic experiences, evaluators can preface the questions with an acknowledgment that having experienced trauma does not automatically make one a "bad parent" or mean that the evaluator perceives them as such. The evaluator can identify patterns and potential triggers and provide resources for the parent to help him understand how his trauma history may be impacting his parenting or current emotional functioning. Similarly, the evaluator can discuss with the child(ren) common fears or reactions that children experience in the midst of family conflict or during periods of major transition. Providing real-time psychoeducation and contextualization in these trauma-informed ways can also serve to increase the perception of procedural justice and therapeutic jurisprudence, as discussed in the previous section.

## *Additional Strategies*

Keeping these broader, overarching approaches in mind, here are some additional guiding principles. The National Child Traumatic Stress Network (NCTSN, 2011) published a fact sheet for child welfare staff who work with parents with trauma histories and emphasized that a history of traumatic experiences may compromise parents' ability to make appropriate judgments about safety, make it difficult for parents to form trusting relationships, impair parents' emotion regulation, and result in triggers, negative coping strategies, impaired decision-making, and increased vulnerability for additional adversity. Accordingly, the NCTSN recommended using specific trauma-informed strategies when assessing parents, such as "Understand that parents' anger, fear, or avoidance may be a reaction to their own past traumatic experiences not the [mental health professional] him/herself…build on parents' desires to be effective in keeping their children safe and reducing their children's challenging behaviors…help parents understand the impact of past trauma on current functioning and parenting…and become knowledgeable about trauma-informed services…and evidence-supported trauma interventions to include in [recommendations]…" (p. 3).

Similarly, the Substance Abuse and Mental Health Services Administration (SAMHSA, 2014) published a comprehensive guide on trauma-informed care, in which they provided recommendations for trauma-informed screening and assessment (see Fig. 9.1).

Taking into account these global and specific recommendations, we will now apply a trauma-informed approach to a sample child custody evaluation scenario.

1. Clarify for the client what to expect in the screening and assessment process.
2. Approach the client in a matter-of-fact, yet supportive manner.
3. Respect the client's personal space.
4. Adjust tone and volume of speech to suit the client's level of engagement and degree of comfort in the interview process.
5. Provide culturally appropriate symbols of safety in the physical environment.
6. Be aware of one's own emotional responses to hearing client's trauma histories.
7. Overcome linguistic barriers via an interpreter.
8. Elicit only the information necessary for determining a history of trauma and the possible existence and extent of traumatic stress symptoms and related disorders.
9. Give the client as much personal control as possible during the assessment.
10. Use self-administered, written checklists rather than interviews when possible to assess trauma.
11. Interview the client if he or she has trouble reading or writing or is otherwise unable to complete a checklist.
12. Allow time for the client to become calm and oriented to the present if he or she has very intense emotional responses when recalling or acknowledging a trauma.
13. Avoid phrases that imply judgment about the trauma.
14. Provide feedback about the results of the screening.
15. Be aware of the possible legal implications of assessment.

**Fig. 9.1** Trauma-Informed Screening and Assessment. (SAMHSA, 2014, pp. 96–98)

## Case Example[1]

The Cavallero family was referred to Dr. Perry for a child custody evaluation by the Family Court Judge. The referral from the Court indicated that the focus of the evaluation is inter-parental conflict, mental status of both parents, disputed visitation/access, the current adjustment of the children, the safety of the children, and the ability of the parents to provide adequate care for the children. Mr. Cavellero (father) and Ms. Fuhrmann (mother) met 11 years ago and have two children, ten-year-old Kirk, and five-year-old Naomi. The parents were never married and had multiple instances of separation and reunification over the course of their relationship. There is an extensive history of conflict between the parents, primarily related to Mr. Cavallero's substance use, and the couple separated for the last time several months after Naomi's birth. The children have been in the primary custody of Ms. Fuhrmann, with occasional periods of supervised visitation between the children and Mr. Cavallero. The current dispute is regarding visitation between the children and Mr. Cavallero.

### Pre-evaluation

Prior to meeting with the family for the first time, Dr. Perry obtained a copy of the court order for the evaluation and sought clarification from the judge about the specific referral questions. She contacted Ms. Fuhrmann's attorney and Mr.

---

[1] All names and case details are fictional. Any similarity to actual parties or legal cases is purely coincidental.

Cavallero (who was pro se) and provided them with a written description of her child custody evaluation process and copies of all relevant consent and release of information forms. She also provided them with written instructions about how to schedule the first evaluation sessions and what to expect in terms of length and quantity of sessions, cost, and who should attend each session. In addition, she asked both parents to complete an internally-created developmental and family history questionnaire and bring it with them to their first evaluation session. Finally, she provided each parent with a brochure that offers suggestions for how to explain to their children the purpose of the evaluation in developmentally-appropriate language and what they can expect regarding their involvement.

During the first evaluation session with each parent, Dr. Perry went through an extensive informed consent process, in which she explained the nature and purpose of the evaluation, what they can expect during each step of the process, collateral sources she will contact and why, the importance of honesty and transparency throughout the process, and her role as a forensic evaluator as distinct from a therapeutic role. She provided some context that it is normal to feel some anxiety or distress when participating in this type of an evaluation and that no parent is perfect. She emphasized that her goal is to evaluate the needs of each child and each parent's strengths in meeting those needs, as well as to provide recommendations and resources that might be helpful to the family. Finally, she described the types of disclosures she might have to immediately report to authorities, as well as how the information provided by each person she interviews will be included in a final report. She provided a similar explanation to each child in developmentally-appropriate language and offered several opportunities for each party to ask questions or seek clarification about the process.

## *During the Evaluation*

Throughout the entire evaluation process, Dr. Perry sought to provide opportunities to empower each individual by letting them select the order of certain steps as much as possible. For example, Mr. Cavallero opted to complete several written questionnaires prior to participating in an interview segment, as he indicated that he preferred to "get the tests over with"; whereas, Ms. Cavallero chose to finish the interview so that she "can relax and take my time with the forms." Ten-year-old Kirk expressed a preference to complete the father-child observation before meeting alone with Dr. Perry because "then you'll see right away what I mean about my dad being a jerk"; whereas, five-year-old Naomi wanted to do the mother-child observation first, as she was not yet comfortable meeting alone with Dr. Perry and needed some time to warm up to her. Dr. Perry tried to give each family member as much control as possible during each meeting, including selecting when breaks were taken and allowing time and space for the individual to regulate his/her emotions following an intense disclosure or reaction.

Dr. Perry was conscious of and intentional about the types of terms she used throughout the evaluation and asked about exposure to various traumatic or adverse experiences in different ways, using both open- and closed-ended questions, developmentally-tailored language, and asking in both direct (e.g., "Have you ever been sexually abused?") and indirect (e.g., "Was there ever a time that someone touched you in a way that you didn't like or that made you feel uncomfortable?") ways. She interpreted responses in developmental context and provided reassurance to each parent and child that exposure to such experiences does not automatically imply one is, for example, seriously mentally ill or a bad parent. She was mindful of cultural or linguistic communication barriers and sought to adjust the tone, rate, and volume of her speech to a comfortable level for each party. She also was careful to elicit only the trauma-related information deemed necessary and relevant to the referral questions, so as to avoid unnecessarily triggering anyone.

In addition to her verbal language, Dr. Perry was conscious of her nonverbal communication and her physical presence. She was careful not to invade the personal space of any family member and to provide notice or ask permission before any physical contact (e.g., "Could I hand you this puzzle to work on with your dad?" "Would it be ok if I stood behind you to look at the question on your form that you wanted me to explain?"). She was also mindful of her facial reactions and was careful to avoid expressions or utterances that might imply shock or judgment about the information being shared by the individual being interviewed.

Prior to the conclusion of each evaluation session, Dr. Perry provided ample time for the party to ask questions or provide additional clarification about any responses given during the session. She checked in with the participants to ensure that they were emotionally contained and safe to leave, particularly if they appeared to have been triggered in any way by content discussed during the evaluation session. If they did not appear safe, Dr. Perry provided local resources for support, crisis management or, in an extreme case, activated emergency response services.

During the final evaluation session with each parent and with each child, Dr. Perry reviewed what would happen next in the process (e.g., she would be talking with collateral sources, reviewing records, and compiling all of the information into a final report) and an approximate timeline. She also provided each party with an opportunity to share any additional information they felt was important and that she had not previously inquired about, as well as to ask any final questions.

## Post-evaluation

The primary considerations for Dr. Perry after the completion of the evaluation are related to how she synthesizes, interprets, and communicates her findings and recommendations. She is thoughtful and intentional about trying to understand and conceptualize emotional and behavioral patterns through a trauma-informed lens. For example, this might include analyzing whether Naomi was truly experiencing developmental delays or, alternatively, is showing regression in several developmental milestones due to the frequent exposure to parental conflict, which has implications for the type of interventions recommended. Dr. Perry may have to provide contextual information about how, for Kirk, witnessing scary or inappropriate behavior was just as traumatizing to him as actually experiencing that behavior firsthand. She may also consider how other, less obvious forms of traumatic exposure have impacted the parent-child relationships and degree of attachment, such as overly harsh or complete lack of discipline, inconsistent or neglectful parenting practices, parent's mental health symptoms or substance abuse, and historical or multigenerational trauma. When appropriate, she may outline her intervention recommendations with a level of specificity, dosage, and prioritization that would be helpful to future individual or family therapists.

In her explanation of the patterns, risks, and strengths of each family member in the report, Dr. Perry is cognizant of how cultural or religious beliefs and values impact what is considered normative child-rearing practices for each of the parents. She provides recommendations that are culturally sensitive and, ideally, not in direct or irreconcilable conflict with the parents' values (though this is not always possible). She also recognizes the potential impact of intergenerational transmission of trauma on each parent's interpersonal style, parenting approach, and personal coping strategies. She seeks to provide a balanced report, in which each family member's strengths and protective factors are highlighted, along with their risks, needs, and deficits.

Finally, assuming the risks and ethical dual role boundaries can be managed appropriately, Dr. Perry offers to meet with each parent and his/her attorney separately or as a group, after they have had a chance to review the report. This feedback meeting provides an opportunity for each parent to obtain clarification about how Dr. Perry arrived at her conclusions, as well as to ask follow-up questions about any of the recommendations outlined in the report. The meeting is not intended to give the parties a chance to add additional information or demand that the report be changed, although Dr. Perry may be willing to entertain information about alleged factual inaccuracies in the report and consider amending the report. Rather, the feedback session is an opportunity to further the goals of therapeutic jurisprudence and procedural justice, such that the parties have a chance to process the results of the evaluation and consider how they might use the recommendations to further their mediation, settlement, and/or parenting plan discussions.

## Conclusion

The overarching goal of considering child custody evaluations through a trauma-informed lens is to further prevention and early intervention efforts, given the frequent overlap of youth involved with the family court, child welfare, and juvenile justice systems. As discussed, many youth that go on to engage in delinquent behavior had earlier contact with family court; thus, the child custody evaluation process can serve as a critical intercept in which to identify areas of risk and strength for each family member, as well as the collective family unit and subunits (following parental separation). This enables early intervention for areas of concern not previously identified, as well as a potentially positive influence on socialization to the legal and mental health systems.

Another potential outcome of viewing child custody evaluation as a means of delinquency prevention is the substantial long-term cost savings if areas of risk and need are identified and addressed before they manifest into delinquent behavior. Depending on whether the child custody evaluation is facilitated through a court clinic, private practice, or other model, Bow and Quinnell (2001) found that evaluations can cost anywhere from $600 to $15,000, with an average cost of $3,335. As that study is now almost 20 years old, these are likely substantial underestimates of current evaluation costs. These evaluations can be an expensive and, thus, inaccessible option for many of the families who would most benefit. However, when contrasted with the average cost of a youth in detention for one year, which is $148,767 or $407.58 per day (Justice Policy Institute, 2014), the economic efficiency of this proposed prevention framework could be considerable. More importantly, juvenile justice policy reform efforts can analyze whether and how financial resources might be better facilitated in collaboration with the family court system to subsidize the cost of child custody evaluations, allowing more families access much earlier in the parental separation process.

A final consideration related to the feasibility of using child custody evaluation as delinquency prevention centers around the ethical and practical implications for the evaluator. Some of the elements and strategies we discussed in this chapter seem to call for the evaluator to cross role boundaries, which could be viewed in conflict with best practices in forensic mental health assessment (APA, 2010, 2013). For example, when using some of the trauma-informed assessment methods, the evaluator may show more empathy, allow the party a modicum of control in the order of operations, and remain acutely aware of how his nonverbal communication and physical positioning may be impacting a parent or child, which is more typical in the rapport-building phases of a non-forensic psychological evaluation (Greenberg & Shuman, 2007). Engaging in a feedback or debriefing session may pose risk for the evaluator to be tempted to crossover into a sort of mediator role (Melton et al., 2018). Asking parents about various early childhood experiences may feel like overreaching or going beyond what is directly relevant for the forensic referral question (Heilbrun, 2001).

However, it is our belief that there are ways to reconcile these potential ethical conflicts and minimize risk while still being trauma-informed in one's assessment approach. This includes being exceedingly transparent, neutral, consistent, and equitable in one's communication with all parties throughout the process (Knapp, Younggren, VandeCreek, Harris, & Martin, 2013) and remaining steadfastly within the boundaries of one's role as a forensic evaluator. In fact, forensic scholars are increasingly identifying the potential benefits and importance of tools like empathy (Brodsky & Wilson, 2013) and trauma-based conceptualizations of problem behaviors (Ko et al., 2008). A trauma-informed approach to forensic assessment is consistent with the overarching call for forensic practitioners to "acknowledge and respect the rights of those they serve" (APA, 2013, p. 7) and to "strive to understand how factors associated with age, gender, gender identity, race, ethnicity, culture, national origin, religion, sexual orientation, disability, language, socioeconomic status, or other relevant individual and cultural differences may affect and be related to the basis for people's contact and involvement with the legal system" (APA, 2013, p. 10). Similar language is found in the *Guidelines for Child Custody Evaluations in Family Law Proceedings* (APA, 2010).

Child custody evaluators have the difficult task of balancing breadth and depth in their evaluation process, efficiency and comprehensiveness, and thorough evaluation of all potentially relevant factors, while not going beyond the scope of the evaluation. It is also an area of forensic mental health assessment in which many of the parties are representing themselves (Shepard, 2010), so there is often a degree of psychoeducation and explanation of legal process with which they are tasked. Even given these complex challenges, child custody evaluations pose unique opportunities for forensic evaluators to make a significant impact on the trajectories of children's lives, as well as to minimize their traumatic experiences. If we do these evaluations wrong, children can suffer, even more than they already have as a result of their family dysfunction. But, if we do them right, using trauma-informed methods, we can potentially mitigate, and maybe even prevent, future long-term consequences.

## Questions/Activities for Further Exploration

1. In what ways has the changing family landscape impacted the effects of parental conflict on children?
2. What does juvenile delinquency have to do with child custody?
3. What potential ethical, legal, or practical challenges might arise when utilizing the suggestions in this chapter?
4. Research child welfare and juvenile justice prevention programs and think about what additional elements might be helpful when thinking about trauma-informed child custody evaluation as delinquency prevention.
5. Reflect on a recent forensic or clinical case you encountered. How could that process and your interactions have been more trauma-informed?

## References

Ackerman, M. J. (2006). *Clinician's guide to child custody evaluations* (3rd ed.). Hoboken, NJ: Wiley.

Ackerman, M. J., & Pritzl, T. B. (2011). Child custody evaluation practices: A 20-year follow-up. *Family Court Review, 49*, 618–628.

American Psychological Association [APA]. (2010). Guidelines for child custody evaluations in family law proceedings. *American Psychologist, 65*, 863–867.

American Psychological Association [APA]. (2013). Specialty guidelines for forensic psychology. *American Psychologist, 68*, 7–19.

Amato, P. R. (2001). Children of divorce in the 1990s: An update of the Amato and Keith (1991) meta-analysis. *Journal of Family Psychology, 15*, 355–370.

Amato, P. R., & Keith, B. (1991). Parental divorce and the well-being of children: A meta-analysis. *Psychological Bulletin, 110*, 26–46.

Association of Family and Conciliation Courts [AFCC]. (2006). *Model standards of practice for child custody evaluation*. Madison, WI: Association of Family and Conciliation Courts.

Babb, B. A. (1997). An interdisciplinary approach to family law jurisprudence: Application of an ecological and therapeutic perspective. *Indiana Law Journal, 72*, 775–808.

Belgrad, H. J. (2003, Fall). An introduction to unified family courts from the American Bar Association's perspective. *Family Law Quarterly, 37*, 329–331.

Bow, J. N., & Quinnell, F. A. (2001). Psychologists' current practices and procedures in child custody evaluations: Five years after American Psychological Association Guidelines. *Professional Psychology: Research & Practice, 32*, 261.

Brodsky, S. L., & Wilson, J. K. (2013). Empathy in forensic evaluations: A systematic reconsideration. *Behavioral Sciences & the Law, 31*, 192–202.

Bryan, P. E. (2006). *Constructive divorce: Procedural justice and sociolegal reform*. Washington, D.C.: American Psychological Association.

Buchanan, A. (2006). Psychiatric evidence on the ultimate issue. *Journal of the American Academy of Psychiatry and the Law, 34*, 14–21.

Burt, S. A., Barnes, A. R., McGue, M., & Iacono, W. G. (2008). Parental divorce and adolescent delinquency: Ruling out the impact of common genes. *Developmental Psychology, 44*, 1668.

Cavanagh, C., & Cauffman, E. (2015). Viewing law and order: Mothers' and sons' justice system attitudes and illegal behavior. *Psychology, Public Policy, and Law, 21*, 432–441. https://doi.org/10.1037/law0000054

Child Welfare Information Gateway. (2013). *How the child welfare system works*. Washington, D.C.: U.S. Department of Health and Human Services, Children's Bureau.

Cook, A., Spinazzola, J., Ford, J., Lanktree, C., Blaustein, M., Cloitre, M., … van der Kolk, B. (2005). Complex trauma in children and adolescents. *Psychiatric Annals, 35*, 390–398.

Danziger, G. (2003). Delinquency jurisdiction in a unified family court: Balancing intervention, prevention, and adjudication. *Family Law Quarterly, 37*, 381–401.

Demuth, S., & Brown, S. L. (2004). Family structure, family processes, and adolescent delinquency: The significance of parental absence versus parental gender. *Journal of Research in Crime and Delinquency, 41*, 58–81.

Emery, R. E., Otto, R. K., & O'Donohue, W. T. (2005). A critical assessment of child custody evaluations: Limited science and a flawed system. *Psychological Science in the Public Interest, 6*, 1–29. https://doi.org/10.1111/j.1529-1006.2005.00020.x

Fraser, M. W. (2004). The ecology of childhood: A multi-systems perspective. In M. W. Fraser (Ed.), *Risk and resilience in childhood* (2nd ed., pp. 1–12). Washington, D.C.: NASW.

Fuhrmann, G. W., & Zibbell, R. A. (2012). *Evaluation for child custody*. New York, NY: Oxford University Press. https://doi.org/10.1093/med:psych/9780199766857.003.0015

Geraghty, A. H., & Mlyniec, W. J. (2002). Unified family courts: Tempering enthusiasm with caution. *Family Court Review, 40*, 435–447.

Gould, J., & Martindale, D. (2007). *The art and science of child custody evaluations*. New York, NY: Guilford Press.

Greacen, J. M. (2008). Confidentiality, due process, and judicial disqualification in the unified family court: Report to the Honorable Stephanie Domitrovich. *Family Court Review, 46*, 340–346.

Greenberg, S. A., & Shuman, D. W. (2007). When worlds collide: Therapeutic and forensic roles. *Professional Psychology: Research and Practice, 38*(2), 129–132.

Grisso, T. (2003). *Evaluating competencies: Forensic assessments and instruments* (2nd ed.). New York, NY: Kluwer Academic/Plenum Press.

Guy, L. S., & Zelechoski, A. D. (2017). Civil forensic assessment. In R. Roesch & A. N. Cook (Eds.), *Handbook of forensic mental health services*. Routledge/Taylor & Francis: New York, NY.

Harland, P., Reijneveld, S., Brugman, E., Verloove-Vanhorick, S. P., & Verhulst, F. C. (2002). Family factors and life events as risk factors for behavioural and emotional problems in children. *European Child & Adolescent Psychiatry, 11*, 176–184.

Harper Browne, C. (2014, September). *The strengthening families approach and protective factors framework™: Branching out and reaching deeper*. Washington, D.C.: Center for the Study of Social Policy.

Heilbrun, K. (2001). *Principles of forensic mental health assessment*. New York, NY: Kluwer Academic/Plenum.

Jaffe, P. G., Johnston, J. R., Crooks, C. V., & Bala, N. (2008). Custody disputes involving allegations of domestic violence: Toward a differentiated approach to parenting plans. *Family Court Review, 46*, 500–522. https://doi.org/10.1111/j.1744-1617.2008.00216.x

Justice Policy Institute. (2014, December). *Sticker shock: Calculating the full price tag for youth incarceration*. Retrieved from http://www.justicepolicy.org/research/8477

Kelly, J. B. (1994). The determination of child custody. *Children and Divorce, 4*, 121–142.

Kelly, J. B., & Emery, R. E. (2003). Children's adjustment following divorce: Risk and resilience perspectives. *Family Relations, 52*, 352–362.

Kerig, P. K. (2013, August). Trauma-informed assessment and intervention. National Child Traumatic Stress Network, Fact Sheet. Accessible at https://www.nctsn.org/resources/trauma-informed-assessment-and-intervention

Kirmayer, L. J., Gone, J. P., & Moses, J. (2014). Rethinking historical trauma. *Transcultural Psychiatry, 51*(3), 299–319.

Kitzmann, K. M., & Emery, R. E. (1993). Procedural justice and parents' satisfaction in a field study of child custody dispute resolution. *Law and Human Behavior, 17*, 553–567.

Knapp, S., Younggren, J. N., VandeCreek, L., Harris, E., & Martin, J. N. (2013). *Assessing and managing risk in psychological practice: An individualized approach*. Rockville, MD: The Trust.

Knowlton, N. A. (2014, October). *The modern family court judge: Knowledge, qualities, and skills for success*. Retrieved from Institute for the Advancement of the American Legal System. https://iaals.du.edu/publications/modern-family-court-judge-knowledge-qualities-skills-success

Ko, S. J., Ford, J. D., Kassam-Adams, N., Berkowitz, S. J., Wilson, C., Wong, M., … Layne, C. M. (2008). Creating trauma-informed systems: Child welfare, education, first responders, health care, juvenile justice. *Professional Psychology: Research and Practice, 39*, 396–404.

Langford, J. (2011, June). *Common ground: One approach, many adaptations*. Retrieved from Center for the Study of Social Policy. www.cssp.org/reform/strengthening-families/ resources/strengthening-families-101

Li, Y., & Lerner, R. M. (2011). Trajectories of school engagement during adolescence: Implications for grades, depression, delinquency, and substance use. *Developmental Psychology, 47*, 233–247.

Lind, E., & Tyler, T. (1988). *The social psychology of procedural justice*. New York, NY: Plenum Press.

Luftman, V. H., Veltkamp, L. J., Clark, J. J., Lannacone, S., & Snooks, H. (2005). Practice guidelines in child custody evaluations for licensed clinical social workers. *Clinical Social Work Journal, 33*, 327–357. https://doi.org/10.1007/s10615-005-4947-4

Lund, M. E. (2015). The place for custody evaluations in family peacemaking. *Family Court Review, 53*, 401–417.

Maccoby, E. E., & Mnookin, R. H. (1992). *Dividing the child: Social and legal dilemmas of custody*. Cambridge, MA: Harvard University Press.

Mallett, C. A., & Stoddard Dare, P. A. (2009). Parental divorce: A protection from later delinquency for maltreated children. *Social Work Faculty Publications, 1*, 388–399. Retrieved from https://engagedscholarship.csuohio.edu/clsowo_facpub/1/

Melton, G. B., Petrila, J., Poythress, N. G., Slobogin, C., Otto, R. K., Mossman, D., & Condie, L. O. (2018). *Psychological evaluations for the courts: A handbook for mental health professionals and lawyers* (4th ed.). New York, NY: Guilford Press.

National Child Traumatic Stress Network [NCTSN]. (2011). *Birth parents with trauma histories and the child welfare system: A guide for child welfare staff*. Retrieved from https://www.nctsn.org/resources/birth-parents-trauma-histories-and-child-welfare-system-guide-resource-parents

Pickar, D. B., & Kaufman, R. L. (2013). The child custody evaluation report: Toward an integrated model of practice. *Journal of Child Custody, 10*, 17–53.

Piquero, A. R., Fagan, J., Mulvey, E. P., Steinberg, L., & Odgers, C. (2005). Developmental trajectories of legal socialization among serious adolescent offenders. *Journal of Criminal Law and Criminology, 96*, 267–298.

Price, C., & Kunz, J. (2003). Rethinking the paradigm of juvenile delinquency as related to divorce. *Journal of Divorce & Remarriage, 39*(1–2), 109–133.

Quinnell, F. A., & Bow, J. N. (2001). Psychological tests used in child custody evaluations. *Behavioral Sciences & the Law, 19*(4), 491–501.

Saini, M. A. (2008). Evidence base of custody and access evaluations. *Brief Treatment and Crisis Intervention, 8*, 111–129.

Sanburn, J. (2010, September 13). Brief history: The American family. *Time*. Retrieved from http://content.time.com/time/magazine/article/0,9171,2015780,00.html

Saunders, D. G. (2015). Research based recommendations for child custody evaluation practices and policies in cases of intimate partner violence. *Journal of Child Custody, 12*, 71–92. https://doi.org/10.1080/15379418.2015.1037052

Schepard, A., & Bozzomo, J. W. (2003). Efficacy, therapeutic justice, mediation, and evaluation: Reflections on a survey of Unified Family Courts. *Family Law Quarterly, 37*(3), 333–359.

Shepard, R. T. (2010). The self-represented litigant: Implications for the bench and bar. *Family Court Review, 48*, 607–618.

Slobogin, C. (2016). Preventive justice for adolescents. In K. Heilbrun, D. DeMatteo, & N. E. S. Goldstein (Eds.), *APA handbook of psychology and juvenile justice* (pp. 45–65). Washington, D.C.: APA.

Snyder, H. N., & Sickmund, M. (1999). *Juvenile offenders and victims: 1999 national report*. Washington, D.C.: U.S. Dept. of Justice, Office of Justice Programs, Office of Juvenile Justice and Delinquency Prevention.

Spatz Widom, C., Czaja, S. J., & DuMont, K. A. (2015). Intergenerational transmission of child abuse and neglect: Real or detection bias? *Science, 347*, 1480–1485.

Substance Abuse and Mental Health Services Administration [SAMHSA]. (2014). *Trauma-informed care in behavioral health services* (Treatment Improvement Protocol (TIP) Series 57. HHS Publication No. (SMA) 13-4801). Rockville, MD: Substance Abuse and Mental Health Services Administration.

Substance Abuse and Mental Health Services Administration [SAMHSA]. (2016, July 21). *Prevention approaches*. Retrieved from https://www.samhsa.gov/capt/practicing-effective-prevention/prevention-approaches

Taylor, S. E., Peplau, L. A., & Sears, D. O. (2006). *Social psychology*. Upper Saddle River, NJ: Prentice Hall.

Thibaut, J., & Walker, L. (1975). *Procedural justice: A psychological analysis*. Hillsdale, NJ: Lawrence Erlbaum.

Tyler, T. R., & Trinker, R. (2017). *Why children follow rules: Legal socialization and the development of legitimacy*. New York, NY: Oxford University Press.

Understanding What to Expect: Custody Evaluation Introduction. (n.d.). Retrieved from https://www.mrcustodycoach.com/blog/custody-evaluation-during-divorce-proceedings

van de Weijer, S. G. A., Thornberry, T. P., Bijleveld, C. C. J. H., & Blokland, A. A. J. (2015). The effects of parental divorce on the intergenerational transmission of crime. *Societies, 5*, 89–108.

Van der Kolk, B. A. (2005). Developmental trauma disorder: Toward a rational diagnosis for children with complex trauma histories. *Psychiatric Annals, 35*, 401–408.

Warmuth, K. A., Cummings, E. M., & Davies, P. T. (2018). Child behavioral dysregulation as a mediator between destructive marital conflict and children's symptoms of psychopathology. *Journal of Child and Family Studies, 27*, 2004–2013.

Weinsten, J. (1997). And never the twain shall meet: The best interests of children and the adversary system. *University of Miami Law Review, 52*, 79–175.

Wexler, D. B. (2000). Therapeutic jurisprudence: An overview. *Thomas M. Cooley Law Review, 17*, 125–134.

Wolfe, S. E., McLean, K., & Pratt, T. C. (2017). I learned it by watching you: Legal socialization and the intergenerational transmission of legitimacy attitudes. *British Journal of Criminology, 57*, 1123–1143.

Zelechoski, A. D. (2015). Trauma, adverse experience, and offending. In K. Heilbrun, D. DeMatteo, & N. S. Goldstein (Eds.), *APA handbook of psychology and juvenile justice* (pp. 325–342). Washington, D.C.: American Psychological Association.

Zelechoski, A. D., Fuhrmann, G. S. W., Zibbell, R. A., & Cavallero, L. M. (2012). Evaluation for child custody: Using best practices in a worst-case scenario. *Journal of Forensic Psychology Practice, 12*, 457–470. https://doi.org/10.1080/15228932.2012.713838

# Chapter 10
# The Impact of Toxic Stress on Refugee Children: Implications for the Asylum Process

**Mary Kelly Persyn and Elizabeth A. Owen**

## Introduction

The consequences of the toxic stress experienced by many asylum-seeking children and minors before, during, and after migration can negatively impact their health, including cognitive and mental health, in ways that can interfere with their ability to meet the legal requirements of the process. Toxic stress, defined by the Center on the Developing Child as "prolonged activation of stress response systems in the absence of protective relationships," has become an area of increasing concern regarding children due to the multiple negative and potentially lifelong effects (Shonkoff & Garner, 2012, p. e235). Stressors include those identified in the Adverse Childhood Experiences Scale (ACEs, including various forms of physical, sexual, and emotional abuse as well as neglect, and family dysfunction), in addition to chronic social stressors such as racism, poverty, and community violence (Center on the Developing Child, n.d.). Toxic stress has been identified as an emergent problem immigrant children face even if they initially come to the United States with adult supervision, as many have been separated from their families (First, & Kemper, 2018).

Since approximately 2010, the influx of migrants from Central America and especially the Northern Triangle countries of El Salvador, Honduras, and Guatemala has increased significantly (Congressional Research Services, 2019). The majority of these are families and unaccompanied children. For that reason, this chapter draws its examples from Northern Triangle-origin refugee children, though the

M. K. Persyn (✉)
Persyn Law & Policy, New Teacher Center, San Francisco, CA, USA
e-mail: marykelly@persynlaw.com

E. A. Owen
Teachers College/Columbia University, New York, NY, USA
e-mail: eao8@tc.columbia.edu

© Springer Nature Switzerland AG 2020
R. A. Javier et al. (eds.), *Assessing Trauma in Forensic Contexts*,
https://doi.org/10.1007/978-3-030-33106-1_10

impact of toxic stress and trauma on refugees is a global phenomenon. We will first begin with a brief overview of the process of seeking asylum in the United States. The chapter then describes the causes and impact of toxic stress in children, including factors specific to migrant children, and concludes with a consideration of the role juvenile forensic experts can play in assisting children with applications for asylum.

## Applying for Asylum in the United States

While asylum is a protection that originated centuries ago, modern asylum was born of the rise in people seeking refuge after World War II. In 1952, the fledgling United Nations created the modern legal framework to provide protection for individuals fleeing violence in their native countries. Table 10.1 provides a summary description of the various categories allowable by these laws for entering into the United States. There are five categories of experiences people may face in their home countries that allow for application for asylum in the United States: persecution experienced because of one's race, religion, nationality, membership in a particular social group, or political opinion. If they have been persecuted, or fear being persecuted for one of those reasons, migrants may apply for asylum in the United States once they are within US borders. The Immigration and Nationality Act states that "Any alien who is physically present in the United States or who arrives in the United States (whether or not at a designated port of arrival and including an alien who is brought to the United States after having been interdicted in international or United States waters), irrespective of such alien's status, may apply for asylum" (8 U.S. Code Sec. 1158(a)(1)). In fiscal year 2017, the most recent year statistics are available, the United States received a total of 205,548 asylum applications. In the same year, 26,568 persons were granted asylum (US Department of Homeland Security Office of Immigration Statistics, 2019). The most common countries of origin of those granted asylum were China, El Salvador, Guatemala, and Honduras (Office of Immigration Statistics, March 2019).

Forensic assessments can make a significant difference in the success of these applications; up to 90% of cases featuring skilled assessments may be granted, compared to 30% without (Physicians for Human Rights, n.d.).

EOIR is the immigration court, where removal proceedings take place. UACs may apply for asylum to the USCIS and proceed via interview with an asylum officer unless they are in active removal proceedings and have not yet filed their form (I-589), in which case they apply to the immigration court and the immigration judge decides whether the immigration court or the USCIS has jurisdiction over it. This is very consequential, as the asylum officer (AO) interviews are not adversarial but the court proceedings are.

**Table 10.1**  Key definitions in modern asylum law

| | |
|---|---|
| Migrant | A person who has temporarily or permanently crossed an international border, is no longer residing in his or her country of origin or habitual residence, and is not recognized as a refugee. The term includes asylum seekers. (Congressional Research Services). |
| Unaccompanied alien child ("UAC") | The United States' term for a migrant under the age of 18 who arrives at the U.S. border alone, or whom the United States separates from their family at the U.S. border. [6 U.S.C. Sec. 279(g)(2)]. |
| Refugee | A person who is unable or unwilling to return to his or her country of nationality because of persecution or a well-founded fear of persecution on account of race, religion, nationality, membership in a particular social group, or political opinion. Persons may apply to the United Nations for refugee status from outside the United States. [8 U.S.C. Sec. 1101(a)(42)(A)]. |
| Asylum | Migrants applying for asylum must prove that they are refugees under the above definition. Migrants may only apply for asylum from within the United States and may apply whether or not they have legal status. [8 U.S.C. Sec. 1158(a)(1), (b)(1)(A)]. |
| Removal | A process authorized by the Immigration and Nationality Act (INA) that denies entry to migrants or seeks to remove migrants who lack legal status from the interior of the United States. (Congressional Research Services; 8 U.S.C. Sec. 1231). |
| Affirmative application for asylum | An application for asylum filed within 1 year of arrival to the United States (there are some exceptions that extend the window). Applicants file Form I-589, Application for Asylum and for the Withholding of Removal, with the United States Citizenship and Immigration Services (USCIS). [8 U.S.C. Sec. 1158(a)(1)]. |
| Defensive application for asylum | A defensive application for asylum happens when migrants request asylum as a defense against removal from the United States. This process takes place through the Executive Office for Immigration Review (EOIR) because that is where removal proceedings take place. |
| EOIR (Executive Office for Immigration Review) | This agency, a part of the Department of Justice, adjudicates all immigration cases in the United States through the immigration courts, presided over by Immigration Judges or IJs. |
| USCIS (U.S. Customs and Immigration Service) | This agency, a part of the Department of Homeland Security, processes immigration and naturalization applications. It hears and decides the asylum cases of most unaccompanied migrant children. |

## *How the Affirmative Asylum Process Works for Adults*

Migrants who arrive at the border, whether they present themselves at a Port of Entry or are apprehended by or present themselves to a Border Patrol agent within the United States, may claim asylum by following these basic steps (Congressional Research Services, 2019):

1. Notify the agent or officer of the intent to apply for asylum.
2. Undergo an interview with a USCIS asylum officer to determine whether the migrant has a credible fear of persecution.

3. If the migrant shows a "substantial and realistic possibility of success on the merits," they will be placed in removal proceedings and may pursue an application for asylum and withholding of removal as part of those proceedings.
4. The migrant must then show a "well-founded" fear of persecution to qualify for asylum. This fear must be demonstrated during an interview with an Asylum Officer (AO).
5. If the AO denies the application, the migrant may appeal to the Immigration Court and continue to appeal to the federal appeals court and the US Supreme Court.
6. Accompanied children are generally treated the same way as noncitizen adults and can be subjected to expedited or formal removal proceedings.

## How the Asylum Process Works for Unaccompanied Children ("UACs")

The asylum process is very different for migrants who are unaccompanied children or "UACs" (Congressional Research Services, 2019). Below are the steps that guide this process:

1. If the Department of Homeland Security determines that a migrant is a UAC, they must transfer the child to the custody of the Office of Refugee Resettlement ("ORR"), an agency of the Department of Health and Human Services, within 72 h.
2. ORR must then place the UAC "in the least restrictive setting that is in the best interest of the child." Children are generally released to individual sponsors who are parents or close relatives within 60 days.
3. The one-year restriction on asylum applications does not apply to UACs. USCIS officers have initial jurisdiction over all UAC asylum applications, whether they are affirmative or defensive.
4. If the AO rejects the UAC's application, the UAC may appeal to the Immigration Court.

DHS has developed an information form for UACs; Fig. 10.1 provides a picture of its first paragraphs.

It is the immigration judge who decides if a UAC case become adversarial (sent to the immigration court for possible deportation) or not adversarial (sent to the Customs and Immigration Service for asylum claims). This decision has significant impact on how long a child's case will take to be resolved. For those applying for asylum, cases can be completed in 6 months (experienced as a very long time in the mind of an unaccompanied 14-year-old child) or can take years (Cepla, 2019). For those whose cases are sent to immigration court, the situation is dire, with a current median of over 2 years (see Table 10.2). In general, UAC guidelines indicate that they should not be held in detention (before being sent to an "appropriate shelter") for more than 72 h (Hauslohner, June 25, 2019). The sheer number of cases (see Table 10.3) has flooded a system so that the 72 h in detention has become weeks if not months (Executive Office for Immigration Review Adjudication Statistics, April 23, 2019).

## INSTRUCTION SHEET FOR AN UNACCOMPANIED ALIEN CHILD IN IMMIGRATION COURT TO SUBMIT A FORM I-589 ASYLUM APPLICATION TO U.S. CITIZENSHIP AND IMMIGRATION SERVICES (USCIS)

You are receiving these instructions from a representative of Immigration and Customs Enforcement (ICE) because you appear to be an unaccompanied alien child (UAC), you are in Immigration Court, and you have indicated your intent to file a Form I-589, Application for Asylum and for Withholding of Removal. This form is not evidence of a previous UAC status determination.

**Attachments to this UAC Instruction Sheet:**
In addition to these instructions, this packet contains a blank Form I-589 asylum application, Instructions for the Form I-589, and a USCIS Form AR-11 (Alien's Change of Address Card). You may request the List of Free Legal Service Providers from the immigration court.

**Fig. 10.1** Information form for UACs (partial)

**Table 10.2** Median unaccompanied alien child (UAC) case completion and case pending time

| Fiscal year | Current median UAC pending time (Days) | FY 19 median UAC completion time (days) |
|---|---|---|
| 2019 (second quarter) | 725 | 586 |

https://www.justice.gov/eoir/page/file/1061551/download

Living in limbo regarding possible deportation or waiting for a decision on an asylum application is difficult for the most resilient adult (Silove, Sinnerbrink, Field & Manicavasagar, 1999). For unaccompanied children, it seems incomprehensibly stressful. Psychologically, it is only marginally less stressful to be "on hold" awaiting decision about being granted asylum as compared to awaiting a decision about deportation. Both instances involve children being held in detainment centers (sometimes in tents, or jail-like conditions) before being shuttled to another facility where they have to wait determination of their fate.

## Toxic Stress, Child Traumatic Stress, and Adverse Childhood Experiences (ACEs)

The popular conception of illness subsequent to psychological trauma usually tends toward posttraumatic stress disorder, or PTSD, an illness initially associated with war veterans (Crocq & Crocq, 2000). In reality, stress illness afflicts many people, including children, with serious impacts that can manifest in both the short and the long term (Bucci, Marques, Oh, & Harris, 2016). Complicating the picture is the

**Table 10.3** Pending
unaccompanied alien child
(UAC) cases

| Fiscal year | Pending |
|---|---|
| 2008 | 3201 |
| 2009 | 3284 |
| 2010 | 4025 |
| 2011 | 4372 |
| 2012 | 5581 |
| 2013 | 6907 |
| 2014 | 18,943 |
| 2015 | 31,597 |
| 2016 | 51,437 |
| 2017 | 70,221 |
| 2018 | 83,852 |
| 2019 (second quarter) | 89,632 |

https://www.justice.gov/eoir/page/file/1060871/download

fact that for many refugees, arrival in a new country does not mean an end to stress; there are many stressful components to the adjustment process, even if the application for asylum is successful. Although children in general are particularly vulnerable to toxic and traumatic stress and their consequences (Center on the Developing Child, n.d.), this is especially true of migrant children who seek asylum. Part of the reason for that is related to the challenges associated with the uncertainty surrounding the whole migration experience.

## *Definitions*

### Toxic Stress

The human body has natural processes enabling it to adapt to and cope with stress (Center on the Developing Child, n.d.). In and of itself, stress is not negative; in fact, a human system must be stressed in order to develop and grow, and many positive life events are also stressful. In its simplest and basic form, it is a condition that propels the individual to respond to a demand from the environment. As the person finds ways to respond in an attempt to minimize possible resulting distress created by the demands, the person is able to grow and develop strategies that are then organized and become part of the person's emotional and behavioral repertoire. Human stress responses are organized as positive, negative or toxic, and tolerable (Center on the Developing Child, n.d.). For example, positive stress encourages a child's body and mind to respond with development and growth. Tolerable stress, although does not require an urgent response, still serves an important intermediary function in understanding a situation that can also become toxic or harmless. Toxic stress, unless buffered, is dangerous to short- and long-term health (Bucci et al., 2016).

These labels do not refer to the stressful event itself, but rather to the human body's response to the event. What is stressful for one person may not be stressful for another. Long-term adverse effects of stress on an individual are not easy to determine as a simple cause-and-effect trajectory because they are influenced by many factors, including genetics, the presence of supportive relationships, and the nature of the stressful experience, including how long it lasts, when it takes place, how intense it is, and where, when, how, and why it happens (Bucci et al., 2016).

Child maltreatment is especially damaging to "executive function," which is responsible for complex reasoning and evaluation of consequences. The negative adaptations characteristic of child abuse and maltreatment victims are a "natural biological reaction to early threats on a person's system" (Cellini, 2004, p. 1), and these abnormal patterns in the brain frequently cause problems with "self-control, memory, emotion, judgement, consequential thinking, and moral reasoning" (p. 3). These aspects of cognition are especially at risk in abused children because damage to the prefrontal cortex is especially prominent in cases of abuse and neglect (p. 1). Since the prefrontal cortex is the "seat of moral development and judgment," damage to this area is likely to affect the child's function in activities requiring judgment and consequential thinking (p. 5). Damage that occurs in childhood and adolescence is particularly significant because that is the period of greatest sensitivity and plasticity for the prefrontal cortex that "extend[s] well into the adolescent period" (Petersen, Joseph, & Feit, 2014, p. 120), and until the mid-20s, according to some findings (Johnson, Blum & Giedd, 2009; Sowell, Thompson, Tessner & Toga, 2001).

The skill set under "executive functioning" is quite extensive and includes higher-order cognitive processes like "holding information in working memory, inhibiting impulses, planning, sustaining attention amid distraction, and flexibly shifting attention to achieve goals" (Petersen et al., 2014, p. 128). It also governs the ability to stay on task and to make complicated decisions with long-term consequences. Maltreated children are at risk for deficits in these essential functions, which are often evidenced by intellectual impairment, decreased IQ, difficulty controlling impulses, and an inability to maintain attention (Petersen et al., 2014).

The reason why toxic stress is especially impactful to children is because "a maladaptive response to stress during childhood…plays an important role in the pathway from early adversity to disease" (Bucci et al., 2016, p. 404). As the American Academy of Pediatrics recently noted in responding to newly developing immigration policies, "fear and stress, particularly prolonged exposure to serious stress – known as toxic stress – can harm the developing brain and negatively impact short- and long-term health" (Stein, 2017). When normal stress becomes chronic and pronounced, it can cause a "dysregulation of the physiologic stress response [that] plays a critical role in the development of negative health outcomes" (Bucci et al., 2016, p. 407). If a child is exposed to severe and/or prolonged trauma without adequate buffering factors, the trauma "can cause lasting changes to the stress response regulation" (p. 415). If the body loses the ability to return to homeostasis, instead remaining in perpetual hyperarousal, chronic stress can damage children's bodies and brains.

## Child Traumatic Stress

About one in every four children will experience a traumatic event before they turn 16 (National Child Traumatic Stress Network, 2005). Child traumatic stress is a term that references toxic stress but is specific to the experience of children. Child traumatic stress refers to the experience of those children who are exposed to one or more traumatic events (an intense event that threatens or causes harm to his or her emotional and physical well-being) and experience persistent symptoms that affect their lives after the event has ended or abated (National Child Traumatic Stress Network, 2005). Some experts characterize traumatic events by a subjective feeling that one's life or the lives of one's primary caretakers are threatened. Events experienced as traumatic can span a broad range, from exposure to a natural disaster to events like war or terrorism to personal experiences like separation from a parent, being the victim of violence, serious injury, abuse, or medical procedures.

Children experience specific symptoms when they are having a traumatic experience, including increased heart rate, sweating, agitation, hyper-alertness and vigilance, "butterflies," and emotional upset (National Child Traumatic Stress Network, 2005). As with positive and tolerable stress, if these feelings are transitory, they do little or no harm (Understanding the effects of maltreatment on brain development, 2015). In the end, child traumatic stress can significantly and negatively impact short- and long-term behavioral, emotional, mental, and physical health, especially when a child's difficult experiences are not buffered by a consistent, safe, close relationship with an adult caregiver.

## Adverse Childhood Experiences (ACEs)

Research into links between childhood stress and adult health made great strides with the publication of the Adverse Childhood Experiences, (ACEs) study in 1997 (Adverse Childhood Experiences, 2019). There were ten original ACEs categories to assess traumatic experience in children: emotional, physical, and sexual abuse; mother treated violently; household substance abuse; mental illness in the household; parental separation or divorce; incarcerated household member; and emotional and physical neglect. In the original study, 15.2% of women and 9.2% of men reported four or more ACEs before the age of 18 (total percent: 12.5%). As the number of ACEs rises, the risk of disease increases, with four or more ACEs as a critical inflection point for increased risk. Buffington, Dierkhising, and Marsh (2010) explain that exposure to complex trauma is cumulative and highly likely to derail a child's development.

These researchers found that adults who had experienced these ten specific types of childhood adversity were at significantly higher risk of a range of adult diseases, including cancer, chronic obstructive pulmonary disease, depression, obesity, suicide attempts, and others (Adverse Childhood Experiences, 2019). Since then, researchers sought to "assess the impact of numerous, interrelated ACEs on a wide variety of health behaviors and outcomes" (Anda et al., 2006, p. 176). They found—

as others have found in allied studies—that "the effects of multiple forms of abuse and related stressors are cumulative and affect a wide variety of outcomes" (Anda et al., 2006, p. 176).

Further research on the impact of ACEs on children has demonstrated that ACEs have short-term as well as long-term impact. Especially in cases of long-term maltreatment and trauma, the impacts of adverse experiences are not isolated, and children do not simply "get over" them (Cellini, 2004, p. 3). Rather, a "dose–response" effect causes multiple forms and instances of abuse to amplify the negative impact that each can have on a child's mental and physical health (Anda et al., 2006, pp. 174, 176).

As we stated earlier, sustained activation of the stress response system without a return to homeostasis can do significant damage to a developing child. Specifically, there is significant evidence that severe child maltreatment (physical, sexual, or emotional abuse as well as neglect) alters brain development and damages cognition, emotional regulation, and moral reasoning (National Institute of Justice, 2016). The scientific research demonstrates that it is not enough to consider particular impacts of child maltreatment in isolation. Rather, different types of early adversity can interact with and reinforce each other in powerfully damaging ways (Finkelhor, Turner, Hamby & Omrod, 2011) that can render traumatized children even *less* capable than developmentally normal children of understanding their rights and speaking for themselves (MacArthur Foundation, 2015).

In part, child traumatic stress has such a significant impact because the brains of children are highly plastic and develop in response to both positive and negative external stimuli. Centuries of evolution have trained the brain to develop in response to its environment, and the most important feature of neurons in the brain is that they "change in response to external signals" (Perry, Pollard, Blakely, Baker, & Vigilante, 1995, p. 274). But when an infant or child is maltreated, the brain "will adapt to a negative environment just as readily as it will adapt to a positive one" (Child Information Gateway, 2015). Such adaptations "can cause permanent, lifelong neurological damage and have a significant negative impact on the developing brain" (Cellini, 2004, p. 10). So while exposure to good experiences benefits the brain, exposure to bad experiences—like severe maltreatment and abuse—can damage the brain (Petersen, et al., 2014).

Although there is strong evidence that severe maltreatment and complex trauma can, and often do, cause temporary or permanent physical brain damage, there is no research on the impact of ACEs on unaccompanied migrant children in this context (Estefan, Ports, & Hipp, 2017, p. 5). There is, however, abundant research on the impact of trauma on refugee children (Gadeberg, Montgomery, Frederiksen, & Norredam, 2017) that can still be helpful to forensic professionals to consider when assessing this population. Given the consistency of evidence demonstrating the link between child traumatic stress and adult health outcomes from studies spanning many countries, professionals working with these children within the asylum system can apply scientific knowledge about child traumatic stress to their practice in order to better serve their clients and the process.

Clinical evaluation of detained mothers and children performed by a team of mental and behavioral health specialists at the South Texas Family Residential Center in Dilley, Texas; at the Greyhound Bus Station in San Antonio; and at Hospitality House, a shelter in San Antonio, from July 22 to July 24, 2015, revealed symptoms indicating widespread trauma experiences before and during detention. Quantitative and qualitative data collection methods were used, including refugee narratives—much like those that an asylum attorney would collect—providing details of conditions in the refugees' native countries, including community violence and violence against children, and conditions experienced during the journey from home (O'Connor, Thomas-Duckwitz & Nuñez-Mchiri, 2015).

## Application: What Does It Mean for Juvenile Asylum Clients?

Juvenile asylum applicants from war- and violence-torn countries run a high risk of complex trauma (repeated chronic traumatic events) from events they experienced in their home countries, on the often-perilous journey to the United States, and upon arrival, including apprehension and detention in centers not built for people their age (Fazel & Stein, 2003). The term "complex trauma" references a child's exposure to multiple traumatic events and the "wide-ranging, long-term effects of this exposure," including impacts that can interfere with participation in legal process, such as dissociation and damage to cognition. The immigration processing system, including credible fear interviews, court hearings, and other proceedings, can retraumatize them and are also not designed for people their age. Cognitively, behaviorally, and emotionally, these vulnerable clients can be at a significant disadvantage when it comes to their eligibility to remain in the United States. But, as the American Academy of Pediatrics has noted, appropriate care can contribute to winning credible asylum cases—an important factor for forensic professionals to bear in mind (Linton, Griffin & Shapiro, 2017).

### *Dangers Faced in the Journey, Especially by Minors Traveling Alone*

Many of the child asylum seekers arriving at our southern border from the Central American countries of El Salvador, Honduras, and Guatemala encounter many dangers and risks on the journey from home. Many dangers are exacerbated at the hands of both criminals and authorities when children travel alone. They are likely to be victims of kidnapping, be held for ransom, and be victims of sexual violence, particularly at "crossing points" during the migration to our border (Estefan et al., 2017, p. 4). Other unaccompanied children have reported suffering violence and exploitation at the hands of immigration authorities at multiple national borders along the way (Estefan et al., 2017).

# Toxic Stress Risk Factors for Migrant and Refugee Children

## Conditions Causing Children and Their Families to Flee Their Home Countries

Most people are heavily impacted by witnessing and experiencing violence and terrorism, but children are uniquely vulnerable to damage from trauma that is highly impactful and difficult to heal. Children are "more vulnerable than adults to the traumatic events, chaos, and disruptions experienced in disasters," and the results can be "serious and persistent even for preschool children" (Williams, 2007, p. 264). Children experience a wide range of feelings and exhibit a broad variety of behaviors in response to war and terrorism. While terrorism may not involve mass casualties, it is a form of mass violence "because of the destructive psychological effects on large numbers of people, including children" (p. 266). Examples include loneliness, disrupted sleep and nightmares, anger, tantrums, reenactment or reliving of distressing experiences, fear of being alone, fear of death, emotional withdrawal, somatic symptoms, and truncated moral development (Williams, 2007).

Exposure to violence is likely the strongest contributor to the "risk of subsequent psychological disturbances" among displaced and refugee children (Reed, Fazel, Jones, Panter-Brick, & Stein, 2012, p. 250). Direct exposure to threat, the cumulative number of violent events, and the duration of exposure "all consistently increase[] the odds of mental health symptoms," whether a child has been the victim of actual or threatened violence or witnessed violence to other people (Reed et al., 2012, p. 257). Thus, the simple fact of trauma exposure does not tell the whole story; both "dose" and co-occurrence of multiple traumas play a role in the damage done to children. Further, the stresses of war and political violence tend to co-occur with "forced displacement; traumatic loss; bereavement or separation; exposure to community violence; and exposure to domestic violence" (Betancourt et al., 2012, p. 682). These combined traumas compound the damage done to children in the midst of key developmental stages in their neurobiology. While the impacts of trauma can be limited to the short term, "negative developmental effects appear more likely if children experience repeated or repetitive 'process' trauma or live in unpredictable climates of fear" (Williams, 2007, p. 274). Posttraumatic stress disorder is more likely to affect children who have been a witness to or victim of violence, have been exposed to shelling or heavy combat, and have lost loved ones.

Many children and minors coming to the United States from El Salvador, Honduras, and Guatemala are trying to escape community and interpersonal violence that their governments are inadequate to prevent or remedy. In one study of unaccompanied minors by the United Nations High Commission for Refugees, children aged 12–17 most often reported exposure to community violence, organized crime, child maltreatment, and interpersonal violence in their homes, and these children most often reported violence as a "primary driver of migration" (Estefan, et al., 2017, p. 3). Data confirm their fears: UNICEF reports that as of 2014, El Salvador and Guatemala had the highest and second-highest rates of homicide among children aged 0–19 in the world. Honduras is one of the most violent countries in the world due to gang violence, and in 2012 it had the highest homicide rate in the world (Estefan et al., 2017).

Exposure to intrapersonal and community violence is a significant and known factor for child traumatic stress and attendant health impacts, including executive and cognitive function harm, damage to concentration, anxiety, depression, and attention-based disorders. The very harms that refugee children and youth are attempting to flee can damage their ability to later present a cogent and convincing case to the American immigration system.

## Impact of Separating Children from Their Parents

According to Jack Shonkoff from Harvard's Center on the Developing Child, "forcibly separating children from their parents is like setting a house on fire. Prolonging that separation is like preventing the first responders from doing their job" (Committee on Energy and Commerce Subcommittee on Oversight and Investigations, February 7, 2019, p. 4). And yet, in 2017 and 2018, United States immigration officials separated untold thousands (the United States "has faced challenges in identifying separated children" US Department of Health & Human Services, 2019) of children from their parents at the border. Parents were taken into custody, so they could be prosecuted for illegal entry and potentially deported. Regardless of age, children—some as young as infants—were taken into custody as "unaccompanied alien children" by the Department of Homeland Security and transferred to the custody of the Office of Refugee Resettlement, part of Health and Human Services. From there, some were released to sponsors within the United States; some were reunited with their parents after a period of time sometimes spanning months; and some remained in detention for an indefinite period of time.

Juvenile asylum seekers who have been separated from their parents are at extremely high risk of trauma, putting them at greatly increased risk of lifelong developmental consequences including generalized anxiety, developmental delay, and chronic physical illness. Separation from parents is most likely to lead to depression, and enforced separation from parents increases the likelihood of poor health in old age by a factor of 3.6. According to the President of the American Academy of Pediatrics, "highly stressful experiences, like family separation, can cause irreparable harm, disrupting a child's brain architecture and affecting his or her short- and long-term health. This type of prolonged exposure to serious stress—known as toxic stress—can carry lifelong consequences for children" (Kraft, 2018). Similarly, the American Psychological Association stated that "the longer that children and parents are separated, the greater the reported symptoms of anxiety and depression for the children. Negative outcomes for children include psychological distress, academic difficulties and disruptions in their development" (Daniel, 2018). The toxic stress referenced here can disrupt developing brain structures that regulate hormone activity in response to environmental stimuli, causing long-term emotional and behavioral pathology and stress-related disease. These effects of separation on children's psychological and emotional well-being often persist for a lifetime. Traumatic separation can also interfere with the development of later healthy attachments and may negatively affect children's capacity to sustain close interpersonal relationships in their lives. Traumatic separation can create general low self-esteem and distrust of others.

Fear of separation can also contribute to trauma. A Board of Immigration Appeals Accredited Representative employed at the family detention center in Dilley, Texas reported the impact of threatened separation in a 2015 declaration. At the ICE holding facilities, women and children report being forcibly separated from other family members without explanation; in the meantime, they report, they are constantly threatened with deportation and loss of their children if they do not comply with immigration officials' and deportation officers' orders (O'Connor et al. 2015). The "terror and existential fear" reported by these women in response to the threat of separation from their children is not only toxic to mothers, but to their children as well.

## Conditions in Detention that Harm Children's Health

The current standards of care for migrant children in US custody are minimal, and experts have recognized that they do not meet best practices standards set by the medical profession. As a result, children held in detention are at high risk of experiencing trauma and compounding the stressful conditions they may have previously experienced.

When minors are apprehended at the border, whether as part of a family unit or not, they are held in Customs and Border Patrol processing centers (see Table 10.1). Federal law requires that unaccompanied children be moved to Office of Refugee Resettlement (ORR) custody within 72 h (United States Government Accountability Office, 2015). Dr. Linton of the American Academy of Pediatrics (AAP) testified to "egregious conditions in many of the centers, including lack of bedding (e.g., sleeping on cement floors), open toilets, no bathing facilities, constant light exposure, confiscation of belongings, insufficient food and water, and lack of legal counsel, and a history of extremely cold temperatures" (Oversight of the Customs and Border Protection's response to the smuggling of persons at the Southern border. Committee on the Judiciary, 2019, p. 2). There are further reports of children held longer than 72 h, denied medical care, separated from their families, and maltreated (Linton et al., 2017). In 2015, a Board of Immigration Appeals Accredited Representative working at the South Texas Residential Family Center in Dilley, Texas filed a sworn declaration recording his client's descriptions of the conditions of confinement in these processing centers. The declaration states that when received in Dilley from ICE holding facilities, the vast majority of clients suffer from fevers, coughing, headaches, and fatigue. Clients report being held in either "iceboxes" or "kennels" while in ICE custody. "Iceboxes" or "hieleras" are "secure facilities that are held at frigid indoor temperatures that shock the body of young children and their mothers into sickness"—without blankets or medical attention, and with only ham sandwiches to eat. "Kennels" are "warehouse-like facilities subdivided by wire fences, so crowded that some children must sleep while standing" (O'Connor et al., 2015).

Unaccompanied children go from CBP centers to ORR shelters. These shelters range in size, type, and level of security. In fiscal year 2018, the average length of stay in ORR facilities was 60 days ("Facts and Data," n.d.). Children who are with their family units either undergo expedited return to their country of origin or go to family residential centers or the family units are released into the community. Family residential centers are administered by Immigration and Customs Enforcement (ICE). In 2015, a federal court found that these centers violated a 1997 settlement agreement that required children to be held in the "least restrictive setting." The American Academy of Pediatrics notes that "despite this order, children continue to be detained, and even with shorter lengths of stay, some were still found to suffer traumatic effects" (Linton, et al., 2017, p. 5). Further, AAP found discrepancies between the standards ICE claims to follow and the actual conditions in the centers, including "inadequate or inappropriate immunizations, delayed medical care, inadequate education services, and limited mental health services" (p. 5).

The bare fact of detention does significant harm to children; "several studies of detained child migrants and asylum seekers have documented extensive mental health issues, including depression, anxiety, and post-traumatic stress disorder, and developmental delays for very young children" (Estefan et al., 2017, p. 4). As noted, the American Academy of Pediatrics has found that Department of Homeland Security detention facilities are categorically unsafe for children; further, the AAP has recognized the potential harm of detaining children in Office of Refugee Resettlement facilities, and has found that family detention centers run by ICE regularly keep children longer than legally permitted; it has called for "longitudinal evaluation of the health consequences of detention of immigrant children in the United States" (Linton, et al., 2017, p. 1). In January 2019, lawyers representing migrant children housed in ORR facilities as part of a decades-long class action suit notified the federal court and the Justice Department's Office of Immigration Litigation that more than a dozen of these facilities are operating without licenses and committing other violations of court orders as well (Kates, 2019).

Beyond the dangers inherent in the basic conditions of detention, migrant children face significant potential harm from other causes. One of the most important is forced administration of medication without parental consent or court order. While against the law, this practice has frequently taken place in detention centers, as documented in active litigation of a court case regarding detained migrant child welfare that has been ongoing for 34 years. In July 2018, the federal court ordered the federal government to stop administering psychotropic medication to children absent court order or parental consent (*Flores v. Sessions*, 2018). The court's order, while specific, applies only to the Shiloh Residential Treatment Center in Texas. As recently as October 2018, lawyers claimed that the government was still administering drugs to children without consent or court order, despite the court's July order (Morel, 2018).

The risk of sexual abuse of migrant children does not end once they reach US custody. Sexual abuse, whether by adults or fellow juvenile migrants, is another widespread danger in detention. According to Health and Human Services (HHS) records, thousands of unaccompanied children have reported sexual abuse and sexual harassment while in detention centers—at least 1000 reports to HHS each year since 2015 (Deutch, 2019). Allegations ranged from watching children shower to fondling, kissing, and raping them. Despite the frequency of reporting to HHS, though, in each year, far fewer allegations were reported out to the Department of Justice (DOJ)—in each of the last two fiscal years, only 49 reports were made to DOJ (Deutch, 2019). From March 2018 to July 2018, the period during which the family separation policy resulted in mass separations, ORR received a record-high 859 complaints, 342 of which were referred to DOJ (Haag, 2019). And according to data from the Office of the Inspector General of the Department of Homeland Security and ICE itself, thousands of migrants have claimed sexual abuse while in ICE custody ("While in ICE custody, thousands of migrants reported sexual abuse," 2018). These reports are not limited to children, but they do reveal that the risk of sexual abuse is present in both DHS and HHS facilities.

## The Role of the Forensic Psychology Expert

While the US asylum process is not well understood by citizens or immigrants alike (and is frequently modified), attorneys are not currently provided in these cases (and there is nothing to suggest that this will be changing anytime soon). When an asylum seeker is fortunate enough to have an attorney (often through a not-for-profit legal agency), it is not certain that a forensic psychologist, psychiatrist, or social worker will be provided and/or available. Some forensic experts will take pro bono or "low bono" (very low pay) cases because there are no or few funds budgeted for these services and personal or professional ethics motivate their engagement. When there are some financial resources earmarked for these much-needed experts, they seldom cover usual fees for forensic assessments. Additionally, an assessment is only the beginning. Collateral information and records must be reviewed, literature research is often needed, reports must be written and edited, and, when needed, the expert will have to testify. One barrier for some experts is the amount of time and energy required for this type of work. Another barrier is the form of testimony. While some courts will allow telephone testimony, it is much less effective than an in-person hearing. However, with the backlog of cases, hearings are frequently held months (or longer) after the assessment is completed and cases are frequently adjourned. Many experts have attended immigration hearings multiple times on the same case before actually testifying (adding to the ripple effect of the backlog and delay of completion of cases). Country experts (so-called because they are experts in the country where the seeker came from and may be returned to) are more readily available, but are limited in that they cannot speak to the specific physical and mental health needs of the applicant. Having both is important for conveying, as much as possible, the effects of the applicant remaining in their home country or being sent back to their home country. In addition, there is the often-present need for an interpreter, even when the client speaks some English. Many psychological and legal nuances are lost on clients who have a low level of English proficiency needed for their daily life. For children, and many adults as well, the level of English skills is important. While testing a client to get a formal reading level is not always feasible, experts can evaluate the reading level of the documents the client is expected to comprehend. Finding competent experts for adults is daunting, and for children it is almost impossible. Inasmuch as every decision has consequences, these legal judgments come with psycho-legal sequalae, often traumatic in nature, no matter the legal outcome. Having an expert not only increases the chances of an appropriate outcome, but in many cases can help mitigate re-traumatization from the process.

## Conclusion

Migrant children fleeing violence and danger in their countries of origin experience a multitude of traumas before departing from their homes, on their way to the United States, and in detention once arrived. As people whose brains and bodies are uniquely sensitive to toxic stress and complex trauma, children applying for asylum face special difficulties. Yet most of these children do not have access to a forensic expert who can examine them and provide the asylum officer or immigration court with an affidavit in support of the asylum application that lays out the evidence of trauma history and expert opinion on its impacts. Interviewing and assessing children for a history of trauma is not straightforward. Specific techniques should be followed to ensure that the child both feels safe and is not unintentionally prompted or encouraged to report trauma or trauma symptoms (Aldridge & Wood, 1998; Cronch, Viljoen, & Hansen, 2005; Lamb, Orbach, Hershkowitz, Horowitz, & Abbott, 2007; Lyon, 2014; Wilson & Powell, 2001). Experts are most helpful in American immigration process when they provide sufficient information about the sequelae of toxic stress in these asylum-seeking individuals, including the neuro-physiological, biological, and psychological range of experiences that can produce it. The comprehensiveness of this forensic assessment is likely to offer the best opportunity for success to asylum seekers.

In light of the extensive research on the effect of ACEs and toxic stress on children seeking asylum, it is critical to introduce this evidence in asylum hearings. There are several ways to increase awareness of the critical role of toxic stress to the attention of immigration courts. First, the use of forensic experts providing high-quality assessments can significantly boost an applicant's chances at being granted asylum. For example, 90% of outcomes in cases involving participation of a volunteer trained in the Physicians for Human Rights Asylum Program are positive, relative to a national average of barely 30%. Research has outlined the most important elements of a successful assessment, including documentation of the evaluation process and all sources of evidence; corroborative evidence unique to the applicant;

description of the psychological consequences of persecution, including the impact of PTSD on the applicant's memory; description and documentation of physical evidence, where possible; and provision of new evidence that supplements prior accounts (Scruggs, Guetterman, Meyer, VanArtsdalen, & Heisler, 2016). Significant training resources ranging from online webinars to multiday workshops are available to assist forensic experts in preparing for this work, including the extensive program run by Physicians for Human Rights, which includes access to volunteer opportunities.

## Questions/Activities for Further Exploration

1. Why are forensic examinations of applicants so important to the asylum process? At what stage of the proceedings can an assessment be done, and why might the timing matter?
2. Why are unaccompanied children uniquely vulnerable to the chaos and stress of migration and asylum proceedings? What are some differences between the way a forensic professional would assess an adult and an unaccompanied child?
3. Describe the impact of trauma and toxic stress on cognition and memory. Why is this important to understand in the case of asylum seekers?
4. You are a forensic professional volunteering in an asylum case. Your client is an unaccompanied child who fled El Salvador and passed through Guatemala and Mexico on the way to the United States. The child traveled with a coyote—a person paid to get groups of people to the United States border—and a group of people of a range of ages.

   (a) What are the possible red flags you see?
   (b) What considerations are most important in examining the child?
   (c) How would you proceed? Explain, step-by-step.

## References

Adverse Childhood Experiences (ACEs). (2019, April 23). Retrieved July 2, 2019, from https://www.cdc.gov/violenceprevention/childabuseandneglect/acestudy/index.html

Aldridge, M., & Wood, J. (1998). *Wiley series in child care and protection. Interviewing children: A guide for child care and forensic practitioners*. New York, NY: Wiley.

Anda, R., Felitti, V., Bremner, J., Walker, J., Whitfield, C., Perry, B., … Giles, W. (2006). The enduring effects of abuse and related adverse experiences in childhood. *European Archives of Psychiatry and Clinical Neuroscience, 256*(3), 174–186.

Betancourt, T. S., Newnham, E. A., Layne, C. M., Kim, S., Steinberg, A. M., Ellis, H., & Birman, D. (2012). Trauma history and psychopathology in war-affected refugee children referred for trauma-related mental health services in the United States. *Journal of Traumatic Stress, 25*(6), 682–690.

Bucci, M., Marques, S. S., Oh, D., & Harris, N. B. (2016). Toxic stress in children and adolescents. *Advances in Pediatrics, 63*(1), 403–428.

Buffington, K., Dierkhising, C. B., & Marsh, S. C. (2010). Ten things every juvenile court judge should know about trauma and delinquency. *Juvenile and Family Court Journal, 61*(3), 13–23.

Center on the Developing Child, Harvard University. (n.d.) Toxic stress. https://developingchild.harvard.edu/science/key-concepts/toxic-stress/

Cellini, H. R. (2004). Child abuse, neglect, and delinquency: The neurological link. *Juvenile and Family Court Journal, 55*(4), 1–14.

Cepla, A. (2019, January 10). Fact sheet: U.S. asylum process. National Immigration Forum. https://immigrationforum.org/article/fact-sheet-u-s-asylum-process/

Child Welfare Information Gateway. (2015). *Understanding the effects of maltreatment on brain development*. Washington, DC: U.S. Department of Health and Human Services, Children's Bureau. https://www.childwelfare.gov/pubs/issue-briefs/brain-development/

Committee on Energy and Commerce Subcommittee on Oversight and Investigations. (2019, February 7). https://energycommerce.house.gov/sites/democrats.energycommerce.house.gov/files/documents/Shonkoff%20testimony%20FINAL_0.pdf

Congressional Research Services. (2019). Recent Migration to the United States from Central America: Frequently Asked Questions. https://fas.org/sgp/crs/row/R45489.pdf

Crocq, M., & Crocq, L. (2000). From shell shock and war neurosis to posttraumatic stress disorder: A history of psychotraumatology. *Dialogues in Clinical Neuroscience, 2*(10), 47–55.

Cronch, L., Viljoen, J., & Hansen, D. (2005). Forensic interviewing in child sexual abuse cases: Current techniques and future directions. *Aggression and Behavior, 11*, 195–207.

Daniel, J. (2018, May 29). *Statement of APA president regarding the traumatic effects of separating immigrant families*. Retrieved from www.apa.org/news/press/releases/2018/05/separating-immigrant-families

Deutch, T. (2019, February 26). *Deutch releases data showing sexual assault of unaccompanied minors in HHS custody*. https://teddeutch.house.gov/news/documentsingle.aspx?DocumentID=399520

Estefan, L., Ports, K., & Hipp, T. (2017). Unaccompanied children migrating from Central America: Public health implications for violence prevention and intervention. *Current Trauma Reports, 3*(2), 97–103.

Executive Office For Immigration Review Adjudication Statistics. (2019, April 23). https://www.justice.gov/eoir/page/file/1061551/download

Facts and Data. (n.d.). Retrieved July 3, 2019, from Office of Refugee Resettlement | ACF website: https://www.acf.hhs.gov/orr/about/ucs/facts-and-data

Fazel, M., & Stein, A. (2003). The mental health of refugee children. *Archives of Disease in Childhood, 87*(5). Retrieved from http://adc.bmj.com/content/87/5/366.full.pdf

Finkelhor, S., Turner, H., Hamby, S. & Ormrod, R. (2011). *Polyvictimization: Children's exposure to multiple types of violence, crime, and abuse*. OJJDP Juvenile Justice Bulletin – NCJ235504 (pp. 1–12). Washington, DC: US Government Printing Office.

First, L., & Kemper, A. (2018, June). The effects of toxic stress and adverse childhood experience at our Southern border: Letting the published evidence speak for itself. *American Academy of Pediatrics Blog*. https://www.aappublications.org/news/2018/06/20/the-effects-of-toxic-stress-and-adverse-childhood-experiences-eg-at-our-southern-border-letting-the-published-evidence-speak-for-itself-pediatrics-6-20-18

Flores v. Sessions. CV 85-4544. (2018, October 30). https://www.leagle.com/decision/infdco20181114715

Gadeberg, A. K., Montgomery, E., Frederiksen, H. W., & Norredam, M. (2017). Assessing trauma and mental health in refugee children and youth: A systematic review of validated screening and measurement tools. *The European Journal of Public Health, 27*(3), 439–446.

Haag, M. (2019, February 27). Thousands of immigrant children said they were sexually abused in U.S. detention centers, report says. *The New York Times*. www.nytimes.com/2019/02/27/us/immigrant-children-sexual-abuse.html

Hauslohner, A. (2019, June 25). U.S. returns 100 migrant children to overcrowded border facility as HHS says it is out of space. *The Washington Post*.

Johnson, S., Blum, R., & Giedd, J. (2009). Adolescent maturity and the brain: The promise and pitfalls of neuroscience research in adolescent health policy. *Journal of Adolescent Health, 45*(3), 216–221.

Kates, G. (2019, January 23). Migrant children in U.S. are being held in unlicensed shelters, lawyers say – CBS News. Retrieved July 3, 2019, from https://www.cbsnews.com/news/migrant-children-in-u-s-are-being-held-in-unlicensed-shelters-lawyers-say/

Kraft, C. (2018, May 8). *AAP statement opposing separation of children and parents at the border*. Retrieved from www.aap.org/en-us/about-the-aap/aap-press-room/Pages/StatementOpposingSeparationofChildrenandParents.aspx

Lamb, M., Orbach, Y., Heshkowitz, I., Horowitz, D., & Abbott, C. (2007). Does the type of prompt affect the accuracy of information provided by alleged victims of abuse in forensic interviews? *Applied Cognitive Psychology, 21*(9), 1117–1130.

Linton, J., Griffin, M., & Shapiro, A. (2017). Detention of immigrant children. *Pediatrics, 139*(4), e20170483. https://doi.org/10.1542/peds.2017-0483

Lyon, T. (2014). Interviewing children. *Annual Review of Law and Social Science, 10*, 73–89.

MacArthur Foundation. (2015). *Juvenile justice in a developmental framework: A 2015 status report.* https://www.macfound.org/media/files/MacArthur_Foundation_2015_Status_Report.pdf

Morel, C. (2018, October 20). *Immigrant children still being drugged at shelter despite judge's order, lawyers say. Reveal.* Retrieved from www.revealnews.org/blog/immigrant-children-still-being-drugged-at-shelter-despite-judges-order-lawyers-say/

National Child Traumatic Stress Network. (2005). *What is child traumatic stress?: (402862005-001)* [Data set]. https://doi.org/10.1037/e402862005-001

National Institute of Justice. (2016). *Children exposed to violence*. Retrieved July 2, 2019, from https://nij.gov:443/topics/crime/children-exposed-to-violence/Pages/welcome.aspx

O'Connor, K., Thomas-Duckwitz, C. & Nuñez-Mchiri, G. (2015). *No safe haven here: mental health assessment of women and children held in U.S. immigration detention.* . Retrieved from https://www.uusc.org/sites/default/files/mental_health_assessment_of_women_and_children_u.s._immigration_detention.pdf

Office of Immigration Statistics. (2019, March). Department of Homeland Security, annual flow report: Refugees and asylees, 2017. https://www.dhs.gov/sites/default/files/publications/Refugees_Asylees_2017.pdf

Oversight of the Customs and Border Protection's response to the smuggling of persons at the southern border. Committee on the Judiciary. (2019, March 6) (testimony of Julie Linton). https://www.judiciary.senate.gov/imo/media/doc/Linton%20Testimony.pdf

Perry, B. D., Pollard, R. A., Blakley, T. L., Baker, W. L., & Vigilante, D. (1995). Childhood trauma, the neurobiology of adaptation, and "use-dependent" development of the brain: How "states" become "traits". *Infant Mental Health Journal, 16*(4), 271–291.

Petersen, A., Joseph, H., & Feit, M. (Eds.). (2014). *New directions in child abuse and neglect research*. Washington, D.C.: National Academies Press.

Physicians for Human Rights. (n.d.). How you can help asylum seekers. https://phr.org/issues/asylum-and-persecution/join-the-asylum-network/

Reed, R. V., Fazel, M., Jones, L., Panter-Brick, C., & Stein, A. (2012). Mental health of displaced and refugee children resettled in low-income and middle-income countries: Risk and protective factors. *The Lancet, 379*(9812), 250–265.

Scruggs, E., Guetterman, T., Meyer, A., VanArtsdalen, H., & Heisler, M. (2016). "An Absolutely Necessary Piece": A qualitative study of legal perspectives on medical affidavits in the asylum process. *Journal of Forensic and Legal Medicine, 44*, 72–78. https://doi.org/10.1016/j.jflm.2016.09.002

Shonkoff, J., & Garner, A. (2012). The lifelong effects of early childhood adversity and toxic stress. *Pediatrics, 129*(1), e232–e246.

Silove, D., Sinnerbrink, I., Field, A., & Manicavasagar, V. (1999). Anxiety, depression and PTSD in asylum seekers: Associations with pre-migration trauma and post-migration stressors. *The British Journal of Psychiatry, 170*(4), 351–357.

Sowell, E., Thompson, P., Tessner, K., & Toga, A. (2001). Mapping continued brain growth and gray matter density reduction in dorsal frontal cortex: Inverse relationships during postadolescent brain maturation. *The Journal of Neuroscience, 21*(22), 8819–8829.

Stein, F. (2017, January 25). *AAP statement on protecting immigrant children.* Retrieved from www.aap.org/en-us/about-the-aap/aap-press-room/Pages/AAPStatementonProtecting ImmigrantChildren.aspx

U.S. Department of Health & Human Services, Office of the Inspector General. (2019, January 17). *Separated Children Placed in Office of Refugee Resettlement Care,* https://oig.hhs.gov/oei/reports/oei-BL-18-00511.asp

U.S. Department of Homeland Security Office of immigration statistics. (2019). Annual flow report refugees and asylees 2017. https://www.dhs.gov/immigration-statistics

Understanding the effects of maltreatment on brain development. (2015, April). https://www.childwelfare.gov/pubPDFs/brain_development.pdf

United States Government Accountability Office. (2015). *Unaccompanied alien children: Actions needed to ensure children receive required care in DHS custody* (No. GAO-15-521). Retrieved from https://www.gao.gov/assets/680/671393.pdf

While in ICE custody, thousands of migrants reported sexual abuse. (2018, July 22). In *PBS News Hour.* Retrieved from www.pbs.org/newshour/show/while-in-ice-custody-thousands-of-migrants-reported-sexual-abuse

Williams, R. (2007). The psychosocial consequences for children of mass violence, terrorism and disasters. *International Review of Psychiatry, 19*(3), 263–277.

Wilson, C., & Powell, M. (2001). *A guide to interviewing children: Essential skills for counsellors, police, lawyers, and social workers.* London, UK: Routledge.

# Chapter 11
# Termination of Parental Rights: Psychological Impact on Children of Immigrants

**Yosef Amrami and Rafael Art. Javier**

## Termination of Parental Rights and Its Contexts

This chapter focuses on psychological impacts that family separation has on migrant and immigrant children. Family separation, in which parents are forcefully removed from their children, can occur in multiple settings and contexts. Immigrants, including undocumented immigrants, are especially vulnerable to encounter family separation. Immigration is an ubiquitous human and cultural experience throughout the history of civilization, although each propelled by different political forces and personal motivations. The most recent data suggest that there are about 71 million migrants globally, including people who are internally displaced and/or seeking asylum in another country (UNHRC, 2019). It is also estimated that about 31 million children were displaced by regional violence and economic hardships during 2018 (UNICEF, 2019). While about half of these displaced children are internally displaced within their country of origin, the remainder are seeking safety in another country (UNICEF, 2018). It is a global phenomenon (see Figs. 11.1, 11.2, and 11.3) made possible by drastic changes in the political and economic landscapes in many countries around the world that is compelling their citizens to migrate to another country, particularly when their own physical and economic safety and/or that of their family becomes seriously compromised due to raging and sectarian-based wars (UNHCR, 2018).

Our concern is not only that the severity of forced migration and its effects on children and their families vary by region, but that their welfare is often determined by their destination's law and policies relating to immigration and asylum (UNHCR, 2018). We see how that very issue is played out in the United States where the

Y. Amrami (✉) · R. A. Javier
St. John's University, Office of Postgraduate Professional Development Programs,
Queens, NY, USA
e-mail: Yosef.Amrami15@stjohns.edu

© Springer Nature Switzerland AG 2020
R. A. Javier et al. (eds.), *Assessing Trauma in Forensic Contexts*,
https://doi.org/10.1007/978-3-030-33106-1_11

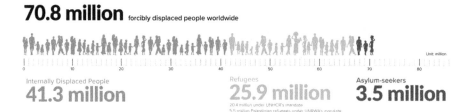

**70.8 million** forcibly displaced people worldwide

Internally Displaced People
**41.3 million**

Refugees
**25.9 million**
20.4 million under UNHCR's mandate
5.5 million Palestinian refugees under UNRWA's mandate

Asylum-seekers
**3.5 million**

**Fig. 11.1** Number of displaced people globally by 2018. (*Source:* UNHRC 2019)

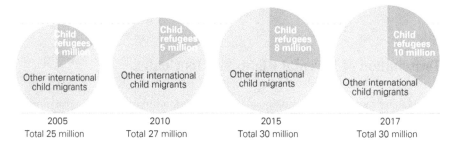

| 2005 | 2010 | 2015 | 2017 |
| Total 25 million | Total 27 million | Total 30 million | Total 30 million |

**Fig. 11.2** Changes in proportion of child refugees relative to total child immigration from 2005 to 2017. (*Source:* UNICEF 2018)

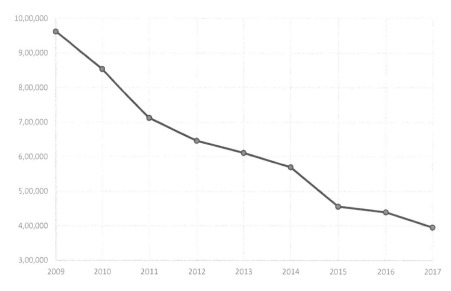

**Fig. 11.3** Deportations of immigrants from the United States Per Year (2009–2017). (*Source:* U.S. Department of Homeland Security 2019)

United States' immigration and asylum-seeking policies can be seen as case studies of how a country's laws can affect the psychological welfare of migrant and immigrant children and families. The United States has a long-standing political history pertaining to migration between the U.S.–Mexican border, with many politicians and media figures attributing domestic economic hardships and crime on the influx of migrants from Central America (Abramitzky & Boustan, 2017). Yet, although the United States can provide an important case study on this topic, many other countries are dealing with an influx of migrants and have used their own regulations to either encourage and/or discourage migrants from being integrated into their countries (UNHCR, 2018).

We recognize that the immigration phenomenon and its consequences is complex and, depending on whether one focuses on the activities of a few individual immigrants who engage in criminal behavior; or one focuses on the consistent findings of the tremendous benefits immigrants tend to bring to the host country at many levels (e.g., filling vital niches in employment; Abramitzky & Boustan, 2017: Peri, 2013); or on anything in between, the argument against or in favor of immigration becomes front and center of the political discourse. This is as true in the United States, as it is around many countries in the world where we find a strong anti-immigrant political discourse taking hold. In the meantime, the most vulnerable and most in need (e.g., children, victims of domestic violence, economic warfare, and gang violence, targets of political and religious persecution, etc.) are furthered victimized/traumatized and their circumstances worsened (e.g., placed in the deportation centers, children separated from parents, returned to their countries of origin, etc.).

Although, there is strong evidence emerging of how much trauma permeates the lives of many immigrants, our focus in this chapter is only to examine the impact of family separation and parental termination on children and the role of forensic professional in understanding and providing services to this population. For this purpose, we will focus on parental termination taking place more specifically in the United States as an example of a larger phenomenon at play in other parts of the world.

## Immigration in the United States

By 2017, there were a reported 10.5 million undocumented immigrants living in the United States, a decline from its peak of 12.2 million a decade previously (Krogstad, Passel, & Cohn, 2019). About half of the total population of undocumented immigrants are from Mexico (Gonzalez-Barrera & Krogstad, 2019). According to these data, about 83% of undocumented immigrants from Mexico and 53% of undocumented immigrants from other countries have lived in the United States for over 10 years, which suggests a development of deep roots in their residing communities (Gonzalez-Barrera & Krogstad, 2019). Therefore, American immigration policies do not solely affect undocumented immigrants but affect their communities and families as well. Data to that effect is found in the fact that about six million U.S. citizen children have at least one family member that is an undocumented immigrant, and four million of those children have one or more parents that are undocumented (American Immigration Council, 2018).

Much of the statistics on immigration apprehension and subsequent family separations in the United States are provided by the Department of Homeland Security (DHS), the federal agency responsible for immigration. The Office of Inspector General of the DHS responsible for auditing the DHS stated in its report that "DHS has struggled to provide accurate, complete, reliable data on family separations and reunification, raising concerns about the accuracy of the reporting" (Kelly, 2018, p. 9). This suggests that much of the information provided regarding family separation is inaccurate, a conclusion also supported by findings from the American Civil Liberties Union which calls the DHS findings an underrepresentation (Rickerd & Drake, 2019). The greatest problem with this underrepresentation is that we are left without a clear and objective perspective of the scope of the problem and with the concern that these statistics may not be emblematic of real migration patterns in the future given how quickly immigration laws and policies have changed and enacted contemporarily. Nevertheless, these statistics provide forensic professionals with at least a glance, albeit not totally accurate, of how changes to immigration policies have resulted in real changes to the lives of immigrants, particularly with regard to immigration detention and family separation.

According to these statistics, the yearly rate of total immigration apprehensions and deportations has fluctuated over the last decade but, over the last decade, has been trending in the downward direction (see Fig. 20.3; U.S. Department of Homeland Security, 2019). The Department of Homeland Security has estimated that 521 thousand people have been apprehended across the U.S.–Mexican border during 2018, which is an increase of over 100 thousand people from the previous year (2019). However, when looking at trends from 2014–2018, the rate of total immigration apprehensions has ranged from about 444 to 569 thousand. In contrast, family separations and the apprehension of unaccompanied minors have increased significantly as of 2019 over previous years. In 2018, the Department of Human Services reported that nearly 2000 children were separated from their parents in a 6-week period at the U.S.–Mexican border (Long, 2018) in separate detention centers for days or weeks at a time.

Immigration policies, such as policies and laws pertaining to parental rights and family separation, have had a strong impact on the American zeitgeist. In addition, the state of such laws has obvious implications for forensic psychologist working with these cases. Broadly speaking, parent–child separation has been found to harm those involved-especially children (Bouza et al., 2018; Wood, 2018). Many national professional and academic organizations have condemned the Zero Tolerance policy enacted in 2018 by the current administration on humanitarian basis, particularly regarding children and their families (e.g., Daniel & Evans, 2018). This policy stipulates that any adult coming into the United States would be considered criminals and detained away from their children, who are then held in separate detention centers. The Society for Research in Child Development (SRCD), an organization representing developmental psychologists, released a "Statement of Evidence" against the family separation policy (Bouza et al., 2018). In a succinct but informative review of literature of family separation, Bouza et al. concluded that family separation incurs short and long-term impairments onto children psychosocial health, such as increasing their vulnerability to anxiety, in addition to making children more predisposed to medical conditions, like obesity (2018). In a similar vein, the American Psychological Association (APA), the American Association for Pediatrics, and the National Education Association (NEA) have adopted resolutions, made public statements, and created petitions condemning the practice of separating migrant children from their parents upon arrival to the United States (Daniel & Evans, 2018; Kraft, 2018; National Education Association, 2019). Furthermore, the American Bar Association, which represents lawyers and sets standards for ethical legal practice, has also condemned family separation as "unnecessarily cruel" (Bass, 2018). Perhaps, one of the most poignant condemnations of this policy came from the APA president at the time, Jessica Henderson Daniel, Ph.D., who said, "The administration's policy of separating children from their families as they attempt to cross into the United States without documentation is not only needless and cruel, it threatens the mental and physical health of both the children and their caregivers" (Daniel & Evans, 2018).

Most of our knowledge about family separation within immigrant has been gained from studying undocumented immigrants who were deported or detained and were subsequently separated from their families after living and raising their families in the county for years. Although an important consideration for forensic psychologists, there are substantially few studies on the psychological ramifications of family separation due to immigrant detention where the parents are still in the country but the children have limited access to them, if any. Nevertheless, scientists point to studies of children of incarcerated guardians or juvenile detention (e.g., Wood, 2018) as an important source of information regarding the impact of separation on children. However, family separation due to immigrant detention at the border raises additional concerns about parent–child separation related to fears immigrants have about family separation and its impact on their psychological well-being. An important consideration for forensic psychologists since immigrants' pervasive fear of legal consequences have been found to result in their discomfort or unwillingness to trust and seek the legal counsel (Dreby, 2012; McFarland & Spangler, 2008), and likely to impact on their willingness to participate in forensic assessments. Finally, this chapter also discusses legal consideration forensic psychologists ought to keep in mind when dealing with litigation concerning immigrant family separation.

## Impact of Parental's Deportation or Retention

The negative impacts that a parent's detention or deportation has on the psychological health of children have been thoroughly investigated by numerous studies (e.g., Chaudry et al., 2010; see Wood, 2018 for a literature review). These studies involve immigrants who immigrated to their country of residence and have often established communities, professional lives, and families in the host countries. In one study, the psychological wellbeing of Children 6–15 years old were examined following parental deportation (Allen, Cisneros, & Tellez, 2015). Most participants were living in mixed-status households (e.g., children were citizens while their parent(s) were not). The participants were segmented into three groups for analyses: A control group, a group of children whose parents were arguing against deportation, and a group of children with parents who were deported. These children's internalizing (e.g., depression and poor self-esteem) and externalizing problems (e.g., noncompliance and aggressiveness) were assessed along with their trauma history and demographics. It was found that compared to the control group, having a deported parent was predictive of greater internalizing (e.g., depressed mood & anxiety) and externalizing problems (e.g., aggression & defiance); no such effect was found for children whose parents were fighting against deportation.

Similar findings were reported when studying the effects that parent deportation and detention had on the occurrence of Post-Traumatic Stress (PTS) and other emotional concerns in children (Rojas-Flores, Clements, Hwang Koo, & London, 2017). In contrast to the study conducted by Allen et al. (2015), Rojas-Flores and associates compiled assessments from multiple sources, such as their teachers and parents, and exclusively studied a pre-adolescent sample. They assessed the prevalence of PTS in children (6–12 years old) who had at least one undocumented immigrant as a parent but varied in whether a parent was separated from them. They found that children with a deported or detained parent experienced greater internalizing problems and PTS compared to other children, according to parents' reports. In addition, children who experienced greater traumas, such as their parent being deported, were reported by their teachers to engage in more externalizing behaviors at school.

Furthermore, comparing children living in the context of family separation to other children with similar demographic characteristics informs us of the added impact that family separation has on a child's wellbeing. Such a study was conducted by Zayas and Bradley (2014) on three samples of 8–15-year-old children. One sample included children from the United States living with deported parents in Mexico; the other sample were children from mixed-status homes in the United States with at least one guardian deported to Mexico; the final sample comprised of children from mixed-status homes in the United States that did not have a deported or detained guardian (the control group). These children's broad psychological functioning and elevations in depression and anxiety were assessed to determine levels of impact, if any, resulting from these different deportation experiences. Initial analyses showed that children who were deported with their parents endorsed more symptoms of depression and less happiness and freedom from anxiety than children in the United States who were living with their parents. Children in the United States who were separated from their family had elevations in inattention and hyperactivity compared to other groups. In a follow-up study, Zayas, Aguilar-Gaxiola, Yoon, and Rey (2015) then separated their sample into two groups for subsequent analyses, which included children affected by deportation and those who were not. They found that children who were affected by deportation were more likely to experience depression, poor-self-concept, diminished happiness, and less freedom from anxiety. These authors raised the issue that, in the end, current immigration law enforcement often forces parents to decide whether to make their children "exiles" or "orphans." By that they meant that a parent who is being deported back to their home country must decide whether they will leave their children to be fostered by relatives or friends or bring their children with them, and thus removing them from their friends, community, and school. It is their view that children of the deported parents may be harmed even if the child is deported alongside their guardian(s); although not as great as when they are separated (Zayas & Bradlee, 2014).

These findings are further supported by a qualitative study conducted on a sample of children of deported parents that looked at the association between deportation and psychological distress – social support (Gulbas et al., 2016). For this study, the authors conducted qualitative analyses on interviews obtained from children who had a parent who was deported. When looking at children who were separated from their parents, they found that these children attributed their depression and negative feelings to having diminished social support. In contrast, children unaffected by deportation were found to be both less likely to experience depression and to associate the loss of social support to their psychological stress. In other words, deportation results in diminishing social support that then contributes to depression and feeling poorly.

Similar findings are found in research conducted on children of incarcerated parents. Although incarceration and deportation are not the same, they both entail that a child is separated from their parents. The general finding from these studies is that incarceration leads to negative impacts on a child's psychological, social, and economic wellbeing (Geller, Garfinkel, Cooper, & Mincy, 2009). An important finding from the University of Minnesota in regard to the impact of social support is that children's perception of parental support buffered against psychological distress in a national sample of children with incarcerated parents (Davis & Shlafer, 2017). The conclusion is that much like children of incarcerated parents, the children of the deported parents experience harm when a primary means of social support, a guardian, is withheld from them.

Findings from large-scale studies with multiple sites are ideal to offer a more comprehensive assessment of the impact of deportation on children. Such an opportunity is offered by the UnidosUS (formally National Council of La Reza) and the Urban Institute which provide informative case-studies on the social and financial impacts of immigration raids (Capps, Castafieda, Chaudry, & Santos, 2007; Chaudry et al., 2010). One of the most salient and relevant finding emerging from these analyses is the intense fears experienced by undocumented immigrants in relation to the prospects of immigration raids or mass arrests. In such incidents, parents are normally removed from their children, often for over 6 months (Capps et al., 2007; Chaudry et al., 2010). These are real fears supported by an increased risk of deportation since 2016. According to the Pew Research Center's recent report, the Immigration and Customs Enforcement agency (ICE) arrested 42% more undocumented immigrants during the first year of Donald Trump's presidency compared to the previous year (Bialik, 2018). To investigate the impacts of this growing concern, some studies have focused on looking at children affected by about ten immigration raids across the United States. They found that over 1000 people were arrested in these raids, and which included parents for 500 children collectively. Most children were 10 years old or younger and had American citizenship. A quarter of these children had both parents arrested while others had only one. In situations where both parents were arrested, ICE allowed only one parent to leave detention the day of their arrest, while the other parent was detained for weeks to months. According to Capps et al. (2007), these raids resulted in "family fragmentation," which they described as being significant and producing lasting adversity for children's health. They found that as consequence of the family fragmentation, parents were unable to provide social and financial support to their children, which resulted in greater social and financial hardships for their children.

The effect of financial hardship resulting from detention and deportation is an important area of concern since a family's income can be determinative of many facets of children's health and wellbeing. There is a consensus that economic privilege, or socioeconomic status (SES), impacts children's development; SS has been shown to impact children's psychosocial wellbeing (Huaqing Qi & Kaiser, 2003), academic achievement (Sirin, 2005), and neurocognitive development (Hackman & Farah, 2009; Sarsour et al., 2011). Part of the reasons for that is costly legal fees resulting from arrests. For example, the Urban Institute estimated that the cost of arrest bonds ranges from $1500 to $32,000 (Chaudry et al., 2010). Furthermore, parents are often their children's primary financial support and their arrest results in substantially less income for their families (Capps et al., 2007). UnidosUS stated that most of the families in their study were struggling financially in the first place, and then further struggled to buy food and baby supplies after the arrest. In addition, The Urban Institute calculated that a family's income decreased by an average of 70% within 6 months of an arrest and 50% 60 months after the arrest. In addition, the fear of further legal repercussions had secondary effects on the financial wellbeing of these families. For example, arrests discourage family members from seeking government assistance, which many need due to their impaired financial state (Capps et al., 2007). Therefore, the lapse in steady income is especially hurtful since most of these families and children were already living with limited financial means and became distrustful of agencies that may have been able to provide help. These tangible immediate effects are in addition to intangible effects, such as feeling anxious about a parent's wellbeing and concern about whether they will see their parents again (Capps et al., 2007; Chaudry et al., 2010).

Finally, children's education is found to be seriously disrupted. Capps et al., (2007) observed greater absentees from school across all three sites upon their parent's arrest. In some cases, children and family members reported that they were reluctant to send children to school because they feared further family fragmentation. It is reasonable to conclude that once children lack parental supervision and monitoring when their parent(s) are detained, the monitoring and supervisory family system normally provided by the parents become immediately eroded, with the outcome that these children are not encouraged to go to school. It leads us to conclude that the scholastic difficulties following these raids can be associated to the broader hardship of family fragmentation. Teachers and other school professions also reported that the children who did come to school appeared distraught and unable to focus in class.

## Impacts of Children's Detention

The large-scale detention of children at the U.S.–Mexico border was the catalyst for the widespread condemnation of family separation by scientists and professions after the Zero Tolerance policy was enacted (e.g., Bouza et al., 2018). According to fact-checking by the Washington Post, the significant increase in detaining immigrant children after the policy was due to their parents being considered criminals and a threat to the society for being undocumented, and thus requiring their detention pending legal action (Rizzo, 2018). Whereas some may argue that people who break the law by coming into the country illegally should be detained and treated as criminals, the notion of detaining non-criminal minors carries substantially less logical or moral legitimacy. The fact that immigration issues have now become criminalized and treated as other violent and dangerous acts is what is making the resolution of family separation resulting from the implementation of such policy a lot more difficult and complicated. In the meantime, we are left with trying to understand the extent to which a brief and/or prolong experience of adversity inherent in their parents' detention and deportation experience may impact these children's psychological development immediately and long term.

In general, immigrant detention centers are resource-poor environments with substantially greater incident rates of abuse. The Office of Inspector General for the DHS released a report on June 2019 describing the poor conditions of detention centers where children of immigrants have been held (Kelly, 2019). The report highlighted the following problems in four detention facilities, "… including nooses in detainee cells, overly restrictive segregation, inadequate medical care, unreported security incidents, and significant food safety issues…" (Kelly, 2019, p. 3). Specifically, Kelly reported that detainees did not have access to safe food, recreational spaces, or clean-living spaces (e.g., pictures in the report show black mold visibly growing around toilets). In addition to resulting in limited access to healthy living conditions, there have been reports that children are vulnerable to assault in detention centers. Investigations by the New York Times found 4500 complaints of sexual assault by minors in immigration detention between October 2014 and July 2018 (Haag, 2019). About one-fifth of these complaints were made in the 3 months following the Zero Tolerance policy. Most of these complaints involved minors allegedly assaulting other minors and about 200 cases reportedly involved adult staff members.

The effects of poor access to resources, safe living condition, and exposure to abuse are salient risk factors for mental health concerns (Ferguson, Cassells, MacAllister, & Evans, 2013; Kisely Abajobir, Mills, Strathearn, Clavarino, & Najman, 2018; Reiss, 2013). These associations are well established in social, medical, and public health literature and, although a full exploration of how resource deprivation and abuse impact mental health and development are outside the scope of this chapter, nevertheless, these should be important issues to consider by forensic psychologists asked to evaluate forensic request related to these issues. This is particularly the case because the practice of family separation can result in children being markedly more at risk to mental health concerns (Wood, 2018).

The fact that these detention facilities' recreational activities, education, and legal counsel continue to be poorly equipped and lack the appropriate personnel to care for these children suggest that the children's detention facilities can continue to be poor environments and not conducive to their adequate functioning (Montoya-Gulvez, 2019). Our concern is that such conditions may have already contributed to the contamination of "the water" in the mind of these children and their families, causing irreparable psychological harms to them. This will be an unfortunate development if whatever levels of suspiciousness and lack of trust of authority figures in the United States that may have resulted from these experiences are spilled over to their reactions to the kind of work forensic psychologists are asked to perform.

## The Psychosocial and Economic Impact of Uncertain Legal Status

Children's psychological wellbeing can be adversely affected by the stress associated with their guardian's insecure legal status, even if not detained and in deportation. Several studies have investigated the effects that a parent's uncertain legal status has on children. In one study, a group of 7–10-years-old Latino children with undocumented parents were found to be more likely to feel anxious than Latino children of documented parents (Brabeck & Sibley, 2016). Furthermore, Brabeck and Sebley (2016) found, in this regard, that the effect of immigration status onto children's anxiety could not be explained by parenting styles, such as how supportive and communicative the parents are with their children, family income, or the child's academic strength. Instead, it was found that their parents' uncertain legal status incrementally contributes to children's anxiety, in addition to other stressors. The effect of uncertainty was further supported by a qualitative analysis of about 200 immigrant parents and children (80 families) which found that these children were significantly fearful of their parent's legal status and what it may incur (Dreby, 2012).

An explanation on how an undocumented status can affect a family, and therefore a child's psychological wellbeing, was posited by Suárez-Orozco, Yoshikawa, Teranishi, and Suárez-Orozco (2011). They used a social–ecological (or bioecological) framework to elucidate how a parent or child's legal status can affect the family's wellbeing and psychological health. Broadly, the social–ecological framework theorizes that there are four dynamic systems within a person's environmental contexts that interact with each other over time to influence one's psychological wellbeing, behaviors, and beliefs (Bronfenbrenner & Morris, 2006). Of note, these systems continue to interact with each other over the course of a person's development. The four primary systems include a person's immediate support systems (Microsystems), the relationships that people within one's microsystem have with each other (Mesosystem), the experiences of people in one's microsystem that indirectly affect an individual (Ecosystem), and the broad societal norms and beliefs (Macrosystems). Suárez-Orozco et al. (2011) posit that documentation status affects a child's ecological systems that then, in turn, influence a child's psychological development. According to Suárez-Orozco et al. (2011) and Rojas-Flores et al., (2017), these systems of compounding stress can affect the child's psychosocial wellbeing and behavioral health. For example, legal policies meant to deter undocumented parents from receiving educational aid, can directly impact their ability to earn a comfortable income. Subsequently, parents may have less time to spend with their children, because they may need to work longer hours, which can impact on how thoroughly they can monitor their child's behaviors and offer emotional support. Furthermore, fears of deportation can deter parents from seeking governmentally provided educational and psychological services, such as public preschool, thus impacting the child's educational trajectory(Suárez-Orozco et al., 2011).

This application of the social–ecological theory has been found to be effective in a recent research on anti-undocumented immigration policies and their effect on people and communities at large. A qualitative analysis of interviews with 21 Mexican undocumented immigrant mothers highlights several obstacles that these mothers face when trying to gain greater social capital or the communal supports one can utilize to improve their or their family's success and wellness (Valdez, Padilla, & Valentine, 2013). This study was conducted in Arizona shortly after the state's government enacted a law that made it easier to stop people for inquiry solely based on suspicion that they are undocumented immigrants (SB1070). Qualitative analyses indicated three prevalent obstacles: Employment stress, detention and deportation, and police intimidation and persecution (Valdez et al., 2013). Concerns of fear of being removed from one's family were found to deter mothers from seeking greater social supports via their friends and schools. For instance, several mothers complained of feeling "locked up" in their home because of their fears of deportation. In addition, these obstacles were also found to have directly affected the kinds of communication that parents had with their children. For example, several mothers recalled speaking with their children about the possibility of being deported and separated from their family. It would be difficult to imagine a child not feeling more concerned or anxious after coming to the realization that their parents might be deported or detained because of their immigration status. Indeed, most of the mothers interviewed had family members who were detained or deported by immigration officials (Valdez et al., 2013).

An important recommendation made to undocumented immigrant families is to have these types of conversations with their children and make the necessary legal arrangements with other adults from the immediate family or from their community at large to take the legal custodial responsibility of these children in case that detention and or deportation were to occur (Brabeck & Sibley, 2016; Thronson, 2008).

## Considerations for Forensic Psychologists

The important consideration for forensic psychologists regarding the psychological impacts of family separation is that it can potentially lead to a Termination of Parental Rights (TPR). Heilbrun, DeMattaeo, Holliday, and LaDuke (2014) in their introduction to Forensic Mental Health Assessment describe the fundamental obligations of forensic psychologists to conduct psychological assessments that are relevant to litigations, provide expert advice to legal professionals, and to make recommendations on effective psychological interventions, if needed. There are two primary fields that intersect with forensic psychology in the case of applying the practice to this population (i.e., children being separated from parents due to immigration law and policies). These include immigration law and enforcement practices and trauma-informed clinical practices (Kerig, 2013; McFarland & Spangler, 2008).

There are a number of landmark cases regarding termination of parental rights that provide a framework and likely to guide the court when adjudicating issues of parental termination in the context of parental deportation and that it should guide the kinds of forensic assessment that may be appropriate. We have summarized these cases in Table 11.1.

**Table 11.1** Landmark legal cases regarding termination of parental rights and immigrants

| Name | Year case was decided | Court | Decision |
| --- | --- | --- | --- |
| Santosky v. Kramer | 1981 | Supreme Court of the United States | Upheld that parental rights may be terminated may proceed if parents have permanently neglected their child |
| Plyer v. Doe (Named and unnamed undocumented children) | 1982 | Supreme Court of the United States | Formally extends the U.S. constitutional right for due process (the 14th Amendment to the U.S. Constitution) to undocumented immigrants since they reside in U.S. jurisdictions |
| Fiallo v. Bell | 1977 | Supreme Court of the United States | Stipulated that the Immigration and Naturalization Act (8 U.S.C. §§ 1101-1178) ensures that undocumented mothers of legal U.S. residents have parental rights but denied that the court can extend said rights to natural fathers |
| Troxel v. Granville | 2000 | Supreme Court of the United States | Due process needs to be maintained before interfering with parental rights, such as a visitation, and custody of children |
| In re Interest of *Angelica L.* | 2009 | Supreme Court of Nebraska | Decided that being an undocumented immigrant does not entail enough harm onto a child to necessitate a termination of parental rights. Reversed lower court's decision that termination of parental rights can occur based on a parent's status as an undocumented immigrant. |

When working with children and parents in the immigration enforcement system, forensic psychologists ought to use trauma-informed assessments and recommendations since the children of undocumented immigrants, who are in immigrant detention facilities or in the process of being deported, are more likely to have experienced traumatic stress and other emotional liabilities (Allen et al., 2015; Rojas-Flores et al., 2017; Suárez-Orozco et al., 2011; Zayas & Bradlee, 2014; see Wood, 2018 for comprehensive review). That calls for forensic psychologists to use principles of trauma-informed (TI) practice when assessing these children and their parents. Indeed, The National Child Traumatic Stress Network has recommended the use of TI assessment and intervention whenever there is speculation that a client has experienced events that can lead to traumatic stress (Kerig, 2013). TI assessment cannot be easily formulated into a set of instructions; however, it entails a few key principles. For one, the psychologist ought to inquire into a child or parent's abuse and maltreatment history and the assessment should include empirically validated measures of traumatic stress. Many people may have experienced multiple traumas associated with immigration and/or family separation, which cannot be attributed to a single incident of discrete abuse and maltreatment (Rojas-Flores et al., 2017). In addition, forensic psychologists should engage in in-depth clinical interviews that inquire about the presence of Post-Traumatic Stress Disorder (PTSD; re: DSM-V, American Psychological Association, 2013, for diagnostic criteria).

TI assessment also entails that psychologists view a person's holistic functioning through the following frame: How has this event, or collection of adversities, affected the person's presenting problems (Kerig, 2013). As indicated earlier, children who have had traumatic experiences are more likely to present with externalizing problems, such as conduct delinquency (Kerig, 2012). Indeed, children with parents undergoing deportation or detention are more likely to have reported externalizing problems in school (Rojas-Flores et al., 2017) and home (Allen et al., 2015). Therefore, even if a child does not meet criteria for PTSD, they can still present with problems related to traumatic stress.

In addition, forensic psychologist would benefit from being informed on immigration law enforcement. Table 11.1 provides brief synopses of landmark common law rulings that have affected family law for undocumented immigrants. Nevertheless, much of the practical implementation of immigration enforcement appears to be under the purview of federal and state governments, which can change every several years based on who has executive control. For instance, the current administration has claimed executive authority over immigration enforcement (Trump, 2017). Furthermore, the laws and policies regarding immigrant enforcement, which has often been the impetus to family separations, have gone through several transformation and changes over the decades. For instance, two federal laws passed in 1996 [the Antiterrorism and Effective Death Penalty Act (AETDPA)] and the Immigration Reform and Immigrant Responsibility Act (IIRIRA) made immigrant deportation more likely and easier, even for lawful residents (Morawetz, 2000). So, an immigrant who commits a serious crime could be deported under this law, even if they are legal residents (i.e., "green card" holders). Subsequently, under the current Trump administration, the implementation of that law has become more intense. This intensification of the law was guided by an executive order on January 2017 where the current administration stipulated that undocumented immigrants could be detained for breaking any state, federal, or immigration law (Trump, 2017). Therefore, family separation could occur, and children may be placed into protective custody simply because a parent has lived in the United States illegally. This is a far cry from the standards needed to prove that a legal U.S. resident is unfit to parent. Therefore, it appears imperative for forensic psychologists to be informed about changes towards immigration enforcement law and, more practically, how said law is implemented by a given executive authority.

In theory, there ought to be no difference in criteria for a TPR regarding undocumented immigrants versus legal residents. American common law suggests that the parental rights of undocumented immigrants is similarly respected than legal residents of the country (Abrams, 2006; Hall, 2011). This notion is reportedly supported by constitutional law and was upheld by SCOTUS in Plyer v. Doe (1982). According to that decision, undocumented immigrants are protected by the same laws as legal residents and have commensurate rights to due process. This decision was based on a reading of the 14th Amendment of the U.S. constitution, which states, "No state shall make or enforce any law which shall abridge the privileges or immunities of citizens of the United States; nor shall any state deprive any person of life, liberty, or property, without due process of law; nor deny to any person within its jurisdiction the equal protection of the laws. In other words, living in a U.S. "jurisdiction" affords one the constitutional right of due process regardless of their citizenship status. Therefore, undocumented immigrants, who live alongside legal residents, should not fear that their parental rights will be arbitrarily violated due to their legal status.

Undocumented parents, nevertheless, experience greater challenges in asserting their parental rights than other U.S. residents. Thronson (2008), in a legal review of immigrant deportation and their harmful effect on children and families, argues that undocumented parents have been held to harsher standard for what behavior incurs termination of parental rights. In addition, immigrant detention and deportation make it more difficult for parents to advocate for their rights to be a part of their children's lives (Rabin, 2011; Thronson, 2008). One of the stories used by Thronson to support this argument is that of Mercedes Santiago-Felipe. Santiago-Felipe was separated from her children for several years after slapping her son on the face, which did not result in any sustained or serious injury. The Nevada state laws where Santiago-Felipe resided, stipulate, among other things, that parental termination occurs in case of "felony assault that resulted in serious bodily injury" (Rev. Stat. § 43–292), which was not the case in this instance. In the end, the decision of the Nebraska's Foster Care Review Board was to vacate the previous decision and to consider that Santiago-Felipe was wrongfully separated from her children since her actions did not seriously harm her children.

Nevertheless, it is within the judges' purview, and the legal system at large, to determine whether a child would be safer in the custody of their parents, the state, or with another family by way of adoption. The question arises, can a parent's immigration status, such as being undocumented or an asylum seeker, warrant a

TPR. Many legal professional and psychologists have stated that the argument that undocumented parents might not be fit to be effective parents because of their lack of legal status it is not only an unfair concern but ultimately very harmful towards children, if implemented (Abram, 2006; McFarland & Spangler, 2008). For example, McFarland and Spangler (2008) argue that this consideration would impair the prestige and trust of that immigrants feel towards legal professionals, which would ultimately disrupt their compliance with those working in legal contexts, such as forensic psychologist. In addition, they state that considering one's undocumented legal status would be tantamount to punishing families due to their immigration status and thus violate the Hague convention, which guarantees fair treatment to immigrants and migrants (McFarland & Spangler, 2008). Abrams (2006) would add that one's immigration status ought not to be considered since the economic and social disparities underlining such a consideration, such as the parents having less economic privilege, are exacerbated by such considerations. Instead, Abram, McFarland, and Spangler (2006; 2008) argue that legal professionals should enable these families to have greater access to resources that can ameliorate their social and economic circumstances, such as access to housing and food stipends and mental health services.

## Assessment for Termination of Parental Rights

The most pertinent legal considerations regarding family separation for forensic psychologists pertain to parental rights, fitness to parent, and consulting on the appropriateness of the termination of parental rights (TPR). Forensic psychologists cannot determine whether a law is fair or argue for or against the application of a law court. However, they can advise legal professionals, including lawyers, and can testify on the psychological impacts of a legal decision. In addition, forensic psychologists can explain the psychological costs and benefits of a single decision with some authority, given their status as a professional psychologist. For example, forensic psychologists can advise on whether executing a TPR would be in the best interest of a child given the risks associated with returning a child to their parents versus an alternative. Furthermore, a discussion on how parental rights are terminated for legal residents and naturalized citizens is warranted before discussing parental rights termination for undocumented parents. This would allow one to contrast the legal caveats of broad parental rights termination with those of undocumented parents.

According to a decision made by the Supreme Court of the United States (SCOTUS), U.S. law and its constitution respects the integrity of family units and seeks to limit the intervention of the state on the cohesion of parents and their children—in theory (Troxel v. Granville, 2000). In addition to prioritizing family cohesion, common law emphasizes the need to ensure a child is safe from potential significant harm if in the custody of their parents. For example, the Adoption and Safe Families Act of 1997 (ASFA) was enacted by the U.S. congress to ensure the long-term safety of children in protective custody. It stipulates that a child's safety should be paramount when determining whether to keep the child in protective custody or to return to the parents once a child is placed in the care of the state, such as into foster care or an immigration detention center. ASFA also instructs family courts to prioritize adoption over reunification with their parents if this child has been in protective custody for 15 out of the past 20 months. ASFA is not the first act to try to ensure the long-term safety of children in protective custody, but it reinforces that a child's safety should be prioritized over parental rights if a child would be exposed to significant abuse or neglect if returned to their parents.

Regardless of a parent's immigration status, parental rights can be legally terminated involuntarily if certain conditions are met. Although the specific laws determining child protective custody are decided by U.S. states, the U.S. congress determined a minimum set of standards for states to follow in the Child Abuse Treatment and Prevention Act (CAPTA; 42 U.S.C.A. § 5106g). For the first one, it applies when a parent or legal guardian has acted in a way that has led to "serious physical and emotional harm, sexual abuse or exploitation." Second, when the parents have failed to prevent serious harm from occurring. CAPTA, however, does not provide specific guidelines for what constitutes serious harm or neglect, other than in case of child's death, is sexually abused, or in the case of medical neglect (i.e., a child's health is compromised because a guardian failed to ensure proper medical treatment). Instead, states and territories are governed by their unique laws that determine how and when a TPR can be enacted, in addition to the minimum standards described in CAPTA. Yet, given federal and state standards for what constitutes fitness to parent, judges ultimately decide whether a parent is fit to be a child's guardian. Normally, forensic psychologists are asked to assess factors relevant to the decision to pursue a TPR, such as whether abuse and neglect likely occurred.

It is useful to consider how a forensic psychologist would assess for the appropriateness of a TPR, in general. Table 11.2 is meant to provide the forensic professional a general guideline to consider in these types of situations. In Forensic Mental Health Assessment: A Casebook, Clark and Budd (2014) describe a case study in which a TPR was considered, delineate a model course for such an assessment, and describe how a psychologist can make recommendations to that end. Their case involves a mother who was seeking to be reunited with her 2-year-old son after he had been placed in foster care for 3 years. The mother had an extensive substance abuse history but had since received treatment. For their assessment, they reviewed: (1) Relevant court records, (2) child protective service records, (3) general service records, and (4) mother's treatment service records, which included records certifying substance abuse treatment and parenting program completion. In addition, they conducted (5) clinical interviews, including abuse/maltreatment assessments with the mother, (6) collateral interviews with relevant parties, such as the child's caseworker and foster parent, (7) observed parent–child interactions, and (8) had the mother complete self-report questionnaires on her parenting related stress and the child's exposure to potential abuse. Of note, the child was young, and a forensic psychologist can conduct clinical interviews and objective measures with the child if they are sufficiently mature.

The question remains, what modification would one make to a typical TPR assessment in the case of undocumented parents and family separation or segmentation?

**Table 11.2** Important components of a TPR assessment

| Assessment component | It's function | Example |
|---|---|---|
| Review of all pertinent legal records | Informs psychologists on the legal context in which this TPR is being considered | Termination hearings, permanency orders, orders of protection |
| Review of service, medical, mental-health, and other treatment and human service records that may be relevant to the case | Informs psychologists of past service recommendations, the compliance with said recommendations, and whether the respondent parent has made significant gains in problem areas | Past mental health reports, certificates of treatment completion, toxicology reports, housing records |
| Clinical interviews | Assesses parent and child's currently psychosocial functioning and history of possible abuse and/or neglect | Semi-structured clinical interviews, such as those assessing for affective and behavioral disorder in children, and |
| Abuse and maltreatment assessment | Assesses if the child has experienced instances that placed them in considerable risk for harm in the past, the parent's involvement in said risks, and whether child's current psychosocial functioning can be attributed to traumatic stress | Refer to guidelines by the American Psychological Association (2013) |
| Collateral interviews | Informs psychologists on child's functioning within protective custody | Interviewing parties on child's wellbeing at the foster home, school, etc. |
| Observations | Assesses parent's ability to affectively parent child, allows psychologists to determine if home environment is sufficiently safe and if child's psychosocial needs are met | In-home observations |
| Questionnaires | To be used *in conjunction with clinical interviews* to assess child and parent's psychosocial functioning | An empirically validated assessment of child's psychosocial functioning, such as the Child Behavior Checklist (CBCL; Achenbach 1999) and an age-appropriate trauma symptom checklist |

*Source:* Gather from Chap. 18 of Forensic mental health assessment (Clark & Budd in Heilbrun, DeMattaeo, Holliday, & LaDuke, 2014)

For one, the parent's and children's primary language may not be English. The importance of language in assessing linguistically and culturally diverse individuals has been addressed by several authors (Dana, 1996; Flanagan, McGrew, & Ortiz, 2000; Javier, 2007) and hence will not be fully developed here. Since the possibility for major mistakes in the outcomes of these types of assessments are so real, including misdiagnosing the condition under consideration, the readers are encouraged to become familiar with their recommendations.

# Conclusion

The purpose of this chapter was to address a poignant issue regarding termination of parental rights in relationship to the immigration experience. This concern is made more urgent by the number of children being separated from their parents for any number of reasons, including issues of detention and deportation of undocumented immigrant parents. According to the United Nations, there are about 30 million displaced children in the world as of 2017 (UNICEF, 2018), representing the single largest global migration crisis since World War II. In this chapter, we examined the impacts suffered by those affected, which include the children themselves as well as family members directly or indirectly involved with these children. We examined, in this context, the relevant laws guiding the decision to terminate the rights of parental involvement and how that could be complicated by a removal of the parental rights as a consequence of a detention and/or deportation. We also examined the impact on these children. It is clear from the many studies examined that these children encounter significant psychological, social, and economic hardships when being separated from their parents (Allen et al., 2015; Rojas-Flores et al., 2017; Suárez-Orozco et al., 2011; Zayas & Bradlee, 2014). Furthermore, even the psychological distress associated with an insecure legal status was found to increase a child's chances of experiencing anxiety and depression relative to their peers (Brabeck & Sibley, 2016; Suárez-Orozco et al., 2011). The concern is that the multiplicity of adversities likely to be experienced by these children as a result of the removal of direct parental involvements will result in the development of *complex trauma* condition manifested in behaviors not typically associated with post-traumatic stress, and contributing to derailing these children's developmental trajectory temporarily or more permanently.

Forensic professionals involved in these types of cases are strongly encouraged to be cognizant of the different stressors faced by those individuals in the midst of parental termination process and to make a careful examination of risks and benefits of the different conditions that each of these individuals will likely have to face. In that context, one of the primary responsibilities of the forensic professional is to address the following question: Does the harm associated with a child living with their parents, which may entail that the child is deported alongside their parent, outweigh the harm associated with family separation? We have some evidence that it can be extremely difficult to make definitive recommendations against the backdrop of family separation. Nevertheless, forensic psychologists can benefit from the use of trauma-informed (TI) practices to ensure that their recommendations are ultimately informed by a prudent course of assessments. The need to use TI assessments for the population of children affected by family separation is supported by evidence-based research findings discussed in the chapter (Kerig, 2013, Rojas-Flores et al., 2017) that confirm that children who are separated from their parents are at risk for post-traumatic stress, sometimes manifested through oppositional defiance or attention deficit behavioral disorders (American Psychiatric Association, 2013; Kerig, 2012).

Although the literature is growing, it is clear that we are in need of more research on the long-term psychological ramifications of detaining children due to family separation. Research examined in this chapter has focused on the impacts that immigration law enforcement, including immigrant raids, detention, and deportation, children's psychological and social-economic wellbeing (Wood, 2018), and how these stressors intensify children's existing trauma and adversity (Androff et al., 2011; UNHCR, 2018). However, there is a relative paucity of research on how children are affected by family separation in border detention facilities. This information can assist forensic psychologists in understanding the psychological underpinnings of clients who were previously detained as children or adolescents. There are several limitations to conducting research on this population; the main one being the inherent difficulty in conducting research in detention centers where access to objective and accurate data can become seriously compromised by bureaucratic and institutional restrictions to direct contacts of the detainees for policy reasons (Rickert & Drake, 2019).

One of the greatest challenges for a forensic psychologist involved in these cases is how best to negotiate the disconnect between what science and the discipline conclude about the consequences of detention and family separation on those affected and the perspective of those responsible for reinforcing an immigration policy that justifies the need for such a decision on non-psychological bases. In the end, our responsibility is to remain faithful to what is revealed in our assessment, following the gold standard of the discipline. We hope that we have provided the necessary information to assist the forensic professional in that regard.

## Questions/Activities for Further Exploration

1. Compare and contrast the legal and ethical consideration regarding the termination of parental rights (TPR) for children of incarcerated parents versus those in immigration detention or who have been deported outside the country.
2. McFarland and Spangler, in their 2008 review, suggested that legal professionals should not consider a parent's immigration status when litigating a TPR or custody since the costs of such a decision, such as hurting the standing of legal professionals within these communities, are too damaging. However, they also make a case for this consideration; for example, people with an uncertain legal status may have more difficulties financially supporting their children. Do you think one's immigration status ought to be used for such litigations? In what contexts would you advise for a TPR in such a scenario?
3. Table 11.2 delineates a prudent course of assessment when a TPR is considered in court. It assumes that a psychologist has access to a plethora of past records, can interview multiple parties, and can conduct in-home observations. Unfortunately, many potential TPR and custody cases may lack these resources for information. Develop an assessment battery for a child in foster care whose father has been detained in immigration detention 15 months and mother currently resides in one

of Latin American countries. Make sure to research at least two empirically validated trauma measures for this child. You will have access to the following:

- Child (6-year-old) who is English and a Spanish bilingual
- Foster parent who primarily speaks Spanish
- One year of school records
- A mental health assessment, which was completed at his intake into foster care 6 months previously.

4. This chapter focused heavily on the U.S. and Hispanic immigrants. However, it provided a frame that can be applied across other cultural groups intersecting family and immigration law, which include being updated in immigration enforcement policies and trauma-informed practices. How might you apply these principals to other immigrant populations? For example, which laws and policies would you seek for asylum seekers from the Middle East? Or, what are culturally relevant questions for such a population when conducting a trauma-informed assessment?

## References

Abramitzky, R., & Boustan, L. (2017). Immigration in American economic history. *Journal of Economic Literature, 55*(4), 1311–1345. https://doi.org/10.1257/jel.20151189

Abrams, K. (2006). Immigration status and the best interests of the child standard. *Social Science Research Network*. Retrieved from https://papers.ssrn.com/abstract=2703513

Achenbach, T. M. (1999). The child behavior checklist and related instruments. In M. E. Maruish (Ed.), *The use of psychological testing for treatment planning and outcomes assessment* (pp. 429–466). Mahwah, NJ: Lawrence Erlbaum Associates Publishers.

Allen, B., Cisneros, E. M., & Tellez, A. (2015). The children left behind: The impact of parental deportation on mental health. *Journal of Child and Family Studies, 24*(2), 386–392. https://doi.org/10.1007/s10826-013-9848-5

American Immigration Council. (2018). Fact sheet: U.S. citizen children impacted by immigration enforcement. Retrieved from https://www.americanimmigrationcouncil.org/research/us-citizen-children-impacted-immigration-enforcement

American Psychiatric Association. (2013). *Diagnostic and statistical manual of mental disorders: DSM-5* (5th ed.). Arlington, VA: Author.

American Psychological Association. (2013). Guidelines for psychological evaluation in child protection matters. *American Psychologist, 63*, 852–862.

Androff, D. K., Ayón, C., Becerra, D., Gurrola, M., Salas, L., Krysik, J., & Segal, E. (2011). U.S. immigration policy and immigrant children's well-being: The impact of policy shifts. *Journal of Sociology and Social Welfare, 38*(1), 77–98.

Bass, H. (2018). *Statement of Hilarie Bass, ABA president Re: Separating immigrant children from parents at the border.* American Bar Association. Retrieved from https://www.americanbar.org/advocacy/governmental_legislative_work/priorities_policy/immigration/familyseparation/

Bialik, K. (2018). *ICE arrests went up in 2017, with biggest increases in Florida, Northern Texas.* Pew Research Center: Oklahoma. Retrieved from: http://www.pewresearch.org/fact-tank/2018/02/08/ice-arrests-went-up-in-2017-with-biggest-increases-in-florida-northern-texas-oklahoma/

Bouza, J., Camacho-Thompson, D. E., Claro, G., Franco, X., Coll, C. G., Halgunseth, L. C., … Stein, G. L. (2018). *The science is clear: Separating families has long-term damaging psycho-*

*logical and health consequences for children, families, and communities.* Society for Research and Child Development: Statement of Research. Retrieved from https://www.srcd.org/sites/default/files/documents/the_science_is_clear.pdf

Brabeck, K. M., & Sibley, E. (2016). Immigrant parent legal status, parent-child relationships, and child social emotional wellbeing: A middle childhood perspective. *Journal of Child and Family Studies, 25*(4), 1155–1167.

Bronfenbrenner, U., & Morris, P. A. (2006). The bioecological model of human development. In *Handbook of child psychology: Theoretical models of human development* (Vol. 1, 6th ed., pp. 793–828). Hoboken, NJ: Wiley.

Capps, R., Castañeda, R. M., Chaudry, A., & Santos, R. (2007). *Paying the price: The impact of immigration raids on America's children.* Washington, DC: Urban Institute and National Council of La Raza.

Chaudry, A., Capps, R., Pedroza, J., Castaneda, R. M., Santos, R., & Scott, M. M. (2010). *Facing our future: Children in the aftermath of immigration enforcement.* The Urban Institute. Retrieved from https://www.urban.org/research/publication/facing-our-future/view/full_report

Clark, J., & Budd, K. (2014). Child protection. In K. Heilbrun, D. DeMatteo, S. B. Holliday, & C. LaDuke (Eds.), *Forensic mental health assessment: A casebook* (2nd ed.). https://doi.org/10.1093/med:psych/9780199941551.001.0001

Dana, R. (1996). Assessment of acculturation in Hispanic populations. *Hispanic Journal of Behavioral Sciences, 18,* 317–328.

Daniel, J. H., & Evans, A. C. (2018). *APA letter to President Donald Trump regarding family separation.* American Psychological Association. Retrieved from https://www.apa.org/images/separating-families-letter_tcm7-236390.pdf

Davis, L., & Shlafer, R. J. (2017). Mental health of adolescents with currently and formerly incarcerated parents. *Journal of Adolescence, 54,* 120–134. https://doi.org/10.1016/j.adolescence.2016.10.006

Dreby, J. (2012). The burden of deportation on children in Mexican immigrant families. *Journal of Marriage and Family, 74*(4), 829–845. https://doi.org/10.1111/j.1741-3737.2012.00989.x

Ferguson, K. T., Cassells, R. C., MacAllister, J. W., & Evans, G. W. (2013). The physical environment and child development: An international review. *International Journal of Psychology: Journal International de Psychologie, 48*(4), 437–468. https://doi.org/10.1080/00207594.2013.804190

Fiallo v. Bell, 430 U.S. 787. (1977).

Flanagan, D. P., McGrew, K. S., & Ortiz, S. O. (2000). *The Wechsler Intelligence Scales and Gf-Gc theory: A contemporary approach to interpretation.* Needham Heights, MA: Allyn & Bacon.

Geller, A., Garfinkel, I., Cooper, C. E., & Mincy, R. B. (2009). Parental incarceration and child well-being: Implications for urban families. *Social Science Quarterly, 90*(5), 1186–1202. https://doi.org/10.1111/j.1540-6237.2009.00653.x

Gonzalez-Barrera, A., & Krogstad, J. M. (2019, June 28). *What we know about illegal immigration from Mexico.* Pew Research Center. Retrieved from https://www.pewresearch.org/fact-tank/2019/06/28/what-we-know-about-illegal-immigration-from-mexico/

Gulbas, L. E., Zayas, L. H., Yoon, H., Szlyk, H., Aguilar-Gaxiola, S., & Natera, G. (2016). A mixed-method study exploring depression in U.S. citizen-children in Mexican immigrant families. *Child: Care, Health and Development, 42*(2), 220–230. https://doi.org/10.1111/cch.12307

Haag, M. (2019, February 27). Thousands of Immigrant Children Said They Were Sexually Abused in U.S. Detention Centers, Report Says. *New York Times.* Retrieved from https://www.nytimes.com/2019/02/27/us/immigrant-children-sexual-abuse.html

Hackman, D. A., & Farah, M. J. (2009). Socioeconomic status and the developing brain. *Trends in Cognitive Sciences, 13*(2), 65–73. https://doi.org/10.1016/j.tics.2008.11.003

Hall, C. E. (2011). Where are my children … and my rights? Parental rights termination as a consequence of deportation. *Duke Law Journal, 60*(6), 1459–1503.

Heilbrun, K., DeMatteo, D., Brooks Holliday, S., & LaDuke, C. (2014). *Forensic mental health assessment: A casebook* (2nd ed.). https://doi.org/10.1093/med:psych/9780199941551.001.0001

Huaqing Qi, C., & Kaiser, A. P. (2003). Behavior problems of preschool children from low-income families: Review of the literature. *Topics in Early Childhood Special Education, 23*(4), 188–216. https://doi.org/10.1177/02711214030230040201

In re Interest of Angelica L., N.W.2d. (2009)

Javier, R. A. (2007). *The bilingual mind: Thinking, feeling and speaking in two languages.* New York: Springer Publications.

Kelly, J. (2018). *Special review – Initial observations regarding family separation issues under the zero tolerance policy.* Washington, D.C.: Department of Homeland Security. Retrieved from https://www.oig.dhs.gov/sites/default/files/assets/2018-10/OIG-18-84-Sep18.pdf

Kelly, J. (2019). *Concerns about ICE detainee treatment and care at four detention facilities.* Washington, D.C.: Office of Inspector General: U.S. Department of Homeland Security. Retrieved from: https://www.oig.dhs.gov/sites/default/files/assets/2019-06/OIG-19-47-Jun19.pdf

Kerig, P. K. (2012). New directions in interventions for trauma and juvenile delinquency. *Journal of Child and Adolescent Trauma, 5*(3), 187–190.

Kerig, P. K. (2013). Trauma-informed assessment and intervention. *National Center for Child Traumatic Stress.* https://doi.org/10.13140/rg.2.1.2474.6482

Kisely, S., Abajobir, A. A., Mills, R., Strathearn, L., Clavarino, A., & Najman, J. M. (2018). Child maltreatment and mental health problems in adulthood: Birth cohort study. *The British Journal of Psychiatry, 213*(6), 698–703. https://doi.org/10.1192/bjp.2018.207

Kraft, C. (2018). AAP statement on executive order on family separation. *American Academic of Pediatrics.* Retrieved from https://www.aap.org/en-us/about-the-aap/aap-press-room/Pages/AAP-Statement-on-Executive-Order-on-Family-Separation.aspx

Krogstad, J. M., Passel, J. S., & Cohn, D. (2019, June 19). *5 facts about illegal immigration in the U.S.* Pew Research Center. Retrieved from: https://www.pewresearch.org/fact-tank/2019/06/12/5-facts-about-illegal-immigration-in-the-u-s/

Long, C. (2018, June 15). *DHS reports about 2,000 minors separated from families.* The Associated Press. Retrieved from https://apnews.com/3361a7d5fa714ea4b028f0a29db1cabc

McFarland, M., & Spangler, E. M. (2008). A parent's undocumented immigration status should not be considered under the best interest of the child standard. *William Mitchell Law Review, 35,* 37.

Montoya-Galvez, C. (2019, June 5). *Trump administration nixes educational, recreational activities for migrant children in U.S. custody.* CBS News. Retrieved from https://www.cbsnews.com/news/trump-administration-nixes-educational-recreational-activities-for-migrant-children-in-u-s-custody/

Morawetz, N. (2000). Understanding the impact of the 1996 deportation laws and the limited scope of proposed reforms. *Harvard Law Review, 113*(8), 1936–1962. https://doi.org/10.2307/1342314

National Education Association (2019). *Families belong together.* Retrieved from https://neaedjustice.org/families-belong-together/

Peri, G. (2013). The economic benefits of immigration. In *Berkley review of Latin American studies.* Berkley, CA: University of California, Berkley. Retrieved from https://clas.berkeley.edu/research/immigration-economic-benefits-immigration

Plyer v. Doe, 457 U.S. 202. (1982)

Rabin, N. (2011). Disappearing Parents: Immigration Enforcement and the Child Welfare System (SSRN Scholarly Paper No. ID 1794263). Retrieved from: https://papers.ssrn.com/abstract=1794263

Reiss, F. (2013). Socioeconomic inequalities and mental health problems in children and adolescents: A systematic review. *Social Science & Medicine, 90,* 24–31. https://doi.org/10.1016/j.socscimed.2013.04.026

Rickert, C., & Drake, S. (2019, March 14). *DHS's own statistics show that it is lying about a border-security crisis.* American Civil Liberties Council. Retrieved from https://www.aclu.org/blog/immigrants-rights/ice-and-border-patrol-abuses/dhss-own-statistics-show-it-lying-about-border

Rizzo, S. (2018, June 15). The facts about Trump's policy of separating families at the border. *The Washington Post*. Retrieved from https://www.washingtonpost.com/news/fact-checker/wp/2018/06/19/the-facts-about-trumps-policy-of-separating-families-at-the-border/?utm_term=.c60f114a6efc

Rojas-Flores, L., Clements, M. L., Hwang Koo, J., & London, J. (2017). Trauma and psychological distress in Latino citizen children following parental detention and deportation. *Psychological Trauma: Theory, Research, Practice, and Policy, 9*(3), 352–361. https://doi.org/10.1037/tra0000177

Santosky v. Kramer, 455 U.S. 745. (1981).

Sarsour, K., Sheridan, M., Jutte, D., Nuru-Jeter, A., Hinshaw, S., & Boyce, W. T. (2011). Family socioeconomic status and child executive functions: The roles of language, home environment, and single parenthood. *Journal of the International Neuropsychological Society, 17*(1), 120–132. https://doi.org/10.1017/S1355617710001335

Sirin, S. R. (2005). Socioeconomic status and academic achievement: A meta-analytic review of research. *Review of Educational Research, 75*(3), 417–453. https://doi.org/10.3102/00346543075003417

Suárez-Orozco, C., Yoshikawa, H., Teranishi, R. T., & Suárez-Orozco, M. M. (2011). Growing up in the shadows: The developmental implications of unauthorized status. *Harvard Educational Review, 81*(3), 438–472.

Thronson, D. B. (2008). Creating crisis: Immigration raids and the destabilization of immigrant families. *Wake Forest Law Review, 43*, 391–420.

Troxel v. Bell, 530 U.S. 57. (2000)

Trump, D. (2017). *Executive order: Border security and immigration enforcement improvements*. Washington D.C.: The White House. Retrieved from https://www.whitehouse.gov/presidential-actions/executive-order-border-security-immigration-enforcement-improvements/

U.S. Department of Homeland Security. (2019). *Immigration data and statistics*. Retrieved from https://www.dhs.gov/immigration-statistics

UNHCR. (2018). *Refugee facts and statistics*. Retrieved from https://www.unrefugees.org/refugee-facts/

UNHRC. (2019). *Figures at a glace*. Retrieved from https://www.unhcr.org/en-us/figures-at-a-glance.html

UNICEF. (2018). *Child displacement*. Retrieved from https://data.unicef.org/topic/child-migration-and-displacement/displacement/

UNICEF. (2019). *Child refugees and migrants*. Retrieved from https://www.unicefusa.org/mission/emergencies/child-refugees

Valdez, C. R., Padilla, B., & Valentine, J. L. (2013). Consequences of Arizona's immigration policy on social capital among Mexican mothers with unauthorized immigration status. *Hispanic Journal of Behavioral Sciences, 35*(3), 303. https://doi.org/10.1177/0739986313488312

Wood, L. C. N. (2018). Impact of punitive immigration policies, parent-child separation and child detention on the mental health and development of children. *BMJ Paediatrics Open, 2*(1), e000338. https://doi.org/10.1136/bmjpo-2018-000338

Zayas, L. H., Aguilar-Gaxiola, S., Yoon, H., & Rey, G. N. (2015). The distress of citizen-children with detained and deported parents. *Journal of Child and Family Studies, 24*(11), 3213–3223. https://doi.org/10.1007/s10826-015-0124-8

Zayas, L. H., & Bradlee, M. H. (2014). Exiling children, creating orphans: When immigration policies hurt citizens. *Social Work, 59*(2), 167–175.

# Chapter 12
# Assessing for Trauma in Psychological Evaluations for Law Enforcement Candidates and Personnel

Michelle Casarella and Amy Beebe

## Assessing for Trauma in Psychological Evaluations for Law Enforcement Candidates and Personnel: Pre-employment Evaluations

Evaluations within the workplace typically fall within two categories: pre-employment psychological evaluations (PPEs) and fitness-for-duty evaluations (FDEs). The former is typically conducted on all job applicants for a specific title, while the latter occurs only when an employee is referred for a specific reason. Within the realm of law enforcement, the International Association of Chiefs of Police (IACP) have set forth specific guidelines for evaluations. It is recommended for clinicians to be extremely familiar with such guidelines and structure their evaluations accordingly. The IACP guidelines assert that clinicians conducting pre-employment and fitness-for-duty evaluations generally be doctoral-level practitioners, except for some jurisdictions that allow for masters-level clinicians.

According to the guidelines, the purpose of a PPE is to "determine whether a public safety applicant meets the minimum requirements for psychological suitability mandated by jurisdictional statutes and regulations, as well as any other criteria established by the hiring agency" (2014, pg. 1). As per the majority of jurisdictions, the minimum requirements for suitability mandate the candidate does not have any emotional or psychological condition that would negatively impact his or her ability to perform the duties inherent to the position.

M. Casarella (✉)
Expert Forensic Psych Consulting, INC., New York City Police Department (NYPD),
New York, NY, USA
e-mail: drcasarella@expertforensicpsych.com

A. Beebe
New York City Police Department (NYPD), New York, NY, USA

© Springer Nature Switzerland AG 2020       271
R. A. Javier et al. (eds.), *Assessing Trauma in Forensic Contexts*,
https://doi.org/10.1007/978-3-030-33106-1_12

The ethics set forth in the guidelines are similar to the practices cited in the American Psychological Association's Ethical Principals of Psychologists and Codes of Conduct. Clinicians should only provide evaluation services within the scope of their competence. This is generally based on education, training, and professional experience. Furthermore, it is imperative to seek supervision and consultation as necessary. Clinicians performing this type of work should have general assessment skills, as well as more specific skills related to assessment of personality, psychopathology, and personnel selection. Just as in any other evaluations, a clinician should avoid circumstances which pose conflicts of interest personally, professionally, financially, or legally. Furthermore, situations that could reasonably expect to impair a clinician's objectivity or pose harm upon the individual should be completely avoided.

Confidentiality issues pose unique challenges given the forensic setting. Generally, the hiring agency or police department is your client rather than the individual who is being evaluated. Despite the fact that confidentiality does not apply, informed consent is still necessary. As per the IACP guidelines, the candidate should be notified in writing of "the nature and objectives of the evaluation, the intended recipients, a statement that the hiring agency is the client, the probable uses of the evaluation, and the information obtained and the limits of confidentiality" (2014, pg. 3).

Prior to the face-to-face interview, the clinician should review the data yielded from the testing battery. While specific tests within the battery may vary, it is imperative to use instruments with documented reliability and validity as well as specific law enforcement norms. Test results should be interpreted in accordance with professionally accepted standards. Cutoff scores should only be used when there is an abundance of evidence indicating it is predictive of issues related to job performance. Of particular importance is that clinicians cannot use different norms or cutoff scores for individuals of protected class. Protected class, as defined by the U.S. federal Civil Rights Act, includes the following nine classes: sex, race, age, disability, color, creed, national origin, religion, or genetic information. Upon reviewing the data, the interview must be conducted face-to-face before making a final determination. Conducting interviews via telehealth is strongly discouraged given the difficulty this medium presents with when evaluating nuanced behavior and interpersonal style. Generally, interviews are semi-structured, with more emphasis placed on specific aspects of an individual's functioning and history. Topics covered include: school and work history, interpersonal relationships, trauma history, legal history, substance use, mental health treatment, and relevant medical treatment.

As part of the hiring process, a background investigation is conducted, and relevant information should be made available to the clinician. If such information is not available at the time of the evaluation, it is recommended for the clinician to make contact with the hiring agency to determine if any issues arose over the course of the investigation. Information made available during the background investigation is especially useful in order to reconcile any discrepancies in the candidate's self-reported history.

It is encouraged that the clinician request records when a determination has been made that it is relevant to their psychological suitability regarding the position. The purpose is to either confirm a suspected issue in which the candidate appeared less than forthcoming or to resolve a concern that arose over the course of the evaluation. However, it is imperative that the clinician carefully evaluate the need for specific records. One must consider an applicant's confidentiality given the private nature of such records and the ethical obligations of a mental health provider. Additionally, requesting unnecessary records adds to a clinician's workload. If records are deemed necessary yet unavailable, it may be helpful to either defer the final determination or resolve the concern in another way.

Once a clinician has yielded a final determination, a report is then generated which should clearly state the candidate's psychological suitability or lack thereof. Some departments or hiring agencies request a dichotomous response: suitable or unsuitable. However, others seek a determination of low, medium, or high risk for hiring. Typically, the risk ratings equate to acceptable, meeting minimum standards, or not recommended for hiring. The main purpose is to answer the referral question of whether or not this candidate is psychologically suitable for the unique demands of the position. If the candidate is deemed suitable, any concerns that arose—and how they were offset—should be addressed. If the outcome is psychologically not suitable, it is helpful to address each concern as it relates to specific job tasks. A unique aspect of these reports is that the clinician is not diagnosing a candidate. Instead, the focus remains on whether or not they present too much risk to safely and effectively carry out the required roles inherent to the position.

One much needed area of development for pre-employment evaluations involves a better screening process for candidates with various racist attitudes toward people of color and protected classes. There are an extremely limited number of psychological tests, if any, geared toward the assessment of such biases within a law enforcement population. Within the psychological evaluation, this is an area assessed during the clinical interview if specific critical items related to bias are endorsed. It may also arise while assessing a candidate's worldview, including issues within the domains of tolerance, social competence, cynicism, and interpersonal interactions. Furthermore, this becomes an area requiring further exploration if concerning issues related to bias are uncovered throughout the course of the background investigation. Specifically, this may be the result of a social media inquiry or polygraph.

## Fitness-for-Duty Evaluations

While a pre-employment evaluation is limited to the assessment of a job candidate, a fitness-for-duty evaluation is focused on an employee experiencing some difficulties at work. The referral question is similar to a pre-employment evaluation, as the main focus is whether a person can safely and effectively perform the essential functions of a particular position. However, a fitness-for-duty evaluation focuses on whether an employee is able to continue to safely perform his or her job functions. According to the guidelines set forth by the IACP, an employee may be referred for a psychological fitness-for-duty evaluation when objective evidence exists that the employee may not be able to safely perform their job functions, and there is a reasonable basis for believing the cause is rooted in a psychological issue.

It is recommended that clinicians conducting such evaluations have an understanding of the essential job functions of the employee's particular title. For officers, this would include awareness of daily responsibilities such as responding to trauma-related calls, interacting with hostile citizens, notifying family members of the deceased, and navigating a bureaucratic organization. Furthermore, clinicians should have some awareness of employment law insofar as it is related to disability requirements, as legal matters such as litigation or arbitration may arise. Given the litigious nature potentially surrounding the evaluations, clinicians should be aware that their work may be subject to scrutiny and practice accordingly. As with any other area of practice, it is crucial to conduct evaluations within one's scope of practice, as based on education, training, and supervised clinical experience. Clinicians should seek out supervision and consultation as needed.

While a fitness-for-duty evaluation may essentially be mandated by the employer, it is imperative to receive both verbal and written informed consent. Given the forensic setting, the limits of confidentiality should be explained to the officer. Furthermore, collateral information will be pivotal in such evaluations to gain a more in-depth understanding of their past and present performance, conduct, and functioning. Specific documents typically requested for the assessment include performance evaluations, any applicable previous remediation plans, internal affairs investigations, formal complaints, use of excessive force reports, disciplinary records, medical records, and prior psychological or substance use evaluations or treatment records. As is the case with pre-employment evaluations, it is crucial that requests for records are limited to being directly related to job performance or the suspected psychological difficulties.

A psychological testing battery consisting of personality and risk assessment measures is typically conducted during the fitness-for-duty evaluation. It is also a helpful practice to obtain the complete pre-employment evaluation file to compare data and review if any related concerns were previously noted. A clinical interview will then be conducted, with a focus on the presenting problem and recent behavior. If deemed appropriate, a clinician may find it useful to conduct collateral interviews with third parties, such as family members or direct supervisors. The final report should assert a clear indication of the clinician's professional opinion regarding whether the officer is fit to return to unrestricted duty, unfit, or requires a specific modification at the time.

## The Importance of Assessing Trauma in Employment Evaluations

The primary purpose of both the pre-employment evaluation and the fitness-for-duty evaluation is to estimate the risk an individual poses "to his or her department, supervisors, and fellow officers, as well as the community in general" (Rostow & Davis, 2004, p. 65). That estimate is broadly "calculated" by comparing the psychological attributes the applicant or member of service exhibits with the traits and behaviors his or her desired position requires. In the evaluation of current or prospective police officers, sound judgment, stress resilience, anger management, and social competence are all psychological characteristics that have been identified by the IACP as critically important to safe and effective law enforcement.

Without question, a history of trauma does not preclude the maintenance or development of any of these key traits—nor does it necessitate an "Unsuitable" or "Unfit for Duty" determination on the part of the evaluating psychologist. Among others, a 2001 longitudinal study by Hodgins et al. found a "lack of association between prior trauma history and subsequent traumatic stress reactions" among law enforcement officers (p. 546). Many recruits who have reported sexual, verbal, or physical abuse in childhood or early adulthood possess the psychological resources to sustain long and impactful careers as law enforcement officers—and may in fact rely on their traumatic experiences to better connect and empathize with those they serve. Similarly, officers are oftentimes exposed to life-threatening situations on the job and very commonly can use those experiences to better navigate comparable circumstances and instruct their peers and subordinates in the future.

With that said, one cannot overlook the fact that a history of trauma (e.g., sexual abuse, physical abuse, exposure to domestic or community violence) *can be* detrimental to individuals' objectivity (particularly when evaluating danger), their ability to self-regulate, and/or their capacity for forging and maintaining positive and trusting relationships (with civilians, partners, and outside social supports). It is for this reason that psychologists must evaluate officers' and applicants' exposure to traumatic incidents and their subsequent responses, both positive and negative, short- and long-term.

When rendering a final determination of suitability for hire or fitness for duty, the psychologist should consider the degree to which past trauma has impacted (and/or continues to impact) the applicant's functioning, in what domains, and for how long. Substantial consideration should also be given to candidates' or current employees' means of coping with triggers, their engagement in high-risk behaviors, and the threat they may pose to themselves or others if placed in an armed position and additional, highly stressful scenarios.

The breadth of research linking the trauma narrative to the constellation and severity of posttraumatic symptoms also supports inquiry into and consideration of the *coherence* of the interviewee's autobiographical account. If the widely held belief among psychologists is true— that "it isn't what happened to you that will determine what you do, [but] how you make sense of what happened to you"—the interviewee's ability to provide an integrated understanding of the incident and its impact can be a key sign of his or her readiness for the inherent dangers and triggers that come with a career in law enforcement (Siegel, 2011).

## *Cultural Considerations*

Cultural and societal considerations are integral components of trauma-related assessments within law enforcement populations. It is helpful to maintain a framework in which the psychological examiner does not consider culture as an "afterthought" to the evaluation. Instead, viewing culture from a constructivist perspective will likely yield a more comprehensive evaluation. Constructivist theory asserts that humans assign meaning to their own experiences. Such meanings shape every aspect of how an individual experiences the world—including internal struggles, coping strategies, interpersonal interactions, behaviors, and cognitions. Thus, having a sense of the individual's cultural influences is highly recommended when conducting such evaluations. It is worth noting that the term "culture" may certainly apply to protected class categories; however, it extends to also include entities such as family and work culture and how both impact the experience and sequelae of trauma.

In psychotherapy, mental health professionals often consider the differences between "process" and "content" (i.e., the difference between a story's narrative/ details and the speaker's nonverbal behavior, emotional reactions, and interpersonal dynamics with the listener). In law enforcement evaluations, the notion that the sequelae of trauma (i.e., "the process") may have a greater impact on job suitability than actual content has been our experience while working with this population. This is an important conceptual foundation when considering cultural and societal aspects of trauma narratives. Such cultural factors contribute to whether a candidate or officer *even* considers their experiences to be traumatic. As with various other concepts, culture influences to what degree an individual will legitimize their internal experiences—or receive validation ranging from the macro to micro levels of society. In other words, an officer's worldview and cultural influences will greatly determine how much they perceive an experience to be traumatic and how he or she responds behaviorally, cognitively, and emotionally.

Western social constructs place great emphasis on the *individual* experience of trauma, with less attention given to the overarching systemic issues that perpetuate trauma. For example, police departments may refer a single officer to psychological services for a fitness-for-duty exam when it appears their drinking may be problematic. That officer will then be evaluated and a determination will be made regarding returning to duty. If necessary, treatment programs and ongoing support will be provided in order for the officer to maintain employment. However, there is little focus on the larger societal and cultural issues contributing to issues with alcohol. Alcohol consumption related to trauma will be discussed in further detail in an upcoming section.

## Assessing Trauma in Pre-employment Evaluations

As previously noted, pre-employment evaluations are typically composed of three parts: (1) a written psychological evaluation, wherein the law enforcement candidate is administered a range of written testing measures (e.g., objective personality measures, projective tests, biopsychosocial questionnaires), (2) a semi-structured clinical interview with a psychologist or Master's level clinician, and (3) a review of collateral records from both the candidate's background investigator and other sources (e.g., medical professionals, previous or contemporary employers) as the psychologist has deemed appropriate and necessary to render a decision. None of the above components should be used in isolation to make a determination of suitability, and in most cases, each step should be used to inform the focus of the next. (In other words, concerns raised by the written testing results should be explored thoroughly in the oral interview with the psychologist; interview responses or behavioral presentations that cast doubts upon the applicant's credibility or true level of functioning should inform which records are requested subsequent to the interview.) Each aspect of the pre-employment evaluation should also be used to develop an understanding of the candidate's trauma history and to ascertain the degree to which that history has and/or may continue to interfere with his or her functioning in the workplace, either directly or indirectly.

## Written Testing Measures

Selected psychological testing instruments vary between law enforcement agencies but typically include objective measures such as the Minnesota Multiphasic Personality Inventory-2-Restructured Form (MMPI-2-RF), the Personality Assessment Inventory (PAI), and/or the California Psychological Inventory (CPI). The MMPI-2-RF and PAI can be particularly helpful in identifying psychopathology among law enforcement candidates in the pre-employment process. Among other attributes, the MMPI-2-RF touts fewer questions than the MMPI-2, greater homogeneity/specificity in its scales, and a complementary Police Candidate Interpretive Report (PCIR) which utilizes the instrument's normative sample of more than two thousand law enforcement officers and validated correlations to post-hire behavior (Corey & Ben-Porath, 2018). The PAI, which has demonstrated good convergent validity with the MMPI-2-RF, may be preferred given its lower reading level and four-point (versus dichotomous, true-false) questions.

In pre-employment evaluations, the CPI oftentimes serves as a complement to the MMPI-2-RF or PAI, as it (1) measures normal-range behaviors such as assertiveness, self-acceptance, tolerance, and flexibility and (2) includes its own Police and Public Safety Selection Report (created by Johnson, Roberts, and Associates, Inc.), which is "based on a normative sample of more than fifty-thousand public safety job applicants" and computes the risk for a variety of issues on the job (e.g., involuntary departure; use of unnecessary force; issues with problem-solving, communication, and citizen relations).

There is no one scale on any of the aforementioned instruments which will inform the evaluating clinician of a history of trauma or generate a conclusion about the applicant's risk of re-experiencing, developing, or abating post-traumatic symptoms after hire. With that said, the results of the MMPI-2-RF, PAI, and CPI can shed light on a candidate's proclivity for anxiety, his or her history of post-traumatic symptoms or reliance on maladaptive coping mechanisms, and his or her current level of emotion regulation and wellbeing. The Demoralization (RCd), Low Positive

Emotions (RC2), and Dysfunctional Negative Emotions (RC7) scales of the MMPI-2-RF, for example, have all been correlated with Post-Traumatic Stress Disorder (PTSD) symptoms and diagnoses (Ben-Porath, 2012). An evaluating psychologist who identifies elevations on these scales may wish to review the specific endorsements which yielded these results and then discuss them in further detail with the candidate in person. The California Psychological Inventory, though not symptom-based, may similarly offer hypotheses and specific items for the psychologist to explore further with the applicant.

Though other assessment instruments do not present the same degree of forensic validity and should be weighted accordingly in one's ultimate determination and report, it is certainly worth considering their inclusion as part of the written testing administration. This is due to the wealth of information an evaluator may gather about the candidate's history even if they are either unable or unwilling to share such information, or if it is occurring at the unconscious level. Projective measures such as the House-Tree-Person, for example, can offer salient indicators of a trauma history (e.g., reinforced walls and barriers on the house, overemphasis on the person's genitals, holes/defects/damage to the tree) which may not have been reported when asked in more direct terms on an objective measure (Buck, 1948). Open-ended prompts, such as those asking the applicant to briefly describe his or her most stressful or threatening event and how he or she responded to it, can also elicit a richer understanding of the psychosocial history, a fragmentation or coherence of the candidate's trauma narrative, and events that could potentially color his or her perceptions and behaviors once in law enforcement.

In our work, we have noted that a basic written history of the applicant's functioning at school and in the workplace can raise important questions for the oral interview and offer supporting data for the psychologist's ultimate determination—either to justify a qualification (in instances where the candidate was functioning well despite stressors and triggers) or to support a disqualification (by illustrating how external stressors or previous traumas impeded his or her ability to meet demands in another setting or at another time).

## The Clinical Interview

The pre-employment interview is fraught with unique challenges and limitations in assessing trauma. First, time constraints and the wide range of domains of functioning that require some level of inquiry allow little time for basic rapport building. (In most agencies, each candidate is allotted one 45- to 60-minute session for the oral interview, a meeting that should result in a reasonably complete conceptualization of the candidate's employment, academic, medical, psychological, and relational history of functioning). Second, the relationship between the evaluator and the law enforcement applicant is inherently strained by a number of extenuating factors: the fact that the agency—and not the interviewee—is the identified "client" and the motivation for the interviewee to present his or her history as unblemished, among others.

In some instances, inquiry into other areas of functioning may naturally elicit discussion of traumatic events. When reviewing a candidate's academic history, for example, concrete questions like "Why do you think your grades were lower that semester?" or "What led you to leave the school?" may reveal their difficulties in the school environment were secondary to a traumatic event (e.g., an incident of sexual assault on campus, an incident wherein they witnessed domestic violence between parents). When the interviewee spontaneously and openly introduces the traumatic incident, the psychologist should aim to both support and focus the discussion, asking follow-up questions about the event itself (e.g., whether it was isolated incident or recurrent, the seriousness of the threat) and the applicant's interpretation of and response to the event. Specific questions about depressive and anxiety symptoms (e.g., anhedonia, irritability, suicidality, panic, flashbacks), maladaptive coping (e.g., high-risk behavior, substance misuse), and/or adaptive coping strategies (e.g., engagement in psychotherapy, reliance on appropriate social supports) should also be included—with focus on the frequency, severity, duration, and most recent occurrence of the former. For those who report a negligible or distant history of post-traumatic symptoms, asking questions about their exposure to triggers and other stressful events in the months or years since can help the evaluator assess their likelihood of symptom recurrence.

More often, the law enforcement candidate will be (understandably) reticent or unwilling to disclose his or her history of abuse or trauma. In circumstances where a history of abuse is known or suspected given information from the background investigator (e.g., police reports, orders of protection) or another collateral source but the applicant appears guarded, exercising clinical judgment is particularly key. If the candidate has already presented a substantial and unambiguous risk that will render him or her unsuitable for the position, to broach the topic of trauma is both unethical and potentially harmful. In other situations, where the candidate's experience of, reaction to, and present insight into a traumatic event or events will in part inform the final determination, the evaluator should introduce the topic empathically and carefully, with the expressly stated goal of understanding the candidate's history and a brief explanation as to the import of this history in the broader evaluation process. (When discussing a history of domestic violence, for example, it may be helpful to remind the candidate that he or she may be tasked with responding to similar incidents as a law enforcement officer.) From there, the clinician should be careful to maintain appropriate boundaries, asking only what is necessary to understand the traumatic event, its impact, and the candidate's understanding of both.

## Collateral Records

Oftentimes, the results of the written testing and the candidate's responses during the semi-structured interview provide sufficient information to render a reliable determination of suitability or unsuitability. In some cases, however, collateral records may be required to clarify historical events and ascertain the veracity of the candidate's self-reports. Potentially helpful collateral records include but are not limited to the following: police reports (e.g., domestic incident reports, civilian complaint reports, arrest reports), orders of protection, medical records (e.g., emergency room visits), and psychotherapy notes.

## Case Example

In the following case example, all identifying information has been altered to ensure the confidentiality and anonymity of the subject.

### Candidate A

Candidate A was an unmarried female candidate in her late-20s when she was evaluated for the position of Police Officer at a large urban police department on the East coast. Though she had left high school at the age of 16—before earning her diploma—she subsequently attained her GED and then an Associate's degree from a local community college with above-average grades. She reported that she was a single mother with two school-aged children who held a number of brief, part-time jobs in retail stores and restaurants and was financially reliant on her parents for most of her 20s. In the 3 years leading up to her pre-employment evaluation, however, she had been working full-time as the office manager of a law firm. According to preliminary background investigation findings, Ms. A was well-liked by her coworkers and supervisors and had no history of disciplinary issues in her current role. She also had no history of arrests, criminal summonses, or moving violations, and the only notable police records wherein Ms. A was named at all were two domestic incident reports wherein she was identified as the victim of physical abuse.

For the written testing, Ms. A was administered the MMPI-2-RF, the CPI, and the House-Tree-Person. She was also asked to write a brief narrative on her most stressful event and to complete a questionnaire about her employment, academic, medical, and psychological history. On the MMPI-2-RF and the CPI, the majority of the candidate's scale scores fell within 1 standard deviation of the mean compared to the test's sample of law enforcement applicants. Neither could be regarded as a valid, reliable measure of Ms. A's true functioning, however, as both showed evidence (or at the very least, raised questions) of her impression management. The candidate's Uncommon Virtues score on the MMPI-2-RF (L-r; T = 95) fell well above the typical range for applicants and suggested she was presenting herself as unusually principled. (Worth noting here, the MMPI-2-RF's L-r scale should not be mistaken for the "Lie" [L] scale of the MMPI-2—but it may be similarly elevated when an individual is presenting herself unrealistically.) Similarly, the candidate's Good Impression score on the CPI (Gi; T = 63) was elevated and suggested she was "faking good" in the hopes of appearing more suitable.

With regard to her most stressful event, Ms. A detailed a week in her mid-20s in which she had several difficult final exams scheduled and her work supervisor assigned her extra hours at the supermarket. Prompted to reflect on how she handled that stressor, Ms. A wrote that she made a "To Do" list and effectively managed all of her responsibilities, albeit with slightly less sleep.

While the candidate's years of inconsistent employment raised some questions about her stability in early adulthood, her 3 years of stable employment—without incident—indicated she was capable of managing and sustaining full-time work. The evaluator's greatest concerns from the outset of the oral interview, then, were Ms. A's credibility (given notable elevations on the L-r and Gi scales) and her apparent involvement in multiple domestic incidents (which was not disclosed anywhere on her self-report questionnaires).

Ms. A arrived to the oral interview on time and neatly groomed. She presented as poised, articulate, and well-prepared, preemptively presenting her evaluator with a letter of recommendation from her employer and referring to a typed resume as she was asked about her work history. When asked about her departures from various jobs, she often stated she had pursued a higher paying position or had moved to another neighborhood and had no choice but to leave given the commute, issues with childcare, etc. Over the course of the evaluation, Ms. A was asked if she had ever filed a police report, had an incident that involved police, or was granted an order of protection, to which she repeatedly and unequivocally stated she hadn't.

Nearing the end of the oral psychological evaluation, the evaluating psychologist began to ask questions about the candidate's relational history: her relationships with immediate family members, her relationship with her children's father, and any other significant or long-term romantic relationships. Ms. A reported that her only notable romantic relationship to date was the one with her children's father. She described it as "on-and-off" and indicated that it spanned nearly 10 years, from her late adolescence until a year-and-a-half before the evaluation itself. Ms. A casually referred to her ex's recurrent infidelity, difficulties sustaining work, and "immaturity" over the course of their dating but stated their ultimate break-up was amicable and described him as an engaged and supportive co-parent.

When Ms. A again denied any history of domestic violence in her relationship with her ex, the undersigned noted that the background investigator had found two police reports wherein the candidate was named; in one, Ms. A was alleged to have been pushed, kicked, punched, and choked by a boyfriend, and in the other (which occurred 2 years before the oral interview), police responded to a call made by a concerned neighbor, who had allegedly witnessed a physical confrontation between Ms. A and this same partner in the street. (According to the report, Ms. A refused to speak with police and/or press charges.)

When presenting these reports, the evaluating psychologist was careful to express understanding of possible discomfort around the topic and to explain the purpose of this line of inquiry (i.e., its relevance to Ms. A's desired career as a Police Officer). Despite these efforts, however, Ms. A became notably guarded, dismissive, and minimizing. With regard to the earlier incident—wherein substantial physical force and injuries were noted—the candidate reported that she had "forgotten" all about what happened (given its temporal distance). Having been reminded of it by the evaluator, though, she could now recall one occasion wherein she and her then-partner were arguing about infidelity and grappling with a cell phone. In the struggle, he lost his grip, let go, and she fell back into a dresser, sustaining a minor bruise. Ms. A insisted this was (1) the only manner in which their altercation was physical and (2) the only occasion on which their arguing escalated and involved physical contact. Referring to the more recent incident, Ms. A reported that she and her ex *had* had a *verbal* disagreement about picking up the children from school a few years earlier but asserted it was in no way physical, that there was no justification for her neighbor's concern, and that the two promptly resolved the conflict (and in fact resumed the relationship shortly thereafter, dating for another 6 months).

Ms. A also reported in a rather defensive tone that neither of these events had any effect on her or her children whatsoever. She reiterated that she and her children's father were "young" and "immature" at the time, that brief engagement in psychotherapy allowed her to move forward and prioritize herself and her career goals over her partner, and that the two had a stable, healthy relationship as co-parents to date.

In this case, the discrepancies between the police department's reports and Ms. A's self-reports to the psychologist substantiated concerns about Ms. A's credibility and, in combination with her marked and abrupt change in demeanor, raised serious questions about the true severity, frequency, duration, and impact of physical abuse in her relationship with her children's father. Ms. A's failure to recall either incident without prompting, her guarded approach to the discussion, her tendency to minimize, and the apparent fact she had reunited with this partner after both documented incidents also raised alarm about the narrative she had constructed for herself, her likelihood of reunification (or development of similarly maladaptive relationships) in the future, and her ability to maintain objectivity and take appropriate action when responding to incidents of domestic violence as a law enforcement officer.

While the above concerns would sufficiently warrant disqualification by themselves, the evaluating psychologist obtained treatment records (with the candidate's consent) from Ms. A's mental health provider subsequent to the oral interview. Somewhat unsurprisingly, the duration of Ms. A's involvement in psychotherapy was substantially longer than she disclosed to her evaluator—and had included discussion of *multiple* instances of domestic violence and notable personal and professional issues: low self-esteem, depressed mood, anxiety, and recurrent tardiness. While, to her credit, Ms. A was apparently managing her responsibilities to her children and her employer at the time of her oral interview, her inability to provide a cohesive narrative of the trauma she experienced, her notable guardedness, her justification and minimizing of her ex's aggressive behavior, and her history of psychological symptoms suggested she was not psychologically suitable for the interpersonally demanding and highly triggering career she was pursuing.

## Assessing Trauma in Fitness-for-Duty Evaluations

Much like the pre-employment evaluation, the fitness-for-duty evaluation typically comprises three components: the completion of objective psychological testing measures (e.g., the PAI, the MMPI-2-RF, the Inward Personality Inventory), a clinical interview by a trained mental health professional, and the integration of information from collateral sources. The overarching goal of the fitness-for-duty evaluation is also comparable, essentially gauging the risk of recurrence in problematic/risk-laden behavior (grounded in a distinctly psychological concern) and/or the interference by psychopathology in specific job-related tasks (International Association Chiefs of Police (2013).

While many of the key approaches of the pre-employment evaluation can be applied here, however, the psychological fitness-for-duty evaluation is also distinctly different in several ways. First, the FFD evaluation is initiated *in response to* a specific incident or concerning behavior—one that denotes either "positive risk… such as threats of harm against others, irrational acts, racist or sexist conduct, explosiveness, or aggression," or "negative risk… [e.g.] dereliction of duty, distractibility because of substance abuse, or rejection of supervision needed to conduct the normal operations associated with his position" (Rostow & Davis, 2004, p. 65). Second, and by extension, the FFD evaluation typically *begins* with collateral data (e.g., a conversation with a superior, an incident report, an alarming record of absences and tardies, a specific complaint filed by a coworker or civilian) and then proceeds to focus on this singular, identified concern.

Third, and of greatest relevance to this particular discussion, is the underlying understanding that the member of service being evaluated, simply by the nature of police work and the responsibilities it entails, is very likely to have been exposed to disturbing, potentially traumatic events at some point (or, more likely, on many occasions) (Liberman, et al., 2002).

The member of service may have experienced or continue to suffer from the well-established symptoms of PTSD (e.g., nightmares, flashbacks, emotional distress, physical reactivity) or from the lesser-known and lesser-discussed signs of secondary post-traumatic stress (e.g., chronic exhaustion, cynicism, numbing, grandiosity, helplessness), if they have been exposed to trauma (Lipsky, 2009). The pervasiveness of traumatic events, the tendency to normalize or dismiss maladaptive reactions to these events by members of service, and the relative usefulness and omnipresence of suspiciousness and hyper masculinity in police culture (discussed in greater detail below) are all important considerations when evaluating the presence, impact, and risk of trauma in an officer (Andersen, Papazoglou, & Koskelainen, 2015; Follette, Polusny, & Milbeck, 1994; Hodgins, Creamer, & Bell, 2001).

### *Vicarious Trauma*

According to Pearlman and Saakvitne (1995), vicarious trauma is the emotional difficulty that is inherent to employment involving exposure to others' trauma on a daily basis. Vicarious trauma is also referred to as compassion fatigue or secondary victimization/traumatic stress. As described by Figley (1982), it is the "cost of caring" for others. It includes bearing witness to traumatic events, hearing stories of traumas, or simply having detailed knowledge of others' trauma. There is long-established literature citing the association between exposure to trauma as part of employment and experience of trauma-related symptoms. Follette et al. (1994) found law enforcement personnel have a greater risk of experiencing psychological symptoms from vicarious trauma than mental health professionals.

Vicarious trauma develops initially as a facet of the officers' ability to have empathy for others. However, it can become consuming and impact their ability to perform the essential functions of the position. It is marked by "increased cynicism, loss of enjoyment of career, and can eventually transform into depression and stress-related illnesses" (Mathieu, 2007, pg. 1). Vicarious trauma can be manifested by avoidance behaviors, a constant state of hyperarousal, or some combination of the two. It is often experienced as a feeling of tension and preoccupation, whether or not this is at the officer's conscious level of awareness.

According to the American Counseling Association (2011), there are ways in which vicarious trauma is manifested emotionally (e.g., symptoms consistent with depression, anxiety, and post-traumatic stress), behaviorally (tardiness, absenteeism, overworking, discontinuing community activities or hobbies), interpersonally (e.g., blaming others, decreasing communication, impatience with others, isolating from colleagues), cognitively (e.g., negative perception of self/others, general apathy, questioning their beliefs/worldview), and within work settings (e.g., perfectionism, increased errors, low motivation).

The risk of experiencing vicarious trauma tends to be higher among those with a personal history of trauma. Other predictors include overall psychological well-being, social support, age, gender, education, socio-economic status, and preference of coping styles. One reason that those with a trauma history are at greater risk is because they may be attempting to manage their own post-traumatic reaction, including active symptoms of depressed mood and anxiety. Furthermore, bearing witness to another person's trauma may alone be a traumatic experience. While officers may believe they "put it in the past," repeated exposure to various traumas or simply being exposed to a specific *type* of trauma can result in the resurgence of numerous symptoms.

## Police Culture

In order to conduct a comprehensive evaluation with any population, it is imperative for the clinician to utilize an approach that considers all aspects of culture. Thus, a trauma-informed evaluation of law enforcement personnel will include knowledge and application of police culture. Police culture is a specific occupational culture that influences the beliefs, behaviors, and motivations of law enforcement personnel. An occupational culture is typically formed when individual members are trained as a unit in the same format and are indoctrinated with specific values. Occupational cultures manifest in several ways, such as language, dress, and coping styles.

One specific manifestation of police culture is the uniform. Wearing the same uniform separates officers from civilians, communicates their rank (e.g., white shirts typically indicate higher ranks), and immediately provides fellow officers with a sense of camaraderie. Regarding the latter, such a sense of devotedness conveys a degree of belonging and support that others without the uniform are not privy to and cannot fully comprehend. An extension of the uniform is the "brotherhood" inherently created by the sheer dangerousness associated with the position. Individuals become both instantaneously and more deeply bonded when sharing experiences that threaten their safety and overall well-being. There is a very valid sense that only others who share this uniform truly understand how it feels to do this type of work.

Another crucial component of police culture is the jargon utilized by members of the police department. Language is often a critical component of any culture, as it is a common thread that reinforces a sense of community. Furthermore, using codes and jargon is necessary in law enforcement as it provides a much more efficient and safe way of communicating over the radio. Specific language features include utilization of military-based language. Examples include referring to 2 p.m. as 1400 hours, or an officer citing their daily shift as a tour-of-duty.      The literature on police culture describes some aspects born from the daily struggles and dangerousness of interacting with the public, as well as a work environment characterized by a bureaucratic system. Current police culture qualities are reflective of the white, heterosexual male dominant culture. While some strides have been made for a more diverse and inclusive police culture, European–American values remain largely ingrained (Addis & Mahalik, 2003; Chan 1997). Specific descriptions include a hyper-masculine culture marked by cynicism, self-reliance, reluctance to change, and expectations for all to express homogenous beliefs (Kingshott, Bailey, & Wolfe, 2004; Prenzler, 1997).

The culture of masculinity is reinforced by the stereotype of a police officer as someone who is strong and brave as well as limited in their emotional expression. While some of these characteristics may be inherently useful to the position, it perpetuates the notion that officers are more like superheroes than actual humans. When a male displays any emotion other than anger, we are indoctrinated to perceive their expression as weakness. This is also the case for police officers, as a significant portion of police culture mandates them to be "stronger and braver" than civilians (Kingshott, Bailey, & Wolfe, 2004). While this may certainly be part of their role as an officer, it contributes to the fact that officers are often reluctant to seek psychological support.

Bureaucratic issues also play a significant role in an officer's potential resistance to psychological treatment. Being referred "to psych" bears a negative connotation as it is viewed as a punishment for wrongdoing or a feeling that they are emotionally unable to handle the role of a police officer. The general consensus is an internal feeling of some degree of incompetency or weakness and subsequently a belief they will be treated unfavorably by the clinician. In our work, our experience has been officers' anticipation of negative employment or treatment outcomes exacerbates the feeling of stigma surrounding psychological services.

## *Occupational Stress and Alcohol Use*

Given the nature of police work, officers are inevitably exposed to high levels of occupational stress. There is a wide range of potential traumatic events or experiences a police officer may be exposed to on any given day. At the lower end, it can include daily interpersonal interactions (e.g., a particularly hostile interaction with a member of the community) or bureaucratic issues out of their control (e.g., limited notice that their command, or the location where they report for duty, has been changed). At the higher end, stressors can include the following: physical injury while on duty, discharging their firearm/officer-involved shooting, fellow officer suicide, terrorism, exposure to dead bodies, hearing accounts of various person-on-person crimes such as rape, domestic violence, and maltreatment of children. Such traumatic events and experiences can be the catalyst for the development of various symptoms consistent with post-traumatic stress. For example, officers involved in shootings commonly report issues such as disturbed perception of time, sleep problems, episodes of tearfulness, and erratic emotions. Of particular importance is that post-traumatic stress symptoms are often accompanied by co-morbid disorders, such as substance abuse (Stewart, Ouimette, & Brown, 2002).

The literature on police officers and alcohol use has been somewhat scarce in the United States over the past two decades. Research during the 1970s and 1980s in the U.S. indicated approximately 25% of police officers had marked difficulties with alcohol (Dietrich & Smith, 1986; Kroes, 1985; Violanti, Marshall, & Howe, 1985). However, notable large studies were conducted more recently in other countries, including Australia and Norway. One study of over 800 police officers in an urban section of Australia indicated nearly half of the male officers, and 40% of the female officers, indicated they engaged in either binge drinking or hazarded/excessive drinking (Richmond, Kehoe, & Heather, 1998). More recently, the Norwegian sample included over 2000 officers from an urban setting. Problematic rates of alcohol use were much lower: approximately 17% of males and 9% of females. While purely speculative, the reason for such discrepancies in problematic use may be accounted for by cultural attitudes toward drinking.

Despite the dearth of research available, we have noted that alcohol use is normalized within police culture. While we believe one possible explanation may be due to the emphasis on "numbing" emotional aspects of the job—which is precisely the behavioral function when individuals turn to alcohol to escape problematic realities. Our anecdotal experiences illustrate the frequent involvement of alcohol in varying capacities during numerous emergency interventions.

### Case Example

In the following case example, all identifying information has been altered to ensure the confidentiality and anonymity of the subject.

***Officer X***   Officer X was a married male police officer in his mid-30s—who had been working in law enforcement for over 10 years—when he was referred for a fitness-for-duty evaluation by his superior. According to the referral, both Officer X and his partner had been involved and injured in a robbery approximately 3 months prior to the evaluation. Though neither sustained life-threatening injuries, Officer X sustained a bullet wound to his left shoulder which required emergency medical attention and necessitated months of recovery. When he returned to work, Officer X was noted to be more distractible and dysphoric. He confided in his partner that he had been experiencing severe sleep difficulties and headaches and that he felt uneasy coming to work each day. His coworkers and superiors also noted a dramatic decline in his social engagement; wherein Officer X used to be the "life of the party," he was now quick to leave and avoid social engagements. Officer X's wife disclosed to his former partner, a close friend of the family, that he had been similarly isolative at home and easily agitated by minor, rather normative disagreements with her and their children.

When administered the MMPI-2-RF, Officer X showed a clinically significant elevation on the Cynicism scale (RC3; $T = 65$) and more moderate elevations on Inefficacy, Stress/Worry, and Disaffiliativeness. In the interview with his evaluating psychologist, he expressed some irritation with his command's referral to "Psych" but a willingness to discuss both the incident and other stressors that were exacerbating his symptoms since. Officer X indicated that he did not believe his current relational or emotional difficulties stemmed from the shooting itself but admitted he often thought about the details of the incident (apropos of nothing) and perseverated on the possibility that he may have been more seriously injured or killed, leaving his wife and children behind.

To his evaluating psychologist, both the timeline and constellation of symptoms provided by the officer, his wife, and his colleagues and superiors suggested the traumatic incident was more impactful than he was either aware of or willing to acknowledge given the context of the evaluation. With that said, as the interview progressed, Officer X appeared increasingly willing to talk about his difficulties (on the job and elsewhere) and motivated to return to his previous level of functioning. Given this, as well as his adamant and seemingly reliable denial of high-risk factors (e.g., suicidality, self-injurious behavior, physical violence, substance misuse), his evaluating psychologist deemed him fit to return to duty with the recommendation that he receive supportive services.

## Emergency Interventions and Trauma Debriefings

Traumatic events of varying degrees occur on a regular basis within the daily interactions of law enforcement. Such events may remain more personal in nature (e.g., an officer in the process of a divorce or custody battle) or may be directly associated with inherent job duties (e.g., an officer-involved shooting, working specialized units such as child abuse or sex crimes). However, there may be blurred lines regarding boundaries, given the permeability of the work. In other words, it is fairly easy for an officer to have difficulty "leaving work at work," given the tendency for such work to "bleed" into thoughts while off-duty, and vice versa. Furthermore, the very nature of police work is highly interpersonal and many interactions may "hit home." For example, an officer going through a divorce may experience increased difficulty responding to domestic calls. Thus, the sequelae of personal or work stressors requires psychological examiners and clinicians to apply emergency response interventions when appropriate. The need for emergency response interventions and trauma debriefings vary greatly by jurisdiction. A larger urban police department will certainly have greater demands than a relatively small suburban location. Furthermore, demands for such services operate on an as-needed basis, given the unpredictable nature of traumatic events.

## Trauma Debriefings

The purpose of a trauma debriefing is to address immediate reactions and concerns of law enforcement personnel in the aftermath of a traumatic event. While the process may include meeting individually with officers, it tends to address officers as a group or unit. Trauma debriefings are typically in response to critical events that impact groups of law enforcement personnel. This could include an officer suicide, an officer being killed, or an act of terrorism. They may be conducted either individually or in teams by mental health professionals or specially-trained peer members. A common practice during the debriefings is to first acknowledge the traumatic event and encourage personnel to share their experiences and reactions. There is also a degree of psycho-education in order to normalize trauma-related symptoms and provide information on what can be expected in the upcoming weeks (Lipsky, 2009). Of particular importance is that members of service receive information on what they can do to mitigate any potential symptoms and steps they should take should the symptoms fail to subside after a specified range of time. Officers are often encouraged to seek out help, both formally and informally, as necessary. Finally, a crucial component of trauma debriefings includes providing information for follow-up resources. A trauma debriefing is not meant to replace treatment, but rather functions as a triage system for members of the department to return to prior functioning before the incident (Lipsky, 2009; Malcolm, Seaton, Perera, Sheehan, & van Hasselt, 2005; Miller 2006).

In our work, it has been the practice that trauma debriefing teams consist of both mental health professionals and peer support officers. As discussed in the Police Culture section, there is a certain inherent degree of mistrust of mental health professionals given the employment context. Peer support officers provide a much-needed sense of relatability and trust, while mental health professionals can offer their clinical expertise. Another crucial component of trauma debriefings includes the need for the team or individual to be mobile and highly responsive. It is strongly recommended to arrive in person for a debriefing, at an appropriate or centralized location. For example, when addressing the officers in the command for an officer who committed suicide, it has been our experience that a centralized and appropriate location is the precinct. Given that officers are in "their own territory," it is more likely that they will feel at least somewhat more open to processing their experience and seeking assistance as necessary. Furthermore, it allows for the team members to become part of the organizational culture.

Regarding timeframe, best practices indicate debriefings should occur within 72 hours after the event. Nonetheless, within 24 hours is strongly recommended (Lipsky, 2009; Malcolm, Seaton, Perera, Sheehan, & van Hasselt, 2005; Miller 2006). As previously mentioned, the response timeframe may vary by jurisdiction given the availability of resources.

## *Emergency Interventions*

It has been our experience that emergency interventions contain many of the components of a trauma debriefing yet tend to focus more on the individual rather than a group. Additionally, they are more likely to involve personal matters and occur while the officer is off-duty. Such interventions are more akin to crisis interventions that a clinician might employ while working with an individual client. The goal of the emergency intervention is not to provide comprehensive treatment; rather, the focus is on stabilization. The first step in an emergency intervention is assessing the individual(s) and current presenting problem(s). This is completed by conducting a semi-structured clinical interview and gathering collateral information. The former involves getting a thorough understanding of the presenting issue. In order to achieve this, the clinician can ask the law enforcement personnel to describe the issue in their own words. Afterward, the clinician's inquiry can be directed toward assessment of various psychopathology, including symptoms consistent with depression, anxiety, mania, and psychosis. Additionally, a major focus of emergency interventions is conducting a thorough risk assessment to include, at minimum, a full suicidal and homicidal risk assessment, including questions regarding thoughts, plans, attempts, access to means, and protective factors. Furthermore, inquiry regarding self-injurious behaviors and coping mechanisms are crucial. While it is generally not the time for an extensive alcohol and drug evaluation, it is imperative to assess if either or both appear problematic for the individual or play a role in the presenting problem. We believe it is beneficial to adopt a forensic mindset when applying emergency interventions. In other words, it is helpful to pay close attention to issues of malingering and not necessarily accept the personnel's narrative without any further prompting or examination. Law enforcement personnel are aware of the confidentiality limits, as well as the possible repercussions given the employment context. Thus, clinical judgment and experience become essential components of the examiner's toolkit.

# Recommendations

There are a variety of recommendations and resources to utilize when working with law enforcement personnel. These are especially helpful to aide in the treatment of work-related stress and trauma.

## *Awareness of Police Culture*

Perhaps of most importance is for the clinician to have an awareness and familiarity with both police culture and the specific challenges associated with policing. This includes knowledge of the values, hierarchies, policies, beliefs, and language within police culture. If you have direct access to police departments, or feel comfortable reaching out to one, you can inquire about ride-along programs offered by many departments. As the name implies, these programs allow civilians to accompany officers on a tour-of-duty to witness their day-to-day responsibilities. One way to gain access without direct contact to police departments is to subscribe to recognized law enforcement journals and magazines. Please see examples under the "Resources" section of the book.

## *Use of Evidence-Based Practices*

As with other populations, it is recommended that clinicians engage in evidence-based practices when working with trauma issues within law enforcement. This includes following the IACP guidelines for both pre-employment and fitness-for-duty evaluations, as well as any provisions set forth by Division 18 (Police and Public Safety) of the American Psychological Association.

## *Including Families in Treatment*

At the end of every shift, an officer arrives home and is expected to change instantaneously to family member. However, this is no easy feat given the nature of policing. They may have witnessed a death or heard detailed accounts of sexual assault during their shift and then been expected to shed all the emotional baggage when they arrive home. From a family systems perspective, the stress and trauma the officers experience will inevitably impact the entire unit to some degree. Research has indicated that communication, daily life activities, and emotion regulation are areas most impacted by the stress of the job. Therefore, it is imperative to include families in the treatment process to the degree to which the officer consents (American Psychological Association, 2002). This may include having open lines of communication with family members or joint sessions from time-to-time.

## Use of Peer Support Programs

Many departments have peer-based programs aimed at supporting the emotional well-being of officers (Klein, 1989). These programs are staffed by specially trained officers within the particular department who offer emotional support in times of both personal and professional crisis. These programs are especially helpful given the ongoing support they provide. As is typical with most major life events, individuals tend to rally around others and offer support immediately following the incident. However, symptoms and challenges will likely persist far beyond that initial time period. Such programs thus serve to support the officer with the emotional and physical sequelae after "the dust settles."

Clinicians can both partner with and refer officers to these programs to offer an additional level of assistance. Officers will likely feel more comfortable talking to a peer who they can relate to prior to meeting with a clinician. This phenomenon is largely due to the nature of police culture, and the encouragement of relying on others in uniform rather than outsiders. Partnership with a peer support program can serve as an introduction to the treatment process as officers will begin to discuss their experiences and emotions with their peers. It can also serve to screen difficulties officers are manifesting in a less formal setting. Additionally, partnering with high-ranking officers or retired personnel who are willing to speak of their experiences may provide exponential benefits. Those at top tiers in the hierarchy will automatically command respect of other officers and serve to dispel the stigma associated with emotional expression and weakness. Hearing these individuals emphasize how crucial psychological support is for overall well-being means others will feel more empowered and validated to reach out in times of need.

## Be Genuine

Research consistently supports the notion of the relationship between the clinician and client as the agent of change in therapy. Thus, it is strongly recommended to build a relationship marked by genuineness, trust, and collaboration. While clinicians will certainly practice from various theoretical orientations, it is recommended to incorporate principles of Carl Rogers' humanistic perspective (Schneider, Pierson, & Bugental, 2015). When the clinician presents with a limited amount of professional façade, they are modeling an authentic interpersonal style that encourages the officer to do the same. Being authentic inevitably results in experiencing basic human emotions and vulnerability—which is emphasized in police culture to be avoided at all costs. Such human connection yields exponential benefits beyond any specific technique or orientation.

It is also important to recognize and discuss the clinician's and officer's inherent differences as a civilian and uniformed member of service, respectively. Due to the hierarchy rankings and police culture, this is likely not a topic that will be raised by the officer, and thus becomes the responsibility of the clinician. Pretending to understand the officer's experience or making assumptions will likely only present as counterproductive in treatment (Mahoney & Granvold, 2005; Pearlman & Saakvitne, 1995). An honest acknowledgement on the part of the clinician that they do not truly understand the daily struggles of policing will serve to build rapport in the relationship and increase the clinician's credibility. These are situations in which certain degrees of self-disclosure may be appropriate. While self-disclosure is a honed skill that is best used with thought and intention of the client's best interest, it can be extremely validating.

# Conclusion

Police psychology is a specialized domain of assessment and clinical treatment that presents unique challenges. Just as a candidate or law enforcement personnel member is being evaluated regarding their capacity to meet the specific demands of the position, the clinician must be competent in this unique role. One major differentiating factor in this work for mental health professionals is the inherent nature of the forensic role. First and foremost, clinicians must be thoroughly familiar with the nature and ethics of such work, including issues related to confidentiality, having a third-party client, and the increased potential for malingering. The clinician must be familiar with the aforementioned practices regarding conducting pre-employment and fitness-for-duty evaluations, as well as trauma debriefings and emergency interventions. Given that risk assessment is the central focus of all law enforcement evaluations, it is imperative for the clinician to be well-versed in this domain. As with other aspects of psychology, acting within one's scope of practice is crucial; therefore, it is always recommended to seek supervision and consultation as needed.

Assessment and treatment of law enforcement personnel requires an understanding of the highly unique occupational culture within a police department. Thus, police culture has a distinct language and systems that influence the behaviors and cognitions of its members. Awareness and adoption of such culture by the clinician increases their trust factor when working with law enforcement personnel. Building trust and being perceived as a genuine, credible person is paramount when working with this population. It is especially critical when assessing for, and treating trauma and stressor-related issues.

Stress and trauma are inherent to police work, and therefore omnipresent in all law enforcement evaluations. While the *types* of traumas and stressors evaluated may differ in pre-employment and fitness-for-duty evaluations, the referral question remains the same: is the individual able to manage the inherent demands of the position?

# Questions/Activities for Further Exploration

## *Questions*

1. What are the clinician's ethical responsibilities and role within the context of Black Lives Matter and Blue Lives Matter?
2. What issues are greatly influenced by the individual clinician's judgment and inherent biases when undertaking pre-employment and fitness-for-duty evaluations?

## *Activities*

While it may vary by jurisdiction, some police departments offer experiential activities in order for citizens to gain a more in-depth understanding of the complexities of police work. For example, some departments offer ride-alongs, where a community member spends the day in the patrol vehicle with officers. The goal is to gain first-hand experience that would otherwise not be available unless actually becoming a police officer.

Experiential trainings related to mental illness and psychopathology. One suggestion is the *Listening to Disturbing Voices* Training. The purpose of this training is to better understand how a person experiencing psychosis must try to function in society while hearing voices. This experiential activity may help the clinician gain a better understanding regarding being "in the shoes" of a person with psychosis. In turn, the clinician can use such knowledge when working with law enforcement personnel who may be triggered or experience stress when interacting with members of the community with mental illnesses.

# References

Addis, M. E., & Mahalik, J. R. (2003). Men, masculinity, and the contexts of help seeking. *American Psychologist, 58*(1), 5.

American Counseling Association. (2011, October). *Vicarious trauma.* Retrieved from https://www.counseling.org/docs/trauma-disaster/fact-sheet-9%2D%2D-vicarious-trauma.pdf

American Psychological Association. (2002, June). Police psychology. *Resources.* Retrieved from https://www.apa.org/monitor/jun02/police

Andersen, J. P., & Papazoglou, K. (2014). Friends under fire: Cross-cultural relationships and trauma exposure among police officers. *Traumatology, 20*(3), 182.

Andersen, J. P., Papazoglou, K., Koskelainen, M., Nyman, M., Gustafsberg, H., & Arnetz, B. B. (2015). Applying resilience promotion training among special forces police officers. Sage Open, 5(2), https://doi.org/10.1177/2158244015590446.

Andersen, J. P., Papazoglou, K., Nyman, M., Koskelainen, M., & Gustafsberg, H. (2015). Fostering resilience among police. *Journal of Law Enforcement, 5*(1), 1–13.

Ben-Porath, Y. (2012). *Interpreting the MMPI-2-RF*. Minneapolis, MN: University of Minnesota Press.

Ben-Porath, Y. S., & Tellegen, A. (2008). *MMPI-2: Restructured form (MMPI-2-RF) manual for administration*. Minneapolis, MN: University of Minnesota Press.

Buck, J. N. (1948). The H-T-P test. *Journal of Clinical Psychology, 4*, 151–159.

Catanese, S. A. (2010). Traumatized by association: The risk of working sex crimes. *Federal Probation, 74*, 36.

Chan, J. (1997). *Changing police culture: Policing in a multicultural society*. Cambridge, MA: Cambridge University Press.

Chopko, B. A. (2010). Posttraumatic distress and growth: An empirical study of police officers. *American Journal of Psychotherapy, 64*(1), 55–72.

Committee on Professional Practice and Standards, & American Psychological Association. (2003). Legal issues in the professional practice of psychology. *Professional Psychology: Research and Practice, 34*(6), 595–600.

Corey, D. M., & Ben-Porath, Y. S. (2018). *Assessing police and other public safety personnel using the MMPI-2-RF*. Minneapolis, MN: University of Minnesota Press.

Dietrich, J. F., & Smith, J. (1986). The nonmedical use of drugs including alcohol among police personnel: A critical literature review. *Journal of Police Science Academy, 14*, 300–306.

Ely, R., & Meyerson, D. (2010). An organizational approach to undoing gender: The unlikely case of offshore oil platforms. *Research in Organizational Behavior, 30*, 3–34.

Figley, C.R. (1982). Traumatization and comfort: Close relationships may be hazardous to your health. Keynote presentation, Families and Close Relationships: Individuals in social interaction. Conference held at the Texas Tech University, Lubbock

Figley, C. R. (1995a). Compassion fatigue as secondary traumatic stress disorder: An overview. In C. R. Figley (Ed.), *Compassion fatigue: Coping with secondary traumatic stress disorder in those who treat the traumatized* (pp. 1–20). New York, NY: Brunner/Mazel.

Figley, C. R. (1995b). Compassion fatigue: Towards a new understanding of the costs of caring. In B. H. Stamm (Ed.), *Secondary traumatic stress: Self-care issues for clinicians, researchers, and educators* (pp. 3–27). Lutherville, MD: Sidran Press.

Figley, C. R., & Stamm, B. H. (1996). Psychometric review of compassion fatigue self-test. In B. H. Stamm (Ed.), *Measurement of stress, trauma and adaptation* (pp. 127–128). Lutherville, MD: Sidran Press.

Fischler, G. L. (2001). Psychological fitness-for-duty evaluations: Practical considerations for public safety department. *Illinois Law Enforcement Executive Forum, 1*, 77–92.

Follette, V. M., Polusny, M. M., & Milbeck, K. (1994). Mental health and law enforcement professionals: Trauma history, psychological symptoms, and impact of providing services to child sexual abuse survivors. *Professional Psychology, Research and Practice, 25*, 275–282.

Gough, H. G., & Bradley, P. (1996). *CPI manual* (3rd ed.). Mountain View, CA: CPP, Inc.

Hodgins, G., Creamer, M., & Bell, R. (2001). Risk factors for post-trauma reactions in police officers: A longitudinal study. *The Journal of Nervous and Mental Disease, 189*(8), 541–547.

International Association Chiefs of Police (2013). *Psychological fitness-for-duty evaluation guidelines*. Retrieved from https://www.theiacp.org/sites/default/files/2018-08/Psych-FitnessforDutyEvaluation0.pdf

International Association Chiefs of Police (2014). *Preemployment psychological evaluation guidelines*. Retrieved from https://www.theiacp.org/sites/default/files/all/p-r/Psych-PreemploymentPsychEval.pdf

Kingshott, B. F., Bailey, K., & Wolfe, S. E. (2004). Police culture, ethics, and entitlement theory. *Criminal Justice Study, 17*(2), 187–202.

Kirschman, E. (2017, September 5). *Pre-employment psychological screening for cops*. Retrieved from https://www.psychologytoday.com/us/blog/cop-doc/201709/pre-employment-psychological-screening-cops

Klein, R. (1989). Police peer counseling: Officers helping officers. *FBI Law Enforcement Bulletin, 58*(10), 1–4.

Kroes, W. H. (1985). *Society's victims – the police: An analysis of job stress in police* (2nd ed.). Springfield, IL: Charles C. Thomas.

Lerias, D., & Byrne, M. K. (2003). Vicarious traumatization: Symptoms and predictors. *Stress and Health: Journal of the International Society for the Investigation of Stress, 19*(3), 129–138.

Liberman, A. M., Best, S. R., Metzler, T. J., Fagan, J. A., Weiss, D. S., & Marmar, C. R. (2002). Routine occupational stress and psychological distress in police. *Policing: An International Journal of Police Strategies & Management, 25*(2), 421–441.

Lipsky, L. V. D. (2009). *Trauma stewardship: An everyday guide to caring for help while caring for others.* San Francisco, CA: Berrett-Koehler Publishers Inc.

MacEachern, A. D., Jindal-Snape, D., & Jackson, S. (2011). Child abuse investigation: Police officers and secondary traumatic stress. *International Journal of Occupational Safety and Ergonomics, 17*(4), 329–339.

Mahoney, M. J., & Granvold, D. K. (2005). Constructivism and psychotherapy. *World Psychiatry, 4*(2), 74.

Malcolm, A. S., Seaton, J., Perera, A., Sheehan, D. C., & Van Hasselt, V. B. (2005). Critical incident stress debriefing and law enforcement: An evaluative review. *Brief Treatment and Crisis Intervention, 5*(3), 261–278.

Mathieu, F. Running on Empty: Compassion Fatigue in Health Professionals. Rehab & Community Care Medicine, Spring 2007.

Miller, L. (2006). Critical incident stress debriefing for law enforcement: Practical models and special applications. *International Journal of Emergency Mental Health, 8*(3), 189–201.

Morey, L. C. (2007). *Personality assessment inventory professional manual* (2nd ed.). Lutz, FL: Psychological Assessment Resources.

Osofsky, J. D., Putnam, F. W., & Lederman, J. C. S. (2008). How to maintain emotional health when working with trauma. *Juvenile and Family Court Journal, 59*(4), 91–102.

Papazoglou, K. (2013). Conceptualizing police complex spiral trauma and its applications in the police field. *Traumatology, 19*(3), 196–209.

Papazoglou, K., & Andersen, J. P. (2014). A guide to utilizing police training as a tool to promote resilience and improve health outcomes among police officers. *Traumatology: An International Journal, 20*(2), 103.

Pearlman, L. A., & Saakvitne, K. W. (1995). *Trauma and the therapist: Countertransference and vicarious traumatization in psychotherapy with incest survivors.* London: W. W. Norton.

Prenzler, T. (1997). Is there a police culture? *Journal of Public Administration, 56*(4), 47–46.

Reiner, R. (2010). *The politics of the police* (4th ed.). Oxford: Oxford University Press.

Reiser, M., & Geiger, S. P. (1984). Police officer as victim. *Professional Psychological Practice, 15*, 315–323.

Richmond, R. L., Wodak, A., Kehoe, L., & Heather, N. (1998). How healthy are the police? A survey of life-style factors. *Addiction, 93*(11), 1729–1737.

Roberts, M. D., & Johnson, M. (2001). *CPI: Police and public safety selection report technical manual.* Los Gatos, CA: Law Enforcement Psychological Services.

Rostow, C., & Davis, R. (2004). *A handbook for psychological fitness-for-duty evaluations in law enforcement.* New York, NY: The Haworth Clinical Practice Press.

Schein, E. (2010). *Organizational culture and leadership* (4th ed.). San Francisco, CA: Jossey-Bass.

Schneider, K. J., Pierson, F., & Bugental, J. F. (Eds.). (2015). *The handbook of humanistic psychology: Theory, research, and practice* (2nd ed.). Thousand Oaks, CA: Sage.

Siegel, D. (2011). Attachment and mindfulness: Relational paths of the developing brain. In R. G. Lee & N. Harris (Eds.), *Relational child, relational brain: Development and therapy in childhood and adolescence.* Santa Cruz, CA: Gestalt Press.

Skolnick, J. H. (1966). *Justice without trial: Law enforcement in democratic society.* New York: Macmillan.

Steiner, C. (2017, January 24). *Ethics for psychologists: Pre-employment evaluations for police and public safety.* Retrieved from https://nationalpsychologist.com/2017/01/ethics-for-psychologists-pre-employment-evaluations-for-police-and-public-safety/103601.html

Stewart, S. H., Ouimette, P., & Brown, P. J. (2002). Gender and the comorbidity of PTSD with substance use disorders. In R. Kimerling, P. Ouimette, & J. Wolfe (Eds.), *Gender and PTSD* (pp. 232–270). New York, NY: The Guilford Press.

U.S. Equal employment opportunity commission. Title VII of the Civil Rights Act of 1964. Retrieved from https://www.eeoc.gov/statutes/titlevii.cfm

Van Raalte, R. (1978). Alcohol as a problem among officers. *Police Chief, 46,* 38–39.

Violanti, J., Marshall, J., & Howe, B. (1985). Stress, coping, and alcohol use: The police connection. *Journal of Police Science Administration, 13,* 106–110.

Westley, W. (1970). *Violence and the police: A sociological study of law, custom, and morality.* Cambridge, MA: MIT Press.

Wright, R., Powell, M. B., & Ridge, D. (2006). Child abuse investigation: An in-depth analysis of how police officers perceive and cope with daily work challenges. *Policing: An International Journal of Police Strategies & Management, 29*(3), 498–512.

# Chapter 13
# Trauma Assessment in Personal Injury and Employment Discrimination Cases

William E. Foote

## Legal Contexts

Traumatic events sometimes become the basis for civil litigation in the United States. These cases are decided in both state and federal courts and may be resolved through administrative systems that aim to avoid litigation (Foote & Lareau, 2013). This chapter focuses on how an examiner can assess PTSD in civil litigation settings and produce information for the court that addresses critical legal issues and assists the court in making decisions about compensation.

This chapter begins with a brief review of how trauma fits into the tort and civil rights legal systems. The focus then turns to an evaluation model designed to provide accurate and usable information for these legal systems. Through this model, this chapter explores issues of causation and legal damages.

### *Two Legal Venues for Trauma*

The American legal system encompasses almost every aspect of life in the United States, including wills and trusts, business agreements and contracts, and a myriad of other fundamentals of daily life. Two of these areas, tort and civil rights law, are venues in which cases involving trauma are most often heard (Foote & Goodman-Delahunty, 1999, 2005; Foote & Lareau, 2013; Goodman-Delahunty & Foote, 1995, 2009; Goodman-Delahunty & Foote, 2013a, 2013b; Kane & Dvoskin, 2011; Kane, Nelson, Dvoskin, & Pitt, 2013; Koch, Douglas, Nicholls, & O'Neill, 2006; Lareau, 2016).

W. E. Foote (✉)
University of New Mexico Department of Psychology, Albuquerque, NM, USA

© Springer Nature Switzerland AG 2020        297
R. A. Javier et al. (eds.), *Assessing Trauma in Forensic Contexts*,
https://doi.org/10.1007/978-3-030-33106-1_13

## Tort Cases

A tort is a method of resolving disputes in which a *plaintiff*, a party alleging injury, files suit against a *defendant*—a party that allegedly caused the injury. In contrast to a criminal act, a tort is a civil wrong that the legal system provides for compensation that is usually monetary. In this system, the plaintiff must prove that the defendant owed a duty to the plaintiff and that the defendant breached that duty in some way (see Foote & Lareau, 2013 for more detailed discussion). For example, a driver has a duty to exercise due care and would have breached that duty by exceeding the posted speed limit.

If the judge or jury (finders of fact) determine that the defendant has breached a legal duty, then two other elements come into play. The next thing the *plaintiff* must prove is a *causal connection* between the breach of duty and legally recognized *damages*. Say, the plaintiff was a passenger in an auto that was struck by a speeding vehicle and claims that she suffered post-traumatic stress disorder (PTSD) from the accident. A mental health professional was asked to determine if there was a diagnosable mental disorder and whether that disorder was caused by the auto accident. That is, the mental health professional was asked to provide the necessary legal element of *causation*.

Once causation is proven, the plaintiff must show that the injuries caused by the plaintiff result in *damages*, usually those that can be addressed through monetary compensation. As Foote and Lareau (2013) note, *damages* "refers to the amount of harm suffered by the plaintiff as a result of the defendant's actions and can include out of pocket costs, lost wages, future earnings, future costs, pain and suffering, loss of companionship and so forth" (Foote & Lareau, 2013, pg. 174).

## Civil Rights Cases

Although civil rights cases find their origin within the US Constitution, it was not until the Civil Rights Act of 1964 (Civil Rights Act of 1964) that the court provided a legal basis for relief in cases of discrimination because of race, color, religion, national origin, and sex (Lareau, 2016). Most of the elements of that landmark legislation focused on equal employment rights for these protected groups, but in the 1980s, the US Supreme Court provided a framework for determining sexual harassment and its impact on harassment targets (see Lareau, 2016).

Unlike tort law, civil rights law did not provide for either emotional damages or significant monetary awards in civil rights cases until the passage of the Civil Rights Act of 1991 (Civil Rights Act of 1991), which allowed plaintiffs to be awarded compensation for mental and emotional damages (Goodman-Delahunty & Foote, 2013a, 2013b). Within a few years, the US Supreme Court ruled on a sexual harassment case (*Harris v. Forklift Systems, Inc.,* 1993) and determined that psychological damages may exist in sexual harassment cases, but that such damages need not be present in order to demonstrate sexual harassment or a hostile work environment, and that the plaintiff need not show that her job performance suffered as a result of the harassment (Goodman-Delahunty & Foote, 2013a, 2013b; Lareau, 2016).

Under the Civil Rights Act of 1964 (Civil Rights Act of 1964) and the Americans with Disabilities Act (Americans with Disability Act of 1990) and other civil rights statutes, the Equal Employment Opportunity Commission (EEOC) was empowered to promulgate rules, regulations, and information concerning the implementation of these laws. In a recent discussion of psychological damages (Equal Employment Opportunity Commission, 2018), the EEOC indicated that the plaintiff in a civil rights lawsuit must prove both that the "claimant actually suffered the damages alleged and that the defendant's unlawful conduct caused the injuries" (Equal Employment Opportunity Commission, 2018, section D.3.a.1).

## *Legal Requirements*

This brief review of damages in both personal injury and civil rights cases provides a framework for the mental health expert's role in these cases. The job is twofold: determine whether the plaintiff has suffered emotional damages and then determine if the source of those damages were actions on the part of the defendant. The first tasks, determining the presence of a mental disorder and associated impairments, are common ones for mental health professionals. Psychologists and psychiatrists are often asked to conduct assessments of patients or clients to determine the nature and impact of their symptoms and to communicate findings to others through the diagnostic system such as the DSM-5 (American Psychiatric Association, 2013), and we have reasonable tools for this task.

The process of determining legal causation is different (Golizadeh & Malcarne, 2015). Mental health professionals recognize that a diagnosable emotional disorder is often a product of multiple factors including genetic predisposition, early childhood experiences and trauma, substance abusing parents, an upbringing marred by domestic violence, and many other influences.

Tort and civil rights law demand simpler explanations. The law recognizes that the events that prompted litigation need not be the only cause of an emotional harm. Pre-existing or subsequent events may in part produce the plaintiff's emotional pattern assessed by the mental health professional who is given the job of opining about the plaintiff's psychological damages.

To simplify the process, the law often applies the "but for" test. That is, "but for" the alleged tort or civil rights violation, the assessed damages would not have occurred, which considerably focuses the mental health professional's job. Tort and civil rights cases don't just demand that we determine the person's symptoms or problems but that we ascertain what caused the problem and rule out or explain other probable sources of causation.

In evaluating PTSD in tort and civil rights litigation, determining the nature and extent of damages and the causation of the emotional harms requires a systematic approach to assessment. Working with Jane Goodman-Delahunty, I developed a system for this kind of assessment of not only PTSD but other emotional disorders that may arise from tort (Goodman-Delahunty & Foote, 1995) and civil rights (Foote & Goodman-Delahunty, 2005; Goodman-Delahunty & Foote, 2013a, 2013b; Goodman-Delahunty, Saunders, & Foote, 2012; Goodman-Delahunty & Foote, 2011) cases. We call this the "five-stage model" (Goodman-Delahunty et al., 2012; Goodman-Delahunty & Foote, 2013a, 2013b).

For the balance of this chapter, I will use the framework of the five-stage model to explain how PTSD may be assessed in both tort and civil rights settings. As the legal requirements for both settings are quite similar, I will refer to both as simply "legal settings" and events that are the basis for litigation as legally relevant events (LREs). The five-stage model is designed to assist the mental health and legal professional to determine damages in legal settings by providing a sequence of steps for gathering and interpreting the sometimes-daunting quantity of information generated in a lawsuit.

The model begins by focusing on the period before the LREs occurred or the "day before" analysis. The second stage examines events during the interval within which the emotional damages occur. The third stage encompasses events in the interval between the LRE and when the assessment occurs. The fourth stage explicates the status of the plaintiff at the time of the assessment. The fifth stage provides an opportunity to discuss the future damages and treatment or other legally available remedies that emotional damages may require. The balance of the chapter will use this framework to discuss how PTSD assessment may be done to assist the legal system in arriving at a just outcome for both the plaintiff and defendant.

## PTSD in Stage 1

### *Impact of Plaintiff's History on Assessment*

Stage 1 of the five-stage model focuses upon the plaintiff's history before the event or events that constitute the basis for the legal action. Examination of this history is critical because things that happen to people over their life span, particularly during the vulnerable period of childhood, can later affect our assessment of those people to determine the impact of the LRE. There are four ways that this can affect the assessment of PTSD: some or all of the PTSD symptoms may be caused by events unrelated to the LRE; prior symptoms or problems may make the plaintiff more vulnerable to experience PTSD following exposure to a given stressor; a pre-existing emotional disorder may be exacerbated by the LRE; and, by eroding social support systems, the later PTSD may be more severe (Gleason, Iida, Shrout, & Bolger, 2008; Goodman-Delahunty & Foote, 2013a, 2013b; King, Taft, King, Hammond, & Stone, 2006).

## PTSD Symptoms Caused by Prior Events

Individuals who later experience PTSD Criterion A events often have histories that include serious adversities and trauma (Beitchman et al., 1992; Brewin, Andrews, & Valentine, 2000; Campbell, Greeson, Bybee, & Raja, 2008; Ehlers, Mayou, & Bryant, 1998; Kessler, Davis, & Kendler, 1997; Monson et al., 1996; Twaite & Rodriguez-Srednicki, 2004). These events produce symptoms that may be mistaken for LRE-generated PTSD symptoms or for comorbid symptoms that may be attributed to the LRE-generated PTSD. For example, a woman who was a victim of "date rape" sexual assault at age 15 was also involved in an auto accident at age 35. The childhood sexual assault generated PTSD symptoms of sufficient severity to warrant a PTSD diagnosis. The teen did not report the rape and never received treatment for that PTSD. Because of the lack of treatment, at the time of the assessment 20 years later, she still showed sufficient traumatic symptoms from that event to warrant a PTSD diagnosis. For the mental health professional, this poses a complicating diagnostic question: Are the PTSD symptoms generated by the 20-year prior rape similar to or distinct from PTSD symptoms produced by the current accident?

The answer is "perhaps." Research has determined that PTSD is a complex diagnosis with symptoms that have been shown to fall into various factorial clusters (Anthony, Lonigan, & Hecht, 1999; Kessler et al., 1997; King et al., 2009; McDonald et al., 2008; Wang et al., 2013; Yufik & Simms, 2010). Some of those symptoms are specific to the source of the trauma, such as intrusive recollections, nightmares, avoidant symptoms, and specific hypervigilance targets (Bowman, 1999; Brewin et al., 2000).

PTSD also includes more general symptoms that are not directly linked with the Criterion A stressor. In this regard, numbing symptoms, anhedonia, social avoidance, increases in irritability, and sleep disorders most likely could not be directly linked to the PTSD instigating events other than through temporal contiguity—the emergence of the symptoms after the traumatic events. This latter group of symptoms have considerable overlap with major depressive disorder and anxiety disorders such as generalized anxiety disorder and panic disorder (Arbona, Fan, & Noor, 2016; Armour et al., 2011; Roth et al., 2006).

If the plaintiff's symptoms are those with "footprints" to the trauma, then it is more straightforward for the examiner to determine that the PTSD symptoms from the earlier traumatic event do not represent sequelae of the current events. If the symptoms generated by the first trauma are more diffuse and overlap with more general symptoms that could be generated by the second trauma, then it would be more difficult for the examiner to determine if current diffuse symptoms are a consequence of the current trauma or represent chronic symptoms stemming from earlier traumatic events. The same logic applies to situations in which the plaintiff has a history of chronic depression or chronic anxiety disorder. Those symptoms could be confused with the diffuse symptoms arising from a LRE.

## Prior Events Create Vulnerability

Researchers have long recognized that a history of traumatic events makes it more likely that a person will later develop PTSD (Beitchman et al., 1992; Campbell et al., 2008; Dhaliwal, Gauzas, Antonowicz, & Ross, 1996; Follette, Polusny, Bechtle, & Naugle, 1996; Jumper, 1995; Lloyd & Turner, 2003; Mireault & Bond, 1992; Neumann, Houskamp, Pollock, & Briere, 1996; Paolucci, Genuis, & Violato, 2001; Polusny & Follette, 1995; Twaite & Rodriguez-Srednicki, 2004; Xue et al., 2015). There are several posited mechanisms for this relationship. The first is that the prior traumatic event, particularly child sexual abuse, has the impact of increasing the probability that the person will experience a later trauma, particularly sexual assault, domestic violence, or sexual harassment (Arata, 2000; Briere & Runtz, 1987; Dansky et al., 1996; Roesler & McKenzie, 1994). The mechanisms underlying this relationship are complex (see Foote & Goodman-Delahunty, 2005, for detailed discussion), but research supports the idea that people who experienced early trauma may be more attractive targets for interpersonal violence (Reed, Collinsworth, Lawson, & Fitzgerald, 2016). Considerable evidence indicates that PTSD symptoms from the earlier trauma may reduce self-protective behaviors or produce re-experiencing symptoms or dissociation that immobilize a potential victim of interpersonal violence or sexual harassment (Briere & Runtz, 1988; Twaite & Rodriguez-Srednicki, 2004).

This increased vulnerability plays out through the long-recognized "eggshell skull" principle in the law (Foote & Lareau, 2013; McQuade, 2001; Ruths, Christiansen, & Vincent, 2013) which says that the tortfeasor (the defendant) "takes the plaintiff as he finds him" (Canterbury v. Spence, 1972, p. 795). That is, even if the pre-existing vulnerability increases the impact of a given stressor, the defendant is still liable for the total damage experienced by the plaintiff (Junker, 2006; Levy & Rosenberg, 2003). This means that the examiner must have a thorough understanding of how this kind of vulnerability contributes to the overall pattern of symptoms and impairments. This is especially so since a common defense strategy is to attribute all the plaintiff's distress to the earlier trauma (Fitzgerald, Collinsworth, & Lawson, 2013; Reed et al., 2016).

## Pre-existing Disorder Is Exacerbated by Recent Trauma

The large literature on the comorbidity (co-occurrence) of mental disorders highlights how life events may worsen the symptoms of a disorder already experienced by a plaintiff (Kessler, Chiu, Dealer, & Walters, 2005; Kessler, Sonnega, Bromet, Hughes, et al., 1995; Roth et al., 2006). For example, a woman who has been treated for chronic depression for a number of years claims she was sexually harassed by her supervisor. Although there may be PTSD symptoms associated with this harassment (Fitzgerald et al., 2013), the most salient impact may be an increase in depressive symptoms such as a sleep disorder, anhedonia, fatigue, or suicidality.

**Eroding Social Support**

Researchers have long observed that the degree of social support provided by friends, family, coworkers, and the community is a critical variable in determining the long-term outcome for people with PTSD (Cohen & Wills, 1985; Kaniasty & Norris, 1993, 2008; Shallcross, Arbisi, Polusny, Kramer, & Erbes, 2016). However, research suggests that PTSD symptoms can erode social support (Lambert, Engh, Hasbun, & Holzer, 2012; Shallcross et al., 2016; Taft et al., 2009). This erosion occurs at multiple levels. PTSD survivors' intimate relationships may experience more conflict and aggression (Monson, Gradus, La Bash, Griffinb, & Resick, 2009; Taft, Watkins, Stafford, Street, & Monson, 2011). Depending on the level of impairment caused by the PTSD, the partners (especially females) may experience caregiver burden and secondary trauma (Lambert et al., 2012).

This negative impact on relationships places the prior PTSD survivor in a vulnerable position when the new Criterion A stressor impacts. The assessment of this social support erosion is obtained through the clinical interview of the plaintiff and collateral interviews of spouses and other family members.

## *Putting Stage 1 Together*

To determine the nature and extent of possible exacerbation of prior symptoms, it is critical to obtain a clear picture of the "day before" status of the plaintiff. A review of medical records particularly focusing on the provision of psychotropic medication is necessary. Additionally, accounts from co-workers, friends, and significant others can provide information about impairment of function caused by the pre-existing disorder. This baseline will allow the examiner to better assess whether the depressed symptoms observed at the time of the evaluation are unchanged or reflect an exacerbation caused by the LRE (Foote & Lareau, 2013; Goodman-Delahunty & Foote, 2013a, 2013b).

**Focus on Function**

At the completion of the Stage 1 "day before" analysis in PTSD cases, the examiner should have a clear idea of the status of the plaintiff at the time the LRE occurs. So far, we have focused on pre-existing disorders and how they play out in setting the stage for the LRE by providing competing hypotheses for symptoms observed following the trauma or by amplifying the impact of the LRE. However, even in assessing pre-existing or comorbid conditions, the examiner must also develop a clear picture of how well the plaintiff was functioning at the time of the LRE. In this regard, as Goodman-Delahunty and Foote (2013a) noted, impaired functioning and diagnosis should not be conflated. Individuals with the same diagnosis may have very different levels of functioning, depending upon the severity and specific impact of their symptoms. The examiner should have an understanding of the "day before" functioning of the plaintiff in four general areas: activities of daily living, work, relationships, and hedonics.

Activities of daily living (ADLs) are those things that people have to do every day in order to live their lives. From the simple tasks of bathing, food preparation, house cleaning, transportation by auto or public transit to the more complex tasks of paying bills, keeping a checkbook, or financial planning, ADLs are the bedrock of life. Impairments of ADL function can be disruptive and may require the assistance of others. The examiner can determine what level of ADL function the plaintiff had before the LRE through the clinical interview, collateral interviews, and reviews of the plaintiff's financial records (Foote, 2016).

The plaintiff's work life is an important focus for the "day before" analysis. As Foote and Goodman-Delahunty (2005) observed, an individual's work life not only allows for organization of time but provides income, social connections, and a source of identity. In addition, impairments of work function that result in decreased earning capacity translate into monetary damages in the form of lost future income, which can be the largest category of damages in a tort or civil rights case (Foote & Goodman-Delahunty, 2005). This means that the examiner should have a thorough understanding of the plaintiff's vocational history, vocational trajectory (whether job sequence showed increasing or decreasing responsibilities and income), job settings, and job duties at the time of the LRE. Remember that individuals who carry a diagnosis of PTSD, major depression, or generalized anxiety disorder may still function sufficiently to go to work every day and earn a living (Kessler & Frank, 1997; Koch & Samra, 2005; Wald, 2009; Wald & Taylor, 2009), so the evaluator may find it necessary to map out how specific pathology-related impairments affect specific tasks. A later section of this chapter will focus on how this can be done, but for the Stage 1 "day before" analysis, the examiner's job is to have a clear understanding of the work-related functions that the plaintiff could and did perform before the LRE.

Relationships with intimate partners, friends, co-workers, neighbors, and co-congregants in a church, synagogue, or mosque are an important area that requires examination in the "day before" analysis. This analysis should again focus on function. Relationships with household members are built on shared activities such as house work, yard maintenance, and other ADLs. Intimate relationships center around sexual functioning shared financial obligations, child-rearing, and similar activities.

*Hedonics* are activities like hobbies, sports, involvement in entertainment, and music that provide sources of enjoyment of life. Enjoying life requires a level of functioning as well. For example, if severe depression or PTSD avoidance symptoms cause a person to rarely leave the house, then hedonics will suffer. The examiner can inquire about the frequency of such activities, and reference to financial records can provide a metric of how much of the plaintiff's resources were committed to enjoyable activities. Loss of enjoyment of life can also be compensated monetarily.

At the end of Stage 1, the examiner should have a full grasp of how the plaintiff was functioning at the time the Criterion A LRE occurred. This knowledge sets the stage for an analysis of what the person experienced during the LRE.

## Stage 2: During the PTSD Criterion A Legally Related Events

Stage 2 focuses on what occurs during the event or events that constitute the DSM-5 Criterion A (American Psychiatric Association, 2013) stressor. In many tort cases involving single events like an auto accident, a "slip and fall" or medical malpractice, the duration of the PTSD generating event may be relatively short—a matter of minutes. In other tort cases and in most civil rights settings, Criterion A stressors may be events of long duration or may be based upon a series of events over days, weeks, months, or even years. For example, if a client was sexually exploited by her psychotherapist over 2 years, these events may generate PTSD symptoms. Fitzgerald and colleagues (Fitzgerald et al., 2013) have observed that although sexually harassing events may not appear to meet Criterion A in part because of multiple instances, targets of sexual harassment and those who endure hostile work environments still manifest significant PTSD symptoms.

Evaluators must be cautioned to avoid assuming that just because the plaintiff was exposed to a Criterion A stressor, PTSD would necessarily follow. In fact, most research suggests that only between 1.3% and 8.8% of people exposed to even extremely traumatic events develop PTSD (Atwoli, Stein, Koenen, & McLaughlin, 2015; Breslau et al., 1998; Kessler et al., 1995; Liu et al., 2017). In a recent and massive ($S = 34,676$) study, Liu et al. determined that some traumatic events are more productive of PTSD symptoms than others. Events that may produce massive dislocation and destruction such as natural disasters (0.2%), toxic chemical exposures (1.6%), and even auto accidents (2.1%) produce relatively low rates of PTSD. In contrast, events involving interpersonal violence such as being kidnapped (11%), witnessing atrocities (8.7%), being raped (17.4%), or being sexually assaulted (11%) generated higher rates of PTSD reactions. This research suggests that it is not just the severity of trauma inflicted by others, but the very fact that enmity is involved that increases the trauma target's emotional reaction (Giourou et al., 2018). Caution about assuming PTSD following an ostensibly traumatic event is tempered by the fact that individuals who report symptoms related to the most severe traumas in their lives report much higher rates of PTSD (Kessler et al., 1995) and that individuals who have more severe PTSD symptoms are also more likely to file lawsuits (Blanchard & Hickling, 2004).

### *Peritraumatic Reactions*

PTSD researchers have determined that what happens during traumatic events has a large impact upon whether PTSD symptoms develop and, if they do, how severe or enduring these symptoms will be (Atwoli et al., 2015; Bovin & Marx, 2011; Hetzel-Riggin & Roby, 2013; Liu et al., 2017; McCanlies, Sarkisian, Andrew, Burchfiel, & Violanti, 2017; Ozer, Best, Lipsey, & Weiss, 2003). Peritraumatic distress captures the fear, horror, dissociation, and other reactions that people have in the midst of terrifying events. In addition, other peritraumatic reactions, such as feeling frozen and unable to react (tonic immobility), occur with some individuals as their reaction to terrifying events (Bovin, Jager-Hyman, Gold, Marx, & Sloan, 2008; Hagenaars, 2016).

If one separates peritraumatic dissociation from other forms of peritraumatic distress, those who experience dissociation during traumatic events are more likely to develop PTSD and comorbid disorders, and those disorders are more likely to be both more severe and long-lasting (Birmes et al., 2003; McCanlies et al., 2017; Vance, Kovachy, Dong, & Bui, 2018). Also, those who are struck by tonic immobility by the traumatic event (about 17%) are more likely to develop PTSD, particularly in response to interpersonal violence (Hagenaars, 2016).

These findings mean that the examiner should query the plaintiff about what happened during the LRE. Because this detailed inquiry is likely to be upsetting to the plaintiff, the examiner should exercise clinical skill in this process, giving the plaintiff time to deal with upsetting experiences, but without acting like a therapist (see Greenberg & Shuman, 1997). This part of the interview will help determine whether peritraumatic distress, dissociation, or tonic immobility occurred. In addition, other sources of information can be helpful. Clinicians can conduct interviews with individuals who were witnesses to the traumatic events who may include fellow passengers in an auto crash or co-workers in a sexual harassment case. A review of police reports or medical notes from emergency personnel can also provide clues about the plaintiff's peritraumatic reactions.

This part of the evaluation will provide information about two legal issues. The first is of *causation*. The research indicates that people who experience peritraumatic distress are more likely to develop serious and disabling PTSD (Birmes et al., 2003; Carleton, Peluso, Abrams, & Asmundson, 2012; McCanlies et al., 2017; Twaite & Rodriguez-Srednicki, 2004). Although peritraumatic reactions are not always present, they can firm up lines of causation and help predict the trajectory of the PTSD (Birmes et al., 2003; McCanlies et al., 2017).

Second, because of the extreme acute symptoms that go along with peritraumatic distress and immobility, the legal issue of *pain and suffering* may be part of the picture. As noted earlier in this chapter, pain and suffering is a separate line item for damages in personal injury cases. These damages may be sought in cases in which the plaintiff has suffered no long-term disability because of the LRE. If the findings of the evaluation warrant, the examiner can help the jury or judge, who must determine whether monetary awards are appropriate, understand the nature and severity of peritraumatic reactions.

## Other Sources of Causation

In addition to attending to the particulars of traumatic events and reactions, the examiner must also attend to other sources of causation that are distinct from those related to the litigation. This is clearly more of an issue in situations in which the trauma occurs over a long period of time, such as recurrent physical assault, sexual harassment or assault, or hostile work environments (Goodman-Delahunty & Foote, 2013a, 2013b). These sources include family problems like domestic violence and marital distress that could be an independent source of PTSD. Family distress may also deprive the plaintiff of essential social support. Financial problems may produce increased anxiety that could masquerade as diffuse PTSD symptoms. More mundane work problems (nasty boss, too much work and not enough time, company bought out) may also be present and increase anxiety and stress symptoms.

In reviewing the events that occurred during the LRE, the examiner should be able to do several things. First, the examiner understands what the plaintiff experienced during the LRE and how the plaintiff reacted to those events. This will contribute to developing a line of causation and anticipating the nature and severity of post-traumatic reactions. Second, it should be possible for the examiner to determine a time line for critical events. This will allow for an understanding of when and how competing sources of causation could contribute to the analysis.

## Stage 3: What Happened in the Interval Between the LRE and the Evaluation

Most cases see a significant time span—often 2 or 3 years—between the occurrence of the LRE and the evaluation. The five-stage model asks the evaluator to attend to what happens during that interval. This attention focuses on three issues: PTSD symptom trajectory, treatment, and competing sources of stress.

### PTSD Symptom Trajectory

The first focus is on immediate post-traumatic symptoms and problems. This window of 3–6 months is critical for determining the trajectory of PTSD symptoms, as it is often within this interval that it is possible to discern the long-term course of the disorder. Several studies (Pietrzak et al., 2014; Sveen, Ekselius, Berdin, & Willebrand, 2011) have determined four different trajectories for PTSD symptoms. The first, labeled as "Resilient" (40%, Sveen et al., 2011) or "Resistant" (77% Pietrzak et al., 2014), begins with few PTSD symptoms of lower severity and continues at that low level over time. The second group is labeled "Delayed" (48%, Sveen et al., 2011) or "Delayed Onset" (8.5% Pietrzak et al., 2014) and begins with a relatively low level of severity and increases to a moderate level over time. The third group, labeled "Recovery" (10%, Sveen et al., 2011) or "Recovering" (8.5% Pietrzak et al., 2014), began with moderate-level symptoms that decreased over time, but never to the low level of the "Resilient" or "Resistant" group. The fourth group, "Chronic" (17%, Sveen et al., 2011) or "Severe Chronic" (5.3%, Pietrzak et al., 2014), initially had quite high levels of symptoms that stayed high over the course of the study.

The job of the examiner is to determine whether the symptoms or problems of the plaintiff follow any of these courses. This is critical, because the groups that never develop PTSD or show recovery within weeks or months following the LRE are unlikely to show long-term damages from the LRE (but may still experience pain and suffering), while the other two groups are likely to have more difficulties that would result in functional limitations and monetary damages. Those will be considered in Stage 4.

## *Treatment*

It is in the days or months following the LRE that the plaintiff may seek treatment for any reactions to the events focal to the lawsuit. From a legal perspective, the plaintiff has an affirmative duty to "mitigate damages." That is, "an injured party cannot recover for damages that he could have reduced or prevented by exercising reasonable care after sustaining his injury" (Kontorovich, 2001, p. 497).

Key to understanding mitigating damages is to grasp what "reasonable care" means in this setting. Legal scholars have defined "reasonable care" as "That degree of care which a person of ordinary prudence would exercise in the same or similar circumstances" (Black, 1991, p. 875). This emphasizes that the context in which the plaintiff lives is critical for determining whether the person's efforts are "reasonable." Although a number of financial, medical, psychological, social, and other considerations may render seeking care difficult, these three illustrate the barriers. First, even those who would desire or benefit from treatment may be so disabled by their psychological or medical symptoms that they cannot imagine leaving the hospital or house to see a therapist (Blanchard & Hickling, 2004). Others, particularly those in the "delayed onset" trajectory, may not believe that their symptoms are of sufficient severity as to warrant treatment (Blanchard & Hickling, 2004). A third group may understand that their therapist's file will be subpoenaed at some point during legal proceedings and do not want to sacrifice their privacy, particularly if their history contains events such as sexual abuse or criminal acts that would be a problem were they to become known to friends, co-workers, and family.

If the plaintiff seeks treatment, it is essential for the examiner to obtain those records and to, if possible, interview the therapists. These interviews are best done after the history has been taken from the plaintiff, and other records have been reviewed. Although those clients who self-pay in cash may avoid a diagnostic label, most record-keeping and reimbursement systems require that therapists provide a diagnosis for each patient or client. The examiner should note that these diagnoses are "working diagnoses" and do not have the same basis as a diagnosis that emerges at the end of a proper forensic mental health evaluation. The therapist's basis for diagnosis is usually what is learned from the plaintiff during sessions and may be incomplete, uncorroborated, and subject to the plaintiff's own biases (Shuman, Greenberg, Heilbrun & Foote, 1998). In contrast, the diagnosis and evaluation of the plaintiff by the forensic examiner in these cases is far more comprehensive and definitive (Shuman, Greenberg, Heilbrun, & Foote, 1998). However, the treatment notes may provide valuable information about the trajectory of the PTSD symptoms, impaired functioning, and the reaction of the plaintiff's social system to this disturbance.

## *Other Sources of Causation*

In the interval between the LRE(s) and the evaluation, other things may happen that could generate symptoms that could affect the evaluation. I delineated the four ways that could happen earlier in the chapter, so I will not recount them here, but only focus on possible sources of distress that could occur in the LRE-evaluation interval.

First, particularly in civil rights cases, the plaintiff may face reprisal or retaliation because of filing an EEOC complaint (a necessary step before filing a lawsuit) or the civil rights lawsuit itself (Foote & Goodman-Delahunty, 2005; Goodman-Delahunty and Foote, 2013a; Owens, Gomes, & Morgan, 2008; Rehg, Miceli, Near, & Van Scotter, 2008; Zimmerle, 2005). Retaliation takes many forms—from blatant firing based on pretexts to changes in work duties or time off. Understanding the impact of retaliation is critical not only because those acts can generate symptoms or problems within the PTSD diagnostic criteria but because these symptoms may be the basis for additional damages. Lareau (2016) noted that retaliation claims can be a basis for a civil rights award even when the jury determines that the underlying civil rights case lacks merit.

Second, PTSD and other symptoms may result in disruption of the plaintiff's intimate relationships (Monson et al., 2009; Taft et al., 2009) that are implicated in separation or divorce, with associated residential changes, financial losses, and disruption of family and friend relationships. These negative events may also occur without PTSD symptoms playing a part. It is the examiner's job to determine whether the symptoms were caused by the LRE and are therefore compensable.

Third, in almost every case, the plaintiff will have filed a lawsuit, and the events that occur as part of the litigation process come into play. Some writers have made much of what has been called "litigation stress," the sources of stress related to filing a suit and going through the interrogatories (sworn answers to questions posed by the defendants) and depositions (sworn testimony before a court reporter) that are integral to the civil litigation process (Binder & Rohling, 1996; Kane et al., 2013; Kane & Dvoskin, 2011; Lees-Haley, 1988; Streseman, 1995; Weissman, 1991). Some commentators (Binder & Rohling, 1996; Lees-Haley, 1988) argue that the stress of litigation accounts for many of the symptoms observed by examiners in plaintiff evaluations.

The best data (Blanchard & Hickling, 2004; Kane & Dvoskin, 2011) supports the notion that many aspects of litigation are stressful for plaintiffs who claim PTSD as a basis for their emotional damages. The most difficult parts are depositions, medical and psychological evaluations, and court testimony that require them to recount the traumatic event(s). This forced confrontation with traumatic events in the context of hard questions by disbelieving and unsympathetic lawyers or mental health professionals is itself likely to be traumatizing. Because of these concerns, the examiner should inquire about litigation-related events and their impact on the plaintiff's functioning.

Fourth, stuff happens. The plaintiff's car is struck in a traffic crash; the plaintiff's child is arrested for drug possession; the plaintiff's husband loses his job; a landslide carries away the plaintiff's home; or a myriad of other events that can cause emotional stress can and do occur in the LRE-evaluation interval. The examiner should ask about other sources of stress during this time and the plaintiff's reactions to those stressors.

At the end of the Stage 3 analysis, the examiner should have a clear understanding of the post-LRE trajectory of any PTSD symptoms and whether that pattern matches those identified in research. If the plaintiff sought treatment in in the post-LRE period, the examiner should know what treatment approaches were utilized and the impact of that treatment on not only the symptoms that the plaintiff may have suffered but on the functions that those symptoms may have impacted. If non-LRE stressors occurred during the interval, the examiner needs a clear picture of how those events may have affected both symptoms and function.

## Stage 4: The Evaluation Process and Its Findings

### The Assessment

#### The Interviews

Information related to the first three stages of this model is gathered from many sources, including medical, vocational, military, and mental health records. Much of the data also comes from the clinical interview with the plaintiff and collateral interviews with family members, co-workers, neighbors, clergy, and others who may have knowledge about the person's status before the LRE, during the LRE, and following those events (Heilbrun, Warren, & Picarello, 2003). All this information is critical for determining the plaintiff's status before the LRE so that a baseline for determining changes in function can be compared to the plaintiff's functioning at the time of the examination.

Since PTSD is a major issue in these cases, a formal assessment of PTSD symptoms should be used. The Clinician-Administered PTSD Scale for DSM-5 (CAPS-5) (Weathers et al., 2013) is a good structured interview for mapping the breadth, detail, and trajectory of PTSD symptoms. A self-report inventory allows for delineation of symptom patterns like the Detailed Assessment of Posttraumatic States (DAPS) (Briere, 2001) and can also be helpful.

**Testing**

Additional assessment should include well accepted personality assessment measures such as the Minnesota Multiphasic Personality Inventory-Second Edition (MMPI-2) (Greene, 2000), the Minnesota Multiphasic Personality Inventory Revised Form (MMPI-2-RF) (Arbisi, Sellbom, & Ben-Porath, 2008), and the Personality Assessment Inventory (PAI) (Morey, 2007). The MMPI-2 can be useful for assessments of plaintiffs who claim PTSD as emotional damages, but it has problems. One major issue is that researchers have not identified a single recognized PTSD profile for the MMPI-2. However, the measure can illuminate particular combinations of PTSD symptoms (Forbes et al., 2003). For example, a plaintiff who has a large number of hypervigilance symptoms may produce a profile with elevated PA and SI scales, while a person with predominant intrusive symptoms may have elevations on the D and PT scales. The most researched PTSD subscale on the MMPI-2, the PK scale (Keane, Malloy, & Fairbank, 1984), was specifically designed for veterans, but has not proved very useful in civilian settings (c.f., Scheibe, Bagby, Miller, & Dorian, 2001).

The revised form of the MMPI-2, the MMPI-2 RF, is sufficiently different from the MMPI-2 to merit consideration for use in lieu of that measure. Considerable research has been done with this measure (Ben-Porath, 2013; Mason et al., 2013; Sellbom, Lee, Ben-Porath, Arbisi, & Gervais, 2012), and it produces a more fine-grained picture of both PTSD symptoms and comorbidity Wolf et al, 2008. The MMPI-2 RF also has shown sensitivity to attempts at feigning and exaggeration (Crisanti, 2015; Sellbom, & Bagby, 2010; Marion et al., 2011; Sobhanian, 2015).

The PAI is a useful measure for assessing PTSD. Not only are the response style measures robust (Thomas, Hopwood, Orlando, Weathers, & McDevitt-Murphy, 2012; Wooley & Rogers, 2015), but the PAI contains items and subscales particularly related to PTSD (Morey, 2007).

The examiner may want to use measures of cognitive functioning such as the Wechsler Adult Intelligence Scale-Fourth Edition (WAIS-IV) (Wechsler, 2008). In cases in which the plaintiff reports problems in memory and concentration, cognitive measures can provide an objective metric of those functional impairments (Scott et al., 2014).

Evaluation of plaintiffs claiming PTSD damages requires the use of measures of response style to determine if the examinee is minimizing, exaggerating, or feigning symptoms (Young, 2017).

Once the record review, plaintiff interview, collateral interviews, and testing are done, it is time to put the data together to produce a report or testimony.

## *Determining Causation*

### Status on Day of Evaluation

The first task for the examiner is to discern if there is a line of causation between the LRE and the symptoms or problems identified in the evaluation. This begins by establishing the plaintiff's status on the day of the evaluation. The procedures the examiner has completed in Stage 4—the record review, interviews, and testing—establish a clear picture of the plaintiff's current emotional and functional status.

## Diagnosis

This process may include establishing a diagnosis for the client. However, there are four good reasons not to provide a diagnosis. First, establishing a diagnosis does not establish causation. Although PTSD is the only diagnosis that requires an event or events as a threshold for initiating the diagnostic process, the examiner is most often not in a position to determine if the LRE occurred as the plaintiff stated it (Bowman, 1999). Also, as discussed earlier in this chapter, emotional reactions similar to PTSD symptoms may arise from an unrelated pre-existing or comorbid disorder. If the examiner assumes that just because the emergence of a symptom after a traumatic event indicates that the traumatic event caused the symptom, the examiner may be engaging in a *post-hoc, propter hoc* (after this, therefore because of this) fallacy.

Second, diagnosis may provide a list of symptoms, but it does not allow for a determination of impairment of function. For example, two people may have evidence of nightmares that are listed as an intrusive PTSD symptom. However, one may have nightmares once a month and is able to return to sleep after the bad dreams. The other may have the nightmares four times a week and is unable to return to sleep, using alcohol to self-medicate for the problem. In this case, the latter person would have significantly more impairment from the same diagnosed PTSD.

Third, a failure to meet all the diagnostic criteria does not mean that the person is not impaired. Partial or subsyndromal PTSD is very common following Criterion A events and accounts for significant functional impairment (Schützwohl & Maercker, 1999; Stein, Walker, Hazen, & Forde, 1997; Varela, Ng, Mauch, & Recklitis, 2013). In the context of DSM-5 criteria, a large World Health Organization study (McLaughlin et al., 2015) showed that individuals who met the criteria for a full diagnosis of PTSD under the DSM-5 were more impaired than those who met the criteria for fewer symptoms. However, that partial PTSD group had significantly more functional impairment than those who neither met the criteria for full or partial PTSD.

Fourth, other actors in the tort or civil rights legal drama—the attorneys—are often more concerned about the presence or absence of a diagnosis than are mental health professionals (Foote & Lareau, 2013), desiring to convince judges or juries either that the diagnosis must exist in order for emotional damages to be present or that the presence of the diagnosis automatically means that the plaintiff is scarred for life. Given our understanding that neither of those perspectives is likely to account for the data, the examining expert is left with the necessity to explain to the court why diagnosis does not matter as much as the lawyers want it to. This explanation can include reference to the four points noted earlier, and the examiner can then hone in on the other issues related to causation.

## Determining Causation

So, if diagnosis alone does not establish diagnosis, and if the emergence of symptoms following a Criterion A event does not clearly establish causation, how does one go about determining causation sufficiently to meet legal standards?

Recall that in tort settings, the standard is that "but for" the LRE, the symptoms or problems would not have occurred. This means that the examiner must account for other sources of causation, which has been part of the process from the beginning of the five-stage procedure. Through this process, competing hypotheses for the causation of symptoms should be examined to determine to what extent, if any, those sources account for the symptoms assessed at Stage 4.

This process begins with the analysis of comorbid conditions. Considerable research indicates that between half and two-thirds of people with full PTSD diagnoses also meet the criteria for one or more other diagnoses (Angelakis & Nixon, 2015; Brunello et al., 2001; Debell et al., 2014; Kessler, Sonnega, & Nelson, 1995; Lockwood & Forbes, 2014; McMillan & Asmundson, 2016; Spinhoven, Penninx, van Hemert, de Rooij, & Elzinga, 2014; Young, Lareau, & Pierre, 2014). These disorders may pre-exist the LRE, may be produced by the LRE, or may emerge as a response or consequence of the PTSD. Whatever the source, the examiner must account for comorbid conditions. If the comorbid symptoms did pre-exist the LRE, then any exacerbation of those symptoms may add to the damages in the case. If the comorbid condition arose either independently in reaction to the LRE or as a result of the LRE caused PTSD, then the comorbid condition may contribute to the damages.

Three other clues to causation are present in PTSD cases. First, although the examiner must avoid *post hoc propter hoc* assumptions, the sudden emergence of PTSD symptoms following the LRE is a good clue that the PTSD was caused by the LRE (McFarlane, 2010). Of course, the examiner must determine if other PTSD generating events were proximal to the LRE to eliminate them as contenders, but the temporal contiguity adds to the examiner's conclusions about causation.

Second, as noted earlier in this chapter, focal PTSD symptoms are uniquely related to the Criterion A stressor and provider "footprints" back to that stressor. The content of intrusive recollections and nightmares, the people, places, and situations that the plaintiff avoids should be related to the LRE. This connection not only provides for substantive clues to causation but allows the judge or jury to see this integral connection.

Third, PTSD symptoms have identifiable trajectories. As noted earlier in this chapter, the pattern of symptom emergence and recovery should follow a "High Chronic," "Recovering," or "Delayed" pattern. That pattern should emerge during the Stage 3 interval between the LRE and the Stage 4 evaluation. Examiners should note that even in the "Delayed" scenario, a subsyndromal pattern should be evident, because what is delayed may be the ability of a mental health professional to diagnose the full PTSD picture. Also, the "Delayed" condition may exhibit significant comorbidity, particularly substance abuse disorders, which provide some degree of self-medication during the interval in which the full PTSD pattern is not evident (Andrews, Brewin, Philpott, & Stewart, 2007; Brewin et al., 2000; McFarlane, 2010).

At the end of the causation analysis, the examiner should be able to determine if there is a causal relationship between the LRE and the observed PTSD symptoms. The next step is to determine the impact of those symptoms.

## Determining Impaired Functions

### Defining Disability

The five-stage model focuses on function through all the stages, because it is the changes in or loss of function that constitute the bulk of monetary damages in tort and civil rights cases. This is a sequential process. By this point in the analysis, the examiner has established the presence of symptoms that have been causally related to the LRE.

However, the existence of symptoms alone does not establish loss or reduction of function (Foote, 2016), but must result in an impairment, which "...constitutes an observational description that should be measurable in some way and related to a health condition" (Gold, 2013, p. 7). Disability is impairment in context. That is, a reduction in function may constitute a disability in some contexts, but not in others. Say, a plaintiff claiming PTSD may have severe agoraphobic symptoms. If that plaintiff worked as a trial attorney, disability related to the symptoms would be significant. If the plaintiff worked as a computer programmer in her own home, the disability would be significantly less.

Some impairments are more significant than others. Impaired ADLs almost always produce disability because ADLs are so fundamental to daily life (Foote, 2016). Impairments that produce disability in work-related functions are important in plaintiff evaluations because loss of work-related abilities results in lost wages, which may account for significant dollar amounts, especially when accrued over time. Impairments that produce disability in hedonic functions are also an important line item for monetary compensation, since loss of enjoyment of life is compensable in most tort contexts.

As discussed earlier in this chapter, PTSD can also produce impairments of social functioning (Brunello et al., 2001; McMIllan & Asmundson, 2016) by way of social isolation and avoidance symptoms that are integral to the disorder. These impairments play out in disrupted intimate relationships and other social functioning (Kessler et al., 1995). In addition, because substance abuse disorders are commonly comorbid with PTSD, the social impact may be multiplied (Debell et al., 2014).

PTSD has been shown to produce significant work-related disability in the form of increased sick days, reduced work performance, and failure to return to work after trauma exposure (Koch et al., 2006; Koch & Samra, 2005; Wald & Taylor, 2009). This disability also extends to workers with partial PTSD (Breslau, Lucia, & Davis, 2004). The severity of these symptoms is directly correlated with the degree of disability, with re-experiencing and hyperarousal symptoms, particularly insomnia, irritability, and concentration problems, producing the greatest degree of disability (Taylor, Wald, & Asmundson, 2006).

Some researchers have identified predictors of disability in individuals with PTSD (Koch & Samara 2005). An inability to function socially with co-workers, supervisors, customers, or the public, characterized by high levels of suspiciousness, hostility, and isolation, contributes to work-related disability. In addition, avoidance and fear-related symptoms may impair the worker's ability to even get to the workplace. Because many workplaces contain their own stresses related to, for example, workload, supervisors' behavior, or co-worker's actions, the reduced stress resilience secondary to PTSD may result in increased sick days, absenteeism, and "presenteeism," when the worker shows up for work, but underperforms the job.

The next step in this Stage 4 process is to translate these reduced functional capacities into concrete losses. When the examiner generates a developed understanding of the plaintiff's disability and places it in the context of the plaintiff's work history, the disability becomes more relevant. Say that the plaintiff had always worked in situations involving high-level social skills, such as sales work. The Stage 2 day before assessment yields evidence that she was doing well on the job as an office manager, in her marriage, in her relationships with friends, and in her ability to enjoy bowling and bridge. After the auto she was driving was struck by another vehicle, she developed PTSD, which was fully evident 1.5 years after the accident. Her main impairments were in social functioning, with strong social withdrawal, impaired connections with others, and agoraphobia, which restricted her to her home. In this case, the fully developed context from Stage 1 allows the examiner to establish the presence of symptoms, determine the impairments that those symptoms produced, and then place those impairments within her life space, which produces a clear picture of loss of function and disability that can be translated into lost wages by an economist.

Stage 4 is when the examiner also assesses changes in the plaintiff's quality of life, the hedonics. By looking at changed activities, particularly those involving sports, hobbies, or social relationships, the examiner can explicate which of those activities have diminished in frequency, duration, or the subjective pleasure derived therefrom. A review of the plaintiff's financial records may reveal reduced trips to the movies, fewer vacations, or camping trips.

Remember that Stage 4 should also capture transitory phenomena. For example, if the plaintiff does develop a diagnosable PTSD in the days or weeks after the LRE but seeks treatment and is largely functional by the time of the evaluation, the examiner may still be in a position to document the compensable "pain and suffering" that the plaintiff experienced during that interval.

## Stage 5: Projecting Damages into the Future

In both tort and civil rights cases, the legal system may ask the examiner to look at future expenses and damages. Even if the plaintiff has been in treatment for PTSD, it may be the case that future treatment is necessary. The examiner can provide testimony on this issue by looking at the status of the plaintiff as determined through the Stage 4 assessment to opine about what treatment is necessary to "make whole" the plaintiff. While this may be an unrealistic goal, the examiner can provide recommendations for effective treatment and a time frame in which that treatment may be accomplished. The examiner can also use this occasion to suggest to what extent the plaintiff will recover from the PTSD caused by the LRE. It may be the case that some symptoms (hypervigilance, nightmares, some avoidances) will remain even after treatment, but therapy will provide ways for the plaintiff to manage those symptoms to reduce functional impairment.

The examiner may also make recommendations about changes in the plaintiff's situation that would result in better outcomes. For example, it may be that the plaintiff suffers anxiety on an almost daily basis because his workplace contains "triggers" for his intrusive recollections and avoidance symptoms. The examiner may recommend a change in job location or employer that would address this problem.

# Conclusion

The five-stage model is an efficient tool for gathering and interpreting information related to PTSD in the context of personal injury and civil rights cases. Using this methodology, the examiner can obtain the records and conduct the interviews and testing necessary for determining emotional damages and what caused them. Paying attention to comorbidity and other possible sources of emotional distress can allow for a diagnostic process that allows not only for a delineation of PTSD symptoms but for an explication of the functional limitations that result from those symptoms. The process is a good model for report writing and testimony and allows for well-founded damages assessment and treatment recommendations. The overall goal is to provide information that is useful to the judge or jury in making more informed and just decisions in the context of civil rights and tort cases.

# Questions/Activities for Further Exploration

1. What is the difference between *causation* as defined by civil law and causation as defined by mental health professionals? What potential conflicts or confusions could this difference produce?
2. If a person had a traumatic experience 10 years ago and then had another traumatic experience recently, would a mental health professional conducting a current evaluation expect the same symptoms from both experiences? Would the assessment yield a diagnosis of PTSD or more than one PTSDs? How might those symptoms differ?
3. The five-stage model described in this chapter is designed to allow an examining mental health professional to develop a solid foundation for testimony. What weakness or omissions do you see in this system? What could be done to solve those problems?

4. Although the five-stage model is designed to assist in conducting, reporting, and testifying about tort and civil rights cases, how could you apply the same method to assessing PTSD in criminal settings? How would the method be modified to reflect the differing legal and factual setting?
5. Trauma makes news and the stories of the victims of trauma find their way into the public eye via such avenues as news stories, blogs, podcasts, social media postings, and fiction. Find a story that has some detail, and with the five-stage model in mind, apply the system to determine the degree of compensable damages the person would have suffered as a result of the events. In the story, are there competing sources that could have resulted in functional disabilities?

# References

American Psychiatric Association. (2013). *Diagnostic and statistical manual of mental disorders* (5th ed.). Arlington, VA: American Psychiatric Publishing.

Americans with Disabilities Act of 1990, 42 U.S.C.A. §12101 *et seq.* (West 1993)

Andrews, B., Brewin, C. R., Philpott, R., & Stewart, L. (2007). Delayed-onset posttraumatic stress disorder: A systematic review of the evidence. *The American Journal of Psychiatry, 164*(9), 1319–1326. https://doi.org/10.1176/appi.ajp.2007.06091491

Angelakis, S., & Nixon, R. D. V. (2015). The comorbidity of PTSD and MDD: Implications for clinical practice and future research. *Behaviour Change, 32*(1), 1–25. https://doi.org/10.1017/bec.2014.26

Anthony, J. L., Lonigan, C. J., & Hecht, S. A. (1999). Dimensionality of posttraumatic stress disorder symptoms in children exposed to disaster: Results from confirmatory factor analyses. *Journal of Abnormal Psychology, 108*(2), 326–336. https://doi.org/10.1037/0021-843X.108.2.326

Arata, C. M. (2000). From child victim to adult victim: A model for predicting sexual revictimization. *Child Maltreatment: Journal of the American Professional Society on the Abuse of Children, 5*(1), 28–38.

Arbisi, P. A., Sellbom, M., & Ben-Porath, Y. S. (2008). Empirical correlates of the MMPI-2 Restructured Clinical (RC) scales in psychiatric inpatients. *Journal of Personality Assessment, 90,* 122–128.

Arbona, C., Fan, W., & Noor, N. (2016). Factor structure and external correlates of posttraumatic stress disorder symptoms among African American firefighters. *Psychology Research and Behavior Management, 9,* 201–209. https://doi.org/10.2147/PRBM.S113615

Armour, C., Layne, C. M., Naifeh, J. A., Shevlin, M., Duraković-Belko, E., Djapo, N., … Elhai, J. D. (2011). Assessing the factor structure of posttraumatic stress disorder symptoms in war-exposed youths with and without criterion A2 endorsement. *Journal of Anxiety Disorders, 25*(1), 80–87. https://doi.org/10.1016/j.janxdis.2010.08.006

Atwoli, L., Stein, D. J., Koenen, K. C., & McLaughlin, K. A. (2015). Epidemiology of posttraumatic stress disorder: Prevalence, correlates and consequences. *Current Opinion in Psychiatry, 28*(4), 307–311. https://doi.org/10.1097/YCO.0000000000000167

Beitchman, J. H., Zucker, K. J., Hood, J. E., daCosta, G. A., Akman, D., & Cassavia, E. (1992). A review of the long-term effects of child sexual abuse. *Child Abuse & Neglect, 16*(1), 101–118.

Ben-Porath, Y. S. (2013). Forensic applications of the Minnesota Multiphasic Personality Inventory-2-Restructured Form. In R. P. Archer & E. M. A. Wheeler (Eds.), *Forensic uses of clinical assessment instruments* (pp. 63–107). New York, NY: Routledge/Taylor & Francis Group.

Binder, L., & Rohling, M. L. (1996). Money matters: A meta-analytic review of the effects of financial incentives on recovery after closed-head injury. *American Journal of Psychiatry, 153,* 7–10.

Briere, J., & Runtz, M. (1988). Symptomatology associated with childhood sexual victimization in a nonclinical adult sample. *Child Abuse & Neglect, 12,* 51–59.

Birmes, P., Brunet, A., Carreras, D., Ducassé, J.-L., Charlet, J.-P., Lauque, D., … Schmitt, L. (2003). The predictive power of peritraumatic dissociation and acute stress symptoms for posttraumatic stress symptoms: A three-month prospective study. *The American Journal of Psychiatry, 160*(7), 1337–1339. https://doi.org/10.1176/appi.ajp.160.7.1337

Black, H. C. (1991). *Black's law dictionary.* St. Paul, MN: West Publishing Company.

Blanchard, E. B., & Hickling, E. J. (2004). *After the crash: Assessment and treatment of motor vehicle accident survivors* (2nd ed.). Washington, D.C.: American Psychological Association.

Bovin, M. J., Jager-Hyman, S., Gold, S. D., Marx, B. P., & Sloan, D. M. (2008). Tonic immobility mediates the influence of peritraumatic fear and perceived inescapability on posttraumatic stress symptom severity among sexual assault survivors. *Journal of Traumatic Stress, 21*(4), 402–409. https://doi.org/10.1002/jts.20354

Bovin, M. J., & Marx, B. P. (2011). The importance of the peritraumatic experience in defining traumatic stress. *Psychological Bulletin, 137*(1), 47–67. https://doi.org/10.1037/a0021353

Bowman, M. L. (1999). Individual differences in posttraumatic distress: Problems with the DSM-IV model. *The Canadian Journal of Psychiatry/La Revue canadienne de psychiatrie, 44*(1), 21–33.

Breslau, N., Kessler, R. C., Chilcoat, H. D., Schultz, L. R., Davis, G. C., & Andreski, P. (1998). Trauma and posttraumatic stress disorder in the community: The 1996 Detroit Area Survey of Trauma. *Archives of General Psychiatry, 55*(7), 626–632. http://dx.doi.org/10.1001/archpsyc.55.7.626

Breslau, N., Lucia, V. C., & Davis, G. C. (2004). Partial PTSD versus full PTSD: An empirical examination of associated impairment. *Psychological Medicine, 34*(7), 1205–1214. https://doi.org/10.1017/S0033291704002594

Brewin, C. R., Andrews, B., & Valentine, J. D. (2000). Meta-analysis of risk factors for posttraumatic stress disorder in trauma-exposed adults. *Journal of Consulting and Clinical Psychology, 68*(5), 748–766. https://doi.org/10.1037/0022-006X.68.5.748

Briere, J. (2001). *Detailed assessment of posttraumatic stress (DAPS).* Odessa, FL: Psychological Assessment Resources.

Briere, J., & Runtz, M. (1987). Post sexual abuse trauma: Data and implications for clinical practice. *Journal of Interpersonal Violence, 2,* 367–379.

Brunello, N., Davidson, J. R. T., Deahl, M., Kessler, R. C., Mendlewicz, J., Racagni, G., … Zohar, J. (2001). Posttraumatic stress disorder: Diagnosis and epidemiology, comorbidity and social consequences, biology and treatment. *Neuropsychobiology, 43*(3), 150–162. https://doi.org/10.1159/000054884

Campbell, R., Greeson, M. R., Bybee, D., & Raja, S. (2008). The co-occurrence of childhood sexual abuse, adult sexual assault, intimate partner violence, and sexual harassment: A mediational model of posttraumatic stress disorder and physical health outcomes. *Journal of Consulting and Clinical Psychology, 76*(2), 194–207. https://doi.org/10.1037/0022-006X.76.2.194

Canterbury v. Spence, 464 F 2d 772 (D.C. Cir. 1972).

Carleton, R. N., Peluso, D. L., Abrams, M. P., & Asmundson, G. J. G. (2012). Absorption, dissociation, and posttraumatic stress: Differential associations among constructs and symptom clusters. *Sleep and Hypnosis, 14*(1–2), 1–12.

Civil Rights Act of 1964, 42 U.S.C. §2000e *et seq.,* as amended (1964) Civil Rights Act of 1964, 42 U.S.C. Sections 2000e et seq., as amended. (1964).

Civil Rights Act of 1991, Pub. L. No. 102–106, §106. (1991).

Cohen, S., & Wills, T. A. (1985). Stress, social support, and the buffering hypothesis. *Psychological Bulletin, 98*(2), 310–357. https://doi.org/10.1037/0033-2909.98.2.310

Crisanti, L. (2015). The ability of the MMPI-2-Rf validity scales to detect feigning of cognitive and posttraumatic stress disorder (ptsd) symptoms. *Dissertation Abstracts International: Section B: The Sciences and Engineering, 75*(11-B(E)).

Dansky, B. S., Brady, K. T., Saladin, M. E., Killeen, T., Becker, S., & Roitzsch, J. (1996). Victimization and PTSD in individuals with substance use disorders: Gender and racial differences. *American Journal of Drug and Alcohol Abuse, 22*(1), 75–93.

Debell, F., Fear, N. T., Head, M., Batt-Rawden, S., Greenberg, N., Wessely, S., & Goodwin, L. (2014). A systematic review of the comorbidity between PTSD and alcohol misuse. *Social Psychiatry and Psychiatric Epidemiology, 49*(9), 1401–1425. https://doi.org/10.1007/s00127-014-0855-7

Dhaliwal, G. K., Gauzas, L., Antonowicz, D. H., & Ross, R. R. (1996). Adult male survivors of childhood sexual abuse: Prevalence, sexual abuse characteristics, and long-term effects. *Clinical Psychology Review, 16*(7), 619–639.

Ehlers, A., Mayou, R. A., & Bryant, B. (1998). Psychological predictors of chronic posttraumatic stress disorder after motor vehicle accidents. *Journal of Abnormal Psychology, 107*(3), 508–519. https://doi.org/10.1037/0021-843X.107.3.5082

Equal Employment Opportunity Commission. (2018, June 18). Nonpecuniary compensatory damages: Issues for review with claimants prior to filing suit. Found at https://www.eeoc.gov/eeoc/litigation/manual/2-2-d_nonpecuniary-comps.cfm

Fitzgerald, L. F., Collinsworth, L. L., & Lawson, A. K. (2013). Sexual harassment, PTSD, and Criterion A: If it walks like a duck…. *Psychological Injury and Law, 6*(2), 81–91. https://doi.org/10.1007/s12207-013-9149-8

Follette, V. M., Polusny, M. A., Bechtle, A., & Naugle, A. (1996). Cumulative trauma: Impact of child sexual abuse, sexual assault, and spouse abuse. *Journal of Traumatic Stress, 9*, 25–35.

Foote, W. E. (2016). Evaluations of individuals for disability in insurance and social security contexts. In R. Jackson & R. Roesch (Eds.), *International perspectives on forensic mental health. Learning forensic assessment: Research and practice* (pp. 413–433). Routledge/Taylor & Francis Group: New York, NY.

Foote, W. E., & Goodman-Delahunty, J. (1999). Same-sex harassment: Implications of the Oncale decision for forensic evaluation of plaintiffs. *Behavioral Sciences & the Law, 17*(1), 123–139. https://doi.org/10.1002/(SICI)1099-798(199901/03)17:1<123::AID-BSL334>3.0.CO;2-

Foote, W. E., & Goodman-Delahunty, J. (2005). *Evaluating sexual harassment: Psychological, social, and legal considerations in forensic examinations.* Washington, D.C.: American Psychological Association. https://doi.org/10.1037/10827-000

Foote, W. E., & Lareau, C. R. (2013). Psychological evaluation of emotional damages in tort cases. In R. K. Otto & I. B. Weiner (Eds.), *Handbook of psychology: Forensic psychology* (pp. 172–200). Hoboken, NJ: Wiley.

Forbes, D., Creamer, M., Allen, N., Elliott, P., McHugh, T., Debenham, P., & Hopwood, M. (2003). MMPI-2 based subgroups of veterans with combat-related PTSD: Differential patterns of symptom change after treatment. *Journal of Nervous and Mental Disease, 191*(8), 531–537. https://doi.org/10.1097/01.nmd.0000082181.79051.83

Giourou, E., Skokou, M., Andrew, S. P., Alexopoulou, K., Gourzis, P., & Jelastopulu, E. (2018). Complex posttraumatic stress disorder: The need to consolidate a distinct clinical syndrome or to reevaluate features of psychiatric disorders following interpersonal trauma? *World Journal of Psychiatry, 8*(1), 12–19.

Gleason, M. E. J., Iida, M., Shrout, P. E., & Bolger, N. (2008). Receiving support as a mixed blessing: Evidence for dual effects of support on psychological outcomes. *Journal of Personality and Social Psychology, 94*(5), 824–838. https://doi.org/10.1037/0022-3514.94.5.824

Gold, L. H. (2013). Mental health disability: A model for assessment. In L. H. Gold & D. L. Vanderpool (Eds.), *Clinical guide to mental disability evaluations* (pp. 3–35). New York, NY: Springer.

Golizadeh, S., & Malcarne, V. L. (2015). Professional and ethical challenges in determinations of causality of psychological disability. *Psychological Injury and Law, 8*, 334–347. https://doi.org/10.1007/s12207-015-9237-z

Goodman-Delahunty, J., & Foote, W. E. (1995). Compensation for pain, suffering, and other psychological injuries: The impact of Daubert on employment discrimination claims. *Behavioral Sciences & the Law, 13*(2), 183–206. https://doi.org/10.1002/bsl.2370130204

Goodman-Delahunty, J., & Foote, W. E. (2009). Forensic evaluations advance scientific theory: Assessing causation of harm. *Pragmatic Case Studies in Psychotherapy, 5*(3), 38–52. https://doi.org/10.14713/pcsp.v5i3.975

Goodman-Delahunty, J., & Foote, W. E. (2011). *Workplace discrimination and harassment*. London, UK: Oxford Press.

Goodman-Delahunty, J., & Foote, W. E. (2013a). Evaluation for harassment and discrimination claims. In R. Roesch & P. A. Zapf (Eds.), *Best practices in forensic mental health assessment. Forensic assessments in criminal and civil law: A handbook for lawyers* (pp. 175–190). New York, NY: Oxford University.

Goodman-Delahunty, J., & Foote, W. E. (2013b). Using a five-stage model to evaluate workplace discrimination injuries. *Psychological Injury and Law, 6*(2), 92–98. https://doi.org/10.1007/s12207-013-9154-y

Goodman-Delahunty, J., Saunders, P., & Foote, W. (2012). Evaluating claims for Workplace Discrimination: A five-stage model. In *Proceedings of the 2011 APS Forensic Psychology Conference*. Sydney, NSW: The Australian Psychological Society Ltd (APS).

Greenberg, S. A., & Shuman, D. W. (1997). Irreconcilable conflict between therapeutic and forensic roles. *Professional Psychology: Research & Practice, 28*(1), 50–57.

Greene, R. L. (2000). *The MMPI-2: An interpretive manual* (2nd ed.). Needham Heights, MA: Allyn & Bacon.

Hagenaars, M. (2016). Tonic immobility and PTSD in a large community sample. *Journal of Experimental Psychopathology, 7*(2), 246–260. https://doi.org/10.5127/jep.051915

Harris, v Forklift Systems, Inc., 510 U.S. 17. (1993).

Heilbrun, K., Warren, J., & Picarello, K. (2003). Third party information in forensic assessment. In A. M. Goldstein (Ed.), *Handbook of psychology: Forensic psychology* (Vol. 11, pp. 69–86). Hoboken, NJ: Wiley.

Hetzel-Riggin, M. D., & Roby, R. P. (2013). Trauma type and gender effects on PTSD, general distress, and peritraumatic dissociation. *Journal of Loss and Trauma, 18*(1), 41–53. http://dx.doi.org/10.1080/15325024.2012.679119

Jumper, S. A. (1995). A meta-analysis of the relationship of child sexual abuse to adult psychological adjustment. *Child Abuse & Neglect, 19*(6), 715–728.

Junker, T. C. (2006). Did the supreme court of Virginia really hold that the "eggshell skull rule" extends to an "eggshell psyche", in its recent decision in *Kondauro v, Kerdasha*? Litigation News, *13*(3), 1–8.

Kane, A. W., & Dvoskin, J. A. (2011). *Best practices in forensic mental health assessment. Evaluation for personal injury claims*. New York, NY: Oxford University Press. https://doi.org/10.1093/med:psych/9780195326079.001.0001

Kane, A. W., Nelson, E. M., Dvoskin, J. A., & Pitt, S. E. (2013). Evaluation for personal injury claims. In R. Roesch & P. A. Zapf (Eds.), *Best practices in forensic mental health assessment. Forensic assessments in criminal and civil law: A handbook for lawyers* (pp. 148–160). New York, NY: Oxford University Pres.

Kaniasty, K., & Norris, F. H. (1993). A test of the social support deterioration model in the context of natural disaster. *Journal of Personality and Social Psychology, 64*(3), 395–408. https://doi.org/10.1037/0022-3514.64.3.395

Kaniasty, K., & Norris, F. H. (2008). Longitudinal linkages between perceived social support and posttraumatic stress symptoms: Sequential roles of social causation and social selection. *Journal of Traumatic Stress, 21*(3), 274–281. https://doi.org/10.1002/jts.20334

Keane, T. M., Malloy, P. F., & Fairbank, J. A. (1984). Empirical development of an MMPI subscale for the assessment of combat-related posttraumatic stress disorder. *Journal of Consulting and Clinical Psychology, 52*(5), 888–891.

Kessler, R. C., Chiu, W. T., Dealer, O., & Walters, E. E. (2005). Prevalence, severity, and comorbidity of 12-month DSM-IV disorders in the National Comorbidity Survey Replication. *Archives of General Psychiatry, 62*(6), 617–627.

Kessler, R. C., Davis, C. G., & Kendler, K. S. (1997). Childhood adversity and adult psychiatric disorder in the US National Comorbidity Survey. *Psychological Medicine, 27*(5), 1101–1119. https://doi.org/10.1017/S0033291797005588

Kessler, R. C., & Frank, R. G. (1997). The impact of psychiatric disorders on work loss days. *Psychological Medicine, 27*(4), 861–873.

Kessler, R. C., Sonnega, A., Bromet, E., Hughes, M., et al. (1995). Posttraumatic stress disorder in the National Comorbidity Survey. *Archives of General Psychiatry, 52*(12), 1048–1060.

King, D. W., Orazem, R. J., Lauterbach, D., King, L. A., Hebenstreit, C. L., & Shalev, A. Y. (2009). Factor structure of posttraumatic stress disorder as measured by the Impact of Event Scale–Revised: Stability across cultures and time. *Psychological Trauma: Theory, Research, Practice, and Policy, 1*(3), 173–187. https://doi.org/10.1037/a0016990

King, D. W., Taft, C., King, L. A., Hammond, C., & Stone, E. R. (2006). Directionality of the association between social support and posttraumatic stress disorder: A longitudinal investigation. *Journal of Applied Social Psychology, 36*(12), 2980–2992. https://doi.org/10.1111/j.0021-9029.2006.00138.x

Koch, W. J., Douglas, K. S., Nicholls, T. L., & O'Neill, M. L. (2006). *Psychological injuries: Forensic assessment, treatment & law.* New York, NY: Oxford Press.

Koch, W. J., & Samra, J. (2005). Posttraumatic stress disability after motor vehicle accidents: Impact on productivity and employment. In I. Z. Schultz & R. J. Gatchel (Eds.), *Handbook of complex occupational disability claims: Early risk identification, intervention, and prevention* (pp. 333–341). https://doi.org/10.1007/0-387-28919-4_18

Kontorovich, E. (2001). The mitigation of emotional distress damages. *University of Chicago Law review, 68*(2), 491–520. https://doi.org/10.2307/1600379

Lambert, J. E., Engh, R., Hasbun, A., & Holzer, J. (2012). Impact of posttraumatic stress disorder on the relationship quality and psychological distress of intimate partners: A meta-analytic review. *Journal of Family Psychology, 26*(5), 729–737. https://doi.org/10.1037/a0029341

Lareau, C. R. (2016). "Because of … sex": The historical development of workplace sexual harassment law in the USA. *Psychological Injury and Law, 9*(3), 206–215. https://doi.org/10.1007/s12207-016-9268-0

Lees-Haley, P. R. (1988). Litigation response syndrome. *American Journal of Forensic Psychology, 6*(1), 3–12.

Levy, M. I., & Rosenberg, S. E. (2003). The "eggshell plaintiff" revisited: Causation of mental damages in civil litigation. *Mental and Physical Disability Law Reporter, 27*, 204–206.

Liu, H., Petukhova, M. V., Sampson, N. A., Aguilar-Gaxiola, S., Alonso, J., Andrade, L. H., World Health Organization World Mental Health Survey Collaborators. (2017). Association of DSM-IV posttraumatic stress disorder with traumatic experience type and history in the World Health Organization World Mental Health Surveys. JAMA Psychiatry, 74(3), 270–281. http://dx.doi.org/10.1001/jamapsychiatry.2016.3783.

Lloyd, D. A., & Turner, R. J. (2003). Cumulative adversity and posttraumatic stress disorder: Evidence from a diverse community sample of young adults. *American Journal of Orthopsychiatry, 73*(4), 381–391. https://doi.org/10.1037/0002-9432.73.4.381

Lockwood, E., & Forbes, D. (2014). Posttraumatic stress disorder and comorbidity: Untangling the Gordian knot. *Psychological Injury and Law, 7*(2), 108–121. https://doi.org/10.1007/s12207-014-9189-8

Marion, B. E., Sellbom, M., & Bagby, R. M. (2011). The detection of feigned psychiatric disorders using the MMPI-2-RF overreporting validity scales: An analog investigation. *Psychological Injury and Law, 4*(1), 1–12. https://doi.org/10.1007/s12207-011-9097-0

Mason, L. H., Shandera-Ochsner, A. L., Williamson, K. D., Harp, J. P., Edmundson, M., Berry, D. T. R., & High, W. M., Jr. (2013). Accuracy of MMPI–2–RF validity scales for identifying feigned PTSD symptoms, random responding, and genuine PTSD. *Journal of Personality Assessment, 95*(6), 585–593.

McCanlies, E. C., Sarkisian, K., Andrew, M. E., Burchfiel, C. M., & Violanti, J. M. (2017). Association of peritraumatic dissociation with symptoms of depression and posttraumatic stress disorder. *Psychological Trauma: Theory, Research, Practice, and Policy, 9*(4), 479–484. https://doi.org/10.1037/tra0000215

McDonald, S. D., Beckham, J. C., Morey, R., Marx, C., Tupler, L. A., & Calhoun, P. S. (2008). Factorial invariance of posttraumatic stress disorder symptoms across three veteran samples. *Journal of Traumatic Stress, 21*(3), 309–317. https://doi.org/10.1002/jts.20344

McFarlane, A. C. (2010). The delayed and cumulative consequences of traumatic stress: Challenges and issues in compensation settings. *Psychological Injury and Law, 3*(2), 100–110. https://doi.org/10.1007/s12207-010-9074-z

McLaughlin, K. A., Koenen, K. C., Friedman, M. J., Ruscio, A. M., Karam, E. G., Shahly, V., … Kessler, R. C. (2015). Subthreshold posttraumatic stress disorder in the World Health Organization world mental health surveys. *Biological Psychiatry, 77*(4), 375–384. https://doi.org/10.1016/j.biopsych.2014.03.028

McMillan, K. A., & Asmundson, G. J. G. (2016). PTSD, social anxiety disorder, and trauma: An examination of the influence of trauma type on comorbidity using a nationally representative sample. *Psychiatry Research, 246*, 561–567. https://doi.org/10.1016/j.psychres.2016.10.036

McQuade, J. S. (2001). The eggshell skull rule and related problems in recovery for mental harm in the law of tors. *Campbell Law Review, 24*(1).

Mireault, G. C., & Bond, L. A. (1992). Parental death in childhood: Perceived vulnerability, and adult depression and anxiety. *American Journal of Orthopsychiatry, 62*(4), 517–524. https://doi.org/10.1037/h0079371

Monson, C. M., Gradus, J. L., La Bash, H. A. J., Griffen, M. G., Resick, P. A., Neumann, D. A., … Briere, J. (1996). The long-term sequelae of childhood sexual abuse in women: A meta-analytic review. *Child Maltreatment: Journal of the American Professional Society on the Abuse of Children, 1*(1), 6–16.

Monson, C. M., Gradus, J. L., La Bash, H. A. J., Griffinb, M. G., & Resick, P. A. (2009). The role of couples interacting world assumptions and relationship adjustment in women's post disaster PTSD symptoms. *Journal of Traumatic Stress, 22*, 276–281. https://doi.org/10.1002/jts.20432

Morey, L. C. (2007). *Personality assessment inventory professional manual* (2nd ed.). Lutz, FL: Psychological Assessment Resources.

Owens, J. M., Gomes, G. M., & Morgan, J. F. (2008). Broadening the definition of unlawful retaliation under Title VII. *Employment Responsibilities and Rights Journal, 20*, 249–260.

Ozer, E. J., Best, S. R., Lipsey, T. L., & Weiss, D. S. (2003). Predictors of posttraumatic stress disorder and symptoms in adults: A meta-analysis. *Psychological Bulletin, 129*, 52–73. PMID: 12555794

Paolucci, E. O., Genuis, M. L., & Violato, C. (2001). A meta-analysis of the published research on the effects of child sexual abuse. *The Journal of Psychology, 135*(1), 17–36.

Pietrzak, R. H., Feder, A., Singh, R., Schechter, C. B., Bromet, E. J., Katz, C. L., ... Southwick, S. M. (2014). Trajectories of PTSD risk and resilience in World Trade Center responders: An 8-year prospective cohort study. *Psychological Medicine, 44*(1), 205–219. http://dx.doi.org/10.1017/S0033291713000597

Polusny, M. A., & Follette, V. M. (1995). Long-term correlates of child sexual abuse: Theory and review of the empirical literature. *Applied & Preventive Psychology, 4*(3), 143–166.

Reed, M. E., Collinsworth, L. L., Lawson, A. K., & Fitzgerald, L. F. (2016). The psychological impact of previous victimization: Examining the "abuse defense" in a sample of harassment litigants. *Psychological Injury and Law, 9*(3), 230–240. https://doi.org/10.1007/s12207-016-9267-1

Rehg, M. T., Miceli, M. P., Near, J. P., & Van Scotter, J. R. (2008). Antecedents and outcomes of retaliation against whistleblowers: Gender differences and power relationships. *Organization Science, 19*, 221–240.

Roesler, T. A., & McKenzie, N. (1994). Effects of childhood trauma on psychological functioning in adults sexually abused as children. *Journal of Nervous & Mental Disease, 182*(3), 145–150.

Roth, T., Jaeger, S., Jin, R., Kalsekar, A., Stang, P. E., & Kessler, R. C. (2006). Sleep problems, comorbid mental disorders, and role functioning in the National Comorbidity Survey Replication. *Biological Psychiatry, 60*(12), 1364–1371. https://doi.org/10.1016/j.biopsych.2006.05.039

Ruths, I. J. I., Christiansen, A. K., & Vincent, J. P. (2013). An assessment of the "Eggshell Psyche" in simulated civil litigation. *Psychological Injury and Law, 6*(2), 144–155. https://doi.org/10.1007/s12207-013-9152-0

Scheibe, S., Bagby, R. M., Miller, L. S., & Dorian, B. J. (2001). Assessing posttraumatic disorder with the MMPI–2 in a sample of workplace accident victims. *Psychological Assessment, 13*(3), 369–374. https://doi.org/10.1037/1040-3590.13.3.369

Schützwohl, M., & Maercker, A. (1999). Effects of varying diagnostic criteria for posttraumatic stress disorder are endorsing the concept of partial PTSD. *Journal of Traumatic Stress, 12*(1), 155–165. https://doi.org/10.1023/A:1024706702133

Scott, J. C., Wrocklage, K. M., Trejo, M., Weisser, V., Southwick, S. M., Krystal, J. H., & Schweinsburg, B. C. (2014, August). Neuropsychological functioning in veterans with post-traumatic stress disorder. In *Conference Proceedings, American Psychological Association*. Washington, D.C.: American Psychological Association. https://doi.org/10.1037/e530432014-001

Sellbom, M., & Bagby, R. M. (2010). Detection of overreported psychopathology with the MMPI-2 RF form validity scales. Psychological Assessment, 22(4), 757–767. http://dx.doi.org/10.1037/a0020825

Sellbom, M., Lee, T. T. C., Ben-Porath, Y. S., Arbisi, P. A., & Gervais, R. O. (2012). Differentiating PTSD symptomatology with the MMPI-2-RF (Restructured Form) in a forensic disability sample. *Psychiatry Research, 197*(1–2), 172–179. https://doi.org/10.1016/j.psychres.2012.02.003

Shallcross, S. L., Arbisi, P. A., Polusny, M. A., Kramer, M. D., & Erbes, C. R. (2016). Social causation versus social erosion: Comparisons of causal models for relations between support and PTSD symptoms. *Journal of Traumatic Stress, 29*(2), 167–175. https://doi.org/10.1002/jts.22086

Shuman, D. W., Greenberg, S., Heilbrun, K., & Foote, W. E. (1998). Special perspective—an immodest proposal: Should treating mental health professionals be barred from testifying about their patients? *Behavioral Sciences & the Law, 16*, 509–523.

Sobhanian, S. (2015). Comparing possible malingered posttraumatic stress disorder symptoms using the Minnesota Multiphasic Personality Inventory-2 and Minnesota Multiphasic Personality Inventory-2 Restructured Form. *Dissertation Abstracts International: Section B: The Sciences and Engineering, 75*(7-B(E)).

Spinhoven, P., Penninx, B. W., van Hemert, A. M., de Rooij, M., & Elzinga, B. M. (2014). Comorbidity of PTSD in anxiety and depressive disorders: Prevalence and shared risk factors. *Child Abuse & Neglect, 38*(8), 1320–1330. https://doi.org/10.1016/j.chiabu.2014.01.017

Stein, M. B., Walker, J. R., Hazen, A. L., & Forde, D. R. (1997). Full and partial posttraumatic stress disorder: Findings from a community survey. *The American Journal of Psychiatry, 154*(8), 1114–1119. https://doi.org/10.1176/ajp.154.8.1114

Streseman, K. N. (1995). Headshrinkers, manmunchers, moneygrubbers, nuts and sluts: Reexamining compelled mental examinations in sexual harassment actions under the Civil Rights Act of 1991. *Cornell Law Review, 80*, 1268–1330.

Sveen, J., Ekselius, L., Berdin, B., & Willebrand, M. (2011). A prospective longitudinal study of posttraumatic stress disorder symptom trajectories after burn injury. *The Journal of Trauma Injury, Infection, and Critical Care, 71*(6), 1808–1815.

Taft, C. T., Monson, C. M., Schumm, J. A., Watkins, L. E., Panuzio, J., & Resick, P. A. (2009). Posttraumatic stress symptoms, relationship adjustment, and relationship aggression in a sample of female flood victims. *Journal of Family Violence, 24*, 389–396. https://doi.org/10.1007/s10896-009-9241-8

Taft, C. T., Watkins, L. E., Stafford, J., Street, A. E., & Monson, C. M. (2011). Posttraumatic stress disorder and intimate relationship problems: A meta-analysis. *Journal of Consulting and Clinical Psychology, 79*, 22–33. https://doi.org/10.1037/a0022196

Taylor, S., Wald, J., & Asmundson, G. J. G. (2006). Factors associated with occupational impairment in people seeking treatment for posttraumatic stress disorder. *Canadian Journal of Community Mental Health, 25*, 289–301.

Thomas, K. M., Hopwood, C. J., Orlando, M. J., Weathers, F. W., & McDevitt-Murphy, M. E. (2012). Detecting feigned PTSD using the personality assessment inventory. *Psychological Injury and Law, 5*(3–4), 192–201. https://doi.org/10.1007/s12207-011-9111-6

Twaite, J. A., & Rodriguez-Srednicki, O. (2004). Childhood sexual and physical abuse and adult vulnerability to PTSD: The mediating effects of attachment and dissociation. *Journal of Child Sexual Abuse, 13*(1), 17–38. https://doi.org/10.1300/J070v13n01_02

Vance, M. C., Kovachy, B., Dong, M., & Bui, E. (2018). Peritraumatic distress: A review and synthesis of 15 years of research. *Journal of Clinical Psychology, 74*(9), 1457–1484. https://doi.org/10.1002/jclp.22612. Advance online publication.

Varela, V. S., Ng, A., Mauch, P., & Recklitis, C. J. (2013). Posttraumatic stress disorder (PTSD) in survivors of Hodgkin's lymphoma: Prevalence of PTSD and partial PTSD compared with sibling controls. *Psycho-Oncology, 22*(2), 434–440.

Wald, J. (2009). Work limitations in employed persons seeking treatment for chronic posttraumatic stress disorder. *Journal of Trauma Stress, 22*(4), 312–315. https://doi.org/10.1002/jts.20430

Wald, J., & Taylor, S. (2009). Work impairment and disability in posttraumatic stress disorder: A review and recommendations for psychological injury research and practice. *Psychological Injury and Law, 2*(3–4), 254–262. https://doi.org/10.1007/s12207-009-9059-y

Wang, M., Armour, C., Li, X., Dai, X., Zhu, X., & Yao, S. (2013). The factorial invariance across gender of three well-supported models: Further evidence for a five-factor model of posttraumatic stress disorder. *Journal of Nervous and Mental Disease, 201*(2), 145–152. https://doi.org/10.1097/NMD.0b013e31827f627

Weathers, F. W., Blake, D. D., Schnurr, P. P., Kaloupek, D. G., Marx, B. P., & Keane, T. M. (2013). *The clinician-administered PTSD scale for DSM-5 (CAPS-5)*. Interview available from the National Center for PTSD at www.ptsd.va.gov

Wechsler, D. (2008). *Wechsler adult intelligence scale (WAIS-IV)* (4th ed.). San Antonio, TX: The Psychological Corporation.

Weissman, H. N. (1991). Forensic psychological assessment and the effects of protracted litigation on impairment in personal injury litigation. *Forensic Reports, 4*(4), 417–429.

Wolf, E. J., Miller, M. W., Orazem, R. J., Weierich, M. R., Castillo, D. T., Milford, J., … Keane, T. M. (2008). The MMPI-2 Restructured Clinical Scales in the assessment of posttraumatic stress disorder and comorbid disorders. *Psychological Assessment, 20*(4), 327–340.

Wooley, C. N., & Rogers, R. (2015). The effectiveness of the personality assessment inventory with feigned PTSD: An initial investigation of Resnick's model of malingering. *Assessment, 22*(4), 449–458. https://doi.org/10.1177/1073191114552076

Xue, C., Ge, Y., Tang, B., Liu, Y., Kang, P., Wang, M., et al. (2015). A meta-analysis of risk factors for combat-related PTSD among military personnel and veterans. *Plos One, 10*(3), e0120270. https://doi.org/10.1371/journal.pone.0120270

Young, G. (2017). PTSD in Court III: Malingering, assessment, and the law. *International Journal of Law and Psychiatry, 52*, 81–102. https://doi.org/10.1016/j.ijlp.2017.03.001

Young, G., Lareau, C., & Pierre, B. (2014). One quintillion ways to have PTSD comorbidity: Recommendations for the disordered DSM-5. *Psychological Injury and Law, 7*(1), 61–74. https://doi.org/10.1007/s12207-014-9186-

Yufik, T., & Simms, L. J. (2010). A meta-analytic investigation of the structure of posttraumatic stress disorder symptoms. *Journal of Abnormal Psychology, 119*(4), 764–776. https://doi.org/10.1037/a0020981

Zimmerle, H. (2005). Common sense vs. the EEOC: Co-worker ostracism and shunning as retaliation under Title VII. *Journal of Corporation Law, 30*, 627–645.

# Chapter 14
# Obstacles to Litigating and Evaluating Trauma in Police Misconduct Cases

**Jemour A. Maddux, Amy Jane Agnew, and I. Bruce Frumkin**

There are a variety of how-to resources available for conducting forensic mental health evaluations in the context of civil rights and personal injury cases (Kane & Dvoskin, 2011; Young, Kane, & Nicholson, 2007). They all describe relevant case law, the typical legal context, and how psychologists go about assessing for damages in relation to an alleged breach of duty. However, assessment procedures can vary based upon the legal context and other case-specific factors. Psychologists may struggle to find specific procedural guidance depending upon the alleged source of harm (e.g., police/correctional officer misconduct) and the suspected nature of the psychological injury (e.g., trauma). Also, psychologists and the public may be unaware of the economic, policy, and legal obstacles that lawyers face when bringing psychological injury cases against defendants for their conduct while operating in a law enforcement capacity.

In recent years, several multimillion-dollar settlements have been reached in civil litigation regarding police misconduct and wrongful death. Sean Bell, Eric Garner, Philando Castile, Michael Brown, Tamir Rice, Walter Scott, Freddie Gray, Akai Gurley, Laquan McDonald, Samuel DuBose, and Christopher Sean Harris have become household names. In each of these cases, civil litigation has resulted in large settlements in connection with claims for misconduct by law enforcement.

During the past few years, the public has had unprecedented access to video footage of police encounters. Some examples include the video of Walter Scott's stride

J. A. Maddux (✉)
Lamb and Maddux, LLC, Hackensack, NJ, USA
e-mail: jm@rule702.com

A. J. Agnew
Law Office of Amy Jane Agnew, P.C, New York, NY, USA
e-mail: aj@ajagnew.com

I. B. Frumkin
Forensic and Clinical Psychology Associates, P.A, South Miami, FL, USA

© Springer Nature Switzerland AG 2020
R. A. Javier et al. (eds.), *Assessing Trauma in Forensic Contexts*,
https://doi.org/10.1007/978-3-030-33106-1_14

as he ran away unarmed from a police officer who shot him in the back and handcuffed him as he died from his injuries, Eric Garner saying "I can't breathe," and Diamond Reynolds saying, "You just killed my boyfriend" as Castile died next to her after being shot by the police during a traffic stop. Her 4-year-old daughter was in the back seat. Today, it is common for the public to view a police officer's deadly use of force on the news and then to opine on the legitimacy of the officer's conduct during our social media exchanges and casual conversations (Wasserman, 2017). In 2015, *The Wall Street Journal* reported that cities with the largest police departments have seen an almost 50% increase in compensation to resolve claims of police misconduct since 2010 (Elinson & Frosch, 2015). This surge has been associated with the increased availability of video capturing these police encounters (Wasserman, 2017). However, video evidence is not ubiquitous in police misconduct cases.

This chapter presents some common legal hurdles in the litigation of psychological injuries sustained from police misconduct. There are economic hurdles, policy restrictions, and legal challenges that decrease the likelihood of successfully litigating claims of psychological injuries (e.g., trauma) from police misconduct. These context-specific hurdles are rarely discussed in published forensic psychology resources.

Notably, the typical victims of police misconduct generally share historical, community, and cultural factors that obscure whether their trauma would not exist but for the misconduct. Therefore, with trauma being central to this book, we present some common assessment challenges faced by psychologists conducting trauma-informed evaluations for police misconduct cases. While specifically focused on trauma, we also endeavor to highlight some of the skills, education, research, and training necessary to conduct helpful, methodical, and culturally intelligent evaluations for the court in these matters. We hope this information will be useful to experts and lawyers on both sides of these cases.

## Police Use of Force

Of all use of force events by the New York City Police Department (NYPD) in 2017 and 2018, 76–82% occurred during the point of arrest (NYPD Use of Force Data Tables, n.d.).These numbers reflect "physical force" incident numbers; the numbers do not reflect the use of chemical spray, tasers, batons, or other weapons during the arrest itself. Researchers have also found that 5% of NYPD officers account for 40% of resisting arrest charges (Lewis & Veltman, 2014). Similarly, Brandl (2017) cited research indicating 5.4% of patrol officers accounted for 40% of all use of force incidents in a particular department. We would expect an officer's use of force to naturally follow an arrestee's efforts to resist. However, some researchers, such as Samuel Walker, have noted that police officers often add a resisting arrest charge to justify their use of force in hindsight (Lewis & Veltman, 2014). It is also notable that these use of force incidents disproportionately befall minority populations (Fryer, 2019; Goff, Lloyd, Geller, Raphael, & Glaser, 2016).

## Police Misconduct as a Criterion-A Event

In 2014, the Substance Abuse and Mental Health Services Administration (SAMHSA), within the US Department of Health and Human Services (HHS), defined trauma as "an event, series of events, or set of circumstances that is experienced by an individual as physically or emotionally harmful or life threatening and that has lasting adverse effects on the individual's functioning and mental, physical, social, emotional, or spiritual well-being" (p.7). Regarding the diagnosis of posttraumatic stress disorder (PTSD), the American Psychiatric Association's (2013) Diagnostic and Statistical Manual of Mental Disorders (DSM-5®) requires the examinee to have experienced a qualifying event characterized by exposure to actual or threatened death, serious injury, or sexual violence. In forensic psychology circles, these are referred to as Criterion-A events.

Notably, an actual or threatened death or serious injury can qualify as a Criterion-A event even if committed by officials during authorized encounters (e.g., waking up during surgery due to physician error). Also, an incident can qualify as a Criterion-A event even if anticipated or previously envisioned (e.g., a soldier becoming a prisoner of war). Therefore, even when looking at the DSM's more restrictive definition of trauma, it is clear that a police officer's misconduct can qualify as a Criterion-A event given the power bestowed upon police officers to arrest people, to use force, and to use deadly force.

## Justice Through Constitutional Torts

When victims petition the court for damages (e.g., monetary compensation) in connection with trauma from police misconduct, these cases generally fall under the umbrella of constitutional torts. Civil cases involving constitutional torts such as excessive force, abuse of process, unlawful arrest, failure to intervene, and a collection of other violations are often perceived as the only form of justice when the criminal justice system fails. A few recent cases are worth note. The death of Freddie Gray in Baltimore, at the hands of police officers, ended with prosecutors dropping all charges against the officers and a 6.4-million-dollar civil settlement to Gray's family. Sam DuBose was fatally shot by a University of Cincinnati officer and two criminal trials ended with hung juries. The University settled with DuBose's family for 5.3 million and free tuition for his children. In the horrific death of Philando Castile, who told police officers who stopped him that there was a weapon in the car to avoid any altercation, the officer who nonetheless shot and killed Mr. Castile was acquitted of all criminal charges. The City of St. Anthony settled with Castile's family for 3.8 million. When an officer leapt from his vehicle and shot Tamir Rice, a 12-year-old with a toy gun, no charges were ever filed against the officer. The City of Cleveland settled with Tamir's family for 6 million.

When victims survive police misconduct, the civil constitutional tort claims are important as a form of justice because of the improbability of criminal charges proceeding against uniformed officers, which is due to a set of obstacles outside of the scope of this chapter. Therefore, monetary damages are the primary recourse for justice when district attorneys fail to file charges against officers, or grand juries fail to indict, or juries acquit. This said, civil constitutional cases are unlikely to drive reform. According to Schwartz (2014), anything less infamous than the highest profile cases do not have an effect on police conduct. Also, recent research by Trinkner, Kerrison, and Goff (2019) suggests that when police officers are concerned about appearing racist, they are less likely to endorse procedurally fair policing. Faced with such concerns, police react by approving unreasonable force and resist restrictions on the use of force (Trinkner et al., 2019).

## Obstacles to Litigating Trauma from Police Misconduct

For several reasons, very few use of force events at the point of arrest lead to lawsuits; but when they do, several factors weigh on decisions to prosecute claims for compensable psychological trauma. The point of tort law is to bring a victim of a civil wrong back to where they would have been if they were not wronged. Without these suits, their trauma is unlikely to be formally addressed by the perpetrator of the injury through monetary compensation for their healthcare needs (e.g., trauma-focused psychotherapy) or emotionally through relational sentiments, such as admissions of wrongdoing or apologies (Reinders Folmer, Desmet, & Van Boom, 2019). Researchers have found psychotherapy for PTSD to be helpful regardless of whether a participant was also in litigation pertaining to their source of trauma (Blanchard et al., 1998; Taylor et al., 2001). Therefore, monetary compensation for treatment is a significant factor when psychotherapy services for trauma symptoms would otherwise be inaccessible. However, victims of excessive force, false arrest, deliberate indifference, and other constitutional torts may be unable to find representation to accept their case on a contingency fee basis if their damages are limited to psychological trauma. The following describes some economic hurdles, policy restrictions, and legal challenges that decrease the likelihood of successfully litigating claims of psychological injuries (e.g., trauma) from police misconduct.

### *Economic Hurdles for the Traumatized*

In 1976, Congress amended 42 U.S.C. § 1988 to allow the award of attorney fees to a prevailing plaintiff or defendant in enumerated civil rights cases (Larson, 1976). As victims of constitutional torts are typically low income, Congress sought to ensure access to competent counsel. This was especially important in cases for injunctive relief – to stop patterns and practices of constitutional torts undertaken by municipal entities (e.g., police departments) – where actual compensatory relief for damages would be low, but the potential benefit to the public might be high (Karlan, 2003; Silver, 1988). Without fee-shifting provisions, plaintiffs would be dependent on already overburdened public interest and pro bono legal services entities. The Civil

Rights Attorneys Fees Act of 1976 sought to rectify the disparate economic power between government entities and victims of constitutional violations.

Despite this great stride toward leveling the playing field, fee-shifting provisions do not allow for the award of expert fees, an often prohibitively expensive component of proving damages in a civil rights case. This fact may surprise forensic psychologists familiar with the number of published resources available for conducting psychological injury evaluations and the monetary settlements that make the news. However, in 1991, the United States Supreme Court decided *West Virginia University Hospital v. Casey* and held that 42 U.S.C. § 1988's fee-shifting provision conveyed no authority to shift expert fees other than the witness appearance fees allowed under 28 U.S.C. § 1920 and 28 U.S.C. § 1821 (Kaufman, 1991). In response, Congress amended § 1988 through the Civil Rights Act of 1991 to include provision for expert fees, but only in suits brought pursuant to 42 U.S.C. § 1981 or § 1981(a) – equal protection claims (Kaufman, 1991). A variety of constitutional torts (e.g., excessive force, false arrest, deliberate indifference, and other violations), which would certainly benefit from a forensic mental health assessment regarding trauma, were left without any provision for recoupment of expert fees by plaintiffs or defendants.

Consequently, fees for experts must come from plaintiffs or well-meaning plaintiff's counsel. This reality demands that lawyers and plaintiffs undertake a cost/benefit analysis before considering whether to retain a forensic psychologist with an expertise in trauma. This obstacle creates an environment where plaintiffs and their lawyers could be making decisions about retaining a forensic psychologist based upon whether the amount of potential monetary compensation for damages justifies the outlay of expert fees.

It could be tempting for a forensic psychologist to provide a potential client with information to guide these conversations and decisions. However, depending upon the information offered by the psychologist, he or she may inadvertently undertake a litigation consulting role, which could prevent the psychologist from ethically proceeding as a neutral and impartial testifying expert in the case. It could also be tempting for a forensic psychologist to enter into an agreement that ties her or his payment to the client's degree of success in seeking or defending against monetary damages. However, such an agreement could threaten the psychologist's impartiality. Therefore, according to the "Specialty Guidelines for Forensic Psychology" (American Psychological Association, 2013), forensic psychologists avoid contingent fee agreements.

## Policy Restrictions

Further complicating the vindication of civil rights violations is the Prison Litigation Reform Act (1996). The Prison Litigation Reform Act (PLRA) creates a cap on attorney's fees for suits brought by detainees or prisoners. The PLRA (1996) fee cap specifically applies to actions brought by prisoners in custody under which an attorney's fees have been authorized. To put this application into context, a civil rights attorney practicing in the Southern District of New York might normally be compensated at $500–$600 per hour for a case. Under the PLRA, the attorney's compensation is limited to $210 per hour; and if the case goes to trial, attorneys' fees can only total up to 150% of any judgment awarded if the case did not involve injunctive relief. If a jury found a constitutional violation, but only awarded nominal damages of $1.00, counsel for the plaintiff would only receive $1.50 for his/her efforts. Therefore, many civil rights attorneys elect to file a notice of claim against the city – preserving the plaintiff's rights to sue – but do not actually file the civil rights lawsuit. A notice of claim must be filed within 90 days of an incident in order to preserve the right to sue the city or its employees. The notice of claim is a thing apart from the actual civil lawsuit complaint. The hope of the plaintiff attorney is that any criminal charges against the plaintiff will be dropped, the plaintiff will be released from custody, and the civil rights lawsuit can then proceed without the shadow of the PLRA.

Alternatively, civil rights attorneys may send the victim the necessary documents for self-filing the notice of claim with a note that says, "please reach out to us if you are acquitted or the charges are dropped." However, many of the most egregious civil rights violations are perpetrated against victims who are ultimately convicted or plead guilty to underlying crimes. The victims end up in jail or prison, diminishing the value and perceived severity of the civil rights violations and their trauma. Many free market civil rights attorneys are only willing to put their time and energy into cases with a high compensation yield. The economic realities imposed by the PLRA mean many civil rights violations go unaddressed, as victims cannot find counsel willing to take on the risk of a low compensation case.

Conviction rates for felonies in Manhattan ("New York State Division of Criminal Justice Services Data for Arrest Dispositions," 2019a) and Queens ("New York State Division of Criminal Justice Services Data for Arrest Dispositions," 2019b) counties hover around 65%. Drug-related charges end in convictions up to 75% of the time. A perfect storm swells when a victim is badly beaten and emotionally traumatized at the point of arrest and is subsequently convicted of his/her underlying crimes. Imprisonment itself, creates its own separate trauma on the victim (DeVeaux, 2013), which a forensic psychologist would have to contend with when assessing the relationships between the victim's trauma, the police misconduct at the time of the arrest, and the victim's subsequent imprisonment. However, once the victim is convicted, the PLRA applies if the victim is in custody at the time of filing, attorney's fees are capped, and expert fees are unavailable (Sutton v. City of Yonkers, 2017; Hall v. Galie, 2009; Robbins v. Chronister, 2006; Jackson v. St. Bd. Of Pardons & Paroles, 2003).Therefore, many civil rights violations that have resulted in trauma are believed to slip through the cracks.

## Legal Obstacles

The legal context for the psychotherapist privilege is straightforward. In 1996, the United States Supreme Court decided *Jaffee v. Redmond* (1996) and found an absolute psychotherapist privilege in federal matters, protecting the notes and impressions of psychiatrists, psychologists, and social workers who treat people for psychological issues. Ironically, in the case, the estate of a victim of police misconduct sought the production of psychiatric notes related to the treatment of the police officer defendant. The Supreme Court found the privilege absolute. Yet, the privilege (like all privileges) can be waived. When a party puts his/her psychological state or injuries *in play*, meaning they are a central part of the lawsuit, then the privilege is waived. When a party claims psychological injury or a defense based on psychological illness or state, the privilege is waived, and all psychological records become relevant.

The psychotherapist privilege becomes incredibly important in the context of prisoner civil rights cases. First, about 15–20 percent of incarcerated people require a psychiatric service while in custody (Fellner, 2015). Victims of civil rights violations being held in correctional settings may accumulate psychological records that reflect negatively on their credibility and call into question the legitimacy of their damages. In part, this reflects the fact that mental health workers can be a lifeline of sorts for prisoners. Should medical and security staff ignore inmates or abuse them, prisoners are likely to turn to mental health professionals, perhaps by feigning a mental health crisis to get necessary health care. Mental health records may mention trauma, but they may also mention malingering, lying, and manipulation. These findings could harm a plaintiff's case even if the manipulative actions were taken in a desperate attempt to get necessary health care, to escape imminent harm by another inmate, or to transfer facilities to be closer to family members unable to visit due to the distance.

Given these circumstances, civil rights attorneys are inclined to limit emotional damage claims to "garden variety" claims in an effort to shield potentially problematic mental health records. "Garden variety" encompasses damages up to $50,000 depending on the jurisdiction. While these plaintiffs may endure great trauma, they are limited in their recovery due to the psychotherapist privilege waiver rules.

It is also worth mentioning the debate about police officer indemnification. According to research conducted by Schwartz (2014), which examined police indemnification throughout the nation, government paid virtually 100% of awards to civil rights plaintiffs irrespective of whether the police officers were prosecuted or terminated. However, while indemnification of police officers permits large monetary awards, some have suggested that civilians will continue to face police misconduct and trauma until police officers are personally held to be financially responsible for damages from their misconduct (Emery & Maazel, 2000). In addition, there are few *causes of action* against the entities that employ law enforcement officers (Fayz, 1994). A cause of action is a required set of facts, which, if accepted as true, would give the plaintiff the right to sue for their trauma.

## Case Example

The following details have been changed to protect the anonymity of the examinee. RM was a 46-year-old Puerto Rican male with a long history of nonviolent property crimes, mostly larceny, burglary, fare evasion, and giving false information to the police– usually suggesting a pseudonym upon arrest. He stole backpacks, laptops, and purses and even once undertook an ambitious scheme to steal a refrigerator only to be thwarted while trying to roll it off the property. These crimes resulted in a series of arrests throughout his life.

RM's first arrest was at 11 years old, not an uncommon occurrence among his peers from his Bronx community. Despite the dozens of arrests since then, he still remembers that first arrest and his fear. Between that first arrest and the present, he has completed several prison sentences in upstate prisons with the associated time at Rikers Island during his trials and sentencing. He was, as we say, "in the system." Yet, none of RM's crimes were violent. The value of the merchandise stolen and the fact that some of the items were removed from college dormitories pushed the charges up to burglary and grand larceny, but RM was a bit rare in that he had never had a weapons or drug-related charge. He worked at a recycling plant and was getting his life together after his second prison sentence ended. At 5'8" and 230 pounds, he was little physical threat and finally realized that he was not terribly good at averting detection or arrest.

One evening, RM made another poor decision. He reconnected with an ex-girlfriend who, years before, had taken out an order of protection against him. The order of protection had not expired, nor had it been withdrawn, and she willingly picked him up from the precinct following his arrest for violating the order. Three years had passed. He went over to her home for dinner and took her children some toys, and hours later a fight erupted. She became furious and called "911." In her first call, the operator asked her if RM had a gun; she said no. As the fight escalated, RM quickly packed his things to leave. The girlfriend called 911 again, this time starting the conversation with, "he has a gun," which was not true. RM left the apartment.

An hour and 22 blocks later, the police caught up with RM. When the lights flashed, he put down his bag and put his hands in the air. Not only did he not have a weapon, he waited passively for the police to take him into custody. He knew how to act during an arrest. Nonetheless, as the four police circled him, they began to beat him – yelling profanities and demanding he tell them where he put the gun. RM was badly beaten and spent 3 days in the hospital with several fractured ribs, contusions, and a concussion. The police charged him with burglary in the second degree, criminal mischief, harassment, and resisting arrest. Because it was his third set of felony offences, his likely sentence was 15 years to life.

## Evaluating Trauma from Police Misconduct: General and Special Considerations

This is the point in the story where any civil case for constitutional torts against the officers may drastically change – the case taking one path if RM is convicted of his underlying crimes and a dramatically different path if he is acquitted. Up to this point, we have discussed the likely path of this case should RM be convicted. If incarcerated, he is likely to struggle to find a lawyer to accept his civil rights case due to the PLRA. If a lawyer takes his case, retaining a psychologist to assess for trauma and psychological damages could be obstructed by: (1) constraints on being awarded expert witness fees and (2) his lawyer limiting the prayer for damages to garden variety so as not to forfeit psychotherapist privilege and potentially reveal damaging medical records by putting his trauma in play.

However, the following describes special considerations, common assessment challenges, and basic information for evaluators undertaking forensic mental health assessments for trauma when evaluating examinees like RM.

## *Assessing for Damages*

Goodman-Delahunty and Foote (2013) developed a five-stage model for evaluating compensable damages in a civil litigation context. The following is a basic overview of their model. First off, the evaluator collects stage one information regarding the examinee's functioning prior to the incident across typical domains of clinical inquiry (e.g., family, school, work, financial, legal, recreational, marital, medical, and mental health functioning). These findings will serve as a baseline to better understand incident and post-incident impairment and their origin. Pre-incident conditions or impairment accounting for current problems in the examinee's functioning, irrespective of the incident, are not compensable. However, pre-incident issues that were exacerbated by the incident or that created a vulnerability for the incident to produce impairment are compensable.

The evaluator also has to collect stage two information regarding the examinee's experiences at the time of the incident. The evaluator explores relevant details of the examinee's experience of the incident, which may reveal information about his or her prognosis. The evaluator also assesses for issues that could have occurred around the same time of the incident and whether current impairment could be explained by these unrelated and non-compensable issues. Regarding stage three, the evaluator explores changes in functioning between the incident and the evaluation, as well as the occurrence of further compensable detriment (e.g., retaliation by the defendant) and non-compensable detriment from unrelated hardships in life coincidentally occurring during this time period.

Stage four refers to the evaluator's assessment of the plaintiff's symptoms and functioning on the day of the evaluation during which a variety of alternative hypotheses and rule-outs should be explored (e.g., malingering) in order to reach a conclusion regarding the most likely explanation(s) for the plaintiff's symptoms and impairment. Stage five refers to our assessment of prognosis and future compensable damages (e.g., pain and suffering and treatment costs).

## *General Cultural Considerations*

As previously indicated, police use of force incidents disproportionately occur in minority populations (Fryer, 2019; Goff et al., 2016). In conducting a forensic evaluation involving trauma, particularly those precipitated by actions of law enforcement, the forensic psychologist needs to consider culture and diversity broadly defined. If the plaintiff is someone from a country of origin other than the United States, there must be consideration of the level of acculturation within mainstream society. Does the mainstream culture marginalize the individual or allow the individual to embrace the host culture while allowing maintenance of one's own cultural identity? How long has the plaintiff or his or her family lived in the United States? Is fluency in English an issue? Even if the plaintiff has lived in the United States for many generations, when interpreting symptoms or behavior, it must be done through the lens of how those from that particular cultural group have historically been adversely impacted in interactions with law enforcement.

One needs to know not only about the particular ethnic group within a country, but the particular region of that country the individual resided, the economic status of the individual and his family within that country of origin, and the role and interactions with law enforcement within that cultural milieu. There are many ways a forensic psychologist can gain expertise in the ways a particular culture may influence evaluation results, such as by reviewing the relevant literature on the specific culture. However, depending upon the complexity of the assignment, the forensic psychologist should seriously consider hiring a cultural consultant. Ideally the cultural consultant would be another psychologist or mental health professional. One may want to look in the American Psychological Association (APA) Membership Directory to get a listing of international affiliates from that country. State psychological associations can also be contacted to obtain contact information for psychologists who might be familiar or who are from that culture. Performing a Google or similar search of key terms may also yield positive results in finding consultative resources.

For example, consider a Spanish-speaking adult male from Peru who immigrated two years ago who has alleged misconduct by the police. It is not enough to speak Spanish and to know about the Peruvian culture in general. Rather, the evaluator must understand what ethnic group, economic status, and region in Peru that person resided in his country of origin. Interactions with law enforcement and psychological responses to police misconduct could differ if one is a Peruvian of Spanish descent living in Lima or if one is a Quechua who resides in a small village in the Andes where law enforcement is based on tribal connections more than anything else. Also, how one is able to process trauma varies based on one's support system, which may differ based on geography. Finding the right cultural consultant can make all of the difference. The consultation will hopefully provide: (a) information regarding the meaning behind normal behavior, (b) the meaning behind abnormal behavior (e.g., whether it is abnormal for that culture), (c) how traumatic events involving law enforcement interact within the cultural context, and (d) the interpretation of psychological test results and/or what psychological tests are best used with someone from that culture.

## *General Interpretation Considerations*

Also, the forensic psychologist needs to understand how language or linguistic issues affect the forensic assessment, both in assessing personality traits and cognitive abilities (e.g., Fletcher-Janzen, Strickland, & Reynolds, 2002). If the forensic evaluation involves an assessment of someone who does not speak English, or if English is not the primary language, a decision needs to be made in conjunction with the retaining attorney, whether to get involved in the case. Is it better to have a forensic psychologist who does not speak the language of the plaintiff but who specializes in the specific trauma-related psycholegal issues or whether it is best for the attorney to obtain a psychologist who speaks the language but is not a forensic practitioner or is not one who specializes in this area? If the former is decided, then the psychologist should utilize the services of a certified interpreter for the evaluation.

Assessing the effects of trauma precipitated by the actions of law enforcement (or in any clinical or forensic evaluation) on culturally and/or linguistically diverse populations creates implicit challenges in how a clinical interview is conducted, the utilization of interpreters, and the use of test instruments. Each evaluation needs to be conducted on a case-by-case basis taking into consideration the extensive literature on cultural and linguistic issues in clinical and forensic assessment. For example, the potential of deportation for victims of crimes (e.g., American Psychological Association, 2018), how distress and emotions are manifested culturally (e.g., Lim, 2016), and the use of psychological testing in the assessment of psychopathology in minority populations (e.g., Gray-Little, 2002) are potential variables when assessing trauma potentially induced by law enforcement. DeJesus, Buigas, and Denny (2012) provide attorneys with a guide on how to evaluate the effectiveness and appropriateness of an expert witness' assessment procedures and resulting opinions with culturally diverse populations in a text designed to help lawyers challenge expert testimony.

Sometimes in order to save money, the retaining attorney prefers to use staff or family members to provide interpretive services. The psychologist should actively refrain from accepting this arrangement (Frumkin & Friedland, 1995). The person evaluated may be uncomfortable revealing trauma-related symptoms to those in the family or may be worried that they initially lied to their counsel and now must continue the lie if the attorney's staff is in the room. Also, the family member or attorney staff interpreter may subconsciously interpret things that present the case in the best possible light. Even if none of the above take place, opposing counsel during cross-examination may argue these points.

Forensic psychologists need to understand how interpretation works. First, it is not translation. Translation pertains to written documents while interpretation involves speech. Psychologists are specially trained to evaluate subtleties of speech patterns. It is often not the content of what is being said but how it is said. Subtle symptoms of anxiety, depression, thought disorder, or other trauma-related symptoms might be discernable based on how information is communicated by the alleged trauma-victim. Thus, it is preferable for the interpreter to interpret verbatim, even if the sentence does not make sense. Paraphrasing what the subject says causes the psychologist to lose the richness of the forensic interview. One is then unable to assess for loose associations, overly complex or stilted vocabulary, and word-finding difficulties (Frumkin, 2015).

The forensic psychologist also needs to decide whether the interpretation should be simultaneous or sequential. Another term for sequential interpretation is consecutive interpretation. Simultaneous interpretation involves the interpreter interpreting at the same time the person speaks. Sequential interpretation involves waiting until the person finishes speaking one or more sentences and then interpreting what was said. Generally, when this is done, more paraphrasing occurs. Simultaneous interpretation allows the interview to proceed at a faster pace. It does not work well though if the speaker has some knowledge of English as well as his or her primary language. There becomes a difficulty in being able to screen out what is being heard in English and their own language simultaneously. Interpretation involves very specific skills and training. (See National Association of Judiciary Interpreters & Translators (NAJIT), 2006 for their position paper on modes of interpreting in the context of court interpretation and translation). Language proficiency is not the only factor that can determine the quality of interpretive services. The same words or phrases might have a different meaning, depending on the culture. For example, an interpreter who is familiar with cultural differences between Cuban Spanish and Argentinian Spanish could provide more accurate renderings of what was actually said when interpreted back to English (see Wagoner, 2017). Likewise, conducting evaluations through interpreters requires various skills and considerations (Maddux, 2010) that cannot be fully summarized here.

## *General Testing Consideration for Non-English Speakers*

Regarding testing, it is tempting for the forensic psychologist, particularly those who speak the language of the victim of trauma, to translate an English version test into the primary language of the accused. With few exceptions, there are problems in arriving at valid results when such a translation is done, even when using a certified translator. There is a complex process used when authorized translations of tests are conducted by test publishing companies. This involves careful translation of the test by multiple bilingual translators, use of key informants to verify linguistic and social appropriateness of items, using translation teams to integrate different renderings of items into an experimental form, a back-translation process into English (because some items do not translate well into English), and pretesting the experimental translation on a bilingual sample in both languages and comparing the results. Even if an appropriate translation of a psychological test exists, this does not mean there are appropriate norms or control groups for the trauma victim. The Wechsler Adult Intelligence Scale-III (WAIS-III) is normed in Spain. It would be inappropriate to give this Spanish version of the test to RM, a Spanish-speaking adult of Puerto Rican descent who lives in the Bronx. The forensic psychologist who is evaluating trauma in alleged victims of police misconduct should consult both the APA's Multicultural Guidelines: An ecological approach to context, identity, and intersectionality (APA, 2017), as well as the Standards for Educational and Psychological Testing (American Educational Research Association et al., 2014).

## Special Areas of Psycholegal Exploration

Minority populations are disproportionately involved in police use of force incidents (Fryer, 2019; Goff et al., 2016). During the pre-incident interval, an examinee from a minority group might have already experienced a race-based trauma in connection with a community injustice (Carter & Forsyth, 2009); an environmental injustice, such as the Flint, Michigan water crisis (Butler, Scammell, & Benson, 2016); or a perceived political injustice, such as an Immigration and Customs Enforcement raid that separated a family (Menjivar & Bejarano, 2004). It is recommended for evaluators to assess for race-based trauma when evaluating minorities in police misconduct cases. Again, pre/post-incident issues accounting for current problems irrespective of the incident are not compensable. However, pre-incident issues that were exacerbated by the incident, or that created a vulnerability for the incident to produce further impairment, are compensable.

Minority status is not a risk factor for PTSD (Koch, Douglas, Nicholls, & O'Neil, 2006). However, in the United States, African Americans report more unfair treatment by the police than Whites (Bjornstrom, 2015). Also, compared to Whites, African Americans report more negative emotions after interactions with the police, and less of a sense of having received procedural justice (Bjornstrom, 2015). These issues require attention when applying Goodman-Delahunty and Foote's (2013) model in police misconduct cases concerning African American plaintiffs seeking damages for trauma. When assessing minorities regarding trauma-related symptoms from police misconduct, Koch et al. (2006) note the importance of doing so from the unique perspective of the plaintiff. Does the plaintiff believe their race was related to the alleged police misconduct; and if so, why?

Some may classify a police officer's particular use of force at the point of arrest as minor even if it was technically misconduct. However, irrespective of the severity of the inappropriate use of force, the incident could play a minor or major role in the plaintiff's ability to function depending upon their pre-incident issues, vulnerabilities, resilience, experiences and appraisal of the event (Carter & Forsyth, 2009). The actual severity of the misconduct will not always correspond with psychological ramifications in a consistent manner across plaintiffs, which is important to know when asked to provide an opinion regarding whether such incidents can be expected to produce the psychological injuries captured by the evaluation and alleged by the plaintiff. Inaccuracy and bias can be introduced when evaluators assess for trauma from police misconduct through their personal culturally informed scope of likely aftereffects. Notably, African Americans are about 13% of the U.S. population, but comprise 47% of defendants that were wrongfully convicted and subsequently exonerated as of October 2016 (Gross, Possley, & Stephens, 2017). Therefore, when addressing the impact of police misconduct, the evaluator should capture the examinee's unique experience of the trauma; whether the plaintiff views the officer's actions as police work or murder. If the wrongfulness of the officer's conduct has yet to be established, then the evaluator should share her opinions with conditional statements pending a future determination by the court about what factually occurred (Carter & Forsyth, 2009).

According to Weitzer and Tuch (2004), evaluators assessing for trauma from police misconduct may find it useful to explore an examinee's pre-incident experiences with police officers, his exposure to news coverage of police brutality, and his experiences living in a high crime neighborhood. Accordingly, an awareness of the following research may assist the evaluator. Per Brunson and Miller (2006), youths growing up in communities, like RM's, are subjected to aggressive policing at the expense of community relations and restoring trust between the police and community members. They found that police officers were not reported to apologize or to assert the suspect's innocence when police searches did not reveal a violation of the law (Brunson & Miller, 2006). In addition to pre-incident exposure to police harassment, any post-complaint retaliation or harassment by the defendants should be noted by the evaluator and considered in an analysis of causation. Likewise, evaluators should explore and evaluate non-compensable detriment from unrelated hardships in life during the stage three interval, such as transportation issues, a lack of childcare, other legal involvement, and lapses in medical insurance. These issues are known to commonly occur in communities with concentrated disadvantage, which is where police misconduct often occurs.

Evaluators in police misconduct cases are often required to explore a number of pre-incident and post-incident threats to well being and mental health in order to reach a conclusion that but for the instant police misconduct experience, psychological trauma would not have manifested. Evaluators in police misconduct cases should be aware of factors characteristic of disadvantaged and minority communities due to societal challenges faced by plaintiffs from communities with aggressive policing (Brunson & Miller, 2006) and how negatively communities of color perceive the police compared to White communities (Cochran & Warren, 2012; Redner-Vera & Galeste, 2015). Again, since police use of force incidents are disproportionately experienced by minorities, their experiences require exploration. The evaluator should have an understanding of how such factors could have affected the examinee's developmental trajectory, functioning and mental health symptoms to ascertain: (a) vulnerabilities to being detrimentally affected or traumatized by the police encounter at issue; and (b) whether the examinee's trauma can be accounted for by pre-incident factors irrespective of whether the police misconduct at issue occurred.

In police misconduct cases, evaluators commonly explore the examinee's history of Adverse Childhood Experiences (ACEs) and exposure to concentrated community disadvantage, which share associations with maladjustment and trauma (Baglivio, Wolff, Epps, & Nelson, 2017). Likewise, the evaluator may wish to explore the examinee's fears of deportation. Becerra, Wagaman, Androff, Messing, and Castillo (2016) found that when people had a greater fear of deportation, they also had less confidence that the police would not engage in misconduct (excessive use of force) at the point of arrest. As previously indicated, evaluators assessing for trauma from police misconduct may find it useful to explore an examinee's pre-incident experiences with police officers (Weitzer & Tuch, 2004). Borrero (2001) surveyed a sample of inner-city youth regarding their experiences of excessive force, police misconduct or both. The sample of 132 youth set forth approximately 400 negative experiences (e.g., physical aggression, verbal degradation, false accusations, being photographed, being threatened, etc.), which may inform the evaluator's assessment; particularly, if the plaintiff is a minor.

According to Bryant-Davis and Ocampo (2006), racist incidents can be traumatic and create persistent impairment in physical, cognitive, emotional and social functioning. Thus, in police misconduct cases where race is at issue for the examinee, the evaluator should assess for a history of racist-incident based trauma un restricted to the examinee's particular experiences with the police. Carter and Forsyth (2009) offered a guide for the forensic assessment of race-based traumatic stress reaction, which can be adapted to fit into the evaluator's procedures in police misconduct cases. Bryant-Davis and Ocampo (2006) also cite research regarding assessment instruments designed for measuring such issues; though, admissibility issues should be explored prior to using them. Goodman-Delahunty and Foote (2013) note the relevance of exploring litigation-related stress during the stage three interval. In police misconduct cases, the evaluator may consider exploring this concept generally, as well as inquiring about race-based stress associated with undergoing depositions and psychological evaluations with professionals from different races and levels of power. The examinee's experiences with law enforcement while attending court for the civil litigation could also yield relevant information. While there is discussion about how to make juvenile justice courts more trauma-informed (Crosby, 2016), we are unaware of any such discussion for youth or adult plaintiffs with trauma presenting in court for civil litigation against the police.

Across these special areas of psycholegal consideration, evaluators must rely upon general forensic mental health assessment skills. For example, the use of psychological testing should be strongly considered in light of the need for a multi-method and multisource analysis of issues relevant to an assessment of causation and the nature and extent of the plaintiff's psychological problems. There is no one psychological test or instrument which definitely answers the psycholegal question regarding causation. Psychological testing may provide data relevant to issues pertaining to causation, but the testing itself does not answer the causation question directly. Intelligence testing might provide information related to adverse cognitive effects potentially caused by the police misconduct. So-called personality tests assess for emotional states and traits that could be relevant to or caused by one of a variety of adverse experiences, including misconduct by law enforcement. Specialized tests or specific embedded scales in tests might be utilized to help assess whether a plaintiff has post-traumatic stress.

Effort testing can be used to assess whether the plaintiff is minimizing or exaggerating cognitive or emotional problems. For example, the evaluator may wish to comment upon the findings of psychological testing, the reporting of unlikely or extreme symptoms during the interview or repeated and significant discrepancies between his reported and observed symptoms. Forensic evaluators should consider if the examinee is willing to deny symptoms during the interview and refrains from indiscriminately making claims of impairment. Commonly, evaluators undertaking this work will consider the following in their analysis of causality.

## Analyzing Causality in Police Misconduct Cases

In the illustrative case of RM, he had a lengthy history of arrests and custodial sentences. This history may lead some to question how his instant arrest could have resulted in trauma. For one, in the case example, RM's prior arrests were not described as eventful. In contrast, the instant arrest was unique in that it appears to fit the characteristics of a Criterion-A event. Since this arrest was wrongful, research suggests his time in custody was likely to be more psychologically detrimental or traumatic than his past experiences in custody for crimes he actually committed (Campbell & Denov, 2004). These possibilities and likelihoods require exploration during the evaluator's interview.

We have reviewed a variety of general and special considerations when conducting evaluations in connection with police misconduct cases. In the preceding section, our description of some of these considerations was not intended to be exhaustive. For police misconduct cases involving inner-city minorities, there is a large number of considerations and alternative hypotheses to be explored. The reader may wonder how causation could be reasonably determined in one of these cases. Therefore, the following brief fictional example concerning RM is provided to illustrate an analysis of causation in one of these cases.

The incident, as alleged by RM, is a qualifying Criterion-A event, which is notable should his allegations be established by the court. RM's evaluation did not reveal pre-incident difficulties that serve to explain his current PTSD apart from the incident. He reported his first arrest was at 11-years-old, and despite the dozens of arrests since then, he still remembers that first arrest and his fear. That said, he has not experienced fear on an ongoing basis since age 11. Rather, he solely reported remembering his fear. No intense fears were found in connection with his subsequent arrests until the one at issue in this evaluation. Regarding his PTSD, his difficulties are not associated with dreams, reminders, memories or triggers about anything unrelated to the current incident. These symptoms had their onset with the incident, and there were no additional traumatic events he experienced around that time. Further, his other posttraumatic symptoms that are not event-specific (e.g., helplessness, sadness, anhedonia, fear, withdrawal, etc.) presented along with the incident. These findings support an association between the incident and his PTSD difficulties in this examiner's opinion. This conclusion is in agreement with the opinions of other professionals that have assessed him, and the collateral interview findings provided by his employer and psychotherapist. On the contrary, RM's personality disorder issues appear to have carried through to the present from the pre-incident interval without being exacerbated by the incident.

Before the incident, RM was working full time at a recycling plant and was getting his life together after his second prison sentence ended. He was 5′8″ and 230 pounds. However, at the time of this evaluation, he was working for a temp agency and was severely overweight at nearly 280 pounds. Since the incident, his functioning has declined across family, employment, financial, recreational and relationship domains with respect to his emotional, cognitive, and interpersonal functioning.

Per RM's description of the incident, he reported believing that the police were going to kill him. He could not adjust when in custody despite previously being able to quickly acclimate to correctional settings. On the contrary, he reported being paranoid, hypervigilant and in physical pain. Facility records corroborate his low activity level and seclusion. By his recollection, it felt like he was outside of his body and was watching the incident like a movie when it occurred. By all accounts, he has not experienced any other potentially traumatizing incidents since the incident at hand.

RM also reported that his sense of seeking justice through this litigation overshadows any litigation stress. RM has a motive to malinger. However, according to the findings of his psychological testing, he did not engage in overreporting of symptoms. He did not describe unlikely or extreme symptoms during his interview. During his interview, there were not repeated and significant discrepancies between his reported and observed symptoms. He also denied a variety of symptoms during his interview and was not indiscriminately making claims of impairment. There is a substantial body of corroborating documentation that has captured the course of his difficulties. Therefore, neither malingering nor overreporting of symptoms were supported in this examiner's opinion.

This examiner considered several alternative hypotheses for RM's development of PTSD symptoms after the incident. For example, this examiner considered his removal and placement in juvenile detention during his childhood. This examiner also considered his adverse childhood experiences, such as his father's incarceration. However, RM never resided with his father and these hypotheses would not account for the timing of his PTSD symptom onset. This examiner considered if concentrated community disadvantage could account for his struggles. However, he denied experiencing crime or violence in his community until the violence of the instant incident. While community factors may account for his pre-incident delinquency and antisocial behavior, it cannot account for the timing or the development of his PTSD. He denied a history of pre-incident race-based trauma, except for being called a racial slur on one occasion by a White youth detention center staff member. However, he viewed the system as just and stated he was deserving of his punishments over the years for his offenses, but not this time. In his view, the incident would not have happened if he was White or wealthy. His resilience (e.g., history of multiple arrests) and strategies to keep himself safe at the point of arrest suddenly and unexpectedly failed, which contributed to his sense that he was going to die. While he denied ever trusting the police given how they have treated him since his youth, he reported becoming overconfident in the police to treat him fairly if he cooperated. He expressed guilt for blaming people in the past for bringing use of force incidents upon themselves by being argumentative and defiant.

The evaluator may conclude that RM's developmental trajectory would have been vastly different if his parents were able to exercise adequate parental control, and if he was not placed in juvenile detention, or if he was provided with a trauma-informed court experience as a juvenile. Indeed, RM appears to have a set of issues that impair his judgment such that he continues to have run-ins with the police. However, this vulnerability to potentially experiencing excessive use of force at the point of an arrest and a resulting PTSD diagnosis does not invalidate his claim or provide an alternative explanation for the onset and nature of his PTSD symptoms. For the purpose of this illustration, we should note that real world examples will rarely allow for analyses of causation that cut so clearly in support of the plaintiff or defense. However, in the fictitious case of RM, the police encounter at issue appears to best explain his PTSD.

## Conclusion

In the case of a claim for police misconduct, plaintiffs and their lawyers undertake a cost/benefit analysis before considering whether to retain a forensic psychologist with an expertise in trauma. Forensic psychologists involved in constitutional tort claims should be highly experienced in the evaluation of harm, and proficiently practicing within the forensic specialty. Also, given the typical parameters of these cases, psychologists undertaking this work should have training, experience and some level of expertise concerning trauma, correctional psychology, disadvantaged communities, and the psychological evaluation of ethnocultural minorities. Hopefully the chapter has refined your understanding of the general and special considerations the forensic psychologist will bring to bear in police misconduct cases.

## Questions/Activities for Further Exploration

1. Indemnification of police officers means that when they are found liable in civil litigation, the municipality (as opposed to the officer) pays the damages. While this allows for the injured to recover larger sums of money than an officer could pay on his or her own, this lack of personal accountability could be a missed opportunity to deter future misconduct. Identify proposed solutions to this dilemma.
2. Civil litigation proceedings are generally open to the public. Take a trip to a courthouse and observe a police misconduct trial and describe your observation in the context of the issues discussed in this chapter.
3. Retaining a forensic psychologist in these cases can be prohibitively expensive. However, according to the APA, psychologists recognize all people should be able to access and receive benefit from our services. Since contingent fee

agreements are prohibited, discuss creative ways psychologists can assist and still earn a living. Consider the ethical issues associated with each solution, including working pro-bono.

# References

American Educational Research Association, American Psychological Association, National Council on Measurement in Education, & Joint Committee on Standards for Educational and Psychological Testing (U.S.). (2014). *Standards for educational and psychological testing*. Washington, DC: AERA.

American Psychiatric Association. (2013). *Diagnostic and statistical manual of mental disorders (DSM-5®)*. Arlington: American Psychiatric Association.

American Psychological Association. (2013). Specialty guidelines for forensic psychology. *American Psychologist, 68*, 7–19.

American Psychological Association. (2017). *Multicultural guidelines: An ecological approach to context, identity, and intersectionality*. Washington, DC: Author.

American Psychological Association. (2018). Statement on the effects of deportation and forced separation of immigrants, their families, and communities. *American Journal of Community Psychology, 62*, 3–12. https://doi.org/10.1002/ajcp.12256

Baglivio, M. T., Wolff, K. T., Epps, N., & Nelson, R. (2017). Predicting adverse childhood experiences: The importance of neighborhood context in youth trauma among delinquent youth. *Crime & Delinquency, 63*(2), 166–188.

Becerra, D., Wagaman, M., Androff, D., Messing, J., & Castillo, J. (2016). Policing immigrants: Fear of deportations and perceptions of law enforcement and criminal justice. *Journal of Social Work, 17*(6), 715–731.

Bjornstrom, E. E. (2015). Race-ethnicity, nativity, neighbourhood context and reports of unfair treatment by police. *Ethnic and Racial Studies, 38*(12), 2019–2036.

Blanchard, E., Hickling, E., Taylor, A., Buckley, T., Loos, W., & Walsh, J. (1998). Effects of litigation settlements on posttraumatic stress symptoms in motor vehicle accident victims. *Journal of Traumatic Stress, 11*(2), 337–354.

Borrero, M. (2001). The widening mistrust between youth and police. Families in society. *The Journal of Contemporary Social Services, 82*(4), 399–408.

Brandl, S. G. (2017). *Police in America*. Thousand Oaks, CA: SAGE Publications.

Brunson, R., & Miller, J. (2006). Gender, race, and urban policing. *Gender & Society, 20*(4), 531–552.

Bryant-Davis, T., & Ocampo, C. (2006). A therapeutic approach to the treatment of racist-incident-based trauma. *Journal of Emotional Abuse, 6*(4), 1–22.

Butler, L. J., Scammell, M. K., & Benson, E. B. (2016). The Flint, Michigan, water crisis: A case study in regulatory failure and environmental injustice. *Environmental Justice, 9*(4), 93–97.

Campbell, K., & Denov, M. (2004). The burden of innocence: Coping with a wrongful imprisonment. *Canadian Journal of Criminology and Criminal Justice, 46*(2), 139–164.

Carter, R., & Forsyth, J. (2009). A guide to the forensic assessment of race-based traumatic stress reactions. *The Journal of the American Academy of Psychiatry and the Law, 37*, 28–40.

Cochran, J. C., & Warren, P. Y. (2012). Racial, ethnic, and gender differences in perceptions of the police. The salience of officer race within the context of racial profiling. *Journal of Contemporary Criminal Justice, 28*, 206–227.

Crosby, S. D. (2016). Trauma-informed approaches to juvenile justice: A critical race perspective. *Juvenile and Family Court Journal, 67*(1), 5–18.

DeJesus, S., Buigas, R., & Denny, R. (2012). Evaluation of culturally diverse populations. In D. Faust (Ed.), *Coping with psychiatric and psychological testimony* (6th ed., pp. 248–265). New York: Oxford University Press.

DeVeaux, M. I. (2013). The trauma of the incarceration experience. *Harvard Civil Rights-Civil Liberties Law Review, 48*, 257.

Elinson, Z., & Frosch, D. (2015, July 15). Cost of police-misconduct cases soars in big US. cities. *The Wall Street Journal.* Retrieved from https://www.wsj.com/articles/cost-of-police-misconduct-cases-soars-in-big-u-s-cities-1437013834

Emery, R., & Maazel, I. M. (2000). Why civil rights lawsuits do not deter police misconduct: The conundrum of indemnification and a proposed solution. *Fordham Urban Law Journal, 28*, 587.

Fayz, M. C. (1994). Fifteenth annual survey of sixth circuit law, "civil rights." *Detroit College of Law Review, 1994*(2), 375–466.

Fellner, J. (2015). *Callous and cruel: Use of force against inmates with mental disabilities in US jails and prisons.* New York: Human Rights Watch.

Fletcher-Janzen, E., Strickland, T., & Reynolds, C. R. (Eds.). (2002). *Handbook of cross-cultural neuropsychology.* New York: Plenum Press.

Frumkin, I. B. (2015). Cross-cultural issues. In *Forensic practitioner's toolbox.* Washington, D.C.: A joint project of divisions 41 and 42 of the American Psychological Association. http://forensictoolbox.com/Sections/cross-cultural-issues

Frumkin, I. B., & Friedland, J. (1995). Forensic evaluations in immigration cases: Evolving issues. *Behavioral Sciences & the Law, 13*(4), 477–489.

Fryer, R. G., Jr. (2019). An empirical analysis of racial differences in police use of force. *Journal of Political Economy, 127*(3), 1210.

Goff, P. A., Lloyd, T., Geller, A., Raphael, S., & Glaser, J. (2016). *The science of justice: Race, arrests, and use of force.* Los Angeles: Center for Policing Equity.

Goodman-Delahunty, J., & Foote, W. E. (2013). Using a five-stage model to evaluate workplace discrimination injuries. *Psychological Injury and Law, 6*(2), 92–98.

Gray-Little, B. (2002). The assessment of psychopathology in racial and ethnic minorities. In J. Butcher (Ed.), *Clinical personality assessment: Practical approaches* (2nd ed., pp. 171–189). New York: Oxford University Press.

Gross, S., Possley, M., & Stephens, K. (2017). *Race and wrongful convictions in the United States.* Irvine: National Registry of Exonerations Newkirk Center For Science And Society. University of California Irvine.

Hall v. Galie (2009) U.S. Dist. LEXIS 21385 (E.D. Penn. Mar 17, 2009)

Jackson v. State. Bd. of Pardons & Paroles, 540 U.S. 880,124 S. Ct. 319 (2003).

Jaffee v. Redmond 518 U.S. (1996).

Kane, A. W., & Dvoskin, J. A. (2011). *Evaluation for personal injury claims.* New York: Oxford University Press.

Karlan, P. S. (2003). Disarming the private attorney general. *University of Illinois Law Review, 2000*, 183.

Kaufman, E. R. (1991). Choosing the insidious path: West Virginia University Hospitals, Inc. v. Casey and the Importance of Experts in Civil Rights Litigation. *N.Y.U. Review of Law & Social Change, 19*, 57.

Koch, W. J., Douglas, K. S., Nicholls, T. L., & O'Neil, M. L. (2006). *American Psychology-Law Society Series. Psychological injuries: Forensic assessment, treatment, and law.* New York: Oxford University Press.

Larson, R. (1976). The civil rights attorneys fees awards act of 1976. *Clearinghouse Review, 10*, 778.

Lewis, R. & Veltman, N. (2014, Dec 5). Can the NYPD spot the abusive cop? WNYC News. Retrieved from https://www.wnyc.org/story/can-the-nypd-spot-the-abusive-cop/

Lim, N. (2016). Cultural differences in emotion: differences in emotional arousal level between the East and the West. *Integrative Medicine Research, 5*(2), 105–109.

Maddux, J. (2010). Recommendations for forensic evaluators conducting interpreter-mediated interviews. *International Journal of Forensic Mental Health, 9*(1), 55–62.

Menjivar, C., & Bejarano, C. (2004). Latino immigrants' perceptions of crime and police authorities in the United States: A case study from the Phoenix Metropolitan area. *Ethnic and Racial Studies, 27*, 120–148.

National Association of Judiciary Interpreters & Translators (NAJIT). (2006). *NAJIT position paper: Modes of interpretation: Simultaneous, consecutive, & sight translation*. Atlanta, GA: NAJIT.

New York State Division of Criminal Justice Services Data for Arrest Dispositions. (2019a, March 22). Retrieved from https://www.criminaljustice.ny.gov/crimnet/ojsa/dispos/newyork.pdf

New York State Division of Criminal Justice Services Data for Arrest Dispositions. (2019b, March 22). Retrieved from https://www.criminaljustice.ny.gov/crimnet/ojsa/dispos/queens.pdf

NYPD Use of Force Data Tables. (n.d.). Retrieved from https://www1.nyc.gov/site/nypd/stats/reports-analysis/use-of-force-data.page

Prison Litigation Reform Act, 42 U.S.C. § 1997e (1996).

Redner-Vera, E., & Galeste, M. A. (2015). Attitudes and marginalization: Examining American Indian perceptions of law enforcement among adolescents. *Journal of Ethnicity in Criminal Justice, 13*(4), 283–308.

Reinders Folmer, C. P., Desmet, P. T. M., & Van Boom, W. H. (2019). Beyond compensation? Examining the role of apologies in the restoration of victims' needs in simulated tort cases. *Law and Human Behavior, 43*(4), 329–341.

Robbins v. Chronister, 435 F. 3d 1238 (10 Cir. 2006).

Schwartz, J. C. (2014). Police indemnification. *New York University Law Review, 89*(3), 885–1005.

Silver, M. A. (1988). Evening the odds: The case for attorneys' fee awards for administrative resolution of Title VI and Title VII disputes. *North Carolina Law Review, 67*, 379.

Substance Abuse and Mental Health Services Administration. (2014). *SAMHSA's concept of trauma and guidance for a trauma-informed approach. HHS Publication No. (SMA) 14–4884*. Rockville, MD: Substance Abuse and Mental Health Services Administration.

Sutton v. City of Yonkers, 2017 U.S. Dist. LEXIS 46853 (S.D.N.Y. Mar. 29, 2017).

Taylor, S., Fedoroff, I. C., Koch, W. J., Thordarson, D. S., Fecteau, G., & Nicki, R. M. (2001). Posttraumatic stress disorder arising after road traffic collisions: Patterns of response to cognitive–behavior therapy. *Journal of Consulting and Clinical Psychology, 69*(3), 541.

Trinkner, R., Kerrison, E., & Goff, P. (2019). The force of fear: Police stereotype threat, self-legitimacy, and support for excessive force. UC Berkeley. https://doi.org/10.1037/lhb0000339. Retrieved from https://escholarship.org/uc/item/1sh5f4fg

Wagoner, R. (2017). The use of an interpreter during a forensic interview: Challenges and considerations. *Psychiatric Services, 68*(5), 507–511.

Wasserman, H. M. (2017). Police misconduct, video recording, and procedural barriers to rights enforcement. *North Carolina Law Review, 96*, 1313.

Weitzer, R., & Tuch, S. A. (2004). Race and perceptions of police misconduct. *Social Problems, 51*(3), 305–325.

Young, G., Kane, A. W., & Nicholson, K. (2007). *Causality of psychological injury: Presenting evidence in court*. New York: Springer Science & Business Media.

# Part III

# Presence of Trauma in Criminal Matters

**Rafael Art. Javier, Elizabeth A. Owen, and Jemour A. Maddux**

## Introduction

In this section, we invite the reader to consider the implications of trauma experiences but now more specifically related to criminal behaviors. As discussed earlier, a history of trauma can complicate ordinary situations in general by obfuscating the individual's capacity to assess the seriousness and severity of interactions with others, where assessing someone's true motivation may be complicated by distorted perceptions of others directly derived from early traumatic experiences. The implication of distorted perceptions reaches its most serious and pernicious consequences in behaviors where serious crimes are committed against other people, some of them sadistically and viciously delivered. It requires from the forensic professional the need to engage in the examination of possible traumatic experiences in perpetrators of crimes, in addition to the victims, to contextualize the criminal act without justifying such acts. It is a difficult but critical task for which we need to keep a firm line if we are going to remain faithful to the standards of forensic practice.

We begin this section by examining intimate partner violence with a thoughtful and empirically well-supported contribution by Paradis, Bowen, and McCullough (Chap. 15) which focuses on exploring the psychological effects and legal defenses used in intimate partner violence victims. This chapter not only reviews research on the prevalence of intimate partner violence (IPV) but also describes the psychological effects of IPV in different populations. In this context, the authors provide a

R. A. Javier
Psychology, St. John's University, Queens, NY, USA

E. A. Owen
Columbia University/Teachers College, New York, NY, USA

J. A. Maddux
Lamb & Maddux, LLC, Hackensack, NJ, USA

thoughtful examination of the evolution of the terms battered woman syndrome
(BWS) and battered person syndrome (BPS) and how these terms can be misunderstood or misused to promote myths and stereotypes about individuals exposed to
IPV. An important issue for the forensic professional is the consideration of the
evolving judicial view about the admissibility of testimony about IPV and the challenges associated with the role of the expert in conducting mental state at the time
of the offense evaluations of defendants charged with assaulting or killing abusive
partners. The included case examples serve to illustrate how expert testimony about
IPV and mental state at the time of the offense can affect the outcome of different
criminal cases.

Another core issue also included in this section is the exploration of not only sex
offenses and victims but also the perpetrators of these offenses. We believe that this
is an area in need of forensic attention as there is too much at stake for the victims
and our society. We also believe that only by considering and exploring all the elements involved in sex offenses will we be in a better position to provide the kind of
response expected of the forensic professional. In this context, we have a contribution by Lamade (Chap. 16) which focuses more specifically on a discussion of
standard assessment tools to be considered when assessing these conditions.
According to this author, sexual offenders represent a heterogeneous group of individuals who are, when appropriate, heavily regulated by complex federal and state
laws. The greatest challenge for the forensic professional is the level of accuracy
required in the evaluation to determine recidivism and dangerousness, in the
assessment of mitigating factors at sentencing, and to determine appropriate management and treatment services in the community. That challenge is made even
more complex as these examinations are done in the context of considering trauma
within this population, which includes looking at antecedents of childhood trauma,
and the impact of trauma incurred in the context of incarceration, commitment, and
legislation regulating sex offender management in the community. This chapter
provides an excellent overview of relevant laws and an examination of standard
forensic tools to assess risk for recidivism and treatment. We also wanted to make
sure that in evaluating and treating this condition, we also consider some important
and emerging information coming from neuropsychological findings about sex
offenders. This is the focus of the contribution by DeMarco and Geller (Chap. 17)
who ask us to consider not only the significance of psychological trauma but also
the possible involvement of traumatic brain injury in some of these cases. The
extent to which TBIs may be the cause of these criminal behaviors, certainly
changes the nature of intervention appropriate for these types of defendants.

The contribution by Shaw, Rogers, and Gefner (Chap. 18) which focuses on a
discussion of the role of resiliency in forensically involved youth with a history of
trauma, becomes quite relevant here if we are going to provide the court with a more
comprehensive understanding of the context in criminal behaviors. This chapter
highlights the importance of understanding childhood trauma as a risk factor for the
youth population, as well as on the need to assess and build upon resilience factors
in working with this population. To that end, the authors first examine concepts of
childhood trauma and adverse childhood experiences. While we still do not have a

definitive consensus as to the definition of resilience and no "gold standard" instrument to use to assess resilience in youth, these authors provide sufficient empirical evidence of various protective factors within the individual, family, and community that practitioners can use to strengthen intervention strategies with youth within the legal system. In that context, they also outline clinical applications and practical techniques and assessment tools that can be used in the evaluation of trauma and resilience with this population. Finally, this chapter covers case examples of how this information can be used in forensic contexts. It is an important contribution which highlights the fact that trauma does not affect everyone or in the same manner and that it is important for the forensic professional to keep that in mind to avoid a biased presentation of the material by also including areas not affected by traumatic experiences, as part of the forensic evaluation of the specific trauma under consideration.

We conclude this section with a discussion on the Treatment Diversion Court in the adjudication of crimes. Forensic psychologists are more and more likely to encounter veterans involved in legal system and in need of forensic services, as well as defendants whose substance abuse may have been implicated in their legal trouble. Thus, we decided to include a few chapters on an important development emerging in some courts around the country. We are referring to specialized treatment diversion courts meant to provide an alternative to traditional court to crime adjudication for a population of defendants for whom alternative approach to punishment may provide the best outcome for the individuals involved and the society. This is particularly the case for returning soldiers (veterans), who find themselves involved in the justice system, where early and deployment-related trauma histories may be involved. The contribution by Lamade and Lee (Chap. 19), in this regard, provides an excellent context to understand the history and basic components of these types of courts and the complexity associated with the implementation of such programs. It is an important but delicate development because there is a lot at stake: to ensure the need to secure the protection of the society at large and to do that while holding the defendants responsible for their crimes in the context of also considering the special circumstances of the crime. It requires a comprehensive and fully integrated approach to crime assessment and contexts, including the active involvement and participations of multiple sectors of our society. The reader is encouraged to become familiar with an example of how such an approach can operate with a description of a program operating in a Queens Court under the direct supervision of Hon. Marcia Hirsch (Chap. 22).

# Chapter 15
# Intimate Partner Violence: Psychological Effects and Legal Defenses

Cheryl Paradis, Monique Bowen, and Gene McCullough

## Introduction

Domestic violence is "a pattern of abusive behavior in any relationship that is used by one partner to gain or maintain power and control over another intimate partner. Domestic violence can be physical, sexual, emotional, economic, or psychological actions or threats of actions that influence another person. This includes any behaviors that intimidate, manipulate, humiliate, isolate, frighten, terrorize, coerce, threaten, blame, hurt, injure, or wound someone" (United States Department of Justice, 2011a, 2011b).

Different terms have been used to describe domestic violence, including spousal abuse, wife battering, and intimate partner violence (IPV). Domestic violence or intimate partner violence (IPV) includes physical and sexual aggression, emotional abuse, stalking, and reproductive coercion. These abusive behaviors are observed in all manner of relationships including former or current same-sex, heterosexual, or gender-nonconforming intimate partners. Males and females can be both perpetrators and victims (Carmo, Grams, & Magalhães, 2011; Messinger, 2011; Morse, 1995). (Note: For the purposes of this paper, the terms spouse or partner will be used for couples who were legally married, common law married, or partnered in a long-term domestic relationship.)

C. Paradis (✉)
State University of New York—Downstate Medical Center, Marymount Manhattan College, New York, NY, USA

State University of New York—Downstate Medical Center, New York, NY, USA

M. Bowen
Antioch University New England, Keene, NH, USA

State University of New York—Downstate Medical Center, New York, NY, USA

G. McCullough
Mount Sinai West Hospital, New York, NY, USA

© Springer Nature Switzerland AG 2020                                    351
R. A. Javier et al. (eds.), *Assessing Trauma in Forensic Contexts*,
https://doi.org/10.1007/978-3-030-33106-1_15

In forensic settings, the terms battered woman syndrome (BWS) and battered person syndrome (BPS) have been widely used. However, since reactions to IPV are so varied, there is some controversy about the use of these terms, with a sense that each one imperfectly and incompletely describes the experience. Moreover, both BWS and BPS can be viewed as implicating the victimized individual as being mentally ill, rather than as someone who has no diagnosable psychiatric illness but may have instead struggled to cope and survive ongoing abuse. Keeping in mind that each person has a unique history and clinical presentation, these terms will be used at times in this paper because they are recognized by the court system.

To illustrate the challenges of mounting a BWS/BPS defense, consider the ways in which the following criminal case demonstrates how testimony about IPV can affect a trial outcome. On February 18, 2008, a 49-year-old school secretary shot and killed her husband, a retired police sergeant, as he shaved in the bathroom of their home. She was charged with murder in the second degree and criminal possession of a weapon. During the month-long trial in Queens, New York, she testified that her husband emotionally and physically abused her for many years of their marriage. She reported that he broke her nose the day before the instant offense. She also testified that, while she received treatment for her injuries at the hospital, "He kept calling me from the parking lot, saying that if he saw the police coming, he would kill me and them, and go down in a blaze of glory." She described how she shot her husband the following day, stating that, as she held the gun in her hand, he picked up a second gun and pointed it at her. She testified that, after shooting him five times with his 0.38-caliber revolver, she then used his semiautomatic, Glock pistol, firing six more bullets at him. The jury acquitted the defendant, Barbara Sheehan, of murder in the second degree and convicted her on the charge of criminal possession of a weapon. Jurors in this case, and other cases with similar testimony about IPV, undoubtedly based their verdicts, in part, on their judgment that the defendant was a victim who took action because she feared for her life (Bilefsky, 2011a, 2011b, 2011c, 2011d; Dwyer, 2011; People v Sheehan, 2013).

## Prevalence Rates of Intimate Partner Violence

Reported prevalence rates of IPV vary greatly, in part, because of how IPV has been defined and measured. While some studies have considered only physical and sexual violence, others have included emotional, psychological, and economic abuses. The rise and immediacy of social media, including near-instant capabilities to connect with others, has changed the nature of and expanded the definition of what constitutes IPV. For example, with the advent of smart home technology (e.g., remote video monitoring; the Echo Dot speaker, with its "Alexa," smart assistant), individuals and groups now have the wherewithal to constantly observe, harass, and control their partners (Bowles, 2018).

Much of the early IPV research focused almost exclusively on heterosexual couples where a male perpetrator abused a female partner. However, IPV occurs in all types of intimate relationships, with both women and men as perpetrators and/or victims (Carmo et al., 2011; Messinger, 2011; Morse, 1995). An early study by Tjaden and Thoennes (2000) included 8000 men and 8000 women (randomly selected) who each completed a telephone interview about their experience of IPV. With regard to lifetime prevalence, the researchers found that approximately 20% of the women and 7% of the men reported being physically abused by a past or current, opposite sex partner (Tjaden & Thoennes, 2000). Researchers have found that IPV increased in both frequency and severity during pregnancy and postpartum periods (Bailey, 2010; Finnbogadóttir & Dykes, 2016).

Complicating the problem of comparing prevalence rates across different studies, some studies use either one or five-year prevalence data, while others report on lifetime occurrences. Moreover, some researchers gather data on self-selected samples, or convenience samples, while others make use of the general population as a representative sample. Research findings estimate that 25–50% of women are abused by their partners at some point in their lives and studies find high rates of mutuality of IPV in heterosexual couples, where both partners act abusively (Browne & Williams, 1993; Ewing, 1987; Hellemans, Loeys, Buysse, Dewaele, & De Smet, 2015; Russell, 2010; Thompson et al., 2006; Tjaden & Thoennes, 2000). Although both men and women are identified as aggressors in intimate relationships, women sustain more severe injuries and are more likely to be killed as a result of relationship violence (Anderson, 2002; Carbone-López, Kruttschnitt, & Macmillan, 2006; Centers of Disease Control, 2017; Paulsen & Brewer, 1999; Puzone, Saltzman, Kresnow, Thompson, & Mercy, 2000; Rennison, 2003; Simmons, Knight, & Menard, 2015; Straus & Gelles, 1990; Tjaden & Thoennes, 2000). Tjaden and Thoennes (2000) found that, compared with men, women were 2.9 times more likely to be physically abused, 8.2 times more likely to be stalked, and 22.5 times more likely to be sexually assaulted by partners. An examination of crime statistics finds that women are both more vulnerable to sexual assaults and less likely to successfully negotiate safe sex practices with their partners. Researchers also find an association between IPV and HIV infection in the female population (Campbell et al., 2008; Prather, Fuller, Marshall, & Jeffries 4th, 2016).

Studies have found the reported lifetime rates of IPV to vary not only by gender but also by social and economic class and by racial and ethnic grouping. Numerous studies found higher rates of IPV reported by non-Hispanic black women as compared with non-Hispanic white women of similar socioeconomic class standing in the United States (Breiding, Chen, & Black, 2014; Catalano, Smith, Snyder, & Rand, 2009; Centers for Disease Control, 2017; Fife, Ebersole, Bigatti, Lane, & Huber, 2008; Hazen & Soriano, 2007; Murdaugh, Hunt, Sowell, & Santana, 2004). Breiding et al. (2014) analyzed data from 16,507 completed phone interviews and found these lifetime IPV prevalence rates: non-Hispanic black women (43.7%), Hispanic women (37.1%), non-Hispanic white women (34.6%), and Asian or Pacific Islander women (19.6%). Furthermore, researchers found that, when compared with poor women of other racial and ethnic groups, non-Hispanic black women reported higher rates of severe IPV not resulting in death (e.g., nonfatal strangulation, rape/sexual assault, and stalking) (Black et al., 2010; West, 2018).

Researchers highlight the importance of systematic racial discrimination and other historical legacies of racial trauma in assessing the widespread prevalence of IPV (Stockman, Hayashi, & Campbell, 2015). Models that use a diathesis-stress formulation illustrate the interrelationships between negative life events and family histories of psychological vulnerability (Mourad, Levendosky, Bogat, & Von Eye, 2008). Stress associated with poverty, housing instability, incarceration, and all manner of community violence (e.g., assaults, robberies, witnessing homicides) exposes non-Hispanic black women and men to higher rates of IPV and overall violence than other racial groups (West, 2018).

Researchers hypothesize that IPV is more prevalent in cultures with traditional gender roles and attitudes, with males viewed as the ultimate decision makers who wield a coercive power to control women and children and to promote their own dominance (Adam & Schewe, 2007; Adames & Campbell, 2005; Breiding et al., 2014; Choi, Elkins, & Disney, 2016; Ellison, Trinitapoli, Anderson, & Johnson, 2007; Eng, 1995; Murdaugh et al., 2004; Raj & Silverman, 2002a, 2002b; Volpp, 2011; Yoshihama & Dabby, 2015). In communities heavily influenced by patriarchal norms, the bodies of women and girls have been, and continue to be, controlled by men, with foreign-born women at higher risk of death from lethal forms of IPV than women born in the United States (Azziz-Baumgartner, McKeown, Melvin, Dang, and Reed (2011). One form of violence against women and girls includes culturally sanctioned, female genital circumcision. An estimated 125 million women around the world have undergone this procedure which is common in many countries, including 29 African nations (Javier, Herron, Pantoja, & De Mucci, 2018).

Published rates underestimate the prevalence of IPV in many populations because victims face multiple barriers to reporting. In addition to realistic concerns for their safety, help-seeking behaviors are greatly influenced by ethnocultural and racial background, socioeconomic level, immigration status, and sexual minority identity (Ard & Makadon, 2011; Azziz-Baumgartner et al., 2011; Crenshaw, 1991; Heavey, 2013; Straus & Gelles, 1990; Tjaden & Thoennes, 2000). Immigrants face many unique barriers to reporting IPV, pressing charges, and/or leaving abusive relationships. Fife et al. (2008) surveyed 100 Latina women, 96 of whom were immigrants (primarily from Mexico); approximately one-half of the sample population reported a lifetime history of IPV. Murdaugh et al. (2004) conducted a study of mostly immigrant Hispanic women in the southeastern US and found that almost three-quarters of the women reported experiencing IPV within the previous year. Similarly, Adam (2001) found in her study that more than half of Indian and Pakistani women immigrants reported experiencing IPV within the previous year. The effects of IPV are compounded by social isolation. Raj and Silverman (2002a, 2002b) conducted a study of South Asian, mostly immigrant, women and found that about 40% reported a history of IPV from their current partners. More than half had no family members living in the United States. Dutton (1994) found that immigrant women who lacked fluency in English were less likely to contact the police.

Undocumented immigrant victims of IPV often face a terrible dilemma: remain in an abusive relationship or risk deportation. In some cases, limited English language proficiency further impedes access to and awareness of services available for victims of IPV (Azziz-Baumgartner et al., 2011; Dutton, 1994). Furthermore, harsher US immigration policy enforcement following the 2016 election also makes it more difficult to estimate prevalence rates as undocumented immigrants are significantly less likely to report IPV to the police for fear of drawing attention to their family members' immigration status (Adams & Campbell, 2012; Gupta et al., 2010). The number of sexual assaults reported by Latinas in the previous year dropped 40% in Houston and 25% in Los Angeles. During the same year the number of IPV reports dropped by 10% in Los Angeles (Medina, 2017). This issue was highlighted in a February 2017 case in El Paso, Texas, where a woman was arrested by Immigration and Customs Enforcement (ICE) in the courthouse where she had just applied for and received an order of protection against an abusive partner (Gonzalez, 2017).

While some studies find higher rates of IPV in patriarchal cultures, others find similarly high rates of IPV in heterosexual couples from other cultural backgrounds and in LGBTQ populations (Balsam, Rothblum, & Beauchaine, 2005; Blosnich & Bossarte, 2009; Carvalho, Lewis, Derlega, Winstead, & Viggiano, 2011; Freedner, Freed, Yang, & Austin, 2002; Hellemans et al., 2015; Merrill & Wolfe, 2000; Murray & Mobley, 2009; Potoczniak, Murot, Crosbie-Burnett, & Potoczniak, 2003; Tjaden, Thoennes, & Allison, 1999). Messinger (2011) analyzed data from the National Violence Against Women Survey and found that, compared to heterosexual individuals, those in same-sex relationships were significantly more likely to report histories of IPV. Waldner-Haugrud, Gratch, and Magruder (1997) reported that, compared with gay men, the lesbian women in their study were more likely to be involved in relationships that involved IPV. Studies also found higher rates of IPV among people who identified as bisexual, as compared with other sexual identity and sexual orientation groups (Breiding et al., 2014; Freedner et al., 2002; Messinger, 2011, 2017). A unique difficulty in estimating prevalence rates in sexual minority populations has been that, compared with the better-studied, male abuser-female victim dyad, researchers have been challenged in determining which member of same-sex couples is the abuser and which the victim (Mize, 2008; Mize, Shackelford, & Shackelford, 2009).

There have been fewer studies of IPV in trans∗ individuals than cisgender research participants (those identifying with their sex assigned at birth). [Note: In line with other scholars, we add an asterisk after the prefix trans (trans∗) to indicate that individuals may identify with several gendered suffixes (e.g., woman, man, genderqueer) (Messinger, 2017).] Research on IPV in trans∗ populations shows that the prevalence rates are similar, if not higher, compared with heterosexuals, gay men, or lesbians (Clements, Katz, & Marx, 1999; Langenderfer-Magruder, Whitfield, Walls, Kattari, & Ramos, 2016; Messinger, 2017). In a study by Langenderfer-Magruder et al. (2016), about 30% of trans∗ individuals reported lifetime histories of IPV or dating violence as compared with about 20% of cisgender individuals. Messinger (2017) found that trans∗ women are more likely to be physically injured by abusive partners compared with trans∗ men.

Underreporting of IPV by members of LGBTQ communities remains a serious concern, due in large part to intra- and interpersonal barriers to reporting and seeking help that are shared by heterosexual and cisgender victims of IPV (e.g., feelings of shame, depression, fear of retaliation by the abuser) (Messinger, 2017). They face additional challenges that are specific to their sexual identity or sexual orientation (e.g., homophobia, transphobia), as well as fewer LGBTQ-specific institutional resources and assistance providers (Ard & Makadon, 2011; Brown & Herman, 2015; Messinger, 2017; Pattavina, Hirschel, Buzawa, Faggiani, & Bentley, 2007). Research also suggests that some lesbian women may not self-identify as IPV victims because images/stereotypes remain based in the male perpetrator-female victim model (Hassouneh & Glass, 2008). Moreover, some in LGBTQ communities may avoid disclosing abuse due to concerns about bringing more stigma or further shame on already oft-stigmatized sexual minorities (Messinger, 2017).

Another issue that complicates obtaining accurate prevalence rates of IPV in LGBTQ communities is that assessment measures were created based on research on heterosexual populations (Stephenson & Finneran, 2013). A recent advance in this area was the creation of the IPV-GBM scale (gay, bisexual, and MSM—men who have sex with men) which assesses IPV among LGBTQ populations. This scale has items (e.g., HIV-related IPV items) that are uniquely sensitive to IPV in relationships in these communities (Stephenson & Finneran, 2013).

The large-scale institutional practices that reflect our society's racist, homophobic, sexist, and transphobic history often interfere with victims' help-seeking behaviors. In a study on police bias, Pattavina et al. (2007) analyzed 2000 NIBRS (National Incident-Based Reporting System) data on 176,488 incidents of IPV. They found that arrests were more likely to occur if the victims were white as compared with minority victims. Furthermore, many victims of IPV report that the police and courts were insensitive and unhelpful. The laws of some states do not guarantee equal protection to all individuals (Grant et al., 2011; Langenderfer-Magruder et al., 2016; VAWA, 2012).

While IPV is present in all cultures and can be found in all types of relationships, some individuals face additional physical challenges or social and institutional barriers and find it especially difficult to leave abusive partners. In terms of prevalence rates, Hahn, McCormick, Silverman, Robinson, and Koenen (2014) interviewed 34,563 American adults and found that prevalence rates of IPV were higher in women with physical and psychiatric impairments. Moreover, providing an accurate estimate of IPV rates within faith-based communities continues to present unique, ongoing barriers to reporting, due in part to within-group social norms and religious values. For example, research shows that married, Orthodox Jewish women are less likely to seek help with IPV because of cultural and religious beliefs about the sanctity of marriage and concerns that their children would be shunned in their close-knit communities (Mills, 2009; Ringel & Bina, 2007).

## Legal-Forensic Issues Related to IPV and BWS

There has been an evolution in how the American legal system views perpetrators and victims of IPV. In the past, husbands were legally permitted to abuse their wives; abuse was regarded as a private family matter. This was reflected in an 1824

United States court ruling which described "moderate chastisement" as the following:

> Family broils and dissensions cannot be investigated before the tribunals of the country, without causing a shade over the character of those who are unfortunately engaged in the controversy. To screen from public reproach those who may be thus unhappily situated, let the husband be permitted to exercise the right of moderate chastisement in cases of great emergency and use salutary restraints in every case of misbehavior without being subjected to vexatious prosecutions, resulting in mutual discredit and shame of all parties concerned. (Bradley v. The State of Mississippi, 1824).

A major shift in how the public and the courts viewed IPV occurred with the advent of the women's rights movement of the 1960s–1970s. In addition to the opening of the first battered women's shelter in St. Paul, Minnesota, in 1974, several police departments were named in class action lawsuits. These lawsuits were later resolved when the departments instituted practice changes to enforce assault laws and to protect victims of IPV (Bruno v. Codd, 1978, 1979; Scott v. Hart, 1976).

The first significant federal legislation on domestic violence, the Violence Against Women Act (VAWA), was passed in 1994; it was reauthorized and expanded in 2000, 2005, and 2013. VAWA recognized that violence directed at women was a crime and authorized funding to protect and provide services for victims of IPV. The VAWA Reauthorization Act of 2005 continued the existing funding, extended protections for immigrant women, and mandated that states enforce existing laws, including one that made it illegal for anyone with a restraining order against them to own a gun (Ortega & Busch-Armendariz, 2013; VAWA, 2005). For nearly 20 years, VAWA did not include protections for persons other than women, nor did it require the federal government to recognize sexual or gender minorities. The VAWA Reauthorization Act of 2013 included this nondiscrimination provision: "explicitly bars discrimination based on actual or perceived gender identity or sexual orientation – as well as race, color, religion, national origin, sex or disability. This groundbreaking provision will ensure that lesbian, gay, bisexual and transgender (LGBT) victims of domestic violence, sexual assault, dating violence and stalking are not denied, on the basis of sexual orientation or gender identity, access to critical services..." (The United States Department of Justice Archives, 2014).

The first criminal case in which the defense sought to introduce expert testimony at trial on the psychological effects of IPV was that of Beverly Ibn-Tamas. In 1979, she shot and killed her husband; she claimed he was abusive and, at the time of the instant offense, had threatened her life (Ibn-Tamas v. United States, 1979). The judge ruled that the defense expert, Dr. Lenore Walker, would not be allowed to testify and Ms. Ibn-Tamas was convicted of murder in the second degree. A second trial was ordered and the new presiding judge also excluded expert testimony. Ms. Ibn-Tamas was convicted again but the trial judge imposed the minimum prison sentence (1–5 years); Ms. Ibn-Tamas' appeal to the DC Court of Appeals was unsuccessful (Ibn-Tamas v. United States, 1979).

In recent decades, US courts became more accepting of expert testimony on the psychological effects of IPV; in fact this testimony often served as the central focus of the legal defense (Browne, 2008; Ewing, 1987; Follingstad, 2003; Kinports, 1988;

Russell, 2010; Walker, 1992, 2016; Wells, 1994). The defense often included research findings indicating that, while many women remained in violent domestic relationships due to realistic concerns about safety, others did not leave their abusive partners because years of prolonged abuse resulted in a pattern of psychological symptoms and behaviors known as battered woman syndrome (BWS) and battered person syndrome (BPS) (Dutton, 1994; Walker, 1979, 1992, 1996, 2016).

Walker (1979, 1992, 1996, 2016) broke new ground on the study of the psychological effects of IPV and coined the term BWS. Unlike a psychiatric diagnosis, a syndrome is a cluster of identifiable features or symptoms. Walker described a battered woman as being "repeatedly subjected to any forceful physical or psychological behavior by a man in order to coerce her to do something he wants her to do without any concern for her rights" (Walker, 1979, p xv). She described how abuse can escalate over a period of years to the point that the woman feels trapped and powerless to escape the relationship. Walker (1979) described a three-phase cycle in which the tension-building phase is followed by an acute battering incident, followed by a period of either loving contrition or absence of threat. During the final phase, also referred to as "the honeymoon phase," the abuser often expresses remorse and promises never to be abusive again. According to Walker (1979), the woman often believes or hopes that her partner will change his behavior, at least in the early stages of the relationship. Walker noted that, in the most violent relationships, the last phase—when the fear or danger has subsided—may not actually exist. Walker found that all defendants did not report experiencing each of these three phases; instead, she determined that all three phases were present in a little more than one-third of the cases reviewed (Walker, 1979, 1992, 1996, 2016). Follingstad (2003) wrote: "The cycle of violence has been considered by numerous commentators to be so flexible and limitless (i.e., no time intervals are ever specified) as to be useless for predicting behavior" (Follingstad, 2003, p.503).

Walker (1979, 1992, 1996, 2016) and other researchers (Ewing, 1987; Ewing, 1990; Fife et al., 2008; Mahoney, 1991) identify IPV-associated psychiatric/psychological symptoms and behaviors similar to posttraumatic stress disorder (PTSD). This includes anxiety, hyperarousal, hypervigilance, flashbacks, depression, sleep disturbances, nightmares, and psychological numbness. Those who suffer more severe abuse typically develop more severe symptoms of psychological disturbance and this prompts some to make suicide attempts (Maguigan, 1991; Morse, 1995; Russell, 2010). Victims of IPV may experience cognitive distortions whereby they view the abuse as their own fault or perceive the abuser as all powerful. Some conclude that whatever they might do will not help or might worsen problems and that their best strategy for avoiding injury is to continually attempt to placate the abuser (Ewing, 1987, 1990; Morse, 1995; Tjaden & Thoennes, 2000; Walker, 1979, 1992, 1996, 2016).

Some scholars in this area use the behavioral research paradigms of "learned helplessness" (Seligman, 1972) and the Stockholm syndrome (Adorjan, Christensen, Kelly, & Pawluch, 2012) as ways of understanding the conditions that lead IPV victims to believe they are powerless and unable to escape. With Stockholm syndrome

(Adorjan et al., 2012), a dependent relationship arises in the context of extended hostage events during which some hostages develop a pathological relationship, or bond, with the hostage taker(s). Mahoney (1991) compares battered women with this mental state with victims of Stockholm syndrome.

Walker's (1979, 1992, 1996, 2016) work in this area and her conceptualization of the term "BWS" have advanced the understanding of the psychological effects of IPV over the past 40 years. However, the term has also been misunderstood and used to promote the misconception that all individuals who experience IPV are the same. These misconceptions are illustrated in a 1984 court decision, which described BWS as "a series of common characteristics that appear in women who are abused physically and psychologically over an extended period of time by the dominant male figure in their lives…" with symptoms and traits of "low self-esteem, traditional beliefs about the home, the family, and the female sex role, tremendous feelings of guilt that their marriages are failing and the tendency to accept responsibility for the batterer's actions" (State v Kelly, 1984). Though individuals may share common or similar experiences of IPV, each victim's experience is unique. The BWS paradigm can sometimes be used to perpetuate the myth that victims of IPV are inherently passive or helpless. In fact, many abused partners employ survival skills and strategies to protect themselves and their children from further harm and victimization (Fleming, Newton, Fernandez-Botran, Miller, & Burns, 2012; Russell, 2010; Russell & Melillo, 2006). They use a variety of coping mechanisms, some more internal/psychological (e.g., becoming more self-reliant, focusing on religious beliefs) and others interpersonal (e.g., fighting back, escaping the relationship, seeking social support). Some manage by completing their educations, finding work, or utilizing community resources (e.g., church and religious organizations, police, domestic violence shelter, restraining orders, and orders of protection) (Schneider, 1986; Walker, 1979, 1992, 1996, 2016).

The impact of IPV on people of color and LGBTQ individuals is compounded by the additional stressors of racism, homophobia, transphobia, and discrimination (Messinger, 2011). Added to the stigma associated with membership in racial and sexual minority groups, many describe feeling forced to cope with IPV-associated stressors in environments that are hostile to their race, sexual identity, and sexual orientation. For example, some non-Hispanic black women report feeling added pressure to not "betray their race" in reporting IPV or to avoid stating their marital status and all the connotations that come with the label: "single, black mother" (Lacey, 2010; Messinger, 2017).

Compared to the general population, many LGBTQ individuals experience high rates of stress and mental health problems such as depression, anxiety, and post-traumatic stress disorder (Descamps, Rothblum, Bradford, & Ryan, 2000). Many report they make efforts to conceal their sexual identity and sexual orientation because of understandable and realistic concerns for their safety (Mays & Cochran, 2001). This additional stress can contribute to the development or worsening of psychological problems (Descamps et al., 2000; Houston & McKirnan, 2007; Mays & Cochran, 2001; Remafedi, French, Story, Resnick, & Blum, 1998).

Research has also found that IPV among gay and bisexual men living with HIV was associated with participation in unprotected sex, higher rates of interruptions of consistent medical care, and higher rates of hospitalizations for HIV-related illnesses (Mays & Cochran, 2001; Siemieniuk, Krentz, & Gill, 2013). Despite modern advances in the treatment of HIV, the psychological stress of HIV infection and related complications and illnesses can be compounded by the additional discrimination and accompanying stigmatization experienced by those with HIV (Siemieniuk, Krentz, & Gill, 2013).

To help IPV victims leave abusive relationships, families can provide psychological support, financial assistance, or physical help. However, compared with heterosexual and cisgender individuals, many LGBTQ individuals report receiving less support of all types from their families (Caman, Kristiansson, Granath, & Sturup, 2017). Estrangement and isolation from families of origin have been shown to increase dependency on abusive partners and lessen victims' ability to leave the relationship (Gupta et al., 2010).

The more marginalized a person's identity, the more difficult it will be for that person to access services. For example, people with physical and psychiatric disabilities experience high rates of IPV but unfortunately face additional barriers to reporting abuse and finding assistance (Chang et al., 2003; Hahn et al., 2014). Those who utilize wheelchairs may be unaware of specialized programs, such as "Barrier Free Living," which operates an accessible domestic violence shelter in New York City called Freedom House ("Barrier Free Living", 2018).

It is particularly difficult for some individuals to access community resources. Those from underrepresented groups, such as US-born individuals from racial and ethnic minority backgrounds, people living with disabilities, non-US citizens, undocumented residents, and people living at or below the poverty line, report unequal treatment in these programs. Staff in shelters or other social service agencies are often viewed as prejudiced against members of these groups and/or insensitive to their basic and social needs. While cisgender women may face the institutional barrier of long waiting lists at shelters, entry into many shelters of this kind is often entirely barred for gay men and trans∗ women and men (Seelman, 2015; Pattavina et al., 2007).

Another often-overlooked group are those IPV victims who seek shelter with their pets (Hageman et al., 2018). There are few pet-friendly shelters for individuals with animals who are attempting to separate from abusive partners (Fleming et al., 2012; Roguski, 2012). Researchers acknowledge the indispensable role animals have in the lives of human beings (Gray, Barrett, Fitzgerald, & Peirone, 2019). Research into the relationships between pet owners and their pets finds that women are more likely to consider pets as members of the family and will often rely on pets for companionship, even more so when their primary human partner behaves violently (Stevenson, Fitzgerald, & Barrett, 2018). Since the animal-human bond is known to be very powerful for many victims of IPV, it is with this knowledge that violent partners often abuse, or threaten to abuse, beloved dogs, cats, birds, or other small animals as a means of coercion or punishment of their partners (Fleming et al., 2012; Roguski, 2012).

## IPV and IPH (Intimate Partner Homicide)

Studies have found that intimate partner homicide (IPH) is associated with IPV, race/ethnicity, substance use, and socioeconomic status and that the majority of women killed by male partners experienced IPV (Belfrage & Rying, 2004; Farooque, Stout, & Ernst, 2005; McFarlane et al., 1999; Moracco, Runyan, & Butts, 1998; Walker, 1979, 1996, 2016; Wilson & Daly, 1992). Studies have also shown that the risk of serious injury or death spikes when and if victims attempt to escape domestic violence (Browne & Williams, 1993; Ewing, 1987; Russell, 2010; Straus & Gelles, 1990; Tjaden & Thoennes, 2000; Walker, 1979, 1984, 1992).

For women under the age of 45, intimate partner homicide continues to be the leading cause of death (Caman et al., 2017; Dugan, Nagin, & Rosenfeld, 2003; Farooque et al., 2005; Ioannou & Hammond, 2015; McFarlane et al., 1999; Rennison, 2003). Researchers found that, between 2003 and 2014, nearly 55% of all female homicide victims in the United States were killed by an intimate partner (CDC, 2017). Petrosky et al. (2017) analyzed data from the National Violent Death Reporting System (NVDRS), which included information on 10,018 female homicide victims from 18 states during the period between 2003 and 2014. Almost a third were young, between the ages of 18 and 29. They found race/ethnicity differences in rates of death, with Non-Hispanic black women having the highest rate, then American Indian/Alaska Native, Hispanic, non-Hispanic white, and Asian/Pacific Islander. In almost half of these cases, there was a documented history of IPV. Puzone et al. (2000) also found that black women were more likely than white women to be killed by their partners. Researchers have found that IPV increased in both frequency and severity during both pregnancy and postpartum periods (Bailey, 2010; Finnbogadóttir & Dykes, 2016). Petrosky et al. (2017) found that, for female homicide victims of reproductive age, approximately 15% were either pregnant or postpartum (less than or equal to 6 weeks). Dugan et al. (2003) observed: "Men's homicidal behavior toward female intimates statistically remain the same regardless of the amount of resources available to battered women" (p. 173).

Compared with men, women are much more likely to be killed by their partners. In 2010, 1095 women were killed in the USA by intimate partners compared with 241 men (US Department of Justice, 2011a, 2011b). In reviewing spousal homicides that occurred in Quebec over a 20-year period, a Canadian study found that women in male-female couples were much more likely to be the victim of IPV compared with men. Of the 276 homicides, 234 were committed by male spouses. (Bourget & Gagné, 2012).

### *Intimate Partner Homicide: Legal Defenses*

Studies show that, although men commit the great majority of homicides, women commit about 10–15% of homicides in the United States and, in about 75% of those cases, the defendant's relationships with the victim involved IPV. A high percentage of female inmates who were convicted of murdering their husbands reported a history of IPV (Browne & Williams, 1993; Huss, Tomkins, Garbin, Schopp, & Kilian, 2006; O'Shea, 1993; Russell, 2010; Straus & Gelles, 1990). Individuals arrested for killing a partner typically face charges of murder in the second degree or manslaughter. To convict a defendant of murder in the second degree, the trier of fact (jury, judge) must conclude that the act was intentional and that the defendant acted with malice. To find a defendant guilty of manslaughter, the jurors must ascribe the defendant's actions to a sudden passion or provocation. Many defendants charged with IPH claim to have acted in self-defense, reporting that they acted in response to an immediate danger (Garner, 2009). In judging guilt, the legal issue rests on whether the defendant faced an immediate danger that required the use of lethal force to protect themselves and/or their children. Studies find that, in the majority of cases, defendants who claimed to be victims of IPV killed their abusive partners during confrontations or acute battering incidents (Browne, 2008; Maguigan, 1991). In these types of cases—those with no provable premeditation— claims of self-defense are most often successful when the triers of fact accept that these defendants faced a legitimate threat.

However, in criminal cases where defendants assaulted or killed a sleeping partner, or on occasions when there was no evidence of immediate threat, their actions do not neatly fit the self-defense paradigm. Their defense may then rely on expert testimony about the psychological effects of IPV. Some therefore view the BWS defense as an imperfect self-defense legal strategy (Kinports, 1988; Schuller & Vidmar, 1992). By considering the totality of the circumstances, the triers of fact may be convinced that the defendants reasonably believed that their actions were necessary to protect their own lives. In this type of case, the defense is more likely to be successful when the expert focuses their testimony on physical rather than emotional abuse and establishes a link between prior or current abuse and the defendant's actions at the time of the instant offense (Ewing, 1990; Ewing & Aubrey, 1987; Kasian, Spanos, Terrance, & Peebles, 1993; Lacey, 2010; Walker, 1979, 1992, 1996, 2016; Wells, 1994).

In some cases, defense teams choose not to include an expert witness and instead rely on the defendants' testimonies about their IPV experiences. For example, in the above-referenced Barbara Sheehan case, she and her children took the stand to describe the abuse she suffered. Although no expert witness testified, she was found not guilty of the most serious charges. The Appeals Court decision in this case included this:

> Moreover, the record in this case - both the trial evidence and the additional evidence put before the court at sentencing - overwhelmingly established that the defendant had been the victim of her husband's constant physical and verbal abuse for almost two decades. (People v. Sheehan, 2013)

In many cases, the evaluations conducted by psychologists, psychiatrists, and social workers have served as essential underpinnings of defense cases. The psychological report and/or testimony about the impact of IPV on the defendant's mental state at the time of the instant offense can have a profound effect on the trajectory of the case at a variety of crucial junctures (e.g., plea negotiations, trial verdicts, sentencing).

During the pretrial period, the expert's report can significantly influence any pleas offered by the prosecution. Persuasive, expert-witness trial testimony has also resulted in acquittals, often on the grounds that the defendant acted in self-defense. This strategy has also resulted in conviction on lesser charges, such as criminally negligent manslaughter rather than murder. Research shows that defendants are more likely to receive more lenient verdicts at trial when expert testimony has been introduced. Even when convicted, mitigating testimony about the abuse the defendant suffered has often resulted in more lenient sentences (Kinports, 1988; Russell, 2010; Schuller & Vidmar, 1992).

The standards of admissibility of expert testimony has continued to evolve over time. Although experts often provide powerful testimony, in some circumstances, they have been precluded from testifying. For many years, the legal standard for admissibility in the United States was based on the Frye v. United States case, in which the defense sought to offer expert testimony based on systolic blood pressure readings that were purported to correlate with lie detector test results. The court excluded this testimony on the following grounds:

> ...The courts will go a long way in admitting experimental testimony deduced from a well-recognized scientific principle or discovery, the thing from which the deduction is made must be sufficiently established to have gained general acceptance in the particular field in which it belongs. (Frye v. United States, 1923)

While some states continue to rely on the Frye standard, the federal system and most state courts have adopted the more rigorous Daubert standard to judge the admissibility of expert testimony (Daubert v. Merrell Dow Pharmaceuticals, Inc., 1993). This US Supreme Court ruling included the following about the admissibility of evidence from studies of the effects of the anti-nausea medication (Bendectin) on pregnant women:

> ...expert opinion based on a scientific technique is inadmissible unless the technique is 'generally accepted' as reliable in the relevant scientific community. (Daubert v. Merrell Dow Pharmaceuticals, Inc., 1993)

The Supreme Court's ruling in the Daubert case underscores that, as gate keepers, judges must decide whether the basis of expert testimony in any particular field has gained general acceptance in the scientific community, that the validity of the theory or scientific technique has been established in peer reviewed publications, and that its potential error rate is known.

In the past, courts ruled that expert testimony about IPV and the BWS syndrome was inadmissible at trial. While some still question whether expert testimony on BWS meets the Daubert standard, it has become more widely accepted by the courts over the past 30 years. Courts have ruled that the average person (i.e., juror) lacks the experience necessary to understand and interpret scientific evidence about the effects of IPV. In fact, excluding this testimony can now be a basis for appeal. In the case of the Commonwealth v. Rodriquez (1994), for example, the defendant's conviction was overturned because the expert witness was not allowed to testify about BWS. Some states have passed laws specifically permitting expert testimony about BWS. For example, the California Code 1107 (2010) includes this language:

> In a criminal action, expert testimony is admissible by either the prosecution or the defense regarding intimate partner battering and its effects, including the nature and effect of physical, emotional, or mental abuse on the beliefs, perceptions, or behavior of victims of domestic violence...

There have been cases in which experts were not allowed to testify about IPV for reasons that were unrelated to the Frye or Daubert standards. For example, in the Sheehan case (discussed earlier), the prosecutor objected to allowing expert testimony, stating that Ms. Sheehan had not fully cooperated with an evaluation by the prosecution's expert despite the fact that she met with the expert for more than 10 hours. The judge sustained the objection and did not allow the defense's expert to testify (Dwyer, 2011).

In the case of Deborah Riker, who was charged with selling drugs to a paid police informant, expert testimony was excluded for a different reason. The defendant claimed that she had agreed to sell the drugs only after the informant threatened her and her children. It was documented that she also was a victim of childhood physical abuse—a fractured skull and two broken wrists; with that knowledge, the defense sought to call an expert to testify that, as a person with BWS, she acted under duress. *Black's Law Dictionary* (9th edition) defines duress as, "a threat of harm made to compel a person to do something against his or her will or judgment...to compel someone to commit an unlawful act...." (Garner, 2009, p. 579). The judge precluded the expert's testimony because Ms. Riker was not in an intimate partner relationship with the informant, and the criminal act was committed in a non-battering context. The court ruled that the expert's testimony failed the Frye test because this novel extension of BWS theory had not yet achieved general scientific acceptance. The appellate court later upheld Ms. Riker's conviction (State v. Riker; Montgomery, 1995).

Defendants have been convicted in cases when expert testimony was admitted and there was uncontroverted evidence of physical abuse. In a 1989 domestic violence case, a wife shot and killed her husband while he slept. A defense expert testified that she was a victim of IPV and that the abuse the defendant experienced amounted to "torture, degradation, and reduction to an animal level of existence where all [her] behavior was marked purely by survival." She was convicted, in part, because the judge instructed the jury that claims of self-defense were justified only when the danger was considered imminent (State v Norman, 1989).

Experts typically testify about IPV in two different ways: general testimony and case-specific testimony. With general testimony, the expert will give a detailed explanation of IPV and its known effects on victims. They will explain the relevant research and the different psychiatric diagnoses associated with trauma exposure. When providing case-specific testimony, experts also include the results of their independent evaluation of the defendant.

When asked to assess a defendant and provide case-specific testimony, the evaluation typically involves four steps: (1) determination of evidence of IPV and assessment of the type and severity of the abuse, (2) assessment of whether the defendant developed BWS or symptoms that fulfill diagnostic criteria for a psychiatric illness, (3) assessment of the defendant's mental state at the time of the offense, and

(4) communication of findings to the referring attorney. Regardless of whether an expert is retained by the court, defense attorney, or the prosecution, the evaluation procedures remain the same (Paradis, 2017).

To conduct a culturally sensitive forensic assessment, it is important to consider the defendant's identity across multiple contexts. It is necessary to recognize how age, ethnicity, socioeconomic status, gender identity, sexual orientation, and relationships within their chosen communities have impacted their help-seeking behaviors and overall psychological functioning. Other identity factors to consider include religion, education, health, disability, and immigration status (West, 2018).

Since a defendant may severely injure or kill their current or former partner for reasons other than domestic abuse (e.g., jealousy, retaliation), the forensic expert must first determine whether there is evidence of IPV. In addition to interviewing the defendant and administering relevant psychological tests, it is necessary to review reports and other collateral sources of information (e.g., police documents, hospital records). Police and court records can provide historical context and often show the couple's history of domestic conflict. Records often illuminate the defendant's efforts to report abuse or obtain restraining orders or orders of protection. Hospital records can be particularly helpful in documenting any injuries a defendant may have sustained at the time of the instant offense or a history of treatment of physical injuries. Important information is also included in records from the Medical Examiner's Office (e.g., autopsy); it can be helpful to interview family members, other witnesses, and individuals who knew the defendant and partner.

The expert conducts in-depth interviews to gather psychosocial data and information about the defendant's relationship with the victim as well as the couple's abuse history. The term victim will be used in the remainder of this paper to refer to the individual who was injured or killed and who was alleged to have abused the defendant. Key information is often obtained when the expert asks for a detailed description of prior episodes of domestic violence. In addition to asking about physical abuse, the expert should inquire as to whether the victim threatened sexual violence or forced the defendant to perform sexual acts. Size and physical strength differentials between the defendant and the victim often become relevant factors that need to be considered. Although experts do not typically interview the victim, collateral sources can provide vitally important examples of physical, verbal, sexual, and emotional abuse. If available, the expert can also refer to any records so as to establish or corroborate the victim's past criminal record of violent offenses. The expert should also inquire about the defendant's previous intimate relationships because it is not uncommon that defendants have been in previous abusive relationships and/or have suffered complex trauma, including childhood abuse, sex trafficking, or sexual assault (Herman, 1992).

In addition to asking about episodes of physical and sexual abuse, the expert should explore with the defendant any instances of emotional or other types of abuse, particularly those which occurred in the context of a power imbalance. The expert may also ask targeted questions, such as: Did the victim have control over all financial resources and make the financial decisions? Did the victim exert psychological control in the relationship through jealousy, intrusiveness, or over-possessiveness? Did the victim isolate the defendant from family or other means of support? Did the victim make direct or veiled threats of harm? (Paradis, 2017; Walker, 1979, 1992, 1996, 2016).

Some of these relevant issues are illustrated in the case of Ms. C., who was evaluated by the first author at the request of a district attorney. Ms. C., who was born and raised in China, was a graduate student living in the United States when she married a man who was also Chinese. She was eight months pregnant when she killed him by striking him with a hammer and repeatedly stabbing him. Her attorney retained a psychiatric expert who concluded that Ms. C had BWS and was not legally responsible for her actions due to a mental disease or defect (Paradis, 2010, 2017).

There was much reliable evidence that supported Ms. C's reports of IPV. Her husband sent her many graphic, threatening emails which demonstrated that the intensity and severity of the abuse was increasing. When evaluated by both the defense expert and the first author, she reported that the beatings became more frequent over time, particularly after she became pregnant. She told of experiences that mirrored the cycle of partner violence first described by Walker (1979). As with many other immigrant victims of IPV, Ms. C had no family members to rely on, as they all resided in China. She indicated that he often monitored her contact with others and, because of his jealousy and constant threats, she felt totally isolated. Furthermore, her husband made it clear in his emails to her that she was totally dependent on him and had no friends or outside means of emotional or financial support (Paradis, 2010, 2017).

If the expert concludes that the defendant was abused by the victim, the next step is to assess whether the defendant struggled with symptoms of a psychiatric illness at the time of the instant offense. The defendant may have met diagnostic criteria for PTSD, depression, or other trauma-related disorders. In Ms. C's case, she reported that she became increasingly depressed and suicidal as her pregnancy progressed (Paradis, 2010, 2017).

Some defendants who experience significant emotional distress do not meet diagnostic criteria for a mental illness and many do not develop the pattern of psychological symptoms and behaviors that have been described in BWS or BPS. People differ in their resilience and access to support outside of the abusive relationship. Specific-trauma related inventories can also be useful (e.g., Trauma Symptom Inventory) (Briere, 1995). Because detection of feigning or malingering should always be part of a forensic examination, many experts administer psychological tests specifically designed for this purpose. Some of the commonly administered tests are the Minnesota Multiphasic Personality Inventory (MMPI-2) (Greene, 2000), the Personality Assessment Inventory (PAI) (Morey, 1991), and the Test of Memory Malingering (TOMM) (Tombaugh, 1996), among others. A comprehensive evaluation must also include an assessment of the defendant's and victim's substance use histories.

The next step is to assess the defendant's state of mind at the time of the offense. The expert needs to determine if the defendant believed the victim was genuinely threatening to kill or seriously injure them and if this was perceived as an imminent threat. Based on the defendant's psychological makeup and history of abuse, the expert needs to determine whether the defendant's beliefs would be considered reasonable. Helpful queries include: Was the abuse increasing in frequency or severity? Had the victim ever threatened use of a weapon before? Was there a weapon in the home? And was the weapon easily accessible to the victim? (Paradis, 2017; Walker, 1979, 1992, 1996, 2016).

In the case of Ms. C, she killed her husband while he slept. She later recounted that he brandished a knife at her on the evening of the instant offense and threatened to kill her and her parents if she allowed them to visit them after the birth of the child. She stated her strong belief that he truly meant to follow through on his threats. She said she was sure there was no other way to protect herself, her parents, or her unborn child. She described how, once he fell asleep, she hit him with a hammer that had been left near the crib he assembled. She then stabbed him with the knife he had kept by the bedside and then cut her own wrists. She later recalled: "I wanted all of us to die. It would be more peaceful to be dead." The self-inflicted wounds reflected her ambivalence about what she had done and led her to then call 911. An ambulance arrived at their home in time, such that she survived and her baby was later delivered by cesarean section (Paradis, 2010, 2017).

After completing the evaluation, the expert communicates findings to the defense attorney or prosecutor and often prepares a forensic report to submit to the court. Typically, opposing counsel will also hire an expert to evaluate the defendant. If the case is not resolved through plea negotiations, a trial will likely ensue, during which all experts testify about their evaluations and conclusions. In the case of Ms. C., the first author concluded that she acted in a state of high emotion and that her actions were not planned in a calm or deliberate manner. After reviewing the forensic report, the prosecutor offered a plea deal, which Ms. C accepted. Because of the amount of time that had passed since her arrest, she was released with time served (Paradis, 2010, 2017).

In preparing a forensic report and in testifying at trial, the expert will often cite relevant research to educate court personnel and/or the triers of fact about the psychological effects of IPV. In providing case-specific opinions/testimony, the expert is often uniquely positioned to "tell the defendant's story." Moreover, the expert is best equipped to describe the defendant's psychological makeup and state of mind at the time of the offense. Although some recommend avoiding using the terms BWS and BPS, these terms can be helpful constructs because they are recognized in most jurisdictions (Russell, 2010). Whether or not an expert chooses to use these terms, focusing on the defendant's unique history and life experience is paramount.

Although a description of the defendant's psychological makeup and mental state at the time of the offense is essential, the effective expert witness must both explain and dispel myths associated with IPV. Film portrayals and highly publicized criminal cases of defendants and victims have raised public awareness about the effects of IPV, but each has also contributed to misattributions about abused individuals. These myths have a powerful effect on how the triers of fact view particular defendants, especially those who do not conform to the stereotype of the battered wife or person. The 1984 television movie, "The Burning Bed," portrayed the life of Francine Hughes who, after years of suffering IPV, killed her abusive husband by pouring gasoline on their bed and then setting it afire (Schreder & Greenwald, 1984). The actor, Farrah Fawcett, rendered a sympathetic portrayal of Ms. Hughes, who was eventually found not guilty of murder by reason of temporary insanity. This widely viewed movie helped mold a stereotypic image of the battered woman as a defenseless, physically frail, mentally ill, financially dependent, heterosexual white woman (Ewing, 1987; Osthoff & Maguigan, 2005; Schneider, 1986; Wells, 1994). Shortly after the film aired, an expert in BWS defenses wrote:

> Regardless of its more complex meaning, the term 'Battered Woman's Syndrome' has been heard to communicate an implicit but powerful view that battered women are all the same, that they are suffering from a psychological disability and this disability prevents them from acting 'normally'. (Schneider, 1986, p 207)

Although public awareness of the effects of IPV has shifted over the past 40+ years, misconceptions about IPV are still quite prevalent. A study by Ewing and Aubrey (1987) found that both men and women in the general public agreed with several myths related to BWS, specifically that a battered woman could "simply leave." With regard to jury selection, one particularly relevant finding of their study was that many female research participants believed battered women were masochistic, emotionally disturbed, and partially responsible for the abuse (Ewing & Aubrey, 1987).

Russell and Melillo (2006) describe the most sympathetic BWS or IPV defendant as an emotionally fragile and depressed mother who was frightened and filled with feelings of guilt at the time of the instant offense. They describe this stereotypical defendant as emotionally and financially dependent on her abusive partner (victim) and isolated from her family and friends from whom she has hidden the extent of the abuse. Before assaulting or killing her abusive partner, she had likely related to him in a passive manner and sought to appease him in innumerable ways.

Oftentimes, experts will reference research findings about defendants who do not fit either the battered woman stereotype or traditional gender roles in their reports or during court testimony. Studies show that defendants who do not fit this stereotype are more likely to be charged with more severe offenses, less likely to be offered lenient pleas or shorter prison sentences, and more likely to be convicted at trial. These biases affect men, people of color, LGBTQ individuals, and working or professional women who typically are not viewed as conforming to conventional ideas of femininity (Eaton & Hyman, 1991; Ferraro, 2003; Henning & Feder, 2005; Russell, 2010; Russell & Melillo, 2006).

These same lingering myths and stereotypes influence police, attorneys, judges, and jurors who frequently hold misconceptions that, in a genuine case of BWS or BPS, the defendant would never fight back or attempt to escape the abusive relationship (Ewing, 1987; Walker, 1979). However, many individuals who suffer IPV do fight back to protect their lives. Experts can frame the defendant's behaviors as survival strategies rather than retribution or worse. The expert may explain that a specific defendant showed resiliency by not passively accepting the tormentor's abuse. Unfortunately, the defendant's resiliency, or even courageous defiance, can be held against them. Thus, it becomes especially important for the expert to dispel gendered myths and racist tropes, including those about women and racial minorities, including African Americans, that simultaneously project indefatigable strength ("strong black woman") and emotional fallibility and lability ("angry black woman") (St. Vil, Sabri, Nwokolo, Alexander, & Campbell, 2017). (Allard, 1991; Gondolf & Fisher, 1988; Walker, 1979, 1992, 1996, 2016; West, 2018).

Another commonly held belief is that defendants could and should have "just left" their abusing partners. The expert is positioned to explain the unique barriers each defendant experienced and what the defendant considered realistic alternatives to combat the dangers they regularly faced, including concerns that their abusive partner could hurt or kill them or their children. In cases where the abused person has children or pets, the sole focus of the abuse victim is often on the safety and welfare of those in their care. Some abusers threatened to kill a beloved pet that served as a proxy for children (Roguski, 2012). The expert could explain how many victims of IPV know that orders of protection do not fully protect them. Tjaden and Thoennes (2000) found that, in 60% of cases, the abusive partner violated the order of protection within the first 12 months.

A defendant sometimes chooses not to leave the relationship because of a desire to avoid other real consequences. When the abuser is the sole wage earner and the defendant has no other means of financial support, a realistic fear of homelessness for her and her children is understandable. At the least, leaving would result in a severe disruption to their lives. In a worst-case scenario, leaving could heighten the risk to herself and her children. If the children were left with the abusive partner, there would be a reasonable fear that no reliable person would be there to protect them. Departure could also result in loss of custody and/or risk to the children during court ordered visitations with the abusive parent (Russell, 2010; Schuller & Vidmar, 1992; Walker, 1979, 1992, 1996, 2016).

For LGBTQ defendants, the expert is often called upon to address different myths. The triers of fact may falsely believe that IPV occurs only in cisgender heterosexual relationships or that the abuse in these relationships is less prevalent or severe. The expert is well-positioned to describe some of the emotional abuse tactics that are unique to these populations, such as threatening to out their partners to family members or co-workers. Psychological abuse against a trans* individual might involve interfering with or blocking their ability to obtain the medical treatments or medications needed to fully express their gender identity. Some defendants may not have sought help because of an expectation that they would be met with homophobic or transphobic responses (Messinger, 2017).

When the defendant is a wealthy individual and/or working professional, the expert can dispel the myth that IPV affects mostly poor, uneducated women. Research has shown that IPV occurs in all socioeconomic groups. Wealthier defendants may have lived in communities that lacked necessary resources, such as battered women shelters; and like other victims of IPV, they were isolated, fearful, and often unaware of their options. Professional defendants may have had realistic concerns that, if an employer learned of the abuse, it could have jeopardized advancement and other job opportunities (West, 2018). When assessing professional or wealthy victims of IPV, the expert might explore whether their high earnings were actually an additional source of tension in their relationships. In some cases, the abusive partner may have actually resented the defendant for being "too successful" and may have attempted to sabotage their career. In addition, financially advantaged abusive partners have been known to hide assets and retain attorneys to wage an unending series of legal battles (e.g., custody, divorce) (Johnson, 1995; Liss & Stahly, 1993).

While the majority of cases in which expert testimony has been introduced at trial has involved women charged with assaulting or killing their partners, there were other types of criminal and civil cases in which the terms battered child syndrome and BPS were used in courts. For example, Carl Colberg, a 62-year-old retired state trooper, was the first man to use a BPS defense in New York State. On April 1, 1999, he shot and killed his son who he claimed was abusive (People v Colberg, 1999). The prosecution sought to exclude expert testimony, but the court ruled it admissible and Mr. Colberg was eventually sentenced to probation.

These issues are also relevant in other types of criminal and civil cases (e.g., duress, child abuse, divorce, child custody). In a duress case, the defendant may claim to have been coerced by their abusive partner to perform or aid in criminal acts. The issue of IPV has also been raised in cases involving deportation and asylum, although former Attorney General Jeffrey Sessions ruled that domestic violence was no longer an accepted basis for an asylum claim in the United States: "An [non-citizen] may suffer threats and violence in a foreign country for any number of reasons relating to her social, economic, family or other personal circumstances… Yet the asylum statute does not provide redress for all misfortune" (Benner & Dickerson, 2018).

## Conclusions

It is estimated that one-quarter to one-third of women have been abused by their partners at some point in their lives. While much of the IPV research has focused on heterosexual couples with a male abuser-female victim dyad, violence occurs in all types of intimate relationships; it is clear that women and men can be perpetrators or victims. People differ in their resiliency and response to IPV, but many do develop IPV-associated psychiatric/psychological symptoms and exhibit behaviors that are similar to those seen in depression and PTSD. For various reasons, these individuals face barriers to reporting abuse and to escaping the relationship. Psychologists and other mental health clinicians can be retained to evaluate defendants arrested for assaulting or killing abusive partners.

Over the last 30 years, expert testimony about the existence of BWS and the effects of IPV has become more accepted in court settings. Because of the growing body of research in this area, experts now focus on the defendant's unique experiences and psychological makeup instead of describing how they fit into specific syndromes like BWS or BPS. Because defendants' histories of abuse and development of psychological reactions/syndromes vary, the expert needs to underscore the uniqueness of each defendant. The terms BWS, BPS, and learned helplessness can be useful constructs because they are widely used and recognized in court settings. However, the expert needs to be mindful of their limitations; they can also be used to perpetuate the myths associated with "the battered woman."

The framework included in this chapter provides a guide for experts to assess defendants whose mental state at the time of the offense has been affected by IPV. When retained to evaluate a defendant who reports a history of IPV, the expert works to determine whether there is evidence of IPV and then assesses whether the defendant developed symptoms that fulfilled diagnostic criteria for a psychiatric illness. To evaluate the defendant's mental state at the time of the offense, the expert will focus on how each defendant was psychologically affected by IPV. There are many myths about the BWS and the effects of IPV; as a result, many people are not aware that IPV occurs in all socioeconomic groups, cultures, and types of relationships. As part of their assessment and testimony, the forensic expert needs to address directly any myths, particularly when a defendant's experience does not fit with the stereotyped view of a battered woman or battered person. The expert is uniquely positioned to challenge these myths while describing each defendant's particular history of abuse.

This chapter illustrates how the forensic expert is in a key position to describe the relationship between the history of IPV and the development of psychological symptoms that made it difficult for the defendant to seek help or to escape the relationship. Furthermore, the expert is uniquely qualified to offer in-depth explanations about a defendant's mental state at the time of the offense so that the triers of fact can better judge whether the defendant feared for their life and whether their actions were necessary or reasonable. It is most important to detail their actions and to make a clear connection between their mental state at the time of the instant offense and their conviction that they were in grave danger. In conclusion, the expert who conducts the forensic evaluation is best able to "tell the defendant's story," so that the triers of fact understand their unique history and the abuse they have endured.

## Questions/Activities for Further Exploration

1. Should expert witness testimony about intimate partner violence (IPV) and battered woman syndrome (BWS) be admitted into court? For what types of cases?
2. How would a forensic expert go about evaluating defendants who are charged with killing their partner and who claim to be a victim of IPV?
3. If you were the expert witness, how would you educate the triers of fact about the myths related to IPV and BWS?
4. Under what circumstances should testimony about syndromes be excluded from the courtroom?

# References

Adam, N. M. (2001). *Domestic violence against women within immigrant Indian and Pakistani communities in the United States* (Doctoral dissertation).

Adam, N. M., & Schewe, P. A. (2007). A multilevel framework exploring domestic violence against immigrant Indian and Pakistani women in the United States. *Journal of Muslim Mental Health, 2*(1), 5–20.

Adames, S. B., & Campbell, R. (2005). Immigrant Latinas' conceptualizations of intimate partner violence. *Violence Against Women, 11*(10), 1341–1364.

Adams, M. E., & Campbell, J. C. (2012). Being undocumented and intimate partner violence (IPV): Multiple vulnerabilities through the lens of feminist intersectionality. *Women's Health and Urban Life, 11*(1), 15–34.

Adorjan, M., Christensen, T., Kelly, B., & Pawluch, D. (2012). Stockholm syndrome as vernacular resource. *The Sociological Quarterly, 53*(3), 454–474.

Allard, S. A. (1991). Rethinking battered woman syndrome: A black feminist perspective. *UCLA Women's Law Journal, 1*, 191.

Anderson, M. J. (2002). Marital immunity, intimate relationships, and improper inferences: A new law on sexual offenses by intimates. *Hastings Law Journal, 54*, 1465.

Ard, K. L., & Makadon, H. J. (2011). Addressing intimate partner violence in lesbian, gay, bisexual, and transgender patients. *Journal of General Internal Medicine, 26*(8), 930–933.

Azziz-Baumgartner, E., McKeown, L., Melvin, P., Dang, Q., & Reed, J. (2011). Rates of femicide in women of different races, ethnicities, and places of birth: Massachusetts, 1993-2007. *Journal of Interpersonal Violence, 26*(5), 1077–1090.

Bailey, B. A. (2010). Partner violence during pregnancy: Prevalence, effects, screening, and management. *International Journal of Women's Health, 2*, 183.

Balsam, K. F., Rothblum, E. D., & Beauchaine, T. P. (2005). Victimization over the life span: A comparison of lesbian, gay, bisexual, and heterosexual siblings. *Journal of Consulting and Clinical Psychology, 73*(3), 477.

Barrier Free Living. (2018). *Services and support for survivors of domestic violence with disabilities*. Retrieved from https://www.bflnyc.org/

Belfrage, H., & Rying, M. (2004). Characteristics of spousal homicide perpetrators: A study of all cases of spousal homicide in Sweden 1990–1999. *Criminal Behaviour and Mental Health, 14*(2), 121–133.

Benner, K., & Dickerson, C. (2018). *Sessions says domestic and gang violence are not grounds for asylum*. Retrieved from https://www.nytimes.com/2018/06/11/us/politics/sessions-domestic-violence-asylum.html

Bilefsky, D. (2011a, September 19). Queens woman testifies she killed her husband in self-defense. *The New York Times*. Retrieved from https://www.nytimes.com/2011/09/20/nyregion/at-murder-trial-barbara-sheehan-testifies-she-killed-her-husband-in-self-defense.html

Bilefsky, D. (2011b, September 21). In mother's trial, man tells of his father's rage. *The New York Times*. Retrieved from https://www.nytimes.com/2011/09/22/nyregion/son-testifies-in-barbara-sheehans-murder-trial.html

Bilefsky, D. (2011c, September 25). An abused wife? or an executioner? *The New York Times*. Retrieved from https://www.nytimes.com/2011/09/26/nyregion/an-abused-wife-or-an-executioner.html

Bilefsky, D. (2011d, October 6). Wife who fired 11 shots is acquitted of murder. *The New York Times*. Retrieved from https://www.nytimes.com/2011/10/07/nyregion/barbara-sheehan-who-killed-husband-is-found-not-guilty-of-murder.html

Black, M. C., Basile, K. C., Breiding, M. J., Smith, S. G., Walters, M. L., Merrick, M. T., & Stevens, M. R. (2010). *The national intimate partner and sexual violence survey: 2010 summary report*. Retrieved from https://www.cdc.gov/violenceprevention/pdf/nisvs_report2010-a.pdf

Blosnich, J. R., & Bossarte, R. M. (2009). Comparisons of intimate partner violence among partners in same-sex and opposite-sex relationships in the United States. *American Journal of Public Health, 99*(12), 2182–2184.

Bourget, D., & Gagné, P. (2012). Women who kill their mates. *Behavioral Sciences & the Law, 30*(5), 598–614.

Bowles, N. (2018, June 23). Thermostats, locks and lights: Digital tools of domestic abuse, *The New York Times.* Retrieved from https://www.nytimes.com/2018/06/23/technology/smart-home-devices-domestic-abuse.html

Bradley v. State, Supreme Court of Mississippi, 1824. 1 Miss. 156, Walker 156

Breiding, M. J., Chen, J., & Black, M. C. (2014). *Intimate partner violence in the United States–2010.* Retrieved from https://stacks.cdc.gov/view/cdc/21961

Briere, J. (1995). *Trauma symptom inventory (TSI): Professional manual.* Odessa, FL: PAR.

Brown, T., & Herman, J. (2015). *Intimate partner violence and sexual abuse among LGBT people.* Los Angeles, CA: The Williams Institute.

Browne, A. (2008). *When battered women kill.* New York, NY: Simon & Schuster.

Browne, A., & Williams, K. R. (1993). Gender, intimacy, and lethal violence: Trends from 1976 through 1987. *Gender & Society, 7*(1), 78–98.

Bruno v. Codd, 64 A.D. 2d 582 (1978)

Bruno v. Codd, 47 N.Y.2d 582 N.Y. (1979).

California Code 1107. (2010). Retrieved from https://law.justia.com/codes/california/2016/code-evid/division-9/chapter-1/Section-1107

Caman, S., Kristiansson, M., Granath, S., & Sturup, J. (2017). Trends in rates and characteristics of intimate partner homicides between 1990 and 2013. *Journal of Criminal Justice, 49*, 14–21.

Campbell, J. C., Baty, M. L., Ghandour, R. M., Stockman, J. K., Francisco, L., & Wagman, J. (2008). The intersection of intimate partner violence against women and HIV/AIDS: A review. *International Journal of Injury Control and Safety Promotion, 15*(4), 221–231.

Carbone-López, K., Kruttschnitt, C., & Macmillan, R. (2006). Patterns of intimate partner violence and their associations with physical health, psychological distress, and substance use. *Public Health Reports, 121*(4), 382–392.

Carmo, R., Grams, A., & Magalhães, T. (2011). Men as victims of intimate partner violence. *Journal of Forensic and Legal Medicine, 18*(8), 355–359.

Carvalho, A. F., Lewis, R. J., Derlega, V. J., Winstead, B. A., & Viggiano, C. (2011). Internalized sexual minority stressors and same-sex intimate partner violence. *Journal of Family Violence, 26*(7), 501–509.

Catalano, S., Smith, E., Snyder, H., & Rand, M. (2009). *Female victims of violence.* Retrieved from https://www.bjs.gov/content/pub/pdf/fvv.pdf

Centers for Disease Control and Prevention. (2017). *Racial and ethnic differences in homicides of adult women and the role of intimate partner violence — United States, 2003–2014.* Retrieved from https://www.cdc.gov/mmwr/volumes/66/wr/mm6628a1.htm?scid=mm6628a1w#suggest edcitation).

Chang, J. C., Martin, S. L., Moracco, K. E., Dulli, L., Scandlin, D., Loucks-Sorrel, M. B., & Bou-Saada, I. (2003). Helping women with disabilities and domestic violence: Strategies, limitations, and challenges of domestic violence programs and services. *Journal of Women's Health, 12*(7), 699–708.

Choi, Y. J., Elkins, J., & Disney, L. (2016). A literature review of intimate partner violence among immigrant populations: Engaging the faith community. *Aggression and Violent Behavior, 29*, 1–9.

Clements, K., Katz, M., & Marx, R. (1999). *The transgender community health project: Descriptive results.* Retrieved from http://hivinsite.ucsf.edu/InSite?page=cftg-02-02

Commonwealth v. Rodriquez, 418 Mass (1994).

Crenshaw, K. (1991). Race, gender, and sexual harassment. *Southern California Law Review., 65*, 1467.

Daubert v. Merrell Dow Pharmaceuticals, Inc. U.S. 579 (1993).

Descamps, M. J., Rothblum, E., Bradford, J., & Ryan, C. (2000). Mental health impact of child sexual abuse, rape, intimate partner violence, and hate crimes in the National Lesbian Health Care Survey. *Journal of Gay & Lesbian Social Services, 11*(1), 27–55.

Dugan, L., Nagin, D. S., & Rosenfeld, R. (2003). Exposure reduction or retaliation? The effects of domestic violence resources on intimate partner homicide. *Law &Society Review, 37*(1), 169–198.

Dutton, D. G. (1994). Patriarchy and wife assault: The ecological fallacy. *Violence and Victims, 9*(2), 167.

Dwyer, J. (2011, April 26). *A court battle over a husband's rage and a wife who'd had enough.* Retrieved from http://www.nytimes.com/2011/04/27/nyregion/barbara-sheehan-murder-trial-battered-wifes-mind.htm

Eaton, S., & Hyman, A. (1991). The domestic violence component of the New York task force report on women in the courts: An evaluation and assessment of nNew York City courts. *Fordham Urban Law Journal, 19*, 391.

Ellison, C. G., Trinitapoli, J. A., Anderson, K. L., & Johnson, B. R. (2007). Race/ethnicity, religious involvement, and domestic violence. *Violence Against Women, 13*(11), 1094–1112.

Eng, P. (1995). Domestic violence in Asian/Pacific island communities. In D. L. Adams (Ed.), *Health issues for women of color: A cultural diversity perspective.* Thousand Oaks, CA: Sage Publications.

Ewing, C. P. (1987). *Battered women who kill: Psychological self-defense as legal justification.* Lexington, MA: Lexington Books.

Ewing, C. P. (1990). Psychological self-defense. *Law and Human Behavior, 14*(6), 579–594.

Ewing, C. P., & Aubrey, M. (1987). Battered woman and public opinion: Some realities about the myths. *Journal of Family Violence, 2*(3), 257–264.

Farooque, R. S., Stout, R. G., & Ernst, F. A. (2005). Heterosexual intimate partner homicide: Review of ten years of clinical experience. *Journal of Forensic Science, 50*(3), 1–4.

Ferraro, K. (2003). The words change, but the melody lingers. *Violence Against Women, 9*(1), 110–129.

Fife, R. S., Ebersole, C., Bigatti, S., Lane, K. A., & Huber, L. B. (2008). Assessment of the relationship of demographic and social factors with intimate partner violence (IPV) among Latinas in Indianapolis. *Journal of Women's Health, 17*(5), 769–775.

Finnbogadóttir, H., & Dykes, A. K. (2016). Increasing prevalence and incidence of domestic violence during the pregnancy and one and a half year postpartum, as well as risk factors: A longitudinal cohort study in Southern Sweden. *BMC Pregnancy and Childbirth, 16*(1), 327.

Fleming, K., Newton, T., Fernandez-Botran, R., Miller, J., & Burns, V. (2012). Intimate partner stalking victimization and posttraumatic stress symptoms in post-abuse women. *Violence Against Women, 18*(12), 1368–1389.

Follingstad, D. R. (2003). Battered woman syndrome in the courts. In A. M. Goldstein (Ed.), *Handbook of psychology: Forensic psychology* (Vol. 11, pp. 485–507). New York, NY: Wiley.

Freedner, N., Freed, L. H., Yang, Y. W., & Austin, S. B. (2002). Dating violence among gay, lesbian, and bisexual adolescents: Results from a community survey. *Journal of Adolescent Health, 31*(6), 469–474.

Frye v. United States 293 F. 1013 (D.C. Cir. (1923).

Garner, B. A. (Ed.). (2009). *Black's law dictionary* (9th ed.). St Paul, MN: West Publishing Co.

Gondolf, E. W., & Fisher, E. R. (1988). *Battered women as survivors: An alternative to treating learned helplessness.* Lanham, MD: Lexington Books.

Gonzalez, R. (2017). *ICE detains alleged victim of domestic abuse at Texas Courthouse.* Retrieved from https://www.npr.org/sections/thetwo-way/2017/02/16/515685385/ice-

Grant, J. M., Mottet, L., Tanis, J. E., Harrison, J., Herman, J., & Keisling, M. (2011). *Injustice at every turn: A report of the national transgender discrimination survey.* Retrieved from https://rhyclearinghouse.acf.hhs.gov/library/2011/injustice-every-turn-report-national-transgender-discrimination-survey

Gray, A., Barrett, B. J., Fitzgerald, A., & Peirone, A. (2019). Fleeing with Fido: An analysis of what Canadian domestic violence shelters are communicating via their websites about leaving an abusive relationship when pets are involved. *Journal of Family Violence, 34*(4), 287–298.

Greene, R. L. (2000). *The MMPI-2: An interpretive manual.* Boston, MA: Allyn & Bacon.

Gupta, J., Acevedo-Garcia, D., Hemenway, D., Decker, M. R., Raj, A., & Silverman, J. G. (2010). Intimate partner violence perpetration, immigration status, and disparities in a community health center-based sample of men. *Public health reports (Washington, D.C.: 1974), 125*(1), 79–87.

Hageman, T., Langenderfer-Magruder, L., Greene, T., Williams, J., St. Mary, J., McDonald, S., & Ascione, F. (2018). Intimate partner violence survivors and pets: Exploring practitioners' experiences in addressing client needs. *Families in Society: The Journal of Contemporary Social Services, 99*(2), 134–145.

Hahn, J. W., McCormick, M. C., Silverman, J. G., Robinson, E. B., & Koenen, K. C. (2014). Examining the impact of disability status on intimate partner violence victimization in a population sample. *Journal of Interpersonal Violence, 29*(17), 3063–3085.

Hassouneh, D., & Glass, N. (2008). The influence of gender role stereotyping on women's experiences of female same-sex intimate partner violence. *Violence Against Women, 14*(3), 310–325.

Hazen, A. L., & Soriano, F. I. (2007). Experiences with intimate partner violence among Latina women. *Violence Against Women, 13*(6), 562–582.

Heavey, S. (2013). *Data show domestic violence, rape an issue for gays.* Retrieved from https://www.reuters.com/article/us-usa-gays-violence/data-shows-domestic-violence-rape-an-issue-for-gays-idUSBRE90O11W20130125

Hellemans, S., Loeys, T., Buysse, A., Dewaele, A., & De Smet, O. (2015). Intimate partner violence victimization among non-heterosexuals: Prevalence and associations with mental and sexual well-being. *Journal of Family Violence, 30*(2), 171–188.

Henning, K., & Feder, L. (2005). Criminal prosecution of domestic violence offenses: An investigation of factors predictive of court outcomes. *Criminal Justice and Behavior, 32*(6), 612–642.

Herman, J. L. (1992). *Trauma and recovery.* New York, NY: Basic Books. (1999).

Houston, E., & McKirnan, D. J. (2007). Intimate partner abuse among gay and bisexual men: Risk correlates and health outcomes. *Journal of Urban Health, 84*(5), 681–690.

Huss, M. T., Tomkins, A. J., Garbin, C. P., Schopp, R. F., & Kilian, A. (2006). Battered women who kill their abusers: An examination of commonsense notions, cognitions, and judgments. *Journal of Interpersonal Violence, 21*(8), 1063–1080.

Ibn-Tamas v. US 407 A.2d 626 (1979).

Ioannou, M., & Hammond, L. (2015). The changing face of homicide research: The shift in empirical focus and emerging research trends. *Journal of Criminal Psychology, 5*(3), 157–162.

Javier, R. A., Herron, W. G., Pantoja, G. A., & De Mucci, J. (2018). Domestic violence in all its contexts. In R. A. Javier & W. G. Herron (Eds.), *Understanding domestic violence: Theories, challenges, and remedies* (pp. 25–48). Lantham, MD: Rowman & Littlefield.

Johnson, H. (1995). The truth about white-collar domestic violence. *Working Woman, 20*(3), 54–57.

Kasian, M., Spanos, N. P., Terrance, C. A., & Peebles, S. (1993). Battered women who kill. *Law and Human Behavior, 17*(3), 289–312.

Kinports, K. (1988). Defending battered women's self-defense claims. *Oregon Law Review, 67*, 393–465.

Lacey, K. K. (2010). When is it enough for me to leave?: Black and Hispanic women's response to violent relationships. *Journal of Family Violence, 25*(7), 669–677.

Langenderfer-Magruder, L., Whitfield, D. L., Walls, N. E., Kattari, S. K., & Ramos, D. (2016). Experiences of intimate partner violence and subsequent police reporting among lesbian, gay, bisexual, transgender, and queer adults in Colorado: Comparing rates of cisgender and transgender victimization. *Journal of Interpersonal Violence, 31*(5), 855–871.

Liss, M. B., & Stahly, G. B. (1993). Domestic violence and child custody. In M. Hansen & M. Harway (Eds.), *Battering and family therapy: A feminist perspective* (pp. 175–187). Thousand Oaks, CA: Sage Publications.

Maguigan, H. (1991). Battered women and self-defense: Myths and misconceptions in current reform proposals. *University of Pennsylvania Law Review, 140*(2), 379–486.

Mahoney, M. R. (1991). Legal images of battered women: Redefining the issue of separation. *Michigan Law Review, 90*(1), 1–94.

Mays, V. M., & Cochran, S. D. (2001). Mental health correlates of perceived discrimination among lesbian, gay, and bisexual adults in the United States. *American Journal of Public Health, 91*(11), 1869–1876.

McFarlane, J. M., Campbell, J. C., Wilt, S., Sachs, C. J., Ulrich, Y., & Xu, X. (1999). Stalking and intimate partner femicide. *Homicide Studies, 3*(4), 300–316.

Medina, J. (2017). Too scared to report sexual abuse. The fear: Deportation. *The New York Times.* https://www.nytimes.com/2017/04/30/us/immigrants-deportation-sexual-abuse.html

Merrill, G. S., & Wolfe, V. A. (2000). Battered gay men: An exploration of abuse, help seeking, and why they stay. *Journal of Homosexuality, 39*(2), 1–30.

Messinger, A. M. (2011). Invisible victims: Same-sex IPV in the national violence against women survey. *Journal of Interpersonal Violence, 26*(11), 2228–2243.

Messinger, A. M. (2017). *LGBTQ intimate partner violence: Lessons for policy, practice, and research.* Oakland, CA: University of California Press.

Mills, L. G. (2009). *Insult to injury: Rethinking our responses to intimate abuse.* Princeton, NJ: Princeton University Press.

Mize, K. D. (2008). Intimate partner homicide methods in heterosexual, gay, and lesbian relationships. *Violence and Victims, 23*(1), 98.

Mize, K. D., Shackelford, T. K., & Shackelford, V. A. (2009). Hands-on killing of intimate partners as a function of sex and relationship status/state. *Journal of Family Violence, 24*(7), 463–470.

Montgomery, A. M. (1995). State v. Riker, battered women under duress: The concept the Washington Supreme Court could not grasp. *Seattle University Law Review, 19*, 385.

Moracco, K. E., Runyan, C. W., & Butts, J. D. (1998). Femicide in North Carolina, 1991-1993: A statewide study of patterns and precursors. *Homicide Studies, 2*(4), 422–446.

Morey, L. C. (1991). *Personality assessment inventory.* Odessa, FL: Psychological Assessment Resources.

Morse, B. J. (1995). Beyond the conflict tactics scale: Assessing gender differences in partner violence. *Violence and Victims, 10*(4), 251.

Mourad, M., Levendosky, A., Bogat, G., & Von Eye, A. (2008). Family psychopathology and perceived stress of both domestic violence and negative life events as predictors of women's mental health symptoms. *Journal of Family Violence, 23*(8), 661–670.

Murdaugh, C., Hunt, S., Sowell, R., & Santana, I. (2004). Domestic violence in Hispanics in the southeastern United States: A survey and needs analysis. *Journal of Family Violence, 19*(2), 107–115.

Murray, C. E., & Mobley, A. K. (2009). Empirical research about same-sex intimate partner violence: A methodological review. *Journal of Homosexuality, 56*(3), 361–386.

O'Shea, K. (1993). Women on death row. In B. R. Fletcher, L. D. E. Shaver, & D. G. Moon (Eds.), *Women prisoners: A forgotten population* (pp. 75–91). Westport, CT: Praeger Publishers/ Greenwood Publishing Group.

Ortega, D., & Busch-Armendariz, N. (2013). *In the name of VAWA.* Retrieved from https://journals. sagepub.com/doi/10.1177/0886109913495644

Osthoff, S., & Maguigan, H. (2005). Explaining without pathologizing: Testimony on battering and its effects. In D. R. Loseke, R. J. Gelles, & M. Cavanaugh (Eds.), *Current controversies on family violence.* Thousand Oaks, CA: Sage Publications.

Paradis, C. (2010). *The measure of madness: The disturbed and disturbing criminal mind.* New York, NY: Citadel Press.

Paradis, C. (2017). Assessment of intimate partner violence and the battered woman syndrome. *Psychiatric Annals, 47*(12), 593–597.

Pattavina, A., Hirschel, D., Buzawa, E., Faggiani, D., & Bentley, H. (2007). A comparison of the police response to heterosexual versus same-sex intimate partner violence. *Violence Against Women, 13*(4), 374–394.

Paulsen, D. J., & Brewer, V. E. (1999). The spousal SROK revisited: A comparison of Chicago and Houston intimate partner homicide ratios. *Gender Issues, 18*(1), 88–100.

People v Colberg, 182 Misc. 2d 798, 701 N.Y.S. 2d 608 (1999).

People v Sheehan 997 N.E. 2d 151 (N.Y. 2013).

Petrosky, E., Blair, J. M., Betz, C. J., Fowler, K. A., Jack, S. P., & Lyons, B. H. (2017). Racial and ethnic differences in homicides of adult women and the role of intimate partner violence— United States, 2003–2014. *Morbidity and Mortality Weekly Report, 66*(28), 741.

Potoczniak, M. J., Murot, J. E., Crosbie-Burnett, M., & Potoczniak, D. J. (2003). Legal and psychological perspectives on same-sex domestic violence: A multisystemic approach. *Journal of Family Psychology, 17*(2), 252.

Prather, C., Fuller, T. R., Marshall, K. J., & Jeffries, W. L., 4th. (2016). The impact of racism on the sexual and reproductive health of African American women. *Journal of Women's Health (2002), 25*(7), 664–671.

Puzone, C. A., Saltzman, L. E., Kresnow, M. J., Thompson, M. P., & Mercy, J. A. (2000). National trends in intimate partner homicide: United States, 1976-1995. *Violence Against Women, 6*(4), 409–426.

Raj, A., & Silverman, J. (2002a). Violence against immigrant women: The roles of culture, context, and legal immigrant status on intimate partner violence. *Violence Against Women, 8*(3), 367–398.

Raj, A., & Silverman, J. G. (2002b). Intimate partner violence against South Asian women in greater Boston. *Journal of the American Medical Women's Association (1972), 57*(2), 111–114.

Remafedi, G., French, S., Story, M., Resnick, M. D., & Blum, R. (1998). The relationship between suicide risk and sexual orientation: Results of a population-based study. *American Journal of Public Health, 88*(1), 57–60.

Rennison, C. M. (2003). *Intimate partner violence, 1993–2001, Bureau of justice statistics crime data brief.* Retrieved from https://www.bjs.gov/content/pub/pdf/ipv01.pd

Ringel, S., & Bina, R. (2007). Understanding causes of and responses to intimate partner violence in a Jewish orthodox community: Survivors' and leaders' perspectives. *Research on Social Work Practice, 17*(2), 277–286.

Roguski, M. (2012). Pets as pawns: The co-existence of animal cruelty and family violence. *Report prepared for Royal New Zealand Society for the Prevention of Cruelty to Animals and The National Collective of Independent Women's Refuges.* Retrieved from http://nationallinkcoalition.org/wp-content/uploads/2013/01/DV-PetsAsPawnsNZ.pdf

Russell, B. L. (2010). *Battered woman syndrome as a legal defense: History, effectiveness and implications.* Jefferson, NC: McFarland & Company.

Russell, B. L., & Melillo, L. S. (2006). Attitudes toward battered women who kill: Defendant typicality and judgments of culpability. *Criminal Justice and Behavior, 33*(2), 219–241.

Schneider, E. M. (1986). Describing and changing: Women's self-defense work and the problem of expert testimony on battering. *Women's Rights Law Reporter., 9,* 195–225.

Schreder, Carol (Producer) & Greenwald, Robert (Director). (October 8, 1984).*The Burning Bed* [Television Broadcast]. NBC.

Schuller, R. A., & Vidmar, N. (1992). Battered woman syndrome evidence in the courtroom: A review of the literature. *Law and Human Behavior, 16*(3), 273.

Scott v. Hart, No. C-76-2395 (N.D. Cal. Filed Oct. 28, 1976).

Seelman, K. L. (2015). Unequal treatment of transgender individuals in domestic violence and rape crisis programs. *Journal of Social Service Research, 41*(3), 307–325.

Seligman, M. E. (1972). Learned helplessness. *Annual Review of Medicine, 23*(1), 407–412.

Siemieniuk, R. A., Krentz, H. B., & Gill, M. J. (2013). Intimate partner violence and HIV: A review. *Current HIV/AIDS Reports, 10*(4), 380–389.

Simmons, S. B., Knight, K. E., & Menard, S. (2015). Consequences of intimate partner violence on substance use and depression for women and men. *Journal of Family Violence, 30*(3), 351–361.

St. Vil, N. M., Sabri, B., Nwokolo, V., Alexander, K. A., & Campbell, J. C. (2017). A qualitative study of survival strategies used by low-income black women who experience intimate partner violence. *Social Work, 62*(1), 63–71.

State v Kelly 97 N.J. 178; 478 A.2d 364 (1984).

State v Norman 324 N.C. 253, 378 S.E.2d 8 (1989).

Stephenson, R., & Finneran, C. (2013). The IPV-GBM scale: A new scale to measure intimate partner violence among gay and bisexual men. *PLoS One, 8*(6), e62592.

Stevenson, R., Fitzgerald, A., & Barrett, B. (2018). Keeping pets safe in the context of intimate partner violence: Insights from domestic violence shelter staff in Canada. *Affilia, 33*(2), 236–252.

Stockman, J. K., Hayashi, H., & Campbell, J. C. (2015). Intimate partner violence and its health impact on ethnic minority women. *Journal of Women's Health, 24*(1), 62–79.

Straus, M. A., & Gelles, R. J. (1990). How violent are American families? Estimates from the National Family Violence Resurvey and other studies. In M. A. Straus & R. J. Gelles (Eds.), *Physical violence in American families: Risk factors and adaptations to violence in 8,145 families* (pp. 95–112). New York, NY: Routledge Taylor and Francis Group.

The United States Department of Justice Archives (2014). *VAWA 2013 Nondiscrimination provision: Making programs accessible to all victims of domestic violence, sexual assault, dating violence and stalking*. Retrieved from https://www.justice.gov/archives/ovw/blog/vawa-2013-nondiscrimination-provision-making-programs-accessible-all-victims-domestic

Thompson, R. S., Bonomi, A. E., Anderson, M., Reid, R. J., Dimer, J. A., Carrell, D., & Rivara, F. P. (2006). Intimate partner violence: Prevalence, types, and chronicity in adult women. *American Journal of Preventive Medicine, 30*(6), 447–457.

Tjaden, P., & Thoennes, N. (2000). Prevalence and consequences of male-to-female and female-to-male intimate partner violence as measured by the National Violence Against Women Survey. *Violence Against Women, 6*(2), 142–161.

Tjaden, P., Thoennes, N., & Allison, C. J. (1999). Comparing violence over the life span in samples of same-sex and opposite-sex cohabitants. *Violence and Victims, 14*(4), 413.

Tombaugh, T. N. (1996). *Test of memory malingering: TOMM*. New York/Toronto, Canada: MHS Assessments.

United States Department of Justice. (2011a). *Office of Justice Programs Fact Sheet*. Retrieved from https://ojp.gov/newsroom/factsheets/ojpfs_domesticviolence.html

United States Department of Justice. (2011b). *Crime in the United States, 2010*. Washington, D.C: Federal Bureau of Investigation, Uniform Crime Reports.

VAWA: Udall celebrates Senate reauthorization of VAWA. (2012). *Lanham, MD: Federal Information & News Dispatch Violence Against Women & Department of Justice Reauthorization Act of 2005*. Retrieved from https://www.govinfo.gov/content/pkg/PLAW-109publ162/pdf/PLAW-109publ162.pdf

Violence Against Women Reauthorization Act of 2005, 42 U.S.C. §§ 13701 (2005). https://www.congress.gov/bill/109th-congress/house-bill/3402

Violence Against Women Reauthorization Act of 2013, 42 U.S.C. §§ 13701 (2013). https://www.justice.gov/tribal/violence-against-women-act-vawa-reauthorization-2013-0

Violence Against Women Act of 1994 (1994). Retrieved from https://legcounsel.house.gov/Comps/DOMVIOL.PDF

Volpp, L. (2011). Framing cultural difference: Immigrant women and discourses of tradition. *Differences, 22*(1), 90–110.

Waldner-Haugrud, L. M., Gratch, L. V., & Magruder, B. (1997). Victimization and perpetration rates of violence in gay and lesbian relationships: Gender issues explored. *Violence and Victims, 12*, 173–184.

Walker, L. E. (1979). *The battered woman*. New York, NY: Harper & Row.

Walker, L. A. (1984) Battered women, psychology, and public policy. *American Psychologist* 39(10):1178–1182.

Walker, L. E. (1992). Battered women syndrome and self-defense. *Notre Dame Journal of Ethics & Public Policy, 6*, 321.

Walker, L. E. (1996). *Assessment of abusive spousal relationships*. New York, NY: Wiley.

Walker, L. E. (2016). *The battered woman syndrome* (4th ed.). New York, NY: Springer.

Wells, C. (1994). Battered woman syndrome and defenses to homicide: Where now? *Legal Studies, 14*(2), 266–276.

West, C. (2018). Intimate partner violence in African American couples. In R. A. Javier & W. G. Herron (Eds.), *Understanding domestic violence: Theories, challenges, and remedies* (pp. 213–236). Lantham, MD: Rowman & Littlefield.

Wilson, M. I., & Daly, M. (1992). Who kills whom in spouse killings? On the exceptional sex ratio of spousal homicides in the United States. *Criminology, 30*(2), 189–216.

Yoshihama, M., & Dabby, C. (2015). *Facts & stats report: Domestic violence in Asian & Pacific Islander homes*. Retrieved from https://s3.amazonaws.com/gbv-wp-uploads/wp-content/uploads/2019/02/01204358/Facts-Stats-Report-DV-API-Communities-2015-formatted2019.pdf

# Chapter 16
# Trauma, Assessment, and Management in Sexual Offender Contexts

Raina V. Lamade

## Introduction

Sexual assault is a pervasive public health issue. One in four women and one in six men have been sexually abused by age 18 (NSVRC, 2015, p. 1), and lifetime rates equate to more than one in three and nearly one in four that have experienced sexual violence involving physical contact (Centers for Disease Control and Prevention, 2019). Sexual assault remains one of the most underreported crimes (NSVRC, 2015), and the majority of sexual assaults are never reported to law enforcement (Kilpatrick, Edmunds, & Seymour, 1992). Sexual offending behaviors range from verbal sexual harassment to noncontact offenses (exposure, public masturbation) to contact offenses, including rape. This also includes the production, distribution, and possession of child pornography that was thought to be almost eradicated, if not at least significantly reduced, through successful law enforcement efforts until the advent of the Internet (United States Department of Justice, 2011).

Other than the fact that the majority of sexual offenders are male, they constitute a heterogeneous group of individuals defined by an illegal behavior (Knight, Rosenberg, & Schneider, 1985), who are regulated and managed by state and federal laws (Lamade & Prentky, 2019). Many laws (e.g., 34 US Code § 20901) were initiated as a result of high-profile crimes and contain the names of the respective victims (e.g., Adam Walsh, Jacob Wetterling, Megan Kanka) and predominantly represent legislators' attempts to assuage the fears of concerned citizens, rather than a comprehensive approach based on research (Lamade & Prentky, 2019).

Over the past 20 years, media coverage has drawn the public's attention to sexual assault, particularly within three specific contexts: Internet child pornography and sexual solicitation of minors, campus sexual assault/misconduct (CSA), and military sexual trauma (MST). The Internet is considered interstate commerce, and therefore,

R. V. Lamade (✉)
University of Massachusetts Dartmouth, North Dartmouth, MA, USA
e-mail: rlamade@umassd.edu

© Springer Nature Switzerland AG 2020
R. A. Javier et al. (eds.), *Assessing Trauma in Forensic Contexts*,
https://doi.org/10.1007/978-3-030-33106-1_16

Internet child pornography production, distribution, and possession fall under federal statutes. Additionally, solicitation of a minor for sexual activity and traveling across state lines to engage in sexual activity with a minor also fall under federal statutes. Military sexual trauma (MST) is the term defined by the Department of Veterans Affairs as "experiences of sexual assault or repeated, threatening sexual harassment that a Veteran experienced during his or her military service" (United States Department of Veterans Affairs, n.d.). Title 38 (38 US Code § 1720D) of federal law provides counseling and treatment benefits for veterans who experienced sexual trauma incurred during service. The Department of Defense's latest report on sexual assault in the military for fiscal year 2018 indicated a 12.6% increase in reports made in fiscal year 2017 (Department of Defense, 2019). Results of this survey sparked congressional action that included the introduction of a new bill, H.R.1092: Servicemembers and Veterans Empowerment and Support Act of 2019 (Bennett, 2019). The literature on campus sexual misconduct dates back to the 1950s with Kanin and Kirkpatrick, who were one of the first teams to examine sexual aggression on college campuses (Kanin, 1957; Kirkpatrick & Kanin, 1957). They found that a significant proportion of college women (20–25%) reported sexually coercive experiences involving their male collegiate peers (Kanin, 1957). Koss and colleagues published a series of landmark studies (1982, 1985, 1987) demonstrating the problem of sexual assault on college campuses, yet it took decades to come to the attention of the general public. Research has shown that both MST and CSA have two common factors, the involvement of alcohol (in MST, alcohol was involved in 62% of victimized women and 49% of victimized men) and familiarity with the perpetrator (Abbey, Jacques-Tiura, & Lebreton, 2011; Abbey, Parkhill, Jacques-Tiura, & Saenz, 2009; Department of Defense, 2019). Additionally, recent reports of sexual abuse perpetrated by celebrities (e.g., Bill Cosby), wealthy businessmen and media moguls (e.g., Harvey Weinstein) resulted in the development or expansion of movements such as "MeToo" (#metoo) and "Time's Up Now" that have raised awareness of the pervasive issue of sexual aggression. Legislation governing sex offenders is driven by public outrage and mobilization which requires awareness that typically stems from high-profile cases and media coverage.

## Legislation

The point of this section and corresponding table (Table 16.1) below is to highlight the numerous laws that pertain to sex crimes, including management law of sex offenders when they return to the community, and the challenges that these laws raise. The earliest state policies regarding sex offenders date back to the 1930s and involve the psychiatric commitment of "sexual psychopaths" (Sutherland, 1950). Beginning in the early 1990s, numerous federal acts were put forth ostensibly to protect the public from sexual assault and exploitation. Currently, the majority of federal criminal laws that pertain to sexual crimes are contained in Title 18 (Crimes and Criminal Procedure) and Title 34 (Crime Control and Law Enforcement) and

**Table 16.1**  List of relevant federal and Uniform Code of Military Justice (UCMJ) laws[a]

| Name of act or statute | Notes |
|---|---|
| The Violence Against Women Act (VAWA) of 1994 H.R.1585 – Violence Against Women Reauthorization Act of 2019 | Codified under Title 42, transferred to Title 34. Reauthorized in 2000, 2005, and 2013<br>The current Reauthorization Act of 2019 passed the house and was in the senate as of April 2019 |
| The Wetterling Act The Wetterling Improvements Act of 1997 (P.L. 105–119) | Passed in 1994 as part of the Violent Crime Control and Law Enforcement Act (42 U.S.C. 14071)<br>Currently under 34 US Code Subchapter I: Sex Offender Registration and Notification<br>34 U.S.C. § 20902: Establishment of program (establishes the Jacob Wetterling, Megan Kanka, and Pam Lychner Sex Offender Registration and Notification Program) |
| The Amended Wetterling Act of 1996, known as "Megan's Law" (P. L. 104–145) | Currently under 34 US Code Subchapter I: Sex Offender Registration and Notification<br>34 U.S.C. § 20902: Establishment of program (establishes the Jacob Wetterling, Megan Kanka, and Pam Lychner Sex Offender Registration and Notification Program) |
| 28a U.S.C. Rule 413. Similar Crimes in Sexual-Assault Cases<br>28a U.S.C. Rule 414. Similar Crimes in Child-Molestation Cases | These are amendments to the Federal Rules of Evidence in 1994/1995 to include prior sex crimes |
| The Pam Lychner Sexual Offender Tracking and Identification Act (42 U.S.C. 14,072) in 1996 | Currently under 34 US Code Subchapter I: Sex Offender Registration and Notification<br>34 U.S.C. § 20902: Establishment of program (establishes the Jacob Wetterling, Megan Kanka, and Pam Lychner Sex Offender Registration and Notification Program) |
| The Victims of Trafficking and Violence Prevention Act of 2000 | Contained under 22 U.S.C. Chapter 78: Trafficking Victims Protection. See Chapter 78 for details. This includes:<br>22 U.S.C. § 7105: Protection and assistance for victims of trafficking<br>22 U.S. Code § 7106: Minimum standards for the elimination of trafficking<br>22 U.S.C. § 7107: Actions against governments failing to meet minimum standards. This requires foreign governments to make minimum standards to eliminate human trafficking and outlines actions against the said governments who fail to comply<br>This also required registered sex offenders to notify the state of any institution of high education where they were enrolled. It also amended the Higher Education Act of 1965 to require institutions that are obligated to disclose campus security policy and campus crime statistics to provide notice on how to obtain this information |
| The Federal Child Abuse Prevention and Treatment Act (CAPTA) of 2003 (reauthorized in 2010) | Contained under *42 U.S.C. Chapter 67*: Child Abuse Prevention and Treatment and Adoption Reform. Title I is found in Subchapter I and Title II of this Act is found in Subchapter II |

(continued)

**Table 16.1** (continued)

| Name of act or statute | Notes |
| --- | --- |
| Prosecutorial Remedies and Other Tools to end the Exploitation of Children Today (PROTECT) Act, Pub. L. 108–21, § 362, 117 Stat. 665 (2003) | Codified at 18 U.S.C. § 2252(B): Misleading Names on the Internet.<br>Established a national Amber Alert coordinator for abducted children.<br>(34 U.S. Code§ 20501.National coordination of AMBER Alert communications network)<br>Amends laws related to sexual tourism, laws related to penalties for child pornography, stricter penalties for sex offenders who perpetrate offenses, and changes to the Tier Sex Offender Registry. |
| The Adam Walsh Child Protection and Safety Act of 2006 (P. L. No. 109–248, 42 U.S.C. 16901) (P. L. No. 109–248, 42 U.S.C. 16971) | This included SORNA (Sex Offender Registration and Notification Act) which was passed in 2006 under Title I of the Adam Walsh Child Protection and Safety Act and established a *comprehensive national system* for the registration of all sex offenders (Title I, §301). While SORNA establishes a basic standard of registration and notification, its implementation occurs at the local level, with each jurisdiction making determinations about who is required to register and what information is included, but all jurisdictions submit all of their information to the National Sex Offender Registry (NSOR) (United States Department of Justice, 2019)<br>The Adam Walsh Child Protection and Safety Act also contained legislation authorizing the federal government to civilly commit "sexually dangerous persons" in federal custody. See 34 U.S.C. § 20971<br>Now contained under 34 U.S.C. Chapter 209: Child Protection and Safety which consists of three subchapters listed below in the next three rows |
| 34 U.S.C. Chapter 209, Subchapter I, Part A: Sex Offender Registration and Notification (consists of §20901–§20962) | 34 U.S.C. § 20911: Relevant definitions<br>Sex Offender Registration and Notification<br>including Amie Zyla expansion of sex offender definition and expanded inclusion of child predators and sets a three-tiered sexual offender registry system. Tier I is the lowest registration level with a mandatory requirement of 15 years that may be dropped to 10 years if the sex offender has a clean record. Tier II requires a 25-year registration period, and Tier III, the highest level, requires lifetime registration, unless the individual is a juvenile, wherein the period is 25 years, if he/she maintains a clean record. Sexual offenses perpetrated against minors are classified as levels II and III. While the understandable goal of registration is to protect society, it is important to remember that this is the only type of crime for which there is a legal requirement to register after having served one's sentence, and that carries serious repercussions for failure to comply |
| 34 U.S.C. § 20971: Commitment of Dangerous Sex Offenders | This is Subchapter II of 34 U.S.C. Chapter 209 |

(continued)

**Table 16.1** (continued)

| Name of act or statute | Notes |
|---|---|
| 34 U.S.C. Chapter 209, Subchapter III: Grants and Other Provisions (consists of §20981–§20991) | Includes: 34 U.S.C. § 20945 which established the SMART (Sex Offender Sentencing, Monitoring, Apprehending, Registering, and Tracking). The SMART Office is the branch of the Department of Justice responsible for all aspects of sex offender apprehension and management and brings together law enforcement and clinical services providers 34 U.S.C. § 20985 established funding for the nonprofit RAINN: Rape, Abuse and Incest National Network |
| The Keeping the Internet Devoid of Sexual Predators Act of 2008 (P.L. No. 110–400) | This was also known as the Kids Act of 2008. Reclassified under: 34 U.S.C. § 20915 and 34 U.S.C. § 20901 |
| Justice for Victims of Trafficking Act, and Military Sex Reporting Act, Title V of the Justice for Victims of Trafficking Act | This amended various laws in Titles 6, 18, 22, 28, 29, 31, 34, 39, and 42. This included legislation to support survivors of human trafficking, such as 18 U.S.C. § 3014: Additional special assessment fine and support to law enforcement to combat human trafficking |
| International Megan's Law to Prevent Child Exploitation and Other Sexual Crimes Through Advanced Notification of Traveling Sex Offenders (P.L. No. 114–119) | Created: 22 U.S. Code § 212b.Unique passport identifiers for covered sex offenders Currently also under 34 U.S. C. § 21501. Findings Amended: 22 U.S. Code § 2152d. Assistance to foreign countries to meet minimum standards for the elimination of trafficking and other laws |
| 18 U.S.C. §1591: Sex trafficking of children or by force, fraud, or coercion | |
| 18 U.S.C. §2241: Aggravated sexual abuse | |
| 18 U.S.C. §2242: Sexual abuse | |
| 18 U.S.C. §2243: Sexual abuse of ward or child | |
| 18 U.S.C. §2244: Abusive sexual contact | |
| 18 U.S.C. §2245: Sexual abuse resulting in death | |
| 18 U.S.C. §2244: Failure to register | |
| 18 U.S.C. §2251: Sexual exploitation of children | |
| 18 U.S.C. §2251A: Selling or buying children | |

(continued)

**Table 16.1** (continued)

| Name of act or statute | Notes |
| --- | --- |
| 18 U.S.C. §2252: Transporting, distributing, or selling child sexually exploitive material | |
| 18 U.S.C. §2252A: Transporting or distributing child pornography | |
| 18 U.S.C. §2252B: Misleading Internet domain names | |
| 18 U.S.C. §2252C: Misleading Internet website source codes | |
| 18 U.S.C. §2260: Making child sexually exploitative material overseas for export to the United States | |
| 18 U.S.C. §2421: Transportation generally | |
| 18 U.S.C. §2422: Coercing or enticing travel for illicit sexual purposes | |
| 18 U.S.C. §2423: Travel involving illicit sexual activity with a child | |
| 18 U.S.C. §2424: Filing false statement concerning an alien for illicit sexual purposes | |
| 18 U.S.C. §2425: Interstate transmission of information about a child relating to illicit sexual activity | |
| UCMJ Art. 120: Rape, sexual assault, aggravated sexual contact, and abusive sexual contact | |
| UCMJ Art. 120b: Rape, sexual assault, and sexual abuse of a child | |
| UCMJ Art. 134 that is conduct that could bring discredit upon the armed forces that are not capital offenders | Sexual offenses can also be charged under a general article (United States Department of Justice, SMART, 2019) |

[a]This table includes the main statues and acts pertaining to sexual offenses/offenders, but is not an exhaustive list.

have been outlined in the table below, along with laws pertaining to sex offenders within the Uniform Code of Military Justice. There are, however, additional laws found under other titles that pertain to sex offenders, for example, 42 US Code § 13663: Ineligibility of dangerous sex offenders for admission to public housing prohibits Tier III (lifetime registered) sex offenders admission to federally assisted housing.

Currently, at the state level, although all states have laws against sexual assault, the definitions and categories vary, but are usually graded according to severity (Lamade & Prentky, 2019). The most significant focus has involved management and civil commitment laws that began in 1990 when the first sexually violent predator (SVP) law was passed in the State of Washington (WA Laws of 1990, ch. 3), with other states soon following suit (Lamade & Prentky, 2019). DeMatteo and colleagues (2015) found that SVP laws differed considerably in terms of standards of proof, commitment procedures, definitions of terms, appeals, and safeguards. LaFond (2000) draws a distinction that SVP laws are different from ordinary civil commitment laws because they do not require the individual to suffer from a serious mental disorder and in some locations, there are no bona fide treatment programs where individuals are committed. Miller (2010) argues that treatment is a constitutional right for individuals who are involuntarily committed. Twenty states and the District of Columbia have laws allowing the involuntary civil commitment of sexual offenders which allow sex offenders to be confined in a secure facility after incarceration when a court has determined that they are likely to be at risk of future sexual violence (Association for the Treatment of Sexual Abusers ATSA, 2010). Concerns regarding the constitutionality (ex post facto and double jeopardy law) of sex offender involuntary commitment as well as due process violations have been raised (DeMatteo et al., 2015; Levenson, 2003). In *Kansas v. Hendricks* (1997), the Supreme Court of the United States upheld that Kansas' definition of "mental abnormality" (including personality disorders) satisfied substantive due process requirements. The United States Supreme Court also decided that civil commitment does not constitute a second prosecution and is not punitive, as its aims are not retribution and deterrence. Punishment is an essential prerequisite for double jeopardy and ex post facto claims, and since civil commitment is nonpunitive, it does not constitute double jeopardy or violate ex post facto laws. The Court noted that treatment, if possible, was an ancillary goal. The Court said that it has upheld involuntary commitment statutes that detain people who are *unable* to control their behavior and therefore pose a danger to themselves or others. As per this ruling, commitment of sex offenders requires a current "mental abnormality," not a "mental illness," which, in this case, included paraphilia, a likelihood of future sexual crimes, and a link between the two. ATSA put forth an amicus brief stating that the "cannot control" standard is untenable and is impossible to assess (ATSA, 2000). In *Kansas v. Crane* (2002), the Court elaborated on *Hendricks* and said that a total or complete lack of control is not required, but merely an abnormality or disorder that makes it difficult for the person to control their behavior (i.e., that there must be a finding of *some* inability to control behavior). The Court, however, left it to legislatures to determine how lack of control is proven in their jurisdiction (*Kansas v. Crane*, 2002).

There are challenges of meeting the legal standards (Harris, 2017), as well as these standards being inconsistent with the empirical science of risk. For example, the *New York v. Donald DD* (2014) ruling found that antisocial personality disorder and psychopathy (conditions closely linked to risk of recidivism) did not meet the standard of "mental abnormality." In *New York v. Kenneth T* (2013), it was decided that the state failed to offer evidence of the defendant's "volitional impairment" or inability to control his sexual misconduct (Harris, 2017). Civil commitment can be costly (Levenson, 2003) with release from commitment for sex offenders being rare (Harris, 2017; Levenson, 2003), particularly since in most states, individuals are committed indefinitely with yearly evaluations until they are no longer considered dangerous to others (Miller, 2010). Texas, however, has an exclusively community-based commitment program (ATSA, 2010) where sex offenders are monitored by GPS, have a supervised case manager, and are subject to polygraphs and penile plethysmographs (Miller, 2010).

## Assessment and Treatment

The primary concern from which most corollary questions emerge about sex offenders is the risk of recidivism (i.e., committing another sexual crime) and treatment/interventions/management strategies to reduce risk. Because the focus of this chapter is about trauma within this population, this section provides only a brief overview that is predominantly based on male contact offenders. Recidivism rates are typically based on record data (e.g., arrests, criminal convictions), and because many sexual offenses are not reported, recidivism rates are a "diluted measure of reoffending" (Przybylski, 2015, p. 1). Research shows that most sex offenders do not re-offend sexually, with recidivism rates for sexual offenders ranging from 5% to 14% and about 13% for child molesters (Hanson & Bussiere, 1998; Hanson & Morton-Bourgon, 2005; Langan, Schmitt, & DuRose, 2003; Schultz, 2014). Perhaps one of the largest studies from the US Department of Justice found a 5.3% recidivism rate (Langan et al., 2003). Rates, however, vary by time period measured (i.e., rates increase as the time period increases because there is more time for recidivism to be detected; Przybylski, 2015) and types of offenders (Harris & Hanson, 2004). For example, incest offenders had the lowest rates of recidivism (13% after 15 years) and extrafamilial boy-victim child molesters had the highest rates (35% after 15 years) across all three periods (5, 10, and 15 years) (Harris & Hanson, 2004).

Comprehensive information about risk factors (see Hanson & Bussiere, 1998; Hanson & Morton-Bourgon, 2005 and Mann, Hanson, & Thornton, 2010), risk assessment, and treatment within this population can be obtained through the resources at the end of this chapter. Risk assessment tools for Internet offenders are still in the nascent stages of development. For a comprehensive overview of Internet sexual offenders, see Seto (2013).

It goes without saying that like any assessment, the validity of risk assessment is dependent upon accurate data. As in most forensic contexts, where confidentiality is typically at best limited, the stakes of disclosing information, particularly for sex offenders, are higher with potentially significant consequences to one's liberty and life. It must therefore be underscored that within this population, because of the crime, personal details about sexual activity, thoughts, and fantasies are asked and the disclosure of such can have major impact on the individual. Sex offenders can be civilly committed and are subject to management laws after they have served their sentences.

The primary assessment question is the level of risk of recidivism. To reiterate, these risk factors and assessment tools are based on samples of adult male offenders. Risk factors that predict recidivism fall into static/historic (i.e., those that are fixed and unchangeable) and dynamic (i.e., those that can change or be modified) (Hanson, 1998). Factors associated with sexual recidivism include sexual deviancy, antisocial orientation, sexual attitudes, intimacy deficits, adverse childhood environment, general psychological problems (e.g., anxiety, mental illness), and clinical presentation (e.g., denial, minimization, low motivation for treatment) (Hanson & Morton-Bourgon, 2005). The two main categories/approaches to sex offender risk assessment used today are actuarial tools (e.g., Static-99/02) and structured professional judgment (SPJ). A third approach, anamnestic, uses behavioral analysis to determine risk factors but is an individualistic approach that is not based on larger nomothetic data. The original approach, unstructured clinical judgment, has been shown to have poor predictive accuracy compared to actuarial and SPJ tools (Heilbrun, Yassuhara, & Shah, 2010). While both actuarial and SPJ tools use variables that are empirically related to outcome (i.e., sexual re-offending), actuarial tools provide a predictive score that is usually associated with a percentage of likelihood or re-offense at some time period (e.g., 5 years), whereas SPJs leave the final judgment (usually low, medium, or high risk) to the evaluator (Heilbrun et al., 2010). Actuarial assessment is based on mathematical formulas, usually regression or discriminative analysis (Prentky, Barbaree, & Janus, 2015), to arrive at a probability (or score) of some outcome (Grove & Meehl, 1996). Actuarial tools consist predominantly of historic variables and therefore provide limited guidance for variables that can be targeted (i.e., changed) through psychological interventions. They include the Static-99/02 (Hanson & Thornton, 1999; Harris, Phenix, Hanson, & Thornton, 2003; Phenix et al., 2012), the Sex Offender Risk Appraisal Guide (SORAG; Quinsey, Harris, Rice, & Cormier, 2006), the Rapid Risk Assessment of Sex Offender Recidivism (RRASOR; Hanson, 1997), MnSOST-R (Epperson, Kaul, Huot, Goldman, & Alexander, 2003), and the Risk Matrix-2000 Sex (Thornton et al., 2003). Structured professional judgment (SPJ) tools include the STABLE (Brankley, Helmus, & Hanson, 2017), ACUTE 2007 (Hanson, Harris, Scott, & Helmus, 2007), SVR-20$^{v3}$ (Boer, Hart, Kropp, & Webster, 2017), and the JSOAP-II (for juveniles; Prentky & Righthand, 2003). Hanson and Morton-Bourgon (2009) found that the best supported instruments for assessing sexual recidivism were the Static-99, Static-2002, MnSOST-R, Risk Matrix-2000 Sex, and the SVR-20.

As part of a comprehensive assessment, in addition to a psychosocial history, including a psychosexual history, physiological or performance-based tools may be used to assess sexual behavior and interest, and include the Abel Assessment for

Sexual Interest (AASI) and the plethysmograph. The Abel is used to measure an individual's sexual interest and obtain information about problematic sexual behavior. The latest version, Abel Assessment for Sexual Interest-3, contains both objective (e.g., visual reaction time to determine sexual interest; measures of cognitive distortions, social desirability) and self-report (sexual fantasies, sexual behaviors, Internet child pornography consumption). See https://abelscreening.com/research-development/for a listing of research papers. Various state departments of corrections and agencies use Abel tools, and they have been accepted in court. However, the Abel and corresponding expert testimony have been challenged under the Daubert standard and Rule 702 (Federal Rules of Evidence) and deemed inadmissible (see *United States v. White Horse* and *U.S. v. Birdsbill*). ATSA (2014) recognizes that phallometry and viewing time may be useful to obtain objective behavioral data about the client that may not be readily obtained through other assessment means, to explore the reliability of self-report, and to explore potential changes (e.g., treatment progress).

Likewise, ATSA recognizes that the polygraph may have utility in facilitating disclosure about offending behaviors, sexual history, and treatment compliance. The polygraph is not admissible in most jurisdictions. Therefore, it is advisable to consider the rules of evidence within the jurisdiction when planning assessments.

Levenson and D'Amora (2007) argue that treatment should be an integral component of any strategy designed to combat sexual violence. Treatment for sex offenders is typically CBT (cognitive behavioral therapy), and initial programs emphasized a relapse prevention approach (similar to substance abuse) (Laws, 1989). Relapse prevention has been replaced with a risk-needs-responsivity (RNR) framework (Andrews & Bonta, 2007). RNR states that treatment targets risk factors and that dose is a function of risk. Those with the greatest risk and need factors get the most intensive treatment, which involves targeting the offenders' specific risk factors. An alternative approach called the Good Lives Model (GLM) focuses on improving interpersonal strengths rather than targeting risk factors (Schultz, 2014). GLM takes the perspective that the major driving focus in treatment should be human well-being and enhancing a client's capabilities to improve quality of life, rather than managing their risk (Ward & Steward, 2003). They argue that targeting risk factors alone is insufficient and will not motivate offenders to make positive change. Ward and Steward (2003) state that RNR and GLM are not mutually exclusive and advocate for using them in conjunction.

As a general rule of thumb, there is a fair amount of denial and minimization within this population. As such, motivational interviewing/enhancement techniques are also employed (see Stinson & Clark, 2017). A treatment paradox exists because successful treatment requires candid discussion of fantasies and past transgressions that are not protected by privilege or confidentiality (Miller, 2010). Sex offender treatment records are the "most relied-upon documentation" and "also play a critical role at each stage of the commitment process" (Miller, 2010, p. 2112). Removing confidentiality, a cornerstone of treatment, can impact treatment and healing, but is particularly significant within commitment and management contexts, wherein information obtained can lead to a loss of civil liberties and have long-standing consequences (Miller, 2010) that are potentially traumatic. Part of the therapeutic process with sex offenders, regardless of approach, is to acknowledge transgressions and problematic behaviors (which may be used against them in future proceedings) and to take accountability and change. Failure to do so or refusal to participate in treatment may tip the balance in favor of commitment (Miller, 2010). Essentially, everything discussed during treatment has the potential to become discoverable, and this presents a huge challenge for successful treatment and necessitates an explicit informed consent about the lack of confidentiality. The incentives, therefore, to withhold information and refuse treatment (Miller, 2010) are understandable. The nature of the information discussed may evoke feelings of embarrassment, shame, or guilt, particularly if the sex offender is empathic or is developing perspective-taking skills (i.e., from the perspective of the victim(s)). Miller (2010) points out that due to these issues, participating in a treatment system is unfair and places participants in a catch-22 situation. If they refuse, it is viewed unfavorably by those making dispositional determinations, and if they genuinely engage, information can be used in future proceedings with unfavorable outcomes. This inadvertently creates the path of superficial engagement (i.e., going through the motions without real commitment) where genuine information is not shared and renders treatment ineffective. This situation may exacerbate feelings of worthlessness and mental illness (e.g., depression, anxiety) (Miller, 2010).

## Childhood Trauma

Adverse childhood experiences are well documented in criminal populations (Garbarino, 2017). Retrospective research demonstrates that adverse, dysfunctional family environments are common among sex offenders (Hanson & Morton-Bourgon, 2005; Lee, Jackson, Pattison, & Ward, 2002; Raymond, Coleman, Ohlerking, Christenson, & Miner, 1999; Smallbone & Dadds, 1998). This includes family environments characterized by instability, abuse, and/or neglect (Prentky, 1999; Prentky et al., 2014). Alexander (1992) opined that it is the overall adversity of the childhood environment that should be considered, rather than the presence or absence of a specific type of childhood trauma (e.g., physical abuse). Childhood sexual abuse, for example, is often accompanied by a range of traumatic experiences (e.g., other types of abuse, neglect, family violence, economic hardships) (Jespersen, Lalumière, & Seto, 2009). When we consider abuse variables, it is therefore important to consider not just whether and what type(s) of abuse had occurred. It is also important to consider contextual factors such as the onset, duration, level of violence, and the family environment within which it occurred (i.e., high level of family dysfunction versus nurturing family environment).

A meta-analysis conducted by Babchishin, Hanson, and Hermann (2011) found that both Internet child pornography and contact offenders reported more childhood abuse compared to males in the general population. There is some evidence that these factors may also be related to recidivism. Hanson and Harris (2000) compared sexual offense recidivists with non-recidivists and found that recidivists had significantly worse family backgrounds (i.e., sexual/emotional abuse, neglect, long-term separations from parents, negative relationships with their mothers) and were significantly more likely to be taken into the care of child protective services.

Sexually victimized child molesters were significantly more likely to have experienced a range of forms of childhood abuse (e.g., neglect, violence, instability) and associated difficulties (Craissati, McClurg, & Browne, 2002). Seghorn, Prentky, and Boucher (1987) similarly found that compared to non-sexually abused child molesters, more than half of the sexually abused child molesters had fathers with a criminal history, three-quarters had fathers with substance abuse problems, more than a third had parents with a psychiatric history, more than three quarters were neglected, and five times as many came from homes in which other family members were sexually abused. Taken together, they concluded that "these data provide clear and unequivocal evidence for the association between childhood sexual victimization and severe parental pathology" (Seghorn et al., 1987, p. 266) and underscore the relevance of the overall level of dysfunction in the family environment.

Childhood adversity/abuse and family dysfunction have been incorporated into models of sexual offending as distal variables, which help set in motion an adverse pattern of interacting with the world (e.g., antisocial orientation), that, without the presence of other protective factors, may lead to more negative consequences (such as sexual offending) (e.g., Marshall & Barbaree, 1990). Childhood trauma seems to disrupt the development of normal attachment, leading to intimacy deficits, and interpersonal deficits that are hypothesized to be a factor related to patterns of sexually deviant behavior (Prentky, 1999). Conversely, children who come from highly nurturing home environments and are sexually assaulted are more likely to have the internal coping mechanisms, as well as external support systems, to recover from the experience relatively unscathed (Seghorn et al., 1987).

## Childhood Physical Abuse

Bard et al. (1987) found that 56% of their overall sample of sex offenders, which included rapists and child molesters, were physically abused and 49% were neglected by their families. Bumby and Hansen (1997) found that 39% of child molesters in their sample reported a history of physical abuse in childhood. Webb, Craissati, and Keen (2007) found that child molesters and Internet child pornography offenders had experienced considerable levels of childhood difficulties, but child molesters reported significantly more physical abuse in childhood than Internet offenders, whereas McCarthy (2010) did not find any significant differences with respect to childhood physical or sexual abuse between contact and Internet offenders. In a meta-analysis of sex offenders that included a non-sexually offending criminal group, Jespersen et al. (2009) found that sex offenders did not differ significantly from non-sex offenders on childhood physical abuse or a history of childhood emotional abuse or neglect. However, they found that compared to child molesters, sex offenders who perpetrate offenses against adults reported significantly more childhood physical abuse (Jespersen et al., 2009).

## Childhood Sexual Abuse

A meta-analysis found that 28.2% of sex offenders reported a history of childhood sexual abuse (Hanson & Slater, 1988) which exceeds the rate (approximately 10%) for nonoffending males in the community. Jespersen et al. (2009) conducted a meta-analysis and found that sex offenders reported significantly more childhood sexual abuse than non-sex offender criminals. Bard et al. (1987) found that one out of six offenders in their overall sample of sex offenders (consisting of rapists and child molesters) was a victim of some type of family sexual deviance (e.g., incest, child pornography) and one-quarter of the sample came from families where promiscuity or unusual sexual practices occurred. Contact and dual (contact and Internet pornography) offenders reported significantly more childhood sexual abuse than Internet offenders (Sheldon & Howitt, 2008).

Childhood sexual abuse is uniquely associated with child molesters (Freund & Kuban, 1994). Sex offenders who perpetrated offenses against children (e.g., child molesters/pedophiles) were significantly more likely to report a history of (Cohen et al., 2002) and had higher prevalence rates of (Jespersen et al., 2009) childhood sexual abuse. Seghorn et al. (1987) compared rapists and child molesters and found that the incidence of childhood sexual assault among child molesters was twice as high as the incidence among rapists. Although many child molesters report a history of sexual abuse during childhood (Ames & Houston, 1990; Finkelhor, 1990; Hall & Hall, 2007; Murray, 2000), estimate ranges from less than 20% (i.e., McCarthy, 2010) in an Internet offender sample, approximately half of which had contact sexual offenses, to as high as over 60% (Cohen et al., 2002) in a small sample consisting of male pedophiles.

Childhood sexual abuse is often cited as an antecedent or precursor for child molestation (Jespersen et al., 2009; Prentky, 1999). Sheldon and Howitt (2008) suggest that while sexual abuse history may be an antecedent, its relevance to committing a sexual offense is either mediated or moderated by other variables. As Finkelhor (1984) pointed out, most victims of childhood sexual abuse do not become perpetrators of sexual abuse (see also Kaufman & Zigler, 1987; Prentky, 1999; Prentky, Knight, & Lee, 1997). Childhood sexual abuse, like other forms of child abuse and other antecedent factors, becomes critical in the presence of other factors, such as age of onset, duration of abuse, child's relationship to the perpetrator, level of violence, and co-occurrence of other types of abuse (Kaufman & Zigler, 1987). The impact of childhood sexual abuse is highly variable (Craissati et al., 2002), and "not all sexually abused children are affected equally and many have factors to mediate or buffer the impact" (Tharinger, 1990, p. 335). Some of the effects of childhood sexual abuse may be due to other premorbid or co-occurring factors such as family conflict, and emotional neglect, that contribute to the individual's vulnerability and exacerbate the trauma (Browne & Finkelhor, 1986).

"When sexual abuse is isolated, noninvasive (e.g., caressing or fondling), without physical violence, and perpetrated by a stranger, the child often can recover without major disruption to normal development" (Prentky, 1999, p.269). Groth (1978) proposed that the greatest trauma from sexual abuse occurs in situations where abuse is protracted, occurs with a more closely related person, involves penetration, and is accompanied by violence, although research findings have not consistently supported this claim (Browne & Finkelhor, 1986).

The impact of childhood sexual abuse can lead to longer-term effects, such as depression, anxiety, shame, poor self-esteem (Alexander, 1992; Murray, 2000), difficulty in regulating affect (Alexander, 1992), isolation, loneliness, emotional immaturity (Hall & Hall, 2007), and problems in interpersonal relationships (Alexander, 1992). Other consequences seen in adulthood include self-destructive behavior, anxiety, isolation, feelings of being stigmatized, negative self-concept/poor self-esteem, problems with substance abuse, difficulty trusting others, hostility, and problems with sexuality and parenting (Browne & Finkelhor, 1986), problems with substance abuse, anger and suicidality (Briere, 1988), and fear, anxiety, aggression, poor self-esteem, and sexually inappropriate behavior (Finkelhor, 1990).

Childhood sexual abuse can impact the process of psychosexual development in inappropriate and interpersonally dysfunctional ways and lead to increased distorted cognitions, attitudes, and behaviors around sex and intimacy (Tharinger, 1990). Urquiza and Crowley (1986) found that sexually abused men expressed a greater desire to hurt others and a greater sexual interest in children. Although there are potential long-term effects of childhood sexual abuse, it generally has not been found to be a significant predictor of recidivism (Hanson & Bussiere, 1998). One study by Lee et al. (2002) found that childhood emotional abuse, family dysfunction, childhood behavioral problems, and childhood sexual abuse were risk factors for developing various paraphilias, including pedophilia, but *only* childhood sexual abuse was a risk factor for pedophilia.

## Stigma and Trauma Associated with Being Convicted of a Sexual Offense

Some argue that any criminal conviction, regardless of how historic and how trivial an offense, can scar one for life (Petersilia, 2003). When considering different disadvantaged groups (e.g., being a prisoner, HIV positive, diagnosed mental health disorder, sexual orientation, etc.), roughly 65% reported discrimination upon release due to being a former prisoner than any other reason and that this was significantly negatively related to self-esteem (LeBel, 2012).

Sex offenders generally face considerably greater stigmatization and are viewed negatively by society at large (Edwards, 2000) which continues throughout incarceration and after they have served their sentence and return to the community (Edwards & Hensley, 2001; Garfinkle, 2003; Levenson, D'Amora, & Hern, 2007; Tewksbury, 2012). "Sex offenders are among the most despised and publicly discussed social deviants in the United States in the past two decades" (Tewksbury, 2012, p. 607). They are perceived as dangerous and uncontrollable, with high rates of recidivism, and should be "avoided, closely monitored and strictly controlled" (Tewksbury, 2012, p. 607), which is inconsistent with the literature that shows that sex offenders have relatively low rates of recidivism (Przybylski, 2015). "In reality, sex offender recidivism is lower than the rate for many other types of criminals" (Prentky et al., 2015, p. 43).

Sex offenders report being recipients of negative, stigmatizing labels in the prison community and civilian population (Tewksbury, 2012). Being stigmatized and a member of a publicly condemned group set an individual up as a prime target for further harassment and social disapproval (Tewksbury, 2012). It is important to underscore the cascading effects of stigma for this population that include social ostracism, insults, emotional distress, loneliness, shame, hopelessness/depression, discrimination, and fear (Tewksbury, 2012) that poses a barrier to treatment (Furst & Evans, 2015). It therefore makes sense that sex offenders conceal their status based on situations in which they anticipate condemnation from others (Furst & Evans, 2015).

There are two additional types of stigma encountered within this population. Courtesy stigma is stigma that extends to immediate family and friends (Goffman, 1963). Within-group stigma due to intragroup hierarchy is stigma against child molesters (pedophiles) who are on the lowest level of the sexual offending group and criminal offender hierarchies and receive the most disdain (Furst & Evans, 2015).

## Stigma and Trauma during Incarceration

Sex offenders, particularly those that have perpetrated crimes against minors (pedophiles/child molesters), are viewed unfavorably by other inmates and correctional staff and often experience stigma that can result in negative treatment (Ireland, 2000; Schwaebe, 2005; Spencer, 2009; Tewksbury, 2012). Pedophiles are often teased and abused by other inmates, are on the lowest level of the prison hierarchy, and are the most vilified subsection of the prison population (James, 2003; Mann, 2012). They are called "chesters," "tree jumpers," "short eyes" (James, 2003), and "baby rapers" (Tewksbury, 2012). Sex offenders face verbal aggression and physical assault from other inmates in prison (Tewksbury, 2012). When their crimes are discovered, they are often at risk of being murdered and require placement in protective custody (James, 2003), isolation, or solitary confinement (Blagden, Winder, & Hames, 2016). Perpetrating harm to a pedophile can bring the perpetrator respect in the prison community. For gang members, going after sex offenders is an easy way to publicly demonstrate strength and earn respect (Ferranti, 2015). They are, therefore, a vulnerable population within the prison system (Mann, 2012). Research has found that sex offenders reported more social isolation while incarcerated compared with nonsexual offenders (van den Berg, Beijersbergen, Nieuwbeerta, & Dirkzwager, 2018).

Social isolation for sex offenders is particularly relevant for this population. Sex offenders have generally been found to have social deficits and deficits in interpersonal functioning and in forming meaningful intimate relationships (Blake & Gannon, 2011; Bumby & Hansen, 1997). Therefore, opportunities for healthy social interactions are particularly important. Loneliness and social isolation have been postulated to be etiological and maintaining factors for sexual aggression (Marshall, 1989, 2010), related to higher levels of aggression in sex offenders (Blake & Gannon, 2011, Ward and Hudson 2000), and are considered to increase the risk of re-offending (Marshall, 1989, 2010).

## *Post-Incarceration Stigma and Trauma*

Generally speaking, regardless of the type of crime, inmates returning to the community from prison face a number of challenges including securing housing and employment, receiving treatment, encountering discrimination, and complying with the requirements of parole/supervision (Edwards & Mottarella, 2015; Kubrin & Stewart, 2006; Rydberg, Grommon, Huebner, & Bynum, 2014; Weir, 2015). When released, they remain largely uneducated and unskilled, with no savings, no immediate rights to unemployment benefits, and few employment prospects (Metcalf, Anderson, & Rolfe, 2001; Petersilia, 2001). Mental health and substance use issues are high in correctional populations (Peters, Wexler, & Lurigio, 2015; Weir, 2015), with rates of serious mental illness being three to four times higher in prisons and four to six times higher in jails (Weir, 2015). Ex-offenders therefore rely on local community resources and services to reintegrate successfully (Kubrin & Stewart, 2006). Even when mental health services are available in the community, however, many fail to use them because they fear institutionalization, deny mental illness, or distrust the health-care system (Petersilia, 2001). Using a general prison population, Kubrin and Stewart (2006) found that living in a disadvantaged neighborhood increases the odds of recidivism above and beyond individual factors (e.g., being male, race, etc.). They concluded that neighborhoods with large concentrations of affluent families or resource-rich neighborhoods "serve a critical protective function in reducing recidivism" (Kubrin & Stewart, 2006, p. 184).

The majority of sex offenders will be managed in the community (Conroy, 2006) as there are nearly 650,000 registered sex offenders in the United States (National Center for Missing and Exploited Children, as cited in Levenson & Tewksbury, 2009). The primary concern is risk of re-offense. A one-size-fits-all model cannot successfully minimize risk to the community (Conroy, 2006). Concerns about risk and public safety add to the amount and stringency of management-related laws. English (1998) recommends the containment approach which is a multidisciplinary, multiagency strategy consisting of a victim-centered/community safety philosophy, multidisciplinary collaboration with consistent policies and protocols across agencies, using specific management tools (i.e., criminal justice supervision, sex offender-specific treatment, and post-conviction polygraph assessment), and program quality control. Ward (2007) and Erooga (2008) argue that effective management strategies are unlikely to be effective if they deprive the individual of individual freedom of movement or prevent the acquisition of factors related to well-being; thus, management should be considered from a human rights perspective.

In addition to the typical burdens and challenges that ex-convicts face, sex offenders have the added challenge of complying with mandatory management laws (Schultz, 2014). More than for any other type of crime, the laws that govern requirements for sex offenders post-incarceration create unintended adverse consequences and challenges for successful community reentry (Rolfe, Tewksbury, & Schroeder, 2017). These laws determine what are considered permissible employment locations, options (e.g., restrictions against certain positions), and populations (e.g., restrictions for working with children) (Brown, Spencer, & Deakin, 2007) and potentially challenge one's ability to engage in treatment and to develop and maintain appropriate social relationships. All of these factors are potentially traumatic and can lead to other negative effects.

The main management laws include SORN/SORNA (Sex Offender Registration and Notification) laws, residency restrictions, and GPS (global positioning system). With GPS, sex offenders wear a transmitter device that is usually attached to their ankle which allows them to be tracked by a computer monitoring system (Levenson & D'Amora, 2007). Passive monitoring sends reports to supervising officers at intervals, whereas active GPS provides continuous real-time surveillance and alerts officers immediately when an offender travels into a forbidden range (Levenson & D'Amora, 2007). Although the effect of GPS is unknown, a report from the Florida legislature based on their use concluded that electronically monitored offenders violated the conditions of probation less frequently than other offenders (Levenson & D'Amora, 2007). Sex offender management legislation also prohibits sex offenders from participating in Halloween activities like handing out candy.

Other less common management strategies include chemical castration and other forms of clear identification (e.g., two states were considering a law that would require registered sex offenders to have distinctive neon green-colored numbered license vehicle plates) (Erooga, 2008), which would have been the equivalent of another scarlet letter (see Farley, 2008). Additional restrictions for Internet child pornography offenders or Internet-facilitated contact offenses extend into the virtual world and include prohibited (no computer, no Internet access) or restricted use, monitoring (installation of monitoring software that track websites visited, download history), and reviewing electronic communications. Additional requirements include submitting computers and electronic devices to searches, and notifying others who use those computers/devices that these may be subject to searchers and monitoring. Given the ubiquitous practical functions that the Internet now serves (e.g., job searches, applications; paying bills), complete restrictions (i.e., no Internet/computer) can further impact other important basic needs. While in some cases complete restrictions may be appropriate, when implemented, economic and pragmatic ways to provide support with these tasks (e.g., finding and applying for suitable jobs) in the absence of the Internet/computer should be considered.

The restrictive nature of these laws makes it difficult to abide by them, resulting in violations and homelessness (Berenson & Appelbaum, 2011; Levenson, Letourneau, Armstrong, & Zgoba, 2010; Socia, Levenson, Ackerman, & Harris, 2015). Homelessness leaves offenders vulnerable to a host of traumatic experiences (e.g., assault, disease). Homeless sex offenders also pose challenges for the public and "not knowing the whereabouts of Registered Sex Offenders (RSOs) directly contradicts such laws' goals of public safety" (Rolfe et al., 2017, p. 1836). For example, the number of sex offenders who could not be located more than doubled within 6 months of implementing SORN laws in Iowa (Rood, 2006).

Although the public wants additional protection from sex offenders in the community, they are not invested in management policies and endorse the belief that SORN is effective in reducing sexual victimization (Brannon, Levenson, Fortney, & Baker, 2007; Call, 2018; Levenson, Brannon, Fortney, & Baker, 2007; Schiavone & Jeglic, 2009). The vast majority of sexual offenders are not arrested for a new sexual crime (Levenson, 2008). The common belief is that management policies will make communities safer, regardless of empirical evidence (Erooga, 2008). In a study on public opinion, 83% of the public believe that community notification was effective in reducing sexual offenses, 58% believe that residency restrictions were effective, 51% believe that chemical castration was effective, and 73% said that they would support these strategies even if they lacked scientific support (Levenson, Brannon, et al., 2007). Most studies have found that sex offender management strategies have had little to no significant effect on sex offender recidivism rates (Ackerman, Sacks, & Greenberg, 2012; Letourneau, Levenson, Bandyopadhyay, Sinha, & Armstrong, 2010; Sandler, Freeman, & Socia, 2008; Tewksbury, Jennings, & Zgoba, 2012; Vasquez, Maddan, & Walker, 2008; Zgoba, Veysey, & Dalessandro, 2010). A few have found modest effects in reducing recidivism under certain conditions such as using SORN for high-risk offenders, as classified by an empirically validated risk assessment tool (Duwe & Donnay, 2008; Prescott & Rockoff, 2011). Zgoba, Jennings, and Salerno (2018) found that SORN had no significant impact on sexual recidivism rates in the past two decades but that there is evidence that it had an impact on the trajectory of offending within 10 years of release in high-rate offenders. Elbogen and colleagues (2003), however, found that in their sample of sex offenders, although they had low familiarity with SORN laws, the majority (72%) felt that these laws provided incentive not to re-offend. Paradoxically, it is the collateral, unintended consequences of these strategies that can increase the risk of re-offending (Edwards & Hensley, 2001; Hanson & Harris, 1998; Schultz, 2014; Tewksbury, 2005; Ward, 2007). Specifically, these laws destabilize offenders and increase transience (Levenson, 2008). For example, challenges to employment and residential stability and social supports can contribute to a major criminogenic risk factor for general and sexual recidivism and lifestyle instability (Andrews & Bonta, 2003; Hanson & Harris, 1998; Hanson & Morton-Bourgon, 2004).

Concerns have been raised about the impact of such policies on sex offenders, that they cause more harm than good (Human Rights Watch, 2007; Zandbergen & Hart, 2006), and Human Rights Watch (2013) has particularly challenged the view that management laws are appropriate for offenses committed by children and juveniles. Sex offender management laws create significant reentry challenges (Blair, 2004; Edwards & Hensley, 2001; Levenson & Cotter, 2005a; Tewksbury, 2005; Zevitz, Crim, & Farkas, 2000a, 2000b) and have "created an environment where isolation and stigmatization are the new norm. By publicly labeling individuals as sex offenders and then by notifying entire communities about their presence, the laws have essentially created a culture of social pariahs that should be permanently excised" (Tolson & Klein, 2015, p. 379). As such, sex offenders will avoid social encounters to conceal their status which leads to social isolation (Evans & Cubellis, 2015). These laws create a punitive atmosphere that diminishes social capital which contributes to recidivism, reentry problems, and mental health issues (Tolson & Klein, 2015). Burchfield and Mingus (2008) found that sex offenders experience four types of barriers to social capital that included individual (i.e., self-imposed isolation due to stigma and shame), community (i.e., fear generated by the sex offender label that limited social interactions in their community), structural (i.e., due to financial and housing issues), and formal (i.e., due to management laws that place restrictions on residency, employment).

## Sex Offender Registration and Notification Laws

Although SORN laws vary across states, every state has had some version of a sexual offender public notification and registration law pursuant to the Federal Wetterling Act of 1996 (Lamade & Prentky, 2019) and which are currently accessible online. Some laws may also vary by municipalities at the county level (e.g., when a specific state law is absent, municipalities pass ordinances). Additionally, there is a National Sex Offender Public Website (NSOPW) that is maintained by the SMART Office of the US Department of Justice and allows the public to search for information from all states for locations and identities of known sex offenders.

The constitutionality of community notification statutes has been successfully challenged, particularly on issues related to privacy rights (Levenson & Cotter, 2005a). Berliner (1996) argued that community notification is a reasonable method to help parents protect their children but that this cannot replace prevention efforts. Others (Freeman-Longo, 1996; Jones, 1999; Levi, 2000; Lotke, 1997; Prentky, 1996) have suggested that this is an emotionally driven response that provides a false sense of security that is not supported by the literature. Freeman-Longo (1996) found that those classified as lower risk (Tier I) were rearrested for sexual offenses at a higher rate than those classified as moderate risk (Tier II) and highest (Tier III) and concluded that SORN was unable to accurately identify high-risk offenders and, therefore, increase public safety. This section will summarize the research demonstrating direct and adverse collateral consequences of SORN laws.

Community notification may exacerbate stressors that may trigger some sex offenders to re-offend (Edwards & Hensley, 2001; Freeman-Longo, 1996). Twenty-three out of the 30 participants interviewed about their experiences with being placed on community notifications reported that they were humiliated in their daily lives, ostracized by neighbors and lifetime acquaintances, and harassed and threatened by nearby residents and strangers (Zevitz & Farkas, 2000). All expressed concerns about their safety (Zevitz & Farkas, 2000). Twenty of the 30 participants said that community notification adversely impacted the lives of their family members (Zevitz & Farkas, 2000). Offenders who attended community notification meetings reported that insults were shouted at them (Zevitz & Farkas, 2000).

Sexual offenders are often required to register and therefore encounter continued punishment following their sentence (Evans & Cubellis, 2015), and this impacts their current relationships and the ability to form future relationships (Tewksbury & Lees, 2006). Registered sex offenders experience stigmatization with friends, family, and parole/probation officers that results in clustering around other sex offenders (Evans & Cubellis, 2015).

Being placed on the registry adversely impacts employment (Tewksbury, 2004; Tewksbury & Lees, 2006), positive social support, and stable housing and contributes to emotional distress (Evans & Porter, 2015; Tewksbury, 2005; Tewksbury & Levenson, 2009; Tewksbury & Zgoba, 2010; Zevitz & Farkas, 2000). Zevitz and colleagues (2000a, 2000b) found that sex offenders reported losing employment due to their high-profile status on SORN. The impact on employment has related consequences for food, clothing, transportation, and housing. Levenson and Cotter (2005a, 2005b) found that over one third of the sex offender participants that they surveyed had experienced negative events such as loss of employment/residence, property damage, and threats/harassment by the neighbors being the highest reported negative consequences (33%) as a result of SORN policies. Additionally, 72% reported less hope for the future now that they are registered sex offenders for life, 71% said that the SORN laws interfered with their recovery by causing more stress in their life, 67% reported that shame and embarrassment kept them from engaging in activities, and 64% reported feeling alone and isolated. Themes about unfairness, particularly with respect to lifetime registration, have also emerged. Levenson and Cotter (2005a) also found positive effects that included motivation to prevent re-offense and increased honesty with friends and family. Results are consistent across samples and states. Tewksbury (2005) used a sample from Kentucky and found similar results. Just under 60% reported losing a friend who discovered the registration, 54.4% reported being harassed in person, 47.4% reported loss of job, 47.4% reported loss of/being denied a place to live, and approximately 45% reported being treated rudely in a public place. Other negative experiences included being denied a promotion at work, asked to leave a business, and assaulted and receiving harassing/threatening calls or mail (Tewksbury, 2005). He also found that those with child victims compared to adult-only victims were less likely to report experiencing seven out of the ten negative consequences (i.e., their reported percentages were lower in seven out of ten conditions). He hypothesized that this finding was due to the fact that those that have child victims are more likely to control who knows about their offenses and registration. Participants also reported high levels of shame, that the registry is an unfair form of punishment, but also that they understood why society wants to have a registry (Tewksbury, 2005).

Sex offenders on the registry have difficulty finding housing (Mustaine, Tewksbury, & Stengel, 2006a, 2006b; Tewksbury, 2004; Zevitz & Farkas, 2000), even in shelters. Rolfe et al. (2017) found that only 12.2% of shelters made exceptions to policies about housing registered sex offenders. Exceptions were typically made for female registered sex offenders or those with statutory rape charges. Nearly half of the shelters prohibit sex offenders. Homeless shelters are generally willing to make exceptions to policies to serve homeless individuals, but are overwhelmingly unwilling to make exceptions to policies regarding registered sexual offenders (Rolfe et al., 2017), regardless of risk. Rolfe and colleagues (2017) attribute the unwillingness to make exceptions to the stigma associated with being a registered sex offender. They argue that depriving sex offenders' access to shelters poses more risk to the public (Rolfe et al., 2017).

Several studies have demonstrated that sex offender registration and notification laws may produce unintended negative consequences such as public anxiety, retaliation, harassment, stigmatization, and retribution (Edwards & Hensley, 2001; Levenson & Cotter, 2005a; Schram & Milloy, 1995; Tewksbury, 2004; Tewksbury & Lees, 2006; Younglove & Vitello, 2003; Zevitz, Crim, & Farkas, 2000a, 2000b) and difficulties in personal and social relationships (Tewksbury, 2004; Tewksbury & Lees, 2006). The registry, like community notification, leaves offenders open to victimization and contributes to social isolation (Levenson & Cotter, 2005a, 2005b; Tewksbury & Levenson, 2009; Tewksbury & Zgoba, 2010). Social isolation from the community and ostracization of offenders drive them "underground" (Edwards & Hensley, 2001; Farley, 2008; Prescott & Rockoff, 2011; Tewksbury, 2005). When isolated and/or ostracized, registered sex offenders will gravitate toward like-minded individuals (e.g., other sex offenders) to decrease isolation, stigma, and guilt and find solace and support (Evans & Cubellis, 2015). The danger in this is the potential to justify, validate, and reinforce their actions, attitudes, feelings, and risk-related behaviors (Mann, 2012). On the other hand, sex offenders who have local family and friends and perceive their neighbors as attached to the local neighborhood are less likely to report feeling stressed about their status or the need to hide their status as a sex offender (Mingus & Burchfield, 2012). They are also less likely to worry about the negative repercussions of their status when they perceive higher levels of neighborhood support (Burchfield & Mingus, 2014).

SORN has also resulted in threats/harassment and employment/financial hardships for family members, including the identification of family victims in cases of incest (Comartin, Kernsmith, & Miles, 2010; Levenson & Cotter, 2005a, 2005b; Levenson & Tewksbury, 2009; Zevitz & Farkas, 2000) and stigma (Burchfield & Mingus, 2014; Farkas & Miller, 2007; Tewksbury & Connor, 2012), causing them to pull away from the sex offender (Tolson & Klein, 2015) during a time of increased trauma.

## Residency Restrictions

Sex offenders have residency restrictions following their sentence and are excluded from government-subsidized housing (Socia, 2011). Many states have legislation that restricts housing opportunities for sex offenders (Rydberg et al., 2014). Residency restrictions (i.e., sex offenders are prohibited to reside within a specific distance that ranges from 500 to 2500 feet) where children congregate have created barriers to where sex offenders can reside (Rolfe et al., 2017). Using data from Orange County, Florida, Zandbergen and Hart (2006) found that housing options for registered sex offenders within urban areas are limited to only 5% of potentially available residences. Bus stops were the most restrictive (93.0% of potential properties fall within 1000 feet of a bus stop and 99.6% within 2500). This results in limiting residency to mostly low-density rural areas. Zgoba, Levenson, and McKee (2009) found similar results in New Jersey. The majority of sex offenders live within 2500 feet of schools (71%) and day cares (80%), and 88% live within any of the four restricted regions (i.e., schools, day care centers, parks, and churches) within Camden County. There are restrictions on permitting sex offenders to access homeless shelters (Goldstein, 2014), and federal law prohibits lifetime registrants (Tier III) from accessing public housing options (42 US Code§ 13663). A few courts, however, have held that once a person has been admitted to a federal housing program, they cannot be terminated from their housing subsequent to a new or newly discovered Tier III registration (United States Department of Justice, 2019).

The consequences place sex offenders outside areas of access to services, included dilapidated areas with limited access to treatment, and therefore place people in these communities at greater risk (Erooga, 2008; Schultz, 2014). Collateral consequences also result in isolation and disrupt or disconnect them from social supports (Erooga, 2008) and bonds that would "facilitate positive reentry transitions" (Rydberg et al., 2014, pg. 423). There is little research on the effect of residential movement on recidivism (Rydberg et al., 2014). Rydberg and colleagues (2014) found that sex offenders paroled after residency restrictions had significantly more address moves than those paroled before residency restrictions. Child molesters had the highest degree of residential movement but the lowest rates following the implementation of residency restriction (Rydberg et al., 2014). Residency restrictions resulted in sex offenders feeling that there was nowhere to live except in minimum-security prisons/correctional centers because of issues with finding suitable housing in the community (Zevitz & Farkas, 2000). Residency restrictions physically isolate sexual offenders from society resulting in clustering of sex offenders in small communities, which essentially deprives them of access to positive social support and increased access to criminal capital (Tolson & Klein, 2015), and reinforce criminogenic thinking.

The top reported consequences of residence restrictions from a Florida sample of sex offenders were difficulty finding a place to live (65%), being unable to live with supportive family members (49%), landlords' refusing to rent (47%), being unable to live with family members who depend on the offender (43%), and being unable to return home (42%) (Levenson, 2008). Additionally, those surveyed spent an average of 63 days homeless due to residency restrictions. Psychosocial consequences in order from highest to lowest include worry that if they have to move, they will not find a place to live in the future; emotional suffering; financial suffering; living further away from family support; being further away from employment opportunities; being further away from social and mental health services; and being further away from public transportation (Levenson, 2008). Younger offenders were particularly affected. Levenson (2008) pointed out that vague terms without guidance on how to define and interpret a "place where children regularly congregate" are problematic (p. 163). Levenson (2008) points out the glaring issue with residency restriction, that is, that they regulate where sex offenders sleep but do not prevent sex offenders from frequenting places where they can potentially cultivate inappropriate, unhealthy relationships (e.g., with children).

Residency restrictions also directly impact family members because those that want to continue to reside with the individual are now also subject to these restrictions. Three-quarters of sex offenders' family members reported being subjected to the same housing restrictions (Schultz, 2014).

## *Professionals' Opinions about the Impact of Sex Offender Management Laws*

Considering the opinions and experiences of professionals who work with sex offenders is important for two reasons. First, they work closely with sex offenders and would be able to offer additional data on the experiences and challenges sex offenders face due to sex offender laws. Second, their opinions about sex offenders can potentially impact services. Interviews of clinical and support service professionals who work with sex offenders found that they generally felt that laws are both over-inclusive and place unfair restrictions on some offenders (Day, Carson, Newton, & Hobbs, 2014). Despite this, participants also expressed broad support for registries as part of a larger plan to contribute to community safety (Day et al., 2014).

Harris, Levenson, Lobanov-Rostovksy, and Walfield (2018) using a mixed-method approach (i.e., face-to-face interviews and survey data) of law enforcement participants consisting of uniformed officers, agency command leaders, and civilian staff found that across all dimensions, civilian staff had the highest overall confidence in SORN's effectiveness, followed by uniformed personnel, and agency leaders expressed the lowest. Participants generally supported citizens' right to know about sex offenders in their communities, but were also circumspect about SORN as a public information tool, expressing concerns about citizens' ability to appropriately understand and contextualize sex offender registry information. Sixty-two percent of participants expressed concerns over registries creating a false sense of security, and almost half (46%) expressed the potential for registries to generate unfounded or misplaced fear within the community (Harris, Levenson, Lobanov-Rostovsky,, & Walfield, 2018). Participants also indicated that SORN was effective as a mechanism of interagency information sharing and assisting law enforcement in monitoring sex offenders residing in the community. They did, however, express concerns around the accuracy of offenders' risk status and the general sentiment that SORN should be more effectively integrated with other elements of the criminal justice system. There was a very small subset of participants that were concerned about collateral consequences including those related to housing that was based on both pragmatic and humanitarian concerns (Harris et al., 2018).

Cubellis, Walfield, and Harris (2018) studied the perspectives of law enforcement agents of SORN on sex offenders. Interviews of law enforcement agents did not specifically ask about collateral effects of SORN; these themes emerged spontaneously and included the stigma that registered sex offenders face due to SORN, the difficulties registered sex offenders have with finding and maintaining housing and employment, and the stress and negativity that can result from registration and community notification (Cubellis et al., 2018). Respondents, however, overwhelmingly believed that SORN was effective and still believed SORN was effective despite these negative consequences (Cubellis et al., 2018). Call (2018) examined professionals' perceptions of collateral consequences of sex offender management policies. Professionals consisted of two groups: corrections, probation, and parole officers and clinicians consisting of psychiatrists, psychologists, and counselors/therapists. There were four factors of collateral consequences. Factor 1 was defined by loss (of job, housing, family, friends); factor 2 consisted of threats and harassment (property damage, harassing/threatening communications, being physically assaulted, threats, harassment, property damage to family members); factor 3 contained emotional and psychological challenges (lonely, isolated, depressed, difficulty forming relationships, shame/embarrassment, stress); and factor 4 was related to residency restrictions. The majority of all professionals agreed or strongly agreed that sex offenders experience each category of collateral consequences when returning to the community, except for factor 2, threats and harassment (Call, 2018). There were significant differences between the two groups of professionals with clinicians endorsing that sex offenders experience collateral consequences for all three other factors (loss, emotional/psychological challenges, and residency restriction) compared to community correctional professionals (Call, 2018). Call (2018) concluded that professionals are more likely than the public to believe that sex offenders experience collateral consequences and that this may be due to having regular contact with sex offenders. Three demographic variables significantly predicted beliefs about sex offenders' collateral consequences (Call, 2018). Political conservatism was a significant predictor of the belief that sex offenders experience collateral consequences involving loss, such that those that are conservative are less likely to believe that sex offenders experienced these collateral consequences (Call, 2018). Females were significantly more likely than males to believe that sex offenders experience collateral consequences involving residency restriction. Race was also significant, as Caucasians were less likely than non-Caucasians to believe that sex offenders experience collateral consequences involving residence restrictions.

## Summary and Recommendations

The focus of this chapter has been on adult sexual offenders. However, one can understand how much more significant and traumatizing unintended collateral consequences are for juvenile sex offenders, and this point cannot be emphasized enough. Separate laws should be considered for juvenile sex offenders, as they should not be subject or subsumed under adult management laws. The knowledge gained from neuroscience and developmental psychology suggest that the impact of laws pertaining to sex offenders and their management in the community is amplified for young offenders. On a positive note, their developmental stage makes them more receptive to psychological interventions and that changes are likely to have a lasting impact.

Sexual violence is a complex public health issue that requires a comprehensive and long-term approach. This includes, as some have suggested, that we view sexual aggression developmentally, as a maladaptive process that unfolds in response to unhealthy childhood adversity or abuse (Levenson, 2014; Prentky et al., 2015). This does not, in any way, diminish the seriousness of the crime, the pain for victims, the potential dangerousness of some sexual offenders, and the paramount goals of public safety. These can remain at the forefront while also providing empirically based assessments to help guide decisions and empirically based treatments and interventions to effect positive behavioral change. This chapter aimed to demonstrate some of the challenges with current policies and how they paradoxically undermine the efforts they are aiming to accomplish while creating potentially traumatic situations for sex offenders. For years, scholars and practitioners have argued that sex offender assessment, treatment, and legislation should be grounded in empirical evidence rather than an emotional reactionary response (Levenson, 2003; Levenson & D'Amora, 2007; Wagner, 2011) and that in doing so, we could achieve better outcomes across the board for all (e.g., victims, public, sex offenders).

Reviewing and revising existing policies (Wagner, 2011) that includes the goals and adverse collateral effects is the first step and likely to receive the most resistance. Nevertheless, it is important to consider what changes will impact goals (increase public safety, reduce recidivism, enhance the ability of offenders to "make it" in the community) and are likely to receive support to become law. Tolson and Klein (2015) suggest that the Supreme Court revisit the idea that these policies are indeed a civil action and not a secondary criminal action. Another important focus should be to consider ways to reinforce positive prosocial behaviors by directly incorporating policies into sex offender management laws that will achieve these goals. For example, Wagner (2011) recommends that offenders with less serious offenses/lower risk with good behavior could be allowed to, over time, provide less detailed information to the public and considers implementing strategies that make the registration process more feasible and provide basic assistance to promote compliance, to help enhance reentry and success in the community. This graduated approach to registry information over time can reinforce positive prosocial behavior and enhance a sense of control. Rather than have residency restrictions, some municipalities have instead implemented child safety zones wherein sex offenders are forbidden from frequenting venues where they can easily cultivate relationships with other children (Zgoba et al., 2009).

Second, it may be beneficial to consider strategies to enhance transitioning into the community. Public safety is enhanced when sex offenders successful reintegrate into the community. One option is to invest in transition/reentry/reintegration planning upfront that includes support and assistance in the community to help with access to housing, employment, and resources that are challenging for sex offenders (Levenson & D'Amora, 2007; Tolson & Klein, 2015). Assistance with transition to the community and support can be managed by a specific PSC (problem-solving court) for sex offenders (LaFond & Winick, 2004). The goal of a sex offender reentry court would be to further promote pro-social change in sex offenders reentering communities, decrease recidivism risk, and increase compliance with sex offender management laws (Budd, Burbrink, & Conner, 2016). PSC can be helpful and offer a nice balance between management and assistance to those in the community. The unique challenges that sex offenders face, coupled with tarnished opinions by staff, have created challenges to PSC sex offender courts in the past. For example, Budd et al. (2016) explored the reasons why a sex offender reentry court failed to succeed and found that some reasons were a function of missing essential components necessary for successful PSC, such as judicial leadership, collaboration with stakeholders, logistics (e.g., having a separate court with scheduling), and training. This includes basic training on trauma-informed care, but also consideration of including trauma questions in assessments. Although trauma variables may not be risk factors per se, it is the mechanism and their relationship to other risk relevant variables that could prove useful. In other words, assessing for trauma history might be useful in determining social and interpersonal deficits, potential relationship to risk factors, and the trajectory of sexual offending behaviors. They found that other main contributors to failure were specific to the unique challenges of working with this population, such as finding services in the community for sex offenders, early case engagement just when they were entering the community (as this is a critical time period), and stigma about sex offenders and possibility of success with this population. These issues are not insurmountable; the majority of them can be addressed with planning and policies.

Regardless of whether or not reintegration is facilitated through a problem-solving court, successful reintegration of sex offenders is best achieved through successful interagency collaboration (Alexander, 2010). In addition, Alexander's (2010) recommendations of developing personnel (staff and counselors) and providing them with the resources and support they need is critical to effectively managing this population and staff retention. This includes specialized caseloads, expertise and training related to sex offender management, and trauma-informed care. Support of staff, particularly counselors who manage caseloads to help reduce secondary (vicarious) trauma (Alexander, 2010), is particularly important for those working with this population. Finally, using empirically validated and known sex offender risk assessment tools and empirically supported treatments is vital. Use of RNR (i.e., more intensive treatment and supervision for higher-risk offenders) and

GLM treatments can be implemented in the community. Given the range of trauma within sex offender populations, perpetrators are among the most in need of trauma-involved services (Levenson, 2014).

## Questions/Activities for Further Exploration

1. What would be effective in shifting public opinion to align with the research of managing sexual offenders to allow for legislative changes consistent with the empirical body of literature?
2. What would be the pros and cons of increasing multidisciplinary/multiagency trainings for those working with sex offenders?
3. How do we promote the development and maintenance of healthy consensual sexual intimacy and relationships across the lifespan in a culture of sexualized marketing, casual "hook ups," and virtually unlimited access to a range of sexual interests vis-à-vis the Internet?
4. What changes to the statutes, if any, and definitions within the statutes should be pursued?

## References

Abbey, A., Jacques-Tiura, A. J., & LeBreton, J. M. (2011). Risk factors for sexual aggression in young men: An expansion of the confluence model. *Aggressive Behavior, 37*(5), 450–464.

Abbey, A., Parkhill, M. R., Jacques-Tiura, A. J., & Saenz, C. (2009). Alcohol's role in men's use of coercion to obtain unprotected sex. *Substance Use & Misuse, 44*(9–10), 1329–1348.

Ackerman, A. R., Sacks, M., & Greenberg, D. (2012). Legislation targeting sex offenders: Are recent policies effective in reducing rape? *Justice Quarterly, 29*(6), 858–887.

Adam Walsh Act, Pub.L. 109–248 (2006).

Alexander, P. C. (1992). Application of attachment theory to the study of sexual abuse. *Journal of Consulting and Clinical Psychology, 60*(2), 185–195.

Alexander, R. (2010). Collaborative supervision strategies for sex offender community management. *Federal Probation, 74*(2), 16–19.

Ames, M. A., & Houston, D. A. (1990). Legal, social, and biological definitions of pedophilia. *Archives of Sexual Behavior, 19*(4), 333–342.

Andrews, D. A., & Bonta, J. (2003). *The psychology of criminal conduct* (3rd ed.). Cincinnati, OH: Anderson.

Andrews, D. A., & Bonta, J. (2007). *The psychology of criminal conduct* (4th ed.). Cincinnati, OH: Anderson.

Association for the Treatment of Sexual Abusers (ATSA). (2000). Brief for the Association for the Treatment of Sexual Abusers as Amicus Curiae in support of petitioner. Kansas v. Crane.

Association for the Treatment of Sexual Abusers (ATSA). (2010). *Civil commitment of sexual violent persons*. Retrieved from: http://www.atsa.com/pdfs/Policy/CivilCommitment.pdf

Association for the Treatment of Sexual Abusers (ATSA). (2014). *Practice guidelines for the assessment, treatment, and management of male adult sexual abusers*. Beaverton, OR: ATSA.

Babchishin, K. M., Hanson, R. K., & Hermann, C. A. (2011). The characteristics of online sex offenders: A meta-analysis. *Sexual Abuse, 23*(1), 92–123.

Bard, L. A., Carter, D. L., Cerce, D. D., Knight, R. A., Rosenberg, R., & Schneider, B. (1987). A descriptive study of rapists and child molesters: Developmental, clinical and criminal characteristics. *Behavioral Sciences & the Law, 5*(2), 203–220.

Bennett, A. (2019). VA incorrectly denied military sexual trauma benefits, Congress calls for change. Retrieved from: https://connectingvets.radio.com/articles/military-sexual-trauma-survivors-denied-benefits-va-congress-wants-change

Berenson, J. A., & Appelbaum, P. S. (2011). A geospatial analysis of the impact of sex offender residency restrictions in two New York counties. *Law and Human Behavior, 35*, 235–246.

Berliner, L. (1996). Community notification: Neither a panacea nor a calamity. *Sexual Abuse: A Journal of Research & Treatment, 8*(2), 101–104.

Blagden, N., Winder, B., & Hames, C. (2016). "They treat us like human beings"—Experiencing a therapeutic sex offenders prison impact on prisoners and staff and implications for treatment. *International Journal of Offender Therapy and Comparative Criminology, 60*, 371–396.

Blair, M. (2004). Wisconsin's sex offender registration and notification laws: Has the Wisconsin Legislature left the criminals and constitution behind? *Marquette Law Review, 87*(5), 939–980.

Blake, E., & Gannon, T. A. (2011). Loneliness in sexual offenders. In S. J. Bevinn (Ed.), *Psychology of loneliness* (pp. 49–68). Hauppauge, NY: Nova Science.

Boer, D. P., Hart, S. D., Kropp, P. R., & Webster, C. D. (2017). *Manual for the sexual violence scale risk–20. Version 2*. Vancouver, BC: Protect International Risk and Safety Services.

Brankley, A. E., Helmus, L.-M., & Hanson, R. K. (2017). *STABLE-2007 evaluator workbook: Updated recidivism rates (includes combinations with Static-99R, Static-2002R, and Risk Matrix 2000)*. Unpublished report. Ottawa, ON: Public Safety Canada.

Brannon, Y. N., Levenson, J. S., Fortney, T., & Baker, J. N. (2007). Attitudes about community notification: A comparison of sexual offenders and the non-offending public. *Sexual Abuse: A Journal of Research and Treatment, 19*, 369–379.

Briere, J. (1988). The long-term clinical correlates of childhood sexual victimization. In R. A. Prentky & V. L. Quinsey (Eds.), *Human sexual aggression* (Vol. 528, pp. 327–344). New York: The New York Academy of Sciences.

Brown, K., Spencer, J., & Deakin, J. (2007). The reintegration of sex offenders: Barriers and opportunities for employment. *The Howard Journal, 46*(1), 32–42.

Browne, A., & Finkelhor, D. (1986). Impact of child sexual abuse: A review of the research. *Psychological Bulletin, 99*(1), 66–77.

Budd, K. M., Burbrink, M. J., & Conner, T. A. (2016). Team member's perceptions on a sex offender reentry court's failure to launch: A pilot study. *Journal of Sexual Aggression, 22*(3), 394–409.

Bumby, K. M., & Hansen, D. J. (1997). Intimacy deficits, fear of intimacy, and loneliness among sexual offenders. *Criminal Justice and Behavior, 24*, 315–331.

Burchfield, K. B. (2012). Assessing community residents' perceptions of local registered sex offenders. *Deviant Behavior, 33*(4), 241–259.

Burchfield, K. B., & Mingus, W. (2008). Not in my neighborhood: Assessing registered sex offenders' experiences with local social capital and social control. *Criminal Justice and Behavior, 35*(3), 356–374.

Burchfield, K. B., & Mingus, W. (2014). Sex offender reintegration: Consequences of the local neighborhood context. *American Journal of Criminal Justice, 39*, 109–124.

Call, C. (2018). The collateral consequences of sex offender management policies: Views from professionals. *International Journal of Offender Therapy and Comparative Criminology, 62*(3), 676–696.

Centers for Disease Control and Prevention (CDC) (2019). *Prevention sexual violence*. Retrieved from: https://www.cdc.gov/features/sexualviolence/index.html

Cohen, L. J., McGeoch, P. G., Gans, S. W., Nikiforov, K., Cullen, K., & Galynker, I. I. (2002). Childhood sexual history of 20 male pedophiles vs. 24 male healthy control subjects. *Journal of Nervous and Mental Disease, 190*(11), 757–766.

Comartin, E., Kernsmith, P., & Miles, B. (2010). Family experiences of young adult sex offender registration. *Journal of Child Sexual Abuse, 19*(2), 204–225.

Conroy, M. A. (2006). Risk management of sex offenders: A model for community intervention. *The Journal of Psychiatry & Law, 34*, 5–23.

Craissati, J., McClurg, G., & Browne, K. (2002). Characteristics of perpetrators of child sexual abuse who have been sexually victimized as children. *Sexual Abuse: Journal of Research and Treatment, 14*(3), 225–239.

Cubellis, M. A., Walfield, S. M., & Harris, A. J. (2018). Collateral consequences and effectiveness of sex offender registration and notification. *International Journal of Offender Therapy and Comparative Criminology, 62*(4), 1080–1106.

Day, A., Carson, E., Newton, D., & Hobbs, G. (2014). Professional views on the management of sex offender in the community. *Journal of Offender Rehabilitation, 53*, 171–189.

DeMatteo, D., Murphy, M., & Galloway, M. (2015). A national survey of United States sexually violent person legislation: Policy, procedures, and practice. *International Journal of Forensic Mental Health, 14*, 245–266.

Department of Defense. (2019). *Department of defense annual report on sexual assault in the military fiscal year 2018.* (Reference ID: 7-1ED0167). Retrieved from: https://int.nyt.com/data/documenthelper/800-dod-annual-report-on-sexual-as/d659d6d0126ad2b19c18/optimized/full.pdf#page=1

Duwe, G., & Donnay, W. (2008). The impact of Megan's law on sex offender recidivism: The Minnesota experience. *Criminology, 46*, 411–446.

Edwards, E. R., & Mottarella, K. (2015). Perceptions of the previously convicted: The influence of convicted type of therapy participation. *International Journal of Offender Therapy and Comparative Criminology, 59*(12), 1358–1377.

Edwards, K. A. (2000). Stigmatizing the stigmatized: A note on the mentally ill prison inmate. *International Journal of Offender Therapy and Comparative Criminology, 44*, 480–489.

Edwards, W., & Hensley, C. (2001). Contextualizing sex offender management legislation and policy: Evaluating the problem of latent consequences in community notification laws. *International Journal of Offender Therapy and Comparative Criminology, 45*(1), 83–101.

Elbogen, E. B., Patry, M., Scalora, M. J. (2003). The impact of community notification laws on sex offender treatment attitudes. *International Journal of Law and Psychiatry, 26*, 207–219.

English, K. (1998). The containment approach: An aggressive strategy for the community management of adult sex offenders. *Psychology, Public Policy, and Law, 4*, 218–235.

Epperson, D. Kaul, J., Huot, S., Goldman, R., & Alexander, W. (2003). Minnesota Sex Offender Screening Tool- Revised (MnSOST-R) technical paper: Development, validation, and recommended risk level cut scores. Retrieved from: https://rsoresearch.files.wordpress.com/2012/01/ia-state-study.pdf

Erooga, M. (2008). A human rights-based approach to sex offender management: The key to effective public protection? *Journal of Sexual Aggression, 14*(3), 171–183.

Evans, D. N., & Cubellis, M. A. (2015). Coping with stigma: How registered sex offenders manage their public identities. *American Journal of Criminal Justice, 40*, 593–619.

Evans, D. N., & Porter, J. R. (2015). Criminal history and landlord rental decisions: A New York quasi-experimental study. *Journal of Experimental Criminology, 11*, 21–42.

Farkas, M. A., & Miller, G. (2007). Reentry and reintegration: Challenges faced by the families of convicted sex offenders. *Federal Sentencing Report, 20*(2), 88–92.

Farley, L. G. (2008). The Adam Walsh Act: The Scarlet Letter of the twenty-first century. *Washburn Law Journal, 47*, 471–503.

Ferranti, S. (February, 18, 2015). *Why are so many sex offenders getting murdered in California's prisons?* Retrieved from: https://www.vice.com/en_us/article/ppmjy8/why-sex-offenders-are-getting-slaughtered-in-california-prisons-218

Finkelhor, D. (1984). *Child sexual abuse: New theory and research.* New York: Free Press.

Finkelhor, D. (1990). Early and long-term effects of child sexual abuse: An update. *Professional Psychology: Research and Practice, 21*(5), 325–330.

Freeman-Longo, R. E. (1996). Prevention or problem. *Sexual Abuse: A Journal of Research & Treatment, 8*(2), 91–100.

Freund, K., & Kuban, M. (1994). The basis of the abused abuser theory of pedophilia: A further elaboration on an earlier study. *Archives of Sexual Behavior, 23*(5), 553–563.

Furst, R. T., & Evans, D. N. (2015). An exploration of stigma in the lives of sex offenders and heroin abusers. *Deviant Behavior, 36*, 130–145.

Garbarino, J. (2017). ACEs in the criminal justice system. *Academic Pediatrics, 17*, S32–S33.

Garfinkle, E. (2003). Coming of age in America: The misapplication of sex-offender registration and community notification to juveniles. *California Law Review, 91*(1), 163–208.

Goffman, E. (1963). *Stigma: Notes on the management of a spoiled identity*. New York: Simon & Shuster.

Goldstein, J. (2014, August). Housing restrictions keeps sex offenders in prison beyond release dates. New York Times. Retrieved from: https://www.nytimes.com/2014/08/22/nyregion/with-new-limits-on-where-they-can-go-sex-offenders-are-held-after-serving-sentences.html

Groth, A. N. (1978). Guidelines for assessment and management of the offender. In N. G. A. Burgess, S. Holmstrom, & S. Sgroi (Eds.), *Sexual assault of children and adolescents* (pp. 25–42). Lexington: Lexington Books.

Grove, M. G., & Meehl, P. E. (1996). Comparative efficiency of informal and formal prediction procedures: The clinical-statistical controversy. *Psychology, Public Policy and Law, 2*(2), 293–323.

H.R.1092: Servicemembers and Veterans Empowerment and Support Act of 2019.

Hall, R. C. W., & Hall, R. C. W. (2007). A profile of pedophilia: Definition, characteristics of offenders, recidivism, treatment outcomes, and forensic issues. *Mayo Clinic Proceedings, 82*(4), 457–471.

Hanson, R. K. (1997). *The development of a brief actuarial risk scale for sexual offense recidivism*. (User Report 97-04). Ottawa, ON: Department of the Solicitor General of Canada.

Hanson, R. K. (1998). What do we know about sex offender risk assessment? *Psychology, Public Policy and Law, 4*, 50–72.

Hanson, R. K., & Bussiere, M. T. (1998). Predicting relapse: A meta-analysis of sexual offender recidivism studies. *Journal of Consulting and Clinical Psychology, 66*, 348–362.

Hanson, R. K. & Harris, A. J. R. (1998). Dynamic predictors of Sexual Recidivism 1998-1. Her Majesty the Queen in Right of Canada, represented by the Sollicitor General of Canada (Minister of Public Safety and Emergency Preparedness). Retrieved from http://static99.org/pdfdocs/hansonandharris1998.pdf

Hanson, R. K., & Harris, A. J. R. (2000). Where should we intervene?: Dynamic predictors of sexual offense recidivism. *Criminal Justice and Behavior, 27*(1), 6–35.

Hanson, R. K., Harris, A. J. R., Scott, T.-L., & Helmus, L. (2007). *Assessing the risk of sexual offenders on community supervision: The Dynamic Supervision Project (User report, Corrections research)*. Ottawa, ON: Public Safety Canada. Retrieved from http://www.static99.org/pdfdocs/hansonharrisscottandhelmus2007.pdf.

Hanson, R. K., & Morton-Bourgon, K. E. (2004). Predictors of sexual recidivism: An updated meta-analysis (Corrections Research User Report No. 2004–02). Ottawa, Ontario, Canada: Public Safety and Emergency Preparedness Canada.

Hanson, R. K., & Morton-Bourgon, K. E. (2005). The characteristics of persistent sexual offenders: A meta-analysis of recidivism studies. *Journal of Consulting and Clinical Psychology, 73*, 1154–1163.

Hanson, R. K. & Morton-Bourgon, K. E. (2009). The accuracy of recidivism risk assessments for sexual offenders: A meta-analysis of 118 prediction studies. *Psychological Assessment, 21*, 1–21.

Hanson, R. K., & Slater, S. (1988). Sexual victimization in the history of sexual abusers: A review. *Annals of sex research, 1*(4), 485–499.

Hanson, R. K., & Thornton, D. (1999). *Static-99: Improving actuarial risk assessments for sex offenders. User Report 99–02*. Ottawa, ON: Department of the Solicitor General of Canada. Department of the Solicitor General of Canada website. www.sgc.gc.ca

Harris, A. J. (2017). Policy implication of New York's sex offender civil management assessment process. *American Society of Criminology, 16*(3), 949–957.

Harris, A. J. R. & Hanson. R. K. (2004). Sex offender recidivism: A simple question 2004-03. Her Majesty the Queen in Right of Canada, represented by the Sollicitor General of Canada (Minister of Public Safety and Emergency Preparedness). Retrieved from http://static99.org/pdfdocs/harrisandhanson2004simpleq.pdf

Harris, A. J., Levenson, J. S., Lobanov-Rostovksy, C., & Walfield, S. M. (2018). Law enforcement perspectives of sex offender registrations and notification: Effectiveness, challenges, and policy priorities. *Criminal Justice Policy Review, 29*(4), 391–420.

Harris, A. J. R., Phenix, A., Hanson, R. K., & Thornton, D. (2003). *Static-99 coding rules: Revised 2003*. Ottawa, ON: Department of the Solicitor General of Canada.

Heilbrun, K., Yassuhara, K., & Shah, S. A. (2010). Approaches to violence risk assessment. Overview and critical analysis. In R. Otto & K. S. Douglas (Eds.), *Handbook of violence risk assessment* (pp. 1–17). New York: Routledge.

Human Rights Watch (2007). *No easy answers: Sex offender laws in the United States*. Vol. 19, No. 4(G). Retrieved from: https://www.hrw.org/report/2007/09/11/no-easy-answers/sex-offender-laws-us

Human Rights Watch (2013). *Raised on the registry: The irreparable harm of placing children on the sex offender registries in the US*. Retrieved from: https://www.hrw.org/report/2013/05/01/raised-registry/irreparable-harm-placing-children-sex-offender-registries-us

Ireland, J. L. (2000). "Bullying" among prisoners: A review of research. *Aggression and Violent Behavior, 5*, 201–215.

Jacob Wetterling Crimes Against Children and Sexually Violent Offender Registration Act, 42 U.S.C. §14071 (1994).

James, M.S. (August, 26, 2003). *Prison is "Living Hell" for Pedophiles*. Retrieved from: https://abcnews.go.com/US/wireStory/talks-resume-sunday-stop-shop-striking-workers-62537511

Jespersen, A. F., Lalumière, M. L., & Seto, M. C. (2009). Sexual abuse history among adult sex offenders and non-sex offenders: A meta-analysis. *Child Abuse & Neglect, 33*, 179–192.

Jones, K. D. (1999). The media and Megan's Law: Is community notification the answer? *Journal of Humanistic Counseling, Education and Development, 38*(2), 80–88.

Kanin, E. J. (1957). Male aggression in dating-courtship relations. *American Journal of Sociology, 63*(2), 197–204.

Kansas v. Crane, 534 U.S. S. Ct. 407 (2002).

Kansas v. Hendricks, 117 S. Ct. 2072 (1997).

Kaufman, J., & Zigler, E. (1987). Do abused children become abusive parents? *American Journal of Orthopsychiatry, 57*(2), 186–192.

Kilpatrick, D. G., Edmunds, C. N., & Seymour, A. (1992). *Rape in America: A report to the nation*. Charleston: Medical University of South Carolina, National Victim Center and Crime Victims Research and Treatment Center.

Kirkpatrick, C., & Kanin, E. (1957). Male sex aggression on a university campus. *American Sociological Review, 22*(1), 52–58.

Knight, R. A., Rosenberg, R., & Schneider, B. (Eds.). (1985). *Classification of sexual offenders: Perspectives, methods, and validation*. New York: Garland Publishing.

Koss, M. P., & Gidycz, C. A. (1985). Sexual experiences survey: Reliability and validity. *Journal of Consulting and Clinical Psychology, 53*(3), 422–423.

Koss, M. P., Gidycz, C. A., & Wisniewski, N. (1987). The scope of rape: Incidence and prevalence of sexual aggression and victimization in a national sample of higher education students. *Journal of Consulting and Clinical Psychology, 55*(2), 162–170.

Koss, M. P., & Oros, C. J. (1982). Sexual experiences survey: A research instrument investigating sexual aggression and victimization. *Journal of Consulting and Clinical Psychology, 50*, 455–457.

Kubrin, C. E., & Stewart, E. A. (2006). Prediction who reoffends: The neglected role of neighborhood context in recidivism studies. *Criminology, 44*(1), 165–197.

LaFond, J. Q. (2000). The future of involuntary civil commitment in the U.S.A. after Kansas v. Hendricks. *Behavioral Sciences & the Law, 18*, 153–167.

LaFond, J. Q., & Winick, B. J. (2004). Sex offender reentry courts: A proposal for managing the risk of returning sex offenders to the community. *Seton Hall Law Review, 34*, 1173–1212.

Lamade, R. V., & Prentky, R. A. (2019). Taxonomic discrimination among sex offenders: Forensic Utility? In D. Bromberg & W. O'Donahue (Eds.), *Sexually violent predators: A clinical science handbook*. New York: Springer.

Langan, P.A., Schmitt, E.L., Durose, M.R. (2003). Recidivism of sex offenders released from prison in 1994. U.S. Department of Justice, Bureau of Justice Programs. NCJ 198281. Retrieved from: https://www.bjs.gov/content/pub/pdf/rsorp94.pdf

Laws, D. R. (1989). *Relapse prevention with sex offenders*. New York: Guilford Press.

LeBel, T. P. (2012). "If one doesn't get you another one will": Formerly incarcerated persons' perceptions of discrimination. *The Prison Journal, 92*(1), 63–87.

Lee, J. K. P., Jackson, H. J., Pattison, P., & Ward, T. (2002). Developmental risk factors for sexual offending. *Child Abuse & Neglect, 26*, 73–92.

Washington Laws of 1990, Chapter 3. Retrieved from: leg.wa.gov/CodeReviser/documents/sessionlaw/1990c3.pdf

Letourneau, E. J., Levenson, J. S., Bandyopadhyay, D., Sinha, D., & Armstrong, K. S. (2010). Effects of South Carolina's sex offender registration and notification policy on adult recidivism. *Criminal Justice Policy Review, 21*, 435–458.

Levenson, J. (2014). Incorporating trauma-informed care into evidence-based sex offender treatment. *Journal of Sexual Aggression, 20*(1), 9–22.

Levenson, J., & Tewksbury, R. (2009). Collateral damage: Family members of registered sex offenders. *American Journal of Criminal Justice, 34*, 54–68.

Levenson, J. S. (2003). Policy interventions designed to combat sexual violence: Community notification and civil commitment. *Journal of Child Sexual Abuse, 12*(3/4), 17–52.

Levenson, J. S. (2008). Collateral consequences of sex offender residence restrictions. *Criminal Justice Studies, 21*(2), 153–166.

Levenson, J. S., Brannon, Y. N., Fortney, T., & Baker, J. (2007). Public perception about sex offenders and community protection policies. *Analysis of Social Issues and Public Policy, 7*, 137–161.

Levenson, J. S., & Cotter, L. P. (2005a). The effect of Megan's law on sex offender reintegration. *Journal of Contemporary Criminal Justice, 21*(1), 49–66.

Levenson, J. S., & Cotter, L. P. (2005b). The impact of sex offender residence restrictions: 1,000 feet from danger or one step from absurd? *International Journal of Offender Therapy and Comparative Criminology, 49*, 168–178.

Levenson, J. S., & D'Amora, D. A. (2007). Social policies designed to prevent sexual violence: The emperor's new clothes? *Criminal Justice Policy Review, 18*, 168–199.

Levenson, J. S., D'Amora, D. A., & Hern, A. L. (2007). Megan's law and its impact on community re-entry for sex offenders. *Behavioral Sciences & the Law, 25*, 587–602.

Levenson, J. S., Letourneau, E., Armstrong, K., & Zgoba, K. (2010). Failure to register as a sex offender: Is it associated with recidivism? *Justice Quarterly, 27*, 305–331.

Levi, R. (2000). Community notification laws: A step toward more effective solutions. *Journal of Interpersonal Violence, 11*(6), 298–300.

Lotke, E. (1997). Politics and irrelevance: Community notification statutes. *Federal Sentencing Reporter, 10*(2), 64–68.

Mann, N. (2012). Ageing child sex offenders in prison: Denial, manipulation and community. *The Howard Journal, 51*(4), 345–358.

Mann, R. E., Hanson, R. K., & Thornton, D. (2010). Assessing risk for sexual recidivism: Some proposals on the nature of psychologically meaningful risk factors. *Sexual Abuse: A Journal of Research and Treatment, 22*(2), 191–217.

Marshall, W. L. (1989). Intimacy, loneliness and sexual offenders. *Behaviour Research and Therapy, 27*(5), 491–503.

Marshall, W. L. (2010). The role of attachments, intimacy, and loneliness in the etiology and maintenance of sexual offending. *Sexual and Relationship Therapy, 25*, 73–85.

Marshall, W. L., & Barbaree, H. E. (1990). An integrated theory of the etiology of sexual offending. In W. L. Marhsall, D. R. Laws & H. E. Barbaree (Eds.). *Handbook of Sexual Assualt:
Issues, Theories, and Treatment of the Offender* (pp. 257–275). New York, NY: Plenum Press.

McCarthy, J. A. (2010). Internet sexual activity: A comparison between contact and non-contact
child pornography offenders. *Journal of Sexual Aggression, 16*(2), 181–195.

Megan's Law, Pub. L. No. 104–145, § 2, 110 Stat. 1345 (1996).

Metcalf, H., Anderson, T., & Rolfe, H. (2001). Barriers to employment for offenders and ex-
offenders (DWP Research Report No. 155), Leeds: Corporate Document Services.

Mingus, W., & Burchfield, K. B. (2012). From prison to integration: Applying modified labeling theory to sex offenders. *Criminal Justice Studies: A Critical Journal of Crime, Law and
Society, 25*(1), 97–109.

Miller, J. A. (2010). Sex offender civil commitment: The treatment paradox. *California Law
Review, 98*, 2093–2128.

Murray, J. B. (2000). Psychological profile of pedophiles and child molesters. *The Journal of
Psychology: Interdisciplinary and Applied, 134*(2), 211–224.

Mustaine, E. E., Tewksbury, R., & Stengel, K. M. (2006a). Residential location and mobility of
registered sex offenders. *American Journal of Criminal Justice, 30*(2), 177–192.

Mustaine, E. E., Tewksbury, R., & Stengel, K. M. (2006b). Social disorganization and residential
locations of registered sex offenders: Is this a collateral consequence? *Deviant Behavior, 27*(3),
329–350.

National Sexual Violence Resource Center (NSVRC). (2015). *Statistics about sexual violence.*
Retrieved from: https://www.nsvrc.org/sites/default/files/publications_nsvrc_factsheet_media-
packet_statistics-about-sexual-violence_0.pdf

Peters, R. H., Wexler, H. K., & Lurigio, A. J. (2015). Co-occurring substance use and mental disorders in the criminal justice system: A new frontier of clinical practice and research. *Psychiatric
Rehabilitation Journal, 38*(1), 1–6.

Petersilia, J. (2001). When prisoners return to communities: Political, economic, and social consequences. U.S. Department of Justice, Office of Justice Programs, National Institute of Justice.
*Sentencing and Corrections: Issues for the 21st Century, 9*, 1–9.

Petersilia, J. (2003). *When prisoners come home: Parole and prisoner reentry.* New York: Oxford
University Press.

Phenix, A., Helmus, L., & Hanson, R. K., (2012). Statis-99R & Static-2002R Evaluators'
Workbook. Retrieved from: http://www.static99.org/pdfdocs/Static-99RandStatic-2002R_
EvaluatorsWorkbook2012-07-26.pdf

Prentky, R. (1996). Community notification and constructive risk reduction. *Journal of
Interpersonal Violence, 11*(2), 295–298.

Prentky, R., Knight, R., & Lee, A. (1997). *Child sexual molestation: Research issues.* (NCJ
163390). Justice Information Center World Wide Web Site U.S. Department of Justice Office
of Justice Programs NIJ.

Prentky, R. A. (1999). Child sexual molestation. In V. B. Van Hasselt & M. Hersen (Eds.),
*Handbook of psychological approaches with violent offenders* (pp. 267–300). New York:
Kluwer Academic/Plenum Publishers.

Prentky, R. A., Barbaree, H. E., & Janus, E. S. (2015). *Sexual predators: Society risk and the law.
New York.* New York: Taylor & Francis.

Prentky, R. A., Lee, A. F., Lamade, R. V., Grossi, L., Schuler, A., Dube, G., … Pond, A. (2014).
Placement instability as a risk factor in proximal sexually inappropriate and aggressive
behaviors in a child welfare sample. *Journal of Child Custody, 11*(4), 251–277.

Prentky, R. A., & Righthand, S. (2003). *Juvenile sex offender assessment protocol-II (J-SOAP-II)
Manual.* Retrieved from: https://www.researchgate.net/publication/239605808

Prescott, J. J., & Rockoff, J. E. (2011). Do sex offender registration and notification laws affect
criminal behavior? *Journal of Law & Economics, 54*(1), 161–206.

Prosecutorial Remedies and Other Tools to End the Exploitation of Children Today (PROTECT)
Act, Pub. L. 108–21, § 362, 117 Stat. 665 (2003).

Przybylski, R. (2015). Recidivism of Adult Sexual Offenders. United States Department of Justice. Office of Justice Programs Office of Sex Offender Sentencing, Monitoring, Apprehending, Registering, and Tracking, SOMAPI Research Brief, 1–6.

Quinsey, V. L., Harris, G. T., Rice, M. E., & Cormier, C. A. (2006). *Violent offenders: Appraising and managing risk* (2nd ed.). The law and public policy. Washington, DC, US: American Psychological Association.

Raymond, N. C., Coleman, E., Ohlerking, F., Christenson, G. A., & Miner, M. (1999). Psychiatric comorbidity in pedophilic sex offenders. *American Journal of Psychiatry, 156*, 786–788.

Rolfe, S. M., Tewksbury, R., & Schroeder, R. D. (2017). Homeless shelters' policies on sex offenders: Is this another collateral consequence? *International Journal of Offender Therapy and Comparative Criminology, 61*(16), 1833–1849.

Rood, L. (2006, January 23). New data shows twice as many sex offenders missing. Des Moines Register. Retrieved from: https://ccoso.org/facts-about-jessica%E2%80%99s-law-and-sex-offenders-residency-restrictions

Rydberg, J., Grommon, E., Huebner, B. M., & Bynum, T. (2014). The effects of statewide residency restrictions on sex offender post-release housing mobility. *Justice Quarterly, 31*(2), 421–444.

Sandler, J. C., Freeman, N. J., & Socia, K. M. (2008). Does a watched pot boil? A time-series analysis of New York State's sex offender registration and notification law. *Psychology, Public Policy, and Law, 14*, 284–302.

Schiavone, S. K., & Jeglic, E. L. (2009). Public perception of sex offender social policies and the impact on sex offenders. *International Journal of Offender Therapy and Comparative Criminology, 53*(6), 679–695.

Schram, D., & Milloy, C. D. (1995). *Community notification: A study of offender characteristics and recidivism.* Olympia, WA: Washington Institute for Public Policy.

Schultz, C. (2014). The stigmatization of individuals convicted of sex offenders: Labeling theory and the sex offense registry. *Themis: Research Journal of Justice Studies and Forensic Science, 2*(4), 64–81.

Schwaebe, C. (2005). Learning to pass: Sex offenders' strategies for establishing a viable identity in the prison general population. *Interpersonal Journal of Offender Therapy and Comparative Criminology, 49*, 614–624.

Seghorn, T. K., Prentky, R. A., & Boucher, R. J. (1987). Childhood sexual abuse in the lives of sexually aggressive offenders. *Journal of the American Academy of Child & Adolescent Psychiatry, 26*(2), 262–267.

Seto, M. C. (2013). *Internet sex offenders.* Washington, DC: American Psychological Association.

Sheldon, K., & Howitt, D. (2008). Sexual fantasy in paedophile offenders: Can any model explain satisfactorily new findings from a study of internet and contact sexual offenders? *Legal and Criminological Psychology, 13*(1), 137–158.

Smallbone, S. W., & Dadds, M. R. (1998). Childhood attachment and adult attachment in incarcerated adult male sex offenders. *Journal of Interpersonal Violence, 13*(5), 555–573.

Socia, K. M. (2011). The policy implications of residence restrictions on sex offender housing in Upstate NY. *Criminology & Public Policy, 10*(2), 351–389.

Socia, K. M., Levenson, J. S., Ackerman, A. R., & Harris, A. J. (2015). "Brothers under the bridge": Factors influencing the transience of registered sex offenders in Florida. *Sexual Abuse: A Journal of Research and Treatment, 27*, 559–586. https://doi.org/10.1177/1079063214521472

Spencer, D. (2009). Sex offender as homo sacer. *Punishment & Society, 11*, 219–240.

State of New York v. Donald DD. 24 N.Y.3d 174 (2014).

State of New York v. Kenneth T. Slip Op 03336 [106AD3d 829] (2013).

Stinson, J. D., & Clark, M. D. (2017). *Motivational interviewing with offenders: Engagement, rehabilitation and reentry.* New York: Guilford Press.

Sutherland, E. H. (1950). The diffusion of sexual psychopath laws. *American Journal of Sociology, 56*, 142–148.

Tewksbury, R. (2004). Experiences and attitudes of registered female sex offenders. *Federal Probation, 68*(3), 30–33.

Tewksbury, R. (2005). Collateral consequences of sex offender registration. *Journal of Contemporary Criminal Justice, 21*(1), 67–81.

Tewksbury, R. (2012). Stigmatization of sex offenders. *Deviant Behavior, 33*, 606–623.

Tewksbury, R., & Connor, D. P. (2012). Incarcerated sex offenders' perceptions of family relationships: Previous experiences and future expectations. *Western Criminology Review, 13*(2), 25–35.

Tewksbury, R., Jennings, W. G., & Zgoba, K. M. (2012). A longitudinal examination of sex offender recidivism prior to and following implementation of SORN. *Behavioral Sciences & the Law, 30*, 308–328.

Tewksbury, R., & Lees, M. B. (2006). Perceptions of sex offender registration: Collateral consequences and community experiences. *Sociological Spectrum, 26*(3), 309–334.

Tewksbury, R., & Levenson, J. S. (2009). Stress experiences of family members of registered sex offenders. *Behavioral Sciences & the Law, 27*, 611–626.

Tewksbury, R., & Zgoba, K. M. (2010). Perceptions and coping with punishment how registered sex offenders respond to stress, internet restrictions, and the collateral consequences of registration. *International Journal of Offender Therapy and Comparative Criminology, 54*, 537–551.

Tharinger, D. (1990). Impact of child sexual abuse on developing sexuality. *Professional Psychology: Research and Practice, 21*(5), 331–337.

The Expanded VAWA Legislation in 2000. (P. L.106–386, 18 U.S.C. 2261).

The Federal Child Abuse Prevention and Treatment Act (CAPTA). of 2003.

The Pam Lychner Sexual Offender Tracking and Identification Act (42 U.S.C. 14072). in 1996.

The Victims of Trafficking and Violence Prevention Act. of 2000.

The Violence Against Women Act. of 1994 (VAWA).

The Wetterling Improvements Act of 1997. (P.L. 105–119).

Thornton, D., Mann, R., Webster, S., Blud, L., Travers, R., Friendship, C., & Erikson, M. (2003). Distinguishing and combining risks for sexual and violent recidivism. In R. Prentky, E. Janus, M. Seto, & A. W. Burgess (Eds.), *Annals of the New York Academy of Sciences* (Vol. 989. Sexually coercive behavior: Understanding and management, pp. 225–235). New York: New York Academy of Sciences.

Tolson, D., & Klein, J. (2015). Registration, residency restrictions and community notification: A social capital perspective on the isolation of registered sex offenders in our communities. *Journal of Human Behavior in the Social Environment, 25*, 375–390.

United States Department of Justice. (2011). *Child exploitation and obscenity section.* Retrieved from: http://www.justice.gov/criminal/ceos/subjectareas/childporn.html

United States Department of Justice. Office of Justice Programs. Office of Sex Offender Sentencing, Tracking, Monitoring, Apprehension, Registration and Tracking (SMART). (2018). *Sex offender registration and notification in the United States current case law and issues — March 2018.* Military registration. Retrieved from: https://www.smart.gov/caselaw/4-Military.pdf

United States Department of Justice. Office of Justice Programs. Office of Sex Offender Sentencing, Tracking, Monitoring, Apprehension, Registration and Tracking (SMART). (2019). Sex offender registration and notification in the United States. Current case law and issues – March 2019. Retrieved from: https://smart.gov/caselaw/10-Miscellaneous.pdf

United States Department of Veterans Affairs. (n.d.). PTSD: National Center for PTSD. *Military Sexual Trauma.* Retrieved from: https://www.ptsd.va.gov/understand/types/sexual_trauma_military.asp

United States v. White Horse, 177 F. Supp. 2d 973. (D.S.D. 2001).

United States v. Birdsbills 243 F.Supp.2d 1128 (2003).

Urquiza, A. J., & Crowley, C. (1986). *Sex differences in the survivors of childhood sexual abuse. Paper presented at the paper presented at the fourth conference on the sexual victimization of children.* LA: New Orleans.

van den Berg, C., Beijersbergen, K., Nieuwbeerta, P., & Dirkzwager, A. (2018). Sexual offenders in prison: Are they socially isolated? *Sexual Abuse, 30*(7), 828–845.

Vasquez, B. E., Maddan, S., & Walker, J. T. (2008). The influence of sex offender registration and notification laws in the United States. *Crime & Delinquency, 54*, 175–192.

Wagner, C. (2011). The good left undone: How to stop sex offender law from causing unnecessary harm at the expense of effectiveness. *American Journal of Criminal Law, 38*, 263–288.

Ward, T. (2007). On a clear day you can see forever: Integrating values and skills in sex offender treatment. *Journal of Sexual Aggression, 13*, 187–201.

Ward, T., & Hudson, S. M. (2000). A self-regulation model of relapse prevention. In D. R. Laws, S. M. Hudson, & T. Ward (Eds.), Remaking relapse prevention with sex offenders: A sourcebook (pp. 79–101). Thousand Oaks, CA: Sage.

Ward, T., & Steward, C. A. (2003). The treatment of sex offenders: Risk management and good lives. *Professional Psychology: Research and Practice, 34*(4), 353–360.

Webb, L., Craissati, J., & Keen, S. (2007). Characteristics of internet child pornography offenders: A comparison with child molesters. *Sexual Abuse: A Journal of Research & Treatment, 19*(4), 449–465. https://doi.org/10.1007/s11194-007-9063-2

Weir, K. (December 2015). Life on the outside. Psychologist are working to increase and improve the reentry services that can help former inmate face the challenges awaiting them outside prison walls. *Monitor on Psychology, 46*(11), 66.

Younglove, J. A., & Vitello, C. J. (2003). Community notification provisions of "Megan's Law" from a therapeutic jurisprudence perspective: A case study. *American Journal of Forensic Psychology, 21*(1), 25–38.

Zandbergen, P., & Hart, T. (2006). Reducing housing options for convicted sex offenders: Investigating the impact of residency restrictions laws using GIS. *Justice Research and Policy, 8*, 1–24.

Zevitz, R. G., Crim, D., & Farkas, M. A. (2000a). Sex offender community notification: Examining the importance of neighborhood meetings. *Behavioral Sciences & the Law, 18*, 393–408.

Zevitz, R. G., Crim, D., & Farkas, M. A. (2000b). Sex offender community notification: Managing high risk criminals or exacting further vengeance? *Behavioral Sciences & the Law, 18*, 375–391.

Zevitz, R. G., & Farkas, M. (2000). Sex offender community notification: Managing high risk criminals or exacting further vengeance? *Behavioral Sciences & the Law, 18*, 375–391.

Zevitz, R. G., & Farkas, M. A. (2000a). The impact of sex offender community notification on probation/parole in Wisconsin. *International Journal of Offender Therapy and Comparative Criminology, 44*(1), 8–21.

Zevitz, R. G., & Farkas, M. A. (2000b). *Sex offender community notification: Assessing the impact in Wisconsin*. Washington, DC: U.S. Department of Justice.

Zgoba, K., Veysey, B., & Dalessandro, M. (2010). An analysis of the effectiveness of community notification and registration: Do the best intentions predict best practices? *Justice Quarterly, 27*, 667–691.

Zgoba, K. M., Jennings, W. G., & Salerno, L. M. (2018). Megan's law 20 years later: An empirical analysis and policy review. *Criminal Justice and Behavior, 45*(7), 1028–1046.

Zgoba, K. M., Levenson, J., & McKee, T. (2009). Residence restrictions on housing availability. *Criminal Justice Review, 20*, 91–110.

# Chapter 17
# The Significance of Psychological Trauma and Brain Injury in the Treatment and Evaluation of Sex Offenders

Sarah DeMarco and Hannah L. Geller

## Psychological Trauma Among Sex Offenders

Traumatic experiences can have lasting effects on individuals. Such experiences often have a major impact when it comes to shaping one's beliefs of the self and one's world view. It is through this lens that individuals interact with their environment. The role that such histories play in the lives of sexual offenders is a prolifically discussed and researched topic. It is commonly purported that most sex offenders have been previously victimized by similar offending behavior. Although this notion has its supporters, the literature offers interesting findings as to how sex offenders differ with regard to their trauma histories, as compared to nonsexual offenders, and moreover, how sex offenders differ in their negative childhood experiences, among each other. Understanding this history is essential in understanding this behavior. It can provide information for the purposes of both the assessment and treatment of sexual offenders. The etiology of sexual offending is an ever growing area of research. Within this literature, the focus has largely been on the contribution of the offender's trauma history. More specifically, the effects of adverse childhood experiences (ACEs) within this population on later sexual offending has gained much attention and consideration.

Hanson and Morton-Bourgon (2005) asserted that adverse family environments are breeding grounds for sexual offending, specifically stating:

> Lacking nurturance and guidance, the potential sex offender develops problems in social functioning (e.g., mistrust, hostility, and insecure attachment) that, in turn, are associated

S. DeMarco (✉)
Private Practice, Verona, NJ, USA
e-mail: Dr.Sarah.DeMarco@gmail.com

H. L. Geller
Private Practice, New York, NY, USA
e-mail: hannahgeller.phd@gmail.com

© Springer Nature Switzerland AG 2020
R. A. Javier et al. (eds.), *Assessing Trauma in Forensic Contexts*,
https://doi.org/10.1007/978-3-030-33106-1_17

with social rejection, loneliness, negative peer associations and delinquent behavior. The form of sexuality that develops in the context of pervasive intimacy deficits is likely to be impersonal and selfish and may even be adversarial. Further contributing to the risk of sexual offending are beliefs that permit nonconsenting sex. Attitudes allowing nonconsenting sex can develop through the individuals' trying to understand their own experiences and adopting the attitudes of their significant others (friends, family, abusers). (p. 1155)

In an effort to explore the long-term impact of ACEs, a collaborative research project began in 1997 between the Center for Disease Control (CDC) and Kaiser Permanente, a managed care consortium. Findings revealed that the prevalence of childhood trauma is pervasive and enduring (CDC, 2013). To illustrate, Felitti et al. (1998) conducted a study wherein 8,506 adults completed the ACE study questionnaire, which included questions about childhood abuse and exposure to forms of household dysfunction. Within this sample, 10.8% reported physical abuse, 11.1% psychological or emotional abuse, and 22% sexual abuse. Nearly 15% experienced emotional neglect and 10% experienced physical neglect. Household challenges, or dysfunctions, were also reported. Namely, 12.5% had a mother who was treated violently, 25.6% had substance abuse in their household, 18.8% had mental illness in the family, 23% had parents who were either separated or divorced, and 3.4% had a household member who was incarcerated. Researchers who have utilized this sample have found that as the range of exposure to abuse or household dysfunction increases in number, the risk for physical and mental health problems in adulthood also increases; a relationship that Felitti et al. described as "strong and cumulative" in nature (p. 251).

Researchers have explored the prevalence of negative childhood experiences in those who later go on to engage in criminal activity. For instance, Weeks and Widom (1998) assessed a group of men incarcerated in New York State prisons for physical abuse, sexual abuse, and neglect. The findings revealed that approximately 68% reported some form of childhood victimization prior to 12 years of age. More specifically, 65% of their total sample reported some type of physical abuse, 14% reported sexual abuse, and 16% reported neglect. A number of researchers have explored, specifically, ACEs among offenders. For instance, Reavis, Looman, Franco, and Rojas (2013) administered the ACE questionnaire to a sample of outpatient male offenders who were mandated to treatment for crimes related to domestic violence, stalking, child physical abuse, general violence, and sexual deviance. Four or more adverse events were reported by 48% of this sample.

## Negative Childhood Experiences Among Sexual Offenders

As previously indicated, it is a common belief that most sex offenders have been victim to similar offending behavior in their past. In an effort to shed light on this assertion, there has been a recent growing body of literature examining this relationship. A number of researchers have analyzed the prevalence of the different types of abuse experienced in the childhoods of those who later go on to sexually offend. To illustrate, Levenson, Willis, and Prescott (2016) found that adult male sexual offenders, as compared to males in the general population, had more than three (3) times the odds of having experienced child sexual abuse, almost twice the odds of having experienced physical abuse, 13 times the odds of verbal abuse, and almost four (4) times the odds of emotional neglect, or having unmarried parents. Weeks and Widom (1998) found a higher prevalence. Specifically, within their sex offender sample, approximately 60% reported physical abuse, 26% reported any type of sexual abuse, and 18% reported any type of childhood neglect. An earlier meta-analysis by Hanson and Slater (1988) revealed that 28% of their sample of 1,717 sex offenders reported having been sexually abused as children. In a later meta-analysis, Jespersen, Lalumiere, and Seto (2009) found a significant difference between sex offenders and nonsex offenders in their histories of sexual abuse. However, such was not observed regarding histories of physical or emotional abuse, or neglect. Jennings, Zgoba, Maschi, and Reingle (2014) looked specifically at the overlap between sex offending and childhood sexual victimization. They found that those who were victims of abusive sexual contact or sexual assault/rape, prior to 16 years old were significantly more likely to be sex offenders, suggesting that these two types of victimization are not mutually exclusive and should be assessed simultaneously. Additionally, having been emotionally abused and neglected was the most robust risk factor for sexual offending found in their study.

Levenson and Socia (2016) examined ACE scores among sex offenders with adult and minor victims. With regard to criminal persistence, it was found that ACE scores were significantly associated with the number of sex crime arrests and total arrests. As such, a higher ACE score was associated with a higher arrest score, which the authors interpreted as a measure of criminal versatility. Sex offenders with adult victims had significantly higher ACE scores and had experienced a wider scope of trauma as children. Accordingly, they were more persistent and versatile in their crimes and had a significantly higher number of nonsexual arrests. Levenson et al. (2016) examined differences in ACE scores among male sex offenders (28% civil commitment; 72% outpatient) and males in the general population. Findings indicated that sex offenders were more likely to have experienced all of the ACE items, as compared to the general population. It was further revealed that ACE scores were not significantly correlated with the number of sex crimes or total number of victims. However, looking more closely at specific offense characteristics, higher mean ACE scores were found in those who had victims under the age of 12, male victims, stranger victims, prepubescent victims, multiple victims, those with contact sex offenses versus noncontact sex offenses, those who used force or violence in the commission of their sex offense, those who used a weapon, and those who injured a victim (see also Levenson & Grady, 2016). Findings also revealed that higher ACE scores were significantly correlated with young victims, contact victims, more nonsexual arrests, and measures of violence and aggression, suggesting that indicators of both sexual deviance and antisociality were associated with early adverse experiences. Based on these findings, Levenson and Socia (2016) asserted, "The ACE literature is therefore relevant to clinicians treating sexually abusive individuals and can inform our understanding of the development of schemas, attitudes, and beliefs that influence risk for sexually aggressive behavior" (p. 352).

Although research has demonstrated commonalities in the histories of sex offenders, findings also indicate differences in past experiences among those who offend against adults or children. For instance, Simons, Wurtele, and Durham (2008) found that significantly more rapists, than child abusers, reported that they witnessed violence between parents. Rapists were also more likely to report physical abuse that was more frequent and severe in nature. Although both types of offenders reported emotional abuse, the frequency of such incidents was reported at a significantly higher rate by rapists. Furthermore, child sexual abusers, who had been sexually abused themselves, were more likely to have reported intra-familial sexual abuse, perpetrated by a male, and having experienced multiple abuse episodes that were more severe in nature. Jespersen et al. (2009), in their study, found that although a history of emotional violence was common among all paraphilic type of offenders, adult rapists were more likely to have experienced physical abuse and parental violence. Furthermore, sex offenders with adult victims were significantly less likely to report a history of sexual abuse as compared to those with child victims. Of note, there were no discernable pattern differences of histories when they compared pedophilic versus nonpedophilic child offenders. In an earlier study by Hanson and Slater (1988), there were no observed differences in abuse histories between incest and extrafamilial child offenders.

In examining the relationship between childhood sexual abuse (CSA) and pedophilic interest, Nunes, Hermann, Malcom, and Lavoie (2013) found that, among child offenders, those who had been sexually abused themselves as children, as compared to those who were not sexually abused, had significantly younger victims and higher scores on the Screening Scale for Pedophilic Interests (SSPI; Seto & Lalumiere, 2001), which measures pedophilic sexual interests among men. Nunes et al. also found that those who had been sexually abused by a male had significantly higher SSPI scores; however, those sexually abused by both a male and female did not differ on the SSPI, as compared to those who were sexually abused by either a male or female. Of note, neither the age at which the person experienced the sexual abuse, nor the relationship of the abuser to the offender, were significantly related to the SSPI score.

With regard to how certain childhood experiences increase the chance of developing a paraphilic interest, Lee, Jackson, Pattison, and Ward (2002) investigated this relationship among four paraphilic groups: Pedophilia, exhibitionism, rape, or multiple paraphilia. They found that childhood emotional abuse and family dysfunction were predictive of all four. Childhood sexual abuse was found to be predictive of pedophilia and multiple paraphilia. Furthermore, for every one standard deviation increase in childhood emotional abuse/family dysfunction and childhood sexual abuse, the odds of receiving a paraphilic diagnosis significantly increased by 3.30 and 3.88, respectively. To examine the differential prediction of childhood emotional abuse and family dysfunction, on each paraphilia, Lee et al. (2002) performed regression analyses on the five variables that constituted the construct of childhood emotional abuse/family dysfunction (i.e., childhood emotional abuse, parental care, parental control, family cohesion, family adaptability). Findings revealed that childhood emotional abuse was the only predictor for a paraphilic diagnosis. The authors also examined the predictors for each paraphilia to ascertain the specific developmental risk factors for each. They found that childhood sexual abuse (CSA) was predictive of pedophilia (compared to nonpedophilia); however, CSA was negatively predictive of exhibitionism (compared to nonexhibitionism paraphilia). More specifically, for every standard deviation increase in CSA, the odds of being in the pedophilic group, compared to the nonsexual offender comparison group increased by 13.43, and by 2.65 when compared to the nonpedophilia paraphilia group. No specific risk factor was identified when similar comparisons were made for the other three paraphilic groups.

Levenson and Grady (2016) sought to examine the influence of ACE scores on two variables: sexual deviance and sexual violence, thus creating scales that measured the two outcomes. The Sexual Deviance Scale included four dichotomous items: Male victim, stranger victim, victim under 12, and multiple victims. The Sexual Violence Scale included whether the offender ever used force, weapons, or caused injury during a sexual crime. Of note, both of these variables were significantly and positively correlated with each other. With sexual deviance as the outcome variable, Levenson and Grady entered the ACE items into a multiple regression model. Results indicated that CSA, emotional neglect, mental illness in the home, and unmarried parents were all predictors of increased sexual deviance – CSA and emotional neglect being the strongest predictors. In a similar model, with sexual violence as the dependent variable, they found that childhood physical abuse, substance abuse in the childhood home, and an incarcerated family member were predictors of increased sexual violence, the latter of which was the strongest predictor, followed by childhood physical abuse and substance abuse in the home. It is important to note, however, that the effect sizes were not substantial and explained only a minority of the variance in the outcome variables. Although this suggests that there are other variables not accounted for in the model that contribute to the outcomes, it is clear that such adverse experiences are related, albeit in conjunction with other factors. Levenson and Grady asserted that these regression analyses provide insight into the different pathways that lead to both sexual deviance and sexual violence. For instance, they suggested that having an incarcerated family member (a predictor of sexual violence) may reinforce a criminal lifestyle, as well as lead to hopelessness and helplessness for such children, and a world view of unfairness leading to a sense of entitlement and control through violence.

## Negative Childhood Experiences and Recidivism

Many professionals are tasked with performing risk assessments with individuals who have sexually offended. When conducting sexual violence risk assessments, the examiner considers case-specific dynamic risk factors associated with risk for engaging in sexual offending behaviors (Thornton, 2002) or psychological meaningful risk factors that can be understood as individual propensities, which may or may not manifest during any particular time period (Mann, Hanson, & Thornton, 2010). These factors not only have some ability to estimate risk of re-offending based on statistical correlations, but also explain the sources of risk.

Among the empirically supported factors, Mann et al. (2010) identified sexual pre-occupation, sexual deviance, lack of emotionally intimate relationships with adults, lifestyle impulsivity, general self-regulation problems, resistance to rules and supervision, poor problem-solving, and others.

In a framework that attempts to describe the factors that perpetuate offending, one can address clinical factors, including emotional problems and/or social difficulties (Beech & Ward, 2004). These clinical factors take place when stable and dynamic risk factors have achieved an acute state. The authors have argued that dynamic risk factors should be understood as psychological traits, vulnerabilities, psychological mechanisms, or psychological predispositions. These factors can be distinguished as traits or states, where states are less permanent and may become acute. In their understanding, for every state there is an underlying trait. Obtaining the history of one's childhood and development may be beneficial for those treating sex offenders, as well as those evaluating them, in that it may inform the evaluator's understanding of the etiology and development of the offender's attitudes and beliefs that play a role in their sexual offending behaviors. Although using such information is important for case conceptualization and implementation of treatment, it is important to determine whether such data should be included while assessing risk. Thus, we look toward the literature to determine if any such experiences have a relationship with sexual recidivism.

For instance, Hanson and Morton-Bourgon (2005) conducted a meta-analysis, finding that the general categories of an adverse childhood environment (e.g., conflict with and separation from parents, neglect, and physical and sexual abuse) had little to no relationship with sexual recidivism ($d = 0.02$). Thus, it may be important to look specifically at the pathways of sexual deviance, as previously reviewed. Of note, however, Hanson and Morton-Bourgon found that sexual deviancy and antisocial orientation were the largest predictors of sexual recidivism. They also noted that, based on their findings, factors that are related to the persistence of sexual offending may be different from those factors that are related to the initiation of such offending. As such, they did not find a relationship between negative family backgrounds and internalization of psychological problems and sexual recidivism, despite previous literature demonstrating that these are common among sex offenders (e.g., Lee et al., 2002). Thus, Hanson and Morton-Bourgon suggested that a prototypical sexual recidivist is one who leads an unstable and antisocial lifestyle, as well as one who may ruminate on sexually deviant themes; instead of one who is upset and lonely.

However, some aspects of an offender's history have demonstrated to be associated with recidivism. When examining the relationship between childhood sexual abuse, pedophilic interest, and risk for sexual recidivism, Nunes et al. (2013) found that being abused by a female was significantly associated with higher rates of recidivism, whereas age of victimization and closeness of the relationship to the abuser was not predictive. Although Nunes et al. found that CSA prior to age 16 was not a significant predictor of sexual recidivism by itself, they did discover that the relationship between CSA and sexual recidivism was moderated by risk as indicated by the Static-99R. Of note, the Static-99R is a widely researched actuarial sexual violence risk assessment instrument that comprises various static (historical) risk factors associated with sexual recidivism (Phenix, Helmus, & Hanson, 2012). Namely, for the lower risk group, CSA was not predictive; in contrast, for the higher risk group, CSA was significantly predictive of sexual recidivism. The authors asserted that although the results of their study indicated a relationship between CSA and pedophilia, sexual deviance did not moderate the relationship between CSA and sexual recidivism; as such, the interaction between CSA and pedophilic interests (as measured by the SSPI) was not predictive of recidivism. The authors suggested that the antisocial orientation of the Static-99R, rather than the sexual deviance component, moderated the relationship between CSA and sexual recidivism.

## *Theories: The Role of Adverse Childhood Events*

A variety of influential models have been proposed in an effort to elucidate the etiology of sexual offending behavior, which have provided the basis for numerous forthcoming theories. The literature summarized herein is a brief overview of the extant theories that consider adverse experiences in childhood.

Jennings et al. (2014) suggested that through a social learning approach, violent and deviant behaviors are learned by observing and imitating, which is then reinforced and results in the perpetration of violence over time. Such a theory can be applied to sexual victimization, leading to later offending of a similar nature. Seto (2008) also suggested that children who are sexually abused, in a compensatory effort toward managing invalidation and powerlessness, may mimic their abuser's behavior and distorted thinking or associate the sexual activity between themselves and their abuser with sexual arousal.

Marshall and Barbaree (1990) proposed an integrated theory that considers the biological bases of aggression and sexual arousal, suggesting that males are biologically inclined toward sexual aggression and must be taught the appropriate skills to inhibit such predisposition. However, the learning of such appropriate skills may not occur in those who experience ongoing adverse conditions in childhood (e.g., poor parenting; inconsistent punishment). Instead, in combination with sociocultural influences, those in such environments may develop schemas that associate sex with aggression, therefore perhaps, enhancing the likelihood of sexual offending. Adolescence is a particularly important period for this development, as sex hormones increase and play a larger role in the development of acknowledging and interpreting sexual cues. As such, those who experience adverse childhood events are predisposed to engaging in antisocial behaviors, and thus the hormones may serve to strengthen the relationship between aggression and sex. Such individuals may also have deficits in social interactions, as well as limited self-regulation, wherein rejection from attempted relationships may lead to low self-esteem and increased negative attitudes toward women. These vulnerability factors, developed throughout childhood, later intersect with situational factors such as intoxication, anger, or stress, which may precipitate sexual offending, depending on whether the man is sexually aroused at that time. It was suggested that offending is thus maintained by the reinforcing effect (either positive or negative reinforcement) of deviant sexual acts and the developed cognitive distortions.

Grady, Levenson, and Bolder (2017) asserted that the growing body of literature has not yet provided a cohesive theoretical model regarding how or why adverse childhood experiences (ACEs) may contribute to the commission of sex offending behaviors. Therefore, Grady et al. posited that such adverse childhood conditions can lead to sexual offending via a number of other psychosocial and behavioral outcomes similar to criminogenic needs that have been demonstrated to be associated with sexually violent acts (e.g., Andrews & Bonta, 2010; Hanson, Bourgon, Helmus, & Hodgson, 2009), such as intimacy deficits, social skills, and emotional regulation. More specifically, they proposed that the link between ACEs and such criminogenic needs may be explained using attachment theory, in that ACEs lead to insecure attachments, which in turn lead to both psychological and social deficits consistent with criminogenic needs.

In an effort to explain how such attachments develop in intimate relationships with adults, Ward, Hudson, and Marshall (1996) proposed a model comprising three distinct styles of insecure attachment: Preoccupied, fearful, and dismissive. While having an insecure relationship is not a unique feature of sex offenders, Ward et al. found a relationship between attachment style and sexual offender type. Marshall and Marshall (2000) later explained that depending on the type of insecure bond formed (e.g., anxious, avoidant, ambivalent), the child may have low self-esteem, poor relationship skills, maintain safe distances from others, be unable to manage stress and life's problems, and have no one on whom they can rely. Such a relationship with a parent may generalize to that of others-for instance, via grooming efforts, an adult may provide a neglected child with affection and care that they may not receive from their own parents. Additionally, inadequate means of managing such stressors may lead to maladaptive coping styles (Marshall & Marshall, 2000). Cortoni and Marshall (2001) demonstrated that sex offenders may be more likely, than other general offenders, to use sex as a means to cope with stress regardless of whether the sex offender is a rapist or child molester.

## Traumatic Brain Injury (TBI) and Sexual Offending

Today, it is still difficult to explain how or predict whether traumatic brain injury may affect one's propensity to commit sexual crimes. Based on the current review of the studies, the scientific community seems to agree that while a damaged brain may contribute to sexual acting out and impact risk factors, it cannot predict sex offending. The difficulty of making definite conclusions lies in the fact in that while our brains are similar in structure, they are different in the exact topography of brain areas, neurophysiological processes, and neuronal connections. Two people with brain damage in the same areas may display different post-lesion symptomatology.

Furthermore, even if both patients struggle with the same sexual effects of a trauma, they may exhibit different behavioral responses. For example, Langevin (2006) discussed differences between sex offenders with and without brain injuries and came to the conclusion that convictions for multiple sexual offenses were comparable between these groups. Nevertheless, the patterns of offending were different and the brain-injured group tended to offend more against adults than children and to exhibit polymorphous sexual behavior.

TBI appears to be associated with general criminality, according to a review by Williams et al. (2018). The authors found that a history of TBIs was associated with an earlier age of incarceration, increased risk of violence, and more convictions, neurological (impulse control and empathy) abnormalities, and other problems. Among those in custody, complicated mild TBI or moderate to severe head injury was prevalent in one to two in ten people.

Neuropsychological dysfunction was found to be linked to violence, prison disciplinary problems, poorer treatment gains, and reconvictions. Life histories of abuse, neglect, and psychological trauma appeared to be elevated in those with TBI versus those without TBI histories, complicated with ongoing mental health and substance use problems. Williams et al. (2018) argued against an assumption that TBI was a coincidental occurrence in the lives of risk takers; instead, they were able to show that the research evidence suggested the opposite. The authors suggest that addressing TBI offers a means to not only improve the lives of those who offend but also to reduce crime. Sexual offenders are no different than general criminals in terms of histories of TBI and interpersonal trauma.

Both clinical and dynamic risk factors frameworks attempt to explain sexual offending, as discussed till now. Meanwhile, neurobiological frameworks attempt to explain how the clinical symptoms arise in the first place; these frameworks include etiological analysis (e.g., influence of genetic factors), brain mechanisms, neuropsychological analysis, and symptom analysis (Pennington, 2002; Ward & Beech, 2006). Luria (1966) and later Pennington (2002) theorized that a human nervous system can be subdivided into three functional networks or systems: Motivational-emotional, memory and perception, and action selection and control. In concert, these three systems, according to Pennington, produce human behaviors. The interactions between these systems are complex and because each system is connected to a different brain network, they can create unique psychological and/or behavioral problems. This part of the chapter will mostly focus on the brain structures and processes that impact an individual's sexual behavior if damage occurs as a result of brain trauma.

## Recency, Severity, and Prevalence

We have gained considerable knowledge about the brain in recent decades, thanks to the advances in medicine, neuroscience, and neuroimaging techniques. Research has uncovered a lot about how our brains function and what may happen if an area of our brain is damaged. We also understand how various brain areas and processes control our sexual desires and behaviors. Sexual activity, like other drives, involves multiple brain areas connected together in a network. Thus, understandably, when any area of this network is damaged due to brain trauma, sexual behavior may be altered. We do not fully understand yet how this network operates as a whole in humans, like many other brain processes. However, science today has uncovered some knowledge about how sexual behavior is wired in our brains.

Traumatic brain injury (TBI) can arise from a closed or an open head injury, acquired as a result of acceleration-deceleration forces (a blow to the head in an assault, a fall, or car crash). Open head injury results in a penetration of the skull. TBIs can range in severity from mild, which may go unnoticed, to severe, which can cause coma and/or death. These injuries can be focal or diffuse. The Glasgow Coma Scale is usually used to determine the severity of the trauma (Rowlett, 2000). The most common areas of TBI appear to be frontal and temporal lobes (Iverson & Lange, 2011a; Scott & Schoenberg, 2011; Williams et al., 2018).

Traumatic brain injury (TBI) is considered to be a significant public-health concern. In the recent years, media and medical professionals have been bringing a lot of attention to the problem of TBI among athletes and children, as specific concerns. TBI is defined as an acute brain injury that results from mechanical energy applied to the head from external physical forces (Gardner & Zafonte, 2016). Thus, TBI may result from falls, assaults, motor vehicle accidents, sports-related traumas. Gardner and Zafonte (2016) reported that the two most commonly identified risk factors for sustaining a traumatic head injury are male sex (males are three times more likely to suffer a TBI than females) and age. In terms of age, they suggested a bimodal age pattern, in which people older than 65 and younger than 14 years are more likely to sustain TBI than other age groups. Gardner and Zafonte estimated that about a third of all deaths in the USA annually can be contributed to TBI. TBI may result in residual symptoms that may persist over time without significant resolution and that include problems in cognition, movement, sensation, and/or emotions.

According to Vaughn, Salas-Wright, Delisi, and Perron (2014), who examined data from two sites in Pennsylvania and Arizona, male youth were almost twice as likely as female youth to report a history of TBI. Overall, one-third (30%) of their entire sample reported TBI, which is almost three times more than TBI rates reported in the general population (12%). They found that such injury was associated with higher impulsivity, negative emotion ratings, and self-reported experience of victimization, even when controlling for demographic factors, such as age, gender, socioeconomic factors, and race/ethnicity, and complications such as psychopathy, substance use, and others.

It is challenging to estimate representative rates of TBI among populations of sex offenders. One of the challenges is that traumatic brain injuries often go unreported. Oftentimes, in my experience, individuals may not realize that have had brain trauma at any point in their lives. An individual may deny any incidents of being hit in the head or loss of consciousness but then inform a doctor that they have lost hearing because their abusive family member repeatedly hit them in the ears.

Another reason that TBI may be underreported is that a person's psychiatric or medical history overshadows the significance of a head trauma. Inquiring about a history of head x-rays, scars on one's head, or participating in a fight and being knocked out could prove useful in determining the history of head injury.

Another challenge is that sex offenders may over-report history of brain injury. Blanchard et al. (2002) discussed limitations of using self-report methodology in studying pedophilia and brain injuries. The authors mentioned a likelihood that sex offenders with pedophilic disorders claim head injuries that never occurred or exaggerate minor occurrences in order to diminish their own responsibility for their sexual conduct. This may be true for other categories of sex offenders as well.

Shiroma, Ferguson, and Pickelsimer (2010) conducted a meta-analysis of prevalence of brain trauma among sex offending population and found that the prevalence of TBI in this population was about 60.25% (95% confidence interval: 48.08 to 72.41). This number is quite significant and indicates that more than a half of all sex offenders may have a history of TBI. Turner, Schöttle, Krueger, and Briken (2015) studied sexual behaviors among individuals who suffered a TBI and observed that a significant number of them show inappropriate sexual behaviors and/or sexual dysfunctions. Additionally, in this study, inappropriate sexual behaviors were linked to younger age, poorer social participation, and more severe injuries.

TBI is a leading cause of disability, and an extensive literature base exists in relation to TBI sequelae and risk factors among the general population (Williams et al., 2018). Much less is known about TBI specifically among sex offenders. Langevin (2006) found that half of the sex offenders among those studied at a university psychiatric hospital for forensic assessment had sustained a head trauma that led to unconsciousness. Moreover, 22.5% of them also sustained significant neurological insults. Among the causes, Langevin noted motor vehicle accidents, as well as substance abuse and history of violence. However, how much TBI is related to sexual offending, is a question with which some of our colleagues grapple when working with sex offenders. Could a known brain injury have affected their brains in such a way that it impacted their sexually deviant and/or sexually violent behaviors, and if so, can the opposite be possible? Can we treat brain abnormalities and help offenders reduce their sexually deviant urges and/or behaviors and hence reduce the rate of their re-offending? To answer these questions, one must consider the relevance of the history of TBI in various assessments of functioning (e.g., risk assessment, disability, cognitive), as well as the implications of such.

A majority of the studies that discuss the connection between deviant sexuality and brain injury involve individual case studies with identifiable disorders. These studies often describe an unusual case or an unexpected result, which varies from the observed norm. As such, it is difficult to make far-reaching or generalizable conclusions based on these case studies. Of note, although many cases do not point to the sole change in sexual desire, many explore the correlation between acquired brain injury and Klüver-Bucy syndrome, which features changes in sexuality as one of its symptoms. Damage to the frontal basal, temporal, and diencephalic structures of the brain have been implicated in changes in sexuality, particularly in hypersexuality.

## *Neuroimaging Studies*

Neuroimaging has been a rapidly advancing field and as such fosters an increase in knowledge about various brain structures and their roles in human behaviors. One of the earlier studies by Miller, Cummings, McIntyre, Ebers, and Grode (1986) discussed eight clinical cases of males and females with various brain injuries and neurological conditions, in which a change of sexual patterns was clearly observed, demonstrating an abrupt change in these individuals' life-long patterns. The researchers reported that, based on data from 1942 to 1981, between 5% and 35% of those individuals that were arrested for exhibitionism were found to be suffering from organic disorders, which at least partially contributed to this sexually inappropriate behavior. Additionally, Miller et al. established that exhibitionism has been consistently described in patients with various neurological conditions, such as Huntington's disease, epilepsy, Tourette's syndrome, and multiple sclerosis. Sexual disinhibition and specifically exhibitionism have been noted among those who showed dysfunction in the basal frontal lobes. Although their sample size was too small to be generalized to larger populations, Miller et al. pinpointed two types of changes in sexual behaviors following traumatic brain events. One group experienced significant increase in their libido along with inappropriate sexually disinhibited behaviors (named the hypersexual group). Another group oddly experienced changes in sexual orientation or interests toward things other than their usual stimuli, such as a sudden interest in children or same sex partners in previously non-paraphilic heterosexual adults (change of preference group).

Among the patients in the study carried out by Miller et al. (1986), in the first hypersexual and disinhibited group, the behavior was often associated with the abrupt cessation of seizures either in the postictal period or following a temporal lobectomy. These types of brain events or injuries were hypothesized to be related to continued limbic electrical discharge (in seizures) or postictal disinhibition of structures in the septum and/or hypothalamus. In the second group, in which patients were observed to turn to children or same sex partners from their normophilic typical interests, no single common anatomical area was implicated, with an exception of the lesions being around the limbic system. However, the most dramatic changes in one's sexual preference followed lesions in the temporal lobe and/or midbrain close to the hypothalamus. The other most marked area of damage in these patients involved the frontal lobe. The same authors implicate the limbic system in the sexual arousal phase of human sexual activity, including the hypothalamus and temporal lobe. Particular significance is attributed to the preoptic nucleus of the hypothalamus. In conclusion, the authors suggested that stimuli leading to sexual arousal vary from person to person and are determined by variances in experience, genetic, and neurological factors. However, the authors do not account for psychological or emotional structures in their study. Paredes (2003) discussed that a medial preoptic area/anterior hypothalamus (MPOA/AH) plays a role in the control of male sexual behavior. Although it is known that the MPOA/AH is involved in the control of sexual behavior in males of all species studied to date, there is little agreement as to what is specifically the role of the MPOA/AH in sexual behavior. Paredes (2003) discussed that this region may be involved in the execution of sexual behavior and in the regulation of sexual motivation in males.

In terms of sexual deviance or anomalous target preference, Schilz et al. (2007) sought to examine whether pedophilic sex offenders demonstrate any structural and/ or neuronal deficits in brain regions that are critical for sexual behaviors. They looked at the amygdalar volume and gray matter of related areas, such as the hypothalamus, septal area, and others, in 15 non-violent male pedophilic offenders. The authors determined that pedophilic offenders had a significantly reduced right amygdalar volume, along with reduced gray matter in the right amygdala and hypothalamus (bilaterally), septal regions, substantia innominata, and bed nucleus of the striae terminals. Additionally, in the majority of the offenders (8 out of 15), they found enlargement of the anterior (frontal) temporal horn of the right lateral ventricle, which adjoins the amygdala. However, the smaller right amygdalar volume correlated with the commission of pedophilic offenses exclusively but not with the perpetrators' age. The authors concluded that these structural abnormalities play a role in formation of pedophilic interests. Thus, development of pedophilia may be impacted by neurobiological factors that influence the size and the volume of gray matter of brain structures that are involved in sexual behavior. Based on the aforementioned research, it appears that pedophilic interests can be congenital as well as acquired (e.g., as a result of TBI). However, the small number of study participants makes it difficult to generalize the conclusions.

A recent study by Darby, Horn, Cushman, and Fox (2018) showed that some previously normal patients, following brain lesions in specific areas, seem to start exhibiting criminal behaviors. The authors identified several brain regions that were observed with various brain lesions in 17 patients. Although the lesion sites were spatially heterogeneous, they included the medial prefrontal cortex, orbitofrontal cortex, and various other locations within the temporal lobes in both hemispheres. The authors noted that no single brain region was damaged in all of the cases. Usually, symptoms of brain dysfunction do not come from the damaged area itself but from the sites connected to the damaged area. Thus, the researchers in this case could pinpoint brain regions functionally connected to each lesion location. One observation of interest is that all lesions were functionally connected to the same network of brain regions. The study concluded that these regions are connected to the brain regions that were involved in the theory of mind, morality, and value-based decision making, while not connected to the regions involved in cognitive control or empathy. Remarkably, studies of recidivism seem to be in line with this discovery, finding that poor victim empathy may not be a risk factor for sexual re-offending, although it sounds counterintuitive (Mann et al., 2010). Finally, Darby et al. concluded that all of the lesions were functionally connected to the orbitofrontal cortex. Additionally, most of the lesions were functionally connected to the anterior temporal lobe, ventromedial prefrontal cortex, mesial temporal lobe/amygdala, and nucleus accumbens. Indeed, according to the functional magnetic resonance imaging (MRI) recorded during masturbation more than a decade earlier, medial amygdala and paraventricular nucleus were found to be involved in human sexual activity (Komisaruk et al., 2004).

The orbitofrontal cortex is an area that deserves some more attention. It is a part of the prefrontal lobes and is located just above the eye sockets. The orbitofrontal cortex is involved in cognitive processing, decision making, social behavior moderation, planning and organization of one's behavior, and personality expressions (Schoenberg & Scott, 2011). After sustaining brain injury in this area, individuals often start displaying symptoms of so-called pseudopsychopathy or orbitofrontal syndrome. The term "pseudopsychopathy" was coined by Blumer and Benson (1975) to describe patients who showed a personality change consistent with psychopathic traits after a brain injury. In contrast to congenital psychopathy (Cleckley, 1988; Hare, 1993), in which psychopathic traits emerge in childhood and adolescence with no gross structural brain lesion, pseudopsychopathic behaviors develop following brain injury, regardless of the age or previous character. Individuals exhibiting pseudopsychopathic behaviors may start engaging in impulsive, disinhibited, self-serving, and antisocial behavior after sustaining brain injury to the orbitofrontal cortex. After the injury, they are noted to lack empathy and awareness, and become sexually preoccupied, disinhibited, and rude. Additionally, due to lack of awareness, they may not even realize what they have done and often express dismay and remorse when confronted with their behaviors (Schoenberg & Scott, 2011).

Psychopathic and pseudopsychopathic behaviors are very similar. Therefore, Kiehl (2006) suggested that the brain dysfunction in these groups is similar based on studies of patients with orbitofrontal cortex damage. Kiehl inferred information regarding areas of potential brain dysfunction in conventional psychopaths. Thus, he suggests the paralimbic system dysfunction model of psychopathy. Psychopathy remains an important risk factor for sexual and generally criminal recidivism, as indicated by several studies. For example, in combination with sexual deviancy, psychopathy appears to be a significant risk factor for sexual recidivism (Hildebrand, de Ruiter, & de Vogel, 2004). Additionally, sexual offense recidivism is predicted by the psychopathic traits that indicate criminal history, while the presence of learning disorders and past history of criminal behavior increases this predictability (Langevin & Curnoe, 2011).

Interestingly, some authors mention changes in sexual orientation after damage to certain areas of the brain as well as potential implication of childhood brain trauma in development of pedophilic and/or hebephilic interests. Alnemari, Mansour, Buehler, and Gaudin (2016) described a male patient in his early twenties, who suffered a brain injury following a horse-riding accident. The patient developed a left epidural hematoma and a CT (computed tomography) scan showed left basal frontal and bilateral temporal contusions. After a craniotomy and evacuation of the hematoma, the patient's functioning mostly returned to premorbid levels in all respects, except for difficulty in sleeping, irritability, and behavioral changes, which included increased sexual desire toward children and teenagers.

Morcos and Guirgis (2014) described an unfortunate incident of a male 39-year-old patient falling off a ladder and presenting with an onset of hypersexuality after this traumatic event. Specifically, they described inappropriate remarks, attempts to touch female staff members, and frequent masturbation. An MRI study showed a signal abnormality in the left temporal lobe. He was diagnosed with acute onset of partial Klüver-Bucy syndrome. Klüver-Bucy syndrome is a clinical syndrome observed in humans and other animals resulting from bilateral lesions of the medial temporal lobe including the amygdaloid nucleus. Furthermore, Pick's disease, Alzheimer's disease, Rett syndrome, carbon monoxide poisoning, and other neurological conditions may contribute to a diagnosis of Klüver–Bucy syndrome (Terzian & Ore, 1955; Salloway, Malloy, & Cummings, 1997). Afifi and Bergman (1998) described how Klüver–Bucy syndrome may present with compulsive eating, hypersexuality, insertion of inappropriate objects in the mouth (hyperorality), visual agnosia, and docility.

Varon, Pritchard III, Wagner, and Topping (2003) in a study of transient Klüver–Bucy syndrome that resulted from complex partial epileptic seizures, described a 19-year-old male patient who suffered from complex partial and rare generalized tonic-clonic seizures that could not be managed with medication. Continuous video-EEG (electroencephalogram) monitoring over the span of 48 hours revealed epileptiform activity in the left temporal convexity or left mesio-basal temporal structures that spread into bilateral temporal structures. When he would return to full alertness, he would make sexually charged statements toward his brother, try to caress his mother's breasts, and act out sexual intercourse using two stuffed animals. He also exhibited hyperorality. Some social neuroscientists have identified changes in the temporal lobe as a cause of anomalous sexual and/or hypersexual behaviors (Marlowe, Mancall, & Thomas, 1975).

Brain lateralization also contributes to some interesting sexual differences associated with right and left hemispheres. First, it is important to keep in mind that in the vast majority of individuals, the left hemisphere is considered dominant for speech, both for left- and right-handed people (Scott & Schoenberg, 2011). Brain topographical studies of normal men showed that sexual excitation is asymmetric as well. Studies have revealed that lesions in the left hemisphere, particularly the temporal lobe, were associated with hyposexual symptoms; while lesions around the right hemisphere, particularly the temporal lobe, were associated with hypersexual symptoms (Braun, Dumont, Duval, Hamel, & Godbout, 2003). Interestingly, the temporal lobes were again particularly implicated in changes of libido intensity. Although Braun et al. (2003) admitted that the limitation of the study was that the libido was considered as a continuously distributed variable and the extreme manifestations of libido could not be precisely identified. The authors reported that patients manifested subtle to significant changes in their sexual feelings overall, which the investigators graded on a scale. Braun et al. found that hypersexuality was associated with post-lesion mania, pseudo-mania, and hyperlalia, all of which more frequently occur in cases of right hemispheric damage. Damage in the left hemisphere often manifested in post-lesion depression, pseudo-depression, as well as hyposexuality. Thus, the authors proposed that there exists a larger phenomenon of *psychic tone*, which includes emotional, motor, moral, language, immunological, and sexual dimensions and is reflected in intellectual representations.

Therefore, it appears that the left hemispheric lesions suppress or subdue this tone, while the right hemispheric lesions tend to stimulate and uplift the psychic tone. The authors further suggest an *approach-avoidance* disposition, in which both hemispheres play opposed roles in the alarm or stress response.

Interestingly, not only do gray matter and brain structures seem to be implicated in sexual deviance, white matter does also. White matter injuries result from axons shearing and tearing in cases of some traumatic brain injuries. Traumatic axonal injuries result from severe rotation or acceleration/ deceleration forces on the brain. This is a gradual process, in which damaged axons stretch and eventually separate. Axons can stretch and twist without being sheared or torn even after repeated stretch injuries and even though internal damage may be sustained. However, axons that change direction, enter the target nuclei, or decussate can be more easily damaged (Iverson & Lange, 2011b).

White matter injury also affects sexual behaviors, according to some data. For example, Cantor et al. (2008) attempted to identify brain regions that could help distinguish pedophilic from non-pedophilic men, using unbiased, automated analyses of the whole brain. MRIs were acquired from men who demonstrated illegal or clinically significant sexual behaviors or interests ($n = 65$) and from men who had histories of nonsexual offenses with no sexual offenses ($n = 62$). They assessed sexual interest in children through the participants' admissions of their pedophilic interest, histories of committing sexual offenses against children, and psychophysiological responses in the laboratory to erotic stimuli depicting children or adults. The analysis of the MRIs revealed significant negative associations between pedophilia and white matter volumes of the temporal and parietal lobes bilaterally. Voxel-based morphometry, which is a neuroimaging analysis technique used to study focal individual differences in brain anatomy, validated the associations and indicated that regions of lower white matter volumes followed, and were limited to, two major fiber bundles: the superior fronto-occipital fasciculus and the right arcuate fasciculus. The superior fronto-occipital and arcuate fasciculi connect the cortical regions that respond to sexual cues. Therefore, the authors suggested that these cortical regions operate as a network for recognizing sexually relevant stimuli and that pedophilia results from a partial disconnection within that network.

In conclusion, various studies pointed out multiple areas and structures of the brain that may be involved in sexual deviant behaviors and/or hypersexuality. Of special importance, in terms of potential sexually inappropriate behaviors, are the medial prefrontal cortex, orbitofrontal cortex, right temporal lobe, amygdala and its volume, white matter volumes of the temporal and parietal lobes bilaterally, medial preoptic area/anterior hypothalamus, and some others. Traumatic brain injury, which involves these areas, may temporarily or permanently impact an individual's libido intensity as well as sexual preference, potentially leading to sex offending. Although brain damage alone may not lead to such a dramatic behavior, it may interact with other socio-emotional factors and cognitive capacities in such a way that it would increase a risk of sex offense or sexual recidivism, especially in those with a criminal history.

## *Traumatic Brain Injury and the Question of Dangerousness*

Of what importance is the history of TBI in the risk assessment of a sex offender? Of course, the answer to this question is anything but simple and depends on multiple factors. The following needs to be taken into account: How significant was the impact of a brain trauma, how did it impact sexual functioning (in terms of hypersexuality, preoccupation, and sexual interest), was it long-term or temporary, and how did TBI affect cognitive and particularly executive functions? Another important consideration is how recent the brain trauma was and how much of recovery has been made. These questions should be considered individually because multiple factors are at play in each clinical case of brain injury.

There are additional issues to ponder. For example, what cognitive areas have been affected by trauma and to what degree? Executive functions help individuals curb sexual preoccupation and/or affect volitional capacity, for example. Hence, damage to the frontal lobes, which house executive functions, can lead to sexually inappropriate, impulsive, unempathic, and disorganized behaviors (Schoenberg & Scott, 2011). It can also result not just in symptoms of hypersexuality but also in social disinhibition, inability to follow rules, and poor moral judgment, all of which may contribute to sexual offending. Oftentimes, an offender reports a remote history of TBI, over decades ago. In this case, we can suppose that the individual's recovery has been completed and any lost function has been compensated for, as it may occur spontaneously in cases of milder brain injuries (Iverson & Lange, 2011a). Although the recovery may be completed, Iverson and Lange warn that it does not mean that the mild TBI cannot cause permanent damage. TBI is a highly individualized injury and most, but not all, people recover relatively quickly and fully. Additionally, the authors reiterate that the term concussion, preferred in sports medicine and research, means mild brain injury. It is often more readily understood by patients; therefore, it is often used by medical practitioners.

Perr (1991) discussed the curious case of "Jerry the Cowboy" of New Jersey, USA, a sex offender whose defense attorney employed an expert to testify that his brain injury at the age of 2 years was responsible for his sexually criminal behavior. Jerry, age 39, was accused of inserting a dildo into the anus of an 8-year-old boy on several occasions. The defense was that Jerry did not have the requisite mental state and therefore committed no crime. Nevertheless, Jerry was able to engage in some goal-directed behaviors, such as have several unskilled jobs, maintain marital relationships to some degree, complete firefighter school and volunteer in firefighting services for 7 years, and other activities. His intelligence was found to be in the borderline range and he exhibited some symptoms of learning disability and/or attention deficits. Moreover, his electroencephalogram was within normal limits; however, his CT showed tissue loss in the left frontal lobe and asymmetry of the lateral ventricles consistent with diffuse tissue loss from the left hemisphere. The doctors agreed that this type of damage could be related to a remote TBI. The defense expert likened the type of damage to frontal lobotomy. Additionally, Jerry abused alcohol and had motor vehicle offenses as an adult. The prosecution expert acknowledged the brain damage found via neuroimaging studies but disagreed with the conclusion about the absence of mens rea. The prosecution expert maintained that the brain defect has been present for 37 years and at that time; Jerry was functioning at a level consistent with borderline to low average intelligence – he was able to socialize and relate, did not have mental illness, and did not have a frontal lobotomy. Thus, Jerry was able to function in society, albeit not at a sophisticated level; and therefore, he had no condition that precluded his knowing the nature and quality of his act or knowing the right from wrong. The jury in this case found Jerry the Cowboy guilty of the charged acts and Perr exemplified how in this case, the legal system of New Jersey facilitated proper application of medical knowledge to a legal issue.

Nevertheless, discussing cases like Jerry's helps our understanding of how one may be interested in over-reporting or exaggerating symptoms of a TBI during a trial. Would Jerry's behavior and academic success be different if he had not sustained a TBI at 2 years old? However, we do not have knowledge of the other factors that contributed to Jerry's development: his family, socioeconomic status, presence of psychological traumas, early sexualization, and/or other factors. We do know that frontal lobes are involved in inhibition of impulses and moral judgment (Geller, 2015; Scott & Schoenberg, 2011) and that temporal lobe damage is associated with changes in libido as well as the moral and emotional domains (Braun et al., 2003). Thus, based on the localization of the damage, we can suppose that Jerry would have sustained some lasting neuropsychological deficits, which would continue into adulthood if he had received no rehabilitative services growing up.

In some cases, when head injury is related to changes in sexual preference, it may potentially increase dangerousness. Blanchard et al. (2003) examined sexual history, phallometric measurement of erotic gender-age preferences, and cognitive functioning of 685 participants. Participants were asked whether they had experienced a traumatic brain injury and if so, at what age. The authors found that pedophilic patients self-reported more head injuries before the age of 13 than non-pedophilic patients but did not report more head injuries after the age of 13. Blanchard et al. hypothesized that subtle brain damage after birth could increase the risk of pedophilia in males or that neurodevelopmental problems before birth increased the risk of accident-proneness and pedophilia. The authors also found that self-reported histories of traumatic brain injuries before the age of 13 years were associated with left-handedness and attentional problems. However, traumatic brain injuries after the age of 13 were associated with promiscuity and drug abuse. The authors concluded that among individuals with primary sexual complaints, childhood head injuries clustered with neuropsychological problems, while head injuries at an older age clustered with lifestyle features. Another interesting finding of Blanchard et al. was that the hebephiles' (those who have sexual preference for early adolescent children) reported rate of childhood head injury was intermediate between that reported by individuals with pedophilia and those who prefer adults as sexual partners.

In contrast, another study suggested that the sexual changes post-TBI actually reflected decrease in quality and frequency of sexual activity (Ponsford, 2003).

The author of this study administered a sexuality questionnaire to 208 participants who experienced a traumatic brain injury. Of the 208 participants, 143 were male and the rest female. A majority (78%) of the participants said that they had been in a sexual relationship prior to the incident (compared to 73% of controls) and only 50% said they were in a relationship at the time of the study (compared to 60% of controls). Interestingly, the author reported that 15% or less of the participants reported increase of frequency and enjoyment on sexual intercourse; nevertheless, increases in these dimensions were no more different than those in the control group who did not suffer a TBI. The results do not include information whether these participants have become interested in non-normophilic sexual activities or if they have become more sexually violent, as the study focused more on such post-TBI issues as self-esteem, importance of sexuality, enjoyment and frequency of sexual activity, ability to become aroused and/or climax, quality of communication with a partner, etc. Additionally, the author did not specifically include those who had criminal involvement.

An important study, albeit involving violent offenders in general (not specifically sex offenders), revealed that individuals with TBI were at a significantly higher risk of committing a violent crime when compared with people with no brain injury (controls) or those suffering with epilepsy. Fazel, Lichtenstein, Grann, and Långström (2011) compared associations of epilepsy ($n$ = 22,947) and TBI ($n$ = 22,914) with violent crimes post-diagnosis, using the Swedish registry between years 1973 and 2009. The study had an additional advantageous element of inclusion of siblings unaffected by epilepsy. Their results showed that for epilepsy, although the risk of committing a violent crime increased significantly after the diagnosis, this association disappeared when the same individuals were compared to their unaffected siblings. However, this was not true with regard to the TBI population, who were compared to general population controls. The TBI population demonstrated a significantly increased risk of committing a violent crime. The authors reported that the heightened risk remained but was attenuated after controlling for substance use and familial factors. This study indicates that there is an observable difference between TBI and acquired but non-traumatic brain injury, with respect to risk for perpetrating violence.

In conclusion, it appears that a history of TBI may be relevant to risk assessment if the trauma encompasses regions of the brain that involve the frontal and temporal lobes, amygdala, and others. At times, moral judgment may not be able to interfere with volitional capacity, as indicated in some cases of pseudopsychopathy, also known as orbitofrontal or disinhibited syndrome (Scott & Schoenberg, 2011). It seems beneficial to consider known dynamic risk factors, which can be associated with some patterns of the brain injury presentations. For example, several studies indicated that general self-regulation problems and life-style impulsivity are significant risk factors for sexual recidivism (Hanson, Harris, Scott, & Helmus, 2007; Mann et al., 2010). Thus, when we ponder the consequences of an individual brain injury, especially the lasting effects of it, it is advisable to consider how the symptoms of TBI play into the risk factors for recidivism, such as compliance with supervision, impulsivity and recklessness, ability for relationship stability, and others.

## Assessment of Traumatic Brain Injury in Sex Offenders

Neuropsychological assessment of sex offenders may be a complicated undertaking, given that there are usually constraints of time and resources. Any assessment should start at the referral question. What is the purpose of such an assessment? How will it benefit an offender himself or would it be useful for risk management or treatment planning? We believe that to answer these questions, we should consider the risk factors themselves and ponder the connection between them and the neuropsychological sequelae of a brain injury. As Mann et al. (2010) discussed, lifestyle impulsivity, general self-regulation problems, and poor cognitive problem solving are well-supported risk factors. To help determine problems in these areas and the degree of dysfunction, a clinician can utilize neuropsychological or cognitive assessment. Another risk factor, resistance to rules and supervision, can also be related or caused in some cases by cognitive difficulties, among other factors. Based on the results of such assessment, decisions can be made regarding the offender's further treatment and supervision needs.

In some cases, an offender becomes a focus of a detailed review due to parole interviews, civil management proceedings, or in the context of sex offender treatment programs, etc. In the process of such evaluative procedures, oftentimes clinicians utilize brief cognitive screens, such as variations of the Mini-Mental State Examination (Folstein, Folstein, & McHugh, 1975) or Montreal Cognitive Assessment (Nasreddine et al., 2005). These brief screenings allow the clinician to determine whether gross cognitive skills are at the expected range for the person's age and education. When an offender presents with gross deficits in cognitive functions, such as attention, executive functions, language, and others and reports a history of TBI, sometimes it may lead to generating a referral for further neuropsychological examination because the impact of a lesion or neurological disease can be objectively quantified via neuropsychological assessment. In other words, what functional deficits an individual sustains and what these deficits mean in terms of their daily life, can be most precisely determined by a neuropsychological assessment.

This assessment may be brief or comprehensive. It can also be either general, or target any specific area of interest, such as memory or executive function. This is where the referral question becomes of utmost importance. Asking, "Something is wrong with Mr. Doe cognitively. Please assess," would be quite unhelpful. This is because cognitive assessment, if not targeted at a specific domain, will turn into a multiple-day fishing expedition. An examiner will waste a lot of time and find deficits that mean nothing in terms of the examinee's life or will find nothing specific at all. Thus, it is always useful to determine what exactly the assessment should focus on and what the purpose of it is. For example, a referral question may ask whether an individual is capable of living alone or following rules of supervision. These could be questions to ask via neuropsychological assessment. Assessment may help determine what, if any, supervision help or compensatory strategies an offender may find useful while residing in the community. Additionally, some offenders with post-TBI cognitive difficulties, such as memory, abstract reasoning, attention, or problem-solving, may require a different approach within the context of the sex offender treatment, to improve the outcome. Finally, determining whether an offender has a neurological disorder, which has been overlooked, can significantly increase their chances of being successful after release and even before it.

For example, treating an individual for ADHD (attention deficit hyperactivity disorder) pharmacologically in the presence of a brain dysfunction could alleviate future criminality. Langevin and Curnoe (2011) examined lifetime recidivism among Hare's Psychopathy Checklist-Revised (PCL-R) scores, attention deficit hyperactivity disorder (ADHD) diagnosis, and brain dysfunction measures in a sample of 1695 adult male sexual, violent, and non-violent offenders. They determined that although sexual offense recidivism was predicted best by the items of PCL-R that focus on criminal history (Factor 2), the presence of learning disorders and past history of criminal behavior increased this predictability. Langevin and Curnoe concluded that when estimating and managing risk for sexual recidivism, it is important to take into consideration a combination of any history of learning difficulties in school and/or potentially ADHD, psychopathy scores and any history of brain dysfunction.

When ADHD, among other factors, is addressed, this may potentially reduce recidivism, as demonstrated by Lichtenstein et al. (2012). The authors reported a reduction in criminality rate among both men and women, 31% and 41% respectively, while being pharmacologically treated for Attention Deficit Hyperactivity Disorder, when compared with non-medication periods. Neurofeedback as a treatment of ADHD is also a promising non-pharmacological treatment and shows potential in reduction of inattention, impulsivity, and hyperactivity (Arns, De Ridder, Strehl, Breteler, & Coenen, 2009). Although it is not known whether neurofeedback could be used effectively as one of the factors that lowers sexual recidivism, it was found to be efficacious and specific based on the meta-analysis by Arns et al. Neurofeedback may potentially offer more lasting effects than medication, as it contributes to forming a skill, not just reduction of symptomatology. However, more research is needed in this area.

In regard to neuropsychological functions of various types of sex offenders, it also of interest to determine whether there could be some markers or variations from the norm. In other words, are sex offenders different from an average person in terms of their cognitive functioning? Langevin, Wortzman, Wright, and Handy (1989) examined pedophiles, including sexually aggressive and incest offenders for brain damage and dysfunction using CT scans, the Halstead-Reitan (HR) neuropsychological test battery, the Wechsler Adult Intelligence Scale-Revised (WAIS-IV), the Wechsler Memory Scale (WMS-IV), and the space relations test (SRT) or the differential aptitude test. The study results suggested that the subgroup of pedophiles showed somewhat different patterns of neuropsychological deficits from other offenders. More specifically, heterosexual and homosexual pedophiles showed verbal deficits and apparent left hemispheric brain dysfunction. However, bisexual pedophiles instead showed right hemispheric visual-spatial deficits. This study shows that there are curious neuropsychological differences between certain types of sex offenders. But it is unlikely that the opposite is true and that based on this specific pattern, one can pinpoint a budding pedophile. Nevertheless, knowing neuropsychological profiles of individuals with pedophilic interest may alert an examiner to the potential presence of such an interest.

Cantor et al. (2004) demonstrated that individuals with pedophilia showed significant negative correlations with intelligence (IQ) and immediate and delayed recall memory. Pedophilia was also related to non-right handedness even after co-varying age and IQ. These results suggested that pedophilia is linked to early neurodevelopmental perturbations. In a later study, Blanchard et al. (2007) confirmed these findings and established the relationship between pedophilia and cognitive function, such as lower IQ, lower education, and more common non-right handedness; this relationship is genuine and not artifactual. The findings were interpreted as evidence for the hypothesis that neurodevelopmental perturbations increase the risk of pedophilia in males.

There are many neuropsychological screening instruments on the market that could aid in assessment. The choice of which one(s) to use depends on the purpose of the assessment itself, available time, and resources. Additionally, neuropsychological assessment in any population should ideally include malingering and/or effort measures, as a general recommendation. Many neuropsychological measures already include embedded effort measures; but they can always be added on.

A brief screening battery, such as the repeatable battery for the assessment of neuropsychological status (RBANS-Update) (Randolph, 2012) only takes about 30 minutes, can be given in English and Spanish to individuals between ages 12 and 90 years old, and has several versions for each language to control for learning effects should the battery be repeated. It offers a glimpse of the overall neuropsychological profile of a person, including language, memory, attention, and visuo-spatial functions. One of the advantages of this instrument is that it can be sensitive enough in cases of lower-functioning individuals. However, in cases when an individual is high-functioning and may exhibit mild deficits, RBANS (Randolph, Tierney, Mohr, & Chase, 1998) would lack sensitivity.

One of the classical batteries developed for traumatic brain injury assessments is the Halstead-Reitan battery (HRB) (Reitan & Wolfson, 1993). The battery assesses most of the cognitive functions, including speech, memory, motor, executive functions, etc. It differentiates well between the brain injured patients and healthy subjects, and it is a highly specialized battery and requires substantial training. It takes a long time to administer, and therefore may not be suitable for a brief assessment in the sex offender population. It is also not suitable for patients with sensory or motor handicaps (Lezak, Howieson, Bigler, & Tranel, 2012).

Another common testing battery is the neuropsychological assessment battery (NAB) (Stern & White, 2003). This assessment battery is considered to have a broad range, comprising 36 different tests that come in two equivalent forms (Lezak et al., 2012). The battery assesses multiple neuropsychological domains and is sensitive to minor changes of the neuropsychological status in high-functioning individuals. One of the benefits of this battery for the population of sex offenders with brain injury is that it specifically assesses executive functions, among other domains.

As we have discussed before, executive functions that are housed in the frontal lobes are responsible for self-directed behavior, problem solving, mental flexibility, executing decisions, and inhibiting impulses. NAB provides norms for individuals between 18 and 97 years of age. It also includes a screening mode, which offers a shorter screen that targets any two domains of interest (memory, language, spatial, attention, or executive) and allows testing at a high and low ability level.

In summary, TBI may alter one's sexual functioning, inhibiting it, increasing libido while decreasing control, or even changing one's sexual interests and orientation. Brain injury can also alter a person's character and increase socially undesirable behaviors. TBI may have a lasting effect on an individual, even years after the injury. At times, these consequences may impact the behaviors of an offender in such a way that their risk of recidivism increases. These consequences can also impact the offender's quality of life, socialization ability, and cognitive capacity in such a way that they may be difficult to supervise, struggle to understand content of sex offender treatment programs, or have trouble adjusting to the society outside the prison walls. It is important to consider assessment for brain injury for offenders who either report this type of injury or appear to have cognitive difficulties. A referral to an appropriate specialist may help develop individualized treatment approach, supervision strategies, and increase adjustment to life in the community. Medication management and cognitive rehabilitation may be utilized in risk management and treatment.

## Conclusion

The relationship between adverse childhood experiences (ACEs) and future sexual offending has gained much consideration recently. Many sex offenders have been victims to similar offending behavior in their past. Various researchers have found a higher rate of childhood sexual abuse in sexual offenders as compared to either the general population (Levenson et al., 2016) or non-sexual offenders (Jespersen et al., 2009). Research in this area has often included the use of the Adverse Childhood Experiences (ACE) questionnaire which includes questions about childhood abuse and exposure to forms of household dysfunction. Findings have revealed higher ACE scores to be associated with a number of sex crime arrests (Levenson & Socia, 2016). Looking closer at specific offense characteristics, higher mean ACE scores were found in those who had victims under the age of 12, male victims, stranger victims, prepubescent victims, multiple victims, those with contact sex offenses versus noncontact sex offenses, those who used force or violence in the commission of their sex offense, those who used a weapon, and those who injured a victim (Levenson et al., 2016; Levenson & Grady, 2016).

Although negative childhood experiences are prevalent among sex offenders, with regard to assessing risk for sexual recidivism, an adverse childhood environment reflects little to no relationship with sexual recidivism, according to a meta-analysis (Hanson & Morton-Bourgon, 2005). As such, it appears that factors that are related to the persistence of sexual offending may be different from those factors that are related to the initiation of such offending. However, some aspects of an offender's history have demonstrated an association with recidivism and may be moderated by risk level (e.g., Nunes et al., 2013; Phenix et al., 2012).

In addition to psychological trauma, traumatic brain injuries of varying severity may alter one's sexual functioning. Brain trauma may increase libido, while decreasing control, or even changing one's sexual interests and orientation; it can also inhibit sexual behavior. Brain injury can also alter a person's character and increase socially undesirable behaviors in such a way that sexual behaviors start presenting a problem for an individual and/or their caregivers. Brain trauma, just like emotional trauma, may have a lasting effect on an individual, impacting his or her quality of life, socialization ability, and cognitive capacity in such a way that it may be difficult to supervise or treat this offender. Various strategies can be recommended, such as neuropsychological assessment, cognitive remediation, modified supervision, medication, and others.

## Questions/Activities for Further Exploration

1. How could sex offenders' histories of psychological and brain trauma impact legal decisions for those who are being considered for civil confinement under sexually violent predator (SVP) laws?
2. Can early detection and addressing of adverse childhood experiences and/or cognitive rehabilitation for brain injury help reduce criminal outcomes?
3. Would cognitive rehabilitation for sex offenders reduce recidivism?
4. Considering that psychological trauma is so pervasive in offenders' histories, how do you determine who would benefit from trauma-related treatment?
5. Do adverse childhood experiences impact juvenile and adult offenders differently?
6. How would trauma-informed treatment be different for adult offenders, as compared to juvenile offenders?

## References

Afifi, A. K., & Bergman, R. A. (1998). *Functional neuroanatomy: Text and atlas* (1st ed.). New York: McGraw-Hill Professional.

Alnemari, A. M., Mansour, T. R., Buehler, M., & Gaudin, D. (2016). Neural basis of pedophilia: Altered sexual preference following traumatic brain injury. *International Journal of Surgery Case Reports, 25*, 221–224.

Andrews, D. A., & Bonta, J. (2010). Rehabilitating criminal justice policy and practice. *Psychology, Public Policy, and Law, 16*, 39–55.

Arns, M., De Ridder, S., Strehl, U., Breteler, M., & Coenen, A. (2009). Efficacy of neurofeedback treatment in ADHD: The effects on inattention, impulsivity, and hyperactivity: A meta-analysis. *Clinical EEG and Neuroscience, 40*(3), 180–189.

Beech, A. R., & Ward, T. (2004). The integration of etiology and risk in sexual offenders: A theoretical framework. *Aggression and Violent Behavior, 10*, 31–63.

Blanchard, R., Christensen, B. K., Strong, S. M., Cantor, J. M., Kuban, M. E., Klassen, P., et al. (2002). Retrospective self-reports of childhood accidents causing unconsciousness in phallometrically diagnosed pedophiles. *Archives of Sexual Behavior, 31*, 511–526.

Blanchard, R., Kolla, N. J., Cantor, J. M., Klassen, P. E., Dickey, R., Kuban, M., & Blak, T. (2007). IQ, handedness, and pedophilia in adult male patients stratified by referral source. *Sexual Abuse: A Journal of Research and Treatment, 19*(3), 285–309.

Blanchard, R., Kuban, M., Klassen, E., Dickey, P., Christensen, R., Cantor, B., & Blak, K. (2003). Self-reported head injuries before and after age 13 in pedophilic and nonpedophilic men referred for clinical assessment. *Archives of Sexual Behavior, 32*(6), 573–581.

Blumer, D., & Benson, D. F. (1975). Personality changes with frontal lobe lesions. In D. F. Benson & D. Blumer (Eds.), *Psychiatric Aspects of Neurological Disease* (pp. 151–170). New York: Gruneand Stratton.

Braun, C. M. J., Dumont, M., Duval, J., Hamel, I., & Godbout, L. (2003). Opposed left and right brain hemisphere contributions to sexual drive: A multiple lesion case study. *Behavioral Neurology, 14*, 55–61.

Cantor, J. M., Blanchard, R., Christensen, B. K., Dickey, R., Klassen, P. E., Beckstead, A. L., et al. (2004). Intelligence, memory, and handedness in pedophilia. *Neuropsychology, 18*(1), 3–14.

Cantor, J. M., Kabani, N., Christensen, B. K., Zipursky, R. B., Barbaree, H. E., Dickey, R., et al. (2008). Cerebral white matter deficiencies in pedophilic men. *Journal of Psychiatric Research, 42*(3), 167–183.

Centers for Disease Control and Prevention. (2013). *Adverse childhood experience study: Prevalence of individual adverse childhood experiences*. Retrieved from http://www.cdc.gov/ace/prevalence.htm

Cleckley, H. (1988). *The mask of sanity: An attempt to clarify some issues about the so-called psychopathic personality* (5th ed.). Retrieved from https://openlibrary.org/books/OL8518405M/The_Mask_of_Sanity

Cortoni, F., & Marshall, W. L. (2001). Sex as a coping strategy and its relationship to juvenile sexual history and intimacy in sexual offenders. *Sexual Abuse: A Journal of Research and Treatment, 13*, 27–43.

Darby, R. R., Horn, A., Cushman, F., & Fox, M. D. (2018). Lesion network localization of criminal behavior. *Proceedings of the National Academy of Sciences of the United States of America, 115*(3), 601–606.

Fazel, S., Lichtenstein, P., Grann, M., & Långström, N. (2011). Risk of violent crime in individuals with epilepsy and traumatic brain injury: A 35-year Swedish population study. *PLoS Medicine, 8*, e1001150. https://doi.org/10.1371/journal.pmed.1001150

Felitti, V. J., Anda, R. F., Nordenberg, D., Williamson, D. F., Spitz, A. M., Marks, J. S., et al. (1998). Relationship of childhood abuse and household dysfunction to many of the leading causes of death in adults: The adverse childhood experiences (ACE) study. *American Journal of Preventive Medicine, 14*(4), 245–355.

Folstein, M. F., Folstein, S. E., & McHugh, P. R. (1975). Mini-mental state. A practical method for grading the cognitive state of patients for the clinician. *Journal of Psychiatrich Research, 12*, 189–198.

Gardner, A. J., & Zafonte, R. (2016). Neuroepidemiology of traumatic brain injury. In M. J. Aminoff, F. Boller, & D. F. Swaab (Eds.), *Handbook of clinical neurology* (Vol. 138, pp. 207–221). London: Elsevier.

Geller, H. L. (2015). Executive functions. In P. Moglia (Ed.), *Salem health: Psychology and behavioral health* (4th ed., pp. 685–688). Amenia: Grey House Publishing. Retrieved from https://www.salempress.com/health_psychology_behavioral_health

Grady, M. D., Levenson, J. S., & Bolder, T. (2017). Linking adverse childhood effects and attachment: A theory of etiology for sexual offending. *Trauma, Violence, & Abuse, 18*(4), 433–444. https://doi.org/10.1177/1524838015627147

Hanson, R. K., Bourgon, G., Helmus, L., & Hodgson, S. (2009). The principles of effective correctional treatment also apply to sexual offenders: A meta-analysis. *Criminal Justice and Behavior, 36*, 865–891.

Hanson, R. K., Harris, A. J. R., Scott, T.-L., & Helmus, L. (2007). *Assessing the risk of sexual offenders on community supervision: The Dynamic Supervision Project.* (Corrections Research User Report No. 2007-05). Ottawa, ON: Public Safety Canada.

Hanson, R. K., & Morton-Bourgon, K. E. (2005). The characteristics of persistent sexual offenders: A meta-analysis of recidivism studies. *Journal of Consulting and Clinical Psychology, 73*(6), 1154–1163. https://doi.org/10.1037/0022-006X.73.6.1154

Hanson, R. K., & Slater, S. (1988). Sexual victimization in the history of sexual abusers: A review. *Annals of Sex Research, 1*, 485–499.

Hare, R. D. (1993). *Without conscience. The disturbing world of the psychopaths among us.* New York: The Guilford Press.

Hildebrand, M., de Ruiter, C., & de Vogel, V. (2004). Psychopathy and sexual deviance in treated rapists: Association with sexual and nonsexual recidivism. *Sexual Abuse: A Journal of Research and Treatment, 16*(1), 1–24.

Iverson, G. L., & Lange, R. T. (2011a). Mild traumatic brain injury. In M. R. Schoenberg & J. G. Scott (Eds.), *The little black book of neuropsychology: A syndrome-based approach* (pp. 697–719). New York: Springer.

Iverson, G. L., & Lange, R. T. (2011b). Moderate and severe traumatic brain injury. In M. R. Schoenberg & J. G. Scott (Eds.), *The little black book of neuropsychology: A syndrome-based approach* (pp. 663–696). New York: Springer.

Jespersen, A. F., Lalumiere, M. L., & Seto, M. C. (2009). Sexual abuse history among adult sex offenders and non-sex offenders: A meta-analysis. *Child Abuse & Neglect, 33*(3), 179. https://doi.org/10.1016/j.chiabu.2008.07.004

Jennings, W. G., Zgoba, K. M., Maschi, T., & Reingle, J. M. (2014). An empirical assessment of the overlap between sexual victimization and sex offending. *International Journal of Offender Therapy and Comparative Criminology, 58*, 1466–1480.

Kiehl, K. A. (2006). A cognitive neuroscience perspective on psychopathy: Evidence for paralimbic system dysfunction. *Psychiatry Research, 142*(2–3), 107–128.

Komisaruk, B. R., Whipple, B., Crawford, A., Grimes, S., Liu, W.-C., Kalnin, A., & Mosier, K. (2004). Brain activation during vaginocervical self-stimulation and orgasm in women with complete spinal cord injury: fMRI evidence of mediation by the vagus nerves. *Brain Research, 1024*, 77–88.

Langevin, R. (2006). Sexual offenses and traumatic brain injury. *Brain and Cognition, 60*(2), 206–207.

Langevin, R., & Curnoe, S. (2011). Psychopathy, ADHD, and brain dysfunction as predictors of lifetime recidivism among sex offenders. *International Journal of Offender Therapy and Comparative Criminology, 55*(1), 5–26.

Langevin, R., Wortzman, G., Wright, P., & Handy, L. (1989). Studies of brain damage and dysfunction in sex offenders. *Annals of Sex Research, 2*(2), 163–179.

Lee, J. K. P., Jackson, H. J., Pattison, P., & Ward, T. (2002). Developmental risk factors for sexual offending. *Child Abuse & Neglect, 26*, 73–92.

Levenson, J. S., & Grady, M. D. (2016). The influence of childhood trauma on sexual violence and sexual deviance in adulthood. *Traumatology, 22*(2), 94–103. https://doi.org/10.1037/trm0000067

Levenson, J. S., & Socia, K. M. (2016). Adverse childhood experiences and arrest patterns in a sample of sexual offenders. *Journal of Interpersonal Violence, 31*(10), 1883–1911. https://doi.org/10.1177/0886260515570751

Levenson, J. S., Willis, G. M., & Prescott, D. S. (2016). Adverse childhood experiences in the lives of male sex offenders: Implications for trauma-informed care. *Sexual Abuse: A Journal of Research and Treatment, 28*(4), 340–359. https://doi.org/10.1177/1079063214535819

Lezak, M. D., Howieson, D. B., Bigler, E. D., & Tranel, D. (2012). *Neuropsychological assessment* (5th ed.). New York: Oxford University Press.

Lichtenstein, P., Halldner, L., Zetterqvist, J., Sjölander, A., Serlachius, E., Fazel, S., & Larsson, H. (2012). Medication for attention deficit-hyperactivity disorder and criminality. *New England Journal of Medicine, 367*, 2006–2014.

Luria, A. R. (1966). *Higher cortical functions in man*. New York: Basic Books.

Mann, R. E., Hanson, R. K., & Thornton, D. (2010). Assessing risk for sexual recidivism: Some proposals on the nature of psychologically meaningful risk factors. *Sexual Abuse: A Journal of Research and Treatment, 22*(2), 191–217.

Marlowe, W. B., Mancall, E. L., & Thomas, J. J. (1975). Complete Klüver-Bucy syndrome in man. *Cortex, 11*(1), 53–59. https://doi.org/10.1016/s0010-9452(75)80020-7. PMID168031

Marshall, W. L., & Barbaree, H. E. (1990). An integrated theory of the etiology of sexual offending. In W. L. Marshall, D. R. Laws, & H. E. Barbaree (Eds.), *Handbook of sexual assault: Issues, theories, and treatment of the offender* (pp. 257–275). New York: Plenum.

Marshall, W. L., & Marshall, L. E. (2000). The origins of sexual offending. *Trauma, Violence, & Abuse, 1*(3), 250–263.

Miller, B. L., Cummings, J. L., McIntyre, H., Ebers, G., & Grode, M. (1986). Hypersexuality or altered sexual preference following brain injury. *Journal of Neurology, Neurosurgery, and Psychiatry, 49*(8), 867–873.

Morcos, N., & Guirgis, H. (2014). A case of acute-onset partial Klüver-Bucy syndrome in a patient with a history of traumatic brain injury. *The Journal of Neuropsychiatry and Clinical Neurosciences, 26*(3), E10–E11.

Nasreddine, Z. S., Phillips, N. A., Bédirian, V., Charbonneau, S., Whitehead, V., Collin, I. ... Chertkow, H. (2005). The montreal cognitive assessment, MoCA: A brief screening tool for mild cognitive impairment. *Journal of the American Geriatrics Society, 53*(4), 695–699.

Nunes, K. L., Hermann, C. A., Malcom, R., & Lavoie, K. (2013). Childhood sexual victimization, pedophilic interest, and sexual recidivism. *Child Abuse & Neglect, 37*, 703–711. https://doi.org/10.1016/j.chiabu.2013.01.008

Paredes, R. G. (2003). Medial preoptic area/anterior hypothalamus and sexual motivation. *Scandinavian Journal of Psychology, 44*(3), 203–212.

Perr, I. N. (1991). Alleged brain damage, diminished capacity, mens rea, and misuse of medical concepts. *Journal of Forensic Sciences, 36*(3), 722–727.

Pennington, B. F. (2002). *The development of psychopathology: Nature and nurture*. New York: Guilford Press.

Phenix, A., Helmus, L., & Hanson, R. K. (2012). Static-99R & Static2002R evaluators' workbook. Retrieved March 5, 2013, from http://www.Static99.org/pdfdocs/Static-99RandStatic-2002R_EvaluatorsWorkbook2012-07-26.pdf

Ponsford, J. (2003). Sexual changes associated with traumatic brain injury. *Neuropsychological Rehabilitation, 13*(1–2), 275–289. https://doi.org/10.1080/09602010244000363

Randolph, C. (2012). *RBANS Manual-Update: Repeatable battery for the assessment of neuropsychological status*. San Antonio, TX: Psychological Corporation.

Randolph, C., Tierney, M. C., Mohr, E., & Chase, T. N. (1998). The repeatable battery for the assessment of neuropsychological status (RBANS): preliminary clinical validity. *Journal of Clinical and Experimental Neuropsychology, 20*(3), 310–319.

Reavis, J. A., Looman, J., Franco, K. A., & Rojas, B. (2013). Adverse childhood experiences and adult criminality: How long must we live before we possess our own lives? *The Permanente Journal, 17*(2), 44–48. https://doi.org/10.7812/TPP/12-072

Reitan, R. M., & Wolfson, D. (1993). *The Halstead-Reitan neuropsychological test battery: Theory and clinical applications* (2nd ed.). Tucson: Neuropsychology Press.

Rowlett, R. (2000). *Glasgow coma scale*. Chapel Hill, NC: University of North Carolina.

Salloway, S., Malloy, P., & Cummings, J. L. (1997). The neuropsychiatry of limbic and subcortical disorders. *Journal of Neuropsychiatry and Clinical Neuroscience, 9*(3), 313–314. ISBN 0-88048-942-1.

Seto, M. C. (2008). Pedophilia and sexual offending against children: Theory, assessment, and intervention. Washington, DC: American Psychological Association.

Seto, M. C., & Lalumiere, M. L. (2001). A brief screening scale to identify pedophilic interests among child molesters. *Sexual Abuse: A Journal of Research and Treatment, 13*(1), 15–25.

Schilz, K., Witzel, J., Northoff, G., Zierhut, K., Gubka, U., Fellmann, H., et al. (2007). Brain pathology in pedophilic offenders. *Archives of General Psychiatry, 64*, 737–746.

Schoenberg, M. R., & Scott, J. G. (Eds.). (2011). *The little black book of neuropsychology: A syndrome-based approach*. New York: Springer.

Scott, J. G., & Schoenberg, M. R. (2011). Frontal lobe/executive functioning. In M. R. Schoenberg & J. G. Scott (Eds.), *The little black book of neuropsychology: A syndrome-based approach* (pp. 219–248). New York: Springer.

Shiroma, E. J., Ferguson, P. L., & Pickelsimer, E. E. (2010). Prevalence of traumatic brain injury in an offender population: A meta-analysis. *Journal of Correctional Health Care, 16*(2), 147–159.

Simons, D. A., Wurtele, S. K., & Durham, R. L. (2008). Developmental experiences of child sexual abusers and rapists. *Child Abuse & Neglect, 32*, 549–560.

Stern, R. A., & White, T. (2003). *Neuropsychological assessment battery (NAB)*. Lutz, FL: Psychological Assessment Resources.

Terzian, H., & Ore, G. D. (1955). Syndrome of Klüver and Bucy; reproduced in man by bilateral removal of the temporal lobes. *Neurology, 5*(6), 373–380.

Thornton, D. (2002). Constructing and testing a framework for dynamic risk assessment. *Sexual Abuse: A Journal of Research and Treatment, 14*, 139–154.

Turner, D., Schöttle, D., Krueger, R., & Briken, P. (2015). Sexual behavior and its correlates after traumatic brain injury. *Current Opinion in Psychiatry, 28*(2), 180–187.

Varon, D., Pritchard, P. B., III, Wagner, M. T., & Topping, K. (2003). Transient Klüver–Bucy syndrome following complex partial status epilepticus. *Epilepsy and Behavior, 4*, 348–351.

Vaughn, M. G., Salas-Wright, C. P., Delisi, M., & Perron, B. (2014). Correlates of traumatic brain injury among juvenile sex offenders: A multi-site study. *Criminal Behaviour and Mental Health, 24*, 188–203.

Ward, T., & Beech, A. R. (2006). An integrated theory of sex offending. *Aggression and Violent Behavior, 11*, 44–63. https://doi.org/10.1016/j.avb.2005.05.002

Ward, T., Hudson, S. M., & Marshall, W. L. (1996). Attachment style in sex offenders: A preliminary study. *The Journal of Sex Research, 33*(1), 17–26. https://www.tandfonline.com/doi/abs/10.1080/00224499609551811

Weeks, R., & Widom, C. S. (1998). Self-reports of early childhood victimization among incarcerated adult male felons. *Journal of Interpersonal Violence, 13*(3), 346–361. https://doi.org/10.1177/088626098013003003

Williams, W. H., Chitsabesan, P., Fazel, S., McMillan, T., Hughes, N., Parsonage, M., & Tonks, J. (2018). Traumatic brain injury: A potential cause of violent crime? *Lancet Psychiatry, 5*, 836–844. Retrieved from https://www.ncbi.nlm.nih.gov/pubmed/29496587

# Chapter 18
# Trauma and Resiliency in Forensically Involved Youth: Applications, Evaluations, and Recommendations

Morgan Shaw, Gimel Rogers, and Robert Geffner

## Introduction

The youth can become involved in the legal system in a number of ways: through the juvenile justice system, juvenile dependency system, or civil courts. Mental health professionals are often being utilized by the court systems to educate the court as to the individualized needs of a youth coming through these systems. Mental health professionals, particularly psychologists, are frequently being asked by juvenile delinquency courts and probation to perform comprehensive psychological evaluations on the youth who interact with the legal system to better clarify the specific psychological and emotional needs of the youth in order to recommend appropriate intervention strategies. Similarly, mental health professionals are frequently used by the juvenile dependency system, including Child Welfare Services (CWS), to evaluate and report on the needs of the individual youth who may be removed from their homes and placed in various state and county programs such as foster care placements, group homes, and residential treatment centers. Often, evaluators need to specifically assess and opine on the mental health functioning of the youth and the level of care necessary to meet the needs of that individual. Additionally, evaluators are often retained in civil cases, particularly personal injury cases, to assess the current functioning of a youth and the impact of the experienced trauma and to provide specific estimates of future care needs for that child.

Research shows that there is an incredibly high prevalence rate of youth coming through these various court systems. In 2017, more than 809,000 minors were arrested by law enforcement agencies in the USA (US; OJJDP, 2017). While lower than the 59% from the 2.11 million youths who were arrested in 2008, it is still a substantial number of minors encountering the juvenile justice system each year.

M. Shaw (✉) · G. Rogers · R. Geffner
Institute on Violence, Abuse, and Trauma, San Diego, CA, USA
e-mail: MorganS@IVATcenters.org; IVATpcfs@IVATcenters.org

© Springer Nature Switzerland AG 2020                                   443
R. A. Javier et al. (eds.), *Assessing Trauma in Forensic Contexts*,
https://doi.org/10.1007/978-3-030-33106-1_18

Additionally, it is estimated that there are currently over 600,000 youths involved in the dependency and foster care system across the USA (DHHS, 2018). While it is more difficult to obtain an accurate estimate, it is known that there are also a substantial number of youths who are involved in the civil court systems at any given year in the USA. Due to these staggering numbers, it is imperative for professionals working with these youths to be appropriately trained on how best to serve the specialized needs that most of them have.

There has been a great deal of research that has examined the unique factors associated with the involvement of forensically involved youth within the legal systems; however, most of that research has specifically examined risk factors associated with court involvement, primarily offending behaviors (Fougere & Daffern, 2011). While an in-depth exploration of risk factors associated with youth who offend is outside of the scope of the current chapter, in general, research has found that young offenders have greater psychosocial and mental health problems (Carswell, Maughan, Davis, Davenport, & Goddard, 2004; Chitsabesan & Bailey, 2006), lower levels of intellectual functioning, and higher incidences of learning disabilities than non-offending youth (Chitsabesan & Bailey, 2006; Katisiyannis, Ryan, Zhang, & Spann, 2008). Recognizing those factors and their connection to trauma, this chapter focuses on childhood trauma, which is a part of most forensically involved youths' histories. In addition, this chapter also explores the concept of resilience and other forms of protective factors for youth.

More recently, protective factors in youth offenders have been more extensively discussed and disseminated in the risk assessment literature as evidenced by an increase in the number of risk assessment tools that incorporate protective factors. These include the Structured Assessment of Violence Risk in Youth (SAVRY; Borum, Bartel, & Forth, 2000) and the Structured Assessment of Protective Factors for Violence Risk – Youth Version (SAPROF-YV; de Vries Robbe, Geers, Stapel, Hilterman, & Vogel, 2015). However, we are encouraging all mental health professionals and other frontline workers who come into contact with youth involved in the court systems to comprehensively assess resilience and other protective factors in order to best serve the youth and their families. Further, it is imperative for the court to better understand how to support and strengthen resilience factors in order to make the most appropriate dispositions and orders for those youth who encounter the legal system.

This chapter provides an overview of childhood trauma and adverse experiences as important risk factors to consider when evaluating youth in any context, but especially within the legal framework. Resiliency in youth is explored by clearly defining resilience and the research associated with those factors. An outline of the different resiliency assessment tools available for evaluators to incorporate in their reports and ways to implement these measures to best evaluate protective factors in a forensic context are also reviewed. Finally, two different case examples are provided to illustrate how to best utilize the information gathered in the context of professional work in the forensic arena.

## Adverse Childhood Experiences

Adverse childhood experiences (ACEs) can be defined as stressful or traumatic events, including abuse and neglect, that negatively impact a child's emotional, mental, and physical well-being. Due to the prevalence of these experiences, a research study was conducted by Kaiser Permanente in California and funded by the Center for Disease Control and Prevention (CDC; Felitti et al., 1998). This study initially examined over 17,000 patients who went in for any type of visits to Kaiser clinics and hospitals throughout the state for over 1.5 years. They were given a 10-item self-report questionnaire (the Adverse Childhood Experience Questionnaire) that measures 10 types of traumatic experiences that a person might have been exposed to in childhood and may be categorized as "traumatic" or "household dysfunction." Recently, there were four extra questions added by researchers to address exposure to poverty, bullying, and community violence, measuring a total of 14 types of traumatic experiences (https://www.acesconnection.com/g/aces-in-pediatrics/blog/who-s-integrating-aces). Presently, the questionnaire asks about traumatic experiences in childhood related to physical abuse, verbal abuse, and sexual abuse, physical neglect, emotional neglect, a parent who had an addiction, a parent who was a victim of domestic violence, an incarcerated family member, a family member who was diagnosed with a mental illness, living in a dangerous or violent neighborhood, economic insecurity or requiring public assistance, and an absent parent due to divorce, death, or abandonment. After the questionnaire is completed, it is scored based on the number of items endorsed as *yes*. The study found on average that the life expectancy of an individual with ACE ≥ four is *almost 20 years less* than that of someone with an ACE of zero (Brown et al., 2009). According to Felitti (2002), "Slightly more than half of our middle-class population... experienced one or more of the categories of adverse childhood experience that we studied. One in four were exposed to two categories... one in 16 were exposed to four categories. Given an exposure to one category, there is an 80% likelihood of exposure to another category.... One may miss the forest for the trees if one studies these categories individually. They do not occur in isolation; for instance, a child does not grow up with an alcoholic parent or with domestic violence in an otherwise well-functioning household" (p. 361).

This study and the expanding body of research suggest that childhood trauma and ACEs can lead to a variety of negative health outcomes, including substance abuse, depressive disorders, heart disease, obesity, cancer, sexually transmitted diseases, intergenerational transmission of abuse, homelessness, prostitution, criminal behavior, unemployment, parenting problems, shortened lifespan, poor attachment, stress hormone dysregulation, intimate partner violent relationships, and attempted suicide among adolescents and adults (Dube et al., 2006; Putnam, Harris, Lieberman, Putnam, & Amaya-Jackson, 2015). One particular study of over 136,000 students in the 6th, 9th, and 12th grades from Minnesota in the USA responded to a questionnaire which included physical abuse, intrafamilial sexual abuse, extrafamilial sexual abuse, and familial alcohol and drug abuse, and it found a correlation to adolescent interpersonal violence perpetration and self-directed violence (Duke, Pettingell, McMorris, & Borowsky, 2010). Furthermore, this study noted that each additional ACE endorsed increased the risk of violence perpetration (Duke et al., 2010). This demonstrates the need to address ACEs and to increase resiliency factors to counter them.

Further, it is important to deal with the effects of ACEs and how most children subsequently develop maladaptive coping mechanisms such as substance abuse and behavioral health problems. Thus, many youths who have interacted with the legal system have comorbid disorders and a variety of substance-related behaviors (Conner & Lochman, 2010; McClelland, Elkington, Teplin, & Abram, 2004). The early initiation of alcohol use is one of the most common substance-related issues that arise in children who are exposed to ACEs (Dube et al., 2006). Research has consistently demonstrated that youths involved in the juvenile justice system demonstrate higher prevalence rates of ACEs and childhood trauma compared to youths in the general population (Dierkhising, Ko, Briggs, Lee, & Pynoos, 2012). Further, research also indicates that these same youths demonstrate higher prevalence rates of poly-victimization, or the experience of multiple forms of trauma (Dierkhising et al., 2012). Similarly, it is known that youths in the dependency system experience high levels of adverse childhood experience and are at increased risk for multiple forms of victimization. One study that surveyed adult women who were in the foster care system as children found that 97% of respondents endorsed at least one ACE, while 70% reported five or more, and 33% reported eight or more (Bruskas, 2013).

Since these experiences occur during peak developmental periods, developmental and social issues can arise. Children exposed to repeated or chronic trauma generally have significantly worse outcomes than those exposed to acute or accidental traumas. Thus, effects of chronic trauma often serve as reminders, which reinforces the negative impact. Further, abuse and neglect of children are extremely common in our society, and their effects are well documented to persist over time (Van der Kolk, Roth, Pelcovitz, Sunday, & Spinazzola, 2005). It is important to note that the exact impact of a particular ACE on a child or adolescent is not known. The research has focused on the number of ACEs and the likelihood of experiencing numerous mental and physical health, social, and behavioral problems throughout a person's lifetime without intervention or countering resiliency factors (Dube et al., 2006; Putnam et al., 2015).

## Neurobiology of Trauma Outcomes

Research has indicated that trauma can begin in utero (Van den Bergh et al., 2017; Yehuda & Meaney, 2018). This suggests that from conception, children who are exposed to chronic stressful events may have their neurodevelopment disrupted. In addition, research has continued to show various emotional, psychological, and neurobiological long-term effects (Mash & Barkley, 2014). Specifically, in children and adolescents, the chronic mobilization of stress in maltreating environments is considered a key cause of persistent negative neurobiological effects. Chronic stress linked with the threat of or actual victimization is thought to damage the body's stress response systems. Some of these include the immune, sympathetic nervous, and neurotransmitter systems. Various brain structures involved include the hippocampus, hypothalamic pituitary adrenal (HPA) axis, amygdala, and the prefrontal cortex. These areas are important to note as they are responsible for learning memory, activation of fight-or-flight response, sleep cycles, extinction of fear response, planning, inhibition, impulsivity, aggressiveness, and other important processes. These neurobiological changes have also been noted in various studies on posttraumatic stress disorder (PTSD; Van der Kolk et al., 2005).

In addition to these specific neurobiological changes, there is also a strong foundation of research supporting an allostatic load (i.e., the wear and tear on the body as a consequence of exposure to repeated or chronic stress in individuals suffering from PTSD (Groer, Kostas-Polston, Dillahunt-Aspilliga, Johnson-Mallard, & Duffy, 2014). Examples of this allostatic load in these individuals include higher cholesterol and triglycerides, higher perceived stress, greater pain, greater fatigue and lower plasma, as well as a propensity for a variety of illnesses later in life when compared to individuals without a history of PTSD (Groer et al., 2014). Furthermore, extreme stress associated with maltreatment can cause changes in both brain development and brain structure (Van der Kolk, et al., 2005). Understanding the neurobiology of trauma in conjunction with ACEs will ultimately inform various systems to provide secondary prevention (i.e., early identification and prompt treatment); it enhances the understanding of the complexities of childhood trauma in forensic cases with youths and ways to counter them (i.e., reducing the residual effects of a chronic issue or minimizing further negative consequences).

## Resilience as a Protective Factor

### Conceptualization of Resilience

Resilience has been identified as an umbrella term to include protective factors for countering ACEs and risk factors. These can help reduce offending and reoffending as evidenced by the inclusion of these factors in more current risk assessment measures. However, despite its identified importance, the way in which scholars and practitioners conceptualize resilience is inconsistent (Fougere & Daffern, 2011). Over the past few decades, the concept of resilience has significantly changed from a trait-oriented to an outcome-oriented approach (Chmitorz et al., 2018). In a trait-oriented approach, resilience is considered an intrinsic and stable attribute that is determined by a certain personality type (i.e., "a hardy personality"), which strengthens the individual's ability to adapt to stress and overcome adversities (Connor, Davidson, & Lee, 2003; Hu, Zhang, & Wang, 2015; Ong, Bergeman, Bisconti, & Wallace, 2006). However, strong empirical support for this conceptualization has not been demonstrated in the literature (Bonanno &

Diminich, 2012; Kalisch et al., 2017), and in fact, personality has been demonstrated to be just one of many risk and protective factors that can affect an individual's mental health (Chmitorz et al., 2018). More recently, an outcome-oriented approach has been increasingly considered and researched, which looks at resilience as the maintenance or recovery of mental or physical health despite significant stress or adversity (Kalisch et al., 2017; Kalisch, Müller, & Tüscher, 2014). In this conceptualization, risk, trauma, or adversity is a central prerequisite of resilience, which means that an individual's level of resilience can only be determined after exposure to stress or trauma (Chmitorz et al., 2018). When viewed this way, resilience is then considered modifiable and can be determined by multiple factors (Bonanno & Diminich, 2012; Chmitorz et al., 2018). These factors can be internal, such as personality traits (e.g., optimism, perseverance), beliefs (e.g., self-efficacy), or can be external, such as access to resources and the presence of positive environmental factors (Chmitorz et al., 2018; Southwick & Charney, 2012).

Other conceptualizations have been used to examine resilience and success as more of an outcome measure. The following conceptualizations are common and will be explored in more depth: sustained competence under threat, recovery from trauma, and achieving positive outcomes despite high-risk status (Masten, Best, & Garmezy, 1990).

**Resilience as Competence Under Threat** The conceptualization of resilience as competence under threat was derived from the literature on stress and coping (Fougere & Daffern, 2011; Masten et al., 1990). In this context, resilience refers to effective coping in response to stress or adversity while the stressor is ongoing or immediately following it. It is important to note that there has been a debate as to whether coping and resilience are separate constructs, with some arguing that coping refers to biological or psychological responses that reduce the impact of stress or trauma, while resilience refers to adaptive outcomes (i.e., success) in response to stress or trauma (Davey, Eaker, & Walters, 2003; Fougere & Daffern, 2011). Davey et al. (2003) attempted to examine the extent to which coping and resilience are two separate constructs by testing whether adolescents who reported themselves as either high or low risk for behavior problems (such as dropping out of school or substance abuse) differed in measures of resilience and coping. Results did indicate that they are likely to be two separate constructs as the youths showed differences in resilience but not in coping abilities. This supports the idea that while they are different constructs, the ability to cope effectively contributes to an individual's level of resilience (Fougere & Daffern, 2011).

**Resilience as Recovery** Similarly, there has been a debate about whether resilience can be defined as the ability to rebound from a trauma or prolonged stressor (Bonanno, 2008; Fougere & Daffern, 2011; Masten et al., 1990). Proponents of this conceptualization argue that nobody is expected to maintain complete competence in the face of severe stressors, and thus resilience would be demonstrated by reduced symptomology or duration of impact (Fougere & Daffern, 2011). However, others argue that resilience and recovery are two separate constructs and that not all individuals experience a significant disruption or impact following a trauma or stressor; those individuals who are not significantly impacted by trauma would be considered the resilient individuals (Bonanno, 2008; Ozer, Best, Lipsey, & Weiss, 2003).

**Resilience as Overcoming the Odds** This conceptualization appears to be the most widely accepted and supported concept despite the fact that there is also debate in this area (Borum et al., 2000; Fougere & Daffern, 2011). Resilience as overcoming the odds is based on risk research and is used to identify individuals who flourish or do not develop a particular negative pattern of behavior or disorder despite being at high risk. An example of a resilient child is one who is at high risk for developing or exhibiting symptoms of a particular disorder based on having a number of identified risk factors but ultimately does not develop or exhibit that disorder. Those who oppose this conceptualization argue that often there are too many confounding factors to fully assess what is contributing to someone not exhibiting a particular behavioral pattern or disorder, and so resilience in this way cannot be fully defined or validated (Olsson, Bond, Burns, Vella-Brodrick, & Sawyer, 2003).

Ultimately, there are many different ways that resilience has been defined and conceptualized, most of which demonstrate a great deal of overlap. However, there still does not always appear to be a clear consensus and standard definition of resilience. It does seem that most agree that resilience includes certain individual personality characteristics, such as high self-efficacy, good social and communication skills, and perseverance, as well as the presence of supportive familial relationships and social environments, including familial factors (Fougere & Daffern, 2011). The Resilience and Healthy Aging Network examined over 250 articles in the resilience literature and settled on the definition of resilience as the process of negotiating, managing, and adapting to significant sources of stress or trauma (Windle, Bennett, & Noyes, 2011). Assets and resources within the individual, their life, and their environment facilitate this capacity for adaptation and "bouncing back" in the face of adversity (Windle et al., 2011).

Despite there still being a lack of clear consensus regarding the conceptualization and definition of resilience, there have been significant longitudinal studies that have examined resilience, protective factors, and positive youth development which have helped to more clearly identify key aspects of resilience research. The Kauai Longitudinal Study helped identify protective factors across the lifespan that differentiated the resilient from the non-resilient individuals (Werner & Smith, 1992, 2001). These included protective factors within the individual, such as good temperament, problem-solving skills, and greater feelings of self-efficacy; protective factors within the family, including a stable, supportive caregiver and a safe and structured living environment; and protective factors within the community, such as prosocial peer and mentor relationships and prosocial activities (Werner & Smith, 2001). Additionally, the National Research Council and Institute of Medicine (2002) identified personal and social assets that promote positive youth development. These included good health habits that strengthen physical development, critical thinking and problem-solving skills that promote intellectual development, healthy coping and self-regulation skills that promote emotional development, and connectedness which strengthens social development. All of these protective factors can be identified, developed, and strengthened in youths to promote positive development and increase resilience.

## Protective Factors

Protective factors, such as the ones described in the previous section, are individual and situational components or aspects that contribute to the decreased likelihood of engaging in a negative or problematic behavior by having either a direct countering effect on the behavior or by moderating the relationship between the behavior and risk factors (Fougere & Daffern, 2011). Research and practical applications have shown that risk factors, such as exposure to early childhood trauma, are really just one component in the overall picture of an individual; it is also necessary to examine and assess protective factors relevant to the youth. This is highlighted in the research on juvenile offenders. Moffitt, Caspi, Harrington, and Milne (2002) seminal research revealed that juvenile offenders can typically be separated into two main groups: (1) those who engage in normative adolescent criminal behavior but who stop offending as they approach adulthood (adolescent-limited offenders) and (2) those who exhibit behavioral problems beginning in childhood and who offend into adulthood (life-course-persistent offenders). Following the establishment of this conceptualization of juvenile offenders, ancillary research began examining how both risk factors *and* protective factors were playing a role in whether a youth continued or ceased offending behaviors. This is highlighted in the creation and utilization of risk assessment tools that specifically involve protective factors, including resilience, to be assessed by the evaluator, such as the SAVRY and the SAPROF-YV.

Research has established the significance of protective factors in violence risk assessment (Carr & Vandiver, 2001; Fougere & Daffern, 2011). One study has demonstrated that with young offenders in the USA, several protective factors were found to significantly distinguish non-repeat from repeat offenders (Carr & Vandiver, 2001). These protective factors included personal characteristics such as high self-esteem and good temperament, structured home environment, parental support, presence of positive adult role models, and prosocial peers, hobbies, and activities.

The SAVRY was the first youth-specific risk assessment tool to incorporate protective factors into the overall judgment of risk, and it includes the following areas: prosocial involvement, strong social support, strong attachments and bonds, positive attitude toward intervention and authority, strong commitment to school, and resilient personality traits. The manual describes markers of resilient traits as "above average intellectual ability and cognitive skills,… ability to develop thoughtful solutions to conflicts and problems, positive responsiveness to others, adaptability to environmental change, capacity to self-soothe or to be soothed by others after a stressful or tension-generating event, calm mood states, and healthy and realistic self-esteem" (Borum et al., 2000, p. 103). It should be noted that the definition provided in the manual is considered to be quite broad, which means that it is likely that individuals with many different characteristics and presentations may receive an endorsement on this factor (Fougere & Daffern, 2011).

The SAPROF-YV is a more recent measure of protective factors, modeled after the well-established adult version (SAPROF; de Vogel, Ruiter, Bouman, & Vries Robbe, 2009), and is meant to be used in conjunction with a risk assessment-specific tool, such as the SAVRY. The measure is comprised of 16 protective factors within four different domains. The first domain encompasses resilience and consists of individual internal factors including social competence, coping, self-control, and perseverance. The second domain is the motivational domain, which is focused on the adolescent's motivation to actively participate in treatment (i.e., future orientation, motivation for treatment, attitude toward agreements and conditions, medication, school/work, and leisure activities). The third is the relation domain, which examines prosocial and supportive relationships (i.e., parents/guardians, peers, and other supportive relationships). The fourth and final domain is the external domain, which focused on external environmental or circumstantial factors (i.e., pedagogical climate, professional care, and court order). Utilizing risk assessment measures that account for protective factors will help professionals conceptualize a client from a resiliency lens.

## *Assessment of Resilience*

Given the significant challenges in conceptualizing and defining resilience, there have been similar issues in developing and implementing a measure to specifically assess for resilience. While there have been a number of tools that have been developed, they are not widely accepted and there does not appear to be one that is more widely used or validated than the others (Ahern, Kiehl, Sole, & Byers, 2006; Windle et al., 2011). The *Resilience Scale* (Wagnild & Young, 1993) was the first instrument designed to specifically measure resilience. It examined factors such as self-efficacy, faith, coping, and perseverance, which have all been associated with resilience. Since then, there have been several different scales and tools that have been developed to measure resilience: some very short, some long, some specific to young children, and some for adolescents. However, a methodological review of 15 different resilience measurement scales in 2011 found that there was no "gold standard" for a resilience measure, and several of those available had questionable psychometric ratings (Windle et al., 2011). Of those included in the review, the *Connor–Davidson Resilience Scale* (CD-RISC; Connor & Davidson, 2003) demonstrated the strongest psychometric properties for tools used with youth. The CD-RISC is a 25-item scale based on the concept of resilience as a measure of coping ability (Fougere & Daffern, 2011), and while originally normed on an adult sample, it has been used with children and adolescents. Other empirically based tools for the measurement of resilience include the *Devereux Early Childhood Assessment* (DECA; LeBuffe & Naglieri, 1999) and the *Resilience Scale for Children and Adolescents* (RSCA; Prince-Embury, 2007). In 2006, Southern Kennebec Healthy Start in Augusta, Maine, also developed a popular 14-item research-informed Resilience Questionnaire that was modeled after the ACE Questionnaire and was meant to be used to educate parents, not conduct research (https://acestoohigh.com/got-your-ace-score/, n.d.). However, it can be used as a helpful screening tool to identify whether protective factors associated with resilience are present, such as a supportive family and/or environment.

In addition to the scales and questionnaires noted earlier, there are also interesting and innovative tools being used across the USA, such as the *Child and Adolescent Needs and Strengths* (CANS) open domain tool (Lyons, 2009). It is a multipurpose tool developed for children's services to "support decision making, including level of care and service planning, to facilitate quality improvement initiatives, and to allow for the monitoring of outcomes of services" (www.praedfoundation.org/tools, n.d.). Versions of the CANS are being used in all 50 states in child welfare, mental health, juvenile justice, and early intervention applications, and it is described by service providers as having dramatic impacts on the service system where it has been utilized (Lyons, 2009).

## *Practical Applications of Resilience*

While few empirical studies have been conducted that specifically examine resilience in youth offender populations, it is clear that it is an important concept to be assessing for and emphasizing when working with this group. Moffitt et al.' (2002) adolescent-limited group was found to have several resilient characteristics such as good temperament, parental support, and high intellectual functioning, which likely contributed to the decrease in offending behaviors. Conversely, life-course-persistent offenders were found to have traits not consistent with resilience, such as difficult temperament, neurological abnormalities, and low intellectual functioning (Fougere & Daffern, 2011; Moffitt et al., 2002). Given this reasoning, it is important for evaluators and providers to identify protective factors in the youth's life with whom they are working in order to promote resiliency within that youth to ultimately decrease the likelihood of re-offending. Further, it is also known that youths being evaluated within the dependency system also require a unique approach to assessment, as there is a high probability that those particular youths do not have strong parental support. Therefore, other protective factors need to be assessed and then emphasized in intervention programs in order to build resilience. Studies have demonstrated that stronger resilience factors in youths transitioning out of the foster care system were correlated with better outcomes after transition (Daining & DePanfilis, 2007). As such, it is crucial to intervene with these youths as early as possible to develop and strengthen protective factors.

## *Assessing for Trauma and Resilience in Forensic Practice*

In forensic work, there are often different referral sources and referral questions that an evaluator is asked to assess and opine on when working with youths. As we are working toward becoming more trauma-informed across the USA, we are seeing certain jurisdictions beginning to implement changes to their procedures to specifically assess for childhood trauma, ACEs, and protective factors associated with resilience. In San Diego County, for example, where the authors of this chapter are located, both the juvenile justice and juvenile dependency systems have taken a trauma-informed approach. The county referral sources, such as juvenile probation or CWS, are specifically asking evaluators to assess for exposure to trauma, the impact of trauma, and protective factors that can be utilized and strengthened in the youth. Similarly, they require providers to use trauma-specific measures in their evaluations, such as the Trauma Symptom Checklist for Children (TSCC; Briere, 1996).

As evidenced by the preceding, evaluating for trauma and resilience in youths is critical. Thus, even if the jurisdiction of practice does not specifically require an assessment of those factors, it is recommended that all evaluators working with youths, particularly in a forensic context, conduct preliminary screenings to ideally be able to more comprehensively evaluate these factors when possible. A screening can be as simple as building in preliminary questions into a standard clinical interview about trauma exposure (such as "Has your family or child experienced any of the following major stressful events...?") or administering more formal screening tools such as the ACE Questionnaire. In a forensic context, it is recommended to conduct both to gain a thorough assessment and to allow the youth multiple opportunities in different contexts to endorse traumatic events or stressors. It is also pivotal when including screening questions in the interview to make sure that the questions are being asked after having built an appropriate level of rapport and in a developmentally appropriate manner. This will help a child who may be more guarded in their disclosures or more concrete in their comprehension to answer the questions (e.g., instead of asking "Have you ever been physically abused?," ask "Has anyone ever hit you or hurt you anywhere on your body?"). It is also very important to obtain as much collateral information as possible in these assessments to gather as many different sources of information as possible.

Once trauma exposure has been assessed, then it is essential to assess for the potential impact of the trauma. This can be accomplished by using trauma-specific tests, such as the TSCC, as well as with other symptomology measures that have indicators for other presentations such as depression or anxiety. Lastly, it is recommended when communicating the findings to the court or other referral sources that psychoeducation is provided on the impact of trauma from a developmental, emotional, and biological perspective, so that they are able to understand and hopefully appreciate the context of the youth's behavior.

Similarly, it is highly recommended that providers not only assess for risk factors (such as trauma or adverse experiences) but also screen for and more thoroughly assess for protective factors and resilience. This will give the referral source a more comprehensive perspective of the youth, and it will better guide intervention recommendations for the youth. Again, this can be done through a combination of interview questions assessing the youth's strengths and available supports in his or her life and specific resilience tools as described in earlier on assessment.

Presently, there is evidence that treatment interventions can strengthen resilience in youths (Arnetz, Nevedal, Lumley, Backman, & Lublin, 2008; Chmitorz et al., 2018; Fougere & Daffern, 2011; Hayman, 2009). While the programs vary in content and structure, and can encompass diverse areas, they typically include strategies for effective coping, emotion regulation, social skills, and strengthening self-efficacy (Chmitorz et al., 2018; Steinhardt & Dolbier, 2008). It is important for evaluators to be aware of various resilience-enhancing intervention strategies that can be recommended or used depending on the specific needs of the youth.

## Case Examples

When working with youths who have interacted with the legal system, understanding their ACE scores assists with framing complex histories of childhood adversity within a clear, empirically based format. It gathers information to glean how life circumstances have impacted the youth and presents illustrative anecdotes. The ACE score and related diagnoses assist with summarizing the youth's life and creating a more robust picture for prognosis and proper interventions. Explaining and presenting the ACEs and resiliency findings in combination with relevant and recent research assists judges and juries to understand behaviors in the developmental context. In the following section are two examples of how to apply the ACE Questionnaire and Resiliency Questionnaire in the context of forensically involved youths.

### *Civil Case Example: Victimization and Recommendations for Future Care Needs*

Susan was referred for a psychological evaluation by her attorney to assess her current psychological functioning and the potential impact from the rape she experienced. To gather information on her functioning, multiple measures were given in the domains of personality, trauma, and protective factors (i.e., resiliency). In reviewing the assessment results and supporting documents, Susan's current experiences and overall psychological functioning suggest impairment due to the multiple traumatic experiences she has had with sexual abuse. The overall experience has impaired her ability to achieve a healthy sense of self and negatively impacts her relationships. The traumatic event has caused ongoing distress within her personal life and her ability to establish healthy interpersonal and romantic relationships. This has led her to internalize problematic symptomology such as hopelessness, overwhelming feelings of sadness, somatic problems, and impulsivity. Her impaired view of herself appears to have developed from many years of sexual anxiety and an inability to understand the fundamentals of healthy sexual relationships. Furthermore, it is likely that increased depression and trauma symptoms and a lack of self-confidence stem from her experiences of being invalidated by authorities and close friends that she had once entrusted to protect her. This has resulted in thoughts of confusion, uncertainty, and a poor sense of self which she struggles to disconnect from day-to-day experiences.

### Adverse Childhood Experience (ACE) Questionnaire Outcome

Susan had a score of one, which is reflective of her experiencing sexual abuse as a child. This score is not unusual for a child, but the experience is.

### Resilience Questionnaire Outcome

The Resilience Questionnaire is a 14-item self-report measure to determine an individual's capacity to adapt positively to pressures, setbacks, challenges, and changes to achieve and sustain peak personal effectiveness. The questionnaire asks the respondent to indicate the most accurate answer using a scale from definitely true to definitely not true during childhood and then at the present time in case additional protective factors were obtained.

Susan endorsed answers mostly in the direction of resiliency, specifically when relating to having support from family. However, it appears that this perception of support wanes when it comes to relying on youth leaders and teachers. In addition, she endorsed not having someone she trusts to talk to when she feels bad. Thus, she may not have a sufficient peer or other support network.

### Application

As a result of her trauma from the sexual assault, she will continue to need ongoing therapy and psychotropic medication to address her present depression and trauma symptoms. In addition, individual therapy is recommended to assist her with building a healthy self-concept and a stronger foundation to enhance positive interpersonal relationships. Also, Susan has an extensive medical history and severe stress can exacerbate some of her somatic complaints. Individual therapy will also provide coping skills to manage present and future developmental stressors. Furthermore, relationship counseling is recommended based upon current stressors in her romantic relationships that if not properly addressed will resurface in future relationships. Lastly, although presently her resiliency score is slightly higher than her ACE score, ongoing treatment at various developmental milestones would be beneficial for Susan's prognosis.

## *Juvenile Delinquency Case Example: Sentencing*

Michael was referred for an evaluation by his attorney to assess psychological functioning and risk for sexual offending. To gather information on his functioning, multiple measures were given in the domains of personality, trauma, risk (SAVRY and JSORRAT-II), and protective factors (i.e., resiliency). Based on the outcome of those measures, there are significant concerns regarding his psychological functioning, particularly his suicidal thoughts and behaviors (i.e., written notes about killing himself). In addition, there is low to mild concern about the potential for Michael to sexually offend. Research indicates some characteristics of male juvenile sexual offenders include negative emotional states, such as loneliness, anger, hostility, and an anxious-ambivalent attachment with their primary caregiver. On the measures, Michael endorsed feelings of loneliness, anger, and an insecure attachment style with his mother due to statements she has made since the surfacing of these allegations.

### Adverse Childhood Experience (ACE) Questionnaire Outcome

Michael's overall ACE score was seven. He indicated his parents were separated, he witnessed his mother being physically abused, he lived with an alcoholic, he lived with a depressed or mentally ill family member, he was threatened or insulted by children, he felt lonely or rejected, and for a period of 2 years or more his family was very poor or on public assistance. His score indicates he may be at an increased risk for later life illness, disease, and a variety of social, behavioral, and emotional problems.

### Resilience Questionnaire Outcome

The Resilience Questionnaire is a 14-item self-report measure to determine an individual's capacity to adapt positively to pressures, setbacks, challenges, and changes and to achieve and sustain peak personal effectiveness. The questionnaire asks the respondent to indicate the most accurate answer using a scale from definitely true to definitely not true during childhood and then at the present time in case additional protective factors were obtained.

Michael endorsed 13 items in the direction of resiliency (in the categories of "definitely true or probably true"). He indicated 6 of the 13 items were still true for him at the time of the evaluation. Some of these items included the belief that when he was little his mother, father, and others cared for him and took part in caring for him. Also, as an infant, someone in his family enjoyed playing with him, and as a child he had relatives in his family who made him feel better if he was sad or worried. He endorsed others in his community seemed to like him and assisted in helping him or offered to assist in improving his life. He also endorsed family members care about his schooling and have rules in his house which he was expected to keep. Michael endorsed having someone to talk to when he felt bad and having teachers, coaches, youth leaders, or ministers available to help him. Michael reported that others noticed he was capable of accomplishing things in his life and he self-identified as a go-getter. He noted that his family, neighbors, and friends talked about making their lives better. He reported he was not sure if life is what you make it.

**Application**

Since Michael has a high risk of committing suicide, it is recommended that he be treated in an inpatient hospital setting. If not and he is committed to a locked facility that is not treatment focused, he will be at higher risk for suicide. In addition, individual psychotherapy with a focus on safety planning, family therapy to rebuild his relationship with his mother, and individual psychotherapy is recommended. The individual psychotherapy should focus on appropriate boundaries and healthy sexual practices. It may be beneficial if the individual psychotherapy is trauma-informed and is based in cognitive behavioral therapy to explore his trauma-related symptoms and the domestic violence he witnessed. Further, it would be critical to explore other possible factors that may be affecting him, particularly since he has a vulnerability due to his mother' and father's histories. Moreover, it is critical that his depressive symptomology is targeted, and a safety plan is implemented due to his risk for suicide. Lastly, although presently his resiliency score is balanced with his ACE score, family therapy may be beneficial for Michael's prognosis and to strengthen his resiliency factors.

# Conclusion

This chapter provided an overview of two key issues when working with youths involved in the legal system: trauma and resilience. As the state of the field is moving toward a much greater recognition of the impact of early childhood trauma and adverse childhood experiences, the importance of identifying and strengthening resilience factors has become more prevalent with both researchers and practitioners. The goal of this chapter was to provide practical applications of the knowledge that has been gained in these key areas in order to educate and support practitioners who are making an impact in the lives of the youths with whom they work. While there is currently no definitive consensus as to the definition of resilience and no "gold standard" instrument to use to assess resilience in youths, there is a great deal of research outlined in this chapter examining the various protective factors within the individual, family, and community that practitioners can use to strengthen intervention strategies with youths within the legal system.

# Questions/Activities for Further Exploration

1. What health or social issue you learned from the research that you were surprised tied back to ACEs and other toxic stressors?
2. How can we better understand negative behaviors exhibited by youth when we look at the biological and emotional impact of childhood trauma? How do we ask the question "What happened to you?" instead of "What's wrong with you?"
3. Based on what you learned in this chapter, what are your thoughts about zero-tolerance policies for "bad behavior" in schools or youth-serving organizations?
4. What are specific interventions that can be used with youths to help them better understand and regulate their trauma responses?
5. What are some of the most important resilience factors that can be fostered and strengthened in youths involved in the juvenile justice system?
6. How can professionals working with youths better understand how the adult's role, words, or behaviors may be triggering or re-traumatizing? How can you as a professional transition to a trauma-focused lens in the work that you do?

# References

Ahern, N. R., Kiehl, E. M., Sole, M. L., & Byers, J. (2006). A review of instruments measuring resilience. *Issues in Comprehensive Pediatric Nursing, 29*(2), 103–125. https://doi.org/10.1080/01460860600677643

Arnetz, B. B., Nevedal, D. C., Lumley, M. A., Backman, L., & Lublin, A. (2008). Trauma resilience training for police: Psychophysiological and performance effects. *Journal of Police and Criminal Psychology, 24*(1), 1–9. https://doi.org/10.1007/s11896-008-9030-y

Bonanno, G. A. (2008). Loss, trauma, and human resilience: Have we underestimated the human capacity to thrive after extremely aversive events? *Psychological Trauma: Theory, Research, Practice, and Policy, 59*(1), 101–113. https://doi.org/10.1037/1942-9681.s.1.101

Bonanno, G. A., & Diminich, E. D. (2012). Annual research review: Positive adjustment to adversity – Trajectories of minimal-impact resilience and emergent resilience. *Journal of Child Psychology and Psychiatry, 54*(4), 378–401. https://doi.org/10.1111/jcpp.12021

Borum, R., Bartel, P., & Forth, A. (2000). *Manual for the structured assessment of violence risk in youth.* Tampa, FL: University of South Florida.

Briere, J. (1996). *Trauma symptom checklist for children (TSCC) professional manual.* Odessa, FL: Psychological Assessment Resources.

Brown, D. W., Anda, R. F., Tiemeier, H., Felitti, V. J., Edwards, V. J., Croft, J. B., & Giles, W. H. (2009). Adverse childhood experiences and the risk of premature mortality. *American Journal of Preventive Medicine, 37*(5), 389–396. https://doi.org/10.1016/j.amepre.2009.06.021

Bruskas, D. (2013). Adverse childhood experiences and psychosocial well-being of women who were in foster care as children. *The Permanente Journal, 17*(3), e131. https://doi.org/10.7812/tpp/12-121

Carr, M., & Vandiver, T. (2001). Risk and protective factors among youth offenders. *Adolescence, 36*(143), 409–426.

Carswell, K., Maughan, B., Davis, H., Davenport, F., & Goddard, N. (2004). The psychosocial needs of young offenders and adolescents from an inner city area. *Journal of Adolescence, 27*(4), 415–428. https://doi.org/10.1016/j.adolescence.2004.04.003

Chitsabesan, P., & Bailey, S. (2006). Mental health, educational and social needs of young offend-ers in custody and in the community. *Current Opinion in Psychiatry, 19*(4), 355–360. https://doi.org/10.1097/01.yco.0000228753.87613.01

Chmitorz, A., Kunzler, A., Helmreich, I., Tüscher, O., Kalisch, R., Kubiak, T., … Lieb, K. (2018). Intervention studies to foster resilience – A systematic review and proposal for a resilience framework in future intervention studies. *Clinical Psychology Review, 59*, 78–100. https://doi.org/10.1016/j.cpr.2017.11.002

Conner, B. T., & Lochman, J. E. (2010). Comorbid conduct disorder and substance use disorders. *Clinical Psychology: Science and Practice, 17*(4), 337–349. https://doi.org/10.1111/j.1468-2850.2010.01225.x

Connor, K. M., & Davidson, J. R. (2003). Development of a new resilience scale: The Connor-Davidson Resilience Scale (CD-RISC). *Depression and Anxiety, 18*(2), 76–82. https://doi.org/10.1002/da.10113

Connor, K. M., Davidson, J. R., & Lee, L. (2003). Spirituality, resilience, and anger in survivors of violent trauma: A community survey. *Journal of Traumatic Stress, 16*(5), 487–494. https://doi.org/10.1023/a:1025762512279

Daining, C., & Depanfilis, D. (2007). Resilience of youth in transition from out-of-home care to adulthood. *Children and Youth Services Review, 29*(9), 1158–1178. https://doi.org/10.1016/j.childyouth.2007.04.006

Davey, M., Eaker, D. G., & Walters, L. H. (2003). Resilience processes in adolescents: Personality profiles, self-worth, and coping. *Journal of Adolescent Research, 18*(4), 347–362. https://doi.org/10.1177/0743558403018004002

de Vogel, V., Ruiter, C., Bouman, Y., & Vries Robbe, M. (2009). *SAPROF. Guidelines for the assessment of protective factors for violence risk. English version*. Utrecht, The Netherlands: Forum Educatief.

de Vries Robbe, Å. L., Geers, M., Stapel, M., Hilterman, E., & Vogel, V. (2015). *SAPROF-YV: Guidelines for the assessment of protective factors for violence risk in youth. Youth version*. Utrecht, The Netherlands: Van der Doeven Kliniek.

Dierkhising, C., Ko, S., Briggs, E., Lee, R., & Pynoos, R. (2012). Trauma histories of youth involved in the Juvenile justice system findings from the NCTSN core data set. *PsycEXTRA Dataset*. https://doi.org/10.1037/e533652013-207

Dube, S. R., Miller, J. W., Brown, D. W., Giles, W. H., Felitti, V. J., Dong, M., & Anda, R. F. (2006). Adverse childhood experiences and the association with ever using alcohol and initiat-ing alcohol use during adolescence. *Journal of Adolescent Health, 38*(4), 444.e1. https://doi.org/10.1016/j.jadohealth.2005.06.006

Duke, N. N., Pettingell, S. L., McMorris, B. J., & Borowsky, I. W. (2010). Adolescent violence perpetration: Association with multiple types of adverse childhood experiences. *Pediatrics, 125*(4), 778–786. https://doi.org/10.1542/peds.2009-0597

Felitti, V. J. (2002). [The relationship of adverse childhood experiences to adult health: Turning gold into lead.] *Zeitschrift fuer Psychosomatische Medizin und Psychotherapie, 48*(4), 359–369.

Felitti, V. J., Anda, R. F., Nordenberg, D., Williamson, D. F., Spitz, A. M., Edwards, V., … Marks, J. S. (1998). Relationship of childhood abuse and household dysfunction to many of the leading causes of death in adults: The Adverse Childhood Experiences (ACE) Study. *American Journal of Preventive Medicine, 14*(4), 245–258.

Fougere, A., & Daffern, M. (2011). Resilience in young offenders. *International Journal of Forensic Mental Health, 10*(3), 244–253. https://doi.org/10.1080/14999013.2011.598602

Groer, M., Kostas-Polston, E., Dillahunt-Aspilliga, C., Johnson-Mallard, V., & Duffy, A. (2014). 23. Allostatic associations in women veterans with histories of childhood sexual assault. *Brain, Behavior, and Immunity, 40*, e7. https://doi.org/10.1016/j.bbi.2014.06.04

Hayman, F. M. (2009). Kids with confidence: A program for adolescents living in families affected by mental illness. *Australian Journal of Rural Health, 17*(5), 268–272. https://doi.org/10.1111/j.1440-1584.2009.01090.x

Hu, T., Zhang, D., & Wang, J. (2015). A meta-analysis of the trait resilience and mental health. *Personality and Individual Differences, 76*, 18–27. https://doi.org/10.1016/j.paid.2014.11.039

Kalisch, R., Baker, D. G., Basten, U., Boks, M. P., Bonanno, G. A., Brummelman, E., … Kleim, B. (2017). The resilience framework as a strategy to combat stress-related disorders. *Nature Human Behaviour, 1*(11), 784–790. https://doi.org/10.1038/s41562-017-0200-8

Kalisch, R., Müller, M. B., & Tüscher, O. (2014). A conceptual framework for the neurobiological study of resilience. *Behavioral and Brain Sciences, 38*(92), 1–49. https://doi.org/10.1017/s0140525x1400082x

Katisiyannis, A., Ryan, J., Zhang, D., & Spann, A. (2008). Juvenile delinquency and recidivism: The impact of academic achievement. *Reading & Writing Quarterly, 24*(2), 177–196.

LeBuffe, P. A., & Naglieri, J. A. (1999). *Devereux early childhood assessment user's guide.* Lewisville, NC: Kaplan Press.

Lyons, J. S. (2009). *Communimetrics: A theory of measurement for human service enterprises.* New York, NY: Springer.

Mash, E. J., & Barkley, R. A. (2014). *Child psychopathology* (3rd ed.). New York, NY: The Guilford Press. ISBN. ISBN:978-1-4625-1668-1.

Masten, A. S., Best, K. M., & Garmezy, N. (1990). Resilience and development: Contributions from the study of children who overcome adversity. *Development and Psychopathology, 2*(04), 425–456. https://doi.org/10.1017/s0954579400005812

Mcclelland, G. M., Elkington, K. S., Teplin, L. A., & Abram, K. M. (2004). Multiple substance use disorders in juvenile detainees. *Journal of the American Academy of Child & Adolescent Psychiatry, 43*(10), 1215–1224. https://doi.org/10.1097/01.chi.0000134489.58054.9c

Moffitt, T. E., Caspi, A., Harrington, H., & Milne, B. J. (2002). Males on the life-course-persistent and adolescence-limited antisocial pathways: Follow-up at age 26 years. *Development and Psychopathology, 14*(1), 179–207. https://doi.org/10.1017/s0954579402001104

National Research Council and Institute of Medicine. (2002). *Community programs to promote youth development.* Washington, D.C.: The National Academies Press. https://doi.org/10.17226/10022

Office of Juvenile Justice and Delinquency Prevention. (2017). *OJJDP statistical briefing book.* Online. Available: https://www.ojjdp.gov/ojstatbb/crime/qa05101.asp?qaDate=2017. Released on 22 Oct 2018.

Olsson, C. A., Bond, L., Burns, J. M., Vella-Brodrick, D. A., & Sawyer, S. M. (2003). Adolescent resilience: A concept analysis. *Journal of Adolescence, 26*(1), 1–11. https://doi.org/10.1016/s0140-1971(02)00118-5

Ong, A. D., Bergeman, C. S., Bisconti, T. L., & Wallace, K. A. (2006). Psychological resilience, positive emotions, and successful adaptation to stress in later life. *Journal of Personality and Social Psychology, 91*(4), 730–749. https://doi.org/10.1037/0022-3514.91.4.730

Ozer, E. J., Best, S. R., Lipsey, T. L., & Weiss, D. S. (2003). Predictors of posttraumatic stress disorder and symptoms in adults: A meta-analysis. *Psychological Bulletin, 129*(1), 52–73. https://doi.org/10.1037//0033-2909.129.1.52

Prince-Embury, S. (2007, 2006). *Resiliency scales for children and adolescents: A profile of personal strengths.* San Antonio, TX: Harcourt Assessment, Inc.

Putnam, F. W., Harris, W., Lieberman, A., Putnam, K., & Amaya-Jackson, L. (2015). Childhood adversity narratives. Retrieved from http://www.canarratives.org

Southwick, S., & Charney, D. (2012). *Resilience: The science of mastering life's greatest challenges.* Cambridge: Cambridge University Press.

Steinhardt, M., & Dolbier, C. (2008). Evaluation of a resilience intervention to enhance coping strategies and protective factors and decrease symptomology. *Journal of American College Health, 56*(4), 445–453.

U.S. Department of Health and Human Services, Administration for Children and Administration on Children, Youth and Families, Children's Bureau. (2018). *Adoption and Foster Care Analysis and Reporting System (AFCARS).*

Van den Bergh, B. R. H., van den Heuvel, M. I., Lahti, M., Braeken, M., de Rooij, S. R., Entringer, S., ... Schwab, M. (2017). Prenatal developmental origins of behavior and mental health: The influence of maternal stress in pregnancy. *Neuroscience and Biobehavioral Reviews*. https://doi.org/10.1016/j.neurobiorev.2017.07.003

Van der Kolk, B. A., Roth, S., Pelcovitz, D., Sunday, S., & Spinazzola, J. (2005). Disorders of extreme stress: The empirical foundation of a complex adaptation to trauma. *Journal of Traumatic Stress, 18*(5), 389–399. https://doi.org/10.1002/jts.20047

Wagnild, W., & Young, H. (1993). Development and psychometric evaluation of the resilience scale. *Journal of Nursing Measurement, 1*, 165–178.

Werner, E. E., & Smith, R. S. (1992). *Overcoming the odds: High-risk children from birth to adulthood*. Ithaca, NY: Cornell University Press.

Werner, E. E., & Smith, R. S. (2001). *Journeys from childhood to midlife: Risk, resilience and recovery*. Ithaca, NY: Cornell University Press.

Windle, G., Bennett, K. M., & Noyes, J. (2011). A methodological review of resilience measurement scales. *Health and Quality of Life Outcomes, 9*(1), 8. https://doi.org/10.1186/1477-7525-9-8

Yehuda, R., & Meaney, M. (2018). Relevance of psychological symptoms in pregnancy to intergenerational effects of preconception trauma. *Biological Psychiatry, 83*, 94–96. https://doi.org/10.1016/j.biopsych.2017.10.027

# Chapter 19
# Trauma in Specialized Treatment Diversion – Problem-Solving Court Contexts (PSCs)

Raina V. Lamade and Rachel M. Lee

## Introduction

The majority of treatment diversion occurs through problem-solving courts (PSCs): specialized courts with dedicated dockets to address a type of offense (e.g., drug court) or the needs of a special population (e.g., veterans) (National Institute of Justice, 2018). They initially developed as an atheoretical (Winick, 2003) response to overwhelmed state courts (Berman & Feinblatt, 2001) aimed at improving the speed and efficiency of processing cases (Lurigio, 2008) while diverting defendants from jail (Acquaviva, 2006). Trauma within the population of PSC defendants/clients should be considered from three broad categories: firstly, existing trauma that is prevalent in this population; secondly, the prevention of potential trauma through successful completion that allows incarceration and the subsequent consequences of criminal convictions to be avoided; finally, engagement in PSCs which can provide this population with resources and services that can promote mental health and well-being (recovery from trauma), and decreased recidivism, all of which can decrease the likelihood of future exposure to potentially traumatic experiences.

### History and Development

Cook County Juvenile Court, formed in 1899, was the precursor to PSCs (Winick, 2003). The first formal, specialized court, or PSC, was a drug treatment court, established in the Eleventh Judicial Circuit in Dade County, Miami, in 1989, with the

R. V. Lamade
University of Massachusetts Dartmouth, North Dartmouth, MA, USA
e-mail: rlamade@umassd.edu

R. M. Lee (✉)
Hunter College, CUNY, Private Practice, New York, NY, USA

© Springer Nature Switzerland AG 2020                        463
R. A. Javier et al. (eds.), *Assessing Trauma in Forensic Contexts*,
https://doi.org/10.1007/978-3-030-33106-1_19

goal of addressing the burgeoning number of drug-related offenses in the criminal justice system (Goldkamp & Weiland, 1993) in the context of the crack epidemic (Landess & Holoyda, 2017). Commonly referred to as the "Miami Drug Court Model," this court was a vast departure from the dominant philosophies of deterrence, incapacitation, and punishment that governed drug-related offenders (Goldkamp & Weiland, 1993) and instead emphasized rehabilitation (Winick, 2003). It was based on the premise that the demand for illicit drugs and resulting criminal involvement could be "reduced through an effective and flexible program of court supervised drug treatment" (Goldkamp & Weiland, 1993, p. 2). DTCs emphasize rehabilitation (Winick, 2003) within an abstinence model that utilizes regular drug testing and judicial compliance monitoring (Roll, Prendergast, Richardson, Burdon, & Ramirez, 2005). Goldkamp and Weiland (1993) identified two distinguishing features of this PSC: a courtroom-based team approach and the central role of the judge, which have continued to be core features of subsequent PSCs. Initial results were promising; they demonstrated that those involved in the Dade County Drug treatment court had fewer rearrests compared to nondrug court defendants (Goldkamp & Weiland, 1993).

Mental health treatment courts (MHCs) were the next type of PSC to develop in the late 1990s (Bureau of Justice Assistance, 2008) "to divert defendants with psychiatric disorders out of the criminal justice system" (Barber-Rioja & Rotter, 2014, p. 272). The first MHCs were founded in Marion County, Indiana, and Broward County, Florida, in 1997 (Redlich, Steadman, Monahan, Robbins, & Petrila, 2006) and developed out of frustration with the "revolving door" of mentally ill individuals within the criminal justice system (Acquaviva, 2006; Wiener, Winick, Georges, & Castro, 2010). MHCs like veterans courts tend to be more understanding of relapses in behavior, provide more chances, adjust treatment plans, use incentives, and use jail less frequently as a sanction (Hiday, Ray, & Wales, 2014). Redlich et al. (2006) identified the following six common features of MHC. They are (1) voluntary, (2) criminal courts with distinct dockets for individuals with mental illness that (3) share a goal of diverting individuals from the criminal justice system into the community, (4) mandate various treatment conditions (e.g., community mental health, prescription medications), (5) provide continuing supervision, and (6) typically offer praise and encouragement for compliance and impose sanctions (most use jail) when individuals are noncompliant (Redlich et al., 2006). Acquaviva (2006) identified three key components of the MHC model. First, MHCs use a multidisciplinary approach to treat the underlying cause of the offender's criminal conduct, that is, mental illness, and therefore the focus is on therapeutic intervention and not prosecution. Second, MHCs are framed within the doctrine of therapeutic jurisprudence. Third, legal court personnel (i.e., judges, attorneys) have nontraditional roles. At the broadest level, MHCs improve individual and social outcomes, increase mental health functioning, and secondarily improve public safety and reduce recidivism (Acquaviva, 2006; Honegger, 2015). Many have argued that MHCs should address criminogenic needs and risk factors (Barber-Rioja, Dewey, Kopelovich, & Kucharski, 2012; Honegger, 2015; Kingston & Oliver, 2018) because of their relationship to noncompliance and recidivism.

Over the past 30 years, PSCs have proliferated in type (e.g., domestic violence, human trafficking courts) and number, with the two largest being mental health treatment and drug treatment courts (Strong, Rantala, & Kyckelhahn, 2016), and the rapidly emerging Veterans Courts (VTC). The first Veterans Courts were established in 2004 in Anchorage, Alaska, and in Buffalo, New York, by Judge Russell (Johnson, Stolar, Wu, Coonan, & Graham, 2015). In 2012, the Department of Justice identified 3052 problem-solving courts in operation in all 50 states, the District of Columbia, and US territories (Strong et al., 2016). In general, increases in PSCs are attributed to a surge in incarceration and, more specifically, a surge in quality-of-life crime (e.g., misdemeanor cases), breakdowns in social and community institutions, advances in therapeutic interventions, rising caseloads, and frustration with the standard court process in state courts (Berman & Feinblatt, 2001). Increases in drug treatment courts are likely to be impacted by the current opioid crisis. Increases in veteran's treatment courts are likely related to mental health problems, mostly post-traumatic stress disorder (PTSD) and substance abuse, from the protracted wars in Iraq (OIF Operation Iraqi Freedom) and Afghanistan (OEF Operation Enduring Freedom) that resulted in multiple and longer deployments with increased exposure to trauma and improvised explosive devices (IEDs) with potential traumatic brain injury (TBI) sequelae.

## *Therapeutic Jurisprudence as an Overarching Framework*

Around the time that PSCs were developing, the doctrine of therapeutic jurisprudence (Wexler, 1990; Wexler, 1992) was emerging. Therapeutic jurisprudence began in the late 1980s as an interdisciplinary approach (Winick, 2003) to studying the "role of the law as a therapeutic agent" and considers how the legal system can potentially help those involved (Wexler, 1992, p.32). It does not, however, suggest that therapeutic objectives trump other considerations such as the values of autonomy. As PSCs have evolved over time, they have been framed in the doctrine of therapeutic jurisprudence to provide an overarching goal/unified principle.

Porter, Rempel, and Mansky (2010) suggest two additional major paradigms of problem-solving courts. These include accountability (i.e., taking responsibility for one's crimes and actions) and community justice (i.e., restorative justice and increasing public trust in the justice system), which vary in degree depending on the type of PSC. For example, therapeutic jurisprudence is more commonly associated with drug and mental health treatment courts because the focus is treatment and rehabilitation, whereas domestic violence and sex offense courts are most commonly associated with the accountability paradigm. PSCs attempt to achieve better outcomes than traditional courts, including reducing recidivism while protecting individual rights (Berman & Feinblatt, 2001).

An example of therapeutic jurisprudence in this context is increased access to services and care (Boothyrod, Poythress, McGaha, & Petrila, 2003; Steadman & Naples, 2005) and decreased time spent in jail (Steadman & Naples, 2005).

For example, defendants in MHC reported more outpatient visits and received more individual counseling, more intense case management, and more varied treatment compared to the TAU sample (Luskin, 2013). At the six-month follow-up, MHC defendants received significantly more outpatient treatment services (Luskin, 2013). Cosden, Ellens, Schnell, and Yamini-Diouf (2005) found that both MHC and TAU groups showed improvements in psychosocial functioning that were maintained through the 24-month follow-up assessment. MHC participants, however, were found to have significantly greater improvements in quality of life, and greater reduction in drug and alcohol problems, and psychological distress.

## Goal and Core Features of PSC

Problem-solving courts allow individuals in the criminal justice system to receive services in the community while being monitored (managed) by the courts. Regardless of the type of problem-solving court, most offer ancillary services to assist with basic needs such as employment, job training, and stable housing (Porter et al., 2010). Addressing basic needs, particularly those that are associated with risk, or are known criminogenic needs, can also potentially reduce risk of future criminal activity. Depending on the court, specific treatment needs (e.g., intensive outpatient programs, drug treatment, individual/group counseling) are provided (Porter et al., 2010). Another benefit of PSCs is that participation could potentially allow for enhanced understanding of an individual's mental health, basic needs, and struggles. This information could serve as mitigating factors at sentencing during a future criminal case (AOPC, 2015).

The goals of problem-solving courts can be viewed from the perspective of the individual and the larger criminal justice population. At the individual level, the goal of a PSC is to offer an alternative to incarceration, to provide help for a particular problem(s), and to prevent reoccurrence (Honegger, 2015; Landess & Holoyda, 2017). As such, it therefore serves as both intervention and a tertiary prevention. It also helps preserve civil liberties by providing a less restrictive environment (i.e., treatment and management in the community as opposed to incarceration) (Porter et al., 2010). At the population level, the goal is to reduce the incarceration level by shifting a proportion of eligible individuals to management in the community where they can receive services. The United States has the world's largest prison population (World Prison Brief, n.d.) and advocates of programs that divert individuals away from incarceration cite humanitarian and economic benefits of diversion (AOPC, 2015).

Although PSCs are heterogenous and vary in policies and practices, Bullard and Thrasher (2016) identified core features of a judge-centered, non-adversarial process that includes treatment, judicial monitoring, and collaboration between the participant (defendant) and team. PSCs espouse a problem-solving orientation, which is led by the judge. It embraces a treatment-focused culture and team approach that emphasizes community (Porter et al., 2010; Winick, 2003). A problem-solving orientation typically refers to solving the underlying problems of the defendant.

Additionally, victims or the community are included to make restorative justice a possibility (Porter et al., 2010). The judge takes an unorthodox role that is non-adversarial and highly active, functioning as a supporter, an encourager, and an enforcer that applies sanctions (e.g., issuing bench warrants and brief jail confinements for motivation) when defendants are noncompliant with treatment (Goldkamp & Weiland, 1993). The judge attends meetings about defendants' treatment progress, listens to defendants' explanations about their noncompliance, and presides over graduation ceremonies (Goldkamp & Weiland, 1993). Interdisciplinary collaboration occurs between criminal justice personnel, such as judges, attorneys, and case managers (Goldkamp & Weiland, 1993). There is also collaboration between external service agencies and criminal justice personnel (Porter et al., 2010). It is common to have a mental health provider, case managers, administrative court staff, the judge, defense attorneys, and assistant district attorneys (ADAs) present at team meetings. This courtroom-based team approach includes active support from the prosecutor and public defender, who also adopt unorthodox roles (Goldkamp & Weiland, 1993). The team takes a non-adversarial role designed to support the judge's role and treatment progress. Defendants also observe the hearings of other defendants (Goldkamp & Weiland, 1993), which can facilitate a sense of community and enhance peer support.

## Criteria

Problem-solving courts generally have eligibility (inclusion) and exclusion criteria. Eligibility criteria typically include that the individual has a particular problem (e.g., mental health or drug addiction), or belongs to a particular group (e.g., veterans), or some combination thereof. For example, in mental health treatment court (MHC), the presence of mental illness is required, and courts will vary as to whether the presence of a serious mental illness (SMI) is required and how this is defined. Often times, in cases where the individual was chronically using a substance that mimics the effects of psychotic symptoms (e.g., chronic K2 use), a period of sobriety, drug treatment, and reevaluation will be recommended to determine/confirm the presence of a mental health disorder. More broadly speaking, both PSCs and diversion programs are usually specific in terms of the type(s) of charges they will take. For example, some PSCs are exclusive to misdemeanor charges; others may take felony charges, but not violent felonies. Other programs, like the Nathaniel Project, in New York City, examine the risk to the public, rather than an automatic exclusion on the basis of charge or history of violence (SAMHSA, 2002/2005). There can be multiple diversion and PSCs for a specific area within a catchment area. For example, within one location/jurisdiction, there may be multiple mental health diversion and MHCs that vary by level of mental health severity and, therefore, level of care (i.e., intensity of psychiatric treatment) and management (i.e., intensity of case management). Therefore, type and severity of mental illness serve to determine eligibility and exclusion for diversion programs/PSCs.

In addition, many PSCs typically require accepting a plea offer. In cases where there is a victim, consent from the victim is typically required. Most MHCs, for example, require the individual to plead guilty and agree to enter court-mandated treatment in the community with supervision and monitoring by MHC staff (Redlich et al., 2006). Depending on the district, for some crimes (e.g., sexual offenses), the district attorney (DA) will not offer a treatment diversion option. If the client completes the court mandate, they avoid incarceration and charges may be reduced or dismissed (Barber-Rioja & Rotter, 2014). If they fail to complete the mandate, they may be sentenced to the term of incarceration agreed upon at the time of the plea (Barber-Rioja et al., 2012).

The main exclusion criterion is if there is risk of harm to self and/or others that cannot be successfully mitigated, such that they cannot be managed in the community. Management in the community includes consideration of available options at the court's disposal, such as services in the community, medications to mitigate risk, etc. In large urban settings with greater resources, management is easier. Smaller communities, however, may have limited intervention resources and management capabilities. Violence risk assessments may be included to determine eligibility. The Department of Justice Census report of problem-solving courts indicated that 56% of problem-solving courts in 2012 did not accept applicants with a history of violent crime and 65% did not accept applicants with a history of sex offenses (Strong et al., 2016). Identifying the specific risk factors that are functionally related to violent behaviors is important to see if there are ways to mitigate, monitor, and manage them in the community. An example is someone who has a serious mental illness (e.g., schizophrenia) and becomes violent when symptomatic, but is responsive to antipsychotic medication that decreases symptoms related to violence.

## Trauma in PSC Populations

SAMHSA defines trauma as "an event, series of events, or set of circumstances that is experienced by an individual as physically or emotionally harmful or life threatening, and that has lasting adverse effects on the individual's functioning and mental, physical, social, emotional, or spiritual well-being" (SAMHSA, n.d.). It is a stressful event that overwhelms one's ability to cope, creating feelings of helplessness and horror (Smyth & Greyber, 2013; Wiechelt, 2014). Not everyone who is exposed to potentially traumatic stimuli becomes traumatized or develops PTSD or a trauma disorder (Smyth & Greyber, 2013; Wiechelt, 2014). There are different types of trauma, such as physical, sexual, or emotional traumas perpetrated by others; trauma incurred due to natural disasters, wars, terrorism, environmental events, witness trauma, grief, traumatic loss, serious illness, loss of functioning, etc. Perhaps less obvious, but particularly relevant for the DTC population, is trauma from neglect, lack of access to proper healthcare and nutrition, systematic trauma (e.g., injustice, bigotry and bias), and historical trauma (e.g., slavery, genocide, and displacement). These traumatic experiences also potentially increase the risk of other types of adverse and traumatic life situations. Generally speaking, risk factors for trauma include a lack of access to mental and physical healthcare, improper nutrition, physical and mental illness, social isolation, a generally negative outlook, substance use disorders, and previous trauma (Sareen, 2014). Protective factors, that is, factors that either buffer against risk of trauma exposure or decrease the likelihood of developing trauma, include external resources such as friends and family, access to appropriate nutrition and healthcare, safe living environments, education, financial resources, etc. Protective factors also include personality factors such as optimism, outlook, a sense of humor, and behavioral factors such as positive self-talk (Yuan et al., 2011).

## Existing Trauma and Mental Illness

Irrespective of the type of PSC, individuals engaged in PSCs are currently involved with the criminal justice system and/or have a history of involvement with the criminal justice system and are a subset of a criminal justice population. It is therefore important to consider the current parameters of the criminal justice population. Individuals with trauma and other mental illness are overrepresented in the criminal justice system, compared to the general population (Lurigio, 2012; Moore & Hiday, 2006; Osher & Steadman, 2007; Prins, 2014).

The deinstitutionalization movement and subsequent closure of state psychiatric hospitals without adequate community resources resulted in jail and prison systems that serve as the new repositories for individuals with mental illness or "the primary mental health institutions in the nation" (Adams & Ferrandino, 2008, p.913). In the late 1990s, it was estimated that the Los Angeles County Jail and Rikers Island Jail in New York City, the largest jails in the United States, also held the largest number of individuals with mental illness (Council of State Governments Justice Center, 2008). Recent estimates are that over half of the people incarcerated within the United States experience current or recent mental health symptoms (James & Glaze, 2006). As many as 40% of the nation's mentally ill are involved with the criminal justice system (Acquaviva, 2006), and two million people with mental illness are booked into jails annually with nearly 15% of men and 30% of women having a serious mental health condition (NAMI, n.d.). Additionally, there is a high prevalence of co-occurring mental and substance use disorders for individuals involved in the criminal justice system (Osher & Steadman, 2007; Steadman & Naples, 2005). Participants of DTCs often have comorbid mental health problems (Smelson et al., 2018) and it is estimated that between approximately 20% and 60% of DTC participants also suffer from a mental health problem (Belenko, 1998).

Briere, Agee, and Dietrich (2016) found that 48% of their prison sample and Harner and colleagues (2015) found that 44% of their female inmate sample met criteria for posttraumatic stress disorder (PTSD). Wolff and colleagues (2014) using a sample of incarcerated men found that rates of current and lifetime PTSD have been found to be significantly higher among incarcerated men (30–60%) than the general nonincarcerated population, and PTSD symptom severity was impacted by different types of traumatic experiences. For example, severe symptoms significantly increased with experiencing sexual assault/molestation or a serious life-threatening illness (Wolff et al., 2014). Additionally, lifetime and current rates of anxiety, mood, and antisocial personality disorders were also elevated in inmates with a PTSD diagnosis (Gibson et al., 1999). Inmates who met lifetime criteria for PTSD were significantly more likely to meet lifetime criteria for major depressive disorder (MDD), generalized anxiety disorder, and antisocial personality disorder. Inmates who met current PTSD criteria were significantly more likely to meet current criteria for MDD, obsessive-compulsive disorder, and generalized anxiety disorder (Gibson et al., 1999).

Using a convenience sample from a public hospital, Donley et al. (2012) found that participants with PTSD were significantly more likely to have encountered the criminal justice system. Donley et al. (2012) also found that those who had a history of illegal activity experienced significantly higher intrusive, avoidance, and arousal symptoms than those that did not have a history of illegal activity. Additionally, participants charged with violent offenses had more symptoms in all three PTSD clusters (intrusive, avoidance, and hyperarousal) than those who were never charged with a violent offense. PTSD symptoms were strongly associated with violent charges, even after adjusting for sex, age, race, education, income, employment, substance abuse, and past trauma history. Participants with more extensive trauma histories and those with a diagnosis of PTSD reported more substantial incarceration records than did those with less extensive trauma histories who did not have the diagnosis.

Sadeh and McNiel (2015) found that PTSD was associated with a greater likelihood of a general arrest and being arrested for a new felony charge, after controlling for risk variables, demographics, and other mental disorders. A PTSD diagnosis increased the odds of being arrested by 1.4 times compared to those without, and the odds of being arrested for a new felony charge was 1.5 times higher in participants with PTSD than those without.

## Childhood Trauma

Self-report rates of childhood trauma and maltreatment are high among inmates. Dutton and Hart (1994) found that 41% of their male inmate sample reported either physical or sexual abuse or neglect. Giarratano, Ford, and Nochajski (2017) found that almost half (49%) of their incarcerated adult sample reported some form of abuse during childhood (approximately 42% of males and 60% of females). Weeks and Widom (1998) found that 68% of their adult male sample reported some form of childhood victimization. Childhood abuse was found to mediate the relationship between gender and complex PTSD, and it partially mediated the relationship between gender and substance-use risk (Giarratano et al., 2017). Childhood trauma and maltreatment are associated with psychological problems, processing deficits and disrupted relationships, as well as long-term effects (Kim, Park, & Kim, 2016). Physical neglect was a significant independent predictor of recidivism, even after controlling for psychiatric disorders (Kim et al., 2016). Zettler and Iratzoqui (2018) found that although childhood maltreatment was not a predictor of DTC failure, it had an indirect effect through its significant positive association with mental health and substance use diagnoses.

Messina, Grella, Burdon, and Prendergast (2007) predicted that the association between childhood trauma and adult physical and mental health problems will be substantially more pronounced among an offender population. Using a large sample of 16,043 incarcerated adults, logistic regression analyses found that adverse childhood experiences increased the risk of various substance abuse outcomes, but childhood sexual abuse increased risk for women only (Marotta, 2017). Research has shown that maltreatment-related adverse childhood experiences (ACEs) are prevalent in justice-involved youth and are associated with recidivism (Kowalski, 2018). Results from the adverse childhood experience (ACE) study of women and men demonstrate significant correlations between childhood abuse and adverse physical and mental health outcomes and social problems (Anda et al., 2002; Dube et al., 2003; Felitti et al., 1998). Specifically, greater ACEs were associated with greater histories of mental health treatment, psychotropic medication use, and early criminal and drug-use behaviors. When ACEs are not addressed through interventions and are protracted, they can set a negative life trajectory.

**Gender Differences in ACEs**

Women are a growing population in the criminal justice system (Harrison & Beck, 2005), with the majority being unmarried parents from minority groups with histories of inconsistent education and employment (Greenfeld & Snell, 1999). Women in the criminal justice system have high rates of childhood and adult physical and sexual abuse (Greenfeld & Snell, 1999; Teplin, Abram, & McClelland, 1996) and higher rates of trauma-related disorders (Pollard, Schuster, Lin, & Frisman, 2007). Women offenders, compared to male inmates, have greater exposure to adverse childhood events, such as abuse and maltreatment (Messina et al., 2007). As such, trauma history should be considered the norm for women within the criminal justice system (Osher & Steadman, 2007) and PSCs.

Furthermore, women offenders with childhood histories of trauma and abuse have an increased likelihood of interpersonal violence in adolescent and adult relationships, conduct disorder diagnoses in adolescence, substance abuse, criminal activities, homelessness, and physical and mental health problems (Messina et al., 2007). Women were significantly more likely than men to have five or more CAEs (childhood averse events) prior to age 16 and significantly more continued sexual abuse past age 16. Some have found that gender differences with childhood abuse and adverse experiences were more strongly related to outcomes in women (Hyman, Garcia, & Sinha, 2006; Messina et al., 2007) and that women inmates were significantly more likely to report emotional abuse and neglect, physical abuse, and sexual abuse compared to male inmates who reported significantly more parental substance abuse and familial incarceration (Messina et al., 2007). Using a sample of incarcerated women, Green et al. (2016) found that trauma items result in three factors consisting of family dysfunction (e.g., violence among family members and family substance abuse), interpersonal violence (e.g., rape and kidnapping), and external events (e.g., witnessing violence) that accounted for 81% of the variance. Interpersonal violence and family dysfunction independently contributed to PTSD, major depressive disorder (MDD), bipolar disorder, and substance use.

Women with moderate to severe PTSD symptoms were more likely to report several physical symptoms (e.g., chest pain, heart palpitations, shortness of breath, etc.) and other mental health conditions than women without PTSD (Harner, Budescu, et al., 2015). Women with severe symptoms were more likely to report a head injury with loss of consciousness in the past year (Harner, Budescu, et al., 2015).

## Gender and Racial Factors

Discussions about trauma, especially within the drug court (DTC) population, would be incomplete without addressing the role that race plays for this population. Although every state is different, there is generally a disproportionate number of incarcerated nonwhites (Osher & Steadman, 2007). Urban drug courts have disproportionate numbers of African American and Hispanic participants (Flores, Lopez, Pemble-Flood, Riegel, & Segura, 2018). Racism and historic injustices related to race are significant sources of trauma for this population (Butler, 2010). Due to the marginalization of minorities in the United States, members of these racial groups are more likely to have grown up in poverty, less likely to have access to appropriate mental and general healthcare, and often are exposed to violence, neglect, and malnutrition (Dearing, McCartney, & Taylor, 2006).

## Complex Trauma

Many of the individuals involved in the criminal justice system, including PSCs, have complex trauma (Briere et al., 2016; Giarratano et al., 2017; Hartwell et al., 2014). Complex or cumulative trauma stems from an accumulation of traumatic events endured or repeated over time. The traumas may be the same or different types and then may be concentrated in time or spread out over time (Briere et al., 2016). Complex trauma for example that includes a history of ACEs with additional adult trauma is highly significant because it is associated with a range of mental health symptoms and increased the likelihood of PTSD (Briere et al., 2016) and can therefore be more challenging to treat.

## Traumatic Brain Injury

Thus far, we have considered psychological, physical, and sexual trauma, but another type of trauma that has psychological sequelae is neurological trauma, more specifically traumatic brain injury (TBI) (Lucas & Addeo, 2006; Horn & Lutz, 2016). There is a correlation between neurological trauma and criminality (Horn & Lutz, 2016), particularly for violent crimes (Colantonio et al., 2014). The presence of traumatic brain injury (TBI) ranges from 25 to 87% in criminal populations (Admire & Mitchell, 2010; Health Resources and Services Administration, 2011; Piccolino & Solberg, 2014; Ray, Sapp, & Kincaid, 2014; Slaughter, Fann, & Ehde, 2003). Additionally, some studies have found TBI to be an independent predictor of criminal behavior, imprisonment, and reoffending behavior (Hawley & Maden, 2003; Leon-Carrion & Ramos, 2003; Ray & Richardson, 2017; Williams et al., 2010). Farrer, Frost, and Hedges (2012) found that the prevalence of TBI among perpetrators of intimate partner violence was significantly higher than the prevalence of TBI in the general population.

TBIs are often overlooked in criminal populations. Individuals that become involved in the criminal justice system have often had preexisting barriers to obtaining medical care (Dearing et al., 2006). More specifically, of those that do access medical care, they typically have difficulty engaging appropriate medical care to identify TBIs, prevent secondary effects, and maintain medical recommendations. The majority of correctional facilities do not utilize basic screening instruments for financial and logistical reasons (Horn & Lutz, 2016). Individuals with TBIs may not have the cognitive skills to understand the adverse consequences of their actions and difficulty with causal relationships (Horn & Lutz, 2016; Kelly & Winkler, 2007). For PSCs this means that sanctions, particularly ones that are thought to facilitate compliance (e.g., jail time), may not be effective for individuals with TBI.

## Veteran's Treatment Court (VTC)

Trauma is probably the most emphasized, if not at the forefront of consideration in VTCs. Beyond the obvious combat trauma, PTSD, and mental health issues facing this population, other forms of trauma such as TBIs (Bullard & Thrasher, 2016), MST (military sexual trauma), as well as reintegration to civilian life challenges (Hartwell et al., 2014) are relevant in this population. Hartwell et al. (2014) found that 93% of participants reported traumatic experiences, and that for the vast majority, their traumatic experiences occurred *before* age 18 (i.e., before they enlisted in the military). They point out that trauma-informed interventions for veterans are included in VTCs; they, however, often focus exclusively on combat or military trauma and not premilitary trauma. They argue that understanding trauma across the life span in VTCs is essential for providing appropriate and holistic treatment and informed policies.

Criminal offending rates are higher in veterans with a PTSD diagnosis than those without (Elbogen et al., 2012). Veterans with likely PTSD who reported anger/irritability were more likely to be arrested than other veterans (Elbogen et al., 2012). They concluded that veterans with PTSD and negative affect may be at increased risk for criminal arrest, but that clinicians should also consider non-PTSD factors when evaluating veterans in the criminal justice system (e.g., age, sex, exposure to family violence, prior history of arrests, and alcohol/drug misuse).

Using a small sample of 86 veterans in VTC with felony and misdemeanor offenses, Knudsen and Wingenfeld (2016) found those that received trauma treatment experienced significantly improved PTSD and depression symptoms and improved functioning, including emotional functioning. They found that receiving peer support predicted improvements in social connections and emotional functioning. Inpatient substance abuse treatment significantly predicted improvements in sleep and substance abuse. Psychiatric medication was significantly related to improvements in depression, emotional lability, psychosis, symptoms, and functioning. The authors emphasized the importance of providing trauma-specific therapy and positive peer role models to veterans with combat exposure who are reintegrating to civilian society.

## Trauma Encumbered as a Function of Interactions with the CJS

Incarceration and interaction with the criminal justice system can potentially result in traumatic experiences. Individuals involved with the criminal justice system are at a higher risk for trauma exposure and developing PTSD than the general population (Sadeh & McNiel, 2015). The conditions of incarceration (e.g., overcrowding, violence, isolation from social networks, limited mental health services, etc.) are not conducive to recovery and are likely to have traumatic or at the very least deleterious effects on mental health (World Health Organization, n.d.). Individuals with mental illness who are involved in the criminal justice system are particularly more vulnerable than the general population and have additional needs which increase their likelihood of adverse impact and trauma from exposure to the criminal justice system (including incarceration and the overall process).

### Effectiveness and Outcome

While the humanitarian and civil liberties merits for PSC and treatment diversion are clear, most funders and oversight agencies are concerned with measuring outcomes, including decreased recidivism. When considering the effectiveness of PSC, one first needs to ask, "effective at achieving what outcome?" There are many outcomes to consider: economic benefits, reducing recidivism, improving mental health, improving quality of life, and solving the primary problem of that PSC's focus (e.g., substance abuse, domestic violence, etc.). Therefore, PSCs use different outcome measures to gauge success.

Honegger (2015) spoke about the idiosyncratic nature of MHC and that the variability of data reported makes large court and cross-article comparisons difficult that pose consequent challenges to generalizing findings (Watson, Hanrahan, Luchins, & Lurigio, 2001), which applies to all PSCs. It should be underscored that there is also variability within PSCs with respect to treatment and service resources. MHCs and DTCs, for example, do not have the funds to purchase treatment and therefore are competing with other clients for public treatment services (Swartz & Robertson, 2016); many clients of MHCs are indigent (Swartz & Robertson, 2016).

Inclusion and exclusion criteria can systematically distort perceived effectiveness of outcome measures (Hiday, Wales, & Ray, 2013; Steadman & Naples, 2005; Wolff and Pogorzelski, 2005). Defendants offered PSC are significantly different from those who were not (Steadman & Naples, 2005). Those offered PSC were more likely to be female, have a primary diagnosis of schizophrenia or a mood disorder with psychotic features, receive SSI/SSDI, have better mental health on a symptom measure, have substance abuse problems, have been arrested/spent time in jail, and less likely to live with a partner (Steadman & Naples, 2005). Whether through known selection criteria or unknown selection bias (Hiday et al., 2013), these factors may account for discrepancies in program performance. Males and racial minorities were more likely to opt out of MHC and to have an increased likelihood of being terminated from MHC (Dirks-Linhorst, Kondrat, Linhorst, & Morani, 2013). That said, the data is mixed concerning the associations between race, compliance, and PSC completion (Redlich et al., 2010).

Methodological limitations of effectiveness studies with PSC populations include limited follow-up periods for recidivism studies and the absence of control groups for comparison (Hiday et al., 2013). Of 20 articles Honegger (2015) reviewed about MHC, only one employed an experimental design, six used a quasi-experimental design, and the remaining used pretest/posttest. The Department of Justice Census of problem-solving courts (2016) indicate that 57% of all problem-solving courts reported that more than half of the exits were successful program completions and that successful completion included dismissal of the case or a suspension of the sentence. It was further indicated that 44% of all PSCs tracked participant progress after program completion (Strong et al., 2016), which is necessary to look at recidivism and long-term treatment effects. Some have concluded that overwhelming scientific evidence reveals that adult drug courts reduce crime and substance abuse, improve family relationships, and increase earning potential (Marlowe, 2010). However, some have criticized the rigor of this research (e.g., Latimer, Morton-Bourgon, & Chretien, 2006; Wilson, Mitchell, & MacKenzie, 2006).

Another outcome measure is economic savings. Some early results indicated cost savings for the criminal justice system in various jurisdictions (Berman & Feinblatt, 2001), but the degree of savings will vary as a function of the expense for the alternative option(s) (Belenko, Patapis, & French, 2005). Regional differences can impact savings as well (Steadman & Naples, 2005). Although there appears to be some economic benefits, depending on the PSC, additional research that weighs this against the cost of court staff is needed. Another perspective is that the real remedy is to address the root cause (i.e., a broken mental health system wherein traumatized and otherwise mentally ill individuals are overrepresented in the criminal justice system) and that the best investment would be in broad reform of community mental health (Seltzer, 2005).

A final important factor to consider when we talk about effectiveness and outcome measures are stakeholder and public perception, particularly since most PSCs require some level of government funding. DTC judges and administrators perceived DTC as relatively successful, with administrators having significantly higher perceptions about success when compared to judges (Nored & Carlan, 2008). Court personnel believed that the strongest support came from local officials, and this was lower from state officials and lowest from federal officials (Nored & Carlan, 2008). Additionally, perceived success was higher for personnel without graduate and professional degrees and those with more experience guiding DTC (Nored & Carlan, 2008). The authors attributed these findings to proximity of state and local officials for perceived court success (Nored & Carlan, 2008). Please see the NIJ link (https://www.crimesolutions.gov/TopicDetails.aspx?ID=49#practice) for a table summary of effectiveness of PSCs.

## *Outcome Data for Drug Treatment Court (DTC)*

Carey, Mackin, and Finigan (2012) identified the following (in order of effect sizes from largest to smallest) essential components of DTCs for reducing recidivism of DTC participants. DTCs with a program caseload (i.e., active participants) of less than 125 had five times greater reductions in recidivism than DTCs with more participants. Those with participants who are expected to have greater than 90 days clean, as measured by drug tests before graduation, had 164% greater reductions in recidivism compared with DTC with less clean time. DTCs where the judge spent an average of three minutes or greater with each participant during court hearings had 153% greater reduction in recidivism compared to DTCs where the judge spent less time per participant. Carey et al. (2012) data shows a direct linear relationship between judge time per participant and positive outcomes. Of note, one MHC study did not find that specific time spent with the judge yielded significant differences (Bullard & Thrasher, 2016). DTCs where treatment providers communicated with the court or team via email had a 119% greater reduction in recidivism. Those where a representative from treatment attended team meetings had 105% greater reductions in recidivism. DTCs that made program modifications based on the data and program statistics had 105% greater reductions in recidivism. DTCs where a treatment representative attended court hearings had 100% greater reductions in recidivism than programs where treatment representatives did not attend. DTCs that allowed nondrug charges had 95% greater reductions in recidivism. Those that had a law enforcement representative on the DTC team had 88% greater reductions in recidivism than programs that did not. DTCs that had independent evaluations and used them to make modifications in operations had 85% greater reductions in recidivism.

Research has found support for reduced recidivism, lower rates of substance use, and significant increases in full-time employment for DTC participants compared to those who did not participate (Latimer et al., 2006; Peters & Murrin, 2000; Smelson et al., 2018). During a 30-month follow-up period, the rates of arrest declined in direct relationship to the duration of drug court involvement (Peters & Murrin, 2000). Age, outpatient treatment, marital status, and the number of times treated for psychiatric problems in a hospital, type of substance use, number of positive drug tests, and receiving any sanctions were associated with two-year post-DTC recidivism (Shannon, Jones, Newell, & Payne, 2018). Mitchell, Wilson, Eggers, and MacKenzie' (2012) meta-analysis found that participants of adult DTCs had lower recidivism than nonparticipants with larger reductions found for those that had higher graduation rates. The authors concluded that DTCs are effective in reducing recidivism but that more experimental evaluations are needed for DWI courts.

## Outcome Data for Mental Health Treatment Court (MHC)

Bullard and Thrasher (2016) examined 11 MHCs in Oklahoma and found that successful courts prioritized intensive monitoring methods; used multiple, tailored treatment options; emphasized program assessment; used a diverse team (i.e., had different positions, different disciplines); visibly differentiated compliant and non-compliant participants in court; and provided tangible symbolic incentives (e.g., certificates).

The outcome metrics for MHC include psychiatric symptoms and results are mixed. Boothroyd, Mercado, Poythress, Christy, and Petrila (2005) found that receiving treatment services alone was in sufficient to produce positive changes in clinical status and concluded that this reflects the chronic nature of their mental disorders and the need for adequate mental health services, rather than the failure of MHC (Boothroyd et al., 2005). Sarteschi, Vaughn, and Kim (2011) found moderate significant aggregate effect sizes for recidivism and improvements of clinical outcomes. Honegger (2015) concluded that research in this area is nascent and that there is insufficient evidence to support the assertion that MHCs improve psychiatric and substance abuse symptoms, frequency and consistency of psychiatric treatment, or case management services but that they appeared to be a promising diversion option for reducing recidivism rates among individuals with mental illness.

In terms of whether MHC reduces recidivism, here too, results are mixed (Hiday & Ray, 2010), with some citing decreased recidivism and drug use, as well as cost-effectiveness (Cross, 2011; Dirks-Linhorst & Linhorst, 2012; Moore & Hiday, 2006; Steadman, Redlich, Callahan, Robbins, & Vesselinov, 2011). Significant reductions of criminal activity in both MHC and TAU (treatment as usual) groups were found only when participants with higher levels of criminal behavior were excluded (Cosden et al., 2005). Moore and Hiday (2006) found that MHC defendants had a lower rearrest rate and those who completed MHC, that is, had the full dose, had an even lower rearrest rate. Factors significantly related to MHC program completion were employment, residential stability, and a concurrent disorder

(Verhaaff & Scott, 2015). Participants who were not employed were significantly more likely than program participants who were employed to successfully complete programs (Verhaaff & Scott, 2015).

Defendants who completed MHC were significantly less likely than those ejected to be rearrested during the post-2-year follow-up period, when defendants were no longer receiving treatment services or monitoring by the court. This sample, however, did not have a control group and overwhelmingly consisted of misdemeanor initial charges (Hiday & Ray, 2010). One study found that MHC participants were significantly less likely to be arrested at the one-year follow-up compared to people in the specialized supervision unit (SSU), an effect that remained even after controlling for confounding variables (Hiday et al., 2013). MHC participation and completion were significant predictors of time to rearrest (Hiday et al., 2013). In a study looking at three outcomes at a MHC, the typical risk factor of having a prior arrest or incarceration record predicted worse outcomes on the three outcome measures of getting a jail sanction, failing MHC, and rearrest (Reich, Pichard-Fritsche, Cerniglia, & Hahn, 2014).

## Outcome Data for Veterans Treatment Court (VTC)

Tsai, Finlay, Flatley, Kasprow, and Clark (2018) found that VTC participants who were older and more educated and had their own residence were significantly less likely to experience a new incarceration. Participants with a history of incarceration were significantly more likely to experience a new incarceration and less likely to be in their own housing or be employed at the end of the program (Tsai et al., 2018). Alcohol and drug-use diagnoses were significant predictors of new incarcerations (Tsai et al., 2018), but Johnson et al. (2015) found that only a history of opioid misuse was associated with subsequent criminal recidivism. Participants with a history of psychiatric hospitalizations, PTSD, or more medical problems were less likely to be employed at the end of the program (Tsai et al., 2018). Those with PTSD and a history of psychiatric hospitalizations were more likely to be receiving VA benefits at the end of the program (Tsai et al., 2018). See Tsai et al. (2018) for details about significant predictors for employment, VA benefits, and housing at the end of the program. The authors concluded that their findings highlight the importance of proper substance abuse treatment as well as employment services for VTC participants in order for them to benefit from the diversion process exit (Tsai et al., 2018).

Using VTCs that excluded felonies, Hartley and Baldwin (2016) found a significant difference in recidivism rates between VTC graduates and the control group (those who opted not to participate in VTC). Specifically, a sub-analysis looking at the time period between entering the program and the start of probation found that VTC graduates had significantly lower recidivism rates than the comparison (control group) across all three time periods (12, 24, or 36 months). Three years after entering VTC, graduates of VTC had the lowest recidivism rates compared to the control group and VTC nongraduates (Hartley & Baldwin, 2016). Inconsistent with the

Risk-Needs-Responsivity (RNR) approach, this study did not find that using intensive treatment programs for low-risk individuals may actually have adverse effects on the achievement of intended outcomes (Hartley & Baldwin, 2016). It is, however, important to recognize that the identification of and assessment of risk and need factors of recidivism in veterans is still in the early stages of research and that other factors may be related to criminal risk.

## Implementing Trauma-Informed Practice in PSCs

Given the likelihood of trauma within this population, as a general rule of practice, all PSCs should implement trauma-informed care. Some have argued, for example, that trauma and substance use are linked and should not be separated (Brown, Harris, & Fallot, 2013). Trauma-informed systems incorporate "knowledge about trauma" in every area of service and interaction with clients (Harris & Fallot, 2001). Trauma-informed care emphasizes client choice, collaboration, safety, respect, empowerment, and resilience while minimizing re-traumatization (Elliott, Bjelajac, Fallot, Markoff, & Reed, 2005). Pollard et al. (2007) found that women in a jail diversion program using motivational interviewing (MI) and trauma treatment produced promising results, with significant decreases in substance use, criminal justice outcomes (e.g., rearrests), and trauma symptoms. They also found significant increases in employment and well-being. This research suggests trauma-informed care within PSCs is important.

Trauma-informed care includes staff education and training in trauma, traumatic reactions, transference, and countertransference. Awareness of how different traumas can manifest is important (e.g., females with sexual trauma inflicted by males may be more reactive with male staff; females abused by their fathers may exhibit a negative transference to male staff). While it is not always feasible to match court staff as a prophylactic, awareness of such reactions and methods to help mitigate them should be considered. In addition to education, clearly defined roles can ensure that staff are not taking on additional responsibilities for which they are not adequately prepared that may potentially exacerbate trauma. For example, today, many VTCs are connected to Veterans Affairs Medical Centers and, like many veterans' programs, have a peer mentor (i.e., fellow veterans) component. Peer mentorship is generally well received by veteran participants, but training is necessary that includes a clear delineation of role identity and purpose. In particular, while there may be psychological benefits to peer mentorship, both mentors and participants need to understand that peer mentors are not providing mental health services.

Trauma-informed care includes an awareness that those with trauma histories are likely to avoid anything that will trigger the trauma (Green et al., 2016), which could include providers, situations (e.g., exposure to court personnel), and treatment itself that might bring about emotional reactions. The mandated monitoring process may not only be triggering for defendants, but could also potentially re-traumatize them. The paradoxical challenge in PSC contexts is minimizing re-traumatization without reinforcing trauma symptoms through avoidance.

Trauma-informed care does not necessarily mean that individuals are receiving trauma-focused therapy, and it is important to understand the difference between the two. Consistent with a trauma-informed approach, trauma should be considered in all problem-solving courts and that includes considering the relevance of trauma for the individual, as well as situations within PSC that could be potentially traumatic – but it is not synonymous with trauma treatment. Trauma treatment can vary in type (e.g., prolonged exposure, cognitive processing therapy, etc.), degree of intensity, and focus. The relevance of trauma should be considered for each participant. In many cases, recommending trauma treatment without having adequately prepared participants for what to expect from treatment and PSC mandates could be detrimental. The decision to recommend trauma-focused treatment while in PSC needs to be considered in the context of diagnostic and mental health functioning, coping skills, ability to tolerate trauma work, duration, and other treatment needs. Regardless of the type, intensity, and focus of trauma treatment, the individual should generally be provided with coping skills to prepare them for therapy and their potential reactions. For example, see stage models like the three-stage model proposed by Landes, Garovoy, and Burkman (2013). Starting intensive trauma work during PSC diversion may not be the optimum time, even for those who have long required therapy to address trauma, because it may be too overwhelming for the participant. Court staff must be mindful to not assign participants to intensive trauma work until the participant is ready. In PSCs, trauma work may need to be tabled in order to establish preparedness.

In general, it can be overwhelming to manage the demands of mandated treatment, which often includes sobriety and learning coping skills, while juggling other life factors (e.g., employment, raising children). It is crucial to remember that even though participants are receiving treatment services, the required compliance conditions of PSCs (e.g., sobriety, negative toxicologies) essentially strip participants of their typical, albeit ineffective, and even harmful coping strategies that they have relied on for many years. Essentially, defendants are being asked not only to deal with mandatory compliance while simultaneously facing trauma triggers, but to do so without being able to utilize any of the tools they have historically employed. The difficulty of this becomes amplified if there is a history of trauma and related symptoms. This is why, in addition to a trauma-informed staff, defendants must receive viable skills (i.e., to manage triggers and cope without access to their typical maladaptive coping strategies, such as substance use, etc.). Incorporating skills from Seeking Safety (Najavits, 2002) or Dialectical Behavior Therapy (Linehan, 1993) early on can provide skills to successfully manage triggers to complete the program. All staff should receive basic training in grounding techniques and coping skills. When possible, we recommend the inclusion of a licensed psychologist with trauma training as part of the PSC team.

Those with trauma histories coupled with either impulsivity, self-injurious behaviors, or borderline personality features need special consideration as management risks are increased. Again, this along with the stressors of mandated conditions can potentially increase self-injurious and suicidal behaviors. They may need more intensive programming or a step type of process. Those with trauma histories from childhood are likely to have attachment issues and transference that are likely to manifest with treatment providers and possibly PSC team members. Those that are securely attached to providers and court staff may have difficulty when the mandate is completed, therefore necessitating a safe transition to a post-PSC provider to reduce the risks of a traumatic separation and loss of treatment gains.

Finally, self-care to avoid burnout and secondary (or vicarious) trauma should be practiced by mental health providers working with individuals with a high level of trauma. Drawing from a DBT team model (Linehan, 1993), the team can be a source of support to minimize potential effects of secondary trauma.

## Recommendations for Best Practice

Establishing and sustaining a PSC requires financial, staff, and community support. Support from the general public, local community, officials, and stakeholders is necessary to sustain and expand PSCs (Acquaviva, 2006). MHCs are primarily funded with grant money (Acquaviva, 2006) and have expanded through federal funding (Steadman & Naples, 2005). Federal legislation to provide grant funding was established under President Clinton in 2000 and expanded by President Bush in 2004 (Acquaviva, 2006). Maintaining existing PSCs and developing new PSCs require adequate and dependable funding resources; and therefore, concerns about the reliance upon grant funding have been raised. Developing a sustainable economic and labor plan is strongly recommended (Acquaviva, 2006). Support and funding require consideration of infrastructure needs, which can be particularly challenging in urban areas where space within the court is limited. Infrastructure and sustainability plans should include what is needed for participant and staff retention, as well as increasing participant compliance and completion. PSC completion is particularly important because it will not only help promote future funding, but because it is associated with improved outcomes, including decreased recidivism. Infrastructure and plans should help increase PSC compliance and completion and address factors that adversely impact them. For example, addressing mental health symptoms and concurrent substance use and residential instability as these have been found to be significantly associated with noncompliance in certain contexts (Reich et al., 2014), partial, and noncompletion (Verhaaff & Scott, 2015).

### *PSC Identity and Goals*

One main criticism of PSCs is that they are vastly heterogenous and lack clear goals and objectives. Best practice starts with developing clear, specific, measurable goals and objectives for the PSC to provide the framework from which policies and practices can then be established. Lack of clear policies and practices poses problems to informed consent and could potentially increase the likelihood of participant failure. Treatments and interventions offered should be evidence based. Likewise, policies and procedures should be rooted in trauma-informed care, based on the treatment court literature of what is effective, and monitoring for negative effects. Policies and procedures should be tracked over time and measured for effectiveness (i.e., how well do they support the goals and objectives, as well as enhance completion). Any policies and procedures that undermine the goals and objectives need to be analyzed and revised. This is likely to be more complex because a procedure might support one goal/objective, but work at cross-purposes to another goal. Additionally, establishing clear criteria, goals, and outcome measures is crucial because states have been developing governing documents to provide oversight and accountability for problem-solving courts, ranging from guidelines to certification checklists (National Center for State Courts, 2015). This requires understanding the target population being served and their needs, such as factors that contribute to compliance and functioning, as well as victims and the community. When considering the direct client, one must establish inclusion and exclusion criteria that are consistent with the goals and objectives. Thompson, Osher, and Tomasini-Joshi (2007) identified the following best practices for MHC:

- Having a broad-based group of stakeholders representing the criminal justice, mental health, substance abuse, and related systems to guide the planning and administration of the court.
- Having a clear definition of the target population, including eligibility criteria.

For example, if the specialized court is for veterans with mental health problems, depending on the goals and objectives, inclusion criteria may be for any veteran with a diagnosed mental health disorder or may be specific, in conjunction with the goals, to combat veterans with a primary diagnosis of PTSD. Exclusion criteria could be excessive history of violence, etc. It is important that inclusion and exclusion criteria consider the goals, populations, and resources available to allow for the greatest number of participants the court can manage. Factors such as trauma history, issues beyond the main PSC problem, and comorbid conditions can represent challenges that require additional support and resources. Areas that are resource rich (i.e., that have internal staff and many external programs and providers) have greater flexibility with inclusion/exclusion criteria. It is important that these be established early on so individuals are not offered PSC when they cannot be appropriately treated and managed in the community. This consideration is especially relevant for individuals with a history of trauma who may need more resources and supports in place to successfully begin trauma-focused care and to complete PSC.

Identifying the required court personnel (e.g., judges, attorneys, case managers) as well as professionals from other disciplines (such as mental health professionals, vocational counselors, etc.) is crucial and should also be determined based on the goals of the PSC, the population, and target outcomes. Having a psychologist as part of the team is a good rule of thumb. The ability for rapid communication between team members is crucial. Procedures about intake, empirically based assessment measures, follow-up, and accommodations for setbacks should be established at the beginning and periodically reviewed and revised when necessary. Reinforcements and therapeutically informed sanction options should be established at the beginning with the proviso that they can be modified as needed. It is crucial to establish regular meetings with core staff, in addition to policies about communication to ensure continuity of care. A training plan for staff to be aware of clinical, trauma, and other relevant issues should be prepared at the outset.

Developing partnerships with treatment providers and community providers, as well as policies for obtaining information about participants' progress, are important to establish at the beginning. Procedures for obtaining status updates on participants from outside treatment providers and programs will help ensure continuity of care and decrease the likelihood of participants falling through the cracks.

## Managing Diagnostic Complexity and Treatment Planning Challenges

Many individuals that come into PSCs, particularly, MHC, DTC, and VTC, have multiple problems that are interrelated and can potentially impact adherence, completion, and outcome measures. Participants often have comorbid conditions and are diagnostically complex. A comprehensive initial assessment should include collateral sources and ascertain diagnostic, risk, and compliance levels and identify potential barriers. Regular assessments and monitoring are recommended.

Many clients/defendants of PSC are often poor reporters of their personal history; and as such, reliance on records and collateral information can provide diagnostic clarity. Diagnostic clarity is essential to determining appropriate treatment and enhancing treatment effectiveness. In MHC, a common example is when a participant presents with psychotic symptoms and chronic K2 use. In this type of scenario, MHCs may require that participants are first treated for substance abuse to attain a period of sobriety and then reevaluated for mental health disorders.

In addition to diagnostic clarification, consideration of the overall clinical picture and assessing, identifying, addressing, and monitoring barriers to treatment and compliance are likely to improve outcomes. Hiday et al. (2014) found that noncompliance had the strongest impact on graduation. Understanding an individual's history can provide information on what has and has not worked and what will likely need to be adjusted for that individual. Consideration of risk factors can be a useful tool in compliance. Barber-Rioja et al. (2012) found that both the HCR-20 and PCL:SV were useful in the context of treatment diversion, but that the HCR-20 was superior to the PCL:SV in predicting noncompliance and reincarceration.

Risk factors should be identified and overall management plans should include mitigation of risk. Consistent with the RNR (Risk-Needs-Responsivity) model (Andrews & Bonta, 2010), determining and targeting risk factors and criminogenic needs will reduce recidivism. Osher and Steadman (2007) recommend that in addition to providing mental health treatment, targeting criminogenic factors and antisocial tendencies is also necessary to reduce recidivism. RNR adjusts the intervention type and/or dose (amount and/or intensity) based on their initial presentation and their responsivity to the intervention. Marlowe et al. (2008) tested an adaptive intervention approach in DTC court and found that this allowed the team to focus on poorly performing participants and address problems earlier rather than allowing such problems to continue developing unabated. Using a sample of mentally disordered offenders, Kingston and Oliver (2017) found that risk relevant factors outlined by the General Personality and Cognitive Social Learning Model (GPCSL) (e.g., criminal history, pro-criminal attitudes, antisocial personality pattern, etc.) predicted general and violent recidivism. They also found that more severe psychiatric symptoms predicted recidivism but that there is overlap between these items and risk factors (e.g., alcohol abuse, physical violence) and therefore this may explain the relevance of this measure (Kingston & Oliver, 2017). They concluded that the GPCSL and RNR principles are important elements of comprehensive treatment programs for offenders with mental illness.

Management of identified risk factors should be included in the overall plan and this could include the use of injectable antipsychotic medication, residential placements, more intensive treatment, and monitoring. Barber-Rioja and Rotter (2014) provide a range of different biopsychosocial explanations for problematic behavior and emphasize the importance of identifying obstacles to compliance in MHC. After a thorough assessment that establishes diagnostic and clinical factors, connecting participants to community service providers as early as possible is strongly recommended. It is recommended that individualized plans are tailored to defendants' risk levels.

## Informed Consent

Clear informed consent that includes understanding the program requirements, the conditions of participation, positive legal outcomes for completion (e.g., misdemeanor instead of felony, or no charges on the record), the consequences of noncompliance, and adverse legal outcomes for failure to complete PSC is important and strongly recommended. This includes the opportunity for prospective participants to consult with legal counsel before agreeing to participate in PSC. A criticism of PSCs is the potential for coercive tactics to drive participation (Berman & Feinblatt, 2001). Another factor is limited privacy about mental health information because of the treatment team approach that includes professionals beyond immediate mental health providers. Seltzer (2005) suggested professional training about keeping information confidential and contained within the team and within appropriate places of discussion. Seltzer also suggested keeping medical and mental health information out of the public record of proceedings.

Critics argue that judges enjoy an increased and inappropriate level of discretionary power and essentially function as social workers in PSC contexts (Redlich et al., 2006). The most intense criticism is that while MHC provides benefits to those in the criminal justice system, they ultimately represent a larger, systemic issue with mental health in our society and that it is ultimately the failure of the mental health system which contributes to individuals ending up in the criminal justice system (Seltzer, 2005). The other major criticism is that although MHC is voluntary, defendants/clients need to understand the consequences of MHC, including potential consequences of not fulfilling treatment mandates (Seltzer, 2005). Related to this issue is that many MHCs require taking a plea or at least taking a no-contest plea in order to participate. Seltzer (2005) has argued that even if the plea is vacated after the mandate is completed, it should never be a prerequisite to participation as it is coercive.

Since participants are often connected to treatment agencies and services within the community that communicate with PSC case managers, it is important that the limits of confidentiality are understood. As much as possible, staff and the PSC team should receive training on confidentiality. Protected health information should be guarded, and confidentiality should be maximized. This includes ongoing training for criminal justice and mental health staff to help mental health court participants achieve treatment and criminal justice goals. Additional training may be required to monitor participants' adherence to court conditions, to modify individualized needs to promote public safety and mental health recovery, and to collect and review data to demonstrate the impact of MHCs and to help inform sustainability plans. It is also recommended that there be a separate regular clinical meeting for clinically trained staff to discuss relevant mental health issues, segregated from the larger team.

Procedures should include informed consent practices and limitations of confidentiality, which is particularly crucial for individuals with trauma. It is also important that defendants know that they have a choice of whether to participate in PSC; and they should be presented with their options and alternatives. When people feel coerced, they are more likely to respond with negative psychological reactions (Winick, 2003), thereby undermining the effectiveness of PSCs. Osher and Steadman (2007) recommend using motivation enhancements (e.g., use of empathy, take a nonjudgmental approach, explore the discrepancy between the client's desired goals/changes and their current behavior) to help reduce perceived coercion and to offset the negative impact of mandated conditions. For those who opt to participate, providing a clear understanding of the limits of confidentiality will enhance trust, decrease confusion, and protect vulnerable populations. Built into this should be an explanation of what measurements will serve as baseline and outcome measures.

## Willingness and Resistance

Resistance to change is a general problem of behavioral change, but it is more of an issue in forensic contexts where participants do not initiate treatment voluntarily and there are mandated conditions. Some courts even include willingness as a key definition of PSC. Pennsylvania courts, for example, state the goal of PSC is to "facilitate rehabilitation of carefully screened and selected defendants who are willing to try to change their behavior" (AOPC, 2015). That said, contrary to common clinical wisdom, an early meta-analysis by Columbia University's National Center of Addiction and Substance Abuse (CASA) examined 59 independent evaluations of 48 drug courts throughout the country and found that drug court participants are more likely to successfully complete mandated substance abuse treatment than comparable participants who sought voluntary treatment (Belenko, 1998). Results also indicated higher retention rates for drug courts compared to voluntary programs (Belenko, 1998).

Tools that address resistance and ambivalence such as motivational interviewing should be readily available to use with participants (Wiener et al., 2010). It is crucial to offer treatments to address trauma, either by treating trauma symptoms directly or by developing strategies for managing trauma symptoms if the client is not ready for treatment. It is important to assess for and consider the impact of all types of trauma (e.g., physical, psychological, and TBIs), particularly with MHC, DTC, and veteran's court populations. Strategies to facilitate engagement, build rapport, and increase compliance may often be creative. For example, a New York VTC used tangible symbolic incentives that included dog tags with positive sayings like "courage," "commitment," etc., that were given by the judge to veterans upon reaching benchmarks of success during court proceedings.

## Conclusion

A basic level of engagement and effort on the part of the participants is imperative, and PSC staff should be trained to understand basic behavioral principles to increase motivation. This includes motivation enhancement techniques, taking a more collaborative approach, respecting autonomy, and being aware of transferential and counter-transferential reactions to increase effectiveness (Winick, 2003). These concepts and recommendations become amplified when working with populations who have a history of trauma. With individuals with a history of trauma, it is likely that there is greater shame, more intense transferential reactions, and greater avoidance due to trauma. Negative interactions with court staff are likely to be perceived as traumatic to individuals, particularly in the context of PSC where the staff reports and enforces consequences for compliance breaches.

Even if the mandate is not completed, the opportunity to re-experience the criminal justice system in a helpful rather than punitive light can provide a new positive association or, in therapeutic terms, a corrective experience. In other words, this is one of the only contexts in which agents of the legal system are all aligned with the goal to help defendants/clients through services. As Winick (2003) has stated, individuals in problem-solving courts may not recognize or might be in denial about their problems. PSCs can provide assistance, resources, and support services, but, ultimately, active participation by the individual is required in order to produce effective problem resolution (Winick, 2003).

## Questions/Activities for Further Exploration

1. What are some potentially adverse effects of trauma-informed care, if any, within the criminal justice system?
2. Does the implementation of trauma-informed care within criminal justice contexts pose potential barriers to the other goals of criminal justice such as retribution, incapacitation, deterrence, or rehabilitation?

    (a) If so, what are potential ways to reconcile these objectives?

3. Within your immediate system, identify potential barriers to developing trauma-informed care.

    (a) What are possible, cost-effective solutions to these challenges?
    (b) How might you implement trauma-informed care within the existing framework of the system such that it becomes integrated and consistently applied?

4. How can one take a trauma-informed approach within the context of forensic assessment, where there is the greater likelihood for symptom exaggeration or malingering?

## References

Acquaviva, G. L. (2006). Mental health courts: No longer experimental. *Seaton Hall Law Review, 36*, 971–1013.

Adams, K., & Ferrandino, J. (2008). Managing mentally ill inmates in prisons. *Criminal Justice and Behavior, 35*(8), 9130927.

Admire, D., & Mitchell, A. (2010). Brain abnormalities in the criminal justice system: Uniting public policy and scientific knowledge. *The International Journal of Interdisciplinary Social Sciences, 5*(2), 343–355.

Anda, R., Whitfield, C., Felitti, V., Chapman, D., Edwards, V., Dube, S., & Williamson, D. (2002). Adverse childhood experiences, alcoholic parents, and later risk of alcoholism and depression. *Psychiatric Services, 53*, 1001–1009.

Andrews, D. A., & Bonta, J. (2010). *The psychology of criminal conduct* (5th ed.). New Providence, NJ: Lexis Nexis.

AOPC Administrative Office of Pennsylvania Courts Office of Communications. (2015). *Problem-solving courts: What are problem-solving courts and how do they benefit Pennsylvanians?* Retrieved from http://www.pacourts.us/assets/files/setting-2236/file-1748.pdf?cb=2953f0

Barber-Rioja, V., Dewey, L., Kopelovich, S., & Kucharski, L. T. (2012). The utility of the HCR-20 and PCL:SV in the prediction of diversion noncompliance and reincarceration in diversion programs. *Criminal Justice and Behavior, 39*(4), 475–492.

Barber-Rioja, V., & Rotter, M. (2014). A therapeutic approach to jurisprudence: A differential thinking model of sanctions and rewards. *International Journal of Forensic Mental Health, 13*(3), 272–278.

Belenko, S. (1998). Research on drug courts: A critical review. *National Drug Court Institute Review, I*(1), 1–42.

Belenko, S. R., Patapis, N., & French, M. (2005). *The economic benefits of drug treatment: A critical review of the evidence for policy makers.* Menomonie: National Rural Alcohol and Drug Abuse Network.

Berman, G., & Feinblatt, J. (2001). Problem-solving courts: A brief primer. *Law & Policy, 23*(2), 125–140.

Boothroyd, R. A., Mercado, C. C., Poythress, N. G., Christy, A., & Petrila, J. (2005). Clinical outcomes of defendants in mental health court. *Psychiatric Services, 56*(7), 829–834.

Boothyrod, R. A., Poythress, N. G., McGaha, A., & Petrila, J. (2003). The Broward County mental health court, process, outcomes and services utilization. *International Journal of Law and Psychiatry, 26*, 55–71.

Briere, J., Agee, E., & Dietrich, A. (2016). Cumulative trauma and current posttraumatic stress disorder status in general population and inmate samples. *Psychological Trauma: Theory, Research, Practice and Policy, 8*(4), 439–446.

Brown, V. B., Harris, M., & Fallot, R. (2013). Moving toward a trauma-informed practice in addiction treatment: A collaborative model of agency assessment. *Journal of Psychoactive Drugs, 45*(5), 386–393.

Bullard, C. E., & Thrasher, R. (2016). Evaluating mental health court by impact on jurisdictional crime rates. *Criminal Justice Policy Review, 27*(3), 227–246.

Bureau of Justice Assistance. (2008). *Mental health courts: A primer for policymakers and practitioners*. Retrieved from https://www.bja.gov/Publications/MHC_Primer.pdf

Butler, P. (2010). One hundred years of race and crime. *Journal of Criminal Law & Criminology, 100*(3), 1043–1060.

Carey, S. M., Mackin, J. R., & Finigan, M. W. (2012). What works? The ten key components of drug court: Research-based best practices. *Drug Court Review, 8*, 6–42.

Carrion, J., & Ramos, F. J. C. (2003). Blows to the head during development can predispose to violent criminal behaviour: Rehabilitation of consequences of head injury is a measure for crime prevention. *Brain Injury, 17*, 207–216.

Colantonio, A., Kim, H., Allen, S., Ashbridge, M., Petgrave, J., & Brochu, S. (2014). Traumatic brain injury and early life experiences among men and women in a prison population. *Journal of Correctional Health Care, 20*(4), 271–279.

Cosden, M., Ellens, J., Schnell, J., & Yamini-Diouf, Y. (2005). Efficacy of a mental health treatment court with assertive community treatment. *Behavioral Sciences & the Law, 23*, 199–214.

Council of State Governments Justice Center. (2008). *Mental health courts: A primer for policymakers and practitioners*. A report prepared by the Council of State Governments Justice Center Criminal Justice/Mental Health Consensus Project New York, New York for the Bureau of Justice Assistance Office of Justice Programs U.S. Department of Justice. Retrieved from: https://csgjusticecenter.org/wp-content/uploads/2012/12/mhc-primer.pdf

Cross, B. (2011). *Mental health courts effectiveness in reducing recidivism and improving clinical outcomes: A meta-analysis*. Graduate Thesis and Dissertations. http://scholarcommons.usf.edu/etd/3052

Dearing, E., McCartney, K., & Taylor, B. A. (2006). Within-child associations between family income and externalizing and internalizing problems. *Developmental Psychology, 42*, 237–252.

Dirks-Linhorst, P. A., Kondrat, D., Linhorst, D. M., & Morani, N. (2013). Factors associated with mental health court nonparticipation and negative termination. *Justice Quarterly, 30*, 681–710. https://doi.org/10.1080/07418825.2011.615756

Dirks-Linhorst, P. A., & Linhorst, D. (2012). Recidivism outcomes for suburban mental health court defendants. *American Journal of Criminal Justice, 37*, 76–91. https://doi.org/10.1007/s12103010-9092-0

Donley, S., Habib, L., Jovanovic, T., Kamkwalala, A., Evec, M., Egan, G., … Ressler, K. J. (2012). Civilian PTSD symptoms and risk for involvement in the criminal justice system. *Journal of the American Academy Psychiatry Law, 40*, 522–529.

Dube, S. R., Felitti, V. J., Dong, M., Chapman, D. P., Giles, W. H., & Anda, R. F. (2003). Childhood abuse, neglect, and household dysfunction and the risk of illicit drug use: The adverse childhood experiences study. *Pediatrics, 111*, 564–572.

Dutton, D. G., & Hart, S. D. (1994). Evidence for long-term, specific effects of childhood abuse and neglect on criminal behavior in men. *International Journal of Offender Therapy and Comparative Criminology, 36*, 129–137.

Elbogen, E. B., Johnson, S. C., Newton, V. M., Straits-Troster, K., Vasterling, J. J., Wagner, H. R., & Beckham, J. C. (2012). Criminal justice involvement, trauma, and negative affect in Iraq and Afghanistan war era veterans. *Journal of Consulting and Clinical Psychology, 80*(6), 1097–1102.

Elliott, D. E., Bjelajac, P., Fallot, R. D., Markoff, L. S., & Reed, B. G. (2005). Trauma-informed or trauma-denied: Principles and implementation of trauma informed services for women. *Journal of Community Psychology, 33*, 429–443.

Farrer, T. J., Frost, R. B., & Hedges, D. W. (2012). Prevalence of traumatic brain injury in intimate partner violence offenders compared to the general population: A meta-analysis. *Trauma, Violence & Abuse, 13*(2), 77–82.

Felitti, V., Anda, R., Nordenberg, D., Williamson, D., Spitz, A., Edwards, V., et al. (1998). Relationship of childhood abuse and household dysfunction to many of the leading causes of death in adults. *American Journal of Preventive Medicine, 14*, 245–258.

Flores, P, Lopez, J, Pemble-Flood, G, Riegel, H, Segura, M (2018). *An Analysis of Drug Treatment Courts in New York State. Rockefeller Institute of Government, Center for Law and Policy Solutions*

Giarratano, P., Ford, J. D., & Nochajski, T. H. (2017). Gender differences in complex posttraumatic stress symptoms, and their relationship to mental health and substance abuse outcomes in incarcerated adults. *Journal of Interpersonal Violence*, 1–25.

Gibson, L. E., Holt, J. C., Fondacaro, K. M., Tang, T. S., Powell, T. A., & Turbitt, E. L. (1999). An examination of antecedent traumas and psychiatric comorbidity among male inmates with PTSD. *Journal of Traumatic Stress, 12*(3), 473–484.

Goldkamp, J. S., & Weiland, D. (1993). *Assessing the impact of Dade County's felony drug court. Executive Summary*. Washington, DC: Crime and Justice Research Institute: National Institute of Justice Research Brief.

Green, B. L., Dass-Brailsford, P., de Mendoz, A. H., Mete, M., Lynch, S. M., DeHart, D. D., & Belknap, J. (2016). Psychological trauma, theory, research. *Practice and Policy, 8*(4), 455–463.

Greenfeld, L. A., & Snell, T. L. (1999). *Bureau of Justice Statistics Special Report: Women Offenders*. Pub no NCJ175688. Washington, DC: US Department of Justice, Office of Justice Programs.

Harner, H.M., Budescu, M., Gillihan, S.J., Riley, S., & Foa, E.B. (2015). Posttraumatic stress disorder in incarcerated women: A call for evidence-based treatment. Psychological Trauma: Theory, Research, Practice, and Policy, 7,1,58–66.

Harris, M., & Fallot, R. (Eds.). (2001). *Using trauma theory to design service systems*. San Francisco, CA: Jossey-Bass.

Harrison, P. M., & Beck, A. J. (2005). *Bureau of Justice Statistics Bulletin: Prison and Jail Inmates t Midyear 2004*. Pub no NCJ 208801. Washington, DC: US Department of Justice, Office of Justice Programs.

Hartley, R. D., & Baldwin, J. M. (2016). Waging war on recidivism among justice-involved veterans: An impact evaluation of a large urban veterans treatment court. *Criminal Justice Policy Review, 30*, 1–27.

Hartwell, S. W., James, A., Chen, J., Pinals, D. A., Marin, M. C., & Smelson, D. (2014). Trauma among justice-involved veterans. *Professional Psychology: Research and Practice, 45*(6), 425–432.

Hawley, C. A., & Maden, A. (2003). Mentally disordered offenders with a history of previous head injury: Are they more difficult to discharge? *Brain Injury, 17*, 743–758.

Health Resources and Service Administration. (2011). *Traumatic brain injury and the U.S. criminal justice system*. [PDF document]. Retrieved from http://www.disabilityrightsohio.org/sites/default/files/ux/hrsa-criminal-justice-fact-sheet.pdf

Hiday, V. A., & Ray, B. (2010). Arrests two years after existing a well-established mental health court. *Psychiatric Services, 61*(5), 463–468.

Hiday, V. A., Ray, B., & Wales, H. W. (2014). Predictors of mental health court graduation. *Psychology Public Policy and Law, 20*(2), 191–199.

Hiday, V. A., Wales, H. W., & Ray, B. (2013). Effectiveness of a short-term mental health court: Criminal recidivism one year postexit. *Law and Human Behavior, 37*, 401–411.

Honegger, L. N. (2015). Does the evidence support the case for mental health courts? A review of the literature. *Law and Human Behavior, 39*(5), 478–488.

Horn, M. L., & Lutz, D. J. (2016). Traumatic brain injury in the criminal justice system: Identification and response to neurological trauma. *Applied Psychology in Criminal Justice, 12*(2), 71–86.

Hyman, S. M., Garcia, M., & Sinha, R. (2006). Gender specific associations between types of childhood maltreatment and the onset, escalation and severity of substance use in cocaine dependent adults. *American Journal of Drug and Alcohol Abuse, 32*, 655–664.

James, D. J., & Glaze, L. E. (2006). *Mental health problems of prison and jail inmates (NCJ 213600)*. Washington, DC: Bureau of Justice Statistics. Retrieved from http://www.prisonpolicy.org/scans/bjs/ mhppji.pdf

Johnson, R. S., Stolar, A. G., Wu, E., Coonan, L. A., & Graham, D. P. (2015). An analysis of successful outcomes and associated contributing factors in veterans' court. *Bulletin of the Menninger Clinic, 7*(2), 166–173.

Kelly, G., & Winkler, D. (2007). Long-term accommodation and support for people with higher levels of challenging behaviour. *Brain Impairment, 8*, 262–275.

Kim, E. Y., Park, J., & Kim, B. (2016). Type of childhood maltreatment and the risk of criminal recidivism in adult probationers: A cross-sectional study. *BMC Psychiatry, 16*, 294–302.

Kingston, D. A., & Olver, M. E. (2017). Psychometric examination of treatment change among mentally disordered offenders. A risk-needs analysis. *Criminal Justice and Behavior, 45*(2), 153–172.

Kingston, D.W., & Oliver, M.E. (2018). Psychometric examination of treatment change among mentally disordered offenders. A risk needs analysis. Criminal Justice and Behavior, 45,2, 153–172.

Knudsen, K., & Wingenfeld, S. (2016). A specialized treatment court for veterans with trauma exposure: Implications for the field. *Community Mental Health, 52*, 127–135.

Kowalski, M. A. (2018). Adverse childhood experiences and justice-involved youth: The effect of trauma and programming on different recidivistic outcomes. *Youth Violence and Juvenile Justice*, 1–31.

Landes, S. J., Garovoy, N. D., & Burkman, K. M. (2013). Treating complex trauma among veterans: Three stage-based treatment models. *Journal of Clinical Psychology: In Session, 69*(5), 523–533.

Landess, J., & Holoyda, B. (2017). Mental health courts and forensic assertive community treatment teams as correctional diversion programs. *Behavioral Sciences Law, 35*, 501–511.

Latimer, J., Morton-Bourgon, K., & Chretien, J. (2006). *A meta-analytic examination of drug treatment courts – do they reduce recidivism?* Ottawa: Research and Statistics Division, Department of Justice.

Linehan, M. M. (1993). *Cognitive-behavioral treatment of borderline personality disorder*. New York: The Guilford Press.

Lucas, J. A., & Addeo, R. (2006). Traumatic brain injury and Postconcussion syndrome. In P. J. Snyder, P. D. Nussbaum, & D. L. Robins (Eds.), *Clinical neuropsychology: A pocket handbook for assessment* (pp. 351–380). Washington, DC: American Psychological Association.

Lurigio, A. (2008). The first 20 years of drug treatment courts: A brief description of their history and impact. *Federal Probation*, 13–17.

Lurigio, A. J. (2012). Responding to the needs of people with mental illness in the criminal justice system: An area ripe for research and community partnerships. *Journal of Crime and Criminal Justice, 35*, 1–12.

Luskin, M. L. (2013). More of the same? Treatment in mental health courts. *Law and Human Behavior, 37*(4), 255–266.

Marlowe, D. B. (2010). *Research update on adult drug courts*. National Association of Drug Court Professionals. Need to know. 1–7.

Marlowe, D. B., Festinger, D. S., Arabia, P. L., Dugosh, K. L., Benasutti, K. M., Croft, J. R., & McKay, J. R. (2008). Adaptive interventions in rug court. A pilot experiment. *Criminal Justice Review, 33*(3), 343–360.

Marotta, P. L. (2017). Childhood adversities and substance misuse among incarcerated: Implications for treatment and practice in correctional settings. *Substance Use & Misuse, 52*(6), 717–733.

Messina, N., Grella, C., Burdon, W., & Prendergast, M. (2007). Childhood adverse events and current traumatic distress. A comparison of men and women drug-dependent prisoners. *Criminal Justice and Behavior, 34*(11), 1385–1404.

Mitchell, O., Wilson, D. B., Eggers, A., & MacKenzie, D. L. (2012). Assessing the effectiveness of drug courts on recidivism: A meta-analytic review of traditional and non-traditional drug courts. *Journal of Criminal Justice, 40*, 60–71.

Moore, M. E., & Hiday, V. A. (2006). Mental health court outcomes: A comparison of re-arrest and re-arrest severity between mental health court and traditional court participants. *Law and Human Behavior, 30*, 659–674.

Najavits, L. M. (2002). *Seeking safety: A treatment manual for PTSD and substance abuse.* New York: The Guilford Press.

NAMI. (n.d.). *Jailing people with mental illness.* Retrieved from: https://www.nami.org/Learn-More/Public-Policy/Jailing-People-with-Mental-Illness

National Center for State Courts. (2015). Statewide efforts for problem-solving courts. Retrieved from https://www.ncsc.org/~/media/Files/PDF/Services%20and%20Experts/Areas%20of%20expertise/Problem%20solving%20courts/Statewide%20Efforts%20in%20PSC%20(2015).ashx

National Institute of Justice. Crime Solutions.gov (2018). *Specialized and problem-solving courts.* Retrieved from: https://www.crimesolutions.gov/TopicDetails.aspx?ID=49#Overview

Nored, L. S., & Carlan, P. E. (2008). Success of drug court programs. Examination of the perceptions of drug court personnel. *Criminal Justice Review, 33*(3), 329–342.

Osher, F. C., & Steadman, H. J. (2007). Adapting evidence-based practices for persons with mental illness involved with the criminal justice system. *Psychiatric Services, 58*, 1472–1478.

Peters, R. H., & Murrin, M. R. (2000). Effectiveness of treatment-based drug courts in reducing criminal recidivism. *Criminal Justice and Behavior, 27*(1), 72–96.

Piccolino, A. L., & Solberg, K. B. (2014). The impact of traumatic brain injury on prison health services and offender management. *Journal of Correctional Health Care, 20*, 203–212.

Pollard, J. M., Schuster, J., Lin, H.-J., & Frisman, L. K. (2007). Evaluation of a gender and trauma specific jail diversion program for female offenders. *American Jails, 21*, 53–63.

Porter, R., Rempel, M., & Mansky, A. (2010). *What makes a court problem-solving.Universal performance indicators for problem-solving justice.* Center for Court Innovation. Retrieved from http://www.courtinnovation.org/sites/default/files/What_Makes_A_Court_P_S.pdf

Prins, S. J. (2014). The prevalence of mental illness in U.S. State Prisons: A systematic review. *Psychiatric Services, 65*(7), 862–872.

Ray, B., Sapp, D., & Kincaid, A. (2014) Traumatic Brain Injury among Indiana State Prisoners. Journal of Forensic Sciences, 59, 1248–1253. https://doi.org/10.1111/1556-4029.12466

Ray, B., & Richardson, N. (2017). Traumatic Brain Injury and Recidivism Among Returning Inmates. Criminal Justice and Behavior, 44. 009385481668663. https://doi.org/10.1177/0093854816686631.

Redlich, A. D., Steadman, H. J., Callahan, L., Robbins, P. C., Vessilinov, R., & Ozdogru, A. A. (2010). The use of mental health court appearances in supervision. *International Journal of Law and Psychiatry, 33*, 272–277. https://doi.org/10.1016/j.ijlp.2010.06.010

Redlich, A. D., Steadman, H. J., Monahan, J., Robbins, P. C., & Petrila, J. (2006). Patterns of practice in mental health courts: A national survey. *Law and Human Behavior, 30*, 347–362.

Reich, W.A., Pichard-Fritsche, S., Cerniglia, L., & Hahn, J.W. (2014). *Predictors of program compliance and re-arrest in the Brooklyn mental health court.* Center for Court Innovation. Retrieved from https://www.courtinnovation.org/sites/default/files/documents/MHC_Brooklyn.pdf

Roll, J. M., Prendergast, M., Richardson, K., Burdon, W., & Ramirez, A. (2005). Identifying predictors of treatment outcome in a drug court program. *The American Journal of Drug and Alcohol Abuse, 31*, 641–656.

Sadeh, N., & McNiel, D. E. (2015). Posttraumatic stress disorder increases risk of criminal recidivism among justice-involved persons with mental disorders. *Criminal Justice and Behavior, 42*(6), 573–586.

Samhsa. (2005). *The Nathaniel project: An alternative to incarceration program for people with serious mental illness who have committed felony offenses.* Retrieved from http://www.antoniocasella.eu/archipsy/nathaniel_project_2002-2005.pdf

Sareen, J. (2014). Posttraumatic stress disorder in adults: Impact, comorbidity, risk factors, and treatment. *Canadian Journal of Psychiatry. Revue Canadienne de Psychiatrie, 59*(9), 460–467. https://doi.org/10.1177/070674371405900902

Sarteschi, C. M., Vaughn, M. G., & Kim, K. (2011). Assessing the effectiveness of mental health courts: A quantitative review. *Journal of Criminal Justice, 39*, 12–20. https://doi.org/10.1016/j.jcrimjus.2010.11.003

Seltzer, T. (2005). Mental health courts: A misguided attempt to address the criminal justice system's unfair treatment of people with mental illness. *Psychology, Publish Policy, Law, 11*(4), 570–586.

Shannon, L. M., Jones, A. J., Newell, J., & Payne, C. (2018). Examining individual characteristics and program performance to understand two-year recidivism rates among drug court participants: Comparing graduates and terminators. *International Journal of Offender Therapy and Comparative Criminology*, 1–25.

Slaughter, B., Fann, J. R., & Ehde, D. (2003). Traumatic brain injury in a county jail population: Prevalence, neuropsychological functioning, and psychiatric disorders. *Brain Injury, 17*, 731–741.

Smelson, D., Farquhar, I., Fisher, W., Pressman, K., Pinals, D. A., Samek, B., … Sawh, L. (2018). Integrating a co-occurring disorders intervention in drug courts: An open pilot trial. *Community Mental Health Journal, 55*, 222–231.

Smyth, N., & Greyber, L. (2013). Trauma-informed practice. In B. Thyer, C. Dulmus, & K. Sowers (Eds.), *Developing evidence-based generalist practice skills* (1st ed., pp. 25–50). Hoboken, NJ: Wiley.

Steadman, H. J., & Naples, M. (2005). Assessing the effectiveness of jail diversion programs for persons with serious mental illness and co-occurring substance use disorders. *Behavioral Sciences & the Law, 23*, 163–170.

Steadman, H. J., Redlich, A., Callahan, L., Robbins, P. C., & Vesselinov, R. (2011). Effect of mental health courts on arrests and jail days: A multisite study. *Archives of General Psychiatry, 68*, 167–172. https://doi.org/10.1001/archgenpsychiatry.2010.134

Strong, S. M., Rantala, R. R., & Kyckelhahn, T. (2016). *Census of problem-solving courts, 2012.* Washington, DC: U.S. Department of Justice, Office of Justice Programs. NCJ 249803. Retrieved from https://www.bjs.gov/content/pub/pdf/cpsc12.pdf

Swartz, M., & Robertson, A. G. (2016). Mental health courts: Does treatment make a difference? *Psychiatric Services, 67*, 363.

Teplin, L. A., Abram, K. M., & McClelland, G. M. (1996). Prevalence of psychiatric disorders among incarcerated women: Pretrial jail detainees. *Archives of General Psychiatry, 53*, 505–512.

Thompson, M., Osher, F., & Tomasini-Joshi, D. (2007). Improving responses to people with mental illnesses: The essential elements of a mental health court. The Council of State Governments Justice Center Criminal Justice/Mental Health Consensus Project for the Bureau of Justice Assistance, Office of Justice Programs U.S. Department of Justice. Retrieved from: https://www.bja.gov/Publications/MHC_Essential_Elements.pdf.

Tsai, J., Finlay, A., Flatley, B., Kasprow, W. J., & Clark, S. (2018). A national study of veterans treatment court participants: Who benefits and who recidivates. *Administrative Policy Mental Health, 45*, 236–244.

Verhaaff, A., & Scott, H. (2015). Individual factors predicting mental health court diversion outcome. *Research on Social Work Practice, 25*(2), 213–228.

Watson, A., Hanrahan, P., Luchins, D., & Lurigio, A. (2001). Mental health courts and the complex issue of mentally ill offenders. *Psychiatric Services, 52*, 477–481. https://doi.org/10.1176/appi.ps.52.4.477

Weeks, R., & Widom, C. S. (1998). Self-reports of early childhood victimization among incarcerated adult male felons. *Journal of Interpersonal Violence, 13*, 346–361.

Wexler, D. (1990). *Therapeutic jurisprudence: The law as a therapeutic agent.* Durham, NC: Carolina Academic Press.

Wexler, D. (1992). Putting mental health into mental health law: Therapeutic jurisprudence. *Law and Human Behavior, 16*(1), 27–38.

Wiechelt, S. (2014). Intersections between trauma and substance misuse: Implications for trauma-informed care. In S. Straussner (Ed.), *Clinical work with substance-abusing clients* (3rd ed., pp. 179–201). New York: Guilford.

Wiener, R. L., Winick, B. J., Georges, L. S., & Castro, A. (2010). A testable theory of problem solving courts: Avoiding past empirical and legal failures. *International Journal of Law and Psychiatry, 33*, 417–427.

Williams, W. H., Mewse, A. J., Tonks, J., Mills, S., Burgess, C. N., & Cordan, G. (2010). Traumatic brain injury in a prison population: Prevalence and risk for re-offending. *Brain Injury, 24*, 1184–1188.

Wilson, D. B., Mitchell, O., & MacKenzie, D. L. (2006). A systematic review of drug court effects on recidivism. *Journal of Experimental Criminology, 2*(4), 459–457.

Winick, B. J. (2003). Therapeutic jurisprudence and problem solving courts. *Fordham Urban Law Journal, 30*, 1055–1090.

Wolff, N., & Pogorzelski, W. (2005). Psychology, Public Policy, and Law, 11,4, 539–569.

Wolff, N., Huening, J., Shi, J., & Frueh, C. (2014). Trauma exposure and posttraumatic stress disorder among incarcerated men. *Journal of Urban Health: Bulletin of the New York Academy of Medicine, 91*(4), 707–719.

World Health Organization. (n.d.). *Mental health and prisons.* Retrieved from https://www.who.int/mental_health/policy/mh_in_prison.pdf

World Prison Brief. (n.d.). *Highest to lowest – prison population total.* Retrieved from http://www.prisonstudies.org/highest-to-lowest/prison-population-total?field_region_taxonomy_tid=All

Yuan, C., Wang, Z., Inslicht, S. S., McCaslin, S. E., Metzler, T. J., Henn-Haase, C., ... Marmar, C. R. (2011). Protective factors for posttraumatic stress disorder symptoms in a prospective study of police officers. *Psychiatry Research, 188*(1), 45–50. https://doi.org/10.1016/j.psychres.2010.10.034

Zettler, H., & Iratzoqui, A. (2018). Investigating the impact of child maltreatment histories on drug court outcomes. *Criminal Justice and Behavior, 45*(6), 799–819.

# Part IV
# Concluding Thoughts and Activities

Rafael Art. Javier, Elizabeth A. Owen, and Jemour A. Maddux

## Introduction

This final sets of chapters are meant not only to highlight the major issues addressed throughout this book but also to provide some perspectives of future directions. There is a general discussion of the emerging issues raised throughout this book and a discussion of specific prescriptions for the forensic professionals (Chap. 20 by Javier, Owen, and Jemour). A particular focus is to encourage more hands-on involvement in the material and in that context, it also includes a chapter entitled "Trauma and Its Trajectory of Criminal Behavior" (Chap. 21 by Javier, Kachersky, Owen, and Jemour). This chapter is set up as "Case Studies" which features not only some of the specific (notorious) crimes committed over the course of history but also some personal history (biographies) of those involved in these crimes. It is set up as a separate chapter to facilitate the use of this section as a teaching tool for class assignments.

The final chapter by Hon. Hirsch (Chap. 22) is meant to provide a case study of how a justice system that considers the multiplicity of factors, which are normally involved in the commission of a crime, can be meaningfully incorporated in the deliberation and adjudication of the crime by the court while still affirming the defendants' personal accountability. It is an interesting and involved process which requires the active participation of many sectors of our society to ensure its success. We are left with the hope that more progress can be made to ensure that the role of

R. A. Javier
Psychology, St. John's University, Queens, NY, USA

E. A. Owen
Columbia University/Teachers College, New York, NY, USA

J. A. Maddux
Lamb & Maddux, LLC, Hackensack, NJ, USA

trauma in those involved in the justice system (as defendants, victims, law enforcement, members of the legal systems, judges, and attorneys) is meaningfully considered in identifying factors that could complicate and confuse the forensic issue under consideration. Failure to do so raises the possibility of miscarriages of justice at all levels.

# Chapter 20
# On the Contextualization of Criminal Behavior: In Search of the Best Practice

**Rafael Art. Javier, Elizabeth A. Owen, and Jemour A. Maddux**

Our main purpose of this book was to highlight the central role and ubiquitous nature of the experience of trauma in the lives of individuals involved in the legal system and, to some extent, also in the general population. We defined trauma as phenomenon along a continuum where the least disruptive aspects of it are likely experienced as mild anxiety when the conditions that triggered it are not considered by the individual as too threatening. The more it is experienced as threatening, the more likely it sets up the likelihood to have a disruptive effect on the individual's general functioning. Since forensic psychologists are often involved in evaluating both victims and perpetrators of crimes, our goal was to encourage an examination of factors in traumatic experiences that may have contributed to the conditions that forensic professionals are asked to assess, whether it is focusing on the victims or the perpetrators. There are important considerations to keep in mind in how to report trauma findings related to perpetrators of crimes as these can be wrongly perceived as providing justification for the crime. Some refer to this consideration as "mitigating factors" which may suggest to others as "finding excuses"; we prefer to view it as part of a "contextualization" based upon the facts on the ground. There is also the consideration that not everyone exposed to trauma will necessarily develop symptoms or a psychological condition.

There is an expressed and unspoken fear that by looking at all the factors involved in a crime; by considering the possible history of trauma, attachment history, and subsequent developmental material of those involved in the justice system as

R. A. Javier (✉)
Psychology, St. John's University, Queens, NY, USA
e-mail: javierr@stjohns.edu

E. A. Owen
Columbia University/Teachers College, New York, NY, USA

J. A. Maddux
Lamb and Maddux, LLC, Hackensack, NJ, USA

© Springer Nature Switzerland AG 2020             497
R. A. Javier et al. (eds.), *Assessing Trauma in Forensic Contexts*,
https://doi.org/10.1007/978-3-030-33106-1_20

defendants; and by considering the specific conditions before, during, and following the commission of a crime, we are basically finding a justification. Behind that perspective is the belief that a crime is a crime for which every criminal should be held accountable and "made to pay for the crime."

The contributors of this volume took great pride and care to include the latest scientific findings guiding psychology as a scientific enterprise. The material presented are meant to encourage "best forensic practice" by ensuring that all pertaining information about the forensic situation under consideration are centrally and meaningfully included in the forensic assessment and in the treatment intervention. That should include trauma-related information as well as information related to resiliency (Almeida, Ramalho, Fernandez, & Guarda, 2019; Courtois & Ford, 2009; Ford & Courtois, 2009). By informing the court of our findings in this context, it may result in a sentence adjudication that, in the mind of some, is considered too lenient for the crime committed and may see the work of the forensic professional as having mainly an advocacy function. That will be an unfortunate conclusion as forensic assessments also routinely include risk assessment of possible recidivism. In that context we communicate findings supporting the difficulty in predicting future crimes, due to the multiplicity of factors normally involved, that are not easily predictable and/or controllable. Improving the predictability of future crimes continues to be a goal of forensic science, but although much improved with the Bootstrapped logistic regression method used by Zagar, Busch, Grove, and Hughes (2009), we still don't have a comfortable level of certainty in this regard. For instance, studying the criterion of violent delinquency, Zagar and his associates suggested that it is possible to arrive to a high level of predictability of violence re-offense (from 39–53% to 69–75% accuracy) when using personality and actuarial probation-parole tests. Because, in the end, we could never be hundred percent certain in our violence prediction, Heilbrun (2009) suggested that we are better off focusing on the management aspects of the risk of reoffending, which may include the judicious application of prison and carefully designed and structured restrictive conditions post release to ensure the protection of society.

There is another fear, but this time coming from forensic professionals: that other professionals may use findings from these types of forensic assessments to advance an ideology regarding the justice system in general and demanding reforms, thus turning the forensic work into advocacy. Although it is not unusual for scientific findings to encourage a change in positions, by helping change long-held beliefs and customary positions that are not justified by the facts on the ground, we have only one goal in mind: to provide the most comprehensive and objective set of information to assist the court in its deliberation. It is clear that some criminal acts require the most severe penalty allowable under the law, while for others, society may be better served with different approaches to the execution of justice. The work of the forensic professional that is guided by considering all factors involved in the criminal condition under consideration (best practice) will be in the best position to assist the court in determining whether the court's intervention should or should not include the treatment of the trauma as a central component in the adjudication process. It may also serve to clarify if the individual accused of the crime may have provided a voluntary or persuaded false confession, and what may have been involved in such an occurrence (e.g., psychopathology, disability, youth, stress, police pressure, cultural factors, etc.) (Leo, 2009; Vaughans & Spielberg, 2014).

## Perception of Motives as Central in Criminal Behavior

We examined or made references to various kinds of crimes and forensic situations in different chapters of this book, ranging from issues related to civil laws to issues more specifically related to criminal laws. Of particular significance is the examination of the different motives guiding the behaviors of those involved with the justice system as defendants. In our examination, we have observed that some of the aggressive and homicidal behaviors involve a level of transformation in those committing the crime, where the people to whom these behaviors are directed are seen as objects deserving what they get and the act itself precipitated by real or perceived personal insults, usually related to intense and severe sensitivity to real or perceived feelings of rejection/dejection. We see multiple examples of these transformations in the list of criminals presented in Chap. 21 of this book on "trauma and its trajectory in criminal behaviors." Considering the level of sensitivity, personal threat, and the enormity and intensity of the crime that it is sometimes unleashed, we come to the conclusion that something is amiss in those individuals.

In our effort to address that very issue, we paid particular attention to the conditions likely to be involved in the development of faulty perceptions and an inability to accurately being able to judge other's motivations. There is an insidious distortion of reality, particularly when negative emotions (anger, rejection, fear, anxiety, etc.) are involved, that, in their mind, require immediate action meant to restore and reconstitute whatever discomfort the situation may have generated. We emphasized that only by examining factors related to early developmental trajectories where the seed of those perceptions are established; by examining relevant aspects of subsequent developmental trajectories where these perceptions are further solidified, and the conditions that may have triggered the development of such faulty perceptions, we will be able to provide the necessary context to understand the psychological factors that may be involved in criminal behaviors. In this context, we discussed the importance of considering the quality of early attachments and how many of those involved in the legal systems are likely to suffer from some attachment and personality disorders and poor mental health conditions (Allen & Fonagy, 2017; Garbarino, 2015); for others, it would be instructive to also consider the environmental, sociopolitical, and socioeconomic factors that may have contributed to such a development. That is particularly the case when dealing with individuals who have been the victims of protracted and severe racism and discrimination (Greene, 2005; Sue et al., 2007; Vaughans & Spielberg, 2014).

We emphasized, in this regard, that something fundamental occurs in the very core of individuals exposed to prolong stress that changes the natural trajectory of how they respond to environmental challenges, even at the most basic biological and neural levels; we discussed relevant data in this context emerging from a variety of sources from neurobiology, neuropsychology, to behavioral sciences. The fact that it has been found to affect the medial prefrontal regions of the brain to the point of rendering ineffective the neurocircuits responsible for regulating a hyperactive amygdala and insula (Liddell et al., 2019; Pitman et al., 2012), highlights the devastating impact sustained trauma could have in such a fundamental and core component of our ability to function effectively and responsibly. It impacts on our ability to function by disrupting the alarm system networks and causing excessive early alertness (hypervigilance) due to excessive prefrontal activity that is unable to filter its response. Some findings suggest a long-lasting effect in various parts of brain function (particularly those responsible for regulating emotions and self-awareness) prolonged trauma exposure have on the individual even in the absence of symptoms. That issue has been amply supported, including most recently by Liddell et al. (2019) in their controlled study with a group of resettled refugees. They found that it is the degree of chronic trauma exposure that tends to increase in "fear-related brain activity" (p. 811) even in a post-displacement environment where the early threats are no longer present.

The fact that the region of the brain mechanism normally highly activated in PTSD and in response to threat in the environment is the one being disrupted explains the insidious and debilitating consequences of this effect. It seriously compromises the individual's perception and disrupts his/her capacity to make proper judgments and interpretations of other's motivations. The complexity and insidiousness of that effect complicate the forensic task by requiring a more comprehensive approach to forensic assessment and intervention that also includes a trauma assessment. Such an assessment approach is meant to offer the court the best opportunity for the adjudication of justice which also includes a consideration of the best course of action to take in terms of the kind of intervention to implement during incarceration that can also address relevant factors involved in the commission of the crime under consideration.

This approach to incarceration was extensively discussed in this volume by Leidenfrost and Antonius, by Lamade and Lee, and by Hon. Hirsch in Chaps. 4, 19, and 21, respectively. It requires a drastic shift in perspectives from the notion of deterrence and punishment as symbol of moral accountability and crime control to a consideration of trauma in the way we understand and manage crime and its rehabilitation process (National Research Council, 2014). Recognizing that the old prison system is not working in deterring crimes but rather it has been found to contribute to recidivism, prison systems in Norway, the UK, Texas, and North Dakota (Leaf, 2015) are all involved in finding and implementing more effective ways to protect our society, while at the same time taking advantage of the prison time to work on a systematic and comprehensive approach to rehabilitation, with reportedly good results. Their approach is considered innovative because it takes into consideration the defendant's unique personal situations (including strengths and deficiencies, skills, educational backgrounds, work history, social support, etc.) and the recognition that it requires the active involvement of all sectors of our society to succeed; that includes securing the necessary financial investment, structural and community resources, and moral support from several sectors of society. It also requires continuous involvement with these individuals after the completion of incarceration and as they engage in reintegration into society. We suggest that for many defendants where the issue of racism and discrimination was also a factor, an intervention that provides ample opportunities to address those issues will likely be more meaningful and contribute to a more positive response. Part of the reason for that is that it provides a recognition and affirmation of the nature of their racial discrimination victimization that may have been central aspects of their experience and contributing to their legal situation.

Chapters 19 by Lamade and Lee and 21 by Hirsch also provide an important discussion with regard to the innovative approaches that some courts are taking as part of the process for the adjudication of justice. These approaches are considered more comprehensive in their focus because they consider all the components in the lives of those convicted of a crime, including addressing the psychological effect of trauma on these individuals and their family. Finally, assistance/close supervision is provided as part of the intervention during the period of reinsertion/reintegration into the society so that they are not left alone to their own devices at those critical times in the rehabilitation process. It is a human approach but with a strong dosage of accountability, as those who are unable to succeed are reintegrated into the prison system to fulfill their prison terms.

The reason for consideration of new approaches to trauma-influenced behaviors is the fact that earlier interventions have had poor or very limited results. For instance, although high rates of PTSD and related disorders are reported among refugees, evidence-based treatment of PTSD has been found not to be as effective as for other populations (Carlsson, Sonne, & Silove, 2014). Similarly, only interventions that focus on specific targeted behaviors have been found to be somewhat effective for incarcerated inmates (Huss, 2014), with the majority of interventions found to have only limited positive outcomes. The issue is that these interventions tend not to be meaningfully effective for a whole range of issues central to the lives of these individuals, which can only happen with treatment models that are more comprehensive in nature and consider the complex quality of complicated and pervasive trauma history (Courtois & Ford, 2009; Ford & Courtois, 2009). As indicated earlier, it should also include intervention opportunities to address victimization issues related to racism and various discriminations (e.g., race, gender, religion, age, intersectionality of mutiple identities, etc.).

## Relevance of Trauma History of Those Enforcing the Law

Considering that findings from the various sources consistently confirm that a legal system focusing only on punishment/deterrence not only fails to address the fundamental reasons for the crime but also ultimately tends to lead to miscarriages of justice, we dedicated Chaps. 12 by Casarella and Beebe, and 14 by Maddux to examining also those working in the justice system responsible for the enforcement of the law. It is a difficult situation to be responsible for protecting society from criminals and for some officers it may become quite a challenge because of their own personal history of trauma. When that is the case, it may impair their perception and response to a threat when dealing with a situation that requires clear ability to make a decision about whether and the extent to which a threat is present and the extent to which it is imminent. Also, an early unresolved trauma history may complicate their relationships with colleagues, immediate superiors, suspects, or community members. These factors may become intricately implicated in the process of a rush to judgment in situations of perceived real or imaginary threat, the most devastating consequence of which is the possibility of making a bad situation even worse. It opens the door to possible corruption of the legal system by forcing a precipitous rush to judgment, with the unintended consequence of also giving a false sense of security (i.e., falsely apprehending an individual who just fits the profile but who has nothing to do with the specific crime).

The consequences of this mental set have been amply reported in the media of individuals being stopped for supposedly suspicious behaviors, mostly people of colors (the stop and frisk police policy and practice); to unarmed individuals with no criminal history being controversially shot and killed; to coerced confessions from innocent individuals, who belong to a potitically and socioeconomically disadvantaged group and overrepresented in the legal system; to the treatment of immigrants and other minority groups, particularly Blacks and Latinos, who are portrayed in the political discourse as criminals and responsible for all the ills affecting our society, etc.

It is quite challenging for officers to have to navigate such a complicated set of messages and expectations while trying to protect our society from criminals and also secretely struggling with their personal trauma history. That mental set may be behind the miscarriage of justice in the case of the "Central Park Jogger" in which a group of youngsters were indicted and convicted of a crime they immediately communicated to the investigating detectives that they did not commit, only to be forced to confess as a condition for their possible release. They were recently exonerated after several years in prison and the crime later proven to be committed by someone else. The successful releases of several individuals cleared by DNA (Zagar et al., 2009) also speak about the danger of that mental set driven by a biased perception that assumes criminality, particularly in reference to some individuals seen as not part of the mainstream and considered part of those "others" in our society who are routinely considered responsible for most of the crimes in the society. The inherent and profound unfairness of this situation is the incarceration of these individuals for crimes assumed to be committed by them but which are later demonstrated to the contrary 20–30 years later. The most painful consequence of these types of legal decisions is the realization that no amount of monetary compensation will ever reconstitute/return those years (now lost forever), with their lives permanently altered in a variety of ways: in relationship to their children in whose lives they could not be meaningful parts of; spouses that have grown apart with the passing of time; community networks which are no longer available once they are released, etc.

Sue and his associates (2007) have provided us with sufficient data describing different types of prejudicial aggression and microaggression judgments that are made by individuals in day-to-day transactions with members of diverse communities, reflecting intended and/or unintended pernicious consequences of these types of transactions on their targets. When expressed by individuals responsible for enforcing the law, they are in effect wittingly or unwittingly exercising their power to detour an individual's personal trajectory by making that individual a defendant in something he/she was not involved but just happen to fit a profile. The other complication here is that by giving the benefit of the doubt to the one making the decision to apprehend (the officer), the assumption is that a reasonable individual understands that *the individual apprehended must have given the officer a reason for the legal action.* A vicious cycle then takes hold of the process with the assumption that once accused, the presumption of innocence does not quite apply, and once in custody, the treatment the individual receives is of an assumed and adjudicated guilty verdict for all practical purposes. Bail reform and reforms requiring evidence sharing by prosecutors now being considered in many states may be seen by some as one avenue to addressing a portion of this quagmire, but time will tell. The sense of helplessness and hopelessness that may engender in the affected individuals is indescribable, particularly if these individuals have already experienced serious and severe trauma prior to that encounter with the law.

That does not mean that there is a conscious and clearly malicious intent in those involved in law enforcement but rather that they too may be influenced in their behaviors and decisions by their own personal trauma history. Hence, our strong recommendation that an assessment of trauma history for law enforcement personnel be an essential aspect of their pre-employment assessment and subsequently in relationship to the discharge of their responsibilities. There is too much at stake by neglecting the mental health condition of officers, whose neglect has already resulted in an increase in domestic violence incidents among officers, in drug and alcohol usage, and even in rising suicide rates (https://www.nytimes.com/2019/08/13/nyregion/nypd-officer-suicide.html) now plaguing those with the task of protecting us. There is some evidence with veterans suffering from PTSD confirming the prevalence of secondary traumatic stress in the partners of these veterans (Diehle, Brooks, & Greenberg, 2017). We consider these findings relevant and pertinent to our discussion because many members of law enforcement also have had at least one tour of duty in recent armed conflicts, and some still active in the military as part of the National Guard Reserve. Our recommendation is to ensure ongoing consultation/treatment opportunities for these officers as a way to help them address the effect of their personal trauma history that may cloud their capacity for a fair discharge of their responsibilities and increase dysfunctionality with their immediate families and friends.

## Bias Consequences in Forensic Professionals

The greatest challenge for the professional is the assumption that the presence of trauma is fully assessed and arrived at with a PTSD diagnosis. The fact of the matter is that we found evidence that assessment of trauma and its vicissitudes can become complicated by a number of factors: The first factor has to do with the intrinsic limitations of symptoms required for a determination of a PTSD diagnosis under the DSM-5. We discussed that issue at length in several chapters of the book (e.g., Chap. 1 by Javier and Owen and Chap. 5 by Caffrey) and suggested the importance of considering the multiple ways traumatic conditions are expressed that include physical and emotional manifestations. The recommendation is to include multiple interrelated diagnoses, the combination of which may represent more accurately the range of symptoms related to traumatic experiences relevant to the person being evaluated, and not to assume that the absence of trauma of PTSD diagnosis as defined by the DSM nomenclature necessarily means that there is no trauma. This is particularly the case, when dealing with individuals from different cultural and linguistic communities than the one on which the assessment tool was normed. In other words, the resulting diagnosis should also consider unique culturally and linguistically specific ways that the clients being assessed use to express the effect of their trauma that may include intensely engaging in dancing, singing, religious rituals, etc.

The second factor is somewhat related to the previous one. It has to do with a series of fallacies that can become particularly damaging and problematic when dealing with the various personal traumatic experiences in multiple cultural contexts, as described by Wells, Wells, and Lawsin (2015). The first fallacy relates to the assumption that identified symptoms in culturally and linguistically different individuals carry the same meaning and significance for those individuals as it is implied in the measurement tools utilized for the assessment. Such a fallacy has resulted in an assumption of symptomatic behaviors in individuals who may primarily see their behaviors as part of a normal response to events in their surroundings. According to these authors, these individuals may be guided by culturally specific norms that inform the ways they process their personal situations, which may include construing these symptoms not as a reflection of some personal psychological condition. The issue here is the unique role of culturally influenced personal perception on the quality, nature, and meaning of their behavioral manifestations. An example given by Wells and associates is the mistake made by researchers and mental health professionals in assuming that a positive endorsement of feelings of hopelessness, fear, and suspiciousness in depression scales necessarily means that these individuals are also endorsing having a subjective experience of depression. This was supported in findings by Nicholas and Whitt (2012) cited by Wells et al. (2015) with a group of Haitian women who did not identify the checklist items of the Beck Depression Inventory as an expression of distress for them.

The other fallacy relates to a circular reasoning that posits that the fact that an individual from a different cultural and linguistic background endorses symptoms of PTSD as listed in an assessment tool (that has been designed based on western thinking's conceptualization), means that it proves positive that the individual has the condition being assessed. This issue is more likely to emerge in the absence of establishing "criterion validity" and contextualization of the instrument used for the assessment. This is a slightly different issue than what we discussed earlier in this section with regard to the inherent limitation with the required list of symptoms necessarily to satisfy a PTSD diagnosis following the DSM-5 criteria, where important symptoms also found to be present in individuals suffering from traumatic experiences are not meaningfully included.

The final fallacy relates to predetermined and premature conclusion suggesting that the fact that someone's environment is described as representing extreme conditions likely to produce a traumatic response in others is an indication that the individuals being assessed from these environments are also suffering from trauma-related disorders and PTSD, even when they are not endorsing it. That assumption implies that trauma and its specific vicissitudes are a universal phenomenon.

## There Is More to Trauma That Should Be Considered

An issue that came across throughout the book as also essential in the forensic assessment of individual behaviors in civil and criminal situations is the role that resilience can play in their resolution, as discussed by Shaw and associates in Chap. 18. This is a complex development which requires of the forensic professional to make sure to include specific ways to assess the extent to which and under what conditions resilience may play a role in the individual's function during and following incarceration in cases of criminal behavior or in employment discrimination and injury.

The importance of focusing on resilience is also a core ingredient in the innovative prison reform initiatives that we discussed earlier. It is in keeping with an earlier insightful and sophisticated analysis by Ungar (2013), who suggests that it is important to examine resilience as a relative construct that also depends on aspects of the individual's social ecology that both promote and protect against the negative effect of exposure to traumatic events. In that context, Unger suggests that there is sufficient evidence that the environment x individual interaction related to resilience can be best understood within the context of three basic principles, as follows: that it is important to recognize that "(1) resilience is not as much an individual construct as it is a quality of the environment and its capacity to facilitate growth…; (2) resilience looks both the same and different within and between populations, with the mechanisms that predict positive growth sensitive to individual, contextual, and cultural variation (differential impact); and (3) the impact that any single factor has on resilience differs by the amount of risk exposure, with the mechanisms that protect against the impact of trauma showing contextual and cultural specificity for particular individuals (cultural variation)" (p. 255). Following Unger's view, a definition and assessment of resilience should highlight components of the environment that facilitate "the navigations and facilitations of individuals for the resources they need to cope with adversity" (p. 255). This is important because "resilience can manifest as either prosocial behaviors or pathological adaptation depending on the quality of the environment" (p. 255), as we see in the lives of criminals discussed in different contributions included in this book.

## Conclusion

We are paying particular attention in this book to the conditions likely to be involved in the development of faulty perceptions and an inability to accurately being able to judge other's motivations because of the inherent dangers in derailing the accuracy of a forensic evaluation. Our goal in this book is to encourage a more comprehensive and flexible approach to the assessment and treatment of traumatic conditions that are made more urgent by the increased number of immigrants traveling to many shores of the world fueled by socioeconomic and sociopolitical instabilities in many countries in Europe, Africa, and Latin America (Rojas-Flores, Clements, Hwang Koo, & London, 2017); to that we should add the devastating consequences of racism and discrimination affecting the lives of so many in our society. The challenges for the professionals responsible for assessing these individuals are fraught with difficulties due to the different cultural and linguistic contexts of the forensic tools normally used for these assessments. If we are interested in reaching an objective, accurate, appropriate, and comprehensive assessment of the condition for which the evaluation is requested, the forensic professional must take into consideration aspects of the individual's personal experiences prior, during, and subsequent to the period of examination that are unique and culturally/linguistically anchored in these individuals' personal psychology. Teasing all these out using instruments not properly validated (criterion validity) renders findings tentative at best.

We hope the book offers sufficient challenges and helps the reader generate important questions that can guide future investigation where issues of trauma and its effects in forensic contexts can be further explored and clarified for the benefit of those affected, whether as a victim or perpetrator, or for society at large.

## References

Allen, J. G., & Fonagy, P. (2017). Trauma. In P. Luyten, L. C. Mayes, P. Fonagy, M. Target, & S. J. Blatt (Eds.), *Handbook of psychodynamic approaches to psychopathology* (pp. 165–198). New York/London: The Guilford Press.

Almeida, I., Ramalho, A., Fernandez, M. B., & Guarda, R. (2019). Adult attachment as a risk factor for intimate partner violence. *Annals of Medicine, 51*(1), 1–5.

Carlsson, J. M., Sonne, C., & Silove, D. (2014). From pioneers to scientists: Challenges in establishing evidence-gathering models in torture and trauma mental health services for refugees. *Journal of Nervous and Mental Disease, 202*, 630–637.

Courtois, C. A., & Ford, J. (Eds.). (2009). *Treating complex traumatic stress disorders: An evidence-based guide*. New York: The Guildford Press.

Diehle, J., Brooks, S. K., & Greenberg, N. (2017). Veterans are not the only ones suffering from posttraumatic stress symptoms: What do we know about dependent's secondary traumatic stress? *Social Psychiatry and Psychiatric Epidemiology, 52*, 35–44. https://doi.org/10.1007/s00127-016-1292-6

Ford, J. D., & Courtois, C. A. (2009). Defining and understanding complex trauma and complex traumatic stress disorders. In C. A. Courtois & J. D. Ford (Eds.), *Treating complex traumatic stress disorders: An evidence-based guide* (pp. 13–30). New York: Guilford Press.

Garbarino, J. (2015). *Listening to killers: Lessons learned from my twenty years as a psychological expert in murder cases*. Los Angeles: University California Press.

Greene, B. (2005). Psychology, cultural diversity & social justice: Beyond heterosexism and across the cultural divide. *Journal of Counseling Psychology Quarterly, 18*, 295–306.

Heilbrun, K. (2009). *Evaluation of risk of violence in adults*. Oxford: New York.

Huss, M. T. (2014). *Forensic psychology. Research, clinical practice, and applications* (2nd ed.). Hoboken: Wiley.

Leo, R. A. (2009). False confessions: Causes, consequences, and implications. *Journal of the American Academy of Psychiatry and Law, 37*, 332–343. Retrieved 11/11/2019 from http://jaapl.org/content/37/3/332

Leaf, S. (2015). *Uncovering treasure in Norway and Texas-Entrepreneurship: Its role in the rehabilitation of offenders and as the foundation of a 'prisoner entrepreneur' programme*. Retrieved 10 Aug 2019 from https://www.wcmt.org.uk/sites/default/files/report-documents/Leaf%20S%20Report%202015%20FINAL.pdf

Liddell, B. J., Cheung, J., Outhred, T., Das, P., Malhi, G. S., Felmingham, K. L., … Bryant, R. A. (2019). Neural correlates of posttraumatic stress disorder symptoms, trauma exposure, and postmigration stress in response to fear faces in resettled refugees. *Clinical Psychological Science, 7*(4), 811–825.

National Research Council. (2014). Chapter 12-The prison in society: Values and principles. In *The Growth of Incarceration in the United States: Exploring Causes and Consequences*. Washington, DC: The National Academies Press. https://doi.org/10.17226/18613.

Nicholas, G., & Whitt, C. L. (2012). Conducting qualitative research with black immigrant sample: Understanding depression among Haitian immigrant women. In D. K. Nagata, L. Kohn-Wood, & L. A. Suzuki (Eds.), *Qualitative strategies for ethno-cultural research* (pp. 199–217). Washington, DC: American Psychological Association.

Pitman, R. K., Rasmussen, A., Koenen, K. C., Shin, L. M., Orr, S. P., Gilbertson, M. W., … Liberzon, I. (2012). Biological studies of posttraumatic stress disorder. *Natural Reviews Neuroscience, 13*, 769–787.

Rojas-Flores, L., Clements, M. L., Hwang Koo, J., & London, J. (2017). Trauma and psychological distress in Latino citizen children following parental detention and deportation. *Psychological Trauma: Theory, Research, Practice, and Policy, 9*(3), 352–361. https://doi.org/10.1037/tra0000177

Sue, D. W., Capodilupo, C. M., Torino, G. C., Bucceri, J. M., Holder, A. M. B., Nadal, K. L., & Esquilin, M. (2007). Racial microaggression in everyday life: Implications for clinical practice. *American Psychologist, 62*(4), 271–286.

Ungar, M. (2013). Resilience, trauma, context, and culture. *Trauma, Violence, & Abuse, 14*(3), 255–266.

Vaughans, K. C., & Spielberg, W. (Eds.). (2014). *The psychology of black boys and adolescents, Vols. 1 & 2*. Santa Barbara: Praeger. ISBN: 978-0313381980.

Wells, R., Wells, D., & Lawsin, C. (2015). Understanding psychological responses to trauma among refugees: The importance of measuring validity in cross-cultural settings. *Journal and Proceedings of the Royal Society of New South Wales, 148*(455–456), 60–69.

Zagar, R. J., Busch, K. G., Grove, W. M., & Hughes, J. R. (2009). Can violent (re)offense be predicted? A review of the role of the clinician and use of actuarial tests in light of new data. *Psychological Reports, 104*, 247–277.

# Chapter 21
# Trauma and Its Trajectory in Criminal Behaviors: Case Study Exercise Assignments

Rafael Art. Javier, Elizabeth A. Owen, and Jemour A. Maddux

## Introduction

This section is meant to provide the reader with opportunities to explore many of the different issues addressed in this book and beyond. For that purpose, we have gathered information about a number of forensic cases that are now part of the public discourse. They are organized as part of the special post-conclusion "Case Study Exercise" Section where we highlight not only specific crimes committed but also the contexts in which the crimes were committed and some aspects of the personal history of the perpetrators. With the exception of the section on "Gang members, Robbers, and Outlaws" that is organized in chronological order by birthdays of the perpetrators, all others are organized chronologically in terms of when the crimes were committed. We also include the sources from where the information was gathered, with the understanding that there are many more cases and information that can be gathered from other sources; thus, we want to encourage the reader interested in a more comprehensive exploration of these cases to pursue other more comprehensive sources.

These cases individually and collectively raise a number of poignant questions; some of them are also likely to generate strong personal reactions because of the enormity and the graphic/gruesome nature of the crimes. Our goal is for the reader to use the information as a point of departure for further exploration/research and inquiry into the nature of the crimes and, more importantly, on the motivation

R. A. Javier (✉)
Psychology, St. John's University, Queens, NY, USA
e-mail: javierr@stjohns.edu

E. A. Owen
Columbia University/Teachers College, New York, NY, USA

J. A. Maddux
Lamb & Maddux, LLC, Hackensack, NJ, USA

© Springer Nature Switzerland AG 2020
R. A. Javier et al. (eds.), *Assessing Trauma in Forensic Contexts*,
https://doi.org/10.1007/978-3-030-33106-1_21

bchind the crimes, the conditions that made these crimes possible, and the personal history that may or may not have contributed to the criminal acts under consideration. As such, it is an ideal document for class assignments to encourage students to continue the exploration of the forensic issues discussed in class by using real-life examples.

There is something to be said about the selection of the crime (e.g., white collars vs more gruesome crimes), the gender and age of the victims, single vs repeated crimes (e.g., serial killers), sites where crimes are committed, how the victims are treated, and whether a crime is planned or impulsively committed. We find that some criminals are cruel to animals, while others are not; some have unstable job histories, while others do not; some come from unstable and abusive home environments, while others come from a relatively stable and normal home settings; there are situations where members from the same family setting end up on different sides of the justice system: One becoming a serious criminal, while the other becoming a well-respected member of society. There are criminals who select children as victims, even infants. Some suffer from neurological difficulties prior to the crime; some are raised by grandparents as if they are the biological parents, something that becomes known to the criminals later in life followed by strong emotional reactions related to feelings of betrayal. Some of the crimes involve killing of the perpetrators' own parents or children. Some decide to steal items from their victims, while others do not. Some decide to eat the flesh and drink the blood of their victims. Some commit crimes as part of a gang, while others do it alone (solitarily); some torture their victims, sometime extremely so, while others are gentle and respectful; some find enjoyment in watching their victims suffer, while others derive their excitement in exposing themselves. Some have history of bedwetting, while others do not; some are very dependent on their mothers, while others are not; some have strong religious beliefs, while others do not; some send notes to the victims' families, while others do not; some have sex with their dead victims (necrophilia), while others do not. Some select either males or females as victims, while others choose only one of the genders; some make relics with their victims' body parts, while others do not.

There are many and various factors involved in a criminal act that a forensic psychologist is expected to consider in order to make a proper determination of the psychological condition of the individual(s) for whom the forensic evaluation is requested. As we invite the readers to engage in an exploration of motives, contextualization of criminal behavior, and other related issues, we want to emphasize that the goal is not about finding a justification for the crime (as that is not an appropriate purview of forensic psychology); it is about offering a contextualization that can provide important information to the court as it adjudicates not only the appropriate penalty to be meted out but also the nature and type of intervention necessary to provide the maximum protection to our society from those committing the crimes. In this manner, forensic experts could perform comprehensive assessments based on careful and evidence-based analyses of the criminal behaviors.

With that in mind, we have organized the material from white collar to more gruesome crimes, as follows:

- Fraud cases
- Gang-bank robberies
- School shooters/School related crimes
- Sexual assaults and murderers
- Crimes committed by female juvenile murderers
- Spree killers/murders
- Serial killers
- Cannibals

We invite the readers to generate questions as part of individual or group assignments. In cases of a course adoption, the instructor may also generate questions related to the specific class assignments. These assignments may be organized around specific types of crimes, specific individuals, or more globally. To assist in that process, we have generated a series of questions to be considered and meant to highlight the extent to which early trauma may or may not have played a role in these crimes:

1. What are the common denominators across the different types of crimes in terms of presence or absence of a trauma experience?
2. In what way the perpetrator's early history might have played a role in the type of crime committed and the selection of the victim(s)?
3. What are the psychological characteristics of individuals involved in the following types of crimes?

   (a) Those who select children as their victims.
   (b) Those who select either males or females or both as victims.
   (c) Those who select elders as victims.
   (d) Those perpetrators who are members of religious institutions, medical, or other health and human service professions (e.g., priests, nuns, rabbis, teachers, medical doctors, nurses, etc.).
   (e) Those who kill family members. Their children. Their parents. Their siblings.
   (f) Those who perpetuate their crimes alone, while others engage with partners or in-groups (e.g., as part of a gang).
   (g) Those who are gentle or sadistic with their victims.
   (h) Those who are cruel to animals and those who show great compassion toward animals.
   (i) Those whose crimes are more impulsive in nature and those who are more planned.
   (j) Those who engage in repeated and ritualistic sexual acts.
   (k) Those who take different types of trophies from the crime scenes (material objects, body parts, and/or specific organs from the victims).
   (l) Those who engage in sexual acts with dead victims (necrophilia).
   (m) Those who drink the blood and other fluids from their victims.
   (n) Those who eat the flesh of their victims.

4. When assessing the psychological condition of perpetrators, what weight should be given to a neurological condition that may be found to be present preceding their crimes? Should that be considered a mitigating factor in the adjudicating of responsibility? What about in cases of low intelligence capability? Should there be a threshold to consider and, if so, what factor (s) should be considered to make such a determination?

5. If you were asked to assess the types and nature of psychopathy in the case studies listed in this section, which criminals would you consider to be part of a primary vs secondary psychopathy category? What factors would you consider for these categories of psychopathy? What tests would you utilize to aid you in the determination? [*Primary psychopathy* refers to someone who "commits antisocial acts, is irresponsible, lacks empathy, and is superficially charming because of some inherent deficits," while *secondary psychopathy is not inherent but instead* is caused "by social disadvantage, low intelligence, neurotic anxiety, or other psychopathology" (Huss, 2014, p. 76)].

6. What condition/factors may be involved in the development of criminality in a situation where one member of the same family ends up a vicious criminal while the other becomes an upstanding/well-respected member of the society?

7. Are there significant differences in the crimes committed by male vs female perpetrators?

8. Are there any types of criminals whose life trajectory (including types of trauma) you would consider beyond redemption (high risk of reoffending) in terms of the possibility of reintegration in society once the penalty phase has been satisfied?

9. Consider the following scenario: You are asked to select a group of inmates from the list included in this "Case Study Exercise" section for whom you are asked to design an intervention meant to prepare them for reintegration into society. What types of inmates would you most likely accept into the group? Which ones would you reject? What factor(s) would you be considering in making the determination?

10. Select one of the cases described in this section for which you are asked by the court to provide a forensic assessment to determine the mental state at the time of the crime (an insanity evaluation). What psychological instruments would you consider to accomplish this task?

**Fraud/Serial Killings**

| Name | Early life | Crimes |
|---|---|---|
| H.H. Holmes | <ul><li>He was born May 16, 1861, in Gilmanton, New Hampshire, USA, into a wealthy family. He showed signs of high intelligence from an early age.</li><li>Always interested in medicine, he allegedly trapped animals and performed surgery on them; some accounts of his life even suggest that he killed a childhood playmate.</li><li>Mudgett attended medical school at the University of Michigan, where he was a mediocre student.</li><li>In 1884 he was nearly prevented from graduating when a widowed hairdresser accused him of making a false promise of marriage to her.</li><li>In 1886, Mudgett moved to Chicago and took a job as a pharmacist under the name "Dr. H.H. Holmes."</li><li>Soon afterward, he apparently began killing people in order to steal their property.</li><li>The house he built for himself, which would become known as "Murder Castle," was equipped with secret passages, trapdoors, soundproof rooms, doors that could be locked from the outside, gas jets to asphyxiate victims, and a kiln to cremate the bodies.</li></ul> | <ul><li>At the reputed peak of his career, during the World's Columbian Exposition in Chicago in 1893, he allegedly seduced and murdered a number of women, typically by becoming engaged to them and then killing them after securing control of their life savings.</li><li>Mudgett also required his employees to carry life insurance policies naming him as beneficiary so that he could collect money after he killed them.</li><li>He sold the bodies of many of his victims to local medical schools.</li><li>In 1893, Mudgett was arrested for insurance fraud after a fire at his home, but he was soon released.</li><li>He then concocted a scheme with an associate, Ben Pitezel, to defraud an insurance company by faking Pitezel's death.</li><li>After Pitezel purchased a $10,000 life insurance policy, he and Mudgett traveled to Colorado, Missouri, New York, Pennsylvania, Tennessee, and Texas, where they committed other acts of fraud (along the way, Mudgett also married).</li><li>In Texas, Mudgett was arrested for attempting to defraud a drug company and was briefly jailed.</li><li>While in jail, he met Marion Hedgepeth, a career criminal who agreed to help Mudgett in the insurance scheme with Pitezel.</li><li>Meanwhile, Pitezel moved to Philadelphia and opened a fake patent office to swindle inventors.</li><li>After his release from jail, Mudgett traveled to Philadelphia and killed Pitezel. He then convinced Pitezel's widow, who had been aware of her husband's involvement in the insurance scheme, that her husband was still alive, later giving her $500 of the money he collected.</li><li>Worried that some of Pitezel's five children might alert the authorities, Mudgett killed three of them.</li><li>Mudgett confessed to 27 murders (he later increased the total to more than 130), though some researchers have suggested that the real number exceeded 200.<ul><li>https://www.britannica.com/biography/H-H-Holmes</li></ul></li></ul> |

(continued)

**Fraud/Serial Killings** (continued)

| Name | Early life | Crimes |
|---|---|---|
| Bruno Richard Hauptmann | • He was born November 26, 1899, in Saxony, Germany.<br>• He served as a teenaged machine gunner in the German infantry on the western front. He lost two brothers in the war.<br>• In post-war Germany, unemployment was rife; food was scarce. With only 8 years of general education and 2 years of trade school where he learned carpentry and machinery, Hauptmann was unable to secure gainful employment.<br>• In March of 1919, he turned to crime.<br>• With the help of a friend, Fritz Petzold, Hauptmann burglarized three homes.<br>• In a more daring daylight robbery, the two accosted two women at gunpoint and stole their food coupons as the women were pushing baby carriages down a city street.<br>• In short order, Hauptmann was tried and convicted. Although he was sentenced to 5 years and 1 week in prison, he was paroled after 4 years.<br>• Soon after being released, he was arrested again and charged with stealing some strips of leather belting. While awaiting trial, Hauptmann escaped from prison.<br>• Hauptmann subsequently made two failed attempts to come to the United States. Both times, he was returned to Germany. On his third attempt, in November of 1923, he successfully entered the United States using a disguise and a stolen landing card.<br>• The following spring, he met Anna Schoeffler, a German immigrant who lived in Queens. In October of 1925, they were married.<br>• Life in the United States was good to the Hauptmanns. Anna worked in a bakery, and Hauptmann was a carpenter. They lived in a comfortable home in the Bronx. | • Charles Augustus Lindbergh, Jr., 20-month-old son of the famous aviator and Anne Morrow Lindbergh, was kidnapped about 9:00 p.m., on March 1, 1932, from the nursery on the second floor of the Lindbergh home near Hopewell, New Jersey.<br>• The child's absence was discovered and reported to his parents, who were then at home, at approximately 10:00 p.m. by the child's nurse, Betty Gow. A search of the premises was immediately made, and a ransom note demanding $50,000 was found on the nursery window sill.<br>• During the search at the kidnapping scene, traces of mud were found on the floor of the nursery. Footprints, impossible to measure, were found under the nursery window. Two sections of the ladder had been used in reaching the window; one of the two sections was split or broken where it joined the other, indicating that the ladder had broken during the ascent or descent. There were no blood stains in or about the nursery nor were there any fingerprints.<br>• A second ransom note was received by Colonel Lindbergh on March 6, 1932, (postmarked Brooklyn, New York, March 4), in which the ransom demand was increased to $70,000.<br>• On May 12, 1932, the body of the kidnapped baby was accidentally found, partly buried, and badly decomposed, about 4.5 miles southeast of the Lindbergh home, 45 feet from the highway, near Mount Rose, New Jersey, in Mercer County. The discovery was made by William Allen, an assistant on a truck driven by Orville Wilson.<br>• The head was crushed, there was a hole in the skull, and some of the body members were missing. The body was positively identified and cremated at Trenton, New Jersey, on May 13, 1932. The coroner's examination showed that the child had been dead for about 2 months and that death was caused by a blow on the head.<br>  ○ https://www.britannica.com/biography/Bruno-Hauptmann<br>  ○ https://www.fbi.gov/history/famous-cases/lindbergh-kidnapping |

| Bernard Madoff | |
|---|---|
| • Bernard Lawrence Madoff was born on April 29, 1938, in Queens, New York, to parents Ralph and Sylvia Madoff. | • The success of Madoff Securities was in part due to a willingness to adapt to changing times; the firm was among the earliest to use computer technology for trading, helping to give rise to the National Association of Securities Dealers Automated Quotations (NASDAQ). Madoff later served as NASDAQ chairman for three 1-year terms. |
| • Ralph, the child of Polish immigrants, worked for many years as a plumber. His wife, Sylvia, was a housewife and the daughter of Romanian and Austrian immigrants. | • As the business expanded, Madoff began employing more family members to help with the company. |
| • Ralph and Sylvia married in 1932, at the height of the Great Depression. After struggling financially for many years, they became involved in finance. | • His younger brother, Peter, joined him in the business in 1970 and became the firm's chief compliance officer. Later, Madoff's sons, Andrew and Mark, also worked for the company as traders. |
| • Records of Madoff's financial dealings show they were less than successful with the trade. | • Peter's daughter, Shana, became a rules-compliance lawyer for the trading division of her uncle's firm, and his son, Roger, joined the firm before his death in 2006. |
| • His mother registered as a broker-dealer in the 1960s, listing the Madoffs' home address in Queens as the office for a company called Gibraltar Securities. | • However, Madoff became famous for a very different reason on December 11, 2008. The day before, the investor informed his sons that he planned to give out several million dollars in bonuses earlier than scheduled, and they demanded to know where the money was coming from. |
| • The SEC forced the closure of the business for failing to report its financial condition. The couple's house also had a tax lien of more than $13,000, which went unpaid from 1956 until 1965. | • Madoff then admitted that a branch of his firm was actually an elaborate Ponzi scheme. Madoff's sons reported their father to federal authorities, and the next day, Madoff was arrested and charged with securities fraud. |
| • Many suggested that the company and the loans were all a front for Ralph's underhanded dealings. | • Madoff reportedly admitted to investigators that he had lost $50 billion of his investors' money, and on March 12, 2009, he pleaded guilty to 11 felony counts: securities fraud, investment adviser fraud, mail fraud, wire fraud, three counts of money laundering, false statements, perjury, false filings with the US Securities and Exchange Commission (SEC), and theft from an employee benefit plan. |
| • Young Madoff showed little interest in finance during this time; he was far more focused on girlfriend, Ruth Alpern, whom he had met at Far Rockaway High School. | • Prosecutors said $170 billion moved through the principal Madoff account over decades and that before his arrest, the firm's statements showed a total of $65 billion in accounts. On June 29, 2009, US District Court Judge Denny Chin sentenced Madoff to 150 years in prison—the maximum possible prison sentence for the 71-year-old defendant. |
| • Madoff's other interest was the school swim team. When Bernie wasn't competing in meets, his swim coach hired him as a lifeguard at the Silver Point Beach Club in Atlantic Beach, Long Island. | |
| • Madoff began saving the money he made on the job for a later investment. | |
| • After graduating from high school in 1956, Madoff headed to the University of Alabama, where he stayed for 1 year before transferring to Hofstra University in Long Island. | |
| • In 1959, he married his high school sweetheart, Ruth, who was attending nearby Queens College. | |

(continued)

**Fraud/Serial Killings**  (continued)

| Name | Early life | Crimes |
|---|---|---|
| | • Madoff earned his bachelor's degree in political science from Hofstra in 1960 and enrolled at Brooklyn Law School, but he didn't last long in that endeavor.<br>• That year, using the $5000 he saved from his lifeguarding job and a side gig installing sprinkler systems, as well as an additional $50,000 borrowed from his in-laws, he and Ruth founded an investment firm called Bernard L. Madoff Investment Securities, LLC.<br>• With the help of Madoff's father-in-law, a retired CPA, the business attracted investors through word of mouth and amassed an impressive client list, including celebrities such as Steven Spielberg, Kevin Bacon, and Kyra Sedgwick.<br>• Madoff Investment Securities grew famous for its reliable annual returns of 10% or more, and by the end of the 1980s, his firm was handling more than 5% of the trading volume on the New York Stock Exchange. | • Madoff was sent to Butner Federal Correctional Complex in North Carolina to serve his sentence, while efforts commenced to reimburse investors through the sale of his assets.<br>   ○ https://www.biography.com/people/bernard-madoff-466366 |
| Kenneth Lay | • Kenneth Lee Lay was born on April 15, 1942, in Tyrone, Missouri. Ken Lay's parents owned a feed store that went out of business; the Lays eventually moved in with relatives on a farm.<br>• Not until he was 11 years old did Kenneth Lay live in a house with indoor plumbing.<br>• His childhood was one of adult responsibilities, as he had to work driving tractors and plowing fields, during which time he would daydream about becoming rich in commerce.<br>• He received both his bachelor and master degrees in economics from the University of Missouri.<br>• With the military draft at its highest level, Lay applied for Navy officers candidate school and was accepted. He served in the US Navy from 1968 to 1971 as an economist.<br>• In 1970, after earning a Ph.D. in economics at the University of Houston, Lay worked as an energy deputy undersecretary for the United States Department of Interior until 1974.<br>• He then went to work for Exxon Corporation's predecessor, Humble Oil and Refining. | • In 1974, Kenneth Lay joined the Florida Gas Company, eventually serving as president of its successor company, Continental Resources Company.<br>• In 1981, he left Continental to join Transco Energy Company in Houston, Texas.<br>• Three years later, Lay joined Houston Natural Gas Co. as chairman and CEO. The company merged with InterNorth in 1985 and was later renamed Enron Corp.<br>• In 1986, Kenneth Lay was appointed chairman and chief executive officer of Enron.<br>• In 2001, Lay sold large amounts of Enron stock in September and October as its share price fell.<br>• He liquidated more than $300 million in Enron stock from 1989 to 2001. Enron filed for bankruptcy in December 2001—the biggest bankruptcy filing in US history at the time, costing 20,000 employees their jobs and many their life savings and losing billions for investors.<br>• In July 2004, Lay was indicted for his role in the company's' collapse, including 11 counts of securities fraud, wire fraud, and making false and misleading statements. On May 25, 2006, Lay was found guilty on all six counts of conspiracy and fraud.<br>   ○ https://www.biography.com/people/kenneth-lay-234611<br>   ○ https://www.referenceforbusiness.com/biography/F-L/Lay-Ken-1942.html |

| Tom Petters | • Thomas J. Petters was born on July 11, 1957. The middle of seven children, Petters grew up in St. Cloud and worked at a fur and fabric shop started by his great-grandfather.<br>• He attended Catholic school and started his first business at age 15, selling electronics out of a rented office. The enterprise had an 18-month run—until his mother found out.<br>• In the 1980s, Petters worked as regional manager for a consumer electronics chain in Colorado and bought five of the chain's stores when it fell into bankruptcy.<br>• The business failed, but by 1988, Petters had made a fresh start—launching a company to buy goods from bankrupt or troubled retailers and then resell them.<br>• In 1995, he started Petters Warehouse Direct to sell goods directly to consumers.<br>• In 2002, he teamed with former Fingerhut Cos. CEO Ted Deikel to buy various assets of the distressed catalog retailer. In 2005, he acquired his best-known company—Polaroid Holding Co.<br>• But Petters knew tragedy, too. In 2004, his son, John, 21, was murdered while vacationing in Italy. That spurred Petters to start a foundation in his son's name to raise money for scholarships for students studying abroad.<br>• In 2006, it was time to buy an airline: Sun Country, the former charter carrier. | • As recently as 2002, Randy Shain investigated Petters for clients who wanted to make sure they were investing in aboveboard entities.<br>• Shain said he found plenty of red flags: lots of lawsuits against Petters for failing to repay money, criminal cases for allegedly writing bad checks, and a biography that falsely claimed a degree from St. Cloud State University.<br>• In one 1989 lawsuit, Shain said Petters contacted Hennepin County court officials and told them to remove the case from the calendar because it had been settled—when it hadn't. In 1989—the year after he started his liquidation business—Petters was charged with theft and forgery in Colorado state court in a case that foreshadowed his legal jam.<br>• Petters was accused of striking a deal to sell 450 refurbished VCRs. But the alleged supplier told police there was no deal. Petters was also accused of using money from investors to pay off debts.<br>• Petters agreed to pay restitution, and the case was dismissed. The court file was sealed in 1995, removing it from the view of anyone who might have dug into Petters' background.<br>• The first public hint anything was amiss in the Petters empire came on September 24, when police raided its headquarters and carted away boxes of documents.<br>• That came just 16 days after Deanna Coleman, a Petters executive, contacted authorities. She outlined a scheme to lure investors by promising big returns in exchange for financing retail transactions that were actually fictitious.<br>• Authorities say investors were given phony papers to document the purchase of merchandise from small vendors and then more phony paperwork showing resale at a profit to big-box retailers like BJ's Wholesale Club and Sam's Club.<br>• On the day of the raid, Petters was interviewed by the FBI at a favorite haunt, the Bellagio Casino in Las Vegas. Court papers filed later in the case described Petters as the casino's "largest comped-room guest," with gambling losses of more than $10 million.<br>• Petters was arrested 9 days later, charged with mail fraud, wire fraud, money laundering, and obstruction of justice.<br>  ○ http://www.startribune.com/petters-timeline/71661967/<br>  ○ https://www.postbulletin.com/minn-businessman-tom-petters-rose-quickly-fell-faster/article_bb5cf23b-d016-5dba-b72d-f25d91a7e802.html<br><br>(continued) |

**Gang members, robbers, and outlaws**

| Name | Early life | Crimes |
|---|---|---|
| Jesse James, a.k.a. "Thomas Howard" | • He was born on September 5, 1847, in Kearney, Missouri.<br>• Jesse and his brother, Frank James, were educated and hailed from a prestigious family of farmers.<br>• Their father, the Reverend Robert James, was a Baptist minister who married Zerelda Cole James and moved from Kentucky to Missouri in 1842.<br>• In the summer of 1863, the James farm was brutally attacked by Union soldiers.<br>• Jesse was 16 when he and Frank became Confederate guerrilla soldiers, riding alongside William Quantrill and "Bloody Bill" Anderson.<br>• Either way, they rebelled against harsh postwar civil legislation and took the law into their own hands. They were popular in Missouri for actively trying to further the Confederate cause.<br>• In 1874, Jesse married his longtime sweetheart and first cousin, Zerelda, and had two children.<br>• Both James brothers were known as good family men who loved their wives and spent time with their children. | • Began robbing trains, stagecoaches, and banks that were owned or operated by a Northern institution.<br>• From 1860 to 1882, the James Gang was the most feared band of outlaws in American history, responsible for more than 20 bank and train robberies and the murders of countless individuals who stood in their way.<br>  ◦ They stole an estimated $200,000.<br>• On December 7, 1869, the gang robbed the Gallatin, Missouri, bank.<br>• Jesse asked to change a $100 bill and, thinking that the banker was responsible for the death of Bloody Bill, shot the man in the heart.<br>  ◦ https://www.biography.com/people/jesse-james-9352646 |
| William Henry McCarty, Jr., a.k.a. "Billy the Kid" | • Billy the Kid was born William Henry McCarty, Jr. on November 23, 1859, in New York City.<br>• Little is known about the early life of William McCarty (also known as Henry Antrim and William H. Bonney), but it is believed that his father died or left the family when Billy was very young.<br>• He was orphaned at 15 when his mother died of tuberculosis. Shortly after, he and his brother got involved in petty theft.<br>• McCarty had a slim physique, sandy blond hair, and blue eyes and wore a signature sugar-loaf sombrero hat with a wide decorative band.<br>• He could be charming and polite one moment and then outraged and violent the next, a quixotic nature he used to great effect during his heists and robberies. | • According to legend, he killed 21 men during his days as an outlaw, one for each year of his life, though he likely killed far fewer than that number.<br>• On the run from the authorities, McCarty moved to Arizona briefly before joining up with a gang of gunfighters called to fight in the Lincoln County War.<br>• Known as the "Kid," McCarty switched to the opposition to fight with John Tunstall as one of the "Regulators."<br>• Barely escaping with his life, McCarty became an outlaw and a fugitive.<br>• He stole horses and cattle until his arrest in 1880 for the killing of Sheriff Brady during the Lincoln County War.<br>• After being sentenced to death, he killed his two guards and escaped in 1881.<br>• He was hunted down and shot dead by Sheriff Pat Garrett on July 14, 1881, in Fort Sumner, New Mexico.<br>  ◦ https://www.biography.com/people/billy-the-kid-278971 |

| Robert Leroy Parker, a.k.a. "Butch Cassidy" | • Butch Cassidy was born Robert Leroy Parker on April 13, 1866, in Beaver, Utah.<br>• The oldest of 13 children in a poor Mormon family.<br>• Parker was a teenager when he left home in the hopes of carving out a better, more prosperous life than what his parents had been able to provide.<br>• He found work on several different ranches and eventually befriended a rancher named Mike Cassidy, who'd had a reputation for stealing cattle and horses.<br>• Young Parker admired the elder Cassidy and, wanting to emulate his friend and not disrespect his family, changed his name to Butch Cassidy | • By all accounts, Cassidy was a charming thief, who was well liked and who never, it's believed, killed anyone.<br>• His first taste of a major robbery came in June 1889, when he and three other cowboys made off with more than $20,000 from the San Miguel Valley Bank in Telluride, Colorado.<br>• After purchasing a ranch of his own in Dubois, Wyoming, in 1890, Cassidy continued to rustle cattle and horses. In 1894 the law caught up to him, and he was jailed for 2 years for the crime.<br>• Despite his criminal background, Cassidy had a reputation for keeping his word. As one story goes, on the night before he was to begin his sentence, Cassidy asked to be released, promising he'd return to jail the following day. Authorities took him at his word and let him go, and Cassidy returned to them the following morning.<br>• Upon his full release in 1896, Cassidy resumed his life as a criminal. With several other well-known outlaws, including Harry Longabaugh (a.k.a. the "Sundance Kid"), William Ellsworth Lay ("Elzy Lay"), Ben Kilpatrick (the "Tall Texan"), and Harvey Logan ("Kid Curry")—a group known as "the Wild Bunch"—Cassidy embarked on what is considered the longest stretch of successful train and bank robberies in American history.<br>• Beginning with an August 1896 bank robbery in Montpelier, Idaho, in which the gang made off with more than $7000, the group hit banks and trains in South Dakota, New Mexico, Nevada, and Wyoming.<br>• Between their robberies, the men hid out at the Hole-in-the-Wall Pass, located in Johnson County, Wyoming, where a number of outlaw gangs had their hideouts.<br>• With each new robbery, the Bunch became better known and better liked by an American public eager to read about their exploits. Their robberies too became bigger.<br>• One of the largest was a $70,000 haul from a train just outside Folsom, New Mexico.<br>• Unable to stop the Bunch, the Union Pacific Railroad went so far as to propose to Cassidy a pardon in exchange for the promise of ending his robberies and coming to work for the company as an express guard. Cassidy turned the offer down.<br>   ○ https://www.biography.com/people/butch-cassidy-9240908 |

(continued)

**Gang members, robbers, and outlaws** (continued)

| Name | Early life | Crimes |
|---|---|---|
| Harry Alonzo Longabaugh, a.k.a. "The Sundance Kid" | • Harry Alonzo Longabaugh was born in 1867 in Mont Clare, Pennsylvania. <br>• He was considered the fastest gunslinger in the Wild Bunch, a well-known gang of robbers and cattle rustlers that roamed the American West during the 1880s and 1890s. <br>• Longabaugh was just 15 when he left home for good. He took his nickname from the Wyoming town of Sundance, where he was arrested for the only time in his life after stealing a horse. <br>• For the crime, Sundance served nearly 2 years in jail. Upon his release in 1889, he attempted to create an honest life for himself as a cowboy | • By the early 1890s, Sundance was back to being an outlaw. <br>• Authorities fingered him for a train robbery in 1892, and 5 years later, for a bank heist that he pulled off with a group that came to be known as 'The Wild Bunch'. <br>• The gang largely consisted of Robert Parker (a.k.a. "Butch Cassidy"), Harry Tracy ("Elzy Lay"), Ben Kilpatrick (the "Tall Texan"), and Harvey Logan ("Kid Curry"). Together, the group embarked on the longest stretch of successful train and bank robberies in the history of the American West. <br>• Among the men, Sundance was considered to be the fastest gunslinger, though historical evidence indicates he never killed anyone during the Wild Bunch's run. <br>• The gang's robberies were scattered around parts of South Dakota. New Mexico, Nevada, and Wyoming. Between robberies, the men hid out at Hole-in-the-Wall Pass, located in Johnson County, Wyoming, where several outlaw gangs had their hideouts. <br>• With each new robbery, the Wild Bunch became better known and well liked by an American public eager to read about their exploits. <br>• Their robberies also became bigger. One of the largest was a $70,000 haul from a train just outside Folsom, New Mexico. <br>   ○ https://www.biography.com/people/sundance-kid-9499214 |

| George Kelly Barnes, a.k.a. "Machine Gun Kelly" | |
|---|---|
| • He was born George Kelly Barnes on July 18, 1895, in Memphis, Tennessee.<br>• Despite the nickname "Machine Gun," Kelly was a relatively minor criminal until a 1933 kidnapping made him infamous.<br>• He was raised by a wealthy traditional family.<br>• He was a "wild child" in school.<br>• Before beginning his life of crime, he was a student at Mississippi A&M College.<br>• He married Geneva Ramsey when he was 19. The couple had two sons together before divorcing.<br>• His first wife told *The New York Times* after his arrest that she divorced him because he was "running in bad company."<br>• Involved in bootlegging as a teenager, Kelly returned to the profitable illegal enterprise after several failed attempts at legitimate work.<br>• He was caught selling illegal liquor in 1927 and spent a few months in jail in New Mexico.<br>• Nabbed again, this time for selling liquor on an Indian reservation, Kelly did time at Leavenworth Prison in Kansas.<br>• While incarcerated, he made friends with several bank robbers, including Charlie Harmon, Frank Nash, Francis Keating, and Thomas Holden, and is believed to have helped Keating and Holden escape. | • After his release from prison in 1930, Kelly traveled to St. Paul, Minnesota, with his girlfriend, Kathryn Thorne. (The two later married in the fall of that year.)<br>• There, he reunited with Keating and Holden and participated in a bank holdup with the pair.<br>• Continuing his crime spree, Kelly was involved in bank robberies in several states, including Iowa, Texas, and Washington.<br>• According to legend, Kelly's wife helped build his reputation, buying him a machine gun and nicknaming him after the weapon.<br>• She also reportedly gave away shell casings from his exploits to people as souvenirs to increase his notoriety.<br>• Along with bank robbing, Kelly made several attempts at kidnapping.<br>• With his wife and longtime associate, Albert L. Bates, Kelly hatched a plan to kidnap wealthy Oklahoma oil man Charles F. Urschel.<br>• On July 22, Bates and Kelly entered Urschel's Oklahoma City home and abducted Urschel and one of his friends, Walter R. Jarrett, leaving their wives behind. Jarrett was soon let go, but Urschel was held for ransom. Kelly and his gang wanted $200,000 for the oil man.<br>• They set up an elaborate system for the handling of their captive and the delivery of the ransom. But they didn't count on Urschel's sharp mind and the authorities keeping track the ransom money's serial numbers.<br>• The ransom was delivered on July 30 in Kansas City, and Urschel was released the next day.<br>• He was unharmed, and, although blindfolded some of the time, he was able to provide a number of clues to authorities.<br>• From Urschel's descriptions of what he heard and saw while being held hostage, the authorities were able to figure out that he must have been near Paradise, Texas. Earlier, there also had been a tip that the Kelly's were involved.<br>   ○ https://www.biography.com/people/machine-gun-kelly-507610<br>   ○ www.svsd.net/cms/lib5/PA01001234/Centricity<br>   ○ /.../George%20Kelly%20Barnes.pptx |

(continued)

# Gang members, robbers, and outlaws (continued)

| Name | Early life | Crimes |
|------|-----------|--------|
| John Dillinger, a.k.a. "Gentleman John" or "The Jackrabbit" | • He was born June 22, 1903, in Indianapolis, Indiana. Dillinger was the younger of two children born to John Wilson Dillinger and Mary Ellen "Molly" Lancaster.<br>• The elder Dillinger was a somber, church-going small businessman who owned a neighborhood grocery store and some rental houses. He was simultaneously a harsh disciplinarian who would beat Johnnie for his insubordination and then turn around and give him money for candy.<br>• Later, when Johnnie was in his teens, Dillinger Sr. would alternate between locking Johnnie in the house all day and then, later in the week, letting him roam the neighborhood for most of the night.<br>• Dillinger's mother, Molly, died of a stroke when he was not quite yet 4 years old.<br>• His sister, Audrey, who was 15 years his senior, raised him until his father remarried in 1912.<br>• As a boy, John Dillinger was constantly getting into trouble. He would commit small-time pranks and petty theft with his neighborhood gang, "the Dirty Dozen."<br>• Most of his neighbors would later say he was generally a cheerful, likable kid who didn't get into any more mischief than other boys.<br>• But there were also accounts of severe juvenile delinquency and malicious behavior as a teenager. To a degree, both of these perceptions are correct and were evident in his adult life.<br>• Like any celebrity, accounts describing his early life were shadowed by his later exploits and added either positively or negatively to his reputation.<br>• Dillinger quit school at age 16, not due to any trouble but because he was bored and wanted to make money on his own.<br>• He was said to be good employee with a talent for working with his hands. His father, however, wasn't pleased with his career choice and tried to talk him out of it. | • Matters reached a head on July 21, 1923, when Dillinger stole a car to impress a girl on a date.<br>• He was later found by a police officer roaming aimlessly through Indianapolis streets. The policeman pulled him over to question him and, suspicious of his vague explanations, placed him under arrest.<br>• Dillinger broke loose and ran. Knowing he couldn't go back home, he joined the United States Navy the next day.<br>• He made it through basic training, but the regimented life of military service was not for him.<br>• While assigned to the USS Utah—the same USS Utah that was sunk at Pearl Harbor in 1941—he jumped from the ship and returned home to Mooresville.<br>• His 5-month military career was over, and he was eventually dishonorably discharged for deserting.<br>• With no job or income, the newlyweds moved into Dillinger's father's farmhouse. Within a few weeks of his wedding, he was arrested for stealing several chickens.<br>• Singleton suggested Dillinger could easily rob the elderly grocer for the cash he would be carrying while Singleton waited for him in a getaway car down the street.<br>• The incident did not go well. Dillinger was armed with a .32-caliber and pistol and a large bolt wrapped in a handkerchief. He came up behind the grocer and clubbed him over the head with the bolt, but the grocer turned and grabbed Dillinger and the gun, forcing it to discharge.<br>• Dillinger thought he had shot the grocer and took off running down the street to meet Singleton's getaway car.<br>• He was caught in the foiled holdup of a Mooresville grocer, and he served much of the next decade in Indiana State Prison.<br>• While incarcerated, he learned the craft of bank robbery from fellow inmates.<br>• Upon parole on May 10, 1933, he turned his knowledge to profit, robbing (with one to four confederates) five Indiana and Ohio banks in 4 months and gaining his first notoriety as a daring, sharply dressed gunman. |

- John showed his obstinacy and refused to go back to school.
- In 1920, hoping a change of venue would provide a more wholesome influence on his son, John Dillinger Sr. sold his grocery store and property to retire to a farm in Mooresville, Indiana.
- Ever defiant, John Jr. kept his job at the Indianapolis machine shop and commuted the 18 miles on his motorcycle.
- His wild and rebellious behavior continued with nightly escapades which included drinking, fighting, and visiting prostitutes.
- Upon his return to Mooresville in April 1924, John Dillinger met and married 16-year-old Beryl Ethel Hovious and attempted to settle down.
- Dillinger and Beryl moved out of their cramped bedroom and into Beryl's parents' home in Martinsville, Indiana. There, he got a job in an upholstery shop.
- During the summer of 1924, Dillinger played shortstop on the Martinsville baseball team. There, he met and befriended Edgar Singleton, a heavy-drinking individual who was a distant relative of Dillinger's stepmother. Singleton became Dillinger's first partner in crime.

- In September 1933, Dillinger was captured and jailed in Ohio. However, the following month, he was rescued by five former convict pals whose own escape from Indiana State Prison he had earlier financed and plotted; a sheriff was killed during the incident.
- Dillinger and his gang next robbed banks in Indiana and Wisconsin and fled south to Florida and then to Tucson, Arizona, where they were discovered and arrested by local police.
- Dillinger was extradited to Indiana and lodged in the Crown Point jail, which was considered escape-proof. However, on March 3, 1934, he executed his most-celebrated breakout. With a razor and a piece of wood, he carved a fake pistol, blackened it with shoe polish, and used it to force his way past a dozen guards to freedom. Dillinger then drove the sheriff's car to Chicago. By taking a stolen vehicle across state lines, he committed a federal offense, and the FBI launched its own manhunt.
- There followed more bank robberies with new confederates, notably Baby Face Nelson. Over the course of Dillinger's yearlong crime spree, several people were killed by his gang, and he barely escaped FBI entrapments and shootouts in Minnesota and Wisconsin.
- He eventually made his way to Chicago, where he reportedly had plastic surgery to alter his appearance.
- His end came through a trap set up by the FBI, Indiana police, and Anna Sage (alias of Ana Cumpanas), a brothel madam who knew Dillinger's girlfriend. Sage informed law officers that she and the couple would be seeing a movie on the night of July 22, 1934. The trio ultimately went to the Biograph Theater.
- After a showing of the crime drama, Manhattan Melodrama (1934), Dillinger emerged to find FBI agents waiting for him. He attempted to escape but was shot to death in the alley.
  - https://www.history.com/topics/crime/john-dillinger
  - https://www.britannica.com/biography/John-Dillinger

(continued)

**Gang members, robbers, and outlaws** (continued)

| Name | Early life | Crimes |
|---|---|---|
| Bugsy Siegel, a.k.a. "Bugz," or "Bugzy Malone" | • He was born in Brooklyn on February 28, 1906, the second of his parents' five children and the most fearless.<br>• The son of Jewish immigrants, Siegel was raised in the crime-ridden section of Williamsburg, where Irish and Italian gangs were prevalent. His father, Max, and mother, Jennie, did some odd jobs to make enough money to survive, and Siegel hated the life he was leading.<br>• He wanted to make big in life at any cost. His neighborhood, infested with antisocial elements and constantly warring Italian and Irish gangs, further pushed him into the world of crime.<br>• As a teenager, he extorted money from pushcart peddlers on New York City's Lower East Side.<br>• In 1918, Siegel befriended fellow hooligan, Meyer Lansky, with whom he established the Bugs-Meyer Gang—a band of ruthless Jewish mobsters that ran a group of contract killers under the name Murder, Inc.<br>• He famously hated his nickname "Bugsy," which was bestowed on him owing to the fact that he was short-tempered and highly intuitive, "like a bedbug." He reportedly threatened everybody who called him by his nickname.<br>• Bugsy Siegel got married to his childhood girlfriend, Esta Krawoker, on January 28, 1929. Siegel was a notorious womanizer so the couple had problems from their initial days.<br>• Esta finally got the divorce in 1946 and left California with her daughters and got settled in New York.<br>• He gave quite a lot of money to charity, and several witnesses claim that he came across as a kindhearted man to average people and said that "they only kill each other," meaning seldom do the gangsters like him harm the commoners.<br>• Siegel's wealth, power, and influence had grown immensely, and he started to hang out with Hollywood film elites. | • Bugsy joined hands with Frank Costello and Luciano and took the charge of killing the mobster, Joe "The Boss" Masseria.<br>• He is believed to be one of the four hit men who showered Joe with bullets in 1931. Salvatore Maranzano was another one of their targets, and slowly, Luciano managed to kill all his rival gang members, which marked the beginning of the modern-day American organized crime scene.<br>• Subsequently, the National Crime Syndicate was formed, followed by "The Commission," which was set up to bring an end to the warring gangs.<br>• All the territories were divided so that no gang interferes into the operation of others. Siegel laid the foundation of Murder Inc. and continued working as a hit man.<br>• He kept evading the law, and the only time he was convicted was in Miami. In 1932, Bugsy had a tussle with the notorious Fabrizzo brothers, who attempted to get him murdered. Lansky and Bugsy hunted down the Fabrizzo brothers.<br>• As a result of this killing, the third Fabrizzo brother, Tony, went to the authorities and exposed the Murder Inc.., which Siegel was running across the country. Siegel made an intricate plan and killed Tony and had an alibi ready for him beforehand. In the mid-1930s, he got the loan shark, Louis and Joseph Amberg, murdered.<br>• By now, Siegel had come to realize that his life wasn't safe anymore, and he had to find a safe hideout.<br>• He chose California for his safe hideout. He collaborated with the local boss, Jack Dragna, and together they started gambling rackets.<br>• He brought his family along with him and started working toward establishing a wide gambling network. Boss Dragna had received special "messages" to cooperate with Siegel, and he did as he was told.<br>• He also had romantic relationships with several actors. One of his affairs even took him to Italy where he befriended Mussolini and offered to sell him weapons. |

|  |  |  |
|---|---|---|
|  | • He was known to be friends with actors Gary Cooper, Clark Gable, and Cary Grant and the studio executive Louis B. Mayer.<br>• His influence grew so much that he got the famous actress Jean Harlow to be his daughter's godmother. | • In late 1930s, he went to Germany and met up with Nazi Germany's Joseph Goebbels and Herman Goring, but he did not like them and even offered to kill them on contract.<br>• He also extorted money from Hollywood stars and studios. It is said that he borrowed more than $400,000 from actors and never paid them back, and nobody ever asked.<br>• He also forced the studios to pay him, as he would get the unions to go on strikes so that the work was stopped until Siegel's demands were met. He was a feared man, and nobody wanted a tussle with him.<br>• In November 1939, Bugsy planned the murder of Harry Greenberg and shot him dead outside his house. Harry was a danger to the syndicate as he had threatened to call their racket off in front of the authorities.<br> ○ https://www.biography.com/people/bugsy-siegel-9542063<br> ○ https://www.thefamouspeople.com/profiles/bugsy-siegel-8946.php |
| Bonnie Parker and Clyde Barrow, a.k.a. "Bonnie and Clyde" | • Bonnie Parker was born on October 1, 1910, in Rowena, Texas, as the second of three children to Henry and Emma Parker.<br>• The family lived somewhat comfortably off Henry Parker's job as a bricklayer, but when he died unexpectedly in 1914, Emma Parker moved the family in with her mother in the small town of Cement City, Texas (now part of Dallas).<br>• From all accounts, Bonnie Parker was beautiful. She stood 4' 11" and weighed a mere 90 pounds. She did well in school and loved to write poetry. (Two poems that she wrote while on the run helped make her famous.)<br>• Bored with her average life, Bonnie dropped out of school at age 16 and married Roy Thornton. The marriage wasn't a happy one, and Roy began to spend a lot of time away from home by 1927. | • A few weeks after they met, Clyde was sentenced to 2 years in prison for past crimes. Bonnie was devastated at his arrest.<br>• On March 11, 1930, Clyde escaped from jail, using the gun Bonnie had smuggled in to him.<br>• A week later, he was recaptured and was then to serve a 14-year sentence in the notoriously brutal Eastham Prison Farm near Weldon, Texas.<br>• On April 21, 1930, Clyde arrived at Eastham. Life was unbearable there for him, and he became desperate to get out.<br>• Hoping that if he was physically incapacitated he might get transferred off of the Eastham farm, he asked a fellow prisoner to chop off some of his toes with an axe.<br>• Although the missing two toes did not get him transferred, Clyde was granted an early parole.<br>• After Clyde was released from Eastham on February 2, 1932, on crutches, he vowed that he would rather die than ever go back to that horrible place. |

(continued)

**Gang members, robbers, and outlaws** (continued)

| Name | Early life | Crimes |
|---|---|---|
|  | • Two years later, Roy was caught for robbery and sentenced to 5 years in prison. They never divorced.<br>• While Roy was away, Bonnie worked as a waitress; however, she was out of a job just as the Great Depression was really getting started at the end of 1929.<br>• Clyde Barrow was born on March 24, 1909, in Telico, Texas, as the sixth of eight children to Henry and Cummie Barrow. Clyde's parents were tenant farmers, often not making enough money to feed their children.<br>• During the rough times, Clyde was frequently sent to live with other relatives.<br>• When Clyde was 12 years old, his parents gave up tenant farming and moved to West Dallas where Henry opened up a gas station.<br>• At that time, West Dallas was a very rough neighborhood, and Clyde fit right in. Clyde and his older brother, Marvin Ivan "Buck" Barrow, were often in trouble with the law for they were frequently stealing things like turkeys and cars.<br>• Clyde stood 5' 7" and weighed about 130 pounds. He had two serious girlfriends (Anne and Gladys) before he met Bonnie, but he never married. In January 1930, Bonnie and Clyde met at a mutual friend's house. The attraction was instantaneous. | • Clyde was released from prison during the Great Depression, when jobs were not easy to come by. Plus, Clyde had little experience holding down a real job. Not surprisingly, as soon as Clyde's foot had healed, he was once again robbing and stealing.<br>• On one of Clyde's first robberies, after he was released, Bonnie went with him. Although she stayed in the car during the robbery, Bonnie was captured and put in the Kaufman, Texas, jail. She was later released for lack of evidence.<br>• While Bonnie was in jail, Clyde and Raymond Hamilton staged another robbery at the end of April 1932. It was supposed to be an easy and quick robbery of a general store, but something went wrong, and the store's owner, John Bucher, was shot and killed.<br>• For the next 2 years, Bonnie and Clyde drove and robbed across five states: Texas, Oklahoma, Missouri, Louisiana, and New Mexico. They usually stayed close to the border to aid their getaway, using the fact that police at that time could not cross state borders to follow a criminal.<br>• Having killed one policeman and mortally wounding another, Bonnie, Clyde, Buck, and W.D. Jones made it to the garage, got into their car, and sped away.<br>• By November 1933, they were back out robbing and stealing.<br>• Rather than get revenge on the lawmen near Dallas who had threatened the lives of his family, Clyde took revenge on the Eastham Prison Farm.<br>• In January 1934, Bonnie and Clyde helped Clyde's old friend, Raymond Hamilton, break out of Eastham. During the escape, a guard was killed, and several extra prisoners hopped into the car with Bonnie and Clyde.<br>• The crime spree continued, including the brutal murder of two motorcycle cops.<br>  ○ https://www.thoughtco.com/bonnie-and-clyde-1779278 |

| Whitey Bulger, a.k.a. "Whitey" | <ul><li>Whitey Bulger was born James Joseph Bulger Jr. on September 3, 1929, in Dorchester, Massachusetts.</li><li>One of six children born to Catholic Irish-American parents, Whitey—a moniker he was given for his white-blond hair—grew up in a South Boston public-housing project.</li><li>His father worked as a longshoreman. Bulger was a troublemaker as a child and even lived out the childhood fantasy of running away with the circus when he was 10 years old.</li><li>Whitey Bulger was first arrested when he was 14 years old, for stealing, and his criminal record continued to escalate from there.</li><li>As a youth, he was arrested for larceny, forgery, assault and battery, and armed robbery and served 5 years in a juvenile reformatory.</li><li>Upon his release, he joined the Air Force where he served time in military jail for assault before being arrested for going AWOL. Nonetheless, he received an honorable discharge in 1952.</li><li>Bulger's brothers would go a very different direction. One of them, William Bulger, would serve as a member of the Massachusetts Senate for 25 years and president of the University of Massachusetts for 7 years.</li></ul> | <ul><li>Bulger was notorious for his readiness to use violence and especially murder to achieve his criminal goals.</li><li>A "Southie," or resident of the tough streets of South Boston, Bulger was attracted to street crime early in life, joining gangs and earning his first arrest at age 14, which sent him to the reformatory.</li><li>As a young man, Whitey was in and out of jail for various assault and theft charges, including military charges during his stint in the Air Force from 1948 to 1952.</li><li>In 1956, he was convicted of federal charges of hijacking and did his first stint in federal prison, landing in penitentiaries in Atlanta, Alcatraz, Leavenworth, and Lewisburg.</li><li>While in the federal system, Bulger volunteered for experiments in which the CIA dosed prisoners with the hallucinatory drug LSD and other drugs in return for lesser sentences.</li><li>According to some biographers, Bulger switched sides and killed the leader of his old gang, although this is disputed by other sources.</li><li>What is not disputed is that by 1972, Bulger and his new allies in the Mullen gang were top dogs among gangsters in Boston.</li><li>During this period, Bulger cemented his reputation for violence by using murder as a means of discipline for wayward Mullen gang members. He was implicated in the deaths of at least three of his cohorts.</li><li>In 1979, the boss and deputy of the Winter Hill Gang, as it became known, were arrested for fixing horse races, and Bulger took over the gang's leadership.</li><li>Bulger was released in 1965, and he went to work for a local Irish-American gang at a time when rival factions were at war.</li><li>Bulger, with the Killeen gang, committed his first homicide during this war. In a case of mistaken identity, Bulger shot and killed the innocent twin brother of a rival gangster.</li><li>On August 12, 2013, after a 2-month trial, a jury of eight men and four women deliberated for 5 days and found Bulger guilty on 31 counts, including federal racketeering, extortion, conspiracy, and 11 of the 19 murders. They found he was not guilty of seven murders and could not reach a verdict on one murder.<ul><li>https://www.biography.com/people/whitey-bulger-328770</li><li>https://themobmuseum.org/notable_names/whitey-bulger/</li></ul></li></ul> |
| --- | --- | --- |

(continued)

R. A. Javier et al.

**Gang members, robbers, and outlaws** (continued)

| Name | Early life | Crimes |
|---|---|---|
| John Joseph Gotti, a.k.a. "The Teflon Don" or "The Dapper Don" | • He was born on October 27, 1940, in the South Bronx, New York. Mother, Fannie, and father, J. Joseph Gotti, were both Italian immigrants.<br>• Gotti was the fifth of 13 children in a family whose only income came from their father's unpredictable work as a day laborer.<br>• Gotti and his family moved frequently before settling in East New York, an area known at the time for its gang activity.<br>• By the age of 12, Gotti was working as an errand boy for an underground club in the neighborhood run by Carmine Fatico.<br>• Fatico was a captain in the local Gambino family, the largest of the five organized crime families in New York City.<br>• Through his activities with the club, Gotti met Aniello Dellacroce, who became his life-long mentor.<br>• Gotti soon became the leader of a gang badge/decoration called the Fulton-Rockaway boys, a group known for their frequent robberies and carjackings.<br>• When he was 14, Gotti's toes were crushed as he tried to steal a cement mixer. The accident gave the mobster-to-be his trademark gait and earned him another on his list of petty crimes.<br>• He was considered a bully and constant discipline problem at Franklin K. Lane High School until he dropped out at 16.<br>• By the age of 18, the police department ranked Gotti as a low-level associate in the Fatico crew.<br>• On March 6, 1962, Gotti married 17-year-old Victoria DiGiorgio. At the time of their marriage, DiGiorgio had already given birth to their first child, Angela, and was pregnant with their second. | • Between 1957 and 1961, Gotti pursued a life of crime on a full-time basis. His arrest record included street fighting, public intoxication, and car theft.<br>• By his 21st birthday, Gotti had been arrested five times, but served little jail time. His crime-free life was brief, however, and Gotti was jailed twice by 1966.<br>• When he and his family made the move to Ozone Park in Queens, New York, the budding criminal quickly became a major player in the Gambino hijacking crew.<br>• In 1968, Gotti served his first major sentence when the FBI charged him and his two accomplices with committing cargo thefts near John F. Kennedy Airport.<br>• All three men were convicted of hijacking and sentenced to 3 years in prison.<br>• While Gotti served his time, the Fatico crew moved from East New York to a storefront near Gotti's home in Queens.<br>• After his release from prison in 1971, Gotti was designated as the temporary leader of Fatico's gang while the captain faced loan-sharking charges.<br>• In May of 1973, while Gotti was captain of Fatico's crew, he committed his first murder: the shooting death of Jimmy McBratney, a rival gang member who kidnapped and murdered a member of the Gambino family.<br>• Gotti was sent to exact revenge, but he was less than discreet, leaving multiple witnesses at the scene of the crime.<br>• Gotti was arrested in 1974 after several bystanders identified him in a photo lineup.<br>• At his trial 3 years later, Gotti cut a deal with the court. In return for a plea of attempted manslaughter, he served only 4 years in prison. |

| | |
|---|---|
| • In the early years of their marriage, the couple fought constantly and separated numerous times.<br>• Gotti briefly tried his hand at legitimate jobs for the sake of his family: first, as a presser in a coat factory, and then as an assistant to a truck driver.<br>• In March of 1980, personal tragedy hit the Gotti family when 12-year-old Frank Gotti (youngest son of John Gotti) was struck by a car driven by neighbor John Favara after the boy steered his bike into traffic.<br>• The death was ruled accidental, but witnesses say Gotti's wife, Victoria, later attacked Favara with a metal baseball bat, sending him to the hospital. Favara decided not to press charges. | • By the early 1980s, John Gotti's prominence in the Gambino family had earned unwanted attention from mob boss Castellano. He considered Gotti's $30,000-a-night gambling habit a liability, and he also disapproved of the Bergin captain's unpredictable behavior.<br>• In 1985, the FBI had gathered enough evidence to place Gotti and Dellacroce under federal indictments for racketeering. Other associates were indicted on heroin trafficking charges.<br>• The FBI then turned the conviction of Gotti into an organizational crusade.<br>• After pressuring the Gambino family's new underboss, Sammy Gravano, into testifying against Gotti, the mob leader was finally convicted of murder and racketeering on April 2, 1992.<br>• It is estimated that, while John Gotti acted as boss, the Gambino family made more than $500 million in revenue from illegal activities such as gambling, drug trafficking, extortion, and stock fraud.<br> ○ https://www.biography.com/people/john-gotti-9542186 |

(continued)

**Gang members, robbers, and outlaws** (continued)

| Name | Early life | Crimes |
|---|---|---|
| Richard Wershe, Jr., a.k.a. "White Boy Rick" | • Richard Wershe Jr. was born on July 18, 1969, in Michigan, to Richard Wershe Sr. and Darlene McCormick. He has a sister, Dawn, 3 years older than him.<br>• Wershe Jr. grew up in a lower middle-class household in the east side of Detroit. When he was 5 years old, his parents decided to separate.<br>• Darlene subsequently moved to the suburbs. Both Wershe Jr. and Dawn chose to live with their father at their small brick house on Hampshire Street at Dickerson Avenue.<br>• The siblings were raised by their father with the help of his own parents who lived across the street from them.<br>• After he turned 12, he briefly stayed with his mother. However, by then, Darlene had remarried, and Wershe Jr. was not fond of his stepfather. About a year later, he moved back in with his father.<br>• He attended a local high school but abandoned his education in 1985, right before his 16th birthday.<br>• Wershe Sr. was a self-admitted hustler and found numerous inventive ways to earn money. He hawked surplus electronics, satellite TV equipment, sporting goods, and devices to pirate cable TV.<br>• In addition to this, he was an amateur inventor. Wershe Sr. was also known as an illegal arms dealer in the black market and spent most of his youth as an FBI informant. | • After the collapse of the Curry brothers' criminal empire, the FBI was done with Wershe Jr. as well. However, he was already accustomed to the affluent life that the steady money from the FBI allowed him to lead. He essentially had two choices at the time, who worked as an FBI informant go back to school or hit the streets. He chose the latter and became a drug dealer.<br>• Wershe Jr. was a "weight man," not a full-fledged kingpin. He directly bought cocaine from a Miami-based supplier named Art Derrick. He had an affair with Johnny's wife, Cathy Volsan, who was an influential figure in Detroit at the time, being the niece of Mayor Coleman Young.<br>• There was even an assassination attempt on Wershe Jr. by former professional hit man, Nathaniel Craft, who later revealed that he was employed by police detective Gil Hill to kill Wershe Jr. to prevent him from speaking about police corruption in Detroit.<br>• During this period, he was earning about $30,000 a month. In May 1987, when he was 17 years old, Wershe Jr. was arrested and charged with the possession of 8 kg of cocaine. He was subsequently sentenced to life imprisonment. In 1998, his case was revisited, and he was granted the chance of parole.<br>• He was unanimously allowed parole in June 2017. Despite this, he was relocated to Florida State Prison to serve another sentence for his involvement in a car theft ring.<br>   o https://www.thefamouspeople.com/profiles/richard-wershe-jr%2D%2D43526.php |

**School shooters/school related crimes**

| Name | Early Life | Crime |
|---|---|---|
| Andrew Kehoe, a.k.a. "The Bath School Murder" | • He was born on February 1, 1872, in Tecumseh, Michigan, 1 of 13 children.<br>• At the age of 5, Kehoe's mother passed away, and his father remarried; however, Kehoe didn't get along well with his stepmother, and both were known for their arguments.<br>• When Kehoe was 14, his stepmother caught fire when an activated stove exploded right in front of her.<br>• Kehoe watched her burn for a few minutes before putting out the flames, but it was too late, for the sustained injuries were fatal.<br>• Kehoe later attended Tecumseh High School and, after graduating, became a student at Michigan State University.<br>• There, he met his future wife, Ellen "Nellie" Price.<br>• In 1911, Kehoe suffered a severe head injury after a fall and drifted in and out of a coma for a course of 2 months.<br>• After recovering, Kehoe returned to Michigan and married Ellen.<br>• Since Ellen was the member of a wealthy family, she and Kehoe were able to purchase a 185-acre farm outside the village of Bath Township.<br>• Kehoe was a strange man, always quick to help others but also prone to anger, criticizing whenever his ways were not met; he was intelligent and articulate but also impatient.<br>• He was also known for his neat and clean habits, as well as his affinity for tinkering with machinery.<br>• Quite disturbingly, Kehoe displayed animal cruelty numerous times, once beating a horse to death. | • On May 18, 1927, Kehoe orchestrated a sinister plot against the people of Bath, especially the town's children.<br>• He killed his wife and set fire to their home and other farm buildings.<br>• The following day, authorities came to what remained of the Kehoe barn and found Ellen's corpse, as well as a message left for them, which read: "CRIMINALS ARE MADE, NOT BORN."<br>• This was a diversion, leading neighbors and others to the farm to fight the blaze.<br>• Meanwhile, Kehoe drove to the Bath Consolidated School—the new school he opposed building—where he had planted hundreds of pounds of dynamite.<br>• An experienced electrician, he had served as the district's volunteer handyman and had unfettered access to the building.<br>• After months of careful planning, Kehoe took his revenge on the town and the school by setting off a bomb at round 8:45 a.m..<br>• Even though not all of the dynamite he had hidden went off, the resulting explosion was catastrophic.<br>• Thirty-seven children, most only 6–8 years old, and two teachers were killed, and scores of others were injured by the blast.<br>• Still, Kehoe's rampage was not complete. His truck was loaded with explosives as well, which he set off during an altercation with the school's superintendent.<br>• This final destructive act killed Kehoe, the school official, and several others. |

(continued)

**School shooters/school related crimes** (continued)

| Name | Early Life | Crime |
|------|-----------|-------|
| | • He was elected to the school board in 1924 and later won another community post to serve as the town clerk.<br>• But 2 years later, he lost the nomination for the clerkship and was having trouble with the school board.<br>• Eventually, Ellen fell chronically ill with tuberculosis and began visiting the local hospital frequently, thrusting Kehoe further into debt.<br>• He was required to pay a special tax to build a new school, a tax he had fought against.<br>• Kehoe finally stopped paying his mortgage and began blaming the Bath Consolidated School for all of his troubles.<br>• Kehoe was now facing the possibility of losing his 80-acre farm. | • In roughly 1 hour's time, the small town of Bath went from being a quiet small town to the site of one of the deadliest school attacks.<br>  ◦ https://criminalminds.fandom.com/wiki/Andrew_Kehoe<br>  ◦ https://www.biography.com/people/andrew-kehoe-235986 |
| Charles Joseph Whitman, a.k.a. "The Texas Tower Sniper" | • He was born on June 24, 1941, in Lake Worth, Florida.<br>• Taught at an early age to handle guns, Whitman was a good student and Eagle Scout who left home to join the Marines immediately after his 18th birthday in 1959.<br>• He grew up with a perfectionist, demanding father who had a violent temper and thus needed an escape.<br>• Whitman underwent boot camp in South Carolina, earning a sharpshooter ranking, and served at Cuba's Guantanamo Navy Base for more than a year.<br>• Via a special military program, he later entered the University of Texas, where he met his future wife, Kathryn Leissner. (They married in 1962.)<br>• After being called back to active service because of poor academic performance, Whitman returned to the Marine Corps in 1963.<br>• By mid-decade, he was honorably discharged. Whitman went back to the University of Texas at Austin in the spring of 1965.<br>• He originally took up mechanical engineering but later switched to architecture. | • On the evening of July 31, Whitman went to his mother's home and stabbed and shot her. In a note left with her body, Whitman explained that he was "truly sorry that this was the only way I could see to relieve her sufferings but I think it was best."<br>• After killing his mother, Whitman went home. Sometime after his wife went to sleep, he stabbed her to death.<br>• He typed a note before her death, stating that he was going to kill her. He said that "I love her dearly…I cannot rationally pinpoint any specific reason for doing this." He thought it might have been his own selfishness or his desire to spare her from facing embarrassment over his actions.<br>• On August 1, 1966, Whitman, along with an assortment of weapons and supplies stored in a trunk, entered the University of Texas tower, wearing overalls.<br>• He headed up to the observation deck, fatally injuring a receptionist and killing two others along the way.<br>• Once he reached the deck, he began shooting at the people below. The rampage lasted less than 2 hours, with most of the deaths and injuries occurring in the first 15–20 minutes. |

- By 1966, Whitman was suffering from severe headaches and consulted a therapist at the university to discuss concerns he had over his mental health.
- The doctor recommended Whitman attend another session the following week, but he never returned.
- In 1966, Whitman's mother finally left his father after suffering years of abuse. She got an apartment in Austin, not far from her son.

- Whitman shot most of his victims near or in the heart. In total, he murdered 14 people and wounded 30 more on the campus before being shot and killed by 2 police officers, with a wide range of civilians assisting authorities during the crisis.
- In one of his writings, Whitman stated that he wanted his brain examined after his death to check for signs of physical cause of mental illness.
- His request was granted in the form of a police autopsy, which showed that he had a brain tumor. But medical experts disagreed over whether it had any influence on Whitman's behavior.
- With the tower observation deck also becoming the site of several suicides, the school closed the area in the mid-1970s. The deck was reopened in 1999 in a special ceremony.
- A 15th victim died in 2001 due to his injuries.
  - https://www.biography.com/political-figure/charles-whitman

(continued)

**School shooters/school related crimes** (continued)

| Name | Early Life | Crime |
|---|---|---|
| Edwards Charles Allaway | • He was born sometime in 1939 in Royal Oak, Michigan, where he remained for most of his childhood. He had one sister.<br>• As an adult, Allaway began exhibiting symptoms of an unstable mentality, attempting suicide at least once, and he was forced to spend a month in a mental institution, where he received shock therapy treatment.<br>• In early 1973, Allaway moved from Michigan to southern California; there, his wife, Carol, divorced him days later.<br>• Allaway was later diagnosed with paranoid schizophrenia, and he began to uphold a delusion that Carol was sleeping with other men and posing for pornographic pictures.<br>• Moving to Orange County, California, he met a woman named Bonnie, an employee of the Anaheim Hilton Inn at Anaheim, California, and later married her. Afterward, they embarked on a cross-country camping trip, trying to find jobs along the way.<br>• Returning to Orange, Allaway landed a job as a custodian in the library of California State University at Fullerton with the help of his sister, who worked as a secretary in the university's sociology department.<br>• At home, his delusions focused on Bonnie, and he believed that his coworkers at the library were producing pornographic films featuring his wife.<br>• Coworkers described him as quiet and keeping to himself but capable of lashing out against others and also racist. Shortly before the massacre, Allaway and Bonnie divorced on Memorial Day weekend of 1976.<br>• Allegedly, he had threatened her with a penknife, saying that he would cut her face if she cheated on him. | • On July 12, 1976, Allaway snapped. Bringing a .22-caliber semiautomatic rifle he apparently purchased, he arrived at the west side of the school library.<br>• Entering the building and going through a stairwell, Allaway made his way down to the basement's Instructional Media Center (IMC).<br>• At around 8:30 a.m., he first opened fire, targeting people in a secretary's office; photographer Paul Herzberg and equipment technician Bruce Jacobsen were killed, while the secretary, Karen Dwinell, survived unharmed.<br>• Allaway then entered the hallway and fired at the graphics department at the opposite end, killing Professor Emeritus Seth Fessenden and fatally wounding graphic artist Frank Teplansky.<br>• He was then confronted by custodians Donald Karges and Deborah Paulsen, both of whom were familiar to him.<br>• Allaway shot and killed both of them before returning to the stairwell to reload his rifle. He then went up the stairs and headed toward the elevators, where he confronted custodial supervisor Maynard Hoffman, wounding him as he fled inside one of the elevators.<br>• Before he could kill Hoffman, Allaway was attacked by assistant librarian Stephen Becker and library supervisor Donald Keran; Becker struck him over the head with a large plate before he and Keran tried to wrestle the rifle out of his grasp, but both were wounded by stray gunshots.<br>• Allaway then fled through an emergency exit that led into a courtyard located on the library's south side. Becker gave chase, but Allaway spotted him and shot him again in the chest, killing him.<br>• He then evaded the university police and driving to the Anaheim Hilton Inn where Bonnie worked. |

- There, he called police, reported his actions, and stated that he was surrendering to them. Officers burst into the banquet room where he was at and arrested him.
- Allaway later went to trial, where the defense alleged that staff members of the school library did indeed screen commercial pornographic movies before opening hours and in break rooms, which could have been where Allaway's delusions concerning his wives starring in them originated.
- However, in 1977, he was eventually found guilty of six counts of first-degree murder and one count of second-degree murder, but the jury deadlocked during the second phase of the trial, and a judge declared him insane after five different mental health professionals diagnosed him with paranoid schizophrenia.
- As a result, he was committed to the California state mental hospital system, starting with Atascadero State Prison.
- Shortly after the trial ended, Allaway's sister committed suicide by shooting herself in the heart. In June 1998, Allaway, supported by a panel of psychiatrists, requested to be transferred into an outpatient counseling program, which essentially would release him back into society.
- His request was met with criticism from several relatives of his victims, who were angered from the outcome of his initial trial and believed that he was still a danger to society.
- Allaway's request was later denied. In 2001, a report compiled by treating physicians recommended his release, but the request was denied.
  - https://criminalminds.fandom.com/wiki/Edward_Allaway

(continued)

**School shooters/school related crimes** (continued)

| Name | Early Life | Crime |
|---|---|---|
| Patrick Purdy | • He was born November 10th, 1964.<br>• His father, Patrick Benjamin Purdy, was stationed at Fort Lewis, Washington. His mother, Kathleen Toscano, filed for divorce when Purdy was 3 years old and moved the family to California after her husband threatened her with a weapon. Toscano then married Albert Gulart, Sr., and the marriage lasted just 6 years. Purdy attended Cleveland Elementary School from kindergarten through third grade.<br>• Twice in December 1973, Child Protective Services took Purdy and his two siblings into custody after a neighbor reported neglect.<br>• As a child, Purdy was described as very quiet and lacking coping skills. Neighbors remember him as weird and violent. Joan Capalla, who lived near Purdy when he was a child, recalled the boy chasing her sons with a wooden-handled butcher knife.<br>• He developed an alcohol problem as a teenager and was kicked out of his mother's home for hitting his mother when he was 13 or 14.<br>• When he was 14 years old, Purdy lived with a foster parent, who told officers she feared him because he had knives and guns.<br>• Purdy lived on the streets for a while, attending high school only sporadically.<br>• Between 1980 and the shooting in 1989, Purdy was arrested numerous times. His first arrest was for prostitution. He also was arrested for selling drugs, possessing illegal weapons, receiving stolen property, and being an accomplice to an armed robbery.<br>• In 1986, he vandalized his mother's car because she refused to give him money for drugs. When he was almost 22, Purdy told a mental health professional that he had destructive thoughts and was considered to have an antisocial personality. | • On January 17, 1989, Purdy dressed himself in a camouflage shirt with the words "PLO," "Libya," and the misspelled "Death to the Great Satin" written on the front.<br>• Before leaving his hotel room, he lined up 100 green plastic soldiers and small tanks, weapons, and jeeps in his hotel room, placing them on shelves, on the refrigerator, and elsewhere.<br>• He had carved the words "Freedom," "Victory," and "Hezbollah" (a Shiite Muslim group) into his bayoneted rifle.<br>• At approximately noon, Purdy parked his car behind Cleveland Elementary School. He set it on fire with a Molotov cocktail, and then entered the school and began to shoot at the students.<br>• When he ran out of ammunition, he shot and killed himself with a pistol.<br>• The California Attorney General concluded that Purdy hated minorities and blamed them for his horrible life.<br>• He selected Southeast Asians simply because he had the most contact with that group.<br>• Captain Dennis Perry of the Stockton Police Department said that Purdy was obsessed with the military.<br>• The school opened the following day, with workmen attempting to patch the 60 bullet holes in the building and scrub the bloodstains from the floors.<br>• Only one-fourth of the school's 970 students were in attendance. The school brought in psychologists and nurses, as well as interpreters, to assist the traumatized students.<br>    ○ http://criminal-justice.iresearchnet.com/crime/school-violence/patrick-purdy/ |

| | |
|---|---|
| • Despite his problems, he never received any long-term mental health intervention. Purdy's friends described him as a nice guy, although they said he was often frustrated and angry.<br>• In fall of 1987, Purdy began taking welding classes at San Joaquin Delta College. He complained that there were too many Southeast Asian students there.<br>• In 1988, Purdy held a series of jobs and drifted from Oregon, to Texas, to Connecticut, to Tennessee, before returning to Stockton and renting a room at the El Rancho Motel on December 26.<br>• It was during these travels, on August 3, that Purdy purchased the AK-47 for $349.95 that he used in the shooting. | • On December 6, 1989 a little after 4 p.m., Marc Lépine arrived at the building housing the École Polytechnique, an engineering school affiliated with the Université de Montréal, armed with a semiautomatic rifle and a hunting knife.<br>• He had purchased a rifle on November 21, 1989, in a Checkmate Sports store in Montreal, telling the clerk that he was going to use it to hunt small game.<br>• Lépine was familiar with the layout of the building since he had been in and around the École Polytechnique at least seven times in the weeks leading up to the event.<br>• Lépine sat for a time in the office of the registrar on the second floor. He was seen rummaging through a plastic bag and did not speak to anyone, even when a staff member asked if he could help him.<br>• He left the office and was subsequently seen in other parts of the building before entering a second-floor mechanical engineering class of about 60 students at about 5:10 p.m.<br>• After approaching the student giving a presentation, he asked everyone to stop everything and ordered the women and men to opposite sides of the classroom. |
| Gamil Gharbi, a.k.a "Marc Lépine" | • Born Gamil Rodrigue Liass Gharbi on October 26, 1964, in Montreal, Quebec, he is the son of Algerian immigrant Rachid Liass Gharbi and Canadian nurse Monique Lépine.<br>• His father, Rachid, who was a mutual funds salesman, was traveling in the Caribbean at the time of his son's birth.<br>• During his absence, his mother, Monique, discovered evidence that her husband had been having an affair.<br>• Rachid was a nonpracticing Muslim, and Monique was a former Catholic nun who had rejected organized religion after she left the convent.<br>• Their son was baptized a Roman Catholic as an infant but received no religious instruction during his childhood; his mother described her son as "a confirmed atheist all his life."<br>• Gamil's sister, Nadia was born in 1967.<br>• Instability and violence marked the family: it moved frequently, and much of Lépine's early childhood was spent in Costa Rica and Puerto Rico, where his father was working for a Swiss mutual funds company.<br>• The family returned to Montreal permanently in 1968, shortly before a stock market crash led to the loss of much of the family's assets.<br>• Rachid was an authoritarian, possessive, and jealous man, frequently violent toward his wife and his children. |

(continued)

**School shooters/school related crimes** (continued)

| Name | Early Life | Crime |
|---|---|---|
|  | • He had contempt for women and believed that they were intended only to serve men.<br>• He required his wife to act as his personal secretary, slapping her if she made any errors in typing and forcing her to retype documents in spite of the cries of their toddler.<br>• He was also neglectful and abusive toward his children, particularly his son, and discouraged any tenderness, as he considered it spoiling.<br>• In 1970, following an incident in which Rachid struck Gamil so hard that the marks on his face were visible a week later, his mother decided to leave.<br>• The legal separation was finalized in 1971 and the divorce in 1976.<br>• Following the separation, Gamil lived with his mother and younger sister, Nadia; soon after, their home and possessions were seized when Rachid defaulted on mortgage payments.<br>• Gamil was afraid of his father and at first saw him on weekly supervised visits. The visits ended quickly, as Rachid ceased contact with his children soon after the separation. Gamil never again saw his father.<br>• Rachid stopped making support payments after paying them twice, and to make ends meet, Monique returned to nursing. She subsequently started taking further courses to advance her career.<br>• During this time, the children lived with other families during the week, seeing their mother only on weekends.<br>• Concerned about her children and parenting skills, she sought help for the family from a psychiatrist at St. Justine's Hospital in 1976; the assessment concluded there was nothing wrong with the shy and withdrawn Gamil but recommended therapy for his sister, Nadia, who was challenging her authority.<br>• After the divorce became final in 1976, the children, then aged 12 and 9, returned to live with their mother, who was director of nursing at a Montreal hospital. | • No one moved at first, believing it to be a joke until he fired a shot into the ceiling.<br>• Lépine then separated the 9 women from the approximately 50 men and ordered the men to leave. Speaking in French, he asked the remaining women whether they knew why they were there, and when one student replied, "no," he answered: "I am fighting feminism."<br>• One of the students, Nathalie Provost, said, "Look, we are just women studying engineering, not necessarily feminists ready to march on the streets to shout we are against men, just students intent on leading a normal life."<br>• Lépine responded, "You're women, you're going to be engineers. You're all a bunch of feminists. I hate feminists."<br>• He then opened fire on the students from left to right, killing six and wounding three others, including Provost. Before leaving the room, he wrote "oh shit" twice on a student project.<br>• Lépine continued into the second-floor corridor and wounded three students before entering another room where he twice attempted to shoot a female student.<br>• When his weapon failed to fire, he entered the emergency staircase where he was seen reloading his gun. He returned to the room he had just left, but the students had locked the door; Lépine failed to unlock it with three shots fired into the door.<br>• Moving along the corridor, he shot at others, wounding one, before moving toward the financial services office where he shot and killed a woman through the window of the door she had just locked.<br>• He next went down to the first-floor cafeteria, in which about a hundred people were gathered. The crowd scattered after he shot a woman standing near the kitchens and wounded another student.<br>• Entering an unlocked storage area at the end of the cafeteria, Lépine shot and killed two more women hiding there.<br>• He told a male and female student to come out from under a table; they complied and were not shot. |

- In 1977, the family moved to a house purchased in the middle-class Montreal suburb of Pierrefonds.
- Gamil Gharbi attended junior high and high school, where he was described as a quiet student who obtained average to above average marks.
- He developed a close friendship with another boy, but he did not fit in with other students.
- Taunted as an Arab because of his name, at the age of 14, he legally changed it to "Marc Lépine," citing his hatred of his father as the reason for taking his mother's surname.
- Lépine was uncommunicative and showed little emotion. He suffered from low self-esteem, exacerbated by his chronic acne.
- Family relations remained difficult; his younger sister, Nadia, publicly humiliated him about his acne and his lack of girlfriends.
- He fantasized about her death and, on one occasion, made a mock grave for her.
- He was overjoyed when in 1981 she was placed in a group home because of her delinquent behavior and drug abuse. Seeking a good male role model for Lépine, his mother arranged for a Big Brother.
- For 2 years, the experience proved positive as Lépine, often with his best friend, enjoyed the time with photography and motocross motorcycles.
- However, in 1979, the meetings ceased abruptly when the Big Brother was detained on suspicion of molesting young boys.
- Both Lépine and his Big Brother denied that any molestation had occurred. Lépine owned an air rifle as a teenager, which he used to shoot pigeons near his home with his friend.

- Lépine then walked up an escalator to the third floor where he shot and wounded one female and two male students in the corridor.
- He entered another classroom and told the three students giving a presentation to "get out," shooting and wounding Maryse Leclair, who was standing on the low platform at the front of the classroom.
- He fired on students in the front row and then killed two women who were trying to escape the room, while other students dived under their desks.
- Lépine moved toward some of the female students, wounding three of them and killing another.
- He changed the magazine in his weapon and moved to the front of the class, shooting in all directions.
- At this point, the wounded Leclair asked for help; Lépine unsheathed his hunting knife and stabbed her three times, killing her.
- He took off his cap, wrapped his coat around his rifle, exclaimed, "Ah shit," and then committed suicide by shooting himself in the head, 20 minutes after having begun his attack.
- About 60 unfired cartridges remained in the boxes he carried with him.
- He had killed 14 women in total (12 engineering students, 1 nursing student, and 1 employee of the university) and injured 14 other people, including 4 men.
- After briefing reporters outside, Montreal Police director of public relations Pierre Leclair entered the building and found his daughter Maryse's stabbed body.
    ◦ https://criminalminds.fandom.com/wiki/Marc_L%C3%A9pine

(continued)

**School shooters/school related crimes** (continued)

| Name | Early Life | Crime |
|---|---|---|
| | • They also enjoyed designing and building electronic gadgets. He developed an interest in World War II and an admiration of Adolf Hitler and enjoyed action and horror movies. | |
| | • Lépine also took considerable responsibility at home, including cleaning and doing repairs while his mother worked. | |
| | • Lépine applied to join the Canadian Forces as an officer cadet in September 1981 at the age of 17 but was rejected during the interview process. | |
| | • He later told his friend it was because of difficulties accepting authority and, in his suicide letter, noted that he had been found to be "antisocial." | |
| | • In 1982, at the age of 18, the family moved to Saint-Laurent, closer to his mother's work and to Lépine's new Cégep. | |
| | • He lost contact with his school friend soon after the move. This period marks the beginning of the 7 years which he described in his suicide note as having "brought [him] no joy." | |
| | • In August 1982, Lépine began a 2-year pre-university course in pure sciences at Cégep de Saint-Laurent, failing two courses in the first semester but improving his grades considerably in the second semester. | |
| | • He worked part-time at a local hospital where his mother was director of nursing, serving food and doing custodial work. He was seen as nervous, hyperactive, and immature by his colleagues. | |
| | • He developed an attraction to another employee, but he was too shy to act on his feelings. | |
| | • After a year at college, he switched to a 3-year technical program geared more toward immediate employment. | |
| | • His teachers remembered him as being a model student, quiet, hardworking, and generally doing well in his classes, particularly those related to electrotechnology. | |
| | • There was an unexplained drop in his marks in the fall 1985 term, and in February 1986, during the last term of the program, he suddenly and without explanation stopped attending classes, as a result failing to complete his diploma. | |

- He moved out of his mother's home into his own apartment, and in 1986, he applied to study engineering at École Polytechnique de Montréal.
- He was admitted on the condition that he completes two compulsory courses, including one in solution chemistry.
- In 1987, Lépine was fired from his job at the hospital for aggressive behavior, as well as disrespect of superiors, and carelessness in his work.
- He was enraged at his dismissal and, at the time, described a plan to commit a murderous rampage and then commit suicide.
- In the fall of 1987, in order to complete his college diploma, Lépine took three courses, obtaining good marks in all of them, and in February 1988, began a course in computer programming at a private college in downtown Montreal, funding his studies with government student loans.
- He moved into a downtown apartment with his old high school friend and, in the winter of 1989, took a CEGEP night course in solution chemistry, a prerequisite course for the École Polytechnique.
- Lépine wanted a girlfriend but was generally ill at ease around women.
- He tended to boss women around and shows off his knowledge in front of them.
- He spoke out to men about his dislike of feminists, career women, and women in traditionally male occupations, such as the police force, stating that women should remain in the home, caring for their families.
- Lépine applied again to the École Polytechnique in 1989; however, his application was rejected as he lacked required courses.
- In March 1989, he abandoned the course in computer programming though he performed well in the CEGEP course, obtaining 100% in his final exam.
- In April 1989, he met with a university admissions officer and complained about how women were taking over the job market from men.
- Nadia Gharbi died in 1996 at age 28 from a drug overdose.

(continued)

**School shooters/school related crimes** (continued)

| Name | Early Life | Crime |
|---|---|---|
| Ralph Tortorici | • He was born sometime in 1968 at Albany Medical Center, of Italian ancestry.<br>• He was described as intelligent, athletic (even being a part of the varsity wrestling team at the seventh grade), a fan of chess, and very popular, as a child.<br>• In his teenage years, however, he became very aggressive and antagonistic toward family members.<br>• In his 20s, the first signs of his schizophrenia began to show, in which he believed the police and several family members were following him through several microchips implanted in his brain, teeth, and penis. The fact is that Tortorici had a deformed urethra that required three surgeries to fix.<br>• After the third surgery, he went to join the National Guard and was recommended for Officer Candidate School but was later honorably discharged.<br>• In 1990, Tortorici entered SUNY-Albany and studied in the fields of world religion, government, and psychology, which reportedly fueled his delusion of a worldwide conspiracy.<br>• In August 1992, the 24-year-old Tortorici went to the University Health Center at SUNY-Albany to complain of a microchip in his penis and asking to be given an X-ray. He was referred to the Capital District Psychiatric Center by a psychiatrist.<br>• Four months later, he went to police barracks in a nearby town to confront authorities about an alleged microchip implanted into his teeth; again, he was referred to the same psychiatric center.<br>• As a result of his delusions and increasing instability, Tortorici became addicted to drugs, including marijuana.<br>• His mother referred him to the Albany County Medical Center, where an evaluation diagnosed him as having cocaine intoxication, suicidal ideation, and depression. On November 29, he was arrested for minor cocaine possession. | • On December 14, 1994, about 10 months after his referral to the Albany County Medical Center, Tortorici, then 26 years old and a senior at the school, snapped and went to SUNY-Albany, wearing a blue sweatshirt and camouflage fatigues.<br>• He was armed with a .270-caliber Remington rifle and a hunting knife and also carried two dozen rounds of ammunition, all of which he acquired through unspecified means. He had the rifle and ammunition stored inside a duffel bag and the knife concealed in his belt. Reportedly, he entered a lecture hall, where Professor Hans Pohlsander was teaching a class of 35 students about the history of ancient Greece. Just after 9:00 a.m., he took everyone inside hostage. Some hostages initially believed it was a surprise test of the internal security system.<br>• Tortorici then ordered several students to barricade the doors to a subterranean room with desks and chairs before forcing 25-year-old Scott Gushlaw to squirt a fire hose into a hallway outside of the classroom, presumably a means to slow down responding tactical units via slippery floor.<br>• In the first few minutes, he released two students when they began crying hysterically. This was soon followed by the release of Pohlsander and three more students, whom he instructed to deliver messages to President *Bill Clinton*, several other officials, and local news reporters.<br>• Pohlsander promptly alerted campus police, and dozens of city and state police officials responded to the scene at about 9:30 a.m.<br>• Three hostage negotiators were eventually deployed to talk with Tortorici, who demanded to speak to President Clinton, the Governor of New York *Mario Cuomo*, the university's president, and financial-aid officials, but made no other specific demands. He threatened to kill the hostages if the demands were not met. |

- He shot at two of the negotiators but missed both. At another point, he stated his belief that doctors implanted a computer chip in his brain during his birth as part of an experiment.
- He was described by hostages as being agitated when speaking to the negotiators but calm and lighthearted toward the students, offering them cigarettes, demanding food for them, and setting up a corner of the classroom as a *latrine*.
- He repeatedly threatened to kill a 19-year-old Jason McEnaney of Hicksville, New York. And at around 11:30 a.m., he separated him from two other students and ordered him to stand behind one of the barricades.
- McEnaney grabbed Tortorici's rifle and wrestled it from his hands, but not before a stray bullet hit him in the upper leg, genital area, and abdomen. As Tortorici reached for his hunting knife, several other students subdued him and held him to a wall as officers entered the classroom to make the arrest. McEnaney survived his gunshot wound. As he was taken away by police, Tortorici shouted at onlooking students, "Stop government experimentation!"
- Tortorici was found guilty on four counts of kidnapping, four of aggravated assault, one of first-degree assault, and one of first-degree criminal use of a firearm. He was ultimately sentenced to 20–47 years in prison, the maximum punishment under New York law for the charges filed against him. His original parole date was October 2, 2011.
- An appeal was filed, citing that the judge had failed to act on Dr. Siegel's assessment, but it was turned down on April 1998.
- The next January, the case was appealed again to the State Court of Appeals, which also turned it down.
- On May, Tortorici's appellate attorney filed to take the case to the US Supreme Court, and a decision to take it up would have been made in October.

(continued)

**School shooters/school related crimes** (continued)

| Name | Early Life | Crime |
|---|---|---|
| | | • In July 1996, months after his sentencing, Tortorici attempted and survived a suicide attempt by hanging himself with a bedsheet.<br>• He spent a year at the Central New York Psychiatric Center, where his condition seemed to improve psychologically.<br>• On July 14, 1999, he was taken to Sullivan Correctional Facility. He was seen daily by mental health staff and received weekly treatment services.<br>• On August 10, 19 months after his release from the Central New York Psychiatric Center, he was found hanging in his cell with a bedsheet at 4:48 a.m. by a correction officer.<br>• Tortorici was pronounced dead in the prison infirmary at 6:47 a.m. by the county coroner.<br>    ○ https://criminalminds.fandom.com/wiki/Ralph_Tortorici |
| Thomas Hamilton, a.k.a. "Mr. Creepy" | • He was born on May 10, 1952, in Glasgow, Scotland. His mother, a hotel chambermaid, was divorced from his father by the time Hamilton was born. Hamilton never knew his father and grew up with his mother's adoptive parents, believing they were his biological parents.<br>• They legally adopted him at age 2. He also thought his biological mother was his sister until he was told the truth when he was 22 years old.<br>• As a boy, Thomas Hamilton did well academically.<br>• He joined a rifle club and the Boys Brigade as a teenager and, at the age of 20, became an assistant leader of his local Boy Scouts club.<br>• Before long, there were complaints from the boys that Hamilton was teaching them to use rifles and handguns, as well as forcing them to engage in perverted activities and then paying them to keep quiet.<br>• Hamilton had briefly been a Scout leader—initially, in July 1973, he was appointed assistant leader with the 4th/6th Stirling of the Scout Association. In the autumn of that year, he was seconded as leader to the 24th Stirlingshire troop, which was being revived. | • On the morning of Wednesday, March 13, 1996, Thomas Hamilton, aged 43, was witnessed scraping ice off his van at approximately 8:15 a.m. outside his home at Kent Road in Stirling.<br>• He left a short time afterward and drove approximately 5 miles (8 km) north to Dunblane in his white van.<br>• He arrived on the grounds of Dunblane Primary School at around 9:30 a.m. and parked his van near to a telegraph pole in the car park of the school.<br>• Hamilton severed the cables at the bottom of the telegraph pole, which served nearby houses, with a set of pliers before making his way across the car park toward the school buildings.<br>• Hamilton headed toward the northwest side of the school to a door near toilets and the school gymnasium.<br>• After gaining entry, he made his way to the gymnasium armed with four legally held handguns; two 9 mm Browning HP pistols and two Smith & Wesson M19.357 Magnum revolvers.<br>• He was also carrying 743 cartridges of ammunition. |

- There had been a number of complaints to police regarding Hamilton's behavior toward the young boys who attended the youth clubs he directed.
- Claims had been made of his having taken photographs of semi-naked boys without parental consent.
- However, several complaints were made about his leadership, including two occasions when scouts were forced to sleep with Hamilton in his van during hill-walking expeditions.
- Within months, on May 13, 1974, Hamilton's scout warrant was withdrawn, with the county commissioner stating that he was "suspicious of his moral intentions towards boys."
- He was asked to leave the scouts in 1974.
- He was blacklisted by the association and thus thwarted in a later attempt he made to become a scout leader in Clackmannanshire.
- In the 1980s, another MP, George Robertson, who lived in Dunblane, complained to Forsyth about Hamilton's local boys' club, which his son had attended.
- He claimed in letters that rumors about him led to the failure of his shop business in 1993, and in the last months of his life he complained again that his attempts to organize a boys' club were subject to persecution by local police and the scout movement.
- Among those to whom he complained were the Queen and the local Member of Parliament, Michael Forsyth.
- On the day following the massacre, Robertson spoke of having argued with Hamilton "in my own home."
- On March 19, 1996, 6 days after the massacre, the body of Thomas Hamilton was cremated in a private ceremony.

- In the gym was a class of 28 Primary 1 pupils preparing for a P.E. lesson in the presence of 3 adult members of staff.
- Before entering the gymnasium, it is believed he fired two shots into the stage of the assembly hall and the girls' toilet.
- Upon entering the gymnasium, Hamilton was about to be confronted by Eileen Harrild, the P.E. teacher in charge of the lesson, before he started shooting rapidly and randomly.
- He shot Harrild, who sustained injuries to her arms and chest as she attempted to protect herself, and continued shooting into the gymnasium.
- Harrild managed to stumble into the open plan store cupboard at the side of the gym along with several injured children. Gwen Mayor, the teacher of the Primary 1 class, was shot and killed instantly.
- The other present adult, Mary Blake, a supervisory assistant, was shot in the head and both legs but also managed to make her way to the store cupboard with several of the children in front of her.
- From entering the gymnasium and walking a few steps, Hamilton had fired 29 shots with one of the pistols and killed one child and injured several others.
- Four injured children had managed to shelter in the store cupboard along with the injured Harrild and Blake.
- Hamilton then advanced up the east side of the gym, firing six shots as he walked and then fired eight shots toward the opposite end of the gym.
- He then proceeded toward the center of the gym, firing 16 shots at point-blank range at a group of children who had been incapacitated by his earlier shots.
- A Primary 7 pupil who was walking along the west side of the gym building at the time heard loud bangs and screams and looked inside the gym.

(continued)

**School shooters/school related crimes** (continued)

| Name | Early Life | Crime |
|---|---|---|
| | | • Hamilton shot in his direction, and the pupil was injured by flying glass before running away. From this position, Hamilton fired 24 cartridges in various directions. |
| | | • He fired shots toward a window next to the fire exit at the southeast end of the gym, possibly at an adult who was walking across the playground, and then fired four more shots in the same direction after opening the fire exit door. |
| | | • Hamilton then exited the gym briefly through the fire exit, firing another four shots toward the cloakroom of the library, striking and injuring Grace Tweddle, another member of staff at the school. |
| | | • In the mobile classroom closest to the fire exit where Hamilton was standing, Catherine Gordon saw him firing shots and instructed her Primary 7 class to get down onto the floor before Hamilton fired nine bullets into the classroom, striking books and equipment. One bullet passed through a chair where a child had been sitting seconds beforehand. |
| | | • Hamilton then reentered the gym, dropped the pistol he was using, and equipped himself with one of the two revolvers. |
| | | • He put the barrel of the gun in his mouth, pointed it upward, and pulled the trigger, killing himself. |
| | | • A total of 32 people sustained gunshot wounds inflicted by Hamilton over a 3–4 minute period, 16 of whom were fatally wounded in the gymnasium, which included Gwen Mayor and 15 of her pupils. One other child died later en route to hospital. |
| | | • The first call to the police was made at 9:41 a.m. by the headmaster of the school, Ronald Taylor, who had been alerted by assistant headmistress Agnes Awlson to the possibility of a gunman on the school premises. |

| | |
|---|---|
| | • Awlson had informed Taylor that she heard screaming inside the gymnasium and had seen what she thought to be cartridges on the ground, while Taylor had been aware of loud noises which he assumed to have been from builders on site that he had not been informed of.<br>• While on his way to the gym, the shooting ended and, when he saw what had happened, ran back to his office and told deputy headmistress Fiona Eadington to call for ambulances, which was made at 9:43 a.m.<br>• By approximately 11:10 a.m., all of the injured victims had been taken to Stirling Royal Infirmary for medical treatment; one victim died en route to the hospital.<br>• Upon examination, several of the patients were transferred to Falkirk and District Royal Infirmary in Falkirk and some to the Royal Hospital for Sick Children in Glasgow.<br>   ◦ https://criminalminds.fandom.com/wiki/Thomas_Hamilton |
| Andrew Golden and Mitchell Johnson, a.k.a 'The 1998 Arkansas School Shooters' | • Mitchell Scott Johnson (born August 11, 1984) and Andrew Douglas Golden (born May 25, 1986).<br>• Mitchell Scott Johnson lived in Jonesboro with his mother, stepfather, and his brother.<br>• His parents divorced when he was seven, and his mother remarried to Terry Woodward, an inmate at the prison where she was a guard.<br>• Johnson had a good relationship with his stepfather, and adults who remember him described him as being quiet and respectful.<br>• Fellow students at Westside Middle School described him as being a bully, who talked of wanting to belong to street gangs and smoke marijuana.<br>• He spoke of "having a lot of killing to do" and holding a bitter grudge against Shannon Wright, his English teacher.<br>• His classmates also commented that he had a fascination with firearms. | • One year prior to the shooting, 12-year-old Johnson was charged with molesting a 3-year-old girl while visiting Minnesota with his family. However, the record of the case was expunged because of Johnson's age.<br>• On the night of March 23, 1998 Golden helped Johnson load his mother's 1991 Dodge Caravan with weapons, snack foods, and camping supplies.<br>• The next day, Johnson stole his mother's keys and drove to the school with Golden. Johnson parked the van in the middle of the woods outside of the backyard of the school, planning to return there once the massacre was over.<br>• Johnson sat on a hill in the backyard of the school, while Golden went inside and pulled the fire alarm. Golden ran back and rejoined him at the hill with his weapon. |

(continued)

**School shooters/school related crimes** (continued)

| Name | Early Life | Crime |
| --- | --- | --- |
| | • Johnson's attorney claimed that he had been sexually abused when he was 6 and 7 years old by a "family member of the day care where he was placed."<br>• Andrew Douglas Golden also lived in the Jonesboro area with his parents.<br>• He came from a stable and loving household, having a good relationship with both his parents, and visiting his grandparents after school.<br>• He was raised to be familiar with guns and their use at an early age; he was given his first firearm by his father when he was 6 years old.<br>• His schoolmates described him as a bully, and faced troublesome behavior; often engaging in fist fights with other students, and would often use profane language. Classmate once accused him of killing her cat with a BB gun. | • As the students and teachers filed out of the building, thinking it was a routine fire drill, Johnson and Golden opened fire on them.<br>• After they fired for 4 minutes, four students and a teacher were killed, and ten more were wounded.<br>• As the police arrived on the scene, Johnson and Golden ran into the woods back to the van. However, they failed to outrun the officers that were pursuing them, and were both arrested by the police officers.<br>   ○ http://murderpedia.org/male.G/g/golden-andrew.htm |
| Kipland Philip Kinkel, a.k.a. "Kip" | • He was born August 30, 1982, in Springfield, Oregon, the second child of Spanish teachers, William Kinkel and Faith Zuranski. His mother taught at Springfield High School and his father at Thurston High School and Lane Community College. He has an older sister.<br>• There was a widespread history of serious mental illnesses in both sides of the family.<br>• According to all accounts, Kinkel's parents were loving and supportive. His sister was a gifted student. The Kinkel family spent a sabbatical year in Spain when Kip was 6, where he attended a Spanish-speaking kindergarten.<br>• When Kinkel returned to Oregon, he attended elementary school in the small community of Walterville. His teachers considered him immature and lacking physical and emotional development. Based on the recommendation of his teachers, Kinkel's parents had him repeat the first grade. He was diagnosed with dyslexia, which became worse, and he was placed in extensive special education classes by the beginning of second grade. | • At home that afternoon on May 20, 1998, Kinkel was told by his father that he would be sent to military school if he did not improve his behavior.<br>• At about 3:00 p.m., Kinkel retrieved his Ruger .22-caliber semiautomatic rifle from his bedroom and ammunition from his parents' bedroom, went to the kitchen where his father was drinking coffee, shot his father once in the back of the head, and then dragged his body into the bathroom and covered it with a sheet.<br>• His mother arrived home at about 6:30 p.m., and he met her in the garage, told her he loved her, and then shot her twice in the back of the head, three times in the face, and once in the heart. He then dragged her body across the floor and covered it with a sheet.<br>• In a note Kinkel left on a coffee table in the living room, he described his motive for killing his parents thus: "I just got two felonies on my record. My parents can't take that! It would destroy them. The embarrassment would be too much for them. They couldn't live with themselves." It also says that, "My head just doesn't work right. God damn these voices inside my head...I have to kill people. I don't know why...I have no other choice." |

- Kinkel had an interest in firearms and explosives from an early age. His father initially discouraged this but later enrolled him at gun safety courses.
- He bought him a .22-caliber long rifle and eventually a 9 mm Glock handgun at the age of 15.
- Classmates described Kinkel as strange and morbid. Others characterized him as psychotic or schizoid and as someone who enjoyed listening to rock bands.
- He constantly talked about committing acts of violence and wanted to join the US Army after graduation to find out what it was like to kill someone.
- He once gave a "how to" speech in bomb making to his speech class and set off "stink bombs" in the lockers of classmates.
- Kinkel's parents enrolled him in anger management and had him evaluated by psychologists. Shortly before being murdered, Kinkel's father confided to a friend that he was "terrified" and had run out of options to help his son.
- Kinkel exhibited signs of paranoid schizophrenia, the full extent of which became apparent only after his trial.
- He went to great lengths to hide any symptoms due to a fear of being labeled abnormal or mentally retarded. His doctors later said that Kinkel had told them of hearing voices in his head from the age of 12.
- He suffered from hallucinations and paranoid delusions—including the belief that the government had implanted a computer chip in his brain. Kinkel described three voices: "Voice A," who commanded Kinkel to commit violent acts; "Voice B," who repeated insulting and depressive statements at the expense of Kinkel; and "Voice C," who constantly echoed what A and B said.
- Kinkel claimed that he was punished by God for being subjected to these voices and that it was Voice A who instigated the killing of his father, mother, and the subsequent attack at Thurston High School.

- On May 21, 1998, he drove his mother's Ford Explorer to Thurston High School in Springfield, Oregon, wearing a trench coat to hide the five weapons he carried: two hunting knives, his rifle, a 9 × 19 mm Glock 19 pistol, and a .22-caliber Ruger MK II pistol. He was carrying 1127 rounds of ammunition.
- He parked on North 61st Street, two blocks from the school, then jogged to the campus, entered the patio area, and fired two shots, one fatally wounding Ben Walker and the other wounding Ryan Atteberry.
- He went to the cafeteria and, walking across it, fired the remaining 48 rounds from his rifle, wounding 24 students and fatally wounding 17-year-old Mikael Nickolauson. Kinkel fired a total of 50 rounds, 37 of which struck students, and killed two.
- He was tackled by wounded student Jacob Ryker, assisted by several other students when his rifle ran out of ammunition and he began to reload. Kinkel then drew the Glock from his belt and fired one shot before he was disarmed, injuring Ryker again as well as another student. A total of seven students were involved in subduing and disarming him.
- He yelled at the students, "Just kill me!" but they restrained Kinkel until the police arrived and arrested him. Even in custody, he tried to get himself killed by retrieving a knife that was secured on his leg and attacking a police officer, begging to be fatally shot. The officer subdued him with pepper spray.
- The shooting left two students, Ben Walker and Mikael Nickolauson, dead and 25 others wounded. Nickolauson died at the scene; Walker died after being transported to the hospital and kept on life support until his parents arrived. The other students, including Ryker, were also taken to the hospital with a variety of wounds. Ryker had a perforated lung, but he made a full recovery. He received the Boy Scouts of America Honor Medal with Crossed Palms for his heroism on the day of the attack.

(continued)

**School shooters/school related crimes** (continued)

| Name | Early Life | Crime |
|---|---|---|
| | • On May 20, 1998, 15-year-old Kinkel was suspended from Thurston High School in Springfield, Oregon, for being in possession of a loaded stolen handgun. Reportedly, a friend had stolen a pistol from the father of one of his friends and arranged to sell the weapon to Kinkel the night before. Kinkel paid $110 for the Beretta Model 90 .32-caliber pistol loaded with a nine-round magazine, which he then placed in a paper bag and left in his locker.<br>• When the father discovered he was missing a handgun, he reported it to the police and supplied the names of students he believed might have stolen the firearm. Kinkel's name was not on the list. The school became aware of his possible involvement and questioned him. Kinkel and his friend were arrested; he was released from police custody and driven home by his father | • Kinkel is currently serving a 111-year sentence without the possibility of parole.<br>  ○ https://en.wikipedia.org/wiki/Thurston_High_School_shooting |
| Dylan Klebold and Eric Harris, a.k.a. "The Columbine High School Massacre Shooters" | • Eric Harris was born on April 9, 1981, in Wichita, Kansas.<br>• The son of an Air Force pilot, Harris moved around several times as a child.<br>• While living in Plattsburgh, New York, he seemed like a regular kid, playing little league baseball.<br>• Harris family moved to Littleton, Colorado, in 1993, after his father retired from the military.<br>• Eric slowly began to change. In his new hometown, he was a decent soccer player and wore preppy-style clothing but had a hard time fitting in at school.<br>• During high school, Harris became close friends with Dylan Klebold, another social outcast. While Harris was talkative and volatile, Klebold was shy and reserved. But they both hated the school and its jock culture and anyone else that they believed had mistreated them—a common bond that would prove deadly. They were computer savvy and enjoyed playing violent video games.<br>• By the second year at Columbine High School, Harris had become visibly different, dressing like the school's outsider clique, the Trench Coat Mafia, by wearing long coats, dark clothes, and boots. | • In 1998, Harris and Klebold, both high school juniors, were arrested after stealing items from a van they broke into.<br>• They were charged with theft, criminal mischief, and criminal trespassing. Since it was their first offense, they were enrolled in a diversion program, which consisted of community service and counseling.<br>• They were released a month early from program in February 1999—only 2 months before their rampage. Both received glowing reports at the end of the program with Harris being called "a bright young man who is likely to succeed in life," according to an article in The Christian Science Monitor.<br>• Sometime after his arrest, he began planning an attack on his school with Klebold. For about a year, the two prepared for what they called "Judgment Day." They wanted to kill hundreds of people at their school, hoping to achieve some lasting fame while metering out their vengeance against the people they hated. Harris wrote about their plans in his diary. |

- Harris was often bullied by other students for his weird looks and odd behavior.
- Both Harris and Klebold studied German and became enamored with Adolf Hitler and the Nazis. They wore swastikas and sometimes gave the "Hail, Hitler" salute. Harris' rage was often visible and apparent. Angry at a friend, he threw an ice ball into his windshield, cracking the glass, and later threatened to kill that same person on his website. The site was filled with violent tirades against anyone and everyone that Harris disliked or thought had done him wrong.
- Harris earned good grades, but his schoolwork often featured violent imagery and gory details.
- Harris had been rejected by the US Marine Corps shortly before the killings because of his psychiatric medication. He was taking Luvox for his depression.

- Dylan Klebold was born on September 11, 1981, in Lakewood, Colorado.
- His father was a geophysicist, and his mother worked with the disabled.
- His parents eventually started their own real estate management company and provided an upper middle-class life.
- Klebold was in a program for gifted students at his elementary school and was described as a shy child who loved baseball.
- He liked violent video games. Klebold also enjoyed bowling and worked behind the scenes for school productions as a sound man.
- He was a quiet teen interested in technology, and although he was bright, he didn't apply himself in school and earned mediocre grades.
- Klebold expressed suicidal thoughts and was deeply saddened by his lack of a romantic relationship.
- His intense rage appeared in the violent essays he wrote for English assignment, which often featured blood, death, and war.
- Klebold and Harris made a video of them acting as vigilantes shooting "jocks" in the school hallways for a school project.

- Harris and Klebold learned to make bombs and acquired guns, posting bomb-making information on his website.
- A friend of Dylan reportedly helped them get three of the weapons and a coworker from the pizza place where Harris had a part-time job assisted in obtaining the fourth gun.
- They made several videotapes in which they discuss their plot, which was filled with rage, racist remarks, and some concern for their parents.
- Harris and Klebold carried out their assault on their school on the morning of April 20, 1999, which was also Adolf Hitler's birthday.
- They planted a bomb in the school's cafeteria, which was supposed to go off around 11:00 a.m., to force everyone to evacuate the building. Harris and Klebold planned on shooting people as they entered the parking lot.
- The bomb failed, so the two entered the school a little after 11:00 a.m. and began shooting. For less than hour, they terrorized the school, killing 12 students and a teacher and wounding more than 20 others.
- Returning to the library, where they had killed and wounded several people, Harris shot himself in the head as did Klebold a few moments later.
- Along with his friend, Dylan Klebold, Harris shot and killed 13 people and wounded more than 20 others at Columbine High School on April 20, 1999.
  - Article Title: Eric Harris Biography Author: Biography.com Editors Website Name: The Biography.com website URL: https://www.biography.com/people/eric-harris-235982. Original Published Date: April 2, 2014
  - Article Title: Dylan Klebold Biography Author: Biography.com Editors Website Name: The Biography.com website URL: https://www.biography.com/people/dylan-klebold-235979. Original Published Date: April 2, 2014

(continued)

**School shooters/school related crimes** (continued)

| Name | Early Life | Crime |
|---|---|---|
| Jeff Weise | • He was born on August 8, 1988, in Minneapolis, Minnesota, a descendant of the Red Lake Native American people Ojibwe.<br>• The only child of an unmarried couple living in Red Lake, Minnesota, Weise was stated to be physically and emotionally abused by his alcoholic mother Joanne.<br>• In November 1988, when he was 3 months old, his father claimed full custody over him; Weise was later reclaimed by his mother when he was 3 years old and taken to the Minneapolis-Saint Paul area.<br>• In 1992, Joanne began dating Timothy Troy DesJarlait, who also allegedly abused Weise; they married after having two children together.<br>• On March 5, 1999, after Joanne and one of her cousins were involved in a car accident, in which Joanne suffered severe brain damage that led to her institutionalization in Bloomington, Weise was placed into the care of his paternal grandmother Shelda but was also cared by his two paternal aunts.<br>• Due to his disrupted family life, Weise attended a number of schools during his early years.<br>• In 2001, Weise was forced to repeat the eighth grade because of his academic grades and truancy, and he enrolled in a special education program at the school called the Learning Center.<br>• Beginning in middle school, Weise was frequently taunted and bullied by the other students, who made fun of his physical appearance and preference of wearing all-black clothing.<br>• Enrolling at Red Lake Senior High School on September 2003, Weise was seen as withdrawn by teachers and a "Goth kid" yet typically nonviolent by fellow students. Despite this, he managed, to maintain an adequate social life, having numerous friends and being capable to relate to girls. | • Finally snapping one day, Weise shot his paternal grandfather Daryl Lussier, Sr., numerous times with a pistol he somehow managed to obtain and keep for unspecified amount of time.<br>• He then stole Lussier's two police-issue weapons and killed Lussier's girlfriend. Driving over to Red Lake Senior High in Lussier's squad car, Weise entered the school and killed an unarmed security guard before shooting into an English classroom, killing four (including the teacher), and wounding three.<br>• At one point, he allegedly asked a student if he believed in God before shooting him, an act that was reminiscent of the Columbine High School shooting.<br>• After exiting the classroom and shooting four more students at the school's main entrance, killing two, Weise engaged in a shootout with the police, during which he was wounded in the abdomen and right arm.<br>• Retreating to an empty classroom, Weise committed suicide by shooting himself under the chin with his shotgun. He was 16 years old when he died<br> ◦ https://criminalminds.fandom.com/wiki/Jeff_Weise |

- He eventually became depressed with life, especially due to his frustrations with living in Red Lake, which he described "as a place where people 'choose alcohol over friendship,' where women neglect 'their own flesh and blood' for relationships with men, where he could not escape 'the grave I'm continually digging for myself'."
- Weise later attempted suicide on May 2004 but allegedly changed his mind.
- However, he attempted suicide again on June 2004, and his aunts arranged with the Red Lake Medical Center for him to be hospitalized at a facility located off of the reservation.
- His continuous treatment included counseling and a prescription for Prozac, an antidepressant.
- One source alleged that his doctor increased Weise's dosage of Prozac in 2005 a week before the shooting, to 60 mg a day
- Weise held a particular set of political views in which he admired Adolf Hitler and Nazism, allegedly posting revelations for intents of persuading other Native Americans to join the Nazi cause.

(continued)

**School shooters/school related crimes** (continued)

| Name | Early Life | Crime |
|------|-----------|-------|
| Charles Carl Roberts | • He was born December 7, 1973, in Lancaster, Pennsylvania.<br>• His father was retired from the local police force. In 2004, his father applied to the state for a special license to provide paratransit service to the Amish.<br>• Roberts earned a diploma through a home-school association, and neither he nor his family was Amish.<br>• In 1990, Roberts worked as a dishwasher at Good 'N Plenty Restaurant in Smoketown, PA.<br>• Two of his coworkers were Lawrence Yunkin and Lisa Michelle Lambert, both of whom would be convicted in the December 20, 1991, murder of 16-year-old Laurie Show in Lancaster, Pennsylvania.<br>• Roberts was a commercial milk tank driver, employed by North West Foods. | • On October 2, 2006, Roberts entered the one-room West Nickel Mines School at approximately 9:51 a.m. with a 9 mm handgun, 12 gauge shotgun, .30–.06 bolt-action rifle, about 600 rounds of ammunition, cans of black powder, a stun gun, two knives, a change of clothes, an apparent truss board, and a box containing a hammer, hacksaw, pliers, wire, screws, bolts, and tape.<br>• He used 2 × 6 and 2 × 4 boards with eye bolts and flex ties to barricade the school doors before binding the arms and legs of the hostages.<br>• He ordered the hostages to line up against the chalkboard and released the 15 male students present, along with a pregnant woman and 3 parents with infants.<br>• He kept the ten remaining female students inside the schoolhouse. The schoolteacher contacted the police upon escaping at approximately 10:36 a.m.<br>• The first police officers arrived about 9 minutes later and attempted (unsuccessfully) to communicate with Roberts using the PA broadcasters in their cruisers.<br>• Police had to break in through the windows when shots were heard. The gunman apparently killed himself along with five school girls.<br>• Three of the girls died at the scene, with two more dying the next morning from related injuries. Five girls were in the hospital in critical condition.<br>• Reports stated that the girls were shot execution style in the head. The ages of the victims ranged from 6 to 13. Roberts fired at least 13 rounds from his 9 mm semiautomatic pistol.<br>• Roberts was last seen by his wife at 8:45 a.m. when they walked their children to the bus stop to go to school in Bart Township.<br>• When his wife returned home at 11:00 a.m., she discovered four notes he had left to her and their children. |

| | |
|---|---|
| | • Roberts reportedly contacted his wife while still in the schoolhouse and stated that he had molested two young female relatives (between the ages of 3 and 5) 20 years ago (when he would have been 12) and had been daydreaming about molesting again.<br>• Both of the relatives in question have denied these claims. Among the items he brought to the school was a tube of KY Jelly, which investigators surmised he might have intended to use as a sexual lubricant.<br>• His suicide notes stated that he was still angry at God for the death of a premature infant daughter 9 years prior.<br>  ○ http://murderpedia.org/male.R/r/roberts-charles.htm |
| Seung-Hui Cho, a.k.a. "The Virginia Tech Shooter" | • Seung-Hui Cho was born in South Korea on January 18, 1984, where he grew up until he was 8 years old.<br>• From the beginning, his mother agonized over his sullen, brooding behavior and empty face. He did not talk with other children or to his own family.<br>• In Seoul, there was never much money. The Cho family occupied a shabby two-room basement apartment, living frugally on the slender proceeds of a used-book shop.<br>• According to relatives, the father, Seung-Tae Cho, had worked in oil fields and on construction sites in Saudi Arabia.<br>• In an arranged marriage, he wed Kim Hwang-Im, the daughter of a farming family that had fled North Korea during the Korean War.<br>• Their son was well behaved, all right, but his pronounced bashfulness deeply worried his parents. Relatives thought he might be a mute or mentally ill.<br>• When Cho was about 8 years old, he and his family came to the USA from South Korea.<br>• They eventually settled in Centreville, Virginia, where they ran a dry-cleaning business.<br>• Cho was known as a shy child who liked basketball and did well in math.<br>• But according to an article in Newsweek magazine, Cho was also bullied by other children, including wealthy members of his church. | • One professor, poet Nikki Giovanni, had him removed from her class for disturbing the other students.<br>• She told TIME magazine that "there was something mean about this boy." She said that he was "a bully" and always came to class wearing sunglasses and a hat, which she would always ask him to remove.<br>• Cho was also photographing the legs and knees of female students in the class. Other members of the English department faculty were concerned about him as well.<br>• Lucinda Roy, the codirector of the school's creative writing program, took him out of class and tutored him individually. She also encouraged Cho to get counseling.<br>• In addition to his odd behavior and dark writings, Cho exhibited other potential warning signs.<br>• He was twice accused of stalking female students in 2005, but neither victim filed charges.<br>• A suicidal statement by Cho to a suitemate led to him being taken to a psychiatric hospital in December of that year.<br>• He was soon released with orders to receive therapy as an outpatient.<br>• Documents released in June 2007 indicate that he did attend at least one court-ordered counseling session at the Cook Counseling Center.<br>• Five weeks before the shooting, Cho bought his first handgun and purchased the second one closer to the date of the attack. |

(continued)

**School shooters/school related crimes** (continued)

| Name | Early Life | Crime |
|---|---|---|
| | • In high school, Cho was described as sullen and aloof.<br>• After graduating in 2003, he went on to study at Virginia Tech University.<br>• Cho stood out as a near-silent loner who wrote gruesome poems, stories, and plays. He sometimes referred to himself as "Question Mark."<br>• In his junior year, Mr. Cho told his then roommates that he had a girlfriend. Her name was Jelly. She was a supermodel who lived in outer space and traveled by spaceship, and she existed only in the dimension of his imagination. | • From evidence found in his dorm room, it was clear that he had been planning the assault on his fellow students and the faculty for quite some time.<br>• On April 16, 2007, Cho began his rampage by killing two students in a dormitory after 7:00 a.m.<br>• He later went to a classroom building and began shooting students and faculty members, killing 32 people and injuring numerous others around 9:45 a.m.<br>• The spree only ended when Cho turned one of his guns on himself, shooting himself in the head.<br>• Up until that point, the largest campus shooting had taken place in 1966, when Charles Whitman killed 15 people on the campus of the University of Texas at Austin.<br>• In between the two sets of attacks, Cho went to the post office to mail a package to NBC News in New York, which was received 2 days after the murders; it contained video clips, photographs of Cho posing with his weapons, and a rambling document.<br>• In one of the video clips, he rails against rich "brats" and talks about being bullied and picked on; he also attacks Christianity and positioned himself as some type of avenger for the weak and defenseless.<br>• Cho even referenced the notorious Columbine school shooters, Eric Harris and Dylan Klebold.<br>• After the shooting, Virginia Tech and many schools across the nation began examining their crisis management plans, as well as how they identify and handle potentially dangerous students.<br>  ○ https://www.biography.com/people/seung-hui-cho-235991<br>  ○ https://www.nytimes.com/2007/04/22/us/22vatech.html |

| | | |
|---|---|---|
| Wellington Menezes de Oliveira, a.k.a. "Pink Elephant" | • He was born July 13, 1987.<br>• Reportedly, he was a target for both verbal and physical bullying during his days at the school; he had a limp leg and was described as "strange."<br>• Although described as kind and friendly, he was once thrown into a garbage bin by students.<br>• Rage and resentment began to build inside him, which lasted until adulthood.<br>• Oliveira was also obsessed with Islam, perceiving it as the "only correct religion."<br>• He also refers to the Virginia Tech shooter, Seung-Hui Cho, as a brother and an icon for those who are oppressed by the majority. | • The day of the shooting on April 7, 2011, Oliveira entered the school, identifying as a former student and lying to the security guard that he was there to give a speech. Instead of giving a speech, Oliveira entered a classroom, and, at first, he was very polite when he put his bag on a table.<br>• Without warning, he took out his revolvers and opened fire. Of the 12 dead, 10 were girls, and 1 boy said that Oliveira only shot at boys to stun them while he tried his best to kill the girls.<br>• However, an alternative explanation can be found in that the population of the class is predominately girls.<br>• Soon, the police arrived; Oliveira shot at them but missed. Soon he was shot in the abdomen and legs, and as a result he fell down a staircase. He then fatally shot himself in the head.<br>  ○ https://real-life-villains.fandom.com/wiki/Wellington_de_Oliveira |
| Adam Lanza, a.k.a. "The Sandy Hook School Shooter" | • Adam Peter Lanza was born in Exeter, New Hampshire, on April 22, 1992.<br>• His mother, Nancy Lanza, was a former stock broker and longtime gun enthusiast. Friends and neighbors said she took her son to the gun range to avoid leaving him alone, but she was responsible with weapons.<br>• Unlike her son, who was quiet and socially awkward, Nancy was outgoing and easily made friends.<br>• Nancy married Peter Lanza, a successful executive, on June 6, 1981; the couple divorced in 2009, when Adam was 16 years old.<br>• Thereafter, Peter Lanza reportedly relocated to Stamford, Connecticut, and agreed to pay an annual alimony of $240,000 with periodic increases.<br>• Adam had one brother, Ryan Lanza, who was 6 years, his senior.<br>• He was described early on by classmates as "fidgety" and "deeply troubled."<br>• According to some of his friends and family members, he had also been diagnosed with Asperger's syndrome.<br>• He had numerous weapons as well as ammunition. Lanza also had a number of books and articles on other mass killings. | • He killed mother, Nancy Lanza, in the head at her home in Newtown, Connecticut, around 9:00 a.m. on December 14, 2012.<br>• He then took her car and drove approximately 5 miles to the Sandy Hook Elementary School, where he shot 27 people: 20 children, between the ages of 5 and 10, as well as 6 teachers and 1 adult worker.<br>• According to reports, most of the shooting occurred in two of the school's first-grade classrooms: 14 students in one classroom and 6 in the other were murdered.<br>• Only two of the victims who were shot by Lanza—both teachers—survived the attack.<br>  ○ https://www.biography.com/people/adam-lanza-21068899 |

(continued)

**School shooters/school related crimes** (continued)

| Name | Early Life | Crime |
|------|-----------|-------|
| Elliot Rodgers, "2014 Isla Vista killings" | • Rodger was born in London, England, UK, on July 24, 1991.<br>• His parents were British filmmaker Peter Rodger (known for his 2009 documentary film *Oh My God* and his work as a second unit director on *The Hunger Games*) and Malaysian research assistant Li Chin Rodger, and he had one younger sister.<br>• His paternal grandfather was photojournalist George Rodger. The family later immigrated to and settled in the USA, with Rodger being raised in Los Angeles, California.<br>• His parents later divorced, and his father remarried to Moroccan actress Soumaya Akaboune, who bore his second son.<br>• Ever since he was 8 years old, Rodger had been seeing therapists and receiving psychiatric treatment, including medication for a variety of mental illnesses and disorders.<br>• However, he refused to take any of the medication that was prescribed to him.<br>• Rodger's mother stated her belief that he suffered from Asperger's syndrome, even though he was never formally diagnosed with the developmental disorder.<br>• In school, Rodger was heavily bullied, and he claimed that he was unable to make any friends, though people later said that he was the one who rebuffed their attempts at being friendly.<br>• At some point, he started and began maintaining a personal YouTube account and online blog, both in which he complained about his loneliness and rejection by others.<br>• He also frequented online communities that fell into the manosphere, which has been commonly associated with misogyny and anti-feminism.<br>• He moved to Isla Vista on June 4, 2011, to attend Santa Barbara City College, but he later dropped out in February of 2012. From 2011 to 2012, Rodger was involved in a series of minor incidents in which he threw or sprayed drinks on couples or groups of people he was jealous of. | • On May 23, 2014, Rodger started his rampage, which he titled "The Day of Retribution," by stabbing three people to death. They were Hong, his other roommate George Chen, and their friend, Weihan "David" Wang.<br>• Police investigators assume he started with Wang and then moved to Hong and finally to Chen and that he killed them in separate events, making efforts to conceal their murders after each time.<br>• At 9:17 p.m., Rodger uploaded his final YouTube video, "Elliot Rodger's Retribution" (in which he described his plans and motivations) and then sent his manifesto a minute later to 34 people, including his parents and other family members, his therapist, former schoolteachers, and childhood friends.<br>• He then went to the Alpha Phi sorority house near the University of California, Santa Barbara, with the intention of massacring all of the occupants inside.<br>• When his knocking on the front door went unanswered, Rodger shot three Delta Delta Delta sorority sisters who were nearby, killing Katherine Cooper and Veronika Weiss and wounding Bianca de Kock.<br>• He then drove further into town and fired into the Isla Vista Deli Mart from inside his BMW, killing a student named Christopher Michaels-Martinez.<br>• After killing Michaels-Martinez, Rodger drove away from the Isla Vista Deli Mart. He was spotted leaving by four responding foot-patrol officers, but they did not suspect him to be the shooter at the time and allowed him to flee.<br>• Rodger continued his rampage, shooting at several pedestrians in drive-by shootings and striking others with his car.<br>• At some points, he drove on the wrong side of the street. He ultimately wounded 12 people in the phase of the rampage, 6 by gunshots and 6 with his vehicle. |

- On July 20, 2013, he attended a party and tried to interact with girls there but was reportedly ignored.
- He then tried to push girls off a 10-foot ledge but failed and was pushed off instead by other men there.
- He left but returned to attempt to retrieve his sunglasses. Instead, Rodger was beaten up by the same assailants.
- He told investigating officers about this, but they determined that he may have been the aggressor. According to him in his manifesto, this caused Rodger to begin planning his rampage.
- Starting in September, Rodger used pocket money from his parents and grandmothers that he had saved up to fund his rampage.
- He visited shooting ranges and bought three handguns from three different cities.
- He also began work on a manifesto, which he would title "My Twisted World: The Story of Elliot Rodger."
- On January 25, 2014, Rodger performed a citizen's arrest on his roommate Cheng Yuan "James" Hong and accused him of stealing a set of candles that belonged to him.
- After being arrested, Hong pleaded guilty to a petty theft charge, but the case was dismissed by police due to insufficient evidence.
- On April 30, Rodger's parents saw his YouTube videos and became alarmed by them, so they contacted police. However, when the officers interviewed Rodger at his apartment, he downplayed the situation.
- They decided "he did not meet the criteria for an involuntary [mental health] hold" nor was there any reason to legally search his residence, so they left.
- At the time, however, Rodger had been planning his killing spree and had two handguns in his possession already; he claimed in his manifesto that a search would have ruined his plans.

- At one point, Rodger got into a brief gunfight with a responding sheriff's deputy and escaped unharmed.
- Near the end of the rampage, Rodger got into another gunfight, this time with three sheriff's deputies near Little Acorn Park, and he suffered a gunshot wound to the left hip.
- He fled but was closely pursued by police. He crashed into a bicyclist named Keith Cheung, seriously wounding him, and then fatally shot himself in the head. He was 22 at the time of his death.
- Police investigated the crashed BMW and handcuffed both Rodger and Cheung, having initially believed Cheung to be a second gunman.
- They later determined him to be an injured victim and released him from police custody. The day after the killing spree, officers went to Rodger's apartment to investigate it and found the bodies of Hong, Chen, and Wang.
  o    https://criminalminds.fandom.com/wiki/Elliot_Rodger

(continued)

**School shooters/school related crimes** (continued)

| Name | Early Life | Crime |
|---|---|---|
| Chris Harper Mercer a.k.a "The Oregon Gunman" | • He was reportedly born in England on July 26, 1989, and arrived in the USA as a young boy.<br>• His parents, Ian Bernard Mercer and Laurel Margaret Harper, married on Valentine's Day 1989, which did not last long, divorce records show. They separated just 11 months later. According to public records, the couple filed for bankruptcy in 1992.<br>• Harper-Mercer's mother moved with the toddler to Harbor Gateway, where they lived in a one-bedroom apartment on 216th Street near Western Avenue on the Torrance border, near Toyota's national headquarters. They lived there for the next 19 years.<br>• Although he spent most of his young life in Harbor Gateway, Los Angeles Unified School District officials said he did not attend their schools. Instead, he attended a "nonpublic" school in Torrance under contract with the LAUSD.<br>Switzer Learning Center, a school for emotionally disturbed students in Torrance, is a nonpublic school that accepts children as young as third grade.<br>• Harper-Mercer lived a lonely life, according to neighbors who watched him grow from a quiet boy to a "mad" teenager who usually wore combat-like black boots and camouflage pants.<br>• As a child, however, he never went out to play downstairs, and, as a teen, he shuffled when he walked and kept his head down, said the Alvarados. He often seemed tense and mad, the Alvarados said.<br>• Their main interaction occurred when they called the property manager because of bad smells coming from their second-floor apartment. Their unit was messy and reeked of cigarettes, they said.<br>At Switzer Learning Center, a former teacher's aide who spoke on the condition of anonymity recalled him as "kind of sweet." She was stunned when she heard his name on the news and recognized his photograph as a former student.<br>• "He was a cute kid," she said. "He cracked me up. He made my days fun sometimes." | • He enrolled at Umpqua Community College in Roseburg, where his rampage erupted in an English class at 10:30 a.m. Thursday on October 1, 2015.<br>• The gunman who opened fire at Oregon's Umpqua Community College targeted Christians specifically, according to the father of a wounded student.<br>• Before going into spinal surgery, Anastasia Boylan told her father and brother the gunman entered her classroom firing. The professor in the classroom was shot point blank. Others were hit, she told her family.<br>• Everyone in the classroom dropped to the ground.<br>• The gunman, while reloading his handgun, ordered the students to stand up if they were Christians, Boylan told her family.<br>• "And they would stand up and he said, 'Good, because you're a Christian, you're going to see God in just about one second,'" Boylan's father, Stacy, told CNN, relaying her account.' And then he shot and killed them."<br>• The shooting appears to have started in one building before the gunman moved to the school's science building, a source with knowledge of the investigation told CNN. Those killed and wounded were found in at least two classrooms.<br>• The instructor and eight students killed in the massacre were Lawrence Levine, 67, of Glide; Quinn Glen Cooper, 18, of Roseburg; Rebecca Ann Carnes, 18, of Myrtle Creek; Lucas Eibel, 18, of Roseburg; Lucero Alcaraz, 19, of Roseburg; Treven Anspach, 20, of Sutherlin; Jason Dale Johnson, 33, of Winston; Sarena Dawn Moore, 44, of Myrtle Creek; and Kim Saltmarsh Dietz, 59, of Roseburg.<br>• Police officers finally shot him to death.<br>   ○ https://www.dailybreeze.com/2015/10/02/details-of-oregon-shooters-troubled-childhood-in-south-bay/<br>   ○ https://www.oregonlive.com/roseburg-oregon-school-shooting/2016/09/umpqua_community_college_shoot.html |

- "He wore glasses and had more than average acne and was a chunky guy," the aide recalled. "He wore mostly black and looked like your average punk rock kid."
- About that time, his father filed for divorce from his mother, citing irreconcilable differences. Although Harper-Mercer lived with his mother, the parents agreed to joint custody. The divorce became final in early 2006.
- Two years later, Harper-Mercer failed basic training following a one-month stint at the US Army Training Center at Fort Jackson, S.C.
- He was discharged for failing to meet the minimum administrative standards, which could have included fitness tests and tests involving math, science, and reading, an Army spokesman said.
- He moved on to classes at El Camino College from 2010 to 2012, a spokeswoman said. His course list was not available, but he passed a remedial English course and enrolled in Breckheimer's freshman composition class.
- About that same time, Harper-Mercer and his mother, a licensed vocational nurse, moved to an apartment on Arlington Avenue near 230th Street in Torrance.
- Neighbors told reporters they largely kept to themselves. His mother complained about loud noises and said a cockroach infestation kept her son awake.
- Neighbors said the pair sometimes carried cases that looked like they contained guns. They said they enjoyed target practice.
- Property and credit records show Harper-Mercer moved with his mother to Winchester, Oregon, in 2013.
- He established accounts on Internet dating sites, expressed anger toward religion, and, after a fired reporter killed two colleagues on live television in August in Virginia, said that the more people you kill, the more notoriety you get.

(continued)

**School shooters/school related crimes** (continued)

| Name | Early Life | Crime |
|---|---|---|
| Nikolas Cruz, a.k.a. "The Parkland School Shooter" | • He was born on September 24, 1998; in February of 2000, Nikolas's brother is born, Zachary.<br>• They were adopted very early in their lives by Lynda and Roger Cruz. Relatives say the boys shared a biological mother but have different fathers.<br>• On Jan. 23, 2002, Nikolas Cruz, at 3 years old, is diagnosed as developmentally delayed.<br>• Cruz's birth mother's life is found largely in the public record: her lengthy criminal history speaks of a devastating battle with addiction and a propensity for violence.<br>• At age 5, Nikolas witnesses his adopted father having a heart attack and die.<br>• On February 5, 2014, at age 15, Nikolas leaves Westglades Middle School in Parkland.<br>• He was diagnosed with a string of disorders and conditions: depression, attention-deficit hyperactivity disorder, emotional behavioral disability, and autism, records from the state Department of Children and Families show.<br>• On February 6, 2014, Nikolas starts at Cross Creek, a school in Pompano Beach, for students with emotional and behavioral disorders.<br>• On June 1, 2015, a school report says Nikolas is at times distracted by inappropriate conversations by classmates about guns, people being killed, or the armed forces.<br>• On August 24, 2015, Nikolas returns to Cross Creek but attends Marjory Stoneman Douglas High School two periods a day, Schools Superintendent Robert Runcie said.<br>• His mother called the police to say he got physical with his brother and with her. The agency responded to 23 calls over 10 years.<br>• On January 11, 2016, Nikolas, now 17, stops attending Cross Creek school. | • On February 14, 2018—the day of the shooting—Cruz told the Sneads he'd be skipping school.<br>• "It's Valentine's Day, and I don't go to school on Valentine's Day," the Sneads said he told them.<br>• At 2:06 p.m., he caught an Uber to Marjory Stoneman Douglas High, arriving when school was letting out.<br>• Security monitor Andrew Medina, an unarmed baseball coach, is riding in a golf cart and unlocking gates 20 minutes before dismissal. He sees Cruz walk through one of those unguarded gates with a rifle bag.<br>• He recognizes Cruz as "Crazy Boy," the former student that he and his colleagues had predicted most likely to shoot up the school. He radios another campus monitor/coach, but he does not pursue Cruz and does not call a code red to lock down the school.<br>• David Taylor, the campus monitor who was alerted by Medina, walks into the first-floor hallway toward Cruz, who goes into the stairwell. At that point, Cruz has yet to pull his gun from the carry bag.<br>• The second chance to lock down the school is missed when freshman Chris McKenna enters the first-floor stairwell and sees Cruz loading his gun.<br>• Cruz tells him, "You'd better get out of here. Things are gonna start getting messy."<br>• McKenna runs from the building and informs Aaron Feis, a football coach and campus monitor, that there is someone with a gun; still no code red is called<br>• At 2:21 p.m., Cruz fires his first shots, killing freshmen Martin Duque, Luke Hoyer, and Gina Montalto in the hallway of the first floor.<br>• Taylor, the campus monitor, hears gunshots and races up to the second floor. He ducks into a janitor's closet. Taylor has a radio but does not call a code red. |

- On January 13, 2016, he starts attending Stoneman Douglas High full time, Runcie said.
- On February 5, 2016, the Broward Sheriff's Office receives a report from a neighbor that Cruz posted on Instagram that he plans to shoot up the school. Police determined he has knives and a BB gun and passed the information along to the school resource officer, who is a sheriff's deputy on campus.
- On August 22, 2016, after the summer break, Nikolas returns to Stoneman Douglas High, and on September 20, 2016, he is suspended for fighting.
- On September 24, 2016, Nikolas turns 18.
- On September 28, 2016, Florida child welfare workers investigate after Nikolas cuts himself while on Snapchat.
- On November 12, 2016, child welfare investigation is closed.
- In November 2016, educational specialists recommend Nikolas transfer back to Cross Creek, but he doesn't want to. Now 18 and legally an adult, Nikolas also refuses to receive further mental health and other services.
- On January 12, 2017, Lynda Cruz, Nikolas' mother, sells the longtime family home at 6166 NW 80th Terrace in Parkland.
- On January 19, 2017, Nikolas receives an internal 1-day suspension for an assault. The school asks the district to conduct a threat assessment on him.
- On February 8, 2017, Nikolas is banished from Stoneman Douglas, according to a discipline file.
- On February 11, 2017, he buys the AR-15 rifle that he will use 1 year later in the Stoneman Douglas massacre.
- For the next calendar year, Nikolas bounces between various alternative schools for at-risk youth: The Off Campus Learning Centers, the Henry D. Perry Education Center, and the Dave Thomas Education Center. His attendance was poor.
- On November 1, 2017, Cruz's mother dies of pneumonia at age 68.

- Cruz stalks the first floor unchallenged. He enters no classrooms and shoots through the windows at people in his line of sight.
- Cruz kills six students in these classrooms—Alyssa Alhadeff, Nicholas Dworet, Alaina Petty, Helena Ramsay, Alex Schachter, and Carmen Schentrup.
- The repeated failures to call a code red become catastrophic when the shooting sets off a fire alarm.
- Instead of hiding in their classrooms, as they would during a code red, some students and teachers stream out of classrooms into hallways, as they would if facing a fire.
- Athletic director and campus monitor Chris Hixon is already at Building 12. He enters the double doors at the west end of the hall and runs toward Cruz.
- Cruz shoots Hixon, who crawls to take cover in a nearby doorway. Cruz finds him about 30 seconds later and shoots him again.
- Feis, the campus monitor and football coach, opens the door to the west stairwell and comes face-to-face with Cruz. Cruz shoots him.
- The carnage is astounding on the first floor, where Cruz kills 11 and wounds 13.
- Cruz heads up the west stairwell to the second floor but finds the hallway empty.
- Cruz fires into two of ten rooms, but no one is hurt.
- Students on the third floor are initially unaware there's a shooter in the building and are crowding the hallways because of the fire alarm. Now hearing the shots, they begin to run back toward classrooms.
- Social studies teacher Ernie Rospierski directs students back into classrooms, but his door locks behind him with his keys inside.
- Cruz goes up the stairwell to the third floor, where about 20 people remain stranded in the middle of the hallway.
- He fires multiple rounds into the crowd.
- Geography teacher Scott Beigel is holding open his classroom door. As he ushers students in, Cruz shoots and kills him.

(continued)

**School shooters/school related crimes** (continued)

| Name | Early Life | Crime |
| --- | --- | --- |
|  | • On November 30, 2017, the Broward Sheriff's Office receives a warning that Nikolas is collecting guns and knives and could be a "school shooter in the making." The caller notes that Nikolas has moved to Palm Beach County and the deputy refers the caller to the Palm Beach County Sheriff's Office. That agency said it has no record of any such incident or threat.<br>• He stays with neighbors but is kicked out after becoming violent/physical. He then goes to stay with family of a friend of his, the Sneads. | • Cruz's assault, which would span 5 minutes and 32 seconds from first shot to last, is half over when someone finally declares a code red.<br>• An earlier decision to lock restrooms because students were vaping in them now traps those who try to find refuge on the third floor. They have nowhere to hide from Cruz and his bullets.<br>• Cruz kills senior Meadow Pollack and freshman Cara Loughran outside a locked classroom; they die huddled together. Cruz shoots senior Joaquin Oliver outside a locked bathroom.<br>• Rospierski flees with ten students toward a stairwell as Cruz fires down the hall.<br>• Two of the students, Jaime Guttenberg and Peter Wang, are hit. Wang dies in the hallway and Guttenberg in the stairwell, but others get away as Rospierski holds the door closed from inside the stairwell to keep Cruz from advancing.<br>• By the time he is done, Cruz kills six and wounds four on the third floor. None of the dead are in classrooms.<br>• Unable to get into the stairwell, Cruz heads to a nearby teachers' lounge.<br>• Cruz shoots at the glass, targeting students and teachers as they flee across the campus below, but the glass won't break, and no one on the ground is hit<br>• The final shot Cruz fires, from inside the teachers' lounge, can be heard at 2:27:10 p.m.<br>• Cruz takes off his rifle vest, drops his AR-15 in a stairwell, heads down the stairs, darts out of the building, and runs across campus—all while police think he's still inside.<br>• The shooting has been over for 5 minutes before any police officers enter the building. |

| | | |
|---|---|---|
| | | • Four Coral Springs officers enter through the west doors, where they see Chris Hixon shot. Two officers pull Hixon out of the building and onto a golf cart. He will not survive.<br>  ○ https://www.sun-sentinel.com/local/broward/parkland/florida-school-shooting/fl-florida-school-shooting-bcps-timeline-20180227-story.html<br>  ○ https://www.washingtonpost.com/graphics/2018/national/timeline-parkland-shooter-nikolas-cruz/?utm_term=.abf0f497afe9<br>  ○ https://www.sun-sentinel.com/local/broward/parkland/florida-school-shooting/fl-florida-school-shooting-nikolas-cruz-life-20180220-story.html<br>  ○ http://projects.sun-sentinel.com/2018/sfl-parkland-school-shooting-critical-moments/ |
| Dimitrious Pagourtzis, a.k.a. "Santa Fe High School Shooter' | • He was born October 12th, 2000, to Greek immigrant parents.<br>• According to students, Dimitrios was an odd character who preferred to wear a trench coat almost every day, even in the heat.<br>• He was also described as a reserved character that kept to himself and didn't talk to many people.<br>• Pagourtzis had indicated in his journals that he was suicidal.<br>• According to at least one witness, Pagourtzis was the victim of bullying by multiple students and coaches. | • On May 18th, 2018, Pagourtzis walked into an art classroom at around 7:40 AM armed with a Remington 870 shotgun and a .38-caliber revolver, both of which were legally owned by his father.<br>• A student who had been injured in the shooting claimed Pagourtzis walked into the classroom, pointed at another student, and shouted "I'm going to kill you," before firing shots.<br>• A number of students had barricaded themselves into a storage closet, to which Pagourtzis tried to breach by firing shotgun rounds through the door.<br>• After Pagourtzis had exited the art room, the students hiding in the closet left to try and barricade that art room door, but before they could, Pagourtzis had kicked open the door, yelled "Surprise" and shot them square in the chest.<br>• The shooting had lasted a total of 25 minutes before police were able to subdue and arrest him.<br>  ○ http://real-life-villains.wikia.com/wiki/Dimitrios_Pagourtzis |

(continued)

**School shooters/school related crimes** (continued)

| Name | Early Life | Crime |
|---|---|---|
| Vladislav Roslyakov | • He was born on May 2, 2000, to parents Igor Roslyakov and Galina Roslyakova in Kerch, Russia. The couple would later divorce 10 years after the birth of their son.<br>• Igor sustained an acute cranial injury and began acting in an aggressive manner toward family members, including Vladislav and Galina.<br>• The unspecified head injury resulted in Igor becoming disabled.<br>• Little is known about Roslyakov's parents. A significant detail that has emerged since the attack is the fact that Galina was/is a member of the Jehovah's Witnesses, a cult that had already been banned in Russia.<br>• Galina enforced restrictive behaviors (possibly picked up from the group) upon her son. As a result, Vladislav was barred from partaking in certain activities such as visiting the cinema and participating in lighthearted school events.<br>• Galina would also frequently search her son's pockets and limit his social interactions (which could very well have contributed to Roslyakov's lack of many friends).<br>• Vladislav was not granted permission to use the computer until he turned 16.<br>• In contrast to his mother's strict religious views, Vladislav Roslyakov developed his own atheistic views as he emerged into adulthood.<br>• On October 16, 2017, only a day before the massacre, Vladislav confided to a friend that he did not believe in an afterlife.<br>• Prior to his enrollment at Kerch Polytechnic Institute, Vladislav attended a local school.<br>• During this time, he expressed no interest in his studies and consequently received poor grades.<br>• It is implied that Roslyakov had a fascination with weapons from a young age and had few friends.<br>• As far as we know, this element of independence was something that would remain consistent throughout his life. | • During the afternoon hours of October 17, 2018, 18-year-old Kerch Polytechnic Institute senior Vladislav Roslyakov entered school grounds, armed with more than 10 homemade explosive, 150 bullets, and a Hatsan Escort Aimguard 12-gauge pump-action shotgun that Roslyakov paid approximately 30,000–40,000 rupies for (or $450–600 USD).<br>• The gun was legally purchased by the perpetrator, as he had obtained a gun/weapon permit earlier that year.<br>• The currency used to acquire the shotgun was allegedly stolen from his grandmother. Roslyakov was donned in black jeans, a black hoodie (which was likely discarded before the events of the massacre), and a white short-sleeved shirt with black text across it, displaying the word "ненависть," when translated to English, means "hatred."<br>• The suspect had also equipped himself with two bags, a gray one and black one.<br>• One of these bags, according to investigators, contained ten homemade bombs.<br>• Although contradictory statements have arisen since the publication of the attack, witnesses claim that Roslyakov began his attack in the canteen before running from room to room, firing his weapon at anyone he spotted.<br>• The suspect also planted two bombs, one in the canteen and another in the institute's dining area.<br>• No deaths, however, have directly resulted from the detonations of these explosives.<br>• Officials claimed that one of the explosives contained unspecified metal objects.<br>• He killed 17 students and left more than 40 people wounded before killing himself. |

| | |
|---|---|
| • In 2015, Vladislav Roslyakov began attending Kerch Polytechnic Institute, with probable hopes of becoming an electrician (evident in both his school records and his liking to video games).<br>• It was around this time that Vladislav began to engage in suspicious behaviors, including carrying a knife bayonet to class and pursuing an interest in weapons and explosives.<br>• If Roslyakov had taken an interest in weapons in his younger years, those interests had almost certainly intensified.<br>• Luckily, there are no reports of the knife having ever been utilized.<br>• Despite this, Vladislav Roslyakov was involved in an incident where he [Roslyakov] ejected the contents from a can of pepper spray into one of his classrooms for unexplained reasons.<br>• A girl claiming to be the perpetrator's ex-girlfriend discloses that Vladislav would confide in her his struggles of bullying he reportedly faced from others, despite contradictory statements from others who knew Roslyakov.<br>• Roslyakov stated that he wanted to exact revenge on "evil professors."<br>• Despite this, the perpetrator reportedly never displayed any sort of aggression toward his peers.<br>• During his freshman year at Kerch Polytechnic Institute, Roslyakov apparently equipped himself with a knife, although there have been no reported incidents regarding any use of the weapon.<br>• Roslyakov and his mother lived in poverty, and the perpetrator claimed to have been bullied for dressing in "poor clothes."<br>• Roslyakov also maintained an unhealthy obsession with murderers and dreamed of recreating the 1999 massacre at Columbine High School in Littleton, Colorado, USA. | • Roslyakov's body was discovered in the library on the second floor of the institute.<br>• Upon further examination, it is extremely likely that Roslyakov died of a self-inflicted gunshot wound.<br>  ◦ https://real-life-villains.fandom.com/wiki/Vladislav_Roslyakov<br>  ◦ https://abc7chicago.com/crimea-school-shooting-gunman-kills-at-least-17-at-kerch-college/4502853/ |

(continued)

**School shooters/school related crimes** (continued)

| Name | Early Life | Crime |
|---|---|---|
| | • Despite his hatred for the Institute, Vladislav Roslyakov received satisfactory grades and was frequently praised by professors as being a model student.<br>• Roslyakov also left behind a social media trail, belonging to multiple online groups centered on the discussion of murderers (specifically serial killers).<br>• Unsurprisingly (as evident from his clothing on the day of the massacre and the attack itself), the perpetrator was enraptured by the Columbine massacre that was carried out 19 years prior by students Eric Harris and Dylan Klebold.<br>• Vladislav was a member of a group dedicated to the teen killers and expressed to friends that "it would be good to have a massacre" [most likely referring to Kerch Polytechnic Institute] | |

**Sexual assault and murder**

| Name | Early life | Crime |
| --- | --- | --- |
| Harvey Louis Carignan | • He was born May 18, 1927. His mother was around age 20 and single.<br>• At age 3–4, his mother remarried and had a second son. Claims he was sexually abused by a babysitter.<br>• At age 6, he was described as having behavior problems, was still undersized, and has a twitch in his face. Carignan was described as a chronic bed-wetter and as having an imaginary friend, Paul.<br>• At age 8, he is sent to live with his aunt and uncle in Cavalier, ND. He is soon sent back home.<br>• At age 10, he is sent to live with his grandmother in Williams, ND. He was then sent to live with another aunt before running home to his mother. He suffers from enuresis and begins stealing.<br>• At age 11, his mother attempted to place him in an orphanage but instead sent to reform school in Mandan, ND, for the next 7 years. He was diagnosed with childhood chorea. From age 12 to 18, Carignan claims female employees sexually abused him.<br>• At age 18, Carignan left the reform school and enlisted in the US Army.<br>• At age 21, he was stationed at Fort Richardson in Anchorage, Alaska.<br>• In 1968, Carignan is paroled from his earlier arrest in 1964.<br>• In 1969, he married Sheila Moran and moved in with her and her daughter.<br>• In 1969, Carignan was arrested for parole violation and suspicion of robbery. He severed 1 year in jail.<br>• In 1970, Sheila divorced him due to physical abuse.<br>• In 1972, Carignan married Alice Johnson and moved in with her and her two children, Billy (11) and Georgia (14).<br>• In 1972, Billy moves out to live with his biological father due to the beatings he received from Carignan.<br>• He was arrested for the assault of his wife Alice. Alice decides to leave Carignan.<br>• He gives up on Alice and begins dating and living with Eileen Hunley, who he picks up hitchhiking, after moving to Minnesota.<br>• Eileen breaks off their relationship.v | • On July 31, 1949, Harvey Carignan raped and killed 57-year-old Laura Showalter. Cause of death was due to several blows to the head.<br>• On September 16, 1949, Dorcas Callen was attacked by Harvey but was able to escape the attempted rape.<br>• She told police she was approached by an intoxicated soldier at around 7:00 a.m. Callen and another eyewitness, John Keith, identified Carignan in a lineup.<br>• In 1950, Carignan was charged and convicted of first-degree murder. He was sentenced to death by hanging. Carignan's lawyers, however, filed an appeal with the Supreme Court.<br>• The Supreme Court ruled that Carignan's confession was unlawfully elicited by an overzealous police officer who assured Carignan that he would not be executed if he confessed.<br>• In 1951, the Supreme Court overruled Carignan's death sentence due the officers' violations of the McNabb rule.<br>• In 1952, Carignan was transferred to Alcatraz.<br>• in 1960, Carignan served 8 more years and was paroled on April 2.<br>• On August 5, 1960, he was arrested in Minnesota for burglary, assault, and attempted rape. He was convicted and sentenced to 2.5 years in a Minnesota State prison and another 2086 days in federal prison in Leavenworth, Kansas.<br>• On March 2, 1964, Carignan is released on parole and moves to Seattle.<br>• On November 22, 1964, he is arrested for second-degree burglary and sentenced to 15 years in the Washington State prison. During his stay, he obtained his high school diploma (GED) and took some college courses.<br>• Mary Townsend was attacked by Carignan waiting at a bus stop. He attacked her from behind knocking her unconscious. She awoke in his vehicle. He began to command sexual favors when she managed to leap from the vehicle and escape.<br>• He then picks up a hitchhiker, Jerri Billings, age 13. He forced her to perform sexual acts on him while he assaulted her with a hammer. After the event, Carignan released her. She did not mention the event until several months later. |

(continued)

**Sexual assault and murder** (continued)

| Name | Early life | Crime |
| --- | --- | --- |
| | | • Eileen Hunley disappeared. Her body was found five weeks later in Shelburne County, her skull imploded by blows to the head. It was determined that she had been raped with a tree branch. |
| | | • June Lynch, 17, and Lisa King, 16, were picked up by Carignan while they were hitching rides in Minneapolis. Carignan offered him money if that would help him fetch another car that had been stranded in a rural area. |
| | | • Once they reach the outskirts of town, Carignan stopped the car and beat June in the head and face with a hammer. Lisa was able to escape. While she was running for help, Carignan sped off leaving June on the roadside to die. |
| | | • Carignan picked up Gwen Burton from a Sears parking lot. He ripped her clothing, choked her into semiconsciousness, and sexually assaulted her with a hammer. Carignan dumped her body in a nearby field. Fortunately, she survived the attack and was able to craw to the roadside for help. |
| | | • Sally Versoi and Diane Flynn were picked up by Carignan. He forced them to perform oral sex and would beat them if they didn't follow a command. The two girls were able to escape when Carignan stopped for fuel. |
| | | • Kathy Shultz did not make it to her classes. Her body was found the next day by hunters in a cornfield 40 miles from Minneapolis. Her skull was imploded. |
| | | • He was pulled over and arrested due to survivor's description of his car. As police search, they found a map of the USA with 181 circles. |
| | | • Some of these circle identified places where he had applied for jobs and purchased cars, but others identify where several bodies were found. |
| | | • They were also associated with areas in which other unsolved crimes against women had taken place. |
| | | • Carignan was arrested for attempted murder of Gwen Burton who identified him in a lineup. |
| | | ◦ http://maamodt.asp.radford.edu/Carignan,%20Harvey.htm |

| Name | Early life | Crime |
|---|---|---|
| Donald Henry Gaskins | • On March 13, 1933, Donald Gaskins was born in Florence County, South Carolina.<br>• At a young age, Gaskins was teased and given the nickname "Pee Wee" as a result of his small body frame.<br>• Violence and ridicule followed him from his home where his stepfather beat him to his school where he fought with the other kids daily.<br>• At age 11, Gaskins quit school and began working on cars at a local garage. While working there, he met two boys, Danny and Marsh.<br>• They were all around the same age and out of school, so they teamed up and called themselves "The Trouble Trio."<br>• The trio burglarized homes, picked up prostitutes, and even sometimes raped little boys.<br>• They would threaten the little boys so they wouldn't go to the police.<br>• Eventually the trio broke up after they were caught for gang-raping Marsh's little sister.<br>• For punishment, the parents beat the boys until they bled. Danny and Marsh left the area shortly after that.<br>• Gaskins continued to burglarize homes alone. In 1946, a girl who knew Gaskins interrupted him while he was burglarizing her home.<br>• She struck him with an ax. He managed to get it away from her, struck her in the head and arm until it before fleeing the scene.<br>• Luckily, the girl survived the attack. Gaskins was arrested and convicted for assault with a deadly weapon and intent to kill.<br>• During the court proceedings, it was the first time he had heard his real name spoken in his whole life.<br>• He was sent to the South Carolina Industrial School for Boys until he turned 18.<br>• At the reform school, Gaskins was almost immediately attacked and raped due to his small stature. | • Crimes committed between 1953 and 1982.<br>• While in prison, Gaskins committed his first murder in an attempt to become a "Power Man."<br>• Power men are the most brutal and feared inmates. Gaskins decided killing a fellow inmate would be enough to keep the other inmates from bothering him.<br>• He was found guilty of manslaughter and sentenced to 6 months of solitary confinement, but he accomplished his goal of becoming a "Power Man."<br>• The newly found status made his life in prison more enjoyable.<br>• In 1955, his wife filed for divorce. Gaskins flipped and escaped from prison. Shortly thereafter, he remarried, but the second marriage only lasted 2 weeks.<br>• Then he became involved with Betty Gates. The two went to Tennessee to bail out Gates' brother, but when Gaskins arrived back at the hotel, he was in for a surprise.<br>• He found out Gates' brother was actually her husband, and he had recently escaped. The police arrived at the hotel, and it didn't take them long to realize that he was an escaped convict.<br>• He was sent back to prison with an extra 9 months for aiding the escape of a prisoner.<br>• Gaskins picked up a female hitchhiker in North Carolina and became angry when she laughed at his sexual propositions. He beat her until she was unconscious. Gaskins raped, sodomized, and tortured her. Then he went to a swamp to sink her weighted body so she would drown.<br>• His "process" of rape, torture, and murder was described by Gaskins as a "vision" into the "bothersome feelings" he experienced throughout his life.<br>• Satisfying these feelings became his driving force in life. He mastered the skill of torture, often keeping his injured victims alive for days.<br>• Sometimes, he would cannibalize their severed body parts and either make them watch him eat them in horror or join in the eating.<br>• Gaskins preferred female victims, but that didn't stop him from doing the same to the males he happened upon. |

(continued)

**Sexual assault and murder** (continued)

| Name | Early life | Crime |
| --- | --- | --- |
| | • He spent his time either accepting protection from the "Boss-Boy" in exchange for sex or attempting to escape.<br>• Eventually, he escaped from the reform school and got on with a traveling carnival.<br>• He married a 13-year-old girl while there but decided to return to the reform school to finish out his sentence.<br>• After he was released from reform school, he began working on a tobacco farm.<br>• There, he got involved in insurance fraud; he worked with a partner by collaborating with local tobacco farmers to burn their barns for a fee.<br>• Around the area, people began to wonder about Gaskins' involvement with the barn fires.<br>• When his employer's daughter questioned him about the barn fires, he panicked and split the girl's skull with the hammer in hand.<br>• He received a 5-year sentence in prison for assault with a deadly weapon and attempted murder.<br>• Throughout Gaskins' life, he described feelings that forced him into criminal activity which he referred to as "aggravated and bothersome feelings." | • By 1975, he had found 80 boys and girls along the highways in North Carolina and killed them. He considered these highway murders as "weekend recreation" and thought killing his personal acquaintances were "serious murders."<br>• Some of the serious murders included his 15-year-old niece and her friend. He lured the two girls off to an abandoned house where he beat, raped, and drowned them.<br>• One of the people who considered Gaskins to be a friend was Doreen Dempsey, a mother of a 2-year-old baby girl and was pregnant with her second child at the time of her death.<br>• She was leaving town and decided to get a ride to the bus station from her old friend. Gaskins took her to a wooded area where he raped and killed her and then raped, sodomized, and killed her baby. He buried the two together.<br>• Gaskins was 42 years old in 1975 and had been killing steadily for the past 6 years. Up until then, he had worked alone and that had helped him avoid being caught.<br>• However, after he murdered three people when their van broke down on the highway, he needed some help. He called up an ex-con, Walter Neely, to drive the victims' van to his garage so he could repaint it and sell it.<br>• Gaskins was also a hired hit man. That same year, Suzanne Kipper paid him $1500 to kill her ex-boyfriend, Silas Yates. On February 12, 1975, Diane Neely lured him out of the house by claiming to have car trouble. Gaskins then kidnapped and murdered Yates.<br>• Diane Neely and her boyfriend decided to blackmail Gaskins. They asked for $5000 in hush money; Gaskins quickly got rid of them after he arranged a meeting for the payoff. Around the same time, Gaskins had tortured and killed other people he knew, such as Kim Ghelkins, a 13-year-old who rejected him. |

- Two locals robbed Gaskins' repair shop without knowing about his bad side. He eventually killed and buried these two with the other locals in his private cemetery.
- Once again, he called on Walter Neely to help him bury the two bodies. While there, Gaskins even showed Neely where he had buried other locals.
- After the disappearance of Kim Ghelkins, the authorities began to become suspicious of Gaskins. After searching his apartment, they found clothing that had been worn by Ghelkins. Gaskins was indicted for "contributing to the delinquency of a minor."
- Neely cracked under pressure while waiting for the trial and showed the police Gaskins' private cemetery.
- In the cemetery, they found the bodies of the following: Sellars, Judy, Howard, Diane Neely, Johnny Knight, Dennis Bellamy, and Doreen Dempsey and her child. On April 27, 1976, Gaskins and Walter Neely were charged with eight counts of murder.
- On May 24, 1976, a jury convicted Gaskins of the murder of Dennis Bellamy, and he was sentenced to death. In an attempt to avoid additional death sentences, he later confessed to seven more murders.
- In November 1976, the Supreme Court ruled that the death penalty was unconstitutional, so his death sentence was converted to life with seven consecutive life sentences.
- In 1978, the death penalty was restored. This didn't mean anything to Gaskins until he was caught and found guilty for being paid to murder fellow prisoner, Rudolph Tyner. This conviction caused him to receive a death sentence.
- Gaskins was placed in the electric chair, with stitched arms, and pronounced dead by electrocution on September 6, 1991.
  ○ https://www.crimemuseum.org/crime-library/serial-killers/donald-pee-wee-gaskins/

(continued)

**Sexual assault and murder**  (continued)

| Name | Early life | Crime |
|---|---|---|
| Gary Leon Ridgway | • Gary Leon Ridgway was born on February 18, 1949, in Salt Lake City, Utah.<br>• His father, Thomas Newton Ridgway, worked as a bus driver who often complained about the prostitutes who frequented the streets on his route.<br>• His mother, Mary Rita Ridgway (née Steinman), ruled the household and was physically and mentally abusive toward Gary and also to his two brothers, Gregory and Thomas Jr., and even her husband.<br>• He was raised near Seattle's Pacific Highway, a deprived neighborhood near SeaTac airport.<br>• Ridgway was a frequent bed-wetter and also tortured animals, locking a cat into a refrigerator until it died on one occasion.<br>• He would also shoot birds with a BB gun with his brothers.<br>• When he was 11, the family moved from Utah to Washington State.<br>• Ridgway was a poor student, with a below average IQ of 82 and dyslexia.<br>• Most of his teenage years were unremarkable.<br>• After graduating from high school in 1969—at the age of 20—he served a 2-year stint in the US Navy. He was sent to Vietnam.<br>• He married his first steady girlfriend, Claudia Barrows, before going to Vietnam.<br>• Ridgway had an insatiable sex drive and spent a lot of time with prostitutes during his military service.<br>• He contracted gonorrhea, and, although it angered him, he didn't stop having unprotected sex with prostitutes.<br>• Claudia began dating while Ridgway was in Vietnam and in less than a year the marriage ended.<br>• In 1973, Marcia Winslow and Ridgway married and had a son. During the marriage, Ridgway became a religious fanatic, proselytizing door-to-door, reading the Bible aloud at work and home, and insisting that Marcia follow the church pastor's strict preaching. | • In 1963, aged 14, Ridgway attempted to kill a 6-year-old boy by stabbing him but was unsuccessful and was never caught for the act.<br>• He claimed to have committed his first murder when he was a teenager, drowning a young boy by wrapping his legs around him while swimming and holding him underwater until he drowned.<br>• In 1980, Ridgway was arrested for allegedly choking a prostitute, but no charges were filed after he claimed that the woman had bit him. Two years later, he was arrested for solicitation.<br>• Ridgway's slayings began in 1982, when young runaways and prostitutes began disappearing from state Route 99 in South King County, Washington.<br>• His first victim was thought to have been a 16-year-old girl who went missing after leaving her foster home in July 1982. Her body was found a week later, in the Green River.<br>• He was brought in for questioning as a person of interest when the first bodies were found and took a polygraph test twice, once in 1982 and once in 1986, passing both times; he was a suspect during the entire investigation.<br>• He came close to being arrested a few times; in 1985, a woman accused him of grabbing her in a choke hold in 1982, and in 1983, a witness saw victim Marie M. Malvar get into his car.<br>• Over the next 2 years, Ridgway raped and killed more than 40 women, many of whom were prostitutes or runaways.<br>• He brought many of them to his home and strangled them and then left them in woodsy, remote sites. The first few bodies turned up along the now-notorious Green River.<br>• The police learned from several prostitutes in the Green River Killer's usual area that they had seen him driving on that strip, which was the route he took to get to work. It was also noted that he had been reported as absent from work on every single occasion that a victim had disappeared.<br>• Dubbed the Green River Killer, Ridgway eluded the law until 2001, when King County sheriff Dave Reichert, the first officer assigned to the case in 1982, called a meeting to re-examine evidence using newly developed DNA testing technology. |

- Ridgway also insisted that Marcia have sex outdoors and in inappropriate places and demanded sex several times a day.
- He continued to hire prostitutes throughout their marriage.
- Marcia, who had a serious weight problem most of her life, decided to have gastric bypass surgery in the late 1970s. She quickly lost weight, and for the first time in her life, men found her attractive, making Ridgway jealous and insecure. The couple began fighting.
- Marcia struggled to accept Ridgway's relationship with his mother, who controlled their spending and made decisions on their purchases, including buying Ridgway's clothing.
- She also accused Marcia of not properly taking care of their son, which Marcia resented. Since Ridgway wouldn't defend her, Marcia was left on her own to compete with her mother-in-law.
- Seven years into the marriage, the couple divorced. Later, Marcia claimed that Ridgway placed her in a choke hold during one of their fights.
- Later, he settled in the Seattle area, where he worked as a truck painter. Over the next 30 years, he married three times and had a son.

- The analysis produced a match between evidence from the victims and Ridgway, and he was charged with four counts of aggravated murder in December 2001. Ridgway eventually pleaded guilty to 48 counts of aggravated first-degree murder.
  - https://www.biography.com/people/gary-ridgway-10073409
  - https://www.britannica.com/biography/Gary-Ridgway
  - https://www.thoughtco.com/green-river-killer-gary-ridgway-973098
  - https://criminalminds.fandom.com/wiki/Gary_Ridgway

(continued)

**Sexual assault and murder** (continued)

| Name | Early life | Crime |
|---|---|---|
| James Edward Wood | • He was born on December 9, 1947, in Louisiana. The only child of his mother (Hazel Godwin).<br>• His father was incarcerated at a federal prison when James was 2 years old; at this time, James and his mother moved to Pocatello, ID. The parent divorced, and his mother remarried. He had another older stepbrother (Earnest Arnold).<br>• His mother died in a fire while working in a potato factory when James was 8 years old.<br>• Wood was in school right across the street and watched the fire.<br>• He was raised by Uncle Gene and Aunt Mildred Wood after mother's death in 1955; due to James' problems, the Wood relatives relinquished their custody, and James became a ward of the state.<br>• James claimed he was physically, psychologically, and sexually abused by his stepfather.<br>• His first sexual experience when he was 9 years old had violent sexual fantasies.<br>• James received counseling at St. Anthony's Youth Correction Center in Idaho (one of three stays).<br>• At 14, he stole a car and set fire to dumpsters.<br>• During most of his teenage years, he was in a youth correction center and attended a reform school in Idaho until 17.<br>• At 17, James was released from reform school under the condition that he leaves the state and lives with his natural father in Louisiana where he began to work in his father's business of selling and installing, chain fences.<br>• At 17, he escaped from prison by threatening a guard's life with a knife; his only successful escape out of seven attempts).<br>• At 19, he killed a colt that was tied to a tree as a Christmas gift.<br>• At 20, he married his first wife, Angie Bell, and had a child. Angie filed for divorce a few months later after learning about James' sentence to prison.<br>• At 22, Wood commits his first rape.<br>• At 27, he remarried Angie and had another child, but a few months later, Angie filed for a final divorce. | • At age 45, he abducted and raped 15-year-old Beth Edwards from a Pizza Hut parking lot.<br>• He robbed a Subway sandwich shop.<br>• Wood raped a 14-year-old, daughter of his girlfriend.<br>• He robbed Sizzler Steak house in Salt Lake City; he then raped a woman after picking her up off the street in Salt Lake City (the same day as the Sizzler Steak house robbery).<br>• For his crimes of armed robbery and rape, he was incarcerated three times before murder conviction; he served 4.5 years in Angola State Penitentiary (1967–1971). He served a second sentence of 6 years out of 10 for robbery and rape. He was released for good behavior.<br>• Jeralee Underwood (Jeralee) resided in Pocatello, Idaho, with her family. On June 29, 1993, James Wood was visiting the home of a customer on Jeralee's paper route when she came by to make a collection. Wood followed her when she left, detained her with a false story, and forced her into his automobile. Wood held Jeralee captive for over a day, during which time he sexually molested her and then shot her in the head with a .22-caliber pistol and hid her body by covering it with brush.<br>• According to the findings of the district court, later, Wood returned to the site of the murder, undressed the corpse, and mutilated the body by removing the sex organs and severing the arms, head, and legs. He threw the clothing and body parts into the Snake River.<br>   ○ http://maamodt.asp.radford.edu/Psyc%20405/serial%20killers/Wood,%20Jame%20 Edward%20_spring%202007_.pdf<br>   ○ http://murderpedia.org/male.W/w/wood-james-edward.htm |

| John Wayne Gacy | <ul><li>He was born March 17, 1942, in Chicago, Illinois.</li><li>The son of Danish and Polish parents, Gacy and his siblings grew up with a drunken father who would beat the children with a razor strap if they were perceived to have misbehaved. His father physically assaulted Gacy's mother as well.</li><li>Gacy's sister, Karen, would later say that the siblings learned to toughen up against the beatings and that Gacy would not cry.</li><li>Gacy suffered further alienation at school, unable to play with other children due to a congenital heart condition that was looked upon by his father as another failing.</li><li>When Gacy was 11, he was playing on a swing set and was hit in the head with one of the swings. The accident caused a blood clot in his brain that was not discovered until he was 16.</li><li>Between the time of the accident and the diagnosis, Gacy suffered from blackouts that were caused by the clot. They were finally treated with medication.</li><li>At 17, he was also diagnosed with a heart ailment that he was hospitalized for several times during his life.</li><li>He complained frequently about it over the years, but no one could ever find a cause for the pain that he claimed to be suffering.</li><li>His family problems extended out into his schoolwork, and after attending four high schools during his senior year and never graduating, Gacy dropped out and left home for Las Vegas.</li><li>He worked part-time as a janitor in a funeral home and saved his money to buy a ticket back to Chicago. Lonely and depressed, he spent 3 months trying to get the money together. His mother and sisters were thrilled to see him when he returned.</li><li>After his return, Gacy enrolled in business college and eventually graduated. While in school, he gained a real talent for salesmanship, and he put these talents to work in a job with the Nunn-Bush Shoe Company.</li></ul> | <ul><li>Rumors were starting to spread around town, and among Jaycees members, about Gacy's sexual preferences. No one could help but notice that young boys always seemed to be in his presence.</li><li>Stories spread that he had made passes at some of the young men who worked in the restaurants, but those close to him refused to believe it, until the rumors were confirmed.</li><li>In May 1968, a grand jury in Black Hawk County indicted Gacy for committing an act of sodomy with a teenage boy named Mark Miller.</li><li>The boy told the courts that Gacy had tricked him into being tied up while visiting Gacy's home, and he had violently raped him. Gacy denied the charges but did say that Miller willingly had sex with him in order to earn extra money.</li><li>Four months later, more charges were filed against Gacy. This time, he was charged with hiring an 18-year-old boy named Dwight Andersson to beat up Mark Miller. Andersson informed the officers who arrested him for the assault that Gacy had hired him to attack the other boy.</li><li>A judge ordered Gacy to undergo a psychiatric evaluation to see if he was mentally competent to stand trial. He was found to be competent, but psychiatrists stated that he was an antisocial personality who would likely not benefit from any known medical treatment.</li><li>Soon after the report was submitted, Gacy entered a guilty plea to the sodomy charge. He received 10 years at the Iowa State Reformatory, the maximum time for the offence, and entered prison for the first time at the age of 26.</li><li>He was released on parole in the summer of 1970 but was arrested again the following year after another teen accused Gacy of sexual assault. The charges were dropped when the boy didn't appear during the trial.</li><li>By the middle of the decade, two more young males accused Gacy of rape, and he would be questioned by police about the disappearances of others.</li><li>In 1976, Gacy divorced for a second time, and it seemed to give him a feeling of personal freedom.</li></ul> |

(continued)

**Sexual assault and murder** (continued)

| Name | Early life | Crime |
|---|---|---|
| | • He excelled as a management trainee, and he was soon transferred to a men's clothing outlet in Springfield, Illinois.<br>• Soon after his move, Gacy's health took a turn for the worse. He gained a great deal of weight and began to suffer more from his mysterious heart ailment. He was hospitalized and, soon after getting out, was back in the hospital again, this time with back problems.<br>• He later realized he was attracted to men and experienced great turmoil over his sexuality.<br>• Gacy worked as a fast-food chain manager during the 1960s and became a self-made building contractor and Democratic precinct captain in the Chicago suburbs in the 1970s.<br>• Well liked in his community, Gacy organized cultural gatherings and worked as a clown at children's parties.<br>• He was married and divorced twice and had biological children and stepchildren.<br>• He was a friendly man who loved to entertain young children. He frequently dressed up as his alter ego, Pogo the Clown, at parties that he hosted for his entire neighborhood. | • Unknown to anyone else at the time, Gacy began to rape and kill young men. Over a period of just a few years, he murdered 33 people, 29 of whom were found underneath Gacy's house—26 in the crawlspace and 3 other bodies in other areas beneath his home.<br>• A young man went to the Chicago police for help in 1977, claiming that he had been kidnapped and molested by John Wayne Gacy. A report was made, but officers failed to follow up on it.<br>• The following year, Gacy murdered a 15-year-old boy who had gone to Gacy's home to ask about a job with his construction company. This time, the Des Plaines police got involved and searched Gacy's home. They found a class ring, clothing for much smaller individuals, and other suspicious items. Upon further investigation, officers discovered that the ring belonged to a teenage boy who was missing, and they found a witness who claimed Gacy had admitted to killing up to 30 people. Gacy was arrested and used an insanity plea in the hopes of a not guilty verdict. The ruse did not work, and he was found guilty. On May 10, 1994, John Wayne Gacy was executed by lethal injection.<br><br> ○ https://www.biography.com/people/john-wayne-gacy-10367544<br> ○ https://www.crimemuseum.org/crime-library/serial-killers/john-wayne-gacy/<br> ○ https://www.prairieghosts.com/gacy.html |

| William Bonin | <ul><li>Bonin was born in Willimantic, Connecticut, on January 8, 1947, as the second of three sons raised by alcoholic parents. They were often neglected by their parents and fed by neighbors.</li><li>Due to their parents' constant absences, Bonin and his brothers were frequently left with his grandfather, a convicted child molester.</li><li>When he was 6 years old, Bonin was sent to live in an orphanage and stayed there until he was 9.</li><li>A year later, he was arrested for stealing license plates and other crimes and sent to a juvenile detention center.</li><li>As a teenager, Bonin began to molest children.</li><li>After graduating from high school in 1965, he became engaged and also joined the US Air Force. He served in the Vietnam War as an aerial gunner, earning a Good Conduct Medal in the process.</li><li>During his service, Bonin risked his life to save another airman but also raped two soldiers at gunpoint, though this crime was apparently never reported.</li><li>He was honorably discharged from the US Air Force in October 1968.</li><li>Afterward, Bonin returned to Connecticut to live with his mother but eventually moved to California.</li><li>A month later, Bonin began abducting and sexually assaulting youths, claiming five victims.</li><li>He was arrested a year later, convicted of kidnapping and sexual assault, and sent to the Atascadero State Hospital to be medically treated.</li><li>He was later moved to a proper prison after it was ruled that he couldn't be treated. However, Bonin was released in May 1974 after doctors concluded he was no longer a danger to others.</li><li>Sixteen months later, he was arrested again and charged with the rape of 14-year-old hitchhiker David McVicker at gunpoint and the attempted abduction of another teenager. He was sentenced to between 1 and 15 years at California Men's Facility.</li></ul> | <ul><li>Bonin's first murder victim was 13-year-old hitchhiker Thomas Glen Lundgren, who was last seen leaving his house before being abducted by both Bonin and Vernon Butts.</li><li>Later, Bonin was arrested again for raping a 17-year-old boy but was released due to an administrative error. After his release, he was driven home by Everett Fraser, to whom he constantly said that no one was going to testify against him again.</li><li>Two months later, Bonin and Butts abducted 17-year-old Mark Shelton; he was raped and entered in a fatal state of shock, which resulted in his death.</li><li>His body was then dumped in San Bernardino County. A day later, they killed 17-year-old hitchhiker Markus Crabs at his home and then dumped his body alongside a Malibu freeway.</li><li>Several days later, they abducted and killed 15-year-old Donald Ray Hyden, and his body was found in a dumpster near the Ventura Freeway.</li><li>Two weeks later, Bonin and Butts abducted 17-year-old David Murillo while he was cycling to a movie theater. He was lured to their van, and there, he was raped, bludgeoned, and strangled to death.</li><li>Eight days later, they abducted and killed 18-year-old Robert Wirostek while he was cycling to work.</li><li>On November 29, Bonin and Butts abducted an unidentified boy, who was beaten and strangled to death before being dumped in Kern County.</li><li>A day later, Bonin abducted, raped, and strangled 17-year-old Frank Dennis Fox, whose nude body was found 2 days later alongside a highway 5 miles east of San Diego.</li><li>Ten days later, 15-year-old John Kilpatrick was abducted and killed, and his body was dumped in Rialto.</li><li>On January 1, 1980, Bonin mutilated and strangled 16-year-old Michael Francis McDonald. Though his body was found soon after, it was not identified until March 24.</li><li>On February 3, with the help of Gregory Miley, Bonin stole the wallet of 15-year-old hitchhiker Charles Miranda before raping and strangling the boy to death with a tire iron.</li></ul> |

(continued)

**Sexual assault and murder** (continued)

| Name | Early life | Crime |
|------|-----------|-------|
| | • He was released on October 11, 1978, and moved to Downey, where he lived in an apartment complex. Bonin eventually found work as a truck driver and began to date a girl.<br>• In Downey, he became acquainted with his neighbor, Everett Fraser, and became an attendee at the parties Fraser held at his apartment.<br>• During one of these parties, he met and became acquainted with a factory worker and part-time magician named Vernon Butts and a Texas native named Gregory Matthews Miley. | • Hours later, they abducted 12-year-old James Macabe while he waited for his bus to show up and take him to Disneyland. The boy was raped, beaten, and strangled to death with his own T-shirt; his body was found days later alongside a dumpster.<br>• On March 14, Bonin abducted 18-year-old Ronald Gatlin. He was beaten and sodomized with an ice pick before being strangled to death, and his body was found a day later in Duarte.<br>• One week later, Bonin lured 14-year-old Glen Barker to his van, where he was raped, beaten, and burned with a lit cigarette before being strangled to death.<br>• Eight days later, they abducted and killed 18-year-old Robert Wirostek while he was cycling to work.<br>• On November 29, Bonin and Butts abducted an unidentified boy, who was beaten and strangled to death before being dumped in Kern County.<br>• A day later, Bonin abducted, raped, and strangled 17-year-old Frank Dennis Fox, whose nude body was found 2 days later alongside a highway 5 miles east of San Diego.<br>• Ten days later, 15-year-old John Kilpatrick was abducted and killed, and his body was dumped in Rialto.<br>• On January 1, 1980, Bonin mutilated and strangled 16-year-old Michael Francis McDonald. Though his body was found soon after, it was not identified until March 24. |

| Name | Early life | Crime |
|---|---|---|
| | | • Hours later, Bonin abducted 15-year-old Russell Rugh from a bus stop in Garden Grove. Like Barker, he was beaten and strangled to death. Both bodies were dumped in the Cleveland National Forest and found on March 23. |
| | | • Days later, Bonin offered a ride home to 17-year-old William Ray Pugh, and he accepted it. Minutes later, Bonin asked Pugh if he wanted to have sex; Pugh panicked and ignored him for several minutes before attempting to leave the van, but he was grabbed by the collar and dragged to the passenger seat. |
| | | • He then said how he enjoyed picking up hitchhikers and strangling them to death, terrifying Pugh even more. Strangely enough, Pugh was driven to his home without being assaulted. Days later, with the help of Pugh himself, Bonin lured 15-year-old Harry Todd Turner to the van, and there, Turner was sodomized by him and savagely beaten and bludgeoned by Pugh before being strangled with his own T-shirt by Bonin. |
| | | • On April 10, he abducted 16-year-old Steven Wood and strangled him to death. |
| | | • Hours later, he abducted and killed an 18-year-old acquaintance of his named Lawrence Sharp, beating and strangling him; his body was found behind a Westminster gas station. |
| | | • Three weeks later, Bonin and Butts lured 19-year-old supermarket employee Darin Kendrick to their van, and there, he was forced to drink hydrochloric acid and then stabbed with an ice pick. His body was dumped near the Artesia Freeway, where it was eventually found. |
| | | • On May 19, Bonin abducted 14-year-old Sean King and strangled him to death and then dumped his body in Yucaipa. |
| | | • Nine days later, Bonin invited 19-year-old homeless drifter James Munro to his house. He did not kill Munro but offered him a chance of employment at the Montebello delivery firm. |
| | | • On June 11, the surveillance team noticed Bonin luring a 15-year-old boy known only as Harold T. The team followed Bonin to a parking lot, where they arrested him in the act of assaulting the boy. In custody, Bonin confessed to abducting, raping, and killing 21 boys and young men, with Butts as his primary accomplice. Despite his confession, police believe that he may have murdered even more people. |
| | | ◦ https://criminalminds.fandom.com/wiki/William_Bonin |

(continued)

**Sexual assault and murder**  (continued)

| Name | Early life | Crime |
|---|---|---|
| Robert Ben Rhoades (The Truck Stop Killer) | • He was born on November 22, 1945, in Council Bluffs, Iowa, and raised alone by his mother until his father eventually returned to live with them.<br>• During high school, he was arrested twice, the first for tampering with a motor vehicle and the second for fighting.<br>• After graduating at Monticello High School, he joined the US Marine Corps but was arrested again for robbery and subsequently dishonorably discharged.<br>• On that same year, his father committed suicide shortly after being arrested for molesting a 12-year-old girl.<br>• After his father's death, he moved out and attended college but dropped out; he attempted to become a police officer but was not hired for unknown reasons (presumably for his prior incarcerations).<br>• A year later, he returned to Council Bluffs and had a son with his first wife, with whom he had a divorce after 4 years of marriage.<br>• He married two more times on the same year and managed to get multiple jobs at different locations, such as supermarkets and warehouses.<br>• Rhoades eventually became a truck driver and took advantage of his constant movements to start serial killing.<br>• Before doing so, he had converted the interior of his truck into a torture chamber in order to get more sexual pleasure from torturing his victims. | • Rhoades' first known victims were two hitchhikers: Douglas Scott Zyskowski and Patricia Candace Walsh.<br>• Crime span was from 1975 to 1990.<br>• Shortly after entering his truck, Douglas was shot and killed while Candace was brutally raped and tortured for 1 week before being killed.<br>• He dumped Douglas' body in Texas and Candace's body in Utah.<br>• One month later, using the same M.O., he killed a teenager named Ricky Lee Jones and abducted his girlfriend, Regina Kay Walters.<br>• She was kept by Rhoades for an unspecified amount of time before dying.<br>• Months later, a state trooper, Mike Miller, investigated Rhoades' truck, which was found lying at the side of Interstate 10 with its hazard lights on.<br>• Inside, he found a handcuffed Miller out of arresting him but failed; he was arrested and charged with aggravated assault, sexual assault, and unlawful imprisonment.<br>• After his arrest, a detective managed to link Rhoades to the Zyskowski-Walsh and Jones-Walters murders.<br>• As a result, a search warrant was requested. Inside Rhoades' house, police found nude photos of Walsh and Walters. The latter's body was found and identified months later.<br>• Four years later, Rhoades was convicted of the first-degree murder of Walters and sentenced to life in prison without parole at Menard Correctional Center.<br>• In 2005, Rhoades was extradited to Utah to be tried for the murders of Zyskowski and Walsh. The charges were dropped 1 year later, and Rhoades was sent back to Menard Correctional Center, where he is currently being held.<br>• Using his trucking logs as clue, further investigation revealed that Rhoades could be responsible for about 50 unsolved murders across the USA.<br>   ◦ https://criminalminds.fandom.com/wiki/Robert_Ben_Rhoades |

| Rodney Alcala | • Rodney Alcala was born on August 23, 1943, in San Antonio, Texas, to Raoul Alcala Buquor and Anna Maria Gutierrez. | • Tali Shapiro was an 8-year-old on her way to school when she was lured into Alcala's car, an act that did not go unnoticed by a nearby motorist who followed the two and contacted police. |
|---|---|---|
| | • He moved to Mexico when he was 8 after his maternal grandmother became ill and wanted to spend her final years in Mexico. His father abandoned the family 3 years later. | • Alcala took Tali into his apartment where he raped, beat, and attempted to strangle her with a 10-pound metal bar. When police arrived, they kicked in the door and found Tali laying on the kitchen floor in a large puddle of blood and not breathing. Because of the brutality of the beating, they thought she was dead and began to search for Alcala in the apartment. |
| | • While in Mexico, Rodney attended his first non-Catholic school. His grandmother passed away. | • A police officer, returning to the kitchen, saw Tali struggling to breathe. All attention went to trying to keep her alive, and at some point, Alcala managed to slip out the back door. |
| | • At around the age of 12, Anna Maria moved the family to Los Angeles. | |
| | • At the age of 17, Alcala joined the Army and remained there until 1964 when he received a medical discharge after being diagnosed with a severe antisocial personality. | • When searching Alcala's apartment, the police found several pictures, many of young girls. They also found out his name and that he had attended UCLA. But it took several months before they would find Alcala. |
| | • At age 19, his father unexpectedly passed away in Tulare County, California. The whole family attended the funeral. | • During the summer months, he worked at an all-girls summer drama camp in New Hampshire. |
| | • Alcala, now out of the Army, enrolled in UCLA School of Fine Arts where he earned his Bachelor of Fine Arts degree in 1968. This is the same year that he kidnapped, raped, beat, and tried to kill his first known victim. | • In 1971, two girls attending the camp recognized Alcala on a wanted poster at the post office. The police were notified, and Alcala was arrested. |
| | • He became an unlikely winner on ABC's long-running game show *The Dating Game*, where he successfully charmed a young lady on television, in front of millions of viewers, while in the middle of a prolific killing spree. | • With Alcala's ability to charm, he was back out on the streets in less than 3 years. |
| | | • Within 8 weeks, he returned to prison for violating his parole for providing marijuana to a 13-year-old girl. She told police that Alcala kidnapped her, but he was not charged. |
| | | • Alcala spent another 2 years behind bars and was released in 1977, again under the "indeterminate sentencing" program. He returned to Los Angeles and got a job as a typesetter for the *Los Angeles Times*. |
| | | • It did not take long for Alcala to get back into his murderous rampage. |
| | | • The news article reads: "The Murder of Jill Barcomb, Los Angeles County in November 1977. Alcala raped, sodomized, and murdered 18-year-old Jill Barcomb, a New York native who had recently moved to California. Alcala used a large rock to smash in her face and strangled her to death by tying her belt and pant leg around her neck. Alcala then left her body in a mountainous area in the foothills near Hollywood, where she was discovered November 10, 1977, posed on her knees with her face in the dirt." |

(continued)

**Sexual assault and murder** (continued)

| Name | Early life | Crime |
|------|-----------|-------|
|  |  | • For the other murder in Los Angeles County in December 1977, Alcala raped, sodomized, and murdered 27-year-old nurse Georgia Wixted. Alcala used a hammer to sexually abuse Georgia and then used the claw end of the hammer to beat and smash her head. He strangled her to death using a nylon stocking and left her body posed in her Malibu apartment. Her body was discovered on December 16, 1977. |
|  |  | • For the murder of Charlotte Lamb, also in Los Angeles County in June 1979, Alcala raped, beat, and murdered this 33-year-old legal secretary. Alcala strangled Charlotte to death using a shoelace from her shoe and left her body posed in a laundry room of an El Segundo apartment complex where it was discovered on June 24, 1979. |
|  |  | • In June 1979, also in Los Angeles County, Alcala raped and murdered 21-year-old Jill Parenteau in her Burbank apartment. He strangled Jill to death using a cord or nylon. Alcala's blood was collected from the scene after he cut himself crawling through a window. Based on a semi-rare blood match, Alcala was linked to the murder. He was charged with murdering Parenteau, but the case was later dismissed. |
|  |  | • On June 20, 1979, Alcala approached 12-year-old Robin Samsoe and her friend Bridget Wilvert at Huntington Beach, Orange County, and asked them to pose for pictures. After posing for a series of photographs, a neighbor intervened and asked if everything was alright, and Samsoe took off. Later, Robin got on a bike and headed to an afternoon dance class. Alcala then kidnapped and murdered Samsoe and dumped her body near the Sierra Madre in the foothills of the San Gabriel Mountains. Her body was scavenged by animals, and her skeletal remains were discovered on July 2, 1979. Her front teeth had been knocked out by Alcala. |
|  |  | ○ https://www.news.com.au/lifestyle/real-life/true-stories/the-serial-killer-that-won-a-tv-dating-show-during-his-murder-spree/news-story/4808e43e9d9e276f4e93d08075103df2 |
|  |  | ○ https://www.thoughtco.com/profile-of-serial-killer-rodney-alcala-973104 |
|  |  | ○ http://maamodt.asp.radford.edu/Psyc%20405/serial%20killers/Alcala.%20Rodney%20_2012_.pdf |

| Ted Bundy | |
|---|---|
| • Ted Bundy was born in Vermont on November 24, 1946, to a young mother, Eleanor Louise Cowell, and an unknown father. | • Ted is suspected to have been the perpetrator of 100+ murders, confessed to 30 before execution. |
| • His maternal grandmother raised him as her own child to avoid scandal, and Bundy grew up believing his biological mother was his older sister. | • He used manipulation and deceit (e.g., feigning an injury, assuming the identity of a police officer) as a technique to kidnap victims. |
| • His grandfather' abusive behavior toward him, and his mother caused them to run away to Tacoma, Washington, when Bundy was 5 years old and find refuge at a cousin's house. | • He described victims as being overtly vulnerable and inviting of victimization. |
| • Eleanor met and married John Bundy shortly after, and John legally adopted Ted to be raised as his own son. They had several more children together. | • He used bludgeoning and strangulation as means of murdering his victims and sexual assault before and after. |
| • Ted was a reckless child, constantly sneaking out and roaming the streets at night | • The first known attack was in January 1974 but was not an actual murder case. Bundy assaulted 18-year-old Karen Sparks, who was a student at the University of Washington. This violent assault left her in a 10-day coma with permanent disabilities. |
| • He was caught spying on women on multiple occasions. | • His second victim, and his first murder, was Lynda Healy, another UW student. |
| • He was well known and well liked as described by people who knew him in high school. | • Shortly after, Bundy started targeting female students in the nearby area. |
| • His intelligence and social skills allowed him to have a successful and enjoyable college career, as well. | • Bundy would often approach them in an arm sling or a cast and ask for their assistance. It was then that he would knock them unconscious and take them into the back of his car to bind, rape, and kill them. |
| • Bundy graduated high school in 1965 and enrolled in the University of Puget Sound but quickly transferred to University of Washington to study Chinese. | • In some cases, Bundy admitted to decapitating his victims and keeping them, sometimes even sleeping with their skulls. |
| • While a student at the University of Washington, Bundy fell in love with a wealthy, pretty young woman from California. She had everything that he wanted: money, class, and influence. He was devastated by their breakup. Many of his later victims resembled his college girlfriend—attractive students with long, dark hair. | ○ Miller, L. (2014). Serial killers: Subtypes, patterns, and motives. *Aggression and Violent Behavior, 19*(1), 1–11. |
| • He dropped out, but re-enrolled as a psychology major in 1968. | ○ Miller, L. (2014). Serial killers: Development, dynamics, and forensics. *Aggression and Violent Behavior, 19*(1), 12–22. |
| • He graduated from the University of Washington with a degree in psychology in 1972 and had been accepted to law school in Utah. | ○ Moes, E. C. (1991). Ted Bundy: A case of schizoid necrophilia. *Melanie Klein & Object Relations, 9*(1), 54–72. |
| • By the mid-1970s, Bundy had transformed himself, becoming more outwardly confident and active in social and political matters. | ○ White, J. H., Lester, D., Gentile, M., & Rosenbleeth, J. (2011). The utilization of forensic science and criminal profiling for capturing serial killers. *Forensic Science International, 209*(1–3), 5–160. |
| • Bundy even got a letter of recommendation from the Republican governor of Washington after working on his campaign. | |

(continued)

**Sexual assault and murder** (continued)

| Name | Early life | Crime |
|---|---|---|
| | • Months later, Bundy stopped showing up for his classes.<br>• In February 1980, Ted Bundy married Carole Ann Boone, a mother of two whom he'd dated before his initial arrest, in a Florida courtroom during the penalty phase of his trial.<br>• When Boone gave birth to a daughter in 1982, she named Ted Bundy as the father.<br>• Boone eventually realized Bundy was guilty of the crimes and stopped visiting him during the last 2 years of his imprisonment. | ○ Keatley, D. A., Golightly, H., Shephard, R., Yaksic, E., & Reid, S. (2018). Using behavior sequence analysis to map serial killers' life histories. *Journal of Interpersonal Violence, 1*(1), 260–886.<br>○ Jenkins, J. P. (2018). *Ted Bundy*. Encyclopædia Britannica. https://www.britannica.com/biography/Ted-Bundy<br>○ Paoletti, G. (2018, October 12). "The very definition of heartless evil": The story of Ted Bundy. Retrieved from https://allthatsinteresting.com/ted-bundy<br>○ Aynesworth, H., & Michaud, S. G. (1989). *Ted Bundy: Conversations with a killer.* Irving, TX: Authorlink Press.<br>○ Aynesworth, H., & Michaud, S. G. (1999). *The only living witness: The true story of serial sex killer Ted Bundy.* Irving, TX: Authorlink Press.<br>○ Rule, A. (2000). *The stranger beside me.* Seattle, WA: W.W. Norton & Company. https://www.biography.com/people/ted-bundy-9231165 |

| Angelo Buono Jr. and Kenneth Bianchi (The Hillside Strangler) | • Angelo Anthony Buono Jr. was born on October 5, 1934, in Rochester, New York. After his parents divorced, Buono was raised by his mother in Glendale, California.<br>• Buono was brought up as Catholic, but he showed no interest in attending church.<br>• He was also a poor student and would often skip school, knowing that his mother, who had a full-time job, could do little to control his activities.<br>• From an early age, he developed a deep loathing for women.<br>• By the age of 14, Buono had been in a reformatory and was bragging about raping and sodomizing young local girls.<br>• Though he married several times and had numerous children, Buono showed nothing but brutality toward the women in his life.<br>• Kenneth Alessio Bianchi was born on May 22, 1951, in Rochester, New York. Bianchi, whose natural mother was an alcoholic prostitute, was adopted at birth and had a love-hate relationship with women even as a young child.<br>• At age 5, Kenneth has frequent lapses into trance-like states of daydreaming. He was evaluated by a physician. These trance-like states of daydreaming were typified by his eyes rolling back in his head and inattentiveness.<br>• He was prone to temper tantrums and quick to anger as well. Doctor diagnosed him with petit mal syndrome and assured the Bianchis that there was nothing to worry about and that Kenneth will eventually grow out of these episodes.<br>• At age 8, he is treated briefly at a psychiatric center in Rochester for mental problems.<br>• At age 9, he begins having involuntary urination.<br>• He became interested in police work but was unable to secure a job; he eventually settled for a post as a security guard<br>• In 1975, Bianchi left Rochester and moved to Los Angeles, where he lived with his older adoptive cousin, Angelo Buono.<br>• Bianchi later moved in with his girlfriend, Kelli Boyd, and had a child.<br>• A chronic liar, he set up a psychology practice with a phony degree and told Boyd he was dying of cancer. | • By 1975, Buono was running an auto upholstery business, where he would lure a steady stream of teenage girls.<br>• In 1977, Angelo and Kenneth discuss the idea of getting young girls to work for them as prostitutes.<br>• It is Angelo's idea as a way for them to get money (as they are short on cash). They purchase a list of names of men who frequent prostitutes from Deborah Noble.<br>• Unbeknownst to Angelo and Kenneth, Deborah delivers a "trick list" and deceives them. Deborah Noble and her friend, Yolanda Washington, deliver the list of men to Angelo. Yolanda is 19 years old, a part-time waitress and a prostitute. Yolanda tells Angelo that she usually works a particular stretch on Sunset Boulevard.<br>• Angelo and Kenneth soon find out that the list is a fake and seek out to get revenge for the money they paid.<br>• He soon teamed with his cousin, Kenneth Bianchi, for a spree of kidnappings, rapes, and murders that claimed 15 victims, mostly in and around Los Angeles, between October 1977 and January 1978.<br>• Posing as policemen, the cousins began with prostitutes, eventually moving on to middle-class girls.<br>• They usually left the bodies on the hillsides of the Glendale-Highland Park area, earning the moniker "The Hillside Strangler."<br>• During the 4-month rampage, Buono and Bianchi inflicted unspeakable horrors on their victims, including injecting them with deadly household chemicals.<br>• In October 1979, police captured Bianchi in Bellingham, Washington, where he had relocated to be with Kelli Boyd. There, he also committed two more murders.<br>  ○ http://maamodt.asp.radford.edu/Psyc%20405/serial%20killers/Bianchi,%20Kenneth.htm<br>  ○ https://www.biography.com/people/angelo-buono-12385174<br>  ○ https://www.biography.com/people/kenneth-bianchi-12385185<br>  ○ https://www.thoughtco.com/angelo-buono-the-hillside-strangler-973111 |

(continued)

**Sexual assault and murder** (continued)

| Name | Early life | Crime |
|------|-----------|-------|
| Randall Woodfield | • He was born on December 26, 1950, in Salem, Oregon, from a middle-class family with no evident signs of dysfunction.<br>• He was popular among his peers and was a football star at Newport High School on the Oregon Coast and at Portland State University.<br>• Beginning in adolescence, however, he began to exhibit antisocial sexual behaviors, primarily a penchant for indecent exposure.<br>• Upon his first arrest for this crime in high school, his football coaches hushed it up so that he wouldn't be kicked off the team.<br>• He was a star wide receiver on PSU's football team, joining the Campus Crusade for Christ and the Fellowship of Christian Athletes.<br>• Three arrests in the early 1970s for petty crimes such as vandalism and public indecency did not prevent Woodfield from being drafted by the Green Bay Packers. In 1974, he was drafted in the 14th round by the Green Bay Packers, but he was dismissed from the team after more than a dozen arrests for indecent exposure.<br>• But there were problems early on, said Ann Rule, the Seattle author who documented Woodfield's case in her bestseller, *The I-5 Killer*. She reported that Woodfield was overshadowed as a youth by his two older sisters who did well in school. One a doctor, the other an attorney.<br>• In an attempt to conceal his identity, he wore tape over his nose to distract his victims, detectives said, thinking they wouldn't recognize him in a lineup without it. | • Woodfield robbed and sexually assaulted several women at knife point.<br>• In 1979, Woodfield embarked upon a 2-year robbery spree, holding up gas stations, ice cream parlors, and homes along the Interstate 5 freeway.<br>• Cherie L. Ayers, 29, was found beaten and stabbed in her southwest Portland home on October 11, 1980.<br>• He murdered Darcey Renee Fix, a 22-year-old he knew from Portland State University, after he went to her home to rape her. But she was with Douglas Keith Altig, 24. Woodfield murdered them both.<br>• Darcey Renee Fix, 22, and Douglas Keith Altig, 24. Found shot to death in their North Portland home on Thanksgiving Day in 1980.<br>• He stole a .32-caliber pistol from the home, which he used to shoot Shari Hull, 20, and a 21-year-old woman, two students working as nighttime janitors in a Salem-area office. The 21-year-old survived, later testifying that Woodfield raped them both at gunpoint and then shot each of them twice in the back of the head. Shari Hull was found shot to death on January 18, 1981, in a Keizer office building where she worked as a cleaner. Woodfield was convicted for killing Hull.<br>• In February 1981, he called his sister in Shasta County, California, asking to have coffee with her. She said her husband didn't want him around. Soon after, Woodfield forced his way into the Shasta home of Jannell Jarvis, 14, and her mother, Donna Eckard, 37, and killed them. They were found shot to death on February 3, 1981.<br>• Julie Reitz, 18, was found shot to death in the Beaverton home she shared with her mother on February 15, 1981. Likely killed close to midnight on Valentine's Day.<br>• While he was charged with four murders, it is estimated that Woodfield committed as many more, as well as upward of 60 sexual assaults.<br><br>○ http://murderpedia.org/male.W/w/woodfield-randall.htm<br>○ https://www.oregonlive.com/portland/2012/05/serial_killer_randy_woodfields.html |

| Andrei Chikatilo | • He was born on October 16, 1936, in the Ukraine state, more specifically in Yablochnoye, a village in the heart of rural Ukraine in the then USSR. Stalin's policies of agricultural collectivization caused widespread hardship and famine that decimated the population.<br>• At the time of Chikatilo's birth, the effects of the famine were still widely felt, and his early childhood was influenced by deprivation.<br>• The situation was made worse still when the USSR entered World War II against Germany, bringing sustained bombing raids on Ukraine.<br>• In addition to the external hardships, Chikatilo is believed to have suffered from hydrocephalus (water on the brain) at birth, which caused him genital-urinary tract problems later in life, including bed-wetting into his late adolescence and, later, the inability to sustain an erection, although he was able to ejaculate.<br>• His home life was disrupted by his father's conscription into the war against Germany, where he was captured, held prisoner, and then vilified by his countrymen for allowing himself to be captured, when he finally returned home. Chikatilo suffered the consequences of his father's "cowardice," making him the focus of school bullying.<br>• Painfully shy as a result of this, his only sexual experience during adolescence occurred at aged 15, when he is reported to have overpowered a young girl, ejaculating immediately during the brief struggle, for which he received even more ridicule.<br>• This humiliation colored all future sexual experiences and cemented his association of sex with violence.<br>• A failure of his entrance exam to Moscow State University was followed by a move to Rodionovo-Nesvetayevsky, a town near Rostov, in 1960, where he became a telephone engineer.<br>• His younger sister moved in with him, and, concerned by his lack of success with the opposite sex, she engineered a meeting with a local girl, Fayina, whom he went on to marry in 1963. | • An eyewitness had seen Chikatilo with the victim, shortly before her disappearance, but his wife provided him with an ironclad alibi that enabled him to evade any further police attention.<br>• Alexsandr Kravchenko, a 25-year-old with a previous rape conviction, was arrested and confessed to the crime under duress, probably as a result of extensive and brutal interrogation. He was tried for the killing of Lena Zakotnova and executed in 1984.<br>• Perhaps as a result of his close brush with the law, there were no more documented victims for the next 3 years.<br>• Still dogged by claims of child abuse, Chikatilo found it impossible to find another teaching post, when he was made redundant from his mining school post, in early 1981.<br>• He took a job as a clerk for a raw materials factory in Rostov, where the travel involved with the position gave him unlimited access to a wide range of young victims over the next 9 years.<br>• Larisa Tkachenko, 17, became his next victim. On September 3, 1981, Chikatilo strangled, stabbed, and gagged her with earth and leaves to prevent her crying out.<br>• The brutal force afforded Chikatilo his sexual release, and he began to develop from a pattern of attack that saw him focusing on young runaways of both sexes.<br>• He befriended them at train stations and bus stops, before luring them into nearby forest areas, where he would attack them, attempt rape, and use his knife, to mutilate them.<br>• In a number of cases, he ate the sexual organs or removed other body parts such as the tips of their noses or tongues.<br>• In the earliest cases, the common pattern was to inflict damage to the eye area, slashing across the sockets and removing the eyeballs in many cases, an act which Chikatilo later attributed to a belief that his victims kept an imprint of his face in their eyes, even after death.<br>• As the body count mounted, rumors of foreign inspired plots, and werewolf attacks, became more prevalent, and public fear and interest grew, despite the lack of any media coverage. |

(continued)

**Sexual assault and murder** (continued)

| Name | Early life | Crime |
|---|---|---|
| | • Despite his sexual problems, and lack of interest in conventional sex, they produced two children and lived an outwardly normal family life.<br>• In 1971, Chikatilo changed careers to become a schoolteacher. A string of complaints about indecent assaults on young children forced him to move from school to school, before he finally settled at a mining school in Shakhty, near Rostov. | • In 1983, Moscow detective Major Mikhail Fetisov assumed control of the investigation. He recognized that a serial killer might be on the loose and assigned a specialist forensic analyst, Viktor Burakov, to head the investigation in the Shakhty area.<br>• The investigation centered on known sex offenders and the mentally ill, but such were the interrogation methods of the local police that they regularly solicited false confessions from prisoners, leaving Burakov skeptical of the majority of these "confessions."<br>• Progress was slow, especially as, at that stage, not all of the victim's bodies had been discovered, so the true body count was unknown to the police.<br>• With each body, the forensic evidence mounted, and police were convinced that the killer had the blood type AB, as evidenced by the semen samples collected from a number of crime scenes. Samples of identical gray hair were also retrieved.<br>• When an additional 15 victims were added during the course of 1984, police efforts were increased drastically, and they mounted massive surveillance operations that canvassed most local transport hubs.<br>• Chikatilo was arrested for behaving suspiciously at a bus station at this time but again avoided suspicion on the murder charges, as his blood type did not match the suspect profile; but he was imprisoned for 3 months for a number of minor outstanding offenses.<br>• What was not realized at the time was that Chikatilo's actual blood type, type A, was different to the type found in his other bodily fluids (type AB), as he was a member of a minority group known as "non-secretors," whose blood type cannot be inferred by anything other than a blood sample.<br>• As police only had a sample of semen, and not blood, from the crime scenes, Chikatilo was able to escape suspicion of murder. Today's sophisticated DNA techniques are not subject to the same fallibility. |

- Following his release, Chikatilo found work as a traveling buyer for a train company, based in Novocherkassk, and managed to keep a low profile until August 1985, when he murdered two women in separate incidents.
- At around the same time as these murders, Burakov, frustrated at the lack of positive progress, engaged the help of psychiatrist, Alexandr Bukhanovsky, who refined the profile of the killer. Bukhanovsky described the killer as a "necro-sadist," or someone who achieves sexual gratification from the suffering and death of others.
- Bukhanovsky also placed the killer's age as between 45 and 50, significantly older than had been believed up to that point. Desperate to catch the killer, Burakov even interviewed a serial killer, Anatoly Slivko, shortly before his execution, in an attempt to gain some insight into his elusive serial killer.
- Coinciding with this attempt to understand the mind of the killer, attacks seemed to dry up, and police suspected that their target might have stopped killing, been incarcerated for other crimes, or died.
- However, early in 1988, Chikatilo again resumed his killing, the majority occurring away from the Rostov area, and victims were no longer taken from local public transport outlets, as police surveillance of these areas continued.
- Over the next 2 years, the body count increased by an additional 19 victims, and it appeared that the killer was taking increasing risks, focusing primarily on young boys and often killing in public places where the risk of detection was far higher.
- Chikatilo was arrested on November 20, 1990, following more suspicious behavior, but he refused at first to confess to any of the killings.
- Burakov decided to allow the psychiatrist, Bukhanovsky, who had prepared the original profile, to talk to Chikatilo, under the guise of trying to understand the mind of a killer from a scientific context.
- Chikatilo, clearly flattered by this approach, opened up to the psychiatrist, providing extensive details of all of his killings and even leading police to the site of bodies previously undiscovered.
- He claimed to have taken the lives of 56 victims, although only 53 of these could be independently verified.

  o   https://www.biography.com/people/andrei-chikatilo-17169648

(continued)

**Sexual assault and murder** (continued)

| Name | Early life | Crime |
|---|---|---|
| Richard Ramirez: The Nightstalker | • Richard Ramirez, full name Ricardo Muñoz Ramirez, was born in El Paso, Texas, on February 29, 1960.<br>• The youngest of five, Richard grew up in an unstable environment, marked by an abusive father.<br>• Ramirez reportedly sustained multiple head injuries at an early age; after he was knocked unconscious by a swing at age 5, he began experiencing epileptic fits.<br>• To avoid his father's temper, Ramirez was known to escape to local cemeteries and pass the time smoking marijuana from an age as young as 10.<br>• When Ramirez was 12 years old, a cousin who was a Vietnamese veteran showed him pictures of Vietnamese women he had allegedly raped, tortured, and killed.<br>• Mike introduced drugs to Ramirez, which consequently resulted in Ramirez committing petty crimes. He also became a Satan worshiper. Because of this rebellion, Ramirez became alienated from his parents.<br>• The following year, Ramirez was a witness to his cousin's fatal shooting of his wife.<br>• Shortly into high school, Ramirez dropped out and moved to Los Angeles.<br>• In 1977, Ramirez was sent to a juvenile detention center for a series of petty crimes. In addition, he was put on probation for marijuana possession in 1982.<br>• Soon after these two crimes, Ramirez moved to California and continued to commit crimes such as burglary and possession of cocaine, as well as a car theft charge, which resulted in a jail sentence.<br>• Around this time, Ramirez began breaking into homes. | • In June, 1984, Richard Ramirez committed his first murder, raping and stabbing a 79-year-old widow.<br>• After waiting 8 months, Ramirez resumed his killings. The majority of the murders occurred in the Los Angeles area and was a result of home invasions. His victims—some of whom survived—were often sexually assaulted and beaten, and Satanic symbols were found at many of the crime scenes.<br>• In just 1 year, Ramirez had murdered over a dozen people and tortured of 25 people.<br>• After many delays, in 1989, Richard Ramirez, age 29, was sentenced to the conviction of 13 murders, 5 attempted murders, 11 sexual assaults, and 14 burglaries. Ramirez was sentenced to die in California's gas chamber. His remarks to this were "Big deal. Death always went with the territory. See you in Disneyland."<br>  ○ "Richard Ramirez: The Night Stalker." *Crime Museum*, www.crimemuseum.org/crime-library/serial-killers/richard-ramirez/.<br>  ○ Britannica, The Editors of Encyclopaedia. "Richard Ramirez." *Encyclopædia Britannica*, Encyclopædia Britannica, Inc., 3 June 2018, www.britannica.com/biography/Richard-Ramirez.<br>  ○ *NYU*, www.nyu.edu/classes/keefer/ww1/grise.html.<br>  ○ https://www.biography.com/people/richard-ramirez-12385163 |

| Steven Brian Pennell | • Not much is known of Pennell's childhood except that for the most apart, he appeared to come from a normal and stable upbringing.<br>• At some point, he ended up in Delaware and applied for numerous positions in the state police department.<br>• Up until this point, he had pursued a career in criminology, having completed several semesters at the University of Delaware.<br>• All of his applications were rejected for various reasons, and he ended up working as an electrician.<br>• He married and settled in New Castle.<br>• He took incredible pleasure in controlling her life and acting as the dominant presence in the household. The Pennells had no children. | • November of 1987, Steven Pennell began what was to become the most appalling case of murder in the history of Small Wonder (Delaware).<br>• For the next 11 months, Pennell drove on Interstates 40 and 13 in search of women that he could torture and rape.<br>• He found the perfect victims in prostitutes. Once engaging in a conversation with a local hooker, Pennell would coerce the unsuspecting woman into his van and then drive to an isolated spot where he would then proceed to subject his new captive to unspeakable amounts of torture and rape.<br>• Inside the van, he carried a so-called rape kit that contained specially chosen devices used to torture his victims. Such items included pliers, a whip, handcuffs, needles, knives, and other types of restraints.<br>• He would bind his victim by the hands and ankles and raped them and beat their buttocks with his whip.<br>• Other times, he would hit them with a hammer until they were battered and bloody (and still alive).<br>• In another case, he used the pliers to squeeze the victim's breasts and cut off her nipples.<br>• Eventually, he would show mercy by strangling them to death and then bashing in their skulls with a blunt object for good measure.<br>• Finally, the bodies would be dumped along wooded areas next to highways 40 and 13.<br>    ○ http://murderpedia.org/male.P/p1/pennell-steven-brian.htm |

(continued)

**Sexual assault and murder** (continued)

| Name | Early life | Crime |
|---|---|---|
| John Eric Armstrong | • He was born in Michigan November 23, 1973.<br>• At age 2, he broke his leg when he fell out of window while his father was supposed to be watching him.<br>• In 1979, his 2-month-old brother, Michael, dies suddenly from infant death syndrome. He then decided to ride his bike into speeding traffic to "be with his brother."<br>• Reportedly, he was physically and sexually abused by his father, who abandoned the family 4 months after Michael's death.<br>• His parents were divorced, and his mother remarried to Ron Pringle.<br>• He spent 30 days in a North Carolina psychiatric hospital because he was distressed due to the fact he was rejected by a girl from his high school with whom he wanted to have sex.<br>• In 1992, he graduated from New Bern high school and then joined the navy in Raleigh, North Carolina.<br>• In 1993, he starts working on the USS Nimitz as a ship's serviceman. He was known for being mild mannered and having an innocent child-like look while in the Navy, so that he was nicknamed "Opie" by his mates.<br>• He received four promotions and earned two Good Conduct medals. In 1995, he was designated a third-class petty officer.<br>• In 1998, he married Katie Rednoske at a church in Redford Township.<br>• He became a father of two.<br>• In April 1999, he was honorably discharged from the Navy.<br>• When he left the Navy in 1999, he and his wife moved to Dearborn Heights, a working-class neighborhood in Michigan.<br>• He got a job with Target retail stores and later with the Detroit Metropolitan Airport refueling airplanes. | • Mr. Armstrong preyed on prostitutes in ports of call where the Nimitz docked during his 8-year Navy career.<br>• Based on interviews, investigators said they thought he committed his first murder in North Carolina, shortly after enlisting there in 1992. A year later, he struck twice in Seattle.<br>• In 1996, Mr. Armstrong is said to have killed two more women, in Thailand and in Seattle.<br>• And in 1997, he is believed to have killed five women in Honolulu, Hong Kong, and Singapore.<br>• He is also suspected of a 1998 murder in Newport News, Va., his last known stop before he left the Navy.<br>• One of the victims was male, a Seattle man whom Mr. Armstrong killed with a pipe.<br>• In Detroit, three prostitutes from that area said that they had sexual encounters with Mr. Armstrong and complained that he had tried to strangle them.<br>• All of the women were strangled. "We initially thought that he was posing the young ladies for a photograph, but he was actually leaving them in the position where he could come back and have sex with them again."<br>• Law enforcement officials have identified two of the five women slain in the Detroit area as Kelly Hood, a 34-year-old mother of three from Detroit, and Wendy Jordan, 39, also from Detroit.<br>  ○ http://murderpedia.org/male.A/a/armstrong-john.htm<br>  ○ https://www.thoughtco.com/serial-killer-john-eric-armstrong-973159<br>  ○ https://www.nytimes.com/2000/04/14/us/ex-sailor-linked-to-slayings-of-prostitutes-worldwide.htm<br>  ○ https://www.svsd.net/cms/lib5/PA01001234/Centricity/Domain/1046/John%20Eric%20Armstrong%205.pdf |

| Israel Keyes | • Keyes was born on January 7, 1978, in Richmond, Utah, to parents who were Mormons, the second oldest of ten children. | • Israel admitted to raping a young girl in Oregon sometime between 1996 and 1998; told FBI agents that he separated a girl from her friends and raped, but not killed her. It was the beginning of a long list of crimes, including burglaries and sexual assaults. |
|---|---|---|
| | • The family moved to Stevens County, Washington, where he attended The Ark, a Christian Identity church, known for racist and anti-Semitic views. | • From his base in Alaska, Keyes ventured out into almost every region of the USA to plan and commit his murders. He traveled many times since 2004, looking for victims and setting up buried caches of money, weapons, and tools needed to kill and dispose of the bodies. |
| | • His parents had by then become fundamentalist Christians, moving from churches Keyes described as "Amish" to a "more militant militia sort of church" when he was a teenager. | • He told the FBI that his crimes were not financed with money from his construction business but from money he got from robbing banks. |
| | • They lived at times without electricity and home-schooled the children. For years, some of the kids slept in a tent. | • He kidnapped 18-year-old Samantha Koenig who was working as a barista at one of the many coffee stands around Anchorage. He took her to a shed at his Anchorage home, sexually assaulted her, and strangled her to death and then immediately left the area and went on a 2-week cruise, leaving her body in the shed. When he returned, he dismembered her body and dumped it in Matanuska Lake north of Anchorage. |
| | • The kids earned money through under-the-table jobs cutting firewood or working on farms. He said he spent time in the woods and hunted "anything with a heartbeat." | • He confessed to the murders of four people in three different incidents in Washington State. He killed two individuals, and he kidnapped and killed a couple. |
| | • Keyes was obsessed with guns from childhood. As an adolescent, Keyes said he shot at houses with BB guns, broke into homes, and started fires in the woods. | • He killed another person on the East Coast and buried the body in New York. |
| | • Later, he slipped into the cabins of neighbors to steal guns, which he secreted in a cache in the family home. When his parents found out, they made him apologize and return the guns. | • He conducted what he called a "blitz" attack on their victims' home, tied them up and, took them to an abandoned house. |
| | • Israel Keyes was childhood friends of Chevie and Cheyne Kehoe, known racists who were later convicted of murder and attempted murder. | |

(continued)

**Sexual assault and murder** (continued)

| Name | Early life | Crime |
|---|---|---|
| | • During his young adult years, he rejected religion completely and proclaimed he was an atheist.<br>• At age 20, Keyes joined the US Army and served at Fort Lewis, Fort Hood, and in Egypt until he was honorably discharged in 2000.<br>• After his deployment, while stationed at Fort Lewis south of Seattle, he met a woman from the Makah Reservation in Neah Bay, on Washington's Olympic Peninsula. She was pregnant with their child when he got out of the Army.<br>• He spent most of the next 6 years living on the reservation with her and their child, working in the parks and recreation department.<br>• By 2007, Keyes established Keyes Construction in Alaska and began working as a construction contractor. | • He shot Bill Currier to death, sexually assaulted Lorraine, and then strangled her.<br><br>  ◦ https://www.thoughtco.com/profile-of-serial-killer-israel-keyes-973103<br>  ◦ https://www.adn.com/alaska-news/crime-courts/2018/05/18/unsealed-interviews-detail-two-lives-of-alaska-serial-killer-israel-keyes/ |
| Luis Garavito | • He was born January 25, 1957, in Génova, Colombia, the eldest of seven children; he was raised in Western Colombia.<br>• He attended school for only a few years and endured a difficult childhood, suffering abuse by his father and several neighbors. | • Garavito's victims were poor children, peasant children, or street children, between the ages of 6 and 16.<br>• Garavito approached them on the street or countryside and offered them gifts or small amounts of money.<br>• After gaining their trust, he took the children for a walk and when they got tired, he would take advantage of them. He then raped them, cut their throats, and usually dismembered their corpses. Most corpses showed signs of torture.<br>• Garavito was captured on April 22, 1999. He confessed to murdering 140 children. However, he is still under investigation for the murder of 172 children in more than 59 towns in Colombia.<br>• He was found guilty in 138 of the 172 cases; the others are ongoing. The sentences for these 138 cases add to 1853 years and 9 days.<br>• Because of Colombian law restrictions, however, he cannot be imprisoned for more than 30 years. In addition, because he helped the authorities in finding the bodies, his sentence has been decreased to 22 years.<br>• The number of his victims, based on the locations of skeletons listed on maps that Garavito drew in prison, could eventually exceed 300.<br><br>  ◦ http://murderpedia.org/male.G/g/garavito.htm<br>  ◦ https://www.britannica.com/biography/Luis-Garavito |

| David Parker Ray | | |
|---|---|---|
| | • Ray was born in Belen, New Mexico, on November 6, 1939.<br>• His parents, Cecil and Nettie Ray, were poor and lived with Nettie's parents on a small ranch where they raised David and his younger sister Peggy.<br>• Cecil was an abusive drunk who lashed out at his wife and children.<br>• He eventually left Nettie and the children when David was 10 years old.<br>• After Cecil divorced Nettie, the decision was made to send David and Peggy to live with their grandparents on their rural ranch in Mountainair, New Mexico.<br>• Life for David and Peggy took a dramatic turn. Their grandfather, Ethan Ray, was nearing 70 years old and lived with strict standards which he expected the grandchildren to follow.<br>• Failure to follow his rules would often result in the children being physically disciplined.<br>• At school, David, who was tall, shy, and awkward, had a hard time fitting in and was often bullied by his classmates.<br>• Much of his spare time was spent alone drinking and using drugs. It was during this time that David Ray began to develop his secret fascination of sadomasochism.<br>• David Ray's sister discovered his collection of erotic photographs of acts of bondage and sadomasochistic drawings.<br>• After high school, he worked as an auto mechanic before joining the Army, where he again worked as a mechanic. He received an honorable discharge from the Army.<br>• Years later, he told his fiancé that his first victim was a woman he tied to a tree and tortured and murdered when he had just become a teenager. Whether this was true or materialized out of his constant fantasies of bondage and torture is unknown. | • On March 22, 1999, in Elephant Butte, New Mexico, a 22-year-old, covered in blood, naked, and with a metal choker collar padlocked around her neck, was running for her life.<br>• She spotted a mobile home and ran inside, pleading for help from the shocked homeowner. The police arrived shortly afterward and listened as Cynthia told her terrifying story of kidnap and torture.<br>• She told them that a man and a woman had kidnapped her and held her as a sex slave for 3 days. There she was raped and tortured with whips, medical instruments, electric shock, and other sexual instruments until she managed to escape.<br>• David Parker Ray and his girlfriend, Cindy Lea Hendy, were apprehended. During questioning, the two stuck to the same story—that Cynthia was a heroin addict and they were trying to help her detoxify.<br>• A search of Ray's property told another story. Inside Ray's mobile home, the police found evidence that backed up Cynthia's story, including the audio tape.<br>• Inside another trailer that sat next to the mobile home was what detectives assumed was the "Toy Box" as Ray called it.<br>• Inside were various instruments of torture, drawn pictures of how Ray would torture his victims, and various restraints, pulleys, whips, and sexual devices. However, the most shocking piece of evidence was a videotape of a woman being tortured by the couple.<br>• Ray and Hendy were arrested and charged with multiple counts including kidnapping.<br>• Once in custody, Cindy Hendy was quick to turn on Ray in a plea deal that included a reduced sentence. She told investigators that Ray told her about 14 murders that he had committed and where some of the bodies had been dumped.<br>• She also told of some of the different ways Ray would torture his victims which included using a mirror which was mounted in the ceiling, above the gynecologist-type table he used to strap his victims to so that they would have to watch was being done to them.<br>• Ray would also put his victims in wooden contraptions that bent them over and immobilized them while he had his dogs rape them and sometimes other friends.<br>   ◦ https://www.thoughtco.com/profile-of-serial-rapist-david-parker-ray-973147 |

**Female murderers**

| Name | Early life | Crimes |
|------|-----------|--------|
| Susan Smith | • Susan Smith was born on September 26, 1971, in Union, South Carolina, to parents Linda and Harry Vaughan.<br>• She was the youngest of three children and the couple's only daughter.<br>• Her parents divorced when Susan was 7, and 5 weeks later Harry, age 37, committed suicide.<br>• Her parents' tumultuous marriage and the death of her father left Susan a sad, empty, and oddly distant child.<br>• Within weeks of the Vaughans' divorce, Linda married Beverly (Bev) Russell, a successful local businessman.<br>• Linda and the children moved from their small modest home into Bev's house located in an exclusive subdivision of Union.<br>• As a teen, Susan was a good student, well liked and outgoing.<br>• In her junior year, she was voted president of the Junior Civitan Club, a club which focused on volunteering in the community.<br>• In her final year of high school, she received the "Friendliest Female" award and was known for her cheerful and fun disposition.<br>• But during those years of enjoying her popularity and positions of leadership, Susan was harboring a family secret.<br>• At the age of 16, her stepfather turned from caretaker to molester. Susan reported the inappropriate behavior to her mother and to the Department of Social Services, and Bev moved out from the home temporarily.<br>• Nothing of any consequence resulted from Susan's report, and after a few family counseling sessions, Bev returned home.<br>• Susan was chastised by her family for making the sexual abuse a public affair and Linda appeared more concerned that the family would be subjected to public embarrassment than protecting her daughter.<br>• Unfortunately for Susan, with Bev back in the house, the sexual molestation continued. | • On October 10, 1991, the Smiths' first son, Michael, was born. David and Susan showered the child with love and attention.<br>• But having a child could not help the differences in the newlywed's backgrounds which began to put a strain on their relationship.<br>• Susan was more materialistic than David and often turned to her mother for financial help.<br>• David found Linda to be intrusive and controlling and resented Susan always doing what Linda wanted her to do, especially when it came to raising Michael. By March 1992, the Smiths were separated, and over the next 7 months, they tried to mend the marriage.<br>• During the breakups, Susan dated a former boyfriend from work which did not help matters.<br>• In November 1992, Susan announced she was pregnant again which seemed to bring David and her into clearer focus, and the two reunited.<br>• The couple borrowed money from Susan's mother for a down payment on a house, believing having their own home would fix their troubles. But over the next 9 months, Susan became more distant and complained continuously about being pregnant.<br>• In June 1993, David felt lonely and isolated in his marriage and began a relationship with a coworker.<br>• After the birth of their second child, Alexander Tyler, on August 5, 1993, David and Susan reunited, but within 3 weeks, David had once again moved out, and the two decided the relationship was over.<br>• Regardless of their broken marriage, both David and Susan were good, attentive, and caring parents who seemed to enjoy the children.<br>• On October 17, 1994, just days before David and Susan's divorce papers were filed, Tom Findlay ended his relationship with Susan through a letter.<br>• His reasons for wanting to end their relationship included the differences in their backgrounds. |

- In her senior year of high school, Susan turned to a school counselor for help. The Department of Social Service was contacted again, but Susan refused to press charges, and the matter was swiftly swept under the proverbial carpet of lawyers' agreements and sealed records, which protected Bev and the family from the feared public humiliation.
- During the summer of 1988, Susan got a job at the local Winn-Dixie grocery store and moved quickly up the ranks from cashier to bookkeeper.
- In her senior year at high school, she was sexually active with three men—a married older man who worked at the store, a younger coworker, and with Bev. Susan became pregnant and had an abortion. The married man ended their relationship, and her reaction to the breakup was to attempt suicide by taking aspirin and Tylenol.
- While being treated in the hospital, she admitted to having tried a similar suicide attempt when she was 13 years old
- At work, another relationship was beginning to form with the coworker and high school friend, David Smith.
- David ended his engagement with another woman and started dating Susan. The two decided to marry when Susan discovered she was pregnant.
- Susan and David Smith married on March 15, 1991, and moved into David's great-grandmother's house.
- David's parents were suffering the recent loss of another son who died from Crohn's disease just 11 days before Susan and David married.
- By May 1991, the strain of the loss of a son proved to be too much for David's parents. His father attempted suicide, and his mother left and moved to another city.
- This kind of family drama fit right into what Susan was used to, and the young couple, both very needy, spent the early months of their marriage comforting one another.

- On October 25, 1994, Susan Smith spent the day obsessing over the breakup with Tom Findlay. As the day progressed, she became increasingly upset and asked to leave work early.
- After picking up her children from daycare, she stopped to talk to a friend in a parking lot and expressed her fears over Tom's reaction to her sleeping with his father. In a last-ditch effort to sway Tom's feelings, she asked her friend to watch the children while she went to Tom's office to tell him the story was a lie.
- According to her friend, Tom did not appear happy to see Susan and quickly got her out of his office. At around 8:00 p.m., Susan put her barefooted sons in the car, strapped them in their car seats, and began driving around.
- In her confession, she stated that she wanted to die and was headed to her mother's house but decided against it.
- Instead, she drove to John D. Long Lake and drove onto a ramp, got out of the car, put the car in drive, released the brake, and watched as her car, with her children sleeping in the back seat, plunged into the lake. The car drifted out then slowly sank.
- Susan Smith ran to a nearby home and hysterically knocked on the door. She told the homeowners, Shirley and Rick McCloud, that a black man had taken her car and her two boys.
- She described how she had stopped at a red light at Monarch Mills when a man with a gun jumped into her car and told her to drive. She drove around some, and then he told her to stop and get out of the car.
- At that point, he told her he wouldn't hurt the kids and then drove off with the boys who she could hear were crying out for her.
- Before breaking the news of Susan's confession, Wells wanted to locate the bodies of the boys.
- A previous search of the lake had failed to turn up Susan's car, but after her confession, she gave police the exact distance the car had floated out before it sank. Divers found the car turned upside down, with the children dangling from their car seats. One diver described that he saw the small hand of one of the children pressed against a window. Also found in the car was the breakup letter Tom Findlay had written.
- An autopsy of the children proved that both boys were still alive when their tiny heads were submerged under water.
  - https://www.thoughtco.com/susan-smith-profile-of-child-killer-972686

(continued)

**Female murderers** (continued)

| Name | Early life | Crimes |
|---|---|---|
| Jodi Arias | <ul><li>She was born on July 9, 1980, in Salinas, California. She had a stable home.</li><li>She has four siblings: an older half-sister, two younger brothers, and a sister.</li><li>She lived with her father and two siblings.</li><li>She was described as a quiet, good, intelligent student who took passion in photography.</li><li>Claimed to be abused since the age of 7, said her parents would hit her with belts and wooden spoons.</li><li>Started to become rebellious during teenage years:<ul><li>At age 14, she got caught growing marijuana on the roof and to teach her a lesson, her parents called the cops on her.</li><li>She started to have an obsession with always having a boyfriend. Dropped out of high school in the 11th grade and moved in with her current boyfriend.</li></ul></li><li>She continued to pursue photography career while also maintaining several part-time jobs.</li><li>Her mother stated how Jodi had shown signs of mental issues and that her friends would call saying how Jodi needs to receive help.</li><li>In September 2006, she met Travis Alexander through a sales conference for her current job, Prepaid Legal Services.</li><li>Jodi believed being with Travis would help her find herself because he was a Mormon.</li><li>She then decided to become a Mormon and had Travis as her sponsor.</li><li>She broke up with her boyfriend of 4 years right after she met Travis.</li><li>Travis lived in Arizona, while she lived in California.</li><li>Mainly a long distant relationship, she would meet up to have dates.</li><li>Their relationship lasted a few months, yet they maintained sexual relations after breakup.</li><li>She moved around only constantly after their breakup. First moved closer to Travis in Arizona to maintain a sexual relationship; one year later, she moved back home to California.</li></ul> | <ul><li>On June 9, 2008, Travis Alexander's body was found in a pool of blood in the shower of his home in Mesa, Arizona.</li><li>Friends discover his body after realizing he's been MIA for about a week.</li><li>He was stabbed over two dozen times and had a deeply, widely slit throat.</li><li>A .25-caliber was used to shoot him in the head.</li><li>He was almost decapitated because his throat was deeply cut from ear to ear.</li></ul><ul><li>https://www.biography.com/people/jodi-arias-21221959</li><li>https://www.psychologytoday.com/us/blog/reading-between-the-headlines/201303/is-jodi-arias-sociopath</li><li>Who is Jodi Arias? Everything You Need to Know. (n.d.). Retrieved from https://www.thefamouspeople.com/profiles/jodi-arias-30978.php</li><li>Press, A. (2013, April 05). Jodi Arias trial: Her parents say their daughter had 'mental problems' as she is tried for murder in Arizona. Retrieved from https://www.dailymail.co.uk/news/article-2304338/Jodi-Arias-trial-Her-parents-say-daughter-mental-problems-tried-murder-Arizona.html</li><li>https://www.youtube.com/watch?v=OMSI2qQ5EX0</li><li>https://www.thoughtco.com/profile-of-jodi-arias-971055</li></ul> |

| Lisa Montgomery | • She was born on February 27, 1968, in Kansas.<br>• She was sexually and physically abused by her stepfather.<br>• At age 16, her parents divorced, and she was blamed for the separation.<br>• She married her stepbrother, Carl Bowman, in 1986 when she was only 18 and had three kids with him from 1987 to 1990.<br>• In 1990, she underwent tubal ligation surgery.<br>• She divorced Bowman and married Kevin Montgomery in 2000.<br>• In 2002, she told friends and family she was receiving prenatal treatment but never let her husband attend to appointments.<br>• Once her due date passed, she told her husband the baby died and she donated its body to science. | • Montgomery met Stinnett online in a dog breeding chatroom, posing as "Darlene Fischer."<br>• Montgomery told Stinnett that she, too, was pregnant.<br>• The two women chatted online and exchanged e-mails about their pregnancies.<br>• Montgomery then arranged a meeting at Stinnett's home under the pretext of wanting to buy a dog.<br>• On December 16, 2004, Montgomery strangled the pregnant woman with a pink neon rope in her home in Skidmore, Missouri, and cut the premature infant from her womb.<br>• She later attempted to pass the infant girl off as her own child.<br>• Stinnett was discovered by her mother, Becky Harper, in a pool of blood about an hour after the assault.<br>• Harper immediately called 911, describing the wounds inflicted upon her daughter as appearing as if her "stomach had exploded."<br>• Attempts by paramedics to revive Stinnett were unsuccessful, and she was pronounced dead at St. Francis Hospital in Maryville, Missouri.<br>• The next day, December 17, 2004, Montgomery was at her farmhouse when she was arrested.<br>• After Montgomery's capture by police, the day-old baby was recovered.<br>• Victoria Jo Stinnett was returned to the care of her father, Zeb Stinnett.<br>  o http://murderpedia.org/female.M/m/montgomery-lisa.htm<br>  o http://www.digitaljournal.com/article/252727 |
| Casey Anthony | • Born on March 19, 1986, in Warren, Ohio, Casey Anthony was one of two children of Cindy and George Anthony, with George having worked in law enforcement.<br>• Casey was a bright, personable young girl with friends and what many thought was an ordinary American family. | • Over the ensuing weeks, Cindy called her daughter to check on Caylee. Each time, Casey told her the little girl was out with a babysitter, Zenaida "Zanny" Fernandez-Gonzalez.<br>• On July 13, 2008, Cindy and George Anthony received a letter saying that Casey's car was in a tow yard. |

(continued)

**Female murderers** (continued)

| Name | Early life | Crimes |
|---|---|---|
| | • However, friends say that a pattern of lying began when Casey was in high school. Cindy and George attended Casey's graduation, along with Casey's grandparents—only to discover that she was several credits short of graduating.<br>• Casey had stopped attending classes toward the end of the school year but led her family to believe she would walk with the graduating class.<br>• When she was 19, Casey gave her family yet another shock.<br>• She had put on weight, and her parents suspected she was pregnant. Casey denied it, claiming she was a virgin.<br>• Months into her pregnancy, she told her parents the truth. The identity of the baby's father, however, remained a mystery.<br>• Casey pointed to different men, including her fiancé, Jesse Grund, as well as a young man she had dated previously, who had died in a car crash. On August 9, 2005, Caylee Anthony was born.<br>• A friend of Casey's said that she had discussed giving the baby up for adoption but was discouraged by her mother.<br>• For the next few years, Casey and Caylee lived with her parents, and Grund acted as the baby's father.<br>• Grund even believed Caylee might be his baby, despite knowing that the timing of her conception made it improbable. A DNA test would later find that Grund was not Caylee's father. The identity of Caylee's father remained unknown.<br>• In mid-June 2008, with her suitability as a mother called into question by Cindy, Casey left her parents' home after a major argument, taking Caylee with her. | • When George went to pick the car up, he found Casey's purse, along with Caylee's car seat and toys.<br>• George noticed a strong smell, like that of organic matter decomposing, coming from the trunk.<br>• Alarmed, Cindy found Casey at the home of her boyfriend, Tony Lazaro, and brought her home.<br>• Casey broke down, telling her mother and brother Lee that she had left Caylee with nanny Zenaida Fernandez-Gonzalez in Orlando on June 16 and that Gonzalez had kidnapped the toddler.<br>• On July 15, 31 days after 2-year-old Caylee's disappearance, Cindy Anthony reported her missing to the Orange County Sheriff's Office.<br>• After questioning Casey, detectives found discrepancies in a signed statement she made about Caylee's disappearance. Casey's friends and family had never heard of Gonzales, and detectives later discovered that, in fact, there was no nanny.<br>• The investigators caught Casey in another lie when she told them she worked at Universal Studios, even leading them around the theme park.<br>• Casey finally admitted she had never returned to work for Universal. She was arrested on July 16.<br>• As the search for Caylee intensified, Casey Anthony came under increasing scrutiny for her actions in the days before Caylee was reported missing—including partying and, in early July, getting a tattoo that reads "Bella Vita," or "beautiful life" in Italian.<br>• Casey returned home on August 21, when bounty hunter/reality TV figure Leonard Padilla posted $500,000 in bail.<br>• Padilla hoped Casey would lead detectives to find Caylee, but he was disappointed when she failed to provide additional clues.<br>• Padilla labeled Casey narcissistic and promiscuous, fueling the fires of public sentiment against the young woman.<br>• Casey Anthony was back in jail only 8 days after being released for identity theft and check forgery.<br>• She was found not guilty on July 5, 2011.<br>  ○ https://www.biography.com/people/casey-anthony-20660183 |

| Sheila Eddy and Rachel Shoaf | • Shelia Rae Eddy (born September 28, 1995) is the only child of Tara Clendenen and Greg Eddy. Shelia was born in Blacksville, West Virginia. Her parents divorced in 2000 when her father got into a car accident that left him with a traumatic brain injury and permanent disability.<br>• Tara struggled as a single mother, working as an accountant for a car dealership. In October 2010, Tara and Shelia moved with Tara's new husband, Jim Clendenen, to Morgantown, West Virginia.<br>• Rachel Shoaf (born June 10, 1996) grew up in Morgantown. She is the only daughter of Rusty and Patricia Shoaf.<br>• Both perpetrators attended University High School along with their victim.<br>• The trio was inseparable and Skylar allegedly served as an emotional rock for the other two girls, as both Eddy and Shoaf came from parents of divorce.<br>• Skylar Neese was an only child, and her parents wanted everything for her. They nurtured her intelligence and encouraged her to be her own person. Eddy, then, was the fun-loving girl in the trio, and David and Mary Neese treated her as if she was one of their own. "Shelia didn't even knock on the door when she came over, she just came on in."<br>• Shoaf, on the other hand, was the opposite of Eddy. Though she was well liked and enjoyed being in school plays, she came from a strict Catholic family and idolized Eddy for her somewhat wild and free attitude.<br>• Neese first met Eddy when the two were in elementary school, and Shoaf arrived during their freshman year of high school. Though Neese and Eddy had formerly been inseparable, Shoaf's arrival allegedly drove a wedge between them. She and Neese began competing to be closest to Eddy, who enjoyed the attention. | • Not only did Eddy and Shoaf plan Neese's murder, but they also outfitted the trunk of Eddy's car with a "serial killer kit" consisting of towels, bleach, a shovel, and a change of clothes for each of them.<br>• In addition, they packed the knives they used to kill Neese. Both girls wore hooded sweatshirts while they stabbed their friend to death.<br>• Their plan was to kill Neese, dispose of her body, change their clothes, and head back home as if nothing had happened.<br>• Following their plan, Eddy and Shoaf drove Neese to a secluded location in Pennsylvania where they frequently went to smoke and hang out.<br>• There, Eddy and Shoaf counted to three and attacked Neese with knives on July 6, 2012. They reportedly stabbed her dozens of times until she stopped making "weird sounds."<br>• After they murdered Neese, Eddy and Shoaf planned to bury her body using the shovel they brought along. However, they found the ground was too rocky for them to make a dent in it. Instead, they dragged Neese's body to a secluded area of the woods next to a large tree and covered her with branches. This is where Neese's body laid for more than 6 months.<br>• Shoaf and Eddy eventually pleaded guilty to Neese's murder, and West Virginia courts tried them as adults.<br>• Shoaf received a sentence of between 10 and 30 years for second-degree murder, while courts charged Eddy with first-degree murder and sentenced her to 15 years to life in prison.<br>  ◦ https://en.wikipedia.org/wiki/Murder_of_Skylar_Neese<br>  ◦ https://www.ranker.com/list/murder-of-skylar-neese/amandasedlakhevener<br>  ◦ https://allthatsinteresting.com/skylar-neese-shelia-eddy |

(continued)

606

**Female murderers**  (continued)

| Name | Early life | Crimes |
|---|---|---|
| Anissa Weier and Morgan Geyser | • Both Weier and Geyser were obsessed with the character, who is often depicted in fan fiction stories online as a horror figure who stalks children.<br>• Anissa's parents were divorced.<br>• Both girls' mothers told "20/20" that they never saw any warning signs from their daughters that they would harm someone else.<br>• "They [Morgan and Payton] would sit up in Morgan's room and they would do each other's nails, and they would laugh, and make a mess," Angie Geyser said. "They were just typical girls."<br>• Morgan's mother said she knew about her daughter's fascination with Slender Man and talked about it with her.<br>• "She would show us some of the pictures, and she would read us some of the stories, and while some of the subject matter was a little dark, I wasn't concerned," Angie Geyser said.<br>• "When I was Morgan's age, I was reading Stephen King novels. I remember being 11 years old and riding home from the library with [the book] *IT* under my arm. And that's a very scary and dark story, so I just thought it was normal for a child of middle school age to be interested in scary stories."<br>• But Anissa's mother, Kristi Weier, said her daughter "never mentioned anything to me about her belief in Slender Man."<br>• Morgan struggled with mental illness.<br>• Morgan received an extraordinarily rare diagnosis for such a young girl: early onset schizophrenia.<br>• Morgan's father has schizophrenia. In fact, according to testimony, Morgan's father had been hospitalized at least four times as a teenager to treat his own schizophrenia.<br>• Morgan had been experiencing visual hallucinations since she was 3 years old.<br>• "One of her hallucinations was a tall, slender, shadowy figure," Geyser said. "And I think that's probably what ultimately solidified her belief in Slender Man."<br>• Anissa was diagnosed with a "shared psychotic disorder." | • The girls revealed they had been planning the attack on Payton for more than 5 months, with Morgan saying "it was necessary" to please "Slender Man."<br>• The girls told police they had originally planned to stab Payton in Morgan's room at the sleepover but changed the plan to stab her in the park the next day instead.<br>• The two then 12-year-old girls, Anissa Weier and Morgan Geyser, were arrested on May 31, 2014, for stabbing then 12-year-old Payton Leutner, with the intent to kill her to appease the online fictional character, "Slender Man."<br>• The victim had been stabbed 19 times.<br>• Payton, now 15, crawled to a nearby road and was helped by a passing bicyclist before she was hospitalized with life-threatening injuries. She survived the attack.<br>• Morgan felt no remorse.<br>• In the aftermath of the stabbing, investigators searched Morgan's room and found disturbing evidence of a deteriorating young mind, which included drawings of Slender Man with children and the words, "I want to die," and "help me escape my mind" scrawled across a page.<br>    ○   https://abcnews.go.com/US/mothers-teens-pleaded-guilty-slender-man-stabbing-case/story?id=52739807 |

**Spree killers/murderers**

| Name | Early life | Crimes |
|---|---|---|
| Charles Manson | • Charles Manson was born November 12, 1934, in Cincinnati, Ohio. His mother was 16 at the time of his birth, and he never knew his father.<br>• His mother was described as an alcoholic and a criminal. She was arrested for armed robbery when Charles was 9 years old, forcing him to move in with an aunt and uncle in West Virginia.<br>• Manson stated that he had another uncle who lived in the Kentucky Mountains. He told him that "they were still rebels" and that school was no good. This uncle most likely began to influence his racist attitudes that would show later in his life. Manson then attempted to set his school on fire and was sent to reformatory school.<br>• Reportedly, he was sold as a child by his mother for a pitch of beer.<br>• He was under the care of multiple people who all were bad experiences.<br>• At age 13, Manson committed his first serious crime of armed robbery and was sent to the Indiana School for Boys. In the same documentary, he reported being raped and beaten at this school and that he ran away 18 times. He also was found being the perpetrator of the rape of another young boy.<br>• He committed petty crimes when he was younger, such as stealing; in 1947, at 12 years old, Manson is sent to Gibault School for stealing. Over the next 20 years, he was in and out of reform schools and prison. | • Manson exited his first juvenile facility at the age of 10 and attempted to live with his mother again; this was unsuccessful.<br>• His crime picked up after this event, and he was eventually sent to a reformatory school where he escaped 3 days later.<br>• Manson was paroled at age 19 in 1954, but by 1961, he was serving a 10-year sentence for check forgery.<br>• From 1956 to 1966, he was in and out of prison:<br>  ○ He stole cars, had his probation revoked, pimped, stole checks, and committed crimes cross state lines.<br>• During this prison stay, he began to study various religious teachings including scientology, as well as continue to study music.<br>• In this period, he began to desire to become a superstar and was heavily influenced by the Beatles and the effects they had on the world.<br>• Manson was released after 7 years on parole and made his way to San Francisco where the counter culture movement was underway.<br>• He became heavily involved in psychedelic drugs and the counterculture (hippie) movement, which provided him with a platform to attract his followers.<br>• He carried out more than 30 killings with his followers, with the first known murder of Gary Hinman on July 25, 1969.<br>• On August 9, 1969, Manson told his followers to kill actress Sharon Tate (who was pregnant at the time) and her husband director Roman Polanski, along with friends of theirs who were at the house.<br>• He was sentenced to death. When the death penalty was ruled unconstitutional in 1972, he was resentenced to life.<br>• He died in prison on November 19, 2017.<br>  ○ A&E. (2018, May 14). Charles Manson. Retrieved November 13, 2018, from https://www.biography.com/people/charles-manson-9397912<br>  ○ Altman, R. (2015). Sympathy for the devil: Charles Manson's exploitation of California's 1960s counter-culture (Undergraduate Honors Theses). 907. https://scholar.colorado.edu/honr_theses/90 |

(continued)

**Spree killers/murderers** (continued)

| Name | Early life | Crimes |
|---|---|---|
| | | ○ Bullis, J. E. (1985). A social-psychological case history: the Manson incident (Dissertations and Theses). Paper 3564. |
| | | ○ *Charles Manson: Helter skelter and beyond.* (n.d.). Place of publication not identified: Filiquarian Pub. LLC. |
| | | ○ Charles Manson [Interview by D. Sawyer]. (1995). *ABC NEWS.* |
| | | ○ Guinn, J. (2014). *Manson the life and times of charles manson.* New York: Simon & Schuster. |
| | | ○ Linder, D. (2007). The Charles Manson (Tate–Labianca Murder) Trial. Available at SSRN: https://ssrn.com/abstract=1029399 or https://doi.org/10.2139/ssrn.1029399 |
| | | ○ Aitchison, A. J., & Heide, K. M. (2010). Charles Manson and the Family. *International Journal of Offender Therapy and Comparative Criminology, 55*(5), 771–798. https://doi.org/10.1177/0306624x10371794 |
| | | ○ TIME-LIFE Killer Cults. (n.d.). Retrieved from https://books.google.com/books?d=9iNIDwAAQBAJ&printsec=frontcover#v=onepage&q&f=false |
| | | ○ People v. Manson. (n.d.). Retrieved from https://law.justia.com/cases/california/court-of-appeal/3d/61/102.html |
| | | ○ Fine, G. (1982). The manson family: The Folklore Traditions of a Small Group. *Journal of the Folklore Institute, 19*(1), 47–60. https://doi.org/10.2307/3813962 |

| Charlie Starkweather and Caril Fugate | |
|---|---|
| • A child of the Great Depression era, Charles Raymond Starkweather was born on November 24, 1938, in Lincoln, Nebraska, the third of seven children of parents Guy and Helen. | • In the early hours of December 1, 1957, Charlie took his first victim, gas station attendant Robert Colvert, for $100. |
| • The Starkweathers were a respectable family with well-behaved children; although his family was of working-class background, the family always had shelter and other resources. | • In 1957, aged 19, Charlie committed his first murder. On November 30, he went to a gas station and tried to buy a stuffed dog toy for Fugate. |
| • Charlie was born with genu varum, a mild birth defect that caused his legs to be misshapen. | • When he found that he wasn't carrying enough money, the manager, Robert Colvert, refused to let him buy it on credit and threw him out. |
| • He also suffered from a speech impediment, which led to constant teasing by classmates. | • At 3:00 a.m. the next day, he returned with a shotgun. First, he entered the store twice and bought first a package of cigarettes and then a package of chewing gum. |
| • He was considered a slow learner and was accused of never applying himself, although in his teens it was discovered that he suffered from severe myopia that had drastically affected his vision for most of his life. | • The third time, he came in dressed with a bandanna and a hat to cover his face and held him at gunpoint with the shotgun. |
| • The sole aspect of school in which Charlie excelled was gym. | • After forcing him to open the store's safe and robbing it, he forced Colvert outside to his own car, made him drive to a nearby remote area, and shot and killed him. |
| • It was gym class wherein he found a physical outlet for his growing rage against those who bullied him. | • On January 21, 1958, Charlie drove to Caril Ann Fugate's house, where he was denied entry by her mother and stepfather, Velda and Marion Bartlett. |
| • Charlie used his newfound physicality to begin bullying those who had once bullied him, and soon his rage stretched beyond those who had bullied him to anyone whom he happened to dislike. | • Following an altercation, he killed both of them, as well as Fugate's 2-year-old half-sister, Betty Jean. |
| • Charlie left school at the age of 16, taking work as a lorry loader for a local newspaper business. | • Charlie and Caril Ann lived in the house for 6 days, telling visitors that the rest of the family was bedridden with the flu; they fled after other family members grew suspicious. |
| • Inspired by the 1955 James Dean movie *Rebel Without a Cause*, he tried to emulate the look and style of its star. | • Charlie drove to the farm of a family friend named August Meyer and killed him, though his car got stuck on the property. |
| • He also became romantically involved with a kindred rebellious spirit, Caril Ann Fugate, who was only 13 years old at the time. | • He and his girlfriend hitched a ride with another teenage couple, Robert Jensen and Carole King, eventually killing them as well and taking the car. |
| • At some point, Caril crashed his car, a 1949 Ford, while he was teaching her how to drive. | • The next day, by which time they had already left the area, the duo's old car, which had gotten stuck in the mud, was found along with the bodies of Meyer and the teenagers. |
| • Guy Starkweather, who was the legal owner of the car, paid for the damages and threw Charles out of the household, no longer willing to put up with his behavior. | • Charles and Caril Ann then fled to a wealthier part of Lincoln with Jensen's car and attacked the home of a wealthy industrialist named C. Lauer Ward. |

(continued)

**Spree killers/murderers** (continued)

| Name | Early life | Crimes |
|---|---|---|
| | • Charles then quit his job at the warehouse and became a garbage collector, using his route to plan bank robberies (though he never actually carried them out).<br>• Charlie later lost his job as a garbage collector and was evicted from where he lived because he couldn't pay his rent.<br><br>• Caril Ann Fugate was born on July 30, 1943 in Lincoln, Nebraska, to William Fugate and Velda Bartlett and had an elder sister named Barbara. Her mother later married Marion Bartlett and had another daughter named Betty Jean. | • Only his wife, Clara Ward, and their maid, Lillian, were home at the time.<br>• After killing Ward and one of the household's two dogs, they forced her to make them breakfast.<br>• When Mr. Ward himself came home that afternoon, he was shot to death. She was then tied to a bed and killed as well.<br>• When Charlie and Caril Ann realized that the Packard they were driving would attract attention, they approached a Buick owned by Merle Collison, a traveling salesman, near the highway close to Douglas, Wyoming, shot him to death, stole the vehicle, and drove away.<br>  ○ https://www.biography.com/people/charles-starkweather-233080<br>  ○ https://criminalminds.fandom.com/wiki/Charles_Starkweather_and_Caril_Ann_Fugate<br>  ○ https://www.thefamouspeople.com/profiles/caril-ann-fugate-34201.php/<br>  ○ http://murderpedia.org/male.S/s/starkweather.htm |
| Robert Chambers | • Born on September 25, 1966, Robert Chambers was raised by his mother, Phyllis (née Shanley), a nurse who emigrated from County Leitrim in Ireland to New York City.<br>• He served as an altar boy and attended a series of prep schools on scholarship, since his mother could not afford to pay private school tuition.<br>• Chambers did not prosper in an environment in which many of his classmates were considerably better off than he and had problems with poor grades and antisocial behavior, including stealing and drug abuse.<br>• Among the schools he attended were Saint David's School (New York City), Choate-Rosemary Hall, The Browning School, and ultimately York Preparatory School.<br>• Chambers also attended Wilbraham Junior High in Massachusetts during middle school.<br>• Chambers was accepted by Boston University, where he completed one semester but was asked to leave because of difficulties, one involving a stolen credit card. He subsequently committed other petty thefts and burglaries in connection with his drug and alcohol abuse. | • Chambers's girlfriend, Alex Kapp, publicly broke up with him at Dorrian's Red Hand bar on the night of Levin's death.<br>• Kapp was heard to express jealousy regarding the presence of Jennifer Levin, Chambers' secret lover, throwing a bag of condoms at him and yelling, "You can take these back because you're not using them with me!" as she ended the relationship. Chambers subsequently left the bar with Levin.<br>• Levin's strangled, half-naked corpse, covered in bruises, bite marks, and cuts, was found by a bicyclist beneath an elm tree on a grassy knoll near Fifth Avenue and 83rd Street, behind the Metropolitan Museum of Art.<br>• Her bra and shirt were pushed up to her neck, and her skirt was around her waist.<br>• The city medical examiner's office said that Levin had died of "asphyxia by strangulation," and police officials had said that there were numerous bruises on her neck, both from the strangulation and from her own fingernails as she clawed at her killer's hands.<br>• Later, Chambers watched from nearby as police officers investigated the scene. The investigators had found Levin's panties some 50 yards (46 m) away. |

| | | |
|---|---|---|
| | • Unable to hold a job, he was issued a summons for disorderly conduct one night after leaving the Upper East Side bar Dorrian's Red Hand, located at 300 East 84th Street in Manhattan.<br>• He later entered and was discharged from the Hazelden Clinic in Minnesota, an addiction treatment center.<br>• He lived with his mother in an apartment in a townhouse at 11 East 90th Street. | • Police were given Chambers' name by patrons at the bar, who had seen him leaving with Levin. When authorities arrived to question him at his home, he had fresh scratches on his face and arms, which he initially said were "cat scratches."<br>  ○ http://murderpedia.org/male.C/c/chambers-robert.htm |
| The Menendez Brothers | • Joseph Lyle Menendez was born on January 10, 1968, in New York City; Erik Galen Menendez, was born November 27, 1970, in Blackwood, New Jersey, to Jose and Mary "Kitty" Menendez.<br>• Jose, a Cuban immigrant, had made himself into a successful entertainment executive, and he exerted tremendous pressure on his boys to succeed as well.<br>• Shy and quiet, Erik grew up emulating his older brother, Lyle.<br>• After the family moved to Southern California in 1986, the boys fell in with more of a troublemaking crowd, and Erik was twice nabbed for burglary in 1988.<br>• In 1987, Lyle returned to New Jersey to attend Princeton University for a year until he was caught for plagiarism.<br>• He also took an interest in screenwriting, ominously creating a script about a son who murders his wealthy parents.<br>• The boys later claimed that they were sexually abused by their father. | • On August 20, 1989 when Lyle was 18 and Erik was 21, they entered the family room of their parents' Beverly Hills mansion and shot their parents Jose and Kitty Menendez a total of 15 times.<br>• Murders were gruesome and violent:<br>  – Wounds at the knees.<br>  – Jose had six wounds inflicted by a 12-gauge shotgun.<br>  – Kitty had ten wounds.<br>• Lyle called 911 and reported the murder saying "someone killed my parents!"<br>• Their alibi was that they were at the movies.<br>• Police initially suspected a Mafia hit.<br>• Early reports of the crime scene describe it as a "gangland-style killing."<br>• Police broke protocol at the crime scene, which compromised the investigation early on: Lyle and Erik performed grief so convincingly that the first responders thought it unnecessary to test their hands and clothing for gunshot residue.<br>• Though they were questioned the night of the murders, police didn't sit down with Lyle and Erik for a formal interview until 2 months after the killing.<br>• For 6 months, they went undetected, traveling, shopping, and partying. |

(continued)

**Spree killers/murderers** (continued)

| Name | Early life | Crimes |
| --- | --- | --- |
|  |  | • Confession came after Erik admitted what he had done to his therapist. Therapists mistress overhead and called the police.<br>• The boys were arrested on March 8 and March 11, 1990.<br>　○ https://www.townandcountrymag.com/society/money-and-power/a12231370/menendez-brothers-murders-trial-why-they-did-it-story/<br>　○ Heide, K. M. (1995). Dangerously antisocial youths who kill their parents. *Journal of Police and Criminal Psychology, 10*(4), 10–14. https://doi.org/10.1007/BF02812864.<br>　○ Mosteller, R. P. (1996). Syndromes and politics in criminal trials and evidence law. *Duke Law Journal, 46*(3), 461. https://doi.org/10.2307/1372940.<br>　○ Mulvey, A., Fournier, A., & Donahue, T. (2006). Murder in the family: The Menendez Brothers. *Victims & Offenders, 1*(3), 213–224. https://doi.org/10.1080/15564880600843677.<br>　○ https://www.biography.com/people/lyle-menendez-10367565 |

**Serial killers**

| Name | Early life | Crimes |
|---|---|---|
| John George Haigh, a.k.a. "The Acid Bath Murderer" | • Haigh was born in 1909 and raised in a highly religious household. | • As the years passed by, Haigh racked up several prison sentences for fraud. In 1936, he moved to London and found work from William McSwann, a wealthy amusement park owner, both as a chauffeur and as a repairman of his park machines. |
| | • His parents, John Robert and Emily, were both members of the Plymouth Brethren, an ultra-puritanical, highly conservative Christian sect. | • They found that they had some interests in common and struck up a friendship. McSwann's parents, Donald and Amy, met Haigh and approved of him immediately. |
| | • His father, who set up a tall fence around the family house in order to lock out the outside world, had a mark on his forehead which he told his son had been branded on him by God as punishment for a past sin and that he too would get marked if he sinned. | • He was then sentenced to 4 years in prison for posing as a lawyer. Less than a year after finishing the sentence, he was arrested again for theft of goods and sentenced to 21 months in prison. |
| | • When John did in fact commit minor sins in the form of pranks and petty thefts and was not marked, he realized that it was in fact possible to commit crimes and go unpunished and grew up a cynic. | • It was during this prison sentence that he began planning a perfect crime. He took a particular interest in the legal term "corpus delicti," a law which basically states that it must be proven that a crime has been committed in order for an accused to be convicted of it (Black's Law Dictionary defines it as "the fact of a crime having actually been committed"). |
| | • John was also told that his mother could not be marked because she was an "angel." | • Haigh, somewhat loosely, interpreted the law as simply "No body, no crime." His fellow inmates even took to calling him "Ol' Corpus Delicti." |
| | • He kept several pets which he cared for deeply, even holding the lives of animals in higher esteem than those of humans. | • In prison, he experimented with disposal of bodies in acid, completely dissolving a rat in a vat of acid in the prison workshop. |
| | • After finishing school, where he kept to himself, he became a car mechanic. Though he loved cars, he absolutely detested dirt and always wore gloves for hygiene purposes. | • After being released from prison for the last time in his life, he set his plan in motion. He rented a workshop at 79 Gloucester Road, London SW7, and placed a 40-gallon (ca. 141 liters) vat of sulfuric acid inside. |
| | • Because it was such dirty work, he left after only a year and became a clerk at the Wakefield Education Community but didn't like that job either. | • His crimes committed from 1944 to 1949. |
| | • John found a career in advertising but was soon arrested as a suspect in the theft of a cash box but was released. | • On September 9, 1944, he lured McSwann to the building, killed him, and placed the body in the vat. After 2 days, the body had completely dissolved, and the sludgy remains were poured down a manhole. |
| | • On July 6, 1934, he married Beatrice Hammer, whom he barely knew. Though his parents disapproved of their union, they allowed them to stay with them. | • Haigh convinced McSwann's parents that he had run off to Scotland to avoid being drafted into the war. He even forged postcards from their son and sent them from Scotland to keep up the illusion. |
| | • A mere 4 months later, John was convicted of fraud for a hire-purchase agreement scam, and they divorced. | • In 1945, after the war had ended, the McSwanns sought Haigh out again. He lured them to his workshop, killed them the same way he had killed their son, and disposed of their bodies the same way as well. |

(continued)

**Serial killers** (continued)

| Name | Early life | Crimes |
|---|---|---|
| | • Hammer later gave birth to his daughter, whom she immediately put up for adoption.<br>• After serving his sentence, John, who lived on as though he had never even been married, ran a dry-cleaning business, which went quite well until his business partner died in a motorcycle accident and World War II began, leading to a decline in business.<br>• He continued committing fraud, forging people's signatures to pay for fake car purchases, before being arrested again and sentenced to 15 months in prison. | • He then forged letters that allowed him to take possession of their estate. Haigh lived off the wealth he got out of the three murders for 3 years.<br>• When the money ran out, he approached another couple, the Hendersons, built a relationship with them over the course of 5 months, lured them to his new workshop on 2 Leopold Road in Crawley, West Sussex, shot and killed them with Dr. Henderson's own .38 Webley service revolver, and dissolved their remains.<br>• After taking over their fortune and spending it in only a year, Haigh pursued yet another victim, a wealthy widow by the name of Olive Durand-Deacon. On February 18, she too was lured to his workshop and shot with a .38 Enfield revolver.<br>• Haigh then took her personal belongings, including her expensive Persian lamb coat, and placed her body in an acid vat.<br>• She was reported missing by a friend 2 days later as well as by Haigh, who fabricated a story that the two had arranged a meeting for which Durand-Deacon never showed up.<br>• When the investigators discovered that Haigh had a long criminal record for fraud, forgery, and theft, he quickly became a suspect.<br>• They searched his workshop and found an attaché case with Haigh's initials, paperwork linking him to the McSwann's and the Henderson's and, a dry cleaner's receipt for Durand-Deacon's coat.<br>• A jewelry store owner also recognized him as the man who had pawned a piece of jewelry belonging to Durand-Deacon the day after her disappearance.<br>• In a more damning scenario, the acid vats also yielded evidence in the form of a great amount of human fat, three human gall stones, fragments of human bones and dentures, and the handle of a red plastic bag and a lipstick container.<br>• After being arrested, Haigh began confessing to his crimes, not just the six murders to which he had been tied but also three additional murders which were never confirmed. |

| | |
|---|---|
| | • He smugly challenged the police to prove his guilt, counting on the absence of a body getting him cleared. He was proven to have made a mistake in his planning and was charged with his six confirmed murders. |
| | • Claiming insanity, he said he had drunk the blood of his victims using a straw before dissolving their bodies and also to have been afflicted by blood-related and sometimes religious nightmares since childhood. |
| | • Another claim was that his craving for human blood had been awakened when he was in a car accident in 1944. He was tested by a dozen of medical examiners, most of who came to the conclusion that he was sane but feigning insanity. |
| | • At the trial, which involved 33 witnesses, Haigh pleaded not guilty. It only took the jury a quarter of an hour to find him otherwise. He was held at the Wandsworth Prison until he was taken to the gallows and hanged on August 10, 1949. <br> ○ https://criminalminds.fandom.com/wiki/John_George_Haigh |
| Ed Gein, a.k.a. "The Plainfield Ghoul" | • Bernice Worden disappeared from her hardware store in November 1957; the store had signs of a forced entry. <br> • Ed Gein was a frequent customer at her hardware store and was seen there the day before. <br> • That night of November 16, 1957, the police headed out to Ed's isolated farm and found the body of Bernice Worden hanging upside down, inside his woodshed, missing her head and gutted similar to a deer carcass. <br> • Ed Gein was taken into custody immediately while police searched his woodshed and home where they found scattered throughout the house human remains: <br> ○ Bowls made from human skulls <br> ○ Bracelets made from body parts <br> ○ Lamp shade made from human skin <br> ○ Furniture covered in human skin |
| • Edward Theodore Gein was born in LaCrosse, Wisconsin, on July 27, 1906, and raised on an isolated farm in Plainville Wisconsin. <br> • He lived with his one brother, Henry, and his parents, George and Augusta. <br> • His mother was a strong-willed God-fearing housewife, and the father was described as having a drinking problem. <br> • His mother was an extremely overbearing and domineering mother. <br> • As a child, Ed was bullied in school due to a slight growth on one eye. <br> • His mother would scold him for trying to make friends at school and preach from the book of revelation, stating women were out to hurt people. He would listen to her and worship her and follow her very closely. | |

(continued)

**Serial killers** (continued)

| Name | Early life | Crimes |
|---|---|---|
| | • He finished school at seventh grade and then continued to work on the farm.<br>• His father passed away of heart failure, and his brother Henry in May 1944 passed away from a brush fire near the property.<br>• Although he claimed to not know where his brother was, he was able to lead police right to his body.<br>• His mother suffered a stroke months later and became paralyzed; Ed was left alone to care for her. In December of 1945, she suffered a second stroke and passed away leaving Ed alone as the only member of his family still alive.<br>• At 39, he was left alone to live on his isolated farm on the outskirts of Plainfield. | ○ Chairs upholstered in human skin<br>○ Face masks hung on the wall from individuals<br>• They found the face of a local bar owner, Mary Hogan, who had been missing for 3 years. Behind a doorway, they noticed a room kept in perfect condition and found it was the room of his deceased mother.<br>○ Borowski, J. (2006). *The Ed Gein file: A psycho's confession and case documents cardiff*. California: Waterfront Productions.<br>○ Dr. Ewing, C. (2008). *Insanity: Murder, Madness, and the Law*. Oxford, England: Oxford University Press.<br>○ Gollmar, R. (1989). *Edward Gein: America's Most Bizarre Murderer*. Minnesota: Pinnacle Publishing. |
| Patrick Wayne Kearney, a.k.a. "The Trash-Bag Killer" | • He was born in East Los Angeles, California, on September 24, 1939.<br>• Kearney was the oldest of three sons and was raised in a stable family. However, because of his appearance, he was a victim of bullying at a young age.<br>• As a teenager, Kearney started to fantasize about killing people.<br>• He lived in Texas for a short time and eventually moved back to California, where he worked as an engineer for the Hughes Aircraft Company.<br>• In his personal life, Kearney was a skilled gay pickup artist and fluent in Spanish, attributes that would later help him during his murders.<br>• After moving to Redondo Beach, he met with a man named David Hill, and they eventually became lovers.<br>• Kearney would go out for long solitary drives after having arguments with Hill.<br>• During these drives, he would pick up male hitchhikers or homosexual men from gay bars. | • Kearney's first known murder victim was an unidentified 19-year-old man in 1962; he took him to a secluded area on his motorcycle and shot him in the head, engaging in acts of necrophilia with the man's corpse.<br>• He proceeded to kill many more victims in the next several years.<br>• Days later, the remains of a victim murdered by Kearney were found, and police discovered that he was last seen with Kearney and Hill.<br>• Both fled to El Paso, Texas, but were arrested after their families convinced them to turn themselves in.<br>• Hill was released after it was deduced that he had no involvement in the murders.<br>• Kearney confessed to 38 murders but was charged with 21 counts of murders.<br>• Police believe that he may be responsible for even more murders. Kearney pleaded guilty and subsequently avoided a death sentence. He is now incarcerated at California State Prison.<br>○ https://criminalminds.fandom.com/wiki/Patrick_Kearney |

| Pedro Rodrigues Filho, a.k.a. "Killer Petey," or "Pedrinho Matador" | • Filho was born in a farm at Santa Rita do Sapucaí, Brazil, on June 17, 1954.<br>• He was born with a damaged skull, which was indirectly inflicted by his father when he physically abused Filho's mother while she was still pregnant with him.<br>• Filho was also physically abused by his father during his childhood.<br>• Filho claimed he first felt the urge to kill at the age of 13 and claimed he attempted to murder his cousin by pushing him into a sugar cane press, but he was unsuccessful. This has yet to be confirmed. | • When Filho was 14 years old, his father was accused of stealing food from the high school kitchen where he worked as a security guard, resulting in him losing his job.<br>• In vengeance, Filho killed the vice mayor of Alfenas with a shotgun, as he was the one who fired his father.<br>• His crimes spanned from 1967 to 2003.<br>• A month later, he killed another guard at the school whom he believed to be the real thief. After killing them, he took refuge in São Paulo, where he started to burglarize local slums.<br>• He also killed a drug dealer during the burglary spree. At São Paulo, Filho met a woman, Maria Aparecida Olympia, who would later become his fiancée. At some point, she was brutally murdered by gang members.<br>• Angered by this, Filho committed a massacre during a wedding organized by the gang's leader, where he and some friends brutally killed 7 people and injured 16 others.<br>• Months after the massacre, he discovered that the boyfriend of his favorite cousin had impregnated her but refused to marry her; he fatally shot him in revenge.<br>• Later, Filho found out that his father was in prison for murdering and dismembering his mother with a machete. Filho visited his father in prison and killed him by stabbing him 22 times. After the murder, he carved his heart out and bit a piece of it.<br>• Filho continued to kill many criminals and was finally arrested on May 24, 1973. After his arrest, Filho was placed in a car with another criminal, a rapist, whom he murdered.<br>• During his incarceration, he continued to kill people in prison, claiming the lives of 47 inmates. He sometimes killed inmates because of his past as a killer of criminals, which caused a majority of the prison population to hate him. | • In one attack by other inmates, Filho was ambushed, but he killed three of his attackers and injured the other two. Other inmates were chosen randomly; one of his victims, a cellmate and career criminal, was killed simply because he snored too much.<br>• Some of his victims were killed because, according to him, the thrill of killing another criminal was wonderful and satisfying.<br>• Filho was almost released from prison in 2003, but the release request was turned down because of his murders inside prison.<br>• He was officially released on April 24, 2007, but he was arrested again at his house on September 15, 2011, and convicted of riot and false imprisonment.<br>• He admitted that his only motivation to being released was the fact that he had a girlfriend out of prison. He was later sentenced to 128 years in prison for these charges. He currently remains incarcerated.<br>   ○ https://criminalminds.fandom.com/wiki/Pedro_Rodrigues_Filho |

(continued)

**Serial killers** (continued)

| Name | Early life | Crimes |
|---|---|---|
| Jerry Brudos, a.k.a. "The Lust Killer" | • Brudos was born on January 31, 1939, in Webster, South Dakota. Reportedly, his mother had wanted a girl and often ignored and belittled him.<br>• He had a fetish for women's shoes from the age of 5 after he rescued a pair of high-heel shoes from the garbage.<br>• As he grew older, his unusual interest in shoes developed into a fetish which he satisfied by breaking into homes to steal shoes and women's underwear.<br>• When he was in his teens, he added violence to his repertoire and began knocking down girls, choking them until they were unconscious, and then stealing their shoes.<br>• At age 17, he was sent to the Oregon State Hospital psychiatric ward after he confessed to holding a girl at knife-point in a hole he dug in the side of a hill for the purpose of keeping sex slaves. There, he forced her to pose nude while he took pictures. Brudos was released from the hospital after 9 months, even though it was clear he had developed a need to act out his violent fantasies toward women. | • Between 1968 and 1969, women in and around the Portland area began to disappear.<br>• In January 1968, Linda Slawson, 19, working as a door-to-door encyclopedia salesperson, happened to knock on Brudos' door. He later confessed to killing her and then cutting off her left foot to use as a model for his collection of stolen shoes.<br>• His next victim was Jan Whitney, 23, whose car broke down while driving home from college in November 1968.<br>   Brudos later admitted to strangling Whitney in her car and then having sex with her body and bringing her corpse back to his workshop where he continued to violate the body for several days while it hung from a hook on his ceiling.<br>   Before disposing of her body, he cut off her right breast in order to make a mold from it in the hopes of making paperweights.<br>• On March 27, 1969, Karen Sprinker, 19, vanished from the parking garage of a department store where she was to meet her mother for lunch.<br>   Brudos later confessed to forcing her into his car at gunpoint and then bringing her to his workshop where he raped her and forced her to put on various women's underwear and pose for pictures. |

|  |  |  |
|---|---|---|
|  | • According to his hospital records, his violence toward women developed from a deep hatred he felt for his mother. Once out of the hospital, he finished high school and became an electronics technician.<br>• Whether he refrained from acting out on his obsessions over the next few years or he just didn't get caught is unknown.<br>• What is known is that he got married, moved to Portland, Oregon, and he and his wife had two children. His mother later joined the family in their small suburban home.<br>• Brudos' relationship with his wife began to falter after he approached her dressed in women's underwear.<br>• Up to that point, she had gone along with his strange bedroom habits, including his request that she walk around the house nude. Rejected by her lack of understanding of his need to wear women's underwear, he retreated to his workshop which was off-limits to the family.<br>• No longer intimate, the two remained married despite his wife discovering pictures of nude women and an odd molded breast among her husband's possessions. | He then killed her by hanging her from the hook in his ceiling. As with his other victims, he violated her corpse and then removed both breasts and disposed of her body.<br>• Linda Salee, 22, became Brudos' next and last known victim. In April 1969, he kidnapped her from a shopping mall, brought her to his home, and raped and then strangled her to death. Like all of his victims, he disposed of her body in a nearby lake.<br>• During the 2-year killing spree, Brudos attacked several other women who managed to escape.<br>• The clues they were able to provide police eventually led them to Brudos' door. While in custody at police headquarters, Brudos gave a detailed confession of the four murders.<br> ○ https://www.thoughtco.com/serial-killer-jerry-brudos-973122<br> ○ http://murderpedia.org/male.B/b/brudos-jerome.htm |
| Donald Harvey, a.k.a. "Angel of Death" | • Born in Butler County, Ohio, in 1952, shortly after, Harvey's parents relocated to Booneville, Kentucky, a small community nestled away on the eastern slopes of the Appalachian Mountains.<br>• In an August 14, 1987, interview with Cincinnati Post reporter Nadine Louthan, Harvey's mother, Goldie Harvey, recalled that her son was brought up in a loving family environment. "My son has always been a good boy," she said. | • During an evening shift, just months after starting at the hospital, Donald Harvey committed his first murder.<br>• Following the murder, Harvey cleaned up the patient and hopped into the shower before notifying the nurses. "No one ever questioned it," he said.<br>• Just 3 weeks after committing his first murder, he killed again when he disconnected an oxygen tank at an elderly woman's bedside.<br>• As the weeks went by and no one detected foul play in his first two murders, Harvey became more brazen. Whether out of boredom, opportunity, or experimentation, his methods varied with each murder. |

(continued)

**Serial killers** (continued)

| Name | Early life | Crimes |
|---|---|---|
| | • Martha D. Turner, who was principal of the elementary school Harvey attended for 8 years, backed up McKinney's comments in her own interview with the Cincinnati Post: "Donnie was a very special child to me," she said. "He was always clean and well dressed with his hair trimmed. He was a happy child, very sociable and well-liked by the other children. He was a handsome boy with big brown eyes and dark curly hair he always had a smile for me. There was never any indication of any abnormality."<br>• Former classmates of Harvey described him as a loner and teacher's pet.<br>• He rarely participated in extracurricular activities, opting instead to read books and dream about the future.<br>• Following his graduation from Sturgeon Elementary School, Harvey entered Booneville High School in 1968.<br>• Earning As and Bs in most classes with little effort, he became bored with the daily routine and dropped out.<br>• Having no real goals, Harvey was not sure what he wanted to do with his newfound freedom.<br>• For unknown reasons, he eventually decided to relocate to Cincinnati, Ohio, where he secured a job at a local factory.<br>• In 1970, work began to slow at the plant, and Harvey was eventually laid off.<br>• His mother called him a few days later and asked him to travel to Kentucky and visit his ailing grandfather, who was recently placed in a hospital there.<br>• Harvey agreed and within days set off for Marymount Hospital in London, Kentucky.<br>• While in Kentucky, Harvey spent much of his time at Marymount Hospital and was soon well known and liked by the nuns who worked there. | • He used various items, such as plastic bags, morphine, and a variety of drugs, to kill more than a dozen patients in a year. In one case, he chose an exceptionally brutal method.<br>• The patient had an argument with Harvey because he thought Harvey was trying to kill him, and during the course of that argument, he reportedly knocked Harvey out with a bedpan.<br>• Upon recovering from the blow, Harvey waited till later that night, snuck into the patient's room, and stuck a coat hanger through his catheter. As a result of the puncture, infection set in and the man died a few days later.<br>• On March 31, 1971, a drunk and disorderly Harvey was arrested for burglary. While being questioned about the crime, Harvey began babbling incoherently about the murders he had committed.<br>• In September 1975, Harvey moved back to Cincinnati, Ohio. Within weeks, he got a job working night shift at the Cincinnati V.A. Medical Hospital.<br>• Over the next 10 years, Harvey murdered at least 15 patients while working at the hospital.<br>• He kept a precise diary of his crimes and took notes on each victim, detailing how he murdered them—pressing a plastic bag and wet towel over the mouth and nose; sprinkling rat poison in a patient's dessert; adding arsenic and cyanide to orange juice; injecting cyanide into an intravenous tube; injecting cyanide into a patient's buttocks.<br>• All the while Harvey was committing his crimes, he was refining his techniques by studying medical journals for underlying hints on how to conceal his crimes.<br>• Over the years, he amassed an astounding 30 pounds of cyanide, which he had slowly pilfered from the hospital and kept at home for safekeeping.<br>• Typically, Harvey would mix a vial of cyanide or arsenic at home and then bring it to work. |

- During one particular conversation, one of the nuns asked Harvey if he would be interested in working there as an orderly. Since he was currently unemployed and didn't want another factory job, Harvey agreed and started work the next day.
- Although he was not a trained nurse or doctor, Harvey's duties required him to spend hours alone with patients. Some of his duties included changing bedpans, inserting catheters, and passing out medications.
- Harvey decided it was time for another change of scenery and enlisted in the US Air Force.
- Harvey served less than a year in the Air Force before he received a general discharge in March 1972. His records list unspecified grounds for the discharge, but it was widely rumored at the time his superiors had learned of his confessions to the Kentucky police and did not want to deal with any similar matters in the future.
- After his release from the military, Harvey dealt with several bouts of depression.
- By July 1972, he was unable to control his inner demons and decided to commit himself to the Veteran's Administration Medical Center in Lexington, Kentucky.
- Harvey remained in the mental ward of the facility until August 25 but then admitted himself again a few weeks later.
- Following a bungled suicide attempt in the hospital, Harvey was placed in restraints and, over the course of the next few weeks, received 21 electroshock therapy treatments.
- On October 17, 1972, Harvey was again released from the hospital. Goldie Harvey later condemned the hospital for releasing her son so abruptly, feeling that he had shown no apparent signs of improvement from the time of his admittance.

- When no one was around, he would slip the mixture into his victim's food or pour it directly into their gastric tube.
- The early 1980s brought about variations in Harvey's methods. He moved in with a gay lover, Carl Hoeweler, and soon began poisoning him out of fear that his mate was cheating on him.
- Harvey would slip small doses of arsenic into Hoeweler's food so that he would be too ill to leave their apartment.
- On one occasion, following an argument with a female neighbor, Harvey laced one of her beverages with hepatitis serum, nearly killing her before the infection was diagnosed and treated.
- Another neighbor, Helen Metzger, was not so lucky. Harvey put arsenic in one of her pies, and she died later that week at a local hospital.
- In April 1983, Harvey had a squabble with Hoeweler's parents and began to poison their food with arsenic. On May 1, 1983, Hoeweler's father, Henry, suffered a stroke and was remitted to Providence Hospital. Harvey visited Henry Hoeweler there and placed arsenic in his pudding before leaving. Hoeweler died later that night.
- Harvey continued to poison Carl's mother, Margaret, off and on for the next year, but was unsuccessful in his attempts to kill her. In January 1984, Hoeweler broke off the relationship with Harvey and asked him to move out.
- Harvey was angry at the rejection and spent the next 2 years trying to kill Hoeweler with his poisonous concoctions.
- At one point, he even tried to kill a female friend of Hoeweler as a way to get his revenge. While neither attempt worked, he did manage to land Hoeweler in the hospital at one point, as a result of the poisons he had unknowingly ingested.
- Authorities became suspicious of Harvey in April 1987, after the death of John Powell, a patient who was comatose for several months, but had since started to recover. During the autopsy, an assistant coroner noticed the faint scent of almonds, the telltale sign of cyanide.
  - http://murderpedia.org/male.H/h/harvey-donald.htm

(continued)

**Serial killers** (continued)

| Name | Early life | Crimes |
|---|---|---|
| Dennis Rader, a.k.a. "The BTK Strangler" | • Dennis Lynn Rader was born on March 9, 1945, in Pittsburg, Kansas, and grew up in Wichita.<br>• The oldest of four sons, he enjoyed a seemingly normal childhood, reportedly masking such disturbing behavior as hanging stray animals.<br>• He claims he was dropped on his head as a youth and that he found his many spankings as a child to be sexually arousing.<br>• The young Rader also developed a fetish for women's panties, frequently stealing them and wearing them himself.<br>• He also claims that a formative influence on him were the True Detective-style magazines popular in the 1960s that described lurid crimes in graphic detail.<br>• He also claims that as a teen, he masturbated to his father's book about Raymond Fernandez, the *Lonely Hearts Killer*.<br>• By the time he reached 18, Rader says his fantasies became focused on women in bondage.<br>• Rader dropped out of college and joined the US Air Force in the mid-1960s.<br>• After returning to Wichita, he married his wife, Paula, in 1971, and worked for an outdoor supply company for about a year.<br>• In 1974, he began a lengthy stint as an employee of ADT Security Services.<br>• Reportedly, an attentive husband, he and his wife had a son in 1975 and a daughter in 1978.<br>• The next year, Rader graduated from Wichita State University with a degree in administration of justice. | • On January 15, 1974, Rader strangled to death four members of the Otero family in their Wichita home—parents Joseph and Julie and two of their children, Josephine and Joseph Jr.—before leaving with a watch and a radio.<br>• Strangulation and souvenir-taking would become part of his modus operandi or pattern of behavior.<br>• He also left semen at the scene and later said that he derived sexual pleasure from killing.<br>• The Oteros' 15-year-old son, Charlie, came home later that day and discovered the bodies.<br>• Rader struck again a few months later: On April 4, 1974, he waited in the apartment of a young woman named Kathryn Bright, before stabbing and strangling her when she returned home.<br>• Rader also shot her brother, Kevin, twice, though he survived. Kevin later described Rader as "an average-sized guy, bushy mustache, 'psychotic' eyes," according to a *TIME* magazine article.<br>• Rader's next known crimes occurred in 1977. In March of that year, he tied up and strangled Shirley Vian, after locking her children in the bathroom.<br>• In December, he strangled Nancy Fox in her home and then called the police to report the homicide.<br>• After several years without a known crime, Rader killed his neighbor, Marine Hedge, on April 27, 1985. Her body was found days later on the side of the road.<br>• The following year, he killed Vicki Wegerle in her home. His final known victim, Dolores Davis, was taken from her home on January 19, 1991.<br>• In each case, he carefully followed and stalked his intended targets before killing them, referring to each new victim as a "project." |

| | |
|---|---|
| | • In many of the murders, he brought along what he called his "Hit Kit"—tools and rope and duct tape from his shed that would enable him to pull off the murders smoothly.<br>• A few of his intended targets in the 1980s got wise to him and filed restraining orders against Rader before he could complete his "project."<br>• And after his arrest he revealed he'd been stalking another woman he'd intended to kill in the spring of 2005—in what he said would be his "opus."<br>• He planned to hang her upside down and mutilate her while alive before burning her house to the ground—but his arrest and conviction made this impossible.<br>   ○ https://www.biography.com/people/dennis-rader-241487<br>   ○ https://thoughtcatalog.com/jim-goad/2018/06/dennis-rader/ |
| Joseph DeAngelo, a.k.a. "The Golden State Killer" | • Born in 1946, he served in the Navy during the Vietnam War.<br>• From 1973 to 1976, he was an officer for Exeter police department and, from 1976 to 1979, served as an officer for the Auburn Police department, where he was fired for stealing a hammer and dog repellent (the same year as his first attack).<br>• DeAngelo married Sharon Marie Huddle and had children.<br>• He was described by his neighbors as having two sides of him: the loving grandfather that took his grandchildren trick or treating, and then there was the creep who screamed at himself in front of his yard and threaten to kill his neighbor's dogs. | • His crimes spanned from 1974 to 1986.<br>• He stalked his victims through drainage ditches and peeped through windows.<br>• He would learn the daily routines of his victims, enter the homes of future victims to unlock windows, unload guns, and plant ligatures for later use.<br>• He frequently phone called some victims before and after the attack saying:<br>   ○ "Your next"<br>   ○ "Merry Christmas, it's me again!"<br>   ○ "Gonna kill you…"<br>   ○ "Remember when we played?"<br>• His initial MO was stalking middle-class neighborhoods at night in search of women who were alone in one-story homes.<br>• Eventually, he preferred attacking couples.<br>• His MO was to break in through a window or sliding glass door and awaken the sleeping occupants with a flashlight, threatening them with a handgun. Victims found tied up with shoelaces, blindfolded, and gagged.<br>• Often raped the woman repeatedly, sometimes for several hours.<br>• He spent hours in the home ransacking closets and drawers, eating food in the kitchen, drinking beer, raping the female again, or making additional threats. |

(continued)

**Serial killers** (continued)

| Name | Early life | Crimes |
|---|---|---|
| | | • Typically stole items, often personal objects, and items of little value but occasionally cash and firearms. He then crept away, leaving victims uncertain if he had left.<br>• First murders: In 1979, he chased down and shot a young couple, Katie and Brian Maggiore, who were walking their dog in the same location where he committed five prior attacks (shoelace was found at the crime scene, which linked GSK).<br>• In 1981, he started killing couples and only leaving one couple behind.<br>• He murdered them by gunshot or bludgeoning.<br><br>○ Delisi, M. (2018). Forensic epidemiology: Harnessing the power of public DNA sources to capture career criminals. *Forensic Science International, 291.* https://doi.org/10.1016/j.forsciint.2018.07.018<br>○ Guerrini, C. J., Robinson, J. O., Petersen, D., & McGuire, A. L. (n.d.). *Should police have access to genetic genealogy databases? Capturing the Golden State Killer and other criminals using a controversial new forensic technique.* Retrieved from https://journals.plos.org/plosbiology/article?id=10.1371/journal.pbio.2006906<br>○ Jouvenal, J. (2018, April 30). *To find alleged Golden State Killer, investigators first found his great-great-grandparents.* Retrieved from https://www.washingtonpost.com/local/public-safety/to-find-alleged-golden-state-killer-investigators-first-found-his-great-great-great-grandparents/2018/04/30/3c865fe7-dfcc-4a0e-b6b2-0bec548d501f_story.html?utm_term=.943b09264fcd<br>○ Golden State Killer Documentary. Youtube<br>○ Selk, Avi. "The Most Disturbing Parts of the 171-Page Warrant for the Golden State Killer Suspect." The Washington Post, WP Company, 2 June 2018. www.washingtonpost.com/news/post-nation/wp/2018/06/02/the-most-disturbing-parts-of-the-171-page-warrants-for-the-golden-state-killer-suspect/?noredirect=on&utm_term=.efa65b5665d1<br>○ Winters, K. (n.d.). *Golden State Killer Trial – The Trial of Joseph DeAngelo.* Retrieved from https://goldenstatekillertrial.com/ |

| Paul John Knowles, a.k.a. "The Casanova Killer" | • He was born on April 17, 1946, in Orlando, Florida, and grew up caring little for authority figures; he felt like he didn't need them. <br> • He habitually refused to do his homework, talked back to adults, stole, and once punched a girl in the face when she rejected him. At the age of 7, he stole a bicycle. <br> • Whenever his parents or teachers reprimanded him, Knowles lashed out in a terrible rage. <br> • Rebellion against authority won him attention from his friends, which encouraged his continued misbehavior. <br> • He idolized criminals who travelled across the country committing crimes, lost their lives in violent shootouts with police, and achieved a level of fame on par with actors and professional athletes. <br> • Knowles was in and out of the Florida School for Boys, a reform school with a terrible history of abusing, torturing, and even murdering its young inmates. <br> • Knowle's love for being at the center of attention egged him to commit worse crimes, and he was in and out of jail for much of his life. <br> • At the age of 19, he stole cars and took a police officer hostage. <br> • After an arrest in 1971, he began corresponding by letter with Angela Covic while in prison. When they made plans to marry, Covic hired a lawyer to get him out early, and Knowles set his heart on turning his life around. <br> • He took college classes, started looking for work as a sign painter, and had full intentions of moving to San Francisco to get away from the bad influences provoking his recidivism in Florida. But Covic broke off the engagement upon his release in 1974. | • After a misspent youth, he was arrested in May of 1968 for attempted burglary and served 3 years in a Florida State prison. <br> • They released him in 1971, but he was quickly re-arrested on similar charges. He escaped from a prison work camp the following year but was recaptured 3 weeks later, earning 3 more years in the big house for the escape and resisting arrest. <br> • He was released in 1974, but after things didn't work out with Angela, she sent him packing, and he returned to Florida where he was arrested in Jacksonville for aggravated assault. <br> • Knowles' first confirmed murder happened on July 26, 1974, 2 months after Covic dumped him. After getting arrested for a bar fight and stabbing a bouncer, Knowles picked the lock to his cell and escaped for the final time. <br> • He went on 4-month crime spree that spanned 37 states. <br> • He was directly linked to the slaying of 18 people, and he later claimed to have taken the lives of 17 more ill-fated souls. <br> • In November of 1974, when he picked up British journalist Sandy Fawkes at a bar in Atlanta, GA, after murdering a man named Carswell Carr and his daughter in nearby Milledgeville. <br> • Knowles swept the infatuated war correspondent off her feet, and they both set off on a romantic road trip down to West Palm Beach, FL, in a car stolen from one of his previous victims. <br> • He soon grew tired of Fawkes but released her unharmed. <br> • As he headed back up the Interstate, Knowles corralled two more unfortunate hostages—one of them was a Florida Highway Patrol Trooper whom the killer overpowered during a routine stop and search. <br> • After that, law enforcement jumped into high gear, and the pursuit swiftly intensified. <br> • By Sunday, November 17, Knowles had brutally executed his two hostages, leaving them handcuffed together to a tree in the woods near Big Indian Creek, just south of Macon. |

(continued)

**Serial killers** (continued)

| Name | Early life | Crimes |
|---|---|---|
| | | • When he was spotted by the police near McDonough, GA, his luck finally ran out. He totaled his Gran Torino after ramming a barricade at the intersection of Highway 42 and Hudson Bridge Rd. and then immediately fled back into the woods. |
| | | • He was still armed and dangerous, but now he was injured and bleeding. |
| | | • Knowles emerged 4 hours later, torn up and exhausted, in the backyard of a Vietnam War veteran who had just returned home from a weekend of hunting. |
| | | • He dropped his jammed shotgun and surrendered. |
| | | • On December 18, 1974, he was riding in the backseat of a marked county car while Douglas County Sheriff Earl Lee drove and FBI Agent Ron Angel rode in the front, allegedly on the way to show them the location of the discarded gun used to murder the Florida Highway Patrol Trooper. |
| | | • According to local authorities, Angel shot Knowles three times in the chest after the killer picked his cuffs with a paperclip and reached over the seat to snatch Lee's gun from its holster. |
| | | ◦ https://www.parcast.com/blog/2017/7/30/the-casanova-killer-profile |
| | | ◦ https://ashevilleoralhistoryproject.com/2014/01/29/casanova-killer/ |

| Tommy Lyn Sells, a.k.a. "The Coast to Coast Killer" | <ul><li>Tommy Lynn Sells and his twin sister, Tammy Jean, were born in Oakland, California on June 28, 1964.</li><li>His mother, Nina Sells, was a single mother with three other children at the time that the twins were born.</li><li>The family moved to St. Louis, Missouri, and at 18 months old, both Sells and Tammy Jean contracted spinal meningitis, which killed Tammy Jean. Tommy survived.</li><li>Soon after his recuperation, Sells was sent to live with his aunt Bonnie Walpole, in Holcomb, Missouri.</li><li>He stayed there until age 5 when he returned to live with his mother after she discovered that Walpole was interested in adopting him.</li><li>Throughout his early childhood years, Sells was left mostly to fend for himself. He rarely attended school, and by the age of 7, he was drinking alcohol.</li><li>Around this same time, Sells began hanging around with a man from a nearby town.</li><li>The man showed him a lot of attention in the form of gifts and frequent outings.</li><li>On several occasions, Sells spent the night at the man's home. Later, this same man was found guilty of child molestation, which came as no surprise to Sells, who had been one of his victims starting when he was just 8 years old.</li><li>From the age of 10 to 13, Sells showed a special knack for staying in trouble. By age 10, he had stopped attending school, choosing instead to smoke pot and drink alcohol.</li><li>Once, when he was 13, he climbed naked into his grandmother's bed. This was the last straw for Tommy's mother.</li><li>Within days, she took his siblings and left Tommy alone, leaving not so much as a forwarding address.</li></ul> | <ul><li>Filled with rage after his abandonment, the teenage Sells attacked his first female victim by pistol whipping her until she was unconscious.</li><li>With no home and no family, Sells began drifting from town to town, picking up odd jobs and stealing what he needed.</li><li>Sells later claimed he committed his first murder at age 16, after breaking into a home and killing a man inside who was performing oral sex on a young boy. There was never any proof to back up his claim about the incident.</li><li>Sells also claimed to have shot and killed John Cade Sr. in July 1979, after Cade caught him burglarizing his home.</li><li>In May 1981, Sells moved to Little Rock, Arkansas, and moved back in with his family. The reunion was short-lived. Nina Sells told him to leave after he attempted to have sex with her while she was taking a shower.</li><li>Back out on the streets, Sells returned to doing what he knew best, robbing and killing, working as a carnival roustabout, and hopping trains to get to his next destination.</li><li>He later confessed to killing two people in Arkansas before heading to St. Louis in 1983. Only the murder of Hal Akins was ever confirmed.</li><li>In May 1984, Sills was convicted of car theft, and he was given a 2-year prison sentence. He was released from prison the following February but failed to follow the terms of his probation.</li><li>While in Missouri, Sells started working a county fair in Forsyth where he met Ena Cordt, 35, and her 4-year-old son. Sells later admitted to killing Cordt and her son.</li><li>According to Sells, Cordt invited him back to her house, but when he caught her going through his knapsack, he beat her to death with a baseball bat. He then did the same to the only witness of the crime, the 4-year-old Rory Cordt. Their bodies were found 3 days later.</li><li>By September 1984, Sells was back in jail for drunk driving after crashing his car. He stayed in jail until May 16, 1986.</li><li>Back in St. Louis, Sells claims he shot a stranger in self-defense. He then headed to Aransas Pass, Texas, where he was hospitalized for an overdose of heroin. Once out of the hospital, he stole a car and headed to Fremont, California.</li></ul> |

(continued)

**Serial killers** (continued)

| Name | Early life | Crimes |
|---|---|---|
| | | • While in Freemont, investigators believe he was responsible for the death of Jennifer Duey, 20, who was shot to death. They also believe he was responsible for murdering Michelle Xavier, 19, who was found dead with her throat cut. |
| | | • Keith Dardeen was the next known unfortunate victim that tried to befriend Sells. He spotted Sells hitchhiking in Ina, Illinois, and offered him a hot meal at his home. In return, Sells shot Dardeen and then mutilated his penis. |
| | | • Next, he murdered Dardeen's 3-year-old son, Pete, by bludgeoning him with a hammer. He then turned his rage on Dardeen's pregnant wife, Elaine, who he attempted to rape. The attack caused Elaine to go into labor, and she gave birth to her daughter. Neither mother nor daughter survived. Sells beat both of them to death with a bat. He then inserted the bat into Elaine's vagina, tucked the children and the mother into bed, and left. |
| | | • For 20 years, Sells was a transient serial killer that managed to stay under the radar as he roamed around the country killing and raping unsuspecting victims of all ages. Investigators believe that Sells is likely responsible for 70 murders across the country. |
| | | ○ https://www.thoughtco.com/serial-killer-tommy-lynn-sells-973154 |

| Ahmad Suradji, a.k.a. "The Sorcerer" | |
|---|---|
| • He was born on January 10, 1949, in Indonesia. Originally a cattle breeder.<br>• He had three wives, who were also arrested for helping him with the killings. One of them received the death sentence as well, though later it was changed to life imprisonment.<br>• He practiced black magic and was a sorcerer as well.<br>• Reportedly, he had committed the murders as a part of a black magic ritual which he believed would increase his magical powers. He said that his deceased father had appeared in a dream and advised him to drink the saliva of 70 dead young women in order to become a mystic healer.<br>• Since it would take him a long time to find 70 dead women, he began to kill women himself so that he could drink their saliva. | • Little is known about his initial victims as he was finally arrested only after the body of his final victim was found.<br>• His crimes spanned from 1986 to 1997.<br>• His last victim was a 21-year-old lady named Sri Kemala Dewi, who had visited him in a rickshaw. She had advised the rickshaw puller to keep her visit a secret. She also never requested to be picked up.<br>• A few days later, her naked and decomposing body was found in a sugarcane field by a man, who dug it up with a group of people.<br>• The police were informed, and soon they learned that she had last visited Suradji. Suradji, however, denied any connection to the killing.<br>• During their investigation, the police found Dewi's handbag, dress, and bracelet in Suradji's home which eventually led to his arrest.<br>• He confessed to his crimes during the interrogation. He said that he had killed up to 42 young women in the same way.<br>• Further excavation was carried out in the sugarcane field where the bodies were buried. Some of them were so badly decomposed that they could not even be identified.<br>• Victims strangled in a cable after being buried up to their waists in the ground as part of a ritual.<br>• Since he was known as a sorcerer, many women came to him in order to receive spiritual advice. He would then take them to the sugarcane field and bury them up to their waists.<br>• Following this, he would kill them by strangulation and drink the saliva that dribbled out of their mouths. He then buried the bodies in a ritualistic fashion in a sugarcane plantation near his house.<br>• He also added that he didn't blame his father for the murders as he hadn't specifically told him to kill anyone. Ahmad Suradji received the death sentence for his crimes. He was finally executed on July 10, 2008, by firing squad.<br>   ○ https://www.thefamouspeople.com/profiles/ahmad-suradji-41485.php<br>   ○ http://www.svsd.net/cms/lib5/PA01001234/Centricity/Domain/1046/Ahmad%20Suradji.pptx |

(continued)

**Serial killers** (continued)

| Name | Early life | Crimes |
|---|---|---|
| Charles Edmund Cullen, a.k.a. "The Angel of Death" | • He was born on February 22, 1960, in West Orange, New Jersey, the youngest of eight children in a deeply religious Catholic family.<br>• His mother stayed at home to raise her children and his father worked as a bus driver and was 58 at the time of his birth; he died when Charles was only 8 months old. Two of his siblings also died in adulthood. Cullen described his childhood as miserable, with report of his father having raped him as a child.<br>• He first attempted suicide was at the age of 9 by drinking chemicals taken from a chemistry set. This would be the first of 20 such suicide attempts throughout his life.<br>• Later, working as a nurse, Cullen fantasized about stealing drugs from the hospital where he worked and using them to commit suicide.<br>• In one attempt, he took a pair of scissors and jabbed them through his head. He was rushed to the hospital to have major surgery done.<br>• When Cullen was 17, Cullen's mother died in an automobile accident; his sister was at the wheel. Devastated by his mother's death, Cullen dropped out of high school and enlisted in the US Navy in 1978.<br>   He was assigned to the submarine corps and served aboard the ballistic missile sub USS Woodrow Wilson. He rose to the rank of petty officer third class as part of the team that operated the ship's Poseidon missiles.<br>• Cullen was showing signs of mental instability by then. He once served a shift in a green surgical gown, surgical mask, and latex gloves stolen from the ship's medical cabinet. He was transferred to the supply ship USS Canopus. | • Cullen committed his first murder on June 11, 1988. Judge John W. Yengo Sr. had been admitted to St. Barnabas Medical Center suffering from an allergic reaction to a blood-thinning drug. Cullen administered a lethal overdose of medication intravenously.<br>• Cullen admitted to killing 11 patients at St. Barnabas, including an AIDS patient who died after being given an overdose of insulin.<br>• Cullen quit his job at St. Barnabas in January 1992 when hospital authorities began investigating who might have tampered with bags of intravenous fluid.<br>• Cullen took a job at Warren Hospital in Phillipsburg, New Jersey, in February 1992. He murdered three elderly women at the hospital by giving them overdoses of the heart medication dioxin.<br>• His final victim said that a "sneaky male nurse" had injected her as she slept, but family members and other healthcare workers dismissed her comments.<br>• In January 1993, Adrienne Cullen filed for divorce. She later filed two domestic violence complaints against him.<br>• The divorce papers and domestic violence complaints depicted Cullen as an alcoholic, someone who abused pets by placing them in bowling bags and trash cans, poured lighter fluid into other people's drinks, and made prank calls to funeral homes.<br>• Cullen had shared custody of his daughters and moved into a basement apartment on Shaffer Avenue in Phillipsburg.<br>• Cullen says he wanted to quit nursing in 1993, but court-ordered child support payments forced him to keep working.<br>• In March 1993, he broke into a coworker's home while she and her young son slept but left without waking them.<br>• Cullen then started phoning her frequently, leaving numerous messages and following her at work and around town. The woman filed a complaint, and Cullen pleaded guilty to trespassing and was placed on a year's probation. |

| | |
|---|---|
| • Cullen tried to kill himself several times over the next few years. His last attempt led to his discharge from the Navy in March 1984. | • The day after his arrest, Cullen attempted suicide. He took 2 months off work and was treated for depression in two psychiatric facilities. He attempted suicide two more times before the end of the year. |
| • After leaving the Navy, Cullen attended Mountainside School of Nursing and got a job at St. Barnabas Medical Center in Livingston, New Jersey, in 1987. | • Cullen left Warren Hospital in December 1993 and took a job at Hunter Medical Center in Rarity Township, New Jersey, early the next year. |
| • That same year, he married Adrienne Taub. The couple had two daughters. | • Cullen worked in the hospital's intensive care/cardiac care unit for 3 years. During his first 2 years, Cullen claims he did not murder anyone. |
| • Cullen became a licensed nurse in Pennsylvania in 1994. | • But hospital records for the time period had already been destroyed at the time of his arrest in 2003, preventing any investigation into his claims. |
| | • However, Cullen did admit to murdering five patients in the first 9 months of 1996. Once more, Cullen administered overdoses of dioxin. |
| | • Cullen found work at Morris Memorial Hospital in Morris, New Jersey. He was fired in August 1997 for poor performance. He remained unemployed for 6 months and stopped making child-support payments. |
| | • In October 1997, Cullen appeared in the Warren Hospital emergency room and sought treatment for depression. He was admitted to a psychiatric facility but left a short time later. |
| | • His treatment had not improved his mental health. Neighbors said that he could be found chasing cats down the street in the dead of night, yelling or talking to himself, and making faces at people when he thought they weren't looking. |
| | • In February 1998, Cullen was hired by Liberty Nursing and Rehabilitation Center in Allentown, Pennsylvania. He worked in a ward for patients who needed ventilators to breathe. |
| | • In May, Cullen filed for bankruptcy, claiming nearly $67,000 in debts. |
| | • Liberty fired Cullen in October 1998 after he was seen entering a patient's room with syringes in his hand. The patient ended up with a broken arm, but apparently no injections were made. Cullen was accused of giving patients drugs at unscheduled times. |

(continued)

**Serial killers** (continued)

| Name | Early life | Crimes |
|------|-----------|--------|
| | | • Cullen worked at Elston Hospital in Elston, Pennsylvania, from November 1998 to March 1999. |
| | | • On December 30, 1998, he murdered yet another patient with dioxin. A coroner's blood test showed lethal amounts of dioxin in the patient's blood, but an investigation was inconclusive, and nothing pointed definitively to Cullen as the murderer. |
| | | • Cullen continued to find work. A nationwide nursing shortage made it difficult for hospitals to recruit nurses, and no reporting mechanisms or other systems existed to identify nurses with mental health issues or employment problems. |
| | | • Cullen took a job at a burn unit at Lehigh Valley Hospital in Allentown, Pennsylvania, in March 1999. During his tenure at Lehigh Valley Hospital, Cullen murdered one patient and attempted to murder another. |
| | | • In April 1999, Cullen voluntarily resigned from Le high Valley Hospital and took a job at St. Luke's Hospital in Bethlehem, Pennsylvania. Cullen worked in St. Luke's cardiac care unit. Over the next 3 years, he murdered five more patients and attempted to murder two. |
| | | • In January 2000, Cullen attempted suicide again. He put a charcoal grill in his bath tub, lit it, and hoped that the carbon monoxide gas would kill him. |
| | | • Neighbors smelled the smoke and called the fire department and police. Cullen was taken to a hospital and a psychiatric facility but was back home the following day. |
| | | • No one suspected Cullen was murdering patients at St. Luke's Hospital until a coworker accidentally found vials of unused medications in a disposal bin. |
| | | • The drugs were not valuable outside the hospital and were not used by recreational drug users, so their theft seemed curious. An investigation showed that Cullen had taken the medication, and he was fired and escorted from the building in June 2002. |
| | | • Seven St. Luke's nurses who worked with Cullen later met with the Le high County district attorney to alert the authorities of their suspicions that Cullen had used drugs to kill patients. |

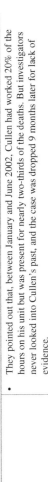

- They pointed out that, between January and June 2002, Cullen had worked 20% of the hours on his unit but was present for nearly two-thirds of the deaths. But investigators never looked into Cullen's past, and the case was dropped 9 months later for lack of evidence.
- In September 2002, Cullen found a job at Somerset Medical Center in Somerset, New Jersey. Cullen worked in Somerset's critical care unit. Cullen's depression worsened, even though he had begun dating a local woman.
- Cullen murdered eight more patients and attempted to murder another by June. Once more, his drugs of choice were dioxin and insulin.
- On June 18, 2003, Cullen attempted to murder Philip Gregor, a patient at Somerset. Gregor survived and was discharged; he died 6 months later of natural causes.
- Soon afterward, the hospital's computer systems showed that Cullen was accessing the records of patients he was not assigned to.
- Coworkers were seeing him in patient's rooms. Computerized drug-dispensing cabinets were showing that Cullen was requesting medications that patients had not been prescribed.
- The executive director of the New Jersey Poison Information and Education System warned Somerset Medical Center officials in July 2003 that at least four of the suspicious overdoses indicated the possibility that an employee was killing patients.
- But the hospital put off contacting authorities until October. By then, Cullen had killed another five patients and attempted to kill a sixth. He then proceeded to have sex with the victims.
- State officials penalized the hospital for failing to report a nonfatal insulin overdose in August. The overdose had been administered by Cullen. When Cullen's final victim died of low blood sugar in October, the medical center alerted state authorities. An investigation into Cullen's employment history revealed past suspicions about his involvement with prior deaths.
- Somerset Medical Center fired Cullen on October 31, 2003, for lying on his job application.
  - http://murderpedia.org/male.C/c/cullen-charles.htm
  - https://criminalminds.fandom.com/wiki/Charles_Cullen

(continued)

**Serial killers** (continued)

| Name | Early life | Crimes |
|---|---|---|
| Aileen Wuornos, a.k.a. "The Florida Highway Killer" | • Abandoned by her mother as babies, Aileen and her brother, Keith, grew up with their grandparents Lauri and Britta Wuornos who adopted them.<br>• She believed they were her parents until the age of 11.<br>• Her biological father was Leo Pittman, a child molester who killed himself in prison.<br>• As a child, she claimed to have been beaten and whipped often by her grandfather. Reportedly, she was forced to lay face down and naked, telling her she was "evil," "wicked," and "worthless" and that she should have never been born; that she wasn't worthy of the air she breathed.<br>• As a teenager, Aileen was known for her temper characterized by unpredictable anger outbursts and usually unprovoked. She was thrown out of parties for being vulgar, drunk, and starting fights. She was arrested multiple times for shoplifting. She performed sexual acts with boys for cigarettes and money.<br>• At age 14, she had a baby and gave him up for adoption. It was unclear who the father was.<br>• Once her grandmother died, she was displaced from her grandparents' home, ending up in Florida at 16 where she began working as a prostitute.<br>• At 20, she married a 70-year-old man. The marriage lasted a month, as Aileen's husband filed for a divorce and a restraining order against her for beating him with his own cane.<br>• After her divorce, she was frequently arrested for more serious crimes. | • Wuornos' crimes spanned from 1989 to 1990.<br>• She continued her work as a prostitute on the highways of Florida, killing seven men between ages 41 and 65.<br>• Aileen procured victims by hitchhiking, and all were victims of opportunity.<br>• She killed her victims with multiple .22-caliber rounds. There were 2–9 gunshots per victim, and at least three were left nude.<br>• She would leave the bodies in wooded areas near state or interstate highways.<br>• The victims' cars were left miles away from their bodies, sometimes in different counties. Money or personal belongings were stolen from almost all her victims.<br>• Aileen testified how all of her victims tried to rape her, but the collected forensic evidence from their bodies and the crime scene never supported her claims.<br>• Her version of what transpired also changed multiple times. In one instance, she would claim what happened was because of her anger, and in another instance, she would say what occurred was because the men were becoming abusive toward her.<br>• She pleaded no contest to the murders of Dick Humphreys, Troy Burress, and David Spears and maintained that Richard Mallory had violently raped her as the reason for killing him; she claimed that the others only tried to rape her. Wuornos was given three death sentences.<br>• Wuornos also pleaded guilty to the killing of Charles Carskaddon for which she received another death sentence.<br>• In 1993, she pleaded guilty to the death of Walter Jeno Antonio and received yet another death sentence.<br>• In the case of Peter Siems, the body was never found, and she could not be tried for his murder. |

| | |
|---|---|
| | • These crimes included possession of a weapon, DUI, assault and battery, and disorderly conduct.<br>• She served 3 years in jail after being convicted of a robbery at a convenience store.<br>• After her release, she continued prostituting herself but more frequently.<br>• She claimed she did this 25–30 times a day just to support herself.<br>• She soon met Tyria Moore, and their relationship lasted 4.5 years.<br>• During the relationship, excessive drinking, grandiosity, prostitution, violence, and unstable living conditions were common themes in Aileen's life. | • She was killed by lethal injection on October 9, 2002, in Florida State prison.<br>   ◦ Arrigo, B. A., & Griffin, A. (2004). Serial murder and the case of Aileen Wuornos: Attachment theory, psychopathy, and predatory aggression. *Behavioral Sciences & the Law, 22*(3), 375–393. https://doi.org/10.1002/bsl.583<br>   ◦ Broomfield, N. (Director). (2014, September 18). *Aileen Wuornos: The Selling of a Serial Killer* [Video file] Retrieved from https://www.youtube.com/watch?v=oPD2hd6y_C8<br>   ◦ Myers, W. C., Gooch, E., & Meloy, J. R. (2005). The role of psychopathy and sexuality in a female serial killer. *Journal of Forensic Sciences, 50*(3), 1–6. https://doi.org/10.1520/jfs2004324<br>   ◦ *Behavioral Sciences and the Law, 22*(3), 375–393. https://doi.org/10.1002/bsl.583<br>   ◦ The Case of Aileen Wuornos - The Facts l Capital Punishment in Context. (n.d.). Retrieved from https://capitalpunishmentincontext.org/node/77454 Aileen Wuornos – The Post-Trial Period l Capital Punishment in Context. (n.d.). Retrieved from https://capitalpunishmentincontext.org/cases/wuornos/posttrial |
| Keith Hunter Jesperson, a.k.a. "The Happy Face Killer" | • Jesperson was born in Chilliwack, British Columbia, Canada, on April 6, 1955.<br>• His father and grandfather were both extremely violent and frequently abused their families.<br>• He moved to Selah, Washington, USA, and because of his large size, he had trouble with making friends and was bullied by his classmates and his own brothers.<br>• Keith's father, Les, drank heavily, dominated his family, looked down on women, and put his kids down with sarcasm and wisecracks; Keith received little attention from his father compared to siblings. | • His crimes spanned between January 22, 1990 and March 16,1995.<br>• Jesperson's first known victim was a woman named Taunja Bennett. He invited her to his house, and after having an argument, she was strangled to death with a rope, and her body was later disposed of.<br>• Her body was found days later, but the case went unsolved until a woman named Laverne Pavlinac claimed that she and her boyfriend, John Sosnovske, were responsible for her death.<br>• They were arrested, and as result, Jesperson wrote a confession on the bathroom wall of a truck stop, signed it with a happy face, and subsequently wrote letters to media outlets and police departments, all signed with a happy face. |

(continued)

**Serial killers** (continued)

| Name | Early life | Crimes |
|---|---|---|
| | • Keith's father shocked him in greenhouse; his father claimed it was only 12 volts, Keith claims 220.<br>• Keith showed signs of being a psychopath at an early age by capturing various animals and then torturing and strangling them to death:<br>  o Bashed in gopher heads.<br>  o Nailed crows to a board and threw knives at them.<br>  o Nailed cats and small dogs to a board and stuck them with nails and needles.<br>  o Favorite thing was to crimp a couple of cats' tails together with wire and hang them. They'd claw each other until one was dead.<br>• His dad witnessed him throw a cat against the pavement and finished it off by strangling it to death, and then his dad bragged about it to others.<br>• His desire to hurt other people first manifested itself in two attempted murders: the first when he attacked a friend, Martin, by beating him, and the second when he attempted to drown a boy at a public school.<br>• He also claimed that he was raped at age of 14, though this was never confirmed.<br>• Although he was not successful with courting girls, he managed to enter into a relationship after high school.<br>• He married a woman named Rose Hucke, and together they had three children. He later became a truck driver to support his family.<br>• Years after marrying, Hucke started to suspect that Jesperson was cheating on her when strange women would call her house. The couple eventually divorced in 1990, devastating Jesperson. His dream was to work as an officer with the Royal Canadian Mounted Police, but he suffered an injury during training, and his dream was destroyed.<br>• He then began to work as an interstate truck driver and took advantage of his job to start serial killing. | • Following this, he was dubbed "The Happy Face Killer" by journalist Phil Stanford. Two-and-a-half years later, he killed his next victim, a woman he claimed to be named Claudia; she was raped by him and then strangled.<br>• A month later, the body of possible prostitute Cynthia Lyn Rose was found. Jesperson's next victim was another possible prostitute, Laurie Ann Pentland; her body was found in November of that year.<br>• More than 6 months later, he murdered another woman, whose name was claimed by him to be Carla or Cindy.<br>• A year later, Jesperson murdered a woman he claimed to be named Susanne. Another year later, he agreed to give a young woman named Angela Subrize a lift from Spokane, Washington, to Indiana.<br>• During the trip, they got into a fight, and in response, Jesperson raped and strangled her before strapping her to the undercarriage of his truck and dragged her face down.<br>• Her body was found only after Jesperson was arrested. Two months later, Jesperson murdered his girlfriend, Julie Ann Winningham, because he felt that she was interested in his money.<br>• He quickly became the prime suspect in her death and was arrested on March 30, 1995, for her murder. He tried to commit suicide twice but failed. Keith subsequently confessed to the murders he committed and also had sent a confession letter to Winningham's brother a week before his arrest.<br>• In prison, he claimed to have killed more than 160 people, though this was never confirmed. He was convicted for all of the murders he had committed in California, Florida, Nebraska, Oregon, Washington, and Wyoming.<br>• Jesperson is now serving three life sentences at the Oregon State Penitentiary. In 2009, he was indicted for murder in Riverside County and was extradited to California to face charges.<br>  o https://criminalminds.fandom.com/wiki/Keith_Hunter_Jespersonhttp://maamodt.asp.radford.edu/Psyc%20405/serial%20killers/Jesperson,%20Keith%20-%20spring,%2006.pdf |

| Henry Louis Wallace, a.k.a. "The Taco Bell Strangler" | • Henry Louis Wallace was born on November 4, 1965, in Barnwell, South Carolina, son of Lottie Mae Wallace, and a married schoolteacher who walked out on his lover when he found out she was pregnant.<br>• Wallace grew up with his mother working long hours as a textile worker. She described as a harsh disciplinarian, constantly criticizing was her son for even the smallest mistakes.<br>• He attended Barnwell High School, where he was elected to student council and was a cheerleader.<br>• Wallace graduated in 1983 and became a DJ for a local radio station in Barnwell.<br>• He went to several colleges before joining the US Navy in 1985. Wallace married his high school sweetheart, the former Maretta Brabham, in 1987.<br>• During his time in the Navy, he began using several drugs, including crack cocaine. In 1988, Wallace was honorably discharged.<br>• In Washington, he was served warrants for several burglaries in and around the Seattle metro area. | • In January 1988, Wallace was arrested for breaking into a hardware store. That June, he pleaded guilty to second-degree burglary.<br>• A judge sentenced him to 2 years of supervised probation. According to Probation Officer Patrick Seaburg, Wallace did not show up for most mandatory meetings.<br>• In early 1990, he murdered Tashonda Bethea and then dumped her in a lake in his hometown. It was not until weeks later that her body was discovered. He was questioned by the police regarding her disappearance and death but was never formally charged in her murder.<br>• He was also questioned in connection with the attempted rape of a 16-year-old Barnwell girl but was never charged for that either.<br>• By that time, his marriage had fallen apart, and he was fired from his job as chemical operator for Sandoz Chemical Co.<br>• In February 1991, he broke into his old high school and the radio station where he once worked. He stole video and recording equipment and was caught trying to pawn them.<br>• In November 1991, he relocated to Charlotte, North Carolina. He found jobs at several fast-food restaurants in East Charlotte.<br>• In May 1992, he picked up Sharon Nance, a convicted drug dealer and prostitute. When she demanded payment for her services, Wallace beat her to death and then dumped her body by the railroad tracks. She was found a few days later.<br>• He then strangled Caroline Love at her apartment and then dumped her body in a wooded area.<br>• After he killed her, he and her sisters filed a missing person's report at the police station.<br>• It would be almost 2 years (March 1994) before her body was discovered in a wooded area in Charlotte.<br>• He murdered Shawna Hawk after visiting her at her home on February 19, 1993, and later went to her funeral. |

(continued)

**Serial killers** (continued)

| Name | Early life | Crimes |
|------|-----------|--------|
|  |  | • In March 1993, Hawk's mother, Dee Sumpter, and her godmother, Judy Williams, founded Mothers of Murder Offspring, a Charlotte-based support group for parents of murdered children. |
|  |  | • On June 22, he killed coworker Audrey Spain. Her body was found 2 days later. |
|  |  | • On August 10, 1993, Wallace killed Valencia M. Jumper and then set her on fire to cover up his crime. A few days after her murder, he and his sister went to Valencia's funeral. |
|  |  | • A month later, in September 1993, he went to the apartment of Michelle Stinson, a struggling college student and single mother of two sons. He strangled and stabbed her in front of her oldest son. That October, his only child was born. |
|  |  | • On February 20, 1994, Wallace killed Vanessa Little Mack in her apartment. Mack had two daughters, aged 7 and 4 months, at the time of her death. |
|  |  | • On March 8, 1994, Wallace robbed and strangled Betty Jean Baucom. Afterward, he took valuables from the house, and then he left the apartment with her car. |
|  |  | • He pawned everything except the car, which he left at a shopping center. |
|  |  | • Wallace went back to the same apartment complex on the night of March 8, 1994, knowing that Vernon Woods would be at work so he could murder his girlfriend, Brandi June Henderson. |
|  |  | • Wallace strangled Henderson and her son, Tarreese, that night. Afterward, he took some valuables from the apartment and left. |
|  |  | • The police beefed up patrols in east Charlotte after two bodies of young black women were found at The Lake apartment complex. |
|  |  | • Even so, Wallace sneaked through to rob, strangle, and stab Deborah Ann Slaughter. Her body was found on March 12, 1994. |
|  |  | • Wallace was arrested on March 13, 1994. For 12 hours, he confessed to the murders of ten women in Charlotte. |
|  |  | • He described in detail, the women's appearances, how he raped, robbed, and killed the women, and of his crack habit. |
|  |  | ◦ http://murderpedia.org/male.W/w/wallace-henry-louis.htm |

| Alexander Pichushkin, a.k.a. "The Chessboard Killer" | • He was born April 9, 1974, in Moscow, Russia.<br>• Little is known of Pichushkin's early years. He had some type of head injury around the age of 4 and spent time in an institute for the disabled as a child.<br>• His parents divorced when he was quite young, and he grew up without a father figure to guide him. His childhood was a difficult and troubled one.<br>• Later, it was found that this injury had damaged a significant part of his brain which led to tendencies of aggression.<br>• Pichushkin was quite close to his maternal grandfather who recognized his intelligence and introduced him to chess.<br>• He became an exceptional player and found a way to channel his aggression by dominating the chessboard.<br>• The death of his beloved grandfather affected him deeply, and he became aggressive and violent toward others soon after. | • His crimes spanned from 1992 to 2006. Pichushkin committed his first murder when he was just a teenager when he pushed a boy out of a window, according to Pichushkin's televised confession.<br>• While the police did question him in the case, it was later declared a suicide. "This first murder, it's like first love, it's unforgettable," he later said.<br>• Pichushkin's murderous impulses lay dormant for years until he began killing people in Moscow's Bittsevsky Park in the early 2000s.<br>• After the loss of his grandfather, with whom he shared a close bond, Pichushkin became depressed.<br>• He got a dog that he often walked in the park. It is unknown whether the dog is actually buried there, however.<br>• Often targeting the elderly or the destitute, he lured his victims to the park to reportedly drink at his dead dog's grave.<br>• Pichushkin waited until his intended victim was intoxicated, and then he hit him or her repeatedly with a blunt instrument—a hammer or a piece of pipe.<br>• To conceal the bodies, he often threw his victims into a sewer pit. Some of them were still alive at the time and ended up drowning.<br>• As the killings progressed, Pichushkin's attacks grew even more savage. He left a broken vodka bottle sticking out of some victims' skulls and seemed to care less about disposing of the bodies, just leaving them out in the open to be discovered.<br>• Authorities finally caught up with Pichushkin in June 2006 after he killed a woman he worked with at a supermarket. She had left a note for her son to tell him that she was taking a walk with Pichushkin. While he was aware of the risks involved in killing his coworker, he still murdered her.<br>• After his arrest, the police discovered a chessboard with dates on 61 or 62 of its 64 squares.<br>• Pichushkin was a fan of the game and had been trying to kill as many people as there were squares on the board. Despite the date references, the police were only able to charge Pichushkin with 51 counts of murder and attempted murder (3 of his victims survived).<br>• "For me, a life without murder is like a life without food for you," Pichushkin reportedly said. Showing no remorse, he later argued that he should be charged with more murders, keeping with his claim of killing 61 or 63 people.<br>   ◦ https://www.biography.com/people/alexander-pichushkin-396824<br>   ◦ https://www.thefamouspeople.com/profiles/alexander-pichushkin-14669.php |

**Cannibals**

| Name | Early life | Crimes |
| --- | --- | --- |
| Albert Fish | • He was born on May 19, 1870, in Washington, D.C., and abandoned by his parents (father aged 75 years old, and mother 32). He lived in an orphanage until the age of 9 years old.<br>• Fish lived a brutal life in the orphanage—reportedly, he was beaten regularly and exposed to sadistic acts of brutality; he was unmercifully whipped and observed other boys engaged in wrong activities.<br>• When he was only 12, he was introduced to urolagnia (drinking urine) and coprophagy (eating feces).<br>• These acts uncovered Fish's paraphilic tendencies through the humiliation of himself or his partner and the intense sexual urges associated with the thought of urine.<br>• He later spent a great part of his weekends lurking public baths, where he would watch other boys undress. This uncovered his voyeuristic affinities (also known as peeping or onlooking).<br>• Fish's paraphilic impulses eventually led him to an obsession with mutilation of self and other. | • Most serious criminal history started in 1919 when Fish's obsession with torture and cannibalism—eating raw meat for dinner and occasionally feeding his children the raw meat as well—led him to plan an actual murder.<br>• Fish molested mostly boys under the age of 6. He would also expose himself to his victims.<br>• Fish often targeted vulnerable children and paid boys to obtain other children for him. He eventually tortured, molested, mutilated, and murdered several young children.<br>• In looking for boys to torture, Albert Fish found 10-year-old Grace Budd after putting up an ad in the news in May of 1928 in the hopes of "hiring" a boy for his farm. Upon visiting the Budd family to interview their son, daughter Grace Budd fell victim to Fish at first sight.<br>• Fish seemed like the typical "loving grandfather" whom occasionally bore gifts. Grace was invited by Fish to a children's party, along with brother Edward, and the unsuspecting parents accepted.<br>• It wasn't until 6 years later that a grotesque letter sent by Fish to the Budd house described the rape, mutilation, and consumption of Grace Budd, after drinking her blood.<br>• Fish was caught, arrested, and immediately began confessing to the killing, mutilation, and molestation of Grace and hundreds of other children.<br>• The jury found him sane, and guilty, and was executed by the electric chair on January 16, 1936, at Sing Sing Prison in New York.<br>○ Blanco, J. I. (2017, June 4). *Albert Hamilton fish.* Retrieved from http://murderpedia.org/male.F/f/fish-albert.htm<br>○ Fink, K. (2015, January 21). *The 8 Scariest psychopaths in history.* Retrieved from https://medium.com/@JeriFink/the-8-scariest-psychopaths-in-history-b5f13b9d9aa2<br>○ Montaldo, C. (2018. August 23). *Biography of serial killer Albert Fish.* Retrieved from https://www.thoughtco.com/serial-killer-albert-fish-973157<br>○ Peters, L. (2017, July 13). *8 suspected psychopaths from history whose stories are still chilling in 2017.* Retrieved from https://www.bustle.com/p/8-suspectedpsychopaths-from-history-whose-stories-are-still-chilling-in-2017-70014<br>○ Serena, K. (2018, Jan 30). *The Gruesome crimes of albert fish, the Brooklyn vampire.* Retrieved from https://allthatsinteresting.com/albert-fish |

| Richard Chase | • Chase was born in Sacramento, California, on May 23, 1950.<br>• His father was physically abusive, which led to him developing a drinking habit and mental illnesses at a young age.<br>• He passed the Macdonald Triad, which is a test used to predict if a child might be a future sociopath.<br>• He had the characteristics of a bed-wetter at the age of 8, and by 10, he was setting fires and killing animals.<br>• He believed that his heart would stop working because of a lack of Vitamin C, so he would hold oranges to his head to absorb the nutrients.<br>• He also thought that the bones in his skull were being detached, so he shaved his hair to monitor the activity.<br>• In his teen years, he couldn't properly function sexually without practicing necrophilia with the corpses of the animals he had killed.<br>• Afterward, he would drink the blood of the animals and eat them raw.<br>• In the 1970s, he was institutionalized after being diagnosed as a schizophrenic and was caught injecting rabbit blood into his veins.<br>• In the hospital, he was nicknamed Dracula by the staff.<br>• After being released, his mother did not want him around because she was afraid of him.<br>• He moved in with his friends in an apartment. Shortly afterward, his friends would be disgusted when he would walk around drunk and naked in front of guests. They asked him to move out, but he refused, so they moved out, leaving him there alone.<br>• Being left alone, he started to capture and kill small animals. He then brought them back to the apartment, stripped them of their organs, and drained their blood. He blended the organs and blood with soda and consumed them. | • Chase took a liking to handguns and played around with them.<br>• That is until December 29, 1977, when he shot and killed Ambrose Griffin during a drive-by shooting.<br>• Chase broke into the home of Teresa Wallin. He then shot her with the same gun that he used on Griffin, raped her dead body, and carved it afterward. He drank the blood and bathed in it. Finally, he stuffed dog feces in her mouth before leaving.<br>• Two days after killing Teresa Wallin, Chase broke into the home of Evelyn Miroth. She was babysitting her 2-year-old nephew David, and her son Jason was also there. The neighbor, Dan Meredith, was also in the house. He shot Dan in the head and murdered Evelyn and the kids. He raped the corpse of Evelyn before drinking her blood from her neck. He then took David's body and consumed his brain matter and drank his blood. He mutilated David's body and left it at a church.<br>• After leaving behind the bodies of Evelyn, Dan, and Jason back at the house, there was enough evidence left (such as the bullet from the gun, to his fingerprints) to arrest Chase.<br>• They also searched his apartment, where they found the body parts of other victims.<br>• He took the insanity plea, but that was unsuccessful. Two psychiatrists deemed him sane mainly because of his motives.<br>• His main reason as to why he committed a murder spree was because he thought that he needed blood to live. However, he was found to know what he was doing.<br>  ○ Markman, R., & Bosco, D. (1989). *Alone with the devil.* NY: Doubleday<br>  ○ Stone, M. (2001). Serial sexual homicide: Biological, psychological, and sociological aspects.<br>  ○ White, J. (2011). The utilization of forensic science and criminal profiling for capturing serial killers. |

(continued)

**Cannibals** (continued)

| Name | Early life | Crimes |
|---|---|---|
| Jeffery Dahmer | • He was born in Milwaukee, Wisconsin, on May 21, 1960, to Lionel and Joyce Dahmer. He has a younger brother, David Dahmer.<br>• He was described as a happy, energetic child until he reached the age of 4.<br>• Several reasons seemed to have contributed to him becoming removed and antisocial:<br>  ○ He had a surgery to correct a double hernia.<br>  ○ He became withdrawn following the birth of his younger brother.<br>  ○ The family moved frequently.<br>  ○ He spent time alone.<br>• At around age 14, he began collecting roadkill, stripped the animal carcasses, and saved the bones.<br>• He started drinking heavily and became an alcoholic by the time he graduated high school.<br>• By 18, he murdered his first victim in June 1978.<br>• He picked up a hitchhiker named Steven Hicks, took him home, and got him drunk; he hit him on the head and strangled him with a bar bell.<br>• He enrolled in college but dropped out due to alcoholism.<br>• His father forced him to join the Army but was discharged after 2 years again because of alcoholism.<br>• He was arrested in 1981 for disorderly conduct and was sent to live with his grandmother. He was arrested again that summer for indecent exposure.<br>• He was arrested in 1986 for masturbating in front of two boys.<br>• He frequented bathhouses but was unsatisfied with his sexual encounters because his partners moved too much.<br>• He began to give his partners sleeping pills and sedatives. "I trained myself to view people as objects of pleasure instead of people." | • He seemed to have the same routine with his victims:<br>  ○ He would find victims at gay bars or malls and persuade them with free alcohol and money if they agreed to pose for photographs. Many of his victims were found to be African-American men.<br>  ○ When they came back with him, he would them drug them, sometimes torture and kill them usually by strangling them.<br>  ○ He would have sex with the corpse, cut up the body, and dispose of the remains.<br>  ○ He usually kept the dismembered body parts in different parts of his home; often body parts were found with intense grips and teeth marks, alluding to his cannibalistic ways.<br>  ○ Or he dismembered the corpse and put the body parts in a plastic bag and buried them behind his parents' home.<br>  ○ He would dig up the bones crush them and scattered the remains.<br>• First murder was in June 1978.<br>• In 1987, he took his second victim, Steven Toumi, checked into a hotel and drank. He woke up the next morning and found Toumi dead, unable to recall the events from the night before. He brought the body to his grandmother's house and masturbated on the corpse before disposing of the remains.<br>• March 1989, he lured Anthony Spears, drugged, strangled, sodomized, and dismembered the body.<br>  ○ Jamet, D. "Offender Profiling – Jeffrey Dahmer." Delphine Jamet: Security Officer / Author / Counter Terrorism Student, 22 Oct. 2012, delphinejamet.wordpress.com/2012/10/22/offender-profiling-jeffrey-dahmer/.<br>  ○ "I Carried It Too Far, That's for Sure'." Psychology Today, Sussex Publishers, www.psychologytoday.com/us/articles/199205/i-carried-it-too-far-thats-sure.<br>Walsh, E. Jury finds Dahmer was sane. *The Washington Post*, WP Company, 16 Feb. 1992, www.washingtonpost.com/archive/politics/1992/02/16/jury-finds-dahmer-was-sane/7ba3ebb0-ec67-4e84-8e02-a75ee4da29bf/?noredirect=on&utm_term=.05f08f151196 |

| | | |
|---|---|---|
| | | ○ https://www.biography.com/people/jeffrey-dahmer-9264755<br>○ https://www.history.com/this-day-in-history/cannibal-and-serial-killer-jeffrey-dahmer-is-caught<br>○ https://www.nytimes.com/1991/08/04/us/17-killed-and-a-life-is-searched-for-clues.html<br>○ https://www.irishtimes.com/culture/film/at-school-with-a-serial-killer-growing-up-with-jeffrey-dahmer-1.3511144 |
| Tsutomu Miyazaki | • He was born on August 21, 1962, in Tokyo, Japan. He was born with deformed hands as result of his premature birth; his hands were fused to his wrists, meaning he would have to move his entire forearm to rotate the hand.<br>• During his elementary school years, he was a quiet and shy student who was rejected by his peers due to his deformity; this rejection caused him to develop an obsession.<br>• Despite his problems with socializing with other people, he was initially one of the best students in his high school class, until his grades began to drop, eventually resulting in him not receiving an admission to Meiji University, a private and prestigious university in Tokyo.<br>• Later, Miyazaki attended a junior college and began studying to become a photo technician, leaving his intentions of becoming a teacher behind.<br>• Miyazaki soon developed an inferiority complex due to the size of his penis and his inability to socialize with women; his hobby was to take pictures of female tennis players, so he could use them to masturbate.<br>• Miyazaki moved into his parents' house and shared a room with his older sister. Miyazaki's family was highly influential in their town, his father owned a newspaper, but he had no desire to take over his job; Miyazaki would later claim that it was during this period that he began to consider suicide. | • On August 22, 1988, just 1 day after his 26th birthday, Miyazaki abducted a young girl named Mari Konno while she was playing at a friend's house and drove her to a wooded area; the two sat in the car under a bridge for several minutes before he strangled her to death and engaged in acts of necrophilia with her corpse, leaving her in hills near his home and taking her clothes with him.<br>• Miyazaki eventually returned to the scene and removed body parts and some of her teeth. He turned Konno's bones into powder and placed them in a box, alongside with her teeth, pictures of her clothes, and a postcard containing the words "Mari. Cremated. Bones. Investigate. Prove," which he then sent to her family; Miyazaki kept her hands and feet on his apartment.<br>• On October 3, Miyazaki spotted Masami Yoshizawa on a rural road, offering her a ride; he took her to the same place where he had killed Konno, repeating the same process of strangling the child, having sex with her corpse, and taking her clothes.<br>• The next month, Miyazaki was returning from a friend's house when he abducted Erika Nanba and drove her to a parking lot, forcing her to undress and allowing him to take pictures of her nude body before killing her.<br>• Miyazaki covered her body with a bedsheet and took her clothes but later disposed of them in a wooded area, leaving the girl's body in the parking lot; Miyazaki would later send a postcard to her family, containing the words "Erika. Cold. Cough. Throat. Rest. Death."<br>• On June 6, 1989, Miyazaki led a girl into his car after taking pictures of her and killed her, leaving her body in his apartment and using it for necrophilia, taking pictures of it in various positions and filming it. |

(continued)

**Cannibals** (continued)

| Name | Early life | Crimes |
|---|---|---|
| | • Miyazaki disliked everyone in his family, except for his grandfather, who died in May 1988; his death worsened Miyazaki's depression, and as a way to "retain something from him," Miyazaki ate part of his grandfather's ashes.<br>• Weeks later, Miyazaki's sister caught him spying on her while she was showering, and when she confronted him, he attacked her and his mother after having an argument with her.<br>• Miyazaki began collecting pornographic anime, adult magazines, violent films, and child porn, gathering a total of 5763 videotapes. | • When her body began decomposing, Miyazaki dismembered it, disposed of the head in a cemetery and the torso in hills, but he would later retrieve the body parts, keeping them in his closet; Miyazaki also drank blood from the girl's hands and ate part of them.<br>• On July 23, Miyazaki attempted to insert zoom lens into the vagina of a girl in a park but was stopped by her father; Miyazaki fled from the area, naked, and on foot but was arrested when he returned to retrieve his car.<br>• Police soon found Miyazaki's disturbing collection and the body parts he had hid. During his trial, Miyazaki blamed the murders on an alter ego called "Rat Man," who coerced him into committing the murders.<br>• The court judged him fit to stand trial, and he was sentenced to death. Miyazaki's father refused to pay for his legal defense and committed suicide in 1994.<br>• Miyazaki was hanged on June 17, 2008, at the age of 45.<br>  ○ https://criminalminds.fandom.com/wiki/Tsutomu_Miyazaki |
| Armin Meiwes | • He was born on December 1, 1961, in Germany. He is a former computer repair technician who achieved international notoriety for killing and eating a voluntary victim whom he had found via the Internet. Because of his acts, Meiwes is also known as the Rotenburg Cannibal or *Der Metzgermeister* (The Master Butcher). | • In March 2001, Meiwes, a then 41-year-old bisexual computer technician, placed an advertisement online on *The Cannibal Cafe* (a defunct forum for people with a cannibalism fetish). The post stated that Meiwes was "looking for a well-built 18- to 30-year-old to be slaughtered and then consumed."<br>• Forty-three year-old-Bernd-Jürgen Brandes, an engineer from Berlin, answered the ad later that month in March 2001.<br>• According to the report, many other people also responded to the advertisement but backed out. Reportedly, Meiwes did not attempt to force them to do anything against their will.<br>• A videotape that they made in Meiwes' home showcased Meiwes amputating Brandes' penis (with his agreement) and the two men attempting to eat it together.<br>• Preceding all this, it was reported that Brandes swallowed 20 sleeping pills and a bottle of cough syrup, something that may have caused slowing of the breathing and extreme tiredness. Brandes initially insisted that Meiwes attempted to bite his penis off, something that he tried unsuccessful. He then decided to use a knife to remove Brandes' penis. |

- Reportedly, Brandes tried to eat some of his own penis raw but was unable to do so because it was too tough and "chewy."
- Meiwes then fried the penis in a pan with salt, pepper, wine, and garlic, using some of Brandes' fat. When it turned too burnt to be consumed, he chopped it up into chunks and fed it to his dog. Meiwes then killed Brandes with Brandes's consent by stabbing him repeatedly in the neck.
- Meiwes then dismembered and ate the corpse over the next 10 months, storing body parts in his freezer under pizza boxes and consuming up to 20 kg (44 lb) of the flesh. According to prosecutors, Meiwes committed the act for sexual pleasure.
- Meiwes was arrested in December 2002, when a college student alerted authorities to new advertisements for victims online. Investigators searched his home and found body parts and the videotape of the killing.
- On January 30, 2004, Meiwes was convicted of manslaughter and sentenced to 8 years in prison. The case attracted considerable media attention.
- Meiwes has admitted cannibalizing Brandes and has expressed regret for his actions. He added he wanted to write a biography to deter anyone who wants to follow his footsteps.
- Apparently, websites dedicated to Meiwes have appeared, with people advertising for willing victims. "They should go for treatment, so it doesn't escalate like it did with me," said Meiwes. While in prison, Meiwes has since become a vegetarian. He believes there are about 800 cannibals in Germany.
  - https://en.wikipedia.org/wiki/Armin_Meiwes

# Reference

Huss, M. T. (2014). *Forensic psychology: Research, clinical practice, and applications.* Hoboken, NJ: Wiley.

# Chapter 22
# Veterans, Trauma, and Trauma-Informed Justice: A View from the Bench

Marcia P. Hirsch

## Overview of Queens Veterans Court

In December 2010, the Queens Veterans Treatment Court (QVTC) opened with great fanfare: a military honor guard, flags from each branch of service, the Pledge of Allegiance, speeches, invited guests, dignitaries, and press coverage. Veteran defendants/participants were already there, too. Our treatment court team had been working with veterans for many years in our Drug Treatment Court, our Mental Health Court, our DWI Treatment Court, and our Drug Diversion Court.

Why the need for a new Veterans Court when we were already serving this population? This court differs from other treatment court models because it specifically focuses on the criminal-justice connected veteran and his/her needs. Our mission statement is "to honor military service and veterans and to assist veterans in fully restoring themselves." Many of our veterans struggle with alcohol dependence, drug abuse, and mental health issues, including posttraumatic stress disorder (PTSD), traumatic brain injury (TBI), as well as physical injuries sustained while serving. We provide linkages to wraparound services for vocational training, higher education, housing, benefits, and entitlements.

Our veteran participants have all committed felony crimes, some having lesser included crimes including misdemeanors. The four major crimes before the QVTC include drugs (both possession and sales), driving while intoxicated (DWI), assaults (oftentimes between family members or "bar room brawl" altercations), and

The author wishes to thank her two wonderful interns, Chaya Dembitzer from CUNY Queens College and Catherine E. Vanech from Hofstra University, for their research and assistance with this chapter.

M. P. Hirsch (✉)
Supreme Court of the State of New York, Kew Gardens, NY, USA

Court of Claims of the State of New York, Saratoga Springs, NY, USA
e-mail: mhirsch@nycourts.gov

© Springer Nature Switzerland AG 2020
R. A. Javier et al. (eds.), *Assessing Trauma in Forensic Contexts*,
https://doi.org/10.1007/978-3-030-33106-1_22

647

weapons charges. After an extensive screening process (see the following texts) and the development of an individualized treatment plan, the veteran takes a plea to the charge(s), admitting guilt, and signs a contract with the court, agreeing to follow the mandates of the court and the treatment plan. As stated in the contract, upon successful completion, the court agrees to dismiss and seal the felony charge in return for his/her compliance over the next year or 18 months. As a comparison, Drug Diversion Court cases mandate a minimum of 18 months, and the other courts usually have a 12-month term. For veterans, sometimes a term of probation is given for a misdemeanor charge, or a conditional discharge is given if the veteran's behavior has been exemplary. This sealing benefit gives the veteran the opportunity to pursue careers, obtain licenses, and take part in civic activities that include voting and serving jury duty, which are normally barred upon felony conviction. Noncompliance by the participant (e.g., missing treatment, repeated relapses, picking up new arrests, absconding from the jurisdiction, failing to make court appearances) can result in additional time being added to the mandate.

The veteran comes to court regularly for status conferences with his/her case manager or the Veterans' Justice Outreach (VJO) coordinator, followed by a court appearance before the judge, with the assistant district attorney, their own attorney, and a veteran mentor.

VJO coordinators are employed by the Veterans Affairs (VA) and case manage those veterans who are eligible for VA treatment, services, and benefits. Our VJO coordinator is a valued member of our team and attends status conferences, court appearances, and team meetings. She will also go to the Rikers Island jails to meet with incarcerated veterans to review their eligibility for services and possible referral to our court.

Veteran mentors are another unique part of Veterans Treatment Courts. They offer peer support to their fellow veterans but also assist with personal recovery plans, transportation, attendance at sober support/recovery meetings, housing, employment linkages, and job training. They provide a shoulder to lean on, someone to talk to or confide in, or a person to check in with if the vet is in crisis. Our court asked a veteran mentor to check in on Saturdays and Sundays with a veteran who was suicidal. The continuity of care, together with the Monday–Friday treatment program, helped this veteran through his depression and allowed him to address his mental health issues, attend drug treatment for his opioid addiction, obtain individual therapy, stay in contact with his teenage daughter, maintain employment, and successfully complete our program.

## Assessment and Evaluation of Trauma

In 2010, the QVTC received a Center for Substance Abuse Treatment (CSAT) grant to provide trauma treatment to all participants who were assessed and suffered from serious trauma symptoms. With this change, the role of forensic psychology within the Veterans Court became apparent. According to the American Board of

Professional Psychology, forensic psychology is the use of psychology to answer questions in relation to the judicial system and the law. For services in connection with the CSAT grant, the question before the court pertained to the veteran's trauma. In order to answer this question, potential participants are evaluated. Their evaluations include a clinical interview and a number of trauma-specific instruments for measuring past trauma. Specifically, these instruments include the Adverse Childhood Experience (ACE) questionnaire, Trauma Symptom Checklist (TSC-40), PTSD Checklist (PCL-C), Impact of Events Scale (IES), Trauma History Screen (THS), and Combat Exposure Scale (CES).

Initially, the QVTC utilized the ACE and TSC-40 scales to assess childhood trauma and current trauma symptoms. The ACE contains 10 items referring to experiences before the age of 18, which are all scored as yes or no. Scores range between 0 and 10. Total ACE scores have been found to have strong relationships to drug use problems, age of drug use initiation, and drug addiction. Compared to people with 0 ACE score, people with 5 or more were 7- to 10-fold more likely to report illicit drug use problems and addiction. Thus, ACE research shows the cumulative effect of multiple traumatic or chaotic childhood experiences.

The TSC-40 is a 40-item self-report measure of symptomatic distress in adults. It asks how often adults experienced symptoms in the previous two months. Ultimately, it produces six subscales (anxiety, depression, dissociation, sexual abuse trauma index, sexual problems, and sleep disturbance) plus a total score (ranging from 0 to 120). However, it is not intended to be diagnostic.

After using the ACE and TSC-40 for several months, the court staff felt that the life experiences and symptoms impacting the participants' recoveries were not being captured. At that point, the QVTC contracted with Policy Research Associates (PRA) to improve the assessment process. PRA recommended adding the PCL-C, IES, THS, and CES evaluation instruments.

The PCL test is a very widely used tool to assess current PTSD symptoms. It is free of charge, has English and Spanish versions, and takes a mere 10 minutes to administer. Containing 17 items, it is self-administered and results in a severity score of PTSD trauma symptoms. Along with this, the IES is a self-administered 22-item measure. It is also free of charge and available in multiple languages. It provides subscale scores for intrusion, avoidance, and hyperarousal. It can also be administered at regular intervals to assess participants' progress. Additionally, the THS is a 13-item measure that asks about 11 events and one general event. This test can be administered to participants with low reading levels and is also free. Psychologists serving at the QVTC have modified this test to ask whether participants are still bothered by the event and whether this type of event has happened in the past month.

It is important to note that the Combat Exposure Scale has been discontinued after the QVTC noticed that it was causing veterans to relive their trauma, producing increased anxiety and agitation. Questions included whether they ever killed anyone, saw anyone be killed or seriously wounded, or handled dead bodies or body parts.

## Research on Veterans and Trauma in Veterans Courts

Again, in 2010, the QVTC started conducting psychological evaluations of its participants to establish whether they suffered from serious trauma symptoms and thereby qualified for trauma treatment. Since that time, every veteran defendant has scored positively for trauma upon psychological evaluation. Some of their trauma predated their military service; some had very traumatic experiences during their military service; and some had additional traumatic events after they returned home.

These findings are consistent with those reported by Elbogen et al. (2010) in a study of 676 veterans of Iraq (OIF, Operation Iraqi Freedom) and Afghanistan (OEF, Operation Enduring Freedom) deployments. The researchers found the following:

- 19% had a history of incarceration
- 8% had at least one parent with a criminal history
- 40% witnessed family violence history
- 34% had been physically or sexually abused when they were under the age of 18
- 81% served in a war zone
- 22% reported traumatic brain injury during combat
- 86% reported war zone trauma

In 2013, the New York State (NYS) Office of Court Administration received a grant from the Bureau of Justice Assistance (BJA) to deepen its understanding of the operation of seven Veterans Treatment Courts in New York State. At the Queens Veterans Treatment Court, interviews were conducted with staff members, veteran participants, and veteran mentors. Quantitative analyses on participant data were collected from the court's management information system. The data showed that over half (58%) of the Queens Veterans Court participants reported having experienced or witnessed a traumatic event during their lifetime. Over one-third (38%) said that they had been threatened by a gun or knife. One-tenth (10%) of the participants said that they had been coerced/forced to engage in a sex act. Over half (52%) reported that they had re-experienced a traumatic event in a distressing way.

Many QVTC veterans had self-medicated their trauma symptoms for years, using a variety of substances. While 29% of veterans in the previously mentioned study identified alcohol as their primary drug, 37% indicated they had a problematic relationship with alcohol. Marijuana (24%), heroin (18%), and crack (11%) use was also significant. In the past 3 years, the QVTC has seen a significant increase in the abuse of prescription drugs (opiates and benzodiazepines) by veterans, oftentimes leading to heroin dependence when their supply of prescription drugs ran out. The national opioid epidemic is taking its toll on our veterans as well.

Women make up more than 7% of the veteran population nationally. The QVTC has only had five female participants. Three had felony DWI charges, one had a drug charge, and one had a serious assault charge for stabbing an acquaintance who allegedly stole money from her. All five had experienced military sexual trauma (MST) and had substance abuse issues. All were deployed to combat zones and experienced war-related trauma. One was diagnosed with a serious mental illness for which she received treatment and medication. All five successfully graduated from the QVTC. It was important that they were able to address their MST, whether in a group setting or through individual therapy sessions.

## Case Example of S.B.

One of my Vietnam era vets told me that he was more affected by the repeated showing of film footage of the 9/11 World Trade Center buildings collapse, where his sister died, than from the battles, deaths, and injuries that he saw first-hand in Vietnam. He visualized his sister dying, over and over again, which was especially difficult for him while he was in treatment in 2011, at the tenth year anniversary of the attack. He was clearly re-traumatized by the news coverage and had to deal with past military trauma and the tragic loss of his sister. He had never disclosed the death of his sister before—not in treatment while living with other veterans in a long-term veteran-specific residential treatment program nor during assessment or in case management appointments. After receiving intensive therapy and trauma treatment, he was finally able to address the heroin addiction that he had battled for 40 years and the past traumatic events that led to general anxiety and isolation. He successfully graduated from our court and his drug felony case was dismissed and sealed.

## Treatment Interventions

Once an eligible veteran is found to have significant trauma, treatment interventions are offered by the QVTC. Three trauma treatment programs have been utilized by QVTC treatment providers; they include Seeking Safety, Helping Men Recover, and Trauma, Addictions, Mental Health and Recovery (TAMAR).

The Seeking Safety Program was developed by Lisa M. Najavits (2002) at Harvard Medical Hospital and is a manualized model that offers coping skills to help clients attain greater safety in their lives. It is present-focused and designed to be inspiring and hopeful. It is also highly versatile and can be used in a group or individual format: for women, men, and adolescents; for all levels of care (e.g., outpatient, inpatient, and residential); and for all types of trauma and substances. It can be administered by any clinician who has received the requisite training and purchased the materials and workbooks.

The Seeking Safety Program contains 25 treatment topics, each representing a safe coping skill relevant to both PTSD and substance use disorder (SUD). All topics are independent and thus can be done in any order, with as few or as many sessions as there is time for. It is not required to do all 25 topics. The model has been successfully implemented with a variety of populations including the incarcerated, homeless, adolescents, veterans, substance abusers, mental health participants, and participants of diverse ethnicities. Additionally, Seeking Safety is the most empirically studied treatment thus far for trauma/PTSD and substance abuse, and it is the only model for PTSD and substance use disorder that meets standard criteria as an effective treatment (Chambless & Hollon, 1998; Najavits, 2002). The model has consistently shown positive outcomes on trauma symptoms and substance abuse as well as for issues such as suicide, HIV risk, and social functioning issues.

Helping Men Recover is a program that integrates a theory of addiction, a theory of trauma, and a theory of male psychosocial development to assist men in their recovery from addiction. It was developed by Dan Griffin (Covington, Griffin, & Dauer, 2011) and there is now a companion program for women. The program is grounded in research, theory, and clinical practice and is administered in 18 sessions in four modules, namely, self, relationships, spirituality, and sexuality. These four areas were chosen after recovering men identified these as triggers for relapse and necessary for growth and healing. The materials for the program are designed to be user-friendly and self-instructive, allowing the Helping Men Recover Program to be implemented by clinicians with a wide range of training and experience.

The TAMAR Program was designed by Dr. Andrea Karfgin (2004) to educate and treat those who have a history of physical and/or sexual abuse, a recent treatment history for a mental health condition, and an alcohol or a drug use or abuse disorder. It is a structured, manualized 15-week intervention combining psychoeducational approaches with expressive therapies designed for women and men with histories of trauma in correctional systems. Groups are run inside detention centers, in state psychiatric hospitals, and in the community.

## *"What Did You Do in the War, Daddy/Mommy?"*

The cases before the QVTC over the past 7 years have made it evident that past traumatic experiences often impact behavior in the following ways. The most obvious is that drugs and alcohol are used often to mask physical pain, to aid in getting to sleep and to stay asleep, and to numb the feelings of past unpleasant experiences that many relive on a daily basis. Vets share personal details about seeing women and children "blown up" by roadside bombs, losing "buddies" in combat, or being the sole survivor when their Humvee was under attack. One veteran told us that he had developed a relationship and shared M&M's with two young Afghan children. Unfortunately, he was there when they died in sniper cross fire. He continued to dream about them, years after the event. He saw their faces and M&M's.

Many veterans use marijuana to "take the edge off" and to get to sleep. With the greater acceptance and legalization of medicinal and/or recreational marijuana, many vets justify its use. In 2018, the New York State legislature added PTSD to the list of chronic conditions for which medical marijuana could be prescribed. Veterans groups had actively lobbied for this amendment to the existing law. New York State has not legalized the recreational use of marijuana, which causes confusion for veterans who may have lived in other states like Colorado that have legalized such use.

Some veterans had noncombat jobs that impacted them as significantly from a trauma perspective as those who were in battle. Medics and medical personnel worked with the gravely injured, amputees, and dying. Other veterans who worked in transport share their stories of bringing the seriously wounded to military hospitals and, sadly, the caskets of the deceased to Dover Air Force Base. These strong men and women are just as vulnerable to suffering PTSD as those who served in infantry. There is also a new body of research that is being conducted on the stress and PTSD suffered by those that operate drones to target and kill the enemy. Even high-tech operations like these, designed and conducted miles away from the point of impact, may have lasting health implications for these veterans (Otto & Webber, 2013).

## *Case Example of T.E.*

At the Manhattan VA, a support group has been formed for combat medics. One of my post 9/11 veterans participated in that group and said repeatedly that it was his favorite part of treatment. He was the youngest member. Many of the others were Vietnam era medics, but their shared experiences formed a bond and helped them put their past trauma in context. My medic veteran recently graduated from our QVTC and plans to come back as a volunteer veteran mentor in the near future after he finishes school.

## The Trauma-Informed Courtroom

At the QVTC, our team is comprised of judges, court officers, and psychologists who are trauma-informed and have received many hours of trauma training. They treat the participants with dignity and respect. They expect the presence of trauma and know that the vets' experiences impact their feelings and behaviors. Pains are taken to avoid re-traumatization of participants. As a trauma-informed court, the QVTC understands that oftentimes, when a person is receiving trauma therapy, this opens a flood of pain and emotions and may trigger relapse to drugs and/or alcohol as a coping mechanism. Adaptations of traditional court-ordered sanctions (e.g., jail or community service) may be necessary as these sanctions are often triggered by lack of compliance with the goal of the program. However, we recognize that trauma therapy can trigger this lack of compliance (e.g., relapse). Writing assignments, journaling, and additional therapy may be required instead of a short-term jail stay or community service.

Also, the QVTC recognizes that what we say and how we say it is supremely important. Words can injure too. Rather than saying, "Your drug screen is dirty," which implies "I'm dirty…There is something wrong with me," a trauma-informed judge would say, "Your drug screen is positive." It is not judgmental, simply states a fact, and may be followed by a discussion of the steps that the person can take when he/she feels like using the next time (Wells & Urff, 2013). Similarly, a judge in a regular courtroom may say, "I'm sending you for a mental evaluation." The trauma survivor hears, "I must be crazy. There is something wrong with me that can't be fixed." A trauma-sensitive judge would say, "I'd like to refer you to a doctor who can help us better understand how to support you." If a veteran is struggling, a trauma-informed veterans court judge may acknowledge that by saying, "I see that you've been struggling with your sobriety (or getting to treatment, or keeping your appointments, etc.). What can we do to help you? What do you need?" This approach is both trauma-informed and offers the elements of voice and choice and an opportunity to tell their side of the story. These are tenets from the procedural justice movement that began with research by Professor Tom Tyler at Yale University (2000). Procedural justice research shows that how people feel they were treated by system actors influences compliance with the law, regardless of whether they *win* or *lose* (LaGratta & Tyler, 2017). It is essential to give court participants an explanation of what is going on, what happens next, and what is expected of them. Trauma-informed veterans court judges will often ask, "Do you understand? Do you have any questions for me?"

At the QVTC, their trauma-informed team is cognizant of anniversaries, birthdays, dates of loss, and anything that could re-trigger a traumatic response. They acknowledge that this could be a difficult time and encourage participants to use the support system built around them. This could mean leaning on their veteran mentor, an AA or NA sponsor, a pastor or priest, a trusted individual counselor, or a professional therapist.

Good calendar management can also ease a veteran's anxiety. Some participants may need to have their cases called first, because the courtroom setting is stressful and may remind them of an unpleasant event that they experienced in the past (e.g., being sentenced to jail.) Some may want to have their cases called last so they can discuss something private and personal (e.g., an abortion, a miscarriage, a recent cancer diagnosis.)

At the QVTC, court officers are also trauma-informed and interact with veterans. The court officers can also give the team a "heads-up" if a defendant is intoxicated or decompensating and might not be taking their prescribed medication. Their team will handle that case first and/or escort the person to appropriate detox, medical, or psychiatric service as needed. Court officers can also relay if the participant comes to court with someone who is threatening, intimidating, or may be abusing them. Intervention services can then be implemented.

## Case Example of R.B.

One of my vets had a service/therapeutic bulldog who accompanied him to court. The service dog was very welcome and improved everyone's spirits when he entered the courtroom. The environment of the trauma-informed courtroom is also important.

For example, at the QVTC, their team wants everyone to feel welcome. They do not have signs telling individuals what not to do (e.g., *no food, no cell phones, no T-shirts or tank tops*). Similarly, if it is upsetting for seated participants to see hand-cuffed persons or jailed defendants wearing prison jump suits, then they call the jail cases last and eliminate that anxiety. Many of these practices developed out of their team's courteous, respectful, and common-sense approach. They applaud the successes and congratulate the veterans for any and all achievements. They look to lift them up and enhance their self-esteem. This, in turn, is meant to foster the vet's resiliency and helps them lead law-abiding, productive, and happy lives. The Queens Veterans Court has a 90% graduation success rate.

## Questions/Activities for Further Exploration

1. Discuss the overarching issue that the trauma-informed justice is attempting to address regarding the ultimate goals of adjudication of crime where factors related to trauma are likely to be present.
2. What is the larger issue about justice and the consideration of mitigating circumstances in the lives of many defendants?
3. What are the personal and legal consequences of not including trauma issues in sentencing decisions?
4. What changes (if any) are needed in the current sentencing guidelines that are likely to lead to a much fairer and humane justice system in this regard while still being able to hold defendants accountable for their crimes?
5. Some may argue that this approach when applied to the general defendant populations runs the risk of encouraging an overly permissive justice system, likely to be abused by skillful defendants. What are your thoughts about that?

## References

Chambless, D. L., & Hollon, S. D. (1998). Defining empirically supported therapies. *Journal of Consulting and Criminal Psychology, 66*(1), 7–18.

Covington, S. S., Griffin, D., & Dauer, R. (2011). *Helping men recover: A man's workbook-Special Edition for Criminal Justice System*. San Francisco, CA: Jossey-Bass.

Elbogen, E. B., Fuller, S., Johnson, S. C., Brooks, S., Kinneer, P., Calhoun, P. S., & Beckham, J. C. (2010). Improving risk assessment of violence among military veterans: An evidence-based approach for clinical decision-making. *Clinical Psychology Review, 30*(6), 595–607.

Karfgin, A. (2004). *TAMAR: Trauma, addictions, mental health, and recovery*. Retrieved 9/4/2019 from https://www.nasmhpd.org/sites/default/files/TAMAR-Introduction-TableofContents_1.pdf

LaGratta, E., & Tyler, T. (2017). To be fair: Conversations about procedural justice. *Center for Court Innovation*. Retrieved from https://www.courtinnovation.org/sites/default/files/documents/To_Be_Fair.pdf

Najavits, L. M. (2002). *Seeking safety: A treatment manual for PTSD and substance abuse*. New York, NY/London, UK: The Guilford Press.

Otto, J. L., & Webber, B. J. (2013). Mental health diagnoses and counseling among pilots of remotely piloted aircraft in the United States Air Force. *Medical Surveillance Monthly Report, 20*(3), 3–8.

Tyler, T. R. (2000). Social justice. *International Journal of Psychology, 35*, 117–125.

Wells, S., & Urff, J. (2013). *Essential components of trauma informed judicial practice: What every judge needs to know about trauma*. Rockville, MD: Substance Abuse and Mental Health Services, Administration's National Center on Trauma-Informed Care and SAMHSA's National GAINS Center for Behavioral Health and Justice.

# List of Additional Resources

## Chapter 1

Garbarino, J. (2015a). *Listening to killers: Lessons learned from my twenty years as a psychological expert in murder cases.* Los Angeles, CA: University California Press.

Koch, W., Douglas, K., Nicholls, T., & O'Neill, M. (2006). *Psychological injuries: Forensic assessment, treatment, and law.* New York: Oxford University Press.

Landay, W. (2013). *Defending Jacob, a novel.* New York: Bantam Books/Random House.

Vaughans, K. C., & Spielberg, W. (Eds.). (2014). *Psychology of black boys and adolescents.* Santa Barbara, CA: Praeger.

## Chapter 2

Garbarino, J. (2015b). *Listening to killers: Lessons learned from my twenty years as a psychological expert witness in murder cases.* Oakland, CA: University of California Press.

Garbarino, J. (2018). *Miller's Children: Why giving teenage killers a second chance matters for all of us.* Oakland, CA: University of California Press.

Greenwald, R. (2012). *Trauma and juvenile delinquency: Theory, research, and interventions.* New York: Routledge.

Kerig, P. K. (2013). *Psychological trauma and juvenile delinquency: New directions in research and intervention.* New York: Routledge.

Nauth, L. (2018). *Lifetrap: From child victim to adult victimizer.* New York: Page Publishing, Inc.

## Chapter 3

American Academy of Psychiatry and the Law website. http://www.aapl.org

American Academy of Psychiatry and the Law Landmark Case List. http://www.aapl.org/landmark_list.htm

American Psychology-Law website. https://www.apadivisions.org/division-41/

© Springer Nature Switzerland AG 2020                                                                         657
R. A. Javier et al. (eds.), *Assessing Trauma in Forensic Contexts*,
https://doi.org/10.1007/978-3-030-33106-1

Find Law Legal Database (including Supreme Court Decisions since 1893). http://www.findlaw.com

Herman, J. L. (1992). Complex PTSD: A syndrome in survivors of prolonged and repeated trauma (PDF). *Journal of Traumatic Stress, 5*(3), 377–391. https://doi.org/10.1007/BF00977235

Perlin, M. (1993). Pretexts and mental disability law: The case of competency. *University of Miami Law, 47*, 625.

Poythress, N., Bonie, R., Monahan, J., Hoge, S., & Otto, R. (2002). *Adjudicative competence: The MacArthur studies*. New York: Springer. Review, 47, 625. https://repository.law.miami.edu/umlr/vol47/iss3/4/Trauma and shock. American Psychological Association. https://www.apa.org/topics/trauma/

Zapf, P,. & Beltrani (January 15, 2019). Competency to stand trial. Oxford Bibliographies. https://doi.org/10.1093/OBO/9780199828340-0229

# Chapter 4

# Trauma-Informed Care in Corrections

National Institute of Corrections: Trauma-Informed Correctional Care: Promising for Prisoners and Facilities. https://community.nicic.gov/blogs/mentalhealth/archive/2013/09/09/trauma-informed-correctional-care-promising-for-prisoners-and-facilities.aspx

U.S. Bureau of Justice Assistance, U.S. Department of Justice: Using Trauma-Informed Practices to Enhance Safety and Security in Women's Correctional Facilities. https://www.bja.gov/Publications/NRCJIW-UsingTraumaInformedPractices.pdf

# Seeking Safety

https://www.treatment-innovations.org/

# Chapter 5

"Diagnosing liability: the legal history of posttraumatic stress disorder". (2011). See Smith, in the chapter's References.

*No More Math Without Subtraction: Deconstructing the Guidelines' Prohibitions and Restrictions on Mitigating Factors*. (2011). See Baron-Evans & Coffin, in the chapter's References.

The American Psychology Association Practice Directorate's "Specialty Guidelines for Forensic Psychology" (2012) and "Clinical Practice Guideline for the treatment of posttraumatic stress disorder (PTSD)" (2017), cited in the References, below.

# Chapter 6

Mothers Against Drunk Driving.
National Center for Victims of Crime.
National Organization for Victim Assistance.
Parents of Murdered Children.
The Compassionate Friends.

# Chapter 7

Anderson, J. A. E., Mak, L., Chahi, A. K., & Bialystok, E. (February, 2018). The language and social background questionnaire: Assessing degree of bilingualism in a diverse population, *Behavior Research Methods, 50*(1), 250–263.
Bialystok, E. (2015). Bilingualism and the development of executive function: The role of attention. *Child Development Perspectives, 9*(2), 117–121. https://doi.org/10.1111/cdep.12116
Evans, F. B., & Hass, G. A. (2018). *Forensic psychological assessment in immigration court- A guidebook for evidence-based and ethical practice. New York*. London: Routledge.
Gopaul-McNicol, S., & Thomas-Presswood, T. (1998). *Working with linguistically and culturally different children: Innovative clinical and educational approaches*. Boston: Allyn & Bacon.

# Chapter 8

## General References for Parenting Evaluations in Child Protection

American Psychological Association. (2013a). Guidelines for psychological evaluations in child protection matters. *American Psychologist, 68*(1), 20–31.
Budd, K. S., Connell, M., & Clark, J. (2011). *Evaluation of parenting capacity in child protection*. New York: Oxford University Press.
Condie, L. O. (2003). *Parenting evaluations for the court: Care and protection matters*. New York: Kluwer Academic/Plenum Publishers.

## Instruments to Assess General Trauma and Racial Trauma

Briere, J. (1998). *Inventory of altered self-capacities*. Lutz, FL: Psychological Assessment Resources.
Briere, J. (2000). *Cognitive distortion scales*. Lutz, FL: Psychological Assessment Resources.
Briere, J. (2001). *Detailed assessment of posttraumatic stress*. Lutz, FL: Psychological Assessment Resources.

Briere, J. (2011). *Trauma symptom inventory-2*. Lutz, FL: Psychological Assessment Resources.

Utsey, S. O. (1999). Development and validation of a short form of the index of race-related stress (IRRS)–brief version. *Measurement and Evaluation in Counseling and Development, 32*(3), 149–167.

Utsey, S. O., & Ponterotto, J. G. (1996). Development and validation of the index of race-related stress (IRRS). *Journal of Counseling Psychology, 43*, 490–501.

Utsey, S. O., Adams, E. P., & Bolden, M. (2000). Development and initial validation of the Africultural coping systems inventory. *Journal of Black Psychology, 26*(2), 194–215.

Utsey, S. O., Belvet, B., Hubbard, R. R., Fischer, N. L., Opare-Henaku, A., & Gladney, L. L. (2013). Development and validation of the prolonged activation and anticipatory race-related stress scale. *Journal of Black Psychology, 39*(6), 532–559.

Williams, D. R., & Mohammed, S. A. (2009). Discrimination and racial disparities in health: Evidence and needed research. *Journal of Behavioral Medicine, 32*, 20–47. https://doi.org/10.1007/s10865-008-9185-0

Williams, D. R., Yu, Y., Jackson, J. S., & Anderson, N. B. (1997). Racial differences in physical and mental health: Socioeconomic status, stress, and discrimination. *Journal of Health Psychology, 2*, 335–351.

# Chapter 9

American Psychological Association (APA). (2010). Guidelines for child custody evaluations in family law proceedings. *American Psychologist, 65*(9), 863–867.

American Psychological Association (APA). (2013). Specialty guidelines for forensic psychology. *American Psychologist, 68*, 7–19.

Association of Family and Conciliation Courts (AFCC). (2006). *Model standards of practice for child custody evaluation*. Madison, WI: Association of Family and Conciliation Courts.

Association of Family and Conciliation Courts (AFCC). (2016). *Guidelines for examining intimate partner violence: A supplement to the AFCC model standards of practice for child custody evaluation*. Madison, WI: Association of Family and Conciliation Courts.

Ferentz, L. (2017). *Trauma-informed assessments* [E-reader Version]. Retrieved from https://www.theferentzinstitute.com/trauma-informed-assessments-e-book-lisa-ferentz/

Fuhrmann, G. W., & Zibbell, R. A. (2012). *Evaluation for child custody*. New York: Oxford University Press. https://doi.org/10.1093/med:psych/9780199766857.003.0015

Heilbrun, K. (2001). *Principles of forensic mental health assessment*. New York: Kluwer Academic/Plenum.

Melton, G. B., Petrila, J., Poythress, N. G., Slobogin, C., Otto, R. K., Mossman, D., & Condie, L. O. (2018). *Psychological evaluations for the courts: A handbook for mental health professionals and lawyers* (4th ed.). New York: Guilford Press.

National Child Traumatic Stress Network. www.nctsn.org

Substance Abuse and Mental Health Services Administration. www.samhsa.gov

# Chapter 10

American Psychological Association, Trauma Psychology Webinar Series. https://www.apatraumadivision.org/527/webinar-series.html

Centers for Disease Control & Prevention, Adverse Childhood Experiences (ACEs). www.cdc.gov/violenceprevention/childabuseandneglect/acestudy/index.html

Executive Office for Immigration Review Adjudication Statistics. https://www.justice.gov/eoir/page/file/1148911/download

National Child Traumatic Stress Network, About Complex Child Trauma: Effects. https://www.nctsn.org/what-is-child-trauma/trauma-types/complex-trauma/effects (useful summary)

National Child Traumatic Stress Network, About Complex Child Trauma: Interventions. https://www.nctsn.org/what-is-child-trauma/trauma-types/complex-trauma/interventions

National Scientific Council on the Developing Child. (2005/2014). *Excessive stress disrupts the architecture of the developing brain: Working Paper No. 3*. Updated Edition. https://developingchild.harvard.edu/resources/wp3/

Physicians for Human Rights, Asylum and Persecution, Guides and Protocols for Clinicians. https://phr.org/issues/asylum-and-persecution/asylum-network-resources-linked/ (find more links to resources on this page)

Physicians for Human Rights, How You Can Help Asylum Seekers. https://phr.org/issues/asylum-and-persecution/join-the-asylum-network/

# Chapter 11

Executive Office for Immigration Review Adjudication Statistics. https://www.justice.gov/eoir/page/file/1148911/download

Forensic experts who work with immigration lawyers to present unaccompanied child and minor asylum applicants to the immigration officials and courts have a crucially important role to play.

Physicians for Human Rights, PHR Asylum Program. https://phr.org/issues/asylum-and-persecution/phr-asylum-program/ ("The results of our program speak for themselves: 90 percent of reported asylum outcomes that include an evaluation performed by a PHR Asylum Network volunteer are successful, compared to a national average of barely 30 percent.").

Physicians for Human Rights, How You Can Help Asylum Seekers. https://phr.org/issues/asylum-and-persecution/join-the-asylum-network/

The Administration for Children and Family, an organization under the U.S. Department of Health and Human Services, provide resources for trauma informed care specific for immigrant and refugee populations. They can be found via the following URL. https://www.acf.hhs.gov/trauma-toolkit/immigrant-or-refugee-populations

The American Bar Association provides resources for immigration law attorneys and other legal professionals via their website. Their resources are especially pertinent in keeping up with changes to immigration enforcement practices. It can be found under the following URL. https://www.americanbar.org/groups/public_interest/immigration/resources/

# Chapter 12

## Journals/Membership

Division 18 (Psychologists in Public Service; Police and Public Safety) of the American Psychological Association (APA) membership and participation is recommended.

International Law Enforcement Educators and Trainers Association Journal. published by the International Law Enforcement Educators and Trainers Association (ILEETA; https://ileeta. org/)

Police Psychological Services Section of the International Association of Chiefs of Police. www. theiacp.org

The Police Chief published by the International Association of Chiefs of Police(IAPC; http://www. policechiefmagazine.org/)

# Books

# The following books are written by individuals who are both retired police officers and university professors, which allows for a unique perspective:

Dying for the Job: Police Work Exposure and Health by John Violanti, Ph.D.

Emotional Survival for Law Enforcement: A Guide for Law Enforcement Officers and their Families, by Kevin Gilmartin, Ph.D.

Working with Traumatized Police Officer-Patients: A Clinician's Guide to Complex PTSD Syndromes in Public Safety Professionals, by Daniel Rudofossi, Ph.D.

# The following books include general primers, as well as information for law enforcement families:

Blau, T. H. (1994). *Psychological services for law enforcement*. New York: John Wiley & Sons.

Kirschman, E. (1997). *I love a cop: What police families need to know*. New York: Guilford Press.

Kurke, M. I., & Scrivner, E. M. (Eds.). (1995). *Police psychology into the 21st century*. Hillsdale, NJ: Lawrence Erlbaum Associates.

# On Compassion Fatigue/Vicarious Trauma

Figley, C. R. (Ed.). (1995). *Compassion fatigue: Coping with secondary traumatic stress disorder in those who treat the traumatized*. New York: Brunner/Mazel.

https://www.tendacademy.ca/

McCann, I. L., & Pearlman, L. A. (1990). Vicarious traumatization: A framework for understanding the psychological effects of working with victims. *Journal of Traumatic Stress, 3*, 131–149.

Stamm, B. H. (Ed.). (1999). *Secondary traumatic stress: Self-care issues for clinicians, researchers, and educators* (2nd ed.). Lutherville, MD: Sidran Press.

## Family Resources

National Institute of Justice's Corrections and Law Enforcement Family Support Program. www.
   ojp.usdoj.gov/nij/clefs
policefamilies.com

## Chapter 13

Foote, W. E., & Lareau, C. R. (2013). Psychological evaluation of emotional damages in tort
   cases. In R. K. Otto & I. B. Weiner (Eds.), *Handbook of psychology: Forensic psychology*
   (pp. 172–200). Hoboken, NJ: John Wiley & Sons Inc.
Goodman-Delahunty, J., & Foote, W. E. (2011). *Workplace discrimination and harassment.*
   London: Oxford Press.
Kane, A. W., & Dvoskin, J. A. (2011). *Best practices in forensic mental health assessment.*
   *Evaluation for personal injury claims.* New York, NY: Oxford University Press. https://doi.
   org/10.1093/med:psych/9780195326079.001.0001

## Chapter 14

## Journals/Membership

The Association for Scientific Advancement in Psychological Injury and Law, which publishes the
   Psychological Injury and Law Journal.
The American Psychological Association, Division 56: Division of Trauma Psychology, which
   publishes Psychological Trauma: Theory, Research, Practice, and Policy.

## Guidelines

American Psychological Association, APA Task Force on Race and Ethnicity Guidelines in
   Psychology. (2019). *Race and Ethnicity Guidelines in Psychology: Promoting Responsiveness
   and Equity.* Retrieved from http://www.apa.org/about/policy/race-and-ethnicity-in-psychol-
   ogy.pdf

## Chapter 15

Barrier Free Living. (2018). Services and support for survivors of domestic violence with disabili-
   ties. Retrieved from https://www.bflnyc.org/
Breiding, M. J., Chen, J., & Black, M. C. (2014). Intimate partner violence in the United
   States—2010. Retrieved from https://stacks.cdc.gov/view/cdc/21961

Centers for Disease Control and Prevention. (2009) Injury-intimate partner violence consequences. Retrieved from http://www.cdc.gov/violenceprevention/intimatepartnerviolence/con-
sequences.html

Centers for Disease Control and Prevention. (2017). Racial and ethnic differences in homicides of
adult women and the role of intimate partner violence — United States, 2003–2014. Retrieved
from https://www.cdc.gov/mmwr/volumes/66/wr/mm6628a1.htm?scid=mm6628a1w#suggest
edcitation

Heavey, S. (2013). Data show domestic violence, rape an issue for gays.
Retrieved from https://www.reuters.com/article/us-usa-gays-violence/
data-shows-domestic-violence-rape-an-issue-for-gays-idUSBRE90O11W20130125

Rennison, C. M. (2003). Intimate partner violence, 1993–2001, Bureau of justice statistics crime
data brief. Retrieved from https://www.bjs.gov/content/pub/pdf/ipv01.pd

The United States Department of Justice Archives. (2014). VAWA 2013 Nondiscrimination
provision: Making programs accessible to all victims of domestic violence, sexual assault,
dating violence and stalking. Retrieved from https://www.justice.gov/archives/ovw/blog/
vawa-2013-nondiscrimination-provision-making-programs-accessible-all-victims-domestic

# Chapter 16

## *presented in alphabetical order

ATSA Association for the Treatment of Sexual Abusers. http://www.atsa.com/
CSOM Center for Sex Offender Management. https://www.csom.org/
International Association for the Treatment of Sexual Offenders (IATSO). https://www.iatso.org/
National Center for Missing and Exploited Children (NCMEC). http://www.missingkids.org/home
National Sexual Violence Resource Center (NSVRC). https://www.nsvrc.org/
New England Adolescent Research Institute (NEARI) Press. https://nearipress.org/
SMART(Office of Sex Offender Monitoring, Apprehending, Registering and Tracking. Department
of Justice. https://www.smart.gov/

# Chapter 17

American Psychological Association. (2013b). Specialty guidelines for forensic psychology.
*American Psychologist, 68*, 7–19. Retrieved from https://doi.org/10.1037/a0029889

Bennett, G. K., Seashore, H. G., & Wesman, A. G. (1974). *Fifth manual for the differential aptitude
tests, forms S and T*. New York: The Psychological Corporation.

Briere, J. (2010). *Trauma Symptom Inventory, 2nd ed. (TSI-2) professional manual*. Odessa, FL:
Psychological Assessment Resources.

Centers for Disease Control and Prevention (2016, April, 1). Retrieved from: www.cdc.gov/violen-
ceprevention/acestudy/index.html.

Doren, D. M. (2002). *Evaluating sex offenders: A manual for civil commitments and beyond*.
Thousand Oaks, CA: Sage Publications.

Hare, R. D. (2003). *Manual for the revised psychopathy checklist* (2nd ed.). Toronto, ON: Multi-Health Systems. Journal of Forensic Neuropsychology. Print ISSN: 1521-1029 Online ISSN: 1540-7136

Lezak, M. D., Howieson, D. B., Bigler, E. D., & Tranel, D. (2012). *Neuropsychological assessment* (5th ed.). New York: Oxford University Press.

Levenson, J. (2013). Incorporating trauma-informed care into evidence-based sex offender treatment. *Journal of Sexual Aggression, 20*(1), 9–22. https://doi.org/10.1080/13552600.2013.861523

Phenix, A., Helmus, L., & Hanson, R. K. (2012). Static-99R & Static2002R evaluators' workbook. Retrieved 5 Mar 2013, from http://www.Static99.org/pdfdocs/Static-99RandStatic-2002R_EvaluatorsWorkbook2012-07-26.pdf

Randolph, C. (1998). *Repeatable battery for the assessment of neuropsychological status manual.* San Antonio, TX: The Psychological Corporation.

Reitan, R. M., & Wolfson, D. (1993). *The halstead-Reitan neuropsychology test battery: Theory and clinical interpretation* (2nd ed.). Tucson, AZ: Neuropsychology Press.

Seto, M. C. (2008). *Pedophilia and sexual offending against children: Theory, assessment, and intervention.* Washington, DC: American Psychological Association.

Seto, M. C., Sandler, J. C., & Freeman, N. J. (2017). The revised screening scale for pedophilic interests: Predictive and concurrent validity. *Sexual Abuse, 29*(7), 636–657. https://doi.org/10.1177/1079063215618375

Stern, R. A., & White, T. (2003). *Neuropsychological assessment battery.* Lutz, FL: Psychological Assessment Resources.

Teasdale, G., Maas, A., Lecky, F., Manley, G., Stocchetti, N., & Murray, G. (2014). The Glasgow Coma Scale at 40 years: Standing the test of time. *The Lancet Neurology, 13*(8), 844–854.

Wechsler, D. (2009). *Wechsler memory scale* (4th ed.). San Antonio, TX: Pearson.

Wechsler, D. (2008). *Wechsler adult intelligence scale* (4th ed.). San Antonio, TX: Pearson.

Zadikoff, C., Fox, S. H., Tang-Wai, D. F., Thmsen, T., de Bie, R. M., Wadia, P., … Marras, C. (2008). A comparison of the mini mental state exam to the montreal cognitive assessment in identifying cognitive deficits in Parkinson's disease. *Movement Disorders, 30, 23*(2), 297–299.

# Chapter 18

Strengthening Families. cssp.org/reform/strengtheningfamilies

The ACEs Connection Home: acesconnection.org.

The ACE Study. cdc.gov/violenceprevention/acestudy

The American Psychological Association on Resilience in Youth. https://www.apa.org/helpcenter/resilience

The Essentials for Childhood. cdc.gov/violenceprevention/childmaltreatment/essentials

The National Child Traumatic Stress Network. https://www.nctsn.org/

The Protective Factors Framework. cssp.org/reform/strengtheningfamilies/about/protective-factors-framework

Website and Awareness toolkit with curriculum by Dr. Linda Chamberlain. connectionsmatter.org

Veto Violence. vetoviolence.cdc.gov

# Chapter19

# PSC Effectiveness Summary

National Institute of Justice Summary of Effectiveness of PSCs. https://www.crimesolutions.gov/
TopicDetails.aspx?ID=49#practice

# Guidelines & Protocols

APA Clinical Practice Guideline for the Treatment of Post-Traumatic Stress Disorder. https://
www.apa.org/ptsd-guideline/assessment/index
APA Division 12: Evidence based Treatments for PTSD. https://www.div12.org/diagnosis/
posttraumatic-stress-disorder
CDC Traumatic Brain Injury in Prisons and Jails. https://www.cdc.gov/traumaticbraininjury/pdf/
prisoner_tbi_prof-a.pdf
SAMHSA's Concept of Trauma and Guidance for a Trauma-Informed Approach. http://www.trau-
mainformedcareproject.org/resources/SAMHSA%20TIC.pdf
SAMHSA Trauma Informed Care in Behavioral Services. https://www.integration.samhsa.gov/
clinical-practice/SAMSA_TIP_Trauma.pdf
Trauma Informed Corrections. https://www.centerforgenderandjustice.org/assets/files/soical-
work-chapter-7-trauma-informed-corrections-final.pdf

# Assessment Instruments

Clinician-Administered PTSD Scale for DSM-5 (CAPS-5). https://www.ptsd.va.gov/professional/
assessment/adult-int/caps.asp
Life Events Checklist. https://www.integration.samhsa.gov/clinical-practice/life-event-checklist-
lec.pdf
PTSD screener – PCL-5. https://www.ptsd.va.gov/professional/assessment/adult-sr/ptsd-checklist.
asp

# Assessment Instruments available for purchase

Childhood Trauma Questionnaire: A Retrospective Self-Report (CTQ).
Davidson Trauma Scale.
Dissociative Experiences Scale.
Structured Clinical Interview for DSM-5 (SCID-5).
TSI-2 Trauma Symptom Inventory 2.

# Chapter 20

Blau, T. H. (1994). *Psychological services for law enforcement*. New York: John Wiley & Sons.

Coutois, A.A. & Ford, J. (2009). *Treating complex trauma stress disorders: An evidence-based guide*. New York, N.Y.: The Guildford Press.

Garbarino, J. (2015). *Listening to killers: Lessons learned from my twenty years as a psychological expert in murder cases*. Los Angeles, CA: University California Press.

Kirschman, E. (1997). *I love a cop: What police families need to know*. New York: Guilford Press.

Walker, L. E. & Jungersen, T. (2018). Essential Elements for an Effective Treat,ment of Domestic Violence in a Complex World. In R.A., Javier & W. Herron (Eds.). *Understanding Domestic Violence: Theories, Challenges, and Remedies* (Pp. 303–322). New York, London: Rowman & Littlefield

# Chapter 22

Sheena Leaf. (2015). *Uncovering treasures in Norway and Texas.*https://www.wcmt.org.uk/sites/default/files/reportdocuments/Leaf%20S%20Report%202015%20FINAL.pdf

# Index

© Springer Nature Switzerland AG 2020
R. A. Javier et al. (eds.), *Assessing Trauma in Forensic Contexts*,
https://doi.org/10.1007/978-3-030-33106-1